The
Poetical Works
of
Longfellow

THE CAMBRIDGE EDITIONS

The Poetical Works of Elizabeth Barrett Browning
The Poetical Works of Robert Browning
The Poetical Works of Burns
The Poetical Works of Byron
The Poetical Works of Dryden
The Poetical Works of Oliver Wendell Holmes
The Poetical Works of Keats
The Poetical Works of Longfellow
The Poetical Works of Amy Lowell
The Poetical Works of Shelley
The Poetical Works of Tennyson
The Selected Works of Thoreau
The Poetical Works of Whittier
The Poetical Works of Wordsworth

The
Poetical Works
of
Longfellow

Cambridge Edition

With a New Introduction
by George Monteiro

Houghton Mifflin Company Boston

Library of Congress Cataloging in Publication Data

Longfellow, Henry Wadsworth, 1807–1882.
The poetical works of Longfellow.
Text of the Cambridge ed. of 1893, which was
edited by H. E. Scudder and published under title:
The complete poetical works of Henry Wadsworth
Longfellow.
Includes indexes.
I. Title.
PS2250.F75   811′.3   75-25976
ISBN 0-395-18487-8

Printed in the United States of America

V 15 14 13 12 11 10 9 8 7 6

TEXTUAL NOTE

THE poetic texts of the present edition, along with headnotes to individual volumes and poems, footnotes to lines and passages, and appendix, with the unimportant exception of the omission of several words, are those of the original Cambridge Edition (1893). That excellent edition was prepared by Horace E. Scudder, who drew upon his own Riverside Edition of Longfellow's complete writings (1886).

G. M.

CONTENTS

INTRODUCTION xvii

VOICES OF THE NIGHT.

Prelude 1
Hymn to the Night . . . 2
A Psalm of Life 2
The Reaper and the Flowers . 3
The Light of Stars . . . 4
Footsteps of Angels . . . 4
Flowers 5
The Beleaguered City . . 5
Midnight Mass for the Dying Year 6

EARLIER POEMS.

An April Day 7
Autumn 8
Woods in Winter . . . 8
Hymn of the Moravian Nuns of
  Bethlehem 9
Sunrise on the Hills . . . 9
The Spirit of Poetry . . . 10
Burial of the Minnisink . . 10
L'Envoi 11

BALLADS AND OTHER POEMS.

The Skeleton in Armor . . 11
The Wreck of the Hesperus . 13
The Village Blacksmith . . 14
Endymion 15
It is not always May . . 15
The Rainy Day . . . 16
God's-Acre 16
To the River Charles . . 16
Blind Bartimeus . . . 17
The Goblet of Life . . . 17
Maidenhood 18
Excelsior 19

POEMS ON SLAVERY.

To William E. Channing . . 20
The Slave's Dream . . . 20
The Good Part, that shall not be
  taken away 21
The Slave in the Dismal Swamp 21
The Slave singing at Midnight 22
The Witnesses 22
The Quadroon Girl . . . 22
The Warning 23

THE SPANISH STUDENT . . 23

THE BELFRY OF BRUGES AND OTHER POEMS.

Introductory Note . . 53
The Belfry of Bruges . . . 54
  Carillon 54
  The Belfry of Bruges . . . 54
A Gleam of Sunshine . . 55
The Arsenal at Springfield . . 56
Nuremberg 57
The Norman Baron . . . 58
Rain in Summer . . . 59
To a Child 60
The Occultation of Orion . . 62
The Bridge 63
To the Driving Cloud . . . 64

Songs.

The Day is Done . . . 64
Afternoon in February . . 65
To an Old Danish Song-Book 65
Walter von der Vogelweid . 66
Drinking Song . . . 67
The Old Clock on the Stairs . 67
The Arrow and the Song . 68

Sonnets.

Mezzo Cammin 68
The Evening Star . . . 69
Autumn 69
Dante 69
Curfew 69

EVANGELINE: A TALE OF ACADIE.

Introductory Note . . . 70
Evangeline 71

THE SEASIDE AND THE FIRESIDE.

Introductory Note . . . 98
Dedication 99

By the Seaside.

The Building of the Ship . 99
Seaweed 103
Chrysaor 104
The Secret of the Sea . . 104
Twilight 105
Sir Humphrey Gilbert . . 105
The Lighthouse . . . 106
The Fire of Drift-Wood . 106

By the Fireside.

Resignation 107
The Builders 108

SAND OF THE DESERT IN AN HOUR-
    GLASS 108
THE OPEN WINDOW 109
KING WITLAF'S DRINKING-HORN 109
GASPAR BECERRA . . . 110
PEGASUS IN POUND . . . 110
TEGNÉR'S DRAPA 111
SONNET, ON MRS. KEMBLE'S READ-
    INGS FROM SHAKESPEARE . 112
THE SINGERS 112
SUSPIRIA 112
HYMN FOR MY BROTHER'S ORDI-
    NATION 112

THE SONG OF HIAWATHA.

INTRODUCTORY NOTE . . . 113
INTRODUCTION 113
    I. THE PEACE-PIPE . . 115
    II. THE FOUR WINDS . . 116
    III. HIAWATHA'S CHILDHOOD . 119
    IV. HIAWATHA AND MUDJEKEEWIS 121
    V. HIAWATHA'S FASTING . 124
    VI. HIAWATHA'S FRIENDS . . 127
    VII. HIAWATHA'S SAILING . 128
    VIII. HIAWATHA'S FISHING . . 130
    IX. HIAWATHA AND THE PEARL-
        FEATHER . . . 132
    X. HIAWATHA'S WOOING . 135
    XI. HIAWATHA'S WEDDING-FEAST 137
    XII. THE SON OF THE EVENING
        STAR 139
    XIII. BLESSING THE CORNFIELDS . 143
    XIV. PICTURE-WRITING. . . 145
    XV. HIAWATHA'S LAMENTATION . 147
    XVI. PAU-PUK-KEEWIS . . 149
    XVII. THE HUNTING OF PAU-PUK-
        KEEWIS . . . 151
    XVIII. THE DEATH OF KWASIND . 155
    XIX. THE GHOSTS 156
    XX. THE FAMINE . . . 158
    XXI. THE WHITE MAN'S FOOT . 160
    XXII. HIAWATHA'S DEPARTURE . 162

THE COURTSHIP OF MILES STANDISH.

INTRODUCTORY NOTE . . . 164
    I. MILES STANDISH . . 165
    II. LOVE AND FRIENDSHIP . 166
    III. THE LOVER'S ERRAND . 168
    IV. JOHN ALDEN . . . 171
    V. THE SAILING OF THE MAY-
        FLOWER . . . 174
    VI. PRISCILLA 177
    VII. THE MARCH OF MILES
        STANDISH . . . 178
    VIII. THE SPINNING-WHEEL . 180

    IX. THE WEDDING-DAY . . 182

BIRDS OF PASSAGE.

FLIGHT THE FIRST.
    BIRDS OF PASSAGE. . . . 184
    PROMETHEUS, OR THE POET'S FORE-
        THOUGHT 185
    EPIMETHEUS, OR THE POET'S AFTER-
        THOUGHT 186
    THE LADDER OF ST. AUGUSTINE . 186
    THE PHANTOM SHIP . . . 187
    THE WARDEN OF THE CINQUE
        PORTS 188
    HAUNTED HOUSES . . . 188
    IN THE CHURCHYARD AT CAM-
        BRIDGE 189
    THE EMPEROR'S BIRD'S-NEST . 189
    THE TWO ANGELS . . . 190
    DAYLIGHT AND MOONLIGHT . 191
    THE JEWISH CEMETERY AT NEW-
        PORT 191
    OLIVER BASSELIN . . . 192
    VICTOR GALBRAITH . . . 193
    MY LOST YOUTH . . . 193
    THE ROPEWALK . . . 195
    THE GOLDEN MILE-STONE . 195
    CATAWBA WINE . . . 196
    SANTA FILOMENA . . . 197
    THE DISCOVERER OF THE NORTH
        CAPE 198
    DAYBREAK 199
    THE FIFTIETH BIRTHDAY OF AG-
        ASSIZ 199
    CHILDREN 200
    SANDALPHON 200
FLIGHT THE SECOND.
    THE CHILDREN'S HOUR . . 201
    ENCELADUS 201
    THE CUMBERLAND. . . . 202
    SNOW-FLAKES 202
    A DAY OF SUNSHINE . . 202
    SOMETHING LEFT UNDONE . 203
    WEARINESS 203

TALES OF A WAYSIDE INN.

INTRODUCTORY NOTE . . . 204
PART FIRST.
    Prelude 204
    THE LANDLORD'S TALE: PAUL
        REVERE'S RIDE . . . 207
    Interlude 209
    THE STUDENT'S TALE: THE FALCON
        OF SER FEDERIGO . . . 209
    Interlude 213
    THE SPANISH JEW'S TALE: THE
        LEGEND OF RABBI BEN LEVI . 214
    Interlude 214

CONTENTS

THE SICILIAN'S TALE: KING ROBERT
  OF SICILY 215
Interlude 218
THE MUSICIAN'S TALE: THE SAGA
  OF KING OLAF.
    I. THE CHALLENGE OF THOR 218
    II. KING OLAF'S RETURN . 219
    III. THORA OF RIMOL . . 220
    IV. QUEEN SIGRID THE
      HAUGHTY . . 220
    V. THE SKERRY OF SHRIEKS 221
    VI. THE WRAITH OF ODIN . 222
    VII. IRON-BEARD . . . 223
    VIII. GUDRUN 224
    IX. THANGBRAND THE PRIEST 225
    X. RAUD THE STRONG . . 226
    XI. BISHOP SIGURD OF SALTEN
      FIORD . . . 226
    XII. KING OLAF'S CHRISTMAS 227
    XIII. THE BUILDING OF THE
      LONG SERPENT . . 228
    XIV. THE CREW OF THE LONG
      SERPENT . . . 229
    XV. A LITTLE BIRD IN THE
      AIR . . . 230
    XVI. QUEEN THYRI AND THE
      ANGELICA STALKS . 230
    XVII. KING SVEND OF THE FORKED
      BEARD 231
    XVIII. KING OLAF AND EARL
      SIGVALD . . . 232
    XIX. KING OLAF'S WAR-HORNS . 233
    XX. EINAR TAMBERSKELVER 233
    XXI. KING OLAF'S DEATH-
      DRINK . . . 234
    XXII. THE NUN OF NIDAROS . 235
Interlude 236
THE THEOLOGIAN'S TALE: TORQUE-
  MADA 236
Interlude 239
THE POET'S TALE: THE BIRDS OF
  KILLINGWORTH . . . 240
Finale 243

PART SECOND.
  Prelude 244
THE SICILIAN'S TALE: THE BELL
  OF ATRI . . . 245
Interlude 247
THE SPANISH JEW'S TALE: KAM-
  BALU 247
Interlude 248
THE STUDENT'S TALE: THE COB-
  BLER OF HAGENAU . . 249
Interlude 251
THE MUSICIAN'S TALE: THE BAL-
  LAD OF CARMILHAN . . 252
Interlude 254

THE POET'S TALE: LADY WENT-
  WORTH 255
Interlude 257
THE THEOLOGIAN'S TALE: THE
  LEGEND BEAUTIFUL . . 257
Interlude 259
THE STUDENT'S SECOND TALE:
  THE BARON OF ST. CASTINE . 259
Finale 262

PART THIRD.
  Prelude 263
THE SPANISH JEW'S TALE:
  AZRAEL 264
Interlude 264
THE POET'S TALE: CHARLEMAGNE 265
Interlude 266
THE STUDENT'S TALE: EMMA AND
  EGINHARD 266
Interlude 269
THE THEOLOGIAN'S TALE: ELIZA-
  BETH 270
Interlude 275
THE SICILIAN'S TALE: THE MONK
  OF CASAL-MAGGIORE . . 275
Interlude 279
THE SPANISH JEW'S SECOND TALE:
  SCANDERBEG 280
Interlude 281
THE MUSICIAN'S TALE: THE MO-
  THER'S GHOST . . . 282
Interlude 283
THE LANDLORD'S TALE: THE
  RHYME OF SIR CHRISTOPHER . 284
Finale 286

FLOWER-DE-LUCE.
  FLOWER-DE-LUCE . . . 287
  PALINGENESIS 287
  THE BRIDGE OF CLOUD . . 288
  HAWTHORNE 289
  CHRISTMAS BELLS . . . 289
  THE WIND OVER THE CHIMNEY . 290
  THE BELLS OF LYNN . . . 290
  KILLED AT THE FORD . . 291
  GIOTTO'S TOWER . . . 291
  TO-MORROW 291
  DIVINA COMMEDIA . . . 292
  NOËL 293

BIRDS OF PASSAGE.
  FLIGHT THE THIRD.
    FATA MORGANA . . . 294
    THE HAUNTED CHAMBER . 294
    THE MEETING . . . 295
    VOX POPULI 295
    THE CASTLE-BUILDER . . . 295

CHANGED 296
THE CHALLENGE 296
THE BROOK AND THE WAVE . . 296
AFTERMATH 297

THE MASQUE OF PANDORA.

THE MASQUE OF PANDORA . . 297
  I. THE WORKSHOP OF HEPHÆS-
     TUS 297
  II. OLYMPUS 298
  III. TOWER OF PROMETHEUS ON
     MOUNT CAUCASUS . . 298
  IV. THE AIR 300
  V. THE HOUSE OF EPIMETHEUS . 301
  VI. IN THE GARDEN . . . 302
  VII. THE HOUSE OF EPIMETHEUS . 305
  VIII. IN THE GARDEN . . . 306

THE HANGING OF THE CRANE . 308

MORITURI SALUTAMUS . . 310

A BOOK OF SONNETS.

THREE FRIENDS OF MINE . . 314
CHAUCER 315
SHAKESPEARE 315
MILTON 315
KEATS 316
THE GALAXY 316
THE SOUND OF THE SEA . . 316
A SUMMER DAY BY THE SEA . 316
THE TIDES 317
A SHADOW 317
A NAMELESS GRAVE . . . 317
SLEEP 317
THE OLD BRIDGE AT FLORENCE . 318
IL PONTE VECCHIO DI FIRENZE . 318
NATURE 318
IN THE CHURCHYARD AT TARRY-
  TOWN 318
ELIOT'S OAK 318
THE DESCENT OF THE MUSES . 319
VENICE 319
THE POETS 319
PARKER CLEAVELAND . . . 319
THE HARVEST MOON . . . 320
TO THE RIVER RHONE . . 320
THE THREE SILENCES OF MOLINOS 320
THE TWO RIVERS . . . 320
BOSTON 321
ST. JOHN'S, CAMBRIDGE . . 321
MOODS 322
WOODSTOCK PARK . . . 322
THE FOUR PRINCESSES AT WILNA 322
HOLIDAYS 322
WAPENTAKE 323
THE BROKEN OAR . . . 323
THE CROSS OF SNOW . . 323

BIRDS OF PASSAGE.

FLIGHT THE FOURTH.
CHARLES SUMNER 324
TRAVELS BY THE FIRESIDE . . 324
CADENABBIA 325
MONTE CASSINO 325
AMALFI 326
THE SERMON OF ST. FRANCIS . 327
BELISARIUS 328
SONGO RIVER 328

KÉRAMOS 329

BIRDS OF PASSAGE.

FLIGHT THE FIFTH.
THE HERONS OF ELMWOOD . . 333
A DUTCH PICTURE . . . 334
CASTLES IN SPAIN . . . 335
VITTORIA COLONNA . . . 336
THE REVENGE OF RAIN-IN-THE
  FACE 336
TO THE RIVER YVETTE . . 337
THE EMPEROR'S GLOVE . . 337
A BALLAD OF THE FRENCH FLEET 337
THE LEAP OF ROUSHAN BEG . 338
HAROUN AL RASCHID . . 339
KING TRISANKU 339
A WRAITH IN THE MIST . . 339
THE THREE KINGS . . . 339
SONG: "STAY, STAY AT HOME MY
  HEART, AND REST" . . 340
THE WHITE CZAR 341
DELIA 341

ULTIMA THULE.

INTRODUCTORY NOTE . . . 341
DEDICATION 342
POEMS.
  BAYARD TAYLOR 342
  THE CHAMBER OVER THE GATE . 342
  FROM MY ARM-CHAIR . . . 343
  JUGURTHA 344
  THE IRON PEN 344
  ROBERT BURNS 344
  HELEN OF TYRE 345
  ELEGIAC 345
  OLD ST. DAVID'S AT RADNOR . 346
FOLK-SONGS.
  THE SIFTING OF PETER . . 346
  MAIDEN AND WEATHERCOCK . 347
  THE WINDMILL 347
  THE TIDE RISES, THE TIDE FALLS 347
SONNETS.
  MY CATHEDRAL 348
  THE BURIAL OF THE POET . 348
  NIGHT 348
L'ENVOI.
  THE POET AND HIS SONGS . . 348

CONTENTS

IN THE HARBOR.

BECALMED 349
THE POET'S CALENDAR . . . 349
AUTUMN WITHIN 351
THE FOUR LAKES OF MADISON . 351
VICTOR AND VANQUISHED . . 351
MOONLIGHT 352
THE CHILDREN'S CRUSADE . . 352
SUNDOWN 353
CHIMES 354
FOUR BY THE CLOCK . . . 354
AUF WIEDERSEHEN . . . 354
ELEGIAC VERSE 354
THE CITY AND THE SEA . . 356
MEMORIES 356
HERMES TRISMEGISTUS . . . 356
TO THE AVON 357
PRESIDENT GARFIELD . . . 357
MY BOOKS 357
MAD RIVER 358
POSSIBILITIES 358
DECORATION DAY 359
A FRAGMENT 359
LOSS AND GAIN 359
INSCRIPTION ON THE SHANKLIN
    FOUNTAIN 359
THE BELLS OF SAN BLAS . . 359

FRAGMENTS.

"NEGLECTED RECORD OF A MIND
    NEGLECTED" 360
"O FAITHFUL, INDEFATIGABLE
    TIDES" 360
"SOFT THROUGH THE SILENT AIR" . 360
"SO FROM THE BOSOM OF DARK-
    NESS" 360

CHRISTUS: A MYSTERY.

INTRODUCTORY NOTE . . . 361
INTROITUS 362

PART I. THE DIVINE TRAGEDY.
THE FIRST PASSOVER.
    I. VOX CLAMANTIS . . . 363
    II. MOUNT QUARANTANIA . . 364
    III. THE MARRIAGE IN CANA . . 366
    IV. IN THE CORNFIELDS . . 368
    V. NAZARETH 369
    VI. THE SEA OF GALILEE . . 370
    VII. THE DEMONIAC OF GADARA . 371
    VIII. TALITHA CUMI . . . 373
    IX. THE TOWER OF MAGDALA . 374
    X. THE HOUSE OF SIMON THE PHAR-
        ISEE 375
THE SECOND PASSOVER.
    I. BEFORE THE GATES OF MACHÆ-
        RUS 376
    II. HEROD'S BANQUET-HALL . . 377

    III. UNDER THE WALLS OF MACHÆ-
        RUS 378
    IV. NICODEMUS AT NIGHT . . 379
    V. BLIND BARTIMEUS . . . 381
    VI. JACOB'S WELL 382
    VII. THE COASTS OF CÆSAREA PHI-
        LIPPI 384
    VIII. THE YOUNG RULER . . . 386
    IX. AT BETHANY . . . 387
    X. BORN BLIND 387
    XI. SIMON MAGUS AND HELEN OF
        TYRE 389
THE THIRD PASSOVER.
    I. THE ENTRY INTO JERUSALEM . 391
    II. SOLOMON'S PORCH . . . 393
    III. LORD, IS IT I? . . . 395
    IV. THE GARDEN OF GETHSEMANE 396
    V. THE PALACE OF CAIAPHAS . 397
    VI. PONTIUS PILATE . . . 399
    VII. BARABBAS IN PRISON . . . 400
    VIII. ECCE HOMO 401
    IX. ACELDAMA 402
    X. THE THREE CROSSES . . 403
    XI. THE TWO MARIES . . . 404
    XII. THE SEA OF GALILEE . . 404
EPILOGUE.
    SYMBOLUM APOSTOLORUM . . 406
FIRST INTERLUDE.
    THE ABBOT JOACHIM . . . 407

PART II. THE GOLDEN LEGEND.
PROLOGUE.
    THE SPIRE OF STRASBURG CATHE-
        DRAL 408
    I. THE CASTLE OF VAUTSBERG
        ON THE RHINE . . . 409
        COURT-YARD OF THE CASTLE . 413
    II. A FARM IN THE ODENWALD 415
        A ROOM IN THE FARM-HOUSE 418
        ELSIE'S CHAMBER . . 420
        THE CHAMBER OF GOTTLIEB
        AND URSULA . . . 420
        A VILLAGE CHURCH . . 422
        A ROOM IN THE FARM-HOUSE 425
        IN THE GARDEN . . . 426
    III. A STREET IN STRASBURG . 427
        SQUARE IN FRONT OF THE CA-
        THEDRAL . . . 429
        IN THE CATHEDRAL . . 430
        THE NATIVITY: A MIRACLE-
        PLAY.
        INTROITUS 431
        I. HEAVEN 431
        II. MARY AT THE WELL . 432
        III. THE ANGELS OF THE
            SEVEN PLANETS . 432
        IV. THE WISE MEN OF THE
            EAST . . . 433

V. The Flight into Egypt 433
VI. The Slaughter of the
Innocents . . 434
VII. Jesus at Play with his
Schoolmates . . 435
VIII. The Village School 435
IX. Crowned with Flow-
ers 436
Epilogue 437
IV. The Road to Hirschau . 437
The Convent of Hirschau in
the Black Forest . . 438
The Scriptorium . . . 439
The Cloisters . . . 440
The Chapel 442
The Refectory . . . 443
The Neighboring Nunnery 446
V. A Covered Bridge at Lu-
cerne 449
The Devil's Bridge . . 450
The St. Gothard Pass . . 451
At the Foot of the Alps . 452
The Inn at Genoa . . . 454
At Sea 455
VI. The School of Salerno . 455
The Farm-house in the Oden-
wald 459
The Castle of Vautsberg
on the Rhine . . . 461
Epilogue.
The Two Recording Angels
ascending 462
Second Interlude.
Martin Luther . . . 463

Part III. The New England Tragedies.
John Endicott.
Prologue 465
Act I. 466
Act II. 471
Act III. 477
Act IV. 484
Act V. 491
Giles Corey of the Salem Farms.
Prologue 495
Act I. 496
Act II. 501
Act III. 507
Act IV. 513
Act V. 519
Finale.
St. John 522

JUDAS MACCABÆUS.
Act I. The Citadel of Antiochus
at Jerusalem . . 523
Act II. The Dungeons in the Cit-
adel 526

Act III. The Battle-Field of Beth-
Horon . . . 529
Act IV. The Outer Courts of the
Temple at Jerusalem 532
Act V. The Mountains of Ecba-
tana 534

MICHAEL ANGELO: A FRAGMENT.
Dedication 537
Part First.
I. Prologue at Ischia . 537
Monologue: The Last
Judgment . . 540
II. San Silvestro . . 541
III. Cardinal Ippolito . 543
IV. Borgo delle Vergine at
Naples . . . 548
V. Vittoria Colonna . 551
Part Second.
I. Monologue . . . 555
II. Viterbo . . . 556
III. Michael Angelo and Ben-
venuto Cellini . 557
IV. Fra Sebastiano del
Piombo . . 560
V. Palazzo Belvedere . 565
VI. Palazzo Cesarini . 567
Part Third.
I. Monologue . . . 569
II. Vigna di Papa Giulio . 570
III. Bindo Altoviti . 574
IV. In the Coliseum . 575
V. Macello de' Corvi . 576
VI. Michael Angelo's Studio 581
VII. The Oaks of Monte Luca 583
VIII. The Dead Christ . 585

TRANSLATIONS.
Introductory Note . . 586
Prelude 587
From the Spanish.
Coplas de Manrique . . 587
Sonnets.
I. The Good Shepherd 592
II. To-Morrow . . 593
III. The Native Land . 593
IV. The Image of God . 593
V. The Brook . . 593
Ancient Spanish Ballads.
I. Rio Verde, Rio Verde . 594
II. Don Nuno, Count of Lara 594
III. The peasant leaves his
plough afield . . 594
Vida de San Millan . . 595
San Miguel, the Convent . 596
Song: She is a maid of artless
grace . . . 596

CONTENTS

SANTA TERESA'S BOOK-MARK . 597
FROM THE CANCIONEROS.
   I. EYES SO TRISTFUL, EYES SO
      TRISTFUL 597
  II. SOME DAY, SOME DAY . 597
 III. COME, O DEATH, SO SILENT
      FLYING 597
  IV. GLOVE OF BLACK IN WHITE
      HAND BARE . . . 597

FROM THE SWEDISH AND DANISH.
INTRODUCTORY NOTE . . . 598
PASSAGES FROM FRITHIOF'S SAGA.
   I. FRITHIOF'S HOMESTEAD . 598
  II. A SLEDGE-RIDE ON THE ICE . 599
 III. FRITHIOF'S TEMPTATION . 599
  IV. FRITHIOF'S FAREWELL . . 600
THE CHILDREN OF THE LORD'S
  SUPPER 600
KING CHRISTIAN 607
THE ELECTED KNIGHT . . 608
CHILDHOOD 608

FROM THE GERMAN.
THE HAPPIEST LAND . . . 609
THE WAVE 609
THE DEAD 610
THE BIRD AND THE SHIP . . 610
WHITHER? 610
BEWARE! 611
SONG OF THE BELL . . . 611
THE CASTLE BY THE SEA . 611
THE BLACK KNIGHT . . 612
SONG OF THE SILENT LAND . 612
THE LUCK OF EDENHALL . 613
THE TWO LOCKS OF HAIR . 613
THE HEMLOCK TREE . . 614
ANNIE OF THARAW . . . 614
THE STATUE OVER THE CATHEDRAL
  DOOR 615
THE LEGEND OF THE CROSSBILL 615
THE SEA HATH ITS PEARLS . 615
POETIC APHORISMS . . . 616
SILENT LOVE 616
BLESSED ARE THE DEAD . 616
WANDERER'S NIGHT-SONGS . 617
REMORSE. 617
FORSAKEN 618
ALLAH 618

FROM THE ANGLO-SAXON.
THE GRAVE 618
BEOWULF'S EXPEDITION TO HEORT 618
THE SOUL'S COMPLAINT AGAINST
  THE BODY 620

FROM THE FRENCH.
SONG: HARK! HARK! . . . 621
SONG: AND WHITHER GOEST THOU,
  GENTLE SIGH 621

THE RETURN OF SPRING . . 621
SPRING. 621
THE CHILD ASLEEP . . . 622
DEATH OF ARCHBISHOP TURPIN . 622
THE BLIND GIRL OF CASTÈL
  CUILLÈ 623
A CHRISTMAS CAROL . . . 628
CONSOLATION 628
TO CARDINAL RICHELIEU . . 629
THE ANGEL AND THE CHILD . 629
ON THE TERRACE OF THE AIGA-
  LADES 630
TO MY BROOKLET 630
BARRÉGES 630
WILL EVER THE DEAR DAYS COME
  BACK AGAIN? 631
AT LA CHAUDEAU . . . 631
A QUIET LIFE 631
THE WINE OF JURANÇON . . 632
FRIAR LUBIN 632
RONDEL 632
MY SECRET. 632
FROM THE ITALIAN.
THE CELESTIAL PILOT . . . 633
THE TERRESTRIAL PARADISE . 633
BEATRICE 634
TO ITALY 635
SEVEN SONNETS AND A CANZONE.
   I. THE ARTIST. . . . 635
  II. FIRE 635
 III. YOUTH AND AGE. . . 636
  IV. OLD AGE 636
   V. TO VITTORIA COLONNA . 636
  VI. TO VITTORIA COLONNA . 636
 VII. DANTE 637
VIII. CANZONE 637
THE NATURE OF LOVE . . 637
FROM THE PORTUGUESE.
SONG: IF THOU ART SLEEPING,
  MAIDEN 637
FROM EASTERN SOURCES.
THE FUGITIVE 638
THE SIEGE OF KAZAN . . . 639
THE BOY AND THE BROOK . 639
TO THE STORK 639
FROM THE LATIN.
VIRGIL'S FIRST ECLOGUE . . 640
OVID IN EXILE 641

APPENDIX.
  I. JUVENILE POEMS.
    The Battle of Lovell's Pond . 645
    To Ianthe 645
    Thanksgiving 645
    Autumnal Nightfall . . 646
    Italian Scenery . . . 646
    The Lunatic Girl . . . 647

The Venetian Gondolier . . 647
The Angler's Song . . . 648
Lover's Rock 648
Dirge over a Nameless Grave . 648
A Song of Savoy . . . 648
The Indian Hunter . . . 649
Ode written for the Commemoration
  at Fryeburg, Maine, of Love-
  well's Fight 649
Jeckoyva 650
The Sea-Diver 650
Musings 650
Song 650
Song of the Birds . . . 651

II. UNACKNOWLEDGED AND UNCOL-
  LECTED TRANSLATIONS.
Let me go warm . . . 651
The Nativity of Christ . 651
The Assumption of the Virgin 652
The Disembodied Spirit . 652
Ideal Beauty . . . 652
The Lover's Complaint . 652
Art and Nature . . 652
The Two Harvests . . . 652
Clear Honor of the Liquid Ele-
  ment 652

Praise of Little Women . . 653
Milagros de Nuestra Señora . 653
Song of the Rhine . . . 653
Elegy written in the Ruins of an
  Old Castle 654
The Stars 654
Rondel 655
The Banks of the Cher . . 655
To the Forest of Gastine . 655
Fontenay 656
Pray for Me . . . 656
Vire 656
A Florentine Song . . 657
A Neapolitan Canzonet . 657
Christmas Carol . . . 657
A Soldier's Song . . . 657
Tell me, tell me, thou pretty bee 658
Sicilian Canzonet . . . 658
The Gleaner of Sapri . 658

III. NOTES AND ILLUSTRATIONS . 658
IV. A CHRONOLOGICAL LIST OF MR.
  LONGFELLOW'S POEMS . . 676

INDEX OF FIRST LINES . . 681

INDEX OF TITLES 686

INTRODUCTION

OF the major nineteenth-century American poets still read by anyone other than the literary historians, none has paid more dearly in abuse and denigration for having achieved popular success in his own time than Henry Wadsworth Longfellow. The first of our "fireside poets" and later the first of our "schoolroom poets," Longfellow has been held up as an author of some singularly mediocre poems. Time and again his most popular pieces have been offered as models of how not to write serious poetry. For I. A. Richards in 1929 the prime specimen was "In the Churchyard at Cambridge"; for Robert Penn Warren, Cleanth Brooks, and their younger contemporary R. W. B. Lewis, writing in 1974, it was almost any poem. To an age nurtured on Herbert J. C. Grierson's studies of English metaphysical verse, the narrow strictures of T. E. Hulme, the Imagists calling for the hard, precise rendering of the curve of an emotion, the critical prescription of a T. S. Eliot clearing the way for the mythic method and the primacy of the impersonal poet, and the practical displays of critics stressing "how" a poem means, not "what" it means — to such an age of critics all of Longfellow's work, except a handful of somehow still appealing, if uncharacteristic, lyrics, failed to pass rigorous examination. Ours has been an age taught early to value the image of the poet embattled, in conflict, and in pain, yet struggling for a transcendent vision. The poet of the barbaric yawp, or the poet-victim valiantly struggling to break through the limitations of a medium pushed further and further away from the center of the literate human being's most meaningful experience, became the rather tentative cynosure of beleaguered readers. Yet as long ago as 1923, the year after the publication of Eliot's *The Waste Land*, Robert Frost deplored the critical changes that devalued the kind of poet Longfellow was. "One of the real American poets of yesterday was Longfellow. No, I am not being sarcastic. I mean it," he insisted. "It is the fashion nowadays to make fun of him. I come across this pose and attitude with people I meet socially, with men and women I meet in the classrooms of colleges where I teach. They laugh at his gentleness, at his lack of worldliness, at his detachment from the world and the meaning thereof. When and where has it been written that a poet must be a club-swinging warrior, a teller of barroom tales, a participant of unspeakable experiences? That, today, apparently is the stamp of poetic integrity." It is somehow fitting that in this century only Frost himself has commanded anything like the veneration and loyalty of the tens of thousands who in Longfellow's own day, both in America and abroad, read his poetry and, somewhat suprisingly, his essays and fiction.

Just how Longfellow achieved such heights of popularity, unheard of in America before and probably unequalled since, is fundamentally a biographical matter. It did not just happen. Granted the possibility that the climate of the times favored the kind of poetry Longfellow wrote, it should not be assumed that what he gave his public was his only alternative. There were many possible strings to his bow, some of which he chose over others for rather hard-headed practical reasons. Not until late in life did he try to convert his readers to poetry welling up out of his most personal needs, and by then he had every reason to believe that he could trade on his great popularity and on his widely accepted public role as sage and bardic spokesman. That he was unable to do so successfully only points to the truth that Longfellow was actually at his best writing for a large public whose interests and tastes he uncannily understood and served through a long professional life. That he understood his constituency, carefully broadened it, and served it well for a lifetime qualifies somewhat the image of the aged, gentle, bearded poet, whose portrait used to adorn the walls of American schoolrooms. Even that last image can be seen as fulfilling the expectations of a populace embued with the sense of progress, manifest destiny, and the rise of the self-made man. America's major poets did not die young and unfulfilled as had the English romantics Byron, Keats, and Shelley, or America's own *poète maudit* Edgar Allan Poe. They lived, as Longfellow did, to a maturity characterized by honor and public reverence. James Russell Lowell, John Greenleaf Whittier, Oliver Wendell Holmes — even, surprisingly, that radical poet who survived both his notoriety and his originality, Walt Whitman — lived long enough to fill this final public role. It was Longfellow, however, who fulfilled it first. As with all innovators, moreover, his journey to that eminence was marked less by inevitability than by conscious and almost daily choices among possibilities and alternatives. What is remarkable about Longfellow's life and professional career is not that from the beginning he knew what he wanted and worked hard to achieve it — notable as that is in itself — but rather that there were almost no false starts and very few mistakes along the way.

Henry Wadsworth Longfellow was to the manner born — such as that manner was in Portland, Maine — in 1807. In Boston the Longfellow family would undoubtedly have been less prominent than it was in the thriving seaport to the northeast. But as the second child of Zilpah Wadsworth, a descendant of the Plymouth Pilgrims, and Stephen Longfellow, a prosperous lawyer educated at Harvard College, the precocious Henry was carefully nurtured and educated. At three he was enrolled in an old-fashioned "dame school." At six he entered the Portland Academy, staying there until the age of fourteen, when he passed entrance examinations for the new Bowdoin College in nearby Brunswick, Maine. (Henry's older brother passed the entrance examination at the same time). There is no doubt that the youth of both boys had something to do with their father's choice of Bowdoin rather than Harvard for his sons. They would not begin college until 1822, at which time they took up residence as sophomores. The college careers of Henry and Stephen Longfellow were in almost every way diametrically opposed.

Henry established a record for high consistency in his studies while Stephen proved to be at best an indifferent scholar and at worst a social delinquent. Both were graduated in 1825, however, in a class that numbered among its members the future romancer Nathaniel Hawthorne.

It was in college that Longfellow made the career plans that would guide the rest of his life. Although his father opted for the law as a profession for his son, Longfellow himself longed for a career in literature. As young as he was, he knew that no American had yet succeeded in earning his living totally as a professional writer, least of all as a poet or a romancer. His strategy with his father, then, was to persuade him that there were certain professions that he would not, indeed could not, follow. During his junior year he wrote in a letter to his father that "in thinking to make a Lawyer of me, I fear you thought more partially than justly. I do not for my own part imagine that such a coat would suit me. I hardly think Nature designed me for the bar, or the pulpit, or the dissecting-room." What, then, could he do? Apparently he had not determined how he could support a literary career, for he presented himself — unconvincingly — as a would-be farmer. "I am altogether in favour of a Farmer's life," he concluded his letter. "Do keep the farmer's boots for me!" Stephen Longfellow could hardly have taken seriously his bookish son's last outburst as in any way indicative of his proclivities, but he did know that Henry did not share his own preferences. All through his years at Bowdoin Longfellow's letters were peppered with references to novels read and poems discovered. On one day he would praise Thomas Gray's "Progress of Poesy." On another he would call his mother's attention to Charles Brockden Brown's *Arthur Mervyn*, lamenting that in his day Brown had suffered great neglect in America yet expressing hope that a proposed collected edition of Brown's work might bring posthumously to this writer the audience he deserved. To anyone who would read the signs it was clear that whatever profession Longfellow chose, that profession would somehow have to fit in with his literary interests. Longfellow's letters to his father at this time are filled with the give and take of bargaining, the father holding out for the law and the son countering in various ways. "For my part, I have already hinted to you what would best please me," wrote Longfellow. "I want to spend one year at Cambridge for the purpose of reading History, and of becoming familiar with the best authors in polite literature: whilst at the same time I can be acquiring a knowledge of the Italian Language, without an acquaintance with which, I shall be shut out from one of the most beautiful departments of letters. The French I mean to understand pretty thoroughly before I leave College. After leaving Cambridge I would attach myself to some literary periodical publication, by which I could maintain myself and still enjoy the advantages of reading . . . the fact is, I most eagerly aspire after future eminence in literature, my whole soul burns most ardently for it, and every earthly thought centers in it." In the same letter he plays a final card. He announces rather proudly that he has recently contributed to the *United States Literary*

Gazette and the *Philadelphia Magazine*, though he is concerned that the editor of the latter has not yet paid him for his contributions. But the father was adamant about the law, and finally it was agreed — rather generously on the father's part — that after Longfellow's year at Harvard he would return to Portland in order to read for the bar. In his euphoria over his father's concession in the matter, Longfellow would say of his practicing law, "This will support my *real* existence, literature an *ideal* one."

But as luck would have it, perhaps aided by some behind-the-scenes maneuvering by his father, a trustee at Bowdoin, something far more congenial than the law was in store for Longfellow. Despite his youth Bowdoin offered him a newly established professorship of modern languages with the condition that he prepare for his duties with a long stay in Europe. Here was the happy, wholly unexpected, solution to his dilemma about a career. Quickly accepting the offer, Longfellow, who until recently had not been "fifty miles from Portland," left for Europe. His stay would extend to three years and would take him to France, Spain, Italy, and Germany. During this scholar's tour of the continent Longfellow dedicated himself assiduously to the study of languages and literature. In addition he found himself for the first time near famous American writers. James Fenimore Cooper, for one, was in Paris when Longfellow was there, and despite Cooper's having "behaved very disgracefully" on departing, Longfellow on his part confessed himself "happy in being near a writer who has gained so much reputation at home and abroad." Rather remarkably during the whole of his European stay his letters give no evidence that his mind was ever on matters pedagogical. Only in the final weeks does he ever refer to the imminence of his forthcoming duties at Bowdoin.

Since his study of languages was a necessary prerequisite to the making of books, the first subject in his letters invariably leads to a consideration of the second. "My familiarity with the modern languages will unlock to me all those springs of literature, which formerly would have been as sealed books to me." Then he leaps naturally to publication: "You see how it is with Washington Irving. He has remained in Spain upwards of three years — and you see what profit he reaps from it. Whoever first makes a Sketch Book of Spain will necessarily make a very interesting book." As he would admit within the month, "My object in visiting Europe has been a literary one." Fortunately, his literary studies had been suitable as well for the long teaching career he would soon begin.

At a salary of eight hundred dollars a year, and a hundred dollars for services with the college library, Longfellow took up his teaching duties in the fall of 1829. To his credit, he plunged in honestly and enthusiastically. Finding a lack of suitable text books and language readers, he set about constructing them himself. By 1830 he had seen through the press four texts: *Elements of French Grammar*, *French Exercises*, *Manuel de Proverbes Dramatiques*, and *Novelas Españolas*. These were followed in 1833 by *Syllabus de la Grammaire Italienne* and *Saggi de' Novellieri Italini d'Ogni Secolo*. Indeed, toward the end of his first year of teaching, Longfellow admitted, "I find such an engrossing interest in the studies of my profession, that I write very seldom, except in connection with those studies." This "engrossing interest" would not sustain him indefinitely, however, for Longfellow soon found Brunswick inadequate to his rather expanded emotional needs and his mounting professional ambition. Even his marriage to Mary Storer Potter of Portland on September 14, 1831, was only a momentary stay against his restlessness. Various schemes for extricating himself from Brunswick — the notion to found a girls' school in New York, the dream of securing the position of Secretary of legation in Madrid, the halfhearted attempt to take over the Round Hill School in Northampton, the tentative candidacies for professorships at the University of Virginia and at New York University (the latter an appointment without salary, such was the magnitude of his disaffection) — all such schemes fell through. Paralleling these abortive attempts were his continuing attempts to write himself out of Brunswick. To the *North American Review* he contributed learned essays on the languages and literatures of France, Spain, Italy and Portugal. From the Spanish he translated the *Coplas de Manrique* to which he appended a professorial essay on the moral and devotional poetry of Spain. He also published over an eighteen month period a series entitled "The Schoolmaster," later recast as *Outre-Mer; a Pilgrimage Beyond the Sea*, a collection of twenty-six prose pieces rather closely modeled on Irving's *Sketch-Book*.

Once again Longfellow's rescue came from an unexpected and unlikely quarter. His five-year stay at Bowdoin ended in 1834 when he accepted an offer from President Josiah Quincy of Harvard College to replace George Ticknor as Smith Professor of Modern Languages. Once again, however, the position, at fifteen hundred dollars per year, carried the further stipulation that Longfellow precede his residence in Cambridge with a stay in Europe of a year or eighteen months "for the purpose of a more perfect attainment of the German." "Good fortune comes at last," he wrote exultantly, "and I certainly shall not reject it."

The "good fortune," as it turned out, was not unalloyed, for that sojourn — undertaken with buoyancy and joy and potentially so significant for his professional career — would be marked by death and sorrow. Within six months of their arrival in Europe his twenty-three year old wife suffered a miscarriage and died a few weeks later in Rotterdam. Longfellow's bereavement at her death was real enough, but it was not disabling. Although he had been forewarned of the possibility of danger to his delicate wife, there is no evidence in his letters at the time that he blamed himself for her death or that he saw it as a ransom paid to his worldly ambition. Indeed he seems not to have considered the possibility of cutting short his European stay. Sorrowladen he might be, but his travels across Europe — to Germany, Switzerland, and France — continued as he sought out the leading literary figures of each nation, forming numerous friendships which would one day result in his being promoted as an international man of letters just as he would promote the reputations of his European friends in the United States. His personal grief gradually turned into a more generalized melanchóly and in that form it lingered for months. In the summer of 1836, however, he met Fanny Appleton and her family in Switzerland. Sentimentally vulnerable, he seems to have fallen in love with Fanny on the spot. The love, however, was then all on his side, and it was to go unrequited for years.

At the end of the year Longfellow arrived in Cambridge to assume his new duties. As his father then discerned, at twenty-nine Longfellow had already accomplished a great deal. "I think your ambition must be satisfied," he wrote, "and your object now will be to fill with eminence and distinction the office in which you are placed, and to become distinguished among the literary men of the age." If his father meant this as advice, it fell on receptive ears. Longfellow's assault on the high parapet of literary fame took several forms. In 1839 he published *Hyperion*, a highly autobiographical novel built around a thinly characterized hero with a predeliction for speaking at people in the manner of literary and travel essays, which draws substantially on Longfellow's recent European experiences. Fanny Appleton, who appears in the book as the free-spirited Mary Ashburton, with whom the hero falls in love, took umbrage at Longfellow's temerity in putting her into his novel. The whole affair appears to have had the effect of putting off for several years any chance of their marrying.

Longfellow, fully in character, continued to write and to publish. "The last year have written a great deal: enough to make volumes," he wrote to a friend. "Have not read much. Have wasted much time on account of the *affaire du coeur*. Shall not go mad. Have a number of literary plans and projects ... Do not like this sedentary life. Want action — want to travel — am too excited — too tumultuous inwardly — and my health suffers from all this." Within days Longfellow would achieve his greatest literary triumph to date. In the *Knickerbocker* for September 1838 appeared what proved to be his most famous poem ever, "A Psalm of Life." Its great success encouraged him to compose other "Psalms" and shortly thereafter he was ready to bring out *Voices of the Night*, his first volume of mature poems. The largely favorable reception accorded these poems coincided, not incidentally, one suspects, with Longfellow's growing disaffection with his increasingly burdensome university duties as lecturer and supervisor of modern language instruction. "I feel all the time, that I am doing wrong to stay here under such circumstances," he complained to his father; "though I know this [my desire to resign] is not *prudent*."

If his university career brought him concern and discomfort, his literary career prospered wonderfully. The success of *Voices of the Night* fostered more poems. Interestingly enough, however, most of the new poems were unlike anything he had hitherto written. He wanted a still larger public audience than he had so far achieved and he was certain that he knew how to reach that audience. "Since the poems," he wrote early in 1840, "I have broken ground in a new field; namely, *Ballads;* beginning with the '*Wreck of the Schooner Hesperus on the Reef of Norman's*

Woe,' in the great storm a fortnight ago. It will be printed in a few days, and I shall send it in [to] some newspaper. I think I shall write more. The *National Ballad* is a virgin soil here in New England; and there are good materials." Beyond this discovery of the poetic possibilities of native material, he had decided that he would become what critics would later call a public poet. "I have a great notion of working upon *people's feelings*," he concluded, "I desire a new sensation, and a new set of critics." Native subjects handled affectively would lead him, he was convinced, to great success. In 1841 he brought out *Ballads and Other Poems,* which collected, among others, such popular individual successes as "The Skeleton in Armor," "The Wreck of the Hesperus," "The Village Blacksmith" and "Excelsior." Although the volume as a whole, judging from sales, proved to be less popular than *Voices of the Night,* the poet's conscious shift from lyric to narrative and dramatic poetry was lasting.

From then on his great successes came with the more public forms of poetry. Though there would always be exceptions, of course, one is notable: *Poems on Slavery* is a set of eight poems written on ship board during his return in 1842 from a six-months rest cure in Europe. The previous year he had followed sympathetically the news of an African slave revolt aboard the Spanish ship *Amistad* and the subsequent trial in which John Quincy Adams successfully defended those slaves. Although Longfellow's poems were sympathetic to the black slave, they exhibited none of the incendiary and righteous anger of Whittier's poems on slavery or Garrison's tracts. Of his own poems he observed, "They are written in a kindly — not a vindictive spirit. Humanity is the chord to be touched. Denuniciation of Slave-holders would do more harm than good; besides, that is not my vein," he acknowledged. "I leave that to more ferocious natures." When the New England Anti-Slavery Association asked his permission to reprint the poems he readily assented. But when Whittier, encouraged by his public stance in *Poems on Slavery,* asked him to run for Congress, Longfellow could only reply, "I cannot for a moment think of entering the political arena. Partizan warfare becomes too violent — too vindicative for my taste; and I should be found but a weak and unworthy champion in public debate."

The next year was momentous for Longfellow. After years of fitful and singularly unsuccessful courtship, Fanny Appleton suddenly agreed to marriage. That event in early summer initiated what was by all imaginable signs the longest period of sustained happiness in Longfellow's life. The equanimity of his sentimental and domestic life was evenly matched by soaring professional prominence. Only that burdensome professorship threatened to mar the satisfaction of his life, and in 1854 he finally resigned his office.

In less than two decades he produced book after book beginning in 1842 with the magazine publication of *The Spanish Student,* a sprightly poetic drama, and ending with the crisp narrative poem, *The Courtship of Myles Standish,* in 1858. The years in between saw the publication of *The Belfrey of Bruges and Other Poems*

(1845), *The Poets and Poetry of Europe* (1845), an innovative and highly influential anthology, *Evangeline* (1847), *Kavanagh* (1849), a novel, *The Seaside and the Fireside* (1849), *The Golden Legend* (1851), and *The Song of Hiawatha* (1855). This was the period of Longfellow's professional consolidation and of his largest popular appeal. Nothing he would write after *Hiawatha* and *Myles Standish* would have the broad appeal of the works of the 1840s and 1850s, and in subsequent years those titles would continue to outsell all new ones.

The rough coincidence of the watershed date with the tragic death by fire of Fanny Longfellow in 1861 suggests that the explanation for this decline in readership for his later work lies principally within Longfellow himself. So disabling was the death of his wife that it was not until nearly six weeks after her death that he could finally answer her sister's letter. "How I am alive after what my eyes have seen, I know not," he wrote. "I am at least patient, if not resigned; and thank God hourly — as I have from the beginning — for the beautiful life we led together, and that I loved her more and more to the end." The death of his first wife had brought him sorrow and melancholy but as an experience of his young manhood the shock was soon effaced by thoughts of literary ambition and the cares and details of his daily existence. At the age of fifty-four, however, no thought of literary ambition could diminish or assuage Longfellow's sorrow. With the exception of *Tales of a Wayside Inn*, begun before his wife's death, he wrote little poetry and published less. Instead he returned to Dante's *Divine Comedy*, the translation of which took up much of his creative energy for several years.

Longfellow would write to the end of his life, but after his wife's death his work became increasingly personal. Even when he tried to write for his popular audience he would no longer celebrate the old virtues, the constancy of Evangeline or the Promethean stance of Hiawatha. Instead his work took on the somber hues of the *New England Tragedies* (1868) and, a year earlier, of *Flower-de-Luce*, which brought together poems such as "Killed at the Ford," "The Bells of Lynn," his elegiac tribute "Hawthorne," and his first set of sonnets on *The Divine Comedy*. While still in college he had written revealingly of the function of religion, as he saw it. "Would it not be better for mankind if we should consider it as a cheerful and social companion, given us to go through life with us from childhood to the grave, and to make us happier here as well as hereafter," he asked; "and not as a stern and chiding task-master, to whom we must cling at last through mere despair, because we have nothing else on earth to which we can cling?" The function of religion was, in his view, similar to the function of literature. In the following passage from the same letter it is instructive to think of the terms "religion" and "Christianity" as interchangeable with "literature" and "poetry."

> I conceive that if religion is ever to benefit us, it must be incorporated with our feelings, and become in every degree identified with our happiness. And hence I love that view of Christianity which sets it in the light of a cheerful, kind-hearted friend, and which gives its thoughts a noble and a liberal turn.

Longfellow was trying to explain why he would not choose to pursue "the profession of Divinity." It would serve just as well, if we make the substitutions suggested, as a justification for the kind of poetry he would write for the next thirty-five years. That justification could no longer serve him, however, after 1861. More revealing of the tragic cast his life now assumed is an observation he quoted with concurrence less than a year after Fanny's death. "This world is only the *negative* of the world to come, and what is dark here will be light hereafter." In the main the poetry of his final phase was written out of the tragic sense of those *negative* truths of human experience. The last two decades of his life are more accurately characterized by the sentiments of *Kéramos and Other Poems* (1878) and *Ultima Thule* (1880) than they are by the then atypical celebration of domesticity in *The Hanging of the Crane* (1874), an anachronistic poem in his earlier vein. Even a final sentimental journey to Europe taken in his early sixties, during which he was honored far beyond the fancies of his youth, could not appreciably restore to him the equanimity of poetic outlook that had sustained him for much of his life.

In his last decade Longfellow carried on in his poetry the task of self-definition and self-assessment. Resuming work he had begun as early as 1850, he wrote and rewrote *Michael Angelo* year in and year out. At his death in 1882 this dramatic poem remained unpublished. Among other possible readings, through its hero the poem can be read as a searching allegory of the poet's own life. Michael Angelo, the Renaissance representative man, as William Charvat has noticed, "asks the unarticulated question of all Longfellow's later poems":

> How will men speak of me when I am gone,
> When all this colorless, sad life is ended,
> And I am dust? They will remember only
> The wrinkled forehead, the marred countenance,
> The rudeness of my speech, and my rough manners,
> And never dream that underneath them all
> There was a woman's heart of tenderness;
> They will not know the secret of my life,
> Locked up in silence, or but vaguely hinted
> In uncouth rhymes, that may perchance survive
> Some little space in memories of men!
> Each one performs his life-work, and then leaves it;
> Those that come after him will estimate
> His influence on the age in which he lived.

If, in the case of Michael Angelo, these questions were already rhetorical in Longfellow's day, history having answered them in his favor, they were not at all rhetorical for the American poet, who late in life repeatedly experienced the sadness of having reprints of his early work greatly outsell *Christus*, a religious work he considered the consummating achievement of a lifetime.

To his credit, the first man in America to commit himself to the profession of poet over an entire career, despite the personal sorrows and the public ironies that would have silenced a lesser being, never abandoned his trade and vocation. "Strange as you may think it," he wrote to his publisher, "I find no longer any pleasure in such things, nor take any interest in going about among men. Whenever I try it, I fail utterly. I had rather be here at my work as long as the day continues; for the night cometh in which no man shall work."

As long ago as 1907, the year of Longfellow's centenary, William Dean Howells put his finger on that characteristic in Longfellow's poetry which would in time bother most modern critics. Writing in the *North American Review*, Howells noted that throughout Longfellow's early career the poet had "loved best the tale which would teach something, or would turn in the telling into a parable." A quarter of a century after Longfellow's death Howells had come to the conclusion, however, that this early penchant for teaching in verse was something that fortunately Longfellow had largely outgrown. Putting aside the question of whether or not he did, as time went by, choose, more and more, "the passages of experience or the plays of fancy which invited no exegesis" (again Howells), we can see that Howells' observation concerning Longfellow's moralism has been transformed into the criticism of his poetry. On the one hand, his moralist's sensibility led him consistently to select themes and subjects reflecting and reinforcing the social attitudes and moral platitudes of his readers. Hence — runs the argument — in *Hiawatha* Longfellow contributed to the ongoing process of sentimentalizing the Indian, while in *Evangeline* he drew on the particularly attractive type of the loyal, constant maiden. In the romantic comedy which is *The Courtship of Miles Standish* he reaffirmed the fireside virtue of domestic love sorted out properly by considerations of chronology and generation. In the twentieth century, however, such themes and messages have not been particularly attractive. Even Howells, the proponent, along with Henry James, of the psychological novel, found the characters in *Evangeline* to be "not persons, but types." But Howells still appreciated the poetry, and despite the psychological thinness of the story he found it very much to his liking.

Not satisfied with impugning Longfellow's subjects and themes, the modern critic set about attacking Longfellow where it was long thought that he was unassailable: in his poetic craft. His lyric poems — a handful of which are generally considered in our day as superior to the narrative and dramatic poems — suffer from the same moralism. Longfellow mars even his best efforts — so it is said — by attaching embarrassing morals to his poems. Critics abound who tell us that such-and-such could have been a good poem had Longfellow left out the fourth stanza, or that having discovered a telling metaphor, he damages it beyond repair by seeing in it a moral applicable to his own life or the lives of others. Such reactions, I would submit, have their source in unrecognized, or at least unacknowledged, shifts in poetic taste. Although Longfellow "is more explicit about drawing the moral than is now the fashion, it may be a false romanticism in the present taste," warns our contemporary, the poet Howard Nemerov, "a desire to indulge the spirit in pseudo-mysteries, which is embarrassed by plain statements and wants everything 'left implicit.'" Are we to rest assured, then, that *mutatis mutandis* poets who do not "explain" their images and metaphors are *ipso facto* superior to those who do? By the assumptions and standards of Modernism even a poem such as the sonnet "The Cross of Snow" might be found wanting. That it has been universally admired, however, despite Longfellow's moralistic analogy of symbol and self, is instructive. In this poem we have the singularly appealing image of the anguished poet, writing out of insistent grief, that our age so often singles out for its greatest approbation.

It is tenable to argue, however, that Longfellow's poetry, if less modern, is nevertheless valuable on its own terms. And those terms were understood by the poet and his audience. Longfellow possessed the great popularity Whitman lacked but so assiduously pursued. He reigned when the poet himself was not only a moral guide but, more important, was considered the single authority — Poe's shrillness notwithstanding — on the meaning of his own emotions, perceptions, and, with important implications for his technique, the images and symbols of his poems. From one point of view, the Imagists can be accused of leading the way to the poet's abdicating the public powers of the poetic role held in America by Longfellow and in England by Tennyson. Longfellow wrote, it should be remembered, long before the reader of poetry was encouraged to become, nay, commandeered as, a collaborator in the creation of the meaning of individual poems. If his contemporaries too readily insisted on his predictable moralizing, modern readers have too easily dismissed his poems solely on the basis of that moralizing. Yet any reader who can accept the idea that there was nothing wrong with the way Longfellow thought and can be tolerant of the moral mission of his poetry will discover an impressively large body of poetry combining suggestive symbol, high technical finish, ethical straightforwardness and a clear, responsible poetic voice.

GEORGE MONTEIRO

The
Poetical Works
of
Longfellow

VOICES OF THE NIGHT

Πότνια, πότνια νύξ,
ὑπνοδώτειρα τῶν πολυπόνων βροτῶν,
Ἐρεβόθεν ἴθι· μόλε μόλε κατάπτερος
Ἀγαμεμνόνιον ἐπὶ δόμον·
ὑπὸ γὰρ ἀλγέων, ὑπό τε συμφορᾶς
διοιχόμεθ', οἰχόμεθα.

EURIPIDES.

PRELUDE

The title *Voices of the Night* originally was used by Mr. Longfellow for the poem *Footsteps of Angels;* then he gave it to the first collected volume of his poetry with special application to the group of eight poems following *Prelude.* Here it is confined to this group.

PLEASANT it was, when woods were green
  And winds were soft and low,
To lie amid some sylvan scene,
Where, the long drooping boughs between,
Shadows dark and sunlight sheen
  Alternate come and go ;

Or where the denser grove receives
  No sunlight from above,
But the dark foliage interweaves
In one unbroken roof of leaves,
Underneath whose sloping eaves
  The shadows hardly move.

Beneath some patriarchal tree
  I lay upon the ground ;
His hoary arms uplifted he,
And all the broad leaves over me
Clapped their little hands in glee,
  With one continuous sound ; —

A slumberous sound, a sound that brings
  The feelings of a dream,
As of innumerable wings,
As, when a bell no longer swings,
Faint the hollow murmur rings
  O'er meadow, lake, and stream.

And dreams of that which cannot die,
  Bright visions, came to me,
As lapped in thought I used to lie.
And gaze into the summer sky,
Where the sailing clouds went by,
  Like ships upon the sea ;

Dreams that the soul of youth engage
  Ere Fancy has been quelled ;
Old legends of the monkish page,
Traditions of the saint and sage,
Tales that have the rime of age,
  And chronicles of eld.

And, loving still these quaint old themes,
  Even in the city's throng
I feel the freshness of the streams,
That, crossed by shades and sunny gleams,
Water the green land of dreams,
  The holy land of song.

Therefore, at Pentecost, which brings
  The Spring, clothed like a bride,
When nestling buds unfold their wings,
And bishop's-caps have golden rings,
Musing upon many things,
  I sought the woodlands wide.

The green trees whispered low and mild ;
  It was a sound of joy !
They were my playmates when a child,
And rocked me in their arms so wild !
Still they looked at me and smiled,
  As if I were a boy ;

And ever whispered, mild and low,
  " Come, be a child once more ! "
And waved their long arms to and fro,
And beckoned solemnly and slow ;
Oh, I could not choose but go
  Into the woodlands hoar, —

Into the blithe and breathing air,
  Into the solemn wood,
Solemn and silent everywhere !
Nature with folded hands seemed there,
Kneeling at her evening prayer !
  Like one in prayer I stood.

Before me rose an avenue
　Of tall and sombrous pines ;
Abroad their fan-like branches grew,
And, where the sunshine darted through,
Spread a vapor soft and blue,
　In long and sloping lines.

And, falling on my weary brain,
　Like a fast-falling shower,
The dreams of youth came back again, —
Low lispings of the summer rain,
Dropping on the ripened grain,
　As once upon the flower.

Visions of childhood ! Stay, oh, stay !
　Ye were so sweet and wild !
And distant voices seemed to say,
"It cannot be ! They pass away !
Other themes demand thy lay ;
　Thou art no more a child !

"The land of Song within thee lies,
　Watered by living springs ;
The lids of Fancy's sleepless eyes
Are gates unto that Paradise ;
Holy thoughts, like stars, arise ;
　Its clouds are angels' wings.

"Learn, that henceforth thy song shall be,
　Not mountains capped with snow,
Nor forests sounding like the sea,
Nor rivers flowing ceaselessly,
Where the woodlands bend to see
　The bending heavens below.

"There is a forest where the din
　Of iron branches sounds !
A mighty river roars between,
And whosoever looks therein
Sees the heavens all black with sin,
　Sees not its depths, nor bounds.

"Athwart the swinging branches cast,
　Soft rays of sunshine pour ;
Then comes the fearful wintry blast ;
Our hopes, like withered leaves, fall fast ;
Pallid lips say, ' It is past !
　We can return no more ! '

"Look, then, into thine heart, and write !
　Yes, into Life's deep stream !
All forms of sorrow and delight,
All solemn Voices of the Night,
That can soothe thee, or affright, —
　Be these henceforth thy theme."

HYMN TO THE NIGHT

'Ασπασίη, τρίλλιστος

Composed in the summer of 1839, "while sitting at
my chamber window, on one of the balmiest nights of
the year. I endeavored to reproduce the impression of
the hour and scene."

I HEARD the trailing garments of the
　　Night
　Sweep through her marble halls !
I saw her sable skirts all fringed with
　　light
　From the celestial walls !

I felt her presence, by its spell of might,
　Stoop o'er me from above ;
The calm, majestic presence of the Night,
　As of the one I love.

I heard the sounds of sorrow and delight,
　The manifold, soft chimes,
That fill the haunted chambers of the
　　Night,
　Like some old poet's rhymes.

From the cool cisterns of the midnight air
　My spirit drank repose ;
The fountain of perpetual peace flows
　　there, —
　From those deep cisterns flows.

O holy Night ! from thee I learn to bear
　What man has borne before !
Thou layest thy finger on the lips of Care,
　And they complain no more.

Peace ! Peace ! Orestes-like I breathe this
　　prayer !
　Descend with broad-winged flight,
The welcome, the thrice-prayed for, the
　　most fair,
　The best-beloved Night !

A PSALM OF LIFE

WHAT THE HEART OF THE YOUNG MAN
SAID TO THE PSALMIST

Mr. Longfellow said of this poem : " I kept it some
time in manuscript, unwilling to show it to any one, it
being a voice from my inmost heart, at a time when I
was rallying from depression." Before it was pub-
lished in the *Knickerbocker Magazine*, October, 1838, it
was read by the poet to his college class at the close
of a lecture on Goethe. Its title, though used now

exclusively for this poem, was originally, in the poet's mind, a generic one. He notes from time to time that he has written a psalm, a psalm of death, or another psalm of life. The "psalmist" is thus the poet himself. When printed in the *Knickerbocker* it bore as a motto the lines from Crashaw : —

> Life that shall send
> A challenge to its end,
> And when it comes say, Welcome, friend.

TELL me not, in mournful numbers,
  Life is but an empty dream ! —
For the soul is dead that slumbers,
  And things are not what they seem.

Life is real ! Life is earnest !
  And the grave is not its goal ;
Dust thou art, to dust returnest,
  Was not spoken of the soul.

Not enjoyment, and not sorrow,
  Is our destined end or way ;
But to act, that each to-morrow
  Find us farther than to-day.

Art is long, and Time is fleeting,
  And our hearts, though stout and brave,
Still, like muffled drums, are beating
  Funeral marches to the grave.

In the world's broad field of battle,
  In the bivouac of Life,
Be not like dumb, driven cattle !
  Be a hero in the strife !

Trust no Future, howe'er pleasant !
  Let the dead Past bury its dead !
Act, — act in the living Present !
  Heart within, and God o'erhead !

Lives of great men all remind us
  We can make our lives sublime,
And, departing, leave behind us
  Footprints on the sands of time ;

Footprints, that perhaps another,
  Sailing o'er life's solemn main,
A forlorn and shipwrecked brother,
  Seeing, shall take heart again.

Let us, then, be up and doing,
  With a heart for any fate ;
Still achieving, still pursuing,
  Learn to labor and to wait.

THE REAPER AND THE FLOWERS

In his diary, under date of December 6, 1838, Mr. Longfellow writes : "A beautiful holy morning within me. I was softly excited, I knew not why, and wrote with peace in my heart, and not without tears in my eyes, *The Reaper and the Flowers, a Psalm of Death* I have had an idea of this kind in my mind for a long time, without finding any expression for it in words. This morning it seemed to crystallize at once, without any effort of my own." This psalm was printed in the *Knickerbocker* for January, 1839, with the sub-title *A Psalm of Death*, and with the familiar stanza from Henry Vaughan, beginning : —

> Dear beauteous death ; the jewel of the just !

THERE is a Reaper, whose name is Death,
  And, with his sickle keen,
He reaps the bearded grain at a breath,
  And the flowers that grow between.

"Shall I have naught that is fair ?" saith
  he ;
  "Have naught but the bearded grain ?
Though the breath of these flowers is
  sweet to me,
  I will give them all back again."

He gazed at the flowers with tearful eyes,
  He kissed their drooping leaves ;
It was for the Lord of Paradise
  He bound them in his sheaves.

"My Lord has need of these flowerets
  gay,"
  The Reaper said, and smiled ;
"Dear tokens of the earth are they,
  Where He was once a child.

"They shall all bloom in fields of light,
  Transplanted by my care,
And saints, upon their garments white,
  These sacred blossoms wear."

And the mother gave, in tears and pain,
  The flowers she most did love ;
She knew she should find them all again
  In the fields of light above.

Oh, not in cruelty, not in wrath,
  The Reaper came that day ;
'T was an angel visited the green earth,
  And took the flowers away.

THE LIGHT OF STARS

"This poem was written on a beautiful summer night. The moon, a little strip of silver, was just set-ting behind the groves of Mount Auburn, and the planet Mars blazing in the southeast. There was a singular light in the sky." H. W. L. It was pub-lished in the same number of the *Knickerbocker* as the last, where it was headed *A Second Psalm of Life*, and prefaced by another stanza from the same poem of Vaughan : —

> It glows and glitters in my cloudy breast,
> Like stars upon some gloomy grove,
> Or those faint beams in which this hill is drest
> After the sun's remove.

THE night is come, but not too soon ;
    And sinking silently,
All silently, the little moon
    Drops down behind the sky.

There is no light in earth or heaven
    But the cold light of stars ;
And the first watch of night is given
    To the red planet Mars.

Is it the tender star of love ?
    The star of love and dreams ?
Oh no ! from that blue tent above
    A hero's armor gleams.

And earnest thoughts within me rise,
    When I behold afar,
Suspended in the evening skies,
    The shield of that red star.

O star of strength ! I see thee stand
    And smile upon my pain ;
Thou beckonest with thy mailèd hand,
    And I am strong again.

Within my breast there is no light
    But the cold light of stars ;
I give the first watch of the night
    To the red planet Mars.

The star of the unconquered will,
    He rises in my breast,
Serene, and resolute, and still,
    And calm, and self-possessed.

And thou, too, whosoe'er thou art,
    That readest this brief psalm,
As one by one thy hopes depart,
    Be resolute and calm.

Oh, fear not in a world like this,
    And thou shalt know erelong,

Know how sublime a thing it is
    To suffer and be strong.

FOOTSTEPS OF ANGELS

The poem in its first form bore the title *Evening Shadows*. The reference in the fourth stanza is to the poet's friend and brother-in-law George W. Pierce, of whom he said long after : "I have never ceased to feel that in his death something was taken from my own life which could never be restored." News of his friend's death reached Mr. Longfellow in Heidelberg on Christ-mas eve, 1835, less than a month after the death of Mrs. Longfellow, who is referred to in the sixth and follow-ing stanzas.

WHEN the hours of Day are numbered,
    And the voices of the Night
Wake the better soul, that slumbered,
    To a holy, calm delight ;

Ere the evening lamps are lighted,
    And, like phantoms grim and tall,
Shadows from the fitful firelight
    Dance upon the parlor wall ;

Then the forms of the departed
    Enter at the open door ;
The beloved, the true-hearted,
    Come to visit me once more ;

He, the young and strong, who cherished
    Noble longings for the strife,
By the roadside fell and perished,
    Weary with the march of life !

They, the holy ones and weakly,
    Who the cross of suffering bore,
Folded their pale hands so meekly,
    Spake with us on earth no more !

And with them the Being Beauteous,
    Who unto my youth was given,
More than all things else to love me,
    And is now a saint in heaven.

With a slow and noiseless footstep
    Comes that messenger divine,
Takes the vacant chair beside me,
    Lays her gentle hand in mine.

And she sits and gazes at me
    With those deep and tender eyes,
Like the stars, so still and saint-like,
    Looking downward from the skies.

Uttered not, yet comprehended,
    Is the spirit's voiceless prayer,

Soft rebukes, in blessings ended,
  Breathing from her lips of air.

Oh, though oft depressed and lonely,
  All my fears are laid aside,
If I but remember only
  Such as these have lived and died !

FLOWERS

"I wrote this poem on the 3d of October, 1837, to send with a bouquet of autumnal flowers. I still remember the great delight I took in its composition, and the bright sunshine that streamed in at the southern windows as I walked to and fro, pausing ever and anon to note down my thoughts." H. W. L. It was probably the first poem written by Mr. Longfellow after his establishment at Cambridge.

SPAKE full well, in language quaint and
    olden,
  One who dwelleth by the castled Rhine,
When he called the flowers, so blue and
    golden,
  Stars, that in earth's firmament do shine.

Stars they are, wherein we read our history,
  As astrologers and seers of eld ;
Yet not wrapped about with awful mystery,
  Like the burning stars, which they beheld.

Wondrous truths, and manifold as won-
    drous,
  God hath written in those stars above ;
But not less in the bright flowerets under
    us
  Stands the revelation of his love.

Bright and glorious is that revelation,
  Written all over this great world of ours ;
Making evident our own creation,
  In these stars of earth, these golden
    flowers.

And the Poet, faithful and far-seeing,
  Sees, alike in stars and flowers, a part
Of the self-same, universal being,
  Which is throbbing in his brain and heart.

Gorgeous flowerets in the sunlight shining,
  Blossoms flaunting in the eye of day,
Tremulous leaves, with soft and silver lining,
  Buds that open only to decay ;

Brilliant hopes, all woven in gorgeous tis-
    sues,
  Flaunting gayly in the golden light ;

Large desires, with most uncertain issues,
  Tender wishes, blossoming at night !

These in flowers and men are more than
    seeming,
  Workings are they of the self - same
    powers,
Which the Poet, in no idle dreaming,
  Seeth in himself and in the flowers.

Everywhere about us are they glowing,
  Some like stars, to tell us Spring is born ;
Others, their blue eyes with tears o'erflow-
    ing,
  Stand like Ruth amid the golden corn ;

Not alone in Spring's armorial bearing,
  And in Summer's green-emblazoned field,
But in arms of brave old Autumn's wearing,
  In the centre of his brazen shield ;

Not alone in meadows and green alleys,
  On the mountain-top, and by the brink
Of sequestered pools in woodland valleys,
  Where the slaves of nature stoop to
    drink ;

Not alone in her vast dome of glory,
  Not on graves of bird and beast alone,
But in old cathedrals, high and hoary,
  On the tombs of heroes, carved in stone;

In the cottage of the rudest peasant,
  In ancestral homes, whose crumbling
    towers,
Speaking of the Past unto the Present,
  Tell us of the ancient Games of Flowers ;

In all places, then, and in all seasons,
  Flowers expand their light and soul-like
    wings,
Teaching us, by most persuasive reasons,
  How akin they are to human things.

And with childlike, credulous affection,
  We behold their tender buds expand ;
Emblems of our own great resurrection,
  Emblems of the bright and better land.

THE BELEAGUERED CITY

Mr. Samuel Longfellow states that the suggestion of the poem came from a note in one of the volumes of Scott's *Border Minstrelsy :* "Similar to this was the *Nacht Lager*, or midnight camp, which seemed nightly to beleaguer the walls of Prague, but which disappeared upon the recitation of [certain] magical words." The title of the poem served also as that of a remarkable prose sketch by Mrs. Oliphant.

I HAVE read, in some old, marvellous tale,
  Some legend strange and vague,
That a midnight host of spectres pale
  Beleaguered the walls of Prague.

Beside the Moldau's rushing stream,
  With the wan moon overhead,
There stood, as in an awful dream,
  The army of the dead.

White as a sea-fog, landward bound,
  The spectral camp was seen,
And, with a sorrowful, deep sound,
  The river flowed between.

No other voice nor sound was there,
  No drum, nor sentry's pace ;
The mist-like banners clasped the air
  As clouds with clouds embrace.

But when the old cathedral bell
  Proclaimed the morning prayer,
The white pavilions rose and fell
  On the alarmèd air.

Down the broad valley fast and far
  The troubled army fled ;
Up rose the glorious morning star,
  The ghastly host was dead.

I have read, in the marvellous heart of man,
  That strange and mystic scroll,
That an army of phantoms vast and wan
  Beleaguer the human soul.

Encamped beside Life's rushing stream,
  In Fancy's misty light,
Gigantic shapes and shadows gleam
  Portentous through the night.

Upon its midnight battle-ground
  The spectral camp is seen,
And, with a sorrowful, deep sound,
  Flows the River of Life between.

No other voice nor sound is there,
  In the army of the grave ;
No other challenge breaks the air,
  But the rushing of Life's wave.

And when the solemn and deep church-bell
  Entreats the soul to pray,

The midnight phantoms feel the spell,
  The shadows sweep away.

Down the broad Vale of Tears afar
  The spectral camp is fled ;
Faith shineth as a morning star,
  Our ghastly fears are dead.

MIDNIGHT MASS FOR THE DYING YEAR

Published in the *Knickerbocker* as *The Fifth Psalm;* the author also calls it in his diary *An Autumnal Chant.*

YES, the Year is growing old,
  And his eye is pale and bleared !
Death, with frosty hand and cold,
  Plucks the old man by the beard,
    Sorely, sorely !

The leaves are falling, falling,
  Solemnly and slow ;
Caw ! caw ! the rooks are calling,
  It is a sound of woe,
    A sound of woe !

Through woods and mountain passes
  The winds, like anthems, roll ;
They are chanting solemn masses,
  Singing, " Pray for this poor soul,
    Pray, pray ! "

And the hooded clouds, like friars,
  Tell their beads in drops of rain,
And patter their doleful prayers ;
  But their prayers are all in vain,
    All in vain !

There he stands in the foul weather,
  The foolish, fond Old Year,
Crowned with wild flowers and with heathe
  Like weak, despisèd Lear,
    A king, a king !

Then comes the summer-like day,
  Bids the old man rejoice !
His joy ! his last ! Oh, the old man gra
  Loveth that ever-soft voice,
    Gentle and low.

To the crimson woods he saith,
  To the voice gentle and low
Of the soft air, like a daughter's breath,
  " Pray do not mock me so !
    Do not laugh at me ! "

And now the sweet day is dead ;
  Cold in his arms it lies ;
No stain from its breath is spread
  Over the glassy skies,
    No mist or stain !

Then, too, the Old Year dieth,
  And the forests utter a moan,
Like the voice of one who crieth
  In the wilderness alone,
    " Vex not his ghost ! "

Then comes, with an awful roar,
  Gathering and sounding on,
The storm-wind from Labrador,

  The wind Euroclydon,
    The storm-wind !

Howl ! howl ! and from the forest
  Sweep the red leaves away !
Would the sins that thou abhorrest,
  O soul ! could thus decay,
    And be swept away !

For there shall come a mightier blast,
  There shall be a darker day ;
And the stars, from heaven down-cast
  Like red leaves be swept away !
    Kyrie, eleyson !
    Christe, eleyson !

EARLIER POEMS

" These poems were written for the most part during my college life, and all of them before the age of nineteen. Some have found their way into schools, and seem to be successful. Others lead a vagabond and precarious existence in the corners of newspapers ; or have changed their names and run away to seek their fortunes beyond the sea. I say, with the Bishop of Avranches on a similar occasion : ' I cannot be displeased to see these children of mine, which I have neglected, and almost exposed, brought from their wanderings in lanes and alleys, and safely lodged, in order to go forth into the world together in a more decorous garb.' " This note was prefixed by Mr. Longfellow to the following group of poems when published in *Voices of the Night*. " The first five " of the following, Mr. Longfellow says elsewhere in a manuscript note, " were written during my last year in college, in No. 27 Maine Hall, whose windows looked out upon the pine groves to which allusion is made in *L'Envoi*." In the appendix may be found a fuller collection of poems of this class.

AN APRIL DAY

WHEN the warm sun, that brings
Seed-time and harvest, has returned again,
'T is sweet to visit the still wood, where
  springs
  The first flower of the plain.

I love the season well,
When forest glades are teeming with bright
  forms,
Nor dark and many-folded clouds foretell
  The coming-on of storms.

From the earth's loosened mould
The sapling draws its sustenance, and
  thrives ;
Though stricken to the heart with winter's
  cold,
  The drooping tree revives.

The softly-warbled song
Comes from the pleasant woods, and colored
  wings
Glance quick in the bright sun, that moves
  along
  The forest openings.

When the bright sunset fills
The silver woods with light, the green slope
  throws
Its shadows in the hollows of the hills,
  And wide the upland glows.

And when the eve is born,
In the blue lake the sky, o'er-reaching
  far,
Is hollowed out, and the moon dips her
  horn,
  And twinkles many a star.

Inverted in the tide
Stand the gray rocks, and trembling shadows throw,
And the fair trees look over, side by
  side,
  And see themselves below.

Sweet April ! many a thought
Is wedded unto thee, as hearts are wed ;
Nor shall they fail, till, to its autumn
  brought,
  Life's golden fruit is shed.

AUTUMN

WITH what a glory comes and goes the
        year !
The buds of spring, those beautiful har-
        bingers
Of sunny skies and cloudless times, enjoy
Life's newness, and earth's garniture
        spread out ;
And when the silver habit of the clouds
Comes down upon the autumn sun, and
        with
A sober gladness the old year takes up
His bright inheritance of golden fruits,
A pomp and pageant fill the splendid
        scene.

There is a beautiful spirit breathing now
Its mellow richness on the clustered trees,
And, from a beaker full of richest dyes,
Pouring new glory on the autumn woods,
And dipping in warm light the pillared
        clouds.
Morn on the mountain, like a summer
        bird,
Lifts up her purple wing, and in the vales
The gentle wind, a sweet and passionate
        wooer,
Kisses the blushing leaf, and stirs up life
Within the solemn woods of ash deep-crim-
        soned,
And silver beech, and maple yellow-leaved,
Where Autumn, like a faint old man, sits
        down
By the wayside a - weary.   Through the
        trees
The golden robin moves.   The purple
        finch,
That on wild cherry and red cedar feeds,
A winter bird, comes with its plaintive
        whistle,
And pecks by the witch-hazel, whilst aloud
From cottage roofs the warbling bluebird
        sings,
And merrily, with oft-repeated stroke,
Sounds from the threshing-floor the busy
        flail.

Oh, what a glory doth this world put
        on
For him who, with a fervent heart, goes
        forth

Under the bright and glorious sky, and
        looks
On duties well performed, and days well
        spent !
For him the wind, ay, and the yellow
        leaves,
Shall have a voice, and give him eloquent
        teachings.
He shall so hear the solemn hymn that
        Death
Has lifted up for all, that he shall go
To his long resting-place without a tear.

WOODS IN WINTER

WHEN winter winds are piercing chill,
        And through the hawthorn blows the
        gale,
With solemn feet I tread the hill,
        That overbrows the lonely vale.

O'er the bare upland, and away
        Through the long reach of desert woods,
The embracing sunbeams chastely play,
        And gladden these deep solitudes.

Where, twisted round the barren oak,
        The summer vine in beauty clung,
And summer winds the stillness broke,
        The crystal icicle is hung.

Where, from their frozen urns, mute
        springs
        Pour out the river's gradual tide,
Shrilly the skater's iron rings,
        And voices fill the woodland side.

Alas ! how changed from the fair scene,
        When birds sang out their mellow lay,
And winds were soft, and woods were
        green,
        And the song ceased not with the day !

But still wild music is abroad,
        Pale, desert woods ! within your crowd ;
And gathering winds, in hoarse accord,
        Amid the vocal reeds pipe loud.

Chill airs and wintry winds ! my ear
        Has grown familiar with your song ;
I hear it in the opening year,
        I listen, and it cheers me long.

HYMN OF THE MORAVIAN NUNS OF BETHLEHEM

AT THE CONSECRATION OF PULASKI'S BANNER

The historical basis of the poem is discussed in a note at the end of this volume.

WHEN the dying flame of day
Through the chancel shot its ray,
Far the glimmering tapers shed
Faint light on the cowlèd head ;
And the censer burning swung,
Where, before the altar, hung
The crimson banner, that with prayer
Had been consecrated there.
And the nuns' sweet hymn was heard the
    while,
Sung low, in the dim, mysterious aisle.

" Take thy banner ! May it wave
  Proudly o'er the good and brave ;
  When the battle's distant wail
  Breaks the sabbath of our vale,
  When the clarion's music thrills
  To the hearts of these lone hills,
  When the spear in conflict shakes,
  And the strong lance shivering breaks.

" Take thy banner ! and, beneath
  The battle-cloud's encircling wreath,
  Guard it, till our homes are free !
  Guard it ! God will prosper thee !
  In the dark and trying hour,
  In the breaking forth of power,
  In the rush of steeds and men,
  His right hand will shield thee then.

" Take thy banner ! But when night
  Closes round the ghastly fight,
  If the vanquished warrior bow,
  Spare him ! By our holy vow,
  By our prayers and many tears,
  By the mercy that endears,
  Spare him ! he our love hath shared !
  Spare him ! as thou wouldst be spared !

" Take thy banner ! and if e'er
  Thou shouldst press the soldier's bier,
  And the muffled drum should beat
  To the tread of mournful feet,
  Then this crimson flag shall be
  Martial cloak and shroud for thee."

The warrior took that banner proud,
And it was his martial cloak and shroud !

SUNRISE ON THE HILLS

I STOOD upon the hills, when heaven's
    wide arch
Was glorious with the sun's returning
    march,
And woods were brightened, and soft gales
Went forth to kiss the sun-clad vales.
The clouds were far beneath me ; bathed
    in light,
They gathered midway round the wooded
    height,
And, in their fading glory, shone
Like hosts in battle overthrown,
As many a pinnacle, with shifting glance,
Through the gray mist thrust up its shat-
    tered lance,
And rocking on the cliff was left
The dark pine blasted, bare, and cleft.
The veil of cloud was lifted, and below
Glowed the rich valley, and the river's flow
Was darkened by the forest's shade,
Or glistened in the white cascade ;
Where upward, in the mellow blush of day,
The noisy bittern wheeled his spiral way.

I heard the distant waters dash,
I saw the current whirl and flash,
And richly, by the blue lake's silver beach,
The woods were bending with a silent
    reach.
Then o'er the vale, with gentle swell,
The music of the village bell
Came sweetly to the echo-giving hills ;
And the wild horn, whose voice the wood-
    land fills,
Was ringing to the merry shout
That faint and far the glen sent out,
Where, answering to the sudden shot, thin
    smoke,
Through thick-leaved branches, from the
    dingle broke.

If thou art worn and hard beset
With sorrows, that thou wouldst forget,
If thou wouldst read a lesson, that will
    keep
Thy heart from fainting and thy soul from
    sleep,
Go to the woods and hills ! No tears
Dim the sweet look that Nature wears.

THE SPIRIT OF POETRY

This and the following poem were written in Portland immediately after Mr. Longfellow left college in the autumn of 1825.

THERE is a quiet spirit in these woods,
That dwells where'er the gentle south-wind
    blows ;
Where, underneath the white-thorn in the
    glade,
The wild flowers bloom, or, kissing the
    soft air,
The leaves above their sunny palms out-
    spread.
With what a tender and impassioned voice
It fills the nice and delicate ear of thought,
When the fast ushering star of morning
    comes
O'er - riding the gray hills with golden
    scarf ;
Or when the cowled and dusky-sandalled
    Eve,
In mourning weeds, from out the western
    gate,
Departs with silent pace ! That spirit
    moves
In the green valley, where the silver brook,
From its full laver, pours the white cas-
    cade ;
And, babbling low amid the tangled woods,
Slips down through moss-grown stones with
    endless laughter.
And frequent, on the everlasting hills,
Its feet go forth, when it doth wrap itself
In all the dark embroidery of the storm,
And shouts the stern, strong wind. And
    here, amid
The silent majesty of these deep woods,
Its presence shall uplift thy thoughts from
    earth,
As to the sunshine and the pure, bright air
Their tops the green trees lift. Hence
    gifted bards
Have ever loved the calm and quiet
    shades.
For them there was an eloquent voice in
    all
The sylvan pomp of woods, the golden sun,
The flowers, the leaves, the river on its
    way,
Blue skies, and silver clouds, and gentle
    winds,
The swelling upland, where the sidelong
    sun

Aslant the wooded slope, at evening,
    goes,
Groves, through whose broken roof the
    sky looks in,
Mountain, and shattered cliff, and sunny
    vale,
The distant lake, fountains, and mighty
    trees,
In many a lazy syllable, repeating
Their old poetic legends to the wind.

And this is the sweet spirit, that doth
    fill
The world ; and, in these wayward days of
    youth,
My busy fancy oft embodies it,
As a bright image of the light and beauty
That dwell in nature ; of the heavenly
    forms
We worship in our dreams, and the soft
    hues
That stain the wild bird's wing, and flush
    the clouds
When the sun sets. Within her tender
    eye
The heaven of April, with its changing
    light,
And when it wears the blue of May, is
    hung,
And on her lip the rich, red rose. Her
    hair
Is like the summer tresses of the trees,
When twilight makes them brown, and on
    her cheek
Blushes the richness of an autumn sky,
With ever - shifting beauty. Then her
    breath,
It is so like the gentle air of Spring,
As, from the morning's dewy flowers, it
    comes
Full of their fragrance, that it is a joy
To have it round us, and her silver voice
Is the rich music of a summer bird,
Heard in the still night, with its passionate
    cadence.

BURIAL OF THE MINNISINK

ON sunny slope and beechen swell,
The shadowed light of evening fell ;
And, where the maple's leaf was brown,
With soft and silent lapse came down,
The glory, that the wood receives,
At sunset, in its golden leaves.

Far upward in the mellow light
Rose the blue hills.   One cloud of white,
Around a far uplifted cone,
In the warm blush of evening shone ;
An image of the silver lakes,
By which the Indian's soul awakes.

But soon a funeral hymn was heard
Where the soft breath of evening stirred
The tall, gray forest ; and a band
Of stern in heart, and strong in hand,
Came winding down beside the wave,
To lay the red chief in his grave.

They sang, that by his native bowers
He stood, in the last moon of flowers,
And thirty snows had not yet shed
Their glory on the warrior's head ;
But, as the summer fruit decays,
So died he in those naked days.

A dark cloak of the roebuck's skin
Covered the warrior, and within
Its heavy folds the weapons, made
For the hard toils of war, were laid ;
The cuirass, woven of plaited reeds,
And the broad belt of shells and beads.

Before, a dark-haired virgin train
Chanted the death dirge of the slain ;
Behind, the long procession came
Of hoary men and chiefs of fame,
With heavy hearts, and eyes of grief,
Leading the war-horse of their chief.

Stripped of his proud and martial dress,
Uncurbed, unreined, and riderless,
With darting eye, and nostril spread,
And heavy and impatient tread,

He came ; and oft that eye so proud
Asked for his rider in the crowd.

They buried the dark chief ; they freed
Beside the grave his battle steed ;
And swift an arrow cleaved its way
To his stern heart !   One piercing neigh
Arose, and, on the dead man's plain,
The rider grasps his steed again.

L'ENVOI

This poem was written as a poetical summary of the volume *Voices of the Night*, which it closed, referring in its three parts to the three divisions of that volume.

YE voices, that arose
After the Evening's close,
And whispered to my restless heart repose !

Go, breathe it in the ear
Of all who doubt and fear,
And say to them, " Be of good cheer ! "

Ye sounds, so low and calm,
That in the groves of balm
Seemed to me like an angel's psalm !

Go, mingle yet once more
With the perpetual roar
Of the pine forest, dark and hoar !

Tongues of the dead, not lost,
But speaking from death's frost,
Like fiery tongues at Pentecost !

Glimmer, as funeral lamps,
Amid the chills and damps
Of the vast plain where Death encamps !

BALLADS AND OTHER POEMS

THE SKELETON IN ARMOR

The volume of *Ballads and other Poems* was published December 19, 1841, and contained all the verse which Mr. Longfellow had written since the publication of *Voices of the Night*, with the important exception of *The Spanish Student*. Besides the pieces here included under this division, the original volume contained two ballads translated from the German, and also *The Children of the Lord's Supper*, which will be found under the general division *Translations* near the close of this volume. The historical basis of *The Skeleton in Armor* is discussed in the *Notes*. This ballad, when first published in the *Knickerbocker* for January, 1841, was furnished with marginal notes after the manner of Coleridge's *The Ancient Mariner*, but in reprinting it in his volume the poet wisely discarded an apparatus, which, unlike Coleridge's, was merely a running index to the poem.

" SPEAK ! speak ! thou fearful guest !
Who, with thy hollow breast
Still in rude armor drest,
    Comest to daunt me !
Wrapt not in Eastern balms,
But with thy fleshless palms
Stretched, as if asking alms,
    Why dost thou haunt me ? "

Then, from those cavernous eyes
Pale flashes seemed to rise,
As when the Northern skies
    Gleam in December ;
And, like the water's flow
Under December's snow,
Came a dull voice of woe
    From the heart's chamber.

" I was a Viking old !
My deeds, though manifold,
No Skald in song has told,
    No Saga taught thee !
Take heed, that in thy verse
Thou dost the tale rehearse,
Else dread a dead man's curse ;
    For this I sought thee.

" Far in the Northern Land,
By the wild Baltic's strand,
I, with my childish hand,
    Tamed the gerfalcon ;
And, with my skates fast-bound,
Skimmed the half-frozen Sound,
That the poor whimpering hound
    Trembled to walk on.

" Oft to his frozen lair
Tracked I the grisly bear,
While from my path the hare
    Fled like a shadow ;
Oft through the forest dark
Followed the were-wolf's bark,
Until the soaring lark
    Sang from the meadow.

" But when I older grew,
Joining a corsair's crew,
O'er the dark sea I flew
    With the marauders.
Wild was the life we led ;
Many the souls that sped,
Many the hearts that bled,
    By our stern orders.

" Many a wassail-bout
Wore the long Winter out ;
Often our midnight shout
    Set the cocks crowing,
As we the Berserk's tale
Measured in cups of ale,
Draining the oaken pail,
    Filled to o'erflowing.

" Once as I told in glee
Tales of the stormy sea,
Soft eyes did gaze on me,
    Burning yet tender ;
And as the white stars shine
On the dark Norway pine,
On that dark heart of mine
    Fell their soft splendor.

" I wooed the blue-eyed maid,
Yielding, yet half afraid,
And in the forest's shade
    Our vows were plighted.
Under its loosened vest
Fluttered her little breast,
Like birds within their nest
    By the hawk frighted.

" Bright in her father's hall
Shields gleamed upon the wall,
Loud sang the minstrels all,
    Chanting his glory ;
When of old Hildebrand
I asked his daughter's hand,
Mute did the minstrels stand
    To hear my story.

" While the brown ale he quaffed,
Loud then the champion laughed,
And as the wind-gusts waft
    The sea-foam brightly,
So the loud laugh of scorn,
Out of those lips unshorn,
From the deep drinking-horn
    Blew the foam lightly.

" She was a Prince's child,
I but a Viking wild,
And though she blushed and smiled,
    I was discarded !
Should not the dove so white
Follow the sea-mew's flight,
Why did they leave that night
    Her nest unguarded ?

" Scarce had I put to sea,
Bearing the maid with me,
Fairest of all was she
    Among the Norsemen !
When on the white sea-strand.
Waving his armèd hand,
Saw we old Hildebrand,
    With twenty horsemen.

" Then launched they to the blast,
Bent like a reed each mast,
Yet we were gaining fast,
    When the wind failed us ;
And with a sudden flaw
Came round the gusty Skaw,
So that our foe we saw
    Laugh as he hailed us.

" And as to catch the gale
Round veered the flapping sail,
'Death !' was the helmsman's hail,
    ' Death without quarter ! '
Mid-ships with iron keel
Struck we her ribs of steel ;
Down her black hulk did reel
    Through the black water !

" As with his wings aslant,
Sails the fierce cormorant,
Seeking some rocky haunt,
    With his prey laden, —
So toward the open main,
Beating to sea again,
Through the wild hurricane,
    Bore I the maiden.

" Three weeks we westward bore,
And when the storm was o'er,
Cloud-like we saw the shore
    Stretching to leeward ;
There for my lady's bower
Built I the lofty tower,
Which, to this very hour,
    Stands looking seaward.

" There lived we many years ;
Time dried the maiden's tears ;
She had forgot her fears,
    She was a mother :
Death closed her mild blue eyes,
Under that tower she lies ;
Ne'er shall the sun arise
    On such another !

" Still grew my bosom then,
Still as a stagnant fen !
Hateful to me were men,
    The sunlight hateful !
In the vast forest here,
Clad in my warlike gear,
Fell I upon my spear,
    Oh, death was grateful !

" Thus, seamed with many scars,
Bursting these prison bars,
Up to its native stars
    My soul ascended !
There from the flowing bowl
Deep drinks the warrior's soul,
Skoal ! to the Northland ! *skoal !* "
    Thus the tale ended.

THE WRECK OF THE HESPERUS

Originally published· in Park Benjamin's mammoth
sheet, *The New World.* Of the composition of the bal-
lad Mr. Longfellow writes as follows in his diary, under
date of December 30, 1839 : " I wrote last evening a no-
tice of Allston's poems. After which I sat till twelve
o'clock by my fire, smoking, when suddenly it came
into my mind to write *The Ballad of the Schooner Hes-
perus ;* which I accordingly did. Then I went to bed,
but could not sleep. New thoughts were running in
my mind, and I got up to add them to the ballad. It
was three by the clock. I then went to bed and fell
asleep. I feel pleased with the ballad. It hardly cost
me an effort. It did not come into my mind by lines,
but by stanzas."

IT was the schooner Hesperus,
    That sailed the wintry sea ;
And the skipper had taken his little .daugh-
        tèr,
    To bear him company.

Blue were her eyes as the fairy-flax,
    Her cheeks like the dawn of day,
And her bosom white as the hawthorn buds,
    That ope in the month of May.

The skipper he stood beside the helm,
    His pipe was in his mouth,
And he watched how the veering flaw did
        blow
    The smoke now West, now South.

Then up and spake an old Sailòr,
    Had sailed to the Spanish Main,
" I pray thee, put into yonder port,
    For I fear a hurricane.

" Last night, the moon had a golden ring,
    And to-night no moon we see ! "
The skipper, he blew a whiff from his pipe,
    And a scornful laugh laughed he.

Colder and louder blew the wind,
    A gale from the Northeast,
The snow fell hissing in the brine,
    And the billows frothed like yeast.

Down came the storm, and smote amain
   The vessel in its strength ;
She shuddered and paused, like a frighted
     steed,
   Then leaped her cable's length.

"Come hither ! come hither ! my little
     daughter,
And do not tremble so ;
For I can weather the roughest gale
   That ever wind did blow."

He wrapped her warm in his seaman's coat
   Against the stinging blast ;
He cut a rope from a broken spar,
   And bound her to the mast.

"O father ! I hear the church-bells ring,
   Oh say, what may it be ? "
" 'T is a fog-bell on a rock-bound coast ! " —
   And he steered for the open sea.

"O father ! I hear the sound of guns,
   Oh say, what may it be ? "
" Some ship in distress, that cannot live
   In such an angry sea ! "

"O father ! I see a gleaming light,
   Oh say, what may it be ? "
But the father answered never a word,
   A frozen corpse was he.

Lashed to the helm, all stiff and stark,
   With his face turned to the skies,
The lantern gleamed through the gleaming
     snow
   On his fixed and glassy eyes.

Then the maiden clasped her hands and
     prayed
   That savèd she might be ;
And she thought of Christ, who stilled the
     wave,
   On the Lake of Galilee.

And fast through the midnight dark and
     drear,
   Through the whistling sleet and snow,
Like a sheeted ghost, the vessel swept
   Tow'rds the reef of Norman's Woe.

And ever the fitful gusts between
   A sound came from the land ;
It was the sound of the trampling surf
   On the rocks and the hard sea-sand.

The breakers were right beneath her bows,
   She drifted a dreary wreck,
And a whooping billow swept the crew
   Like icicles from her deck.

She struck where the white and fleecy waves
   Looked soft as carded wool,
But the cruel rocks, they gored her side
   Like the horns of an angry bull.

Her rattling shrouds, all sheathed in ice,
   With the masts went by the board ;
Like a vessel of glass, she stove and sank,
   Ho ! ho ! the breakers roared !

At daybreak, on the bleak sea-beach,
   A fisherman stood aghast,
To see the form of a maiden fair,
   Lashed close to a drifting mast.

The salt sea was frozen on her breast,
   The salt tears in her eyes ;
And he saw her hair, like the brown sea-
     weed,
   On the billows fall and rise.

Such was the wreck of the Hesperus,
   In the midnight and the snow !
Christ save us all from a death like this,
   On the reef of Norman's Woe !

THE VILLAGE BLACKSMITH

In the autumn of 1839 Mr. Longfellow was writing
psalms, as seen above, and he notes in his diary, October
5th : " Wrote a new Psalm of Life. It is *The Village
Blacksmith.*" A year later he was thinking of ballads,
and he writes to his father, October 25th : " My pen
has not been very prolific of late ; only a little poetry
has trickled from it. There will be a kind of ballad on
a Blacksmith in the next *Knickerbocker* [November,
1840], which you may consider, if you please, as a song
in praise of your ancestor at Newbury [the first Stephen
Longfellow]." It is hardly to be supposed, however,
that the form of the poem had been changed during the
year. The suggestion of the poem came from the
smithy which the poet passed daily, and which stood
beneath a horse-chestnut tree not far from his house in
Cambridge. The tree, against the protests of Mr. Long-
fellow and others, was removed in 1876, on the ground
that it imperilled drivers of heavy loads who passed
under it.

UNDER a spreading chestnut-tree
   The village smithy stands ;
The smith, a mighty man is he,
   With large and sinewy hands ;
And the muscles of his brawny arms
   Are strong as iron bands.

His hair is crisp, and black, and long,
  His face is like the tan ;
His brow is wet with honest sweat,
  He earns whate'er he can,
And looks the whole world in the face,
  For he owes not any man.

Week in, week out, from morn till night,
  You can hear his bellows blow ;
You can hear him swing his heavy sledge,
  With measured beat and slow,
Like a sexton ringing the village bell,
  When the evening sun is low.

And children coming home from school
  Look in at the open door ;
They love to see the flaming forge,
  And hear the bellows roar,
And catch the burning sparks that fly
  Like chaff from a threshing-floor.

He goes on Sunday to the church,
  And sits among his boys ;
He hears the parson pray and preach,
  He hears his daughter's voice,
Singing in the village choir,
  And it makes his heart rejoice.

It sounds to him like her mother's voice,
  Singing in Paradise !
He needs must think of her once more,
  How in the grave she lies ;
And with his hard, rough hand he wipes
  A tear out of his eyes.

Toiling, — rejoicing, — sorrowing,
  Onward through life he goes ;
Each morning sees some task begin,
  Each evening sees it close ;
Something attempted, something done,
  Has earned a night's repose.

Thanks, thanks to thee, my worthy friend,
  For the lesson thou hast taught !
Thus at the flaming forge of life
  Our fortunes must be wrought ;
Thus on its sounding anvil shaped
  Each burning deed and thought.

ENDYMION

THE rising moon has hid the stars ;
  Her level rays, like golden bars,

Lie on the landscape green,
  With shadows brown between.

And silver white the river gleams,
As if Diana, in her dreams
  Had dropt her silver bow
  Upon the meadows low.

On such a tranquil night as this,
She woke Endymion with a kiss,
  When, sleeping in the grove,
  He dreamed not of her love.

Like Dian's kiss, unasked, unsought,
Love gives itself, but is not bought ;
  Nor voice, nor sound betrays
  Its deep, impassioned gaze.

It comes, — the beautiful, the free,
The crown of all humanity, —
  In silence and alone
  To seek the elected one.

It lifts the boughs, whose shadows deep
Are Life's oblivion, the soul's sleep,
  And kisses the closed eyes
  Of him who slumbering lies.

O weary hearts ! O slumbering eyes !
O drooping souls, whose destinies
  Are fraught with fear and pain,
  Ye shall be loved again !

No one is so accursed by fate,
No one so utterly desolate,
  But some heart, though unknown,
  Responds unto his own.

Responds, — as if with unseen wings,
An angel touched its quivering strings ;
  And whispers, in its song,
  "Where hast thou stayed so long ? "

IT IS NOT ALWAYS MAY

No hay pájaros en los nidos de antaño.
  Spanish Proverb;

THE sun is bright, — the air is clear,
  The darting swallows soar and sing,
And from the stately elms I hear
  The bluebird prophesying Spring.

So blue yon winding river flows,
  It seems an outlet from the sky,

Where, waiting till the west wind blows,
  The freighted clouds at anchor lie.

All things are new ; — the buds, the leaves,
  That gild the elm-tree's nodding crest,
And even the nest beneath the eaves ; —
  There are no birds in last year's nest !

All things rejoice in youth and love,
  The fulness of their first delight !
And learn from the soft heavens above
  The melting tenderness of night.

Maiden, that read'st this simple rhyme,
  Enjoy thy youth, it will not stay ;
Enjoy the fragrance of thy prime,
  For oh, it is not always May !

Enjoy the Spring of Love and Youth,
  To some good angel leave the rest ;
For Time will teach thee soon the truth,
  There are no birds in last year's nest !

THE RAINY DAY

Written at the old home in Portland.

The day is cold, and dark, and dreary ;
It rains, and the wind is never weary ;
The vine still clings to the mouldering
    wall,
But at every gust the dead leaves fall,
  And the day is dark and dreary.

My life is cold, and dark, and dreary ;
It rains, and the wind is never weary ;
My thoughts still cling to the mouldering
    Past,
But the hopes of youth fall thick in the
    blast,
  And the days are dark and dreary.

Be still, sad heart ! and cease repining ;
Behind the clouds is the sun still shining ;
Thy fate is the common fate of all,
Into each life some rain must fall,
  Some days must be dark and dreary.

GOD'S-ACRE

"I would like to be *burned*, not *buried*," Mr. Long-
fellow notes, and in a letter to Mr. Ward, who had the
poem in his hands for publication, he writes: "I here
add a concluding stanza for *God's-Acre*, which I think

improves the piece and rounds it off more perfectly than
before, — the thought no longer resting on the cold
furrow, but on the waving harvest beyond : —

  Green gate of Paradise ! let in the sun !
    Unclose thy portals, that we may behold
  Those fields elysian, where bright rivers run,
    And waving harvests bend like seas of gold.

The poem was published with this additional stanza in
The Democratic Review for December, 1841, but when
it came to be added to the volume the stanza was
dropped.

I like that ancient Saxon phrase, which
    calls
  The burial-ground God's-Acre ! It is
    just ;
It consecrates each grave within its walls,
  And breathes a benison o'er the sleeping
    dust.

God's-Acre ! Yes, that blessed name im-
    parts
  Comfort to those who in the grave have
    sown
The seed that they had garnered in their
    hearts,
  Their bread of life, alas ! no more their
    own.

Into its furrows shall we all be cast,
  In the sure faith, that we shall rise again
At the great harvest, when the archangel's
    blast
  Shall winnow like a fan, the chaff and
    grain.

Then shall the good stand in immortal
    bloom,
  In the fair gardens of that second birth ;
And each bright blossom mingle its perfume
  With that of flowers, which never bloomed
    on earth.

With thy rude ploughshare, Death, turn
    up the sod,
  And spread the furrow for the seed we
    sow ;
This is the field and Acre of our God,
  This is the place where human harvests
    grow.

TO THE RIVER CHARLES

The three friends hinted at in the eighth stanza were
Charles Sumner, Charles Folsom, and Charles Amory.

River ! that in silence windest
  Through the meadows, bright and free,

Till at length thy rest thou findest
  In the bosom of the sea !

Four long years of mingled feeling,
  Half in rest, and half in strife,
I have seen thy waters stealing
  Onward, like the stream of life

Thou hast taught me, Silent River !
  Many a lesson, deep and long ;
Thou hast been a generous giver ;
  I can give thee but a song.

Oft in sadness and in illness,
  I have watched thy current glide,
Till the beauty of its stillness
  Overflowed me, like a tide.

And in better hours and brighter,
  When I saw thy waters gleam,
I have felt my heart beat lighter,
  And leap onward with thy stream.

Not for this alone I love thee,
  Nor because thy waves of blue
From celestial seas above thee
  Take their own celestial hue.

Where yon shadowy woodlands hide thee,
  And thy waters disappear,
Friends I love have dwelt beside thee,
  And have made thy margin dear.

More than this ; — thy name reminds me
  Of three friends, all true and tried ;
And that name, like magic, binds me
  Closer, closer to thy side.

Friends my soul with joy remembers !
  How like quivering flames they start,
When I fan the living embers
  On the hearth-stone of my heart !

T is for this, thou Silent River !
  That my spirit leans to thee ;
Thou hast been a generous giver,
  Take this idle song from me.

BLIND BARTIMEUS

Written November 3, 1841. Mr. Longfellow writes under that date to Mr. Ward : "I was reading this morning, just after breakfast, the tenth chapter of Mark, in Greek, the last seven verses of which contain the story of blind Bartimeus, and always seemed to me remarkable for their beauty. At once the whole scene presented itself to my mind in lively colors, — the walls of Jericho, the cold wind through the gateway, the ragged, blind beggar, his shrill cry, the tumultuous crowd, the serene Christ, the miracle ; and these things took the form I have given them above, where, perforce, I have retained the striking Greek expressions of entreaty, comfort, and healing ; though I am well aware that Greek was not spoken at Jericho. . . . I think I shall add to the title, 'supposed to be written by a monk of the Middle Ages,' as it is in the legend style."

BLIND Bartimeus at the gates
Of Jericho in darkness waits ;
He hears the crowd ; — he hears a breath
Say, " It is Christ of Nazareth ! "
And calls, in tones of agony,
Ἰησοῦ, ἐλέησόν με !

The thronging multitudes increase ;
Blind Bartimeus, hold thy peace !
But still, above the noisy crowd,
The beggar's cry is shrill and loud ;
Until they say, " He calleth thee ! "
Θάρσει· ἔγειραι, φωνεῖ σε !

Then saith the Christ, as silent stands
The crowd, " What wilt thou at my
    hands ? "
And he replies, " Oh, give me light !
Rabbi, restore the blind man's sight."
And Jesus answers, Ὕπαγε·
Ἡ πίστις σου σέσωκέ σε !

Ye that have eyes, yet cannot see, —
In darkness and in misery,
Recall those mighty Voices Three,
Ἰησοῦ, ἐλέησόν με !
Θάρσει· ἔγειραι, ὕπαγε !
Ἡ πίστις σου σέσωκέ σε !

THE GOBLET OF LIFE

Mr. Longfellow, writing to Mr. Ward, November 3, 1841, says : "I shall send him [Mr. Benjamin] a new poem, called simply Fennel, which I do not copy here on account of its length. It is as good, perhaps, as Excelsior. Hawthorne, who is passing the night with me, likes it better." He afterward changed the title to that which the poem now bears.

FILLED is Life's goblet to the brim ;
And though my eyes with tears are dim,
I see its sparkling bubbles swim,
    And chant a melancholy hymn
    With solemn voice and slow.

No purple flowers, — no garlands green,
Conceal the goblet's shade or sheen,

Nor maddening draughts of Hippocrene,
Like gleams of sunshine, flash between
　　Thick leaves of mistletoe.

This goblet, wrought with curious art,
Is filled with waters, that upstart,
When the deep fountains of the heart,
By strong convulsions rent apart,
　　Are running all to waste.

And as it mantling passes round,
With fennel is it wreathed and crowned,
Whose seed and foliage sun-imbrowned
Are in its waters steeped and drowned,
　　And give a bitter taste.

Above the lowly plants it towers,
The fennel, with its yellow flowers,
And in an earlier age than ours
Was gifted with the wondrous powers,
　　Lost vision to restore.

It gave new strength, and fearless mood ;
And gladiators, fierce and rude,
Mingled it in their daily food ;
And he who battled and subdued,
　　A wreath of fennel wore.

Then in Life's goblet freely press
The leaves that give it bitterness,
Nor prize the colored waters less,
For in thy darkness and distress
　　New light and strength they give !

And he who has not learned to know
How false its sparkling bubbles show,
How bitter are the drops of woe,
With which its brim may overflow,
　　He has not learned to live.

The prayer of Ajax was for light ;
Through all that dark and desperate
　　fight,
The blackness of that noonday night,
He asked but the return of sight,
　　To see his foeman's face.

Let our unceasing, earnest prayer
Be, too, for light, — for strength to bear
Our portion of the weight of care,
That crushes into dumb despair
　　One half the human race.

O suffering, sad humanity !
O ye afflicted ones, who lie

Steeped to the lips in misery,
Longing, and yet afraid to die,
　　Patient, though sorely tried !

I pledge you in this cup of grief,
Where floats the fennel's bitter leaf !
The Battle of our Life is brief,
The alarm, — the struggle, — the relief,
　　Then sleep we side by side.

MAIDENHOOD

When writing to his father of the appearance of his
new volume of poems, Mr. Longfellow said : " I think
the last two pieces the best, — perhaps as good as any-
thing I have written." These pieces were the following
and *Excelsior*.

MAIDEN ! with the meek, brown eyes,
In whose orbs a shadow lies
Like the dusk in evening skies !

Thou whose locks outshine the sun,
Golden tresses, wreathed in one,
As the braided streamlets run !

Standing, with reluctant feet,
Where the brook and river meet,
Womanhood and childhood fleet !

Gazing, with a timid glance,
On the brooklet's swift advance,
On the river's broad expanse !

Deep and still, that gliding stream
Beautiful to thee must seem,
As the river of a dream.

Then why pause with indecision,
When bright angels in thy vision
Beckon thee to fields Elysian ?

Seest thou shadows sailing by,
As the dove, with startled eye,
Sees the falcon's shadow fly ?

Hearest thou voices on the shore,
That our ears perceive no more,
Deafened by the cataract's roar ?

Oh, thou child of many prayers !
Life hath quicksands, — Life hath snares !
Care and age come unawares !

Like the swell of some sweet tune,
Morning rises into noon,
May glides onward into June.

Childhood is the bough, where slumbered
Birds and blossoms many-numbered ; —
Age, that bough with snows encumbered.

Gather, then, each flower that grows,
When the young heart overflows,
To embalm that tent of snows.

Bear a lily in thy hand ;
Gates of brass cannot withstand
One touch of that magic wand.

Bear through sorrow, wrong, and ruth,
In thy heart the dew of youth,
On thy lips the smile of truth.

Oh, that dew, like balm, shall steal
Into wounds that cannot heal,
Even as sleep our eyes doth seal ;

And that smile, like sunshine, dart
Into many a sunless heart,
For a smile of God thou art.

EXCELSIOR

The original manuscript of *Excelsior*, showing the several drafts and interlineations, is preserved in the library of Harvard University. It was written on the back of a note from Mr. Sumner, and is dated at the close : "September 28, 1841. Half past 3 o'clock, morning. Now to bed." The suggestion of the poem came to Mr. Longfellow from a scrap of newspaper, a part of the heading of one of the New York journals, bearing the seal of the State, — a shield, with a rising sun, and the motto *Excelsior*. The intention of the poem was intimated in a letter from Mr. Longfellow written some time after to Mr. C. K. Tuckerman : —

"I have had the pleasure of receiving your note in regard to the poem *Excelsior* and very willingly give you my intention in writing it. This was no more than to display, in a series of pictures, the life of a man of genius, resisting all temptations, laying aside all fears, heedless of all warnings, and pressing right on to accomplish his purpose. His motto is Excelsior — 'higher.' He passes through the Alpine village — through the rough, cold paths of the world — where the peasants cannot understand him, and where his watchword is in an 'unknown tongue.' He disregards the happiness of domestic peace and sees the glaciers — his fate — before him. He disregards the warning of the old man's wisdom and the fascinations of woman's love. He answers to all, 'Higher yet!' The monks of St. Bernard are the representatives of religious forms and ceremonies, and with their oft-repeated prayer mingles the sound of his voice, telling them there is something higher than forms and ceremonies. Filled with these aspirations, he perishes; without having reached the perfection he longed for; and the voice heard in the air is the promise of immortality and progress ever upward. You will perceive that *Excelsior*, an adjective of the comparative degree, is used adverbially ; a use justified by the best Latin writers." This he afterwards found to be a mistake, and explained *excelsior* as the last word of the phrase *Scopus meus est excelsior*.

Five years after writing this poem, Mr. Longfellow made the following entry in his diary : "December 8,

1846. Looking over Brainard's poems, I find, in a piece called *The Mocking-Bird*, this passage : —
> Now his note
> Mounts to the play-ground of the lark, high up
> Quite to the sky. And then again it falls
> *As a lost star falls* down into the marsh.

Now, when in *Excelsior* I said,
> A voice fell, like a falling star,

Brainard's poem was not in my mind, nor had I in all probability ever read it. Felton said at the time that the same image was in Euripides, or Pindar, I forget which. Of a truth, one cannot strike a spade into the soil of Parnassus, without disturbing the bones of some dead poet."

Dr. Holmes remarks of *Excelsior* that " the repetition of the aspiring exclamation which gives its name to the poem, lifts every stanza a step higher than the one which preceded it."

THE shades of night were falling fast,
As through an Alpine village passed
A youth, who bore, 'mid snow and ice,
A banner with the strange device,
    Excelsior !

His brow was sad ; his eye beneath,
Flashed like a falchion from its sheath,
And like a silver clarion rung
The accents of that unknown tongue,
    Excelsior !

In happy homes he saw the light
Of household fires gleam warm and bright;
Above, the spectral glaciers shone,
And from his lips escaped a groan,
    Excelsior !

" Try not the Pass ! " the old man said;
" Dark lowers the tempest overhead,
The roaring torrent is deep and wide ! "
And loud that clarion voice replied,
    Excelsior !

" Oh stay," the maiden said, " and rest
Thy weary head upon this breast ! "
A tear stood in his bright blue eye,
But still he answered, with a sigh,
    Excelsior !

" Beware the pine-tree's withered branch !
Beware the awful avalanche ! "
This was the peasant's last Good-night,
A voice replied, far up the height,
    Excelsior !

At break of day, as heavenward
The pious monks of Saint Bernard
Uttered the oft-repeated prayer,
A voice cried through the startled air,
    Excelsior !

A traveller, by the faithful hound,
Half-buried in the snow was found,
Still grasping in his hand of ice
That banner with the strange device,
    Excelsior !

There in the twilight cold and gray,
Lifeless, but beautiful, he lay,
And from the sky, serene and far,
A voice fell, like a falling star,
    Excelsior !

POEMS ON SLAVERY

In the spring of 1842 Mr. Longfellow obtained leave of absence from college duties for six months and went abroad to try the virtues of the water-cure at Marienberg on the Rhine. When absent in Europe in the summer of 1842 Mr. Longfellow made an acquaintance with Ferdinand Freiligrath, the poet, which ripened into a life-long friendship. It was to this friend that he wrote shortly after his return to America [on leaving Bristol for New York] : "We sailed (or rather, paddled) out in the very teeth of a violent west wind, which blew for a week,—'Frau die alte sass gekehrt rückwärts nach Osten' with a vengeance. We had a very boisterous passage. I was not out of my berth more than twelve hours for the first twelve days. I was in the forward part of the vessel, where all the great waves struck and broke with voices of thunder. There, 'cribbed, cabined, and confined,' I passed fifteen days. During this time I wrote seven poems on slavery ; I meditated upon them in the stormy, sleepless nights, and wrote them down with a pencil in the morning. A small window in the side of the vessel admitted light into my berth, and there I lay on my back and soothed my soul with songs. I send you some copies."

He had published the poems at once on his arrival in America in December, 1842, in a thin volume of thirty-one pages in glazed paper covers, adding to the seven an eighth, previously written, poem, The Warning. It is possible that his immediate impulse to write came from his recent association with Dickens, whose American Notes, with its " grand chapter on slavery," he speaks of having read in London.

The book naturally received attention out of all proportion to its size. It was impossible for one at that time to range himself on one side or other of the great controversy without inviting criticism, not so much of literary art as of ethical position. To his father, Mr. Longfellow wrote : "How do you like the Slavery Poems? I think they make an impression ; I have received many letters about them, which I will send to you by the first good opportunity. Some persons regret that I should have written them, but for my own part I am glad of what I have done. My feelings prompted me, and my judgment approved, and still approves." The poem on Dr. Channing was written when the poet was ignorant of the great preacher's death.

" Since that event," he says in his prefatory note to the volume, " the poem addressed to him is no longer appropriate. I have decided, however, to let it remain as it was written, in testimony of my admiration for a great and good man."

TO WILLIAM E. CHANNING

The pages of thy book I read,
  And as I closed each one,
My heart, responding, ever said,
  " Servant of God ! well done ! "

Well done ! Thy words are great and bold;
  At times they seem to me,
Like Luther's, in the days of old,
  Half-battles for the free.

Go on, until this land revokes
  The old and chartered Lie,
The feudal curse, whose whips and yokes
  Insult humanity.

A voice is ever at thy side
  Speaking in tones of might,
Like the prophetic voice, that cried
  To John in Patmos, " Write ! "

Write ! and tell out this bloody tale ;
  Record this dire eclipse,
This Day of Wrath, this Endless Wail,
  This dread Apocalypse !

THE SLAVE'S DREAM

Beside the ungathered rice he lay,
  His sickle in his hand ;
His breast was bare, his matted hair
  Was buried in the sand.
Again, in the mist and shadow of sleep,
  He saw his Native Land.

Wide through the landscape of his dreams
  The lordly Niger flowed ;
Beneath the palm-trees on the plain
  Once more a king he strode ;
And heard the tinkling caravans
  Descend the mountain road.

He saw once more his dark-eyed queen
  Among her children stand ;
They clasped his neck, they kissed his
    cheeks,
  They held him by the hand ! —
A tear burst from the sleeper's lids
  And fell into the sand.

And then at furious speed he rode
  Along the Niger's bank :

His bridle-reins were golden chains,
  And, with a martial clank,
At each leap he could feel his scabbard of
    steel
  Smiting his stallion's flank.

Before him, like a blood-red flag,
  The bright flamingoes flew ;
From morn till night he followed their
    flight,
  O'er plains where the tamarind grew,
Till he saw the roofs of Caffre huts,
  And the ocean rose to view.

At night he heard the lion roar,
  And the hyena scream,
And the river-horse, as he crushed the
    reeds
  Beside some hidden stream ;
And it passed, like a glorious roll of drums,
  Through the triumph of his dream.

The forests, with their myriad tongues,
  Shouted of liberty ;
And the Blast of the Desert cried aloud,
  With a voice so wild and free,
That he started in his sleep and smiled
  At their tempestuous glee.

He did not feel the driver's whip,
  Nor the burning heat of day ;
For Death had illumined the Land of
    Sleep,
  And his lifeless body lay
A worn-out fetter, that the soul
  Had broken and thrown away !

THE GOOD PART

THAT SHALL NOT BE TAKEN AWAY

She dwells by Great Kenhawa's side,
  In valleys green and cool ;
And all her hope and all her pride
  Are in the village school.

Her soul, like the transparent air
  That robes the hills above,
Though not of earth, encircles there
  All things with arms of love.

And thus she walks among her girls
  With praise and mild rebukes ;

Subduing e'en rude village churls
  By her angelic looks.

She reads to them at eventide
  Of One who came to save ;
To cast the captive's chains aside
  And liberate the slave.

And oft the blessed time foretells
  When all men shall be free ;
And musical, as silver bells,
  Their falling chains shall be.

And following her beloved Lord,
  In decent poverty,
She makes her life one sweet record
  And deed of charity.

For she was rich, and gave up all
  To break the iron bands
Of those who waited in her hall,
  And labored in her lands.

Long since beyond the Southern Sea
  Their outbound sails have sped,
While she, in meek humility,
  Now earns her daily bread.

It is their prayers, which never cease,
  That clothe her with such grace ;
Their blessing is the light of peace
  That shines upon her face.

THE SLAVE IN THE DISMAL SWAMP

In dark fens of the Dismal Swamp
  The hunted Negro lay ;
He saw the fire of the midnight camp,
And heard at times a horse's tramp
  And a bloodhound's distant bay.

Where will-o'-the-wisps and glow-worms
    shine,
  In bulrush and in brake ;
Where waving mosses shroud the pine,
And the cedar grows, and the poisonous
    vine
  Is spotted like the snake ;

Where hardly a human foot could pass,
  Or a human heart would dare,
On the quaking turf of the green morass

He crouched in the rank and tangled grass,
  Like a wild beast in his lair.

A poor old slave, infirm and lame ;
  Great scars deformed his face ;
On his forehead he bore the brand of
    shame,
And the rags, that hid his mangled frame,
  Were the livery of disgrace.

All things above were bright and fair,
  All things were glad and free ;
Lithe squirrels darted here and there,
And wild birds filled the echoing air
  With songs of Liberty !

On him alone was the doom of pain,
  From the morning of his birth ;
On him alone the curse of Cain
Fell, like a flail on the garnered grain,
  And struck him to the earth !

THE SLAVE SINGING AT MIDNIGHT

Loud he sang the psalm of David !
He, a Negro and enslavèd,
Sang of Israel's victory,
Sang of Zion, bright and free.

In that hour, when night is calmest,
Sang he from the Hebrew Psalmist,
In a voice so sweet and clear
That I could not choose but hear,

Songs of triumph, and ascriptions,
Such as reached the swart Egyptians,
When upon the Red Sea coast
Perished Pharaoh and his host.

And the voice of his devotion
Filled my soul with strange emotion ;
For its tones by turns were glad,
Sweetly solemn, wildly sad.

Paul and Silas, in their prison,
Sang of Christ, the Lord arisen.
And an earthquake's arm of might
Broke their dungeon-gates at night.

But, alas ! what holy angel
Brings the Slave this glad evangel ?
And what earthquake's arm of might
Breaks his dungeon-gates at night ?

THE WITNESSES

In Ocean's wide domains,
  Half buried in the sands,
Lie skeletons in chains,
  With shackled feet and hands.

Beyond the fall of dews,
  Deeper than plummet lies,
Float ships, with all their crews,
  No more to sink nor rise.

There the black Slave-ship swims,
  Freighted with human forms,
Whose fettered, fleshless limbs
  Are not the sport of storms.

These are the bones of Slaves ;
  They gleam from the abyss ;
They cry, from yawning waves,
  "We are the Witnesses ! "

Within Earth's wide domains
  Are markets for men's lives ;
Their necks are galled with chains,
  Their wrists are cramped with gyves.

Dead bodies, that the kite
  In deserts makes its prey ;
Murders, that with affright
  Scare school-boys from their play !

All evil thoughts and deeds ;
  Anger, and lust, and pride ;
The foulest, rankest weeds,
  That choke Life's groaning tide !

These are the woes of Slaves ;
  They glare from the abyss ;
They cry, from unknown graves,
  "We are the Witnesses ! "

THE QUADROON GIRL

The Slaver in the broad lagoon
  Lay moored with idle sail ;
He waited for the rising moon,
  And for the evening gale.

Under the shore his boat was tied,
  And all her listless crew
Watched the gray alligator slide
  Into the still bayou.

Odors of orange-flowers, and spice,
  Reached them from time to time,
Like airs that breathe from Paradise
  Upon a world of crime.

The Planter, under his roof of thatch,
  Smoked thoughtfully and slow ;
The Slaver's thumb was on the latch,
  He seemed in haste to go.

He said, " My ship at anchor rides
  In yonder broad lagoon ;
I only wait the evening tides,
  And the rising of the moon."

Before them, with her face upraised,
  In timid attitude,
Like one half curious, half amazed,
  A Quadroon maiden stood.

Her eyes were large, and full of light,
  Her arms and neck were bare ;
No garment she wore save a kirtle bright,
  And her own long, raven hair.

And on her lips there played a smile
  As holy, meek, and faint,
As lights in some cathedral aisle
  The features of a saint.

" The soil is barren, — the farm is old,"
  The thoughtful planter said ;
Then looked upon the Slaver's gold,
  And then upon the maid.

His heart within him was at strife
  With such accursèd gains :
For he knew whose passions gave her life,
  Whose blood ran in her veins.

But the voice of nature was too weak ;
  He took the glittering gold !
Then pale as death grew the maiden's cheek,
  Her hands as icy cold.

The Slaver led her from the door,
  He led her by the hand,
To be his slave and paramour
  In a strange and distant land !

THE WARNING

Beware ! The Israelite of old, who tore
  The lion in his path, — when, poor and
    blind,
He saw the blessed light of heaven no more,
  Shorn of his noble strength and forced to
    grind
In prison, and at last led forth to be
A pander to Philistine revelry, —

Upon the pillars of the temple laid
  His desperate hands, and in its overthrow
Destroyed himself, and with him those who
    made
  A cruel mockery of his sightless woe ;
The poor, blind Slave, the scoff and jest of
    all,
Expired, and thousands perished in the fall !

There is a poor, blind Samson in this land,
  Shorn of his strength and bound in bonds
    of steel,
Who may, in some grim revel, raise his hand,
  And shake the pillars of this Common-
    weal,
Till the vast Temple of our liberties
A shapeless mass of wreck and rubbish lies.

THE SPANISH STUDENT

The first form of this comedy was serial publication in *Graham's Magazine*, September, October, and November, 1842. It was afterward carefully revised and published in book form in 1843, with the following preface : —

" The subject of the following play is taken in part from the beautiful tale of Cervantes, *La Gitanilla*. To this source, however, I am indebted for the main incident only, the love of a Spanish student for a Gypsy Girl, and the name of the heroine, Preciosa. I have not followed the story in any of its details.

" In Spain this subject has been twice handled dramatically ; first by Juan Perez de Montalvan, in *La Gitanilla*, and afterwards by Antonio de Solís y Rivadeneira in *La Gitanilla de Madrid*.

" The same subject has also been made use of by Thomas Middleton, an English dramatist of the seventeenth century. His play is called *The Spanish Gypsy*. The main plot is the same as in the Spanish pieces ; but there runs through it a tragic underplot of the loves of Rodrigo and Doña Clara, which is taken from another tale of Cervantes, *La Fuerza de la Sangre*.

" The reader who is acquainted with *La Gitanilla* of Cervantes, and the plays of Montalvan, Solís, and Middleton will perceive that my treatment of the subject differs entirely from theirs."

The book bore upon its title-page a motto from Burns : —

  " What 's done we partly may compute,
    But know not what 's resisted."

It had been the poet's intention at first to have the drama put on the stage, but this plan was abandoned. A German version was performed at the Ducal Court-Theatre in Dessau, January 28, 1855.

DRAMATIS PERSONÆ

VICTORIAN } . . . .   *Students of Alcalá.*
HYPOLITO }
THE COUNT OF LARA } . . . *Gentlemen of Madrid.*
DON CARLOS }
THE ARCHBISHOP OF TOLEDO.
A CARDINAL.
BELTRAN CRUZADO . . . . . *Count of the Gypsies.*
BARTOLOMÉ ROMÁN . . . . *A young Gypsy.*
THE PADRE CURA OF GUADARRAMA.
PEDRO CRESPO . . . . . . *Alcalde.*
PANCHO . . . . *Alguacil.*
FRANCISCO . . . . *Lara's Servant.*
CHISPA . . . . *Victorian's Servant.*
BALTASAR . . . . *Innkeeper.*
PRECIOSA . . . . *A Gypsy Girl.*
ANGELICA . . . . *A poor Girl.*
MARTINA . . . . *The Padre Cura's Niece.*
DOLORES . . . . *Preciosa's Maid.*
        Gypsies, Musicians, etc.

ACT I

SCENE I. — *The* COUNT OF LARA's *chambers. Night. The* COUNT *in his dressing-gown, smoking and conversing with* DON CARLOS.

Lara. You were not at the play to-night,
     Don Carlos ;
How happened it ?
     Don C.   I had engagements elsewhere.
Pray who was there ?
     Lara.   Why, all the town and court.
The house was crowded ; and the busy fans
Among the gayly dressed and perfumed ladies
Fluttered like butterflies among the flowers.
There was the Countess of Medina Celi ;
The Goblin Lady with her Phantom Lover,
Her Lindo Don Diego ; Doña Sol,
And Doña Serafina, and her cousins.
     Don C. What was the play ?
     Lara.   It was a dull affair ;
One of those comedies in which you see,
As Lope says, the history of the world
Brought down from Genesis to the day of Judgment.
There were three duels fought in the first act,
Three gentlemen receiving deadly wounds,
Laying their hands upon their hearts, and saying,
" Oh, I am dead ! " a lover in a closet,
An old hidalgo, and a gay Don Juan,
A Doña Inez with a black mantilla,
Followed at twilight by an unknown lover,

Who looks intently where he knows she is
     not !
     Don C. Of course, the Preciosa danced
     to-night ?
     Lara. And never better. Every foot-
     step fell
As lightly as a sunbeam on the water.
I think the girl extremely beautiful.
     Don C. Almost beyond the privilege of
     woman !
I saw her in the Prado yesterday.
Her step was royal, — queen-like, — and
her face
As beautiful as a saint's in Paradise.
     Lara. May not a saint fall from her
     Paradise,
And be no more a saint ?
     Don C.   Why do you ask ?
     Lara. Because I have heard it said this
     angel fell,
And though she is a virgin outwardly,
Within she is a sinner ; like those panels
Of doors and altar-pieces the old monks
Painted in convents, with the Virgin Mary
On the outside, and on the inside Ve-
     nus !
     Don C. You do her wrong ; indeed, you
     do her wrong !
She is as virtuous as she is fair.
     Lara. How credulous you are ! Why,
     look you, friend,
There 's not a virtuous woman in Madrid,
In this whole city ! And would you per-
     suade me
That a mere dancing-girl, who shows
     herself,
Nightly, half naked, on the stage, for
     money,
And with voluptuous motions fires the
     blood
Of inconsiderate youth, is to be held
A model for her virtue ?
     Don C.   You forget
She is a Gypsy girl.
     Lara.   And therefore won
The easier.
     Don C.   Nay, not to be won at all !
The only virtue that a Gypsy prizes
Is chastity. That is her only virtue.
Dearer than life she holds it. I remem-
     ber
A Gypsy woman, a vile, shameless bawd,
Whose craft was to betray the young and
     fair ;
And yet this woman was above all bribes.

And when a noble lord, touched by her
beauty,
The wild and wizard beauty of her race,
Offered her gold to be what she made
others,
She turned upon him, with a look of scorn,
And smote him in the face !
Lara.   And does that prove
That Preciosa is above suspicion ?
Don C. It proves a nobleman may be
repulsed
When he thinks conquest easy. I believe
That woman, in her deepest degradation,
Holds something sacred, something unde-
filed,
Some pledge and keepsake of her higher
nature,
And, like the diamond in the dark, retains
Some quenchless gleam of the celestial
light !
Lara. Yet Preciosa would have taken
the gold.
Don C. (rising). I do not think so.
Lara.   I am sure of it.
But why this haste ? Stay yet a little
longer,
And fight the battles of your Dulcinea.
Don C. 'T is late. I must begone, for
if I stay
You will not be persuaded.
Lara.   Yes ; persuade me.
Don C. No one so deaf as he who will
not hear !
Lara. No one so blind as he who will not
see !
Don C. And so good night. I wish you
pleasant dreams,
And greater faith in woman.   [Exit.
Lara.   Greater faith !
I have the greatest faith ; for I believe
Victorian is her lover. I believe
That I shall be to-morrow ; and thereafter
Another, and another, and another,
Chasing each other through her zodiac,
As Taurus chases Aries.
(Enter FRANCISCO with a casket.)
                    Well, Francisco,
What speed with Preciosa ?
Fran.   None, my lord.
She sends your jewels back, and bids me
tell you
She is not to be purchased by your gold.
Lara. Then I will try some other way to
win her.
Pray, dost thou know Victorian ?

Fran.   Yes, my lord ;
I saw him at the jeweller's to-day.
Lara. What was he doing there ?
Fran.   I saw him buy
A golden ring, that had a ruby in it.
Lara. Was there another like it ?
Fran.   One so like it
I could not choose between them.
Lara.   It is well.
To-morrow morning bring that ring to me.
Do not forget. Now light me to my bed.
                    [Exeunt.

SCENE II. — A street in Madrid.   Enter CHISPA, fol-
lowed by musicians, with a bagpipe, guitars, and
other instruments.

Chispa. Abernuncio Satanas : and a
plague on all lovers who ramble about at
night drinking the elements, instead of
sleeping quietly in their beds. Every
dead man to his cemetery, say I ; and
every friar to his monastery. Now, here 's
my master, Victorian, yesterday a cow-
keeper, and to-day a gentleman ; yesterday
a student, and to-day a lover ; and I must
be up later than the nightingale, for as the
abbot sings so must the sacristan respond.
God grant he may soon be married, for
then shall all this serenading cease. Ay,
marry ! marry ! marry ! Mother, what
does marry mean ? It means to spin, to
bear children, and to weep, my daughter !
And, of a truth, there is something more
in matrimony than the wedding-ring. (To
the musicians.) And now, gentlemen, Pax
vobiscum ! as the ass said to the cabbages.
Pray, walk this way ; and don't hang down
your heads. It is no disgrace to have an
old father and a ragged shirt. Now, look
you, you are gentlemen who lead the life
of crickets ; you enjoy hunger by day and
noise by night. Yet, I beseech you, for
this once be not loud, but pathetic ; for it
is a serenade to a damsel in bed, and not to
the Man in the Moon. Your object is not
to arouse and terrify, but to soothe and
bring lulling dreams. Therefore, each
shall not play upon his instrument as if it
were the only one in the universe, but
gently, and with a certain modesty, ac-
cording with the others. Pray, how may I
call thy name, friend ?
First Mus. Gerónimo Gil, at your ser-
vice.
Chispa. Every tub smells of the wine

that is in it. Pray, Gerónimo, is not Saturday an unpleasant day with thee?

First Mus. Why so?

Chispa. Because I have heard it said that Saturday is an unpleasant day with those who have but one shirt. Moreover, I have seen thee at the tavern, and if thou canst run as fast as thou canst drink, I should like to hunt hares with thee. What instrument is that?

First Mus. An Aragonese bagpipe.

Chispa. Pray, art thou related to the bagpiper of Bujalance, who asked a maravedi for playing, and ten for leaving off?

First Mus. No, your honor.

Chispa. I am glad of it. What other instruments have we?

Second and Third Musicians. We play the bandurria.

Chispa. A pleasing instrument. And thou ?

Fourth Mus. The fife.

Chispa. I like it ; it has a cheerful, soul-stirring sound, that soars up to my lady's window like the song of a swallow. And you others ?

Other Mus. We are the singers, please your honor.

Chispa. You are too many. Do you think we are going to sing mass in the cathedral of Córdova? Four men can make but little use of one shoe, and I see not how you can all sing in one song. But follow me along the garden wall. That is the way my master climbs to the lady's window. It is by the Vicar's skirts that the Devil climbs into the belfry. Come, follow me, and make no noise. [*Exeunt.*

SCENE III. — PRECIOSA's *chamber. She stands at the open window.*

Prec. How slowly through the lilac-scented air
Descends the tranquil moon ! Like thistle-down
The vapory clouds float in the peaceful sky ;
And sweetly from yon hollow vaults of shade
The nightingales breathe out their souls in song.
And hark ! what songs of love, what soul-like sounds,
Answer them from below !

SERENADE

Stars of the summer night!
  Far in yon azure deeps,
Hide, hide your golden light!
  She sleeps!
My lady sleeps!
  Sleeps!

Moon of the summer night!
  Far down yon western steeps,
Sink, sink in silver light!
  She sleeps!
My lady sleeps!
  Sleeps!

Wind of the summer night!
  Where yonder woodbine creeps,
Fold, fold thy pinions light!
  She sleeps!
My lady sleeps!
  Sleeps!

Dreams of the summer night!
  Tell her, her lover keeps
Watch! while in slumbers light
  She sleeps!
My lady sleeps!
  Sleeps!

(*Enter* VICTORIAN *by the balcony.*)

Vict. Poor little dove ! Thou tremblest like a leaf !

Prec. I am so frightened ! 'T is for thee I tremble !
I hate to have thee climb that wall by night !
Did no one see thee ?

Vict.   None, my love, but thou.

Prec. 'T is very dangerous ; and when thou art gone
I chide myself for letting thee come here
Thus stealthily by night. Where hast thou been ?
Since yesterday I have no news from thee.

Vict. Since yesterday I have been in Alcalá.
Erelong the time will come, sweet Preciosa,
When that dull distance shall no more divide us ;
And I no more shall scale thy wall by night
To steal a kiss from thee, as I do now.

Prec. An honest thief, to steal but what thou givest.

Vict. And we shall sit together unmolested,
And words of true love pass from tongue to tongue,
As singing birds from one bough to another.

Prec. That were a life to make time
    envious !
I knew that thou wouldst come to me to-
    night.
I saw thee at the play.
    Vict.   Sweet child of air !
Never did I behold thee so attired
And garmented in beauty as to-night !
What hast thou done to make thee look so
    fair ?
    Prec. Am I not always fair ?
    Vict.   Ay, and so fair
That I am jealous of all eyes that see thee,
And wish that they were blind.
    Prec.   I heed them not ;
When thou art present, I see none but
    thee !
    Vict. There 's nothing fair nor beautiful,
    but takes
Something from thee, that makes it beauti-
    ful.
    Prec. And yet thou leavest me for those
    dusty books.
    Vict. Thou comest between me and those
    books too often !
I see thy face in everything I see !
The paintings in the chapel wear thy looks,
The canticles are changed to sarabands,
And with the learned doctors of the schools
I see thee dance cachuchas.
    Prec.   In good sooth,
I dance with learned doctors of the schools
To-morrow morning.
    Vict. And with whom, I pray ?
    Prec. A grave and reverend Cardinal,
    and his Grace
The Archbishop of Toledo.
    Vict.   What mad jest
Is this ?
    Prec.   It is no jest ; indeed it is not.
    Vict. Prithee, explain thyself.
    Prec.   Why, simply thus.
Thou knowest the Pope has sent here into
    Spain
To put a stop to dances on the stage.
    Vict. I have heard it whispered.
    Prec.   Now the Cardinal,
Who for this purpose comes, would fain
    behold
With his own eyes these dances ; and the
    Archbishop
Has sent for me —
    Vict. That thou mayest dance before
    them !
Now viva la cachucha !   It will breathe

The fire of youth into these gray old men !
'T will be thy proudest conquest !
    Prec.   Saving one.
And yet I fear these dances will be stopped,
And Preciosa be once more a beggar.
    Vict. The sweetest beggar that e'er asked
    for alms ;
With such beseeching eyes, that when I
    saw thee
I gave my heart away !
    Prec.   Dost thou remember
When first we met ?
    Vict.   It was at Córdova,
In the cathedral garden. Thou wast sit-
    ting
Under the orange trees, beside a fountain.
    Prec. 'T was Easter Sunday. The full-
    blossomed trees
Filled all the air with fragrance and with
    joy.
The priests were singing, and the organ
    sounded,
And then anon the great cathedral bell.
It was the elevation of the Host.
We both of us fell down upon our knees,
Under the orange boughs, and prayed to-
    gether.
I never had been happy till that moment.
    Vict. Thou blessed angel !
    Prec.   And when thou wast gone
I felt an aching here. I did not speak
To any one that day. But from that day
Bartolomé grew hateful unto me.
    Vict. Remember him no more. Let not
    his shadow
Come between thee and me. Sweet Pre-
    ciosa !
I loved thee even then, though I was silent!
    Prec. I thought I ne'er should see **thy**
    face again.
Thy farewell had a sound of sorrow in it.
    Vict. That was the first sound in the
    song of love !
Scarce more than silence is, and yet **a**
    sound.
Hands of invisible spirits touch the strings
Of that mysterious instrument, the soul,
And play the prelude of our fate. We hear
The voice prophetic, and are not alone.
    Prec. That is my faith. Dost thou be-
    lieve these warnings ?
    Vict. So far as this. Our feelings and
    our thoughts
Tend ever on, and rest not in the Present.
As drops of rain fall into some dark well,

And from below comes a scarce audible
sound,
So fall our thoughts into the dark Here-
after,
And their mysterious echo reaches us.
   Prec. I have felt it so, but found no
      words to say it !
I cannot reason ; I can only feel !
But thou hast language for all thoughts
   and feelings.
Thou art a scholar; and sometimes I think
We cannot walk together in this world !
The distance that divides us is too great !
Henceforth thy pathway lies among the
   stars ;
I must not hold thee back.
   Vict.   Thou little sceptic !
Dost thou still doubt ? What I most prize
   in woman
Is her affections, not her intellect !
The intellect is finite ; but the affections
Are infinite, and cannot be exhausted.
Compare me with the great men of the
   earth ;
What am I ? Why, a pygmy among
   giants !
But if thou lovest, — mark me ! I say
   lovest, —
The greatest of thy sex excels thee not !
The world of the affections is thy world,
Not that of man's ambition. In that still-
   ness
Which most becomes a woman, calm and
   holy,
Thou sittest by the fireside of the heart,
Feeding its flame. The element of fire
Is pure. It cannot change nor hide its na-
   ture,
But burns as brightly in a Gypsy camp
As in a palace hall. Art thou convinced ?
   Prec. Yes, that I love thee, as the good
      love heaven ;
But not that I am worthy of that heaven.
How shall I more deserve it ?
   Vict.   Loving more.
   Prec. I cannot love thee more; my heart
   is full.
   Vict. Then let it overflow, and I will
   drink it,
As in the summer-time the thirsty sands
Drink the swift waters of the Manzanares,
And still do thirst for more.
   A Watchman (*in the street*). Ave Maria
Purissima ! 'T is midnight and serene !
   Vict. Hear'st thou that cry ?

   Prec.   It is a hateful sound,
To scare thee from me !
   Vict.   As the hunter's horn
Doth scare the timid stag, or bark of
   hounds
The moor-fowl from his mate.
   Prec.   Pray, do not go !
   Vict. I must away to Alcalá to-night.
Think of me when I am away.
   Prec.   Fear not !
I have no thoughts that do not think of
   thee.
   Vict. (*giving her a ring*). And to remind
      thee of my love, take this ;
A serpent, emblem of Eternity ;
A ruby, — say, a drop of my heart's blood.
   Prec. It is an ancient saying, that the
   ruby
Brings gladness to the wearer, and pre-
   serves
The heart pure, and, if laid beneath the
   pillow,
Drives away evil dreams. But then, alas !
It was a serpent tempted Eve to sin.
   Vict. What convent of barefooted Car-
   melites
Taught thee so much theology ?
   Prec. (*laying her hand upon his mouth*).
               Hush ! hush !
Good night ! and may all holy angels guard
   thee !
   Vict. Good night ! good night ! Thou
      art my guardian angel !
I have no other saint than thou to pray to !
      (*He descends by the balcony.*)
   Prec. Take care, and do not hurt thee.
   Art thou safe ?
   Vict. (*from the garden*). Safe as my
      love for thee ! But art thou safe ?
Others can climb a balcony by moonlight
As well as I. Pray shut thy window close;
I am jealous of the perfumed air of night
That from this garden climbs to kiss thy
   lips.
   Prec. (*throwing down her handkerchief*).
      Thou silly child ! Take this to blind
      thine eyes.
It is my benison !
   Vict.   And brings to me
Sweet fragrance from thy lips, as the soft
   wind
Wafts to the out-bound mariner the breath
Of the beloved land he leaves behind.
   Prec. Make not thy voyage long.
   Vict.   To-morrow night

Shall see me safe returned. Thou art the
    star
To guide me to an anchorage. Good night!
My beauteous star! My star of love, good
    night!
Prec. Good night!
Watchman (at a distance). Ave Maria
    Purissima!

SCENE IV. — *An inn on the road to Alcalá.* BALTASAR
    asleep on a bench. Enter CHISPA.

Chispa. And here we are, half-way to
Alcalá, between cocks and midnight. Body
o' me! what an inn this is! The lights
out, and the landlord asleep. Holá! an-
cient Baltasar!
Bal. (waking). Here I am.
Chispa. Yes, there you are, like a one-
eyed Alcalde in a town without inhabitants.
Bring a light, and let me have supper.
Bal. Where is your master?
Chispa. Do not trouble yourself about
him. We have stopped a moment to
breathe our horses; and if he chooses to
walk up and down in the open air, looking
into the sky as one who hears it rain, that
does not satisfy my hunger, you know. But
be quick, for I am in a hurry, and every
man stretches his legs according to the
length of his coverlet. What have we
here?
Bal. (setting a light on the table). Stewed
rabbit.
Chispa (eating). Conscience of Portale-
gre! Stewed kitten, you mean!
Bal. And a pitcher of Pedro Ximenes,
with a roasted pear in it.
Chispa (drinking). Ancient Baltasar,
amigo! You know how to cry wine and
sell vinegar. I tell you this is nothing but
Vinto Tinto of La Mancha, with a tang of
the swine-skin.
Bal. I swear to you by Saint Simon and
Judas, it is all as I say.
Chispa. And I swear to you by Saint
Peter and Saint Paul, that it is no such
thing. Moreover, your supper is like the
hidalgo's dinner, very little meat and a
great deal of tablecloth.
Bal. Ha! ha! ha!
Chispa. And more noise than nuts.
Bal. Ha! ha! ha! You must have your
joke, Master Chispa. But shall I not ask
Don Victorian in, to take a draught of the
Pedro Ximenes?

Chispa. No; you might as well say,
"Don't-you-want-some?" to a dead man.
Bal. Why does he go so often to Madrid?
Chispa. For the same reason that he
eats no supper. He is in love. Were you
ever in love, Baltasar?
Bal. I was never out of it, good Chispa.
It has been the torment of my life.
Chispa. What! are you on fire, too, old
haystack? Why, we shall never be able
to put you out.
Vict. (without). Chispa!
Chispa. Go to bed, Pero Grullo, for the
cocks are crowing.
Vict. Ea! Chispa! Chispa!
Chispa. Ea! Señor. Come with me,
ancient Baltasar, and bring water for the
horses. I will pay for the supper to-
morrow.   [*Exeunt.*

SCENE V. — VICTORIAN'S *chambers at Alcalá.* HYPOLITO
    asleep in an arm-chair. He awakes slowly.

Hyp. I must have been asleep! ay, sound
    asleep!
And it was all a dream. O sleep, sweet
    sleep!
Whatever form thou takest, thou art fair,
Holding unto our lips thy goblet filled
Out of Oblivion's well, a healing draught!
The candles have burned low; it must be
    late.
Where can Victorian be? Like Fray Car-
    rillo,
The only place in which one cannot find him
Is his own cell. Here's his guitar, that
    seldom
Feels the caresses of its master's hand.
Open thy silent lips, sweet instrument!
And make dull midnight merry with a
    song.

      (He plays and sings.)

      Padre Francisco!
      Padre Francisco!
What do you want of Padre Francisco?
    Here is a pretty young maiden
    Who wants to confess her sins!
Open the door and let her come in,
I will shrive her of every sin.

      (Enter VICTORIAN.)

Vict. Padre Hypolito! Padre Hypolito!
Hyp. What do you want of Padre Hy-
    polito?
Vict. Come, shrive me straight; for, if
    love be a sin,

I am the greatest sinner that doth live.
I will confess the sweetest of all crimes,
A maiden wooed and won.
   Hyp.   The same old tale
Of the old woman in the chimney-corner,
Who, while the pot boils, says, " Come
   here, my child ;
I 'll tell thee a story of my wedding-day."
   Vict. Nay, listen, for my heart is full ;
   so full
That I must speak.
   Hyp.   Alas ! that heart of thine
Is like a scene in the old play ; the curtain
Rises to solemn music, and lo ! enter
The eleven thousand virgins of Cologne !
   Vict. Nay, like the Sibyl's volumes, thou
   shouldst say ;
Those that remained, after the six were
   burned,
Being held more precious than the nine
   together.
But listen to my tale. Dost thou remember
The Gypsy girl we saw at Córdova
Dance the Romalis in the market-place ?
   Hyp. Thou meanest Preciosa.
   Vict.   Ay, the same.
Thou knowest how her image haunted me
Long after we returned to Alcalá.
She 's in Madrid.
   Hyp.   I know it.
   Vict.   And I 'm in love.
   Hyp. And therefore in Madrid when
   thou shouldst be
In Alcalá.
   Vict.   Oh pardon me, my friend,
If I so long have kept this secret from
   thee ;
But silence is the charm that guards such
   treasures,
And, if a word be spoken ere the time,
They sink again, they were not meant for us.
   Hyp. Alas ! alas ! I see thou art in love.
Love keeps the cold out better than a cloak.
It serves for food and raiment. Give a
   Spaniard
His mass, his olla, and his Doña Luisa —
Thou knowest the proverb. But pray tell
   me, lover,
How speeds thy wooing ? Is the maiden
   coy ?
Write her a song, beginning with an *Ave ;*
Sing as the monk sang to the Virgin Mary,

      Ave! cujus calcem clare
      Nec centenni commendare
      Sciret Seraph studio !

   Vict. Pray, do not jest ! This is no time
   for it !
I am in earnest !
   Hyp.   Seriously enamored ?
What, ho ! The Primus of great Alcalá
Enamored of a Gypsy ? Tell me frankly,
How meanest thou ?
   Vict.   I mean it honestly.
   Hyp. Surely thou wilt not marry her !
   Vict.   Why not ?
   Hyp. She was betrothed to one Bartol-
   omé,
If I remember rightly, a young Gypsy
Who danced with her at Córdova.
   Vict.   They quarrelled,
And so the matter ended.
   Hyp.   But in truth
Thou wilt not marry her.
   Vict.   In truth I will.
The angels sang in heaven when she was
   born !
She is a precious jewel I have found
Among the filth and rubbish of the world.
I 'll stoop for it ; but when I wear it
   here,
Set on my forehead like the morning star,
The world may wonder, but it will not
   laugh.
   Hyp. If thou wear'st nothing else upon
   thy forehead,
'T will be indeed a wonder.
   Vict.   Out upon thee
With thy unseasonable jests ! Pray tell
   me,
Is there no virtue in the world ?
   Hyp.   Not much.
What, think'st thou, is she doing at this
   moment ;
Now, while we speak of her ?
   Vict.   She lies asleep,
And from her parted lips her gentle breath
Comes like the fragrance from the lips of
   flowers.
Her tender limbs are still, and on her
   breast
The cross she prayed to, ere she fell asleep,
Rises and falls with the soft tide of dreams,
Like a light barge safe moored.
   Hyp.   Which means, in prose,
She 's sleeping with her mouth a little open !
   Vict. Oh, would I had the old magician's
   glass
To see her as she lies in child-like sleep !
   Hyp. And wouldst thou venture ?
   Vict.   Ay, indeed I would!

Hyp. Thou art courageous. Hast thou
  e'er reflected
How much lies hidden in that one word,
  now?
Vict. Yes; all the awful mystery of Life!
I oft have thought, my dear Hypolito,
That could we, by some spell of magic,
  change
The world and its inhabitants to stone,
In the same attitudes they now are in,
What fearful glances downward might we
  cast
Into the hollow chasms of human life!
What groups should we behold about the
  death-bed,
Putting to shame the group of Niobe!
What joyful welcomes, and what sad fare-
  wells!
What stony tears in those congealèd eyes!
What visible joy or anguish in those
  cheeks!
What bridal pomps, and what funereal
  shows!
What foes, like gladiators, fierce and strug-
  gling!
What lovers with their marble lips to-
  gether!
  Hyp. Ay, there it is! and, if I were in
  love,
That is the very point I most should dread.
This magic glass, these magic spells of
  thine,
Might tell a tale were better left untold.
For instance, they might show us thy fair
  cousin,
The Lady Violante, bathed in tears
Of love and anger, like the maid of Col-
  chis,
Whom thou, another faithless Argonaut,
Having won that golden fleece, a woman's
  love,
Desertest for this Glaucè.
  Vict.   Hold thy peace!
She cares not for me. She may wed an-
  other,
Or go into a convent, and, thus dying,
Marry Achilles in the Elysian Fields.
  Hyp. (*rising*). And so, good night!
  Good morning, I should say.
       (*Clock strikes three.*)
Hark! how the loud and ponderous mace
  of Time
Knocks at the golden portals of the day!
And so, once more, good night! We'll
  speak more largely

Of Preciosa when we meet again.
Get thee to bed, and the magician, Sleep,
Shall show her to thee, in his magic glass,
In all her loveliness. Good night!   [*Exit.*
  Vict.   Good night!
But not to bed; for I must read awhile.

(*Throws himself into the arm-chair which* HYPOLITO
has left, and lays a large book open upon his knees.)

Must read, or sit in revery and watch
The changing color of the waves that break
Upon the idle sea-shore of the mind!
Visions of Fame! that once did visit me,
Making night glorious with your smile,
  where are ye?
Oh, who shall give me, now that ye are
  gone,
Juices of those immortal plants that bloom
Upon Olympus, making us immortal?
Or teach me where that wondrous man-
  drake grows
Whose magic root, torn from the earth with
  groans,
At midnight hour, can scare the fiends
  away,
And make the mind prolific in its fancies?
I have the wish, but want the will, to act!
Souls of great men departed! Ye whose
  words
Have come to light from the swift river of
  Time,
Like Roman swords found in the Tagus'
  bed,
Where is the strength to wield the arms ye
  bore?
From the barred visor of Antiquity
Reflected shines the eternal light of Truth,
As from a mirror! All the means of
  action —
The shapeless masses, the materials —
Lie everywhere about us. What we need
Is the celestial fire to change the flint
Into transparent crystal, bright and clear.
That fire is genius! The rude peasant sits
At evening in his smoky cot, and draws
With charcoal uncouth figures on the wall.
The son of genius comes, foot-sore with
  travel,
And begs a shelter from the inclement
  night.
He takes the charcoal from the peasant's
  hand,
And, by the magic of his touch at once
Transfigured, all its hidden virtues shine,
And, in the eyes of the astonished clown,

It gleams a diamond! Even thus trans-
    formed,
Rude popular traditions and old tales
Shine as immortal poems, at the touch
Of some poor, houseless, homeless, wander-
    ing bard,
Who had but a night's lodging for his
    pains.
But there are brighter dreams than those
    of Fame,
Which are the dreams of Love! Out of
    the heart
Rises the bright ideal of these dreams,
As from some woodland fount a spirit rises
And sinks again into its silent deeps,
Ere the enamored knight can touch her
    robe!
'T is this ideal that the soul of man,
Like the enamored knight beside the foun-
    tain,
Waits for upon the margin of Life's
    stream ;
Waits to behold her rise from the dark
    waters,
Clad in a mortal shape! Alas! how many
Must wait in vain! The stream flows ever-
    more,
But from its silent deeps no spirit rises!
Yet I, born under a propitious star,
Have found the bright ideal of my dreams.
Yes! she is ever with me. I can feel,
Here, as I sit at midnight and alone,
Her gentle breathing! on my breast can
    feel
The pressure of her head! God's benison
Rest ever on it! Close those beauteous
    eyes,
Sweet Sleep! and all the flowers that bloom
    at night
With balmy lips breathe in her ears my
    name!
    (*Gradually sinks asleep.*)

ACT II

Scene I. — Preciosa's *chamber. Morning.* Preciosa
    and Angelica.

Prec. Why will you go so soon? Stay
    yet awhile.
The poor too often turn away unheard
From hearts that shut against them with a
    sound
That will be heard in heaven. Pray, tell
    me more

Of your adversities. Keep nothing from
    me.
What is your landlord's name?
    Ang.   The Count of Lara.
    Prec. The Count of Lara? Oh, beware
        that man!
Mistrust his pity, — hold no parley with
    him!
And rather die an outcast in the streets
Than touch his gold.
    Ang.   You know him, then!
    Prec.   As much
As any woman may, and yet be pure.
As you would keep your name without a
    blemish,
Beware of him!
    Ang.   Alas! what can I do?
I cannot choose my friends. Each word of
    kindness,
Come whence it may, is welcome to the poor.
    Prec. Make me your friend. A girl so
        young and fair
Should have no friends but those of her
    own sex.
What is your name?
    Ang.   Angelica.
    Prec.   That name
Was given you, that you might be an angel
To her who bore you! When your infant
    smile
Made her home Paradise, you were her
    angel.
Oh, be an angel still! She needs that smile.
So long as you are innocent, fear nothing.
No one can harm you! I am a poor girl,
Whom chance has taken from the public
    streets.
I have no other shield than mine own
    virtue.
That is the charm which has protected me!
Amid a thousand perils, I have worn it
Here on my heart! It is my guardian angel.
    Ang. (*rising*). I thank you for this
        counsel, dearest lady.
    Prec. Thank me by following it.
    Ang.   Indeed I will.
    Prec. Pray, do not go. I have much
        more to say.
    Ang. My mother is alone. I dare not
        leave her.
    Prec. Some other time, then, when we
        meet again.
You must not go away with words alone.
        (*Gives her a purse.*)
Take this. Would it were more.

Ang.   I thank you, lady.
Prec. No thanks. To-morrow come to
   me again.
I dance to-night, — perhaps for the last
   time.
But what I gain, I promise shall be yours,
If that can save you from the Count of
   Lara.
   Ang. Oh, my dear lady! how shall I be
   grateful
For so much kindness?
   Prec.   I deserve no thanks.
Thank Heaven, not me.
   Ang.   Both Heaven and you.
   Prec.   Farewell.
Remember that you come again to-morrow.
   Ang. I will. And may the Blessed Vir-
   gin guard you,
And all good angels.   [*Exit.*
   Prec.   May they guard thee too,
And all the poor; for they have need of
   angels.
Now bring me, dear Dolores, my basquina,
My richest maja dress, — my dancing dress,
And my most precious jewels! Make me
   look
Fairer than night e'er saw me! I 've a
   prize
To win this day, worthy of Preciosa!
      (*Enter* BELTRAN CRUZADO.)
   Cruz. Ave Maria!
   Prec.   O God! my evil genius!
What seekest thou here to-day?
   Cruz.   Thyself, — my child.
   Prec. What is thy will with me?
   Cruz.   Gold! gold!
   Prec. I gave thee yesterday; I have no
   more.
   Cruz. The gold of the Busné, — give me
   his gold!
   Prec. I gave the last in charity to-day.
   Cruz. That is a foolish lie.
   Prec.   It is the truth.
   Cruz. Curses upon thee! Thou art not
   my child!
Hast thou given gold away, and not to me?
Not to thy father? To whom, then?
   Prec.   To one
Who needs it more.
   Cruz.   No one can need it more.
   Prec. Thou art not poor.
   Cruz.   What, I, who lurk about
In dismal suburbs and unwholesome lanes;
I, who am housed worse than the galley
   slave;

I, who am fed worse than the kennelled
   hound;
I, who am clothed in rags, — Beltran Cru-
   zado, —
Not poor!
   Prec. Thou hast a stout heart and strong
   hands.
Thou canst supply thy wants; what wouldst
   thou more?
   Cruz. The gold of the Busné! give me
   his gold!
   Prec. Beltran Cruzado! hear me once
   for all.
I speak the truth. So long as I had gold,
I gave it to thee freely, at all times,
Never denied thee; never had a wish
But to fulfil thine own. Now go in peace!
Be merciful, be patient, and erelong
Thou shalt have more.
   Cruz.   And if I have it not,
Thou shalt no longer dwell here in rich
   chambers,
Wear silken dresses, feed on dainty food,
And live in idleness; but go with me,
Dance the Romalis in the public streets,
And wander wild again o'er field and
   fell;
For here we stay not long.
   Prec.   What! march again?
   Cruz. Ay, with all speed. I hate the
   crowded town!
I cannot breathe shut up within its gates!
Air, — I want air, and sunshine, and blue
   sky,
The feeling of the breeze upon my face,
The feeling of the turf beneath my feet,
And no walls but the far-off mountain-
   tops.
Then I am free and strong, — once more
   myself,
Beltran Cruzado, Count of the Calés!
   Prec. God speed thee on thy march! —
   I cannot go.
   Cruz. Remember who I am, and who
   thou art!
Be silent and obey! Yet one thing more.
Bartolomé Román —
   Prec. (with emotion). Oh, I beseech thee!
If my obedience and blameless life,
If my humility and meek submission
In all things hitherto, can move in thee
One feeling of compassion; if thou art
Indeed my father, and canst trace in me
One look of her who bore me, or one tone
That doth remind thee of her, let it plead

In my behalf, who am a feeble girl,
Too feeble to resist, and do not force me
To wed that man ! I am afraid of him !
I do not love him ! On my knees I beg
    thee
To use no violence, nor do in haste
What cannot be undone !
    Cruz.   O child, child, child !
Thou hast betrayed thy secret, as a bird
Betrays her nest, by striving to conceal it.
I will not leave thee in the great city
To be a grandee's mistress. Make thee
    ready
To go with us ; and until then remember
A watchful eye is on thee.   [*Exit.*
    Prec.   Woe is me !
I have a strange misgiving in my heart !
But that one deed of charity I 'll do,
Befall what may ; they cannot take that
    from me.

SCENE II. — *A room in the* ARCHBISHOP'S *Palace. The*
ARCHBISHOP *and a* CARDINAL *seated.*

    Arch. Knowing how near it touched the
        public morals,
And that our age is grown corrupt and
    rotten
By such excesses, we have sent to Rome,
Beseeching that his Holiness would aid
In curing the gross surfeit of the time,
By seasonable stop put here in Spain
To bull-fights and lewd dances on the stage.
All this you know.
    Card.   Know and approve.
    Arch.   And further,
That, by a mandate from his Holiness,
The first have been suppressed.
    Card.   I trust forever.
It was a cruel sport.
    Arch.   A barbarous pastime,
Disgraceful to the land that calls itself
Most Catholic and Christian.
    Card.   Yet the people
Murmur at this ; and, if the public dances
Should be condemned upon too slight occa-
    sion,
Worse ills might follow than the ills we cure.
As *Panem et Circenses* was the cry
Among the Roman populace of old,
So *Pan y Toros* is the cry in Spain.
Hence I would act advisedly herein ;
And therefore have induced your Grace to
    see
These national dances, ere we interdict
    them.

    (Enter a Servant.)
    Serv. The dancing-girl, and with her the
        musicians
Your Grace was pleased to order, wait
    without.
    Arch. Bid them come in. Now shall
        your eyes behold
In what angelic, yet voluptuous shape
The Devil came to tempt Saint Anthony.

(Enter PRECIOSA, *with a mantle thrown over her head.*
She advances slowly, in modest, half-timid attitude.)

    Card. (*aside*). Oh, what a fair and min-
        istering angel
Was lost to heaven when this sweet woman
    fell !
    Prec. (*kneeling before the* ARCHBISHOP).
        I have obeyed the order of your
        Grace.
If I intrude upon your better hours,
I proffer this excuse, and here beseech
Your holy benediction.
    Arch.   May God bless thee,
And lead thee to a better life. Arise.
    Card. (*aside*). Her acts are modest, and
        her words discreet !
I did not look for this ! Come hither,
    child.
Is thy name Preciosa ?
    Prec.   Thus I am called.
    Card. That is a Gypsy name. Who is
        thy father ?
    Prec. Beltran Cruzado, Count of the
        Calés.
    Arch. I have a dim remembrance of
        that man ;
He was a bold and reckless character,
A sun-burnt Ishmael !
    Card.   Dost thou remember
Thy earlier days ?
    Prec.   Yes ; by the Darro's side
My childhood passed. I can remember
    still
The river, and the mountains capped with
    snow ;
The villages, where, yet a little child,
I told the traveller's fortune in the street ;
The smuggler's horse, the brigand and the
    shepherd ;
The march across the moor ; the halt at
    noon ;
The red fire of the evening camp, that
    lighted
The forest where we slept ; and, further
    back,

As in a dream or in some former life,
Gardens and palace walls.

Arch. 'T is the Alhambra,
Under whose towers the Gypsy camp was
     pitched.
But the time wears ; and we would see thee
dance.

Prec. Your Grace shall be obeyed.

(*She lays aside her mantilla. The music of the cachu-
cha is played, and the dance begins. The ARCH-
BISHOP and the CARDINAL look on with gravity and
an occasional frown ; then make signs to each other ;
and, as the dance continues, become more and more
pleased and excited ; and at length rise from their
seats, throw their caps in the air, and applaud vehe-
mently as the scene closes.*)

SCENE III. — *The Prado. A long avenue of trees lead-
ing to the gate of Atocha. On the right the dome and
spires of a convent. A fountain. Evening.* DON
CARLOS *and* HYPOLITO *meeting.*

Don C. Holá ! good evening, Don Hypo-
lito.

Hyp. And a good evening to my friend,
Don Carlos.
Some lucky star has led my steps this way.
I was in search of you.

Don C. Command me always.

Hyp. Do you remember, in Quevedo's
Dreams,
The miser, who, upon the Day of Judg-
ment,
Asks if his money-bags would rise ?

Don C. I do ;
But what of that ?

Hyp. I am that wretched man.

Don C. You mean to tell me yours have
risen empty ?

Hyp. And amen ! said my Cid Campe-
ador.

Don C. Pray, how much need you ?

Hyp. Some half-dozen ounces,
Which, with due interest —

Don C. (*giving his purse*). What, am I
a Jew
To put my moneys out at usury ?
Here is my purse.

Hyp. Thank you. A pretty purse.
Made by the hand of some fair Madrileña ;
Perhaps a keepsake.

Don C. No, 't is at your service.

Hyp. Thank you again. Lie there, good
Chrysostom,
And with thy golden mouth remind me
often,
I am the debtor of my friend.

Don C. But tell me,
Come you to-day from Alcalá ?

Hyp. This moment.

Don C. And pray, how fares the brave
Victorian ?

Hyp. Indifferent well ; that is to say, not
well.
A damsel has ensnared him with the glances
Of her dark, roving eyes, as herdsmen catch
A steer of Andalusia with a lazo.
He is in love.

Don C. And is it faring ill
To be in love ?

Hyp. In his case very ill.

Don C. Why so ?

Hyp. For many reasons. First and fore-
most,
Because he is in love with an ideal ;
A creature of his own imagination ;
A child of air ; an echo of his heart ;
And, like a lily on a river floating,
She floats upon the river of his thoughts !

Don C. A common thing with poets. But
who is
This floating lily ? For, in fine, some wo-
man,
Some living woman, — not a mere ideal, —
Must wear the outward semblance of his
thought.
Who is it ? Tell me.

Hyp. Well, it is a woman !
But, look you, from the coffer of his heart
He brings forth precious jewels to adorn
her,
As pious priests adorn some favorite saint
With gems and gold, until at length she
gleams
One blaze of glory. Without these, you
know,
And the priest's benediction, 't is a doll.

Don C. Well, well ! who is this doll ?

Hyp. Why, who do you think ?

Don C. His cousin Violante.

Hyp. Guess again.
To ease his laboring heart, in the last storm
He threw her overboard, with all her in-
gots.

Don C. I cannot guess ; so tell me who
it is.

Hyp. Not I.

Don C. Why not ?

Hyp. (*mysteriously*). Why ? Because
Mari Franca
Was married four leagues out of Sala-
manca !

Don C. Jesting aside, who is it?
Hyp.   Preciosa.
Don C. Impossible ! The Count of Lara
     tells me
She is not virtuous.
Hyp.   Did I say she was ?
The Roman Emperor Claudius had a wife
Whose name was Messalina, as I think ;
Valeria Messalina was her name.
But hist ! I see him yonder through the
     trees,
Walking as in a dream.
Don C.   He comes this way.
Hyp. It has been truly said by some wise
     man,
That money, grief, and love cannot be hid-
     den.
          (*Enter* VICTORIAN *in front.*)
Vict. Where'er thy step has passed is
     holy ground !
These groves are sacred ! I behold thee
     walking
Under these shadowy trees, where we have
     walked
At evening, and I feel thy presence now ;
Feel that the place has taken a charm from
     thee,
And is forever hallowed.
Hyp.   Mark him well !
See how he strides away with lordly air,
Like that odd guest of stone, that grim
     Commander
Who comes to sup with Juan in the play.
Don C. What ho ! Victorian !
Hyp.   Wilt thou sup with us ?
Vict. Holá ! amigos ! Faith, I did not
     see you.
How fares Don Carlos ?
Don C.   At your service ever.
Vict. How is that young and green-eyed
     Gaditana
That you both wot of ?
Don C.   Ay, soft, emerald eyes !
She has gone back to Cadiz.
Hyp.   Ay de mí !
Vict. You are much to blame for letting
     her go back.
A pretty girl ; and in her tender eyes
Just that soft shade of green we sometimes
     see
In evening skies.
Hyp.   But, speaking of green eyes,
Are thine green ?
Vict.   Not a whit. Why so ?
Hyp.   I think

The slightest shade of green would be be-
     coming,
For thou art jealous.
Vict.   No, I am not jealous.
Hyp. Thou shouldst be.
Vict.   Why ?
Hyp.   Because thou art in love.
And they who are in love are always jealous.
Therefore thou shouldst be.
Vict.   Marry, is that all ?
Farewell ; I am in haste. Farewell, Don
     Carlos.
Thou sayest I should be jealous ?
Hyp.   Ay, in truth
I fear there is reason. Be upon thy guard.
I hear it whispered that the Count of Lara
Lays siege to the same citadel.
Vict.   Indeed !
Then he will have his labor for his pains.
Hyp. He does not think so, and Don
     Carlos tells me
He boasts of his success.
Vict.   How 's this, Don Carlos ?
Don C. Some hints of it I heard from
     his own lips.
He spoke but lightly of the lady's virtue,
As a gay man might speak.
Vict.   Death and damnation !
I 'll cut his lying tongue out of his mouth,
And throw it to my dog ! But, no, no, no !
This cannot be. You jest, indeed you jest.
Trifle with me no more. For otherwise
We are no longer friends. And so, fare-
     well !   [*Exit.*
Hyp. Now what a coil is here ! The
     Avenging Child
Hunting the traitor Quadros to his death,
And the great Moor Calaynos, when he
     rode
To Paris for the ears of Oliver,
Were nothing to him !   O hot - headed
     youth !
But come; we will not follow. Let us join
The crowd that pours into the Prado. There
We shall find merrier company ; I see
The Marialonzos and the Almavivas,
And fifty fans, that beckon me already.
                                    [*Exeunt.*

SCENE IV. — PRECIOSA'S *chamber. She is sitting, with
     a book in her hand, near a table, on which are flow-
     ers. A bird singing in its cage.* The COUNT OF
     LARA *enters behind unperceived.*

Prec. (*reads*).

     All are sleeping, weary heart !
     Thou, thou only sleepless art !

Heigho! I wish Victorian were here.
I know not what it is makes me so restless!
(The bird sings.)
Thou little prisoner with thy motley coat,
That from thy vaulted, wiry dungeon sing-
   est,
Like thee I am a captive, and, like thee,
I have a gentle jailer. Lack-a-day!

> All are sleeping, weary heart!
> Thou, thou only sleepless art!
> All this throbbing, all this aching,
> Evermore shall keep thee waking,
> For a heart in sorrow breaking
> Thinketh ever of its smart!

Thou speakest truly, poet! and methinks
More hearts are breaking in this world of
   ours
Than one would say. In distant villages
And solitudes remote, where winds have
   wafted
The barbèd seeds of love, or birds of pas-
   sage
Scattered them in their flight, do they take
   root,
And grow in silence, and in silence perish.
Who hears the falling of the forest leaf?
Or who takes note of every flower that
   dies?
Heigho! I wish Victorian would come.
Dolores!

(Turns to lay down her book, and perceives the Count.*)*

       Ha!
Lara.   Señora, pardon me!
Prec. How's this? Dolores!
Lara.   Pardon me —
Prec.   Dolores!
Lara. Be not alarmed; I found no one
   in waiting.
If I have been too bold —
  Prec. (turning her back upon him). You
   are too bold!
Retire! retire, and leave me!
Lara.   My dear lady,
First hear me! I beseech you, let me
   speak!
'T is for your good I come.
  Prec. (turning toward him with indigna-
   tion). Begone! begone!
You are the Count of Lara, but your deeds
Would make the statues of your ancestors
Blush on their tombs! Is it Castilian
   honor,
Is it Castilian pride, to steal in here
Upon a friendless girl, to do her wrong?

Oh shame! shame! shame! that you, a
   nobleman,
Should be so little noble in your thoughts
As to send jewels here to win my love,
And think to buy my honor with your gold!
I have no words to tell you how I scorn
   you!
Begone! The sight of you is hateful to me!
Begone, I say!
  Lara.   Be calm; I will not harm you.
  Prec. Because you dare not.
  Lara.   I dare anything!
Therefore beware! You are deceived in
   me.
In this false world, we do not always know
Who are our friends and who our enemies.
We all have enemies, and all need friends.
Even you, fair Preciosa, here at court
Have foes, who seek to wrong you.
  Prec.   If to this
I owe the honor of the present visit,
You might have spared the coming. Hav-
   ing spoken,
Once more I beg you, leave me to myself.
  Lara. I thought it but a friendly part to
   tell you
What strange reports are current here in
   town.
For my own self, I do not credit them;
But there are many who, not knowing you,
Will lend a readier ear.
  Prec.   There was no need
That you should take upon yourself the
   duty
Of telling me these tales.
  Lara.   Malicious tongues
Are ever busy with your name.
  Prec.   Alas!
I've no protectors. I am a poor girl,
Exposed to insults and unfeeling jest.
They wound me, yet I cannot shield my-
   self.
I give no cause for these reports. I live
Retired; am visited by none.
  Lara.   By none?
Oh, then, indeed, you are much wronged!
  Prec.   How mean you?
  Lara. Nay, nay; I will not wound your
   gentle soul
By the report of idle tales.
  Prec.   Speak out!
What are these idle tales? You need not
   spare me.
  Lara. I will deal frankly with you. Par-
   don me;

This window, as I think, looks towards the street,
And this into the Prado, does it not ?
In yon high house, beyond the garden wall, —
You see the roof there just above the trees, —
There lives a friend, who told me yesterday,
That on a certain night, — be not offended
If I too plainly speak, — he saw a man
Climb to your chamber window. You are silent !
I would not blame you, being young and fair —

(*He tries to embrace her. She starts back, and draws a dagger from her bosom.*)

Prec. Beware ! beware ! I am a Gypsy girl !
Lay not your hand upon me. One step nearer
And I will strike !
Lara.   Pray you, put up that dagger.
Fear not.
Prec. I do not fear. I have a heart
In whose strength I can trust.
Lara.   Listen to me.
I come here as your friend, — I am your friend, —
And by a single word can put a stop
To all those idle tales, and make your name
Spotless as lilies are. Here on my knees,
Fair Preciosa ! on my knees I swear,
I love you even to madness, and that love
Has driven me to break the rules of custom,
And force myself unasked into your presence.

(VICTORIAN *enters behind.*)

Prec. Rise, Count of Lara ! That is not the place
For such as you are. It becomes you not
To kneel before me. I am strangely moved
To see one of your rank thus low and humbled ;
For your sake I will put aside all anger,
All unkind feeling, all dislike, and speak
In gentleness, as most becomes a woman,
And as my heart now prompts me. I no more
Will hate you, for all hate is painful to me.
But if, without offending modesty
And that reserve which is a woman's glory,
I may speak freely, I will teach my heart
To love you.

Lara.   O sweet angel !
Prec.   Ay, in truth,
Far better than you love yourself or me.
Lara. Give me some sign of this, — the slightest token.
Let me but kiss your hand !
Prec.   Nay, come no nearer.
The words I utter are its sign and token.
Misunderstand me not ! Be not deceived !
The love wherewith I love you is not such
As you would offer me. For you come here
To take from me the only thing I have,
My honor. You are wealthy, you have friends
And kindred, and a thousand pleasant hopes
That fill your heart with happiness ; but I.
Am poor, and friendless, having but one treasure,
And you would take that from me, and for what ?
To flatter your own vanity, and make me
What you would most despise. Oh, sir, such love,
That seeks to harm me, cannot be true love.
Indeed it cannot. But my love for you
Is of a different kind. It seeks your good.
It is a holier feeling. It rebukes
Your earthly passion, your unchaste desires,
And bids you look into your heart, and see
How you do wrong that better nature in you,
And grieve your soul with sin.
Lara.   I swear to you,
I would not harm you ; I would only love you.
I would not take your honor, but restore it,
And in return I ask but some slight mark
Of your affection. If indeed you love me,
As you confess you do, oh, let me thus
With this embrace —
Vict. (*rushing forward*). Hold ! hold !
This is too much.
What means this outrage ?
Lara.   First, what right have you
To question thus a nobleman of Spain ?
Vict. I too am noble, and you are no more !
Out of my sight !
Lara.   Are you the master here ?
Vic. Ay, here and elsewhere, when the wrong of others
Gives me the right !

Prec. (*to* LARA). Go! I beseech you,
    go!
Vict. I shall have business with you,
    Count, anon!
Lara. You cannot come too soon! [*Exit.*
Prec.   Victorian!
Oh, we have been betrayed!
Vict.   Ha! ha! betrayed!
'T is I have been betrayed, not we!—not
    we!
Prec. Dost thou imagine—
Vict.   I imagine nothing;
I see how 't is thou whilest the time away
When I am gone!
Prec.   Oh, speak not in that tone!
It wounds me deeply.
Vict.   'T was not meant to flatter.
Prec. Too well thou knowest the pres-
    ence of that man
Is hateful to me!
Vict.   Yet I saw thee stand
And listen to him, when he told his love.
Prec. I did not heed his words.
Vict.   Indeed thou didst,
And answeredst them with love.
Prec.   Hadst thou heard all—
Vict. I heard enough.
Prec.   Be not so angry with me.
Vict. I am not angry; I am very calm.
Prec. If thou wilt let me speak—
Vict.   Nay, say no more.
I know too much already. Thou art false!
I do not like these Gypsy marriages!
Where is the ring I gave thee?
Prec.   In my casket.
Vict. There let it rest! I would not
    have thee wear it:
I thought thee spotless, and thou art pol-
    luted!
Prec. I call the Heavens to witness—
Vict.   Nay, nay, nay!
Take not the name of Heaven upon thy
    lips!
They are forsworn!
Prec.   Victorian! dear Victorian!
Vict. I gave up all for thee; myself, my
    fame,
My hopes of fortune, ay, my very soul!
And thou hast been my ruin! Now, go on!
Laugh at my folly with thy paramour
And, sitting on the Count of Lara's knee,
Say what a poor, fond fool Victorian was!
    (*He casts her from him and rushes out.*)
Prec. And this from thee!
    (*Scene closes.*)

SCENE V.—*The* COUNT OF LARA'S *rooms.* *Enter the*
    COUNT.

Lara. There 's nothing in this world so
    sweet as love,
And next to love the sweetest thing is hate!
I 've learned to hate, and therefore am re-
    venged.
A silly girl to play the prude with me!
The fire that I have kindled—
    (*Enter* FRANCISCO.)
            Well, Francisco,
What tidings from Don Juan?
Fran.   Good, my lord;
He will be present.
Lara.   And the Duke of Lermos!
Fran. Was not at home.
Lara.   How with the rest?
Fran.   I 've found
The men you wanted. They will all be there,
And at the given signal raise a whirlwind
Of such discordant noises, that the dance
Must cease for lack of music.
Lara.   Bravely done.
Ah! little dost thou dream, sweet Preciosa,
What lies in wait for thee. Sleep shall not
    close
Thine eyes this night! Give me my cloak
    and sword.   [*Exeunt.*

SCENE VI.—*A retired spot beyond the city gates.* *En-*
    ter VICTORIAN *and* HYPOLITO.

Vict. Oh shame! Oh shame! Why do
    I walk abroad
By daylight, when the very sunshine mocks
    me,
And voices, and familiar sights and sounds
Cry, "Hide thyself!" Oh, what a thin
    partition
Doth shut out from the curious world the
    knowledge
Of evil deeds that have been done in dark-
    ness!
Disgrace has many tongues. My fears are
    windows,
Through which all eyes seem gazing.
    Every face
Expresses some suspicion of my shame.
And in derision seems to smile at me!
Hyp. Did I not caution thee? Did I
    not tell thee
I was but half persuaded of her virtue?
Vict. And yet, Hypolito, we may be
    wrong,
We may be over-hasty in condemning!
The Count of Lara is a cursèd villain.

Hyp. And therefore is she cursèd, loving
   him.
Vict. She does not love him! 'T is for
   gold! for gold!
Hyp. Ay, but remember, in the public
   streets
He shows a golden ring the Gypsy gave
   him,
A serpent with a ruby in its mouth.
Vict. She had that ring from me! God!
   she is false;
But I will be revenged! The hour is
   passed.
Where stays the coward?
Hyp.   Nay, he is no coward;
A villain, if thou wilt, but not a coward.
I've seen him play with swords; it is his
   pastime.
And therefore be not over-confident,
He'll task thy skill anon. Look, here he
   comes.

(*Enter* LARA *followed by* FRANCISCO)

Lara. Good evening, gentlemen.
Hyp.   Good evening, Count.
Lara. I trust I have not kept you long
   in waiting.
Vict. Not long, and yet too long. Are
   you prepared?
Lara. I am.
Hyp.   It grieves me much to see this
   quarrel
Between you, gentlemen. Is there no way
Left open to accord this difference,
But you must make one with your swords?
Vict.   No! none!
I do entreat thee, dear Hypolito,
Stand not between me and my foe. Too
   long
Our tongues have spoken. Let these
   tongues of steel
End our debate. Upon your guard, Sir
   Count.

(*They fight.* VICTORIAN *disarms the* COUNT.)

Your life is mine; and what shall now
   withhold me
From sending your vile soul to its ac-
   count?
Lara. Strike! strike!
Vict. You are disarmed. I will not
   kill you.
I will not murder you. Take up your
   sword.

(FRANCISCO *hands the* COUNT *his sword, and* HYPOLITO
interposes.)

Hyp. Enough! Let it end here! The
   Count of Lara.
Has shown himself a brave man, and Vic-
   torian
A generous one, as ever. Now be friends.
Put up your swords; for, to speak frankly
   to you,
Your cause of quarrel is too slight a thing
To move you to extremes.
Lara.   I am content.
I sought no quarrel. A few hasty words,
Spoken in the heat of blood, have led to
   this.
Vict. Nay, something more than that.
Lara.   I understand you.
Therein I did not mean to cross your path.
To me the door stood open, as to others.
But, had I known the girl belonged to
   you,
Never would I have sought to win her from
   you.
The truth stands now revealed; she has
   been false
To both of us.
Vict.   Ay, false as hell itself!
Lara. In truth, I did not seek her; she
   sought me;
And told me how to win her, telling me
The hours when she was oftenest left
   alone.
Vict. Say, can you prove this to me?
   Oh, pluck out
These awful doubts, that goad me into
   madness!
Let me know all! all! all!
Lara.   You shall know all.
Here is my page, who was the messenger
Between us. Question him. Was it not so,
   Francisco?
Fran.   Ay, my lord.
Lara.   If further proof
Is needful, I have here a ring she gave me.
Vict. Pray let me see that ring! It is
   the same!

(*Throws it upon the ground, and tramples upon it.*)

Thus may she perish who once wore that
   ring!
Thus do I spurn her from me; do thus
   trample
Her memory in the dust! O Count of
   Lara,
We both have been abused, been much
   abused!
I thank you for your courtesy and frank-
   ness.

Though, like the surgeon's hand, yours
    gave me pain,
Yet it has cured my blindness, and I thank
    you.
I now can see the folly I have done,
Though 't is, alas! too late. So fare you
    well!
To-night I leave this hateful town forever.
Regard me as your friend. Once more
    farewell!
    Hyp. Farewell, Sir Count.

                    [*Exeunt* VICTORIAN *and* HYPOLITO.

    Lara. Farewell! farewell! farewell!
Thus have I cleared the field of my worst
    foe!
I have none else to fear; the fight is done,
The citadel is stormed, the victory won!

                    [*Exit with* FRANCISCO.

SCENE VII. — *A lane in the suburbs. Night. Enter*
    CRUZADO *and* BARTOLOMÉ.

    Cruz. And so, Bartolomé, the expedition
failed. But where wast thou for the most
part?
    Bart. In the Guadarrama mountains,
near San Ildefonso.
    Cruz. And thou bringest nothing back
with thee? Didst thou rob no one?
    Bart. There was no one to rob, save a
party of students from Segovia, who looked
as if they would rob us; and a jolly little
friar, who had nothing in his pockets but
a missal and a loaf of bread.
    Cruz. Pray, then, what brings thee back
to Madrid?
    Bart. First tell me what keeps thee here?
    Cruz. Preciosa.
    Bart. And she brings me back. Hast
thou forgotten thy promise?
    Cruz. The two years are not passed yet.
Wait patiently. The girl shall be thine.
    Bart. I hear she has a Busné lover.
    Cruz. That is nothing.
    Bart. I do not like it. I hate him, —
the son of a Busné harlot. He goes in
and out, and speaks with her alone, and I
must stand aside, and wait his pleasure.
    Cruz. Be patient, I say. Thou shalt have
thy revenge. When the time comes, thou
shalt waylay him.
    Bart. Meanwhile, show me her house.
    Cruz. Come this way. But thou wilt not
find her. She dances at the play to-night.
    Bart. No matter. Show me the house.
                    [*Exeunt.*

SCENE VIII. — *The Theatre. The orchestra plays the
cachucha. Sound of castanets behind the scenes.
The curtain rises, and discovers* PRECIOSA *in the
attitude of commencing the dance. The cachucha.
Tumult; hisses; cries of* "*Brava!*" *and* "*Afuera!*"
*She falters and pauses. The music stops. General
confusion.* PRECIOSA *faints.*

SCENE IX. — *The* COUNT OF LARA'S *chambers.* LARA
    and his friends at supper.

    Lara. So, Caballeros, once more many
    thanks!
You have stood by me bravely in this mat-
    ter.
Pray fill your glasses.
    Don J.   Did you mark, Don Luis,
How pale she looked, when first the noise
    began,
And then stood still, with her large eyes
    dilated!
Her nostrils spread! her lips apart! her
    bosom
Tumultuous as the sea!
    Don L.   I pitied her.
    Lara. Her pride is humbled; and this
    very night
I mean to visit her.
    Don J.   Will you serenade her?
    Lara. No music! no more music!
    Don L.   Why not music?
It softens many hearts.
    Lara.   Not in the humor
She now is in. Music would madden
    her.
    Don J. Try golden cymbals.
    Don L.   Yes, try Don Dinero;
A mighty wooer is your Don Dinero.
    Lara. To tell the truth, then, I have
    bribed her maid.
But, Caballeros, you dislike this wine.
A bumper and away; for the night wears.
A health to Preciosa.

            (*They rise and drink.*)

    All.   Preciosa.
    Lara (*holding up his glass*). Thou bright
    and flaming minister of Love!
Thou wonderful magician! who hast stolen
My secret from me, and 'mid sighs of pas-
    sion
Caught from my lips, with red and fiery
    tongue,
Her precious name! Oh nevermore hence-
    forth
Shall mortal lips press thine; and never-
    more

A mortal name be whispered in thine ear.
Go ! keep my secret !
(*Drinks and dashes the goblet down.*)
Don J.   Ite ! missa est !
(*Scene closes.*)

SCENE X. — *Street and garden wall. Night. Enter* CRUZADO *and* BARTOLOMÉ.

Cruz. This is the garden wall, and above it, yonder, is her house. The window in which thou seest the light is her window. But we will not go in now.

Bart. Why not ?

Cruz. Because she is not at home.

Bart. No matter ; we can wait. But how is this ? The gate is bolted. (*Sound of guitars and voices in a neighboring street.*) Hark ! There comes her lover with his infernal serenade ! · Hark !

SONG

Good night ! Good night, beloved !
I come to watch o'er thee !
To be near thee, — to be near thee,
Alone is peace for me.

Thine eyes are stars of morning,
Thy lips are crimson flowers !
Good night ! Good night, beloved,
While I count the weary hours.

Cruz. They are not coming this way.

Bart. Wait, they begin again.

SONG (*coming nearer*)

Ah ! thou moon that shinest
Argent-clear above !
All night long enlighten
My sweet lady-love ;
Moon that shinest,
All night long enlighten !

Bart. Woe be to him, if he comes this way !

Cruz. Be quiet, they are passing down the street.

SONG (*dying away*)

The nuns in the cloister
Sang to each other ;
For so many sisters
Is there not one brother !
Ay, for the partridge, mother !
The cat has run away with the partridge !
Puss ! puss ! puss !

Bart. Follow that ! follow that ! Come with me. Puss ! puss !

[*Exeunt. On the opposite side enter the* COUNT OF LARA *and gentlemen with* FRANCISCO.)

Lara. The gate is fast. Over the wall, Francisco,
And draw the bolt. There, so, and so, and over.
Now, gentlemen, come in, and help me scale
Yon balcony. How now ? Her light still burns.
Move warily. Make fast the gate, Francisco.
(*Exeunt. Reënter* CRUZADO *and* BARTOLOMÉ.)

Bart. They went in at the gate. Hark !
I hear them in the garden. (*Tries the gate.*) Bolted again ! Vive Cristo ! Follow me over the wall.
(*They climb the wall.*)

SCENE XI. — PRECIOSA'S *bedchamber. Midnight. She is sleeping in an arm-chair, in an undress.* DOLORES *watching her.*

Dol. She sleeps at last !
(*Opens the window, and listens.*)
All silent in the street,
And in the garden. Hark !

Prec. (*in her sleep*). I must go hence !
Give me my cloak !

Dol. He comes ! I hear his footsteps.

Prec. Go tell them that I cannot dance to-night ;
I am too ill ! Look at me ! See the fever
That burns upon my cheek ! I must go hence.
I am too weak to dance.
(*Signal from the garden.*)

Dol. (*from the window*). Who 's there ?

Voice (*from below*).   A friend.

Dol. I will undo the door. Wait till I come.

Prec. I must go hence. I pray you do not harm me !
Shame ! shame ! to treat a feeble woman thus !
Be you but kind, I will do all things for you.
I 'm ready now, — give me my castanets.
Where is Victorian ? Oh, those hateful lamps !
They glare upon me like an evil eye.
I cannot stay. Hark ! how they mock at me !
They hiss at me like serpents ! Save me !
save me !
(*She wakes.*)
How late is it, Dolores ?

Dol. It is midnight.

Prec. We must be patient. Smooth this pillow for me.

(*She sleeps again. Noise from the garden, and voices.*)

Voice. Muera!

Another voice. O villains! villains!

Lara. So! have at you!

Voice. Take that!

Lara. Oh, I am wounded!

Dol. (*shutting the window*). Jesu Maria!

ACT III

Scene I. — *A cross-road through a wood. In the background a distant village spire.* Victorian *and* Hypolito, *as travelling students, with guitars, sitting under the trees.* Hypolito *plays and sings.*

SONG

Ah, Love!
Perjured, false, treacherous Love!
Enemy
Of all that mankind may not rue!
Most untrue
To him who keeps most faith with thee.
Woe is me!
The falcon has the eyes of the dove.
Ah, Love!
Perjured, false, treacherous Love!

Vict. Yes, Love is ever busy with his shuttle,
Is ever weaving into life's dull warp
Bright, gorgeous flowers and scenes Arcadian;
Hanging our gloomy prison-house about
With tapestries, that make its walls dilate
In never-ending vistas of delight.

Hyp. Thinking to walk in those Arcadian pastures,
Thou hast run thy noble head against the wall.

SONG (continued)

Thy deceits
Give us clearly to comprehend,
Whither tend
All thy pleasures, all thy sweets!
They are cheats,
Thorns below and flowers above.
Ah, Love!
Perjured, false, treacherous Love!

Vict. A very pretty song. I thank thee for it.

Hyp. It suits thy case.

Vict. Indeed, I think it does.
What wise man wrote it?

Hyp. Lopez Maldonado.

Vict. In truth, a pretty song.

Hyp. With much truth in it.
I hope thou wilt profit by it; and in earnest
Try to forget this lady of thy love.

Vict. I will forget her! All dear recollections
Pressed in my heart, like flowers within a book,
Shall be torn out, and scattered to the winds!
I will forget her! But perhaps hereafter,
When she shall learn how heartless is the world,
A voice within her will repeat my name,
And she will say, "He was indeed my friend!"
Oh, would I were a soldier, not a scholar,
That the loud march, the deafening beat of drums,
The shattering blast of the brass-throated trumpet,
The din of arms, the onslaught and the storm,
And a swift death, might make me deaf forever
To the upbraidings of this foolish heart!

Hyp. Then let that foolish heart upbraid no more!
To conquer love, one need but will to conquer.

Vict. Yet, good Hypolito, it is in vain
I throw into Oblivion's sea the sword
That pierces me; for, like Excalibar,
With gemmed and flashing hilt, it will not sink.
There rises from below a hand that grasps it,
And waves it in the air; and wailing voices
Are heard along the shore.

Hyp. And yet at last
Down sank Excalibar to rise no more.
This is not well. In truth, it vexes me.
Instead of whistling to the steeds of Time,
To make them jog on merrily with life's burden,
Like a dead weight thou hangest on the wheels.
Thou art too young, too full of lusty health
To talk of dying.

Vict. Yet I fain would die!
To go through life, unloving and unloved;
To feel that thirst and hunger of the soul
We cannot still; that longing, that wild impulse,
And struggle after something we have not

And cannot have ; the effort to be strong ;
And, like the Spartan boy, to smile, and
smile,
While secret wounds do bleed beneath our
cloaks ;
All this the dead feel not, — the dead
alone !
Would I were with them !
Hyp. We shall all be soon.
Vict. It cannot be too soon ; for I am
weary
Of the bewildering masquerade of Life,
Where strangers walk as friends, and
friends as strangers ;
Where whispers overheard betray false
hearts ;
And through the mazes of the crowd we
chase
Some form of loveliness, that smiles, and
beckons,
And cheats us with fair words, only to leave
us
A mockery and a jest ; maddened, — con-
fused, —
Not knowing friend from foe.
Hyp. Why seek to know ?
Enjoy the merry shrove-tide of thy youth !
Take each fair mask for what it gives it-
self,
Nor strive to look beneath it.
Vict. I confess,
That were the wiser part. But Hope no
longer
Comforts my soul. I am a wretched man,
Much like a poor and shipwrecked mariner,
Who, struggling to climb up into the boat,
Has both his bruised and bleeding hands
cut off,
And sinks again into the weltering sea,
Helpless and hopeless !
Hyp. Yet thou shalt not perish.
The strength of thine own arm is thy salva-
tion.
Above thy head, through rifted clouds,
there shines
A glorious star. Be patient. Trust thy
star !
(*Sound of a village bell in the distance.*)
Vict. Ave Maria ! I hear the sacristan
Ringing the chimes from yonder village
belfry !
A solemn sound, that echoes far and wide
Over the red roofs of the cottages,
And bids the laboring hind afield, the shep-
herd,

Guarding his flock, the lonely muleteer,
And all the crowd in village streets, stand
still,
And breathe a prayer unto the blessed Vir-
gin !
Hyp. Amen ! amen ! Not half a league
from hence
The village lies.
Vict. This path will lead us to it,
Over the wheat-fields, where the shadows
sail
Across the running sea, now green, now
blue,
And, like an idle mariner on the main,
Whistles the quail. Come, let us hasten
on. [*Exeunt.*

SCENE II. — *Public square in the village of Guadar-*
rama. The Ave Maria still tolling. A crowd of vil-
lagers, with their hats in their hands, as if in prayer.
In front, a group of Gypsies. The bell rings a mer-
rier peal. A Gypsy dance. Enter PANCHO, *followed*
by PEDRO CRESPO.

Pancho. Make room, ye vagabonds and
Gypsy thieves !
Make room for the Alcalde and for me !
Pedro C. Keep silence all ! I have an
edict here
From our most gracious lord, the King of
Spain,
Jerusalem, and the Canary Islands,
Which I shall publish in the market-place.
Open your ears and listen !
(*Enter the* PADRE CURA *at the door of his cottage.*)
Padre Cura,
Good day ! and, pray you, hear this edict
read.
Padre C. Good day, and God be with
you !
Pray, what is it ?
Pedro C. An act of banishment against
the Gypsies !
(*Agitation and murmurs in the crowd.*)
Pancho. Silence !
Pedro C. (*reads*). " I hereby order and
command,
That the Egyptian and Chaldean stran-
gers,
Known by the name of Gypsies, shall
henceforth
Be banished from the realm, as vagabonds
And beggars ; and if, after seventy days,
Any be found within our kingdom's bounds,
They shall receive a hundred lashes each ;
The second time, shall have their ears cut
off ;

The third, be slaves for life to him who
    takes them,
Or burnt as heretics. Signed, I, the King."
Vile miscreants and creatures unbaptized !
You hear the law ! Obey and disappear !
  Pancho. And if in seventy days you are
    not gone,
Dead or alive I make you all my slaves.
(*The Gypsies go out in confusion, showing signs of fear
and discontent.* PANCHO *follows.*)
  Padre C. A righteous law ! A very
    righteous law !
Pray you, sit down.
  Pedro C.   I thank you heartily.

(*They seat themselves on a bench at the* PADRE CURA'S
*door. Sound of guitars heard at a distance, ap-
proaching during the dialogue which follows.*)

A very righteous judgment, as you say.
Now tell me, Padre Cura, — you know all
    things, —
How came these Gypsies into Spain ?
  Padre C.   Why, look you ;
They came with Hercules from Palestine,
And hence are thieves and vagrants, Sir
    Alcalde,
As the Simoniacs from Simon Magus.
And, look you, as Fray Jayme Bleda says,
There are a hundred marks to prove a
    Moor
Is not a Christian, so 't is with the Gypsies.
They never marry, never go to mass,
Never baptize their children, nor keep
    Lent,
Nor see the inside of a church, — nor —
    nor —
  Pedro C. Good reasons, good, substan-
    tial reasons all !
No matter for the other ninety-five.
They should be burnt, I see it plain enough,
They should be burnt.
    (*Enter* VICTORIAN *and* HYPOLITO *playing.*)
  Padre C. And pray, whom have we here ?
  Pedro C. More vagrants ! By Saint
    Lazarus, more vagrants !
  Hyp. Good evening, gentlemen ! Is this
    Guadarrama ?
  Padre C. Yes, Guadarrama, and good
    evening to you.
  Hyp. We seek the Padre Cura of the
    village ;
And, judging from your dress and rev-
    erend mien,
You must be he.
  Padre C. I am. Pray, what 's your
    pleasure ?

  Hyp. We are poor students travelling in
    vacation.
You know this mark ?
    (*Touching the wooden spoon in his hat-band.*)
  Padre C. (*joyfully*). Ay, know it, and
    have worn it.
  Pedro C. (*aside*). Soup-eaters ! by the
    mass ! The worst of vagrants !
And there 's no law against them. Sir,
    your servant.   [*Exit.*
  Padre C. Your servant, Pedro Crespo.
  Hyp.   Padre Cura,
From the first moment I beheld your face,
I said within myself, " This is the man ! "
There is a certain something in your looks,
A certain scholar-like and studious some-
    thing, —
You understand, — which cannot be mis-
    taken ;
Which marks you as a very learned man,
In fine, as one of us.
  Vict. (*aside*).   What impudence !
  Hyp. As we approached, I said to my
    companion,
" That is the Padre Cura ; mark my
    words ! "
Meaning your Grace. " The other man,"
    said I,
" Who sits so awkwardly upon the bench,
Must be the sacristan."
  Padre C.   Ah ! said you so ?
Why, that was Pedro Crespo, the alcalde !
  Hyp. Indeed ! you much astonish me !
    His air
Was not so full of dignity and grace
As an alcalde's should be.
  Padre C.   That is true,
He 's out of humor with some vagrant
    Gypsies,
Who have their camp here in the neighbor-
    hood.
There 's nothing so undignified as anger.
  Hyp. The Padre Cura will excuse our
    boldness,
If, from his well-known hospitality,
We crave a lodging for the night.
  Padre C.   I pray you !
You do me honor ! I am but too happy
To have such guests beneath my humble
    roof.
It is not often that I have occasion
To speak with scholars ; and *Emollit mores,*
Nec sinit esse feros, Cicero says.
  Hyp. 'T is Ovid, is it not ?
  Padre C.   No, Cicero.

Hyp. Your Grace is right. You are the
better scholar.
Now what a dunce was I to think it Ovid !
But hang me if it is not ! (*Aside.*)
Padre C. Pass this way.
He was a very great man, was Cicero !
Pray you, go in, go in ! no ceremony.
[*Exeunt.*

SCENE III. — *A room in the* PADRE CURA'S *house.
Enter the* PADRE *and* HYPOLITO.

Padre C. So then, Señor, you come from
Alcalá.
I am glad to hear it. It was there I studied.
Hyp. And left behind an honored name,
no doubt.
How may I call your Grace ?
Padre C. Gerónimo
De Santillana, at your Honor's service.
Hyp. Descended from the Marquis San-
tillana ?
From the distinguished poet ?
Padre C. From the Marquis,
Not from the poet.
Hyp. Why, they were the same.
Let me embrace you ! Oh, some lucky star
Has brought me hither ! Yet once more !
— once more !
Your name is ever green in Alcalá,
And our professor, when we are unruly,
Will shake his hoary head, and say, " Alas !
It was not so in Santillana's time ! "
Padre C. I did not think my name re-
membered there.
Hyp. More than remembered ; it is idol-
ized.
Padre C. Of what professor speak you ?
Hyp. Timoneda.
Padre C. I don't remember any Timo-
neda.
Hyp. A grave and sombre man, whose
beetling brow
O'erhangs the rushing current of his speech
As rocks o'er rivers hang. Have you for-
gotten ?
Padre C. Indeed, I have. Oh, those
were pleasant days,
Those college days ! I ne'er shall see the
like !
I had not buried then so many hopes !
I had not buried then so many friends !
I 've turned my back on what was then
before me ;
And the bright faces of my young com-
panions

Are wrinkled like my own, or are no more.
Do you remember Cueva ?
Hyp. Cueva ? Cueva ?
Padre C. Fool that I am ! He was be-
fore your time.
You 're a mere boy, and I am an old man.
Hyp. I should not like to try my strength
with you.
Padre C. Well, well. But I forget ; you
must be hungry.
Martina ! ho ! Martina ! 'T is my niece.
(*Enter* MARTINA.)
Hyp. You may be proud of such a niece
as that.
I wish I had a niece. *Emollit mores.*
(*Aside.*)
He was a very great man, was Cicero !
Your servant, fair Martina.
Mart. Servant, sir.
Padre C. This gentleman is hungry. See
thou to it.
Let us have supper.
Mart. 'T will be ready soon.
Padre C. And bring a bottle of my Val-
de-Peñas
Out of the cellar. Stay ; I 'll go myself.
Pray you, Señor, excuse me. [*Exit.*
Hyp. Hist ! Martina !
One word with you. Bless me ! what hand-
some eyes !
To-day there have been Gypsies in the vil-
lage.
Is it not so ?
Mart. There have been Gypsies here.
Hyp. Yes, and have told your fortune.
Mart. (*embarrassed*). Told my fortune ?
Hyp. Yes, yes ; I know they did. Give
me your hand.
I 'll tell you what they said. They said, —
they said,
The shepherd boy that loved you was a
clown,
And him you should not marry. Was it
not ?
Mart. (*surprised*). How know you that ?
Hyp. Oh, I know more than that.
What a soft, little hand ! And then they
said,
A cavalier from court, handsome, and tall
And rich, should come one day to marry
you,
And you should be a lady. Was it not ?
He has arrived, the handsome cavalier.
(*Tries to kiss her. She runs off. Enter* VICTORIAN,
with a letter.)

Vict. The muleteer has come.
Hyp. So soon?
Vict. I found him
Sitting at supper by the tavern door,
And, from a pitcher that he held aloft
His whole arm's length, drinking the blood-
red wine.
Hyp. What news from Court?
Vict. He brought this letter only.
(*Reads.*)
Oh, cursèd perfidy! Why did I let
That lying tongue deceive me! Preciosa,
Sweet Preciosa! how art thou avenged!
Hyp. What news is this, that makes thy
cheek turn pale,
And thy hand tremble?
Vict. Oh, most infamous!
The Count of Lara is a worthless villain!
Hyp. That is no news, forsooth.
Vict. He strove in vain
To steal from me the jewel of my soul,
The love of Preciosa. Not succeeding,
He swore to be revenged; and set on foot
A plot to ruin her, which has succeeded.
She has been hissed and hooted from the
stage,
Her reputation stained by slanderous lies
Too foul to speak of; and, once more a
beggar,
She roams a wanderer over God's green
earth,
Housing with Gypsies!
Hyp. To renew again
The Age of Gold, and make the shepherd
swains
Desperate with love, like Gasper Gil's
Diana.
Redit et Virgo!
Vict. Dear Hypolito,
How have I wronged that meek, confiding
heart!
I will go seek for her; and with my tears
Wash out the wrong I 've done her!
Hyp. Oh, beware!
Act not that folly o'er again.
Vict. Ay, folly,
Delusion, madness, call it what thou wilt,
I will confess my weakness, — I still love
her!
Still fondly love her!
(*Enter the* PADRE CURA.)
Hyp. Tell us, Padre Cura,
Who are these Gypsies in the neighbor-
hood?
Padre C. Beltran Cruzado and his crew.

Vict. Kind Heaven,
I thank thee! She is found! is found
again!
Hyp. And have they with them a pale,
beautiful girl,
Called Preciosa?
Padre C. Ay, a pretty girl.
The gentleman seems moved.
Hyp. Yes, moved with hunger,
He is half famished with this long day's
journey.
Padre C. Then, pray you, come this way.
The supper waits. [*Exeunt.*

SCENE IV. — *A post-house on the road to Segovia, not
far from the village of Guadarrama. Enter* CHISPA,
cracking a whip, and singing the cachucha.

Chispa. Halloo! Don Fulano! Let us
have horses, and quickly. Alas, poor Chis-
pa! what a dog's life dost thou lead! I
thought, when I left my old master Victo-
rian, the student, to serve my new master
Don Carlos, the gentleman, that I, too,
should lead the life of a gentleman; should
go to bed early, and get up late. For when
the abbot plays cards, what can you expect
of the friars? But, in running away from
the thunder, I have run into the lightning.
Here I am in hot chase after my master
and his Gypsy girl. And a good beginning
of the week it is, as he said who was hanged
on Monday morning.
(*Enter* DON CARLOS.)
Don C. Are not the horses ready yet?
Chispa. I should think not, for the host-
ler seems to be asleep. Ho! within there!
Horses! horses! horses! (*He knocks at
the gate with his whip, and enter* MOSQUITO,
putting on his jacket.)
Mosq. Pray, have a little patience. I 'm
not a musket.
Chispa. Health and pistareens! I 'm
glad to see you come on dancing, padre!
Pray, what 's the news?
Mosq. You cannot have fresh horses;
because there are none.
Chispa. Cachiporra! Throw that bone
to another dog. Do I look like your aunt?
Mosq. No; she has a beard.
Chispa. Go to! go to!
Mosq. Are you from Madrid?
Chispa. Yes; and going to Estramadura.
Get us horses.
Mosq. What 's the news at Court?
Chispa. Why, the latest news is, that I

am going to set up a coach, and I have already bought the whip.

(*Strikes him round the legs.*)

Mosq. Oh! oh! you hurt me!

Don C. Enough of this folly. Let us have horses. (*Gives money to* Mosquito.) It is almost dark; and we are in haste. But tell me, has a band of Gypsies passed this way of late?

Mosq. Yes; and they are still in the neighborhood.

Don C. And where?

Mosq. Across the fields yonder, in the woods near Guadarrama. [*Exit.*

Don C. Now this is lucky. We will visit the Gypsy camp.

Chispa. Are you not afraid of the evil eye? Have you a stag's horn with you?

Don C. Fear not. We will pass the night at the village.

Chispa. And sleep like the Squires of Hernan Daza, nine under one blanket.

Don C. I hope we may find the Preciosa among them.

Chispa. Among the Squires?

Don C. No; among the Gypsies, blockhead!

Chispa. I hope we may; for we are giving ourselves trouble enough on her account. Don't you think so? However, there is no catching trout without wetting one's trousers. Yonder come the horses.

[*Exeunt.*

Scene V. — *The Gypsy camp in the forest. Night. Gypsies working at a forge. Others playing cards by the firelight.*

Gypsies (*at the forge sing*).

On the top of a mountain I stand,
With a crown of red gold in my hand,
Wild Moors come trooping over the lea,
Oh how from their fury shall I flee, flee, flee?
Oh how from their fury shall I flee?

First Gypsy (*playing*). Down with your John - Dorados, my pigeon. Down with your John-Dorados, and let us make an end.

Gypsies (*at the forge sing*).

Loud sang the Spanish cavalier,
And thus his ditty ran;
God send the Gypsy lassie here,
And not the Gypsy man.

First Gypsy (*playing*). There you are in your morocco!

Second Gypsy. One more game. The

Alcalde's doves against the Padre Cura's new moon.

First Gypsy. Have at you, Chirelin.

Gypsies (*at the forge sing*).

At midnight, when the moon began
To show her silver flame,
There came to him no Gypsy man,
The Gypsy lassie came.

(*Enter* Beltran Cruzado.)

Cruz. Come hither, Murcigalleros and Rastilleros; leave work, leave play; listen to your orders for the night. (*Speaking to the right.*) You will get you to the village, mark you, by the stone cross.

Gypsies. Ay!

Cruz. (*to the left*). And you, by the pole with the hermit's head upon it.

Gypsies. Ay!

Cruz. As soon as you see the planets are out, in with you, and be busy with the ten commandments, under the sly, and Saint Martin asleep. D' ye hear?

Gypsies. Ay!

Cruz. Keep your lanterns open, and, if you see a goblin or a papagayo, take to your trampers. Vineyards and Dancing John is the word. Am I comprehended?

Gypsies. Ay! ay!

Cruz. Away, then!

(*Exeunt severally.* Cruzado *walks up the stage, and disappears among the trees. Enter* Preciosa.)

Prec. How strangely gleams through the gigantic trees,
The red light of the forge! Wild, beckoning shadows
Stalk through the forest, ever and anon
Rising and bending with the flickering flame,
Then flitting into darkness! So within me
Strange hopes and fears do beckon to each other,
My brightest hopes giving dark fears a being
As the light does the shadow. Woe is me!
How still it is about me, and how lonely!

(Bartolomé *rushes in.*)

Bart. Ho! Preciosa!

Prec.   O Bartolomé!
Thou here?

Bart.   Lo! I am here.

Prec.   Whence comest thou?

Bart. From the rough ridges of the wild Sierra,
From caverns in the rocks, from hunger, thirst.

And fever! Like a wild wolf to the sheep-
fold
Come I for thee my lamb.
    Prec.   Oh, touch me not!
The Count of Lara's blood is on thy hands!
The Count of Lara's curse is on thy soul!
Do not come near me! Pray, begone from
here!
Thou art in danger! They have set a price
Upon thy head!
    Bart.   Ay, and I've wandered long
Among the mountains; and for many days
Have seen no human face, save the rough
swineherd's.
The wind and rain have been my sole com-
panions.
I shouted to them from the rocks thy
name,
And the loud echo sent it back to me,
Till I grew mad. I could not stay from
thee,
And I am here! Betray me, if thou wilt.
    Prec. Betray thee? I betray thee?
    Bart.   Preciosa!
I come for thee! for thee I thus brave
death!
Fly with me o'er the borders of this realm!
Fly with me!
    Prec. Speak of that no more. I cannot.
I'm thine no longer.
    Bart.   Oh, recall the time
When we were children! how we played
together,
How we grew up together; how we plighted
Our hearts unto each other, even in child-
hood!
Fulfil thy promise, for the hour has come.
I'm hunted from the kingdom, like a wolf!
Fulfil thy promise.
    Prec.   'T was my father's promise,
Not mine. I never gave my heart to
thee,
Nor promised thee my hand!
    Bart.   False tongue of woman!
And heart more false!
    Prec.   Nay, listen unto me.
I will speak frankly. I have never loved
thee;
I cannot love thee. This is not my fault,
It is my destiny. Thou art a man
Restless and violent. What wouldst thou
with me,
A feeble girl, who have not long to live,
Whose heart is broken? Seek another
wife,

Better than I, and fairer; and let not
Thy rash and headlong moods estrange her
from thee.
Thou art unhappy in this hopeless passion.
I never sought thy love; never did aught
To make thee love me. Yet I pity thee,
And most of all I pity thy wild heart,
That hurries thee to crimes and deeds of
blood.
Beware, beware of that.
    Bart.   For thy dear sake
I will be gentle. Thou shalt teach me
patience.
    Prec. Then take this farewell, and depart
in peace.
Thou must not linger here.
    Bart.   Come, come with me.
    Prec. Hark! I hear footsteps.
    Bart.   I entreat thee, come!
    Prec. Away! It is in vain.
    Bart.   Wilt thou not come?
    Prec. Never!
    Bart. Then woe, eternal woe, upon thee!
Thou shalt not be another's. Thou shalt
die.   [*Exit.*
    Prec. All holy angels keep me in this
hour!
Spirit of her who bore me, look upon me!
Mother of God, the glorified, protect me!
Christ and the saints, be merciful unto me!
Yet why should I fear death? What is it
to die?
To leave all disappointment, care, and sor-
row,
To leave all falsehood, treachery, and un-
kindness,
All ignominy, suffering, and despair,
And be at rest forever! O dull heart,
Be of good cheer! When thou shalt cease
to beat,
Then shalt thou cease to suffer and com-
plain!
    (*Enter* VICTORIAN *and* HYPOLITO *behind.*)
    Vict. 'T is she! Behold, how beautiful
she stands
Under the tent-like trees!
    Hyp.   A woodland nymph!
    Vict. I pray thee, stand aside. Leave me.
    Hyp.   Be wary.
Do not betray thyself too soon.
    Vict. (*disguising his voice*). Hist! Gypsy!
    Prec. (*aside, with emotion*). That voice!
that voice from heaven! Oh, speak
again!
Who is it calls?

Vict.   A friend.
Prec. (*aside*).   'T is he ! 'T is he !
I thank thee, Heaven, that thou hast heard
     my prayer,
And sent me this protector ! Now be
     strong,
Be strong, my heart ! I must dissemble
     here.
False friend or true ?
     Vict.   A true friend to the true ;
Fear not ; come hither. So ; can you tell
     fortunes ?
     Prec. Not in the dark. Come nearer to
     the fire.
Give me your hand. It is not crossed, I
     see.
     Vict. (*putting a piece of gold into her
     hand*). There is the cross.
     Prec.   Is 't silver ?
     Vict.   No, 't is gold.
     Prec. There 's a fair lady at the Court,
     who loves you,
And for yourself alone.
     Vict.   Fie ! the old story !
Tell me a better fortune for my money ;
Not this old woman's tale !
     Prec.   You are passionate ;
And this same passionate humor in your
     blood
Has marred your fortune. Yes ; I see it
     now ;
The line of life is crossed by many marks.
Shame ! shame ! Oh, you have wronged
     the maid who loved you !
How could you do it ?
     Vict.   I never loved a maid ;
For she I loved was then a maid no more.
     Prec. How know you that ?
     Vict.   A little bird in the air
Whispered the secret.
     Prec.   There, take back your gold !
Your hand is cold, like a deceiver's hand !
There is no blessing in its charity !
Make her your wife, for you have been
     abused ;
And you shall mend your fortunes, mend-
     ing hers.
     Vict. (*aside*). How like an angel's speaks
     the tongue of woman,
When pleading in another's cause her
     own !
That is a pretty ring upon your finger.
Pray give it me. (*Tries to take the ring.*)
     Prec.   No ; never from my hand
Shall that be taken !

Vict.   Why, 't is but a ring.
I 'll give it back to you ; or, if I keep it,
Will give you gold to buy you twenty
     such.
     Prec. Why would you have this ring ?
     Vict.   A traveller's fancy,
A whim, and nothing more. I would fain
     keep it
As a memento of the Gypsy camp
In Guadarrama, and the fortune-teller
Who sent me back to wed a widowed
     maid.
Pray, let me have the ring.
     Prec.   No, never ! never !
I will not part with it, even when I die ;
But bid my nurse fold my pale fingers
     thus,
That it may not fall from them. 'T is a
     token
Of a beloved friend, who is no more.
     Vict.   How ? dead ?
     Prec. Yes ; dead to me ; and worse than
     dead.
He is estranged ! And yet I keep this
     ring.
I will rise with it from my grave here-
     after,
To prove to him that I was never false.
     Vict. (*aside*). Be still, my swelling
     heart ! one moment, still !
Why, 't is the folly of a love-sick girl.
Come, give it me, or I will say 't is mine,
And that you stole it.
     Prec.   Oh, you will not dare
To utter such a falsehood !
     Vict.   I not dare ?
Look in my face, and say if there is
     aught
I have not dared, I would not dare for
     thee !

(*She rushes into his arms.*)

Prec. 'T is thou ! 't is thou ! Yes; yes;
     my heart's elected !
My dearest-dear Victorian ! my soul's
     heaven !
Where hast thou been so long ? Why
     didst thou leave me ?
     Vict. Ask me not now, my dearest Pre-
     ciosa.
Let me forget we ever have been parted !
     Prec. Hadst thou not come —
     Vict.   I pray thee, do not chide me !
     Prec. I should have perished here among
     these Gypsies.

Vict. Forgive me, sweet! for what I
made thee suffer.
Think'st thou this heart could feel a mo-
ment's joy,
Thou being absent? Oh, believe it not!
Indeed, since that sad hour I have not
slept,
For thinking of the wrong I did to thee!
Dost thou forgive me? Say, wilt thou
forgive me?
Prec. I have forgiven thee. Ere those
words of anger
Were in the book of Heaven writ down
against thee,
I had forgiven thee.
Vict. I'm the veriest fool
That walks the earth, to have believed
thee false.
It was the Count of Lara —
Prec. That bad man
Has worked me harm enough. Hast thou
not heard —
Vict. I have heard all. And yet speak
on, speak on!
Let me but hear thy voice, and I am
happy;
For every tone, like some sweet incanta-
tion,
Calls up the buried past to plead for me.
Speak, my beloved, speak into my heart,
Whatever fills and agitates thine own.
(*They walk aside.*)
Hyp. All gentle quarrels in the pastoral
poets,
All passionate love-scenes in the best ro-
mances,
All chaste embraces on the public stage,
All soft adventures, which the liberal stars
Have winked at, as the natural course of
things,
Have been surpassed here by my friend,
the student,
And this sweet Gypsy lass, fair Preciosa!
Prec. Señor Hypolito! I kiss your hand.
Pray, shall I tell your fortune?
Hyp. Not to-night;
For, should you treat me as you did Vic-
torian,
And send me back to marry maids forlorn,
My wedding day would last from now till
Christmas.
Chispa (*within*). What ho! the Gyp-
sies, ho! Beltran Cruzado!
Halloo! halloo! halloo! halloo!
(*Enters booted, with a whip and lantern.*)

Vict. What now?
Why such a fearful din? Hast thou been
robbed?
Chispa. Ay, robbed and murdered; and
good evening to you,
My worthy masters.
Vict. Speak; what brings thee here?
Chispa (*to* PRECIOSA). Good news from
Court; good news! Beltran Cru-
zado,
The Count of the Calés, is not your father,
But your true father has returned to Spain
Laden with wealth. You are no more a
Gypsy.
Vict. Strange as a Moorish tale!
Chispa. And we have all
Been drinking at the tavern to your health,
As wells drink in November, when it rains.
Vict. Where is the gentleman?
Chispa. As the old song says,

His body is in Segovia,
His soul is in Madrid.

Prec. Is this a dream? Oh, if it be a
dream,
Let me sleep on, and do not wake me yet!
Repeat thy story! Say I'm not deceived!
Say that I do not dream! I am awake;
This is the Gypsy camp; this is Victorian,
And this his friend, Hypolito! Speak!
speak!
Let me not wake and find it all a dream!
Vict. It is a dream, sweet child! a
waking dream,
A blissful certainty, a vision bright
Of that rare happiness, which even on
earth
Heaven gives to those it loves. Now art
thou rich,
As thou wast ever beautiful and good;
And I am now the beggar.
Prec. (*giving him her hand*). I have still
A hand to give.
Chispa (*aside*). And I have two to take.
I've heard my grandmother say, that
Heaven gives almonds
To those who have no teeth. That's nuts
to crack.
I've teeth to spare, but where shall I find
almonds?
Vict. What more of this strange story?
Chispa. Nothing more.
Your friend, Don Carlos, is now at the vil-
lage
Showing to Pedro Crespo, the Alcalde,

The proofs of what I tell you. The old
    hag,
Who stole you in your childhood, has con-
    fessed ;
And probably they'll hang her for the
    crime,
To make the celebration more complete.
    Vict. No ; let it be a day of general joy ;
Fortune comes well to all, that comes not
    late.
Now let us join Don Carlos.
    Hyp.   So farewell,
The student's wandering life ! Sweet ser-
    enades,
Sung under ladies' windows in the night,
And all that makes vacation beautiful !
To you, ye cloistered shades of Alcalá,
To you, ye radiant visions of romance,
Written in books, but here surpassed by
    truth,
The Bachelor Hypolito returns,
And leaves the Gypsy with the Spanish
    Student.

SCENE VI. — *A pass in the Guadarrama mountains.*
Early morning. A muleteer crosses the stage, sitting
sideways on his mule, and lighting a paper cigar with
flint and steel.

SONG

If thou art sleeping, maiden,
    Awake and open thy door,
'T is the break of day, and we must away
    O'er meadow, and mount, and moor.

Wait not to find thy slippers,
    But come with thy naked feet ;
We shall have to pass through the dewy grass,
    And waters wide and fleet.

(*Disappears down the pass. Enter a Monk. A Shep-*
herd appears on the rocks above.)

    Monk. Ave Maria, gratia plena. Olá !
good man !
    Shep. Olá !
    Monk. Is this the road to Segovia ?
    Shep. It is, your reverence.
    Monk. How far is it ?
    Shep. I do not know.
    Monk. What is that yonder in the val-
ley ?
    Shep. San Ildefonso.
    Monk. A long way to breakfast.
    Shep. Ay, marry.
    Monk. Are there robbers in these moun-
tains ?
    Shep. Yes, and worse than that.
    Monk. What ?

    Shep. Wolves.
    Monk. Santa Maria ! Come with me to
San Ildefonso, and thou shalt be well re-
warded.
    Shep. What wilt thou give me ?
    Monk. An Agnus Dei and my benedic-
tion.

(*They disappear. A mounted Contrabandista passes,*
wrapped in his cloak, and a gun at his saddle-bow.
He goes down the pass singing.)

SONG

Worn with speed is my good steed,
    And I march me hurried, worried ;
Onward, caballito mio,
    With the white star in thy forehead !
Onward, for here comes the Ronda,
    And I hear their rifles crack !
Ay, jaléo ! Ay, ay, jaléo !
    Ay, jaléo ! They cross our track.

(*Song dies away. Enter* PRECIOSA, *on horseback, at-*
tended by VICTORIAN, HYPOLITO, DON CARLOS, *and*
CHISPA, *on foot and armed.*)

    Vict. This is the highest point. Here let
    us rest.
See, Preciosa, see how all about us
Kneeling, like hooded friars, the misty
    mountains
Receive the benediction of the sun !
O glorious sight !
    Prec.   Most beautiful indeed !
    Hyp. Most wonderful !
    Vict.   And in the vale below,
Where yonder steeples flash like lifted hal-
    berds,
San Ildefonso, from its noisy belfries,
Sends up a salutation to the morn,
As if an army smote their brazen shields,
And shouted victory !
    Prec.   And which way lies
Segovia ?
    Vict.   At a great distance yonder.
Dost thou not see it ?
    Prec.   No. I do not see it.
    Vict. The merest flaw that dents the
    horizon's edge,
There, yonder !
    Hyp.   'T is a notable old town,
Boasting an ancient Roman aqueduct,
And an Alcázar, builded by the Moors,
Wherein, you may remember, poor Gil Blas
Was fed on *Pan del Rey.* Oh, many a time
Out of its grated windows have I looked
Hundreds of feet plumb down to the
    Eresma,

That, like a serpent through the valley
  creeping,
Glides at its foot.
   Prec.   Oh yes ! I see it now,
Yet rather with my heart than with mine
  eyes,
So faint it is.   And all my thoughts sail
  thither,
Freighted with prayers and hopes, and for-
  ward urged
Against all stress of accident, as in
The Eastern Tale, against the wind and tide
Great ships were drawn to the Magnetic
  Mountains,
And there were wrecked, and perished in
  the sea ! (*She weeps.*)
  Vict. O gentle spirit ! Thou didst bear
  unmoved
Blasts of adversity and frosts of fate !
But the first ray of sunshine that falls on
  thee
Melts thee to tears ! Oh, let thy weary heart
Lean upon mine ! and it shall faint no
  more,
Nor thirst, nor hunger ; but be comforted
And filled with my affection.
  Prec.   Stay no longer !
My father waits.   Methinks I see him
  there,
Now looking from the window, and now
  watching

Each sound of wheels or footfall in the
  street,
And saying, "Hark ! she comes !" O
  father ! father !
  (*They descend the pass.* CHISPA *remains behind.*)
  Chispa. I have a father, too, but he is a
dead one. Alas and alack-a-day ! Poor
was I born, and poor do I remain. I neither
win nor lose. Thus I wag through the
world, half the time on foot, and the other
half walking ; and always as merry as a
thunder-storm in the night. And so we
plough along, as the fly said to the ox.
Who knows what may happen ? Patience,
and shuffle the cards ! I am not yet so bald
that you can see my brains ; and perhaps,
after all, I shall some day go to Rome, and
come back Saint Peter. Benedicite ! [*Exit.*
  (*A pause. Then enter* BARTOLOMÉ *wildly, as if in pur-
suit, with a carbine in his hand.*)
  Bart. They passed this way. I hear their
  horses' hoofs !
Yonder I see them ! Come, sweet cara-
  millo,
This serenade shall be the Gypsy's last !
                (*Fires down the pass.*)
Ha ! ha ! Well whistled, my sweet cara-
  millo !
Well whistled ! — I have missed her ! — O
  my God !
  (*The shot is returned.* BARTOLOMÉ *falls.*)

THE BELFRY OF BRUGES AND OTHER POEMS

The Belfry of Bruges and other Poems was published
December 23, 1845, but the greater part of the volume
had already appeared in the illustrated edition of Mr.
Longfellow's poems published earlier in the year in
Philadelphia, as well as in the pages of *Graham's Mag-
azine*, which at this time was the most frequent vehicle
of his writing.

The poem which gives the title to the volume was the
product of his excursion in Europe in the summer of
1842. While on his way to the watercure at Marien-
berg on the Rhine, he spent a few days in Belgium, and
here is the entry which he makes in his diary : —

May 30. In the evening took the railway from Ghent
to Bruges. Stopped at *La Fleur de Blé* attracted by
the name, and found it a good hotel. It was not yet
night ; and I strolled through the fine old streets and
felt myself a hundred years old. The chimes seemed
to be ringing incessantly ; and the air of repose and an-
tiquity was delightful. . . . Oh, those chimes, those
chimes ! how deliciously they lull one to sleep ! The
little bells, with their clear, liquid notes, like the voices
of boys in a choir, and the solemn bass of the great bell
tolling in, like the voice of a friar !

May 31. Rose before five and climbed the high bel-

fry which was once crowned by the gilded copper drag-
on now at Ghent. The carillon of forty-eight bells ;
the little chamber in the tower ; the machinery, like a
huge barrel-organ, with keys like a musical instrument
for the *carilloneur ;* the view from the tower ; the sing-
ing of swallows with the chimes ; the fresh morning
air ; the mist in the horizon ; the red roofs far below ;
the canal, like a silver clasp, linking the city with the
sea, — how much to remember !

From some expressions in a letter to Freiligrath it
would seem that this poem and *Nuremberg* formed part
of a plan which the poet had designed of a series of
travel-sketches in verse, a plan which in a desultory
way he may be said to have been executing all his days
and to have carried out systematically in another shape
in his collection of *Poems of Places.*

The contents of this division are the same as in the
volume so entitled, except that a group of six trans-
lations has been withheld, to be placed with the other
translated pieces at the end of the volume ; except also
that to the Sonnets is added the personal one entitled
Mezzo Cammin, written at this time and first printed
in the *Life.*

THE BELFRY OF BRUGES

CARILLON

In the ancient town of Bruges,
In the quaint old Flemish city,
As the evening shades descended,
Low and loud and sweetly blended,
Low at times and loud at times,
And changing like a poet's rhymes,
Rang the beautiful wild chimes
From the Belfry in the market
Of the ancient town of Bruges.

Then, with deep sonorous clangor
Calmly answering their sweet anger,
When the wrangling bells had ended,
Slowly struck the clock eleven,
And, from out the silent heaven,
Silence on the town descended.
Silence, silence everywhere,
On the earth and in the air,
Save that footsteps here and there
Of some burgher home returning,
By the street lamps faintly burning,
For a moment woke the echoes
Of the ancient town of Bruges.

But amid my broken slumbers
Still I heard those magic numbers,
As they loud proclaimed the flight
And stolen marches of the night;
Till their chimes in sweet collision
Mingled with each wandering vision,
Mingled with the fortune-telling
Gypsy-bands of dreams and fancies,
Which amid the waste expanses
Of the silent land of trances
Have their solitary dwelling;
All else seemed asleep in Bruges,
In the quaint old Flemish city.

And I thought how like these chimes
Are the poet's airy rhymes,
All his rhymes and roundelays,
His conceits, and songs, and ditties,
From the belfry of his brain,
Scattered downward, though in vain,
On the roofs and stones of cities!
For by night the drowsy ear
Under its curtains cannot hear,
And by day men go their ways,
Hearing the music as they pass,
But deeming it no more, alas!
Than the hollow sound of brass.

Yet perchance a sleepless wight,
Lodging at some humble inn
In the narrow lanes of life,
When the dusk and hush of night
Shut out the incessant din
Of daylight and its toil and strife,
May listen with a calm delight
To the poet's melodies,
Till he hears, or dreams he hears,
Intermingled with the song,
Thoughts that he has cherished long;
Hears amid the chime and singing
The bells of his own village ringing,
And wakes, and finds his slumberous
    eyes
Wet with most delicious tears.

Thus dreamed I, as by night I lay
In Bruges, at the Fleur-de-Blé,
Listening with a wild delight
To the chimes that, through the night,
Rang their changes from the Belfry
Of that quaint old Flemish city.

THE BELFRY OF BRUGES

In the market-place of Bruges stands the
    belfry old and brown;
Thrice consumed and thrice rebuilded, still
    it watches o'er the town.

As the summer morn was breaking, on that
    lofty tower I stood,
And the world threw off the darkness, like
    the weeds of widowhood.

Thick with towns and hamlets studded,
    and with streams and vapors gray,
Like a shield embossed with silver, round
    and vast the landscape lay.

At my feet the city slumbered. From its
    chimneys, here and there,
Wreaths of snow-white smoke, ascending,
    vanished, ghost-like, into air.

Not a sound rose from the city at that
    early morning hour,
But I heard a heart of iron beating in the
    ancient tower.

From their nests beneath the rafters sang
    the swallows wild and high;
And the world, beneath me sleeping,
    seemed more distant than the sky.

Then most musical and solemn, bringing
    back the olden times,
With their strange, unearthly changes
    rang the melancholy chimes,

Like the psalms from some old cloister,
    when the nuns sing in the choir ;
And the great bell tolled among them, like
    the chanting of a friar.

Visions of the days departed, shadowy
    phantoms filled my brain ;
They who live in history only seemed to
    walk the earth again ;

All the Foresters of Flanders, — mighty
    Baldwin Bras de Fer,
Lyderick du Bucq and Cressy, Philip, Guy
    de Dampierre.

I beheld the pageants splendid that adorned
    those days of old ;
Stately dames, like queens attended, knights
    who bore the Fleece of Gold ;

Lombard and Venetian merchants with
    deep-laden argosies ;
Ministers from twenty nations ; more than
    royal pomp and ease.

I beheld proud Maximilian, kneeling hum-
    bly on the ground ;
I beheld the gentle Mary, hunting with her
    hawk and hound ;

And her lighted bridal-chamber, where a
    duke slept with the queen,
And the armèd guard around them, and
    the sword unsheathed between.

I beheld the Flemish weavers, with Namur
    and Juliers bold,
Marching homeward from the bloody battle
    of the Spurs of Gold ;

Saw the fight at Minnewater, saw the White
    Hoods moving west,
Saw great Artevelde victorious scale the
    Golden Dragon's nest.

And again the whiskered Spaniard all the
    land with terror smote ;
And again the wild alarum sounded from
    the tocsin's throat ;

Till the bell of Ghent responded o'er lagoon
    and dike of sand,
" I am Roland ! I am Roland ! there is
    victory in the land ! "

Then the sound of drums aroused me.   The
    awakened city's roar
Chased the phantoms I had summoned
    back into their graves once more.

Hours had passed away like minutes ; and,
    before I was aware,
Lo ! the shadow of the belfry crossed the
    sun-illumined square.

A GLEAM OF SUNSHINE

The scene of this poem is mentioned in the poet's
diary, under date of August 31, 1846. " In the afternoon
a delicious drive with F. and C. through Brookline, by
the church and ' the green lane,' and homeward through
a lovelier lane, with barberries and wild vines cluster-
ing over the old stone walls."

THIS is the place.   Stand still, my steed,
    Let me review the scene,
And summon from the shadowy Past
    The forms that once have been.

The Past and Present here unite
    Beneath Time's flowing tide,
Like footprints hidden by a brook,
    But seen on either side.

Here runs the highway to the town ;
    There the green lane descends,
Through which I walked to church with
    thee,
    O gentlest of my friends !

The shadow of the linden-trees
    Lay moving on the grass ;
Between them and the moving boughs,
    A shadow, thou didst pass.

Thy dress was like the lilies,
    And thy heart as pure as they :
One of God's holy messengers
    Did walk with me that day.

I saw the branches of the trees
    Bend down thy touch to meet,
The clover-blossoms in the grass
    Rise up to kiss thy feet.

" Sleep, sleep to-day, tormenting cares,
    Of earth and folly born ! "
Solemnly sang the village choir
    On that sweet Sabbath morn.

Through the closed blinds the golden sun
    Poured in a dusty beam,
Like the celestial ladder seen
    By Jacob in his dream.

And ever and anon, the wind
    Sweet-scented with the hay,
Turned o'er the hymn - book's fluttering
        leaves
    That on the window lay.

Long was the good man's sermon,
    Yet it seemed not so to me ;
For he spake of Ruth the beautiful,
    And still I thought of thee.

Long was the prayer he uttered,
    Yet it seemed not so to me ;
For in my heart I prayed with him,
    And still I thought of thee.

But now, alas ! the place seems changed ;
    Thou art no longer here :
Part of the sunshine of the scene
    With thee did disappear.

Though thoughts, deep-rooted in my heart,
    Like pine-trees dark and high,
Subdue the light of noon, and breathe
    A low and ceaseless sigh ;

This memory brightens o'er the past,
    As when the sun, concealed
Behind some cloud that near us hangs,
    Shines on a distant field.

THE ARSENAL AT SPRINGFIELD

On his wedding journey in the summer of 1843, Mr.
Longfellow passed through Springfield, Massachusetts,
and visited the United States arsenal there, in com-
pany with Mr. Charles Sumner. " While Mr. Sumner
was endeavoring," says Mr. S. Longfellow, " to impress
upon the attendant that the money expended upon
these weapons of war would have been much better
spent upon a great library, Mrs. Longfellow pleased her
husband by remarking how like an organ looked the
ranged and shining gun - barrels which covered the
walls from floor to ceiling, and suggesting what mourn-
ful music Death would bring from them. ' We grew
quite warlike against war,' she wrote, ' and I urged
H. to write a peace poem.' " The poem was written
some months later.

THIS is the Arsenal.   From floor to ceil-
        ing,
    Like a huge organ, rise the burnished
        arms ;
But from their silent pipes no anthem peal-
        ing
    Startles the villages with strange alarms.

Ah ! what a sound will rise, how wild and
        dreary,
    When the death-angel touches those swift
        keys !
What loud lament and dismal Miserere
    Will mingle with their awful sympho-
        nies !

I hear even now the infinite fierce chorus,
    The cries of agony, the endless groan,
Which, through the ages that have gone
        before us,
    In long reverberations reach our own.

On helm and harness rings the Saxon ham-
        mer,
    Through Cimbric forest roars the Norse-
        man's song,
And loud, amid the universal clamor,
    O'er distant deserts sounds the Tartar
        gong.

I hear the Florentine, who from his pal-
        ace
    Wheels out his battle-bell with dreadful
        din,
And Aztec priests upon their teocallis
    Beat the wild war-drums made of ser-
        pent's skin ;

The tumult of each sacked and burning
        village ;
    The shout that every prayer for mercy
        drowns ;
The soldiers' revels in the midst of pil-
        lage ;
    The wail of famine in beleaguered towns ;

The bursting shell, the gateway wrenched
        asunder,
    The rattling musketry, the clashing
        blade ;
And ever and anon, in tones of thunder
    The diapason of the cannonade.

Is it, O man, with such discordant noises,
    With such accursed instruments as these,

Thou drownest Nature's sweet and kindly
    voices,
And jarrest the celestial harmonies?

Were half the power that fills the world
    with terror,
Were half the wealth bestowed on camps
    and courts,
Given to redeem the human mind from error,
    There were no need of arsenals or forts:

The warrior's name would be a name ab-
    horrèd!
And every nation, that should lift again
Its hand against a brother, on its forehead
    Would wear forevermore the curse of
    Cain!

Down the dark future, through long gener-
    ations,
    The echoing sounds grow fainter and then
      cease;
And like a bell, with solemn, sweet vibra-
    tions,
    I hear once more the voice of Christ say,
      " Peace ! "

Peace ! and no longer from its brazen por-
    tals
    The blast of War's great organ shakes
      the skies !
But beautiful as songs of the immortals,
    The holy melodies of love arise.

NUREMBERG

In a letter to Freiligrath, printed in the *Life*, I. 436,
Mr. Longfellow describes with enthusiasm a day at
Nuremberg, from the memory of which this poem
sprang.

IN the valley of the Pegnitz, where across
    broad meadow-lands
Rise the blue Franconian mountains, Nu-
    remberg, the ancient, stands.

Quaint old town of toil and traffic, quaint
    old town of art and song,
Memories haunt thy pointed gables, like
    the rooks that round them throng :

Memories of the Middle Ages, when the
    emperors, rough and bold,
Had their dwelling in thy castle, time-
    defying, centuries old ;

And thy brave and thrifty burghers boasted,
    in their uncouth rhyme,
That their great imperial city stretched its
    hand through every clime.

In the court-yard of the castle, bound with
    many an iron band,
Stands the mighty linden planted by Queen
    Cunigunde's hand ;

On the square the oriel window, where in
    old heroic days
Sat the poet Melchior singing Kaiser Maxi-
    milian's praise.

Everywhere I see around me rise the won-
    drous world of Art :
Fountains wrought with richest sculpture
    standing in the common mart ;

And above cathedral doorways saints and
    bishops carved in stone,
By a former age commissioned as apostles
    to our own.

In the church of sainted Sebald sleeps en-
    shrined his holy dust,
And in bronze the Twelve Apostles guard
    from age to age their trust ;

In the church of sainted Lawrence stands a
    pix of sculpture rare,
Like the foamy sheaf of fountains, rising
    through the painted air.

Here, when Art was still religion, with a
    simple, reverent heart,
Lived and labored Albrecht Dürer, the
    Evangelist of Art ;

Hence in silence and in sorrow, toiling still
    with busy hand,
Like an emigrant he wandered, seeking for
    the Better Land.

Emigravit is the inscription on the tomb-
    stone where he lies ;
Dead he is not, but departed, — for the
    artist never dies.

Fairer seems the ancient city, and the sun-
    shine seems more fair,
That he once has trod its pavement, that
    he once has breathed its air !

Through these streets so broad and stately,
    these obscure and dismal lanes,
Walked of yore the Mastersingers, chanting
    rude poetic strains.

From remote and sunless suburbs came
    they to the friendly guild,
Building nests in Fame's great temple, as
    in spouts the swallows build.

As the weaver plied the shuttle, wove he
    too the mystic rhyme,
And the smith his iron measures hammered
    to the anvil's chime ;

Thanking God, whose boundless wisdom
    makes the flowers of poesy bloom
In the forge's dust and cinders, in the tis-
    sues of the loom.

Here Hans Sachs, the cobbler-poet, laureate
    of the gentle craft,
Wisest of the Twelve Wise Masters, in
    huge folios sang and laughed.

But his house is now an ale-house, with a
    nicely sanded floor,
And a garland in the window, and his face
    above the door ;

Painted by some humble artist, as in Adam
    Puschman's song,
As the old man gray and dove-like, with
    his great beard white and long.

And at night the swart mechanic comes to
    drown his cark and care,
Quaffing ale from pewter tankards, in the
    master's antique chair.

Vanished is the ancient splendor, and be-
    fore my dreamy eye
Wave these mingled shapes and figures,
    like a faded tapestry.

Not thy Councils, not thy Kaisers, win for
    thee the world's regard ;
But thy painter, Albrecht Dürer, and Hans
    Sachs thy cobbler bard.

Thus, O Nuremberg, a wanderer from a
    region far away,
As he paced thy streets and court-yards,
    sang in thought his careless lay :

Gathering from the pavement's crevice,
    as a floweret of the soil,
The nobility of labor, — the long pedigree
    of toil.

THE NORMAN BARON

The following passage from Thierry was sent to Mr.
Longfellow by an unknown correspondent, who sug-
gested it as a theme for a poem.

Dans les moments de la vie où la réflexion devient plus
calme et plus profonde, où l'intérêt et l'avarice parlent
moins haut que la raison, dans les instants de chagrin
domestique, de maladie, et de péril de mort, les nobles
se repentirent de posséder des serfs, comme d'une
chose peu agréable à Dieu, qui avait créé tous les
hommes à son image. — *Conquête de l'Angleterre.*

In his chamber, weak and dying,
Was the Norman baron lying ;
Loud, without, the tempest thundered,
    And the castle-turret shook.

In this fight was Death the gainer,
Spite of vassal and retainer,
And the lands his sires had plundered,
    Written in the Doomsday Book.

By his bed a monk was seated,
Who in humble voice repeated
Many a prayer and pater-noster,
    From the missal on his knee ;

And, amid the tempest pealing,
Sounds of bells came faintly stealing,
Bells, that from the neighboring kloster
    Rang for the Nativity.

In the hall, the serf and vassal
Held, that night, their Christmas wassail
Many a carol, old and saintly,
    Sang the minstrels and the waits;

And so loud these Saxon gleemen
Sang to slaves the songs of freemen,
That the storm was heard but faintly,
    Knocking at the castle-gates.

Till at length the lays they chanted
Reached the chamber terror-haunted,
Where the monk, with accents holy,
    Whispered at the baron's ear.

Tears upon his eyelids glistened,
As he paused awhile and listened,
And the dying baron slowly
    Turned his weary head to hear.

" Wassail for the kingly stranger
Born and cradled in a manger !
King, like David, priest, like Aaron,
    Christ is born to set us free ! "

And the lightning showed the sainted
Figures on the casement painted,
And exclaimed the shuddering baron,
    " Miserere, Domine ! "

In that hour of deep contrition
He beheld, with clearer vision,
Through all outward show and fashion,
    Justice, the Avenger, rise.

All the pomp of earth had vanished,
Falsehood and deceit were banished,
Reason spake more loud than passion,
    And the truth wore no disguise.

Every vassal of his banner,
Every serf born to his manor,
All those wronged and wretched crea-
    tures,
    By his hand were freed again.

And, as on the sacred missal
He recorded their dismissal,
Death relaxed his iron features,
    And the monk replied, " Amen ! "

Many centuries have been numbered
Since in death the baron slumbered
By the convent's sculptured portal,
    Mingling with the common dust :

But the good deed, through the ages
Living in historic pages,
Brighter grows and gleams immortal,
    Unconsumed by moth or rust.

RAIN IN SUMMER

How beautiful is the rain !
After the dust and heat,
In the broad and fiery street,
In the narrow lane,
How beautiful is the rain !

How it clatters along the roofs,
Like the tramp of hoofs !
How it gushes and struggles out
From the throat of the overflowing spout !

Across the window-pane
It pours and pours ;
And swift and wide,
With a muddy tide,
Like a river down the gutter roars
The rain, the welcome rain !

The sick man from his chamber looks
At the twisted brooks ;
He can feel the cool
Breath of each little pool ;
His fevered brain
Grows calm again,
And he breathes a blessing on the rain.

From the neighboring school
Come the boys,
With more than their wonted noise
And commotion ;
And down the wet streets
Sail their mimic fleets,
Till the treacherous pool
Ingulfs them in its whirling
And turbulent ocean.

In the country, on every side,
Where far and wide,
Like a leopard's tawny and spotted hide,
Stretches the plain,
To the dry grass and the drier grain
How welcome is the rain !

In the furrowed land
The toilsome and patient oxen stand ;
Lifting the yoke-encumbered head,
With their dilated nostrils spread,
They silently inhale
The clover-scented gale,
And the vapors that arise
From the well-watered and smoking soil.
For this rest in the furrow after toil
Their large and lustrous eyes
Seem to thank the Lord,
More than man's spoken word.

Near at hand,
From under the sheltering trees,
The farmer sees
His pastures, and his fields of grain,
As they bend their tops
To the numberless beating drops
Of the incessant rain.
He counts it as no sin
That he sees therein
Only his own thrift and gain.

These, and far more than these,
The Poet sees !
He can behold
Aquarius old
Walking the fenceless fields of air ;
And from each ample fold
Of the clouds about him rolled
Scattering everywhere
The showery rain,
As the farmer scatters his grain.

He can behold
Things manifold
That have not yet been wholly told, —
Have not been wholly sung nor said.
For his thought, that never stops,
Follows the water-drops
Down to the graves of the dead,
Down through chasms and gulfs profound,
To the dreary fountain-head
Of lakes and rivers under ground ;
And sees them, when the rain is done,
On the bridge of colors seven
Climbing up once more to heaven,
Opposite the setting sun.

Thus the Seer,
With vision clear,
Sees forms appear and disappear,
In the perpetual round of strange,
Mysterious change
From birth to death, from death to birth,
From earth to heaven, from heaven to
         earth ;
Till glimpses more sublime
Of things unseen before,
Unto his wondering eyes reveal
The Universe, as an immeasurable wheel
Turning forevermore
In the rapid and rushing river of Time.

TO A CHILD

This poem was begun October 2, 1845, and on the 13th of the next month Mr. Longfellow noted in his diary : " Walked in the garden and tried to finish the *Ode to a Child ;* but could not find the exact expressions I wanted, to round and complete the whole." After the publication of the volume containing it, he wrote : " The poem *To a Child* and *The Old Clock on the Stairs* seem to be the favorites. This is the best answer to my assailants." Possibly the charge was made then as frequently afterward that his poetry was an echo of foreign scenes. It is at any rate noticeable that in this poem he first strongly expressed that domestic sentiment which was to be so conspicuous in his after work. It will be remembered that he was married to Miss Appleton in July, 1843, and his second

child was born at the time when he was writing this ode. Five years later he made the following entry in his diary : " Some years ago, writing an *Ode to a Child,* I spoke of

The buried treasures of the miser, Time.

What was my astonishment to-day, in reading for the first time in my life Wordsworth's beautiful ode *On the Power of Sound,* to read

All treasures hoarded by the miser, Time."

DEAR child ! how radiant on thy mother's
         knee,
With   merry - making eyes and jocund
         smiles,
Thou gazest at the painted tiles,
Whose figures grace,
With many a grotesque form and face,
The ancient chimney of thy nursery !
The lady with the gay macaw,
The dancing girl, the grave bashaw
With bearded lip and chin ;
And, leaning idly o'er his gate,
Beneath the imperial fan of state,
The Chinese mandarin.

With what a look of proud command
Thou shakest in thy little hand
The coral rattle with its silver bells,
Making a merry tune !
Thousands of years in Indian seas
That coral grew, by slow degrees,
Until some deadly and wild monsoon
Dashed it on Coromandel's sand !
Those silver bells
Reposed of yore,
As shapeless ore,
Far down in the deep-sunken wells
Of darksome mines,
In some obscure and sunless place,
Beneath huge Chimborazo's base,
Or Potosí's o'erhanging pines !
And thus for thee, O little child,
Through many a danger and escape,
The tall ships passed the stormy cape ;
For thee in foreign lands remote,
Beneath a burning, tropic clime,
The Indian peasant, chasing the wild goat,
Himself as swift and wild,
In falling, clutched the frail arbute,
The fibres of whose shallow root,
Uplifted from the soil, betrayed
The silver veins beneath it laid,
The buried treasures of the miser, Time.

But, lo ! thy door is left ajar !
Thou hearest footsteps from afar !

And, at the sound,
Thou turnest round
With quick and questioning eyes,
Like one, who, in a foreign land,
Beholds on every hand
Some source of wonder and surprise !
And, restlessly, impatiently,
Thou strivest, strugglest, to be free.

The four walls of thy nursery
Are now like prison walls to thee.
No more thy mother's smiles,
No more the painted tiles,
Delight thee, nor the playthings on the
    floor,
That won thy little, beating heart before ;
Thou strugglest for the open door.

Through these once solitary halls
Thy pattering footstep falls.
The sound of thy merry voice
Makes the old walls
Jubilant, and they rejoice
With the joy of thy young heart,
O'er the light of whose gladness
No shadows of sadness
From the sombre background of memory
    start.

Once, ah, once, within these walls,
One whom memory oft recalls,
The Father of his Country, dwelt.
And yonder meadows broad and damp
The fires of the besieging camp
Encircled with a burning belt.
Up and down these echoing stairs,
Heavy with the weight of cares,
Sounded his majestic tread ;
Yes, within this very room
Sat he in those hours of gloom,
Weary both in heart and head.

But what are these grave thoughts to thee ?
Out, out ! into the open air !
Thy only dream is liberty,
Thou carest little how or where.
I see thee eager at thy play,
Now shouting to the apples on the tree,
With cheeks as round and red as they ;
And now among the yellow stalks,
Among the flowering shrubs and plants,
As restless as the bee.
Along the garden walks,
The tracks of thy small carriage-wheels I
    trace ;

And see at every turn how they efface
Whole villages of sand-roofed tents,
That rise like golden domes
Above the cavernous and secret homes
Of wandering and nomadic tribes of ants.
Ah, cruel little Tamerlane,
Who, with thy dreadful reign,
Dost persecute and overwhelm
These hapless Troglodytes of thy realm !

What ! tired already ! with those suppliant
    looks,
And voice more beautiful than a poet's
    books
Or murmuring sound of water as it flows,
Thou comest back to parley with re-
    pose !
This rustic seat in the old apple-tree,
With its o'erhanging golden canopy
Of leaves illuminate with autumnal hues,
And shining with the argent light of dews,
Shall for a season be our place of rest.
Beneath us, like an oriole's pendent nest,
From which the laughing birds have taken
    wing,
By thee abandoned, hangs thy vacant
    swing.
Dream-like the waters of the river gleam ;
A sailless vessel drops adown the stream,
And like it, to a sea as wide and deep,
Thou driftest gently down the tides of
    sleep.

O child ! O new-born denizen
Of life's great city ! on thy head
The glory of the morn is shed,
Like a celestial benison !
Here at the portal thou dost stand,
And with thy little hand
Thou openest the mysterious gate
Into the future's undiscovered land.
I see its valves expand,
As at the touch of Fate !
Into those realms of love and hate,
Into that darkness blank and drear,
By some prophetic feeling taught,
I launch the bold, adventurous thought,
Freighted with hope and fear ;
As upon subterranean streams,
In caverns unexplored and dark,
Men sometimes launch a fragile bark,
Laden with flickering fire,
And watch its swift-receding beams,
Until at length they disappear,
And in the distant dark expire.

By what astrology of fear or hope
Dare I to cast thy horoscope !
Like the new moon thy life appears ;
A little strip of silver light,
And widening outward into night
The shadowy disk of future years ;
And yet upon its outer rim,
A luminous circle, faint and dim,
And scarcely visible to us here,
Rounds and completes the perfect sphere ;
A prophecy and intimation,
A pale and feeble adumbration,
Of the great world of light, that lies
Behind all human destinies.

Ah ! if thy fate, with anguish fraught,
Should be to wet the dusty soil
With the hot tears and sweat of toil, —
To struggle with imperious thought,
Until the overburdened brain,
Weary with labor, faint with pain,
Like a jarred pendulum, retain
Only its motion, not its power, —
Remember, in that perilous hour,
When most afflicted and oppressed,
From labor there shall come forth rest.

And if a more auspicious fate
On thy advancing steps await,
Still let it ever be thy pride
To linger by the laborer's side ;
With words of sympathy or song
To cheer the dreary march along
Of the great army of the poor,
O'er desert sand, o'er dangerous moor.
Nor to thyself the task shall be
Without reward ; for thou shalt learn
The wisdom early to discern
True beauty in utility ;
As great Pythagoras of yore,
Standing beside the blacksmith's door,
And hearing the hammers, as they smote
The anvils with a different note,
Stole from the varying tones, that hung
Vibrant on every iron tongue,
The secret of the sounding wire,
And formed the seven-chorded lyre.

Enough ! I will not play the Seer ;
I will no longer strive to ope
The mystic volume, where appear
The herald Hope, forerunning Fear,
And Fear, the pursuivant of Hope.
Thy destiny remains untold ;
For, like Acestes' shaft of old,

The swift thought kindles as it flies,
And burns to ashes in the skies.

THE OCCULTATION OF ORION

Mr. Longfellow says : " Astronomically speaking, this title is incorrect ; as I apply to a constellation what can properly be applied to some of its stars only. But my observation is made from the hill of song, and not from that of science ; and will, I trust, be found sufficiently accurate for the present purpose."

I saw, as in a dream sublime,
The balance in the hand of Time.
O'er East and West its beam impended ;
And Day, with all its hours of light,
Was slowly sinking out of sight,
While, opposite, the scale of Night
Silently with the stars ascended.

Like the astrologers of eld,
In that bright vision I beheld
Greater and deeper mysteries.
I saw, with its celestial keys,
Its chords of air, its frets of fire,
The Samian's great Æolian lyre,
Rising through all its sevenfold bars,
From earth unto the fixèd stars.
And through the dewy atmosphere,
Not only could I see, but hear,
Its wondrous and harmonious strings,
In sweet vibration, sphere by sphere,
From Dian's circle light and near,
Onward to vaster and wider rings,
Where, chanting through his beard of
      snows,
Majestic, mournful, Saturn goes,
And down the sunless realms of space
Reverberates the thunder of his bass.

Beneath the sky's triumphal arch
This music sounded like a march,
And with its chorus seemed to be
Preluding some great tragedy.
Sirius was rising in the east ;
And, slow ascending one by one,
The kindling constellations shone.
Begirt with many a blazing star,
Stood the great giant Algebar,
Orion, hunter of the beast !
His sword hung gleaming by his side,
And, on his arm, the lion's hide
Scattered across the midnight air
The golden radiance of its hair.

The moon was pallid, but not faint ;
And beautiful as some fair saint,
Serenely moving on her way
In hours of trial and dismay.
As if she heard the voice of God,
Unharmed with naked feet she trod
Upon the hot and burning stars,
As on the glowing coals and bars,
That were to prove her strength and try
Her holiness and her purity.

Thus moving on, with silent pace,
And triumph in her sweet, pale face,
She reached the station of Orion.
Aghast he stood in strange alarm !
And suddenly from his outstretched arm
Down fell the red skin of the lion
Into the river at his feet.
His mighty·club no longer beat
The forehead of the bull ; but he
Reeled as of yore beside the sea,
When, blinded by Œnopion,
He sought the blacksmith at his forge,
And, climbing up the mountain gorge,
Fixed his blank eyes upon the sun.

Then, through the silence overhead,
An angel with a trumpet said,
" Forevermore, forevermore,
The reign of violence is o'er ! "
And, like an instrument that flings
Its music on another's strings,
The trumpet of the angel cast
Upon the heavenly lyre its blast,
And on from sphere to sphere the words
Reëchoed down the burning chords, —
" Forevermore, forevermore,
The reign of violence is o'er ! "

THE BRIDGE

At first localized as *The Bridge over the Charles*, the
river which separates Cambridge from Boston.

I STOOD on the bridge at midnight,
　As the clocks were striking the hour,
And the moon rose o'er the city,
　Behind the dark church-tower.

I saw her bright reflection
　In the waters under me,
Like a golden goblet falling
　And sinking into the sea.

And far in the hazy distance
　Of that lovely night in June,
The blaze of the flaming furnace
　Gleamed redder than the moon.

Among the long, black rafters
　The wavering shadows lay,
And the current that came from the ocean
　Seemed to lift and bear them away ;

As, sweeping and eddying through them,
　Rose the belated tide,
And, streaming into the moonlight,
　The seaweed floated wide.

And like those waters rushing
　Among the wooden piers,
A flood of thoughts came o'er me
　That filled my eyes with tears.

How often, oh how often,
　In the days that had gone by,
I had stood on that bridge at midnight
　And gazed on that wave and sky !

How often, oh how often,
　I had wished that the ebbing tide
Would bear me away on its bosom
　O'er the ocean wild and wide !

For my heart was hot and restless,
　And my life was full of care,
And the burden laid upon me
　Seemed greater than I could bear.

But now it has fallen from me,
　It is buried in the sea ;
And only the sorrow of others
　Throws its shadow over me.

Yet whenever I cross the river
　On its bridge with wooden piers,
Like the odor of brine from the ocean
　Comes the thought of other years.

And I think how many thousands
　Of care-encumbered men,
Each bearing his burden of sorrow,
　Have crossed the bridge since then.

I see the long procession
　Still passing to and fro,
The young heart hot and restless,
　And the old subdued and slow !

And forever and forever,
    As long as the river flows,
As long as the heart has passions,
    As long as life has woes ;

The moon and its broken reflection
    And its shadows shall appear,
As the symbol of love in heaven,
    And its wavering image here.

TO THE DRIVING CLOUD

GLOOMY and dark art thou, O chief of the
        mighty Omahas ;
Gloomy and dark as the driving cloud,
        whose name thou hast taken !
Wrapped in thy scarlet blanket, I see thee
        stalk through the city's
Narrow and populous streets, as once by
        the margin of rivers
Stalked those birds unknown, that have left
        us only their footprints.
What, in a few short years, will remain of
        thy race but the footprints ?

How canst thou walk these streets, who
        hast trod the green turf of the
        prairies ?
How canst thou breathe this air, who hast
        breathed the sweet air of the moun-
        tains ?
Ah ! 't is in vain that with lordly looks of
        disdain thou dost challenge
Looks of disdain in return, and question
        these walls and these pavements,
Claiming the soil for thy hunting-grounds,
        while down-trodden millions
Starve in the garrets of Europe, and cry
        from its caverns that they, too,
Have been created heirs of the earth, and
        claim its division !

Back, then, back to thy woods in the regions
        west of the Wabash !
There as a monarch thou reignest. In au-
        tumn the leaves of the maple
Pave the floors of thy palace-halls with
        gold, and in summer
Pine-trees waft through its chambers the
        odorous breath of their branches.
There thou art strong and great, a hero, a
        tamer of horses !
There thou chasest the stately stag on the
        banks of the Elkhorn,

Or by the roar of the Running-Water, or
        where the Omaha
Calls thee, and leaps through the wild ra-
        vine like a brave of the Blackfeet !

Hark ! what murmurs arise from the heart
        of those mountainous deserts ?
Is it the cry of the Foxes and Crows, or the
        mighty Behemoth,
Who, unharmed, on his tusks once caught
        the bolts of the thunder,
And now lurks in his lair to destroy the
        race of the red man ?
Far more fatal to thee and thy race than
        the Crows and the Foxes,
Far more fatal to thee and thy race than
        the tread of Behemoth,
Lo ! the big thunder-canoe, that steadily
        breasts the Missouri's
Merciless current ! and yonder, afar on the
        prairies, the camp-fires
Gleam through the night ; and the cloud of
        dust in the gray of the daybreak
Marks not the buffalo's track, nor the Man-
        dan's dexterous horse-race ;
It is a caravan, whitening the desert where
        dwell the Camanches !
Ha ! how the breath of these Saxons and
        Celts, like the blast of the east-wind,
Drifts evermore to the west the scanty
        smokes of thy wigwams !

SONGS

THE DAY IS DONE

Written in the fall of 1844 as proem to *The Waif*, a
small volume of poems selected by Mr. Longfellow and
published at Christmas of that year.

THE day is done, and the darkness
    Falls from the wings of Night,
As a feather is wafted downward
    From an eagle in his flight.

I see the lights of the village
    Gleam through the rain and the mist,
And a feeling of sadness comes o'er me
    That my soul cannot resist :

A feeling of sadness and longing,
    That is not akin to pain,
And resembles sorrow only
    As the mist resembles the rain.

Come, read to me some poem,
  Some simple and heartfelt lay,
That shall soothe this restless feeling,
  And banish the thoughts of day.

Not from the grand old masters,
  Not from the bards sublime,
Whose distant footsteps echo
  Through the corridors of Time.

For, like strains of martial music,
  Their mighty thoughts suggest
Life's endless toil and endeavor ;
  And to-night I long for rest.

Read from some humbler poet,
  Whose songs gushed from his heart,
As showers from the clouds of sum-
      mer,
  Or tears from the eyelids start ;

Who, through long days of labor,
  And nights devoid of ease,
Still heard in his soul the music
  Of wonderful melodies.

Such songs have power to quiet
  The restless pulse of care,
And come like the benediction
  That follows after prayer.

Then read from the treasured volume
  The poem of thy choice,
And lend to the rhyme of the poet
  The beauty of thy voice.

And the night shall be filled with music,
  And the cares, that infest the day,
Shall fold their tents, like the Arabs,
  And as silently steal away.

AFTERNOON IN FEBRUARY

  THE day is ending,
  The night is descending ;
  The marsh is frozen,
  The river dead.

  Through clouds like ashes
  The red sun flashes
  On village windows
  That glimmer red.

The snow recommences ;
The buried fences
Mark no longer
The road o'er the plain ;

While through the meadows,
Like fearful shadows,
Slowly passes
A funeral train.

The bell is pealing,
And every feeling
Within me responds
To the dismal knell ;

Shadows are trailing,
My heart is bewailing
And tolling within
Like a funeral bell.

TO AN OLD DANISH SONG BOOK

Mr. Longfellow upon Andersen's *Story of my Life*, notes in his diary : " Autumn always brings back very freshly my autumnal sojourn in Copenhagen, delightfully mingled with bracing air and yellow falling leaves. I have tried to record the impression in the song *To an Old Danish Song Book*."

WELCOME, my old friend,
Welcome to a foreign fireside,
While the sullen gales of autumn
Shake the windows.

The ungrateful world
Has, it seems, dealt harshly with thee,
Since, beneath the skies of Denmark,
First I met thee.

There are marks of age,
There are thumb-marks on thy margin,
Made by hands that clasped thee rudely,
At the alehouse.

Soiled and dull thou art ;
Yellow are thy time-worn pages,
As the russet, rain-molested
Leaves of autumn.

Thou art stained with wine
Scattered from hilarious goblets,
As the leaves with the libations
Of Olympus.

Yet dost thou recall
Days departed, half-forgotten,
When in dreamy youth I wandered
By the Baltic, —

When I paused to hear
The old ballad of King Christian
Shouted from suburban taverns
In the twilight.

Thou recallest bards,
Who, in solitary chambers,
And with hearts by passion wasted,
Wrote thy pages.

Thou recallest homes
Where thy songs of love and friendship
Made the gloomy Northern winter
Bright as summer.

Once some ancient Scald,
In his bleak, ancestral Iceland,
Chanted staves of these old ballads
To the Vikings.

Once in Elsinore,
At the court of old King Hamlet,
Yorick and his boon companions
Sang these ditties.

Once Prince Frederick's Guard
Sang them in their smoky barracks ; —
Suddenly the English cannon
Joined the chorus !

Peasants in the field,
Sailors on the roaring ocean,
Students, tradesmen, pale mechanics,
All have sung them.

Thou hast been their friend ;
They, alas ! have left thee friendless !
Yet at least by one warm fireside
Art thou welcome.

And, as swallows build
In these wide, old-fashioned chimneys,
So thy twittering song shall nestle
In my bosom, —

Quiet, close, and warm,
Sheltered from all molestation,
And recalling by their voices
Youth and travel.

WALTER VON DER VOGEL-WEID

Vogelweid the Minnesinger,
  When he left this world of ours,
Laid his body in the cloister,
  Under Würtzburg's minster towers.

And he gave the monks his treasures,
  Gave them all with this behest :
They should feed the birds at noontide
  Daily on his place of rest ;

Saying, " From these wandering minstrels
  I have learned the art of song ;
Let me now repay the lessons
  They have taught so well and long."

Thus the bard of love departed ;
  And, fulfilling his desire,
On his tomb the birds were feasted
  By the children of the choir.

Day by day, o'er tower and turret,
  In foul weather and in fair,
Day by day, in vaster numbers,
  Flocked the poets of the air.

On the tree whose heavy branches
  Overshadowed all the place,
On the pavement, on the tombstone,
  On the poet's sculptured face,

On the cross-bars of each window,
  On the lintel of each door,
They renewed the War of Wartburg,
  Which the bard had fought before.

There they sang their merry carols,
  Sang their lauds on every side ;
And the name their voices uttered
  Was the name of Vogelweid.

Till at length the portly abbot
  Murmured, " Why this waste of food ?
Be it changed to loaves henceforward
  For our fasting brotherhood."

Then in vain o'er tower and turret,
  From the walls and woodland nests,
When the minster bells rang noontide,
  Gathered the unwelcome guests.

Then in vain, with cries discordant,
  Clamorous round the Gothic spire,
Screamed the feathered Minnesingers
  For the children of the choir.

Time has long effaced the inscriptions
  On the cloister's funeral stones,
And tradition only tells us
  Where repose the poet's bones.

But around the vast cathedral,
  By sweet echoes multiplied,
Still the birds repeat the legend,
  And the name of Vogelweid.

DRINKING SONG

INSCRIPTION FOR AN ANTIQUE PITCHER

Come, old friend ! sit down and listen !
  From the pitcher, placed between us,
How the waters laugh and glisten
  In the head of old Silenus !

Old Silenus, bloated, drunken,
  Led by his inebriate Satyrs ;
On his breast his head is sunken,
  Vacantly he leers and chatters.

Fauns with youthful Bacchus follow ;
  Ivy crowns that brow supernal
As the forehead of Apollo,
  And possessing youth eternal.

Round about him, fair Bacchantes,
  Bearing cymbals, flutes, and thyrses,
Wild from Naxian groves, or Zante's
  Vineyards, sing delirious verses.

Thus he won, through all the nations,
  Bloodless victories, and the farmer
Bore, as trophies and oblations,
  Vines for banners, ploughs for armor.

Judged by no o'erzealous rigor,
  Much this mystic throng expresses :
Bacchus was the type of vigor,
  And Silenus of excesses.

These are ancient ethnic revels,
  Of a faith long since forsaken ;
Now the Satyrs, changed to devils,
  Frighten mortals wine-o'ertaken.

Now to rivulets from the mountains
  Point the rods of fortune-tellers ;
Youth perpetual dwells in fountains, —
  Not in flasks, and casks, and cellars.

Claudius, though he sang of flagons
  And huge tankards filled with Rhenish,
From that fiery blood of dragons
  Never would his own replenish.

Even Redi, though he chaunted
  Bacchus in the Tuscan valleys,
Never drank the wine he vaunted
  In his dithyrambic sallies.

Then with water fill the pitcher
  Wreathed about with classic fables ;
Ne'er Falernian threw a richer
  Light upon Lucullus' tables.

Come, old friend, sit down and listen !
  As it passes thus between us,
How its wavelets laugh and glisten
  In the head of old Silenus !

THE OLD CLOCK ON THE STAIRS

The house commemorated in the poem is the Gold house, now known as the Plunkett mansion, in Pittsfield, Massachusetts, the homestead of Mrs. Longfellow's maternal grandfather, whither Mr. Longfellow went after his marriage in the summer of 1843. The poem was not written, however, till November, 1845, when, under date of the 12th of the month, he wrote in his diary : " Began a poem on a clock, with the words 'Forever, never,' as the burden ; suggested by the words of Bridaine, the old French missionary, who said of eternity, *C'est une pendule dont le balancier dit et redit sans cesse ces deux mots seulement dans le silence des tombeaux, — Toujours, jamais ! Jamais, toujours ! Et pendant ces effrayables révolutions, un réprouvé s' écrie, 'Quelle heure est-il?' et la voix d'un autre misérable lui répond, 'L'Eternité.'* "

Somewhat back from the village street
Stands the old-fashioned country-seat.
Across its antique portico
Tall poplar-trees their shadows throw ;
And from its station in the hall
An ancient timepiece says to all, —
    " Forever — never !
    Never — forever ! "

Half-way up the stairs it stands,
And points and beckons with its hands
From its case of massive oak,
Like a monk, who, under his cloak,

Crosses himself, and sighs, alas !
With sorrowful voice to all who pass, —
    " Forever — never !
      Never — forever ! "

By day its voice is low and light ;
But in the silent dead of night,
Distinct as a passing footstep's fall,
It echoes along the vacant hall,
Along the ceiling, along the floor,
And seems to say, at each chamber-door, —
    " Forever — never !
      Never — forever ! "

Through days of sorrow and of mirth,
Through days of death and days of birth,
Through every swift vicissitude
Of changeful time, unchanged it has
    stood,
And as if, like God, it all things saw,
It calmly repeats those words of awe, —
    " Forever — never !
      Never — forever ! "

In that mansion used to be
Free-hearted Hospitality ;
His great fires up the chimney roared ;
The stranger feasted at his board ;
But, like the skeleton at the feast,
That warning timepiece never ceased, —
    " Forever — never !
      Never — forever ! "

There groups of merry children played,
There youths and maidens dreaming
    strayed ;
O precious hours ! O golden prime,
And affluence of love and time !
Even as a miser counts his gold,
Those hours the ancient timepiece told, —
    " Forever — never !
      Never — forever ! "

From that chamber, clothed in white,
The bride came forth on her wedding
    night ;
There, in that silent room below,
The dead lay in his shroud of snow ;
And in the hush that followed the prayer,
Was heard the old clock on the stair, —
    " Forever — never !
      Never — forever ! "

All are scattered now and fled,
Some are married, some are dead ;

And when I ask, with throbs of pain,
" Ah ! when shall they all meet again ? "
As in the days long since gone by,
The ancient timepiece makes reply, —
    " Forever — never !
      Never — forever ! "

Never here, forever there,
Where all parting, pain, and care,
And death, and time shall disappear, —
Forever there, but never here !
The horologe of Eternity
Sayeth this incessantly, —
    " Forever — never !
      Never — forever ! "

THE ARROW AND THE SONG

" October 16, 1845. Before church, wrote *The Arrow and the Song*, which came into my mind as I stood with my back to the fire, and glanced on to the paper with arrow's speed. Literally an improvisation."

I shot an arrow into the air,
It fell to earth, I knew not where ;
For, so swiftly it flew, the sight
Could not follow it in its flight.

I breathed a song into the air,
It fell to earth, I knew not where ;
For who has sight so keen and strong,
That it can follow the flight of song ?

Long, long afterward, in an oak
I found the arrow, still unbroke ;
And the song, from beginning to end,
I found again in the heart of a friend.

SONNETS

MEZZO CAMMIN

Written at Boppard on the Rhine, August 25, 1842
just before leaving for home.

HALF of my life is gone, and I have let
    The years slip from me and have not
      fulfilled
    The aspiration of my youth, to build
Some tower of song with lofty parapet.
Not indolence, nor pleasure, nor the fret
    Of restless passions that would not be
      stilled,
    But sorrow, and a care that almost killed,
Kept me from what I may accomplish
    yet ;

Though, half-way up the hill, I see the Past
  Lying beneath me with its sounds and
      sights, —
  A city in the twilight dim and vast,
With smoking roofs, soft bells, and gleam-
      ing lights, —
  And hear above me on the autumnal
      blast
  The cataract of Death far thundering
      from the heights.

THE EVENING STAR

"October 30, 1845. The Indian summer still in its
glory. Wrote the sonnet *Hesperus* in the rustic seat of
the old apple-tree." This sonnet, addressed to his wife,
and afterward given its present title, "is noticeable,"
says his biographer, "as being the only love-poem among
Mr. Longfellow's verses."

Lo ! in the painted oriel of the West,
  Whose panes the sunken sun incarna-
      dines,
  Like a fair lady at her casement, shines
  The evening star, the star of love and
      rest !
And then anon she doth herself divest
  Of all her radiant garments, and reclines
  Behind the sombre screen of yonder pines,
  With slumber and soft dreams of love
      oppressed.
O my beloved, my sweet Hesperus !
  My morning and my evening star of love !
  My best and gentlest lady ! even thus,
As that fair planet in the sky above,
  Dost thou retire unto thy rest at night,
  And from thy darkened window fades
      the light.

AUTUMN

Thou comest, Autumn, heralded by the
      rain,
  With banners, by great gales incessant
      fanned,
  Brighter than brightest silks of Samar-
      cand,
  And stately oxen harnessed to thy wain !
Thou standest, like imperial Charlemagne,
  Upon thy bridge of gold ; thy royal
      hand
  Outstretched with benedictions o'er the
      land,
  Blessing the farms through all thy vast
      domain !

Thy shield is the red harvest moon, sus-
      pended
  So long beneath the heaven's o'erhanging
      eaves ;
  Thy steps are by the farmer's prayers
      attended ;
Like flames upon an altar shine the sheaves ;
  And, following thee, in thy ovation
      splendid,
  Thine almoner, the wind, scatters the
      golden leaves !

DANTE

Tuscan, that wanderest through the realms
      of gloom,
  With thoughtful pace, and sad, majestic
      eyes,
  Stern thoughts and awful from thy soul
      arise,
  Like Farinata from his fiery tomb.
Thy sacred song is like the trump of doom ;
  Yet in thy heart what human sympa-
      thies,
  What soft compassion glows, as in the
      skies
  The tender stars their clouded lamps re-
      lume !
Methinks I see thee stand with pallid
      cheeks
  By Fra Hilario in his diocese,
  As up the convent-walls, in golden
      streaks,
The ascending sunbeams mark the day's
      decrease ;
  And, as he asks what there the stranger
      seeks,
  Thy voice along the cloister whispers
      " Peace ! "

CURFEW

I

Solemnly, mournfully,
  Dealing its dole,
The Curfew Bell
  Is beginning to toll.

Cover the embers,
  And put out the light ;

Toil comes with the morning,
And rest with the night.

Dark grow the windows,
And quenched is the fire ;
Sound fades into silence, —
All footsteps retire.

No voice in the chambers,
No sound in the hall !
Sleep and oblivion
Reign over all !

II

The book is completed,
And closed, like the day ;

And the hand that has written it
Lays it away.

Dim grow its fancies ;
Forgotten they lie ;
Like coals in the ashes,
They darken and die.

Song sinks into silence,
The story is told,
The windows are darkened,
The hearth-stone is cold.

Darker and darker
The black shadows fall ;
Sleep and oblivion
Reign over all.

EVANGELINE

A TALE OF ACADIE

In Hawthorne's *American Note-Books* is the following passage : —
" H. L. C. heard from a French Canadian a story of a young couple in Acadie. On their marriage-day all the men of the Province were summoned to assemble in the church to hear a proclamation. When assembled, they were all seized and shipped off to be distributed through New England, — among them the new bridegroom. His bride set off in search of him — wandered about New England all her life-time, and at last, when she was old, she found her bridegroom on his death-bed. The shock was so great that it killed her likewise."

This is the story as set down by the romancer, which his friend, Rev. H. L. Conolly, had heard from a parishioner. Mr. Conolly saw in it a fine theme for a romance, but for some reason Hawthorne was disinclined to undertake it. One day the two were dining with Mr. Longfellow, and Mr. Conolly told the story again and wondered that Hawthorne did not care for it. " If you really do not want this incident for a tale," said Mr. Longfellow to his friend, " let me have it for a poem." Just when the conversation took place we cannot say, but the poem was begun apparently soon after the completion of the volume, *The Belfry of Bruges and other Poems*, and published October 30, 1847. Hawthorne, who had taken a lively interest in the poem, wrote a few days after, to say that he had read it " with more pleasure than it would be decorous to express." Mr. Longfellow, in replying, thanked him for a friendly notice which he had written for a Salem paper, and added : " Still more do I thank you for resigning to me that legend of Acady. This success I owe entirely to you, for being willing to forego the pleasure of writing a prose tale which many people would have

taken for poetry, that I might write a poem which many people take for prose."

In preparing for his poem Mr. Longfellow drew upon the nearest, most accessible materials, which at that time were to be found in Haliburton's *An Historical and Statistical Account of Nova Scotia*, with its liberal quotations from the Abbé Raynal's emotional account of the French settlers. He may have examined Winslow's narrative of the expedition under his command, in the cabinet of the Massachusetts Historical Society, not then printed but since that time made easily accessible. He did not visit Grand-Pré nor the Mississippi, but trusted to descriptions and Banvard's diorama. At the time of the publication of *Evangeline* the actual history of the deportation of the Acadians had scarcely been investigated. It is not too much to say that this tale was itself the cause of the frequent studies since made, studies which have resulted in a revision of the accepted rendering of the facts.

Mr. Longfellow gave to a Philadelphia journalist a reminiscence of his first notice of the material which was used in the conclusion of the poem : " I was passing down Spruce Street one day toward my hotel, after a walk, when my attention was attracted to a large building with beautiful trees about it, inside of a high enclosure.[1] I walked along until I came to the great gate, and then stepped inside, and looked carefully over the place. The charming picture of lawn, flowerbeds, and shade which it presented made an impression which has never left me, and when I came to write *Evangeline* I placed the final scene, the meeting between Evangeline and Gabriel, and the death, at the poor-house, and the burial in an old Catholic graveyard not far away, which I found by chance in another of my walks."

[1] The Pennsylvania Hospital.

From the outset Mr. Longfellow had no hesitation in the choice of a metre. He had before experimented in it in his translation of *The Children of the Lord's Supper*, and in his lines *To the Driving Cloud*. While engaged upon *Evangeline* he chanced upon a specimen in *Blackwood* of a hexameter translation of the Iliad, and expressed himself very emphatically on its fitness. "Took down Chapman's *Homer*," he writes later, "and read the second book. Rough enough ; and though better than Pope, how inferior to the books in hexameter in *Blackwood!* The English world is not yet awake to the beauty of that metre." After his poem was published, he wrote : "The public takes more kindly to hexameters than I could have imagined," and referring to a criticism on *Evangeline* by Mr. Felton, in which the metre was considered, he said : "I am more than ever glad that I chose this metre for my poem." Again he notes in his diary : "Talked with Theophilus Parsons about English hexameters ; and 'almost persuaded him to be a Christian.'" While his mind was thus dwelling on the subject, he fell into the measure in his journal entries, and in these lines under date of December 18, 1847.

Soft through the silent air descend the feathery snow-
    flakes ;
White are the distant hills, white are the neighboring
    fields ;
Only the marshes are brown, and the river rolling
    among them
Weareth the leaden hue seen in the eyes of the blind.

Especially interesting is the experiment which he made, while in the process of his work, in another metre. "Finished second canto of Part II. of *Evangeline*. I then tried a passage of it in the common rhymed English pentameter. It is the song of the mocking-bird : —

Upon a spray that overhung the stream,
The mocking-bird, awaking from his dream,
Poured such delirious music from his throat
That all the air seemed listening to his note.
Plaintive at first the song began, and slow ;
It breathed of sadness, and of pain and woe ;
Then, gathering all his notes, abroad he flung
The multitudinous music from his tongue, —
As, after showers, a sudden gust again
Upon the leaves shakes down the rattling rain."

As the story of *Evangeline* was the incentive to historical inquiry, so the successful use of the hexameter had much to do both with the revival of the measure and with a critical discussion upon its value. "Of the longer poems of our chief singer," says Dr. Holmes, "I should not hesitate to select *Evangeline* as the masterpiece, and I think the general verdict of

opinion would confirm my choice. The German model which it follows in its measure and the character of its story was itself suggested by an earlier idyl. If Dorothea was the mother of Evangeline, Luise was the mother of Dorothea. And what a beautiful creation is the Acadian maiden ! From the first line of the poem, from its first words, we read as we would float down a broad and placid river, murmuring softly against its banks, heaven over it, and the glory of the unspoiled wilderness all around, —

This is the forest primeval.

The words are already as familiar as

Μῆνιν ἄειδε, θεά,

or

Arma virumque cano.

The hexameter has been often criticised, but I do not believe any other measure could have told that lovely story with such effect, as we feel when carried along the tranquil current of these brimming, slow-moving, soul-satisfying lines. Imagine for one moment a story like this minced into octosyllabics. The poet knows better than his critics the length of step which best befits his muse."

The publication of *Evangeline* doubtless marks the period of Mr. Longfellow's greatest accession of fame, as it probably is the poem which the majority of readers would first name if called upon to indicate the poet's most commanding work. It was finished upon his fortieth birthday. Two days before, the following lines were written by Mr. Longfellow in his diary : —

EPIGRAMME.

Par un ci-devant jeune homme en approchant de la quarantaine.

"Sous le firmament
Tout n'est que changement,
    Tout passe ; "
Le cantique le dit,
Il est ainsi écrit
Il est sans contredit,
    Tout passe.

O douce vie humaine !
O temps qui nous entraine !
Destinée souveraine !
    Tout change.
Moi qui, poète rêveur,
Ne fus jamais friseur.
Je frise, — oh, quelle horreur !
    La quarantaine !

EVANGELINE

THIS is the forest primeval. The murmuring pines and the hemlocks,
Bearded with moss, and in garments green, indistinct in the twilight,
Stand like Druids of eld, with voices sad and prophetic,
Stand like harpers hoar, with beards that rest on their bosoms.

Loud from its rocky caverns, the deep-voiced neighboring ocean
Speaks, and in accents disconsolate answers the wail of the forest.

This is the forest primeval ; but where are the hearts that beneath it
Leaped like the roe, when he hears in the woodland the voice of the huntsman ?

Where is the thatch-roofed village, the
home of Acadian farmers, —
Men whose lives glided on like rivers that
water the woodlands,
Darkened by shadows of earth, but reflect-
ing an image of heaven ?
Waste are those pleasant farms, and the
farmers forever departed !
Scattered like dust and leaves, when the
mighty blasts of October
Seize them, and whirl them aloft, and
sprinkle them far o'er the ocean.
Naught but tradition remains of the beau-
tiful village of Grand-Pré.

Ye who believe in affection that hopes,
and endures, and is patient,
Ye who believe in the beauty and strength
of woman's devotion,
List to the mournful tradition, still sung by
the pines of the forest ;
List to a Tale of Love in Acadie, home of
the happy.

PART THE FIRST

I

In the Acadian land, on the shores of the
Basin of Minas,
Distant, secluded, still, the little village of
Grand-Pré
Lay in the fruitful valley. Vast meadows
stretched to the eastward,
Giving the village its name, and pasture
to flocks without number.
Dikes, that the hands of the farmers had
raised with labor incessant,
Shut out the turbulent tides ; but at stated
seasons the flood-gates
Opened, and welcomed the sea to wander
at will o'er the meadows.
West and south there were fields of flax,
and orchards and cornfields
Spreading afar and unfenced o'er the plain ;
and away to the northward
Blomidon rose, and the forests old, and
aloft on the mountains
Sea-fogs pitched their tents, and mists from
the mighty Atlantic
Looked on the happy valley, but ne'er
from their station descended.
There, in the midst of its farms, reposed
the Acadian village.

Strongly built were the houses, with frames
of oak and of hemlock,
Such as the peasants of Normandy built in
the reign of the Henries.
Thatched were the roofs, with dormer-win-
dows ; and gables projecting
Over the basement below protected and
shaded the doorway.
There in the tranquil evenings of summer,
when brightly the sunset
Lighted the village street, and gilded the
vanes on the chimneys,
Matrons and maidens sat in snow-white
caps and in kirtles
Scarlet and blue and green, with distaffs
spinning the golden
Flax for the gossiping looms, whose noisy
shuttles within doors
Mingled their sounds with the whir of the
wheels and the songs of the maidens.
Solemnly down the street came the parish
priest, and the children
Paused in their play to kiss the hand he
extended to bless them.
Reverend walked he among them ; and up
rose matrons and maidens,
Hailing his slow approach with words of
affectionate welcome.
Then came the laborers home from the
field, and serenely the sun sank
Down to his rest, and twilight prevailed.
Anon from the belfry
Softly the Angelus sounded, and over the
roofs of the village
Columns of pale blue smoke, like clouds of
incense ascending,
Rose from a hundred hearths, the homes
of peace and contentment.
Thus dwelt together in love these simple
Acadian farmers, —
Dwelt in the love of God and of man.
Alike were they free from
Fear, that reigns with the tyrant, and envy,
the vice of republics.
Neither locks had they to their doors, nor
bars to their windows ;
But their dwellings were open as day and
the hearts of the owners ;
There the richest was poor, and the poorest
lived in abundance.

Somewhat apart from the village, and
nearer the Basin of Minas,
Benedict Bellefontaine, the wealthiest
farmer of Grand-Pré,

Dwelt on his goodly acres ; and with him,
directing his household,
Gentle Evangeline lived, his child, and the
pride of the village.
Stalworth and stately in form was the man
of seventy winters ;
Hearty and hale was he, an oak that is
covered with snow-flakes ;
White as the snow were his locks, and his
cheeks as brown as the oak-leaves.
Fair was she to behold, that maiden of
seventeen summers.
Black were her eyes as the berry that
grows on the thorn by the wayside,
Black, yet how softly they gleamed be-
neath the brown shade of her tresses !
Sweet was her breath as the breath of kine
that feed in the meadows.
When in the harvest heat she bore to the
reapers at noontide
Flagons of home-brewed ale, ah ! fair in
sooth was the maiden.
Fairer was she when, on Sunday morn,
while the bell from its turret
Sprinkled with holy sounds the air, as the
priest with his hyssop
Sprinkles the congregation, and scatters
blessings upon them,
Down the long street she passed, with her
chaplet of beads and her missal,
Wearing her Norman cap, and her kirtle
of blue, and the ear-rings,
Brought in the olden time from France,
and since, as an heirloom,
Handed down from mother to child,
through long generations.
But a celestial brightness — a more ethe-
real beauty —
Shone on her face and encircled her form,
when, after confession,
Homeward serenely she walked with God's
benediction upon her.
When she had passed, it seemed like the
ceasing of exquisite music.

Firmly builded with rafters of oak, the
house of the farmer
Stood on the side of a hill commanding the
sea ; and a shady
Sycamore grew by the door, with a wood-
bine wreathing around it.
Rudely carved was the porch, with seats
beneath ; and a footpath
Led through an orchard wide, and disap-
peared in the meadow.

Under the sycamore-tree were hives over-
hung by a penthouse,
Such as the traveller sees in regions remote
by the roadside,
Built o'er a box for the poor, or the blessed
image of Mary.
Farther down, on the slope of the hill, was
the well with its moss-grown
Bucket, fastened with iron, and near it a
trough for the horses.
Shielding the house from storms, on the
north, were the barns and the farm-
yard.
There stood the broad-wheeled wains and
the antique ploughs and the har-
rows ;
There were the folds for the sheep ; and
there, in his feathered seraglio,
Strutted the lordly turkey, and crowed the
cock, with the selfsame
Voice that in ages of old had startled the
penitent Peter.
Bursting with hay were the barns, them-
selves a village. In each one
Far o'er the gable projected a roof of
thatch ; and a staircase,
Under the sheltering eaves, led up to the
odorous corn-loft.
There too the dove-cot stood, with its meek
and innocent inmates
Murmuring ever of love ; while above in
the variant breezes
Numberless noisy weathercocks rattled and
sang of mutation.

Thus, at peace with God and the world,
the farmer of Grand-Pré
Lived on his sunny farm, and Evangeline
governed his household.
Many a youth, as he knelt in church and
opened his missal,
Fixed his eyes upon her as the saint of his
deepest devotion ;
Happy was he who might touch her hand
or the hem of her garment !
Many a suitor came to her door, by the
darkness befriended,
And, as he knocked and waited to hear the
sound of her footsteps,
Knew not which beat the louder, his heart
or the knocker of iron ;
Or at the joyous feast of the Patron Saint
of the village,
Bolder grew, and pressed her hand in the
dance as he whispered

Hurried words of love, that seemed a part
of the music.
But, among all who came, young Gabriel
only was welcome ;
Gabriel Lajeunesse, the son of Basil the
blacksmith,
Who was a mighty man in the village, and
honored of all men ;
For, since the birth of time, throughout all
ages and nations,
Has the craft of the smith been held in
repute by the people.
Basil was Benedict's friend. Their children
from earliest childhood
Grew up together as brother and sister ;
and Father Felician,
Priest and pedagogue both in the village,
had taught them their letters
Out of the selfsame book, with the hymns
of the church and the plain-song.
But when the hymn was sung, and the
daily lesson completed,
Swiftly they hurried away to the forge of
Basil the blacksmith.
There at the door they stood, with wonder-
ing eyes to behold him
Take in his leathern lap the hoof of the
horse as a plaything,
Nailing the shoe in its place ; while near
him the tire of the cart-wheel
Lay like a fiery snake, coiled round in a
circle of cinders.
Oft on autumnal eves, when without in the
gathering darkness
Bursting with light seemed the smithy,
through every cranny and crevice,
Warm by the forge within they watched
the laboring bellows,
And as its panting ceased, and the sparks
expired in the ashes,
Merrily laughed, and said they were nuns
going into the chapel.
Oft on sledges in winter, as swift as the
swoop of the eagle,
Down the hillside bounding, they glided
away o'er the meadow.
Oft in the barns they climbed to the popu-
lous nests on the rafters,
Seeking with eager eyes that wondrous
stone, which the swallow
Brings from the shore of the sea to restore
the sight of its fledglings ;
Lucky was he who found that stone in the
nest of the swallow !

Thus passed a few swift years, and they no
longer were children.
He was a valiant youth, and his face, like
the face of the morning,
Gladdened the earth with its light, and
ripened thought into action.
She was a woman now, with the heart and
hopes of a woman.
"Sunshine of Saint Eulalie" was she
called ; for that was the sunshine
Which, as the farmers believed, would load
their orchards with apples ;
She, too, would bring to her husband's
house delight and abundance,
Filling it with love and the ruddy faces of
children.

II

Now had the season returned, when the
nights grow colder and longer,
And the retreating sun the sign of the
Scorpion enters.
Birds of passage sailed through the leaden
air, from the ice-bound,
Desolate northern bays to the shores of
tropical islands.
Harvests were gathered in ; and wild with
the winds of September
Wrestled the trees of the forest, as Jacob
of old with the angel.
All the signs foretold a winter long and
inclement.
Bees, with prophetic instinct of want, had
hoarded their honey
Till the hives overflowed ; and the Indian
hunters asserted
Cold would the winter be, for thick was the
fur of the foxes.
Such was the advent of autumn. Then
followed that beautiful season,
Called by the pious Acadian peasants the
Summer of All-Saints !
Filled was the air with a dreamy and magi-
cal light ; and the landscape
Lay as if new-created in all the freshness
of childhood.
Peace seemed to reign upon earth, and the
restless heart of the ocean
Was for a moment consoled. All sounds
were in harmony blended.
Voices of children at play, the crowing of
cocks in the farm-yards,

Whir of wings in the drowsy air, and the cooing of pigeons,
All were subdued and low as the murmurs of love, and the great sun
Looked with the eye of love through the golden vapors around him ;
While arrayed in its robes of russet and scarlet and yellow,
Bright with the sheen of the dew, each glittering tree of the forest
Flashed like the plane-tree the Persian adorned with mantles and jewels.

Now recommenced the reign of rest and affection and stillness.
Day with its burden and heat had departed, and twilight descending
Brought back the evening star to the sky, and the herds to the homestead.
Pawing the ground they came, and resting their necks on each other,
And with their nostrils distended inhaling the freshness of evening.
Foremost, bearing the bell, Evangeline's beautiful heifer,
Proud of her snow-white hide, and the ribbon that waved from her collar,
Quietly paced and slow, as if conscious of human affection.
Then came the shepherd back with his bleating flocks from the seaside,
Where was their favorite pasture. Behind them followed the watch-dog,
Patient, full of importance, and grand in the pride of his instinct,
Walking from side to side with a lordly air, and superbly
Waving his bushy tail, and urging forward the stragglers ;
Regent of flocks was he when the shepherd slept ; their protector,
When from the forest at night, through the starry silence the wolves howled.
Late, with the rising moon, returned the wains from the marshes,
Laden with briny hay, that filled the air with its odor.
Cheerily neighed the steeds, with dew on their manes and their fetlocks,
While aloft on their shoulders the wooden and ponderous saddles,
Painted with brilliant dyes, and adorned with tassels of crimson,

Nodded in bright array, like hollyhocks heavy with blossoms.
Patiently stood the cows meanwhile, and yielded their udders
Unto the milkmaid's hand ; whilst loud and in regular cadence
Into the sounding pails the foaming streamlets descended.
Lowing of cattle and peals of laughter were heard in the farm-yard,
Echoed back by the barns. Anon they sank into stillness ;
Heavily closed, with a jarring sound, the valves of the barn-doors,
Rattled the wooden bars, and all for a season was silent.

In - doors, warm by the wide - mouthed fireplace, idly the farmer
Sat in his elbow-chair and watched how the flames and the smoke-wreaths
Struggled together like foes in a burning city. Behind him,
Nodding and mocking along the wall, with gestures fantastic,
Darted his own huge shadow, and vanished away into darkness.
Faces, clumsily carved in oak, on the back of his arm-chair
Laughed in the flickering light ; and the pewter plates on the dresser
Caught and reflected the flame, as shields of armies the sunshine.
Fragments of song the old man sang, and carols of Christmas,
Such as at home, in the olden time, his fathers before him
Sang in their Norman orchards and bright Burgundian vineyards.
Close at her father's side was the gentle Evangeline seated,
Spinning flax for the loom, that stood in the corner behind her.
Silent awhile were its treadles, at rest was its diligent shuttle,
While the monotonous drone of the wheel, like the drone of a bagpipe,
Followed the old man's song and united the fragments together.
As in a church, when the chant of the choir at intervals ceases,
Footfalls are heard in the aisles, or words of the priest at the altar,
So, in each pause of the song, with measured motion the clock clicked.

Thus as they sat, there were footsteps heard, and, suddenly lifted,
Sounded the wooden latch, and the door swung back on its hinges.
Benedict knew by the hob-nailed shoes it was Basil the blacksmith,
And by her beating heart Evangeline knew who was with him.
"Welcome!" the farmer exclaimed, as their footsteps paused on the threshold,
"Welcome, Basil, my friend! Come, take thy place on the settle
Close by the chimney-side, which is always empty without thee;
Take from the shelf overhead thy pipe and the box of tobacco;
Never so much thyself art thou as when through the curling
Smoke of the pipe or the forge thy friendly and jovial face gleams
Round and red as the harvest moon through the mist of the marshes."
Then, with a smile of content, thus answered Basil the blacksmith,
Taking with easy air the accustomed seat by the fireside: —
"Benedict Bellefontaine, thou hast ever thy jest and thy ballad!
Ever in cheerfullest mood art thou, when others are filled with
Gloomy forebodings of ill, and see only ruin before them.
Happy art thou, as if every day thou hadst picked up a horseshoe."
Pausing a moment, to take the pipe that Evangeline brought him,
And with a coal from the embers had lighted, he slowly continued: —
"Four days now are passed since the English ships at their anchors
Ride in the Gaspereau's mouth, with their cannon pointed against us.
What their design may be is unknown; but all are commanded
On the morrow to meet in the church, where his Majesty's mandate
Will be proclaimed as law in the land. Alas! in the mean time
Many surmises of evil alarm the hearts of the people."
Then made answer the farmer: "Perhaps some friendlier purpose
Brings these ships to our shores. Perhaps the harvests in England
By untimely rains or untimelier heat have been blighted,
And from our bursting barns they would feed their cattle and children."
"Not so thinketh the folk in the village," said, warmly, the blacksmith,
Shaking his head, as in doubt; then, heaving a sigh, he continued: —
"Louisburg is not forgotten, nor Beau Séjour, nor Port Royal.
Many already have fled to the forest, and lurk on its outskirts,
Waiting with anxious hearts the dubious fate of to-morrow.
Arms have been taken from us, and warlike weapons of all kinds;
Nothing is left but the blacksmith's sledge and the scythe of the mower."
Then with a pleasant smile made answer the jovial farmer: —
"Safer are we unarmed, in the midst of our flocks and our cornfields,
Safer within these peaceful dikes, besieged by the ocean,
Than our fathers in forts, besieged by the enemy's cannon.
Fear no evil, my friend, and to-night may no shadow of sorrow
Fall on this house and hearth; for this is the night of the contract.
Built are the house and the barn. The merry lads of the village
Strongly have built them and well; and, breaking the glebe round about them,
Filled the barn with hay, and the house with food for a twelvemonth.
René Leblanc will be here anon, with his papers and inkhorn.
Shall we not then be glad, and rejoice in the joy of our children?"
As apart by the window she stood, with her hand in her lover's,
Blushing Evangeline heard the words that her father had spoken,
And, as they died on his lips, the worthy notary entered.

III

Bent like a laboring oar, that toils in the surf of the ocean,
Bent, but not broken, by age was the form of the notary public;

Shocks of yellow hair, like the silken floss
    of the maize, hung
Over his shoulders ; his forehead was high ;
    and glasses with horn bows
Sat astride on his nose, with a look of
    wisdom supernal.
Father of twenty children was he, and
    more than a hundred
Children's children rode on his knee, and
    heard his great watch tick.
Four long years in the times of the war
    had he languished a captive,
Suffering much in an old French fort as
    the friend of the English.
Now, though warier grown, without all
    guile or suspicion,
Ripe in wisdom was he, but patient, and
    simple, and childlike.
He was beloved by all, and most of all by
    the children ;
For he told them tales of the Loup-garou
    in the forest,
And of the goblin that came in the night
    to water the horses,
And of the white Létiche, the ghost of a
    child who unchristened
Died, and was doomed to haunt unseen the
    chambers of children ;
And how on Christmas eve the oxen talked
    in the stable,
And how the fever was cured by a spider
    shut up in a nutshell,
And of the marvellous powers of four-
    leaved clover and horseshoes,
With whatsoever else was writ in the lore
    of the village.
Then up rose from his seat by the fireside
    Basil the blacksmith,
Knocked from his pipe the ashes, and
    slowly extending his right hand,
"Father Leblanc," he exclaimed, "thou
    hast heard the talk in the village,
And, perchance, canst tell us some news
    of these ships and their errand."
Then with modest demeanor made answer
    the notary public, —
"Gossip enough have I heard, in sooth, yet
    am never the wiser ;
And what their errand may be I know not
    better than others.
Yet am I not of those who imagine some
    evil intention
Brings them here, for we are at peace ;
    and why then molest us ? "

"God's name ! " shouted the hasty and
    somewhat irascible blacksmith ;
"Must we in all things look for the how,
    and the why, and the wherefore ?
Daily injustice is done, and might is the
    right of the strongest ! "
But without heeding his warmth, continued
    the notary public, —
"Man is unjust, but God is just ; and
    finally justice
Triumphs ; and well I remember a story,
    that often consoled me,
When as a captive I lay in the old French
    fort at Port Royal."
This was the old man's favorite tale, and
    he loved to repeat it
When his neighbors complained that any
    injustice was done them.
"Once in an ancient city, whose name I no
    longer remember,
Raised aloft on a column, a brazen statue
    of Justice
Stood in the public square, upholding the
    scales in its left hand,
And in its right a sword, as an emblem
    that justice presided
Over the laws of the land, and the hearts
    and homes of the people.
Even the birds had built their nests in the
    scales of the balance,
Having no fear of the sword that flashed
    in the sunshine above them.
But in the course of ·time the laws of the
    land were corrupted ;
Might took the place of right, and the weak
    were oppressed, and the mighty
Ruled with an iron rod. Then it chanced
    in a nobleman's palace
That a necklace of pearls was lost, and
    erelong a suspicion
Fell on an orphan girl who lived as a maid
    in the household.
She, after form of trial condemned to die
    on the scaffold,
Patiently met her doom at the foot of the
    statue of Justice.
As to her Father in heaven her innocent
    spirit ascended,
Lo ! o'er the city a tempest rose ; and the
    bolts of the thunder
Smote the statue of bronze, and hurled in
    wrath from its left hand
Down on the pavement below the clattering
    scales of the balance,

And in the hollow thereof was found the nest of a magpie,
Into whose clay-built walls the necklace of pearls was inwoven."
Silenced, but not convinced, when the story was ended, the blacksmith
Stood like a man who fain would speak, but findeth no language ;
All his thoughts were congealed into lines on his face, as the vapors
Freeze in fantastic shapes on the window-panes in the winter.

Then Evangeline lighted the brazen lamp on the table,
Filled, till it overflowed, the pewter tankard with home-brewed
Nut-brown ale, that was famed for its strength in the village of Grand-Pré ;
While from his pocket the notary drew his papers and inkhorn,
Wrote with a steady hand the date and the age of the parties,
Naming the dower of the bride in flocks of sheep and in cattle.
Orderly all things proceeded, and duly and well were completed,
And the great seal of the law was set like a sun on the margin.
Then from his leathern pouch the farmer threw on the table
Three times the old man's fee in solid pieces of silver ;
And the notary rising, and blessing the bride and the bridegroom,
Lifted aloft the tankard of ale and drank to their welfare,
Wiping the foam from his lip, he solemnly bowed and departed,
While in silence the others sat and mused by the fireside,
Till Evangeline brought the draught-board out of its corner.
Soon was the game begun. In friendly contention the old men
Laughed at each lucky hit, or unsuccessful manœuvre,
Laughed when a man was crowned, or a breach was made in the king-row.
Meanwhile apart, in the twilight gloom of a window's embrasure,
Sat the lovers, and whispered together, beholding the moon rise

Over the pallid sea, and the silvery mists of the meadows.
Silently one by one, in the infinite meadows of heaven,
Blossomed the lovely stars, the forget-me-nots of the angels.

Thus was the evening passed. Anon the bell from the belfry
Rang out the hour of nine, the village curfew, and straightway
Rose the guests and departed ; and silence reigned in the household.
Many a farewell word and sweet good-night on the door-step
Lingered long in Evangeline's heart, and filled it with gladness.
Carefully then were covered the embers that glowed on the hearth-stone,
And on the oaken stairs resounded the tread of the farmer.
Soon with a soundless step the foot of Evangeline followed.
Up the staircase moved a luminous space in the darkness,
Lighted less by the lamp than the shining face of the maiden.
Silent she passed the hall, and entered the door of her chamber.
Simple that chamber was, with its curtains of white, and its clothes-press
Ample and high, on whose spacious shelves were carefully folded
Linen and woollen stuffs, by the hand of Evangeline woven.
This was the precious dower she would bring to her husband in marriage,
Better than flocks and herds, being proofs of her skill as a housewife.
Soon she extinguished her lamp, for the mellow and radiant moonlight
Streamed through the windows, and lighted the room, till the heart of the maiden
Swelled and obeyed its power, like the tremulous tides of the ocean.
Ah ! she was fair, exceeding fair to behold, as she stood with
Naked snow-white feet on the gleaming floor of her chamber !
Little she dreamed that below, among the trees of the orchard,
Waited her lover and watched for the gleam of her lamp and her shadow.

Yet were her thoughts of him, and at times
a feeling of sadness
Passed o'er her soul, as the sailing shade of
clouds in the moonlight
Flitted across the floor and darkened the
room for a moment.
And, as she gazed from the window, she
saw serenely the moon pass
Forth from the folds of a cloud, and one
star follow her footsteps,
As out of Abraham's tent young Ishmael
wandered with Hagar !

IV

Pleasantly rose next morn the sun on the
village of Grand-Pré.
Pleasantly gleamed in the soft, sweet air
the Basin of Minas,
Where the ships, with their wavering shad-
ows, were riding at anchor.
Life had long been astir in the village, and
clamorous labor
Knocked with its hundred hands at the
golden gates of the morning.
Now from the country around, from the
farms and neighboring hamlets,
Came in their holiday dresses the blithe
Acadian peasants.
Many a glad good-morrow and jocund laugh
from the young folk
Made the bright air brighter, as up from
the numerous meadows,
Where no path could be seen but the track
of wheels in the greensward,
Group after group appeared, and joined, or
passed on the highway.
Long ere noon, in the village all sounds of
labor were silenced.
Thronged were the streets with people ;
and noisy groups at the house-doors
Sat in the cheerful sun, and rejoiced and
gossiped together.
Every house was an inn, where all were
welcomed and feasted ;
For with this simple people, who lived like
brothers together,
All things were held in common, and what
one had was another's.
Yet under Benedict's roof hospitality
seemed more abundant :
For Evangeline stood among the guests of
her father ;

Bright was her face with smiles, and words
of welcome and gladness
Fell from her beautiful lips, and blessed
the cup as she gave it.

Under the open sky, in the odorous air of
the orchard,
Stript of its golden fruit, was spread the
feast of betrothal.
There in the shade of the porch were the
priest and the notary seated ;
There good Benedict sat, and sturdy Basil
the blacksmith.
Not far withdrawn from these, by the cider-
press and the beehives,
Michael the fiddler was placed, with the
gayest of hearts and of waistcoats.
Shadow and light from the leaves alter-
nately played on his snow-white
Hair, as it waved in the wind ; and the
jolly face of the fiddler
Glowed like a living coal when the ashes
are blown from the embers.
Gayly the old man sang to the vibrant
sound of his fiddle,
Tous les Bourgeois de Chartres, and *Le
Carillon de Dunquerque*,
And anon with his wooden shoes beat time
to the music.
Merrily, merrily whirled the wheels of the
dizzying dances
Under the orchard-trees and down the path
to the meadows ;
Old folk and young together, and children
mingled among them.
Fairest of all the maids was Evangeline,
Benedict's daughter !
Noblest of all the youths was Gabriel, son
of the blacksmith !

So passed the morning away. And lo !
with a summons sonorous
Sounded the bell from its tower, and over
the meadows a drum beat.
Thronged erelong was the church with
men. Without, in the churchyard,
Waited the women. They stood by the
graves, and hung on the headstones
Garlands of autumn-leaves and evergreens
fresh from the forest.
Then came the guard from the ships, and
marching proudly among them
Entered the sacred portal. With loud and
dissonant clangor

Echoed the sound of their brazen drums
from ceiling and casement, —
Echoed a moment only, and slowly the
ponderous portal
Closed, and in silence the crowd awaited
the will of the soldiers.
Then uprose their commander, and spake
from the steps of the altar,
Holding aloft in his hands, with its seals,
the royal commission.
"You are convened this day," he said, "by
his Majesty's orders.
Clement and kind has he been; but how
you have answered his kindness,
Let your own hearts reply! To my nat-
ural make and my temper
Painful the task is I do, which to you I
know must be grievous.
Yet must I bow and obey, and deliver the
will of our monarch;
Namely, that all your lands, and dwellings,
and cattle of all kinds
Forfeited be to the crown; and that you
yourselves from this province
Be transported to other lands. God grant
you may dwell there
Ever as faithful subjects, a happy and
peaceable people!
Prisoners now I declare you; for such is
his Majesty's pleasure!"
As, when the air is serene in sultry solstice
of summer,
Suddenly gathers a storm, and the deadly
sling of the hailstones
Beats down the farmer's corn in the field
and shatters his windows,
Hiding the sun, and strewing the ground
with thatch from the house-roofs,
Bellowing fly the herds, and seek to break
their enclosures;
So on the hearts of the people descended the
words of the speaker.
Silent a moment they stood in speechless
wonder, and then rose
Louder and ever louder a wail of sorrow
and anger,
And, by one impulse moved, they madly
rushed to the door-way.
Vain was the hope of escape; and cries
and fierce imprecations
Rang through the house of prayer;
and high o'er the heads of the oth-
ers
Rose, with his arms uplifted, the figure of
Basil the blacksmith,

As, on a stormy sea, a spar is tossed by the
billows.
Flushed was his face and distorted with
passion; and wildly he shouted, —
"Down with the tyrants of England! we
never have sworn them allegiance!
Death to these foreign soldiers, who seize
on our homes and our harvests!"
More he fain would have said, but the
merciless hand of a soldier
Smote him upon the mouth, and dragged
him down to the pavement.

In the midst of the strife and tumult of
angry contention,
Lo! the door of the chancel opened, and
Father Felician
Entered, with serious mien, and ascended
the steps of the altar.
Raising his reverend hand, with a gesture
he awed into silence
All that clamorous throng; and thus he
spake to his people;
Deep were his tones and solemn; in accents
measured and mournful
Spake he, as, after the tocsin's alarum, dis-
tinctly the clock strikes.
"What is this that ye do, my children?
what madness has seized you?
Forty years of my life have I labored
among you, and taught you,
Not in word alone, but in deed, to love one
another!
Is this the fruit of my toils, of my vigils
and prayers and privations?
Have you so soon forgotten all lessons of
love and forgiveness?
This is the house of the Prince of Peace,
and would you profane it
Thus with violent deeds and hearts over-
flowing with hatred?
Lo! where the crucified Christ from his
cross is gazing upon you!
See! in those sorrowful eyes what meek-
ness and holy compassion!
Hark! how those lips still repeat the
prayer, 'O Father, forgive them!'
Let us repeat that prayer in the hour when
the wicked assail us,
Let us repeat it now, and say, 'O Father,
forgive them!'"
Few were his words of rebuke, but deep in
the hearts of his people
Sank they, and sobs of contrition succeeded
the passionate outbreak,

While they repeated his prayer, and said,
  "O Father, forgive them ! "

Then came the evening service. The
  tapers gleamed from the altar.
Fervent and deep was the voice of the
  priest, and the people responded,
Not with their lips alone, but their hearts ;
  and the Ave Maria
Sang they, and fell on their knees, and
  their souls, with devotion translated,
Rose on the ardor of prayer, like Elijah
  ascending to heaven.

Meanwhile had spread in the village the
  tidings of ill, and on all sides
Wandered, wailing, from house to house
  the women and children.
Long at her father's door Evangeline stood,
  with her right hand
Shielding her eyes from the level rays of
  the sun, that, descending,
Lighted the village street with mysterious
  splendor, and roofed each
Peasant's cottage with golden thatch, and
  emblazoned its windows.
Long within had been spread the snow-
  white cloth on the table ;
There stood the wheaten loaf, and the
  honey fragrant with wild-flowers ;
There stood the tankard of ale, and
  the cheese fresh brought from the
  dairy,
And, at the head of the board, the great
  arm-chair of the farmer.
Thus did Evangeline wait at her father's
  door, as the sunset
Threw the long shadows of trees o'er the
  broad ambrosial meadows.
Ah ! on her spirit within a deeper shadow
  had fallen,
And from the fields of her soul a fragrance
  celestial ascended, —
Charity, meekness, love, and hope, and
  forgiveness, and patience !
Then, all-forgetful of self, she wandered
  into the village,
Cheering with looks and words the mourn-
  ful hearts of the women,
As o'er the darkening fields with lingering
  steps they departed,
Urged by their household cares, and the
  weary feet of their children.
Down sank the great red sun, and in
  golden, glimmering vapors

Veiled the light of his face, like the
  Prophet descending from Sinai.
Sweetly over the village the bell of the
  Angelus sounded.

Meanwhile, amid the gloom, by the
  church Evangeline lingered.
All was silent within ; and in vain at the
  door and the windows
Stood she, and listened and looked, till,
  overcome by emotion,
"Gabriel ! " cried she aloud with tremulous
  voice ; but no answer
Came from the graves of the dead, nor the
  gloomier grave of the living.
Slowly at length she returned to the tenant-
  less house of her father.
Smouldered the fire on the hearth, on the
  board was the supper untasted,
Empty and drear was each room, and
  haunted with phantoms of terror.
Sadly echoed her step on the stair and the
  floor of her chamber.
In the dead of the night she heard the dis-
  consolate rain fall
Loud on the withered leaves of the syca-
  more-tree by the window.
Keenly the lightning flashed ; and the voice
  of the echoing thunder
Told her that God was in heaven, and gov-
  erned the world he created !
Then she remembered the tale she had
  heard of the justice of Heaven ;
Soothed was her troubled soul, and she
  peacefully slumbered till morning.

V

Four times the sun had risen and set ; and
  now on the fifth day
Cheerily called the cock to the sleeping
  maids of the farm-house.
Soon o'er the yellow fields, in silent and
  mournful procession,
Came from the neighboring hamlets and
  farms the Acadian women,
Driving in ponderous wains their house-
  hold goods to the sea-shore,
Pausing and looking back to gaze once
  more on their dwellings,
Ere they were shut from sight by the
  winding road and the woodland.
Close at their sides their children ran, and
  urged on the oxen,

While in their little hands they clasped
some fragments of playthings.

Thus to the Gaspereau's mouth they hur-
ried ; and there on the sea-beach
Piled in confusion lay the household goods
of the peasants.
All day long between the shore and the
ships did the boats ply ;
All day long the wains came laboring down
from the village.
Late in the afternoon, when the sun was
near to his setting,
Echoed far o'er the fields came the roll of
drums from the churchyard.
Thither the women and children thronged.
On a sudden the church-doors
Opened, and forth came the guard, and
marching in gloomy procession
Followed the long-imprisoned, but patient,
Acadian farmers.
Even as pilgrims, who journey afar from
their homes and their country,
Sing as they go, and in singing forget they
are weary and wayworn,
So with songs on their lips the Acadian
peasants descended
Down from the church to the shore, amid
their wives and their daughters.
Foremost the young men came ; and, raising
together their voices,
Sang with tremulous lips a chant of the
Catholic Missions : —
"Sacred heart of the Saviour !   O inex-
haustible fountain !
Fill our hearts this day with strength and
submission and patience ! "
Then the old men, as they marched, and
the women that stood by the way-
side
Joined in the sacred psalm, and the birds
in the sunshine above them
Mingled their notes therewith, like voices
of spirits departed.

Half-way down to the shore Evangeline
waited in silence,
Not overcome with grief, but strong in the
hour of affliction, —
Calmly and sadly she waited, until the pro-
cession approached her,
And she beheld the face of Gabriel pale
with emotion.
Tears then filled her eyes, and, eagerly run-
ning to meet him,

Clasped she his hands, and laid her head on
his shoulder, and whispered, —
"Gabriel ! be of good cheer ! for if we
love one another
Nothing, in truth, can harm us, whatever
mischances may happen ! "
Smiling she spake these words ; then sud-
denly paused, for her father
Saw she slowly advancing.   Alas ! how
changed was his aspect !
Gone was the glow from his cheek, and the
fire from his eye, and his footstep
Heavier seemed with the weight of the
heavy heart in his bosom.
But with a smile and a sigh, she clasped
his neck and embraced him,
Speaking words of endearment where words
of comfort availed not.
Thus to the Gaspereau's mouth moved on
that mournful procession.

There disorder prevailed, and the tumult
and stir of embarking.
Busily plied the freighted boats ; and in
the confusion
Wives were torn from their husbands, and
mothers, too late, saw their children
Left on the land, extending their arms, with
wildest entreaties.
So unto separate ships were Basil and
Gabriel carried,
While in despair on the shore Evangeline
stood with her father.
Half the task was not done when the sun
went down, and the twilight
Deepened and darkened around ; and in
haste the refluent ocean
Fled away from the shore, and left the line
of the sand-beach
Covered with waifs of the tide, with kelp
and the slippery sea-weed.
Farther back in the midst of the household
goods and the wagons,
Like to a gypsy camp, or a leaguer after a
battle,
All escape cut off by the sea, and the senti-
nels near them,
Lay encamped for the night the houseless
Acadian farmers.
Back to its nethermost caves retreated the
bellowing ocean,
Dragging adown the beach the rattling
pebbles, and leaving
Inland and far up the shore the stranded
boats of the sailors.

Then, as the night descended, the herds returned from their pastures ;
Sweet was the moist still air with the odor of milk from their udders ;
Lowing they waited, and long, at the well-known bars of the farm-yard, —
Waited and looked in vain for the voice and the hand of the milk-maid.
Silence reigned in the streets ; from the church no Angelus sounded,
Rose no smoke from the roofs, and gleamed no lights from the windows.

But on the shores meanwhile the evening fires had been kindled,
Built of the drift-wood thrown on the sands from wrecks in the tempest.
Round them shapes of gloom and sorrowful faces were gathered,
Voices of women were heard, and of men, and the crying of children.
Onward from fire to fire, as from hearth to hearth in his parish,
Wandered the faithful priest, consoling and blessing and cheering,
Like unto shipwrecked Paul on Melita's desolate sea-shore.
Thus he approached the place where Evangeline sat with her father,
And in the flickering light beheld the face of the old man,
Haggard and hollow and wan, and without either thought or emotion,
E'en as the face of a clock from which the hands have been taken.
Vainly Evangeline strove with words and caresses to cheer him,
Vainly offered him food ; yet he moved not, he looked not, he spake not,
But, with a vacant stare, ever gazed at the flickering fire-light.
"*Benedicite !*" murmured the priest, in tones of compassion.
More he fain would have said, but his heart was full, and his accents
Faltered and paused on his lips, as the feet of a child on a threshold,
Hushed by the scene he beholds, and the awful presence of sorrow.
Silently, therefore, he laid his hand on the head of the maiden,
Raising his tearful eyes to the silent stars that above them
Moved on their way, unperturbed by the wrongs and sorrows of mortals.

Then sat he down at her side, and they wept together in silence.

Suddenly rose from the south a light, as in autumn the blood-red
Moon climbs the crystal walls of heaven, and o'er the horizon
Titan-like stretches its hundred hands upon the mountain and meadow,
Seizing the rocks and the rivers and piling huge shadows together.
Broader and ever broader it gleamed on the roofs of the village,
Gleamed on the sky and sea, and the ships that lay in the roadstead.
Columns of shining smoke uprose, and flashes of flame were
Thrust through their folds and withdrawn, like the quivering hands of a martyr.
Then as the wind seized the gleeds and the burning thatch, and, uplifting,
Whirled them aloft through the air, at once from a hundred house-tops
Started the sheeted smoke with flashes of flame intermingled.

These things beheld in dismay the crowd on the shore and on shipboard.
Speechless at first they stood, then cried aloud in their anguish,
"We shall behold no more our homes in the village of Grand-Pré !"
Loud on a sudden the cocks began to crow in the farm-yards,
Thinking the day had dawned ; and anon the lowing of cattle
Came on the evening breeze, by the barking of dogs interrupted.
Then rose a sound of dread, such as startles the sleeping encampments
Far in the western prairies or forests that skirt the Nebraska,
When the wild horses affrighted sweep by with the speed of the whirlwind,
Or the loud bellowing herds of buffaloes rush to the river.
Such was the sound that arose on the night, as the herds and the horses
Broke through their folds and fences, and madly rushed o'er the meadows.

Overwhelmed with the sight, yet speechless, the priest and the maiden
Gazed on the scene of terror that reddened and widened before them :

And as they turned at length to speak
to their silent companion,
Lo ! from his seat he had fallen, and
stretched abroad on the sea-shore
Motionless lay his form, from which the
soul had departed.
Slowly the priest uplifted the lifeless head,
and the maiden
Knelt at her father's side, and wailed aloud
in her terror.
Then in a swoon she sank, and lay with her
head on his bosom.
Through the long night she lay in deep, ob-
livious slumber ;
And when she awoke from the trance, she
beheld a multitude near her.
Faces of friends she beheld, that were
mournfully gazing upon her,
Pallid, with tearful eyes, and looks of sad-
dest compassion.
Still the blaze of the burning village illu-
mined the landscape,
Reddened the sky overhead, and gleamed
on the faces around her,
And like the day of doom it seemed to her
wavering senses.
Then a familiar voice she heard, as it said
to the people, —
"Let us bury him here by the sea.   When
a happier season
Brings us again to our homes from the un-
known land of our exile,
Then shall his sacred dust be piously laid
in the churchyard."
Such were the words of the priest.   And
there in haste by the sea-side,
Having the glare of the burning village
for funeral torches,
But without bell or book, they buried the
farmer of Grand-Pré.
And as the voice of the priest repeated the
service of sorrow,
Lo ! with a mournful sound, like the voice
of a vast congregation,
Solemnly answered the sea, and mingled its
roar with the dirges.
'T was the returning tide, that afar from
the waste of the ocean,
With the first dawn of the day, came heav-
ing and hurrying landward.
Then recommenced once more the stir and
noise of embarking ;
And with the ebb of the tide the ships
sailed out of the harbor,
Leaving behind them the dead on the shore,
and the village in ruins.

PART THE SECOND

I

MANY a weary year had passed since the
burning of Grand-Pré,
When on the falling tide the freighted ves-
sels departed,
Bearing a nation, with all its household
gods, into exile,
Exile without an end, and without an ex-
ample in story.
Far asunder, on separate coasts, the Aca-
dians landed ;
Scattered were they, like flakes of snow,
when the wind from the north-
east
Strikes aslant through the fogs that darken
the Banks of Newfoundland.
Friendless, homeless, hopeless, they wan-
dered from city to city,
From the cold lakes of the North to sultry
Southern savannas, —
From the bleak shores of the sea to the
lands where the Father of Waters
Seizes the hills in his hands, and drags them
down to the ocean,
Deep in their sands to bury the scattered
bones of the mammoth.
Friends they sought and homes ; and many,
despairing, heart-broken,
Asked of the earth but a grave, and no
longer a friend nor a fireside.
Written their history stands on tablets of
stone in the churchyards.
Long among them was seen a maiden who
waited and wandered,
Lowly and meek in spirit, and patiently
suffering all things.
Fair was she and young : but, alas ! before
her extended,
Dreary and vast and silent, the desert of
life, with its pathway
Marked by the graves of those who had
sorrowed and suffered before her,
Passions long extinguished, and hopes long
dead and abandoned,
As the emigrant's way o'er the Western
desert is marked by
Camp-fires long consumed, and bones that
bleach in the sunshine.
Something there was in her life incomplete,
imperfect, unfinished ;
As if a morning of June, with all its music
and sunshine,

Suddenly paused in the sky, and, fading, slowly descended
Into the east again, from whence it late had arisen.
Sometimes she lingered in towns, till, urged by the fever within her,
Urged by a restless longing, the hunger and thirst of the spirit,
She would commence again her endless search and endeavor ;
Sometimes in churchyards strayed, and gazed on the crosses and tombstones,
Sat by some nameless grave, and thought that perhaps in its bosom
He was already at rest, and she longed to slumber beside him.
Sometimes a rumor, a hearsay, an inarticulate whisper,
Came with its airy hand to point and beckon her forward.
Sometimes she spake with those who had seen her beloved and known him,
But it was long ago, in some far-off place or forgotten.
" Gabriel Lajeunesse ! " they said ; " Oh yes ! we have seen him.
He was with Basil the blacksmith, and both have gone to the prairies ;
Coureurs-des-Bois are they, and famous hunters and trappers."
" Gabriel Lajeunesse ! " said others ; " Oh yes ! we have seen him.
He is a Voyageur in the lowlands of Louisiana."
Then would they say, " Dear child ! why dream and wait for him longer ?
Are there not other youths as fair as Gabriel ? others
Who have hearts as tender and true, and spirits as loyal ?
Here is Baptiste Leblanc, the notary's son, who has loved thee
Many a tedious year ; come, give him thy hand and be happy !
Thou art too fair to be left to braid St. Catherine's tresses."
Then would Evangeline answer, serenely but sadly, " I cannot !
Whither my heart has gone, there follows my hand, and not elsewhere.
For when the heart goes before, like a lamp, and illumines the pathway,
Many things are made clear, that else lie hidden in darkness."

Thereupon the priest, her friend and father-confessor,
Said, with a smile, " O daughter ! thy God thus speaketh within thee !
Talk not of wasted affection, affection never was wasted ;
If it enrich not the heart of another, its waters, returning
Back to their springs, like the rain, shall fill them full of refreshment ;
That which the fountain sends forth returns again to the fountain.
Patience ; accomplish thy labor ; accomplish thy work of affection !
Sorrow and silence are strong, and patient endurance is godlike.
Therefore accomplish thy labor of love, till the heart is made godlike,
Purified, strengthened, perfected, and rendered more worthy of heaven ! "
Cheered by the good man's words, Evangeline labored and waited.
Still in her heart she heard the funeral dirge of the ocean,
But with its sound there was mingled a voice that whispered, " Despair not ! "
Thus did that poor soul wander in want and cheerless discomfort,
Bleeding, barefooted, over the shards and thorns of existence.
Let me essay, O Muse ! to follow the wanderer's footsteps ; —
Not through each devious path, each changeful year of existence,
But as a traveller follows a streamlet's course through the valley :
Far from its margin at times, and seeing the gleam of its water
Here and there, in some open space, and at intervals only ;
Then drawing nearer its banks, through sylvan glooms that conceal it,
Though he behold it not, he can hear its continuous murmur ;
Happy, at length, if he find the spot where it reaches an outlet.

II

It was the month of May. Far down the Beautiful River,
Past the Ohio shore and past the mouth of the Wabash,

Into the golden stream of the broad and
    swift Mississippi,
Floated a cumbrous boat, that was rowed
    by Acadian boatmen.
It was a band of exiles : a raft, as it were,
    from the shipwrecked
Nation, scattered along the coast, now
    floating together,
Bound by the bonds of a common belief and
    a common misfortune ;
Men and women and children, who, guided
    by hope or by hearsay,
Sought for their kith and their kin among
    the few-acred farmers
On the Acadian coast, and the prairies of
    fair Opelousas.
With them Evangeline went, and her guide,
    the Father Felician.
Onward o'er sunken sands, through a wil-
    derness sombre with forests,
Day after day they glided adown the turbu-
    lent river ;
Night after night, by their blazing fires,
    encamped on its borders.
Now through rushing chutes, among green
    islands, where plumelike
Cotton-trees nodded their shadowy crests,
    they swept with the current,
Then emerged into broad lagoons, where
    silvery sand-bars
Lay in the stream, and along the wimpling
    waves of their margin,
Shining with snow - white plumes, large
    flocks of pelicans waded.
Level the landscape grew, and along the
    shores of the river,
Shaded by china-trees, in the midst of lux-
    uriant gardens,
Stood the houses of planters, with negro-
    cabins and dove-cots.
They were approaching the region where
    reigns perpetual summer,
Where through the Golden Coast, and
    groves of orange and citron,
Sweeps with majestic curve the river away
    to the eastward.
They, too, swerved from their course ; and
    entering the Bayou of Plaque-
    mine,
Soon were lost in a maze of sluggish and
    devious waters,
Which, like a network of steel, extended in
    every direction.
Over their heads the towering and tene-
    brous boughs of the cypress

Met in a dusky arch, and trailing mosses
    in mid-air
Waved like banners that hang on the walls
    of ancient cathedrals.
Deathlike the silence seemed, and unbroken,
    save by the herons
Home to their roosts in the cedar-trees re-
    turning at sunset,
Or by the owl, as he greeted the moon with
    demoniac laughter.
Lovely the moonlight was as it glanced and
    gleamed on the water,
Gleamed on the columns of cypress and
    cedar sustaining the arches,
Down through whose broken vaults it fell
    as through chinks in a ruin.
Dreamlike, and indistinct, and strange were
    all things around them ;
And o'er their spirits there came a feeling
    of wonder and sadness, —
Strange forebodings of ill, unseen and that
    cannot be compassed.
As, at the tramp of a horse's hoof on the
    turf of the prairies,
Far in advance are closed the leaves of the
    shrinking mimosa,
So, at the hoof-beats of fate, with sad fore-
    bodings of evil,
Shrinks and closes the heart, ere the stroke
    of doom has attained it.
But Evangeline's heart was sustained by a
    vision, that faintly
Floated before her eyes, and beckoned her
    on through the moonlight.
It was the thought of her brain that as-
    sumed the shape of a phantom.
Through those shadowy aisles had Gabriel
    wandered before her,
And every stroke of the oar now brought
    him nearer and nearer.

Then in his place, at the prow of the
    boat, rose one of the oarsmen,
And, as a signal sound, if others like them
    peradventure
Sailed on those gloomy and midnight
    streams, blew a blast on his bugle.
Wild through the dark colonnades and cor-
    ridors leafy the blast rang,
Breaking the seal of silence, and giving
    tongues to the forest.
Soundless above them the banners of moss
    just stirred to the music.
Multitudinous echoes awoke and died in
    the distance,

Over the watery floor, and beneath the re-
verberant branches ;
But not a voice replied ; no answer came
from the darkness ;
And, when the echoes had ceased, like a
sense of pain was the silence.
Then Evangeline slept ; but the boatmen
rowed through the midnight,
Silent at times, then singing familiar Cana-
dian boat-songs,
Such as they sang of old on their own Aca-
dian rivers,
While through the night were heard the
mysterious sounds of the desert,
Far off, — indistinct, — as of wave or wind
in the forest,
Mixed with the whoop of the crane and
the roar of the grim alligator.

Thus ere another noon they emerged
from the shades ; and before them
Lay, in the golden sun, the lakes of the
Atchafalaya.
Water-lilies in myriads rocked on the
slight undulations
Made by the passing oars, and, resplendent
in beauty, the lotus
Lifted her golden crown above the heads
of the boatmen.
Faint was the air with the odorous breath
of magnolia blossoms,
And with the heat of noon ; and number-
less sylvan islands,
Fragrant and thickly embowered with blos-
soming hedges of roses,
Near to whose shores they glided along,
invited to slumber.
Soon by the fairest of these their weary
oars were suspended.
Under the boughs of Wachita willows, that
grew by the margin,
Safely their boat was moored ; and scat-
tered about on the greensward,
Tired with their midnight toil, the weary
travellers slumbered.
Over them vast and high extended the cope
of a cedar.
Swinging from its great arms, the trumpet-
flower and the grapevine
Hung their ladder of ropes aloft like the
ladder of Jacob,
On whose pendulous stairs the angels
ascending, descending,
Were the swift humming-birds, that flitted
from blossom to blossom.

Such was the vision Evangeline saw as she
slumbered beneath it.
Filled was her heart with love, and the
dawn of an opening heaven
Lighted her soul in sleep with the glory of
regions celestial.

Nearer, and ever nearer, among the
numberless islands,
Darted a light, swift boat, that sped away
o'er the water,
Urged on its course by the sinewy arms of
hunters and trappers.
Northward its prow was turned, to the land
of the bison and beaver.
At the helm sat a youth, with countenance
thoughtful and careworn.
Dark and neglected locks overshadowed his
brow, and a sadness
Somewhat beyond his years on his face was
legibly written.
Gabriel was it, who, weary with waiting, un-
happy and restless,
Sought in the Western wilds oblivion of
self and of sorrow.
Swiftly they glided along, close under the
lee of the island,
But by the opposite bank, and behind a
screen of palmettos,
So that they saw not the boat, where it lay
concealed in the willows ;
All undisturbed by the dash of their oars,
and unseen, were the sleepers.
Angel of God was there none to awaken
the slumbering maiden.
Swiftly they glided away, like the shade of
a cloud on the prairie.
After the sound of their oars on the tholes
had died in the distance,
As from a magic trance the sleepers awoke,
and the maiden
Said with a sigh to the friendly priest, " O
Father Felician !
Something says in my heart that near me
Gabriel wanders.
Is it a foolish dream, an idle and vague
superstition ?
Or has an angel passed, and revealed the
truth to my spirit ? "
Then, with a blush, she added, " Alas for
my credulous fancy !
Unto ears like thine such words as these
have no meaning."
But made answer the reverend man, and
he smiled as he answered, —

" Daughter, thy words are not idle ; nor are
    they to me without meaning.
Feeling is deep and still ; and the word
    that floats on the surface
Is as the tossing buoy, that betrays where
    the anchor is hidden.
Therefore trust to thy heart, and to what
    the world calls illusions.
Gabriel truly is near thee ; for not far away
    to the southward,
On the banks of the Têche, are the towns
    of St. Maur and St. Martin.
There the long-wandering bride shall be
    given again to her bridegroom,
There the long-absent pastor regain his
    flock and his sheepfold.
Beautiful is the land, with its prairies and
    forests of fruit-trees ;
Under the feet a garden of flowers, and the
    bluest of heavens
Bending above, and resting its dome on the
    walls of the forest.
They who dwell there have named it the
    Eden of Louisiana ! "

With these words of cheer they arose and
    continued their journey.
Softly the evening came. The sun from
    the western horizon
Like a magician extended his golden wand
    o'er the landscape ;
Twinkling vapors arose ; and sky and water
    and forest
Seemed all on fire at the touch, and melted
    and mingled together.
Hanging between two skies, a cloud with
    edges of silver,
Floated the boat, with its dripping oars, on
    the motionless water.
Filled was Evangeline's heart with inex-
    pressible sweetness.
Touched by the magic spell, the sacred
    fountains of feeling
Glowed with the light of love, as the skies
    and waters around her.
Then from a neighboring thicket the mock-
    ing-bird, wildest of singers,
Swinging aloft on a willow spray that hung
    o'er the water,
Shook from his little throat such floods of
    delirious music,
That the whole air and the woods and
    the waves seemed silent to listen.
Plaintive at first were the tones and sad :
    then soaring to madness

Seemed they to follow or guide the revel
    of frenzied Bacchantes.
Single notes were then heard, in sorrowful,
    low lamentation ;
Till, having gathered them all, he flung
    them abroad in derision,
As when, after a storm, a gust of wind
    through the tree-tops
Shakes down the rattling rain in a crystal
    shower on the branches.
With such a prelude as this, and hearts
    that throbbed with emotion,
Slowly they entered the Têche, where it
    flows through the green Opelousas,
And, through the amber air, above the
    crest of the woodland,
Saw the column of smoke that arose from
    a neighboring dwelling ; —
Sounds of a horn they heard, and the dis-
    tant lowing of cattle.

III

Near to the bank of the river, o'ershad-
    owed by oaks, from whose branches
Garlands of Spanish moss and of mystic
    mistletoe flaunted,
Such as the Druids cut down with golden
    hatchets at Yule-tide,
Stood, secluded and still, the house of the
    herdsman. A garden
Girded it round about with a belt of luxuri-
    ant blossoms,
Filling the air with fragrance. The house
    itself was of timbers
Hewn from the cypress-tree, and carefully
    fitted together.
Large and low was the roof; and on slender
    columns supported,
Rose-wreathed, vine-encircled, a broad and
    spacious veranda,
Haunt of the humming-bird and the bee,
    extended around it.
At each end of the house, amid the flowers
    of the garden,
Stationed the dove-cots were, as love's per-
    petual symbol,
Scenes of endless wooing, and endless con-
    tentions of rivals.
Silence reigned o'er the place. The line of
    shadow and sunshine
Ran near the tops of the trees ; but the
    house itself was in shadow,
And from its chimney-top, ascending and
    slowly expanding

Into the evening air, a thin blue column of
smoke rose.
In the rear of the house, from the garden
gate, ran a pathway
Through the great groves of oak to the
skirts of the limitless prairie,
Into whose sea of flowers the sun was
slowly descending.
Full in his track of light, like ships with
shadowy canvas
Hanging loose from their spars in a motion-
less calm in the tropics,
Stood a cluster of trees, with tangled cord-
age of grape-vines.

Just where the woodlands met the flowery
surf of the prairie,
Mounted upon his horse, with Spanish sad-
dle and stirrups,
Sat a herdsman, arrayed in gaiters and
doublet of deerskin.
Broad and brown was the face that from
under the Spanish sombrero
Gazed on the peaceful scene, with the
lordly look of its master.
Round about him were numberless herds
of kine, that were grazing
Quietly in the meadows, and breathing the
vapory freshness
That uprose from the river, and spread
itself over the landscape.
Slowly lifting the horn that hung at his side,
and expanding
Fully his broad, deep chest, he blew a blast,
that resounded
Wildly and sweet and far, through the still
damp air of the evening.
Suddenly out of the grass the long white
horns of the cattle
Rose like flakes of foam on the adverse cur-
rents of ocean.
Silent a moment they gazed, then bellow-
ing rushed o'er the prairie,
And the whole mass became a cloud, a
shade in the distance.
Then, as the herdsman turned to the
house, through the gate of the gar-
den
Saw he the forms of the priest and the
maiden advancing to meet him.
Suddenly down from his horse he sprang
in amazement, and forward
Rushed with extended arms and exclama-
tions of wonder;

When they beheld his face, they recognized
Basil the blacksmith.
Hearty his welcome was, as he led his
guests to the garden.
There in an arbor of roses with endless
question and answer
Gave they vent to their hearts, and renewed
their friendly embraces,
Laughing and weeping by turns, or sitting
silent and thoughtful.
Thoughtful, for Gabriel came not; and now
dark doubts and misgivings
Stole o'er the maiden's heart; and Basil,
somewhat embarrassed,
Broke the silence and said, "If you came
by the Atchafalaya,
How have you nowhere encountered my
Gabriel's boat on the bayous?"
Over Evangeline's face at the words of
Basil a shade passed.
Tears came into her eyes, and she said,
with a tremulous accent,
"Gone? is Gabriel gone?" and, conceal-
ing her face on his shoulder,
All her o'erburdened heart gave way, and
she wept and lamented.
Then the good Basil said, — and his voice
grew blithe as he said it, —
"Be of good cheer, my child; it is only to-
day he departed.
Foolish boy! he has left me alone with my
herds and my horses.
Moody and restless grown, and tried and
troubled, his spirit
Could no longer endure the calm of this
quiet existence,
Thinking ever of thee, uncertain and sor-
rowful ever,
Ever silent, or speaking only of thee and his
troubles,
He at length had become so tedious to men
and to maidens,
Tedious even to me, that at length I be-
thought me, and sent him
Unto the town of Adayes to trade for mules
with the Spaniards.
Thence he will follow the Indian trails to
the Ozark Mountains,
Hunting for furs in the forests, on rivers
trapping the beaver.
Therefore be of good cheer; we will follow
the fugitive lover;
He is not far on his way, and the Fates and
the streams are against him.

Up and away to-morrow, and through the
  red dew of the morning
We will follow him fast, and bring him
  back to his prison."

Then glad voices were heard, and up
  from the banks of the river,
Borne aloft on his comrades' arms, came
  Michael the fiddler.
Long under Basil's roof had he lived like a
  god on Olympus,
Having no other care than dispensing
  music to mortals.
Far renowned was he for his silver locks
  and his fiddle.
"Long live Michael," they cried, "our
  brave Acadian minstrel!"
As they bore him aloft in triumphal pro-
  cession; and straightway
Father Felician advanced with Evangeline,
  greeting the old man
Kindly and oft, and recalling the past,
  while Basil, enraptured,
Hailed with hilarious joy his old compan-
  ions and gossips,
Laughing loud and long, and embracing
  mothers and daughters.
Much they marvelled to see the wealth of
  the ci-devant blacksmith,
All his domains and his herds, and his pa-
  triarchal demeanor;
Much they marvelled to hear his tales of
  the soil and the climate,
And of the prairies, whose numberless herds
  were his who would take them;
Each one thought in his heart, that he, too,
  would go and do likewise.
Thus they ascended the steps, and crossing
  the breezy veranda,
Entered the hall of the house, where al-
  ready the supper of Basil
Waited his late return; and they rested
  and feasted together.

Over the joyous feast the sudden dark-
  ness descended.
All was silent without, and, illuming the
  landscape with silver,
Fair rose the dewy moon and the myriad
  stars; but within doors,
Brighter than these, shone the faces of
  friends in the glimmering lamp-
  light.
Then from his station aloft, at the head of
  the table, the herdsman

Poured forth his heart and his wine to-
  gether in endless profusion.
Lighting his pipe, that was filled with sweet
  Natchitoches tobacco,
Thus he spake to his guests, who listened,
  and smiled as they listened : —
"Welcome once more, my friends, who
  long have been friendless and home-
  less,
Welcome once more to a home, that is
  better perchance than the old one!
Here no hungry winter congeals our blood
  like the rivers;
Here no stony ground provokes the wrath
  of the farmer.
Smoothly the ploughshare runs through
  the soil, as a keel through the wa-
  ter.
All the year round the orange-groves are
  in blossom; and grass grows
More in a single night than a whole Cana-
  dian summer.
Here, too, numberless herds run wild and
  unclaimed in the prairies;
Here, too, lands may be had for the asking,
  and forests of timber
With a few blows of the axe are hewn and
  framed into houses.
After your houses are built, and your fields
  are yellow with harvests,
No King George of England shall drive
  you away from your homesteads,
Burning your dwellings and barns, and
  stealing your farms and your
  cattle."
Speaking these words, he blew a wrathful
  cloud from his nostrils,
While his huge, brown hand came thunder-
  ing down on the table,
So that the guests all started; and Father
  Felician, astounded,
Suddenly paused, with a pinch of snuff
  half-way to his nostrils.
But the brave Basil resumed, and his
  words were milder and gayer : —
"Only beware of the fever, my friends,
  beware of the fever!
For it is not like that of our cold Acadian
  climate,
Cured by wearing a spider hung round
  one's neck in a nutshell!"
Then there were voices heard at the door.
  and footsteps approaching
Sounded upon the stairs and the floor of
  the breezy veranda.

It was the neighboring Creoles and small
    Acadian planters,
Who had been summoned all to the house
    of Basil the Herdsman.
Merry the meeting was of ancient com-
    rades and neighbors :
Friend clasped friend in his arms ; and
    they who before were as strangers,
Meeting in exile, became straightway as
    friends to each other,
Drawn by the gentle bond of a common
    country together.
But in the neighboring hall a strain of
    music, proceeding
From the accordant strings of Michael's
    melodious fiddle,
Broke up all further speech. Away, like
    children delighted,
All things forgotten beside, they gave
    themselves to the maddening
Whirl of the giddy dance, as it swept and
    swayed to the music,
Dreamlike, with beaming eyes and the rush
    of fluttering garments.

Meanwhile, apart, at the head of the
    hall, the priest and the herdsman
Sat, conversing together of past and present
    and future ;
While Evangeline stood like one entranced,
    for within her
Olden memories rose, and loud in the midst
    of the music
Heard she the sound of the sea, and an
    irrepressible sadness
Came o'er her heart, and unseen she stole
    forth into the garden.
Beautiful was the night. Behind the black
    wall of the forest,
Tipping its summit with silver, arose the
    moon. On the river
Fell here and there through the branches a
    tremulous gleam of the moonlight,
Like the sweet thoughts of love on a dark-
    ened and devious spirit.
Nearer and round about her, the manifold
    flowers of the garden
Poured out their souls in odors, that were
    their prayers and confessions
Unto the night, as it went its way, like a
    silent Carthusian.
Fuller of fragrance than they, and as heavy
    with shadows and night-dews,
Hung the heart of the maiden. The calm
    and the magical moonlight

Seemed to inundate her soul with indefin-
    able longings,
As, through the garden-gate, and beneath
    the shade of the oak-trees,
Passed she along the path to the edge of
    the measureless prairie.
Silent it lay, with a silvery haze upon it,
    and fire-flies
Gleamed and floated away in mingled and
    infinite numbers.
Over her head the stars, the thoughts of
    God in the heavens,
Shone on the eyes of man, who had ceased
    to marvel and worship,
Save when a blazing comet was seen on the
    walls of that temple,
As if a hand had appeared and written
    upon them, "Upharsin."
And the soul of the maiden, between the
    stars and the fire-flies,
Wandered alone, and she cried, "O Gabriel!
    O my beloved !
Art thou so near unto me, and yet I cannot
    behold thee ?
Art thou so near unto me, and yet thy voice
    does not reach me ?
Ah! how often thy feet have trod this path
    to the prairie !
Ah ! how often thine eyes have looked on
    the woodlands around me !
Ah ! how often beneath this oak, returning
    from labor,
Thou hast lain down to rest, and to dream
    of me in thy slumbers !
When shall these eyes behold, these arms
    be folded about thee ? "
Loud and sudden and near the notes of a
    whippoorwill sounded
Like a flute in the woods ; and anon,
    through the neighboring thickets,
Farther and farther away it floated and
    dropped into silence.
" Patience ! " whispered the oaks from orac-
    ular caverns of darkness :
And, from the moonlit meadow, a sigh re-
    sponded, " To-morrow ! "

Bright rose the sun next day ; and all the
    flowers of the garden
Bathed his shining feet with their tears,
    and anointed his tresses
With the delicious balm that they bore in
    their vases of crystal.
" Farewell ! " said the priest, as he stood at
    the shadowy threshold ;

" See that you bring us the Prodigal Son
    from his fasting and famine,
And, too, the Foolish Virgin, who slept when
    the bridegroom was coming."
" Farewell ! " answered the maiden, and,
    smiling, with Basil descended
Down to the river's brink, where the boat-
    men already were waiting.
Thus beginning their journey with morn-
    ing, and sunshine, and gladness,
Swiftly they followed the flight of him who
    was speeding before them,
Blown by the blast of fate like a dead leaf
    over the desert.
Not that day, nor the next, nor yet the day
    that succeeded,
Found they the trace of his course, in lake
    or forest or river,
Nor, after many days, had they found him ;
    but vague and uncertain
Rumors alone were their guides through a
    wild and desolate country ;
Till, at the little inn of the Spanish town of
    Adayes,
Weary and worn, they alighted, and learned
    from the garrulous landlord,
That on the day before, with horses and
    guides and companions,
Gabriel left the village, and took the road
    of the prairies.

IV

Far in the West there lies a desert land,
    where the mountains
Lift, through perpetual snows, their lofty
    and luminous summits.
Down from their jagged, deep ravines,
    where the gorge, like a gateway,
Opens a passage rude to the wheels of the
    emigrant's wagon,
Westward the Oregon flows and the Walle-
    way and Owyhee.
Eastward, with devious course, among the
    Wind-river Mountains,
Through the Sweet-water Valley precipi-
    tate leaps the Nebraska ;
And to the south, from Fontaine-qui-bout
    and the Spanish sierras,
Fretted with sands and rocks, and swept
    by the wind of the desert,
Numberless torrents, with ceaseless sound,
    descend to the ocean,
Like the great chords of a harp, in loud
    and solemn vibrations.

Spreading between these streams are the
    wondrous, beautiful prairies ;
Billowy bays of grass ever rolling in shadow
    and sunshine,
Bright with luxuriant clusters of roses and
    purple amorphas.
Over them wandered the buffalo herds, and
    the elk and the roebuck ;
Over them wandered the wolves, and herds
    of riderless horses ;
Fires that blast and blight, and winds that
    are weary with travel ;
Over them wander the scattered tribes of
    Ishmael's children,
Staining the desert with blood ; and above
    their terrible war-trails
Circles and sails aloft, on pinions majestic,
    the vulture,
Like the implacable soul of a chieftain
    slaughtered in battle,
By invisible stairs ascending and scaling
    the heavens.
Here and there rise smokes from the camps
    of these savage marauders ;
Here and there rise groves from the mar-
    gins of swift-running rivers ;
And the grim, taciturn bear, the anchorite
    monk of the desert,
Climbs down their dark ravines to dig for
    roots by the brook-side,
And over all is the sky, the clear and crys-
    talline heaven,
Like the protecting hand of God inverted
    above them.

Into this wonderful land, at the base of
    the Ozark Mountains,
Gabriel far had entered, with hunters and
    trappers behind him.
Day after day, with their Indian guides, the
    maiden and Basil
Followed his flying steps, and thought each
    day to o'ertake him.
Sometimes they saw, or thought they saw,
    the smoke of his camp-fire
Rise in the morning air from the distant
    plain ; but at nightfall,
When they had reached the place they
    found only embers and ashes.
And, though their hearts were sad at times
    and their bodies were weary,
Hope still guided them on, as the magic
    Fata Morgana
Showed them her lakes of light, that re-
    treated and vanished before them.

Once, as they sat by their evening fire,
  there silently entered
Into their little camp an Indian woman,
  whose features
Wore deep traces of sorrow, and patience
  as great as her sorrow.
She was a Shawnee woman returning home
  to her people,
From the far-off hunting-grounds of the
  cruel Camanches,
Where her Canadian husband, a Coureur-
  des-Bois, had been murdered.
Touched were their hearts at her story,
  and warmest and friendliest wel-
  come
Gave they, with words of cheer, and she
  sat and feasted among them
On the buffalo-meat and the venison cooked
  on the embers.
But when their meal was done, and Basil
  and all his companions,
Worn with the long day's march and the
  chase of the deer and the bison,
Stretched themselves on the ground, and
  slept where the quivering fire-light
Flashed on their swarthy cheeks, and their
  forms wrapped up in their blankets,
Then at the door of Evangeline's tent she
  sat and repeated
Slowly, with soft, low voice, and the charm
  of her Indian accent,
All the tale of her love, with its pleasures,
  and pains, and reverses.
Much Evangeline wept at the tale, and to
  know that another
Hapless heart like her own had loved and
  had been disappointed.
Moved to the depths of her soul by pity
  and woman's compassion,
Yet in her sorrow pleased that one who had
  suffered was near her,
She in turn related her love and all its dis-
  asters.
Mute with wonder the Shawnee sat, and
  when she had ended
Still was mute ; but at length, as if a mys-
  terious horror
Passed through her brain, she spake, and
  repeated the tale of the Mowis ;
Mowis, the bridegroom of snow, who won
  and wedded a maiden,
But, when the morning came, arose and
  passed from the wigwam,
Fading and melting away and dissolving
  into the sunshine,

Till she beheld him no more, though she
  followed far into the forest.
Then, in those sweet, low tones, that seemed
  like a weird incantation,
Told she the tale of the fair Lilinau, who
  was wooed by a phantom,
That through the pines o'er her father's
  lodge, in the hush of the twilight,
Breathed like the evening wind, and whis-
  pered love to the maiden,
Till she followed his green and waving
  plume through the forest,
And nevermore returned, nor was seen
  again by her people.
Silent with wonder and strange surprise,
  Evangeline listened
To the soft flow of her magical words, till
  the region around her
Seemed like enchanted ground, and her
  swarthy guest the enchantress.
Slowly over the tops of the Ozark Moun-
  tains the moon rose,
Lighting the little tent, and with a mys-
  terious splendor
Touching the sombre leaves, and embracing
  and filling the woodland.
With a delicious sound the brook rushed
  by, and the branches
Swayed and sighed overhead in scarcely
  audible whispers.
Filled with the thoughts of love was Evan-
  geline's heart, but a secret,
Subtile sense crept in of pain and indefinite
  terror,
As the cold, poisonous snake creeps into
  the nest of the swallow.
It was no earthly fear. A breath from the
  region of spirits
Seemed to float in the air of night ; and
  she felt for a moment
That, like the Indian maid, she, too, was
  pursuing a phantom.
With this thought she slept, and the fear
  and the phantom had vanished.

Early upon the morrow the march was
  resumed ; and the Shawnee
Said, as they journeyed along, "On the
  western slope of these mountains
Dwells in his little village the Black Robe
  chief of the Mission.
Much he teaches the people, and tells them
  of Mary and Jesus.
Loud laugh their hearts with joy, and weep
  with pain, as they hear him."

Then, with a sudden and secret emotion,
    Evangeline answered,
"Let us go to the Mission, for there good
    tidings await us ! "
Thither they turned their steeds ; and be-
    hind a spur of the mountains,
Just as the sun went down, they heard a
    murmur of voices,
And in a meadow green and broad, by the
    bank of a river,
Saw the tents of the Christians, the tents
    of the Jesuit Mission.
Under a towering oak, that stood in the
    midst of the village,
Knelt the Black Robe chief with his chil-
    dren. A crucifix fastened
High on the trunk of the tree, and over-
    shadowed by grapevines,
Looked with its agonized face on the multi-
    tude kneeling beneath it.
This was their rural chapel. Aloft, through
    the intricate arches
Of its aerial roof, arose the chant of their
    vespers,
Mingling its notes with the soft susurrus
    and sighs of the branches.
Silent, with heads uncovered, the travellers,
    nearer approaching,
Knelt on the swarded floor, and joined in
    the evening devotions.
But when the service was done, and the
    benediction had fallen
Forth from the hands of the priest, like seed
    from the hands of the sower,
Slowly the reverend man advanced to the
    strangers, and bade them
Welcome ; and when they replied, he smiled
    with benignant expression,
Hearing the homelike sounds of his mother-
    tongue in the forest,
And, with words of kindness, conducted
    them into his wigwam.
There upon mats and skins they reposed,
    and on cakes of the maize-ear
Feasted, and slaked their thirst from the
    water-gourd of the teacher.
Soon was their story told ; and the priest
    with solemnity answered: —
"Not six suns have risen and set since
    Gabriel, seated
On this mat by my side, where now the
    maiden reposes,
Told me this same sad tale ; then arose
    and continued his journey ! "

Soft was the voice of the priest, and he
    spake with an accent of kindness ;
But on Evangeline's heart fell his words as
    in winter the snow-flakes
Fall into some lone nest from which the
    birds have departed.
"Far to the north he has gone," continued
    the priest ; "but in autumn,
When the chase is done, will return again
    to the Mission."
Then Evangeline said, and her voice was
    meek and submissive,
"Let me remain with thee, for my soul is
    sad and afflicted."
So seemed it wise and well unto all ; and
    betimes on the morrow,
Mounting his Mexican steed, with his Indian
    guides and companions,
Homeward Basil returned, and Evangeline
    stayed at the Mission.

Slowly, slowly, slowly the days succeeded
    each other, —
Days and weeks and months ; and the fields
    of maize that were springing
Green from the ground when a stranger
    she came, now waving above her,
Lifted their slender shafts, with leaves
    interlacing, and forming
Cloisters for mendicant crows and granaries
    pillaged by squirrels.
Then in the golden weather the maize was
    husked, and the maidens
Blushed at each blood-red ear, for that be-
    tokened a lover,
But at the crooked laughed, and called it a
    thief in the corn-field.
Even the blood-red ear to Evangeline
    brought not her lover.
"Patience !" the priest would say ; "have
    faith, and thy prayer will be an-
    swered !
Look at this vigorous plant that lifts its
    head from the meadow,
See how its leaves are turned to the north,
    as true as the magnet ;
This is the compass-flower, that the finger
    of God has planted
Here in the houseless wild, to direct the
    traveller's journey
Over the sea-like, pathless, limitless waste
    of the desert.
Such in the soul of man is faith. The
    blossoms of passion,

Gay and luxuriant flowers, are brighter and
    fuller of fragrance,
But they beguile us, and lead us astray, and
    their odor is deadly.
Only this humble plant can guide us here,
    and hereafter
Crown us with asphodel flowers, that are
    wet with the dews of nepenthe."

So came the autumn, and passed, and the
    winter, — yet Gabriel came not ;
Blossomed the opening spring, and the notes
    of the robin and bluebird
Sounded sweet upon wold and in wood, yet
    Gabriel came not.
But on the breath of the summer winds a
    rumor was wafted
Sweeter than song of bird, or hue or odor
    of blossom.
Far to the north and east, it said, in the
    Michigan forests,
Gabriel had his lodge by the banks of the
    Saginaw River.
And, with returning guides, that sought the
    lakes of St. Lawrence,
Saying a sad farewell, Evangeline went
    from the Mission.
When over weary ways, by long and peril-
    ous marches,
She had attained at length the depths of
    the Michigan forests,
Found she the hunter's lodge deserted and
    fallen to ruin !

Thus did the long sad years glide on,
    and in seasons and places
Divers and distant far was seen the wan-
    dering maiden ; —
Now in the Tents of Grace of the meek
    Moravian Missions,
Now in the noisy camps and the battle-fields
    of the army,
Now in secluded hamlets, in towns and
    populous cities.
Like a phantom she came, and passed away
    unremembered.
Fair was she and young, when in hope
    began the long journey ;
Faded was she and old, when in disappoint-
    ment it ended.
Each succeeding year stole something away
    from her beauty,
Leaving behind it, broader and deeper, the
    gloom and the shadow.

Then there appeared and spread faint
    streaks of gray o'er her forehead,
Dawn of another life, that broke o'er her
    earthly horizon,
As in the eastern sky the first faint streaks
    of the morning.

V

In that delightful land which is washed by
    the Delaware waters,
Guarding in sylvan shades the name of
    Penn the apostle,
Stands on the banks of its beautiful stream
    the city he founded.
There all the air is balm, and the peach is
    the emblem of beauty,
And the streets still reëcho the names of
    the trees of the forest,
As if they fain would appease the Dryads
    whose haunts they molested.
There from the troubled sea had Evange-
    line landed, an exile,
Finding among the children of Penn a home
    and a country.
There old René Leblanc had died ; and
    when he departed,
Saw at his side only one of all his hundred
    descendants.
Something at least there was in the friendly
    streets of the city,
Something that spake to her heart, and
    made her no longer a stranger ;
And her ear was pleased with the Thee and
    Thou of the Quakers,
For it recalled the past, the old Acadian
    country,
Where all men were equal, and all were
    brothers and sisters.
So, when the fruitless search, the disap-
    pointed endeavor,
Ended, to recommence no more upon earth,
    uncomplaining,
Thither, as leaves to the light, were turned
    her thoughts and her footsteps.
As from the mountain's top the rainy mists
    of the morning
Roll away, and afar we behold the land-
    scape below us,
Sun-illumined, with shining rivers and cities
    and hamlets,
So fell the mists from her mind, and she
    saw the world far below her,

Dark no longer, but all illumined with love ;
and the pathway
Which she had climbed so far, lying smooth
and fair in the distance.
Gabriel was not forgotten. Within her
heart was his image,
Clothed in the beauty of love and youth, as
last she beheld him,
Only more beautiful made by his death-like
silence and absence.
Into her thoughts of him time entered not,
for it was not.
Over him years had no power ; he was not
changed, but transfigured ;
He had become to her heart as one who is
dead, and not absent ;
Patience and abnegation of self, and devo-
tion to others,
This was the lesson a life of trial and sor-
row had taught her.
So was her love diffused, but, like to some
odorous spices,
Suffered no waste nor loss, though filling
the air with aroma.
Other hope had she none, nor wish in life,
but to follow
Meekly, with reverent steps, the sacred
feet of her Saviour.
Thus many years she lived as a Sister of
Mercy ; frequenting
Lonely and wretched roofs in the crowded
lanes of the city,
Where distress and want concealed them-
selves from the sunlight,·
Where disease and sorrow in garrets lan-
guished neglected.
Night after night, when the world was
asleep, as the watchman repeated
Loud, through the gusty streets, that all
was well in the city,
High at some lonely window he saw the
light of her taper.
Day after day, in the gray of the dawn, as
slow through the suburbs
Plodded the German farmer, with flowers
and fruits for the market,
Met he that meek, pale face, returning home
from its watchings.

Then it came to pass that a pestilence
fell on the city,
Presaged by wondrous signs, and mostly
by flocks of wild pigeons,
Darkening the sun in their flight, with
naught in their craws but an acorn.

And, as the tides of the sea arise in the
month of September,
Flooding some silver stream, till it spreads
to a lake in the meadow,
So death flooded life, and, o'erflowing its
natural margin,
Spread to a brackish lake, the silver
stream of existence.
Wealth had no power to bribe, nor beauty
to charm, the oppressor ;
But all perished alike beneath the scourge
of his anger ; —
Only, alas ! the poor, who had neither
friends nor attendants,
Crept away to die in the almshouse, home
of the homeless.
Then in the suburbs it stood, in the midst
of meadows and woodlands ; —
Now the city surrounds it ; but still, with
its gateway and wicket
Meek, in the midst of splendor, its humble
walls seemed to echo
Softly the words of the Lord : " The poor
ye always have with you."
Thither, by night and by day, came the
Sister of Mercy. The dying
Looked up into her face, and thought, in-
deed, to behold there
Gleams of celestial light encircle her fore-
head with splendor,
Such as the artist paints o'er the brows of
saints and apostles,
Or such as hangs by night o'er a city seen
at a distance.
Unto their eyes it seemed the lamps of the
city celestial,
Into whose shining gates erelong their
spirits would enter.

Thus, on a Sabbath morn, through the
streets, deserted and silent,
Wending her quiet way, she entered the
door of the almshouse.
Sweet on the summer air was the odor of
flowers in the garden ;
And she paused on her way to gather the
fairest among them,
That the dying once more might rejoice in
their fragrance and beauty.
Then, as she mounted the stairs to the cor-
ridors, cooled by the east-wind,
Distant and soft on her ear fell the chimes
from the belfry of Christ Church,
While, intermingled with these, across the
meadows were wafted

Sounds of psalms, that were sung by
    the Swedes in their church at Wi-
    caco.
Soft as descending wings fell the calm of
    the hour on her spirit :
Something within her said, " At length thy
    trials are ended ; "
And, with light in her looks, she entered
    the chambers of sickness.
Noiselessly moved about the assiduous,
    careful attendants,
Moistening the feverish lip, and the aching
    brow, and in silence
Closing the sightless eyes of the dead, and
    concealing their faces,
Where on their pallets they lay, like drifts
    of snow by the roadside.
Many a languid head, upraised as Evange-
    line entered,
Turned on its pillow of pain to gaze while
    she passed, for her presence
Fell on their hearts like a ray of the sun on
    the walls of a prison.
And, as she looked around, she saw how
    Death, the consoler,
Laying his hand upon many a heart, had
    healed it forever.
Many familiar forms had disappeared in the
    night time ;
Vacant their places were, or filled already
    by strangers.

Suddenly, as if arrested by fear or a feel-
    ing of wonder,
Still she stood, with her colorless lips apart,
    while a shudder
Ran through her frame, and, forgotten,
    the flowerets dropped from her fin-
    gers,
And from her eyes and cheeks the light
    and bloom of the morning.
Then there escaped from her lips a cry of
    such terrible anguish,
That the dying heard it, and started up
    from their pillows.
On the pallet before her was stretched the
    form of an old man.
Long, and thin, and gray were the locks
    that shaded his temples ;
But, as he lay in the morning light, his
    face for a moment
Seemed to assume once more the forms of
    its earlier manhood ;
So are wont to be changed the faces of
    those who are dying.

Hot and red on his lips still burned the
    flush of the fever,
As if life, like the Hebrew, with blood had
    besprinkled its portals,
That the Angel of Death might see the
    sign, and pass over.
Motionless, senseless, dying, he lay, and
    his spirit exhausted
Seemed to be sinking down through infi-
    nite depths in the darkness,
Darkness of slumber and death, forever
    sinking and sinking.
Then through those realms of shade, in mul-
    tiplied reverberations,
Heard he that cry of pain, and through the
    hush that succeeded
Whispered a gentle voice, in accents tender
    and saint-like,
" Gabriel ! O my beloved ! " and died away
    into silence.
Then he beheld, in a dream, once more the
    home of his childhood ;
Green Acadian meadows, with sylvan
    rivers among them,
Village, and mountain, and woodlands ; and,
    walking under their shadow,
As in the days of her youth, Evangeline
    rose in his vision.
Tears came into his eyes ; and as slowly he
    lifted his eyelids,
Vanished the vision away, but Evangeline
    knelt by his bedside.
Vainly he strove to whisper her name, for
    the accents unuttered
Died on his lips, and their motion revealed
    what his tongue would have spoken.
Vainly he strove to rise ; and Evangeline,
    kneeling beside him,
Kissed his dying lips, and laid his head on
    her bosom.
Sweet was the light of his eyes ; but it sud-
    denly sank into darkness,
As when a lamp is blown out by a gust of
    wind at a casement.

All was ended now, the hope, and the
    fear, and the sorrow,
All the aching of heart, the restless, unsat-
    isfied longing,
All the dull, deep pain, and constant an-
    guish of patience !
And, as she pressed once more the lifeless
    head to her bosom,
Meekly she bowed her own, and murmured,
    " Father, I thank thee ! "

Still stands the forest primeval ; but far
　away from its shadow,
Side by side, in their nameless graves, the
　lovers are sleeping.
Under the humble walls of the little Catho-
　lic churchyard,
In the heart of the city, they lie, unknown
　and unnoticed.
Daily the tides of life go ebbing and flow-
　ing beside them,
Thousands of throbbing hearts, where
　theirs are at rest and forever,
Thousands of aching brains, where theirs
　no longer are busy,
Thousands of toiling hands, where theirs
　have ceased from their labors,
Thousands of weary feet, where theirs have
　completed their journey !

Still stands the forest primeval ; but un-
　der the shade of its branches
Dwells another race, with other customs
　and language.
Only along the shore of the mournful and
　misty Atlantic
Linger a few Acadian peasants, whose fa-
　thers from exile
Wandered back to their native land to die
　in its bosom.
In the fisherman's cot the wheel and the
　loom are still busy ;
Maidens still wear their Norman caps and
　their kirtles of homespun,
And by the evening fire repeat Evangeline's
　story,
While from its rocky caverns the deep-
　voiced, neighboring ocean
Speaks, and in accents disconsolate answers
　the wail of the forest.

THE SEASIDE AND THE FIRESIDE

After the publication of *Evangeline*, there was a pe-
riod when Mr. Longfellow's mood was not a poetic one.
He pleased himself with writing the tale of *Kavanagh*,
but there are frequent laments in his diary at his un-
productiveness ; that the golden days of October, usu-
ally so fruitful in verse, faded away and left no lines
written ; that his growing fame brought him numberless
interruptions, and that the routine of his college work
was becoming intolerable. Now and then a poem came
to him, and he even made headway with a dramatic
romance of the age of Louis XIV., but abandoned the
work finally. It was two years after finishing *Evan-
geline* before he had accumulated sufficient material
to warrant him in planning a new volume of poems.
The Seaside and the Fireside was published in Novem-
ber, 1849, with *The Building of the Ship* as the leading
piece.

The form of the poem was clearly suggested by
Schiller's *Song of the Bell*, which has more than once
served poets as a model. Schiller may be said to have
introduced a new artistic form, and Mr. Longfellow, in
adopting the general scheme, showed his apprehension
of its capacity by the skill with which he moved from
one passage to another, using the short lines to express
the quicker, more sudden, or hurried action, the longer
to indicate lingering, moderate action or reflection.
The oratorical character of the poem, so to speak, has
always caught the ear, and it is interesting to read in
the poet's diary shortly after the publication of the
book, this entry : —

"February 12, 1850. In the evening Mrs. Kemble
read before the Mercantile Library Association, to an
audience of more than three thousand, portions of *As
You Like It ;* then *The Building of the Ship*, standing
out upon the platform, book in hand, trembling, palpi-
tating, and weeping, and giving every word its true
weight and emphasis. She prefaced the recital by a
few words, to this effect ; that when she first saw the
poem, she desired to read it before a Boston audience ;

and she hoped she would be able to make every word
audible to that great multitude."

By this graceful action Mrs. Kemble may well have
thrown into concrete form the lines with which Mr.
Longfellow closed the sonnet commemorating her read-
ings, —

　　O happy Poet ! . . .
　　How must thy listening spirit now rejoice
　　To be interpreted by such a voice !

But it is to be suspected that the vast multitude was
stirred to its depths not so much by the artistic com-
pleteness of the rendition, as by the impassioned burst
with which the poem closes, and which fell upon no
listless ears in the deep agitation of the eventful year
1850. Mr. Noah Brooks in his paper on *Lincoln's Im-
agination* (*Scribner's Monthly*, August, 1879) mentions
that he found the President one day attracted by these
stanzas, quoted in a political speech. "Knowing the
whole poem," he adds, "as one of my early exercises
in recitation, I began, at his request, with the descrip-
tion of the launch of the ship, and repeated it to the
end. As he listened to the last lines, his eyes filled
with tears, and his cheeks were wet. He did not speak
for some minutes, but finally said, with simplicity : 'It
is a wonderful gift to be able to stir men like that.'"
Dr. William Everett, in his remarks before the Massa-
chusetts Historical Society, after the death of Mr.
Longfellow, called attention to the striking contrast in
these spirited, hopeful lines to Horace's timid, trem-
ulous *O navis*.

In his diary, under date of March 23, 1850, Mr. Long-
fellow writes : "Cast lead flat-irons for the children, to
their great delight. C. in great and joyous excitement,
which he showed by the most voluble speech. E.
showed his only in his eyes, and looked on in silence.
The casting was to them as grand as the casting of a
bell to grown-up children. Why not write for them a
Song of the Lead Flat-Iron ? "

DEDICATION

As one who, walking in the twilight gloom,
  Hears round about him voices as it
    darkens,
And seeing not the forms from which they
    come,
  Pauses from time to time, and turns and
    hearkens ;

So walking here in twilight, O my friends !
  I hear your voices, softened by the dis-
    tance,
And pause, and turn to listen, as each sends
  His words of friendship, comfort, and
    assistance.

If any thought of mine, or sung or told,
  Has ever given delight or consolation,
Ye have repaid me back a thousand-fold,
  By every friendly sign and salutation.

Thanks for the sympathies that ye have
    shown !
  Thanks for each kindly word, each silent
    token,
That teaches me, when seeming most alone,
  Friends are around us, though no word
    be spoken.

Kind messages, that pass from land to
    land ;
  Kind letters, that betray the heart's deep
    history,
In which we feel the pressure of a hand, —
  One touch of fire, — and all the rest is
    mystery !

The pleasant books, that silently among
  Our household treasures take familiar
    places,
And are to us as if a living tongue
  Spake from the printed leaves or pictured
    faces !

Perhaps on earth I never shall behold,
  With eye of sense, your outward form
    and semblance ;
Therefore to me ye never will grow old,
  But live forever young in my remem-
    brance !

Never grow old, nor change, nor pass away !
  Your gentle voices will flow on forever,
When life grows bare and tarnished with
    decay,
  As through a leafless landscape flows a
    river.

Not chance of birth or place has made us
    friends,
  Being oftentimes of different tongues and
    nations,
But the endeavor for the selfsame ends,
  With the same hopes, and fears, and as-
    pirations.

Therefore I hope to join your seaside walk,
  Saddened, and mostly silent, with emo-
    tion ;
Not interrupting with intrusive talk
  The grand, majestic symphonies of ocean.

Therefore I hope, as no unwelcome guest,
  At your warm fireside, when the lamps
    are lighted,
To have my place reserved among the
    rest,
  Nor stand as one unsought and unin-
    vited !

BY THE SEASIDE

THE BUILDING OF THE SHIP

" BUILD me straight, O worthy Master !
  Stanch and strong, a goodly vessel,
That shall laugh at all disaster,
  And with wave and whirlwind wrestle ! "

The merchant's word
Delighted the Master heard ;
For his heart was in his work, and the
    heart
Giveth grace unto every Art.
A quiet smile played round his lips,
As the eddies and dimples of the tide
Play round the bows of ships,
That steadily at anchor ride.
And with a voice that was full of glee,
He answered, " Erelong we will launch
A vessel as goodly, and strong, and stanch,
As ever weathered a wintry sea ! "
And first with nicest skill and art,
Perfect and finished in every part,
A little model the Master wrought,
Which should be to the larger plan
What the child is to the man,

Its counterpart in miniature ;
That with a hand more swift and sure
The greater labor might be brought
To answer to his inward thought.
And as he labored, his mind ran o'er
The various ships that were built of yore,
And above them all, and strangest of all
Towered the Great Harry, crank and tall,
Whose picture was hanging on the wall,
With bows and stern raised high in air,
And balconies hanging here and there,
And signal lanterns and flags afloat,
And eight round towers, like those that
    frown
From some old castle, looking down
Upon the drawbridge and the moat.
And he said with a smile, " Our ship, I wis,
Shall be of another form than this ! "
It was of another form, indeed ;
Built for freight, and yet for speed,
A beautiful and gallant craft ;
Broad in the beam, that the stress of the
    blast,
Pressing down upon sail and mast,
Might not the sharp bows overwhelm ;
Broad in the beam, but sloping aft
With graceful curve and slow degrees,
That she might be docile to the helm,
And that the currents of parted seas,
Closing behind, with mighty force,
Might aid and not impede her course.

In the ship-yard stood the Master,
With the model of the vessel,
That should laugh at all disaster,
And with wave and whirlwind wrestle !

Covering many a rood of ground,
Lay the timber piled around ;
Timber of chestnut, and elm, and oak,
And scattered here and there, with these,
The knarred and crooked cedar knees ;
Brought from regions far away,
From Pascagoula's sunny bay,
And the banks of the roaring Roanoke !
Ah ! what a wondrous thing it is
To note how many wheels of toil
One thought, one word, can set in motion !
There 's not a ship that sails the ocean,
But every climate, every soil,
Must bring its tribute, great or small,
And help to build the wooden wall !

The sun was rising o'er the sea,
And long the level shadows lay,
As if they, too, the beams would be

Of some great, airy argosy,
Framed and launched in a single day.
That silent architect, the sun,
Had hewn and laid them every one,
Ere the work of man was yet begun.
Beside the Master, when he spoke,
A youth, against an anchor leaning,
Listened, to catch his slightest meaning.
Only the long waves, as they broke
In ripples on the pebbly beach,
Interrupted the old man's speech.

Beautiful they were, in sooth,
The old man and the fiery youth !
The old man, in whose busy brain
Many a ship that sailed the main
Was modelled o'er and o'er again ; —
The fiery youth, who was to be
The heir of his dexterity,
The heir of his house, and his daughter's
    hand,
When he had built and launched from
    land
What the elder head had planned.

" Thus," said he, " will we build this ship !
Lay square the blocks upon the slip,
And follow well this plan of mine.
Choose the timbers with greatest care ;
Of all that is unsound beware ;
For only what is sound and strong
To this vessel shall belong.
Cedar of Maine and Georgia pine
Here together shall combine.
A goodly frame, and a goodly fame,
And the UNION be her name !
For the day that gives her to the sea
Shall give my daughter unto thee ! "

The Master's word
Enraptured the young man heard ;
And as he turned his face aside,
With a look of joy and a thrill of pride
Standing before
Her father's door,
He saw the form of his promised bride.
The sun shone on her golden hair,
And her cheek was glowing fresh and
    fair,
With the breath of morn and the soft sea
    air.
Like a beauteous barge was she,
Still at rest on the sandy beach,
Just beyond the billow's reach ;
But he
Was the restless, seething, stormy sea !

Ah, how skilful grows the hand
That obeyeth Love's command !
It is the heart, and not the brain,
That to the highest doth attain,
And he who followeth Love's behest
Far excelleth all the rest !

Thus with the rising of the sun
Was the noble task begun,
And soon throughout the ship-yard's bounds
Were heard the intermingled sounds
Of axes and of mallets, plied
With vigorous arms on every side ;
Plied so deftly and so well,
That, ere the shadows of evening fell,
The keel of oak for a noble ship,
Scarfed and bolted, straight and strong,
Was lying ready, and stretched along
The blocks, well placed upon the slip.
Happy, thrice happy, every one
Who sees his labor well begun,
And not perplexed and multiplied,
By idly waiting for time and tide !

And when the hot, long day was o'er,
The young man at the Master's door
Sat with the maiden calm and still,
And within the porch, a little more
Removed beyond the evening chill,
The father sat, and told them tales
Of wrecks in the great September gales,
Of pirates coasting the Spanish Main,
And ships that never came back again,
The chance and change of a sailor's life,
Want and plenty, rest and strife,
His roving fancy, like the wind,
That nothing can stay and nothing can
    bind,
And the magic charm of foreign lands,
With shadows of palms, and shining sands,
Where the tumbling surf,
O'er the coral reefs of Madagascar,
Washes the feet of the swarthy Lascar,
As he lies alone and asleep on the turf.
And the trembling maiden held her breath
At the tales of that awful, pitiless sea,
With all its terror and mystery,
The dim, dark sea, so like unto Death,
That divides and yet unites mankind !
And whenever the old man paused, a
    gleam
From the bowl of his pipe would awhile
    illume
The silent group in the twilight gloom,
And thoughtful faces, as in a dream ;

And for a moment one might mark
What had been hidden by the dark,
That the head of the maiden lay at rest,
Tenderly, on the young man's breast !

Day by day the vessel grew,
With timbers fashioned strong and true,
Stemson and keelson and sternson-knee,
Till, framed with perfect symmetry,
A skeleton ship rose up to view !
And around the bows and along the side
The heavy hammers and mallets plied,
Till after many a week, at length,
Wonderful for form and strength,
Sublime in its enormous bulk,
Loomed aloft the shadowy hulk !
And around it columns of smoke, upwreath-
    ing,
Rose from the boiling, bubbling, seething
Caldron, that glowed,
And overflowed
With the black tar, heated for the sheath-
    ing.
And amid the clamors
Of clattering hammers,
He who listened heard now and then
The song of the Master and his men : —

" Build me straight, O worthy Master,
    Stanch and strong, a goodly vessel,
That shall laugh at all disaster,
    And with wave and whirlwind wrestle ! "

With oaken brace and copper band,
Lay the rudder on the sand,
That, like a thought, should have control
Over the movement of the whole ;
And near it the anchor, whose giant hand
Would reach down and grapple with the
    land,
And immovable and fast
Hold the great ship against the bellowing
    blast !
And at the bows an image stood,
By a cunning artist carved in wood,
With robes of white, that far behind
Seemed to be fluttering in the wind.
It was not shaped in a classic mould,
Not like a Nymph or Goddess of old,
Or Naiad rising from the water,
But modelled from the Master's daugh-
    ter !
On many a dreary and misty night,
'T will be seen by the rays of the signal
    light,

Speeding along through the rain and the
 dark,
Like a ghost in its snow-white sark,
The pilot of some phantom bark,
Guiding the vessel, in its flight,
By a path none other knows aright !

Behold, at last,
Each tall and tapering mast
Is swung into its place ;
Shrouds and stays
Holding it firm and fast !

Long ago,
In the deer-haunted forests of Maine,
When upon mountain and plain
Lay the snow,
They fell, — those lordly pines !
Those grand, majestic pines !
'Mid shouts and cheers
The jaded steers,
Panting beneath the goad,
Dragged down the weary, winding road
Those captive kings so straight and tall,
To be shorn of their streaming hair,
And naked and bare,
To feel the stress and the strain
Of the wind and the reeling main,
Whose roar
Would remind them forevermore
Of their native forests they should not see
 again.

And everywhere
The slender, graceful spars
Poise aloft in the air,
And at the mast-head,
White, blue, and red,
A flag unrolls the stripes and stars.
Ah ! when the wanderer, lonely, friendless,
In foreign harbors shall behold
That flag unrolled,
'T will be as a friendly hand
Stretched out from his native land,
Filling his heart with memories sweet and
 endless !

All is finished ! and at length
Has come the bridal day
Of beauty and of strength.
To-day the vessel shall be launched !
With fleecy clouds the sky is blanched,
And o'er the bay,
Slowly, in all his splendors dight,
The great sun rises to behold the sight.

The ocean old,
Centuries old,
Strong as youth, and as uncontrolled,
Paces restless to and fro,
Up and down the sands of gold.
His beating heart is not at rest ;
And far and wide,
With ceaseless flow,
His beard of snow
Heaves with the heaving of his breast.
He waits impatient for his bride.
There she stands,
With her foot upon the sands,
Decked with flags and streamers gay,
In honor of her marriage day,
Her snow-white signals fluttering, blend-
 ing,
Round her like a veil descending,
Ready to be
The bride of the gray old sea.

On the deck another bride
Is standing by her lover's side.
Shadows from the flags and shrouds,
Like the shadows cast by clouds,
Broken by many a sudden fleck,
Fall around them on the deck.

The prayer is said,
The service read,
The joyous bridegroom bows his head ;
And in tears the good old Master
Shakes the brown hand of his son,
Kisses his daughter's glowing cheek
In silence, for he cannot speak,
And ever faster
Down his own the tears begin to run.
The worthy pastor —
The shepherd of that wandering flock,
That has the ocean for its wold,
That has the vessel for its fold,
Leaping ever from rock to rock —
Spake, with accents mild and clear,
Words of warning, words of cheer,
But tedious to the bridegroom's ear.
He knew the chart
Of the sailor's heart,
All its pleasures and its griefs,
All its shallows and rocky reefs,
All those secret currents, that flow
With such resistless undertow,
And lift and drift, with terrible force,
The will from its moorings and its course.
Therefore he spake, and thus said
 he : —

" Like unto ships far off at sea,
Outward or homeward bound, are we.
Before, behind, and all around,
Floats and swings the horizon's bound,
Seems at its distant rim to rise
And climb the crystal wall of the skies,
And then again to turn and sink,
As if we could slide from its outer brink.
Ah ! it is not the sea,
It is not the sea that sinks and shelves,
But ourselves
That rock and rise
With endless and uneasy motion,
Now touching the very skies,
Now sinking into the depths of ocean.
Ah ! if our souls but poise and swing
Like the compass in its brazen ring,
Ever level and ever true
To the toil and the task we have to do,
We shall sail securely, and safely reach
The Fortunate Isles, on whose shining
    beach
The sights we see, and the sounds we
    hear,
Will be those of joy and not of fear ! "

Then the Master,
With a gesture of command,
Waved his hand ;
And at the word,
Loud and sudden there was heard,
All around them and below,
The sound of hammers, blow on blow,
Knocking away the shores and spurs.
And see ! she stirs !
She starts, — she moves, — she seems to
    feel
The thrill of life along her keel,
And, spurning with her foot the ground,
With one exulting, joyous bound,
She leaps into the ocean's arms !

And lo ! from the assembled crowd
There rose a shout, prolonged and loud,
That to the ocean seemed to say,
" Take her, O bridegroom, old and gray,
Take her to thy protecting arms,
With all her youth and all her charms ! "

How beautiful she is ! How fair
She lies within those arms, that press
Her form with many a soft caress
Of tenderness and watchful care !
Sail forth into the sea, O ship !

Through wind and wave, right onward steer!
The moistened eye, the trembling lip,
Are not the signs of doubt or fear.

Sail forth into the sea of life,
O gentle, loving, trusting wife,
And safe from all adversity
Upon the bosom of that sea
Thy comings and thy goings be !
For gentleness and love and trust
Prevail o'er angry wave and gust ;
And in the wreck of noble lives
Something immortal still survives !

Thou, too, sail on, O Ship of State !
Sail on, O Union, strong and great !
Humanity with all its fears,
With all the hopes of future years,
Is hanging breathless on thy fate !
We know what Master laid thy keel,
What Workmen wrought thy ribs of steel,
Who made each mast, and sail, and rope,
What anvils rang, what hammers beat,
In what a forge and what a heat
Were shaped the anchors of thy hope !
Fear not each sudden sound and shock,
'T is of the wave and not the rock ;
'T is but the flapping of the sail,
And not a rent made by the gale !
In spite of rock and tempest's roar,
In spite of false lights on the shore,
Sail on, nor fear to breast the sea !
Our hearts, our hopes, are all with thee,
Our hearts, our hopes, our prayers, our
    tears,
Our faith triumphant o'er our fears,
Are all with thee, — are all with thee !

SEAWEED

WHEN descends on the Atlantic
    The gigantic
Storm-wind of the equinox,
Landward in his wrath he scourges
    The toiling surges,
Laden with seaweed from the rocks :

From Bermuda's reefs ; from edges
    Of sunken ledges,
In some far-off, bright Azore ;
From Bahama, and the dashing,
    Silver-flashing
Surges of San Salvador ;

From the tumbling surf, that buries
 The Orkneyan skerries,
Answering the hoarse Hebrides ;
And from wrecks of ships, and drifting
 Spars, uplifting
On the desolate, rainy seas ; —

Ever drifting, drifting, drifting
 On the shifting
Currents of the restless main ;
Till in sheltered coves, and reaches
 Of sandy beaches,
All have found repose again.

So when storms of wild emotion
 Strike the ocean
Of the poet's soul, erelong
From each cave and rocky fastness,
 In its vastness,
Floats some fragment of a song :

From the far-off isles enchanted,
 Heaven has planted
With the golden fruit of Truth ;
From the flashing surf, whose vision
 Gleams Elysian
In the tropic clime of Youth ;

From the strong Will, and the Endeavor
 That forever
Wrestle with the tides of Fate ;
From the wreck of Hopes far-scattered,
 Tempest-shattered,
Floating waste and desolate ; —

Ever drifting, drifting, drifting
 On the shifting
Currents of the restless heart ;
Till at length in books recorded,
 They, like hoarded
Household words, no more depart.

CHRYSAOR

In the first edition of *The Seaside and the Fireside*
this poem bore the title of *The Evening Star*.

JUST above yon sandy bar,
 As the day grows fainter and dimmer,
Lonely and lovely, a single star
 Lights the air with a dusky glimmer.

Into the ocean faint and far
 Falls the trail of its golden splendor,

And the gleam of that single star
 Is ever refulgent, soft, and tender.

Chrysaor, rising out of the sea,
 Showed thus glorious and thus emulous,
Leaving the arms of Callirrhoë,
 Forever tender, soft, and tremulous.

Thus o'er the ocean faint and far
 Trailed the gleam of his falchion brightly;
Is it a God, or is it a star
 That, entranced, I gaze on nightly !

THE SECRET OF THE SEA

AH ! what pleasant visions haunt me
 As I gaze upon the sea !
All the old romantic legends,
 All my dreams, come back to me.

Sails of silk and ropes of sandal,
 Such as gleam in ancient lore ;
And the singing of the sailors,
 And the answer from the shore !

Most of all, the Spanish ballad
 Haunts me oft, and tarries long,
Of the noble Count Arnaldos
 And the sailor's mystic song.

Like the long waves on a sea-beach,
 Where the sand as silver shines,
With a soft, monotonous cadence,
 Flow its unrhymed lyric lines ; —

Telling how the Count Arnaldos,
 With his hawk upon his hand,
Saw a fair and stately galley,
 Steering onward to the land ; —

How he heard the ancient helmsman
 Chant a song so wild and clear,
That the sailing sea-bird slowly
 Poised upon the mast to hear,

Till his soul was full of longing,
 And he cried, with impulse strong, —
" Helmsman ! for the love of heaven,
 Teach me, too, that wondrous song ! "

" Wouldst thou," — so the helmsman an-
 swered,
 " Learn the secret of the sea ?

Only those who brave its dangers
　Comprehend its mystery ! "

In each sail that skims the horizon,
　In each landward-blowing breeze,
I behold that stately galley,
　Hear those mournful melodies ;

Till my soul is full of longing
　For the secret of the sea,
And the heart of the great ocean
　Sends a thrilling pulse through me.

TWILIGHT

THE twilight is sad and cloudy,
　The wind blows wild and free,
And like the wings of sea-birds
　Flash the white caps of the sea.

But in the fisherman's cottage
　There shines a ruddier light,
And a little face at the window
　Peers out into the night.

Close, close it is pressed to the window,
　As if those childish eyes
Were looking into the darkness
　To see some form arise.

And a woman's waving shadow
　Is passing to and fro,
Now rising to the ceiling,
　Now bowing and bending low.

What tale do the roaring ocean,
　And the night-wind, bleak and wild,
As they beat at the crazy casement,
　Tell to that little child ?

And why do the roaring ocean,
　And the night-wind, wild and bleak,
As they beat at the heart of the mother
　Drive the color from her cheek ?

SIR HUMPHREY GILBERT

SOUTHWARD with fleet of ice
　Sailed the corsair Death ;

Wild and fast blew the blast,
　And the east-wind was his breath.

His lordly ships of ice
　Glisten in the sun ;
On each side, like pennons wide,
　Flashing crystal streamlets run.

His sails of white sea-mist
　Dripped with silver rain ;
But where he passed there were cast
　Leaden shadows o'er the main.

Eastward from Campobello
　Sir Humphrey Gilbert sailed ;
Three days or more seaward he bore,
　Then, alas ! the land-wind failed.

Alas ! the land-wind failed,
　And ice-cold grew the night ;
And nevermore, on sea or shore,
　Should Sir Humphrey see the light.

He sat upon the deck,
　The Book was in his hand ;
" Do not fear ! Heaven is as near,"
　He said, " by water as by land ! "

In the first watch of the night,
　Without a signal's sound,
Out of the sea, mysteriously,
　The fleet of Death rose all around.

The moon and the evening star
　Were hanging in the shrouds ;
Every mast, as it passed,
　Seemed to rake the passing clouds.

They grappled with their prize,
　At midnight black and cold !
As of a rock was the shock ;
　Heavily the ground-swell rolled.

Southward through day and dark,
　They drift in close embrace,
With mist and rain, o'er the open main ;
　Yet there seems no change of place.

Southward, forever southward,
　They drift through dark and day ;
And like a dream, in the Gulf-Stream
　Sinking, vanish all away.

THE LIGHTHOUSE

THE rocky ledge runs far into the sea,
    And on its outer point, some miles away,
The Lighthouse lifts its massive masonry,
    A pillar of fire by night, of cloud by day.

Even at this distance I can see the tides,
    Upheaving, break unheard along its base,
A speechless wrath, that rises and subsides
    In the white lip and tremor of the face.

And as the evening darkens, lo ! how bright,
    Through the deep purple of the twilight
       air,
Beams forth the sudden radiance of its light
    With strange, unearthly splendor in the
       glare !

Not one alone ; from each projecting cape
    And perilous reef along the ocean's verge,
Starts into life a dim, gigantic shape,
    Holding its lantern o'er the restless surge.

Like the great giant Christopher it stands
    Upon the brink of the tempestuous wave,
Wading far out among the rocks and sands,
    The night-o'ertaken mariner to save.

And the great ships sail outward and return,
    Bending and bowing o'er the billowy
       swells,
And ever joyful, as they see it burn,
    They wave their silent welcomes and
       farewells.

They come forth from the darkness, and
       their sails
    Gleam for a moment only in the blaze,
And eager faces, as the light unveils,
    Gaze at the tower, and vanish while they
       gaze.

The mariner remembers when a child,
    On his first voyage, he saw it fade and
       sink ;
And when, returning from adventures wild,
    He saw it rise again o'er ocean's brink.

Steadfast, serene, immovable, the same
    Year after year, through all the silent
       night
Burns on forevermore that quenchless flame,
    Shines on that inextinguishable light !

It sees the ocean to its bosom clasp
    The rocks and sea-sand with the kiss of
       peace ;
It sees the wild winds lift it in their grasp,
    And hold it up, and shake it like a fleece.

The startled waves leap over it ; the storm
    Smites it with all the scourges of the rain,
And steadily against its solid form
    Press the great shoulders of the hurri-
       cane.

The sea-bird wheeling round it, with the
       din
    Of wings and winds and solitary cries,
Blinded and maddened by the light within,
    Dashes himself against the glare, and
       dies.

A new Prometheus, chained upon the rock,
    Still grasping in his hand the fire of Jove,
It does not hear the cry, nor heed the
       shock,
    But hails the mariner with words of love.

"Sail on !" it says, "sail on, ye stately
       ships !
    And with your floating bridge the ocean
       span ;
Be mine to guard this light from all eclipse.
    Be yours to bring man nearer unto
       man ! "

THE FIRE OF DRIFT-WOOD

DEVEREUX FARM, NEAR MARBLEHEAD

"September 29, 1846   A delicious drive with F. through Malden and Lynn to Marblehead, to visit E. W. at the Devereux Farm by the sea-side.   Drove across the beautiful sand.   What a delicious scene ! The ocean in the sunshine changing from the silvery hue of the thin waves upon the beach, through the lighter and the deeper green, to a rich purple in the horizon.   We recalled the times past, and the days when we were at Nahant.   The Devereux Farm is by the sea, some miles from Lynn.   An old-fashioned farm-house, with low rooms, and narrow windows rattling in the sea-breeze." From this visit sprang the poem that follows.   In a letter in 1879 to a correspondent who had raised a matter-of-fact objection, Mr. Longfellow readily admitted that the harbor and lighthouse, which he visited the same day, could not be seen from the windows of the farm-house.

WE sat within the farm-house old,
    Whose windows, looking o'er the bay,
Gave to the sea-breeze damp and cold
    An easy entrance, night and day.

Not far away we saw the port,
  The strange, old-fashioned, silent town,
The lighthouse, the dismantled fort,
  The wooden houses, quaint and brown.

We sat and talked until the night,
  Descending, filled the little room ;
Our faces faded from the sight,
  Our voices only broke the gloom.

We spake of many a vanished scene,
  Of what we once had thought and said,
Of what had been, and might have been,
  And who was changed, and who was
      dead ;

And all that fills the hearts of friends,
  When first they feel, with secret pain,
Their lives thenceforth have separate ends,
  And never can be one again ;

The first slight swerving of the heart,
  That words are powerless to express,
And leave it still unsaid in part,
  Or say it in too great excess.

The very tones in which we spake
  Had something strange, I could but
     mark ;
The leaves of memory seemed to make
  A mournful rustling in the dark.

Oft died the words upon our lips,
  As suddenly, from out the fire
Built of the wreck of stranded ships,
  The flames would leap and then expire.

And, as their splendor flashed and failed,
  We thought of wrecks upon the main,
Of ships dismasted, that were hailed
  And sent no answer back again.

The windows, rattling in their frames,
  The ocean, roaring up the beach,
The gusty blast, the bickering flames,
  All mingled vaguely in our speech ;

Until they made themselves a part
  Of fancies floating through the brain,
The long-lost ventures of the heart,
  That send no answers back again.

O flames that glowed ! O hearts that
    yearned !
  They were indeed too much akin,

The drift-wood fire without that burned,
  The thoughts that burned and glowed
    within.

BY THE FIRESIDE

RESIGNATION

Written in the autumn of 1848, after the death of his little daughter Fanny. There is a passage in the poet's diary, under date of November 12, in which he says : " I feel very sad to-day. I miss very much my dear little Fanny. An inappeasable longing to see her comes over me at times, which I can hardly control."

THERE is no flock, however watched and
    tended,
  But one dead lamb is there !
There is no fireside, howsoe'er defended,
  But has one vacant chair !

The air is full of farewells to the dying,
  And mournings for the dead ;
The heart of Rachel, for her children crying,
  Will not be comforted !

Let us be patient ! These severe afflictions
  Not from the ground arise,
But oftentimes celestial benedictions
  Assume this dark disguise.

We see but dimly through the mists and
    vapors ;
  Amid these earthly damps
What seem to us but sad, funereal tapers
  May be heaven's distant lamps.

There is no Death ! What seems so is
    transition ;
  This life of mortal breath
Is but a suburb of the life elysian,
  Whose portal we call Death.

She is not dead, — the child of our affec-
    tion, —
  But gone unto that school
Where she no longer needs our poor pro-
    tection,
  And Christ himself doth rule.

In that great cloister's stillness and seclu-
    sion,
  By guardian angels led,
Safe from temptation, safe from sin's pollu-
    tion,
  She lives, whom we call dead.

Day after day we think what she is doing
  In those bright realms of air ;
Year after year, her tender steps pursuing,
  Behold her grown more fair.

Thus do we walk with her, and keep unbroken
  The bond which nature gives,
Thinking that our remembrance, though unspoken,
  May reach her where she lives.

Not as a child shall we again behold her ;
  For when with raptures wild
In our embraces we again enfold her,
  She will not be a child ;

But a fair maiden, in her Father's mansion,
  Clothed with celestial grace ;
And beautiful with all the soul's expansion
  Shall we behold her face.

And though at times impetuous with emotion
  And anguish long suppressed,
The swelling heart heaves moaning like the ocean,
  That cannot be at rest, —

We will be patient, and assuage the feeling
  We may not wholly stay ;
By silence sanctifying, not concealing,
  The grief that must have way.

THE BUILDERS

ALL are architects of Fate,
  Working in these walls of Time ;
Some with massive deeds and great,
  Some with ornaments of rhyme.

Nothing useless is, or low ;
  Each thing in its place is best ;
And what seems but idle show
  Strengthens and supports the rest.

For the structure that we raise,
  Time is with materials filled ;
Our to-days and yesterdays
  Are the blocks with which we build.

Truly shape and fashion these ;
  Leave no yawning gaps between ;
Think not, because no man sees,
  Such things will remain unseen.

In the elder days of Art,
  Builders wrought with greatest care
Each minute and unseen part ;
  For the Gods see everywhere.

Let us do our work as well,
  Both the unseen and the seen ;
Make the house, where Gods may dwell,
  Beautiful, entire, and clean.

Else our lives are incomplete,
  Standing in these walls of Time,
Broken stairways, where the feet
  Stumble as they seek to climb.

Build to-day, then, strong and sure,
  With a firm and ample base ;
And ascending and secure
  Shall to-morrow find its place.

Thus alone can we attain
  To those turrets, where the eye
Sees the world as one vast plain,
  And one boundless reach of sky.

SAND OF THE DESERT IN AN HOUR-GLASS

A HANDFUL of red sand, from the hot clime
  Of Arab deserts brought,
Within this glass becomes the spy of Time,
  The minister of Thought.

How many weary centuries has it been
  About those deserts blown !
How many strange vicissitudes has seen,
  How many histories known !

Perhaps the camels of the Ishmaelite
  Trampled and passed it o'er,
When into Egypt from the patriarch's sight
  His favorite son they bore.

Perhaps the feet of Moses, burnt and bare,
  Crushed it beneath their tread,
Or Pharaoh's flashing wheels into the air
  Scattered it as they sped ;

Or Mary, with the Christ of Nazareth
  Held close in her caress,
Whose pilgrimage of hope and love and faith
  Illumed the wilderness ;

Or anchorites beneath Engaddi's palms
  Pacing the Dead Sea beach,
And singing slow their old Armenian psalms
  In half-articulate speech ;

Or caravans, that from Bassora's gate
  With westward steps depart ;
Or Mecca's pilgrims, confident of Fate,
  And resolute in heart !

These have passed over it, or may have
      passed !
  Now in this crystal tower
Imprisoned by some curious hand at last,
  It counts the passing hour.

And as I gaze, these narrow walls ex-
      pand ; —
  Before my dreamy eye
Stretches the desert with its shifting sand,
  Its unimpeded sky.

And borne aloft by the sustaining blast,
  This little golden thread
Dilates into a column high and vast,
  A form of fear and dread.

And onward, and across the setting sun,
  Across the boundless plain,
The column and its broader shadow run,
  Till thought pursues in vain.

The vision vanishes ! These walls again
  Shut out the lurid sun,
Shut out the hot, immeasurable plain ;
  The half-hour's sand is run !

THE OPEN WINDOW

The old house by the lindens is what was known as the
Lechmere house which formerly stood on Brattle Street,
corner of Sparks Street, in Cambridge. It was in this
house that Baron Riedesel was quartered as prisoner of
war after the surrender of Burgoyne, and the window-
pane used to be shown on which the Baroness wrote
her name with a diamond.

THE old house by the lindens
  Stood silent in the shade,
And on the gravelled pathway
  The light and shadow played.

I saw the nursery windows
  Wide open to the air ;
But the faces of the children,
  They were no longer there.

The large Newfoundland house-dog
  Was standing by the door ;
He looked for his little playmates,
  Who would return no more.

They walked not under the lindens,
  They played not in the hall ;
But shadow, and silence, and sadness
  Were hanging over all.

The birds sang in the branches,
  With sweet, familiar tone ;
But the voices of the children
  Will be heard in dreams alone !

And the boy that walked beside me,
  He could not understand
Why closer in mine, ah ! closer,
  I pressed his warm, soft hand !

KING WITLAF'S DRINKING—HORN

"September 30, 1848. Worked upon *Kavanagh* all
the morning ; and wound up with *King Witlaf's
Drinking-Horn*, which I painted with a sweep of the
pencil just before dinner."

WITLAF, a king of the Saxons,
  Ere yet his last he breathed,
To the merry monks of Croyland
  His drinking-horn bequeathed, —

That, whenever they sat at their revels,
  And drank from the golden bowl,
They might remember the donor,
  And breathe a prayer for his soul.

So sat they once at Christmas,
  And bade the goblet pass ;
In their beards the red wine glistened
  Like dew-drops in the grass.

They drank to the soul of Witlaf,
  They drank to Christ the Lord,
And to each of the Twelve Apostles,
  Who had preached his holy word.

They drank to the Saints and Martyrs
  Of the dismal days of yore,
And as soon as the horn was empty
  They remembered one Saint more.

And the reader droned from the pulpit,
  Like the murmur of many bees,

The legend of good Saint Guthlac,
  And Saint Basil's homilies ;

Till the great bells of the convent,
  From their prison in the tower,
Guthlac and Bartholomæus,
  Proclaimed the midnight hour.

And the Yule-log cracked in the chimney,
  And the Abbot bowed his head,
And the flamelets flapped and flickered,
  But the Abbot was stark and dead.

Yet still in his pallid fingers
  He clutched the golden bowl,
In which, like a pearl dissolving,
  Had sunk and dissolved his soul.

But not for this their revels
  The jovial monks forbore,
For they cried, " Fill high the goblet !
  We must drink to one Saint more ! "

GASPAR BECERRA

This poem appears to have been suggested by a passage in Sterling's *Spanish Painters*, which Mr. Longfellow was reading at the time with great pleasure. He had some thought of writing a drama based on Sterling's account of Murillo's life in Seville.

By his evening fire the artist
  Pondered o'er his secret shame ;
Baffled, weary, and disheartened,
  Still he mused, and dreamed of fame.

'T was an image of the Virgin
  That had tasked his utmost skill ;
But, alas ! his fair ideal
  Vanished and escaped him still.

From a distant Eastern island
  Had the precious wood been brought ;
Day and night the anxious master
  At his toil untiring wrought ;

Till, discouraged and desponding,
  Sat he now in shadows deep,
And the day's humiliation
  Found oblivion in sleep.

Then a voice cried, " Rise, O master !
  From the burning brand of oak
Shape the thought that stirs within thee ! " —
  And the startled artist woke, —

Woke, and from the smoking embers
  Seized and quenched the glowing wood ;
And therefrom he carved an image,
  And he saw that it was good.

O thou sculptor, painter, poet !
  Take this lesson to thy heart :
That is best which lieth nearest ;
  Shape from that thy work of art.

PEGASUS IN POUND

Written as proem to *The Estray*, a collection of poems edited by Mr. Longfellow.

ONCE into a quiet village,
  Without haste and without heed,
In the golden prime of morning,
  Strayed the poet's wingèd steed.

It was Autumn, and incessant
  Piped the quails from shocks and sheaves,
And, like living coals, the apples
  Burned among the withering leaves.

Loud the clamorous bell was ringing
  From its belfry gaunt and grim ;
'T was the daily call to labor,
  Not a triumph meant for him.

Not the less he saw the landscape,
  In its gleaming vapor veiled ;
Not the less he breathed the odors
  That the dying leaves exhaled.

Thus, upon the village common,
  By the school-boys he was found ;
And the wise men, in their wisdom,
  Put him straightway into pound.

Then the sombre village crier,
  Ringing loud his brazen bell,
Wandered down the street proclaiming
  There was an estray to sell.

And the curious country people,
  Rich and poor, and young and old,
Came in haste to see this wondrous
  Wingèd steed, with mane of gold.

Thus the day passed, and the evening
  Fell, with vapors cold and dim ;
But it brought no food nor shelter,
  Brought no straw nor stall, for him.

Patiently, and still expectant,
  Looked he through the wooden bars,
Saw the moon rise o'er the landscape,
  Saw the tranquil, patient stars ;

Till at length the bell at midnight
  Sounded from its dark abode,
And, from out a neighboring farm-yard,
  Loud the cock Alectryon crowed.

Then, with nostrils wide distended,
  Breaking from his iron chain,
And unfolding far his pinions,
  To those stars he soared again.

On the morrow, when the village
  Woke to all its toil and care,
Lo ! the strange steed had departed.
  And they knew not when nor where.

But they found, upon the greensward
  Where his struggling hoofs had trod,
Pure and bright, a fountain flowing
  From the hoof-marks in the sod.

From that hour, the fount unfailing
  Gladdens the whole region round,
Strengthening all who drink its waters,
  While it soothes them with its sound.

TEGNÉR'S DRAPA

"October 14, 1847. Went to town, after finishing a poem on Tegnér's death, in the spirit of the old Norse poetry." In the first edition, the poem bore the title *Tegnér's Death.* The word *drapa* signifies death-song, or dirge.

I HEARD a voice, that cried,
" Balder the Beautiful
Is dead, is dead ! "
And through the misty air
Passed like the mournful cry
Of sunward sailing cranes.

I saw the pallid corpse
Of the dead sun
Borne through the Northern sky.
Blasts from Niffelheim
Lifted the sheeted mists
Around him as he passed.

And the voice forever cried,
" Balder the Beautiful
Is dead, is dead ! "

And died away
Through the dreary night,
In accents of despair.

Balder the Beautiful,
God of the summer sun,
Fairest of all the Gods !
Light from his forehead beamed,
Runes were upon his tongue,
As on the warrior's sword.

All things in earth and air
Bound were by magic spell
Never to do him harm ;
Even the plants and stones ;
All save the mistletoe,
The sacred mistletoe !

Hœder, the blind old God,
Whose feet are shod with silence,
Pierced through that gentle breast
With his sharp spear, by fraud,
Made of the mistletoe,
The accursed mistletoe !

They laid him in his ship,
With horse and harness,
As on a funeral pyre.
Odin placed
A ring upon his finger,
And whispered in his ear.

They launched the burning ship !
It floated far away
Over the misty sea,
Till like the sun it seemed,
Sinking beneath the waves.
Balder returned no more !

So perish the old Gods !
But out of the sea of Time
Rises a new land of song,
Fairer than the old.
Over its meadows green
Walk the young bards and sing.

Build it again,
O ye bards,
Fairer than before !
Ye fathers of the new race,
Feed upon morning dew,
Sing the new Song of Love !

The law of force is dead !
The law of love prevails !

Thor, the thunderer,
Shall rule the earth no more,
No more, with threats,
Challenge the meek Christ.

Sing no more,
O ye bards of the North,
Of Vikings and of Jarls !
Of the days of Eld
Preserve the freedom only,
Not the deeds of blood !

SONNET

ON MRS. KEMBLE'S READINGS FROM SHAKESPEARE

In the winter of 1849 Mrs. Fanny Kemble Butler was reading Shakespeare in Boston, and Mr. Longfellow was a constant attendant. He notes in his diary under date of February 20 : " We did not go last night to hear *Othello*. I wrote this morning a sonnet on Mrs. Butler's readings." A week later the poet entertained Mrs. Butler after a reading in Cambridge, and read his sonnet at the close of the supper.

O PRECIOUS evenings ! all too swiftly sped !
Leaving us heirs to amplest heritages
Of all the best thoughts of the greatest
    sages,
And giving tongues unto the silent dead !
How our hearts glowed and trembled as she
    read,
Interpreting by tones the wondrous pages
Of the great poet who foreruns the ages,
Anticipating all that shall be said !
O happy Reader ! having for thy text
The magic book, whose Sibylline leaves
    have caught
The rarest essence of all human thought !
O happy Poet ! by no critic vext !
How must thy listening spirit now rejoice
To be interpreted by such a voice !

THE SINGERS

"November 6, 1849. Wrote *The Singers* to show the excellence of different kinds of song." No individual poets were intended.

GOD sent his Singers upon earth
With songs of sadness and of mirth,
That they might touch the hearts of men,
And bring them back to heaven again.

The first, a youth with soul of fire,
Held in his hand a golden lyre ;

Through groves he wandered, and by
    streams,
Playing the music of our dreams.

The second, with a bearded face,
Stood singing in the market-place,
And stirred with accents deep and loud
The hearts of all the listening crowd.

A gray old man, the third and last,
Sang in cathedrals dim and vast,
While the majestic organ rolled
Contrition from its mouths of gold.

And those who heard the Singers three
Disputed which the best might be ;
For still their music seemed to start
Discordant echoes in each heart.

But the great Master said, " I see
No best in kind, but in degree ;
I gave a various gift to each,
To charm, to strengthen, and to teach.

" These are the three great chords of might,
And he whose ear is tuned aright
Will hear no discord in the three,
But the most perfect harmony."

SUSPIRIA

TAKE them, O Death ! and bear away
    Whatever thou canst call thine own !
Thine image, stamped upon this clay,
    Doth give thee that, but that alone !

Take them, O Grave ! and let them lie
    Folded upon thy narrow shelves,
As garments by the soul laid by,
    And precious only to ourselves !

Take them, O great Eternity !
    Our little life is but a gust
That bends the branches of thy tree,
    And trails its blossoms in the dust !

HYMN

FOR MY BROTHER'S ORDINATION

The brother was the Rev. Samuel Longfellow, the poet's biographer. In his diary, February 8, 1848, Mr. Longfellow wrote : " S. returned from Portland. Read to him the chant I wrote for his ordination, — a midnight thought. He likes it, and will have it sung."

CHRIST to the young man said : " Yet one thing more ;
If thou wouldst perfect be,
Sell all thou hast and give it to the poor,
And come and follow me ! "

Within this temple Christ again, unseen,
Those sacred words hath said
And his invisible hands to-day have been
Laid on a young man's head.

And evermore beside him on his way
The unseen Christ shall move,

That he may lean upon his arm and say,
" Dost thou, dear Lord, approve ? "

Beside him at the marriage feast shall be,
To make the scene more fair ;
Beside him in the dark Gethsemane
Of pain and midnight prayer.

O holy trust ! O endless sense of rest !
Like the beloved John
To lay his head upon the Saviour's breast
And thus to journey on !

THE SONG OF HIAWATHA

The general purpose to make use of Indian material appears to have been in the poet's mind for some time, but the conception as finally wrought in *Hiawatha* was formed in the summer of 1854. He writes in his diary under date of June 22," I have at length hit upon a plan for a poem on the American Indians, which seems to me the right one and the only. It is to weave together their beautiful traditions into a whole. I have hit upon a measure, too, which I think the right and only one for such a theme." A few days before, he had been reading with great delight the Finnish epic *Kalevala*, and this poem suggested the measure and may well have reminded him also of the Indian legends, which have that likeness to the Finnish that springs from a common intellectual stage of development and a general community of habits and occupation.

An interest in the Indians had long been felt by Mr. Longfellow, and in his early plans for prose sketches tales about the Indians had a place. He had seen a few of the straggling remainder of the Algonquins in Maine, and had read Heckewelder while in college ; he had witnessed the spectacle of Black Hawk and his Sacs and Foxes on Boston Common ; and a few years before, he had made the acquaintance of the fine-tempered Kah-ge-ga-gah-bowh, the Ojibway chief, and had entertained him at his house, trusting not unlikely that he might derive from the Indian some helpful suggestion. His authority for the legends and the material generally of his poem was in the main Schoolcraft's great, ill-digested work, with probably the same author's more literary composition *Algic Researches*, and Heckewelder's narrative. He soon took Manabozho's other and more euphonic name, Hiawatha, into his service, and gave himself up to a thorough enjoyment of the task.

Mr. Longfellow began writing *Hiawatha* June 25, 1854. It was finished March 29, 1855, and published November 10. It is doubtful if the poet wrote any of his longer works with more abandonment, with more thorough enjoyment of his task, with a keener sense of the originality of his venture, and by consequence, with more perplexity when he thought of his readers. He tried the poem on his friends more freely than had been customary with him, and with varied results. His own mind, as he neared the test of publication, wavered a little in its moods. " Proof sheets of *Hiawatha*," he wrote in June, 1855. " I am growing idiotic about this song, and no longer know whether it is good or bad ; " and later still : " In great doubt about a canto of *Hiawatha*, — whether to retain or suppress it. It is odd how confused one's mind becomes about such matters from long looking at the same subject."

No sooner was the poem published than its popularity was assured, and it was subjected to the most searching tests. It was read by public readers to large audiences, and a few years later was set to music by Stoepel and given at the Boston Theatre with explanatory readings by Matilda Heron. It was parodied, — one of the surest signs of popularity, — and it lived its parodies down, a surer sign still of intrinsic uncopyableness. It was criticised with heated words, and made the occasion for controversy. The elemental nature of the poetry led to vehement charges of plagiarism, and altogether the poet found himself in the midst of a violent war of words which recalled his experience with *Hyperion*. He felt keenly the unreasonableness of the attack upon his honesty in the charge that he had borrowed metre and incidents both from the *Kalevala*. He made no secret of the suggestion of the metre, — he had used an acknowledged form, which was not exclusively Finnish ; and as for the legends, he openly confessed his indebtedness to Schoolcraft in the notes to the poem.

Meanwhile the book had an unexampled sale, and the letters which the poet received from Emerson, Hawthorne, Parsons, Taylor, and others showed the judgment passed upon his work by those whose poetic perception was not blunted by habits of professional criticism nor taken captive by mere novelty. Several years after, a translation into Latin of a portion of the poem was made for use as a school-book, by Professor Francis W. Newman. A suggestive criticism, by Dr. Holmes, upon the measure of the poem will be found in the *Proceedings* of the Massachusetts Historical Society for April 13, 1882.

INTRODUCTION

SHOULD you ask me, whence these stories ?
Whence these legends and traditions,
With the odors of the forest,
With the dew and damp of meadows,

With the curling smoke of wigwams,
With the rushing of great rivers,
With their frequent repetitions,
And their wild reverberations,
As of thunder in the mountains ?
I should answer, I should tell you,

" From the forests and the prairies,
From the great lakes of the Northland,
From the land of the Ojibways,
From the land of the Dacotahs,
From the mountains, moors, and fen-
lands
Where the heron, the Shuh-shuh-gah,
Feeds among the reeds and rushes.
I repeat them as I heard them
From the lips of Nawadaha,
The musician, the sweet singer."
Should you ask where Nawadaha
Found these songs so wild and wayward,
Found these legends and traditions,
I should answer, I should tell you,
" In the bird's-nests of the forest,
In the lodges of the beaver,
In the hoof-prints of the bison,
In the eyry of the eagle !
" All the wild-fowl sang them to him,
In the moorlands and the fen-lands,
In the melancholy marshes ;
Chetowaik, the plover, sang them,
Mahng, the loon, the wild-goose, Wawa,
The blue heron, the Shuh-shuh-gah,
And the grouse, the Mushkodasa ! "
If still further you should ask me,
Saying, " Who was Nawadaha ?
Tell us of this Nawadaha,"
I should answer your inquiries
Straightway in such words as follow.
" In the vale of Tawasentha,
In the green and silent valley,
By the pleasant water-courses,
Dwelt the singer Nawadaha.
Round about the Indian village
Spread the meadows and the corn-fields,
And beyond them stood the forest,
Stood the groves of singing pine-trees,
Green in Summer, white in Winter,
Ever sighing, ever singing.
" And the pleasant water-courses,
You could trace them through the val-
ley,
By the rushing in the Spring-time,
By the alders in the Summer,
By the white fog in the Autumn,
By the black line in the Winter ;
And beside them dwelt the singer,
In the vale of Tawasentha,
In the green and silent valley.
" There he sang of Hiawatha,
Sang the Song of Hiawatha,
Sang his wondrous birth and being,

How he prayed and how he fasted,
How he lived, and toiled, and suffered,
That the tribes of men might prosper,
That he might advance his people ! "
Ye who love the haunts of Nature,
Love the sunshine of the meadow,
Love the shadow of the forest,
Love the wind among the branches,
And the rain-shower and the snow-storm,
And the rushing of great rivers
Through their palisades of pine-trees,
And the thunder in the mountains,
Whose innumerable echoes
Flap like eagles in their eyries ; —
Listen to these wild traditions,
To this Song of Hiawatha !
Ye who love a nation's legends,
Love the ballads of a people,
That like voices from afar off
Call to us to pause and listen,
Speak in tones so plain and childlike,
Scarcely can the ear distinguish
Whether they are sung or spoken ; —
Listen to this Indian Legend,
To this Song of Hiawatha !
Ye whose hearts are fresh and simple,
Who have faith in God and Nature,
Who believe that in all ages
Every human heart is human,
That in even savage bosoms
There are longings, yearnings, strivings
For the good they comprehend not,
That the feeble hands and helpless,
Groping blindly in the darkness,
Touch God's right hand in that dark-
ness
And are lifted up and strengthened ; —
Listen to this simple story,
To this Song of Hiawatha !
Ye, who sometimes, in your rambles
Through the green lanes of the country,
Where the tangled barberry-bushes
Hang their tufts of crimson berries
Over stone walls gray with mosses,
Pause by some neglected graveyard,
For a while to muse, and ponder
On a half-effaced inscription,
Written with little skill of song-craft,
Homely phrases, but each letter
Full of hope and yet of heart-break,
Full of all the tender pathos
Of the Here and the Hereafter ; —
Stay and read this rude inscription,
Read this Song of Hiawatha !

I

THE PEACE-PIPE

On the Mountains of the Prairie,
On the great Red Pipe-stone Quarry,
Gitche Manito, the mighty,
He the Master of Life, descending,
On the red crags of the quarry
Stood erect, and called the nations,
Called the tribes of men together.

From his footprints flowed a river,
Leaped into the light of morning,
O'er the precipice plunging downward
Gleamed like Ishkoodah, the comet.
And the Spirit, stooping earthward,
With his finger on the meadow
Traced a winding pathway for it,
Saying to it, " Run in this way ! "
From the red stone of the quarry
With his hand he broke a fragment,
Moulded it into a pipe-head,
Shaped and fashioned it with figures ;
From the margin of the river
Took a long reed for a pipe-stem,
With its dark green leaves upon it ;
Filled the pipe with bark of willow,
With the bark of the red willow ;
Breathed upon the neighboring forest,
Made its great boughs chafe together,
Till in flame they burst and kindled ;
And erect upon the mountains,
Gitche Manito, the mighty,
Smoked the calumet, the Peace-Pipe,
As a signal to the nations.

And the smoke rose slowly, slowly,
Through the tranquil air of morning,
First a single line of darkness,
Then a denser, bluer vapor,
Then a snow-white cloud unfolding,
Like the tree-tops of the forest,
Ever rising, rising, rising,
Till it touched the top of heaven,
Till it broke against the heaven,
And rolled outward all around it.

From the Vale of Tawasentha,
From the Valley of Wyoming,
From the groves of Tuscaloosa,
From the far-off Rocky Mountains,
From the Northern lakes and rivers
All the tribes beheld the signal,
Saw the distant smoke ascending,
The Pukwana of the Peace-Pipe.

And the Prophets of the nations

Said : " Behold it, the Pukwana !
By this signal from afar off,
Bending like a wand of willow,
Waving like a hand that beckons,
Gitche Manito, the mighty,
Calls the tribes of men together,
Calls the warriors to his council ! "

Down the rivers, o'er the prairies,
Came the warriors of the nations,
Came the Delawares and Mohawks,
Came the Choctaws and Camanches,
Came the Shoshonies and Blackfeet,
Came the Pawnees and Omahas,
Came the Mandans and Dacotahs,
Came the Hurons and Ojibways,
All the warriors drawn together
By the signal of the Peace-Pipe,
To the Mountains of the Prairie,
To the great Red Pipe-stone Quarry.

And they stood there on the meadow,
With their weapons and their war-gear,
Painted like the leaves of Autumn,
Painted like the sky of morning,
Wildly glaring at each other ;
In their faces stern defiance,
In their hearts the feuds of ages,
The hereditary hatred,
The ancestral thirst of vengeance.

Gitche Manito, the mighty,
The creator of the nations,
Looked upon them with compassion,
With paternal love and pity ;
Looked upon their wrath and wrangling
But as quarrels among children,
But as feuds and fights of children !

Over them he stretched his right hand,
To subdue their stubborn natures,
To allay their thirst and fever,
By the shadow of his right hand ;
Spake to them with voice majestic
As the sound of far-off waters,
Falling into deep abysses,
Warning, chiding, spake in this wise : —
" O my children ! my poor children !
Listen to the words of wisdom,
Listen to the words of warning,
From the lips of the Great Spirit,
From the Master of Life, who made you !

" I have given you lands to hunt in,
I have given you streams to fish in,
I have given you bear and bison,
I have given you roe and reindeer,
I have given you brant and beaver,
Filled the marshes full of wild-fowl,
Filled the rivers full of fishes :

Why then are you not contented ?
Why then will you hunt each other ?
"I am weary of your quarrels,
Weary of your wars and bloodshed,
Weary of your prayers for vengeance,
Of your wranglings and dissensions ;
All your strength is in your union,
All your danger is in discord ;
Therefore be at peace henceforward,
And as brothers live together.
"I will send a Prophet to you,
A Deliverer of the nations,
Who shall guide you and shall teach you,
Who shall toil and suffer with you.
If you listen to his counsels,
You will multiply and prosper ;
If his warnings pass unheeded,
You will fade away and perish !
"Bathe now in the stream before you,
Wash the war-paint from your faces,
Wash the blood-stains from your fingers,
Bury your war-clubs and your weapons,
Break the red stone from this quarry,
Mould and make it into Peace-Pipes,
Take the reeds that grow beside you,
Deck them with your brightest feathers,
Smoke the calumet together,
And as brothers live henceforward ! "
Then upon the ground the warriors
Threw their cloaks and shirts of deer-skin,
Threw their weapons and their war-gear,
Leaped into the rushing river,
Washed the war-paint from their faces.
Clear above them flowed the water,
Clear and limpid from the footprints
Of the Master of Life descending ;
Dark below them flowed the water,
Soiled and stained with streaks of crimson,
As if blood were mingled with it !
From the river came the warriors,
Clean and washed from all their war-paint ;
On the banks their clubs they buried,
Buried all their warlike weapons.
Gitche Manito, the mighty,
The Great Spirit, the creator,
Smiled upon his helpless children !
And in silence all the warriors
Broke the red stone of the quarry,
Smoothed and formed it into Peace-Pipes,
Broke the long reeds by the river,
Decked them with their brightest feathers,
And departed each one homeward,
While the Master of Life, ascending,
Through the opening of cloud-curtains,
Through the doorways of the heaven,

Vanished from before their faces,
In the smoke that rolled around him,
The Pukwana of the Peace-Pipe !

II

THE FOUR WINDS

"HONOR be to Mudjekeewis ! "
Cried the warriors, cried the old men,
When he came in triumph homeward
With the sacred Belt of Wampum,
From the regions of the North-Wind,
From the kingdom of Wabasso,
From the land of the White Rabbit.
He had stolen the Belt of Wampum
From the neck of Mishe-Mokwa,
From the Great Bear of the mountains,
From the terror of the nations,
As he lay asleep and cumbrous
On the summit of the mountains,
Like a rock with mosses on it,
Spotted brown and gray with mosses.
Silently he stole upon him
Till the red nails of the monster
Almost touched him, almost scared him,
Till the hot breath of his nostrils
Warmed the hands of Mudjekeewis,
As he drew the Belt of Wampum
Over the round ears, that heard not,
Over the small eyes, that saw not,
Over the long nose and nostrils,
The black muffle of the nostrils,
Out of which the heavy breathing
Warmed the hands of Mudjekeewis.
Then he swung aloft his war-club,
Shouted loud and long his war-cry,
Smote the mighty Mishe-Mokwa
In the middle of the forehead,
Right between the eyes he smote him.
With the heavy blow bewildered,
Rose the Great Bear of the mountains ;
But his knees beneath him trembled,
And he whimpered like a woman,
As he reeled and staggered forward,
As he sat upon his haunches ;
And the mighty Mudjekeewis,
Standing fearlessly before him,
Taunted him in loud derision,
Spake disdainfully in this wise : —
"Hark you, Bear ! you are a coward ;
And no Brave, as you pretended ;
Else you would not cry and whimper
Like a miserable woman !

Bear ! you know our tribes are hostile,
Long have been at war together ;
Now you find that we are strongest,
You go sneaking in the forest,
You go hiding in the mountains !
Had you conquered me in battle
Not a groan would I have uttered ;
But you, Bear ! sit here and whimper,
And disgrace your tribe by crying,
Like a wretched Shaugodaya,
Like a cowardly old woman ! "
Then again he raised his war-club,
Smote again the Mishe-Mokwa
In the middle of his forehead,
Broke his skull, as ice is broken
When one goes to fish in Winter.
Thus was slain the Mishe-Mokwa,
He the Great Bear of the mountains,
He the terror of the nations.
" Honor be to Mudjekeewis ! "
With a shout exclaimed the people,
" Honor be to Mudjekeewis !
Henceforth he shall be the West-Wind,
And hereafter and forever
Shall he hold supreme dominion
Over all the winds of heaven.
Call him no more Mudjekeewis,
Call him Kabeyun, the West-Wind ! "
Thus was Mudjekeewis chosen
Father of the Winds of Heaven.
For himself he kept the West-Wind,
Gave the others to his children ;
Unto Wabun gave the East-Wind,
Gave the South to Shawondasee,
And the North-Wind, wild and cruel,
To the fierce Kabibonokka.
Young and beautiful was Wabun ;
He it was who brought the morning,
He it was whose silver arrows
Chased the dark o'er hill and valley ;
He it was whose cheeks were painted
With the brightest streaks of crimson,
And whose voice awoke the village,
Called the deer, and called the hunter.
Lonely in the sky was Wabun ;
Though the birds sang gayly to him,
Though the wild-flowers of the meadow
Filled the air with odors for him ;
Though the forests and the rivers
Sang and shouted at his coming,
Still his heart was sad within him,
For he was alone in heaven.
But one morning, gazing earthward,
While the village still was sleeping,
And the fog lay on the river,

Like a ghost, that goes at sunrise,
He beheld a maiden walking
All alone upon a meadow,
Gathering water-flags and rushes
By a river in the meadow.
Every morning, gazing earthward,
Still the first thing he beheld there
Was her blue eyes looking at him,
Two blue lakes among the rushes.
And he loved the lonely maiden,
Who thus waited for his coming ;
For they both were solitary,
She on earth and he in heaven.
And he wooed her with caresses,
Wooed her with his smile of sunshine,
With his flattering words he wooed her,
With his sighing and his singing,
Gentlest whispers in the branches,
Softest music, sweetest odors,
Till he drew her to his bosom,
Folded in his robes of crimson,
Till into a star he changed her,
Trembling still upon his bosom ;
And forever in the heavens
They are seen together walking,
Wabun and the Wabun-Annung,
Wabun and the Star of Morning.
But the fierce Kabibonokka
Had his dwelling among icebergs,
In the everlasting snow-drifts,
In the kingdom of Wabasso,
In the land of the White Rabbit.
He it was whose hand in Autumn
Painted all the trees with scarlet,
Stained the leaves with red and yellow ;
He it was who sent the snow-flakes,
Sifting, hissing through the forest,
Froze the ponds, the lakes, the rivers,
Drove the loon and sea-gull southward,
Drove the cormorant and curlew
To their nests of sedge and sea-tang
In the realms of Shawondasee.
Once the fierce Kabibonokka
Issued from his lodge of snow-drifts,
From his home among the icebergs,
And his hair, with snow besprinkled,
Streamed behind him like a river,
Like a black and wintry river,
As he howled and hurried southward,
Over frozen lakes and moorlands.
There among the reeds and rushes
Found he Shingebis, the diver,
Trailing strings of fish behind him,
O'er the frozen fens and moorlands,
Lingering still among the moorlands,

Though his tribe had long departed
To the land of Shawondasee.
    Cried the fierce Kabibonokka,
" Who is this that dares to brave me ?
Dares to stay in my dominions,
When the Wawa has departed,
When the wild-goose has gone southward,
And the heron, the Shuh-shuh-gah,
Long ago departed southward ?
I will go into his wigwam,
I will put his smouldering fire out ! "
    And at night Kabibonokka
To the lodge came wild and wailing,
Heaped the snow in drifts about it,
Shouted down into the smoke-flue,
Shook the lodge-poles in his fury,
Flapped the curtain of the door-way.
Shingebis, the diver, feared not,
Shingebis, the diver, cared not ;
Four great logs had he for firewood,
One for each moon of the winter,
And for food the fishes served him.
By his blazing fire he sat there,
Warm and merry, eating, laughing,
Singing, " O Kabibonokka,
You are but my fellow-mortal ! "
    Then Kabibonokka entered,
And though Shingebis, the diver,
Felt his presence by the coldness,
Felt his icy breath upon him,
Still he did not cease his singing,
Still he did not leave his laughing,
Only turned the log a little,
Only made the fire burn brighter,
Made the sparks fly up the smoke-flue.
    From Kabibonokka's forehead,
From his snow-besprinkled tresses,
Drops of sweat fell fast and heavy,
Making dints upon the ashes,
As along the eaves of lodges,
As from drooping boughs of hemlock,
Drips the melting snow in spring-time,
Making hollows in the snow-drifts.
    Till at last he rose defeated,
Could not bear the heat and laughter,
Could not bear the merry singing,
But rushed headlong through the door-way,
Stamped upon the crusted snow-drifts,
Stamped upon the lakes and rivers,
Made the snow upon them harder,
Made the ice upon them thicker,
Challenged Shingebis, the diver,
To come forth and wrestle with him,
To come forth and wrestle naked
On the frozen fens and moorlands.

    Forth went Shingebis, the diver,
Wrestled all night with the North-Wind,
Wrestled naked on the moorlands
With the fierce Kabibonokka,
Till his panting breath grew fainter,
Till his frozen grasp grew feebler,
Till he reeled and staggered backward,
And retreated, baffled, beaten,
To the kingdom of Wabasso,
To the land of the White Rabbit,
Hearing still the gusty laughter,
Hearing Shingebis, the diver,
Singing, " O Kabibonokka,
You are but my fellow-mortal ! "
    Shawondasee, fat and lazy,
Had his dwelling far to southward,
In the drowsy, dreamy sunshine,
In the never-ending Summer.
He it was who sent the wood-birds,
Sent the robin, the Opechee,
Sent the bluebird, the Owaissa,
Sent the Shawshaw, sent the swallow,
Sent the wild-goose, Wawa, northward,
Sent the melons and tobacco,
And the grapes in purple clusters.
    From his pipe the smoke ascending
Filled the sky with haze and vapor,
Filled the air with dreamy softness,
Gave a twinkle to the water,
Touched the rugged hills with smoothness,
Brought the tender Indian Summer
To the melancholy north-land,
In the dreary Moon of Snow-shoes.
    Listless, careless Shawondasee !
In his life he had one shadow,
In his heart one sorrow had he.
Once, as he was gazing northward,
Far away upon a prairie
He beheld a maiden standing,
Saw a tall and slender maiden
All alone upon a prairie ;
Brightest green were all her garments,
And her hair was like the sunshine.
    Day by day he gazed upon her,
Day by day he sighed with passion,
Day by day his heart within him
Grew more hot with love and longing
For the maid with yellow tresses.
But he was too fat and lazy
To bestir himself and woo her.
Yes, too indolent and easy
To pursue her and persuade her ;
So he only gazed upon her,
Only sat and sighed with passion
For the maiden of the prairie.

Till one morning, looking northward,
He beheld her yellow tresses
Changed and covered o'er with whiteness,
Covered as with whitest snow-flakes.
" Ah ! my brother from the North-land,
From the kingdom of Wabasso,
From the land of the White Rabbit !
You have stolen the maiden from me,
You have laid your hand upon her,
You have wooed and won my maiden,
With your stories of the North-land ! "

Thus the wretched Shawondasee
Breathed into the air his sorrow ;
And the South-Wind o'er the prairie
Wandered warm with sighs of passion,
With the sighs of Shawondasee,
Till the air seemed full of snow-flakes,
Full of thistle-down the prairie,
And the maid with hair like sunshine
Vanished from his sight forever ;
Never more did Shawondasee
See the maid with yellow tresses !

Poor, deluded Shawondasee !
'T was no woman that you gazed at,
'T was no maiden that you sighed for,
'T was the prairie dandelion
That through all the dreamy Summer
You had gazed at with such longing,
You had sighed for with such passion,
And had puffed away forever,
Blown into the air with sighing.
Ah ! deluded Shawondasee !

Thus the Four Winds were divided ;
Thus the sons of Mudjekeewis
Had their stations in the heavens,
At the corners of the heavens ;
For himself the West-Wind only
Kept the mighty Mudjekeewis.

III

HIAWATHA'S CHILDHOOD

DOWNWARD through the evening twilight,
In the days that are forgotten,
In the unremembered ages,
From the full moon fell Nokomis,
Fell the beautiful Nokomis,
She a wife, but not a mother.

She was sporting with her women,
Swinging in a swing of grape-vines,
When her rival the rejected,
Full of jealousy and hatred,
Cut the leafy swing asunder,

Cut in twain the twisted grape-vines,
And Nokomis fell affrighted
Downward through the evening twilight,
On the Muskoday, the meadow,
On the prairie full of blossoms.
" See ! a star falls ! " said the people ;
" From the sky a star is falling ! "

There among the ferns and mosses,
There among the prairie lilies,
On the Muskoday, the meadow,
In the moonlight and the starlight,
Fair Nokomis bore a daughter.
And she called her name Wenonah,
As the first-born of her daughters.
And the daughter of Nokomis
Grew up like the prairie lilies,
Grew a tall and slender maiden,
With the beauty of the moonlight,
With the beauty of the starlight.

And Nokomis warned her often,
Saying oft, and oft repeating,
" Oh, beware of Mudjekeewis,
Of the West-Wind, Mudjekeewis ;
Listen not to what he tells you ;
Lie not down upon the meadow,
Stoop not down among the lilies,
Lest the West-Wind come and harm
      you ! "
But she heeded not the warning,
Heeded not those words of wisdom,
And the West-Wind came at evening,
Walking lightly o'er the prairie,
Whispering to the leaves and blossoms,
Bending low the flowers and grasses,
Found the beautiful Wenonah,
Lying there among the lilies,
Wooed her with his words of sweetness,
Wooed her with his soft caresses,
Till she bore a son in sorrow,
Bore a son of love and sorrow.

Thus was born my Hiawatha,
Thus was born the child of wonder ;
But the daughter of Nokomis,
Hiawatha's gentle mother,
In her anguish died deserted
By the West-Wind, false and faithless,
By the heartless Mudjekeewis.

For her daughter long and loudly
Wailed and wept the sad Nokomis ;
" Oh that I were dead ! " she murmured,
" Oh that I were dead, as thou art !
No more work, and no more weeping,
Wahonowin ! Wahonowin ! "

By the shores of Gitche Gumee,
By the shining Big-Sea-Water,

Stood the wigwam of Nokomis,
Daughter of the Moon, Nokomis.
Dark behind it rose the forest,
Rose the black and gloomy pine-trees,
Rose the firs with cones upon them ;
Bright before it beat the water,
Beat the clear and sunny water,
Beat the shining Big-Sea-Water.
    There the wrinkled old Nokomis
Nursed the little Hiawatha,
Rocked him in his linden cradle,
Bedded soft in moss and rushes,
Safely bound with reindeer sinews ;
Stilled his fretful wail by saying,
" Hush ! the Naked Bear will hear thee ! "
Lulled him into slumber, singing,
" Ewa-yea ! my little owlet !
Who is this, that lights the wigwam ?
With his great eyes lights the wigwam ?
Ewa-yea ! my little owlet ! "
    Many things Nokomis taught him
Of the stars that shine in heaven ;
Showed him Ishkoodah, the comet,
Ishkoodah, with fiery tresses ;
Showed the Death-Dance of the spirits,
Warriors with their plumes and war-clubs,
Flaring far away to northward
In the frosty nights of Winter ;
Showed the broad white road in heaven,
Pathway of the ghosts, the shadows,
Running straight across the heavens,
Crowded with the ghosts, the shadows.
    At the door on summer evenings
Sat the little Hiawatha ;
Heard the whispering of the pine-trees,
Heard the lapping of the waters,
Sounds of music, words of wonder ;
" Minne-wawa ! " said the pine-trees,
" Mudway-aushka ! " said the water.
    Saw the fire-fly, Wah-wah-taysee,
Flitting through the dusk of evening,
With the twinkle of its candle
Lighting up the brakes and bushes,
And he sang the song of children,
Sang the song Nokomis taught him :
" Wah-wah-taysee, little fire-fly,
Little, flitting, white-fire insect,
Little, dancing, white-fire creature,
Light me with your little candle,
Ere upon my bed I lay me,
Ere in sleep I close my eyelids ! "
    Saw the moon rise from the water
Rippling, rounding from the water,
Saw the flecks and shadows on it,
Whispered, " What is that, Nokomis ? "

And the good Nokomis answered :
" Once a warrior, very angry,
Seized his grandmother, and threw her
Up into the sky at midnight ;
Right against the moon he threw her ;
'T is her body that you see there."
    Saw the rainbow in the heaven,
In the eastern sky, the rainbow,
Whispered, " What is that, Nokomis ? "
And the good Nokomis answered :
" 'T is the heaven of flowers you see there ;
All the wild-flowers of the forest,
All the lilies of the prairie,
When on earth they fade and perish,
Blossom in that heaven above us."
    When he heard the owls at midnight,
Hooting, laughing in the forest,
" What is that ? " he cried in terror,
" What is that," he said, " Nokomis ? "
And the good Nokomis answered :
" That is but the owl and owlet,
Talking in their native language,
Talking, scolding at each other."
    Then the little Hiawatha
Learned of every bird its language,
Learned their names and all their secrets,
How they built their nests in Summer,
Where they hid themselves in Winter,
Talked with them whene'er he met them,
Called them " Hiawatha's Chickens."
    Of all beasts he learned the language,
Learned their names and all their secrets,
How the beavers built their lodges,
Where the squirrels hid their acorns,
How the reindeer ran so swiftly,
Why the rabbit was so timid,
Talked with them whene'er he met them,
Called them " Hiawatha's Brothers."
    Then Iagoo, the great boaster,
He the marvellous story-teller,
He the traveller and the talker,
He the friend of old Nokomis,
Made a bow for Hiawatha ;
From a branch of ash he made it,
From an oak-bough made the arrows,
Tipped with flint, and winged with feathers,
And the cord he made of deer-skin.
    Then he said to Hiawatha :
" Go, my son, into the forest,
Where the red deer herd together,
Kill for us a famous roebuck,
Kill for us a deer with antlers ! "
    Forth into the forest straightway
All alone walked Hiawatha
Proudly, with his bow and arrows ;

And the birds sang round him, o'er him,
"Do not shoot us, Hiawatha!"
Sang the robin, the Opechee,
Sang the bluebird, the Owaissa,
"Do not shoot us, Hiawatha!"
  Up the oak-tree, close beside him,
Sprang the squirrel, Adjidaumo,
In and out among the branches,
Coughed and chattered from the oak-tree,
Laughed, and said between his laughing,
"Do not shoot me, Hiawatha!"
  And the rabbit from his pathway
Leaped aside, and at a distance
Sat erect upon his haunches,
Half in fear and half in frolic,
Saying to the little hunter,
"Do not shoot me, Hiawatha!"
  But he heeded not, nor heard them,
For his thoughts were with the red deer;
On their tracks his eyes were fastened,
Leading downward to the river,
To the ford across the river,
And as one in slumber walked he.
  Hidden in the alder-bushes,
There he waited till the deer came,
Till he saw two antlers lifted,
Saw two eyes look from the thicket,
Saw two nostrils point to windward,
And a deer came down the pathway,
Flecked with leafy light and shadow.
And his heart within him fluttered,
Trembled like the leaves above him,
Like the birch-leaf palpitated,
As the deer came down the pathway.
  Then, upon one knee uprising,
Hiawatha aimed an arrow;
Scarce a twig moved with his motion,
Scarce a leaf was stirred or rustled,
But the wary roebuck started,
Stamped with all his hoofs together,
Listened with one foot uplifted,
Leaped as if to meet the arrow;
Ah! the singing, fatal arrow,
Like a wasp it buzzed and stung him!
  Dead he lay there in the forest,
By the ford across the river;
Beat his timid heart no longer,
But the heart of Hiawatha
Throbbed and shouted and exulted,
As he bore the red deer homeward,
And Iagoo and Nokomis
Hailed his coming with applauses.
  From the red deer's hide Nokomis
Made a cloak for Hiawatha,
From the red deer's flesh Nokomis

Made a banquet to his honor.
All the village came and feasted,
All the guests praised Hiawatha,
Called him Strong-Heart, Soan-ge-taha!
Called him Loon-Heart, Mahn-go-taysee!

IV

HIAWATHA AND MUDJEKEEWIS

OUT of childhood into manhood
Now had grown my Hiawatha,
Skilled in all the craft of hunters,
Learned in all the lore of old men,
In all youthful sports and pastimes,
In all manly arts and labors.
  Swift of foot was Hiawatha;
He could shoot an arrow from him,
And run forward with such fleetness,
That the arrow fell behind him!
Strong of arm was Hiawatha;
He could shoot ten arrows upward,
Shoot them with such strength and swift-
    ness,
That the tenth had left the bow-string
Ere the first to earth had fallen!
He had mittens, Minjekahwun,
Magic mittens made of deer-skin;
When upon his hands he wore them,
He could smite the rocks asunder,
He could grind them into powder.
He had moccasins enchanted,
Magic moccasins of deer-skin;
When he bound them round his ankles,
When upon his feet he tied them,
At each stride a mile he measured!
  Much he questioned old Nokomis
Of his father Mudjekeewis;
Learned from her the fatal secret
Of the beauty of his mother,
Of the falsehood of his father;
And his heart was hot within him,
Like a living coal his heart was.
  Then he said to old Nokomis,
"I will go to Mudjekeewis,
See how fares it with my father,
At the doorways of the West-Wind,
At the portals of the Sunset!"
  From his lodge went Hiawatha,
Dressed for travel, armed for hunting;
Dressed in deer-skin shirt and leggings,
Richly wrought with quills and wampum;
On his head his eagle-feathers,
Round his waist his belt of wampum,

In his hand his bow of ash-wood,
Strung with sinews of the reindeer ;
In his quiver oaken arrows,
Tipped with jasper, winged with feathers ;
With his mittens, Minjekahwun,
With his moccasins enchanted.
  Warning said the old Nokomis,
" Go not forth, O Hiawatha !
To the kingdom of the West-Wind,
To the realms of Mudjekeewis,
Lest he harm you with his magic,
Lest he kill you with his cunning ! "
  But the fearless Hiawatha
Heeded not her woman's warning ;
Forth he strode into the forest,
At each stride a mile he measured ;
Lurid seemed the sky above him,
Lurid seemed the earth beneath him,
Hot and close the air around him,
Filled with smoke and fiery vapors,
As of burning woods and prairies,
For his heart was hot within him,
Like a living coal his heart was.
  So he journeyed westward, westward,
Left the fleetest deer behind him,
Left the antelope and bison ;
Crossed the rushing Esconaba,
Crossed the mighty Mississippi,
Passed the Mountains of the Prairie,
Passed the land of Crows and Foxes,
Passed the dwellings of the Blackfeet,
Came unto the Rocky Mountains,
To the kingdom of the West-Wind,
Where upon the gusty summits
Sat the ancient Mudjekeewis,
Ruler of the winds of heaven.
  Filled with awe was Hiawatha
At the aspect of his father.
On the air about him wildly
Tossed and streamed his cloudy tresses,
Gleamed like drifting snow his tresses,
Glared like Ishkoodah, the comet,
Like the star with fiery tresses.
  Filled with joy was Mudjekeewis
When he looked on Hiawatha,
Saw his youth rise up before him
In the face of Hiawatha,
Saw the beauty of Wenonah
From the grave rise up before him.
  " Welcome ! " said he, " Hiawatha,
To the kingdom of the West-Wind !
Long have I been waiting for you !
Youth is lovely, age is lonely,
Youth is fiery, age is frosty ;
You bring back the days departed,

You bring back my youth of passion,
And the beautiful Wenonah ! "
  Many days they talked together,
Questioned, listened, waited, answered ;
Much the mighty Mudjekeewis
Boasted of his ancient prowess,
Of his perilous adventures,
His indomitable courage,
His invulnerable body.
  Patiently sat Hiawatha,
Listening to his father's boasting ;
With a smile he sat and listened,
Uttered neither threat nor menace,
Neither word nor look betrayed him,
But his heart was hot within him,
Like a living coal his heart was.
  Then he said, " O Mudjekeewis,
Is there nothing that can harm you ?
Nothing that you are afraid of ? "
And the mighty Mudjekeewis,
Grand and gracious in his boasting,
Answered, saying, " There is nothing,
Nothing but the black rock yonder,
Nothing but the fatal Wawbeek ! "
  And he looked at Hiawatha
With a wise look and benignant,
With a countenance paternal,
Looked with pride upon the beauty
Of his tall and graceful figure,
Saying, " O my Hiawatha !
Is there anything can harm you ?
Anything you are afraid of ? "
  But the wary Hiawatha
Paused awhile, as if uncertain,
Held his peace, as if resolving,
And then answered, " There is nothing,
Nothing but the bulrush yonder,
Nothing but the great Apukwa ! "
  And as Mudjekeewis, rising,
Stretched his hand to pluck the bulrush,
Hiawatha cried in terror,
Cried in well-dissembled terror,
" Kago ! kago ! do not touch it ! "
" Ah, kaween ! " said Mudjekeewis,
" No indeed, I will not touch it ! "
  Then they talked of other matters ;
First of Hiawatha's brothers,
First of Wabun, of the East-Wind,
Of the South-Wind, Shawondasee,
Of the North, Kabibonokka ;
Then of Hiawatha's mother,
Of the beautiful Wenonah,
Of her birth upon the meadow,
Of her death, as old Nokomis
Had remembered and related.

And he cried, " O Mudjekeewis,
It was you who killed Wenonah,
Took her young life and her beauty,
Broke the Lily of the Prairie,
Trampled it beneath your footsteps ;
You confess it ! you confess it ! "
And the mighty Mudjekeewis
Tossed upon the wind his tresses,
Bowed his hoary head in anguish,
With a silent nod assented.
    Then up started Hiawatha,
And with threatening look and gesture
Laid his hand upon the black rock,
On the fatal Wawbeek laid it,
With his mittens, Minjekahwun,
Rent the jutting crag asunder,
Smote and crushed it into fragments,
Hurled them madly at his father,
The remorseful Mudjekeewis,
For his heart was hot within him,
Like a living coal his heart was.
    But the ruler of the West-Wind
Blew the fragments backward from him,
With the breathing of his nostrils,
With the tempest of his anger,
Blew them back at his assailant ;
Seized the bulrush, the Apukwa,
Dragged it with its roots and fibres
From the margin of the meadow,
From its ooze the giant bulrush ;
Long and loud laughed Hiawatha !
    Then began the deadly conflict,
Hand to hand among the mountains ;
From his eyry screamed the eagle,
The Keneu, the great war-eagle,
Sat upon the crags around them,
Wheeling flapped his wings above them.
    Like a tall tree in the tempest
Bent and lashed the giant bulrush ;
And in masses huge and heavy
Crashing fell the fatal Wawbeek ;
Till the earth shook with the tumult
And confusion of the battle,
And the air was full of shoutings,
And the thunder of the mountains,
Starting, answered, " Baim-wawa ! "
    Back retreated Mudjekeewis,
Rushing westward o'er the mountains,
Stumbling westward down the mountains,
Three whole days retreated fighting,
Still pursued by Hiawatha
To the doorways of the West-Wind,
To the portals of the Sunset,
To the earth's remotest border,
Where into the empty spaces

Sinks the sun, as a flamingo
Drops into her nest at nightfall
In the melancholy marshes.
    " Hold ! " at length cried Mudjekeewis,
" Hold, my son, my Hiawatha !
'T is impossible to kill me,
For you cannot kill the immortal
I have put you to this trial,
But to know and prove your courage ;
Now receive the prize of valor !
    " Go back to your home and people,
Live among them, toil among them,
Cleanse the earth from all that harms it,
Clear the fishing-grounds and rivers,
Slay all monsters and magicians,
All the Wendigoes, the giants,
All the serpents, the Kenabeeks,
As I slew the Mishe-Mokwa,
Slew the Great Bear of the mountains.
    " And at last when Death draws near you,
When the awful eyes of Pauguk
Glare upon you in the darkness,
I will share my kingdom with you,
Ruler shall you be thenceforward
Of the Northwest-Wind, Keewaydin,
Of the home-wind, the Keewaydin."
    Thus was fought that famous battle
In the dreadful days of Shah-shah,
In the days long since departed,
In the kingdom of the West-Wind.
Still the hunter sees its traces
Scattered far o'er hill and valley ;
Sees the giant bulrush growing
By the ponds and water-courses,
Sees the masses of the Wawbeek
Lying still in every valley.
    Homeward now went Hiawatha ;
Pleasant was the landscape round him,
Pleasant was the air above him,
For the bitterness of anger
Had departed wholly from him,
From his brain the thought of vengeance,
From his heart the burning fever.
    Only once his pace he slackened,
Only once he paused or halted,
Paused to purchase heads of arrows
Of the ancient Arrow-maker,
In the land of the Dacotahs,
Where the Falls of Minnehaha
Flash and gleam among the oak-trees,
Laugh and leap into the valley.
    There the ancient Arrow-maker
Made his arrow-heads of sandstone,
Arrow-heads of chalcedony,
Arrow-heads of flint and jasper,

Smoothed and sharpened at the edges,
Hard and polished, keen and costly.
    With him dwelt his dark-eyed daughter,
Wayward as the Minnehaha,
With her moods of shade and sunshine,
Eyes that smiled and frowned alternate,
Feet as rapid as the river,
Tresses flowing like the water,
And as musical a laughter :
And he named her from the river,
From the water-fall he named her,
Minnehaha, Laughing Water.
    Was it then for heads of arrows,
Arrow-heads of chalcedony,
Arrow-heads of flint and jasper,
That my Hiawatha halted
In the land of the Dacotahs ?
    Was it not to see the maiden,
See the face of Laughing Water
Peeping from behind the curtain,
Hear the rustling of her garments
From behind the waving curtain,
As one sees the Minnehaha
Gleaming, glancing through the branches,
As one hears the Laughing Water
From behind its screen of branches ?
    Who shall say what thoughts and visions
Fill the fiery brains of young men ?
Who shall say what dreams of beauty
Filled the heart of Hiawatha ?
All he told to old Nokomis,
When he reached the lodge at sunset,
Was the meeting with his father,
Was his fight with Mudjekeewis ;
Not a word he said of arrows,
Not a word of Laughing Water.

V

HIAWATHA'S FASTING

You shall hear how Hiawatha
Prayed and fasted in the forest,
Not for greater skill in hunting,
Not for greater craft in fishing,
Not for triumphs in the battle,
And renown among the warriors,
But for profit of the people,
For advantage of the nations.
    First he built a lodge for fasting,
Built a wigwam in the forest,
By the shining Big-Sea-Water,
In the blithe and pleasant Spring-time,
In the Moon of Leaves he built it,

And, with dreams and visions many,
Seven whole days and nights he fasted.
    On the first day of his fasting
Through the leafy woods he wandered ;
Saw the deer start from the thicket,
Saw the rabbit in his burrow,
Heard the pheasant, Bena, drumming,
Heard the squirrel, Adjidaumo,
Rattling in his hoard of acorns,
Saw the pigeon, the Omeme,
Building nests among the pine-trees,
And in flocks the wild-goose, Wawa,
Flying to the fen-lands northward,
Whirring, wailing far above him.
" Master of Life ! " he cried, desponding,
" Must our lives depend on these things ? "
    On the next day of his fasting
By the river's brink he wandered,
Through the Muskoday, the meadow,
Saw the wild rice, Mahnomonee,
Saw the blueberry, Meenahga,
And the strawberry, Odahmin,
And the gooseberry, Shahbomin,
And the grape-vine, the Bemahgut,
Trailing o'er the alder-branches,
Filling all the air with fragrance !
" Master of Life ! " he cried, desponding,
" Must our lives depend on these things ? "
    On the third day of his fasting
By the lake he sat and pondered,
By the still, transparent water ;
Saw the sturgeon, Nahma, leaping,
Scattering drops like beads of wampum,
Saw the yellow perch, the Sahwa,
Like a sunbeam in the water,
Saw the pike, the Maskenozha,
And the herring, Okahahwis,
And the Shawgashee, the craw-fish !
" Master of Life ! " he cried, desponding,
" Must our lives depend on these things ? "
    On the fourth day of his fasting
In his lodge he lay exhausted ;
From his couch of leaves and branches
Gazing with half-open eyelids,
Full of shadowy dreams and visions,
On the dizzy, swimming landscape,
On the gleaming of the water,
On the splendor of the sunset.
    And he saw a youth approaching,
Dressed in garments green and yellow,
Coming through the purple twilight,
Through the splendor of the sunset ;
Plumes of green bent o'er his forehead,
And his hair was soft and golden.
    Standing at the open doorway,

Long he looked at Hiawatha,
Looked with pity and compassion
On his wasted form and features,
And, in accents like the sighing
Of the South-Wind in the tree-tops,
Said he, " O my Hiawatha !
All your prayers are heard in heaven,
For you pray not like the others ;
Not for greater skill in hunting,
Not for greater craft in fishing,
Not for triumph in the battle,
Nor renown among the warriors,
But for profit of the people,
For advantage of the nations.
" From the Master of Life descending,
I, the friend of man, Mondamin,
Come to warn you and instruct you,
How by struggle and by labor
You shall gain what you have prayed for.
Rise up from your bed of branches,
Rise, O youth, and wrestle with me ! "
Faint with famine, Hiawatha
Started from his bed of branches,
From the twilight of his wigwam
Forth into the flush of sunset
Came, and wrestled with Mondamin ;
At his touch he felt new courage
Throbbing in his brain and bosom,
Felt new life and hope and vigor
Run through every nerve and fibre.
So they wrestled there together
In the glory of the sunset,
And the more they strove and struggled,
Stronger still grew Hiawatha ;
Till the darkness fell around them,
And the heron, the Shuh-shuh-gah,
From her nest among the pine-trees,
Gave a cry of lamentation,
Gave a scream of pain and famine.
" 'T is enough ! " then said Mondamin,
Smiling upon Hiawatha,
" But to-morrow, when the sun sets,
I will come again to try you."
And he vanished, and was seen not ;
Whether sinking as the rain sinks,
Whether rising as the mists rise,
Hiawatha saw not, knew not,
Only saw that he had vanished,
Leaving him alone and fainting,
With the misty lake below him,
And the reeling stars above him.
On the morrow and the next day,
When the sun through heaven descending,
Like a red and burning cinder
From the hearth of the Great Spirit,

Fell into the western waters,
Came Mondamin for the trial,
For the strife with Hiawatha ;
Came as silent as the dew comes,
From the empty air appearing,
Into empty air returning,
Taking shape when earth it touches,
But invisible to all men
In its coming and its going.
Thrice they wrestled there together
In the glory of the sunset,
Till the darkness fell around them,
Till the heron, the Shuh-shuh-gah,
From her nest among the pine-trees,
Uttered her loud cry of famine,
And Mondamin paused to listen.
Tall and beautiful he stood there,
In his garments green and yellow ;
To and fro his plumes above him
Waved and nodded with his breathing,
And the sweat of the encounter
Stood like drops of dew upon him.
And he cried, " O Hiawatha !
Bravely have you wrestled with me,
Thrice have wrestled stoutly with me,
And the Master of Life, who sees us,
He will give to you the triumph ! "
Then he smiled, and said : " To-morrow
Is the last day of your conflict,
Is the last day of your fasting.
You will conquer and o'ercome me ;
Make a bed for me to lie in,
Where the rain may fall upon me,
Where the sun may come and warm me ;
Strip these garments, green and yellow,
Strip this nodding plumage from me,
Lay me in the earth, and make it
Soft and loose and light above me.
" Let no hand disturb my slumber,
Let no weed nor worm molest me,
Let not Kahgahgee, the raven,
Come to haunt me and molest me,
Only come yourself to watch me,
Till I wake, and start, and quicken,
Till I leap into the sunshine."
And thus saying, he departed ;
Peacefully slept Hiawatha,
But he heard the Wawonaissa,
Heard the whippoorwill complaining,
Perched upon his lonely wigwam ;
Heard the rushing Sebowisha,
Heard the rivulet rippling near him,
Talking to the darksome forest ;
Heard the sighing of the branches,
As they lifted and subsided

At the passing of the night-wind,
Heard them, as one hears in slumber
Far-off murmurs, dreamy whispers :
Peacefully slept Hiawatha.
　On the morrow came Nokomis,
On the seventh day of his fasting,
Came with food for Hiawatha,
Came imploring and bewailing,
Lest his hunger should o'ercome him,
Lest his fasting should be fatal.
　But he tasted not, and touched not,
Only said to her, " Nokomis,
Wait until the sun is setting,
Till the darkness falls around us,
Till the heron, the Shuh-shuh-gah,
Crying from the desolate marshes,
Tells us that the day is ended."
　Homeward weeping went Nokomis,
Sorrowing for her Hiawatha,
Fearing lest his strength should fail him,
Lest his fasting should be fatal.
He meanwhile sat weary waiting
For the coming of Mondamin,
Till the shadows, pointing eastward,
Lengthened over field and forest,
Till the sun dropped from the heaven,
Floating on the waters westward,
As a red leaf in the Autumn
Falls and floats upon the water,
Falls and sinks into its bosom.
　And behold ! the young Mondamin,
With his soft and shining tresses,
With his garments green and yellow,
With his long and glossy plumage,
Stood and beckoned at the doorway.
And as one in slumber walking,
Pale and haggard, but undaunted,
From the wigwam Hiawatha
Came and wrestled with Mondamin.
　Round about him spun the landscape,
Sky and forest reeled together,
And his strong heart leaped within him,
As the sturgeon leaps and struggles
In a net to break its meshes.
Like a ring of fire around him
Blazed and flared the red horizon,
And a hundred suns seemed looking
At the combat of the wrestlers.
　Suddenly upon the greensward
All alone stood Hiawatha,
Panting with his wild exertion,
Palpitating with the struggle ;
And before him breathless, lifeless,
Lay the youth, with hair dishevelled,
Plumage torn, and garments tattered,

Dead he lay there in the sunset.
　And victorious Hiawatha
Made the grave as he commanded,
Stripped the garments from Mondamin,
Stripped his tattered plumage from him,
Laid him in the earth, and made it
Soft and loose and light above him ;
And the heron, the Shuh-shuh-gah,
From the melancholy moorlands,
Gave a cry of lamentation,
Gave a cry of pain and anguish !
　Homeward then went Hiawatha
To the lodge of old Nokomis,
And the seven days of his fasting
Were accomplished and completed.
But the place was not forgotten
Where he wrestled with Mondamin ;
Nor forgotten nor neglected
Was the grave where lay Mondamin,
Sleeping in the rain and sunshine,
Where his scattered plumes and garments
Faded in the rain and sunshine.
　Day by day did Hiawatha
Go to wait and watch beside it ;
Kept the dark mould soft above it,
Kept it clean from weeds and insects,
Drove away, with scoffs and shoutings,
Kahgahgee, the king of ravens.
　Till at length a small green feather
From the earth shot slowly upward,
Then another and another,
And before the Summer ended
Stood the maize in all its beauty,
With its shining robes about it,
And its long, soft, yellow tresses ;
And in rapture Hiawatha
Cried aloud, " It is Mondamin !
Yes, the friend of man, Mondamin !"
　Then he called to old Nokomis
And Iagoo, the great boaster,
Showed them where the maize was growing,
Told them of his wondrous vision,
Of his wrestling and his triumph,
Of this new gift to the nations,
Which should be their food forever.
　And still later, when the Autumn
Changed the long, green leaves to yellow,
And the soft and juicy kernels
Grew like wampum hard and yellow,
Then the ripened ears he gathered,
Stripped the withered husks from off them,
As he once had stripped the wrestler,
Gave the first Feast of Mondamin,
And made known unto the people
This new gift of the Great Spirit.

VI

HIAWATHA'S FRIENDS

Two good friends had Hiawatha,
Singled out from all the others,
Bound to him in closest union,
And to whom he gave the right hand
Of his heart, in joy and sorrow;
Chibiabos, the musician,
And the very strong man, Kwasind.

Straight between them ran the pathway,
Never grew the grass upon it;
Singing birds, that utter falsehoods,
Story-tellers, mischief-makers,
Found no eager ear to listen,
Could not breed ill-will between them,
For they kept each other's counsel,
Spake with naked hearts together,
Pondering much and much contriving
How the tribes of men might prosper.

Most beloved by Hiawatha
Was the gentle Chibiabos,
He the best of all musicians,
He the sweetest of all singers.
Beautiful and childlike was he,
Brave as man is, soft as woman,
Pliant as a wand of willow,
Stately as a deer with antlers.

When he sang, the village listened;
All the warriors gathered round him,
All the women came to hear him;
Now he stirred their souls to passion,
Now he melted them to pity.

From the hollow reeds he fashioned
Flutes so musical and mellow,
That the brook, the Sebowisha,
Ceased to murmur in the woodland,
That the wood-birds ceased from singing,
And the squirrel, Adjidaumo,
Ceased his chatter in the oak-tree,
And the rabbit, the Wabasso,
Sat upright to look and listen.

Yes, the brook, the Sebowisha,
Pausing, said, "O Chibiabos,
Teach my waves to flow in music,
Softly as your words in singing!"

Yes, the bluebird, the Owaissa,
Envious, said, "O Chibiabos,
Teach me tones as wild and wayward,
Teach me songs as full of frenzy!"

Yes, the robin, the Opechee,
Joyous, said, "O Chibiabos,
Teach me tones as sweet and tender,
Teach me songs as full of gladness!"

And the whippoorwill, Wawonaissa,
Sobbing, said, "O Chibiabos,
Teach me tones as melancholy,
Teach me songs as full of sadness!"

All the many sounds of nature
Borrowed sweetness from his singing;
All the hearts of men were softened
By the pathos of his music;
For he sang of peace and freedom,
Sang of beauty, love, and longing;
Sang of death, and life undying
In the Islands of the Blessed,
In the kingdom of Ponemah,
In the land of the Hereafter.

Very dear to Hiawatha
Was the gentle Chibiabos,
He the best of all musicians,
He the sweetest of all singers;
For his gentleness he loved him,
And the magic of his singing.

Dear, too, unto Hiawatha
Was the very strong man, Kwasind,
He the strongest of all mortals,
He the mightiest among many;
For his very strength he loved him,
For his strength allied to goodness.

Idle in his youth was Kwasind,
Very listless, dull, and dreamy,
Never played with other children,
Never fished and never hunted,
Not like other children was he;
But they saw that much he fasted,
Much his Manito entreated,
Much besought his Guardian Spirit.

"Lazy Kwasind!" said his mother,
"In my work you never help me!
In the Summer you are roaming
Idly in the fields and forests;
In the Winter you are cowering
O'er the firebrands in the wigwam!
In the coldest days of Winter
I must break the ice for fishing;
With my nets you never help me!
At the door my nets are hanging,
Dripping, freezing with the water;
Go and wring them, Yenadizze!
Go and dry them in the sunshine!"

Slowly, from the ashes, Kwasind
Rose, but made no angry answer;
From the lodge went forth in silence,
Took the nets, that hung together,
Dripping, freezing at the doorway;
Like a wisp of straw he wrung them,

Like a wisp of straw he broke them,
Could not wring them without breaking,
Such the strength was in his fingers.
 "Lazy Kwasind!" said his father,
"In the hunt you never help me ;
Every bow you touch is broken,
Snapped asunder every arrow ;
Yet come with me to the forest,
You shall bring the hunting homeward."
 Down a narrow pass they wandered,
Where a brooklet led them onward,
Where the trail of deer and bison
Marked the soft mud on the margin,
Till they found all further passage
Shut against them, barred securely
By the trunks of trees uprooted,
Lying lengthwise, lying crosswise,
And forbidding further passage.
 "We must go back," said the old man,
"O'er these logs we cannot clamber ;
Not a woodchuck could get through them,
Not a squirrel clamber o'er them !"
And straightway his pipe he lighted,
And sat down to smoke and ponder.
But before his pipe was finished,
Lo ! the path was cleared before him ;
All the trunks had Kwasind lifted,
To the right hand, to the left hand,
Shot the pine-trees swift as arrows,
Hurled the cedars light as lances.
 "Lazy Kwasind!" said the young men,
As they sported in the meadow :
"Why stand idly looking at us,
Leaning on the rock behind you ?
Come and wrestle with the others,
Let us pitch the quoit together !"
 Lazy Kwasind made no answer,
To their challenge made no answer,
Only rose, and slowly turning,
Seized the huge rock in his fingers,
Tore it from its deep foundation,
Poised it in the air a moment,
Pitched it sheer into the river,
Sheer into the swift Pauwating,
Where it still is seen in Summer.
 Once as down that foaming river,
Down the rapids of Pauwating,
Kwasind sailed with his companions,
In the stream he saw a beaver,
Saw Ahmeek, the King of Beavers,
Struggling with the rushing currents,
Rising, sinking in the water.
 Without speaking, without pausing,
Kwasind leaped into the river,
Plunged beneath the bubbling surface,

Through the whirlpools chased the beaver,
Followed him among the islands,
Stayed so long beneath the water,
That his terrified companions
Cried, "Alas ! good-by to Kwasind !
We shall never more see Kwasind !"
But he reappeared triumphant,
And upon his shining shoulders
Brought the beaver, dead and dripping,
Brought the King of all the Beavers.
 And these two, as I have told you,
Were the friends of Hiawatha,
Chibiabos, the musician,
And the very strong man, Kwasind.
Long they lived in peace together,
Spake with naked hearts together,
Pondering much and much contriving
How the tribes of men might prosper.

VII

HIAWATHA'S SAILING

"GIVE me of your bark, O Birch-tree !
Of your yellow bark, O Birch-tree !
Growing by the rushing river,
Tall and stately in the valley !
I a light canoe will build me,
Build a swift Cheemaun for sailing,
That shall float upon the river,
Like a yellow leaf in Autumn,
Like a yellow water-lily !
 "Lay aside your cloak, O Birch-tree !
Lay aside your white-skin wrapper,
For the Summer-time is coming,
And the sun is warm in heaven,
And you need no white-skin wrapper !"
 Thus aloud cried Hiawatha
In the solitary forest,
By the rushing Taquamenaw,
When the birds were singing gayly,
In the Moon of Leaves were singing,
And the sun, from sleep awaking,
Started up and said, "Behold me !
Gheezis, the great Sun, behold me !"
 And the tree with all its branches
Rustled in the breeze of morning,
Saying, with a sigh of patience,
"Take my cloak, O Hiawatha !"
 With his knife the tree he girdled ;
Just beneath its lowest branches,
Just above the roots, he cut it,
Till the sap came oozing outward ;
Down the trunk, from top to bottom,

Sheer he cleft the bark asunder,
With a wooden wedge he raised it,
Stripped it from the trunk unbroken.
" Give me of your boughs, O Cedar !
Of your strong and pliant branches,
My canoe to make more steady,
Make more strong and firm beneath me ! "
Through the summit of the Cedar
Went a sound, a cry of horror,
Went a murmur of resistance ;
But it whispered, bending downward,
" Take my boughs, O Hiawatha ! "
Down he hewed the boughs of cedar,
Shaped them straightway to a frame-work,
Like two bows he formed and shaped
them,
Like two bended bows together.
" Give me of your roots, O Tamarack !
Of your fibrous roots, O Larch-tree !
My canoe to bind together,
So to bind the ends together
That the water may not enter,
That the river may not wet me ! "
And the Larch, with all its fibres,
Shivered in the air of morning,
Touched his forehead with its tassels,
Said, with one long sigh of sorrow,
" Take them all, O Hiawatha ! "
From the earth he tore the fibres,
Tore the tough roots of the Larch-tree,
Closely sewed the bark together,
Bound it closely to the frame-work.
" Give me of your balm, O Fir-tree !
Of your balsam and your resin,
So to close the seams together
That the water may not enter,
That the river may not wet me ! "
And the Fir-tree, tall and sombre,
Sobbed through all its robes of darkness,
Rattled like a shore with pebbles,
Answered wailing, answered weeping,
" Take my balm, O Hiawatha ! "
And he took the tears of balsam,
Took the resin of the Fir-tree,
Smeared therewith each seam and fissure,
Made each crevice safe from water.
" Give me of your quills, O Hedgehog !
All your quills, O Kagh, the Hedgehog !
I will make a necklace of them,
Make a girdle for my beauty,
And two stars to deck her bosom ! "
From a hollow tree the Hedgehog
With his sleepy eyes looked at him,
Shot his shining quills, like arrows,
Saying with a drowsy murmur,

Through the tangle of his whiskers,
" Take my quills, O Hiawatha ! "
From the ground the quills he gathered,
All the little shining arrows,
Stained them red and blue and yellow,
With the juice of roots and berries ;
Into his canoe he wrought them,
Round its waist a shining girdle,
Round its bows a gleaming necklace,
On its breast two stars resplendent.
Thus the Birch Canoe was builded
In the valley, by the river,
In the bosom of the forest ;
And the forest's life was in it,
All its mystery and its magic,
All the lightness of the birch-tree,
All the toughness of the cedar,
All the larch's supple sinews ;
And it floated on the river
Like a yellow leaf in Autumn,
Like a yellow water-lily.
Paddles none had Hiawatha,
Paddles none he had or needed,
For his thoughts as paddles served him,
And his wishes served to guide him ;
Swift or slow at will he glided,
Veered to right or left at pleasure.
Then he called aloud to Kwasind,
To his friend, the strong man, Kwasind,
Saying, " Help me clear this river
Of its sunken logs and sand-bars."
Straight into the river Kwasind
Plunged as if he were an otter,
Dived as if he were a beaver,
Stood up to his waist in water,
To his arm-pits in the river,
Swam and shouted in the river,
Tugged at sunken logs and branches,
With his hands he scooped the sand-bars,
With his feet the ooze and tangle.
And thus sailed my Hiawatha
Down the rushing Taquamenaw,
Sailed through all its bends and windings,
Sailed through all its deeps and shallows,
While his friend, the strong man, Kwasind,
Swam the deeps, the shallows waded.
Up and down the river went they,
In and out among its islands,
Cleared its bed of root and sand-bar,
Dragged the dead trees from its channel,
Made its passage safe and certain,
Made a pathway for the people,
From its springs among the mountains,
To the waters of Pauwating,
To the bay of Taquamenaw.

VIII

HIAWATHA'S FISHING

FORTH upon the Gitche Gumee,
On the shining Big-Sea-Water,
With his fishing-line of cedar,
Of the twisted bark of cedar,
Forth to catch the sturgeon Nahma,
Mishe-Nahma, King of Fishes,
In his birch canoe exulting
All alone went Hiawatha.

Through the clear, transparent water
He could see the fishes swimming
Far down in the depths below him ;
See the yellow perch, the Sahwa,
Like a sunbeam in the water,
See the Shawgashee, the craw-fish,
Like a spider on the bottom,
On the white and sandy bottom.

At the stern sat Hiawatha,
With his fishing-line of cedar ;
In his plumes the breeze of morning
Played as in the hemlock branches ;
On the bows, with tail erected,
Sat the squirrel, Adjidaumo ;
In his fur the breeze of morning
Played as in the prairie grasses.

On the white sand of the bottom
Lay the monster Mishe-Nahma,
Lay the sturgeon, King of Fishes ;
Through his gills he breathed the water,
With his fins he fanned and winnowed,
With his tail he swept the sand-floor.

There he lay in all his armor ;
On each side a shield to guard him,
Plates of bone upon his forehead,
Down his sides and back and shoulders
Plates of bone with spines projecting !
Painted was he with his war-paints,
Stripes of yellow, red, and azure,
Spots of brown and spots of sable ;
And he lay there on the bottom,
Fanning with his fins of purple,
As above him Hiawatha
In his birch canoe came sailing,
With his fishing-line of cedar.

" Take my bait," cried Hiawatha,
Down into the depths beneath him,
" Take my bait, O Sturgeon, Nahma !
Come up from below the water,
Let us see which is the stronger ! "
And he dropped his line of cedar
Through the clear, transparent water,

Waited vainly for an answer,
Long sat waiting for an answer,
And repeating loud and louder,
" Take my bait, O King of Fishes ! "

Quiet lay the sturgeon, Nahma,
Fanning slowly in the water,
Looking up at Hiawatha,
Listening to his call and clamor,
His unnecessary tumult,
Till he wearied of the shouting ;
And he said to the Kenozha,
To the pike, the Maskenozha,
" Take the bait of this rude fellow,
Break the line of Hiawatha ! "

In his fingers Hiawatha
Felt the loose line jerk and tighten ;
As he drew it in, it tugged so
That the birch canoe stood endwise,
Like a birch log in the water,
With the squirrel, Adjidaumo,
Perched and frisking on the summit.

Full of scorn was Hiawatha
When he saw the fish rise upward,
Saw the pike, the Maskenozha,
Coming nearer, nearer to him,
And he shouted through the water,
" Esa ! esa ! shame upon you !
You are but the pike, Kenozha,
You are not the fish I wanted,
You are not the King of Fishes ! "

Reeling downward to the bottom
Sank the pike in great confusion,
And the mighty sturgeon, Nahma,
Said to Ugudwash, the sun-fish,
To the bream, with scales of crimson,
" Take the bait of this great boaster,
Break the line of Hiawatha ! "

Slowly upward, wavering, gleaming,
Rose the Ugudwash, the sun-fish,
Seized the line of Hiawatha,
Swung with all his weight upon it,
Made a whirlpool in the water,
Whirled the birch canoe in circles,
Round and round in gurgling eddies,
Till the circles in the water
Reached the far-off sandy beaches,
Till the water-flags and rushes
Nodded on the distant margins.

But when Hiawatha saw him
Slowly rising through the water,
Lifting up his disk refulgent,
Loud he shouted in derision,
" Esa ! esa ! shame upon you !
You are Ugudwash, the sun-fish,
You are not the fish I wanted,

You are not the King of Fishes ! "
Slowly downward, wavering, gleaming,
Sank the Ugudwash, the sun-fish,
And again the sturgeon, Nahma,
Heard the shout of Hiawatha,
Heard his challenge of defiance,
The unnecessary tumult,
Ringing far across the water.

From the white sand of the bottom
Up he rose with angry gesture,
Quivering in each nerve and fibre,
Clashing all his plates of armor,
Gleaming bright with all his war-paint ;
In his wrath he darted upward,
Flashing leaped into the sunshine,
Opened his great jaws, and swallowed
Both canoe and Hiawatha.

Down into that darksome cavern
Plunged the headlong Hiawatha,
As a log on some black river
Shoots and plunges down the rapids,
Found himself in utter darkness,
Groped about in helpless wonder,
Till he felt a great heart beating,
Throbbing in that utter darkness.

And he smote it in his anger,
With his fist, the heart of Nahma,
Felt the mighty King of Fishes
Shudder through each nerve and fibre,
Heard the water gurgle round him
As he leaped and staggered through it,
Sick at heart, and faint and weary.

Crosswise then did Hiawatha
Drag his birch-canoe for safety,
Lest from out the jaws of Nahma,
In the turmoil and confusion,
Forth he might be hurled and perish.
And the squirrel, Adjidaumo,
Frisked and chattered very gayly,
Toiled and tugged with Hiawatha
Till the labor was completed.

Then said Hiawatha to him,
" O my little friend, the squirrel,
Bravely have you toiled to help me ;
Take the thanks of Hiawatha,
And the name which now he gives you ;
For hereafter and forever
Boys shall call you Adjidaumo,
Tail-in-air the boys shall call you ! "

And again the sturgeon, Nahma,
Gasped and quivered in the water,
Then was still, and drifted landward
Till he grated on the pebbles,
Till the listening Hiawatha
Heard him grate upon the margin,

Felt him strand upon the pebbles,
Knew that Nahma, King of Fishes,
Lay there dead upon the margin.

Then he heard a clang and flapping,
As of many wings assembling,
Heard a screaming and confusion,
As of birds of prey contending,
Saw a gleam of light above him,
Shining through the ribs of Nahma,
Saw the glittering eyes of sea-gulls,
Of Kayoshk, the sea-gulls, peering,
Gazing at him through the opening,
Heard them saying to each other,
" 'T is our brother, Hiawatha ! "

And he shouted from below them,
Cried exulting from the caverns :
" O ye sea-gulls !   O my brothers !
I have slain the sturgeon, Nahma ;
Make the rifts a little larger,
With your claws the openings widen,
Set me free from this dark prison,
And henceforward and forever
Men shall speak of your achievements,
Calling you Kayoshk, the sea-gulls,
Yes, Kayoshk, the Noble Scratchers ! "

And the wild and clamorous sea-gulls
Toiled with beak and claws together,
Made the rifts and openings wider
In the mighty ribs of Nahma,
And from peril and from prison,
From the body of the sturgeon,
From the peril of the water,
They released my Hiawatha.

He was standing near his wigwam,
On the margin of the water,
And he called to old Nokomis,
Called and beckoned to Nokomis,
Pointed to the sturgeon, Nahma,
Lying lifeless on the pebbles,
With the sea-gulls feeding on him.

" I have slain the Mishe-Nahma,
Slain the King of Fishes ! " said he ;
" Look ! the sea-gulls feed upon him,
Yes, my friends Kayoshk, the sea-gulls;
Drive them not away, Nokomis,
They have saved me from great peril
In the body of the sturgeon,
Wait until their meal is ended,
Till their craws are full with feasting,
Till they homeward fly, at sunset,
To their nests among the marshes ;
Then bring all your pots and kettles,
And make oil for us in Winter."

And she waited till the sun set,
Till the pallid moon, the Night-sun,

Rose above the tranquil water,
Till Kayoshk, the sated sea-gulls,
From their banquet rose with clamor,
And across the fiery sunset
Winged their way to far-off islands,
To their nests among the rushes.

To his sleep went Hiawatha,
And Nokomis to her labor,
Toiling patient in the moonlight,
Till the sun and moon changed places,
Till the sky was red with sunrise,
And Kayoshk, the hungry sea-gulls,
Came back from the reedy islands,
Clamorous for their morning banquet.

Three whole days and nights alternate
Old Nokomis and the sea-gulls
Stripped the oily flesh of Nahma,
Till the waves washed through the rib-bones,
Till the sea-gulls came no longer,
And upon the sands lay nothing
But the skeleton of Nahma.

IX

HIAWATHA AND THE PEARL-FEATHER

On the shores of Gitche Gumee,
Of the shining Big-Sea-Water,
Stood Nokomis, the old woman,
Pointing with her finger westward,
O'er the water pointing westward,
To the purple clouds of sunset.

Fiercely the red sun descending
Burned his way along the heavens,
Set the sky on fire behind him,
As war-parties, when retreating,
Burn the prairies on their war-trail;
And the moon, the Night-sun, eastward,
Suddenly starting from his ambush,
Followed fast those bloody footprints,
Followed in that fiery war-trail,
With its glare upon his features.

And Nokomis, the old woman,
Pointing with her finger westward,
Spake these words to Hiawatha:
"Yonder dwells the great Pearl-Feather,
Megissogwon, the Magician,
Manito of Wealth and Wampum,
Guarded by his fiery serpents,
Guarded by the black pitch-water.
You can see his fiery serpents,
The Kenabeek, the great serpents,
Coiling, playing in the water;
You can see the black pitch-water

Stretching far away beyond them,
To the purple clouds of sunset!
"He it was who slew my father,
By his wicked wiles and cunning,
When he from the moon descended,
When he came on earth to seek me.
He, the mightiest of Magicians,
Sends the fever from the marshes,
Sends the pestilential vapors,
Sends the poisonous exhalations,
Sends the white fog from the fen-lands,
Sends disease and death among us!
"Take your bow, O Hiawatha,
Take your arrows, jasper-headed,
Take your war-club, Puggawaugun,
And your mittens, Minjekahwun,
And your birch-canoe for sailing,
And the oil of Mishe-Nahma,
So to smear its sides, that swiftly
You may pass the black pitch-water;
Slay this merciless magician,
Save the people from the fever
That he breathes across the fen-lands,
And avenge my father's murder!"

Straightway then my Hiawatha
Armed himself with all his war-gear,
Launched his birch-canoe for sailing;
With his palm its sides he patted,
Said with glee, "Cheemaun, my darling,
O my Birch-canoe! leap forward,
Where you see the fiery serpents,
Where you see the black pitch-water!"

Forward leaped Cheemaun exulting,
And the noble Hiawatha
Sang his war-song wild and woful,
And above him the war-eagle,
The Keneu, the great war-eagle,
Master of all fowls with feathers,
Screamed and hurtled through the heavens

Soon he reached the fiery serpents,
The Kenabeek, the great serpents,
Lying huge upon the water,
Sparkling, rippling in the water,
Lying coiled across the passage,
With their blazing crests uplifted,
Breathing fiery fogs and vapors,
So that none could pass beyond them.

But the fearless Hiawatha
Cried aloud, and spake in this wise,
"Let me pass my way, Kenabeek,
Let me go upon my journey!"
And they answered, hissing fiercely,
With their fiery breath made answer:
"Back, go back! O Shaugodaya!
Back to old Nokomis, Faint-heart!"

Then the angry Hiawatha
Raised his mighty bow of ash-tree,
Seized his arrows, jasper-headed,
Shot them fast among the serpents ;
Every twanging of the bow-string
Was a war-cry and a death-cry,
Every whizzing of an arrow
Was a death-song of Kenabeek.
    Weltering in the bloody water,
Dead lay all the fiery serpents,
And among them Hiawatha
Harmless sailed, and cried exulting :
" Onward, O Cheemaun, my darling !
Onward to the black pitch-water ! "
    Then he took the oil of Nahma,
And the bows and sides anointed,
Smeared them well with oil, that swiftly
He might pass the black pitch-water.
    All night long he sailed upon it,
Sailed upon that sluggish water,
Covered with its mould of ages,
Black with rotting water-rushes,
Rank with flags and leaves of lilies,
Stagnant, lifeless, dreary, dismal,
Lighted by the shimmering moonlight,
And by will-o'-the-wisps illumined,
Fires by ghosts of dead men kindled,
In their weary night-encampments.
    All the air was white with moonlight,
All the water black with shadow,
And around him the Suggema,
The mosquito, sang his war-song,
And the fire-flies, Wah-wah-taysee,
Waved their torches to mislead him ;
And the bull-frog, the Dahinda,
Thrust his head into the moonlight,
Fixed his yellow eyes upon him,
Sobbed and sank beneath the surface ;
And anon a thousand whistles,
Answered over all the fen-lands,
And the heron, the Shuh-shuh-gah,
Far off on the reedy margin,
Heralded the hero's coming.
    Westward thus fared Hiawatha,
Toward the realm of Megissogwon,
Toward the land of the Pearl-Feather,
Till the level moon stared at him,
In his face stared pale and haggard,
Till the sun was hot behind him,
Till it burned upon his shoulders,
And before him on the upland
He could see the Shining Wigwam
Of the Manito of Wampum,
Of the mightiest of Magicians.
    Then once more Cheemaun he patted,

To his birch-canoe said, " Onward ! "
And it stirred in all its fibres,
And with one great bound of triumph
Leaped across the water-lilies,
Leaped through tangled flags and rushes,
And upon the beach beyond them
Dry-shod landed Hiawatha.
    Straight he took his bow of ash-tree,
On the sand one end he rested,
With his knee he pressed the middle,
Stretched the faithful bow-string tighter,
Took an arrow, jasper-headed,
Shot it at the Shining Wigwam,
Sent it singing as a herald,
As a bearer of his message,
Of his challenge loud and lofty :
" Come forth from your lodge, Pearl-
        Feather !
Hiawatha waits your coming ! "
    Straightway from the Shining Wigwam
Came the mighty Megissogwon,
Tall of stature, broad of shoulder,
Dark and terrible in aspect,
Clad from head to foot in wampum,
Armed with all his warlike weapons,
Painted like the sky of morning,
Streaked with crimson, blue, and yellow,
Crested with great eagle-feathers,
Streaming upward, streaming outward.
    " Well I know you, Hiawatha ! "
Cried he in a voice of thunder,
In a tone of loud derision.
" Hasten back, O Shaugodaya !
Hasten back among the women,
Back to old Nokomis, Faint-heart !
I will slay you as you stand there,
As of old I slew her father ! "
    But my Hiawatha answered,
Nothing daunted, fearing nothing :
" Big words do not smite like war-clubs,
Boastful breath is not a bow-string,
Taunts are not so sharp as arrows,
Deeds are better things than words are,
Actions mightier than boastings ! "
    Then began the greatest battle
That the sun had ever looked on,
That the war-birds ever witnessed.
All a Summer's day it lasted,
From the sunrise to the sunset ;
For the shafts of Hiawatha
Harmless hit the shirt of wampum,
Harmless fell the blows he dealt it
With his mittens, Minjekahwun,
Harmless fell the heavy war-club ;
It could dash the rocks asunder,

But it could not break the meshes
Of that magic shirt of wampum.
  Till at sunset Hiawatha,
Leaning on his bow of ash-tree,
Wounded, weary, and desponding,
With his mighty war-club broken,
With his mittens torn and tattered,
And three useless arrows only,
Paused to rest beneath a pine-tree,
From whose branches trailed the mosses,
And whose trunk was coated over
With the Dead-man's Moccasin-leather,
With the fungus white and yellow.
  Suddenly from the boughs above him
Sang the Mama, the woodpecker :
" Aim your arrows, Hiawatha,
At the head of Megissogwon,
Strike the tuft of hair upon it,
At their roots the long black tresses ;
There alone can he be wounded ! "
  Winged with feathers, tipped with jasper,
Swift flew Hiawatha's arrow,
Just as Megissogwon, stooping,
Raised a heavy stone to throw it.
Full upon the crown it struck him,
At the roots of his long tresses,
And he reeled and staggered forward,
Plunging like a wounded bison,
Yes, like Pezhekee, the bison,
When the snow is on the prairie.
  Swifter flew the second arrow,
In the pathway of the other,
Piercing deeper than the other,
Wounding sorer than the other ;
And the knees of Megissogwon
Shook like windy reeds beneath him,
Bent and trembled like the rushes.
  But the third and latest arrow
Swiftest flew, and wounded sorest,
And the mighty Megissogwon
Saw the fiery eyes of Pauguk,
Saw the eyes of Death glare at him,
Heard his voice call in the darkness ;
At the feet of Hiawatha
Lifeless lay the great Pearl-Feather,
Lay the mightiest of Magicians.
  Then the grateful Hiawatha·
Called the Mama, the woodpecker,
From his perch among the branches
Of the melancholy pine-tree,
And, in honor of his service,
Stained with blood the tuft of feathers
On the little head of Mama ;

Even to this day he wears it,
Wears the tuft of crimson feathers,
As a symbol of his service.
  Then he stripped the shirt of wampum
From the back of Megissogwon,
As a trophy of the battle,
As a signal of his conquest.
On the shore he left the body,
Half on land and half in water,
In the sand his feet were buried,
And his face was in the water.
And above him, wheeled and clamored
The Keneu, the great war-eagle,
Sailing round in narrower circles,
Hovering nearer, nearer, nearer.
  From the wigwam Hiawatha
Bore the wealth of Megissogwon,
All his wealth of skins and wampum,
Furs of bison and of beaver,
Furs of sable and of ermine,
Wampum belts and strings and pouches,
Quivers wrought with beads of wampum,
Filled with arrows, silver-headed.
  Homeward then he sailed exulting,
Homeward through the black pitch-water,
Homeward through the weltering serpents
With the trophies of the battle,
With a shout and song of triumph.
On the shore stood old Nokomis,
On the shore stood Chibiabos,
And the very strong man, Kwasind,
Waiting for the hero's coming,
Listening to his songs of triumph.
And the people of the village
Welcomed him with songs and dances,
Made a joyous feast, and shouted :
" Honor be to Hiawatha !
He has slain the great Pearl-Feather,
Slain the mightiest of Magicians,
Him, who sent the fiery fever,
Sent the white fog from the fen-lands,
Sent disease and death among us ! "
  Ever dear to Hiawatha
Was the memory of Mama !
And in token of his friendship,
As a mark of his remembrance,
He adorned and decked his pipe-stem
With the crimson tuft of feathers,
With the blood-red crest of Mama.
But the wealth of Megissogwon,
All the trophies of the battle,
He divided with his people,
Shared it equally among them.

X

HIAWATHA'S WOOING

" As unto the bow the cord is,
So unto the man is woman ;
Though she bends him, she obeys him,
Though she draws him, yet she follows ;
Useless each without the other ! "
　　Thus the youthful Hiawatha
Said within himself and pondered,
Much perplexed by various feelings,
Listless, longing, hoping, fearing,
Dreaming still of Minnehaha,
Of the lovely Laughing Water,
In the land of the Dacotahs.
　　" Wed a maiden of your people,"
Warning said the old Nokomis ;
" Go not eastward, go not westward,
For a stranger, whom we know not !
Like a fire upon the hearth-stone
Is a neighbor's homely daughter,
Like the starlight or the moonlight
Is the handsomest of strangers ! "
　　Thus dissuading spake Nokomis,
And my Hiawatha answered
Only this : " Dear old Nokomis,
Very pleasant is the firelight,
But I like the starlight better,
Better do I like the moonlight ! "
　　Gravely then said old Nokomis :
" Bring not here an idle maiden,
Bring not here a useless woman,
Hands unskilful, feet unwilling ;
Bring a wife with nimble fingers,
Heart and hand that move together,
Feet that run on willing errands ! "
　　Smiling answered Hiawatha :
" In the land of the Dacotahs
Lives the Arrow-maker's daughter,
Minnehaha, Laughing Water,
Handsomest of all the women.
I will bring her to your wigwam,
She shall run upon your errands,
Be your starlight, moonlight, firelight,
Be the sunlight of my people ! "
　　Still dissuading said Nokomis :
" Bring not to my lodge a stranger
From the land of the Dacotahs !
Very fierce are the Dacotahs,
Often is there war between us,
There are feuds yet unforgotten,
Wounds that ache and still may open ! "
　　Laughing answered Hiawatha :

" For that reason, if no other,
Would I wed the fair Dacotah,
That our tribes might be united,
That old feuds might be forgotten,
And old wounds be healed forever ! "
　　Thus departed Hiawatha
To the land of the Dacotahs,
To the land of handsome women ;
Striding over moor and meadow,
Through interminable forests,
Through uninterrupted silence.
　　With his moccasins of magic,
At each stride a mile he measured ;
Yet the way seemed long before him,
And his heart outran his footsteps ;
And he journeyed without resting,
Till he heard the cataract's laughter,
Heard the Falls of Minnehaha
Calling to him through the silence.
" Pleasant is the sound ! " he murmured,
" Pleasant is the voice that calls me ! "
　　On the outskirts of the forests,
'Twixt the shadow and the sunshine,
Herds of fallow deer were feeding,
But they saw not Hiawatha ;
To his bow he whispered, " Fail not ! "
To his arrow whispered, " Swerve not ! "
Sent it singing on its errand,
To the red heart of the roebuck ;
Threw the deer across his shoulder,
And sped forward without pausing.
　　At the doorway of his wigwam
Sat the ancient Arrow-maker,
In the land of the Dacotahs,
Making arrow-heads of jasper,
Arrow-heads of chalcedony.
At his side, in all her beauty,
Sat the lovely Minnehaha,
Sat his daughter, Laughing Water,
Plaiting mats of flags and rushes ;
Of the past the old man's thoughts were,
And the maiden's of the future.
　　He was thinking, as he sat there,
Of the days when with such arrows
He had struck the deer and bison,
On the Muskoday, the meadow ;
Shot the wild goose, flying southward
On the wing, the clamorous Wawa ;
Thinking of the great war-parties,
How they came to buy his arrows,
Could not fight without his arrows.
Ah, no more such noble warriors
Could be found on earth as they were !
Now the men were all like women,
Only used their tongues for weapons !

She was thinking of a hunter,
From another tribe and country,
Young and tall and very handsome,
Who one morning, in the Spring-time,
Came to buy her father's arrows,
Sat and rested in the wigwam,
Lingered long about the doorway,
Looking back as he departed.
She had heard her father praise him,
Praise his courage and his wisdom ;
Would he come again for arrows
To the Falls of Minnehaha ?
On the mat her hands lay idle,
And her eyes were very dreamy.
    Through their thoughts they heard a
        footstep,
Heard a rustling in the branches,
And with glowing cheek and forehead,
With the deer upon his shoulders,
Suddenly from out the woodlands
Hiawatha stood before them.
    Straight the ancient Arrow-maker
Looked up gravely from his labor,
Laid aside the unfinished arrow,
Bade him enter at the doorway,
Saying, as he rose to meet him,
" Hiawatha, you are welcome ! "
    At the feet of Laughing Water
Hiawatha laid his burden,
Threw the red deer from his shoulders ;
And the maiden looked up at him,
Looked up from her mat of rushes,
Said with gentle look and accent,
" You are welcome, Hiawatha ! "
    Very spacious was the wigwam,
Made of deer-skins dressed and whitened,
With the Gods of the Dacotahs
Drawn and painted on its curtains,
And so tall the doorway, hardly
Hiawatha stooped to enter,
Hardly touched his eagle-feathers
As he entered at the doorway.
    Then uprose the Laughing Water,
From the ground fair Minnehaha,
Laid aside her mat unfinished,
Brought forth food and set before them,
Water brought them from the brooklet,
Gave them food in earthen vessels,
Gave them drink in bowls of bass-wood,
Listened while the guest was speaking,
Listened while her father answered,
But not once her lips she opened,
Not a single word she uttered.
    Yes, as in a dream she listened
To the words of Hiawatha,

As he talked of old Nokomis,
Who had nursed him in his childhood,
As he told of his companions,
Chibiabos, the musician,
And the very strong man, Kwasind,
And of happiness and plenty
In the land of the Ojibways,
In the pleasant land and peaceful.
    " After many years of warfare,
Many years of strife and bloodshed,
There is peace between the Ojibways
And the tribe of the Dacotahs."
Thus continued Hiawatha,
And then added, speaking slowly,
" That this peace may last forever,
And our hands be clasped more closely,
And our hearts be more united,
Give me as my wife this maiden,
Minnehaha, Laughing Water,
Loveliest of Dacotah women ! "
    And the ancient Arrow-maker
Paused a moment ere he answered,
Smoked a little while in silence,
Looked at Hiawatha proudly,
Fondly looked at Laughing Water,
And made answer very gravely :
" Yes, if Minnehaha wishes ;
Let your heart speak, Minnehaha ! "
    And the lovely Laughing Water
Seemed more lovely as she stood there,
Neither willing nor reluctant,
As she went to Hiawatha,
Softly took the seat beside him,
While she said, and blushed to say it,
" I will follow you, my husband ! "
    This was Hiawatha's wooing !
Thus it was he won the daughter
Of the ancient Arrow-maker,
In the land of the Dacotahs !
    From the wigwam he departed,
Leading with him Laughing Water ;
Hand in hand they went together,
Through the woodland and the meadow,
Left the old man standing lonely
At the doorway of his wigwam,
Heard the Falls of Minnehaha
Calling to them from the distance,
Crying to them from afar off,
" Fare thee well, O Minnehaha ! "
    And the ancient Arrow-maker
Turned again unto his labor,
Sat down by his sunny doorway,
Murmuring to himself, and saying :
" Thus it is our daughters leave us,
Those we love, and those who love us !

Just when they have learned to help us,
When we are old and lean upon them,
Comes a youth with flaunting feathers,
With his flute of reeds, a stranger
Wanders piping through the village,
Beckons to the fairest maiden,
And she follows where he leads her,
Leaving all things for the stranger !"
　Pleasant was the journey homeward,
Through interminable forests,
Over meadow, over mountain,
Over river, hill, and hollow.
Short it seemed to Hiawatha,
Though they journeyed very slowly,
Though his pace he checked and slackened
To the steps of Laughing Water.
　Over wide and rushing rivers
In his arms he bore the maiden ;
Light he thought her as a feather,
As the plume upon his head-gear ;
Cleared the tangled pathway for her,
Bent aside the swaying branches,
Made at night a lodge of branches,
And a bed with boughs of hemlock,
And a fire before the doorway
With the dry cones of the pine-tree.
　All the travelling winds went with them,
O'er the meadows, through the forest ;
All the stars of night looked at them,
Watched with sleepless eyes their slumber;
From his ambush in the oak-tree
Peeped the squirrel, Adjidaumo,
Watched with eager eyes the lovers ;
And the rabbit, the Wabasso,
Scampered from the path before them,
Peering, peeping from his burrow,
Sat erect upon his haunches,
Watched with curious eyes the lovers.
　Pleasant was the journey homeward !
All the birds sang loud and sweetly
Songs of happiness and heart's-ease ;
Sang the bluebird, the Owaissa,
"Happy are you, Hiawatha,
Having such a wife to love you !"
Sang the robin, the Opechee,
"Happy are you, Laughing Water,
Having such a noble husband !"
　From the sky the sun benignant
Looked upon them through the branches,
Saying to them, "O my children,
Love is sunshine, hate is shadow,
Life is checkered shade and sunshine,
Rule by love, O Hiawatha !"
　From the sky the moon looked at them,
Filled the lodge with mystic splendors,

Whispered to them, "O my children,
Day is restless, night is quiet,
Man imperious, woman feeble ;
Half is mine, although I follow ;
Rule by patience, Laughing Water !"
　Thus it was they journeyed homeward ;
Thus it was that Hiawatha
To the lodge of old Nokomis
Brought the moonlight, starlight, firelight,
Brought the sunshine of his people,
Minnehaha, Laughing Water,
Handsomest of all the women
In the land of the Dacotahs,
In the land of handsome women.

XI

HIAWATHA'S WEDDING-FEAST

You shall hear how Pau-Puk-Keewis,
How the handsome Yenadizze
Danced at Hiawatha's wedding ;
How the gentle Chibiabos,
He the sweetest of musicians,
Sang his songs of love and longing ;
How Iagoo, the great boaster,
He the marvellous story-teller,
Told his tales of strange adventure,
That the feast might be more joyous,
That the time might pass more gayly,
And the guests be more contented.
　Sumptuous was the feast Nokomis
Made at Hiawatha's wedding ;
All the bowls were made of bass-wood,
White and polished very smoothly,
All the spoons of horn of bison,
Black and polished very smoothly.
　She had sent through all the village
Messengers with wands of willow,
As a sign of invitation,
As a token of the feasting ;
And the wedding guests assembled,
Clad in all their richest raiment,
Robes of fur and belts of wampum,
Splendid with their paint and plumage,
Beautiful with beads and tassels.
　First they ate the sturgeon, Nahma,
And the pike, the Maskenozha,
Caught and cooked by old Nokomis ;
Then on pemican they feasted,
Pemican and buffalo marrow,
Haunch of deer and hump of bison,
Yellow cakes of the Mondamin,
And the wild rice of the river.

But the gracious Hiawatha,
And the lovely Laughing Water,
And the careful old Nokomis,
Tasted not the food before them,
Only waited on the others,
Only served their guests in silence.
And when all the guests had finished,
Old Nokomis, brisk and busy,
From an ample pouch of otter,
Filled the red-stone pipes for smoking
With tobacco from the South-land,
Mixed with bark of the red willow,
And with herbs and leaves of fragrance.
Then she said, " O Pau-Puk-Keewis,
Dance for us your merry dances,
Dance the Beggar's Dance to please us,
That the feast may be more joyous,
That the time may pass more gayly,
And our guests' be more contented ! "
Then the handsome Pau-Puk-Keewis,
He the idle Yenadizze,
He the merry mischief-maker,
Whom the people called the Storm-Fool,
Rose among the guests assembled.
Skilled was he in sports and pastimes,
In the merry dance of snow-shoes,
In the play of quoits and ball-play ;
Skilled was he in games of hazard,
In all games of skill and hazard,
Pugasaing, the Bowl and Counters,
Kuntassoo, the Game of Plum-stones.
Though the warriors called him Faint-
    Heart,
Called him coward, Shaugodaya,
Idler, gambler, Yenadizze,
Little heeded he their jesting,
Little cared he for their insults,
For the women and the maidens
Loved the handsome Pau-Puk-Keewis.
He was dressed in shirt of doeskin,
White and soft, and fringed with ermine,
All inwrought with beads of wampum ;
He was dressed in deer-skin leggings,
Fringed with hedgehog quills and ermine,
And in moccasins of buck-skin,
Thick with quills and beads embroidered.
On his head were plumes of swan's down,
On his heels were tails of foxes,
In one hand a fan of feathers,
And a pipe was in the other.
Barred with streaks of red and yellow,
Streaks of blue and bright vermilion,
Shone the face of Pau-Puk-Keewis.
From his forehead fell his tresses,
Smooth, and parted like a woman's,

Shining bright with oil, and plaited,
Hung with braids of scented grasses,
As among the guests assembled,
To the sound of flutes and singing,
To the sound of drums and voices,
Rose the handsome Pau-Puk-Keewis,
And began his mystic dances.
First he danced a solemn measure,
Very slow in step and gesture,
In and out among the pine-trees,
Through the shadows and the sunshine,
Treading softly like a panther.
Then more swiftly and still swifter,
Whirling, spinning round in circles,
Leaping o'er the guests assembled,
Eddying round and round the wigwam,
Till the leaves went whirling with him,
Till the dust and wind together
Swept in eddies round about him.
Then along the sandy margin
Of the lake, the Big-Sea-Water,
On he sped with frenzied gestures,
Stamped upon the sand, and tossed it
Wildly in the air around him ;
Till the wind became a whirlwind,
Till the sand was blown and sifted
Like great snowdrifts o'er the landscape,
Heaping all the shores with Sand Dunes,
Sand Hills of the Nagow Wudjoo !
Thus the merry Pau-Puk-Keewis
Danced his Beggar's Dance to please them,
And, returning, sat down laughing
There among the guests assembled,
Sat and fanned himself serenely
With his fan of turkey-feathers.
Then they said to Chibiabos,
To the friend of Hiawatha,
To the sweetest of all singers,
To the best of all musicians,
" Sing to us, O Chibiabos !
Songs of love and songs of longing,
That the feast may be more joyous,
That the time may pass more gayly,
And our guests be more contented ! "
And the gentle Chibiabos
Sang in accents sweet and tender,
Sang in tones of deep emotion,
Songs of love and songs of longing ;
Looking still at Hiawatha,
Looking at fair Laughing Water,
Sang he softly, sang in this wise :
"Onaway ! Awake, beloved !
Thou the wild-flower of the forest !
Thou the wild-bird of the prairie !
Thou with eyes so soft and fawn-like !

"If thou only lookest at me,
I am happy, I am happy,
As the lilies of the prairie,
When they feel the dew upon them!
"Sweet thy breath is as the fragrance
Of the wild-flowers in the morning,
As their fragrance is at evening,
In the Moon when leaves are falling.
"Does not all the blood within me
Leap to meet thee, leap to meet thee,
As the springs to meet the sunshine,
In the Moon when nights are brightest?
"Onaway! my heart sings to thee,
Sings with joy when thou art near me,
As the sighing, singing branches
In the pleasant Moon of Strawberries!
"When thou art not pleased, beloved,
Then my heart is sad and darkened,
As the shining river darkens
When the clouds drop shadows on it!
"When thou smilest, my beloved,
Then my troubled heart is brightened,
As in sunshine gleam the ripples
That the cold wind makes in rivers.
"Smiles the earth, and smile the waters,
Smile the cloudless skies above us,
But I lose the way of smiling
When thou art no longer near me!
"I myself, myself! behold me!
Blood of my beating heart, behold me!
Oh awake, awake, beloved!
Onaway! awake, beloved!"

Thus the gentle Chibiabos
Sang his song of love and longing;
And Iagoo, the great boaster,
He the marvellous story-teller,
He the friend of old Nokomis,
Jealous of the sweet musician,
Jealous of the applause they gave him,
Saw in all the eyes around him,
Saw in all their looks and gestures,
That the wedding guests assembled
Longed to hear his pleasant stories,
His immeasurable falsehoods.

Very boastful was Iagoo;
Never heard he an adventure
But himself had met a greater;
Never any deed of daring
But himself had done a bolder;
Never any marvellous story
But himself could tell a stranger.

Would you listen to his boasting,
Would you only give him credence,
No one ever shot an arrow
Half so far and high as he had;

Ever caught so many fishes,
Ever killed so many reindeer,
Ever trapped so many beaver!
None could run so fast as he could,
None could dive so deep as he could,
None could swim so far as he could;
None had made so many journeys,
None had seen so many wonders,
As this wonderful Iagoo,
As this marvellous story-teller!
Thus his name became a by-word
And a jest among the people;
And whene'er a boastful hunter
Praised his own address too highly,
Or a warrior, home returning,
Talked too much of his achievements,
All his hearers cried, "Iagoo!
Here's Iagoo come among us!"

He it was who carved the cradle
Of the little Hiawatha,
Carved its framework out of linden,
Bound it strong with reindeer sinews;
He it was who taught him later
How to make his bows and arrows,
How to make the bows of ash-tree,
And the arrows of the oak-tree.
So among the guests assembled
At my Hiawatha's wedding
Sat Iagoo, old and ugly,
Sat the marvellous story-teller.

And they said, "O good Iagoo,
Tell us now a tale of wonder,
Tell us of some strange adventure,
That the feast may be more joyous,
That the time may pass more gayly,
And our guests be more contented!"

And Iagoo answered straightway,
"You shall hear a tale of wonder,
You shall hear the strange adventures
Of Osseo, the Magician,
From the Evening Star descended."

XII

THE SON OF THE EVENING STAR

CAN it be the sun descending
O'er the level plain of water?
Or the Red Swan floating, flying,
Wounded by the magic arrow,
Staining all the waves with crimson,
With the crimson of its life-blood,
Filling all the air with splendor,
With the splendor of its plumage?

Yes ; it is the sun descending,
Sinking down into the water ;
All the sky is stained with purple,
All the water flushed with crimson !
No ; it is the Red Swan floating,
Diving down beneath the water ;
To the sky its wings are lifted,
With its blood the waves are reddened !
Over it the Star of Evening
Melts and trembles through the purple,
Hangs suspended in the twilight.
No ; it is a bead of wampum
On the robes of the Great Spirit
As he passes through the twilight,
Walks in silence through the heavens.
This with joy beheld Iagoo
And he said in haste : " Behold it !
See the sacred Star of Evening !
You shall hear a tale of wonder,
Hear the story of Osseo,
Son of the Evening Star, Osseo !
" Once, in days no more remembered,
Ages nearer the beginning,
When the heavens were closer to us,
And the Gods were more familiar,
In the North-land lived a hunter,
With ten young and comely daughters,
Tall and lithe as wands of willow ;
Only Oweenee, the youngest,
She the wilful and the wayward,
She the silent, dreamy maiden,
Was the fairest of the sisters.
" All these women married warriors,
Married brave and haughty husbands ;
Only Oweenee, the youngest,
Laughed and flouted all her lovers,
All her young and handsome suitors,
And then married old Osseo,
Old Osseo, poor and ugly,
Broken with age and weak with coughing,
Always coughing like a squirrel.
" Ah, but beautiful within him
Was the spirit of Osseo,
From the Evening Star descended,
Star of Evening, Star of Woman,
Star of tenderness and passion !
All its fire was in his bosom,
All its beauty in his spirit,
All its mystery in his being,
All its splendor in his language !
" And her lovers, the rejected,
Handsome men with belts of wampum,
Handsome men with paint and feathers,
Pointed at her in derision,
Followed her with jest and laughter.

But she said : ' I care not for you,
Care not for your belts of wampum,
Care not for your paint and feathers,
Care not for your jests and laughter ;
I am happy with Osseo ! '
" Once to some great feast invited,
Through the damp and dusk of evening,
Walked together the ten sisters,
Walked together with their husbands ;
Slowly followed old Osseo,
With fair Oweenee beside him ;
All the others chatted gayly,
These two only walked in silence.
" At the western sky Osseo
Gazed intent, as if imploring,
Often stopped and gazed imploring
At the trembling Star of Evening,
At the tender Star of Woman ;
And they heard him murmur softly,
' Ah, showain nemeshin, Nosa !
Pity, pity me, my father ! '
" ' Listen ! ' said the eldest sister,
' He is praying to his father !
What a pity that the old man
Does not stumble in the pathway,
Does not break his neck by falling ! '
And they laughed till all the forest
Rang with their unseemly laughter.
" On their pathway through the wood-
    lands
Lay an oak, by storms uprooted,
Lay the great trunk of an oak-tree,
Buried half in leaves and mosses,
Mouldering, crumbling, huge and hollow.
And Osseo, when he saw it,
Gave a shout, a cry of anguish,
Leaped into its yawning cavern,
At one end went in an old man,
Wasted, wrinkled, old, and ugly ;
From the other came a young man,
Tall and straight and strong and handsome.
" Thus Osseo was transfigured,
Thus restored to youth and beauty ;
But, alas for good Osseo,
And for Oweenee, the faithful !
Strangely, too, was she transfigured.
Changed into a weak old woman,
With a staff she tottered onward,
Wasted, wrinkled, old, and ugly !
And the sisters and their husbands
Laughed until the echoing forest
Rang with their unseemly laughter.
" But Osseo turned not from her,
Walked with slower step beside her,
Took her hand, as brown and withered

As an oak-leaf is in Winter,
Called her sweetheart, Nenemoosha,
Soothed her with soft words of kindness,
Till they reached the lodge of feasting,
Till they sat down in the wigwam,
Sacred to the Star of Evening,
To the tender Star of Woman.
    " Wrapt in visions, lost in dreaming,
At the banquet sat Osseo ;
All were merry, all were happy,
All were joyous but Osseo.
Neither food nor drink he tasted,
Neither did he speak nor listen,
But as one bewildered sat he,
Looking dreamily and sadly,
First at Oweenee, then upward
At the gleaming sky above them.
    " Then a voice was heard, a whisper,
Coming from the starry distance,
Coming from the empty vastness,
Low, and musical, and tender ;
And the voice said : ' O Osseo !
O my son, my best beloved !
Broken are the spells that bound you,
All the charms of the magicians,
All the magic powers of evil ;
Come to me ; ascend, Osseo !
    " ' Taste the food that stands before
            you :
It is blessed and enchanted,
It has magic virtues in it,
It will change you to a spirit.
All your bowls and all your kettles
Shall be wood and clay no longer ;
But the bowls be changed to wampum,
And the kettles shall be silver ;
They shall shine like shells of scarlet,
Like the fire shall gleam and glimmer.
    " ' And the women shall no longer
Bear the dreary doom of labor,
But be changed to birds, and glisten
With the beauty of the starlight,
Painted with the dusky splendors
Of the skies and clouds of evening ! '
    " What Osseo heard as whispers,
What as words he comprehended,
Was but music to the others,
Music as of birds afar off,
Of the whippoorwill afar off,
Of the lonely Wawonaissa
Singing in the darksome forest.
    " Then the lodge began to tremble,
Straight began to shake and tremble,
And they felt it rising, rising,
Slowly through the air ascending,

From the darkness of the tree-tops
Forth into the dewy starlight,
Till it passed the topmost branches ;
And behold ! the wooden dishes
All were changed to shells of scarlet !
And behold ! the earthen kettles
All were changed to bowls of silver !
And the roof-poles of the wigwam
Were as glittering rods of silver,
And the roof of bark upon them
As the shining shards of beetles.
    " Then Osseo gazed around him,
And he saw the nine fair sisters,
All the sisters and their husbands,
Changed to birds of various plumage.
Some were jays and some were magpies,
Others thrushes, others blackbirds ;
And they hopped, and sang, and twittered,
Perked and fluttered all their feathers,
Strutted in their shining plumage,
And their tails like fans unfolded.
    " Only Oweenee, the youngest,
Was not changed, but sat in silence,
Wasted, wrinkled, old, and ugly,
Looking sadly at the others ;
Till Osseo, gazing upward,
Gave another cry of anguish,
Such a cry as he had uttered
By the oak-tree in the forest.
    " Then returned her youth and beauty,
And her soiled and tattered garments
Were transformed to robes of ermine,
And her staff became a feather,
Yes, a shining silver feather !
    " And again the wigwam trembled,
Swayed and rushed through airy currents,
Through transparent cloud and vapor,
And amid celestial splendors
On the Evening Star alighted,
As a snow-flake falls on snow-flake,
As a leaf drops on a river,
As the thistle-down on water.
    " Forth with cheerful words of welcome
Came the father of Osseo,
He with radiant locks of silver,
He with eyes serene and tender.
And he said : ' My son, Osseo,
Hang the cage of birds you bring there,
Hang the cage with rods of silver,
And the birds with glistening feathers,
At the doorway of my wigwam.'
    " At the door he hung the bird-cage,
And they entered in and gladly
Listened to Osseo's father,
Ruler of the Star of Evening,

As he said : ' O my Osseo !
I have had compassion on you,
Given you back your youth and beauty,
Into birds of various plumage
Changed your sisters and their husbands ;
Changed them thus because they mocked
          you
In the figure of the old man,
In that aspect sad and wrinkled,
Could not see your heart of passion,
Could not see your youth immortal ;
Only Oweenee, the faithful,
Saw your naked heart and loved you.
   " ' In the lodge that glimmers yonder,
In the little star that twinkles
Through the vapors, on the left hand,
Lives the envious Evil Spirit,
The Wabeno, the magician,
Who transformed you to an old man.
Take heed lest his beams fall on you,
For the rays he darts around him
Are the power of his enchantment,
Are the arrows that he uses.'
   " Many years, in peace and quiet,
On the peaceful Star of Evening
Dwelt Osseo with his father ;
Many years, in song and flutter,
At the doorway of the wigwam,
Hung the cage with rods of silver,
And fair Oweenee, the faithful,
Bore a son unto Osseo,
With the beauty of his mother,
With the courage of his father.
   " And the boy grew up and prospered,
And Osseo, to delight him,
Made him little bows and arrows,
Opened the great cage of silver,
And let loose his aunts and uncles,
All those birds with glossy feathers,
For his little son to shoot at.
   " Round and round they wheeled and
          darted,
Filled the Evening Star with music,
With their songs of joy and freedom ;
Filled the Evening Star with splendor,
With the fluttering of their plumage ;
Till the boy, the little hunter,
Bent his bow and shot an arrow,
Shot a swift and fatal arrow,
And a bird, with shining feathers,
At his feet fell wounded sorely.
   " But, O wondrous transformation !
'T was no bird he saw before him,
'T was a beautiful young woman,
With the arrow in her bosom !

   " When her blood fell on the planet,
On the sacred Star of Evening,
Broken was the spell of magic,
Powerless was the strange enchantment,
And the youth, the fearless bowman,
Suddenly felt himself descending,
Held by unseen hands, but sinking
Downward through the empty spaces,
Downward through the clouds and vapors,
Till he rested on an island,
On an island, green and grassy,
Yonder in the Big-Sea-Water.
   " After him he saw descending
All the birds with shining feathers,
Fluttering, falling, wafted downward,
Like the painted leaves of Autumn ;
And the lodge with poles of silver,
With its roof like wings of beetles,
Like the shining shards of beetles,
By the winds of heaven uplifted,
Slowly sank upon the meadow,
Bringing back the good Osseo,
Bringing Oweenee, the faithful.
   " Then the birds, again transfigured,
Reassumed the shape of mortals,
Took their shape, but not their stature ;
They remained as Little People,
Like the pygmies, the Puk-Wudjies,
And on pleasant nights of Summer,
When the Evening Star was shining,
Hand in hand they danced together
On the island's craggy headlands,
On the sand-beach low and level.
   " Still their glittering lodge is seen
          there,
On the tranquil Summer evenings,
And upon the shore the fisher
Sometimes hears their happy voices,
Sees them dancing in the starlight ! "
   When the story was completed,
When the wondrous tale was ended,
Looking round upon his listeners,
Solemnly Iagoo added :
" There are great men, I have known such,
Whom their people understand not,
Whom they even make a jest of,
Scoff and jeer at in derision.
From the story of Osseo
Let us learn the fate of jesters ! "
   All the wedding guests delighted
Listened to the marvellous story,
Listened laughing and applauding,
And they whispered to each other :
" Does he mean himself, I wonder ?
And are we the aunts and uncles ? "

Then again sang Chibiabos,
Sang a song of love and longing,
In those accents sweet and tender,
In those tones of pensive sadness,
Sang a maiden's lamentation
For her lover, her Algonquin.
  " When I think of my beloved,
Ah me ! think of my beloved,
When my heart is thinking of him,
O my sweetheart, my Algonquin !
  " Ah me ! when I parted from him,
Round my neck he hung the wampum,
As a pledge, the snow-white wampum,
O my sweetheart, my Algonquin !
  " I will go with you, he whispered,
Ah me ! to your native country ;
Let me go with you, he whispered,
O my sweetheart, my Algonquin !
  " Far away, away, I answered,
Very far away, I answered,
Ah me ! is my native country,
O my sweetheart, my Algonquin !
  " When I looked back to behold him,
Where we parted, to behold him,
After me he still was gazing,
O my sweetheart, my Algonquin !
  " By the tree he still was standing,
By the fallen tree was standing,
That had dropped into the water,
O my sweetheart, my Algonquin !
  " When I think of my beloved,
Ah me ! think of my beloved,
When my heart is thinking of him,
O my sweetheart, my Algonquin ! "
  Such was Hiawatha's Wedding,
Such the dance of Pau-Puk-Keewis,
Such the story of Iagoo,
Such the songs of Chibiabos ;
Thus the wedding banquet ended,
And the wedding guests departed,
Leaving Hiawatha happy
With the night and Minnehaha.

XIII

BLESSING THE CORNFIELDS

SING, O Song of Hiawatha,
Of the happy days that followed,
In the land of the Ojibways,
In the pleasant land and peaceful !
Sing the mysteries of Mondamin,
Sing the Blessing of the Cornfields !
  Buried was the bloody hatchet,

Buried was the dreadful war-club,
Buried were all warlike weapons,
And the war-cry was forgotten.
There was peace among the nations ;
Unmolested roved the hunters,
Built the birch canoe for sailing,
Caught the fish in lake and river,
Shot the deer and trapped the beaver ;
Unmolested worked the women,
Made their sugar from the maple,
Gathered wild rice in the meadows,
Dressed the skins of deer and beaver.
  All around the happy village
Stood the maize-fields, green and shining,
Waved the green plumes of Mondamin,
Waved his soft and sunny tresses,
Filling all the land with plenty.
'T was the women who in Spring-time
Planted the broad fields and fruitful,
Buried in the earth Mondamin ;
'T was the women who in Autumn
Stripped the yellow husks of harvest,
Stripped the garments from Mondamin,
Even as Hiawatha taught them.
  Once, when all the maize was planted,
Hiawatha, wise and thoughtful,
Spake and said to Minnehaha,
To his wife, the Laughing Water :
" You shall bless to-night the cornfields,
Draw a magic circle round them,
To protect them from destruction,
Blast of mildew, blight of insect,
Wagemin, the thief of cornfields,
Paimosaid, who steals the maize-ear !
  " In the night, when all is silence,
In the night, when all is darkness,
When the Spirit of Sleep, Nepahwin,
Shuts the doors of all the wigwams,
So that not an ear can hear you,
So that not an eye can see you,
Rise up from your bed in silence,
Lay aside your garments wholly,
Walk around the fields you planted,
Round the borders of the cornfields,
Covered by your tresses only,
Robed with darkness as a garment.
  " Thus the fields shall be more fruitful,
And the passing of your footsteps
Draw a magic circle round them,
So that neither blight nor mildew,
Neither burrowing worm nor insect,
Shall pass o'er the magic circle ;
Not the dragon-fly, Kwo-ne-she,
Nor the spider, Subbekashe,
Nor the grasshopper, Pah-puk-keena,

Nor the mighty caterpillar,
Way-muk-kwana, with the bear-skin,
King of all the caterpillars ! "
   On the tree-tops near the cornfields
Sat the hungry crows and ravens,
Kahgahgee, the King of Ravens,
With his band of black marauders.
And they laughed at Hiawatha,
Till the tree-tops shook with laughter,
With their melancholy laughter,
At the words of Hiawatha.
" Hear him ! " said they ; " hear the Wise
   Man,
Hear the plots of Hiawatha ! "
   When the noiseless night descended
Broad and dark o'er field and forest,
When the mournful Wawonaissa
Sorrowing sang among the hemlocks,
And the Spirit of Sleep, Nepahwin,
Shut the doors of all the wigwams,
From her bed rose Laughing Water,
Laid aside her garments wholly,
And with darkness clothed and guarded,
Unashamed and unaffrighted,
Walked securely round the cornfields,
Drew the sacred, magic circle
Of her footprints round the cornfields.
   No one but the Midnight only
Saw her beauty in the darkness,
No one but the Wawonaissa
Heard the panting of her bosom ;
Guskewau, the darkness, wrapped her
Closely in his sacred mantle,
So that none might see her beauty,
So that none might boast, " I saw her ! "
   On the morrow, as the day dawned,
Kahgahgee, the King of Ravens,
Gathered all his black marauders,
Crows and blackbirds, jays and ravens,
Clamorous on the dusky tree-tops,
And descended, fast and fearless,
On the fields of Hiawatha,
On the grave of the Mondamin.
   " We will drag Mondamin," said they,
" From the grave where he is buried,
Spite of all the magic circles
Laughing Water draws around it,
Spite of all the sacred footprints
Minnehaha stamps upon it ! "
   But the wary Hiawatha,
Ever thoughtful, careful, watchful,
Had o'erheard the scornful laughter
When they mocked him from the tree-tops.
" Kaw ! " he said, " my friends the ravens !
Kahgahgee, my King of Ravens !

I will teach you all a lesson
That shall not be soon forgotten ! "
   He had risen before the daybreak,
He had spread o'er all the cornfields
Snares to catch the black marauders,
And was lying now in ambush
In the neighboring grove of pine-trees,
Waiting for the crows and blackbirds,
Waiting for the jays and ravens.
   Soon they came with caw and clamor,
Rush of wings and cry of voices,
To their work of devastation,
Settling down upon the cornfields,
Delving deep with beak and talon,
For the body of Mondamin.
And with all their craft and cunning,
All their skill in wiles of warfare,
They perceived no danger near them,
Till their claws became entangled,
Till they found themselves imprisoned
In the snares of Hiawatha.
   From his place of ambush came he,
Striding terrible among them,
And so awful was his aspect
That the bravest quailed with terror.
Without mercy he destroyed them
Right and left, by tens and twenties,
And their wretched, lifeless bodies
Hung aloft on poles for scarecrows
Round the consecrated cornfields,
As a signal of his vengeance,
As a warning to marauders.
   Only Kahgahgee, the leader,
Kahgahgee, the King of Ravens,
He alone was spared among them
As a hostage for his people.
With his prisoner-string he bound him,
Led him captive to his wigwam,
Tied him fast with cords of elm-bark
To the ridge-pole of his wigwam.
   " Kahgahgee, my raven ! " said he,
" You the leader of the robbers,
You the plotter of this mischief,
The contriver of this outrage,
I will keep you, I will hold you,
As a hostage for your people,
As a pledge of good behavior ! "
   And he left him, grim and sulky,
Sitting in the morning sunshine
On the summit of the wigwam,
Croaking fiercely his displeasure,
Flapping his great sable pinions,
Vainly struggling for his freedom,
Vainly calling on his people !
   Summer passed, and Shawondasee

Breathed his sighs o'er all the landscape,
From the South-land sent his ardors,
Wafted kisses warm and tender ;
And the maize-field grew and ripened,
Till it stood in all the splendor
Of its garments green and yellow,
Of its tassels and its plumage,
And the maize-ears full and shining
Gleamed from bursting sheaths of verdure.

Then Nokomis, the old woman,
Spake, and said to Minnehaha :
"'T is the Moon when leaves are falling ;
All the wild rice has been gathered,
And the maize is ripe and ready ;
Let us gather in the harvest,
Let us wrestle with Mondamin,
Strip him of his plumes and tassels,
Of his garments green and yellow ! "

And the merry Laughing Water
Went rejoicing from the wigwam,
With Nokomis, old and wrinkled,
And they called the women round them,
Called the young men and the maidens,
To the harvest of the cornfields,
To the husking of the maize-ear.

On the border of the forest,
Underneath the fragrant pine-trees,
Sat the old men and the warriors
Smoking in the pleasant shadow.
In uninterrupted silence
Looked they at the gamesome labor
Of the young men and the women ;
Listened to their noisy talking,
To their laughter and their singing,
Heard them chattering like the magpies,
Heard them laughing like the blue-jays,
Heard them singing like the robins.

And whene'er some lucky maiden
Found a red ear in the husking,
Found a maize-ear red as blood is,
"Nushka ! " cried they all together,
"Nushka ! you shall have a sweetheart,
You shall have a handsome husband ! "
"Ugh ! " the old men all responded
From their seats beneath the pine-trees.

And whene'er a youth or maiden
Found a crooked ear in husking,
Found a maize-ear in the husking
Blighted, mildewed, or misshapen,
Then they laughed and sang together,
Crept and limped about the cornfields,
Mimicked in their gait and gestures
Some old man, bent almost double,
Singing singly or together :
"Wagemin, the thief of cornfields !

Paimosaid, who steals the maize-ear ! "
Till the cornfields rang with laughter,
Till from Hiawatha's wigwam
Kahgahgee, the King of Ravens,
Screamed and quivered in his anger,
And from all the neighboring tree-tops
Cawed and croaked the black marauders.
"Ugh ! " the old men all responded,
From their seats beneath the pine-trees !

XIV

PICTURE-WRITING

In those days said Hiawatha,
"Lo ! how all things fade and perish !
From the memory of the old men
Pass away the great traditions,
The achievements of the warriors,
The adventures of the hunters,
All the wisdom of the Medas,
All the craft of the Wabenos,
All the marvellous dreams and visions
Of the Jossakeeds, the Prophets !

"Great men die and are forgotten,
Wise men speak ; their words of wisdom
Perish in the ears that hear them,
Do not reach the generations
That, as yet unborn, are waiting
In the great, mysterious darkness
Of the speechless days that shall be !

"On the grave-posts of our fathers
Are no signs, no figures painted ;
Who are in those graves we know not,
Only know they are our fathers.
Of what kith they are and kindred,
From what old, ancestral Totem,
Be it Eagle, Bear, or Beaver,
They descended, this we know not,
Only know they are our fathers.

"Face to face we speak together,
But we cannot speak when absent,
Cannot send our voices from us
To the friends that dwell afar off ;
Cannot send a secret message,
But the bearer learns our secret,
May pervert it, may betray it,
May reveal it unto others."

Thus said Hiawatha, walking
In the solitary forest,
Pondering, musing in the forest,
On the welfare of his people.

From his pouch he took his colors,
Took his paints of different colors,

On the smooth bark of a birch-tree
Painted many shapes and figures,
Wonderful and mystic figures,
And each figure had a meaning,
Each some word or thought suggested.
    Gitche Manito the Mighty,
He, the Master of Life, was painted
As an egg, with points projecting
To the four winds of the heavens.
Everywhere is the Great Spirit,
Was the meaning of this symbol.
    Mitche Manito the Mighty,
He the dreadful Spirit of Evil,
As a serpent was depicted,
As Kenabeek, the great serpent.
Very crafty, very cunning,
Is the creeping Spirit of Evil,
Was the meaning of this symbol.
    Life and Death he drew as circles,
Life was white, but Death was darkened ;
Sun and moon and stars he painted,
Man and beast, and fish and reptile,
Forests, mountains, lakes, and rivers.
    For the earth he drew a straight line,
For the sky a bow above it ;
White the space between for daytime,
Filled with little stars for night-time ;
On the left a point for sunrise,
On the right a point for sunset,
On the top a point for noontide,
And for rain and cloudy weather
Waving lines descending from it.
    Footprints pointing towards a wigwam
Were a sign of invitation,
Were a sign of guests assembling ;
Bloody hands with palms uplifted
Were a symbol of destruction,
Were a hostile sign and symbol.
    All these things did Hiawatha
Show unto his wondering people,
And interpreted their meaning,
And he said : " Behold, your grave-posts
Have no mark, no sign, nor symbol,
Go and paint them all with figures ;
Each one with its household symbol,
With its own ancestral Totem ;
So that those who follow after
May distinguish them and know them."
    And they painted on the grave-posts
On the graves yet unforgotten,
Each his own ancestral Totem,
Each the symbol of his household ;
Figures of the Bear and Reindeer,
Of the Turtle, Crane, and Beaver,
Each inverted as a token

That the owner was departed,
That the chief who bore the symbol
Lay beneath in dust and ashes.
    And the Jossakeeds, the Prophets,
The Wabenos, the Magicians,
And the Medicine-men, the Medas,
Painted upon bark and deer-skin
Figures for the songs they chanted,
For each song a separate symbol,
Figures mystical and awful,
Figures strange and brightly colored ;
And each figure had its meaning,
Each some magic song suggested.
    The Great Spirit, the Creator,
Flashing light through all the heaven ;
The Great Serpent, the Kenabeek,
With his bloody crest erected,
Creeping, looking into heaven ;
In the sky the sun, that listens,
And the moon eclipsed and dying ;
Owl and eagle, crane and hen-hawk,
And the cormorant, bird of magic ;
Headless men, that walk the heavens,
Bodies lying pierced with arrows,
Bloody hands of death uplifted,
Flags on graves, and great war-captains
Grasping both the earth and heaven !
    Such as these the shapes they painted
On the birch-bark and the deer-skin ;
Songs of war and songs of hunting,
Songs of medicine and of magic,
All were written in these figures,
For each figure had its meaning,
Each its separate song recorded.
    Nor forgotten was the Love-Song,
The most subtle of all medicines,
The most potent spell of magic,
Dangerous more than war or hunting !
Thus the Love-Song was recorded,
Symbol and interpretation.
    First a human figure standing,
Painted in the brightest scarlet ;
'T is the lover, the musician,
And the meaning is, " My painting
Makes me powerful over others."
    Then the figure seated, singing,
Playing on a drum of magic,
And the interpretation, " Listen !
'T is my voice you hear, my singing !'
    Then the same red figure seated
In the shelter of a wigwam,
And the meaning of the symbol,
" I will come and sit beside you
In the mystery of my passion ! "
    Then two figures, man and woman,

Standing hand in hand together
With their hands so clasped together
That they seemed in one united,
And the words thus represented
Are, " I see your heart within you,
And your cheeks are red with blushes ! "
    Next the maiden on an island,
In the centre of an island ;
And the song this shape suggested
Was, " Though you were at a distance,
Were upon some far-off island,
Such the spell I cast upon you,
Such the magic power of passion,
I could straightway draw you to me ! "
    Then the figure of the maiden
Sleeping, and the lover near her,
Whispering to her in her slumbers,
Saying, " Though you were far from me
In the land of Sleep and Silence,
Still the voice of love would reach you ! "
    And the last of all the figures
Was a heart within a circle,
Drawn within a magic circle ;
And the image had this meaning :
" Naked lies your heart before me,
To your naked heart I whisper ! "
    Thus it was that Hiawatha,
In his wisdom, taught the people
All the mysteries of painting,
All the art of Picture-Writing,
On the smooth bark of the birch-tree,
On the white skin of the reindeer,
On the grave-posts of the village.

XV

HIAWATHA'S LAMENTATION

In those days the Evil Spirits,
All the Manitos of mischief,
Fearing Hiawatha's wisdom,
And his love for Chibiabos,
Jealous of their faithful friendship,
And their noble words and actions,
Made at length a league against them,
To molest them and destroy them.
    Hiawatha, wise and wary,
Often said to Chibiabos,
" O my brother ! do not leave me,
Lest the Evil Spirits harm you ! "
Chibiabos, young and heedless,
Laughing shook his coal-black tresses,
Answered ever sweet and childlike,

" Do not fear for me, O brother !
Harm and evil come not near me ! "
    Once when Peboan, the Winter,
Roofed with ice the Big-Sea-Water,
When the snow-flakes, whirling downward,
Hissed among the withered oak-leaves,
Changed the pine-trees into wigwams,
Covered all the earth with silence, —
Armed with arrows, shod with snow-shoes,
Heeding not his brother's warning,
Fearing not the Evil Spirits,
Forth to hunt the deer with antlers
All alone went Chibiabos.
    Right across the Big-Sea-Water
Sprang with speed the deer before him.
With the wind and snow he followed,
O'er the treacherous ice he followed,
Wild with all the fierce commotion
And the rapture of the hunting.
    But beneath, the Evil Spirits
Lay in ambush, waiting for him,
Broke the treacherous ice beneath him,
Dragged him downward to the bottom,
Buried in the sand his body.
Unktahee, the god of water,
He the god of the Dacotahs,
Drowned him in the deep abysses
Of the lake of Gitche Gumee.
    From the headlands Hiawatha
Sent forth such a wail of anguish,
Such a fearful lamentation,
That the bison paused to listen,
And the wolves howled from the prairies,
And the thunder in the distance
Starting answered " Baim-wawa ! "
    Then his face with black he painted,
With his robe his head he covered,
In his wigwam sat lamenting,
Seven long weeks he sat lamenting,
Uttering still this moan of sorrow : —
    " He is dead, the sweet musician !
He the sweetest of all singers !
He has gone from us forever,
He has moved a little nearer
To the Master of all music,
To the Master of all singing !
O my brother, Chibiabos ! "
    And the melancholy fir-trees
Waved their dark green fans above him,
Waved their purple cones above him,
Sighing with him to console him,
Mingling with his lamentation
Their complaining, their lamenting.
    Came the Spring, and all the forest
Looked in vain for Chibiabos ;

Sighed the rivulet, Sebowisha,
Sighed the rushes in the meadow.
From the tree-tops sang the bluebird,
Sang the bluebird, the Owaissa,
"Chibiabos! Chibiabos!
He is dead, the sweet musician!"
From the wigwam sang the robin,
Sang the robin, the Opechee,
"Chibiabos! Chibiabos!
He is dead, the sweetest singer!"
And at night through all the forest
Went the whippoorwill complaining,
Wailing went the Wawonaissa,
"Chibiabos! Chibiabos!
He is dead, the sweet musician!
He the sweetest of all singers!"
Then the Medicine-men, the Medas,
The magicians, the Wabenos,
And the Jossakeeds, the Prophets,
Came to visit Hiawatha;
Built a Sacred Lodge beside him,
To appease him, to console him,
Walked in silent, grave procession,
Bearing each a pouch of healing,
Skin of beaver, lynx, or otter,
Filled with magic roots and simples,
Filled with very potent medicines.
When he heard their steps approaching,
Hiawatha ceased lamenting,
Called no more on Chibiabos;
Naught he questioned, naught he answered,
But his mournful head uncovered,
From his face the mourning colors
Washed he slowly and in silence,
Slowly and in silence followed
Onward to the Sacred Wigwam.
There a magic drink they gave him,
Made of Nahma-wusk, the spearmint,
And Wabeno-wusk, the yarrow,
Roots of power, and herbs of healing;
Beat their drums, and shook their rattles;
Chanted singly and in chorus,
Mystic songs like these, they chanted.
"I myself, myself! behold me!
'T is the great Gray Eagle talking;
Come, ye white crows, come and hear him!
The loud-speaking thunder helps me;
All the unseen spirits help me;
I can hear their voices calling,
All around the sky I hear them!
I can blow you strong, my brother,
I can heal you, Hiawatha!"
"Hi-au-ha!" replied the chorus,
"Way-ha-way!" the mystic chorus.
"Friends of mine are all the serpents!

Hear me shake my skin of hen-hawk!
Mahng, the white loon, I can kill him;
I can shoot your heart and kill it!
I can blow you strong, my brother,
I can heal you, Hiawatha!"
"Hi-au-ha!" replied the chorus.
"Way-ha-way!" the mystic chorus.
"I myself, myself! the prophet!
When I speak the wigwam trembles,
Shakes the Sacred Lodge with terror,
Hands unseen begin to shake it!
When I walk, the sky I tread on
Bends and makes a noise beneath me!
I can blow you strong, my brother!
Rise and speak, O Hiawatha!"
"Hi-au-ha!" replied the chorus,
"Way-ha-way!" the mystic chorus.
Then they shook their medicine-pouches
O'er the head of Hiawatha,
Danced their medicine-dance around him;
And upstarting wild and haggard,
Like a man from dreams awakened,
He was healed of all his madness,
As the clouds are swept from heaven,
Straightway from his brain departed
All his moody melancholy;
As the ice is swept from rivers,
Straightway from his heart departed
All his sorrow and affliction.
Then they summoned Chibiabos
From his grave beneath the waters,
From the sands of Gitche Gumee
Summoned Hiawatha's brother.
And so mighty was the magic
Of that cry and invocation,
That he heard it as he lay there
Underneath the Big-Sea-Water;
From the sand he rose and listened,
Heard the music and the singing,
Came, obedient to the summons,
To the doorway of the wigwam,
But to enter they forbade him.
Through a chink a coal they gave him,
Through the door a burning fire-brand;
Ruler in the Land of Spirits,
Ruler o'er the dead, they made him,
Telling him a fire to kindle
For all those that died thereafter,
Camp-fires for their night encampments
On their solitary journey
To the kingdom of Ponemah,
To the land of the Hereafter.
From the village of his childhood,
From the homes of those who knew him,
Passing silent through the forest,

Like a smoke-wreath wafted sideways,
Slowly vanished Chibiabos !
Where he passed, the branches moved not,
Where he trod, the grasses bent not,
And the fallen leaves of last year
Made no sound beneath his footsteps.

Four whole days he journeyed onward
Down the pathway of the dead men ;
On the dead-man's strawberry feasted,
Crossed the melancholy river,
On the swinging log he crossed it,
Came unto the Lake of Silver,
In the Stone Canoe was carried
To the Islands of the Blessed,
To the land of ghosts and shadows.

On that journey, moving slowly,
Many weary spirits saw he,
Panting under heavy burdens,
Laden with war-clubs, bows and arrows,
Robes of fur, and pots and kettles,
And with food that friends had given
For that solitary journey.

" Ay ! why do the living," said they,
" Lay such heavy burdens on us !
Better were it to go naked,
Better were it to go fasting,
Than to bear such heavy burdens
On our long and weary journey ! "

Forth then issued Hiawatha,
Wandered eastward, wandered westward,
Teaching men the use of simples
And the antidotes for poisons,
And the cure of all diseases.
Thus was first made known to mortals
All the mystery of Medamin,
All the sacred art of healing.

XVI

PAU-PUK-KEEWIS

YOU shall hear how Pau-Puk-Keewis,
He, the handsome Yenadizze,
Whom the people called the Storm-Fool,
Vexed the village with disturbance;
You shall hear of all his mischief,
And his flight from Hiawatha,
And his wondrous transmigrations,
And the end of his adventures.

On the shores of Gitche Gumee,
On the dunes of Nagow Wudjoo,
By the shining Big-Sea-Water
Stood the lodge of Pau-Puk-Keewis.
It was he who in his frenzy

Whirled these drifting sands together,
On the dunes of Nagow Wudjoo,
When, among the guests assembled,
He so merrily and madly
Danced at Hiawatha's wedding,
Danced the Beggar's Dance to please
    them.

Now, in search of new adventures,
From his lodge went Pau-Puk-Keewis,
Came with speed into the village,
Found the young men all assembled
In the lodge of old Iagoo,
Listening to his monstrous stories,
To his wonderful adventures.

He was telling them the story
Of Ojeeg, the Summer-Maker,
How he made a hole in heaven,
How he climbed up into heaven,
And let out the summer-weather,
The perpetual, pleasant Summer ;
How the Otter first essayed it ;
How the Beaver, Lynx, and Badger
Tried in turn the great achievement,
From the summit of the mountain
Smote their fists against the heavens,
Smote against the sky their foreheads,
Cracked the sky, but could not break it ;
How the Wolverine, uprising,
Made him ready for the encounter,
Bent his knees down, like a squirrel,
Drew his arms back, like a cricket.

" Once he leaped," said old Iagoo,
" Once he leaped, and lo ! above him
Bent the sky, as ice in rivers
When the waters rise beneath it ;
Twice he leaped, and lo ! above him
Cracked the sky, as ice in rivers
When the freshet is at highest !
Thrice he leaped, and lo ! above him
Broke the shattered sky asunder,
And he disappeared within it,
And Ojeeg, the Fisher Weasel,
With a bound went in behind him ! "

" Hark you ! " shouted Pau-Puk-Keewis
As he entered at the doorway ;
" I am tired of all this talking,
Tired of old Iagoo's stories,
Tired of Hiawatha's wisdom.
Here is something to amuse you,
Better than this endless talking."

Then from out his pouch of wolf-skin
Forth he drew, with solemn manner,
All the game of Bowl and Counters,
Pugasaing, with thirteen pieces.
White on one side were they painted,

And vermilion on the other ;
Two Kenabeeks or great serpents,
Two Ininewug or wedge-men,
One great war-club, Pugamaugun,
And one slender fish, the Keego,
Four round pieces, Ozawabeeks,
And three Sheshebwug or ducklings.
All were made of bone and painted,
All except the Ozawabeeks ;
These were brass, on one side burnished,
And were black upon the other.
    In a wooden bowl he placed them,
Shook and jostled them together,
Threw them on the ground before him,
Thus exclaiming and explaining :
" Red side up are all the pieces,
And one great Kenabeek standing
On the bright side of a brass piece,
On a burnished Ozawabeek ;
Thirteen tens and eight are counted."
    Then again he shook the pieces,
Shook and jostled them together,
Threw them on the ground before him,
Still exclaiming and explaining :
" White are both the great Kenabeeks,
White the Ininewug, the wedge-men,
Red are all the other pieces ;
Five tens and an eight are counted."
    Thus he taught the game of hazard,
Thus displayed it and explained it,
Running through its various chances,
Various changes, various meanings :
Twenty curious eyes stared at him,
Full of eagerness stared at him.
    " Many games," said old Iagoo,
" Many games of skill and hazard
Have I seen in different nations,
Have I played in different countries.
He who plays with old Iagoo
Must have very nimble fingers ;
Though you think yourself so skilful,
I can beat you, Pau-Puk-Keewis,
I can even give you lessons
In your game of Bowl and Counters ! "
    So they sat and played together,
All the old men and the young men,
Played for dresses, weapons, wampum,
Played till midnight, played till morning,
Played until the Yenadizze,
Till the cunning Pau-Puk-Keewis,
Of their treasures had despoiled them,
Of the best of all their dresses,
Shirts of deer-skin, robes of ermine,
Belts of wampum, crests of feathers,
Warlike weapons, pipes and pouches.

Twenty eyes glared wildly at him,
Like the eyes of wolves glared at him.
    Said the lucky Pau-Puk-Keewis :
" In my wigwam I am lonely,
In my wanderings and adventures
I have need of a companion,
Fain would have a Meshinauwa,
An attendant and pipe-bearer.
I will venture all these winnings,
All these garments heaped about me,
All this wampum, all these feathers,
On a single throw will venture
All against the young man yonder ! "
'T was a youth of sixteen summers,
'T was a nephew of Iagoo ;
Face-in-a-Mist, the people called him.
    As the fire burns in a pipe-head
Dusky red beneath the ashes,
So beneath his shaggy eyebrows
Glowed the eyes of old Iagoo.
" Ugh ! " he answered very fiercely ;
" Ugh ! " they answered all and each one.
    Seized the wooden bowl the old man,
Closely in his bony fingers
Clutched the fatal bowl, Onagon,
Shook it fiercely and with fury,
Made the pieces ring together
As he threw them down before him.
    Red were both the great Kenabeeks,
Red the Ininewug, the wedge-men,
Red the Sheshebwug, the ducklings,
Black the four brass Ozawabeeks,
White alone the fish, the Keego ;
Only five the pieces counted !
    Then the smiling Pau-Puk-Keewis
Shook the bowl and threw the pieces ;
Lightly in the air he tossed them,
And they fell about him scattered ;
Dark and bright the Ozawabeeks,
Red and white the other pieces,
And upright among the others
One Ininewug was standing,
Even as crafty Pau-Puk-Keewis
Stood alone among the players,
Saying, " Five tens ! mine the game is ! "
    Twenty eyes glared at him fiercely,
Like the eyes of wolves glared at him,
As he turned and left the wigwam,
Followed by his Meshinauwa,
By the nephew of Iagoo,
By the tall and graceful stripling,
Bearing in his arms the winnings,
Shirts of deer-skin, robes of ermine,
Belts of wampum, pipes and weapons.
    " Carry them," said Pau-Puk-Keewis,

Pointing with his fan of feathers,
"To my wigwam far to eastward,
On the dunes of Nagow Wudjoo!"
    Hot and red with smoke and gambling
Were the eyes of Pau-Puk-Keewis
As he came forth to the freshness
Of the pleasant Summer morning.
All the birds were singing gayly,
All the streamlets flowing swiftly,
And the heart of Pau-Puk-Keewis
Sang with pleasure as the birds sing,
Beat with triumph like the streamlets,
As he wandered through the village,
In the early gray of morning,
With his fan of turkey-feathers,
With his plumes and tufts of swan's down,
Till he reached the farthest wigwam,
Reached the lodge of Hiawatha.
    Silent was it and deserted;
No one met him at the doorway,
No one came to bid him welcome;
But the birds were singing round it,
In and out and round the doorway,
Hopping, singing, fluttering, feeding,
And aloft upon the ridge-pole
Kahgahgee, the King of Ravens,
Sat with fiery eyes, and, screaming,
Flapped his wings at Pau-Puk-Keewis.
    "All are gone! the lodge is empty!"
Thus it was spake Pau-Puk-Keewis,
In his heart resolving mischief;—
"Gone is wary Hiawatha,
Gone the silly Laughing Water,
Gone Nokomis, the old woman,
And the lodge is left unguarded!"
    By the neck he seized the raven,
Whirled it round him like a rattle,
Like a medicine-pouch he shook it,
Strangled Kahgahgee, the raven,
From the ridge-pole of the wigwam
Left its lifeless body hanging,
As an insult to its master,
As a taunt to Hiawatha.
    With a stealthy step he entered,
Round the lodge in wild disorder
Threw the household things about him,
Piled together in confusion
Bowls of wood and earthen kettles,
Robes of buffalo and beaver,
Skins of otter, lynx, and ermine,
As an insult to Nokomis,
As a taunt to Minnehaha.
    Then departed Pau-Puk-Keewis,
Whistling, singing through the forest,
Whistling gayly to the squirrels,

Who from hollow boughs above him
Dropped their acorn-shells upon him,
Singing gayly to the wood birds,
Who from out the leafy darkness
Answered with a song as merry.
    Then he climbed the rocky headlands,
Looking o'er the Gitche Gumee,
Perched himself upon their summit,
Waiting full of mirth and mischief
The return of Hiawatha.
    Stretched upon his back he lay there;
Far below him plashed the waters,
Plashed and washed the dreamy waters;
Far above him swam the heavens,
Swam the dizzy, dreamy heavens;
Round him hovered, fluttered, rustled
Hiawatha's mountain chickens,
Flock-wise swept and wheeled about him,
Almost brushed him with their pinions.
    And he killed them as he lay there,
Slaughtered them by tens and twenties,
Threw their bodies down the headland,
Threw them on the beach below him,
Till at length Kayoshk, the sea-gull,
Perched upon a crag above them,
Shouted: "It is Pau-Puk-Keewis!
He is slaying us by hundreds!
Send a message to our brother,
Tidings send to Hiawatha!"

XVII

THE HUNTING OF PAU-PUK-KEEWIS

FULL of wrath was Hiawatha
When he came into the village,
Found the people in confusion,
Heard of all the misdemeanors,
All the malice and the mischief,
Of the cunning Pau-Puk-Keewis.
    Hard his breath came through his nostrils,
Through his teeth he buzzed and muttered
Words of anger and resentment,
Hot and humming, like a hornet.
"I will slay this Pau-Puk-Keewis,
Slay this mischief-maker!" said he.
"Not so long and wide the world is,
Not so rude and rough the way is,
That my wrath shall not attain him,
That my vengeance shall not reach him!"
    Then in swift pursuit departed
Hiawatha and the hunters
On the trail of Pau-Puk-Keewis,

Through the forest, where he passed it,
To the headlands where he rested ;
But they found not Pau-Puk-Keewis,
Only in the trampled grasses,
In the whortleberry-bushes,
Found the couch where he had rested,
Found the impress of his body.

From the lowlands far beneath them,
From the Muskoday, the meadow,
Pau-Puk-Keewis, turning backward,
Made a gesture of defiance,
Made a gesture of derision ;
And aloud cried Hiawatha,
From the summit of the mountains :
"Not so long and wide the world is,
Not so rude and rough the way is,
But my wrath shall overtake you,
And my vengeance shall attain you !"

Over rock and over river,
Thorough bush, and brake, and forest,
Ran the cunning Pau-Puk-Keewis ;
Like an antelope he bounded,
Till he came unto a streamlet
In the middle of the forest,
To a streamlet still and tranquil,
That had overflowed its margin,
To a dam made by the beavers,
To a pond of quiet water,
Where knee-deep the trees were standing,
Where the water-lilies floated,
Where the rushes waved and whispered.

On the dam stood Pau-Puk-Keewis,
On the dam of trunks and branches,
Through whose chinks the water spouted,
O'er whose summit flowed the streamlet.
From the bottom rose the beaver,
Looked with two great eyes of wonder,
Eyes that seemed to ask a question,
At the stranger, Pau-Puk-Keewis.

On the dam stood Pau-Puk-Keewis,
O'er his ankles flowed the streamlet,
Flowed the bright and silvery water,
And he spake unto the beaver,
With a smile he spake in this wise :
"O my friend Ahmeek, the beaver,
Cool and pleasant is the water ;
Let me dive into the water,
Let me rest there in your lodges ;
Change me, too, into a beaver !"

Cautiously replied the beaver,
With reserve he thus made answer :
"Let me first consult the others,
Let me ask the other beavers."
Down he sank into the water,
Heavily sank he, as a stone sinks,

Down among the leaves and branches,
Brown and matted at the bottom.

On the dam stood Pau-Puk-Keewis,
O'er his ankles flowed the streamlet,
Spouted through the chinks below him,
Dashed upon the stones beneath him,
Spread serene and calm before him,
And the sunshine and the shadows
Fell in flecks and gleams upon him,
Fell in little shining patches,
Through the waving, rustling branches

From the bottom rose the beavers,
Silently above the surface
Rose one head and then another,
Till the pond seemed full of beavers,
Full of black and shining faces.

To the beavers Pau-Puk-Keewis
Spake entreating, said in this wise :
"Very pleasant is your dwelling,
O my friends ! and safe from danger ;
Can you not, with all your cunning,
All your wisdom and contrivance,
Change me, too, into a beaver ?"

"Yes !" replied Ahmeek, the beaver,
He the King of all the beavers,
"Let yourself slide down among us,
Down into the tranquil water."

Down into the pond among them
Silently sank Pau-Puk-Keewis ;
Black became his shirt of deer-skin,
Black his moccasins and leggings,
In a broad black tail behind him
Spread his fox-tails and his fringes ;
He was changed into a beaver.

"Make me large," said Pau-Puk-Keewis,
"Make me large and make me larger,
Larger than the other beavers."
"Yes," the beaver chief responded,
"When our lodge below you enter,
In our wigwam we will make you
Ten times larger than the others."

Thus into the clear, brown water
Silently sank Pau-Puk-Keewis :
Found the bottom covered over
With the trunks of trees and branches,
Hoards of food against the winter,
Piles and heaps against the famine ;
Found the lodge with arching doorway,
Leading into spacious chambers.

Here they made him large and larger,
Made him largest of the beavers,
Ten times larger than the others.
"You shall be our ruler," said they ;
"Chief and King of all the beavers."
But not long had Pau-Puk-Keewis

Sat in state among the beavers,
When there came a voice of warning
From the watchman at his station
In the water-flags and lilies,
Saying, "Here is Hiawatha!
Hiawatha with his hunters!"
　　Then they heard a cry above them,
Heard a shouting and a tramping,
Heard a crashing and a rushing,
And the water round and o'er them
Sank and sucked away in eddies,
And they knew their dam was broken.
　　On the lodge's roof the hunters
Leaped, and broke it all asunder;
Streamed the sunshine through the crevice,
Sprang the beavers through the doorway,
Hid themselves in deeper water,
In the channel of the streamlet;
But the mighty Pau-Puk-Keewis
Could not pass beneath the doorway;
He was puffed with pride and feeding,
He was swollen like a bladder.
　　Through the roof looked Hiawatha,
Cried aloud, "O Pau-Puk-Keewis!
Vain are all your craft and cunning,
Vain your manifold disguises!
Well I know you, Pau-Puk-Keewis!"
With their clubs they beat and bruised
　　him,
Beat to death poor Pau-Puk-Keewis,
Pounded him as maize is pounded,
Till his skull was crushed to pieces.
　　Six tall hunters, lithe and limber,
Bore him home on poles and branches,
Bore the body of the beaver;
But the ghost, the Jeebi in him,
Thought and felt as Pau-Puk-Keewis,
Still lived on as Pau-Puk-Keewis.
　　And it fluttered, strove, and struggled,
Waving hither, waving thither,
As the curtains of a wigwam
Struggle with their thongs of deer-skin,
When the wintry wind is blowing;
Till it drew itself together,
Till it rose up from the body,
Till it took the form and features
Of the cunning Pau-Puk-Keewis
Vanishing into the forest.
　　But the wary Hiawatha
Saw the figure ere it vanished,
Saw the form of Pau-Puk-Keewis
Glide into the soft blue shadow
Of the pine-trees of the forest;
Toward the squares of white beyond it,
Toward an opening in the forest.

Like a wind it rushed and panted,
Bending all the boughs before it,
And behind it, as the rain comes,
Came the steps of Hiawatha.
　　To a lake with many islands
Came the breathless Pau-Puk-Keewis,
Where among the water-lilies
Pishnekuh, the brant, were sailing;
Through the tufts of rushes floating,
Steering through the reedy islands.
Now their broad black beaks they lifted,
Now they plunged beneath the water,
Now they darkened in the shadow,
Now they brightened in the sunshine.
　　"Pishnekuh!" cried Pau-Puk-Keewis,
"Pishnekuh! my brothers!" said he,
"Change me to a brant with plumage,
With a shining neck and feathers,
Make me large, and make me larger,
Ten times larger than the others."
　　Straightway to a brant they changed him,
With two huge and dusky pinions,
With a bosom smooth and rounded,
With a bill like two great paddles,
Made him larger than the others,
Ten times larger than the largest,
Just as, shouting from the forest,
On the shore stood Hiawatha.
　　Up they rose with cry and clamor,
With a whir and beat of pinions,
Rose up from the reedy islands,
From the water-flags and lilies.
And they said to Pau-Puk-Keewis:
"In your flying, look not downward,
Take good heed and look not downward,
Lest some strange mischance should hap-
　　pen,
Lest some great mishap befall you!"
　　Fast and far they fled to northward,
Fast and far through mist and sunshine,
Fed among the moors and fen-lands,
Slept among the reeds and rushes.
　　On the morrow as they journeyed,
Buoyed and lifted by the South-wind,
Wafted onward by the South-wind,
Blowing fresh and strong behind them,
Rose a sound of human voices,
Rose a clamor from beneath them,
From the lodges of a village,
From the people miles beneath them.
　　For the people of the village
Saw the flock of brant with wonder,
Saw the wings of Pau-Puk-Keewis
Flapping far up in the ether,
Broader than two doorway curtains.

Pau-Puk-Keewis heard the shouting,
Knew the voice of Hiawatha,
Knew the outcry of Iagoo,
And, forgetful of the warning,
Drew his neck in, and looked downward,
And the wind that blew behind him
Caught his mighty fan of feathers,
Sent him wheeling, whirling downward !

All in vain did Pau-Puk-Keewis
Struggle to regain his balance !
Whirling round and round and downward,
He beheld in turn the village
And in turn the flock above him,
Saw the village coming nearer,
And the flock receding farther,
Heard the voices growing louder,
Heard the shouting and the laughter ;
Saw no more the flocks above him,
Only saw the earth beneath him ;
Dead out of the empty heaven,
Dead among the shouting people,
With a heavy sound and sullen,
Fell the brant with broken pinions.

But his soul, his ghost, his shadow,
Still survived as Pau-Puk-Keewis,
Took again the form and features
Of the handsome Yenadizze,
And again went rushing onward,
Followed fast by Hiawatha,
Crying : " Not so wide the world is,
Not so long and rough the way is,
But my wrath shall overtake you,
But my vengeance shall attain you ! "

And so near he came, so near him,
That his hand was stretched to seize him,
His right hand to seize and hold him,
When the cunning Pau-Puk-Keewis
Whirled and spun about in circles,
Fanned the air into a whirlwind,
Danced the dust and leaves about him,
And amid the whirling eddies
Sprang into a hollow oak-tree,
Changed himself into a serpent,
Gliding out through root and rubbish.

With his right hand Hiawatha
Smote amain the hollow oak-tree,
Rent it into shreds and splinters,
Left it lying there in fragments.
But in vain ; for Pau-Puk-Keewis,
Once again in human figure,
Full in sight ran on before him,
Sped away in gust and whirlwind,
On the shores of Gitche Gumee,
Westward by the Big-Sea-Water,
Came unto the rocky headlands,

To the Pictured Rocks of sandstone,
Looking over lake and landscape.

And the Old Man of the Mountain,
He the Manito of Mountains,
Opened wide his rocky doorways,
Opened wide his deep abysses,
Giving Pau-Puk-Keewis shelter
In his caverns dark and dreary,
Bidding Pau-Puk-Keewis welcome
To his gloomy lodge of sandstone.

There without stood Hiawatha,
Found the doorways closed against him,
With his mittens, Minjekahwun,
Smote great caverns in the sandstone,
Cried aloud in tones of thunder,
" Open ! I am Hiawatha ! "
But the Old Man of the Mountain
Opened not, and made no answer
From the silent crags of sandstone,
From the gloomy rock abysses.

Then he raised his hands to heaven,
Called imploring on the tempest,
Called Waywassimo, the lightning,
And the thunder, Annemeekee ;
And they came with night and darkness,
Sweeping down the Big-Sea-Water
From the distant Thunder Mountains ;
And the trembling Pau-Puk-Keewis
Heard the footsteps of the thunder,
Saw the red eyes of the lightning,
Was afraid, and crouched and trembled.

Then Waywassimo, the lightning,
Smote the doorways of the caverns,
With his war-club smote the doorways,
Smote the jutting crags of sandstone,
And the thunder, Annemeekee,
Shouted down into the caverns,
Saying, " Where is Pau-Puk-Keewis ! "
And the crags fell, and beneath them
Dead among the rocky ruins
Lay the cunning Pau-Puk-Keewis,
Lay the handsome Yenadizze,
Slain in his own human figure.

Ended were his wild adventures,
Ended were his tricks and gambols,
Ended all his craft and cunning,
Ended all his mischief-making,
All his gambling and his dancing,
All his wooing of the maidens.

Then the noble Hiawatha
Took his soul, his ghost, his shadow,
Spake and said : " O Pau-Puk-Keewis,
Never more in human figure
Shall you search for new adventures ;
Never more with jest and laughter

Dance the dust and leaves in whirlwinds ;
But above there in the heavens
You shall soar and sail in circles ;
I will change you to an eagle,
To Keneu, the great war-eagle,
Chief of all the fowls with feathers,
Chief of Hiawatha's chickens."
  And the name of Pau-Puk-Keewis
Lingers still among the people,
Lingers still among the singers,
And among the story-tellers ;
And in Winter, when the snow-flakes
Whirl in eddies round the lodges,
When the wind in gusty tumult
O'er the smoke-flue pipes and whistles,
"There," they cry, "comes Pau-Puk-Kee-
    wis ;
He is dancing through the village,
He is gathering in his harvest ! "

XVIII

THE DEATH OF KWASIND

FAR and wide among the nations
Spread the name and fame of Kwasind ;
No man dared to strive with Kwasind,
No man could compete with Kwasind.
But the mischievous Puk-Wudjies,
They the envious Little People,
They the fairies and the pygmies,
Plotted and conspired against him.
  " If this hateful Kwasind," said they,
" If this great, outrageous fellow
Goes on thus a little longer,
Tearing everything he touches,
Rending everything to pieces,
Filling all the world with wonder,
What becomes of the Puk-Wudjies ?
Who will care for the Puk-Wudjies ?
He will tread us down like mushrooms,
Drive us all into the water,
Give our bodies to be eaten
By the wicked Nee-ba-naw-baigs,
By the Spirits of the water ! "
  So the angry Little People
All conspired against the Strong Man,
All conspired to murder Kwasind,
Yes, to rid the world of Kwasind,
The audacious, overbearing,
Heartless, haughty, dangerous Kwasind !
  Now this wondrous strength of Kwasind
In his crown alone was seated ;
In his crown too was his weakness ;

There alone could he be wounded,
Nowhere else could weapon pierce him,
Nowhere else could weapon harm him.
  Even there the only weapon
That could wound him, that could slay him,
Was the seed-cone of the pine-tree,
Was the blue cone of the fir-tree.
This was Kwasind's fatal secret,
Known to no man among mortals ;
But the cunning Little People,
The Puk-Wudjies, knew the secret,
Knew the only way to kill him.
  So they gathered cones together,
Gathered seed-cones of the pine-tree,
Gathered blue cones of the fir-tree,
In the woods by Taquamenaw,
Brought them to the river's margin,
Heaped them in great piles together,
Where the red rocks from the margin
Jutting overhang the river.
There they lay in wait for Kwasind,
The malicious Little People.
  'T was an afternoon in Summer ;
Very hot and still the air was,
Very smooth the gliding river,
Motionless the sleeping shadows :
Insects glistened in the sunshine,
Insects skated on the water,
Filled the drowsy air with buzzing,
With a far resounding war-cry.
  Down the river came the Strong Man,
In his birch canoe came Kwasind,
Floating slowly down the current
Of the sluggish Taquamenaw,
Very languid with the weather,
Very sleepy with the silence.
  From the overhanging branches,
From the tassels of the birch-trees,
Soft the Spirit of Sleep descended ;
By his airy hosts surrounded,
His invisible attendants,
Came the Spirit of Sleep, Nepahwin ;
Like a burnished Dush-kwo-ne-she,
Like a dragon-fly, he hovered
O'er the drowsy head of Kwasind.
  To his ear there came a murmur
As of waves upon a sea-shore,
As of far-off tumbling waters,
As of winds among the pine-trees ;
And he felt upon his forehead
Blows of little airy war-clubs,
Wielded by the slumbrous legions
Of the Spirit of Sleep, Nepahwin,
As of some one breathing on him.
  At the first blow of their war-clubs,

Fell a drowsiness on Kwasind ;
At the second blow they smote him,
Motionless his paddle rested ;
At the third, before his vision
Reeled the landscape into darkness,
Very sound asleep was Kwasind.
  So he floated down the river,
Like a blind man seated upright,
Floated down the Taquamenaw,
Underneath the trembling birch-trees,
Underneath the wooded headlands,
Underneath the war encampment
Of the pygmies, the Puk-Wudjies.
  There they stood, all armed and waiting,
Hurled the pine-cones down upon him,
Struck him on his brawny shoulders,
On his crown defenceless struck him.
"Death to Kwasind ! " was the sudden
War-cry of the Little People.
  And he sideways swayed and tumbled,
Sideways fell into the river,
Plunged beneath the sluggish water
Headlong, as an otter plunges ;
And the birch canoe, abandoned,
Drifted empty down the river,
Bottom upward swerved and drifted :
Nothing more was seen of Kwasind.
  But the memory of the Strong Man
Lingered long among the people,
And whenever through the forest
Raged and roared the wintry tempest,
And the branches, tossed and troubled,
Creaked and groaned and split asunder,
"Kwasind ! " cried they ; " that is Kwasind !
He is gathering in his fire-wood ! "

XIX

THE GHOSTS

NEVER stoops the soaring vulture
On his quarry in the desert,
On the sick or wounded bison,
But another vulture, watching
From his high aerial look-out,
Sees the downward plunge, and follows ;
And a third pursues the second,
Coming from the invisible ether,
First a speck, and then a vulture,
Till the air is dark with pinions.
  So disasters come not singly ;
But as if they watched and waited,
Scanning one another's motions,
When the first descends, the others

Follow, follow, gathering flock-wise
Round their victim, sick and wounded,
First a shadow, then a sorrow,
Till the air is dark with anguish.
  Now, o'er all the dreary North-land,
Mighty Peboan, the Winter,
Breathing on the lakes and rivers,
Into stone had changed their waters.
From his hair he shook the snow-flakes,
Till the plains were strewn with whiteness,
One uninterrupted level,
As if, stooping, the Creator
With his hand had smoothed them over.
  Through the forest, wide and wailing,
Roamed the hunter on his snow-shoes ;
In the village worked the women,
Pounded maize, or dressed the deer-skin ;
And the young men played together
On the ice the noisy ball-play,
On the plain the dance of snow-shoes.
  One dark evening, after sundown,
In her wigwam Laughing Water
Sat with old Nokomis, waiting
For the steps of Hiawatha
Homeward from the hunt returning.
  On their faces gleamed the firelight,
Painting them with streaks of crimson,
In the eyes of old Nokomis
Glimmered like the watery moonlight,
In the eyes of Laughing Water
Glistened like the sun in water ;
And behind them crouched their shadows
In the corners of the wigwam,
And the smoke in wreaths above them
Climbed and crowded through the smoke-
    flue.
  Then the curtain of the doorway
From without was slowly lifted ;
Brighter glowed the fire a moment,
And a moment swerved the smoke-wreath,
As two women entered softly,
Passed the doorway uninvited,
Without word of salutation,
Without sign of recognition,
Sat down in the farthest corner,
Crouching low among the shadows.
  From their aspect and their garments,
Strangers seemed they in the village ;
Very pale and haggard were they,
As they sat there sad and silent,
Trembling, cowering with the shadows.
  Was it the wind above the smoke-flue,
Muttering down into the wigwam ?
Was it the owl, the Koko-koho,
Hooting from the dismal forest ?

Sure a voice said in the silence :
"These are corpses clad in garments,
These are ghosts that come to haunt you,
From the kingdom of Ponemah,
From the land of the Hereafter ! "
    Homeward now came Hiawatha
From his hunting in the forest,
With the snow upon his tresses,
And the red deer on his shoulders.
At the feet of Laughing Water
Down he threw his lifeless burden ;
Nobler, handsomer she thought him,
Than when first he came to woo her,
First threw down the deer before her,
As a token of his wishes,
As a promise of the future.
    Then he turned and saw the strangers,
Cowering, crouching with the shadows ;
Said within himself, "Who are they ?
What strange guests has Minnehaha ? "
But he questioned not the strangers,
Only spake to bid them welcome
To his lodge, his food, his fireside.
    When the evening meal was ready,
And the deer had been divided,
Both the pallid guests, the strangers,
Springing from among the shadows,
Seized upon the choicest portions,
Seized the white fat of the roebuck,
Set apart for Laughing Water,
For the wife of Hiawatha ;
Without asking, without thanking,
Eagerly devoured the morsels,
Flitted back among the shadows
In the corner of the wigwam.
    Not a word spake Hiawatha,
Not a motion made Nokomis,
Not a gesture Laughing Water ;
Not a change came o'er their features ;
Only Minnehaha softly
Whispered, saying, "They are famished ;
Let them do what best delights them ;
Let them eat, for they are famished."
    Many a daylight dawned and darkened,
Many a night shook off the daylight
As the pine shakes off the snow-flakes
From the midnight of its branches ;
Day by day the guests unmoving
Sat there silent in the wigwam ;
But by night, in storm or starlight,
Forth they went into the forest,
Bringing fire-wood to the wigwam,
Bringing pine-cones for the burning,
Always sad and always silent.
    And whenever Hiawatha

Came from fishing or from hunting,
When the evening meal was ready,
And the food had been divided,
Gliding from their darksome corner,
Came the pallid guests, the strangers,
Seized upon the choicest portions
Set aside for Laughing Water,
And without rebuke or question
Flitted back among the shadows.
    Never once had Hiawatha
By a word or look reproved them ;
Never once had old Nokomis
Made a gesture of impatience ;
Never once had Laughing Water
Shown resentment at the outrage.
All had they endured in silence,
That the rights of guest and stranger,
That the virtue of free-giving,
By a look might not be lessened,
By a word might not be broken.
    Once at midnight Hiawatha,
Ever wakeful, ever watchful,
In the wigwam, dimly lighted
By the brands that still were burning,
By the glimmering, flickering firelight,
Heard a sighing, oft repeated,
Heard a sobbing, as of sorrow.
From his couch rose Hiawatha,
From his shaggy hides of bison,
Pushed aside the deer-skin curtain,
Saw the pallid guests, the shadows,
Sitting upright on their couches,
Weeping in the silent midnight.
    And he said : "O guests ! why is it
That your hearts are so afflicted,
That you sob so in the midnight ?
Has perchance the old Nokomis,
Has my wife, my Minnehaha,
Wronged or grieved you by unkindness,
Failed in hospitable duties ? "
    Then the shadows ceased from weeping,
Ceased from sobbing and lamenting,
And they said, with gentle voices :
"We are ghosts of the departed,
Souls of those who once were with you.
From the realms of Chibiabos
Hither have we come to try you,
Hither have we come to warn you.
    "Cries of grief and lamentation
Reach us in the Blessed Islands ;
Cries of anguish from the living,
Calling back their friends departed,
Sadden us with useless sorrow.
Therefore have we come to try you ;
No one knows us, no one heeds us.

We are but a burden to you,
And we see that the departed
Have no place among the living.
  " Think of this, O Hiawatha !
Speak of it to all the people,
That henceforward and forever
They no more with lamentations
Sadden the souls of the departed
In the Islands of the Blessed.
  " Do not lay such heavy burdens
In the graves of those you bury,
Not such weight of furs and wampum,
Not such weight of pots and kettles,
For the spirits faint beneath them.
Only give them food to carry,
Only give them fire to light them.
  " Four days is the spirit's journey
To the land of ghosts and shadows,
Four its lonely night encampments ;
Four times must their fires be lighted.
Therefore, when the dead are buried,
Let a fire, as night approaches,
Four times on the grave be kindled,
That the soul upon its journey
May not lack the cheerful firelight,
May not grope about in darkness.
  " Farewell, noble Hiawatha !
We have put you to the trial,
To the proof have put your patience,
By the insult of our presence,
By the outrage of our actions.
We have found you great and noble.
Fail not in the greater trial,
Faint not in the harder struggle."
  When they ceased, a sudden darkness
Fell and filled the silent wigwam.
Hiawatha heard a rustle
As of garments trailing by him,
Heard the curtain of the doorway
Lifted by a hand he saw not,
Felt the cold breath of the night air,
For a moment saw the starlight ;
But he saw the ghosts no longer,
Saw no more the wandering spirits
From the kingdom of Ponemah,
From the land of the Hereafter.

XX

THE FAMINE

Oh the long and dreary Winter !
Oh the cold and cruel Winter !
Ever thicker, thicker, thicker

Froze the ice on lake and river,
Ever deeper, deeper, deeper
Fell the snow o'er all the landscape,
Fell the covering snow, and drifted
Through the forest, round the village.
  Hardly from his buried wigwam
Could the hunter force a passage ;
With his mittens and his snow-shoes
Vainly walked he through the forest,
Sought for bird or beast and found none,
Saw no track of deer or rabbit,
In the snow beheld no footprints,
In the ghastly, gleaming forest
Fell, and could not rise from weakness,
Perished there from cold and hunger.
  Oh the famine and the fever !
Oh the wasting of the famine !
Oh the blasting of the fever !
Oh the wailing of the children !
Oh the anguish of the women !
  All the earth was sick and famished ;
Hungry was the air around them,
Hungry was the sky above them,
And the hungry stars in heaven
Like the eyes of wolves glared at them !
  Into Hiawatha's wigwam
Came two other guests, as silent
As the ghosts were, and as gloomy,
Waited not to be invited,
Did not parley at the doorway,
Sat there without word of welcome
In the seat of Laughing Water ;
Looked with haggard eyes and hollow
At the face of Laughing Water.
  And the foremost said : " Behold me !
I am Famine, Bukadawin ! "
And the other said : " Behold me !
I am Fever, Ahkosewin ! "
  And the lovely Minnehaha
Shuddered as they looked upon her,
Shuddered at the words they uttered,
Lay down on her bed in silence,
Hid her face, but made no answer ;
Lay there trembling, freezing, burning
At the looks they cast upon her,
At the fearful words they uttered.
  Forth into the empty forest
Rushed the maddened Hiawatha ;
In his heart was deadly sorrow,
In his face a stony firmness ;
On his brow the sweat of anguish
Started, but it froze and fell not.
  Wrapped in furs and armed for hunting,
With his mighty bow of ash-tree,
With his quiver full of arrows,

With his mittens, Minjekahwun,
Into the vast and vacant forest
On his snow-shoes strode he forward.
"Gitche Manito, the Mighty!"
Cried he with his face uplifted
In that bitter hour of anguish,
"Give your children food, O father!
Give us food, or we must perish!
Give me food for Minnehaha,
For my dying Minnehaha!"
Through the far-resounding forest,
Through the forest vast and vacant
Rang that cry of desolation,
But there came no other answer
Than the echo of his crying,
Than the echo of the woodlands,
"Minnehaha! Minnehaha!"
All day long roved Hiawatha
In that melancholy forest,
Through the shadow of whose thickets,
In the pleasant days of Summer,
Of that ne'er forgotten Summer,
He had brought his young wife homeward
From the land of the Dacotahs;
When the birds sang in the thickets,
And the streamlets laughed and glistened,
And the air was full of fragrance,
And the lovely Laughing Water
Said with voice that did not tremble,
"I will follow you, my husband!"
In the wigwam with Nokomis,
With those gloomy guests that watched her,
With the Famine and the Fever,
She was lying, the Beloved,
She, the dying Minnehaha.
"Hark!" she said; "I hear a rushing,
Hear a roaring and a rushing,
Hear the Falls of Minnehaha
Calling to me from a distance!"
"No, my child!" said old Nokomis,
"'T is the night-wind in the pine-trees!"
"Look!" she said; "I see my father
Standing lonely at his doorway,
Beckoning to me from his wigwam
In the land of the Dacotahs!"
"No, my child!" said old Nokomis.
"'T is the smoke, that waves and beck-
ons!"
"Ah!" said she, "the eyes of Pauguk
Glare upon me in the darkness,
I can feel his icy fingers
Clasping mine amid the darkness!
Hiawatha! Hiawatha!"
And the desolate Hiawatha,
Far away amid the forest,

Miles away among the mountains,
Heard that sudden cry of anguish,
Heard the voice of Minnehaha
Calling to him in the darkness,
"Hiawatha! Hiawatha!"
Over snow-fields waste and pathless,
Under snow-encumbered branches,
Homeward hurried Hiawatha,
Empty-handed, heavy-hearted,
Heard Nokomis moaning, wailing:
"Wahonowin! Wahonowin!
Would that I had perished for you,
Would that I were dead as you are!
Wahonowin! Wahonowin!"
And he rushed into the wigwam,
Saw the old Nokomis slowly
Rocking to and fro and moaning,
Saw his lovely Minnehaha
Lying dead and cold before him,
And his bursting heart within him
Uttered such a cry of anguish,
That the forest moaned and shuddered,
That the very stars in heaven
Shook and trembled with his anguish.
Then he sat down, still and speechless,
On the bed of Minnehaha,
At the feet of Laughing Water,
At those willing feet, that never
More would lightly run to meet him,
Never more would lightly follow.
With both hands his face he covered,
Seven long days and nights he sat there,
As if in a swoon he sat there,
Speechless, motionless, unconscious
Of the daylight or the darkness.
Then they buried Minnehaha;
In the snow a grave they made her,
In the forest deep and darksome,
Underneath the moaning hemlocks;
Clothed her in her richest garments,
Wrapped her in her robes of ermine,
Covered her with snow, like ermine;
Thus they buried Minnehaha.
And at night a fire was lighted,
On her grave four times was kindled,
For her soul upon its journey
To the Islands of the Blessed.
From his doorway Hiawatha
Saw it burning in the forest,
Lighting up the gloomy hemlocks;
From his sleepless bed uprising,
From the bed of Minnehaha,
Stood and watched it at the doorway,
That it might not be extinguished,
Might not leave her in the darkness.

" Farewell ! " said he, " Minnehaha !
Farewell, O my Laughing Water !
All my heart is buried with you,
All my thoughts go onward with you !
Come not back again to labor,
Come not back again to suffer,
Where the Famine and the Fever
Wear the heart and waste the body.
Soon my task will be completed,
Soon your footsteps I shall follow
To the Islands of the Blessed,
To the Kingdom of Ponemah,
To the Land of the Hereafter ! "

XXI

THE WHITE MAN'S FOOT

In his lodge beside a river,
Close beside a frozen river,
Sat an old man, sad and lonely.
White his hair was as a snow-drift ;
Dull and low his fire was burning,
And the old man shook and trembled,
Folded in his Waubewyon,
In his tattered white-skin-wrapper,
Hearing nothing but the tempest
As it roared along the forest,
Seeing nothing but the snow-storm,
As it whirled and hissed and drifted.
    All the coals were white with ashes,
And the fire was slowly dying,
As a young man, walking lightly,
At the open doorway entered.
Red with blood of youth his cheeks were,
Soft his eyes, as stars in Spring-time,
Bound his forehead was with grasses ;
Bound and plumed with scented grasses,
On his lips a smile of beauty,
Filling all the lodge with sunshine,
In his hand a bunch of blossoms
Filling all the lodge with sweetness.
    " Ah, my son ! " exclaimed the old man,
" Happy are my eyes to see you.
Sit here on the mat beside me,
Sit here by the dying embers,
Let us pass the night together,
Tell me of your strange adventures,
Of the lands where you have travelled ;
I will tell you of my prowess,
Of my many deeds of wonder."
    From his pouch he drew his peace-pipe,
Very old and strangely fashioned ;
Made of red stone was the pipe-head,

And the stem a reed with feathers ;
Filled the pipe with bark of willow,
Placed a burning coal upon it,
Gave it to his guest, the stranger,
And began to speak in this wise :
" When I blow my breath about me,
When I breathe upon the landscape,
Motionless are all the rivers,
Hard as stone becomes the water ! "
    And the young man answered, smiling :
" When I blow my breath about me,
When I breathe upon the landscape,
Flowers spring up o'er all the meadows,
Singing, onward rush the rivers ! "
    " When I shake my hoary tresses,"
Said the old man darkly frowning,
" All the land with snow is covered ;
All the leaves from all the branches
Fall and fade and die and wither,
For I breathe, and lo ! they are not.
From the waters and the marshes
Rise the wild goose and the heron,
Fly away to distant regions,
For I speak, and lo ! they are not.
And where'er my footsteps wander,
All the wild beasts of the forest
Hide themselves in holes and caverns,
And the earth becomes as flintstone ! "
    " When I shake my flowing ringlets,"
Said the young man, softly laughing,
" Showers of rain fall warm and wel-
    come,
Plants lift up their heads rejoicing,
Back into their lakes and marshes
Come the wild goose and the heron,
Homeward shoots the arrowy swallow,
Sing the bluebird and the robin,
And where'er my footsteps wander,
All the meadows wave with blossoms,
All the woodlands ring with music,
All the trees are dark with foliage ! "
    While they spake, the night departed :
From the distant realms of Wabun,
From his shining lodge of silver,
Like a warrior robed and painted,
Came the sun, and said, " Behold me
Gheezis, the great sun, behold me ! "
    Then the old man's tongue was speech
    less
And the air grew warm and pleasant,
And upon the wigwam sweetly
Sang the bluebird and the robin,
And the stream began to murmur,
And a scent of growing grasses
Through the lodge was gently wafted.

And Segwun, the youthful stranger,
More distinctly in the daylight
Saw the icy face before him ;
It was Peboan, the Winter !
    From his eyes the tears were flowing,
As from melting lakes the streamlets,
And his body shrunk and dwindled
As the shouting sun ascended,
Till into the air it faded,
Till into the ground it vanished,
And the young man saw before him,
On the hearth-stone of the wigwam,
Where the fire had smoked and smoul-
    dered,
Saw the earliest flower of Spring-time,
Saw the Beauty of the Spring-time,
Saw the Miskodeed in blossom.
    Thus it was that in the North-land
After that unheard-of coldness,
That intolerable Winter,
Came the Spring with all its splendor,
All its birds and all its blossoms,
All its flowers and leaves and grasses.
    Sailing on the wind to northward,
Flying in great flocks, like arrows,
Like huge arrows shot through heaven,
Passed the swan, the Mahnahbezee,
Speaking almost as a man speaks ;
And in long lines waving, bending
Like a bow-string snapped asunder,
Came the white goose, Waw-be-wawa ;
And in pairs, or singly flying,
Mahng the loon, with clangorous pinions,
The blue heron, the Shuh-shuh-gah,
And the grouse, the Mushkodasa.
    In the thickets and the meadows
Piped the bluebird, the Owaissa,
On the summit of the lodges
Sang the robin, the Opechee,
In the covert of the pine-trees
Cooed the pigeon, the Omemee ;
And the sorrowing Hiawatha,
Speechless in his infinite sorrow,
Heard their voices calling to him,
Went forth from his gloomy doorway,
Stood and gazed into the heaven,
Gazed upon the earth and waters.
    From his wanderings far to eastward,
From the regions of the morning,
From the shining land of Wabun,
Homeward now returned Iagoo,
The great traveller, the great boaster,
Full of new and strange adventures,
Marvels many and many wonders.
    And the people of the village

Listened to him as he told them
Of his marvellous adventures,
Laughing answered him in this wise :
"Ugh ! it is indeed Iagoo !
No one else beholds such wonders ! "
    He had seen, he said, a water
Bigger than the Big-Sea-Water,
Broader than the Gitche Gumee,
Bitter so that none could drink it !
At each other looked the warriors,
Looked the women at each other,
Smiled, and said, " It cannot be so !
Kaw ! " they said, " it cannot be so ! "
    O'er it, said he, o'er this water
Came a great canoe with pinions,
A canoe with wings came flying,
Bigger than a grove of pine-trees,
Taller than the tallest tree-tops !
And the old men and the women
Looked and tittered at each other ;
"Kaw ! " they said, " we don't believe
    it ! "
    From its mouth, he said, to greet him,
Came Waywassimo, the lightning,
Came the thunder, Annemeekee !
And the warriors and the women
Laughed aloud at poor Iagoo ;
"Kaw ! " they said, " what tales you tell
    us ! "
    In it, said he, came a people,
In the great canoe with pinions
Came, he said, a hundred warriors ;
Painted white were all their faces
And with hair their chins were covered !
And the warriors and the women
Laughed and shouted in derision,
Like the ravens on the tree-tops,
Like the crows upon the hemlocks.
"Kaw ! " they said, " what lies you tell
    us !
Do not think that we believe them ! "
    Only Hiawatha laughed not,
But he gravely spake and answered
To their jeering and their jesting :
"True is all Iagoo tells us ;
I have seen it in a vision,
Seen the great canoe with pinions,
Seen the people with white faces,
Seen the coming of this bearded
People of the wooden vessel
From the regions of the morning,
From the shining land of Wabun.
    " Gitche Manito, the Mighty,
The Great Spirit, the Creator,
Sends them hither on his errand.

Sends them to us with his message.
Wheresoe'er they move, before them
Swarms the stinging fly, the Ahmo,
Swarms the bee, the honey-maker ;
Wheresoe'er they tread, beneath them
Springs a flower unknown among us,
Springs the White-man's Foot in blossom.
     " Let us welcome, then, the strangers,
Hail them as our friends and brothers,
And the heart's right hand of friendship
Give them when they come to see us.
Gitche Manito, the Mighty,
Said this to me in my vision.
     " I beheld, too, in that vision
All the secrets of the future,
Of the distant days that shall be.
I beheld the westward marches
Of the unknown, crowded nations.
All the land was full of people,
Restless, struggling, toiling, striving,
Speaking many tongues, yet feeling
But one heart-beat in their bosoms.
In the woodlands rang their axes,
Smoked their towns in all the valleys,
Over all the lakes and rivers
Rushed their great canoes of thunder.
     " Then a darker, drearier vision
Passed before me, vague and cloud-like ;
I beheld our nation scattered,
All forgetful of my counsels,
Weakened, warring with each other :
Saw the remnants of our people
Sweeping westward, wild and woful,
Like the cloud-rack of a tempest,
Like the withered leaves of Autumn ! "

XXII

HIAWATHA'S DEPARTURE

By the shore of Gitche Gumee,
By the shining Big-Sea-Water,
At the doorway of his wigwam,
In the pleasant Summer morning,
Hiawatha stood and waited.
All the air was full of freshness,
All the earth was bright and joyous,
And before him, through the sunshine,
Westward toward the neighboring forest
Passed in golden swarms the Ahmo,
Passed the bees, the honey-makers,
Burning, singing in the sunshine.
     Bright above him shone the heavens,
Level spread the lake before him ;

From its bosom leaped the sturgeon,
Sparkling, flashing in the sunshine ;
On its margin the great forest
Stood reflected in the water,
Every tree-top had its shadow,
Motionless beneath the water.
     From the brow of Hiawatha
Gone was every trace of sorrow,
As the fog from off the water,
As the mist from off the meadow.
With a smile of joy and triumph,
With a look of exultation,
As of one who in a vision
Sees what is to be, but is not,
Stood and waited Hiawatha.
     Toward the sun his hands were lifted,
Both the palms spread out against it,
And between the parted fingers
Fell the sunshine on his features,
Flecked with light his naked shoulders,
As it falls and flecks an oak-tree
Through the rifted leaves and branches.
     O'er the water floating, flying,
Something in the hazy distance,
Something in the mists of morning,
Loomed and lifted from the water,
Now seemed floating, now seemed flying,
Coming nearer, nearer, nearer.
     Was it Shingebis the diver ?
Or the pelican, the Shada ?
Or the heron, the Shuh-shuh-gah ?
Or the white goose, Waw-be-wawa,
With the water dripping, flashing,
From its glossy neck and feathers ?
     It was neither goose nor diver,
Neither pelican nor heron,
O'er the water floating, flying,
Through the shining mist of morning,
But a birch canoe with paddles,
Rising, sinking on the water,
Dripping, flashing in the sunshine ;
And within it came a people
From the distant land of Wabun,
From the farthest realms of morning
Came the Black-Robe chief, the Prophet,
He the Priest of Prayer, the Pale-face,
With his guides and his companions.
     And the noble Hiawatha,
With his hands aloft extended,
Held aloft in sign of welcome,
Waited, full of exultation,
Till the birch canoe with paddles
Grated on the shining pebbles,
Stranded on the sandy margin,
Till the Black-Robe chief, the Pale-face,

With the cross upon his bosom,
Landed on the sandy margin.
Then the joyous Hiawatha
Cried aloud and spake in this wise :
" Beautiful is the sun, O strangers,
When you come so far to see us !
All our town in peace awaits you,
All our doors stand open for you ;
You shall enter all our wigwams,
For the heart's right hand we give you.
" Never bloomed the earth so gayly,
Never shone the sun so brightly,
As to-day they shine and blossom
When you come so far to see us !
Never was our lake so tranquil,
Nor so free from rocks and sand-bars ;
For your birch canoe in passing
Has removed both rock and sand-bar.
" Never before had our tobacco
Such a sweet and pleasant flavor,
Never the broad leaves of our cornfields
Were so beautiful to look on,
As they seem to us this morning,
When you come so far to see us ! "
And the Black-Robe chief made answer,
Stammered in his speech a little,
Speaking words yet unfamiliar :
" Peace be with you, Hiawatha,
Peace be with you and your people,
Peace of prayer, and peace of pardon,
Peace of Christ, and joy of Mary ! "
Then the generous Hiawatha
Led the strangers to his wigwam,
Seated them on skins of bison,
Seated them on skins of ermine,
And the careful old Nokomis
Brought them food in bowls of basswood,
Water brought in birchen dippers,
And the calumet, the peace-pipe,
Filled and lighted for their smoking.
All the old men of the village,
All the warriors of the nation,
All the Jossakeeds, the Prophets,
The magicians, the Wabenos,
And the Medicine-men, the Medas,
Came to bid the strangers welcome ;
" It is well," they said, " O brothers,
That you come so far to see us ! "
In a circle round the doorway,
With their pipes they sat in silence,
Waiting to behold the strangers,
Waiting to receive their message ;
Till the Black-Robe chief, the Pale-face,
From the wigwam came to greet them,
Stammering in his speech a little,

Speaking words yet unfamiliar ;
" It is well," they said, " O brother,
That you come so far to see us ! "
Then the Black-Robe chief, the Prophet,
Told his message to the people,
Told the purport of his mission,
Told them of the Virgin Mary,
And her blessed Son, the Saviour,
How in distant lands and ages
He had lived on earth as we do ;
How he fasted, prayed, and labored ;
How the Jews, the tribe accursed,
Mocked him, scourged him, crucified him ;
How he rose from where they laid him,
Walked again with his disciples,
And ascended into heaven.
And the chiefs made answer, saying :
" We have listened to your message,
We have heard your words of wisdom,
We will think on what you tell us.
It is well for us, O brothers,
That you come so far to see us ! "
Then they rose up and departed
Each one homeward to his wigwam,
To the young men and the women
Told the story of the strangers
Whom the Master of Life had sent them
From the shining land of Wabun.
Heavy with the heat and silence
Grew the afternoon of Summer ;
With a drowsy sound the forest
Whispered round the sultry wigwam,
With a sound of sleep the water
Rippled on the beach below it ;
From the cornfields shrill and ceaseless
Sang the grasshopper, Pah-puk-keena ;
And the guests of Hiawatha,
Weary with the heat of Summer,
Slumbered in the sultry wigwam.
Slowly o'er the simmering landscape
Fell the evening's dusk and coolness,
And the long and level sunbeams
Shot their spears into the forest,
Breaking through its shields of shadow,
Rushed into each secret ambush,
Searched each thicket, dingle, hollow ;
Still the guests of Hiawatha
Slumbered in the silent wigwam.
From his place rose Hiawatha,
Bade farewell to old Nokomis,
Spake in whispers, spake in this wise,
Did not wake the guests, that slumbered ;
" I am going, O Nokomis,
On a long and distant journey,
To the portals of the Sunset,

To the regions of the home-wind,
Of the Northwest-Wind, Keewaydin.
But these guests I leave behind me,
In your watch and ward I leave them ;
See that never harm comes near them,
See that never fear molests them,
Never danger nor suspicion,
Never want of food or shelter,
In the lodge of Hiawatha ! ”
　Forth into the village went he,
Bade farewell to all the warriors,
Bade farewell to all the young men,
Spake persuading, spake in this wise :
　“ I am going, O my people,
On a long and distant journey ;
Many moons and many winters
Will have come, and will have vanished,
Ere I come again to see you.
But my guests I leave behind me ;
Listen to their words of wisdom,
Listen to the truth they tell you,
For the Master of Life has sent them
From the land of light and morning ! ”
　On the shore stood Hiawatha,
Turned and waved his hand at parting ;
On the clear and luminous water
Launched his birch canoe for sailing,
From the pebbles of the margin
Shoved it forth into the water ;
Whispered to it, “ Westward ! westward ! ”
And with speed it darted forward.
　And the evening sun descending
Set the clouds on fire with redness,
Burned the broad sky, like a prairie,

Left upon the level water
One long track and trail of splendor,
Down whose stream, as down a river,
Westward, westward Hiawatha
Sailed into the fiery sunset,
Sailed into the purple vapors,
Sailed into the dusk of evening.
　And the people from the margin
Watched him floating, rising, sinking,
Till the birch canoe seemed lifted
High into that sea of splendor,
Till it sank into the vapors
Like the new moon slowly, slowly
Sinking in the purple distance.
　And they said, “ Farewell forever ! ”
Said, “ Farewell, O Hiawatha ! ”
And the forests, dark and lonely,
Moved through all their depths of darkness
Sighed, “ Farewell, O Hiawatha ! ”
And the waves upon the margin
Rising, rippling on the pebbles,
Sobbed, “ Farewell, O Hiawatha ! ”
And the heron, the Shuh-shuh-gah,
From her haunts among the fen-lands,
Screamed, “ Farewell, O Hiawatha ! ”
　Thus departed Hiawatha,
Hiawatha the Beloved,
In the glory of the sunset,
In the purple mists of evening,
To the regions of the home-wind,
Of the Northwest-Wind, Keewaydin,
To the Islands of the Blessed,
To the Kingdom of Ponemah,
To the Land of the Hereafter !

THE COURTSHIP OF MILES STANDISH

It is possible that the unmistakable success of *Hiawatha* made Mr. Longfellow more ready to occupy himself with another subject of American life. At any rate, a few weeks after the publication of that poem one of his friends urged him to write a poem on the Puritans and Quakers. “ A good subject for a tragedy,” he remarks, and began looking over books which would give him incidents. The first outcome was the beginning of *The New England Tragedies*. Then he appears to have begun as an alternative, lighter work a drama, *The Courtship of Miles Standish*. This was December 2, 1856. Exactly a year later he writes in his diary: “ Soft as spring. I begin a new poem, *Priscilla*, to be a kind of Puritan pastoral ; the subject, the courtship of Miles Standish. This, I think, will be a better treatment of the subject than the dramatic one I wrote some time ago ; ” and the next day : “ My poem is in hexameters ; an idyl of the Old Colony times. What it will turn out I do not know ; but it gives me pleasure to write it ; and that I count for something.”
　He seems to have made a fresh start on the poem, January 29, 1858, and then to have carried it rapidly forward to completion, for the first draft was finished March 22d, although the book, which contained besides a collection of his recent short poems, was not published until September. When midway in the writing he changed the title to that which the poem now bears. The incident of Priscilla's reply, on which the story turns, was a tradition, and John Alden was a maternal ancestor of the poet. For the rest, he drew his material from the easily accessible historical resources. Dr. Young had published his valuable *Chronicles of the Pilgrim Fathers*, and Mr. Charles Wyllis Elliott his entertaining *History of New England*, in which he had attempted to reconstruct the interior, household life in greater detail than had other learned writers. Mr. Longfellow did not think it necessary to follow the early Plymouth history with scrupulous reference to chronology ; it was sufficient for him to catch the broad features of the colonial life and to reproduce the spirit of the relations existing between Plymouth and the Indians. The hexameter verse differs in its general effect from that produced by the more stately form used in *Evangeline*, through its greater elasticity. A crispness of touch is gained by a more varying accent and a freer use of trochees.

THE COURTSHIP OF MILES STANDISH

I

MILES STANDISH

In the Old Colony days, in Plymouth the
land of the Pilgrims,
To and fro in a room of his simple and
primitive dwelling,
Clad in doublet and hose, and boots of Cor-
dovan leather,
Strode, with a martial air, Miles Standish
the Puritan Captain.
Buried in thought he seemed, with his
hands behind him, and pausing
Ever and anon to behold his glittering
weapons of warfare,
Hanging in shining array along the walls
of the chamber, —
Cutlass and corselet of steel, and his trusty
sword of Damascus,
Curved at the point and inscribed with its
mystical Arabic sentence,
While underneath, in a corner, were fowl-
ing-piece, musket, and matchlock.
Short of stature he was, but strongly built
and athletic,
Broad in the shoulders, deep-chested, with
muscles and sinews of iron ;
Brown as a nut was his face, but his russet
beard was already
Flaked with patches of snow, as hedges
sometimes in November.
Near him was seated John Alden, his friend
and household companion,
Writing with diligent speed at a table of
pine by the window ;
Fair-haired, azure-eyed, with delicate Saxon
complexion,
Having the dew of his youth, and the
beauty thereof, as the captives
Whom Saint Gregory saw, and exclaimed,
"Not Angles, but Angels."
Youngest of all was he of the men who
came in the Mayflower.

Suddenly breaking the silence, the dili-
gent scribe interrupting,
Spake, in the pride of his heart, Miles
Standish the Captain of Plymouth.
"Look at these arms," he said, "the war-
like weapons that hang here
Burnished and bright and clean, as if for
parade or inspection !
This is the sword of Damascus I fought
with in Flanders ; this breastplate,
Well I remember the day ! once saved my
life in a skirmish ;
Here in front you can see the very dint of
the bullet
Fired point-blank at my heart by a Spanish
arcabucero.
Had it not been of sheer steel, the for-
gotten bones of Miles Standish
Would at this moment be mould, in their
grave in the Flemish morasses."
Thereupon answered John Alden, but
looked not up from his writing :
"Truly the breath of the Lord hath slack-
ened the speed of the bullet ;
He in his mercy preserved you, to be our
shield and our weapon ! "
Still the Captain continued, unheeding the
words of the stripling :
"See, how bright they are burnished, as if
in an arsenal hanging ;
That is because I have done it myself, and
not left it to others.
Serve yourself, would you be well served,
is an excellent adage ;
So I take care of my arms, as you of your
pens and your inkhorn.
Then, too, there are my soldiers, my great,
invincible army,
Twelve men, all equipped, having each his
rest and his matchlock,
Eighteen shillings a month, together with
diet and pillage,
And, like Cæsar, I know the name of each
of my soldiers ! "
This he said with a smile, that danced in
his eyes, as the sunbeams
Dance on the waves of the sea, and vanish
again in a moment.
Alden laughed as he wrote, and still the
Captain continued :
" Look ! you can see from this window my
brazen howitzer planted
High on the roof of the church, a preacher
who speaks to the purpose,
Steady, straightforward, and strong, with
irresistible logic,
Orthodox, flashing conviction right into the
hearts of the heathen.
Now we are ready, I think, for any assault
of the Indians ;

Let them come, if they like, and the sooner
    they try it the better, —
Let them come, if they like, be it sagamore,
    sachem, or pow-wow,
Aspinet, Samoset, Corbitant, Squanto, or
    Tokamahamon ! "

Long at the window he stood, and wist-
    fully gazed on the landscape,
Washed with a cold gray mist, the vapory
    breath of the east-wind,
Forest and meadow and hill, and the steel-
    blue rim of the ocean,
Lying silent and sad, in the afternoon shad-
    ows and sunshine.
Over his countenance flitted a shadow like
    those on the landscape,
Gloom intermingled with light ; and his
    voice was subdued with emotion,
Tenderness, pity, regret, as after a pause
    he proceeded :
" Yonder there, on the hill by the sea, lies
    buried Rose Standish ;
Beautiful rose of love, that bloomed for me
    by the wayside !
She was the first to die of all who came in
    the Mayflower !
Green above her is growing the field of
    wheat we have sown there,
Better to hide from the Indian scouts the
    graves of our people,
Lest they should count them and see how
    many already have perished ! "
Sadly his face he averted, and strode up
    and down, and was thoughtful.

Fixed to the opposite wall was a shelf of
    books, and among them
Prominent three, distinguished alike for
    bulk and for binding ;
Bariffe's Artillery Guide, and the Com-
    mentaries of Cæsar
Out of the Latin translated by Arthur
    Goldinge of London,
And, as if guarded by these, between them
    was standing the Bible.
Musing a moment before them, Miles
    Standish paused, as if doubtful
Which of the three he should choose for
    his consolation and comfort,
Whether the wars of the Hebrews, the fa-
    mous campaigns of the Romans,
Or the Artillery practice, designed for bel-
    ligerent Christians.

Finally down from its shelf he dragged the
    ponderous Roman,
Seated himself at the window, and opened
    the book, and in silence
Turned o'er the well-worn leaves, where
    thumb-marks thick on the margin,
Like the trample of feet, proclaimed the
    battle was hottest.
Nothing was heard in the room but the
    hurrying pen of the stripling,
Busily writing epistles important, to go by
    the Mayflower,
Ready to sail on the morrow, or next day
    at latest, God willing !
Homeward bound with the tidings of all
    that terrible winter,
Letters written by Alden, and full of the
    name of Priscilla !
Full of the name and the fame of the Pu-
    ritan maiden Priscilla !

II

LOVE AND FRIENDSHIP

NOTHING was heard in the room but the
    hurrying pen of the stripling,
Or an occasional sigh from the laboring
    heart of the Captain,
Reading the marvellous words and achieve-
    ments of Julius Cæsar.
After a while he exclaimed, as he smote
    with his hand, palm downwards,
Heavily on the page : " A wonderful man
    was this Cæsar !
You are a writer, and I am a fighter, but
    here is a fellow
Who could both write and fight, and in
    both was equally skilful ! "
Straightway answered and spake John
    Alden, the comely, the youthful :
" Yes, he was equally skilled, as you say,
    with his pen and his weapons.
Somewhere have I read, but where I for-
    get, he could dictate
Seven letters at once, at the same time
    writing his memoirs."
" Truly," continued the Captain, not heed-
    ing or hearing the other,
" Truly a wonderful man was Caius Julius
    Cæsar !
Better be first, he said, in a little Iberian
    village,

Than be second in Rome, and I think he
  was right when he said it.
Twice was he married before he was
  twenty, and many times after ;
Battles five hundred he fought, and a
  thousand cities he conquered ;
He, too, fought in Flanders, as he himself
  has recorded ;
Finally he was stabbed by his friend, the
  orator Brutus !
Now, do you know what he did on a cer-
  tain occasion in Flanders,
When the rear-guard of his army retreated,
  the front giving way too,
And the immortal Twelfth Legion was
  crowded so closely together
There was no room for their swords ?
  Why, he seized a shield from a sol-
  dier,
Put himself straight at the head of his
  troops, and commanded the captains,
Calling on each by his name, to order for-
  ward the ensigns ;
Then to widen the ranks, and give more
  room for their weapons ;
So he won the day, the battle of something-
  or-other.
That 's what I always say ; if you wish a
  thing to be well done,
You must do it yourself, you must not
  leave it to others ! "

All was silent again ; the Captain con-
  tinued his reading.
Nothing was heard in the room but the
  hurrying pen of the stripling
Writing epistles important to go next day
  by the Mayflower,
Filled with the name and the fame of the
  Puritan maiden Priscilla ;
Every sentence began or closed with the
  name of Priscilla,
Till the treacherous pen, to which he con-
  fided the secret,
Strove to betray it by singing and shouting
  the name of Priscilla !
Finally closing his book, with a bang of the
  ponderous cover,
Sudden and loud as the sound of a soldier
  grounding his musket,
Thus to the young man spake Miles Stan-
  dish the Captain of Plymouth :
" When you have finished your work, I have
  something important to tell you.

Be not however in haste ; I can wait ; I
  shall not be impatient ! "
Straightway Alden replied, as he folded the
  last of his letters,
Pushing his papers aside, and giving re-
  spectful attention :
" Speak ; for whenever you speak, I am
  always ready to listen,
Always ready to hear whatever pertains to
  Miles Standish."
Thereupon answered the Captain, embar-
  rassed, and culling his phrases :
" 'T is not good for a man to be alone, say
  the Scriptures.
This I have said before, and again and
  again I repeat it ;
Every hour in the day, I think it, and feel
  it, and say it.
Since Rose Standish died, my life has been
  weary and dreary ;
Sick at heart have I been, beyond the heal-
  ing of friendship ;
Oft in my lonely hours have I thought of
  the maiden Priscilla.
She is alone in the world ; her father and
  mother and brother
Died in the winter together ; I saw her
  going and coming,
Now to the grave of the dead, and now to
  the bed of the dying,
Patient, courageous, and strong, and said
  to myself, that if ever
There were angels on earth, as there are
  angels in heaven,
Two have I seen and known ; and the angel
  whose name is Priscilla
Holds in my desolate life the place which
  the other abandoned.
Long have I cherished the thought, but
  never have dared to reveal it,
Being a coward in this though valiant
  enough for the most part.
Go to the damsel Priscilla, the loveliest
  maiden of Plymouth,
Say that a blunt old Captain, a man not
  of words but of actions,
Offers his hand and his heart, the hand and
  heart of a soldier.
Not in these words, you know, but this in
  short is my meaning ;
I am a maker of war, and not a maker of
  phrases.
You, who are bred as a scholar, can say it
  in elegant language,

Such as you read in your books of the
    pleadings and wooings of lovers,
Such as you think best adapted to win the
    heart of a maiden."

When he had spoken, John Alden, the
    fair-haired, taciturn stripling,
All aghast at his words, surprised, embar-
    rassed, bewildered,
Trying to mask his dismay by treating the
    subject with lightness,
Trying to smile, and yet feeling his heart
    stand still in his bosom,
Just as a timepiece stops in a house that is
    stricken by lightning,
Thus made answer and spake, or rather
    stammered than answered :
"Such a message as that, I am sure I
    should mangle and mar it ;
If you would have it well done, — I am
    only repeating your maxim, —
You must do it yourself, you must not leave
    it to others ! "
But with the air of a man whom nothing
    can turn from his purpose,
Gravely shaking his head, made answer the
    Captain of Plymouth :
"Truly the maxim is good, and I do not
    mean to gainsay it ;
But we must use it discreetly, and not
    waste powder for nothing.
Now, as I said before, I was never a maker
    of phrases.
I can march up to a fortress and summon
    the place to surrender,
But march up to a woman with such a pro-
    posal, I dare not.
I 'm not afraid of bullets, nor shot from the
    mouth of a cannon,
But of a thundering 'No!' point-blank
    from the mouth of a woman,
That I confess ı 'm afraid of, nor am I
    ashamed to confess it !
So you must grant my request, for you are
    an elegant scholar,
Having the graces of speech, and skill in
    the turning of phrases."
Taking the hand of his friend, who still
    was reluctant and doubtful,
Holding it long in his own, and pressing it
    kindly, he added :
"Though I have spoken thus lightly, yet
    deep is the feeling that prompts me ;
Surely you cannot refuse what I ask in the
    name of our friendship ! "

Then made answer John Alden : "The
    name of friendship is sacred ;
What you demand in that name, I have not
    the power to deny you ! "
So the strong will prevailed, subduing and
    moulding the gentler,
Friendship prevailed over love, and Alden
    went on his errand.

III

THE LOVER'S ERRAND

So the strong will prevailed, and Alden
    went on his errand,
Out of the street of the village, and into
    the paths of the forest,
Into the tranquil woods, where bluebirds
    and robins were building
Towns in the populous trees, with hanging
    gardens of verdure,
Peaceful, aerial cities of joy and affection
    and freedom.
All around him was calm, but within him
    commotion and conflict,
Love contending with friendship, and self
    with each generous impulse.
To and fro in his breast his thoughts were
    heaving and dashing,
As in a foundering ship, with every roll of
    the vessel,
Washes the bitter sea, the merciless surge
    of the ocean !
"Must I relinquish it all," he cried with a
    wild lamentation, —
"Must I relinquish it all, the joy, the hope,
    the illusion ?
Was it for this I have loved, and waited,
    and worshipped in silence ?
Was it for this I have followed the flying
    feet and the shadow
Over the wintry sea, to the desolate shores
    of New England ?
Truly the heart is deceitful, and out of its
    depths of corruption
Rise, like an exhalation, the misty phan-
    toms of passion ;
Angels of light they seem, but are only
    delusions of Satan.
All is clear to me now ; I feel it, I see it
    distinctly !
This is the hand of the Lord ; it is laid upon
    me in anger,

For I have followed too much the heart's
desires and devices,
Worshipping Astaroth blindly, and impious
idols of Baal.
This is the cross I must bear ; the sin and
the swift retribution."

So through the Plymouth woods John
Alden went on his errand ;
Crossing the brook at the ford, where it
brawled over pebble and shallow,
Gathering still, as he went, the May-flowers
blooming around him,
Fragrant, filling the air with a strange and
wonderful sweetness,
Children lost in the woods, and covered
with leaves in their slumber.
" Puritan flowers," he said, " and the type
of Puritan maidens,
Modest and simple and sweet, the very
type of Priscilla !
So I will take them to her ; to Priscilla the
Mayflower of Plymouth,
Modest and simple and sweet, as a parting
gift will I take them ;
Breathing their silent farewells, as they
fade and wither and perish,
Soon to be thrown away as is the heart of
the giver."
So through the Plymouth woods John
Alden went on his errand ;
Came to an open space, and saw the disk
of the ocean,
Sailless, sombre and cold with the comfort-
less breath of the east-wind ;
Saw the new-built house, and people at
work in a meadow ;
Heard, as he drew near the door, the mu-
sical voice of Priscilla
Singing the hundredth Psalm, the grand
old Puritan anthem,
Music that Luther sang to the sacred words
of the Psalmist,
Full of the breath of the Lord, consoling
and comforting many.
Then, as he opened the door, he beheld the
form of the maiden
Seated beside her wheel, and the carded
wool like a snow-drift
Piled at her knee, her white hands feeding
the ravenous spindle,
While with her foot on the treadle she
guided the wheel in its motion.
Open wide on her lap lay the well-worn
psalm-book of Ainsworth,

Printed in Amsterdam, the words and the
music together,
Rough-hewn, angular notes, like stones in
the wall of a churchyard,
Darkened and overhung by the running
vine of the verses.
Such was the book from whose pages she
sang the old Puritan anthem,
She, the Puritan girl, in the solitude of the
forest,
Making the humble house and the modest
apparel of homespun
Beautiful with her beauty, and rich with
the wealth of her being !
Over him rushed, like a wind that is keen
and cold and relentless,
Thoughts of what might have been, and
the weight and woe of his errand ;
All the dreams that had faded, and all the
hopes that had vanished,
All his life henceforth a dreary and tenant-
less mansion,
Haunted by vain regrets, and pallid, sorrow-
ful faces.
Still he said to himself, and almost fiercely
he said it,
"Let not him that putteth his hand to the
plough look backwards ;
Though the ploughshare cut through the
flowers of life to its fountains,
Though it pass o'er the graves of the dead
and the hearths of the living,
It is the will of the Lord ; and his mercy
endureth forever ! "

So he entered the house : and the hum of
the wheel and the singing
Suddenly ceased ; for Priscilla, aroused by
his step on the threshold,
Rose as he entered, and gave him her hand,
in signal of welcome,
Saying, " I knew it was you, when I heard
your step in the passage ;
For I was thinking of you, as I sat there
singing and spinning."
Awkward and dumb with delight, that a
thought of him had been mingled
Thus in the sacred psalm, that came from
the heart of the maiden,
Silent before her he stood, and gave her
the flowers for an answer,
Finding no words for his thought. He re-
membered that day in the winter,
After the first great snow, when he broke
a path from the village,

Reeling and plunging along through the
   drifts that encumbered the doorway,
Stamping the snow from his feet as he en-
   tered the house, and Priscilla
Laughed at his snowy locks, and gave him
   a seat by the fireside,
Grateful and pleased to know he had
   thought of her in the snow-storm.
Had he but spoken then ! perhaps not in
   vain had he spoken ;
Now it was all too late ; the golden mo-
   ment had vanished !
So he stood there abashed, and gave her
   the flowers for an answer.

Then they sat down and talked of the
   birds and the beautiful Spring-time,
Talked of their friends at home, and the
   Mayflower that sailed on the mor-
   row.
" I have been thinking all day," said gently
   the Puritan maiden,
" Dreaming all night, and thinking all day,
   of the hedge-rows of England, —
They are in blossom now, and the country
   is all like a garden :
Thinking of lanes and fields, and the song
   of the lark and the linnet,
Seeing the village street, and familiar faces
   of neighbors
Going about as of old, and stopping to gos-
   sip together,
And, at the end of the street, the village
   church, with the ivy
Climbing the old gray tower, and the quiet
   graves in the churchyard.
Kind are the people I live with, and dear
   to me my religion ;
Still my heart is so sad, that I wish myself
   back in Old England.
You will say it is wrong, but I cannot help
   it : I almost
Wish myself back in Old England, I feel
   so lonely and wretched."

Thereupon answered the youth : " In-
   deed I do not condemn you ;
Stouter hearts than a woman's have quailed
   in this terrible winter.
Yours is tender and trusting, and needs
   a stronger to lean on ;
So I have come to you now, with an offer
   and proffer of marriage
Made by a good man and true, Miles Stan-
   dish the Captain of Plymouth ! "

Thus he delivered his message, the dex-
   terous writer of letters, —
Did not embellish the theme, nor array it
   in beautiful phrases,
But came straight to the point, and blurted
   it out like a school-boy ;
Even the Captain himself could hardly
   have said it more bluntly.
Mute with amazement and sorrow, Priscilla
   the Puritan maiden
Looked into Alden's face, her eyes dilated
   with wonder,
Feeling his words like a blow, that stunned
   her and rendered her speechless ;
Till at length she exclaimed, interrupting
   the ominous silence :
" If the great Captain of Plymouth is so
   very eager to wed me,
Why does he not come himself, and take
   the trouble to woo me ?
If I am not worth the wooing, I surely am
   not worth the winning ! "
Then John Alden began explaining and
   smoothing the matter,
Making it worse as he went, by saying the
   Captain was busy, —
Had no time for such things — such things !
   the words grating harshly
Fell on the ear of Priscilla ; and swift as a
   flash she made answer :
" Has he no time for such things, as you
   call it, before he is married,
Would he be likely to find it, or make it,
   after the wedding ?
That is the way with you men ; you don't
   understand us, you cannot.
When you have made up your minds,
   after thinking of this one and that
   one,
Choosing, selecting, rejecting, comparing
   one with another,
Then you make known your desire, with
   abrupt and sudden avowal,
And are offended and hurt, and indignant
   perhaps, that a woman
Does not respond at once to a love that she
   never suspected,
Does not attain at a bound the height to
   which you have been climbing.
This is not right nor just : for surely a
   woman's affection
Is not a thing to be asked for, and had for
   only the asking.
When one is truly in love, one not only
   says it, but shows it.

Had he but waited awhile, had he only
    showed that he loved me,
Even this Captain of yours — who knows ?
    — at last might have won me,
Old and rough as he is ; but now it never
    can happen."

Still John Alden went on, unheeding the
    words of Priscilla,
Urging the suit of his friend, explaining,
    persuading, expanding ;
Spoke of his courage and skill, and of all
    his battles in Flanders,
How with the people of God he had chosen
    to suffer affliction ;
How, in return for his zeal, they had made
    him Captain of Plymouth ;
He was a gentleman born, could trace his
    pedigree plainly
Back to Hugh Standish of Duxbury Hall,
    in Lancashire, England,
Who was the son of Ralph, and the grand-
    son of Thurston de Standish ;
Heir unto vast estates, of which he was
    basely defrauded,
Still bore the family arms, and had for his
    crest a cock argent,
Combed and wattled gules, and all the rest
    of the blazon.
He was a man of honor, of noble and gen-
    erous nature ;
Though he was rough, he was kindly ; she
    knew how during the winter
He had attended the sick, with a hand as
    gentle as woman's ;
Somewhat hasty and hot, he could not deny
    it, and headstrong,
Stern as a soldier might be, but hearty, and
    placable always,
Not to be laughed at and scorned, because
    he was little of stature ;
For he was great of heart, magnanimous,
    courtly, courageous ;
Any woman in Plymouth, nay, any woman
    in England,
Might be happy and proud to be called the
    wife of Miles Standish !

But as he warmed and glowed, in his
    simple and eloquent language,
Quite forgetful of self, and full of the praise
    of his rival,
Archly the maiden smiled, and, with eyes
    overrunning with laughter,
Said, in a tremulous voice, " Why don't you
    speak for yourself, John ? "

IV

JOHN ALDEN

INTO the open air John Alden, perplexed
    and bewildered,
Rushed like a man insane, and wandered
    alone by the sea-side ;
Paced up and down the sands, and bared
    his head to the east-wind,
Cooling his heated brow, and the fire and
    fever within him.
Slowly as out of the heavens, with apocalyp-
    tical splendors,
Sank the City of God, in the vision of John
    the Apostle,
So, with its cloudy walls of chrysolite,
    jasper, and sapphire,
Sank the broad red sun, and over its turrets
    uplifted
Glimmered the golden reed of the angel
    who measured the city.

" Welcome, O wind of the East ! " he
    exclaimed in his wild exultation,
" Welcome, O wind of the East, from the
    caves of the misty Atlantic !
Blowing o'er fields of dulse, and measure-
    less meadows of sea-grass,
Blowing o'er rocky wastes, and the grottoes
    and gardens of ocean !
Lay thy cold, moist hand on my burning
    forehead, and wrap me
Close in thy garments of mist, to allay the
    fever within me ! "

Like an awakened conscience, the sea
    was moaning and tossing,
Beating remorseful and loud the mutable
    sands of the sea-shore.
Fierce in his soul was the struggle and tu-
    mult of passions contending ;
Love triumphant and crowned, and friend-
    ship wounded and bleeding,
Passionate cries of desire, and importunate
    pleadings of duty !
" Is it my fault," he said, " that the maiden
    has chosen between us ?
Is it my fault that he failed, — my fault
    that I am the victor ? "
Then within him there thundered a voice,
    like the voice of the Prophet :
" It hath displeased the Lord ! " — and he
    thought of David's transgression,
Bathsheba's beautiful face, and his friend
    in the front of the battle !

Shame and confusion of guilt, and abasement and self-condemnation,
Overwhelmed him at once ; and he cried in the deepest contrition :
" It hath displeased the Lord ! It is the temptation of Satan ! "

Then, uplifting his head, he looked at the sea, and beheld there
Dimly the shadowy form of the Mayflower riding at anchor,
Rocked on the rising tide, and ready to sail on the morrow ;
Heard the voices of men through the mist, the rattle of cordage
Thrown on the deck, the shouts of the mate, and the sailors' " Ay, ay, Sir ! "
Clear and distinct, but not loud, in the dripping air of the twilight.
Still for a moment he stood, and listened, and stared at the vessel,
Then went hurriedly on, as one who, seeing a phantom,
Stops, then quickens his pace, and follows the beckoning shadow.
" Yes, it is plain to me now," he murmured ; " the hand of the Lord is
Leading me out of the land of darkness, the bondage of error,
Through the sea, that shall lift the walls of its waters around me,
Hiding me, cutting me off, from the cruel thoughts that pursue me.
Back will I go o'er the ocean, this dreary land will abandon,
Her whom I may not love, and him whom my heart has offended.
Better to be in my grave in the green old churchyard in England,
Close by my mother's side, and among the dust of my kindred ;
Better be dead and forgotten, than living in shame and dishonor ;
Sacred and safe and unseen, in the dark of the narrow chamber
With me my secret shall lie, like a buried jewel that glimmers
Bright on the hand that is dust, in the chambers of silence and darkness, —
Yes, as the marriage ring of the great espousal hereafter ! "

Thus as he spake, he turned, in the strength of his strong resolution,
Leaving behind him the shore, and hurried along in the twilight,
Through the congenial gloom of the forest silent and sombre,
Till he beheld the lights in the seven houses of Plymouth,
Shining like seven stars in the dusk and mist of the evening.
Soon he entered his door, and found the redoubtable Captain
Sitting alone, and absorbed in the martial pages of Cæsar,
Fighting some great campaign in Hainault or Brabant or Flanders.
" Long have you been on your errand," he said with a cheery demeanor,
Even as one who is waiting an answer, and fears not the issue.
" Not far off is the house, although the woods are between us ;
But you have lingered so long, that while you were going and coming
I have fought ten battles and sacked and demolished a city.
Come, sit down, and in order relate to me all that has happened."

Then John Alden spake, and related the wondrous adventure,
From beginning to end, minutely, just as it happened ;
How he had seen Priscilla, and how he had sped in his courtship,
Only smoothing a little, and softening down her refusal.
But when he came at length to the words Priscilla had spoken,
Words so tender and cruel : " Why don't you speak for yourself, John ? "
Up leaped the Captain of Plymouth, and stamped on the floor, till his armor
Clanged on the wall, where it hung, with a sound of sinister omen.
All his pent-up wrath burst forth in a sudden explosion,
E'en as a hand-grenade, that scatters destruction around it.
Wildly he shouted, and loud : " John Alden ! you have betrayed me !
Me, Miles Standish, your friend ! have supplanted, defrauded, betrayed me !
One of my ancestors ran his sword through the heart of Wat Tyler ;
Who shall prevent me from running my own through the heart of a traitor ?

Yours is the greater treason, for yours is a
   treason to friendship !
You, who lived under my roof, whom I
   cherished and loved as a brother ;
You, who have fed at my board, and drunk
   at my cup, to whose keeping
I have intrusted my honor, my thoughts
   the most sacred and secret, —
You too, Brutus ! ah woe to the name of
   friendship hereafter !
Brutus was Cæsar's friend, and you were
   mine, but henceforward
Let there be nothing between us save war,
   and implacable hatred ! "

So spake the Captain of Plymouth, and
   strode about in the chamber,
Chafing and choking with rage ; like cords
   were the veins on his temples.
But in the midst of his anger a man ap-
   peared at the doorway,
Bringing in uttermost haste a message of
   urgent importance,
Rumors of danger and war and hostile in-
   cursions of Indians !
Straightway the Captain paused, and, with-
   out further question or parley,
Took from the nail on the wall his sword
   with its scabbard of iron,
Buckled the belt round his waist, and,
   frowning fiercely, departed.
Alden was left alone.   He heard the clank
   of the scabbard
Growing fainter and fainter, and dying
   away in the distance.
Then he arose from his seat, and looked
   forth into the darkness,
Felt the cool air blow on his cheek, that
   was hot with the insult,
Lifted his eyes to the heavens, and, folding
   his hands as in childhood,
Prayed in the silence of night to the Father
   who seeth in secret.

Meanwhile the choleric Captain strode
   wrathful away to the council,
Found it already assembled, impatiently
   waiting his coming ;
Men in the middle of life, austere and grave
   in deportment,
Only one of them old, the hill that was
   nearest to heaven,
Covered with snow, but erect, the excellent
   Elder of Plymouth.

God had sifted three kingdoms to find the
   wheat for this planting,
Then had sifted the wheat, as the living
   seed of a nation ;
So say the chronicles old, and such is the
   faith of the people !
Near them was standing an Indian, in atti-
   tude stern and defiant,
Naked down to the waist, and grim and
   ferocious in aspect ;
While on the table before them was lying
   unopened a Bible,
Ponderous, bound in leather, brass-studded,
   printed in Holland,
And beside it outstretched the skin of a
   rattlesnake glittered,
Filled, like a quiver, with arrows ; a signal
   and challenge of warfare,
Brought by the Indian, and speaking with
   arrowy tongues of defiance.
This Miles Standish beheld, as he entered,
   and heard them debating
What were an answer befitting the hostile
   message and menace,
Talking of this and of that, contriving, sug-
   gesting, objecting ;
One voice only for peace, and that the
   voice of the Elder,
Judging it wise and well that some at least
   were converted,
Rather than any were slain, for this was
   but Christian behavior !
Then out spake Miles Standish, the stal-
   wart Captain of Plymouth,
Muttering deep in his throat, for his voice
   was husky with anger,
" What ! do you mean to make war with
   milk and the water of roses ?
Is it to shoot red squirrels you have your
   howitzer planted
There on the roof of the church, or is it to
   shoot red devils ?
Truly the only tongue that is understood
   by a savage
Must be the tongue of fire that speaks from
   the mouth of the cannon ! "
Thereupon answered and said the excellent
   Elder of Plymouth,
Somewhat amazed and alarmed at this ir-
   reverent language ;
" Not so thought St. Paul, nor yet the other
   Apostles ;
Not from the cannon's mouth were the
   tongues of fire they spake with ! "

But unheeded fell this mild rebuke on the
    Captain,
Who had advanced to the table, and thus
    continued discoursing :
" Leave this matter to me, for to me by
    right it pertaineth.
War is a terrible trade ; but in the cause
    that is righteous,
Sweet is the smell of powder ; and thus I
    answer the challenge ! "

Then from the rattlesnake's skin, with
    a sudden, contemptuous gesture,
Jerking the Indian arrows, he filled it with
    powder and bullets
Full to the very jaws, and handed it back
    to the savage,
Saying, in thundering tones : " Here, take
    it ! this is your answer ! "
Silently out of the room then glided the
    glistening savage,
Bearing the serpent's skin, and seeming
    himself like a serpent,
Winding his sinuous way in the dark to the
    depths of the forest.

V

THE SAILING OF THE MAYFLOWER

JUST in the gray of the dawn, as the mists
    uprose from the meadows,
There was a stir and a sound in the slum-
    bering village of Plymouth ;
Clanging and clicking of arms, and the
    order imperative, " Forward ! "
Given in tone suppressed, a tramp of feet,
    and then silence.
Figures ten, in the mist, marched slowly
    out of the village.
Standish the stalwart it was, with eight of
    his valorous army,
Led by their Indian guide, by Hobomok,
    friend of the white men,
Northward marching to quell the sudden
    revolt of the savage.
Giants they seemed in the mist, or the
    mighty men of King David ;
Giants in heart they were, who believed in
    God and the Bible, —
Ay, who believed in the smiting of Midian-
    ites and Philistines.
Over them gleamed far off the crimson
    banners of morning ;

Under them loud on the sands, the serried
    billows, advancing,
Fired along the line, and in regular order
    retreated.

Many a mile had they marched, when at
    length the village of Plymouth
Woke from its sleep, and arose, intent on
    its manifold labors.
Sweet was the air and soft ; and slowly the
    smoke from the chimneys
Rose over roofs of thatch, and pointed
    steadily eastward ;
Men came forth from the doors, and paused
    and talked of the weather,
Said that the wind had changed, and was
    blowing fair for the Mayflower ;
Talked of their Captain's departure, and
    all the dangers that menaced,
He being gone, the town, and what should
    be done in his absence.
Merrily sang the birds, and the tender
    voices of women
Consecrated with hymns the common cares
    of the household.
Out of the sea rose the sun, and the billows
    rejoiced at his coming ;
Beautiful were his feet on the purple tops
    of the mountains ;
Beautiful on the sails of the Mayflower
    riding at anchor,
Battered and blackened and worn by all
    the storms of the winter.
Loosely against her masts was hanging and
    flapping her canvas,
Rent by so many gales, and patched by the
    hands of the sailors.
Suddenly from her side, as the sun rose
    over the ocean,
Darted a puff of smoke, and floated sea-
    ward ; anon rang
Loud over field and forest the cannon's
    roar, and the echoes
Heard and repeated the sound, the signal-
    gun of departure !
Ah ! but with louder echoes replied the
    hearts of the people !
Meekly, in voices subdued, the chapter was
    read from the Bible,
Meekly the prayer was begun, but ended
    in fervent entreaty !
Then from their houses in haste came forth
    the Pilgrims of Plymouth,
Men and women and children, all hurrying
    down to the sea-shore.

Eager, with tearful eyes, to say farewell to
  the Mayflower,
Homeward bound o'er the sea, and leaving
  them here in the desert.

Foremost among them was Alden. All
  night he had lain without slum-
  ber,
Turning and tossing about in the heat and
  unrest of his fever.
He had beheld Miles Standish, who came
  back late from the council,
Stalking into the room, and heard him mut-
  ter and murmur ;
Sometimes it seemed a prayer, and some-
  times it sounded like swearing.
Once he had come to the bed, and stood
  there a moment in silence ;
Then he had turned away, and said : "I
  will not awake him ;
Let him sleep on, it is best ; for what is the
  use of more talking ! "
Then he extinguished the light, and threw
  himself down on his pallet,
Dressed as he was, and ready to start at
  the break of the morning, —
Covered himself with the cloak he had
  worn in his campaigns in Flan-
  ders, —
Slept as a soldier sleeps in his bivouac,
  ready for action.
But with the dawn he arose ; in the twilight
  Alden beheld him
Put on his corselet of steel, and all the rest
  of his armor,
Buckle about his waist his trusty blade of
  Damascus,
Take from the corner his musket, and so
  stride out of the chamber.
Often the heart of the youth had burned
  and yearned to embrace him,
Often his lips had essayed to speak, im-
  ploring for pardon ;
All the old friendship came back, with its
  tender and grateful emotions ;
But his pride overmastered the nobler na-
  ture within him, —
Pride, and the sense of his wrong, and the
  burning fire of the insult.
So he beheld his friend departing in anger,
  but spake not,
Saw him go forth to danger, perhaps to
  death, and he spake not !
Then he arose from his bed, and heard
  what the people were saying,

Joined in the talk at the door, with Stephen
  and Richard and Gilbert,
Joined in the morning prayer, and in the
  reading of Scripture,
And, with the others, in haste went hurry-
  ing down to the sea-shore,
Down to the Plymouth Rock, that had been
  to their feet as a doorstep
Into a world unknown, — the corner-stone
  of a nation !

There with his boat was the Master,
  already a little impatient
Lest he should lose the tide, or the wind
  might shift to the eastward,
Square-built, hearty, and strong, with an
  odor of ocean about him,
Speaking with this one and that, and cram-
  ming letters and parcels
Into his pockets capacious, and messages
  mingled together
Into his narrow brain, till at last he was
  wholly bewildered.
Nearer the boat stood Alden, with one foot
  placed on the gunwale,
One still firm on the rock, and talking at
  times with the sailors.
Seated erect on the thwarts, all ready and
  eager for starting.
He too was eager to go, and thus put an
  end to his anguish,
Thinking to fly from despair, that swifter
  than keel is or canvas,
Thinking to drown in the sea the ghost
  that would rise and pursue him.
But as he gazed on the crowd, he beheld
  the form of Priscilla
Standing dejected among them, unconscious
  of all that was passing.
Fixed were her eyes upon his, as if she di-
  vined his intention,
Fixed with a look so sad, so reproachful,
  imploring, and patient,
That with a sudden revulsion his heart re-
  coiled from its purpose,
As from the verge of a crag, where one
  step more is destruction.
Strange is the heart of man, with its quick,
  mysterious instincts !
Strange is the life of man, and fatal or
  fated are moments,
Whereupon turn, as on hinges, the gates of
  the wall adamantine !
"Here I remain ! " he exclaimed, as he
  looked at the heavens above him,

Thanking the Lord whose breath had scat-
  tered the mist and the madness,
Wherein, blind and lost, to death he was
  staggering headlong.
" Yonder snow-white cloud, that floats in
  the ether above me,
Seems like a hand that is pointing and beck-
  oning over the ocean.
There is another hand, that is not so spec-
  tral and ghost-like,
Holding me, drawing me back, and clasp-
  ing mine for protection.
Float, O hand of cloud, and vanish away in
  the ether !
Roll thyself up like a fist, to threaten and
  daunt me ; I heed not
Either your warning or menace, or any
  omen of evil !
There is no land so sacred, no air so pure
  and so wholesome,
As is the air she breathes, and the soil that
  is pressed by her footsteps.
Here for her sake will I stay, and like an
  invisible presence
Hover around her forever, protecting, sup-
  porting her weakness ;
Yes ! as my foot was the first that stepped
  on this rock at the landing,
So, with the blessing of God, shall it be the
  last at the leaving ! "

Meanwhile the Master alert, but with dig-
  nified air and important,
Scanning with watchful eye the tide and
  the wind and the weather,
Walked about on the sands, and the people
  crowded around him
Saying a few last words, and enforcing his
  careful remembrance.
Then, taking each by the hand, as if he
  were grasping a tiller,
Into the boat he sprang, and in haste
  shoved off to his vessel,
Glad in his heart to get rid of all this worry
  and flurry,
Glad to be gone from a land of sand and
  sickness and sorrow,
Short allowance of victual, and plenty of
  nothing but Gospel !
Lost in the sound of the oars was the last
  farewell of the Pilgrims.
O strong hearts and true ! not one went
  back in the Mayflower !
No, not one looked back, who had set his
  hand to this ploughing !

Soon were heard on board the shouts
  and songs of the sailors
Heaving the windlass round, and hoisting
  the ponderous anchor.
Then the yards were braced, and all sails
  set to the west-wind,
Blowing steady and strong ; and the May-
  flower sailed from the harbor,
Rounded the point of the Gurnet, and leav-
  ing far to the southward
Island and cape of sand, and the Field of
  the First Encounter,
Took the wind on her quarter, and stood
  for the open Atlantic,
Borne on the send of the sea, and the swell-
  ing hearts of the Pilgrims.

Long in silence they watched the reced-
  ing sail of the vessel,
Much endeared to them all, as something
  living and human ;
Then, as if filled with the spirit, and wrapt
  in a vision prophetic,
Baring his hoary head, the excellent Elder
  of Plymouth
Said, " Let us pray ! " and they prayed,
  and thanked the Lord and took
  courage.
Mournfully sobbed the waves at the base
  of the rock, and above them
Bowed and whispered the wheat on the
  hill of death, and their kindred
Seemed to awake in their graves, and to
  join in the prayer that they ut-
  tered.
Sun-illumined and white, on the eastern
  verge of the ocean
Gleamed the departing sail, like a marble
  slab in a graveyard ;
Buried beneath it lay forever all hope of
  escaping.
Lo ! as they turned to depart, they saw the
  form of an Indian,
Watching them from the hill ; but while
  they spake with each other,
Pointing with outstretched hands, and say-
  ing, " Look ! " he had vanished.
So they returned to their homes ; but Alden
  lingered a little,
Musing alone on the shore, and watching
  the wash of the billows
Round the base of the rock, and the sparkle
  and flash of the sunshine,
Like the spirit of God, moving visibly over
  the waters.

VI

PRISCILLA

THUS for a while he stood, and mused by
    the shore of the ocean,
Thinking of many things, and most of all
    of Priscilla ;
And as if thought had the power to draw
    to itself, like the loadstone,
Whatsoever it touches, by subtile laws of
    its nature,
Lo ! as he turned to depart, Priscilla was
    standing beside him.

"Are you so much offended, you will not
    speak to me ? " said she.
"Am I so much to blame, that yesterday,
    when you were pleading
Warmly the cause of another, my heart,
    impulsive and wayward,
Pleaded your own, and spake out, forgetful
    perhaps of decorum ?
Certainly you can forgive me for speaking
    so frankly, for saying
What I ought not to have said, yet now I
    can never unsay it ;
For there are moments in life, when the
    heart is so full of emotion,
That if by chance it be shaken, or into its
    depths like a pebble
Drops some careless word, it overflows, and
    its secret,
Spilt on the ground like water, can never
    be gathered together.
Yesterday I was shocked, when I heard
    you speak of Miles Standish,
Praising his virtues, transforming his very
    defects into virtues,
Praising his courage and strength, and even
    his fighting in Flanders,
As if by fighting alone you could win the
    heart of a woman,
Quite overlooking yourself and the rest, in
    exalting your hero.
Therefore I spake as I did, by an irre-
    sistible impulse.
You will forgive me, I hope, for the sake
    of the friendship between us,
Which is too true and too sacred to be so
    easily broken ! "
Thereupon answered John Alden, the
    scholar, the friend of Miles Stan-
    dish :

"I was not angry with you, with myself
    alone I was angry,
Seeing how badly I managed the matter
    I had in my keeping."
"No ! " interrupted the maiden, with answer
    prompt and decisive ;
"No ; you were angry with me, for speak-
    ing so frankly and freely.
It was wrong, I acknowledge ; for it is the
    fate of a woman
Long to be patient and silent, to wait like
    a ghost that is speechless,
Till some questioning voice dissolves the
    spell of its silence.
Hence is the inner life of so many suffering
    women
Sunless and silent and deep, like subter-
    ranean rivers
Running through caverns of darkness, un-
    heard, unseen, and unfruitful,
Chafing their channels of stone, with end-
    less and profitless murmurs."
Thereupon answered John Alden, the young
    man, the lover of women :
"Heaven forbid it, Priscilla ; and truly
    they seem to me always
More like the beautiful rivers that watered
    the garden of Eden,
More like the river Euphrates, through
    deserts of Havilah flowing,
Filling the land with delight, and memories
    sweet of the garden ! "
"Ah, by these words, I can see," again in-
    terrupted the maiden,
"How very little you prize me, or care for
    what I am saying.
When from the depths of my heart, in pain
    and with secret misgiving,
Frankly I speak to you, asking for sym-
    pathy only and kindness,
Straightway you take up my words, that
    are plain and direct and in ear-
    nest,
Turn them away from their meaning, and
    answer with flattering phrases.
This is not right, is not just, is not true to
    the best that is in you ;
For I know and esteem you, and feel that
    your nature is noble,
Lifting mine up to a higher, a more ethereal
    level.
Therefore I value your friendship, and feel
    it perhaps the more keenly
If you say aught that implies I am only as
    one among many,

If you make use of those common and com-
   plimentary phrases
Most men think so fine, in dealing and
   speaking with women,
But which women reject as insipid, if not
   as insulting."

Mute and amazed was Alden ; and lis-
   tened and looked at Priscilla,
Thinking he never had seen her more fair,
   more divine in her beauty.
He who but yesterday pleaded so glibly the
   cause of another,
Stood there embarrassed and silent, and
   seeking in vain for an answer.
So the maiden went on, and little divined
   or imagined
What was at work in his heart, that made
   him so awkward and speechless.
" Let us, then, be what we are, and speak
   what we think, and in all things
Keep ourselves loyal to truth, and the sa-
   cred professions of friendship.
It is no secret I tell you, nor am I ashamed
   to declare it :
I have liked to be with you, to see you, to
   speak with you always.
So I was hurt at your words, and a little
   affronted to hear you
Urge me to marry your friend, though
   he were the Captain Miles Stan-
   dish.
For I must tell you the truth : much more
   to me is your friendship
Than all the love he could give, were he
   twice the hero you think him."
Then she extended her hand, and Alden,
   who eagerly grasped it,
Felt all the wounds in his heart, that were
   aching and bleeding so sorely,
Healed by the touch of that hand, and he
   said, with a voice full of feeling :
" Yes, we must ever be friends ; and of all
   who offer you friendship
Let me be ever the first, the truest, the
   nearest and dearest ! "

Casting a farewell look at the glimmer-
   ing sail of the Mayflower,
Distant, but still in sight, and sinking be-
   low the horizon,
Homeward together they walked, with a
   strange, indefinite feeling,
That all the rest had departed and left
   them alone in the desert.

But, as they went through the fields in the
   blessing and smile of the sunshine,
Lighter grew their hearts, and Priscilla
   said very archly :
" Now that our terrible Captain has gone
   in pursuit of the Indians,
Where he is happier far than he would be
   commanding a household,
You may speak boldly, and tell me of all
   that happened between you,
When you returned last night, and said
   how ungrateful you found me."
Thereupon answered John Alden, and told
   her the whole of the story, —
Told her his own despair, and the direful
   wrath of Miles Standish.
Whereat the maiden smiled, and said be-
   tween laughing and earnest,
" He is a little chimney, and heated hot in
   a moment ! "
But as he gently rebuked her, and told her
   how he had suffered, —
How he had even determined to sail that
   day in the Mayflower,
And had remained for her sake, on hearing
   the dangers that threatened, —
All her manner was changed, and she said
   with a faltering accent,
" Truly I thank you for this : how good
   you have been to me always ! "

Thus, as a pilgrim devout, who toward
   Jerusalem journeys,
Taking three steps in advance, and one
   reluctantly backward,
Urged by importunate zeal, and withheld
   by pangs of contrition ;
Slowly but steadily onward, receding yet
   ever advancing,
Journeyed this Puritan youth to the Holy
   Land of his longings,
Urged by the fervor of love, and withheld
   by remorseful misgivings.

VII

THE MARCH OF MILES STANDISH

MEANWHILE the stalwart Miles Standish
   was marching steadily northward,
Winding through forest and swamp, and
   along the trend of the sea-shore,
All day long, with hardly a halt, the fire of
   his anger

Burning and crackling within, and the sulphurous odor of powder
Seeming more sweet to his nostrils than all the scents of the forest.
Silent and moody he went, and much he revolved his discomfort ;
He who was used to success, and to easy victories always,
Thus to be flouted, rejected, and laughed to scorn by a maiden,
Thus to be mocked and betrayed by the friend whom most he had trusted !
Ah ! 't was too much to be borne, and he fretted and chafed in his armor !

" I alone am to blame," he muttered, " for mine was the folly.
What has a rough old soldier, grown grim and gray in the harness,
Used to the camp and its ways, to do with the wooing of maidens ?
'T was but a dream, — let it pass, — let it vanish like so many others !
What I thought was a flower, is only a weed, and is worthless ;
Out of my heart will I pluck it, and throw it away, and henceforward
Be but a fighter of battles, a lover and wooer of dangers ! "
Thus he revolved in his mind his sorry defeat and discomfort,
While he was marching by day or lying at night in the forest,
Looking up at the trees, and the constellations beyond them.

After a three days' march he came to an Indian encampment
Pitched on the edge of a meadow, between the sea and the forest ;
Women at work by the tents, and warriors, horrid with war-paint,
Seated about a fire, and smoking and talking together ;
Who, when they saw from afar the sudden approach of the white men,
Saw the flash of the sun on breastplate and sabre and musket,
Straightway leaped to their feet, and two, from among them advancing,
Came to parley with Standish, and offer him furs as a present ;
Friendship was in their looks, but in their hearts there was hatred.

Braves of the tribe were these, and brothers, gigantic in stature,
Huge as Goliath of Gath, or the terrible Og, king of Bashan ;
One was Pecksuot named, and the other was called Wattawamat.
Round their necks were suspended their knives in scabbards of wampum,
Two-edged, trenchant knives, with points as sharp as a needle.
Other arms had they none, for they were cunning and crafty.
" Welcome, English ! " they said, — these words they had learned from the traders
Touching at times on the coast, to barter and chaffer for peltries.
Then in their native tongue they began to parley with Standish,
Through his guide and interpreter, Hobomok, friend of the white man,
Begging for blankets and knives, but mostly for muskets and powder,
Kept by the white man, they said, concealed, with the plague, in his cellars,
Ready to be let loose, and destroy his brother the red man !
But when Standish refused, and said he would give them the Bible,
Suddenly changing their tone, they began to boast and to bluster.
Then Wattawamat advanced with a stride in front of the other,
And, with a lofty demeanor, thus vauntingly spake to the Captain :
" Now Wattawamat can see, by the fiery eyes of the Captain,
Angry is he in his heart ; but the heart of the brave Wattawamat
Is not afraid at the sight.   He was not born of a woman,
But on a mountain at night, from an oak-tree riven by lightning,
Forth he sprang at a bound, with all his weapons about him,
Shouting, ' Who is there here to fight with the brave Wattawamat ? ' "
Then he unsheathed his knife, and, whetting the blade on his left hand,
Held it aloft and displayed a woman's face on the handle ;
Saying, with bitter expression and look of sinister meaning :

"I have another at home, with the face of
    a man on the handle ;
By and by they shall marry ; and there
    will be plenty of children !"

Then stood Pecksuot forth, self-vaunt-
    ing, insulting Miles Standish :
While with his fingers he patted the knife
    that hung at his bosom,
Drawing it half from its sheath, and plung-
    ing it back, as he muttered,
"By and by it shall see ; it shall eat ; ah,
    ha ! but shall speak not !
This is the mighty Captain the white men
    have sent to destroy us !
He is a little man ; let him go and work
    with the women !"

Meanwhile Standish had noted the faces
    and figures of Indians
Peeping and creeping about from bush to
    tree in the forest,
Feigning to look for game, with arrows set
    on their bow-strings,
Drawing about him still closer and closer
    the net of their ambush.
But undaunted he stood, and dissembled
    and treated them smoothly ;
So the old chronicles say, that were writ in
    the days of the fathers.
But when he heard their defiance, the boast,
    the taunt, and the insult,
All the hot blood of his race, of Sir Hugh
    and of Thurston de Standish,
Boiled and beat in his heart, and swelled in
    the veins of his temples.
Headlong he leaped on the boaster, and,
    snatching his knife from its scab-
    bard,
Plunged it into his heart, and, reeling back-
    ward, the savage
Fell with his face to the sky, and a fiend-
    like fierceness upon it.
Straight there arose from the forest the
    awful sound of the war-whoop.
And, like a flurry of snow on the whistling
    wind of December,
Swift and sudden and keen came a flight
    of feathery arrows.
Then came a cloud of smoke, and out of
    the cloud came the lightning,
Out of the lightning thunder ; and death
    unseen ran before it.
Frightened the savages fled for shelter in
    swamp and in thicket,

Hotly pursued and beset ; but their sachem,
    the brave Wattawamat,
Fled not ; he was dead. Unswerving and
    swift had a bullet
Passed through his brain, and he fell with
    both hands clutching the green-
    sward,
Seeming in death to hold back from his foe
    the land of his fathers.

There on the flowers of the meadow the
    warriors lay, and above them,
Silent, with folded arms, stood Hobomok,
    friend of the white man.
Smiling at length he exclaimed to the stal-
    wart Captain of Plymouth : —
"Pecksuot bragged very loud, of his cour-
    age, his strength, and his stature, —
Mocked the great Captain, and called him
    a little man ; but I see now
Big enough have you been to lay him
    speechless before you !"

Thus the first battle was fought and won
    by the stalwart Miles Standish.
When the tidings thereof were brought to
    the village of Plymouth,
And as a trophy of war the head of the
    brave Wattawamat
Scowled from the roof of the fort, which at
    once was a church and a fortress,
All who beheld it rejoiced, and praised the
    Lord, and took courage.
Only Priscilla averted her face from this
    spectre of terror,
Thanking God in her heart that she had not
    married Miles Standish ;
Shrinking, fearing almost, lest, coming
    home from his battles,
He should lay claim to her hand, as the
    prize and reward of his valor.

VIII

THE SPINNING-WHEEL

MONTH after month passed away, and in
    Autumn the ships of the merchants
Came with kindred and friends, with cattle
    and corn for the Pilgrims.
All in the village was peace ; the men were
    intent on their labors,
Busy with hewing and building, with
    garden-plot and with merestead,

Busy with breaking the glebe, and mowing
  the grass in the meadows,
Searching the sea for its fish, and hunting
  the deer in the forest.
All in the village was peace ; but at times
  the rumor of warfare
Filled the air with alarm, and the appre-
  hension of danger.
Bravely the stalwart Standish was scouring
  the land with his forces,
Waxing valiant in fight and defeating the
  alien armies,
Till his name had become a sound of fear
  to the nations.
Anger was still in his heart, but at times
  the remorse and contrition
Which in all noble natures succeed the pas-
  sionate outbreak,
Came like a rising tide, that encounters the
  rush of a river,
Staying its current awhile, but making it
  bitter and brackish.

Meanwhile Alden at home had built him
  a new habitation,
Solid, substantial, of timber rough - hewn
  from the firs of the forest.
Wooden-barred was the door, and the roof
  was covered with rushes ;
Latticed the windows were, and the win-
  dow-panes were of paper,
Oiled to admit the light, while wind and
  rain were excluded.
There too he dug a well, and around
  it planted an orchard :
Still may be seen to this day some trace of
  the well and the orchard.
Close to the house was the stall, where, safe
  and secure from annoyance,
Raghorn, the snow-white bull, that had
  fallen to Alden's allotment
In the division of cattle, might ruminate in
  the night-time
Over the pastures he cropped, made fra-
  grant by sweet pennyroyal.

Oft when his labor was finished, with
  eager feet would the dreamer
Follow the pathway that ran through the
  woods to the house of Priscilla,
Led by illusions romantic and subtile
  deceptions of fancy,
Pleasure disguised as duty, and love in the
  semblance of friendship.

Ever of her he thought, when he fashioned
  the walls of his dwelling ;
Ever of her he thought, when he delved
  in the soil of his garden ;
Ever of her he thought, when he read in
  his Bible on Sunday
Praise of the virtuous woman, as she is
  described in the Proverbs, —
How the heart of her husband doth safely
  trust in her always,
How all the days of her life she will do him
  good, and not evil,
How she seeketh the wool and the flax and
  worketh with gladness,
How she layeth her hand to the spindle and
  holdeth the distaff,
How she is not afraid of the snow for her-
  self or her household,
Knowing her household are clothed with
  the scarlet cloth of her weaving !

So as she sat at her wheel one afternoon
  in the Autumn,
Alden, who opposite sat, and was watching
  her dexterous fingers,
As if the thread she was spinning were that
  of his life and his fortune,
After a pause in their talk, thus spake to
  the sound of the spindle.
" Truly, Priscilla," he said, " when I see
  you spinning and spinning,
Never idle a moment, but thrifty and
  thoughtful of others,
Suddenly you are transformed, are visibly
  changed in a moment ;
You are no longer Priscilla, but Bertha
  the Beautiful Spinner."
Here the light foot on the treadle grew
  swifter and swifter ; the spindle
Uttered an angry snarl, and the thread
  snapped short in her fingers ;
While the impetuous speaker, not heeding
  the mischief, continued :
" You are the beautiful Bertha, the spinner,
  the queen of Helvetia ;
She whose story I read at a stall in the
  streets of Southampton,
Who, as she rode on her palfrey, o'er
  valley and meadow and moun-
  tain,
Ever was spinning her thread from a distaff
  fixed to her saddle.
She was so thrifty and good, that her name
  passed into a proverb.

So shall it be with your own, when the spinning-wheel shall no longer
Hum in the house of the farmer, and fill its chambers with music.
Then shall the mothers, reproving, relate how it was in their childhood,
Praising the good old times, and the days of Priscilla the spinner ! "
Straight uprose from her wheel the beautiful Puritan maiden,
Pleased with the praise of her thrift from him whose praise was the sweetest,
Drew from the reel on the table a snowy skein of her spinning,
Thus making answer, meanwhile, to the flattering phrases of Alden :
" Come, you must not be idle ; if I am a pattern for housewives,
Show yourself equally worthy of being the model of husbands.
Hold this skein on your hands, while I wind it, ready for knitting ;
Then who knows but hereafter, when fashions have changed and the manners,
Fathers may talk to their sons of the good old times of John Alden ! "
Thus, with a jest and a laugh, the skein on his hands she adjusted,
He sitting awkwardly there, with his arms extended before him,
She standing graceful, erect, and winding the thread from his fingers,
Sometimes chiding a little his clumsy manner of holding,
Sometimes touching his hands, as she disentangled expertly
Twist or knot in the yarn, unawares — for how could she help it ? —
Sending electrical thrills through every nerve in his body.

Lo ! in the midst of this scene, a breathless messenger entered,
Bringing in hurry and heat the terrible news from the village.
Yes ; Miles Standish was dead ! — an Indian had brought them the tidings, —
Slain by a poisoned arrow, shot down in the front of the battle,
Into an ambush beguiled, cut off with the whole of his forces ;
All the town would be burned, and all the people be murdered !
Such were the tidings of evil that burst on the hearts of the hearers.

Silent and statue-like stood Priscilla, her face looking backward
Still at the face of the speaker, her arms uplifted in horror ;
But John Alden, upstarting, as if the barb of the arrow
Piercing the heart of his friend had struck his own, and had sundered
Once and forever the bonds that held him bound as a captive,
Wild with excess of sensation, the awful delight of his freedom,
Mingled with pain and regret, unconscious of what he was doing,
Clasped, almost with a groan, the motionless form of Priscilla,
Pressing her close to his heart, as forever his own, and exclaiming :
" Those whom the Lord hath united, let no man put them asunder ! "

Even as rivulets twain, from distant and separate sources,
Seeing each other afar, as they leap from the rocks, and pursuing
Each one its devious path, but drawing nearer and nearer,
Rush together at last, at their trysting-place in the forest ;
So these lives that had run thus far in separate channels,
Coming in sight of each other, then swerving and flowing asunder,
Parted by barriers strong, but drawing nearer and nearer,
Rushed together at last, and one was lost in the other.

IX

THE WEDDING-DAY

FORTH from the curtain of clouds, from the tent of purple and scarlet,
Issued the sun, the great High-Priest, in his garments resplendent,
Holiness unto the Lord, in letters of light, on his forehead,
Round the hem of his robe the golden bells and pomegranates.
Blessing the world he came, and the bars of vapor beneath him
Gleamed like a grate of brass, and the sea at his feet was a laver !

This was the wedding morn of Priscilla
  the Puritan maiden.
Friends were assembled together ; the
  Elder and Magistrate also
Graced the scene with their presence, and
  stood like the Law and the Gospel,
One with the sanction of earth and one with
  the blessing of heaven.
Simple and brief was the wedding, as that
  of Ruth and of Boaz.
Softly the youth and the maiden repeated
  the words of betrothal,
Taking each other for husband and wife in
  the Magistrate's presence,
After the Puritan way, and the laudable
  custom of Holland.
Fervently then, and devoutly, the excellent
  Elder of Plymouth
Prayed for the hearth and the home, that
  were founded that day in affection,
Speaking of life and of death, and implor-
  ing Divine benedictions.

Lo ! when the service was ended, a form
  appeared on the threshold,
Clad in armor of steel, a sombre and sor-
  rowful figure !
Why does the bridegroom start and stare
  at the strange apparition ?
Why does the bride turn pale, and hide her
  face on his shoulder ?
Is it a phantom of air, — a bodiless, spectral
  illusion ?
Is it a ghost from the grave, that has come
  to forbid the betrothal ?
Long had it stood there unseen, a guest
  uninvited, unwelcomed ;
Over its clouded eyes there had passed at
  times an expression
Softening the gloom and revealing the warm
  heart hidden beneath them,
As when across the sky the driving rack of
  the rain-cloud
Grows for a moment thin, and betrays the
  sun by its brightness.
Once it had lifted its hand, and moved its
  lips, but was silent,
As if an iron will had mastered the fleeting
  intention.
But when were ended the troth and the
  prayer and the last benediction,
Into the room it strode, and the people be-
  held with amazement
Bodily there in his armor Miles Standish,
  the Captain of Plymouth !

Grasping the bridegroom's hand, he said
  with emotion, " Forgive me !
I have been angry and hurt, — too long
  have I cherished the feeling ;
I have been cruel and hard, but now, thank
  God ! it is ended.
Mine is the same hot blood that leaped in
  the veins of Hugh Standish,
Sensitive, swift to resent, but as swift in
  atoning for error.
Never so much as now was Miles Standish
  the friend of John Alden."
Thereupon answered the bridegroom : " Let
  all be forgotten between us, —
All save the dear old friendship, and that
  shall grow older and dearer ! "
Then the Captain advanced, and, bowing,
  saluted Priscilla,
Gravely, and after the manner of old-fash-
  ioned gentry in England,
Something of camp and of court, of town
  and of country, commingled,
Wishing her joy of her wedding, and loudly
  lauding her husband.
Then he said with a smile : " I should have
  remembered the adage, —
If you would be well served, you must serve
  yourself ; and moreover,
No man can gather cherries in Kent at the
  season of Christmas ! "

Great was the people's amazement, and
  greater yet their rejoicing,
Thus to behold once more the sunburnt
  face of their Captain,
Whom they had mourned as dead ; and they
  gathered and crowded about him,
Eager to see him and hear him, forgetful
  of bride and of bridegroom,
Questioning, answering, laughing, and each
  interrupting the other,
Till the good Captain declared, being quite
  overpowered and bewildered,
He had rather by far break into an Indian
  encampment,
Than come again to a wedding to which he
  had not been invited.

Meanwhile the bridegroom went forth
  and stood with the bride at the
  doorway,
Breathing the perfumed air of that warm
  and beautiful morning.
Touched with autumnal tints, but lonely
  and sad in the sunshine,

Lay extended before them the land of toil
    and privation ;
There were the graves of the dead, and the
    barren waste of the sea-shore,
There the familiar fields, the groves of
    pine, and the meadows ;
But to their eyes transfigured, it seemed
    as the Garden of Eden,
Filled with the presence of God, whose
    voice was the sound of the ocean.

Soon was their vision disturbed by the
    noise and stir of departure,
Friends coming forth from the house, and
    impatient of longer delaying,
Each with his plan for the day, and the
    work that was left uncompleted.
Then from a stall near at hand, amid ex-
    clamations of wonder,
Alden the thoughtful, the careful, so happy,
    so proud of Priscilla,
Brought out his snow-white bull, obeying
    the hand of its master,
Led by a cord that was tied to an iron ring
    in its nostrils,
Covered with crimson cloth, and a cushion
    placed for a saddle.
She should not walk, he said, through the
    dust and heat of the noonday ;
Nay, she should ride like a queen, not plod
    along like a peasant.
Somewhat alarmed at first, but reassured
    by the others,
Placing her hand on the cushion, her foot
    in the hand of her husband,

Gayly, with joyous laugh, Priscilla mounted
    her palfrey.
" Nothing is wanting now," he said with a
    smile, " but the distaff ;
Then you would be in truth my queen, my
    beautiful Bertha ! "

Onward the bridal procession now
    moved to their new habitation,
Happy husband and wife, and friends con-
    versing together.
Pleasantly murmured the brook, as they
    crossed the ford in the forest,
Pleased with the image that passed, like a
    dream of love, through its bosom,
Tremulous, floating in air, o'er the depths
    of the azure abysses.
Down through the golden leaves the sun
    was pouring his splendors,
Gleaming on purple grapes, that, from
    branches above them suspended,
Mingled their odorous breath with the balm
    of the pine and the fir-tree,
Wild and sweet as the clusters that grew
    in the valley of Eshcol.
Like a picture it seemed of the primitive,
    pastoral ages,
Fresh with the youth of the world, and re-
    calling Rebecca and Isaac,
Old and yet ever new, and simple and beau-
    tiful always,
Love immortal and young in the endless
    succession of lovers.
So through the Plymouth woods passed
    onward the bridal procession.

BIRDS OF PASSAGE

. . . come i gru van cantando lor lai,
Facendo in aer di sè lunga riga.
              DANTE.

FLIGHT THE FIRST

BIRDS OF PASSAGE.

This poem, originally published in *The Seaside and
the Fireside*, afforded the poet a convenient title under
which to group successively poems contributed to vari-
ous periodicals, especially *Putnam's Monthly* and *The
Atlantic Monthly*; it has therefore been made the in-
troductory poem. The several *Flights* were printed as
the miscellaneous poems in volumes containing longer
works. The first was contained in the volume which
held *The Courtship of Miles Standish*.

BLACK shadows fall
From the lindens tall,
That lift aloft their massive wall
    Against the southern sky ;

And from the realms
Of the shadowy elms
A tide-like darkness overwhelms
    The fields that round us lie.

But the night is fair,
And everywhere
A warm, soft vapor fills the air,
  And distant sounds seem near ;

And above, in the light
Of the star-lit night,
Swift birds of passage wing their flight
  Through the dewy atmosphere.

I hear the beat
Of their pinions fleet,
As from the land of snow and sleet
  They seek a southern lea.

I hear the cry
Of their voices high
Falling dreamily through the sky,
  But their forms I cannot see.

Oh, say not so !
Those sounds that flow
In murmurs of delight and woe
  Come not from wings of birds.

They are the throngs
Of the poet's songs,
Murmurs of pleasures, and pains, and
      wrongs,
  The sound of wingèd words.

This is the cry
Of souls, that high
On toiling, beating pinions, fly,
  Seeking a warmer clime.

From their distant flight
Through realms of light
It falls into our world of night,
  With the murmuring sound of rhyme.

PROMETHEUS

OR THE POET'S FORETHOUGHT

The two poems *Prometheus* and *Epimetheus* were originally conceived as a single poem, bearing both the names in the title.

OF Prometheus, how undaunted
  On Olympus' shining bastions
His audacious foot he planted,
Myths are told and songs are chanted,
  Full of promptings and suggestions.

Beautiful is the tradition
  Of that flight through heavenly portals,
The old classic superstition
Of the theft and the transmission
  Of the fire of the Immortals !

First the deed of noble daring,
  Born of heavenward aspiration,
Then the fire with mortals sharing,
Then the vulture, — the despairing
  Cry of pain on crags Caucasian.

All is but a symbol painted
  Of the Poet, Prophet, Seer ;
Only those are crowned and sainted
Who with grief have been acquainted,
  Making nations nobler, freer.

In their feverish exultations,
  In their triumph and their yearning,
In their passionate pulsations,
In their words among the nations,
  The Promethean fire is burning.

Shall it, then, be unavailing,
  All this toil for human culture ?
Through the cloud-rack, dark and trailing,
Must they see above them sailing
  O'er life's barren crags the vulture ?

Such a fate as this was Dante's,
  By defeat and exile maddened ;
Thus were Milton and Cervantes,
Nature's priests and Corybantes,
  By affliction touched and saddened.

But the glories so transcendent
  That around their memories cluster,
And, on all their steps attendant,
Make their darkened lives resplendent
  With such gleams of inward lustre !

All the melodies mysterious,
  Through the dreary darkness chanted ;
Thoughts in attitudes imperious,
Voices soft, and deep, and serious,
  Words that whispered, songs that
      haunted !

All the soul in rapt suspension,
  All the quivering, palpitating
Chords of life in utmost tension,
With the fervor of invention,
  With the rapture of creating !

Ah, Prometheus ! heaven-scaling !
   In such hours of exultation
Even the faintest heart, unquailing,
Might behold the vulture sailing
   Round the cloudy crags Caucasian !

Though to all there be not given
   Strength for such sublime endeavor,
Thus to scale the walls of heaven,
And to leaven with fiery leaven,
   All the hearts of men forever ;

Yet all bards, whose hearts unblighted
   Honor and believe the presage,
Hold aloft their torches lighted,
Gleaming through the realms benighted,
   As they onward bear the message !

EPIMETHEUS

OR THE POET'S AFTERTHOUGHT

HAVE I dreamed ? or was it real,
   What I saw as in a vision,
When to marches hymeneal
In the land of the Ideal
   Moved my thought o'er Fields Elysian ?

What ! are these the guests whose glances
   Seemed like sunshine gleaming round me?
These the wild, bewildering fancies,
That with dithyrambic dances
   As with magic circles bound me ?

Ah ! how cold are their caresses !
   Pallid cheeks, and haggard bosoms !
Spectral gleam their snow-white dresses,
And from loose, dishevelled tresses
   Fall the hyacinthine blossoms !

O my songs ! whose winsome measures
   Filled my heart with secret rapture !
Children of my golden leisures !
Must even your delights and pleasures
   Fade and perish with the capture ?

Fair they seemed, those songs sonorous,
   When they came to me unbidden ;
Voices single, and in chorus,
Like the wild birds singing o'er us
   In the dark of branches hidden.

Disenchantment ! Disillusion !
   Must each noble aspiration

Come at last to this conclusion,
Jarring discord, wild confusion,
   Lassitude, renunciation ?

Not with steeper fall nor faster,
   From the sun's serene dominions,
Not through brighter realms nor vaster,
In swift ruin and disaster,
   Icarus fell with shattered pinions !

Sweet Pandora ! dear Pandora !
   Why did mighty Jove create thee
Coy as Thetis, fair as Flora,
Beautiful as young Aurora,
   If to win thee is to hate thee ?

No, not hate thee ! for this feeling
   Of unrest and long resistance
Is but passionate appealing,
A prophetic whisper stealing
   O'er the chords of our existence.

Him whom thou dost once enamor,
   Thou, beloved, never leavest ;
In life's discord, strife, and clamor,
Still he feels thy spell of glamour ;
   Him of Hope thou ne'er bereavest.

Weary hearts by thee are lifted,
   Struggling souls by thee are strength-
      ened,
Clouds of fear asunder rifted,
Truth from falsehood cleansed and sifted,
   Lives, like days in summer, lengthened !

Therefore art thou ever dearer,
   O my Sibyl, my deceiver !
For thou makest each mystery clearer,
And the unattained seems nearer,
   When thou fillest my heart with fever !

Muse of all the Gifts and Graces !
   Though the fields around us wither,
There are ampler realms and spaces,
Where no foot has left its traces :
   Let us turn and wander thither !

THE LADDER OF SAINT AUGUSTINE

SAINT AUGUSTINE ! well hast thou said,
   That of our vices we can frame
A ladder, if we will but tread
   Beneath our feet each deed of shame !

All common things, each day's events,
  That with the hour begin and end,
Our pleasures and our discontents,
  Are rounds by which we may ascend.

The low desire, the base design,
  That makes another's virtues less ;
The revel of the ruddy wine,
  And all occasions of excess ;

The longing for ignoble things ;
  The strife for triumph more than truth ;
The hardening of the heart, that brings
  Irreverence for the dreams of youth ;

All thoughts of ill ; all evil deeds,
  That have their root in thoughts of ill ;
Whatever hinders or impedes
  The action of the nobler will ; —

All these must first be trampled down
  Beneath our feet, if we would gain
In the bright fields of fair renown
  The right of eminent domain.

We have not wings, we cannot soar ;
  But we have feet to scale and climb
By slow degrees, by more and more,
  The cloudy summits of our time.

The mighty pyramids of stone
  That wedge-like cleave the desert airs,
When nearer seen, and better known,
  Are but gigantic flights of stairs.

The distant mountains, that uprear
  Their solid bastions to the skies,
Are crossed by pathways, that appear
  As we to higher levels rise.

The heights by great men reached and
    kept
  Were not attained by sudden flight,
But they, while their companions slept,
  Were toiling upward in the night.

Standing on what too long we bore
  With shoulders bent and downcast eyes,
We may discern — unseen before —
  A path to higher destinies,

Nor deem the irrevocable Past
  As wholly wasted, wholly vain,
If, rising on its wrecks, at last
  To something nobler we attain.

THE PHANTOM SHIP

In Mather's Magnalia Christi,
  Of the old colonial time,
May be found in prose the legend
  That is here set down in rhyme.

A ship sailed from New Haven,
  And the keen and frosty airs,
That filled her sails at parting,
  Were heavy with good men's prayers.

"O Lord ! if it be thy pleasure " —
  Thus prayed the old divine —
" To bury our friends in the ocean,
  Take them, for they are thine ! "

But Master Lamberton muttered,
  And under his breath said he,
" This ship is so crank and walty,
  I fear our grave she will be ! "

And the ships that came from England,
  When the winter months were gone,
Brought no tidings of this vessel
  Nor of Master Lamberton.

This put the people to praying
  That the Lord would let them hear
What in his greater wisdom
  He had done with friends so dear.

And at last their prayers were answered :
  It was in the month of June,
An hour before the sunset
  Of a windy afternoon,

When, steadily steering landward,
  A ship was seen below,
And they knew it was Lamberton, Master,
  Who sailed so long ago.

On she came, with a cloud of canvas,
  Right against the wind that blew,
Until the eye could distinguish
  The faces of the crew.

Then fell her straining topmasts,
  Hanging tangled in the shrouds,
And her sails were loosened and lifted,
  And blown away like clouds.

And the masts, with all their rigging,
  Fell slowly, one by one,

And the hulk dilated and vanished,
As a sea-mist in the sun !

And the people who saw this marvel
Each said unto his friend,
That this was the mould of their vessel,
And thus her tragic end.

And the pastor of the village
Gave thanks to God in prayer,
That, to quiet their troubled spirits,
He had sent this Ship of Air.

THE WARDEN OF THE CINQUE PORTS

Written in October, 1852. The Warden was the Duke of Wellington, who died September 13.

A MIST was driving down the British Channel,
The day was just begun,
And through the window-panes, on floor
and panel,
Streamed the red autumn sun.

It glanced on flowing flag and rippling
pennon,
And the white sails of ships ;
And, from the frowning rampart, the black
cannon
Hailed it with feverish lips.

Sandwich and Romney, Hastings, Hithe,
and Dover
Were all alert that day,
To see the French war-steamers speeding
over,
When the fog cleared away.

Sullen and silent, and like couchant lions,
Their cannon, through the night,
Holding their breath, had watched, in grim
defiance,
The sea-coast opposite.

And now they roared at drum-beat from
their stations
On every citadel ;
Each answering each, with morning saluta-
tions,
That all was well.

And down the coast, all taking up the
burden,
Replied the distant forts,

As if to summon from his sleep the Warden
And Lord of the Cinque Ports.

Him shall no sunshine from the fields of
azure,
No drum-beat from the wall,
No morning gun from the black fort's
embrasure,
Awaken with its call !

No more, surveying with an eye impartial
The long line of the coast,
Shall the gaunt figure of the old Field
Marshal
Be seen upon his post !

For in the night, unseen, a single warrior,
In sombre harness mailed,
Dreaded of man, and surnamed the De-
stroyer,
The rampart wall had scaled.

He passed into the chamber of the sleeper,
The dark and silent room,
And as he entered, darker grew, and
deeper,
The silence and the gloom.

He did not pause to parley or dissemble,
But smote the Warden hoar ;
Ah ! what a blow ! that made all England
tremble
And groan from shore to shore.

Meanwhile, without, the surly cannon
waited,
The sun rose bright o'erhead ;
Nothing in Nature's aspect intimated
That a great man was dead.

HAUNTED HOUSES

ALL houses wherein men have lived and
died
Are haunted houses. Through the open
doors
The harmless phantoms on their errands
glide,
With feet that make no sound upon the
floors.

We meet them at the doorway, on the
stair,
Along the passages they come and go,

Impalpable impressions on the air,
A sense of something moving to and fro.

There are more guests at table than the
hosts
Invited ; the illuminated hall
Is thronged with quiet, inoffensive ghosts,
As silent as the pictures on the wall.

The stranger at my fireside cannot see
The forms I see, nor hear the sounds I
hear ;
He but perceives what is ; while unto me
All that has been is visible and clear.

We have no title-deeds to house or lands ;
Owners and occupants of earlier dates
From graves forgotten stretch their dusty
hands,
And hold in mortmain still their old
estates.

The spirit-world around this world of sense
Floats like an atmosphere, and every-
where
Wafts through these earthly mists and
vapors dense
A vital breath of more ethereal air.

Our little lives are kept in equipoise
By opposite attractions and desires ;
The struggle of the instinct that enjoys,
And the more noble instinct that aspires.

These perturbations, this perpetual jar
Of earthly wants and aspirations high,
Come from the influence of an unseen
star,
An undiscovered planet in our sky.

And as the moon from some dark gate of
cloud
Throws o'er the sea a floating bridge of
light,
Across whose trembling planks our fancies
crowd
Into the realm of mystery and night, —

So from the world of spirits there descends
A bridge of light, connecting it with this,
O'er whose unsteady floor, that sways and
bends,
Wander our thoughts above the dark
abyss.

IN THE CHURCHYARD AT CAM-
BRIDGE

In the village churchyard she lies,
Dust is in her beautiful eyes,
No more she breathes, nor feels, nor
stirs ;
At her feet and at her head
Lies a slave to attend the dead,
But their dust is white as hers.

Was she, a lady of high degree,
So much in love with the vanity
And foolish pomp of this world of ours ?
Or was it Christian charity,
And lowliness and humility,
The richest and rarest of all dowers ?

Who shall tell us ? No one speaks ;
No color shoots into those cheeks,
Either of anger or of pride,
At the rude question we have asked ;
Nor will the mystery be unmasked
By those who are sleeping at her side.

Hereafter ? — And do you think to look
On the terrible pages of that Book
To find her failings, faults, and errors ?
Ah, you will then have other cares,
In your own shortcomings and despairs,
In your own secret sins and terrors !

THE EMPEROR'S BIRD'S-NEST

Once the Emperor Charles of Spain,
With his swarthy, grave commanders,
I forget in what campaign,
Long besieged, in mud and rain,
Some old frontier town of Flanders.

Up and down the dreary camp,
In great boots of Spanish leather,
Striding with a measured tramp,
These Hidalgos, dull and damp,
Cursed the Frenchmen, cursed the
weather.

Thus as to and fro they went
Over upland and through hollow,
Giving their impatience vent,
Perched upon the Emperor's tent,
In her nest, they spied a swallow.

Yes, it was a swallow's nest,
  Built of clay and hair of horses,
Mane, or tail, or dragoon's crest,
Found on hedge-rows east and west,
  After skirmish of the forces.

Then an old Hidalgo said,
  As he twirled his gray mustachio,
" Sure this swallow overhead
Thinks the Emperor's tent a shed,
  And the Emperor but a Macho ! "

Hearing his imperial name
  Coupled with those words of malice,
Half in anger, half in shame,
Forth the great campaigner came
  Slowly from his canvas palace.

" Let no hand the bird molest,"
  Said he solemnly, " nor hurt her ! "
Adding then, by way of jest,
" Golondrina is my guest,
  'T is the wife of some deserter ! "

Swift as bowstring speeds a shaft,
  Through the camp was spread the rumor,
And the soldiers, as they quaffed
Flemish beer at dinner, laughed
  At the Emperor's pleasant humor.

So unharmed and unafraid
  Sat the swallow still and brooded,
Till the constant cannonade
Through the walls a breach had made,
  And the siege was thus concluded.

Then the army, elsewhere bent,
  Struck its tents as if disbanding,
Only not the Emperor's tent,
For he ordered, ere he went,
  Very curtly, " Leave it standing ! "

So it stood there all alone,
  Loosely flapping, torn and tattered,
Till the brood was fledged and flown,
Singing o'er those walls of stone
  Which the cannon-shot had shattered.

THE TWO ANGELS

In a letter to a correspondent written April 25, 1855,
Mr. Longfellow says: " I have only time this morning
to enclose you a poem . . . written on the birth of my
younger daughter, and the death of the young and beau-
tiful wife of my neighbor and friend, the poet Lowell.
It will serve as an answer to one of your questions
about life and its many mysteries. To these dark prob-
lems there is no other solution possible, except the one
word *Providence*."

Two angels, one of Life and one of Death,
  Passed o'er our village as the morning
    broke ;
The dawn was on their faces, and beneath,
  The sombre houses hearsed with plumes
    of smoke.

Their attitude and aspect were the same,
  Alike their features and their robes of
    white ;
But one was crowned with amaranth, as
    with flame,
  And one with asphodels, like flakes of
    light.

I saw them pause on their celestial way ;
  Then said I, with deep fear and doubt
    oppressed,
" Beat not so loud, my heart, lest thou be-
    tray
  The place where thy beloved are at
    rest ! "

And he who wore the crown of asphodels,
  Descending, at my door began to knock,
And my soul sank within me, as in wells
  The waters sink before an earthquake's
    shock.

I recognized the nameless agony,
  The terror and the tremor and the pain,
That oft before had filled or haunted me,
  And now returned with threefold
    strength again.

The door I opened to my heavenly guest,
  And listened, for I thought I heard God's
    voice ;
And, knowing whatsoe'er he sent was best,
  Dared neither to lament nor to rejoice.

Then with a smile, that filled the house
    with light,
  " My errand is not Death, but Life," he
    said ;
And ere I answered, passing out of sight,
  On his celestial embassy he sped.

'T was at thy door, O friend ! and not at
    mine,
  The angel with the amaranthine wreath,

Pausing, descended, and with voice divine
  Whispered a word that had a sound like
    Death.

Then fell upon the house a sudden gloom,
  A shadow on those features fair and
    thin ;
And softly, from that hushed and darkened
    room,
  Two angels issued, where but one went
    in.

All is of God ! If he but wave his hand,
  The mists collect, the rain falls thick
    and loud,
Till, with a smile of light on sea and
    land,
  Lo ! he looks back from the departing
    cloud.

Angels of Life and Death alike are his ;
  Without his leave they pass no threshold
    o'er ;
Who, then, would wish or dare, believing
    this,
  Against his messengers to shut the door ?

DAYLIGHT AND MOONLIGHT

  In broad daylight, and at noon,
  Yesterday I saw the moon
  Sailing high, but faint and white,
  As a school-boy's paper kite.

  In broad daylight, yesterday,
  I read a Poet's mystic lay ;
  And it seemed to me at most
  As a phantom, or a ghost.

  But at length the feverish day
  Like a passion died away,
  And the night, serene and still,
  Fell on village, vale, and hill.

  Then the moon, in all her pride,
  Like a spirit glorified,
  Filled and overflowed the night
  With revelations of her light.

  And the Poet's song again
  Passed like music through my brain ;
  Night interpreted to me
  All its grace and mystery.

THE JEWISH CEMETERY AT NEWPORT

How strange it seems ! These Hebrews
  in their graves,
  Close by the street of this fair seaport
    town,
Silent beside the never-silent waves,
  At rest in all this moving up and
    down !

The trees are white with dust, that o'er
  their sleep
  Wave their broad curtains in the south-
    wind's breath,
While underneath these leafy tents they
  keep
  The long, mysterious Exodus of Death.

And these sepulchral stones, so old and
  brown,
  That pave with level flags their burial-
    place,
Seem like the tablets of the Law, thrown
  down
  And broken by Moses at the mountain's
    base.

The very names recorded here are strange,
  Of foreign accent, and of different
    climes ;
Alvares and Rivera interchange
  With Abraham and Jacob of old times.

"Blessed be God, for he created Death !"
  The mourners said, "and Death is rest
    and peace ;"
Then added, in the certainty of faith,
  "And giveth Life that nevermore shall
    cease."

Closed are the portals of their Synagogue,
  No Psalms of David now the silence
    break,
No Rabbi reads the ancient Decalogue
  In the grand dialect the Prophets spake.

Gone are the living, but the dead remain,
  And not neglected ; for a hand un-
    seen,
Scattering its bounty, like a summer rain,
  Still keeps their graves and their remem-
    brance green.

How came they here ?   What burst of
    Christian hate,
What persecution, merciless and blind,
Drove o'er the sea — that desert deso-
    late —
    These Ishmaels and Hagars of mankind ?

They lived in narrow streets and lanes ob-
    scure,
    Ghetto and Judenstrass, in mirk and
    mire ;
Taught in the school of patience to endure
    The life of anguish and the death of
    fire.

All their lives long, with the unleavened
    bread
And bitter herbs of exile and its fears,
The wasting famine of the heart they fed,
    And slaked its thirst with marah of their
    tears.

Anathema maranatha ! was the cry
    That rang from town to town, from
    street to street :
At every gate the accursed Mordecai
    Was mocked and jeered, and spurned by
    Christian feet.

Pride and humiliation hand in hand
    Walked with them through the world
    where'er they went ;
Trampled and beaten were they as the
    sand,
    And yet unshaken as the continent.

For in the background figures vague and
    vast
    Of patriarchs and of prophets rose sub-
    lime,
And all the great traditions of the Past
    They saw reflected in the coming time.

And thus forever with reverted look
    The mystic volume of the world they
    read,
Spelling it backward, like a Hebrew book,
    Till life became a Legend of the Dead.

But ah ! what once has been shall be no
    more !
    The groaning earth in travail and in pain
Brings forth its races, but does not re-
    store,
And the dead nations never rise again.

OLIVER BASSELIN

In the Valley of the Vire
    Still is seen an ancient mill,
With its gables quaint and queer,
    And beneath the window-sill,
      On the stone,
      These words alone :
" Oliver Basselin lived here."

Far above it, on the steep,
    Ruined stands the old Château ;
Nothing but the donjon-keep
    Left for shelter or for show.
      Its vacant eyes
      Stare at the skies,
Stare at the valley green and deep.

Once a convent, old and brown,
    Looked, but ah ! it looks no more,
From the neighboring hillside down
    On the rushing and the roar
      Of the stream
      Whose sunny gleam
Cheers the little Norman town.

In that darksome mill of stone,
    To the water's dash and din,
Careless, humble, and unknown,
    Sang the poet Basselin
      Songs that fill
      That ancient mill
With a splendor of its own.

Never feeling of unrest
    Broke the pleasant dream he dreamed;
Only made to be his nest,
    All the lovely valley seemed ;
      No desire
      Of soaring higher
Stirred or fluttered in his breast.

True, his songs were not divine ;
    Were not songs of that high art,
Which, as winds do in the pine,
    Find an answer in each heart ;
      But the mirth
      Of this green earth
Laughed and revelled in his line.

From the alehouse and the inn,
    Opening on the narrow street,
Came the loud, convivial din,
    Singing and applause of feet,

The laughing lays
That in those days
Sang the poet Basselin.

In the castle, cased in steel,
  Knights, who fought at Agincourt,
Watched and waited, spur on heel ;
  But the poet sang for sport
    Songs that rang
    Another clang,
Songs that lowlier hearts could feel.

In the convent, clad in gray,
  Sat the monks in lonely cells,
Paced the cloisters, knelt to pray,
  And the poet heard their bells ;
    But his rhymes
    Found other chimes,
Nearer to the earth than they.

Gone are all the barons bold,
  Gone are all the knights and squires,
Gone the abbot stern and cold,
  And the brotherhood of friars ;
    Not a name
    Remains to fame,
From those mouldering days of old !

But the poet's memory here
  Of the landscape makes a part ;
Like the river, swift and clear,
  Flows his song through many a heart ;
    Haunting still
    That ancient mill
In the Valley of the Vire.

VICTOR GALBRAITH

UNDER the walls of Monterey
At daybreak the bugles began to play,
    Victor Galbraith !
In the mist of the morning damp and
    gray,
These were the words they seemed to say :
    "Come forth to thy death,
    Victor Galbraith ! "

Forth he came, with a martial tread ;
Firm was his step, erect his head ;
    Victor Galbraith,
He who so well the bugle played,
Could not mistake the words it said :
    "Come forth to thy death,
    Victor Galbraith ! "

He looked at the earth, he looked at the
    sky,
He looked at the files of musketry,
    Victor Galbraith !
And he said, with a steady voice and eye,
    "Take good aim ; I am ready to die !"
    Thus challenges death
    Victor Galbraith.

Twelve fiery tongues flashed straight and
    red,
Six leaden balls on their errand sped ;
    Victor Galbraith
Falls to the ground, but he is not dead :
His name was not stamped on those balls of
    lead,
    And they only scath
    Victor Galbraith.

Three balls are in his breast and brain,
But he rises out of the dust again,
    Victor Galbraith !
The water he drinks has a bloody stain ;
    "Oh kill me, and put me out of my
    pain ! "
    In his agony prayeth
    Victor Galbraith.

Forth dart once more those tongues of
    flame,
And the bugler has died a death of shame,
    Victor Galbraith !
His soul has gone back to whence it came,
And no one answers to the name,
    When the Sergeant saith,
    " Victor Galbraith ! "

Under the walls of Monterey
By night a bugle is heard to play,
    Victor Galbraith !
Through the mist of the valley damp and
    gray
The sentinels hear the sound, and say,
    "That is the wraith
    Of Victor Galbraith ! "

MY LOST YOUTH

During one of his visits to Portland in 1846, Mr.
Longfellow relates how he took a long walk round
Munjoy's hill and down to the old Fort Lawrence.
"I lay down," he says, "in one of the embrasures and
listened to the lashing, lulling sound of the sea just at
my feet. It was a beautiful afternoon, and the harbor
was full of white sails, coming and departing. Med-
itated a poem on the Old Fort." It does not appear

that any poem was then written, but the theme remained, and in 1855, when in Cambridge, he notes in his diary, March 29 : "A day of pain ; cowering over the fire. At night, as I lie in bed, a poem comes into my mind, — a memory of Portland, — my native town, the city by the sea.

Siede la terra dove nato fui
Sulla marina.

"March 30. Wrote the poem ; and am rather pleased with it, and with the bringing in of the two lines of the old Lapland song,

A boy's will is the wind's will,
And the thoughts of youth are long, long thoughts."

OFTEN I think of the beautiful town
  That is seated by the sea ;
Often in thought go up and down
The pleasant streets of that dear old town,
  And my youth comes back to me.
    And a verse of a Lapland song
    Is haunting my memory still :
    " A boy's will is the wind's will,
And the thoughts of youth are long, long
    thoughts."

I can see the shadowy lines of its trees,
  And catch, in sudden gleams,
The sheen of the far-surrounding seas,
And islands that were the Hesperides
  Of all my boyish dreams.
    And the burden of that old song,
    It murmurs and whispers still :
    " A boy's will is the wind's will,
And the thoughts of youth are long, long
    thoughts."

I remember the black wharves and the
    slips,
  And the sea-tides tossing free ;
And Spanish sailors with bearded lips,
And the beauty and mystery of the ships,
  And the magic of the sea.
    And the voice of that wayward song
    Is singing and saying still :
    " A boy's will is the wind's will,
And the thoughts of youth are long, long
    thoughts."

I remember the bulwarks by the shore,
  And the fort upon the hill ;
The sunrise gun, with its hollow roar,
The drum-beat repeated o'er and o'er,
  And the bugle wild and shrill.
    And the music of that old song
    Throbs in my memory still :
    " A boy's will is the wind's will,
And the thoughts of youth are long, long
    thoughts."

I remember the sea-fight far away,
  How it thundered o'er the tide !
And the dead captains, as they lay
In their graves, o'erlooking the tranquil bay
  Where they in battle died.
    And the sound of that mournful song
    Goes through me with a thrill :
    " A boy's will is the wind's will,
And the thoughts of youth are long, long
    thoughts."

I can see the breezy dome of groves,
  The shadows of Deering's Woods ;
And the friendships old and the early
    loves
Come back with a Sabbath sound, as of
    doves
  In quiet neighborhoods.
    And the verse of that sweet old song,
    It flutters and murmurs still :
    " A boy's will is the wind's will,
And the thoughts of youth are long, long
    thoughts."

I remember the gleams and glooms that
    dart
  Across the school-boy's brain ;
The song and the silence in the heart,
That in part are prophecies, and in part
  Are longings wild and vain.
    And the voice of that fitful song
    Sings on, and is never still :
    " A boy's will is the wind's will,
And the thoughts of youth are long, long
    thoughts."

There are things of which I may not
    speak ;
  There are dreams that cannot die ;
There are thoughts that make the strong
    heart weak,
And bring a pallor into the cheek,
  And a mist before the eye.
    And the words of that fatal song
    Come over me like a chill :
    " A boy's will is the wind's will,
And the thoughts of youth are long, long
    thoughts."

Strange to me now are the forms I meet
  When I visit the dear old town ;
But the native air is pure and sweet,
And the trees that o'ershadow each well-
    known street,
  As they balance up and down,

Are singing the beautiful song,
Are sighing and whispering still :
" A boy's will is the wind's will,
And the thoughts of youth are long, long
    thoughts."

And Deering's Woods are fresh and fair,
  And with joy that is almost pain
My heart goes back to wander there,
And among the dreams of the days that
    were,
  I find my lost youth again.
    And the strange and beautiful song,
    The groves are repeating it still :
" A boy's will is the wind's will,
And the thoughts of youth are long, long
    thoughts."

THE ROPEWALK

In that building, long and low,
With its windows all a-row,
  Like the port-holes of a hulk,
Human spiders spin and spin,
Backward down their threads so thin
  Dropping, each a hempen bulk.

At the end, an open door ;
Squares of sunshine on the floor
  Light the long and dusky lane ;
And the whirring of a wheel,
Dull and drowsy, makes me feel
  All its spokes are in my brain.

As the spinners to the end
Downward go and reascend,
  Gleam the long threads in the sun ;
While within this brain of mine
Cobwebs brighter and more fine
  By the busy wheel are spun.

Two fair maidens in a swing,
Like white doves upon the wing,
  First before my vision pass ;
Laughing, as their gentle hands
Closely clasp the twisted strands,
  At their shadow on the grass.

Then a booth of mountebanks,
With its smell of tan and planks,
  And a girl poised high in air
On a cord, in spangled dress,
With a faded loveliness,
  And a weary look of care.

Then a homestead among farms,
And a woman with bare arms
  Drawing water from a well ;
As the bucket mounts apace,
With it mounts her own fair face,
  As at some magician's spell.

Then an old man in a tower,
Ringing loud the noontide hour,
  While the rope coils round and round
Like a serpent at his feet,
And again, in swift retreat,
  Nearly lifts him from the ground.

Then within a prison-yard,
Faces fixed, and stern, and hard,
  Laughter and indecent mirth ;
Ah ! it is the gallows-tree !
Breath of Christian charity,
  Blow, and sweep it from the earth !

Then a school-boy, with his kite
Gleaming in a sky of light,
  And an eager, upward look ;
Steeds pursued through lane and field ;
Fowlers with their snares concealed ;
  And an angler by a brook.

Ships rejoicing in the breeze,
Wrecks that float o'er unknown seas,
  Anchors dragged through faithless
    sand ;
Sea-fog drifting overhead,
And, with lessening line and lead,
  Sailors feeling for the land.

All these scenes do I behold,
These, and many left untold,
  In that building long and low ;
While the wheel goes round and round,
With a drowsy, dreamy sound,
  And the spinners backward go.

THE GOLDEN MILE-STONE

" December 20, 1854. The weather is ever so cold.
The landscape looks dreary ; but the sunset and twilight
are resplendent. Sketch out a poem, *The Golden Mile-
Stone*."

LEAFLESS are the trees ; their purple
    branches
Spread themselves abroad, like reefs of
    coral,
        Rising silent
In the Red Sea of the winter sunset.

From the hundred chimneys of the village,
Like the Afreet in the Arabian story,
    Smoky columns
Tower aloft into the air of amber.

At the window winks the flickering fire-
    light ;
Here and there the lamps of evening glim-
    mer,
    Social watch-fires
Answering one another through the dark-
    ness.

On the hearth the lighted logs are glowing,
And like Ariel in the cloven pine-tree
    For its freedom
Groans and sighs the air imprisoned in
    them.

By the fireside there are old men seated,
Seeing ruined cities in the ashes,
    Asking sadly
Of the Past what it can ne'er restore them.

By the fireside there are youthful dreamers,
Building castles fair, with stately stairways,
    Asking blindly
Of the Future what it cannot give them.

By the fireside tragedies are acted
In whose scenes appear two actors only,
    Wife and husband,
And above them God the sole spectator.

By the fireside there are peace and comfort,
Wives and children, with fair, thoughtful
    faces,
    Waiting, watching
For a well-known footstep in the passage.

Each man's chimney is his Golden Mile-
    Stone ;
Is the central point, from which he mea-
    sures
    Every distance
Through the gateways of the world around
    him.

In his farthest wanderings still he sees it ;
Hears the talking flame, the answering
    night-wind,
    As he heard them
When he sat with those who were, but are
    not.

Happy he whom neither wealth nor fash-
    ion,
Nor the march of the encroaching city,
    Drives an exile
From the hearth of his ancestral home-
    stead.

We may build more splendid habitations,
Fill our rooms with paintings and with
    sculptures,
    But we cannot
Buy with gold the old associations !

CATAWBA WINE

Written on the receipt of a gift of Catawba wine from
the vineyards of Nicholas Longworth on the Ohio River.

THIS song of mine
Is a Song of the Vine,
To be sung by the glowing embers
    Of wayside inns,
    When the rain begins
To darken the drear Novembers.

    It is not a song
    Of the Scuppernong,
From warm Carolinian valleys,
    Nor the Isabel
    And the Muscadel
That bask in our garden alleys.

    Nor the red Mustang,
    Whose clusters hang
O'er the waves of the Colorado,
    And the fiery flood
    Of whose purple blood
Has a dash of Spanish bravado.

    For richest and best
    Is the wine of the West,
That grows by the Beautiful River ;
    Whose sweet perfume
    Fills all the room
With a benison on the giver.

    And as hollow trees
    Are the haunts of bees,
Forever going and coming ;
    So this crystal hive
    Is all alive
With a swarming and buzzing and hum
    ming.

Very good in its way
Is the Verzenay,
Or the Sillery soft and creamy;
But Catawba wine
Has a taste more divine,
More dulcet, delicious, and dreamy.

There grows no vine
By the haunted Rhine,
By Danube or Guadalquivir,
Nor on island or cape,
That bears such a grape
As grows by the Beautiful River.

Drugged is their juice
For foreign use,
When shipped o'er the reeling Atlantic,
To rack our brains
With the fever pains,
That have driven the Old World frantic.

To the sewers and sinks
With all such drinks,
And after them tumble the mixer ;
For a poison malign
Is such Borgia wine,
Or at best but a Devil's Elixir.

While pure as a spring
Is the wine I sing,
And to praise it, one needs but name it ;
For Catawba wine
Has need of no sign,
No tavern-bush to proclaim it.

And this Song of the Vine,
This greeting of mine,
The winds and the birds shall deliver
To the Queen of the West,
In her garlands dressed,
On the banks of the Beautiful River.

SANTA FILOMENA

Published in the first number of the *Atlantic Monthly*, November, 1857. "For the legend," Mr. Longfellow writes to Mr. Sumner, "see Mrs. Jameson's *Legendary Art*. The modern application you will not miss. In Italian, one may say *Filomela* or *Filomena*." The reference is to Miss Florence Nightingale, who rendered great service in the hospitals during the Crimean War.

WHENE'ER a noble deed is wrought,
Whene'er is spoken a noble thought,

Our hearts, in glad surprise,
To higher levels rise.

The tidal wave of deeper souls
Into our inmost being rolls,
And lifts us unawares
Out of all meaner cares.

Honor to those whose words or deeds
Thus help us in our daily needs,
And by their overflow
Raise us from what is low !

Thus thought I, as by night I read
Of the great army of the dead,
The trenches cold and damp,
The starved and frozen camp, —

The wounded from the battle-plain,
In dreary hospitals of pain,
The cheerless corridors,
The cold and stony floors.

Lo ! in that house of misery
A lady with a lamp I see
Pass through the glimmering gloom,
And flit from room to room.

And slow, as in a dream of bliss,
The speechless sufferer turns to kiss
Her shadow, as it falls
Upon the darkening walls.

As if a door in heaven should be
Opened and then closed suddenly,
The vision came and went,
The light shone and was spent.

On England's annals, through the long
Hereafter of her speech and song,
That light its rays shall cast
From portals of the past.

A Lady with a Lamp shall stand
In the great history of the land,
A noble type of good,
Heroic womanhood.

Nor even shall be wanting here
The palm, the lily, and the spear,
The symbols that of yore
Saint Filomena bore.

THE DISCOVERER OF THE NORTH CAPE

A LEAF FROM KING ALFRED'S OROSIUS

OTHERE, the old sea-captain,
　Who dwelt in Helgoland,
To King Alfred, the Lover of Truth,
Brought a snow-white walrus-tooth,
　Which he held in his brown right hand.

His figure was tall and stately,
　Like a boy's his eye appeared ;
His hair was yellow as hay,
But threads of a silvery gray
　Gleamed in his tawny beard.

Hearty and hale was Othere,
　His cheek had the color of oak ;
With a kind of a laugh in his speech,
Like the sea-tide on a beach,
　As unto the King he spoke.

And Alfred, King of the Saxons,
　Had a book upon his knees,
And wrote down the wondrous tale
Of him who was first to sail
　Into the Arctic seas.

" So far I live to the northward,
　No man lives north of me ;
To the east are wild mountain-chains,
And beyond them meres and plains ;
　To the westward all is sea.

" So far I live to the northward,
　From the harbor of Skeringes-hale,
If you only sailed by day,
With a fair wind all the way,
　More than a month would you sail.

" I own six hundred reindeer,
　With sheep and swine beside ;
I have tribute from the Finns,
Whalebone and reindeer-skins,
　And ropes of walrus-hide.

" I ploughed the land with horses,
　But my heart was ill at ease,
For the old seafaring men
Came to me now and then,
　With their sagas of the seas ; —

" Of Iceland and of Greenland,
　And the stormy Hebrides,
And the undiscovered deep ; —
Oh I could not eat nor sleep
　For thinking of those seas.

" To the northward stretched the des-
　ert,
　How far I fain would know ;
So at last I sallied forth,
And three days sailed due north,
　As far as the whale-ships go.

" To the west of me was the ocean,
　To the right the desolate shore,
But I did not slacken sail
For the walrus or the whale,
　Till after three days more.

" The days grew longer and longer,
　Till they became as one,
And northward through the haze
I saw the sullen blaze
　Of the red midnight sun.

" And then uprose before me,
　Upon the water's edge,
The huge and haggard shape
Of that unknown North Cape,
　Whose form is like a wedge.

" The sea was rough and stormy,
　The tempest howled and wailed,
And the sea-fog, like a ghost,
Haunted that dreary coast,
　But onward still I sailed.

" Four days I steered to eastward,
　Four days without a night :
Round in a fiery ring
Went the great sun, O King,
　With red and lurid light."

Here Alfred, King of the Saxons,
　Ceased writing for a while ;
And raised his eyes from his book,
With a strange and puzzled look,
　And an incredulous smile.

But Othere, the old sea-captain,
　He neither paused nor stirred,
Till the King listened, and then
Once more took up his pen,
　And wrote down every word.

" And now the land," said Othere,
  " Bent southward suddenly,
And I followed the curving shore
And ever southward bore
  Into a nameless sea.

" And there we hunted the walrus,
  The narwhale, and the seal ;
Ha ! 't was a noble game !
And like the lightning's flame
  Flew our harpoons of steel.

" There were six of us all together,
  Norsemen of Helgoland ;
In two days and no more
We killed of them threescore,
  And dragged them to the strand ! "

Here Alfred the Truth-teller
  Suddenly closed his book,
And lifted his blue eyes,
With doubt and strange surmise
  Depicted in their look.

And Othere the old sea-captain
  Stared at him wild and weird,
Then smiled, till his shining teeth
Gleamed white from underneath
  His tawny, quivering beard.

And to the King of the Saxons,
  In witness of the truth,
Raising his noble head,
He stretched his brown hand, and said,
  " Behold this walrus-tooth ! "

DAYBREAK

A WIND came up out of the sea,
And said, " O mists, make room for me."

It hailed the ships, and cried, " Sail on,
Ye mariners, the night is gone."

And hurried landward far away,
Crying, " Awake ! it is the day."

It said unto the forest, " Shout !
Hang all your leafy banners out ! "

It touched the wood-bird's folded wing,
And said, " O bird, awake and sing."

And o'er the farms, " O chanticleer,
Your clarion blow ; the day is near."

It whispered to the fields of corn,
" Bow down, and hail the coming morn."

It shouted through the belfry-tower,
" Awake, O bell ! proclaim the hour."

It crossed the churchyard with a sigh,
And said, " Not yet ! in quiet lie."

THE FIFTIETH BIRTHDAY OF AGASSIZ

MAY 28, 1857

Read by Mr. Longfellow at a dinner, at which he presided, given to Agassiz on the occasion.

IT was fifty years ago
  In the pleasant month of May,
In the beautiful Pays de Vaud,
  A child in its cradle lay.

And Nature, the old nurse, took
  The child upon her knee,
Saying : " Here is a story-book
  Thy Father has written for thee."

" Come, wander with me," she said,
  " Into regions yet untrod ;
And read what is still unread
  In the manuscripts of God."

And he wandered away and away
  With Nature, the dear old nurse,
Who sang to him night and day
  The rhymes of the universe.

And whenever the way seemed long,
  Or his heart began to fail,
She would sing a more wonderful song,
  Or tell a more marvellous tale.

So she keeps him still a child,
  And will not let him go,
Though at times his heart beats wild
  For the beautiful Pays de Vaud ;

Though at times he hears in his dreams
  The Ranz des Vaches of old,
And the rush of mountain streams
  From glaciers clear and cold ;

And the mother at home says, " Hark !
　For his voice I listen and yearn ;
It is growing late and dark,
　And my boy does not return ! "

CHILDREN

COME to me, O ye children !
　For I hear you at your play,
And the questions that perplexed me
　Have vanished quite away.

Ye open the eastern windows,
　That look towards the sun,
Where thoughts are singing swallows
　And the brooks of morning run.

In your hearts are the birds and the sun-
　　shine,
In your thoughts the brooklet's flow,
But in mine is the wind of Autumn
　And the first fall of the snow.

Ah ! what would the world be to us
　If the children were no more ?
We should dread the desert behind us
　Worse than the dark before.

What the leaves are to the forest,
　With light and air for food,
Ere their sweet and tender juices
　Have been hardened into wood, —

That to the world are children ;
　Through them it feels the glow
Of a brighter and sunnier climate
　Than reaches the trunks below.

Come to me, O ye children !
　And whisper in my ear
What the birds and the winds are sing-
　　ing
In your sunny atmosphere.

For what are all our contrivings,
　And the wisdom of our books,
When compared with your caresses,
　And the gladness of your looks ?

Ye are better than all the ballads
　That ever were sung or said ;
For ye are living poems,
　And all the rest are dead.

SANDALPHON

HAVE you read in the Talmud of old,
In the Legends the Rabbins have told
　Of the limitless realms of the air,
Have you read it, — the marvellous story
Of Sandalphon, the Angel of Glory,
　Sandalphon, the Angel of Prayer ?

How, erect, at the outermost gates
Of the City Celestial he waits,
　With his feet on the ladder of light,
That, crowded with angels unnumbered,
By Jacob was seen, as he slumbered
　Alone in the desert at night ?

The Angels of Wind and of Fire
Chant only one hymn, and expire
　With the song's irresistible stress ;
Expire in their rapture and wonder,
As harp-strings are broken asunder
　By music they throb to express.

But serene in the rapturous throng,
Unmoved by the rush of the song,
　With eyes unimpassioned and slow,
Among the dead angels, the deathless
Sandalphon stands listening breathless
　To sounds that ascend from below ; —

From the spirits on earth that adore,
From the souls that entreat and implore
　In the fervor and passion of prayer ;
From the hearts that are broken with losses,
And weary with dragging the crosses
　Too heavy for mortals to bear.

And he gathers the prayers as he stands,
And they change into flowers in his hands,
　Into garlands of purple and red ;
And beneath the great arch of the portal,
Through the streets of the City Immortal
　Is wafted the fragrance they shed.

It is but a legend, I know, —
A fable, a phantom, a show,
　Of the ancient Rabbinical lore ;
Yet the old mediæval tradition,
The beautiful, strange superstition,
　But haunts me and holds me the more.

When I look from my window at night,
And the welkin above is all white,
　All throbbing and panting with stars,

Among them majestic is standing
Sandalphon the angel, expanding
  His pinions in nebulous bars.

And the legend, I feel, is a part
Of the hunger and thirst of the heart,
  The frenzy and fire of the brain,
That grasps at the fruitage forbidden,
The golden pomegranates of Eden,
  To quiet its fever and pain.

FLIGHT THE SECOND

Included in the volume which contained the first
series of *Tales of a Wayside Inn*, 1863.

THE CHILDREN'S HOUR

BETWEEN the dark and the daylight,
  When the night is beginning to lower,
Comes a pause in the day's occupations,
  That is known as the Children's Hour.

I hear in the chamber above me
  The patter of little feet,
The sound of a door that is opened,
  And voices soft and sweet.

From my study I see in the lamplight,
  Descending the broad hall stair,
Grave Alice, and laughing Allegra,
  And Edith with golden hair.

A whisper, and then a silence :
  Yet I know by their merry eyes
They are plotting and planning together
  To take me by surprise.

A sudden rush from the stairway,
  A sudden raid from the hall !
By three doors left unguarded
  They enter my castle wall !

They climb up into my turret
  O'er the arms and back of my chair ;
If I try to escape, they surround me ;
  They seem to be everywhere.

They almost devour me with kisses,
  Their arms about me entwine,
Till I think of the Bishop of Bingen
  In his Mouse-Tower on the Rhine !

Do you think, O blue-eyed banditti,
  Because you have scaled the wall,
Such an old mustache as I am
  Is not a match for you all !

I have you fast in my fortress,
  And will not let you depart,
But put you down into the dungeon
  In the round-tower of my heart.

And there will I keep you forever,
  Yes, forever and a day,
Till the walls shall crumble to ruin,
  And moulder in dust away !

ENCELADUS

Written February 3, 1859. "I have written," says
Mr. Longfellow in a letter to Mr. Sumner, " a lyric on
Italy, entitled *Enceladus*, from which title your imagi-
nation can construct the poem. It is not a war-song,
but a kind of lament for the woes of the country."
Mr. Longfellow used the money paid him for the poem,
which appeared in the *Atlantic Monthly*, August, 1859,
in aid of the Italian widows and the soldiers wounded
in the war then going on for the deliverance of Italy
from Austrian rule.

UNDER Mount Etna he lies,
  It is slumber, it is not death ;
For he struggles at times to arise,
And above him the lurid skies
  Are hot with his fiery breath.

The crags are piled on his breast,
  The earth is heaped on his head ;
But the groans of his wild unrest,
Though smothered and half suppressed,
  Are heard, and he is not dead.

And the nations far away
  Are watching with eager eyes ;
They talk together and say,
" To-morrow, perhaps to-day,
  Enceladus will arise ! "

And the old gods, the austere
  Oppressors in their strength,
Stand aghast and white with fear
At the ominous sounds they hear,
  And tremble, and mutter, "At length ! "

Ah me ! for the land that is sown
  With the harvest of despair !
Where the burning cinders, blown
From the lips of the overthrown
  Enceladus, fill the air ;

Where ashes are heaped in drifts
　　Over vineyard and field and town,
Whenever he starts and lifts
His head through the blackened rifts
　　Of the crags that keep him down.

See, see ! the red light shines !
　　'T is the glare of his awful eyes !
And the storm - wind shouts through the
　　　pines
Of Alps and of Apennines,
　　" Enceladus, arise ! "

THE CUMBERLAND

At anchor in Hampton Roads we lay,
　　On board of the Cumberland, sloop-of-
　　　war ;
And at times from the fortress across the
　　bay
　　The alarum of drums swept past,
　　Or a bugle blast
From the camp on the shore.

Then far away to the south uprose
　　A little feather of snow-white smoke,
And we knew that the iron ship of our
　　foes
　　Was steadily steering its course
　　To try the force
Of our ribs of oak.

Down upon us heavily runs,
　　Silent and sullen, the floating fort ;
Then comes a puff of smoke from her
　　guns,
　　And leaps the terrible death,
　　With fiery breath,
From each open port.

We are not idle, but send her straight
　　Defiance back in a full broadside !
As hail rebounds from a roof of slate,
　　Rebounds our heavier hail
　　From each iron scale
Of the monster's hide.

" Strike your flag ! " the rebel cries,
　　In his arrogant old plantation strain.
" Never ! " our gallant Morris replies ;
　　" It is better to sink than to yield ! "
　　And the whole air pealed
With the cheers of our men.

Then, like a kraken huge and black,
　　She crushed our ribs in her iron grasp !
Down went the Cumberland all a wrack,
　　With a sudden shudder of death,
　　And the cannon's breath
For her dying gasp.

Next morn, as the sun rose over the bay,
　　Still floated our flag at the mainmast head.
Lord, how beautiful was Thy day !
　　Every waft of the air
　　Was a whisper of prayer,
Or a dirge for the dead.

Ho ! brave hearts that went down in the
　　seas !
　　Ye are at peace in the troubled stream ;
Ho ! brave land ! with hearts like these,
　　Thy flag, that is rent in twain,
　　Shall be one again,
And without a seam !

SNOW-FLAKES

Out of the bosom of the Air,
　　Out of the cloud-folds of her garments
　　　shaken,
Over the woodlands brown and bare,
　　Over the harvest-fields forsaken,
　　Silent, and soft, and slow
　　Descends the snow.

Even as our cloudy fancies take
　　Suddenly shape in some divine expres-
　　　sion,
Even as the troubled heart doth make
　　In the white countenance confession,
　　The troubled sky reveals
　　The grief it feels.

This is the poem of the air,
　　Slowly in silent syllables recorded ;
This is the secret of despair,
　　Long in its cloudy bosom hoarded,
　　Now whispered and revealed
　　To wood and field.

A DAY OF SUNSHINE

O gift of God ! O perfect day :
Whereon shall no man work, but play ;
Whereon it is enough for me,
Not to be doing, but to be !

Through every fibre of my brain,
Through every nerve, through every
        vein,
I feel the electric thrill, the touch
Of life, that seems almost too much.

I hear the wind among the trees
Playing celestial symphonies ;
I see the branches downward bent,
Like keys of some great instrument.

And over me unrolls on high
The splendid scenery of the sky,
Where through a sapphire sea the sun
Sails like a golden galleon,

Towards yonder cloud-land in the West,
Towards yonder Islands of the Blest,
Whose steep sierra far uplifts
Its craggy summits white with drifts.

Blow, winds ! and waft through all the
        rooms
The snow-flakes of the cherry-blooms !
Blow, winds ! and bend within my reach
The fiery blossoms of the peach !

O Life and Love ! O happy throng
Of thoughts, whose only speech is song !
O heart of man ! canst thou not be
Blithe as the air is, and as free ?

SOMETHING LEFT UNDONE

LABOR with what zeal we will,
    Something still remains undone,
Something uncompleted still
    Waits the rising of the sun.

By the bedside, on the stair,
    At the threshold, near the gates,
With its menace or its prayer,
    Like a mendicant it waits ;

Waits, and will not go away ;
    Waits, and will not be gainsaid ;
By the cares of yesterday
    Each to-day is heavier made ;

Till at length the burden seems
    Greater than our strength can bear,
Heavy as the weight of dreams,
    Pressing on us everywhere.

And we stand from day to day,
    Like the dwarfs of times gone by,
Who, as Northern legends say,
    On their shoulders held the sky.

WEARINESS

O LITTLE feet ! that such long years
Must wander on through hopes and fears,
    Must ache and bleed beneath your load ;
I, nearer to the wayside inn
Where toil shall cease and rest begin,
    Am weary, thinking of your road !

O little hands ! that, weak or strong,
Have still to serve or rule so long,
    Have still so long to give or ask ;
I, who so much with book and pen
Have toiled among my fellow-men,
    Am weary, thinking of your task.

O little hearts ! that throb and beat
With such impatient, feverish heat,
    Such limitless and strong desires ;
Mine, that so long has glowed and burned,
With passions into ashes turned,
    Now covers and conceals its fires.

O little souls ! as pure and white
And crystalline as rays of light
    Direct from heaven, their source divine ;
Refracted through the mist of years,
How red my setting sun appears,
    How lurid looks this soul of mine !

TALES OF A WAYSIDE INN

The plan for a group of stories under the fiction of a company of story-tellers at an inn appears to have visited Mr. Longfellow after he had made some progress with the separate tales. The considerable collection under the title of *The Saga of King Olaf* was indeed written at first with the design of independent publication. Nearly two years passed before he took up the task in earnest; then, in November, 1860, "with all kinds of interruptions," he says, he wrote fifteen of the lyrics in as many days, and a few days afterward completed the whole of the *Saga.* Meanwhile he had written and published *Paul Revere's Ride,* and before the publication of his volume he had printed one of the lyrics of the *Saga* and *The Legend of Rabbi Ben Levi.* Just when he determined upon the framework of *The Wayside Inn* does not appear; it is quite possible that he had connected *The Saga of King Olaf,* which had been lying by for two or three years, with his friend Ole Bull, and that the desire to use so picturesque a figure had suggested a group of which the musician should be one. Literature had notable precedents for the general plan of a company at an inn, but whether the actual inn at Sudbury came to localize his conception, or was itself the cause of the plan, is not quite clear.

He sent the book to the printer in April, 1863, under the title of *The Sudbury Tales,* but in August wrote to Mr. Fields: "I am afraid we have made a mistake in calling the new volume *The Sudbury Tales.* Now that I see it announced I do not like the title. Sumner cries out against it and has persuaded me, as I think he will you, to come back to *The Wayside Inn.* Pray think as we do."

The book as originally planned consisted of the first part only, and was published November 25, 1863, in an edition of fifteen thousand copies, — an indication of the confidence which the publishers had in the poet's popularity.

The disguises of characters were so slight that readers easily recognized most of them at once, and Mr. Longfellow himself never made any mystery of their identity. Just after the publication of the volume he wrote to a correspondent in England : —

"*The Wayside Inn* has more foundation in fact than you may suppose. The town of Sudbury is about twenty miles from Cambridge. Some two hundred years ago, an English family by the name of Howe built there a country house, which has remained in the family down to the present time, the last of the race dying but two years ago. Losing their fortune, they became inn-keepers; and for a century the Red-Horse Inn has flourished, going down from father to son. The place is just as I have described it, though no longer an inn. All this will account for the landlord's coat-of-arms, and his being a justice of the peace, and his being known as 'the Squire,' — things that must sound strange in English ears. All the characters are real. The musician is Ole Bull ; the Spanish Jew, Israel Edrehi, whom I have seen as I have painted him, etc., etc."

It is easy to fill up the etc. of Mr. Longfellow's catalogue. The poet is T. W. Parsons, the translator of Dante ; the Sicilian, Luigi Monti, whose name occurs often in Mr. Longfellow's *Life* as a familiar friend ; the theologian, Professor Daniel Treadwell, a physicist of genius who had also a turn for theology ; the student, Henry Ware Wales, a scholar of promise who had travelled much, who died early, and whose tastes appeared in the collection of books which he left to the library of Harvard College. This group was collected by the poet's fancy ; in point of fact three of them, Parsons, Monti, and Treadwell, were wont to spend their summer months at the inn.

The form was so agreeable that it was easy to extend it afterward so as to include the tales which the poet found it in his mind to write. *The Second Day* was published in 1872 ; *The Third Part* formed the principal portion of *Aftermath* in 1873, and subsequently the three parts were brought together, into a complete volume.

TALES OF A WAYSIDE INN

PART FIRST

PRELUDE

THE WAYSIDE INN

ONE Autumn night, in Sudbury town,
Across the meadows bare and brown,
The windows of the wayside inn
Gleamed red with fire-light through the
    leaves
Of woodbine, hanging from the eaves
Their crimson curtains rent and thin.

As ancient is this hostelry
As any in the land may be,
Built in the old Colonial day,
When men lived in a grander way,
With ampler hospitality ;
A kind of old Hobgoblin Hall,

Now somewhat fallen to decay,
With weather-stains upon the wall,
And stairways worn, and crazy doors,
And creaking and uneven floors,
And chimneys huge, and tiled and tall.

A region of repose it seems,
A place of slumber and of dreams,
Remote among the wooded hills !
For there no noisy railway speeds,
Its torch-race scattering smoke and gleeds ;
But noon and night, the panting teams
Stop under the great oaks, that throw
Tangles of light and shade below,
On roofs and doors and window-sills.
Across the road the barns display
Their lines of stalls, their mows of hay,
Through the wide doors the breezes blow,
The wattled cocks strut to and fro,
And, half effaced by rain and shine,
The Red Horse prances on the sign.
Round this old-fashioned, quaint abode
Deep silence reigned, save when a gust

Went rushing down the county road,
And skeletons of leaves, and dust,
A moment quickened by its breath,
Shuddered and danced their dance of
    death,
And through the ancient oaks o'erhead
Mysterious voices moaned and fled.

But from the parlor of the inn
A pleasant murmur smote the ear,
Like water rushing through a weir:
Oft interrupted by the din
Of laughter and of loud applause,
And, in each intervening pause,
The music of a violin.
The fire-light, shedding over all
The splendor of its ruddy glow,
Filled the whole parlor large and low;
It gleamed on wainscot and on wall,
It touched with more than wonted grace
Fair Princess Mary's pictured face;
It bronzed the rafters overhead,
On the old spinet's ivory keys
It played inaudible melodies,
It crowned the sombre clock with flame,
The hands, the hours, the maker's name,
And painted with a livelier red
The Landlord's coat-of-arms again;
And, flashing on the window-pane,
Emblazoned with its light and shade
The jovial rhymes, that still remain,
Writ near a century ago,
By the great Major Molineaux,
Whom Hawthorne has immortal made.

Before the blazing fire of wood
Erect the rapt musician stood;
And ever and anon he bent
His head upon his instrument,
And seemed to listen, till he caught
Confessions of its secret thought, —
The joy, the triumph, the lament,
The exultation and the pain;
Then, by the magic of his art,
He soothed the throbbings of its heart,
And lulled it into peace again.

Around the fireside at their ease
There sat a group of friends, entranced
With the delicious melodies;
Who from the far-off noisy town
Had to the wayside inn come down,
To rest beneath its old oak trees.
The fire-light on their faces glanced,
Their shadows on the wainscot danced,

And, though of different lands and speech,
Each had his tale to tell, and each
Was anxious to be pleased and please.
And while the sweet musician plays,
Let me in outline sketch them all,
Perchance uncouthly as the blaze
With its uncertain touch portrays
Their shadowy semblance on the wall.

But first the Landlord will I trace;
Grave in his aspect and attire;
A man of ancient pedigree,
A Justice of the Peace was he,
Known in all Sudbury as "The Squire."
Proud was he of his name and race,
Of old Sir William and Sir Hugh,
And in the parlor, full in view,
His coat-of-arms, well framed and glazed,
Upon the wall in colors blazed;
He beareth gules upon his shield,
A chevron argent in the field,
With three wolf's-heads, and for the crest
A Wyvern part-per-pale addressed
Upon a helmet barred; below
The scroll reads, "By the name of Howe."
And over this, no longer bright,
Though glimmering with a latent light,
Was hung the sword his grandsire bore
In the rebellious days of yore,
Down there at Concord in the fight.

A youth was there, of quiet ways,
A Student of old books and days,
To whom all tongues and lands were
    known,
And yet a lover of his own;
With many a social virtue graced,
And yet a friend of solitude;
A man of such a genial mood
The heart of all things he embraced,
And yet of such fastidious taste,
He never found the best too good.
Books were his passion and delight,
And in his upper room at home
Stood many a rare and sumptuous tome,
In vellum bound, with gold bedight,
Great volumes garmented in white,
Recalling Florence, Pisa, Rome.
He loved the twilight that surrounds
The border-land of old romance;
Where glitter hauberk, helm, and lance,
And banner waves, and trumpet sounds,
And ladies ride with hawk on wrist,
And mighty warriors sweep along,
Magnified by the purple mist,

The dusk of centuries and of song.
The chronicles of Charlemagne,
Of Merlin and the Mort d'Arthure,
Mingled together in his brain
With tales of Flores and Blanchefleur,
Sir Ferumbras, Sir Eglamour,
Sir Launcelot, Sir Morgadour,
Sir Guy, Sir Bevis, Sir Gawain.

A young Sicilian, too, was there ;
In sight of Etna born and bred,
Some breath of its volcanic air
Was glowing in his heart and brain,
And, being rebellious to his liege,
After Palermo's fatal siege,
Across the western seas he fled,
In good King Bomba's happy reign.
His face was like a summer night,
All flooded with a dusky light ;
His hands were small ; his teeth shone
                                    white
As sea-shells, when he smiled or spoke ;
His sinews supple and strong as oak ;
Clean shaven was he as a priest,
Who at the mass on Sunday sings,
Save that upon his upper lip
His beard, a good palm's length at least,
Level and pointed at the tip,
Shot sideways, like a swallow's wings.
The poets read he o'er and o'er,
And most of all the Immortal Four
Of Italy ; and next to those,
The story-telling bard of prose,
Who wrote the joyous Tuscan tales
Of the Decameron, that make
Fiesole's green hills and vales
Remembered for Boccaccio's sake.
Much too of music was his thought ;
The melodies and measures fraught
With sunshine and the open air,
Of vineyards and the singing sea
Of his beloved Sicily ;
And much it pleased him to peruse
The songs of the Sicilian muse, —
Bucolic songs by Meli sung
In the familiar peasant tongue,
That made men say, " Behold ! once more
The pitying gods to earth restore
Theocritus of Syracuse ! "

A Spanish Jew from Alicant
With aspect grand and grave was there ;
Vender of silks and fabrics rare,
And attar of rose from the Levant.
Like an old Patriarch he appeared,

Abraham or Isaac, or at least
Some later Prophet or High-Priest ;
With lustrous eyes, and olive skin,
And, wildly tossed from cheeks and chin,
The tumbling cataract of his beard.
His garments breathed a spicy scent
Of cinnamon and sandal blent,
Like the soft aromatic gales
That meet the mariner, who sails
Through the Moluccas, and the seas
That wash the shores of Celebes.
All stories that recorded are
By Pierre Alphonse he knew by heart,
And it was rumored he could say
The Parables of Sandabar,
And all the Fables of Pilpay,
Or if not all, the greater part !
Well versed was he in Hebrew books,
Talmud and Targum, and the lore
Of Kabala ; and evermore
There was a mystery in his looks ;
His eyes seemed gazing far away,
As if in vision or in trance
He heard the solemn sackbut play,
And saw the Jewish maidens dance.

A Theologian, from the school
Of Cambridge on the Charles, was there ;
Skilful alike with tongue and pen,
He preached to all men everywhere
The Gospel of the Golden Rule,
The New Commandment given to men,
Thinking the deed, and not the creed,
Would help us in our utmost need.
With reverent feet the earth he trod,
Nor banished nature from his plan,
But studied still with deep research
To build the Universal Church,
Lofty as is the love of God,
And ample as the wants of man.

A Poet, too, was there, whose verse
Was tender, musical, and terse ;
The inspiration, the delight,
The gleam, the glory, the swift flight
Of thoughts so sudden, that they seem
The revelations of a dream,
All these were his ; but with them came
No envy of another's fame ;
He did not find his sleep less sweet,
For music in some neighboring street
Nor rustling hear in every breeze
The laurels of Miltiades.
Honor and blessings on his head
While living, good report when dead,

Who, not too eager for renown,
Accepts, but does not clutch, the crown !

Last the Musician, as he stood
Illumined by that fire of wood ;
Fair-haired, blue-eyed, his aspect blithe,
His figure tall and straight and lithe,
And every feature of his face
Revealing his Norwegian race ;
A radiance, streaming from within,
Around his eyes and forehead beamed,
The Angel with the violin,
Painted by Raphael, he seemed.
He lived in that ideal world
Whose language is not speech, but song ;
Around him evermore the throng
Of elves and sprites their dances whirled ;
The Strömkarl sang, the cataract hurled
Its headlong waters from the height ;
And mingled in the wild delight
The scream of sea-birds in their flight,
The rumor of the forest trees,
The plunge of the implacable seas,
The tumult of the wind at night,
Voices of eld, like trumpets blowing,
Old ballads, and wild melodies
Through mist and darkness pouring forth,
Like Elivagar's river flowing
Out of the glaciers of the North.

The instrument on which he played
Was in Cremona's workshops made,
By a great master of the past,
Ere yet was lost the art divine ;
Fashioned of maple and of pine,
That in Tyrolean forests vast
Had rocked and wrestled with the blast :
Exquisite was it in design,
Perfect in each minutest part,
A marvel of the lutist's art ;
And in its hollow chamber, thus,
The maker from whose hands it came
Had written his unrivalled name, —
" Antonius Stradivarius."

And when he played, the atmosphere
Was filled with magic, and the ear
Caught echoes of that Harp of Gold,
Whose music had so weird a sound,
The hunted stag forgot to bound,
The leaping rivulet backward rolled,
The birds came down from bush and tree,
The dead came from beneath the sea,
The maiden to the harper's knee !

The music ceased ; the applause was loud,
The pleased musician smiled and bowed ;
The wood-fire clapped its hands of flame,
The shadows on the wainscot stirred,
And from the harpsichord there came
A ghostly murmur of acclaim,
A sound like that sent down at night
By birds of passage in their flight,
From the remotest distance heard.

Then silence followed ; then began
A clamor for the Landlord's tale, —
The story promised them of old,
They said, but always left untold ;
And he, although a bashful man,
And all his courage seemed to fail,
Finding excuse of no avail,
Yielded ; and thus the story ran.

THE LANDLORD'S TALE

PAUL REVERE'S RIDE

LISTEN, my children, and you shall hear
Of the midnight ride of Paul Revere,
On the eighteenth of April, in Seventy-
    five ;
Hardly a man is now alive
Who remembers that famous day and year.

He said to his friend, " If the British
    march
By land or sea from the town to-night,
Hang a lantern aloft in the belfry arch
Of the North Church tower as a signal
    light, —
One, if by land, and two, if by sea ;
And I on the opposite shore will be,
Ready to ride and spread the alarm
Through every Middlesex village and
    farm,
For the country folk to be up and to arm."

Then he said, " Good night ! " and with
    muffled oar
Silently rowed to the Charlestown shore,
Just as the moon rose over the bay,
Where swinging wide at her moorings lay
The Somerset, British man-of-war ;
A phantom ship, with each mast and spar
Across the moon like a prison bar,
And a huge black hulk, that was magnified
By its own reflection in the tide.

Meanwhile, his friend, through alley and
  street,
Wanders and watches with eager ears,
Till in the silence around him he hears
The muster of men at the barrack door,
The sound of arms, and the tramp of feet,
And the measured tread of the grenadiers,
Marching down to their boats on the shore.

Then he climbed the tower of the Old North
  Church,
By the wooden stairs, with stealthy tread,
To the belfry-chamber overhead,
And startled the pigeons from their perch
On the sombre rafters, that round him
  made
Masses and moving shapes of shade, —
By the trembling ladder, steep and tall,
To the highest window in the wall,
Where he paused to listen and look down
A moment on the roofs of the town,
And the moonlight flowing over all.

Beneath, in the churchyard, lay the dead,
In their night-encampment on the hill,
Wrapped in silence so deep and still
That he could hear, like a sentinel's tread,
The watchful night-wind, as it went
Creeping along from tent to tent,
And seeming to whisper, "All is well!"
A moment only he feels the spell
Of the place and the hour, and the secret
  dread
Of the lonely belfry and the dead;
For suddenly all his thoughts are bent
On a shadowy something far away,
Where the river widens to meet the bay, —
A line of black that bends and floats
On the rising tide, like a bridge of boats.

Meanwhile, impatient to mount and ride,
Booted and spurred, with a heavy stride
On the opposite shore walked Paul Revere.
Now he patted his horse's side,
Now gazed at the landscape far and near,
Then, impetuous, stamped the earth,
And turned and tightened his saddle-
  girth;
But mostly he watched with eager search
The belfry-tower of the Old North Church,
As it rose above the graves on the hill,
Lonely and spectral and sombre and still.
And lo! as he looks, on the belfry's height
A glimmer, and then a gleam of light!
He springs to the saddle, the bridle he turns,

But lingers and gazes, till full on his sight
A second lamp in the belfry burns!

A hurry of hoofs in a village street,
A shape in the moonlight, a bulk in the
  dark,
And beneath, from the pebbles, in passing,
  a spark
Struck out by a steed flying fearless and
  fleet:
That was all! And yet, through the gloom
  and the light,
The fate of a nation was riding that night;
And the spark struck out by that steed, in
  his flight,
Kindled the land into flame with its heat.

He has left the village and mounted the
  steep,
And beneath him, tranquil and broad and
  deep,
Is the Mystic, meeting the ocean tides;
And under the alders that skirt its edge,
Now soft on the sand, now loud on the ledge,
Is heard the tramp of his steed as he rides.

It was twelve by the village clock,
When he crossed the bridge into Medford
  town.
He heard the crowing of the cock,
And the barking of the farmer's dog,
And felt the damp of the river fog,
That rises after the sun goes down.

It was one by the village clock,
When he galloped into Lexington.
He saw the gilded weathercock
Swim in the moonlight as he passed,
And the meeting-house windows, blank and
  bare,
Gaze at him with a spectral glare,
As if they already stood aghast
At the bloody work they would look upon.

It was two by the village clock,
When he came to the bridge in Concord
  town.
He heard the bleating of the flock,
And the twitter of birds among the trees,
And felt the breath of the morning breeze
Blowing over the meadows brown.
And one was safe and asleep in his bed
Who at the bridge would be first to fall,
Who that day would be lying dead,
Pierced by a British musket-ball.

You know the rest.   In the books you have
 read,
How the British Regulars fired and
 fled, —
How the farmers gave them ball for ball,
From behind each fence and farm-yard
 wall,
Chasing the red-coats down the lane,
Then crossing the fields to emerge again
Under the trees at the turn of the road,
And only pausing to fire and load.

So through the night rode Paul Revere ;
And so through the night went his cry of
 alarm
To every Middlesex village and farm, —
A cry of defiance and not of fear,
A voice in the darkness, a knock at the
 door,
And a word that shall echo forevermore !
For, borne on the night-wind of the Past,
Through all our history, to the last,
In the hour of darkness and peril and
 need,
The people will waken and listen to hear
The hurrying hoof-beats of that steed,
And the midnight message of Paul Revere.

INTERLUDE

THE Landlord ended thus his tale,
Then rising took down from its nail
The sword that hung there, dim with dust,
And cleaving to its sheath with rust,
And said, " This sword was in the fight."
The Poet seized it, and exclaimed,
" It is the sword of a good knight.
Though homespun was his coat-of-mail ;
What matter if it be not named
Joyeuse, Colada, Durindale,
Excalibar, or Aroundight,
Or other name the books record ?
Your ancestor, who bore this sword
As Colonel of the Volunteers,
Mounted upon his old gray mare,
Seen here and there and everywhere,
To me a grander shape appears
Than old Sir William, or what not,
Clinking about in foreign lands
With iron gauntlets on his hands,
And on his head an iron pot ! "

All laughed ; the Landlord's face grew red
As his escutcheon on the wall ;

He could not comprehend at all
The drift of what the Poet said ;
For those who had been longest dead
Were always greatest in his eyes ;
And he was speechless with surprise
To see Sir William's plumèd head
Brought to a level with the rest,
And made the subject of a jest.
And this perceiving, to appease
The Landlord's wrath, the others' fears,
The Student said, with careless ease,
" The ladies and the cavaliers,
The arms, the loves, the courtesies,
The deeds of high emprise, I sing !
Thus Ariosto says, in words
That have the stately stride and ring
Of armèd knights and clashing swords.
Now listen to the tale I bring ;
Listen ! though not to me belong
The flowing draperies of his song,
The words that rouse, the voice that
 charms.
The Landlord's tale was one of arms,
Only a tale of love is mine,
Blending the human and divine,
A tale of the Decameron, told
In Palmieri's garden old,
By Fiametta, laurel-crowned,
While her companions lay around,
And heard the intermingled sound
Of airs that on their errands sped,
And wild birds gossiping overhead,
And lisp of leaves, and fountain's fall,
And her own voice more sweet than all,
Telling the tale, which, wanting these,
Perchance may lose its power to please."

THE STUDENT'S TALE

THE FALCON OF SER FEDERIGO

ONE summer morning, when the sun was
 hot,
Weary with labor in his garden-plot,
On a rude bench beneath his cottage
 eaves,
Ser Federigo sat among the leaves
Of a huge vine, that, with its arms out-
 spread,
Hung its delicious clusters overhead.
Below him, through the lovely valley,
 flowed
The river Arno, like a winding road,
And from its banks were lifted high in air

The spires and roofs of Florence called the
    Fair ;
To him a marble tomb, that rose above
His wasted fortunes and his buried love.
For there, in banquet and in tournament,
His wealth had lavished been, his substance
    spent,
To woo and lose, since ill his wooing sped,
Monna Giovanna, who his rival wed,
Yet ever in his fancy reigned supreme,
The ideal woman of a young man's dream.

Then he withdrew, in poverty and pain,
To this small farm, the last of his domain,
His only comfort and his only care
To prune his vines, and plant the fig and
    pear ;
His only forester and only guest.
His falcon, faithful to him, when the rest,
Whose willing hands had found so light of
    yore
The brazen knocker of his palace door,
Had now no strength to lift the wooden
    latch,
That entrance gave beneath a roof of
    thatch.
Companion of his solitary ways,
Purveyor of his feasts on holidays,
On him this melancholy man bestowed
The love with which his nature overflowed.

And so the empty-handed years went
    round,
Vacant, though voiceful with prophetic
    sound,
And so, that summer morn, he sat and
    mused
With folded, patient hands, as he was used,
And dreamily before his half-closed sight
Floated the vision of his lost delight.
Beside him, motionless, the drowsy bird
Dreamed of the chase, and in his slumber
    heard
The sudden, scythe-like sweep of wings,
    that dare
The headlong plunge through eddying
    gulfs of air,
Then, starting broad awake upon his perch,
Tinkled his bells, like mass-bells in a
    church,
And looking at his master, seemed to say,
" Ser Federigo, shall we hunt to-day ? "

Ser Federigo thought not of the chase ;
The tender vision of her lovely face,

I will not say he seems to see, he sees
In the leaf-shadows of the trellises,
Herself, yet not herself ; a lovely child
With flowing tresses, and eyes wide and
    wild,
Coming undaunted up the garden walk,
And looking not at him, but at the hawk.
" Beautiful falcon ! " said he, " would that I
Might hold thee on my wrist, or see thee
    fly ! "
The voice was hers, and made strange
    echoes start
Through all the haunted chambers of his
    heart,
As an æolian harp through gusty doors
Of some old ruin its wild music pours.

" Who is thy mother, my fair boy ? " he
    said,
His hand laid softly on that shining head.
" Monna Giovanna.   Will you let me stay
A little while, and with your falcon play ?
We live there, just beyond your garden
    wall,
In the great house behind the poplars tall."

So he spake on ; and Federigo heard
As from afar each softly uttered word,
And drifted onward through the golden
    gleams
And shadows of the misty sea of dreams,
As mariners becalmed through vapors
    drift,
And feel the sea beneath them sink and
    lift,
And hear far off the mournful breakers
    roar,
And voices calling faintly from the shore !
Then waking from his pleasant reveries,
He took the little boy upon his knees,
And told him stories of his gallant bird,
Till in their friendship he became a
    third.

Monna Giovanna, widowed in her prime,
Had come with friends to pass the summer
    time
In her grand villa, half-way up the hill,
O'erlooking Florence, but retired and still ;
With iron gates, that opened through long
    lines
Of sacred ilex and centennial pines,
And terraced gardens, and broad steps of
    stone,
And sylvan deities, with moss o'ergrown.

And fountains palpitating in the heat,
And all Val d'Arno stretched beneath its
    feet.
Here in seclusion, as a widow may,
The lovely lady whiled the hours away,
Pacing in sable robes the statued hall,
Herself the stateliest statue among all,
And seeing more and more, with secret
    joy,
Her husband risen and living in her boy,
Till the lost sense of life returned again,
Not as delight, but as relief from pain.
Meanwhile the boy, rejoicing in his
    strength,
Stormed down the terraces from length to
    length ;
The screaming peacock chased in hot pur-
    suit,
And climbed the garden trellises for fruit.
But his chief pastime was to watch the
    flight,
Of a gerfalcon, soaring into sight,
Beyond the trees that fringed the garden
    wall,
Then downward stooping at some distant
    call ;
And as he gazed full often wondered he
Who might the master of the falcon be,
Until that happy morning, when he found
Master and falcon in the cottage ground.

And now a shadow and a terror fell
On the great house, as if a passing-bell
Tolled from the tower, and filled each
    spacious room
With secret awe and preternatural gloom ;
The petted boy grew ill, and day by day
Pined with mysterious malady away.
The mother's heart would not be com-
    forted ;
Her darling seemed to her already dead,
And often, sitting by the sufferer's side,
"What can I do to comfort thee ? " she
    cried.
At first the silent lips made no reply,
But, moved at length by her importunate
    cry,
"Give me," he answered, with imploring
    tone,
"Ser Federigo's falcon for my own ! "

No answer could the astonished mother
    make ;
How could she ask, e'en for her darling's
    sake,

Such favor at a luckless lover's hand,
Well knowing that to ask was to command ?
Well knowing, what all falconers con-
    fessed,
In all the land that falcon was the best,
The master's pride and passion and de-
    light,
And the sole pursuivant of this poor
    knight.
But yet, for her child's sake, she could no
    less
Than give assent, to soothe his restlessness,
So promised, and then promising to keep
Her promise sacred, saw him fall asleep.

The morrow was a bright September morn ;
The earth was beautiful as if new-born ;
There was that nameless splendor every-
    where,
That wild exhilaration in the air,
Which makes the passers in the city street
Congratulate each other as they meet.
Two lovely ladies, clothed in cloak and
    hood,
Passed through the garden gate into the
    wood,
Under the lustrous leaves, and through the
    sheen
Of dewy sunshine showering down be-
    tween.
The one, close-hooded, had the attractive
    grace
Which sorrow sometimes lends a woman's
    face ;
Her dark eyes moistened with the mists
    that roll
From the gulf-stream of passion in the
    soul ;
The other with her hood thrown back, her
    hair
Making a golden glory in the air,
Her cheeks suffused with an auroral
    blush,
Her young heart singing louder than the
    thrush,
So walked, that morn, through mingled
    light and shade,
Each by the other's presence lovelier made,
Monna Giovanna and her bosom friend,
Intent upon their errand and its end.

They found Ser Federigo at his toil,
Like banished Adam, delving in the soil ;
And when he looked and these fair women
    spied,

The garden suddenly was glorified ;
His long-lost Eden was restored again,
And the strange river winding through the
    plain
No longer was the Arno to his eyes,
But the Euphrates watering Paradise !

Monna Giovanna raised her stately head,
And with fair words of salutation said :
"Ser Federigo, we come here as friends,
Hoping in this to make some poor amends
For past unkindness.   I who ne'er before
Would even cross the threshold of your
    door,
I who in happier days such pride main-
    tained,
Refused your banquets, and your gifts dis-
    dained,
This morning come, a self-invited guest,
To put your generous nature to the test,
And breakfast with you under your own
    vine."
To which he answered : "Poor desert of
    mine,
Not your unkindness call it, for if aught
Is good in me of feeling or of thought,
From you it comes, and this last grace out-
    weighs
All sorrows, all regrets of other days."

And after further compliment and talk,
Among the asters in the garden walk
He left his guests ; and to his cottage
    turned,
And as he entered for a moment yearned
For the lost splendors of the days of old,
The ruby glass, the silver and the gold,
And felt how piercing is the sting of pride,
By want embittered and intensified.
He looked about him for some means or
    way
To keep this unexpected holiday ;
Searched every cupboard, and then searched
    again,
Summoned the maid, who came, but came
    in vain ;
"The Signor did not hunt to-day," she
    said,
"There's nothing in the house but wine
    and bread."
Then suddenly the drowsy falcon shook
His little bells, with that sagacious look,
Which said, as plain as language to the
    ear,
"If anything is wanting, I am here !"

Yes, everything is wanting, gallant bird !
The master seized thee without further
    word.
Like thine own lure, he whirled thee round ;
    ah me !
The pomp and flutter of brave falconry,
The bells, the jesses, the bright scarlet
    hood,
The flight and the pursuit o'er field and
    wood,
All these forevermore are ended now ;
No longer victor, but the victim thou !

Then on the board a snow-white cloth he
    spread,
Laid on its wooden dish the loaf of bread,
Brought purple grapes with autumn sun-
    shine hot,
The fragrant peach, the juicy bergamot ;
Then in the midst a flask of wine he placed
And with autumnal flowers the banquet
    graced.
Ser Federigo, would not these suffice
Without thy falcon stuffed with cloves and
    spice ?

When all was ready, and the courtly dame
With her companion to the cottage came,
Upon Ser Federigo's brain there fell
The wild enchantment of a magic spell !
The room they entered, mean and low and
    small,
Was changed into a sumptuous banquet-
    hall,
With fanfares by aerial trumpets blown ;
The rustic chair she sat on was a throne ;
He ate celestial food, and a divine
Flavor was given to his country wine,
And the poor falcon, fragrant with his spice,
A peacock was, or bird of paradise !

When the repast was ended, they arose
And passed again into the garden-close.
Then said the lady, "Far too well I know,
Remembering still the days of long ago,
Though you betray it not, with what sur-
    prise
You see me here in this familiar wise.
You have no children, and you cannot
    guess
What anguish, what unspeakable distress
A mother feels, whose child is lying ill,
Nor how her heart anticipates his will.
And yet for this, you see me lay aside
All womanly reserve and check of pride,

And ask the thing most precious in your
    sight,
Your falcon, your sole comfort and delight,
Which if you find it in your heart to give,
My poor, unhappy boy perchance may
    live."

Ser Federigo listens, and replies,
With tears of love and pity in his eyes:
"Alas, dear lady! there can be no task
So sweet to me, as giving when you ask.
One little hour ago, if I had known
This wish of yours, it would have been my
    own.
But thinking in what manner I could best
Do honor to the presence of my guest,
I deemed that nothing worthier could be
Than what most dear and precious was to
    me ;
And so my gallant falcon breathed his last
To furnish forth this morning our repast."

In mute contrition, mingled with dismay,
The gentle lady turned her eyes away,
Grieving that he such sacrifice should
    make
And kill his falcon for a woman's sake,
Yet feeling in her heart a woman's pride,
That nothing she could ask for was denied ;
Then took her leave, and passed out at the
    gate
With footstep slow and soul disconsolate.

Three days went by, and lo ! a passing-
    bell
Tolled from the little chapel in the dell ;
Ten strokes Ser Federigo heard, and said,
Breathing a prayer, "Alas ! her child is
    dead !"
Three months went by ; and lo ! a merrier
    chime
Rang from the chapel bells at Christmas-
    time ;
The cottage was deserted, and no more
Ser Federigo sat beside its door,
But now, with servitors to do his will,
In the grand villa, half-way up the hill,
Sat at the Christmas feast, and at his side
Monna Giovanna, his beloved bride,
Never so beautiful, so kind, so fair,
Enthroned once more in the old rustic
    chair,
High-perched upon the back of which there
    stood
The image of a falcon carved in wood,

And underneath the inscription, with a
    date,
"All things come round to him who will
    but wait."

INTERLUDE

Soon as the story reached its end,
One, over eager to commend,
Crowned it with injudicious praise ;
And then the voice of blame found vent,
And fanned the embers of dissent
Into a somewhat lively blaze.

The Theologian shook his head ;
"These old Italian tales," he said,
"From the much-praised Decameron down
Through all the rabble of the rest,
Are either trifling, dull, or lewd ;
The gossip of a neighborhood
In some remote provincial town,
A scandalous chronicle at best !
They seem to me a stagnant fen,
Grown rank with rushes and with reeds,
Where a white lily, now and then,
Blooms in the midst of noxious weeds
And deadly nightshade on its banks !"

To this the Student straight replied,
"For the white lily, many thanks !
One should not say, with too much pride,
Fountain, I will not drink of thee !
Nor were it grateful to forget
That from these reservoirs and tanks
Even imperial Shakespeare drew
His Moor of Venice, and the Jew,
And Romeo and Juliet,
And many a famous comedy."

Then a long pause ; till some one said,
"An Angel is flying overhead !"
At these words spake the Spanish Jew,
And murmured with an inward breath :
"God grant, if what you say be true,
It may not be the Angel of Death !"
And then another pause ; and then,
Stroking his beard, he said again :
"This brings back to my memory
A story in the Talmud told,
That book of gems, that book of gold,
Of wonders many and manifold,
A tale that often comes to me,
And fills my heart, and haunts my brain,
And never wearies nor grows old."

THE SPANISH JEW'S TALE

THE LEGEND OF RABBI BEN LEVI

RABBI BEN LEVI, on the Sabbath, read
A volume of the Law, in which it said,
"No man shall look upon my face and
    live."
And as he read, he prayed that God would
    give
His faithful servant grace with mortal eye
To look upon His face and yet not die.

Then fell a sudden shadow on the page,
And, lifting up his eyes, grown dim with
    age,
He saw the Angel of Death before him
    stand,
Holding a naked sword in his right hand.
Rabbi Ben Levi was a righteous man,
Yet through his veins a chill of terror ran.
With trembling voice he said, "What wilt
    thou here?"
The Angel answered, "Lo! the time draws
    near
When thou must die; yet first, by God's
    decree,
Whate'er thou askest shall be granted
    thee."
Replied the Rabbi, "Let these living eyes
First look upon my place in Paradise."

Then said the Angel, "Come with me and
    look."
Rabbi Ben Levi closed the sacred book,
And rising, and uplifting his gray head,
"Give me thy sword," he to the Angel
    said,
"Lest thou shouldst fall upon me by the
    way."
The Angel smiled and hastened to obey,
Then led him forth to the Celestial Town,
And set him on the wall, whence, gazing
    down,
Rabbi Ben Levi, with his living eyes,
Might look upon his place in Paradise.

Then straight into the city of the Lord
The Rabbi leaped with the Death-Angel's
    sword,
And through the streets there swept a
    sudden breath
Of something there unknown, which men
    call death.

Meanwhile the Angel stayed without, and
    cried,
"Come back!" To which the Rabbi's
    voice replied,
"No! in the name of God, whom I adore,
I swear that hence I will depart no
    more!"

Then all the Angels cried, "O Holy One,
See what the son of Levi here hath done!
The kingdom of Heaven he takes by
    violence,
And in Thy name refuses to go hence!"
The Lord replied, "My Angels, be not
    wroth;
Did e'er the son of Levi break his oath?
Let him remain; for he with mortal eye
Shall look upon my face and yet not die."

Beyond the outer wall the Angel of Death
Heard the great voice, and said, with pant-
    ing breath,
"Give back the sword, and let me go my
    way."
Whereat the Rabbi paused, and answered,
    "Nay!
Anguish enough already hath it caused
Among the sons of men." And while he
    paused
He heard the awful mandate of the Lord
Resounding through the air, "Give back
    the sword!"

The Rabbi bowed his head in silent prayer,
Then said he to the dreadful Angel,
    "Swear
No human eye shall look on it again;
But when thou takest away the souls of
    men,
Thyself unseen, and with an unseen sword,
Thou wilt perform the bidding of the
    Lord."
The Angel took the sword again, and
    swore,
And walks on earth unseen forevermore.

INTERLUDE

HE ended: and a kind of spell
Upon the silent listeners fell.
His solemn manner and his words
Had touched the deep, mysterious chords
That vibrate in each human breast
Alike, but not alike confessed.

The spiritual world seemed near ;
And close above them, full of fear,
Its awful adumbration passed,
A luminous shadow, vague and vast.
They almost feared to look, lest there,
Embodied from the impalpable air,
They might behold the Angel stand,
Holding the sword in his right hand.

At last, but in a voice subdued,
Not to disturb their dreamy mood,
Said the Sicilian : " While you spoke,
Telling your legend marvellous,
Suddenly in my memory woke
The thought of one, now gone from us, —
An old Abate, meek and mild,
My friend and teacher, when a child,
Who sometimes in those days of old
The legend of an Angel told,
Which ran, as I remember thus."

THE SICILIAN'S TALE

KING ROBERT OF SICILY

ROBERT of Sicily, brother of Pope Urbane
And Valmond, Emperor of Allemaine,
Apparelled in magnificent attire,
With retinue of many a knight and squire,
On St. John's eve, at vespers, proudly
      sat
And heard the priests chant the Magnifi-
      cat.
And as he listened, o'er and o'er again
Repeated, like a burden or refrain,
He caught the words, " *Deposuit potentes
De sede, et exaltavit humiles ;* "
And slowly lifting up his kingly head
He to a learned clerk beside him said,
" What mean these words ? "   The clerk
      made answer meet,
" He has put down the mighty from their
      seat,
And has exalted them of low degree."
Thereat King Robert muttered scornfully,
" 'T is well that such seditious words are
      sung
Only by priests and in the Latin tongue ;
For unto priests and people be it known,
There is no power can push me from my
      throne ! "
And leaning back, he yawned and fell
      asleep,
Lulled by the chant monotonous and deep.

When he awoke, it was already night ;
The church was empty, and there was no
      light,
Save where the lamps, that glimmered few
      and faint,
Lighted a little space before some saint.
He started from his seat and gazed around,
But saw no living thing and heard no
      sound.
He groped towards the door, but it was
      locked ;
He cried aloud, and listened, and then
      knocked,
And uttered awful threatenings and com-
      plaints,
And imprecations upon men and saints.
The sounds reëchoed from the roof and
      walls
As if dead priests were laughing in their
      stalls.

At length the sexton, hearing from with-
      out
The tumult of the knocking and the shout,
And thinking thieves were in the house of
      prayer,
Came with his lantern, asking, " Who is
      there ? "
Half choked with rage, King Robert fiercely
      said,
" Open : 't is I, the King ! Art thou
      afraid ? "
The frightened sexton, muttering, with a
      curse,
" This is some drunken vagabond, or
      worse ! "
Turned the great key and flung the portal
      wide ;
A man rushed by him at a single stride,
Haggard, half naked, without hat or cloak,
Who neither turned, nor looked at him, nor
      spoke,
But leaped into the blackness of the night,
And vanished like a spectre from his
      sight.

Robert of Sicily, brother of Pope Urbane
And Valmond, Emperor of Allemaine,
Despoiled of his magnificent attire,
Bareheaded, breathless, and besprent with
      mire,
With sense of wrong and outrage desper-
      ate,
Strode on and thundered at the palace
      gate ;

Rushed through the courtyard, thrusting in his rage
To right and left each seneschal and page,
And hurried up the broad and sounding stair,
His white face ghastly in the torches' glare.
From hall to hall he passed with breathless speed ;
Voices and cries he heard, but did not heed,
Until at last he reached the banquet-room,
Blazing with light, and breathing with perfume.

There on the dais sat another king,
Wearing his robes, his crown, his signet-ring,
King Robert's self in features, form, and height,
But all transfigured with angelic light !
It was an Angel ; and his presence there
With a divine effulgence filled the air,
An exaltation, piercing the disguise,
Though none the hidden Angel recognize.

A moment speechless, motionless, amazed,
The throneless monarch on the Angel gazed,
Who met his look of anger and surprise
With the divine compassion of his eyes ;
Then said, " Who art thou ? and why com'st thou here ? "
To which King Robert answered with a sneer,
" I am the King, and come to claim my own
From an impostor, who usurps my throne ! "
And suddenly, at these audacious words,
Up sprang the angry guests, and drew their swords ;
The Angel answered, with unruffled brow,
" Nay, not the King, but the King's Jester, thou
Henceforth shalt wear the bells. and scalloped cape,
And for thy counsellor shalt lead an ape ;
Thou shalt obey my servants when they call,
And wait upon my henchmen in the hall ! "

Deaf to King Robert's threats and cries and prayers,
They thrust him from the hall and down the stairs ;

A group of tittering pages ran before,
And as they opened wide the folding-door,
His heart failed, for he heard, with strange alarms,
The boisterous laughter of the men-at-arms,
And all the vaulted chamber roar and ring
With the mock plaudits of " Long live the King ! "

Next morning, waking with the day's first beam,
He said within himself, " It was a dream ! "
But the straw rustled as he turned his head,
There were the cap and bells beside his bed,
Around him rose the bare, discolored walls,
Close by, the steeds were champing in their stalls,
And in the corner, a revolting shape,
Shivering and chattering sat the wretched ape.
It was no dream ; the world he loved so much
Had turned to dust and ashes at his touch !

Days came and went ; and now returned again
To Sicily the old Saturnian reign ;
Under the Angel's governance benign
The happy island danced with corn and wine,
And deep within the mountain's burning breast
Enceladus, the giant, was at rest.

Meanwhile King Robert yielded to his fate,
Sullen and silent and disconsolate.
Dressed in the motley garb that Jesters wear,
With look bewildered and a vacant stare,
Close shaven above the ears, as monks are shorn,
By courtiers mocked, by pages laughed to scorn,
His only friend the ape, his only food
What others left, — he still was unsubdued.
And when the Angel met him on his way,
And half in earnest, half in jest, would say,
Sternly, though tenderly, that he might feel
The velvet scabbard held a sword of steel,
" Art thou the King ? " the passion of his woe
Burst from him in resistless overflow,

And, lifting high his forehead, he would
    fling
The haughty answer back, " I am, I am the
    King ! "

Almost three years were ended ; when
    there came
Ambassadors of great repute and name
From Valmond, Emperor of Allemaine,
Unto King Robert, saying that Pope Ur-
    bane
By letter summoned them forthwith to come
On Holy Thursday to his city of Rome.
The Angel with great joy received his
    guests,
And gave them presents of embroidered
    vests,
And velvet mantles with rich ermine lined,
And rings and jewels of the rarest kind.
Then he departed with them o'er the sea
Into the lovely land of Italy,
Whose loveliness was more resplendent
    made
By the mere passing of that cavalcade,
With plumes, and cloaks, and housings, and
    the stir
Of jewelled bridle and of golden spur.
And lo ! among the menials, in mock state,
Upon a piebald steed, with shambling gait,
His cloak of fox-tails flapping in the wind,
The solemn ape demurely perched behind,
King Robert rode, making huge merriment
In all the country towns through which
    they went.

The Pope received them with great pomp
    and blare
Of bannered trumpets, on Saint Peter's
    square,
Giving his benediction and embrace,
Fervent, and full of apostolic grace.
While with congratulations and with
    prayers
He entertained the Angel unawares,
Robert, the Jester, bursting through the
    crowd,
Into their presence rushed, and cried aloud,
" I am the King ! Look, and behold in
    me
Robert, your brother, King of Sicily !
This man, who wears my semblance to your
    eyes,
Is an impostor in a king's disguise.
Do you not know me ? does no voice within
Answer my cry, and say we are akin ? "

The Pope in silence, but with troubled
    mien,
Gazed at the Angel's countenance serene ;
The Emperor, laughing, said, " It is strange
    sport
To keep a madman for thy Fool at court ! "
And the poor, baffled Jester in disgrace
Was hustled back among the populace.

In solemn state the Holy Week went by,
And Easter Sunday gleamed upon the sky ;
The presence of the Angel, with its light,
Before the sun rose, made the city bright,
And with new fervor filled the hearts of
    men,
Who felt that Christ indeed had risen
    again.
Even the Jester, on his bed of straw,
With haggard eyes the unwonted splendor
    saw,
He felt within a power unfelt before,
And, kneeling humbly on his chamber floor,
He heard the rushing garments of the Lord
Sweep through the silent air, ascending
    heavenward.

And now the visit ending, and once more
Valmond returning to the Danube's shore,
Homeward the Angel journeyed, and again
The land was made resplendent with his
    train,
Flashing along the towns of Italy
Unto Salerno, and from thence by sea.
And when once more within Palermo's
    wall,
And, seated on the throne in his great hall,
He heard the Angelus from convent
    towers,
As if the better world conversed with ours,
He beckoned to King Robert to draw
    nigher,
And with a gesture bade the rest retire ;
And when they were alone, the Angel said,
" Art thou the King ? " Then, bowing
    down his head,
King Robert crossed both hands upon his
    breast,
And meekly answered him : " Thou know-
    est best !
My sins as scarlet are ; let me go hence,
And in some cloister's school of penitence,
Across those stones, that pave the way to
    heaven,
Walk barefoot, till my guilty soul be
    shriven ! "

The Angel smiled, and from his radiant
    face
A holy light illumined all the place,
And through the open window, loud and
    clear,
They heard the monks chant in the chapel
    near,
Above the stir and tumult of the street :
" He has put down the mighty from their
    seat,
And has exalted them of low degree ! ' '
And through the chant a second melody
Rose like the throbbing of a single string :
" I am an Angel, and thou art the King ! "

King Robert, who was standing near the
    throne,
Lifted his eyes, and lo ! he was alone !
But all apparelled as in days of old,
With ermined mantle and with cloth of
    gold ;
And when his courtiers came, they found
    him there
Kneeling upon the floor, absorbed in silent
    prayer.

INTERLUDE

AND then the blue-eyed Norseman told
A Saga of the days of old.
" There is," said he, " a wondrous book
Of Legends in the old Norse tongue,
Of the dead kings of Norroway, —
Legends that once were told or sung
In many a smoky fireside nook
Of Iceland, in the ancient day,
By wandering Saga-man or Scald ;
' Heimskringla ' is the volume called ;
And he who looks may find therein
The story that I now begin."

And in each pause the story made
Upon his violin he played,
As an appropriate interlude,
Fragments of old Norwegian tunes
That bound in one the separate runes,
And held the mind in perfect mood,
Entwining and encircling all
The strange and antiquated rhymes
With melodies of olden times ;
As over some half-ruined wall,
Disjointed and about to fall,
Fresh woodbines climb and interlace,
And keep the loosened stones in place.

THE MUSICIAN'S TALE

THE SAGA OF KING OLAF

I

THE CHALLENGE OF THOR

I AM the God Thor,
I am the War God,
I am the Thunderer !
Here in my Northland,
My fastness and fortress,
Reign I forever !

Here amid icebergs
Rule I the nations ;
This is my hammer,
Miölner the mighty ;
Giants and sorcerers
Cannot withstand it !

These are the gauntlets
Wherewith I wield it,
And hurl it afar off ;
This is my girdle ;
Whenever I brace it,
Strength is redoubled !

The light thou beholdest
Stream through the heavens,
In flashes of crimson,
Is but my red beard
Blown by the night-wind,
Affrighting the nations !

Jove is my brother ;
Mine eyes are the lightning ;
The wheels of my chariot
Roll in the thunder,
The blows of my hammer
Ring in the earthquake !

Force rules the world still,
Has ruled it, shall rule it ;
Meekness is weakness,
Strength is triumphant,
Over the whole earth
Still is it Thor's-Day !

Thou art a God too,
O Galilean !
And thus single-handed

Unto the combat,
Gauntlet or Gospel,
Here I defy thee !

II

KING OLAF'S RETURN

And King Olaf heard the cry,
Saw the red light in the sky,
  Laid his hand upon his sword,
As he leaned upon the railing,
And his ships went sailing, sailing
  Northward into Drontheim fiord.

There he stood as one who dreamed ;
And the red light glanced and gleamed
  On the armor that he wore ;
And he shouted, as the rifted
Streamers o'er him shook and shifted,
  " I accept thy challenge, Thor ! "

To avenge his father slain,
And reconquer realm and reign,
  Came the youthful Olaf home,
Through the midnight sailing, sailing,
Listening to the wild wind's wailing,
  And the dashing of the foam.

To his thoughts the sacred name
Of his mother Astrid came,
  And the tale she oft had told
Of her flight by secret passes
Through the mountains and morasses,
  To the home of Hakon old.

Then strange memories crowded back
Of Queen Gunhild's wrath and wrack,
  And a hurried flight by sea ;
Of grim Vikings, and the rapture
Of the sea-fight, and the capture,
  And the life of slavery.

How a stranger watched his face
In the Esthonian market-place,
  Scanned his features one by one,
Saying, " We should know each other ;
I am Sigurd, Astrid's brother,
  Thou art Olaf, Astrid's son ! "

Then as Queen Allogia's page,
Old in honors, young in age,
  Chief of all her men-at-arms ;

Till vague whispers, and mysterious,
Reached King Valdemar, the imperious,
  Filling him with strange alarms.

Then his cruisings o'er the seas,
Westward to the Hebrides
  And to Scilly's rocky shore ;
And the hermit's cavern dismal,
Christ's great name and rites baptismal
  In the ocean's rush and roar.

All these thoughts of love and strife
Glimmered through his lurid life,
  As the stars' intenser light
Through the red flames o'er him trail-
    ing,
As his ships went sailing, sailing
  Northward in the summer night.

Trained for either camp or court,
Skilful in each manly sport,
  Young and beautiful and tall ;
Art of warfare, craft of chases,
Swimming, skating, snow-shoe races,
  Excellent alike in all.

When at sea, with all his rowers,
He along the bending oars
  Outside of his ship could run.
He the Smalsor Horn ascended,
And his shining shield suspended
  On its summit, like a sun.

On the ship-rails he could stand,
Wield his sword with either hand,
  And at once two javelins throw ;
At all feasts where ale was strongest
Sat the merry monarch longest,
  First to come and last to go.

Norway never yet had seen
One so beautiful of mien,
  One so royal in attire,
When in arms completely furnished,
Harness gold-inlaid and burnished,
  Mantle like a flame of fire.

Thus came Olaf to his own,
When upon the night-wind blown
  Passed that cry along the shore ;
And he answered, while the rifted
Streamers o'er him shook and shifted,
  " I accept thy challenge, Thor ! "

III

THORA OF RIMOL

"Thora of Rimol ! hide me ! hide me !
Danger and shame and death betide me !
For Olaf the King is hunting me down
Through field and forest, through thorp
    and town ! "
    Thus cried Jarl Hakon
    To Thora, the fairest of women.

" Hakon Jarl ! for the love I bear thee
Neither shall shame nor death come near
    thee !
But the hiding-place wherein thou must
    lie
Is the cave underneath the swine in the
    sty."
    Thus to Jarl Hakon
    Said Thora, the fairest of women.

So Hakon Jarl and his base thrall Karker
Crouched in the cave, than a dungeon
    darker,
As Olaf came riding, with men in mail,
Through the forest roads into Orkadale,
    Demanding Jarl Hakon
    Of Thora, the fairest of women.

" Rich and honored shall be whoever
The head of Hakon Jarl shall dissever ! "
Hakon heard him, and Karker the slave,
Through the breathing-holes of the dark-
    some cave.
    Alone in her chamber
    Wept Thora, the fairest of women.

Said Karker, the crafty, " I will not slay
    thee !
For all the king's gold I will never betray
    thee ! "
" Then why dost thou turn so pale, O
    churl,
And then again black as the earth ? " said
    the Earl.
    More pale and more faithful
    Was Thora, the fairest of women.

From a dream in the night the thrall
    started, saying,
" Round my neck a gold ring King Olaf
    was laying ! "

And Hakon answered, " Beware of the
    king !
He will lay round thy neck a blood-red
    ring."
    At the ring on her finger
    Gazed Thora, the fairest of women.

At daybreak slept Hakon, with sorrows
    encumbered,
But screamed and drew up his feet as he
    slumbered ;
The thrall in the darkness plunged with his
    knife,
And the Earl awakened no more in this
    life.
    But wakeful and weeping
    Sat Thora, the fairest of women.

At Nidarholm the priests are all singing,
Two ghastly heads on the gibbet are swing-
    ing ;
One is Jarl Hakon's and one is his thrall's,
And the people are shouting from windows
    and walls ;
    While alone in her chamber
    Swoons Thora, the fairest of women.

IV

QUEEN SIGRID THE HAUGHTY

Queen Sigrid the Haughty sat proud and
    aloft
In her chamber, that looked over meadow
    and croft.
    Heart's dearest,
    Why dost thou sorrow so ?

The floor with tassels of fir was besprent,
Filling the room with their fragrant scent.

She heard the birds sing, she saw the sun
    shine,
The air of summer was sweeter than wine.

Like a sword without scabbard the bright
    river lay
Between her own kingdom and Norroway.

But Olaf the King had sued for her hand,
The sword would be sheathed, the river
    be spanned.

Her maidens were seated around her knee,
Working bright figures in tapestry.

And one was singing the ancient rune
Of Brynhilda's love and the wrath of
Gudrun.

And through it, and round it, and over it
all
Sounded incessant the waterfall.

The Queen in her hand held a ring of
gold,
From the door of Ladé's Temple old.

King Olaf had sent her this wedding gift,
But her thoughts as arrows were keen and
swift.

She had given the ring to her goldsmiths
twain,
Who smiled, as they handed it back again.

And Sigrid the Queen, in her haughty
way,
Said, "Why do you smile, my goldsmiths,
say?"

And they answered: "O Queen! if the
truth must be told,
The ring is of copper, and not of gold!"

The lightning flashed o'er her forehead and
cheek,
She only murmured, she did not speak:

"If in his gifts he can faithless be,
There will be no gold in his love to me."

A footstep was heard on the outer stair,
And in strode King Olaf with royal air.

He kissed the Queen's hand, and he whis-
pered of love,
And swore to be true as the stars are above.

But she smiled with contempt as she an-
swered: "O King,
Will you swear it, as Odin once swore, on
the ring?"

And the King: "Oh speak not of Odin to
me,
The wife of King Olaf a Christian must
be."

Looking straight at the King, with her
level brows,
She said, "I keep true to my faith and my
vows."

Then the face of King Olaf was darkened
with gloom,
He rose in his anger and strode through
the room.

"Why, then, should I care to have thee?"
he said, —
"A faded old woman, a heathenish jade!"

His zeal was stronger than fear or love,
And he struck the Queen in the face with
his glove.

Then forth from the chamber in anger he
fled,
And the wooden stairway shook with his
tread.

Queen Sigrid the Haughty said under her
breath,
"This insult, King Olaf, shall be thy
death!"
    Heart's dearest,
    Why dost thou sorrow so?

V

THE SKERRY OF SHRIEKS

Now from all King Olaf's farms
    His men-at-arms
Gathered on the Eve of Easter;
To his house at Angvalds-ness
    Fast they press,
Drinking with the royal feaster.

Loudly through the wide-flung door
    Came the roar
Of the sea upon the Skerry;
And its thunder loud and near
    Reached the ear,
Mingling with their voices merry.

"Hark!" said Olaf to his Scald,
    Halfred the Bald,
"Listen to that song, and learn it!
Half my kingdom would I give,
    As I live,
If by such songs you would earn it!

" For of all the runes and rhymes
 Of all times,
Best I like the ocean's dirges,
When the old harper heaves and rocks,
 His hoary locks
Flowing and flashing in the surges ! "

Halfred answered : " I am called
 The Unappalled !
Nothing hinders me or daunts me.
Hearken to me, then, O King,
 While I sing
The great Ocean Song that haunts me."

" I will hear your song sublime
 Some other time,"
Says the drowsy monarch, yawning,
And retires ; each laughing guest
 Applauds the jest ;
Then they sleep till day is dawning.

Pacing up and down the yard,
 King Olaf's guard
Saw the sea-mist slowly creeping
O'er the sands, and up the hill,
 Gathering still
Round the house where they were sleeping.

It was not the fog he saw,
 Nor misty flaw,
That above the landscape brooded ;
It was Eyvind Kallda's crew
 Of warlocks blue
With their caps of darkness hooded !

Round and round the house they go,
 Weaving slow
Magic circles to encumber
And imprison in their ring
 Olaf the King,
As he helpless lies in slumber.

Then athwart the vapors dun
 The Easter sun
Streamed with one broad track of splendor !
In their real forms appeared
 The warlocks weird,
Awful as the Witch of Endor.

Blinded by the light that glared,
 They groped and stared,
Round about with steps unsteady ;
From his window Olaf gazed,
 And, amazed,
" Who are these strange people ? " said he,

" Eyvind Kallda and his men ! "
 Answered then
From the yard a sturdy farmer ;
While the men-at-arms apace
 Filled the place,
Busily buckling on their armor.

From the gates they sallied forth,
 South and north,
Scoured the island coast around them,
Seizing all the warlock band,
 Foot and hand
On the Skerry's rocks they bound them.

And at eve the king again
 Called his train,
And, with all the candles burning,
Silent sat and heard once more
 The sullen roar
Of the ocean tides returning.

Shrieks and cries of wild despair
 Filled the air,
Growing fainter as they listened ;
Then the bursting surge alone
 Sounded on ; —
Thus the sorcerers were christened !

" Sing, O Scald, your song sublime,
 Your ocean-rhyme,"
Cried King Olaf : " it will cheer me ! "
Said the Scald, with pallid cheeks,
 " The Skerry of Shrieks
Sings too loud for you to hear me ! "

VI

THE WRAITH OF ODIN

The guests were loud, the ale was strong,
King Olaf feasted late and long ;
The hoary Scalds together sang ;
O'erhead the smoky rafters rang.
 Dead rides Sir Morten of Fogelsang.

The door swung wide, with creak and din ;
A blast of cold night-air came in,
And on the threshold shivering stood
A one-eyed guest, with cloak and hood.
 Dead rides Sir Morten of Fogelsang.

The King exclaimed, " O graybeard pale !
Come warm thee with this cup of ale."

The foaming draught the old man quaffed,
The noisy guests looked on and laughed.
   Dead rides Sir Morten of Fogelsang.

Then spake the King: "Be not afraid :
Sit here by me." The guest obeyed,
And, seated at the table, told
Tales of the sea, and Sagas old.
   Dead rides Sir Morten of Fogelsang.

And ever, when the tale was o'er,
The King demanded yet one more ;
Till Sigurd the Bishop smiling said,
" 'T is late, O King, and time for bed."
   Dead rides Sir Morten of Fogelsang.

The King retired ; the stranger guest
Followed and entered with the rest ;
The lights were out, the pages gone,
But still the garrulous guest spake on.
   Dead rides Sir Morten of Fogelsang.

As one who from a volume reads,
He spake of heroes and their deeds,
Of lands and cities he had seen,
And stormy gulfs that tossed between.
   Dead rides Sir Morten of Fogelsang.

Then from his lips in music rolled
The Havamal of Odin old,
With sounds mysterious as the roar
Of billows on a distant shore.
   Dead rides Sir Morten of Fogelsang.

" Do we not learn from runes and rhymes
Made by the gods in elder times,
And do not still the great Scalds teach
That silence better is than speech ? "
   Dead rides Sir Morten of Fogelsang.

Smiling at this, the King replied,
" Thy lore is by thy tongue belied ;
For never was I so enthralled
Either by Saga-man or Scald."
   Dead rides Sir Morten of Fogelsang.

The Bishop said, " Late hours we keep !
Night wanes, O King ! 't is time for
   sleep ! "
Then slept the King, and when he woke
The guest was gone, the morning broke.
   Dead rides Sir Morten of Fogelsang.

They found the doors securely barred,
They found the watch-dog in the yard,

There was no footprint in the grass,
And none had seen the stranger pass.
   Dead rides Sir Morten of Fogelsang.

King Olaf crossed himself and said :
" I know that Odin the Great is dead ;
Sure is the triumph of our Faith,
The one-eyed stranger was his wraith."
   Dead rides Sir Morten of Fogelsang.

VII

IRON-BEARD

Olaf the King, one summer morn,
Blew a blast on his bugle-horn,
Sending his signal through the land of
   Drontheim.

And to the Hus-Ting held at Mere
Gathered the farmers far and near,
With their war weapons ready to confront
   him.

Ploughing under the morning star,
Old Iron-Beard in Yriar
Heard the summons, chuckling with a low
   laugh.

He wiped the sweat-drops from his brow,
Unharnessed his horses from the plough,
And clattering came on horseback to King
   Olaf.

He was the churliest of the churls ;
Little he cared for king or earls ;
Bitter as home-brewed ale were his foam-
   ing passions.

Hodden-gray was the garb he wore,
And by the Hammer of Thor he swore ;
He hated the narrow town, and all its
   fashions.

But he loved the freedom of his farm,
His ale at night, by the fireside warm,
Gudrun his daughter, with her flaxen
   tresses.

He loved his horses and his herds,
The smell of the earth, and the song of
   birds,
His well-filled barns, his brook with its
   watercresses.

Huge and cumbersome was his frame ;
His beard, from which he took his name,
Frosty and fierce, like that of Hymer the
　　Giant.

So at the Hus-Ting he appeared,
The farmer of Yriar, Iron-Beard,
On horseback, in an attitude defiant.

And to King Olaf he cried aloud,
Out of the middle of the crowd,
That tossed about him like a stormy
　　ocean :

" Such sacrifices shalt thou bring
To Odin and to Thor, O King,
As other kings have done in their devotion ! "

King Olaf answered :　" I command
This land to be a Christian land ;
Here is my Bishop who the folk baptizes !

" But if you ask me to restore
Your sacrifices, stained with gore,
Then will I offer human sacrifices !

" Not slaves and peasants shall they be,
But men of note and high degree,
Such men as Orm of Lyra and Kar of
　　Gryting ! "

Then to their Temple strode he in,
And loud behind him heard the din
Of his men-at-arms and the peasants fiercely
　　fighting.

There in the Temple, carved in wood,
The image of great Odin stood,
And other gods, with Thor supreme among
　　them.

King Olaf smote them with the blade
Of his huge war-axe, gold inlaid,
And downward shattered to the pavement
　　flung them.

At the same moment rose without,
From the contending crowd, a shout,
A mingled sound of triumph and of wailing.

And there upon the trampled plain
The farmer Iron-Beard lay slain,
Midway between the assailed and the
　　assailing.

King Olaf from the doorway spoke ·
" Choose ye between two things, my
　　folk,
To be baptized or given up to slaugh-
　　ter ! "

And seeing their leader stark and dead,
The people with a murmur said,
" O King, baptize us with thy holy water."

So all the Drontheim land became
A Christian land in name and fame,
In the old gods no more believing and
　　trusting.

And as a blood-atonement, soon
King Olaf wed the fair Gudrun ;
And thus in peace ended the Drontheim
　　Hus-Ting !

VIII

GUDRUN

On King Olaf's bridal night
Shines the moon with tender light,
And across the chamber streams
　　Its tide of dreams.

At the fatal midnight hour,
When all evil things have power,
In the glimmer of the moon
　　Stands Gudrun.

Close against her heaving breast
Something in her hand is pressed ;
Like an icicle, its sheen
　　Is cold and keen.

On the cairn are fixed her eyes
Where her murdered father lies,
And a voice remote and drear
　　She seems to hear.

What a bridal night is this !
Cold will be the dagger's kiss ;
Laden with the chill of death
　　Is its breath.

Like the drifting snow she sweeps
To the couch where Olaf sleeps ;
Suddenly he wakes and stirs,
　　His eyes meet hers.

"What is that," King Olaf said,
"Gleams so bright above my head?
Wherefore standest thou so white
    In pale moonlight?"

"'T is the bodkin that I wear
When at night I bind my hair;
It woke me falling on the floor;
    'T is nothing more."

"Forests have ears, and fields have eyes;
Often treachery lurking lies
Underneath the fairest hair!
    Gudrun beware!"

Ere the earliest peep of morn
Blew King Olaf's bugle-horn;
And forever sundered ride
    Bridegroom and bride!

IX

THANGBRAND THE PRIEST

Short of stature, large of limb,
    Burly face and russet beard,
All the women stared at him,
    When in Iceland he appeared.
        "Look!" they said,
        With nodding head,
"There goes Thangbrand, Olaf's Priest."

All the prayers he knew by rote,
    He could preach like Chrysostome,
From the Fathers he could quote,
    He had even been at Rome.
        A learned clerk,
        A man of mark,
Was this Thangbrand, Olaf's Priest.

He was quarrelsome and loud,
    And impatient of control,
Boisterous in the market crowd,
    Boisterous at the wassail-bowl,
        Everywhere
        Would drink and swear,
Swaggering Thangbrand, Olaf's Priest.

In his house this malcontent
    Could the King no longer bear,
So to Iceland he was sent
    To convert the heathen there,
        And away
        One summer day
Sailed this Thangbrand, Olaf's Priest.

There in Iceland, o'er their books
    Pored the people day and night,
But he did not like their looks,
    Nor the songs they used to write.
        "All this rhyme
        Is waste of time!"
Grumbled Thangbrand, Olaf's Priest.

To the alehouse, where he sat,
    Came the Scalds and Saga-men;
Is it to be wondered at
    That they quarrelled now and then,
        When o'er his beer
        Began to leer
Drunken Thangbrand, Olaf's Priest?

All the folk in Altafiord
    Boasted of their island grand;
Saying in a single word,
    "Iceland is the finest land
        That the sun
        Doth shine upon!"
Loud laughed Thangbrand, Olaf's Priest.

And he answered: "What 's the use
    Of this bragging up and down,
When three women and one goose
    Make a market in your town!"
        Every Scald
        Satires drawled
On poor Thangbrand, Olaf's Priest.

Something worse they did than that;
    And what vexed him most of all
Was a figure in shovel hat,
    Drawn in charcoal on the wall;
        With words that go
        Sprawling below,
"This is Thangbrand, Olaf's Priest."

Hardly knowing what he did,
    Then he smote them might and main,
Thorvald Veile and Veterlid
    Lay there in the alehouse slain.
        "To-day we are gold,
        To-morrow mould!"
Muttered Thangbrand, Olaf's Priest.

Much in fear of axe and rope,
    Back to Norway sailed he then.
"O King Olaf! little hope
    Is there of these Iceland men!"
        Meekly said,
        With bending head,
Pious Thangbrand, Olaf's Priest.

X

RAUD THE STRONG

" All the old gods are dead,
All the wild warlocks fled ;
But the White Christ lives and reigns,
And throughout my wide domains
His Gospel shall be spread ! "
    On the Evangelists
    Thus swore King Olaf.

But still in dreams of the night
Beheld he the crimson light,
And heard the voice that defied
Him who was crucified,
And challenged him to the fight.
    To Sigurd the Bishop
    King Olaf confessed it.

And Sigurd the Bishop said,
" The old gods are not dead,
For the great Thor still reigns,
And among the Jarls and Thanes
The old witchcraft still is spread."
    Thus to King Olaf
    Said Sigurd the Bishop.

" Far north in the Salten Fiord,
By rapine, fire, and sword,
Lives the Viking, Raud the Strong ;
All the Godoe Isles belong
To him and his heathen horde."
    Thus went on speaking
    Sigurd the Bishop.

" A warlock, a wizard is he,
And the lord of the wind and the sea ;
And whichever way he sails,
He has ever favoring gales,
By his craft in sorcery."
    Here the sign of the cross
    Made devoutly King Olaf.

" With rites that we both abhor,
He worships Odin and Thor ;
So it cannot yet be said,
That all the old gods are dead,
And the warlocks are no more,"
    Flushing with anger
    Said Sigurd the Bishop.

Then King Olaf cried aloud :
" I will talk with this mighty Raud,

And along the Salten Fiord
Preach the Gospel with my sword,
Or be brought back in my shroud ! "
    So northward from Drontheim
    Sailed King Olaf !

XI

BISHOP SIGURD OF SALTEN FIORD

Loud the angry wind was wailing
As King Olaf's ships came sailing
Northward out of Drontheim haven
    To the mouth of Salten Fiord.

Though the flying sea-spray drenches
Fore and aft the rowers' benches,
Not a single heart is craven
    Of the champions there on board.

All without the Fiord was quiet,
But within it storm and riot,
Such as on his Viking cruises
    Raud the Strong was wont to ride.

And the sea through all its tide-ways
Swept the reeling vessels sideways,
As the leaves are swept through sluices,
    When the flood-gates open wide.

" 'T is the warlock ! 't is the demon
Raud ! " cried Sigurd to the seamen ;
" But the Lord is not affrighted
    By the witchcraft of his foes."

To the ship's bow he ascended,
By his choristers attended,
Round him were the tapers lighted,
    And the sacred incense rose.

On the bow stood Bishop Sigurd,
In his robes, as one transfigured,
And the Crucifix he planted
    High amid the rain and mist.

Then with holy water sprinkled
All the ship ; the mass-bells tinkled :
Loud the monks around him chanted,
    Loud he read the Evangelist.

As into the Fiord they darted,
On each side the water parted ;
Down a path like silver molten
    Steadily rowed King Olaf's ships ;

Steadily burned all night the tapers,
And the White Christ through the vapors
Gleamed across the Fiord of Salten,
    As through John's Apocalypse, —

Till at last they reached Raud's dwelling
On the little isle of Gelling ;
Not a guard was at the doorway,
    Not a glimmer of light was seen.

But at anchor, carved and gilded,
Lay the dragon-ship he builded ;
'T was the grandest ship in Norway,
    With its crest and scales of green.

Up the stairway, softly creeping,
To the loft where Raud was sleeping,
With their fists they burst asunder
    Bolt and bar that held the door.

Drunken with sleep and ale they found
        him,
Dragged him from his bed and bound him,
While he stared with stupid wonder
    At the look and garb they wore.

Then King Olaf said : " O Sea-King !
Little time have we for speaking,
Choose between the good and evil ;
    Be baptized ! or thou shalt die ! "

But in scorn the heathen scoffer
Answered : " I disdain thine offer;
Neither fear I God nor Devil ;
    Thee and thy Gospel I defy ! "

Then between his jaws distended,
When his frantic struggles ended,
Through King Olaf's horn an adder,
    Touched by fire, they forced to glide.

Sharp his tooth was as an arrow,
As he gnawed through bone and marrow ;
But without a groan or shudder,
    Raud the Strong blaspheming died.

Then baptized they all that region,
Swarthy Lap and fair Norwegian,
Far as swims the salmon, leaping,
    Up the streams of Salten Fiord.

In their temples Thor and Odin
Lay in dust and ashes trodden,

As King Olaf, onward sweeping,
    Preached the Gospel with his sword.

Then he took the carved and gilded
Dragon-ship that Raud had builded,
And the tiller single-handed
    Grasping, steered into the main.

Southward sailed the sea-gulls o'er him,
Southward sailed the ship that bore him,
Till at Drontheim haven landed
    Olaf and his crew again.

XII

KING OLAF'S CHRISTMAS

At Drontheim, Olaf the King
Heard the bells of Yule-tide ring,
    As he sat in his banquet-hall,
Drinking the nut-brown ale,
With his bearded Berserks hale
    And tall.

Three days his Yule-tide feasts
He held with Bishops and Priests,
    And his horn filled up to the brim ;
But the ale was never too strong,
Nor the Saga-man's tale too long,
    For him.

O'er his drinking-horn, the sign
He made of the cross divine,
    As he drank, and muttered his prayers;
But the Berserks evermore
Made the sign of the Hammer of Thor
    Over theirs.

The gleams of the fire-light dance
Upon helmet and hauberk and lance,
    And laugh in the eyes of the King;
And he cries to Halfred the Scald,
Gray-bearded, wrinkled, and bald,
    " Sing ! "

" Sing me a song divine,
With a sword in every line,
    And this shall be thy reward."
And he loosened the belt at his waist,
And in front of the singer placed
    His sword.

" Quern-biter of Hakon the Good,
Wherewith at a stroke he hewed
    The millstone through and through,
And Foot-breadth of Thoralf the Strong,
Were neither so broad nor so long,
    Nor so true."

Then the Scald took his harp and sang,
And loud through the music rang
    The sound of that shining word ;
And the harp-strings a clangor made,
As if they were struck with the blade
    Of a sword.

And the Berserks round about
Broke forth into a shout
    That made the rafters ring :
They smote with their fists on the board,
And shouted, " Long live the Sword,
    And the King !"

But the King said, "O my son,
I miss the bright word in one
    Of thy measures and thy rhymes."
And Halfred the Scald replied,
" In another 't was multiplied
    Three times."

Then King Olaf raised the hilt
Of iron, cross-shaped and gilt,
    And said, " Do not refuse ;
Count well the gain and the loss,
Thor's hammer or Christ's cross :
    Choose !"

And Halfred the Scald said, " This
In the name of the Lord I kiss,
    Who on it was crucified !"
And a shout went round the board,
" In the name of Christ the Lord,
    Who died !"

Then over the waste of snows
The noonday sun uprose,
    Through the driving mists revealed,
Like the lifting of the Host,
By incense-clouds almost
    Concealed.

On the shining wall a vast
And shadowy cross was cast
    From the hilt of the lifted sword,
And in foaming cups of ale
The Berserks drank " Was-hael !
    To the Lord !"

XIII

THE BUILDING OF THE LONG SERPENT

Thorberg Skafting, master-builder,
    In his ship-yard by the sea,
Whistling, said, " It would bewilder
Any man but Thorberg Skafting,
    Any man but me !"

Near him lay the Dragon stranded,
    Built of old by Raud the Strong,
And King Olaf had commanded
He should build another Dragon,
    Twice as large and long.

Therefore whistled Thorberg Skafting,
    As he sat with half-closed eyes,
And his head turned sideways, drafting
That new vessel for King Olaf
    Twice the Dragon's size.

Round him busily hewed and hammered
    Mallet huge and heavy axe ;
Workmen laughed and sang and clam-
    ored ;
Whirred the wheels, that into rigging
    Spun the shining flax !

All this tumult heard the master, —
    It was music to his ear ;
Fancy whispered all the faster,
" Men shall hear of Thorberg Skaft
    ing
    For a hundred year !"

Workmen sweating at the forges
    Fashioned iron bolt and bar,
Like a warlock's midnight orgies
Smoked and bubbled the black caldron
    With the boiling tar.

Did the warlocks mingle in it,
    Thorberg Skafting, any curse ?
Could you not be gone a minute
But some mischief must be doing,
    Turning bad to worse ?

'T was an ill wind that came wafting
    From his homestead words of woe ;
To his farm went Thorberg Skafting,
Oft repeating to his workmen,
    Build ye thus and so.

After long delays returning
    Came the master back by night ;
To his ship-yard longing, yearning,
Hurried he, and did not leave it
    Till the morning's light.

" Come and see my ship, my darling ! "
    On the morrow said the King ;
" Finished now from keel to carling ;
Never yet was seen in Norway
    Such a wondrous thing ! "

In the ship-yard, idly talking,
    At the ship the workmen stared :
Some one, all their labor balking,
Down her sides had cut deep gashes,
    Not a plank was spared !

" Death be to the evil-doer ! "
    With an oath King Olaf spoke ;
" But rewards to his pursuer ! "
And with wrath his face grew redder
    Than his scarlet cloak.

Straight the master-builder, smiling,
    Answered thus the angry King :
" Cease blaspheming and reviling,
Olaf, it was Thorberg Skafting
    Who has done this thing ! "

Then he chipped and smoothed the plank-
    ing,
    Till the King, delighted, swore,
With much lauding and much thanking,
" Handsomer is now my Dragon
    Than she was before ! "

Seventy ells and four extended
    On the grass the vessel's keel ;
High above it, gilt and splendid,
Rose the figure-head ferocious
    With its crest of steel.

Then they launched her from the tressels,
    In the ship-yard by the sea ;
She was the grandest of all vessels,
Never ship was built in Norway
    Half so fine as she !

The Long Serpent was she christened,
    'Mid the roar of cheer on cheer !
They who to the Saga listened
Heard the name of Thorberg Skafting
    For a hundred year !

XIV

THE CREW OF THE LONG SERPENT

Safe at anchor in Drontheim bay
King Olaf's fleet assembled lay,
    And, striped with white and blue,
Downward fluttered sail and banner,
As alights the screaming lanner ;
Lustily cheered, in their wild manner,
    The Long Serpent's crew.

Her forecastle man was Ulf the Red ;
Like a wolf's was his shaggy head,
    His teeth as large and white ;
His beard, of gray and russet blended,
Round as a swallow's nest descended ;
As standard-bearer he defended
    Olaf's flag in the fight.

Near him Kolbiorn had his place,
Like the King in garb and face,
    So gallant and so hale ;
Every cabin-boy and varlet
Wondered at his cloak of scarlet ;
Like a river, frozen and star-lit,
    Gleamed his coat of mail.

By the bulkhead, tall and dark,
Stood Thrand Rame of Thelemark,
    A figure gaunt and grand ;
On his hairy arm imprinted
Was an anchor, azure-tinted ;
Like Thor's hammer, huge and dinted
    Was his brawny hand.

Einar Tamberskelver, bare
To the winds his golden hair,
    By the mainmast stood ;
Graceful was his form, and slender,
And his eyes were deep and tender
As a woman's, in the splendor
    Of her maidenhood.

In the fore-hold Biorn and Bork
Watched the sailors at their work :
    Heavens ! how they swore !
Thirty men they each commanded,
Iron-sinewed, horny-handed,
Shoulders broad, and chests expanded,
    Tugging at the oar.

These, and many more like these,
With King Olaf sailed the seas,

Till the waters vast
Filled them with a vague devotion,
With the freedom and the motion,
With the roll and roar of ocean
   And the sounding blast.

When they landed from the fleet,
How 'they roared through Drontheim's
   street,
   Boisterous as the gale !
How they laughed and stamped and
   pounded,
Till the tavern roof resounded
And the host looked on astounded
   As they drank the ale !

Never saw the wild North Sea
Such a gallant company
   Sail its billows blue !
Never, while they cruised and quarrelled,
Old King Gorm, or Blue-Tooth Harald,
Owned a ship so well apparelled,
   Boasted such a crew !

XV

A LITTLE BIRD IN THE AIR

A little bird in the air
Is singing of Thyri the fair,
   The sister of Svend the Dane ;
And the song of the garrulous bird
In the streets of the town is heard,
   And repeated again and again.
     Hoist up your sails of silk,
     And flee away from each other.

To King Burislaf, it is said,
Was the beautiful Thyri wed,
   And a sorrowful bride went she ;
And after a week and a day
She has fled away and away
   From his town by the stormy sea.
     Hoist up your sails of silk,
     And flee away from each other.

They say, that through heat and through
   cold,
Through weald, they say, and through
   wold,
   By day and by night, they say,
She has fled ; and the gossips report
She has come to King Olaf's court,
   And the town is all in dismay.

Hoist up your sails of silk,
   And flee away from each other.

It is whispered King Olaf has seen,
Has talked with the beautiful Queen ;
   And they wonder how it will end ;
For surely, if here she remain,
It is war with King Svend the Dane,
   And King Burislaf the Vend !
     Hoist up your sails of silk,
     And flee away from each other.

Oh, greatest wonder of all !
It is published in hamlet and hall,
   It roars like a flame that is fanned !
The King — yes, Olaf the King —
Has wedded her with his ring,
   And Thyri is Queen in the land !
     Hoist up your sails of silk,
     And flee away from each other.

XVI

QUEEN THYRI AND THE ANGELICA STALKS

Northward over Drontheim,
Flew the clamorous sea-gulls,
Sang the lark and linnet
   From the meadows green ;

Weeping in her chamber,
Lonely and unhappy,
Sat the Drottning Thyri,
   Sat King Olaf's Queen.

In at all the windows
Streamed the pleasant sunshine,
On the roof above her
   Softly cooed the dove ;

But the sound she heard not,
Nor the sunshine heeded,
For the thoughts of Thyri
   Were not thoughts of love.

Then King Olaf entered,
Beautiful as morning,
Like the sun at Easter
   Shone his happy face ;

In his hand he carried
Angelicas uprooted,
With delicious fragrance
   Filling all the place.

Like a rainy midnight
Sat the Drottning Thyri,
Even the smile of Olaf
   Could not cheer her gloom ;

Nor the stalks he gave her
With a gracious gesture,
And with words as pleasant
   As their own perfume.

In her hands he placed them,
And her jewelled fingers
Through the green leaves glistened
   Like the dews of morn ;

But she cast them from her,
Haughty and indignant,
On the floor she threw them
   With a look of scorn.

" Richer presents," said she,
" Gave King Harald Gormson
To the Queen, my mother,
   Than such worthless weeds ;

" When he ravaged Norway,
Laying waste the kingdom,
Seizing scatt and treasure
   For her royal needs.

" But thou darest not venture
Through the Sound to Vendland,
My domains to rescue
   From King Burislaf ;

" Lest King Svend of Denmark,
Forked Beard, my brother,
Scatter all thy vessels
   As the wind the chaff."

Then up sprang King Olaf,
Like a reindeer bounding,
With an oath he answered
   Thus the luckless Queen :

" Never yet did Olaf
Fear King Svend of Denmark ;
This right hand shall hale him
   By his forked chin ! "

Then he left the chamber,
Thundering through the doorway,
Loud his steps resounded
   Down the outer stair.

Smarting with the insult,
Through the streets of Drontheim
Strode he red and wrathful,
   With his stately air.

All his ships he gathered,
Summoned all his forces,
Making his war levy
   In the region round.

Down the coast of Norway,
Like a flock of sea-gulls,
Sailed the fleet of Olaf
   Through the Danish Sound.

With his own hand fearless
Steered he the Long Serpent,
Strained the creaking cordage,
   Bent each boom and gaff ;

Till in Vendland landing,
The domains of Thyri
He redeemed and rescued
   From King Burislaf.

Then said Olaf, laughing,
" Not ten yoke of oxen
Have the power to draw us
   Like a woman's hair !

" Now will I confess it,
Better things are jewels
Than angelica stalks are
   For a queen to wear."

XVII

KING SVEND OF THE FORKED BEARD

Loudly the sailors cheered
Svend of the Forked Beard,
As with his fleet he steered
   Southward to Vendland ;
Where with their courses hauled
All were together called,
Under the Isle of Svald
   Near to the mainland.

After Queen Gunhild's death,
So the old Saga saith,
Plighted King Svend his faith
   To Sigrid the Haughty ;

And to avenge his bride,
Soothing her wounded pride,
Over the waters wide
   King Olaf sought he.

Still on her scornful face,
Blushing with deep disgrace,
Bore she the crimson trace
   Of Olaf's gauntlet ;
Like a malignant star,
Blazing in heaven afar,
Red shone the angry scar
   Under her frontlet.

Oft to King Svend she spake,
" For thine own honor's sake
Shalt thou swift vengeance take
   On the vile coward ! "
Until the King at last,
Gusty and overcast,
Like a tempestuous blast
   Threatened and lowered.

Soon as the Spring appeared,
Svend of the Forked Beard
High his red standard reared,
   Eager for battle ;
While every warlike Dane,
Seizing his arms again,
Left all unsown the grain,
   Unhoused the cattle.

Likewise the Swedish King
Summoned in haste a Thing,
Weapons and men to bring
   In aid of Denmark ;
Eric the Norseman, too,
As the war-tidings flew,
Sailed with a chosen crew
   From Lapland and Finmark.

So upon Easter day
Sailed the three kings away,
Out of the sheltered bay,
   In the bright season ;
With them Earl Sigvald came,
Eager for spoil and fame ;
Pity that such a name
   Stooped to such treason !

Safe under Svald at last,
Now were their anchors cast,
Safe from the sea and blast,
   Plotted the three kings ;

While, with a base intent,
Southward Earl Sigvald went,
On a foul errand bent,
   Unto the Sea-kings.

Thence to hold on his course
Unto King Olaf's force,
Lying within the hoarse
   Mouths of Stet-haven ;
Him to ensnare and bring
Unto the Danish king,
Who his dead corse would fling
   Forth to the raven !

XVIII

KING OLAF AND EARL SIGVALD

On the gray sea-sands
King Olaf stands,
Northward and seaward
He points with his hands.

With eddy and whirl
The sea-tides curl,
Washing the sandals
Of Sigvald the Earl.

The mariners shout,
The ships swing about,
The yards are all hoisted,
The sails flutter out.

The war-horns are played,
The anchors are weighed,
Like moths in the distance
The sails flit and fade.

The sea is like lead,
The harbor lies dead,
As a corse on the sea-shore,
Whose spirit has fled !

On that fatal day,
The histories say,
Seventy vessels
Sailed out of the bay.

But soon scattered wide
O'er the billows they ride,
While Sigvald and Olaf
Sail side by side.

Cried the Earl : "Follow me !
I your pilot will be,
For I know all the channels
Where flows the deep sea ! "

So into the strait
Where his foes lie in wait,
Gallant King Olaf
Sails to his fate !

Then the sea-fog veils
The ships and their sails ;
Queen Sigrid the Haughty,
Thy vengeance prevails !

XIX

KING OLAF'S WAR-HORNS

"Strike the sails ! " King Olaf said ;
" Never shall men of mine take flight ;
Never away from battle I fled,
Never away from my foes !
    Let God dispose
Of my life in the fight ! "

"Sound the horns ! " said Olaf the King ;
And suddenly through the drifting brume
The blare of the horns began to ring,
Like the terrible trumpet shock
    Of Regnarock,
On the Day of Doom !

Louder and louder the war-horns sang
Over the level floor of the flood ;
All the sails came down with a clang,
And there in the midst overhead
    The sun hung red
As a drop of blood.

Drifting down on the Danish fleet
Three together the ships were lashed,
So that neither should turn and retreat ;
In the midst, but in front of the rest,
    The burnished crest
Of the Serpent flashed.

King Olaf stood on the quarter-deck,
With bow of ash and arrows of oak,
His gilded shield was without a fleck,
His helmet inlaid with gold,
    And in many a fold
Hung his crimson cloak.

On the forecastle Ulf the Red
Watched the lashing of the ships ;
"If the Serpent lie so far ahead,
We shall have hard work of it here,"
    Said he with a sneer
On his bearded lips.

King Olaf laid an arrow on string,
"Have I a coward on board ? " said he.
"Shoot it another way, O King ! "
Sullenly answered Ulf,
    The old sea-wolf ;
"You have need of me ! "

In front came Svend, the King of the
        Danes,
Sweeping down with his fifty rowers ;
To the right, the Swedish king with his
        thanes ;
And on board of the Iron Beard
    Earl Eric steered
To the left with his oars.

"These soft Danes and Swedes," said the
        King,
"At home with their wives had better stay,
Than come within reach of my Serpent's
        sting :
But where Eric the Norseman leads
    Heroic deeds
Will be done to-day ! "

Then as together the vessels crashed,
Eric severed the cables of hide,
With which King Olaf's ships were lashed,
And left them to drive and drift
    With the currents swift
Of the outward tide.

Louder the war-horns growl and snarl,
Sharper the dragons bite and sting !
Eric the son of Hakon Jarl
A death-drink salt as the sea
    Pledges to thee,
Olaf the King !

XX

EINAR TAMBERSKELVER

It was Einar Tamberskelver
    Stood beside the mast ;
From his yew-bow, tipped with silver,
    Flew the arrows fast ;

Aimed at Eric unavailing,
  As he sat concealed,
Half behind the quarter-railing,
  Half behind his shield.

First an arrow struck the tiller,
  Just above his head ;
" Sing, O Eyvind Skaldaspiller,"
  Then Earl Eric said.
" Sing the song of Hakon dying,
  Sing his funeral wail ! "
And another arrow flying
  Grazed his coat of mail.

Turning to a Lapland yeoman,
  As the arrow passed,
Said Earl Eric, " Shoot that bowman
  Standing by the mast."
Sooner than the word was spoken
  Flew the yeoman's shaft ;
Einar's bow in twain was broken,
  Einar only laughed.

" What was that ? " said Olaf, standing
  On the quarter-deck.
" Something heard I like the stranding
  Of a shattered wreck."
Einar then, the arrow taking
  From the loosened string,
Answered, " That was Norway breaking
  From thy hand, O King ! "

" Thou art but a poor diviner,"
  Straightway Olaf said ;
" Take my bow, and swifter, Einar,
  Let thy shafts be sped."
Of his bows the fairest choosing,
  Reached he from above ;
Einar saw the blood-drops oozing
  Through his iron glove.

But the bow was thin and narrow ;
  At the first assay,
O'er its head he drew the arrow,
  Flung the bow away ;
Said, with hot and angry temper
  Flushing in his cheek,
" Olaf ! for so great a Kämper
  Are thy bows too weak ! "

Then, with smile of joy defiant
  On his beardless lip,
Scaled he, light and self-reliant,
  Eric's dragon-ship.

Loose his golden locks were flowing,
  Bright his armor gleamed ;
Like Saint Michael overthrowing
  Lucifer he seemed.

XXI

KING OLAF'S DEATH-DRINK

All day has the battle raged,
All day have the ships engaged,
But not yet is assuaged
  The vengeance of Eric the Earl.

The decks with blood are red,
The arrows of death are sped,
The ships are filled with the dead,
  And the spears the champions hurl.

They drift as wrecks on the tide,
The grappling-irons are plied,
The boarders climb up the side,
  The shouts are feeble and few.

Ah ! never shall Norway again
See her sailors come back o'er the main ;
They all lie wounded or slain,
  Or asleep in the billows blue !

On the deck stands Olaf the King,
Around him whistle and sing
The spears that the foemen fling,
  And the stones they hurl with their hands

In the midst of the stones and the spears,
Kolbiorn, the marshal, appears,
His shield in the air he uprears,
  By the side of King Olaf he stands.

Over the slippery wreck
Of the Long Serpent's deck
Sweeps Eric with hardly a check,
  His lips with anger are pale ;

He hews with his axe at the mast,
Till it falls, with the sails overcast,
Like a snow-covered pine in the vast
  Dim forests of Orkadale.

Seeking King Olaf then,
He rushes aft with his men,
As a hunter into the den
  Of the bear, when he stands at bay.

"Remember Jarl Hakon!" he cries;
When lo! on his wondering eyes,
Two kingly figures arise,
    Two Olafs in warlike array!

Then Kolbiorn speaks in the ear
Of King Olaf a word of cheer,
In a whisper that none may hear,
    With a smile on his tremulous lip;

Two shields raised high in the air,
Two flashes of golden hair,
Two scarlet meteors' glare,
    And both have leaped from the ship.

Earl Eric's men in the boats
Seize Kolbiorn's shield as it floats,
And cry, from their hairy throats,
    "See! it is Olaf the King!"

While far on the opposite side
Floats another shield on the tide,
Like a jewel set in the wide
    Sea-current's eddying ring.

There is told a wonderful tale,
How the King stripped off his mail,
Like leaves of the brown sea-kale,
    As he swam beneath the main;

But the young grew old and gray,
And never, by night or by day,
In his kingdom of Norroway
    Was King Olaf seen again!

XXII

THE NUN OF NIDAROS

In the convent of Drontheim,
Alone in her chamber
Knelt Astrid the Abbess,
At midnight, adoring,
Beseeching, entreating
The Virgin and Mother.

She heard in the silence
The voice of one speaking,
Without in the darkness,
In gusts of the night-wind,
Now louder, now nearer,
Now lost in the distance.

The voice of a stranger
It seemed as she listened,
Of some one who answered
Beseeching, imploring,
A cry from afar off
She could not distinguish.

The voice of Saint John,
The beloved disciple,
Who wandered and waited
The Master's appearance,
Alone in the darkness,
Unsheltered and friendless.

"It is accepted,
The angry defiance,
The challenge of battle!
It is accepted,
But not with the weapons
Of war that thou wieldest!

"Cross against corselet,
Love against hatred,
Peace-cry for war-cry!
Patience is powerful;
He that o'ercometh
Hath power o'er the nations!

"As torrents in summer,
Half dried in their channels,
Suddenly rise, though the
Sky is still cloudless,
For rain has been falling
Far off at their fountains;

"So hearts that are fainting
Grow full to o'erflowing,
And they that behold it
Marvel, and know not
That God at their fountains
Far off has been raining!

"Stronger than steel
Is the sword of the Spirit;
Swifter than arrows
The light of the truth is,
Greater than anger
Is love, and subdueth!

"Thou art a phantom,
A shape of the sea-mist,
A shape of the brumal
Rain, and the darkness
Fearful and formless;
Day dawns and thou art not!

"The dawn is not distant,
Nor is the night starless ;
Love is eternal !
God is still God, and
His faith shall not fail us ;
Christ is eternal ! "

INTERLUDE

A STRAIN of music closed the tale,
A low, monotonous, funeral wail,
That with its cadence, wild and sweet,
Made the long Saga more complete.

"Thank God," the Theologian said,
" The reign of violence is dead,
Or dying surely from the world ;
While Love triumphant reigns instead,
And in a brighter sky o'erhead
His blessed banners are unfurled.
And most of all thank God for this :
The war and waste of clashing creeds
Now end in words, and not in deeds,
And no one suffers loss, or bleeds,
For thoughts that men call heresies.

" I stand without here in the porch,
I hear the bell's melodious din,
I hear the organ peal within,
I hear the prayer, with words that scorch
Like sparks from an inverted torch,
I hear the sermon upon sin,
With threatenings of the last account.
And all, translated in the air,
Reach me but as our dear Lord's Prayer,
And as the Sermon on the Mount.

"Must it be Calvin, and not Christ?
Must it be Athanasian creeds,
Or holy water, books, and beads ?
Must struggling souls remain content
With councils and decrees of Trent ?
And can it be enough for these
The Christian Church the year embalms
With evergreens and boughs of palms,
And fills the air with litanies ?

"I know that yonder Pharisee
Thanks God that he is not like me ;
In my humiliation dressed,
I only stand and beat my breast,
And pray for human charity.

"Not to one church alone, but seven,
The voice prophetic spake from heaven ;
And unto each the promise came,
Diversified, but still the same ;
For him that overcometh are
The new name written on the stone,
The raiment white, the crown, the throne,
And I will give him the Morning Star !

"Ah ! to how many Faith has been
No evidence of things unseen,
But a dim shadow, that recasts
The creed of the Phantasiasts,
For whom no Man of Sorrows died,
For whom the Tragedy Divine
Was but a symbol and a sign,
And Christ a phantom crucified !

"For others a diviner creed
Is living in the life they lead.
The passing of their beautiful feet
Blesses the pavement of the street,
And all their looks and words repeat
Old Fuller's saying, wise and sweet,
Not as a vulture, but a dove,
The Holy Ghost came from above.

" And this brings back to me a tale
So sad the hearer well may quail,
And question if such things can be ;
Yet in the chronicles of Spain
Down the dark pages runs this stain,
And naught can wash them white again,
So fearful is the tragedy."

THE THEOLOGIAN'S TALE

TORQUEMADA

"December 5 [at midnight]. Finished *Torquemada*,
— a dismal story of fanaticism ; but in its main points
historic. See De Castro, *Protestantes Españolas*, page
310."

IN the heroic days when Ferdinand
And Isabella ruled the Spanish land,
And Torquemada, with his subtle brain,
Ruled them as Grand Inquisitor of Spain,
In a great castle near Valladolid,
Moated and high and by fair woodlands
    hid,
There dwelt, as from the chronicles we
    learn,
An old Hidalgo proud and taciturn,

Whose name has perished, with his towers
  of stone,
And all his actions save this one alone ;
This one, so terrible, perhaps 't were best
If it, too, were forgotten with the rest ;
Unless, perchance, our eyes can see therein
The martyrdom triumphant o'er the sin ;
A double picture, with its gloom and glow,
The splendor overhead, the death below.

This sombre man counted each day as lost
On which his feet no sacred threshold
  crossed ;
And when he chanced the passing Host to
  meet,
He knelt and prayed devoutly in the
  street ;
Oft he confessed ; and with each mutinous
  thought,
As with wild beasts at Ephesus, he fought.
In deep contrition scourged himself in
  Lent,
Walked in processions, with his head down
  bent,
At plays of Corpus Christi oft was seen,
And on Palm Sunday bore his bough of
  green.
His sole diversion was to hunt the boar
Through tangled thickets of the forest
  hoar,
Or with his jingling mules to hurry down
To some grand bull-fight in the neighbor-
  ing town,
Or in the crowd with lighted taper stand,
When Jews were burned, or banished from
  the land.
Then stirred within him a tumultuous joy ;
The demon whose delight is to destroy
Shook him, and shouted with a trumpet
  tone,
"Kill ! kill ! and let the Lord find out his
  own ! "

And now, in that old castle in the wood,
His daughters, in the dawn of womanhood,
Returning from their convent school, had
  made
Resplendent with their bloom the forest
  shade,
Reminding him of their dead mother's
  face,
When first she came into that gloomy
  place, —
A memory in his heart as dim and sweet
As moonlight in a solitary street,

Where the same rays, that lift the sea, are
  thrown
Lovely but powerless upon walls of stone.
These two fair daughters of a mother dead
Were all the dream had left him as it fled.
A joy at first, and then a growing care,
As if a voice within him cried, " Beware ! "
A vague presentiment of impending doom,
Like ghostly footsteps in a vacant room,
Haunted him day and night ; a formless
  fear
That death to some one of his house was
  near,
With dark surmises of a hidden crime,
Made life itself a death before its time.
Jealous, suspicious, with no sense of shame,
A spy upon his daughters he became ;
With velvet slippers, noiseless on the floors,
He glided softly through half-open doors ;
Now in the room, and now upon the stair,
He stood beside them ere they were aware;
He listened in the passage when they
  talked,
He watched them from the casement when
  they walked,
He saw the gypsy haunt the river's side,
He saw the monk among the cork-trees
  glide ;
And, tortured by the mystery and the
  doubt
Of some dark secret, past his finding out,
Baffled he paused ; then reassured again
Pursued the flying phantom of his brain.
He watched them even when they knelt in
  church ;
And then, descending lower in his search,
Questioned the servants, and with eager
  eyes
Listened incredulous to their replies ;
The gypsy ? none had seen her in the
  wood !
The monk ? a mendicant in search of food !

At length the awful revelation came,
Crushing at once his pride of birth and
  name ;
The hopes his yearning bosom forward cast
And the ancestral glories of the past,
All fell together, crumbling in disgrace,
A turret rent from battlement to base.
His daughters talking in the dead of night
In their own chamber, and without a light,
Listening, as he was wont, he overheard,
And learned the dreadful secret, word by
  word ;

And hurrying from his castle, with a cry
He raised his hands to the unpitying sky,
Repeating one dread word, till bush and
    tree
Caught it, and shuddering answered,
    " Heresy ! "

Wrapped in his cloak, his hat drawn o'er
    his face,
Now hurrying forward, now with lingering
    pace,
He walked all night the alleys of his park,
With one unseen companion in the dark,
The demon who within him lay in wait
And by his presence turned his love to
    hate,
Forever muttering in an undertone,
" Kill ! kill ! and let the Lord find out his
    own ! "

Upon the morrow, after early Mass,
While yet the dew was glistening on the
    grass,
And all the woods were musical with birds,
The old Hidalgo, uttering fearful words,
Walked homeward with the Priest, and in
    his room
Summoned his trembling daughters to their
    doom.
When questioned, with brief answers they
    replied,
Nor when accused evaded or denied ;
Expostulations, passionate appeals,
All that the human heart most fears or
    feels,
In vain the Priest with earnest voice
    essayed ;
In vain the father threatened, wept, and
    prayed ;
Until at last he said, with haughty mien,
" The Holy Office, then, must intervene ! "

And now the Grand Inquisitor of Spain,
With all the fifty horsemen of his train,
His awful name resounding, like the blast
Of funeral trumpets, as he onward passed,
Came to Valladolid, and there began
To harry the rich Jews with fire and ban.
To him the Hidalgo went, and at the gate
Demanded audience on affairs of state,
And in a secret chamber stood before
A venerable graybeard of fourscore,
Dressed in the hood and habit of a friar ;
Out of his eyes flashed a consuming fire,
And in his hand the mystic horn he held,

Which poison and all noxious charms dis-
    pelled.
He heard in silence the Hidalgo's tale,
Then answered in a voice that made him
    quail :
" Son of the Church ! when Abraham of old
To sacrifice his only son was told,
He did not pause to parley nor protest,
But hastened to obey the Lord's behest.
In him it was accounted righteousness ;
The Holy Church expects of thee no less ! "

A sacred frenzy seized the father's brain,
And Mercy from that hour implored in
    vain.
Ah ! who will e'er believe the words I say ?
His daughters he accused, and the same
    day
They both were cast into the dungeon's
    gloom,
That dismal antechamber of the tomb,
Arraigned, condemned, and sentenced to
    the flame,
The secret torture and the public shame.

Then to the Grand Inquisitor once more
The Hidalgo went more eager than before,
And said : " When Abraham offered up his
    son,
He clave the wood wherewith it might be
    done.
By his example taught, let me too bring
Wood from the forest for my offering ! "
And the deep voice, without a pause, re-
    plied :
" Son of the Church ! by faith now justified,
Complete thy sacrifice, even as thou wilt ;
The Church absolves thy conscience from
    all guilt ! "

Then this most wretched father went his
    way
Into the woods, that round his castle lay,
Where once his daughters in their child-
    hood played
With their young mother in the sun and
    shade.
Now all the leaves had fallen ; the branches
    bare
Made a perpetual moaning in the air,
And screaming from their eyries overhead
The ravens sailed athwart the sky of lead.
With his own hands he lopped the boughs
    and bound
Fagots, that crackled with foreboding sound,

And on his mules, caparisoned and gay
With bells and tassels, sent them on their
    way.

Then with his mind on one dark purpose
    bent,
Again to the Inquisitor he went,
And said : "Behold, the fagots I have
    brought,
And now, lest my atonement be as naught,
Grant me one more request, one last de-
    sire, —
With my own hand to light the funeral
    fire ! "
And Torquemada answered from his seat,
"Son of the Church ! Thine offering is
    complete ;
Her servants through all ages shall not
    cease
To magnify thy deed. Depart in peace ! "

Upon the market-place, builded of stone
The scaffold rose, whereon Death claimed
    his own.
At the four corners, in stern attitude,
Four statues of the Hebrew Prophets stood,
Gazing with calm indifference in their
    eyes
Upon this place of human sacrifice,
Round which was gathering fast the eager
    crowd,
With clamor of voices dissonant and loud,
And every roof and window was alive
With restless gazers, swarming like a hive.

The church-bells tolled, the chant of monks
    drew near,
Loud trumpets stammered forth their notes
    of fear,
A line of torches smoked along the street,
There was a stir, a rush, a tramp of feet,
And, with its banners floating in the air,
Slowly the long procession crossed the
    square,
And, to the statues of the Prophets bound,
The victims stood, with fagots piled around.
Then all the air a blast of trumpets shook,
And louder sang the monks with bell and
    book,
And the Hidalgo, lofty, stern, and proud,
Lifted his torch, and, bursting through the
    crowd,
Lighted in haste the fagots, and then fled,
Lest those imploring eyes should strike him
    dead !

O pitiless skies ! why did your clouds re-
    tain
For peasants' fields their floods of hoarded
    rain ?
O pitiless earth ! why opened no abyss
To bury in its chasm a crime like this ?

That night, a mingled column of fire and
    smoke
From the dark thickets of the forest broke,
And, glaring o'er the landscape leagues
    away,
Made all the fields and hamlets bright as
    day.
Wrapped in a sheet of flame the castle
    blazed,
And as the villagers in terror gazed,
They saw the figure of that cruel knight
Lean from a window in the turret's height,
His ghastly face illumined with the glare,
His hands upraised above his head in
    prayer,
Till the floor sank beneath him, and he fell
Down the black hollow of that burning
    well.

Three centuries and more above his bones
Have piled the oblivious years like funeral
    stones ;
His name has perished with him, and no
    trace
Remains on earth of his afflicted race ;
But Torquemada's name, with clouds o'er-
    cast,
Looms in the distant landscape of the Past,
Like a burnt tower upon a blackened heath,
Lit by the fires of burning woods beneath !

INTERLUDE

THUS closed the tale of guilt and gloom,
That cast upon each listener's face
Its shadow, and for some brief space
Unbroken silence filled the room.
The Jew was thoughtful and distressed ;
Upon his memory thronged and pressed
The persecution of his race,
Their wrongs and sufferings and disgrace ;
His head was sunk upon his breast,
And from his eyes alternate came
Flashes of wrath and tears of shame.

The Student first the silence broke,
As one who long has lain in wait,

With purpose to retaliate,
And thus he dealt the avenging stroke.
" In such a company as this,
A tale so tragic seems amiss,
That by its terrible control
O'ermasters and drags down the soul
Into a fathomless abyss.
The Italian Tales that you disdain,
Some merry Night of Straparole,
Or Machiavelli's Belphagor,
Would cheer us and delight us more,
Give greater pleasure and less pain
Than your grim tragedies of Spain ! "

And here the Poet raised his hand,
With such entreaty and command,
It stopped discussion at its birth,
And said : " The story I shall tell
Has meaning in it, if not mirth ;
Listen, and hear what once befell
The merry birds of Killingworth ! "

THE POET'S TALE

THE BIRDS OF KILLINGWORTH

It was the season, when through all the
land
The merle and mavis build, and build-
ing sing
Those lovely lyrics, written by His hand,
Whom Saxon Cædmon calls the Blithe-
heart King ;
When on the boughs the purple buds ex-
pand,
The banners of the vanguard of the
Spring,
And rivulets, rejoicing, rush and leap,
And wave their fluttering signals from the
steep.

The robin and the bluebird, piping loud,
Filled all the blossoming orchards with
their glee ;
The sparrows chirped as if they still were
proud
Their race in Holy Writ should men-
tioned be ;
And hungry crows, assembled in a crowd,
Clamored their piteous prayer inces-
santly,
Knowing who hears the ravens cry, and said :
" Give us, O Lord, this day, our daily
bread ! "

Across the Sound the birds of passage
sailed,
Speaking some unknown language
strange and sweet
Of tropic isle remote, and passing hailed
The village with the cheers of all their
fleet ;
Or quarrelling together, laughed and
railed
Like foreign sailors, landed in the street
Of seaport town, and with outlandish noise
Of oaths and gibberish frightening girls
and boys.

Thus came the jocund Spring in Killing-
worth,
In fabulous days, some hundred years
ago ;
And thrifty farmers, as they tilled the
earth,
Heard with alarm the cawing of the
crow,
That mingled with the universal mirth,
Cassandra-like, prognosticating woe ;
They shook their heads, and doomed with
dreadful words
To swift destruction the whole race of
birds.

And a town-meeting was convened straight-
way
To set a price upon the guilty heads
Of these marauders, who, in lieu of pay,
Levied black - mail upon the garden
beds
And cornfields, and beheld without dis-
may
The awful scarecrow, with his fluttering
shreds ;
The skeleton that waited at their feast,
Whereby their sinful pleasure was in-
creased.

Then from his house, a temple painted
white,
With fluted columns, and a roof of red,
The Squire came forth, august and splen-
did sight !
Slowly descending, with majestic tread,
Three flights of steps, nor looking left nor
right,
Down the long street he walked, as one
who said,
" A town that boasts inhabitants like me
Can have no lack of good society ! "

The Parson, too, appeared, a man austere,
  The instinct of whose nature was to
    kill ;
The wrath of God he preached from year
    to year,
  And read, with fervor, Edwards on the
    Will ;
His favorite pastime was to slay the deer
  In Summer on some Adirondac hill ;
E'en now, while walking down the rural
    lane,
He lopped the wayside lilies with his cane.

From the Academy, whose belfry crowned
  The hill of Science with its vane of
    brass,
Came the Preceptor, gazing idly round,
  Now at the clouds, and now at the green
    grass,
And all absorbed in reveries profound
  Of fair Almira in the upper class,
Who was, as in a sonnet he had said,
As pure as water, and as good as bread.

And next the Deacon issued from his door,
  In his voluminous neck-cloth, white as
    snow ;
A suit of sable bombazine he wore ;
  His form was ponderous, and his step
    was slow ;
There never was so wise a man before ;
  He seemed the incarnate " Well, I told
    you so ! "
And to perpetuate his great renown
There was a street named after him in
    town.

These came together in the new town-hall,
  With sundry farmers from the region
    round.
The Squire presided, dignified and tall,
  His air impressive and his reasoning
    sound ;
Ill fared it with the birds, both great and
    small ;
  Hardly a friend in all that crowd they
    found,
But enemies enough, who every one
Charged them with all the crimes beneath
    the sun.

When they had ended, from his place
    apart
  Rose the Preceptor, to redress the
    wrong,

And, trembling like a steed before the
    start,
  Looked round bewildered on the expect-
    ant throng ;
Then thought of fair Almira, and took
    heart
  To speak out what was in him, clear and
    strong,
Alike regardless of their smile or frown,
And quite determined not to be laughed
    down.

" Plato, anticipating the Reviewers,
  From his Republic banished without pity
The Poets ; in this little town of yours,
  You put to death, by means of a Com-
    mittee,
The ballad-singers and the Troubadours,
  The street-musicians of the heavenly
    city,
The birds, who make sweet music for us
    all
In our dark hours, as David did for Saul.

" The thrush that carols at the dawn of
    day
  From the green steeples of the piny
    wood ;
The oriole in the elm ; the noisy jay,
  Jargoning like a foreigner at his food ;
The bluebird balanced on some topmost
    spray,
  Flooding with melody the neighbor-
    hood ;
Linnet and meadow-lark, and all the throng
That dwell in nests, and have the gift of
    song.

" You slay them all ! and wherefore ? for
    the gain
  Of a scant handful more or less of
    wheat,
Or rye, or barley, or some other grain,
  Scratched up at random by industrious
    feet,
Searching for worm or weevil after rain !
  Or a few cherries, that are not so sweet
As are the songs these uninvited guests
Sing at their feast with comfortable
    breasts.

" Do you ne'er think what wondrous beings
    these ?
  Do you ne'er think who made them, and
    who taught

The dialect they speak, where melodies
  Alone are the interpreters of thought ?
Whose household words are songs in many
    keys,
  Sweeter than instrument of man e'er
    caught !
Whose habitations in the tree-tops even
Are half-way houses on the road to
    heaven !

" Think, every morning when the sun peeps
    through
  The dim, leaf-latticed windows of the
    grove,
How jubilant the happy birds renew
  Their old, melodious madrigals of love !
And when you think of this, remember
    too
  'T is always morning somewhere, and
    above
The awakening continents, from shore to
    shore,
Somewhere the birds are singing evermore.

" Think of your woods and orchards without
    birds !
  Of empty nests that cling to boughs and
    beams
As in an idiot's brain remembered words
  Hang empty 'mid the cobwebs of his
    dreams !
Will bleat of flocks or bellowing of herds
  Make up for the lost music, when your
    teams
Drag home the stingy harvest, and no
    more
The feathered gleaners follow to your
    door ?

" What ! would you rather see the incessant
    stir
  Of insects in the windrows of the hay,
And hear the locust and the grasshopper
  Their melancholy hurdy-gurdies play ?
Is this more pleasant to you than the whir
  Of meadow-lark, and her sweet rounde-
    lay,
Or twitter of little field-fares, as you take
Your nooning in the shade of bush and
    brake ?

" You call them thieves and pillagers ; but
    know,
  They are the wingèd wardens of your
    farms,

Who from the cornfields drive the insidious
    foe,
  And from your harvests keep a hundred
    harms ;
Even the blackest of them all, the crow,
  Renders good service as your man-at-
    arms,
Crushing the beetle in his coat of mail,
And crying havoc on the slug and snail.

" How can I teach your children gentle-
    ness,
  And mercy to the weak, and reverence
For Life, which, in its weakness or excess,
  Is still a gleam of God's omnipotence,
Or Death, which, seeming darkness, is no
    less
  The selfsame light, although averted
    hence,
When by your laws, your actions, and your
    speech,
You contradict the very things I teach ? "

With this he closed ; and through the au-
    dience went
  A murmur, like the rustle of dead
    leaves ;
The farmers laughed and nodded, and some
    bent
  Their yellow heads together like their
    sheaves ;
Men have no faith in fine-spun sentiment
  Who put their trust in bullocks and in
    beeves.
The birds were doomed ; and, as the record
    shows,
A bounty offered for the heads of crows.

There was another audience out of reach,
  Who had no voice nor vote in making
    laws,
But in the papers read his little speech,
  And crowned his modest temples with
    applause ;
They made him conscious, each one more
    than each,
  He still was victor, vanquished in their
    cause.
Sweetest of all the applause he won from
    thee,
O fair Almira at the Academy !

And so the dreadful massacre began ;
  O'er fields and orchards, and o'er wood-
    land crests,

The ceaseless fusillade of terror ran.
  Dead fell the birds, with blood-stains on
    their breasts,
Or wounded crept away from sight of
    man,
  While the young died of famine in their
    nests ;
A slaughter to be told in groans, not words,
The very St. Bartholomew of Birds !

The Summer came, and all the birds were
    dead ;
  The days were like hot coals ; the very
    ground
Was burned to ashes ; in the orchards fed
  Myriads of caterpillars, and around
The cultivated fields and garden beds
  Hosts of devouring insects crawled, and
    found
No foe to check their march, till they had
    made
The land a desert without leaf or shade.

Devoured by worms, like Herod, was the
    town,
  Because, like Herod, it had ruthlessly
Slaughtered the Innocents. From the trees
    spun down
  The canker-worms upon the passers-by,
Upon each woman's bonnet, shawl, and
    gown,
  Who shook them off with just a little
    cry ;
They were the terror of each favorite walk,
The endless theme of all the village talk.

The farmers grew impatient, but a few
  Confessed their error, and would not
    complain,
For after all, the best thing one can do
  When it is raining, is to let it rain.
Then they repealed the law, although they
    knew
  It would not call the dead to life again ;
As school-boys, finding their mistake too
    late,
Draw a wet sponge across the accusing
    slate.

That year in Killingworth the Autumn
    came
  Without the light of his majestic look,
The wonder of the falling tongues of flame,
  The illumined pages of his Doom's-Day
    book.

A few lost leaves blushed crimson with
    their shame,
  And drowned themselves despairing in
    the brook,
While the wild wind went moaning every-
    where,
  Lamenting the dead children of the air !

But the next Spring a stranger sight was
    seen,
  A sight that never yet by bard was sung,
As great a wonder as it would have been
  If some dumb animal had found a tongue !
A wagon, overarched with evergreen,
  Upon whose boughs were wicker cages
    hung,
All full of singing birds, came down the
    street,
  Filling the air with music wild and sweet.

From all the country round these birds
    were brought,
  By order of the town, with anxious quest,
And, loosened from their wicker prisons,
    sought
  In woods and fields the places they loved
    best,
Singing loud canticles, which many thought
  Were satires to the authorities addressed,
While others, listening in green lanes,
    averred
Such lovely music never had been heard !

But blither still and louder carolled they
  Upon the morrow, for they seemed to
    know
It was the fair Almira's wedding-day,
  And everywhere, around, above, below,
When the Preceptor bore his bride away,
  Their songs burst forth in joyous over-
    flow,
And a new heaven bent over a new earth
Amid the sunny farms of Killingworth.

FINALE

THE hour was late ; the fire burned low,
The Landlord's eyes were closed in sleep,
And near the story's end a deep,
Sonorous sound at times was heard,
As when the distant bagpipes blow.
At this all laughed ; the Landlord stirred,
As one awaking from a swound,
And, gazing anxiously around,

Protested that he had not slept,
But only shut his eyes, and kept
His ears attentive to each word.

Then all arose, and said " Good Night."
Alone remained the drowsy Squire
To rake the embers of the fire,
And quench the waning parlor light ;
While from the windows, here and there,
The scattered lamps a moment gleamed,
And the illumined hostel seemed
The constellation of the Bear,
Downward, athwart the misty air,
Sinking and setting toward the sun.
Far off the village clock struck one.

PART SECOND

PRELUDE

A COLD, uninterrupted rain,
That washed each southern window-pane,
And made a river of the road ;
A sea of mist that overflowed
The house, the barns, the gilded vane,
And drowned the upland and the plain,
Through which the oak-trees, broad and
    high,
Like phantom ships went drifting by ;
And, hidden behind a watery screen,
The sun unseen, or only seen
As a faint pallor in the sky ; —
Thus cold and colorless and gray,
The morn of that autumnal day,
As if reluctant to begin,
Dawned on the silent Sudbury Inn,
And all the guests that in it lay.

Full late they slept. They did not hear
The challenge of Sir Chanticleer,
Who on the empty threshing-floor,
Disdainful of the rain outside,
Was strutting with a martial stride,
As if upon his thigh he wore
The famous broadsword of the Squire,
And said, " Behold me, and admire ! "

Only the Poet seemed to hear,
In drowse or dream, more near and near
Across the border-land of sleep,
The blowing of a blithesome horn,
That laughed the dismal day to scorn ;
A splash of hoofs and rush of wheels
Through sand and mire like stranding keels,

As from the road with sudden sweep
The Mail drove up the little steep,
And stopped beside the tavern door ;
A moment stopped, and then again
With crack of whip and bark of dog
Plunged forward through the sea of fog,
And all was silent as before, —
All silent save the dripping rain.

Then one by one the guests came down,
And greeted with a smile the Squire,
Who sat before the parlor fire,
Reading the paper fresh from town.
First the Sicilian, like a bird,
Before his form appeared, was heard
Whistling and singing down the stair ;
Then came the Student. with a look
As placid as a meadow-brook ;
The Theologian, still perplexed
With thoughts of this world and the next;
The Poet then, as one who seems
Walking in visions and in dreams ;
Then the Musician, like a fair
Hyperion from whose golden hair
The radiance of the morning streams ;
And last the aromatic Jew
Of Alicant, who, as he threw
The door wide open, on the air
Breathed round about him a perfume
Of damask roses in full bloom,
Making a garden of the room.

The breakfast ended, each pursued
The promptings of his various mood ;
Beside the fire in silence smoked
The taciturn, impassive Jew,
Lost in a pleasant revery ;
While, by his gravity provoked,
His portrait the Sicilian drew,
And wrote beneath it " Edrehi,
At the Red Horse in Sudbury."

By far the busiest of them all,
The Theologian in the hall
Was feeding robins in a cage, —
Two corpulent and lazy birds,
Vagrants and pilferers at best,
If one might trust the hostler's words,
Chief instrument of their arrest ;
Two poets of the Golden Age,
Heirs of a boundless heritage
Of fields and orchards, east and west,
And sunshine of long summer days,
Though outlawed now and dispossessed ! —
Such was the Theologian's phrase.

Meanwhile the Student held discourse
With the Musician, on the source
Of all the legendary lore
Among the nations, scattered wide
Like silt and seaweed by the force
And fluctuation of the tide ;
The tale repeated o'er and o'er,
With change of place and change of name,
Disguised, transformed, and yet the same
We've heard a hundred times before.

The Poet at the window mused,
And saw, as in a dream confused,
The countenance of the Sun, discrowned,
And haggard with a pale despair,
And saw the cloud-rack trail and drift
Before it, and the trees uplift
Their leafless branches, and the air
Filled with the arrows of the rain,
And heard amid the mist below,
Like voices of distress and pain,
That haunt the thoughts of men insane,
The fateful cawings of the crow.

Then down the road, with mud besprent,
And drenched with rain from head to hoof,
The rain-drops dripping from his mane
And tail as from a pent-house roof,
A jaded horse, his head down bent,
Passed slowly, limping as he went.

The young Sicilian — who had grown
Impatient longer to abide
A prisoner, greatly mortified
To see completely overthrown
His plans for angling in the brook,
And, leaning o'er the bridge of stone,
To watch the speckled trout glide by,
And float through the inverted sky,
Still round and round the baited hook —
Now paced the room with rapid stride,
And, pausing at the Poet's side,
Looked forth, and saw the wretched steed,
And said : " Alas for human greed,
That with cold hand and stony eye
Thus turns an old friend out to die,
Or beg his food from gate to gate !
This brings a tale into my mind,
Which, if you are not disinclined
To listen, I will now relate."

All gave assent ; all wished to hear,
Not without many a jest and jeer,
The story of a spavined steed ;
And even the Student with the rest

Put in his pleasant little jest
Out of Malherbe, that Pegasus
Is but a horse that with all speed
Bears poets to the hospital ;
While the Sicilian, self-possessed,
After a moment's interval
Began his simple story thus.

THE SICILIAN'S TALE

THE BELL OF ATRI

At Atri in Abruzzo, a small town
Of ancient Roman date, but scant renown,
One of those little places that have run
Half up the hill, beneath a blazing sun,
And then sat down to rest, as if to say,
" I climb no farther upward, come what
          may," —
The Re Giovanni, now unknown to fame,
So many monarchs since have borne the
          name,
Had a great bell hung in the market-place,
Beneath a roof, projecting some small space
By way of shelter from the sun and rain.
Then rode he through the streets with all
          his train,
And, with the blast of trumpets loud and
          long,
Made proclamation, that whenever wrong
Was done to any man, he should but ring
The great bell in the square, and he, the
          King,
Would cause the Syndic to decide thereon.
Such was the proclamation of King John.

How swift the happy days in Atri sped,
What wrongs were righted, need not here
          be said.
Suffice it that, as all things must decay,
The hempen rope at length was worn away,
Unravelled at the end, and, strand by
          strand,
Loosened and wasted in the ringer's hand,
Till one, who noted this in passing by,
Mended the rope with braids of briony,
So that the leaves and tendrils of the vine
Hung like a votive garland at a shrine.

By chance it happened that in Atri dwelt
A knight, with spur on heel and sword in
          belt,
Who loved to hunt the wild-boar in the
          woods,

Who loved his falcons with their crimson
   hoods,
Who loved his hounds and horses, and all
   sports
And prodigalities of camps and courts ; —
Loved, or had loved them ; for at last,
   grown old,
His only passion was the love of gold.

He sold his horses, sold his hawks and
   hounds,
Rented his vineyards and his garden-
   grounds,
Kept but one steed, his favorite steed of
   all,
To starve and shiver in a naked stall,
And day by day sat brooding in his chair,
Devising plans how best to hoard and spare.

At length he said : " What is the use or
   need
To keep at my own cost this lazy steed,
Eating his head off in my stables here,
When rents are low and provender is dear ?
Let him go feed upon the public ways ;
I want him only for the holidays."
So the old steed was turned into the heat
Of the long, lonely, silent, shadeless street ;
And wandered in suburban lanes forlorn,
Barked at by dogs, and torn by brier and
   thorn.

One afternoon, as in that sultry clime
It is the custom in the summer time,
With bolted doors and window-shutters
   closed,
The inhabitants of Atri slept or dozed ;
When suddenly upon their senses fell
The loud alarm of the accusing bell !
The Syndic started from his deep repose,
Turned on his couch, and listened, and then
   rose
And donned his robes, and with reluctant
   pace
Went panting forth into the market-place,
Where the great bell upon its cross-beams
   swung,
Reiterating with persistent tongue,
In half-articulate jargon, the old song :
" Some one hath done a wrong, hath done
   a wrong ! "

But ere he reached the belfry's light arcade
He saw, or thought he saw, beneath its
   shade,

No shape of human form of woman born,
But a poor steed dejected and forlorn,
Who with uplifted head and eager eye
Was tugging at the vines of briony.
" Domeneddio ! " cried the Syndic straight,
" This is the Knight of Atri's steed of state !
He calls for justice, being sore distressed,
And pleads his cause as loudly as the best."

Meanwhile from street and lane a noisy
   crowd
Had rolled together like a summer cloud,
And told the story of the wretched beast
In five-and-twenty different ways at least,
With much gesticulation and appeal
To heathen gods, in their excessive zeal.
The Knight was called and questioned ; in
   reply
Did not confess the fact, did not deny ;
Treated the matter as a pleasant jest,
And set at naught the Syndic and the rest,
Maintaining, in an angry undertone,
That he should do what pleased him with
   his own.

And thereupon the Syndic gravely read
The proclamation of the King ; then said :
" Pride goeth forth on horseback grand and
   gay,
But cometh back on foot, and begs its way ;
Fame is the fragrance of heroic deeds,
Of flowers of chivalry and not of weeds !
These are familiar proverbs ; but I fear
They never yet have reached your knightly
   ear.
What fair renown, what honor, what re-
   pute
Can come to you from starving this poor
   brute ?
He who serves well and speaks not, merits
   more
Than they who clamor loudest at the door.
Therefore the law decrees that as this steed
Served you in youth, henceforth you shall
   take heed
To comfort his old age, and to provide
Shelter in stall, and food and field beside."

The Knight withdrew abashed ; the people
   all
Led home the steed in triumph to his stall.
The King heard and approved, and laughed
   in glee,
And cried aloud : " Right well it pleaseth
   me !

Church-bells at best but ring us to the
    door ;
But go not in to mass ; my bell doth more :
It cometh into court and pleads the cause
Of creatures dumb and unknown to the
    laws ;
And this shall make, in every Christian
    clime,
The Bell of Atri famous for all time."

INTERLUDE

" YES, well your story pleads the cause
Of those dumb mouths that have no speech,
Only a cry from each to each
In its own kind, with its own laws ;
Something that is beyond the reach
Of human power to learn or teach, —
An inarticulate moan of pain,
Like the immeasurable main
Breaking upon an unknown beach."

Thus spake the Poet with a sigh ;
Then added, with impassioned cry,
As one who feels the words he speaks,
The color flushing in his cheeks,
The fervor burning in his eye :
" Among the noblest in the land,
Though he may count himself the least,
That man I honor and revere
Who without favor, without fear,
In the great city dares to stand
The friend of every friendless beast,
And tames with his unflinching hand
The brutes that wear our form and face,
The were-wolves of the human race ! "
Then paused, and waited with a frown,
Like some old champion of romance,
Who, having thrown his gauntlet down,
Expectant leans upon his lance ;
But neither Knight nor Squire is found
To raise the gauntlet from the ground,
And try with him the battle's chance.

"Wake from your dreams, O Edrehi !
Or dreaming speak to us, and make
A feint of being half awake,
And tell us what your dreams may be.
Out of the hazy atmosphere
Of cloud-land deign to reappear
Among us in this Wayside Inn ;
Tell us what visions and what scenes
Illuminate the dark ravines
In which you grope your way.   Begin ! "

Thus the Sicilian spake.   The Jew
Made no reply, but only smiled,
As men unto a wayward child,
Not knowing what to answer, do.
As from a cavern's mouth, o'ergrown
With moss and intertangled vines,
A streamlet leaps into the light
And murmurs over root and stone
In a melodious undertone ;
Or as amid the noonday night
Of sombre and wind-haunted pines
There runs a sound as of the sea ;
So from his bearded lips there came
A melody without a name,
A song, a tale, a history,
Or whatsoever it may be,
Writ and recorded in these lines.

THE SPANISH JEW'S TALE

KAMBALU

INTO the city of Kambalu,
By the road that leadeth to Ispahan,
At the head of his dusty caravan,
Laden with treasure from realms afar,
Baldacca and Kelat and Kandahar,
Rode the great captain Alau.

The Khan from his palace-window gazed,
And saw in the thronging street beneath,
In the light of the setting sun, that blazed
Through the clouds of dust by the caravan
    raised,
The flash of harness and jewelled sheath,
And the shining scimitars of the guard,
And the weary camels that bared their
    teeth,
As they passed and passed through the
    gates unbarred
Into the shade of the palace-yard.

Thus into the city of Kambalu
Rode the great captain Alau ;
And he stood before the Khan, and said :
" The enemies of my lord are dead ;
All the Kalifs of all the West
Bow and obey thy least behest ;
The plains are dark with the mulberry-
    trees,
The weavers are busy in Samarcand,
The miners are sifting the golden sand,
The divers plunging for pearls in the seas,
And peace and plenty are in the land.

" Baldacca's Kalif, and he alone,
Rose in revolt against thy throne :
His treasures are at thy palace-door,
With the swords and the shawls and the
    jewels he wore ;
His body is dust o'er the desert blown.

" A mile outside of Baldacca's gate
I left my forces to lie in wait,
Concealed by forests and hillocks of sand,
And forward dashed with a handful of
    men,
To lure the old tiger from his den
Into the ambush I had planned.
Ere we reached the town the alarm was
    spread,
For we heard the sound of gongs from
    within ;
And with clash of cymbals and warlike din
The gates swung wide ; and we turned and
    fled ;
And the garrison sallied forth and pur-
    sued,
With the gray old Kalif at their head,
And above them the banner of Mohammed:
So we snared them all, and the town was
    subdued.

" As in at the gate we rode, behold,
A tower that is called the Tower of Gold !
For there the Kalif had hidden his wealth,
Heaped and hoarded and piled on high,
Like sacks of wheat in a granary ;
And thither the miser crept by stealth
To feel of the gold that gave him health,
And to gaze and gloat with his hungry
    eye
On jewels that gleamed like a glow-worm's
    spark,
Or the eyes of a panther in the dark.

" I said to the Kalif : ' Thou art old,
Thou hast no need of so much gold.
Thou shouldst not have heaped and hidden
    it here,
Till the breath of battle was hot and near,
But have sown through the land these use-
    less hoards
To spring into shining blades of swords,
And keep thine honor sweet and clear.
These grains of gold are not grains of
    wheat ;
These bars of silver thou canst not eat ;
These jewels and pearls and precious stones
Cannot cure the aches in thy bones,

Nor keep the feet of Death one hour
From climbing the stairways of thy tower !'

" Then into his dungeon I locked the drone,
And left him to feed there all alone
In the honey-cells of his golden hive ;
Never a prayer, nor a cry, nor a groan
Was heard from those massive walls of
    stone,
Nor again was the Kalif seen alive !

" When at last we unlocked the door,
We found him dead upon the floor ;
The rings had dropped from his withered
    hands,
His teeth were like bones in the desert
    sands :
Still clutching his treasure he had died ;
And as he lay there, he appeared
A statue of gold with a silver beard,
His arms outstretched as if crucified."

This is the story, strange and true,
That the great captain Alau
Told to his brother the Tartar Khan,
When he rode that day into Kambalu
By the road that leadeth to Ispahan.

INTERLUDE

" I THOUGHT before your tale began,"
The Student murmured, " we should have
Some legend written by Judah Rav
In his Gemara of Babylon ;
Or something from the Gulistan, —
The tale of the Cazy of Hamadan,
Or of that King of Khorasan
Who saw in dreams the eyes of one
That had a hundred years been dead
Still moving restless in his head,
Undimmed, and gleaming with the lust
Of power, though all the rest was dust.

" But lo ! your glittering caravan
On the road that leadeth to Ispahan
Hath led us farther to the East
Into the regions of Cathay.
Spite of your Kalif and his gold,
Pleasant has been the tale you told,
And full of color ; that at least
No one will question or gainsay.
And yet on such a dismal day
We need a merrier tale to clear
The dark and heavy atmosphere.

So listen, Lordlings, while I tell,
Without a preface, what befell
A simple cobbler, in the year —
No matter ; it was long ago ;
And that is all we need to know."

THE STUDENT'S TALE

THE COBBLER OF HAGENAU

I TRUST that somewhere and somehow
You all have heard of Hagenau,
A quiet, quaint, and ancient town
Among the green Alsatian hills,
A place of valleys, streams, and mills,
Where Barbarossa's castle, brown
With rust of centuries, still looks down
On the broad, drowsy land below, —
On shadowy forests filled with game,
And the blue river winding slow
Through meadows, where the hedges grow
That give this little town its name.

It happened in the good old times,
While yet the Master-singers filled
The noisy workshop and the guild
With various melodies and rhymes,
That here in Hagenau there dwelt
A cobbler, — one who loved debate,
And, arguing from a postulate,
Would say what others only felt ;
A man of forecast and of thrift,
And of a shrewd and careful mind
In this world's business, but inclined
Somewhat to let the next world drift.

Hans Sachs with vast delight he read,
And Regenbogen's rhymes of love,
For their poetic fame had spread
Even to the town of Hagenau ;
And some Quick Melody of the Plough,
Or Double Harmony of the Dove
Was always running in his head.
He kept, moreover, at his side,
Among his leathers and his tools,
Reynard the Fox, the Ship of Fools,
Or Eulenspiegel, open wide ;
With these he was much edified :
He thought them wiser than the Schools.

His good wife, full of godly fear,
Liked not these worldly themes to hear;
The Psalter was her book of songs ;
The only music to her ear

Was that which to the Church belongs,
When the loud choir on Sunday chanted,
And the two angels carved in wood,
That by the windy organ stood,
Blew on their trumpets loud and clear,
And all the echoes, far and near,
Gibbered as if the church were haunted.

Outside his door, one afternoon,
This humble votary of the muse
Sat in the narrow strip of shade
By a projecting cornice made,
Mending the Burgomaster's shoes,
And singing a familiar tune : —

" Our ingress into the world
    Was naked and bare ;
Our progress through the world
    Is trouble and care ;
Our egress from the world
    Will be nobody knows where :
But if we do well here
    We shall do well there ;
And I could tell you no more,
    Should I preach a whole year ! "

Thus sang the cobbler at his work ;
And with his gestures marked the time,
Closing together with a jerk
Of his waxed thread the stitch and rhyme.

Meanwhile his quiet little dame
Was leaning o'er the window-sill,
Eager, excited, but mouse-still,
Gazing impatiently to see
What the great throng of folk might be
That onward in procession came,
Along the unfrequented street,
With horns that blew, and drums that
    beat,
And banners flying, and the flame
Of tapers, and, at times, the sweet
Voices of nuns ; and as they sang
Suddenly all the church-bells rang.

In a gay coach, above the crowd,
There sat a monk in ample hood,
Who with his right hand held aloft
A red and ponderous cross of wood,
To which at times he meekly bowed.
In front three horsemen rode, and oft,
With voice and air importunate,
A boisterous herald cried aloud :
" The grace of God is at your gate ! "
So onward to the church they passed.

The cobbler slowly turned his last,
And, wagging his sagacious head,
Unto his kneeling housewife said :
" 'T is the monk Tetzel.   I have heard
The cawings of that reverend bird.
Don't let him cheat you of your gold ;
Indulgence is not bought and sold."

The church of Hagenau, that night,
Was full of people, full of light ;
An odor of incense filled the air,
The priest intoned, the organ groaned
Its inarticulate despair ;
The candles on the altar blazed,
And full in front of it upraised
The red cross stood against the glare.
Below, upon the altar-rail
Indulgences were set to sale,
Like ballads at a country fair.
A heavy strong-box, iron-bound
And carved with many a quaint device,
Received, with a melodious sound,
The coin that purchased Paradise.

Then from the pulpit overhead,
Tetzel the monk, with fiery glow,
Thundered upon the crowd below.
" Good people all, draw near ! " he said ;
" Purchase these letters, signed and sealed,
By which all sins, though unrevealed
And unrepented, are forgiven !
Count but the gain, count not the loss !
Your gold and silver are but dross,
And yet they pave the way to heaven.
I hear your mothers and your sires
Cry from their purgatorial fires,
And will ye not their ransom pay ?
O senseless people ! when the gate
Of heaven is open, will ye wait ?
Will ye not enter in to-day ?
To-morrow it will be too late ;
I shall be gone upon my way.
Make haste ! bring money while ye may ! "

The women shuddered, and turned pale ;
Allured by hope or driven by fear,
With many a sob and many a tear,
All crowded to the altar-rail.
Pieces of silver and of gold
Into the tinkling strong-box fell
Like pebbles dropped into a well ;
And soon the ballads were all sold.
The cobbler's wife among the rest
Slipped into the capacious chest
A golden florin ; then withdrew,

Hiding the paper in her breast ;
And homeward through the darkness went
Comforted, quieted, content ;
She did not walk, she rather flew,
A dove that settles to her nest,
When some appalling bird of prey
That scared her has been driven away.

The days went by, the monk was gone,
The summer passed, the winter came ;
Though seasons changed, yet still the same
The daily round of life went on ;
The daily round of household care,
The narrow life of toil and prayer.
But in her heart the cobbler's dame
Had now a treasure beyond price,
A secret joy without a name,
The certainty of Paradise.
Alas, alas ! Dust unto dust !
Before the winter wore away,
Her body in the churchyard lay,
Her patient soul was with the Just !
After her death, among the things
That even the poor preserve with care, —
Some little trinkets and cheap rings,
A locket with her mother's hair,
Her wedding gown, the faded flowers
She wore upon her wedding day, —
Among these memories of past hours,
That so much of the heart reveal,
Carefully kept and put away,
The Letter of Indulgence lay
Folded, with signature and seal.

Meanwhile the Priest, aggrieved **and**
　　pained,
Waited and wondered that no word
Of mass or requiem he heard,
As by the Holy Church ordained :
Then to the Magistrate complained,
That as this woman had been dead
A week or more, and no mass said,
It was rank heresy, or at least
Contempt of Church ; thus said the Priest.
And straight the cobbler was arraigned.

He came, confiding in his cause,
But rather doubtful of the laws.
The Justice from his elbow-chair
Gave him a look that seemed to say :
" Thou standest before a Magistrate,
Therefore do not prevaricate ! "
Then asked him in a business way,
Kindly but cold : " Is thy wife dead ? "
The cobbler meekly bowed his head ·

"She is," came struggling from his throat
Scarce audibly. The Justice wrote
The words down in a book, and then
Continued, as he raised his pen ;
"She is ; and hath a mass been said
For the salvation of her soul ?
Come, speak the truth ! confess the whole !"
The cobbler without pause replied :
"Of mass or prayer there was no need ;
For at the moment when she died
Her soul was with the glorified !"
And from his pocket with all speed
He drew the priestly title-deed,
And prayed the Justice he would read.

The Justice read, amused, amazed ;
And as he read his mirth increased ;
At times his shaggy brows he raised,
Now wondering at the cobbler gazed,
Now archly at the angry Priest.
"From all excesses, sins, and crimes
Thou hast committed in past times
Thee I absolve ! And furthermore,
Purified from all earthly taints,
To the communion of the Saints
And to the sacraments restore !
All stains of weakness, and all trace
Of shame and censure I efface ;
Remit the pains thou shouldst endure,
And make thee innocent and pure,
So that in dying, unto thee
The gates of heaven shall open be !
Though long thou livest, yet this grace
Until the moment of thy death
Unchangeable continueth ! "

Then said he to the Priest : " I find
This document is duly signed
Brother John Tetzel, his own hand.
At all tribunals in the land
In evidence it may be used ;
Therefore acquitted is the accused."
Then to the cobbler turned : " My friend,
Pray tell me, didst thou ever read
Reynard the Fox ? " — " Oh yes, in-
       deed ! " —
" I thought so. Don't forget the end."

INTERLUDE

" WHAT was the end ? I am ashamed
Not to remember Reynard's fate ;
I have not read the book of late ;
Was he not hanged ? " the Poet said.

The Student gravely shook his head,
And answered : " You exaggerate.
There was a tournament proclaimed,
And Reynard fought with Isegrim
The Wolf, and having vanquished him,
Rose to high honor in the State,
And Keeper of the Seals was named ! "
At this the gay Sicilian laughed :
" Fight fire with fire, and craft with
       craft ;
Successful cunning seems to be
The moral of your tale," said he.
" Mine had a better, and the Jew's
Had none at all, that I could see ;
His aim was only to amuse."

Meanwhile from out its ebon case
His violin the Minstrel drew,
And having tuned its strings anew,
Now held it close in his embrace,
And poising in his outstretched hand
The bow, like a magician's wand,
He paused, and said, with beaming face ;
" Last night my story was too long ;
To-day I give you but a song,
An old tradition of the North ;
But first, to put you in the mood,
I will a little while prelude,
And from this instrument draw forth
Something by way of overture."

He played ; at first the tones were pure
And tender as a summer night,
The full moon climbing to her height,
The sob and ripple of the seas,
The flapping of an idle sail ;
And then by sudden and sharp degrees
The multiplied, wild harmonies
Freshened and burst into a gale ;
A tempest howling through the dark,
A crash as of some shipwrecked bark,
A loud and melancholy wail.

Such was the prelude to the tale
Told by the Minstrel ; and at times
He paused amid its varying rhymes,
And at each pause again broke in
The music of his violin,
With tones of sweetness or of fear,
Movements of trouble or of calm,
Creating their own atmosphere ;
As sitting in a church we hear
Between the verses of the psalm
The organ playing soft and clear,
Or thundering on the startled ear.

THE MUSICIAN'S TALE

THE BALLAD OF CARMILHAN

I

At Stralsund, by the Baltic Sea,
  Within the sandy bar,
At sunset of a summer's day,
Ready for sea, at anchor lay
  The good ship Valdemar.

The sunbeams danced upon the waves,
  And played along her side ;
And through the cabin windows streamed
In ripples of golden light, that seemed
  The ripple of the tide.

There sat the captain with his friends,
  Old skippers brown and hale,
Who smoked and grumbled o'er their
    grog,
And talked of iceberg and of fog,
  Of calm and storm and gale.

And one was spinning a sailor's yarn
  About Klaboterman,
The Kobold of the sea ; a spright
Invisible to mortal sight,
  Who o'er the rigging ran.

Sometimes he hammered in the hold,
  Sometimes upon the mast,
Sometimes abeam, sometimes abaft,
Or at the bows he sang and laughed,
  And made all tight and fast.

He helped the sailors at their work,
  And toiled with jovial din ;
He helped them hoist and reef the sails,
He helped them stow the casks and bales,
  And heave the anchor in.

But woe unto the lazy louts,
  The idlers of the crew ;
Them to torment was his delight,
And worry them by day and night,
  And pinch them black and blue.

And woe to him whose mortal eyes
  Klaboterman behold.
It is a certain sign of death ! —
The cabin-boy here held his breath,
  He felt his blood run cold.

II

The jolly skipper paused awhile,
  And then again began ;
"There is a Spectre Ship," quoth he,
"A ship of the Dead that sails the sea,
  And is called the Carmilhan.

"A ghostly ship, with a ghostly crew,
  In tempests she appears ;
And before the gale, or against the gale,
She sails without a rag of sail,
  Without a helmsman steers.

"She haunts the Atlantic north and south,
  But mostly the mid-sea,
Where three great rocks rise bleak and
    bare
Like furnace chimneys in the air,
  And are called the Chimneys Three.

"And ill betide the luckless ship
  That meets the Carmilhan ;
Over her decks the seas will leap,
She must go down into the deep,
  And perish mouse and man."

The captain of the Valdemar
  Laughed loud with merry heart.
"I should like to see this ship," said he ;
"I should like to find these Chimneys Three
  That are marked down in the chart.

"I have sailed right over the spot," he said,
  "With a good stiff breeze behind,
When the sea was blue, and the sky was
    clear, —
You can follow my course by these pinholes
    here, —
  And never a rock could find."

And then he swore a dreadful oath,
  He swore by the Kingdoms Three,
That, should he meet the Carmilhan,
He would run her down, although he ran
  Right into Eternity !

All this, while passing to and fro,
  The cabin-boy had heard ;
He lingered at the door to hear,
And drank in all with greedy ear,
  And pondered every word.

He was a simple country lad,
  But of a roving mind.

" Oh, it must be like heaven," thought he,
" Those far-off foreign lands to see,
  And fortune seek and find ! "

But in the fo'castle, when he heard
  The mariners blaspheme,
He thought of home, he thought of God,
And his mother under the churchyard
  sod,
  And wished it were a dream.

One friend on board that ship had he ;
  'T was the Klaboterman,
Who saw the Bible in his chest,
And made a sign upon his breast,
  All evil things to ban.

                    III

The cabin windows have grown blank
  As eyeballs of the dead ;
No more the glancing sunbeams burn
On the gilt letters of the stern,
  But on the figure-head ;

On Valdemar Victorious,
  Who looketh with disdain
To see his image in the tide
Dismembered float from side to side,
  And reunite again.

" It is the wind," those skippers said,
  " That swings the vessel so ;
It is the wind ; it freshens fast,
'T is time to say farewell at last,
  'T is time for us to go."

They shook the captain by the hand,
  "Good luck ! good luck ! " they cried ;
Each face was like the setting sun,
As, broad and red, they one by one
  Went o'er the vessel's side.

The sun went down, the full moon rose,
  Serene o'er field and flood ;
And all the winding creeks and bays
And broad sea-meadows seemed ablaze,
  The sky was red as blood.

The southwest wind blew fresh and fair,
  As fair as wind could be ;
Bound for Odessa, o'er the bar,
With all sail set, the Valdemar
  Went proudly out to sea.

The lovely moon climbs up the sky
  As one who walks in dreams ;
A tower of marble in her light,
A wall of black, a wall of white,
  The stately vessel seems.

Low down upon the sandy coast
  The lights begin to burn ;
And now, uplifted high in air,
They kindle with a fiercer glare,
  And now drop far astern.

The dawn appears, the land is gone,
  The sea is all around ;
Then on each hand low hills of sand
Emerge and form another land ;
  She steereth through the Sound.

Through Kattegat and Skager-rack
  She flitteth like a ghost ;
By day and night, by night and day,
She bounds, she flies upon her way
  Along the English coast.

Cape Finisterre is drawing near,
  Cape Finisterre is past ;
Into the open ocean stream
She floats, the vision of a dream
  Too beautiful to last.

Suns rise and set, and rise, and yet
  There is no land in sight ;
The liquid planets overhead
Burn brighter now the moon is dead,
  And longer stays the night.

                    IV

And now along the horizon's edge
  Mountains of cloud uprose,
Black as with forests underneath,
Above, their sharp and jagged teeth
  Were white as drifted snows.

Unseen behind them sank the sun,
  But flushed each snowy peak
A little while with rosy light,
That faded slowly from the sight
  As blushes from the cheek.

Black grew the sky, — all black, all black ;
  The clouds were everywhere ;
There was a feeling of suspense
In nature, a mysterious sense
  Of terror in the air.

And all on board the Valdemar
  Was still as still could be ;
Save when the dismal ship-bell tolled,
As ever and anon she rolled,
  And lurched into the sea.

The captain up and down the deck
  Went striding to and fro ;
Now watched the compass at the wheel,
Now lifted up his hand to feel
  Which way the wind might blow.

And now he looked up at the sails,
  And now upon the deep ;
In every fibre of his frame
He felt the storm before it came,
  He had no thought of sleep.

Eight bells ! and suddenly abaft,
  With a great rush of rain,
Making the ocean white with spume,
In darkness like the day of doom,
  On came the hurricane.

The lightning flashed from cloud to cloud,
  And rent the sky in two ;
A jagged flame, a single jet
Of white fire, like a bayonet,
  That pierced the eyeballs through.

Then all around was dark again,
  And blacker than before ;
But in that single flash of light
He had beheld a fearful sight,
  And thought of the oath he swore.

For right ahead lay the Ship of the Dead,
  The ghostly Carmilhan !
Her masts were stripped, her yards were
    bare,
And on her bowsprit, poised in air,
  Sat the Klaboterman.

Her crew of ghosts was all on deck
  Or clambering up the shrouds ;
The boatswain's whistle, the captain's
    hail
Were like the piping of the gale,
  And thunder in the clouds.

And close behind the Carmilhan
  There rose up from the sea,
As from a foundered ship of stone,
Three bare and splintered masts alone :
  They were the Chimneys Three.

And onward dashed the Valdemar
  And leaped into the dark ;
A denser mist, a colder blast,
A little shudder, and she had passed
  Right through the Phantom Bark.

She cleft in twain the shadowy hulk,
  But cleft it unaware ;
As when, careering to her nest,
The sea-gull severs with her breast
  The unresisting air.

Again the lightning flashed ; again
  They saw the Carmilhan,
Whole as before in hull and spar ;
But now on board of the Valdemar
  Stood the Klaboterman.

And they all knew their doom was sealed ;
  They knew that death was near ;
Some prayed who never prayed before,
And some they wept, and some they
    swore,
  And some were mute with fear.

Then suddenly there came a shock,
  And louder than wind or sea
A cry burst from the crew on deck,
As she dashed and crashed, a hopeless
    wreck,
  Upon the Chimneys Three.

The storm and night were passed, the light
  To streak the east began ;
The cabin-boy, picked up at sea,
Survived the wreck, and only he,
  To tell of the Carmilhan.

INTERLUDE

When the long murmur of applause
That greeted the Musician's lay
Had slowly buzzed itself away,
And the long talk of Spectre Ships
That followed died upon their lips
And came unto a natural pause,
" These tales you tell are one and all
Of the Old World," the Poet said,
" Flowers gathered from a crumbling wall,
Dead leaves that rustle as they fall ;
Let me present you in their stead
Something of our New England earth,
A tale, which, though of no great worth,
Has still this merit, that it yields

A certain freshness of the fields,
A sweetness as of home-made bread."

The Student answered : " Be discreet ;
For if the flour be fresh and sound,
And if the bread be light and sweet,
Who careth in what mill 't was ground,
Or of what oven felt the heat,
Unless, as old Cervantes said,
You are looking after better bread
Than any that is made of wheat ?
You know that people nowadays
To what is old give little praise ;
All must be new in prose and verse ;
They want hot bread, or something worse,
Fresh every morning, and half baked ;
The wholesome bread of yesterday,
Too stale for them, is thrown away,
Nor is their thirst with water slaked."

As oft we see the sky in May
Threaten to rain, and yet not rain,
The Poet's face, before so gay,
Was clouded with a look of pain,
But suddenly brightened up again ;
And without further let or stay
He told his tale of yesterday.

THE POET'S TALE

LADY WENTWORTH

ONE hundred years ago, and something
        more,
In Queen Street, Portsmouth, at her tav-
        ern door,
Neat as a pin, and blooming as a rose,
Stood Mistress Stavers in her furbelows,
Just as her cuckoo-clock was striking nine.
Above her head, resplendent on the sign,
The portrait of the Earl of Halifax,
In scarlet coat and periwig of flax,
Surveyed at leisure all her varied charms,
Her cap, her bodice, her white folded arms,
And half resolved, though he was past his
        prime,
And rather damaged by the lapse of time,
To fall down at her feet, and to declare
The passion that had driven him to de-
        spair.
For from his lofty station he had seen
Stavers, her husband, dressed in bottle-
        green,

Drive his new Flying Stage-coach, four in
        hand,
Down the long lane, and out into the land,
And knew that he was far upon the way
To Ipswich and to Boston on the Bay !

Just then the meditations of the Earl
Were interrupted by a little girl,
Barefooted, ragged, with neglected hair,
Eyes full of laughter, neck and shoulders
        bare,
A thin slip of a girl, like a new moon,
Sure to be rounded into beauty soon,
A creature men would worship and adore,
Though now in mean habiliments she bore
A pail of water, dripping through the street,
And bathing, as she went, her naked feet.

It was a pretty picture, full of grace, —
The slender form, the delicate, thin face ;
The swaying motion, as she hurried by ;
The shining feet, the laughter in her eye,
That o'er her face in ripples gleamed and
        glanced,
As in her pail the shifting sunbeam danced :
And with uncommon feelings of delight
The Earl of Halifax beheld the sight.
Not so Dame Stavers, for he heard her say
These words, or thought he did, as plain as
        day :
" O Martha Hilton !   Fie ! how dare you
        go
About the town half dressed, and looking
        so ! "
At which the gypsy laughed, and straight
        replied :
" No matter how I look ; I yet shall ride
In my own chariot, ma'am." And on the
        child
The Earl of Halifax benignly smiled,
As with her heavy burden she passed on,
Looked back, then turned the corner, and
        was gone.

What next, upon that memorable day,
Arrested his attention was a gay
And brilliant equipage, that flashed and
        spun,
The silver harness glittering in the sun,
Outriders with red jackets, lithe and lank,
Pounding the saddles as they rose and sank,
While all alone within the chariot sat
A portly person with three-cornered hat,
A crimson velvet coat, head high in air,
Gold-headed cane, and nicely powdered hair,

And diamond buckles sparkling at his knees,
Dignified, stately, florid, much at ease.
Onward the pageant swept, and as it passed,
Fair Mistress Stavers courtesied low and fast ;
For this was Governor Wentworth, driving down
To Little Harbor, just beyond the town,
Where his Great House stood looking out to sea,
A goodly place, where it was good to be.

It was a pleasant mansion, an abode
Near and yet hidden from the great high-road,
Sequestered among trees, a noble pile,
Baronial and colonial in its style ;
Gables and dormer-windows everywhere,
And stacks of chimneys rising high in air, —
Pandæan pipes, on which all winds that blew
Made mournful music the whole winter through.
Within, unwonted splendors met the eye,
Panels, and floors of oak, and tapestry ;
Carved chimney-pieces, where on brazen dogs
Revelled and roared the Christmas fires of logs ;
Doors opening into darkness unawares,
Mysterious passages, and flights of stairs ;
And on the walls, in heavy gilded frames,
The ancestral Wentworths with Old-Scripture names.

Such was the mansion where the great man dwelt,
A widower and childless ; and he felt
The loneliness, the uncongenial gloom,
That like a presence haunted every room ;
For though not given to weakness, he could feel
The pain of wounds, that ache because they heal.

The years came and the years went, — seven in all,
And passed in cloud and sunshine o'er the Hall ;
The dawns their splendor through its chambers shed,
The sunsets flushed its western windows red ;

The snow was on its roofs, the wind, the rain ;
Its woodlands were in leaf and bare again ;
Moons waxed and waned, the lilacs bloomed and died,
In the broad river ebbed and flowed the tide,
Ships went to sea, and ships came home from sea,
And the slow years sailed by and ceased to be.

And all these years had Martha Hilton served
In the Great House, not wholly unob-served :
By day, by night, the silver crescent grew,
Though hidden by clouds, her light still shining through ;
A maid of all work, whether coarse or fine,
A servant who made service seem divine !
Through her each room was fair to look upon ;
The mirrors glistened, and the brasses shone,
The very knocker on the outer door,
If she but passed, was brighter than be-fore.

And now the ceaseless turning of the mill
Of time, that never for an hour stands still,
Ground out the Governor's sixtieth birth-day,
And powdered his brown hair with silver-gray.
The robin, the forerunner of the spring,
The bluebird with his jocund carolling,
The restless swallows building in the eaves,
The golden buttercups, the grass, the leaves,
The lilacs tossing in the winds of May,
All welcomed this majestic holiday !
He gave a splendid banquet, served on plate,
Such as became the Governor of the State,
Who represented England and the King,
And was magnificent in everything.
He had invited all his friends and peers, —
The Pepperels, the Langdons, and the Lears,
The Sparhawks, the Penhallows, and the rest ;
For why repeat the name of every guest ?

But I must mention one in bands and gown,
The rector there, the Reverend Arthur
    Brown
Of the Established Church ; with smiling
    face
He sat beside the Governor and said grace ;
And then the feast went on, as others do,
But ended as none other I e'er knew.

When they had drunk the King, with many
    a cheer,
The Governor whispered in a servant's ear,
Who disappeared, and presently there stood
Within the room, in perfect womanhood,
A maiden, modest and yet self-possessed,
Youthful and beautiful, and simply dressed.
Can this be Martha Hilton ?   It must be !
Yes, Martha Hilton, and no other she !
Dowered with the beauty of her twenty
    years,
How ladylike, how queenlike she appears ;
The pale, thin crescent of the days gone by
Is Dian now in all her majesty !
Yet scarce a guest perceived that she was
    there,
Until the Governor, rising from his chair,
Played slightly with his ruffles, then looked
    down,
And said unto the Reverend Arthur
    Brown :
" This is my birthday : it shall likewise be
My wedding-day ; and you shall marry
    me ! "

The listening guests were greatly mystified,
None more so than the rector, who replied :
" Marry you ?   Yes, that were a pleasant
    task,
Your Excellency ; but to whom ? I ask."
The Governor answered : " To this lady
    here ; "
And beckoned Martha Hilton to draw near.
She came and stood, all blushes, at his side.
The rector paused.   The impatient Gov-
    ernor cried :
" This is the lady ; do you hesitate ?
Then I command you as Chief Magistrate."
The rector read the service loud and clear :
" Dearly beloved, we are gathered here,"
And so on to the end.   At his command
On the fourth finger of her fair left hand
The Governor placed the ring ; and that
    was all :
Martha was Lady Wentworth of the Hall !

INTERLUDE

WELL pleased the audience heard the tale.
The Theologian said : " Indeed,
To praise you there is little need ;
One almost hears the farmer's flail
Thresh out your wheat, nor does there
    fail
A certain freshness, as you said,
And sweetness as of home-made bread.
But not less sweet and not less fresh
Are many legends that I know,
Writ by the monks of long-ago,
Who loved to mortify the flesh,
So that the soul might purer grow,
And rise to a diviner state ;
And one of these — perhaps of all
Most beautiful — I now recall,
And with permission will narrate ;
Hoping thereby to make amends
For that grim tragedy of mine,
As strong and black as Spanish wine,
I told last night, and wish almost
It had remained untold, my friends ;
For Torquemada's awful ghost
Came to me in the dreams I dreamed,
And in the darkness glared and gleamed
Like a great lighthouse on the coast."

The Student laughing said :   " Far more
Like to some dismal fire of bale
Flaring portentous on a hill ;
Or torches lighted on a shore
By wreckers in a midnight gale.
No matter ; be it as you will,
Only go forward with your tale."

THE THEOLOGIAN'S TALE

THE LEGEND BEAUTIFUL

" HADST thou stayed, I must have fled ! "
That is what the Vision said.

In his chamber all alone,
Kneeling on the floor of stone,
Prayed the Monk in deep contrition
For his sins of indecision,
Prayed for greater self-denial
In temptation and in trial ;
It was noonday by the dial,
And the Monk was all alone.

Suddenly, as if it lightened,
An unwonted splendor brightened
All within him and without him
In that narrow cell of stone ;
And he saw the Blessed Vision
Of our Lord, with light Elysian
Like a vesture wrapped about Him,
Like a garment round Him thrown.

Not as crucified and slain,
Not in agonies of pain,
Not with bleeding hands and feet,
Did the Monk his Master see ;
But as in the village street,
In the house or harvest-field,
Halt and lame and blind He healed,
When He walked in Galileê.

In an attitude imploring,
Hands upon his bosom crossed,
Wondering, worshipping, adoring,
Knelt the Monk in rapture lost.
Lord, he thought, in heaven that reignest,
Who am I, that thus thou deignest
To reveal thyself to me ?
Who am I, that from the centre
Of thy glory thou shouldst enter
This poor cell, my guest to be ?

Then amid his exaltation,
Loud the convent bell appalling,
From its belfry calling, calling,
Rang through court and corridor
With persistent iteration
He had never heard before.
It was now the appointed hour
When alike in shine or shower,
Winter's cold or summer's heat,
To the convent portals came
All the blind and halt and lame,
All the beggars of the street,
For their daily dole of food
Dealt them by the brotherhood ;
And their almoner was he
Who upon his bended knee,
Rapt in silent ecstasy
Of divinest self-surrender,
Saw the Vision and the Splendor.
Deep distress and hesitation
Mingled with his adoration ;
Should he go or should he stay ?
Should he leave the poor to wait
Hungry at the convent gate,
Till the Vision passed away ?

Should he slight his radiant guest,
Slight this visitant celestial,
For a crowd of ragged, bestial
Beggars at the convent gate ?
Would the Vision there remain ?
Would the Vision come again ?
Then a voice within his breast
Whispered, audible and clear
As if to the outward ear :
" Do thy duty ; that is best ;
Leave unto thy Lord the rest ! "

Straightway to his feet he started,
And with longing look intent
On the Blessed Vision bent,
Slowly from his cell departed,
Slowly on his errand went.

At the gate the poor were waiting,
Looking through the iron grating,
With that terror in the eye
That is only seen in those
Who amid their wants and woes
Hear the sound of doors that close,
And of feet that pass them by ;
Grown familiar with disfavor,
Grown familiar with the savor
Of the bread by which men die !
But to-day, they know not why,
Like the gate of Paradise
Seemed the convent gate to rise,
Like a sacrament divine
Seemed to them the bread and wine.
In his heart the Monk was praying,
Thinking of the homeless poor,
What they suffer and endure ;
What we see not, what we see ;
And the inward voice was saying :
" Whatsoever thing thou doest
To the least of mine and lowest,
That thou doest unto me ! "

Unto me ! but had the Vision
Come to him in beggar's clothing,
Come a mendicant imploring,
Would he then have knelt adoring,
Or have listened with derision,
And have turned away with loathing ?

Thus his conscience put the question,
Full of troublesome suggestion,
As at length, with hurried pace,
Towards his cell he turned his face,
And beheld the convent bright

With a supernatural light,
Like a luminous cloud expanding
Over floor and wall and ceiling.

But he paused with awe-struck feeling
At the threshold of his door,
For the Vision still was standing
As he left it there before,
When the convent bell appalling,
From its belfry calling, calling,
Summoned him to feed the poor.
Through the long hour intervening
It had waited his return,
And he felt his bosom burn,
Comprehending all the meaning,
When the Blessed Vision said,
" Hadst thou stayed, I must have fled ! "

INTERLUDE

ALL praised the Legend more or less ;
Some liked the moral, some the verse ;
Some thought it better, and some worse
Than other legends of the past ;
Until, with ill-concealed distress
At all their cavilling, at last
The Theologian gravely said :
" The Spanish proverb, then, is right ;
Consult your friends on what you do,
And one will say that it is white,
And others say that it is red."
And " Amen ! " quoth the Spanish Jew.

" Six stories told ! We must have seven,
A cluster like the Pleiades,
And lo ! it happens, as with these,
That one is missing from our heaven.
Where is the Landlord ? Bring him
here ;
Let the Lost Pleiad reappear."

Thus the Sicilian cried, and went
Forthwith to seek his missing star,
But did not find him in the bar,
A place that landlords most frequent,
Nor yet beside the kitchen fire,
Nor up the stairs, nor in the hall ;
It was in vain to ask or call,
There were no tidings of the Squire.

So he came back with downcast head,
Exclaiming : " Well, our bashful host
Hath surely given up the ghost.
Another proverb says the dead

Can tell no tales ; and that is true.
It follows, then, that one of you
Must tell a story in his stead.
You must," he to the Student said,
" Who know so many of the best,
And tell them better than the rest."

Straight, by these flattering words be-
guiled,
The Student, happy as a child
When he is called a little man,
Assumed the double task imposed,
And without more ado unclosed
His smiling lips, and thus began.

THE STUDENT'S SECOND TALE

THE BARON OF ST. CASTINE

BARON CASTINE of St. Castine
Has left his château in the Pyrenees,
And sailed across the western seas.
When he went away from his fair demesne
The birds were building, the woods were
green ;
And now the winds of winter blow
Round the turrets of the old château,
The birds are silent and unseen,
The leaves lie dead in the ravine,
And the Pyrenees are white with snow.

His father, lonely, old, and gray,
Sits by the fireside day by day,
Thinking ever one thought of care ;
Through the southern windows, narrow and
tall,
The sun shines into the ancient hall,
And makes a glory round his hair.
The house-dog, stretched beneath his
chair,
Groans in his sleep, as if in pain,
Then wakes, and yawns, and sleeps again,
So silent is it everywhere, —
So silent you can hear the mouse
Run and rummage along the beams
Behind the wainscot of the wall ;
And the old man rouses from his dreams,
And wanders restless through the house,
As if he heard strange voices call.

His footsteps echo along the floor
Of a distant passage, and pause awhile ;
He is standing by an open door
Looking long, with a sad, sweet smile,

Into the room of his absent son.
There is the bed on which he lay,
There are the pictures bright and gay,
Horses and hounds and sun-lit seas ;
There are his powder-flask and gun,
And his hunting-knives in shape of a fan ;
The chair by the window where he sat,
With the clouded tiger-skin for a mat,
Looking out on the Pyrenees,
Looking out on Mount Marboré
And the Seven Valleys of Lavedan.
Ah me ! he turns away and sighs ;
There is a mist before his eyes.

At night, whatever the weather be,
Wind or rain or starry heaven,
Just as the clock is striking seven,
Those who look from the windows see
The village Curate, with lantern and maid,
Come through the gateway from the park
And   cross   the   courtyard   damp   and
      dark, —
A ring of light in a ring of shade.

And now at the old man's side he stands,
His voice is cheery, his heart expands,
He gossips pleasantly, by the blaze
Of the fire of fagots, about old days,
And Cardinal Mazarin and the Fronde,
And the Cardinal's nieces fair and fond,
And what they did, and what they said,
When they heard his Eminence was dead.

And after a pause the old man says,
His mind still coming back again
To the one sad thought that haunts his
      brain,
" Are there any tidings from over sea ?
Ah, why has that wild boy gone from
      me ? "
And the Curate answers, looking down,
Harmless and docile as a lamb,
" Young blood ! young blood !   It must so
      be ! "
And draws from the pocket of his gown
A handkerchief like an oriflamb,
And wipes his spectacles, and they play
Their little game of lansquenet
In silence for an hour or so,
Till the clock at nine strikes loud and clear
From the village lying asleep below,
And across the courtyard, into the dark
Of the winding pathway in the park,
Curate and lantern disappear,
And darkness reigns in the old château.

The ship has come back from over sea,
She has been signalled from below,
And into the harbor of Bordeaux
She sails with her gallant company.
But among them is nowhere seen
The brave young Baron of St. Castine ;
He hath tarried behind, I ween,
In the beautiful land of Acadie !

And the father paces to and fro
Through the chambers of the old château,
Waiting, waiting to hear the hum
Of wheels on the road that runs below,
Of servants hurrying here and there,
The voice in the courtyard, the step on the
      stair,
Waiting for some one who doth not come !
But letters there are, which the old man
      reads
To the Curate, when he comes at night,
Word by word, as an acolyte
Repeats his prayers and tells his beads ;
Letters full of the rolling sea,
Full of a young man's joy to be
Abroad in the world, alone and free ;
Full of adventures and wonderful scenes
Of hunting the deer through forests vast
In the royal grant of Pierre du Gast ;
Of nights in the tents of the Tarratines ;
Of Madocawando the Indian chief,
And his daughters, glorious as queens,
And beautiful beyond belief ;
And so soft the tones of their native
      tongue,
The words are not spoken, they are sung !

And the Curate listens, and smiling says :
" Ah yes, dear friend ! in our young days
We should have liked to hunt the deer
All day amid those forest scenes,
And to sleep in the tents of the Tarratines ;
But now it is better sitting here
Within four walls, and without the fear
Of losing our hearts to Indian queens ;
For man is fire and woman is tow,
And the Somebody comes and begins to
      blow."
Then a gleam of distrust and vague sur-
      mise
Shines in the father's gentle eyes,
As fire-light on a window-pane
Glimmers and vanishes again ;
But naught he answers ; he only sighs,
And for a moment bows his head ;
Then, as their custom is, they play

Their little game of lansquenet,
And another day is with the dead.

Another day, and many a day
And many a week and month depart,
When a fatal letter wings its way
Across the sea, like a bird of prey,
And strikes and tears the old man's heart.
Lo! the young Baron of St. Castine,
Swift as the wind is, and as wild,
Has married a dusky Tarratine,
Has married Madocawando's child!

The letter drops from the father's hand;
Though the sinews of his heart are wrung,
He utters no cry, he breathes no prayer,
No malediction falls from his tongue;
But his stately figure, erect and grand,
Bends and sinks like a column of sand
In the whirlwind of his great despair.
Dying, yes, dying! His latest breath
Of parley at the door of death
Is a blessing on his wayward son.
Lower and lower on his breast
Sinks his gray head; he is at rest;
No longer he waits for any one.

For many a year the old château
Lies tenantless and desolate;
Rank grasses in the courtyard grow,
About its gables caws the crow;
Only the porter at the gate
Is left to guard it, and to wait
The coming of the rightful heir;
No other life or sound is there;
No more the Curate comes at night,
No more is seen the unsteady light,
Threading the alleys of the park;
The windows of the hall are dark,
The chambers dreary, cold, and bare!

At length, at last, when the winter is past,
And birds are building, and woods are
        green,
With flying skirts is the Curate seen
Speeding along the woodland way,
Humming gayly, "No day is so long
But it comes at last to vesper-song."
He stops at the porter's lodge to say
That at last the Baron of St. Castine
Is coming home with his Indian queen,
Is coming without a week's delay;
And all the house must be swept and clean,
And all things set in good array!
And the solemn porter shakes his head;

And the answer he makes is: "Lackaday!
We will see, as the blind man said!"

Alert since first the day began,
The cock upon the village church
Looks northward from his airy perch,
As if beyond the ken of man
To see the ships come sailing on,
And pass the Isle of Oléron,
And pass the Tower of Cordouan.

In the church below is cold in clay
The heart that would have leaped for joy —
O tender heart of truth and trust! —
To see the coming of that day;
In the church below the lips are dust;
Dust are the hands, and dust the feet
That would have been so swift to meet
The coming of that wayward boy.

At night the front of the old château
Is a blaze of light above and below;
There's a sound of wheels and hoofs in the
        street,
A cracking of whips, and scamper of feet,
Bells are ringing, and horns are blown,
And the Baron hath come again to his own.
The Curate is waiting in the hall,
Most eager and alive of all
To welcome the Baron and Baroness;
But his mind is full of vague distress,
For he hath read in Jesuit books
Of those children of the wilderness,
And now, good, simple man! he looks
To see a painted savage stride
Into the room, with shoulders bare,
And eagle feathers in her hair,
And around her a robe of panther's hide.

Instead, he beholds with secret shame
A form of beauty undefined,
A loveliness without a name,
Not of degree, but more of kind;
Nor bold nor shy, nor short nor tall,
But a new mingling of them all.
Yes, beautiful beyond belief,
Transfigured and transfused, he sees
The lady of the Pyrenees,
The daughter of the Indian chief.
Beneath the shadow of her hair
The gold-bronze color of the skin
Seems lighted by a fire within,
As when a burst of sunlight shines
Beneath a sombre grove of pines, —
A dusky splendor in the air.

The two small hands, that now are pressed
In his, seem made to be caressed,
They lie so warm and soft and still,
Like birds half hidden in a nest,
Trustful, and innocent of ill.
And ah ! he cannot believe his ears
When her melodious voice he hears
Speaking his native Gascon tongue ;
The words she utters seem to be
Part of some poem of Goudouli,
They are not spoken, they are sung !
And the Baron smiles, and says, " You see,
I told you but the simple truth ;
Ah, you may trust the eyes of youth ! "

Down in the village day by day
The people gossip in their way,
And stared to see the Baroness pass
On Sunday morning to early mass ;
And when she kneeleth down to pray,
They wonder, and whisper together, and say
" Surely this is no heathen lass ! "
And in course of time they learn to bless
The Baron and the Baroness.

And in course of time the Curate learns
A secret so dreadful, that by turns
He is ice and fire, he freezes and burns.
The Baron at confession hath said,
That though this woman be his wife,
He hath wed her as the Indians wed,
He hath bought her for a gun and a knife !
And the Curate replies : " O profligate,
O Prodigal Son ! return once more
To the open arms and the open door
Of the Church, or ever it be too late.
Thank God, thy father did not live
To see what he could not forgive ;
On thee, so reckless and perverse,
He left his blessing, not his curse.
But the nearer the dawn the darker the
      night,
And by going wrong all things come right ;
Things have been mended that were worse,
And the worse, the nearer they are to mend.
For the sake of the living and the dead,
Thou shalt be wed as Christians wed,
And all things come to a happy end."

O sun, that followest the night,
In yon blue sky, serene and pure,
And pourest thine impartial light
Alike on mountain and on moor,
Pause for a moment in thy course,
And bless the bridegroom and the bride !

O Gave, that from thy hidden source
In yon mysterious mountain-side
Pursuest thy wandering way alone,
And leaping down its steps of stone,
Along the meadow-lands demure
Stealest away to the Adour,
Pause for a moment in thy course
To bless the bridegroom and the bride !

The choir is singing the matin song,
The doors of the church are opened wide,
The people crowd, and press, and throng
To see the bridegroom and the bride.
They enter and pass along the nave ;
They stand upon the father's grave ;
The bells are ringing soft and slow ;
The living above and the dead below
Give their blessing on one and twain ;
The warm wind blows from the hills of
      Spain,
The birds are building, the leaves are
      green,
And Baron Castine of St. Castine
Hath come at last to his own again.

FINALE

" *Nunc plaudite !* " the Student cried,
When he had finished ; " now applaud,
As Roman actors used to say
At the conclusion of a play ; "
And rose, and spread his hands abroad,
And smiling bowed from side to side,
As one who bears the palm away.

And generous was the applause and loud,
But less for him than for the sun,
That even as the tale was done
Burst from its canopy of cloud,
And lit the landscape with the blaze
Of afternoon on autumn days,
And filled the room with light, and made
The fire of logs a painted shade.

A sudden wind from out the west
Blew all its trumpets loud and shrill ;
The windows rattled with the blast,
The oak-trees shouted as it passed,
And straight, as if by fear possessed,
The cloud encampment on the hill
Broke up, and fluttering flag and tent
Vanished into the firmament,
And down the valley fled amain
The rear of the retreating rain.

Only far up in the blue sky
A mass of clouds, like drifted snow
Suffused with a faint Alpine glow,
Was heaped together, vast and high,
On which a shattered rainbow hung,
Not rising like the ruined arch
Of some aerial aqueduct,
But like a roseate garland plucked
From an Olympian god, and flung
Aside in his triumphal march.

Like prisoners from their dungeon gloom,
Like birds escaping from a snare,
Like school-boys at the hour of play,
All left at once the pent-up room,
And rushed into the open air ;
And no more tales were told that day.

PART THIRD

PRELUDE

THE evening came ; the golden vane
A moment in the sunset glanced,
Then darkened, and then gleamed again,
As from the east the moon advanced
And touched it with a softer light ;
While underneath, with flowing mane,
Upon the sign the Red Horse pranced,
And galloped forth into the night.

But brighter than the afternoon
That followed the dark day of rain,
And brighter than the golden vane
That glistened in the rising moon,
Within, the ruddy fire-light gleamed ;
And every separate window-pane,
Backed by the outer darkness, showed
A mirror, where the flamelets gleamed
And flickered to and fro, and seemed
A bonfire lighted in the road.

Amid the hospitable glow,
Like an old actor on the stage,
With the uncertain voice of age,
The singing chimney chanted low
The homely songs of long ago.

The voice that Ossian heard of yore,
When midnight winds were in his hall ;
A ghostly and appealing call,
A sound of days that are no more !
And dark as Ossian sat the Jew,
And listened to the sound, and knew

The passing of the airy hosts,
The gray and misty cloud of ghosts
In their interminable flight ;
And listening muttered in his beard,
With accent indistinct and weird,
" Who are ye, children of the Night ? "

Beholding his mysterious face,
" Tell me," the gay Sicilian said,
" Why was it that in breaking bread
At supper, you bent down your head
And, musing, paused a little space,
As one who says a silent grace ? "

The Jew replied, with solemn air,
" I said the Manichæan's prayer.
It was his faith, — perhaps is mine, —
That life in all its forms is one,
And that its secret conduits run
Unseen, but in unbroken line,
From the great fountain-head divine
Through man and beast, through grain and
              grass.
Howe'er we struggle, strive, and cry,
From death there can be no escape,
And no escape from life, alas !
Because we cannot die, but pass
From one into another shape :
It is but into life we die.

" Therefore the Manichæan said
This simple prayer on breaking bread,
Lest he with hasty hand or knife
Might wound the incarcerated life,
The soul in things that we call dead :
' I did not reap thee, did not bind thee,
I did not thrash thee, did not grind thee,
Nor did I in the oven bake thee !
It was not I, it was another
Did these things unto thee, O brother ;
I only have thee, hold thee, break thee ! ' "

" That birds have souls I can concede,"
The Poet cried, with glowing cheeks ;
" The flocks that from their beds of reed
Uprising north or southward fly,
And flying write upon the sky
The biforked letter of the Greeks,
As hath been said by Rucellai ;
All birds that sing or chirp or cry,
Even those migratory bands,
The minor poets of the air,
The plover, peep, and sanderling,
That hardly can be said to sing,
But pipe along the barren sands, —

All these have souls akin to ours ;
So hath the lovely race of flowers :
Thus much I grant, but nothing more.
The rusty hinges of a door
Are not alive because they creak ;
This chimney, with its dreary roar,
These rattling windows, do not speak ! "
" To me they speak," the Jew replied ;
" And in the sounds that sink and soar,
I hear the voices of a tide
That breaks upon an unknown shore ! "

Here the Sicilian interfered :
" That was your dream, then, as you dozed
A moment since, with eyes half-closed,
And murmured something in your beard."
The Hebrew smiled, and answered, " Nay ;
Not that, but something very near ;
Like, and yet not the same, may seem
The vision of my waking dream ;
Before it wholly dies away,
Listen to me, and you shall hear."

THE SPANISH JEW'S TALE

AZRAEL

KING SOLOMON, before his palace gate
At evening, on the pavement tessellate
Was walking with a stranger from the
    East,
Arrayed in rich attire as for a feast,
The mighty Runjeet-Sing, a learned man,
And Rajah of the realms of Hindostan.
And as they walked the guest became
    aware
Of a white figure in the twilight air,
Gazing intent, as one who with surprise
His form and features seemed to recog-
    nize ;
And in a whisper to the king he said :
" What is yon shape, that, pallid as the
    dead,
Is watching me, as if he sought to trace
In the dim light the features of my face ? "

The king looked, and replied : " I know
    him well ;
It is the Angel men call Azrael,
'T is the Death Angel ; what hast thou to
    fear ? "
And the guest answered : " Lest he should
    come near,

And speak to me, and take away my
    breath !
Save me from Azrael, save me from
    death !
O king, that hast dominion o'er the wind,
Bid it arise and bear me hence to Ind."

The king gazed upward at the cloudless
    sky,
Whispered a word, and raised his hand on
    high,
And lo ! the signet-ring of chrysoprase
On his uplifted finger seemed to blaze
With hidden fire, and rushing from the
    west
There came a mighty wind, and seized the
    guest
And lifted him from earth, and on they
    passed,
His shining garments streaming in the
    blast,
A silken banner o'er the walls upreared,
A purple cloud, that gleamed and disap-
    peared.
Then said the Angel, smiling : " If this
    man
Be Rajah Runjeet-Sing of Hindostan,
Thou hast done well in listening to his
    prayer ;
I was upon my way to seek him there."

INTERLUDE

" O EDREHI, forbear to-night
Your ghostly legends of affright,
And let the Talmud rest in peace ;
Spare us your dismal tales of death
That almost take away one's breath ;
So doing, may your tribe increase."

Thus the Sicilian said ; then went
And on the spinet's rattling keys
Played Marianina, like a breeze
From Naples and the Southern seas,
That brings us the delicious scent
Of citron and of orange trees,
And memories of soft days of ease
At Capri and Amalfi spent.

" Not so," the eager Poet said ;
" At least, not so before I tell
The story of my Azrael,
An angel mortal as ourselves,
Which in an ancient tome I found

Upon a convent's dusty shelves,
Chained with an iron chain, and bound
In parchment, and with clasps of brass,
Lest from its prison, some dark day,
It might be stolen or steal away,
While the good friars were singing mass.

" It is a tale of Charlemagne,
When like a thunder-cloud, that lowers
And sweeps from mountain-crest to coast,
With lightning flaming through its show-
ers,
He swept across the Lombard plain,
Beleaguering with his warlike train
Pavia, the country's pride and boast,
The City of the Hundred Towers."

Thus heralded the tale began,
And thus in sober measure ran.

THE POET'S TALE

CHARLEMAGNE

OLGER the Dane and Desiderio,
King of the Lombards, on a lofty tower
Stood gazing northward o'er the rolling
plains,
League after league of harvests, to the
foot
Of the snow-crested Alps, and saw ap-
proach
A mighty army, thronging all the roads
That led into the city. And the King
Said unto Olger, who had passed his youth
As hostage at the court of France, and
knew
The Emperor's form and face : " Is Char-
lemagne
Among that host ? " And Olger answered :
" No."

And still the innumerable multitude
Flowed onward and increased, until the
King
Cried in amazement : " Surely Charle-
magne
Is coming in the midst of all these
knights ! "
And Olger answered slowly : " No ; not
yet ;
He will not come so soon." Then much
disturbed
King Desiderio asked : " What shall we do,

If he approach with a still greater army ? "
And Olger answered : " When he shall
appear,
You will behold what manner of man he is ;
But what will then befall us I know not."

Then came the guard that never knew
repose,
The Paladins of France ; and at the sight
The Lombard King o'ercome with terror
cried :
" This must be Charlemagne ! " and as
before
Did Olger answer : " No ; not yet, not
yet."

And then appeared in panoply complete
The Bishops and the Abbots and the
Priests
Of the imperial chapel, and the Counts ;
And Desiderio could no more endure
The light of day, nor yet encounter death,
But sobbed aloud and said : " Let us go
down
And hide us in the bosom of the earth,
Far from the sight and anger of a foe
So terrible as this ! " And Olger said :
" When you behold the harvests in the
fields
Shaking with fear, the Po and the Ticino
Lashing the city walls with iron waves,
Then may you know that Charlemagne is
come."
And even as he spake, in the northwest,
Lo ! there uprose a black and threatening
cloud,
Out of whose bosom flashed the light of
arms
Upon the people pent up in the city ;
A light more terrible than any darkness,
And Charlemagne appeared ; — a Man of
Iron !

His helmet was of iron, and his gloves
Of iron, and his breastplate and his greaves
And tassets were of iron, and his shield.
In his left hand he held an iron spear,
In his right hand his sword invincible.
The horse he rode on had the strength of
iron,
And color of iron. All who went before
him,
Beside him and behind him, his whole host,
Were armed with iron, and their hearts
within them

Were stronger than the armor that they
   wore.
The fields and all the roads were filled
   with iron,
And points of iron glistened in the sun
And shed a terror through the city streets.

This at a single glance Olger the Dane
Saw from the tower, and turning to the
   King
Exclaimed in haste : "Behold ! this is the
   man
You looked for with such eagerness !" and
   then
Fell as one dead at Desiderio's feet.

INTERLUDE

WELL pleased all listened to the tale,
That drew, the Student said, its pith
And marrow from the ancient myth
Of some one with an iron flail ;
Or that portentous Man of Brass
Hephæstus made in days of yore,
Who stalked about the Cretan shore,
And saw the ships appear and pass,
And threw stones at the Argonauts,
Being filled with indiscriminate ire
That tangled and perplexed his thoughts ;
But, like a hospitable host,
When strangers landed on the coast,
Heated himself red-hot with fire,
And hugged them in his arms, and pressed
Their bodies to his burning breast.

The Poet answered : "No, not thus
The legend rose ; it sprang at first
Out of the hunger and the thirst
In all men for the marvellous.
And thus it filled and satisfied
The imagination of mankind,
And this ideal to the mind
Was truer than historic fact.
Fancy enlarged and multiplied
The terrors of the awful name
Of Charlemagne, till he became
Armipotent in every act,
And, clothed in mystery, appeared
Not what men saw, but what they feared.

"Besides, unless my memory fail,
Your some one with an iron flail
Is not an ancient myth at all,
But comes much later on the scene

As Talus in the Faërie Queene,
The iron groom of Artegall,
Who threshed out falsehood and deceit,
And truth upheld, and righted wrong,
And was, as is the swallow, fleet,
And as the lion is, was strong."

The Theologian said : "Perchance
Your chronicler in writing this
Had in his mind the Anabasis,
Where Xenophon describes the advance
Of Artaxerxes to the fight ;
At first the low gray cloud of dust,
And then a blackness o'er the fields
As of a passing thunder-gust,
Then flash of brazen armor bright,
And ranks of men, and spears up-thrust,
Bowmen and troops with wicker shields,
And cavalry equipped in white,
And chariots ranged in front of these
With scythes upon their axle-trees."

To this the Student answered : "Well,
I also have a tale to tell
Of Charlemagne ; a tale that throws
A softer light, more tinged with rose,
Than your grim apparition cast
Upon the darkness of the past.
Listen, and hear in English rhyme
What the good Monk of Lauresheim
Gives as the gossip of his time,
In mediæval Latin prose."

THE STUDENT'S TALE

EMMA AND EGINHARD

WHEN Alcuin taught the sons of Charle-
   magne,
In the free schools of Aix, how kings should
   reign,
And with them taught the children of the
   poor
How subjects should be patient and endure,
He touched the lips of some, as best befit,
With honey from the hives of Holy Writ ;
Others intoxicated with the wine
Of ancient history, sweet but less divine ;
Some with the wholesome fruits of grammar
   fed ;
Others with mysteries of the stars o'erhead,
That hang suspended in the vaulted sky
Like lamps in some fair palace vast and
   high.

In sooth, it was a pleasant sight to see
That Saxon monk, with hood and rosary,
With inkhorn at his belt, and pen and book,
And mingled love and reverence in his look,
Or hear the cloister and the court repeat
The measured footfalls of his sandaled feet,
Or watch him with the pupils of his school,
Gentle of speech, but absolute of rule.

Among them, always earliest in his place,
Was Eginhard, a youth of Frankish race,
Whose face was bright with flashes that
    forerun
The splendors of a yet unrisen sun.
To him all things were possible, and seemed
Not what he had accomplished, but had
    dreamed,
And what were tasks to others were his
    play,
The pastime of an idle holiday.

Smaragdo, Abbot of St. Michael's, said,
With many a shrug and shaking of the
    head,
Surely some demon must possess the lad,
Who showed more wit than ever school-boy
    had,
And learned his Trivium thus without the
    rod ;
But Alcuin said it was the grace of God.

Thus he grew up, in Logic point-device,
Perfect in Grammar, and in Rhetoric nice ;
Science of Numbers, Geometric art,
And lore of Stars, and Music knew by
    heart ;
A Minnesinger, long before the times
Of those who sang their love in Suabian
    rhymes.

The Emperor, when he heard this good
    report
Of Eginhard much buzzed about the court,
Said to himself, " This stripling seems to be
Purposely sent into the world for me ;
He shall become my scribe, and shall be
    schooled
In all the arts whereby the world is ruled."
Thus did the gentle Eginhard attain
To honor in the court of Charlemagne ;
Became the sovereign's favorite, his right
    hand,
So that his fame was great in all the land,
And all men loved him for his modest grace
And comeliness of figure and of face.

An inmate of the palace, yet recluse,
A man of books, yet sacred from abuse
Among the armèd knights with spur on
    heel,
The tramp of horses and the clang of steel ;
And as the Emperor promised he was
    schooled
In all the arts by which the world is ruled.
But the one art supreme, whose law is fate,
The Emperor never dreamed of till too
    late.

Home from her convent to the palace came
The lovely Princess Emma, whose sweet
    name,
Whispered by seneschal or sung by bard,
Had often touched the soul of Eginhard.
He saw her from his window, as in state
She came, by knights attended through the
    gate ;
He saw her at the banquet of that day,
Fresh as the morn, and beautiful as May ;
He saw her in the garden, as she strayed
Among the flowers of summer with her
    maid,
And said to him, " O Eginhard, disclose
The meaning and the mystery of the rose ; "
And trembling he made answer : " In good
    sooth,
Its mystery is love, its meaning youth ! "

How can I tell the signals and the signs
By which one heart another heart divines ?
How can I tell the many thousand ways
By which it keeps the secret it betrays ?

O mystery of love !   O strange romance !
Among the Peers and Paladins of France,
Shining in steel, and prancing on gay steeds,
Noble by birth, yet nobler by great deeds,
The Princess Emma had no words nor looks
But for this clerk, this man of thought and
    books.

The summer passed, the autumn came ; the
    stalks
Of lilies blackened in the garden walks ;
The leaves fell, russet-golden and blood-red,
Love-letters thought the poet fancy-led,
Or Jove descending in a shower of gold
Into the lap of Danaë of old ;
For poets cherish many a strange conceit,
And love transmutes all nature by its heat.
No more the garden lessons, nor the dark
And hurried meetings in the twilight park ;

But now the studious lamp, and the de-
lights
Of firesides in the silent winter nights,
And watching from his window hour by
hour
The light that burned in Princess Emma's
tower.

At length one night, while musing by the
fire,
O'ercome at last by his insane desire, —
For what will reckless love not do and
dare ?
He crossed the court, and climbed the wind-
ing stair,
With some feigned message in the Em-
peror's name ;
But when he to the lady's presence came
He knelt down at her feet, until she laid
Her hand upon him, like a naked blade,
And whispered in his ear : " Arise, Sir
Knight,
To my heart's level, O my heart's delight."

And there he lingered till the crowing
cock,
The Alectryon of the farmyard and the
flock,
Sang his aubade with lusty voice and clear,
To tell the sleeping world that dawn was
near.
And then they parted ; but at parting, lo !
They saw the palace courtyard white with
snow,
And, placid as a nun, the moon on high
Gazing from cloudy cloisters of the sky.
" Alas ! " he said, " how hide the fatal line
Of footprints leading from thy door to
mine,
And none returning ! " Ah, he little knew
What woman's wit, when put to proof, can
do !

That night the Emperor, sleepless with the
cares
And troubles that attend on state affairs,
Had risen before the dawn, and musing
gazed
Into the silent night, as one amazed
To see the calm that reigned o'er all
supreme,
When his own reign was but a troubled
dream.
The moon lit up the gables capped with
snow,

And the white roofs, and half the court
below,
And he beheld a form, that seemed to
cower
Beneath a burden, come from Emma's
tower, —
A woman, who upon her shoulders bore
Clerk Eginhard to his own private door,
And then returned in haste, but still
essayed
To tread the footprints she herself had
made ;
And as she passed across the lighted space,
The Emperor saw his daughter Emma's
face !

He started not ; he did not speak or moan,
But seemed as one who hath been turned to
stone ;
And stood there like a statue, nor awoke
Out of his trance of pain, till morning
broke,
Till the stars faded, and the moon went
down,
And o'er the towers and steeples of the
town
Came the gray daylight ; then the sun, who
took
The empire of the world with sovereign
look,
Suffusing with a soft and golden glow
All the dead landscape in its shroud of
snow,
Touching with flame the tapering chapel
spires,
Windows and roofs, and smoke of house-
hold fires,
And kindling park and palace as he came ;
The stork's nest on the chimney seemed in
flame.
And thus he stood till Eginhard appeared,
Demure and modest with his comely beard
And flowing flaxen tresses, come to ask,
As was his wont, the day's appointed task.
The Emperor looked upon him with a
smile,
And gently said : "My son, wait yet
awhile ;
This hour my council meets upon some
great
And very urgent business of the state.
Come back within the hour. On thy re-
turn
The work appointed for thee shalt thou
learn."

Having dismissed this gallant Troubadour,
He summoned straight his council, and secure
And steadfast in his purpose, from the throne
All the adventure of the night made known ;
Then asked for sentence ; and with eager breath
Some answered banishment, and others death.

Then spake the king : " Your sentence is not mine ;
Life is the gift of God, and is divine ;
Nor from these palace walls shall one depart
Who carries such a secret in his heart ;
My better judgment points another way.
Good Alcuin, I remember how one day
When my Pepino asked you, ' What are men ? '
You wrote upon his tablets with your pen,
' Guests of the grave and travellers that pass ! '
This being true of all men, we, alas !
Being all fashioned of the selfsame dust,
Let us be merciful as well as just ;
This passing traveller who hath stolen away
The brightest jewel of my crown to-day,
Shall of himself the precious gem restore ;
By giving it, I make it mine once more.
Over those fatal footprints I will throw
My ermine mantle like another snow."

Then Eginhard was summoned to the hall,
And entered, and in presence of them all,
The Emperor said : " My son, for thou to me
Hast been a son, and evermore shalt be,
Long hast thou served thy sovereign, and thy zeal
Pleads to me with importunate appeal,
While I have been forgetful to requite
Thy service and affection as was right.
But now the hour is come, when I, thy Lord,
Will crown thy love with such supreme reward,
A gift so precious kings have striven in vain
To win it from the hands of Charlemagne."

Then sprang the portals of the chamber wide,
And Princess Emma entered, in the pride
Of birth and beauty, that in part o'ercame
The conscious terror and the blush of shame.
And the good Emperor rose up from his throne,
And taking her white hand within his own
Placed it in Eginhard's, and said : " My son,
This is the gift thy constant zeal hath won ;
Thus I repay the royal debt I owe,
And cover up the footprints in the snow."

INTERLUDE

THUS ran the Student's pleasant rhyme
Of Eginhard and love and youth ;
Some doubted its historic truth,
But while they doubted, ne'ertheless
Saw in it gleams of truthfulness,
And thanked the Monk of Lauresheim.

This they discussed in various mood ;
Then in the silence that ensued
Was heard a sharp and sudden sound
As of a bowstring snapped in air ;
And the Musician with a bound
Sprang up in terror from his chair,
And for a moment listening stood,
Then strode across the room, and found
His dear, his darling violin
Still lying safe asleep within
Its little cradle, like a child
That gives a sudden cry of pain,
And wakes to fall asleep again ;
And as he looked at it and smiled,
By the uncertain light beguiled,
Despair ! two strings were broken in twain.

While all lamented and made moan,
With many a sympathetic word
As if the loss had been their own,
Deeming the tones they might have heard
Sweeter than they had heard before,
They saw the Landlord at the door,
The missing man, the portly Squire !
He had not entered, but he stood
With both arms full of seasoned wood,
To feed the much-devouring fire,
That like a lion in a cage
Lashed its long tail and roared with rage.

The missing man ! Ah, yes, they said,
Missing, but whither had he fled ?
Where had he hidden himself away ?
No farther than the barn or shed ;
He had not hidden himself, nor fled ;
How should he pass the rainy day
But in his barn with hens and hay,
Or mending harness, cart, or sled ?
Now, having come, he needs must stay
And tell his tale as well as they.

The Landlord answered only : " These
Are logs from the dead apple-trees
Of the old orchard planted here
By the first Howe of Sudbury.
Nor oak nor maple has so clear
A flame, or burns so quietly,
Or leaves an ash so clean and white ; "
Thinking by this to put aside
The impending tale that terrified ;
When suddenly, to his delight,
The Theologian interposed,
Saying that when the door was closed,
And they had stopped that draft of cold,
Unpleasant night air, he proposed
To tell a tale world-wide apart
From that the Student had just told ;
World-wide apart, and yet akin,
As showing that the human heart
Beats on forever as of old,
As well beneath the snow-white fold
Of Quaker kerchief, as within
Sendal or silk or cloth of gold,
And without preface would begin.

And then the clamorous clock struck eight,
Deliberate, with sonorous chime
Slow measuring out the march of time,
Like some grave Consul of Old Rome
In Jupiter's temple driving home
The nails that marked the year and
    date.
Thus interrupted in his rhyme,
The Theologian needs must wait ;
But quoted Horace, where he sings
The dire Necessity of things,
That drives into the roofs sublime
Of new-built houses of the great
The adamantine nails of Fate.

When ceased the little carillon
To herald from its wooden tower
The important transit of the hour,
The Theologian hastened on,
Content to be allowed at last
To sing his Idyl of the Past.

THE THEOLOGIAN'S TALE

ELIZABETH

I

" Ah, how short are the days ! How soon
    the night overtakes us !
In the old country the twilight is longer ;
    but here in the forest
Suddenly comes the dark, with hardly a
    pause in its coming,
Hardly a moment between the two lights,
    the day and the lamplight ;
Yet how grand is the winter ! How spot-
    less the snow is, and perfect ! "

Thus spake Elizabeth Haddon at night-
    fall to Hannah the housemaid,
As in the farm-house kitchen, that served
    for kitchen and parlor,
By the window she sat with her work, and
    looked on the landscape
White as the great white sheet that Peter
    saw in his vision,
By the four corners let down and descend-
    ing out of the heavens.
Covered with snow were the forests of pine,
    and the fields and the meadows.
Nothing was dark but the sky, and the dis-
    tant Delaware flowing
Down from its native hills, a peaceful and
    bountiful river.

Then with a smile on her lips made an-
    swer Hannah the housemaid :
" Beautiful winter ! yea, the winter is beau-
    tiful, surely,
If one could only walk like a fly with one's
    feet on the ceiling.
But the great Delaware River is not like
    the Thames, as we saw it
Out of our upper windows in Rotherhithe
    Street in the Borough,
Crowded with masts and sails of vessels
    coming and going ;
Here there is nothing but pines, with
    patches of snow on their branches.
There is snow in the air, and see ! it is fall-
    ing already ;
All the roads will be blocked, and I pity
    Joseph to-morrow,
Breaking his way through the drifts, with
    his sled and oxen ; and then, too,
How in all the world shall we get to Meet-
    ing on First-Day ? "

But Elizabeth checked her, and answered,
    mildly reproving :
" Surely the Lord will provide ; for unto
    the snow He sayeth,
Be thou on the earth, the good Lord sayeth ;
    He is it
Giveth snow like wool, like ashes scatters
    the hoar-frost."
So she folded her work and laid it away in
    her basket.

Meanwhile Hannah the housemaid had
    closed and fastened the shutters,
Spread the cloth, and lighted the lamp on
    the table, and placed there
Plates and cups from the dresser, the brown
    rye loaf, and the butter
Fresh from the dairy, and then, protecting
    her hand with a holder,
Took from the crane in the chimney the
    steaming and simmering kettle,
Poised it aloft in the air, and filled up the
    earthen teapot,
Made in Delft, and adorned with quaint
    and wonderful figures.

Then Elizabeth said, " Lo ! Joseph is
    long on his errand.
I have sent him away with a hamper of food
    and of clothing
For the poor in the village. A good lad
    and cheerful is Joseph ;
In the right place is his heart, and his hand
    is ready and willing."

Thus in praise of her servant she spake,
    and Hannah the housemaid
Laughed with her eyes, as she listened, but
    governed her tongue and was silent,
While her mistress went on : " The house
    is far from the village ;
We should be lonely here, were it not for
    Friends that in passing
Sometimes tarry o'ernight, and make us
    glad by their coming."

Thereupon answered Hannah the house-
    maid, the thrifty, the frugal :
" Yea, they come and they tarry, as if thy
    house were a tavern ;
Open to all are its doors, and they come
    and go like the pigeons
In and out of the holes of the pigeon-house
    over the hayloft,
Cooing and smoothing their feathers and
    basking themselves in the sunshine."

But in meekness of spirit, and calmly,
    Elizabeth answered :
" All I have is the Lord's, not mine to give
    or withhold it ;
I but distribute his gifts to the poor, and to
    those of his people
Who in journeyings often surrender their
    lives to his service.
His, not mine, are the gifts, and only so far
    can I make them
Mine, as in giving I add my heart to what-
    ever is given.
Therefore my excellent father first built
    this house in the clearing ;
Though he came not himself, I came ; for
    the Lord was my guidance,
Leading me here for this service. We
    must not grudge, then, to others
Ever the cup of cold water, or crumbs that
    fall from our table."

Thus rebuked, for a season was silent the
    penitent housemaid ;
And Elizabeth said in tones even sweeter
    and softer :
" Dost thou remember, Hannah, the great
    May-Meeting in London,
When I was still a child, how we sat in the
    silent assembly,
Waiting upon the Lord in patient and pas-
    sive submission ?
No one spake, till at length a young man,
    a stranger, John Estaugh,
Moved by the Spirit, rose, as if he were
    John the Apostle,
Speaking such words of power that they
    bowed our hearts, as a strong
    wind
Bends the grass of the fields, or grain that
    is ripe for the sickle.
Thoughts of him to-day have been oft borne
    inward upon me,
Wherefore I do not know ; but strong is
    the feeling within me
That once more I shall see a face I have
    never forgotten."

II

E'en as she spake they heard the musical
    jangle of sleigh-bells,
First far off, with a dreamy sound and faint
    in the distance,
Then growing nearer and louder. and turn-
    ing into the farmyard,

Till it stopped at the door, with sudden
creaking of runners.
Then there were voices heard as of two
men talking together,
And to herself, as she listened, upbraiding
said Hannah the housemaid,
"It is Joseph come back, and I wonder
what stranger is with him."

Down from its nail she took and lighted
the great tin lantern
Pierced with holes, and round, and roofed
like the top of a lighthouse,
And went forth to receive the coming guest
at the doorway,
Casting into the dark a network of glimmer
and shadow
Over the falling snow, the yellow sleigh,
and the horses,
And the forms of men, snow-covered, loom-
ing gigantic.
Then giving Joseph the lantern, she en-
tered the house with the stranger.
Youthful he was and tall, and his cheeks
aglow with the night air ;
And as he entered, Elizabeth rose, and, going
to meet him,
As if an unseen power had announced and
preceded his presence,
And he had come as one whose coming had
long been expected,
Quietly gave him her hand, and said,
"Thou art welcome, John Estaugh."
And the stranger replied, with staid and
quiet behavior,
"Dost thou remember me still, Elizabeth?
After so many
Years have passed, it seemeth a wonderful
thing that I find thee.
Surely the hand of the Lord conducted me
here to thy threshold.
For as I journeyed along, and pondered
alone and in silence
On his ways, that are past finding out, I
saw in the snow-mist,
Seemingly weary with travel, a wayfarer,
who by the wayside
Paused and waited. Forthwith I remem-
bered Queen Candace's eunuch,
How on the way that goes down from
Jerusalem unto Gaza,
Reading Esaias the Prophet, he journeyed,
and spake unto Philip,
Praying him to come up and sit in his
chariot with him.

So I greeted the man, and he mounted the
sledge beside me,
And as we talked on the way he told me of
thee and thy homestead,
How, being led by the light of the Spirit,
that never deceiveth,
Full of zeal for the work of the Lord, thou
hadst come to this country.
And I remembered thy name, and thy
father and mother in England,
And on my journey have stopped to see
thee, Elizabeth Haddon,
Wishing to strengthen thy hand in the
labors of love thou art doing."

And Elizabeth answered with confident
voice, and serenely
Looking into his face with her innocent
eyes as she answered,
"Surely the hand of the Lord is in it ; his
Spirit hath led thee
Out of the darkness and storm to the light
and peace of my fireside."

Then, with stamping of feet the door
was opened, and Joseph
Entered, bearing the lantern, and, care-
fully blowing the light out,
Hung it up on its nail, and all sat down to
their supper ;
For underneath that roof was no distinction
of persons,
But one family only, one heart, one hearth,
and one household.

When the supper was ended they drew
their chairs to the fireplace,
Spacious, open-hearted, profuse of flame
and of firewood,
Lord of forests unfelled, and not a gleaner
of fagots,
Spreading its arms to embrace with inex-
haustible bounty
All who fled from the cold, exultant, laugh-
ing at winter !
Only Hannah the housemaid was busy in
clearing the table,
Coming and going, and bustling about in
closet and chamber.

Then Elizabeth told her story again to
John Estaugh,
Going far back to the past, to the early
days of her childhood ;

How she had waited and watched, in all
    her doubts and besetments,
Comforted with the extendings and holy,
    sweet inflowings
Of the spirit of love, till the voice impera-
    tive sounded,
And she obeyed the voice, and cast in her
    lot with her people
Here in the desert land, and God would
    provide for the issue.

Meanwhile Joseph sat with folded hands,
    and demurely
Listened, or seemed to listen, and in the
    silence that followed
Nothing was heard for a while but the step
    of Hannah the housemaid
Walking the floor overhead, and setting the
    chambers in order.
And Elizabeth said, with a smile of com-
    passion, " The maiden
Hath a light heart in her breast, but her
    feet are heavy and awkward."
Inwardly Joseph laughed, but governed his
    tongue, and was silent.

Then came the hour of sleep, death's
    counterfeit, nightly rehearsal
Of the great Silent Assembly, the Meeting
    of shadows, where no man
Speaketh, but all are still, and the peace
    and rest are unbroken !
Silently over that house the blessing of
    slumber descended.
But when the morning dawned, and the sun
    uprose in his splendor,
Breaking his way through clouds that
    encumbered his path in the hea-
    vens,
Joseph was seen with his sled and oxen
    breaking a pathway
Through the drifts of snow ; the horses
    already were harnessed,
And John Estaugh was standing and taking
    leave at the threshold,
Saying that he should return at the Meet-
    ing in May ; while above them
Hannah the housemaid, the homely, was
    looking out of the attic,
Laughing aloud at Joseph, then suddenly
    closing the casement,
As the bird in a cuckoo-clock peeps out of
    its window,
Then disappears again, and closes   the
    shutter behind it.

III

Now was the winter gone, and the snow ;
    and Robin the Redbreast
Boasted on bush and tree it was he, it was
    he and no other
That had covered with leaves the Babes in
    the Wood, and blithely
All the birds sang with him, and little cared
    for his boasting,
Or for his Babes in the Wood, or the Cruel
    Uncle, and only
Sang for the mates they had chosen, and
    cared for the nests they were build-
    ing.
With them, but more sedately and meekly,
    Elizabeth Haddon
Sang in her inmost heart, but her lips were
    silent and songless.
Thus came the lovely spring with a rush of
    blossoms and music,
Flooding the earth with flowers, and the
    air with melodies vernal.

Then it came to pass, one pleasant morn-
    ing, that slowly
Up the road there came a cavalcade, as of
    pilgrims,
Men and women, wending their way to the
    Quarterly Meeting
In the neighboring town ; and with them
    came riding John Estaugh.
At Elizabeth's door they stopped to rest,
    and alighting
Tasted the currant wine, and the bread of
    rye, and the honey
Brought from the hives, that stood by the
    sunny wall of the garden ;
Then remounted their horses, refreshed,
    and continued their journey,
And Elizabeth with them, and Joseph, and
    Hannah the housemaid.
But, as they started, Elizabeth lingered a
    little, and leaning
Over her horse's neck, in a whisper said to
    John Estaugh :
" Tarry awhile behind, for I have some-
    thing to tell thee,
Not to be spoken lightly, nor in the pres-
    ence of others ;
Them it concerneth not, only thee and me
    it concerneth."
And they rode slowly along through the
    woods, conversing together.

It was a pleasure to breathe the fragrant
 air of the forest ;
It was a pleasure to live on that bright
 and happy May morning !

Then Elizabeth said, though still with a
 certain reluctance,
As if impelled to reveal a secret she fain
 would have guarded :
" I will no longer conceal what is laid upon
 me to tell thee ;
I have received from the Lord a charge to
 love thee, John Estaugh."

And John Estaugh made answer, sur-
 prised at the words she had spo-
 ken,
" Pleasant to me are thy converse, thy
 ways, thy meekness of spirit ;
Pleasant thy frankness of speech, and thy
 soul's immaculate whiteness,
Love without dissimulation, a holy and in-
 ward adorning.
But I have yet no light to lead me, no voice
 to direct me.
When the Lord's work is done, and the
 toil and the labor completed
He hath appointed to me, I will gather
 into the stillness
Of my own heart awhile, and listen and
 wait for his guidance."

Then Elizabeth said, not troubled nor
 wounded in spirit,
" So is it best, John Estaugh. We will not
 speak of it further.
It hath been laid upon me to tell thee this,
 for to-morrow
Thou art going away, across the sea, and
 I know not
When I shall see thee more ; but if the
 Lord hath decreed it,
Thou wilt return again to seek me here and
 to find me."
And they rode onward in silence, and en-
 tered the town with the others.

IV

Ships that pass in the night, and speak each
 other in passing,
Only a signal shown and a distant voice in
 the darkness ;

So on the ocean of life, we pass and speak
 one another,
Only a look and a voice, then darkness
 again and a silence.

Now went on as of old the quiet life of
 the homestead.
Patient and unrepining Elizabeth labored,
 in all things
Mindful not of herself, but bearing the bur-
 dens of others,
Always thoughtful and kind and untrou-
 bled ; and Hannah the housemaid
Diligent early and late, and rosy with
 washing and scouring,
Still as of old disparaged the eminent mer-
 its of Joseph,
And was at times reproved for her light
 and frothy behavior,
For her shy looks, and her careless words,
 and her evil surmisings,
Being pressed down somewhat, like a cart
 with sheaves overladen,
As she would sometimes say to Joseph,
 quoting the Scriptures.

Meanwhile John Estaugh departed across
 the sea, and departing
Carried hid in his heart a secret sacred and
 precious,
Filling its chambers with fragrance, and
 seeming to him in its sweetness
Mary's ointment of spikenard, that filled
 all the house with its odor.
O lost days of delight, that are wasted in
 doubting and waiting !
O lost hours and days in which we might
 have been happy !
But the light shone at last, and guided his
 wavering footsteps,
And at last came the voice, imperative,
 questionless, certain.

Then John Estaugh came back o'er the
 sea for the gift that was offered,
Better than houses and lands, the gift of a
 woman's affection.
And on the First-Day that followed, he rose
 in the Silent Assembly,
Holding in his strong hand a hand that
 trembled a little,
Promising to be kind and true and faithful
 in all things.
Such were the marriage rites of John and
 Elizabeth Estaugh.

And not otherwise Joseph, the honest,
   the diligent servant,
Sped in his bashful wooing with homely
   Hannah the housemaid ;
For when he asked her the question, she
   answered, " Nay ; " and then added :
" But thee may make believe, and see what
   will come of it, Joseph."

INTERLUDE

" A PLEASANT and a winsome tale,"
The Student said, " though somewhat pale
And quiet in its coloring,
As if it caught its tone and air
From the gray suits that Quakers wear ;
Yet worthy of some German bard,
Hebel, or Voss, or Eberhard,
Who love of humble themes to sing,
In humble verse ; but no more true
Than was the tale I told to you."

The Theologian made reply,
And with some warmth, " That I deny ;
'T is no invention of my own,
But something well and widely known
To readers of a riper age,
Writ by the skilful hand that wrote
The Indian tale of Hobomok,
And Philothea's classic page.
I found it like a waif afloat,
Or dulse uprooted from its rock,
On the swift tides that ebb and flow
In daily papers, and at flood
Bear freighted vessels to and fro,
But later, when the ebb is low,
Leave a long waste of sand and mud."

" It matters little," quoth the Jew ;
" The cloak of truth is lined with lies,
Sayeth some proverb old and wise ;
And Love is master of all arts,
And puts it into human hearts
The strangest things to say and do."

And here the controversy closed
Abruptly, ere 't was well begun ;
For the Sicilian interposed
With, " Lordlings, listen, every one
That listen may, unto a tale
That 's merrier than the nightingale ;
A tale that cannot boast, forsooth,
A single rag or shred of truth ;
That does not leave the mind in doubt

As to the with it or without ;
A naked falsehood and absurd
As mortal ever told or heard.
Therefore I tell it ; or, maybe,
Simply because it pleases me."

THE SICILIAN'S TALE

THE MONK OF CASAL—MAGGIORE

ONCE on a time, some centuries ago,
   In the hot sunshine two Franciscan friars
Wended their weary way, with footsteps
   slow,
   Back to their convent, whose white walls
     and spires
Gleamed on the hillside like a patch of
   snow ;
   Covered with dust they were, and torn
     by briers,
And bore like sumpter-mules upon their
   backs
The badge of poverty, their beggar's sacks.

The first was Brother Anthony, a spare
   And silent man, with pallid cheeks and
     thin,
Much given to vigils, penance, fasting,
   prayer,
   Solemn and gray, and worn with disci-
     pline,
As if his body but white ashes were,
   Heaped on the living coals that glowed
     within ;
A simple monk, like many of his day,
Whose instinct was to listen and obey.

A different man was Brother Timothy,
   Of larger mould and of a coarser paste ;
A rubicund and stalwart monk was he,
   Broad in the shoulders, broader in the
     waist,
Who often filled the dull refectory
   With noise by which the convent was dis-
     graced,
But to the mass-book gave but little heed,
By reason he had never learned to read.

Now, as they passed the outskirts of a
   wood,
   They saw, with mingled pleasure and
     surprise,
Fast tethered to a tree an ass, that stood
   Lazily winking his large, limpid eyes.

The farmer Gilbert, of that neighborhood,
  His owner was, who, looking for sup-
    plies
Of fagots, deeper in the wood had strayed,
Leaving his beast to ponder in the shade.

As soon as Brother Timothy espied
  The patient animal, he said : " Good-
    lack !
Thus for our needs doth Providence pro-
    vide ;
  We 'll lay our wallets on the creature's
    back."
This being done, he leisurely untied
  From head and neck the halter of the
    jack,
And put it round his own, and to the tree
Stood tethered fast as if the ass were he.

And, bursting forth into a merry laugh,
  He cried to Brother Anthony : " Away !
And drive the ass before you with your
    staff ;
  And when you reach the convent you
    may say
You left me at a farm, half tired and half
Ill with a fever, for a night and day,
And that the farmer lent this ass to bear
Our wallets, that are heavy with good fare."

Now Brother Anthony, who knew the
    pranks
  Of Brother Timothy, would not persuade
Or reason with him on his quirks and
    cranks,
  But, being obedient, silently obeyed ;
And, smiting with his staff the ass's flanks,
  Drove him before him over hill and
    glade,
Safe with his provend to the convent gate,
Leaving poor Brother Timothy to his fate.

Then Gilbert, laden with fagots for his fire,
  Forth issued from the wood, and stood
    aghast
To see the ponderous body of the friar
  Standing where he had left his donkey
    last.
Trembling he stood, and dared not venture
    nigher,
  But stared, and gaped, and crossed him-
    self full fast ;
For, being credulous and of little wit,
He thought it was some demon from the
    pit.

While speechless and bewildered thus he
    gazed,
  And dropped his load of fagots on the
    ground,
Quoth Brother Timothy : " Be not amazed
  That where you left a donkey should be
    found
A poor Franciscan friar, half-starved and
    crazed,
  Standing demure and with a halter
    bound ;
But set me free, and hear the piteous story
Of Brother Timothy of Casal-Maggiore.

" I am a sinful man, although you see
  I wear the consecrated cowl and cape ;
You never owned an ass, but you owned
    me,
  Changed and transformed from my own
    natural shape
All for the deadly sin of gluttony,
  From which I could not otherwise es-
    cape,
Than by this penance, dieting on grass,
And being worked and beaten as an ass.

" Think of the ignominy I endured ;
  Think of the miserable life I led,
The toil and blows to which I was inured,
  My wretched lodging in a windy shed,
My scanty fare so grudgingly procured,
  The damp and musty straw that formed
    my bed !
But, having done this penance for my sins,
My life as man and monk again begins."

The simple Gilbert, hearing words like
    these,
  Was conscience-stricken, and fell down
    apace
Before the friar upon his bended knees,
  And with a suppliant voice implored his
    grace ;
And the good monk, now very much at
    ease,
  Granted him pardon with a smiling face,
Nor could refuse to be that night his guest,
It being late, and he in need of rest.

Upon a hillside, where the olive thrives,
  With figures painted on its whitewashed
    walls,
The cottage stood ; and near the humming
    hives
  Made murmurs as of far-off waterfalls ;

A place where those who love secluded
    lives
Might live content, and, free from noise
    and brawls,
Like Claudian's Old Man of Verona here
Measure by fruits the slow-revolving year.

And, coming to this cottage of content,
    They found his children, and the buxom
    wench
His wife, Dame Cicely, and his father, bent
    With years and labor, seated on a bench,
Repeating over some obscure event
In the old wars of Milanese and French ;
All welcomed the Franciscan, with a sense
Of sacred awe and humble reverence.

When Gilbert told them what had come to
    pass,
    How beyond question, cavil, or surmise,
Good Brother Timothy had been their ass,
    You should have seen the wonder in
    their eyes ;
You should have heard them cry " Alas !
    alas ! "
    Have heard their lamentations and their
    sighs !
For all believed the story, and began
To see a saint in this afflicted man.

Forthwith there was prepared a grand
    repast,
    To satisfy the craving of the friar
After so rigid and prolonged a fast ;
    The bustling housewife stirred the kitch-
    en fire ;
Then her two barn-yard fowls, her best and
    last,
Were put to death, at her express desire,
And served up with a salad in a bowl,
And flasks of country wine to crown the
    whole.

It would not be believed should I repeat
    How hungry Brother Timothy appeared ;
It was a pleasure but to see him eat,
    His white teeth flashing through his
    russet beard,
His face aglow and flushed with wine and
    meat,
    His roguish eyes that rolled and laughed
    and leered !
Lord ! how he drank the blood-red country
    wine
As if the village vintage were divine !

And all the while he talked without sur-
    cease,
    And told his merry tales with jovial glee
That never flagged, but rather did in-
    crease,
    And laughed aloud as if insane were he,
And wagged his red beard, matted like a
    fleece,
    And cast such glances at Dame Cicely
That Gilbert now grew angry with his guest,
And thus in words his rising wrath ex-
    pressed.

" Good father," said he, " easily we see
    How needful in some persons, and how
    right,
Mortification of the flesh may be.
    The indulgence you have given it to-
    night,
After long penance, clearly proves to me
    Your strength against temptation is but
    slight,
And shows the dreadful peril you are in
Of a relapse into your deadly sin.

" To-morrow morning, with the rising sun,
    Go back unto your convent, nor refrain
From fasting and from scourging, for you
    run
Great danger to become an ass again,
Since monkish flesh and asinine are one ;
    Therefore be wise, nor longer here re-
    main,
Unless you wish the scourge should be ap-
    plied
By other hands, that will not spare your
    hide."

When this the monk had heard, his color
    fled
    And then returned, like lightning in the
    air,
Till he was all one blush from foot to
    head,
    And even the bald spot in his russet hair
Turned from its usual pallor to bright
    red !
    The old man was asleep upon his chair.
Then all retired, and sank into the deep
And helpless imbecility of sleep.

They slept until the dawn of day drew
    near,
    Till the cock should have crowed, but
    did not crow,

For they had slain the shining chanticleer
And eaten him for supper, as you know.
The monk was up betimes and of good
  cheer,
And, having breakfasted, made haste to
  go,
As if he heard the distant matin bell,
And had but little time to say farewell.

Fresh was the morning as the breath of
  kine ;
Odors of herbs commingled with the
  sweet
Balsamic exhalations of the pine ;
A haze was in the air presaging heat ;
Uprose the sun above the Apennine,
And all the misty valleys at its feet
Were full of the delirious song of birds,
Voices of men, and bells, and low of herds.

All this to Brother Timothy was naught ;
He did not care for scenery, nor here
His busy fancy found the thing it sought ;
But when he saw the convent walls ap-
  pear,
And smoke from kitchen chimneys upward
  caught
And whirled aloft into the atmosphere,
He quickened his slow footsteps, like a
  beast
That scents the stable a league off at least.

And as he entered through the convent
  gate
He saw there in the court the ass, who
  stood
Twirling his ears about, and seemed to
  wait,
Just as he found him waiting in the
  wood ;
And told the Prior that, to alleviate
The daily labors of the brotherhood,
The owner, being a man of means and
  thrift,
Bestowed him on the convent as a gift.

And thereupon the Prior for many days
Revolved this serious matter in his
  mind,
And turned it over many different ways,
Hoping that some safe issue he might
  find ;
But stood in fear of what the world would
  say,
If he accepted presents of this kind,

Employing beasts of burden for the packs
That lazy monks should carry on their
  backs.

Then, to avoid all scandal of the sort,
And stop the mouth of cavil, he decreed
That he would cut the tedious matter
  short,
And sell the ass with all convenient
  speed,
Thus saving the expense of his support,
And hoarding something for a time of
  need.
So he despatched him to the neighboring
  Fair,
And freed himself from cumber and from
  care.

It happened now by chance, as some
  might say,
Others perhaps would call it destiny,
Gilbert was at the Fair ; and heard a bray,
And nearer came, and saw that it was
  he,
And whispered in his ear, " Ah, lackaday !
Good father, the rebellious flesh, I see,
Has changed you back into an ass again,
And all my admonitions were in vain."

The ass, who felt this breathing in his ear,
Did not turn round to look, but shook his
  head,
As if he were not pleased these words to
  hear,
And contradicted all that had been said.
And this made Gilbert cry in voice more
  clear,
" I know you well ; your hair is russet-
  red ;
Do not deny it ; for you are the same
Franciscan friar, and Timothy by name."

The ass, though now the secret had come out,
Was obstinate, and shook his head
  again ;
Until a crowd was gathered round about
To hear this dialogue between the
  twain ;
And raised their voices in a noisy shout
When Gilbert tried to make the matter
  plain,
And flouted him and mocked him all day
  long
With laughter and with jibes and scraps
  of song.

"If this be Brother Timothy," they cried,
  " Buy him, and feed him on the tenderest
      grass ;
Thou canst not do too much for one so
      tried
  As to be twice transformed into an ass."
So simple Gilbert bought him, and untied
  His halter, and o'er mountain and mo-
      rass
He led him homeward, talking as he went
Of good behavior and a mind content.

The children saw them coming, and ad-
      vanced,
  Shouting with joy, and hung about his
      neck, —
Not Gilbert's, but the ass's, — round him
      danced,
  And wove green garlands wherewithal
      to deck
His sacred person ; for again it chanced
  Their childish feelings, without rein or
      check,
Could not discriminate in any way
A donkey from a friar of Orders Gray.

" O Brother Timothy," the children said,
  " You have come back to us just as
      before ;
We were afraid, and thought that you were
      dead,
  And we should never see you any more."
And then they kissed the white star on his
      head,
  That like a birth-mark or a badge he
      wore,
And patted him upon the neck and face,
And said a thousand things with childish
      grace.

Thenceforward and forever he was known
  As Brother Timothy, and led alway
A life of luxury, till he had grown
  Ungrateful, being stuffed with corn and
      hay,
And very vicious. Then in angry tone,
  Rousing himself, poor Gilbert said one
      day,
" When simple kindness is misunderstood
A little flagellation may do good."

His many vices need not here be told ;
  Among them was a habit that he had
Of flinging up his heels at young and old,
  Breaking his halter, running off like mad

O'er pasture-lands and meadow, wood and
      wold,
  And other misdemeanors quite as bad ;
But worst of all was breaking from his
      shed
At night, and ravaging the cabbage-bed.

So Brother Timothy went back once more
  To his old life of labor and distress ;
Was beaten worse than he had been
      before ;
  And now, instead of comfort and ca-
      ress,
Came labors manifold and trials sore ;
  And as his toils increased his food grew
      less,
Until at last the great consoler, Death,
Ended his many sufferings with his breath.

Great was the lamentation when he died ;
  And mainly that he died impenitent ;
Dame Cicely bewailed, the children cried,
  The old man still remembered the event
In the French war, and Gilbert magni-
      fied
  His many virtues, as he came and went,
And said : " Heaven pardon Brother Tim-
      othy,
And keep us from the sin of gluttony."

INTERLUDE

" Signor Luigi," said the Jew,
  When the Sicilian's tale was told,
" The were-wolf is a legend old,
  But the were-ass is something new,
  And yet for one I think it true.
  The days of wonder have not ceased ;
  If there are beasts in forms of men,
  As sure it happens now and then,
  Why may not man become a beast,
  In way of punishment at least ?

" But this I will not now discuss ;
  I leave the theme, that we may thus
  Remain within the realm of song.
  The story that I told before,
  Though not acceptable to all,
  At least you did not find too long.
  I beg you, let me try again,
  With something in a different vein,
  Before you bid the curtain fall.
  Meanwhile keep watch upon the door,
  Nor let the Landlord leave his chair,

Lest he should vanish into air,
And so elude our search once more."

Thus saying, from his lips he blew
A little cloud of perfumed breath,
And then, as if it were a clew
To lead his footsteps safely through,
Began his tale as followeth.

THE SPANISH JEW'S SECOND TALE

SCANDERBEG

THE battle is fought and won
By King Ladislaus, the Hun,
In fire of hell and death's frost,
On the day of Pentecost.
And in rout before his path
From the field of battle red
Flee all that are not dead
Of the army of Amurath.

In the darkness of the night
Iskander, the pride and boast
Of that mighty Othman host,
With his routed Turks, takes flight
From the battle fought and lost
On the day of Pentecost ;
Leaving behind him dead
The army of Amurath,
The vanguard as it led,
The rearguard as it fled,
Mown down in the bloody swath
Of the battle's aftermath.

But he cared not for Hospodars,
Nor for Baron or Voivode,
As on through the night he rode
And gazed at the fateful stars,
That were shining overhead ;
But smote his steed with his staff,
And smiled to himself, and said :
"This is the time to laugh."

In the middle of the night,
In a halt of the hurrying flight,
There came a Scribe of the King
Wearing his signet ring,
And said in a voice severe :
"This is the first dark blot
On thy name, George Castriot !
Alas ! why art thou here,
And the army of Amurath slain,
And left on the battle plain ?"

And Iskander answered and said :
"They lie on the bloody sod
By the hoofs of horses trod ;
But this was the decree
Of the watchers overhead ;
For the war belongeth to God,
And in battle who are we,
Who are we, that shall withstand
The wind of his lifted hand ?"

Then he bade them bind with chains
This man of books and brains ;
And the Scribe said : "What misdeed
Have I done, that, without need,
Thou doest to me this thing ?"
And Iskander answering
Said unto him : "Not one
Misdeed to me hast thou done ;
But for fear that thou shouldst run
And hide thyself from me,
Have I done this unto thee.

"Now write me a writing, O Scribe,
And a blessing be on thy tribe !
A writing sealed with thy ring,
To King Amurath's Pasha
In the city of Croia,
The city moated and walled,
That he surrender the same
In the name of my master, the King ;
For what is writ in his name
Can never be recalled."

And the Scribe bowed low in dread,
And unto Iskander said :
"Allah is great and just,
But we are as ashes and dust ;
How shall I do this thing,
When I know that my guilty head
Will be forfeit to the King ?"

Then swift as a shooting star
The curved and shining blade
Of Iskander's scimetar
From its sheath, with jewels bright,
Shot, as he thundered : "Write !"
And the trembling Scribe obeyed,
And wrote in the fitful glare
Of the bivouac fire apart,
With the chill of the midnight air
On his forehead white and bare,
And the chill of death in his heart.

Then again Iskander cried :
"Now follow whither I ride,

For here thou must not stay.
Thou shalt be as my dearest friend,
And honors without end
Shall surround thee on every side,
And attend thee night and day."
But the sullen Scribe replied :
" Our pathways here divide ;
Mine leadeth not thy way."

And even as he spoke
Fell a sudden scimetar stroke,
When no one else was near ;
And the Scribe sank to the ground,
As a stone, pushed from the brink
Of a black pool, might sink
With a sob and disappear ;
And no one saw the deed ;
And in the stillness around
No sound was heard but the sound
Of the hoofs of Iskander's steed,
As forward he sprang with a bound.

Then onward he rode and afar,
With scarce three hundred men,
Through river and forest and fen,
O'er the mountains of Argentar ;
And his heart was merry within,
When he crossed the river Drin,
And saw in the gleam of the morn
The White Castle Ak-Hissar,
The city Croia called,
The city moated and walled,
The city where he was born, —
And above it the morning star.

Then his trumpeters in the van
On their silver bugles blew,
And in crowds about him ran
Albanian and Turkoman,
That the sound together drew.
And he feasted with his friends,
And when they were warm with wine,
He said : " O friends of mine,
Behold what fortune sends,
And what the fates design !
King Amurath commands
That my father's wide domain,
This city and all its lands,
Shall be given to me again."

Then to the Castle White
He rode in regal state,
And entered in at the gate
In all his arms bedight,
And gave to the Pasha

Who ruled in Croia
The writing of the King,
Sealed with his signet ring.
And the Pasha bowed his head,
And after a silence said :
" Allah is just and great !
I yield to the will divine,
The city and lands are thine ;
Who shall contend with fate ? "

Anon from the castle walls
The crescent banner falls,
And the crowd beholds instead,
Like a portent in the sky,
Iskander's banner fly,
The Black Eagle with double head ;
And a shout ascends on high,
For men's souls are tired of the Turks,
And their wicked ways and works,
That have made of Ak-Hissar
A city of the plague ;
And the loud, exultant cry
That echoes wide and far
Is : " Long live Scanderbeg ! "

It was thus Iskander came
Once more unto his own ;
And the tidings, like the flame
Of a conflagration blown
By the winds of summer, ran,
Till the land was in a blaze,
And the cities far and near,
Sayeth Ben Joshua Ben Meir,
In his Book of the Words of the Days,
" Were taken as a man
Would take the tip of his ear."

INTERLUDE

" Now that is after my own heart,"
The Poet cried ; " one understands
Your swarthy hero Scanderbeg,
Gauntlet on hand and boot on leg,
And skilled in every warlike art,
Riding through his Albanian lands,
And following the auspicious star
That shone for him o'er Ak-Hissar."

The Theologian added here
His word of praise not less sincere,
Although he ended with a jibe ;
" The hero of romance and song
Was born," he said, " to right the wrong ;
And I approve ; but all the same

That bit of treason with the Scribe
Adds nothing to your hero's fame."

The Student praised the good old times,
And liked the canter of the rhymes,
That had a hoofbeat in their sound ;
But longed some further word to hear
Of the old chronicler Ben Meir,
And where his volume might be found.

The tall Musician walked the room
With folded arms and gleaming eyes,
As if he saw the Vikings rise,
Gigantic shadows in the gloom ;
And much he talked of their emprise
And meteors seen in Northern skies,
And Heimdal's horn, and day of doom.
But the Sicilian laughed again ;
" This is the time to laugh," he said,
For the whole story he well knew
Was an invention of the Jew,
Spun from the cobwebs in his brain,
And of the same bright scarlet thread
As was the Tale of Kambalu.

Only the Landlord spake no word ;
'T was doubtful whether he had heard
The tale at all, so full of care
Was he of his impending fate,
That, like the sword of Damocles,
Above his head hung blank and bare,
Suspended by a single hair,
So that he could not sit at ease,
But sighed and looked disconsolate,
And shifted restless in his chair,
Revolving how he might evade
The blow of the descending blade.

The Student came to his relief
By saying in his easy way
To the Musician : " Calm your grief,
My fair Apollo of the North,
Balder the Beautiful and so forth ;
Although your magic lyre or lute
With broken strings is lying mute,
Still you can tell some doleful tale
Of shipwreck in a midnight gale,
Or something of the kind to suit
The mood that we are in to-night
For what is marvellous and strange ;
So give your nimble fancy range,
And we will follow in its flight."

But the Musician shook his head ;
" No tale I tell to-night," he said,

" While my poor instrument lies there,
Even as a child with vacant stare
Lies in its little coffin dead."

Yet, being urged, he said at last :
" There comes to me out of the Past
A voice, whose tones are sweet and wild,
Singing a song almost divine,
And with a tear in every line ;
An ancient ballad, that my nurse
Sang to me when I was a child,
In accents tender as the verse ;
And sometimes wept, and sometimes smiled
While singing it, to see arise
The look of wonder in my eyes,
And feel my heart with terror beat.
This simple ballad I retain
Clearly imprinted on my brain,
And as a tale will now repeat."

THE MUSICIAN'S TALE

THE MOTHER'S GHOST

SVEND DYRING he rideth adown the glade ;
I myself was young !
There he hath wooed him so winsome a
    maid ;
    Fair words gladden so many a heart.

Together were they for seven years,
And together children six were theirs.

Then came Death abroad through the land,
And blighted the beautiful lily-wand.

Svend Dyring he rideth adown the glade,
And again hath he wooed him another maid.

He hath wooed him a maid and brought
    home a bride,
But she was bitter and full of pride.

When she came driving into the yard,
There stood the six children weeping so
    hard.

There stood the small children with sorrow-
    ful heart ;
From before her feet she thrust them apart.

She gave to them neither ale nor bread ;
" Ye shall suffer hunger and hate," she
    said.

She took from them their quilts of blue,
And said : " Ye shall lie on the straw we
    strew."

She took from them the great waxlight :
" Now ye shall lie in the dark at night."

In the evening late they cried with cold ;
The mother heard it under the mould.

The woman heard it the earth below :
" To my little children I must go."

She standeth before the Lord of all :
" And may I go to my children small ? "

She prayed him so long, and would not
    cease,
Until he bade her depart in peace.

" At cock-crow thou shalt return again ;
Longer thou shalt not there remain ! "

She girded up her sorrowful bones,
And rifted the walls and the marble
    stones.

As through the village she flitted by,
The watch-dogs howled aloud to the sky.

When she came to the castle gate,
There stood her eldest daughter in wait.

" Why standest thou here, dear daughter
    mine ?
How fares it with brothers and sisters
    thine ? "

" Never art thou mother of mine,
For my mother was both fair and fine.

" My mother was white, with cheeks of
    red,
But thou art pale, and like to the dead."

" How should I be fair and fine ?
I have been dead ; pale cheeks are mine.

" How should I be white and red,
So long, so long have I been dead ? "

When she came in at the chamber door,
There stood the small children weeping
    sore.

One she braided, another she brushed,
The third she lifted, the fourth she hushed.

The fifth she took on her lap and pressed,
As if she would suckle it at her breast.

Then to her eldest daughter said she,
" Do thou bid Svend Dyring come hither
    to me."

Into the chamber when he came
She spake to him in anger and shame.

" I left behind me both ale and bread ;
My children hunger and are not fed.

" I left behind me quilts of blue ;
My children lie on the straw ye strew.

" I left behind me the great waxlight ;
My children lie in the dark at night.

" If I come again unto your hall,
As cruel a fate shall you befall !

" Now crows the cock with feathers red ;
Back to the earth must all the dead.

" Now crows the cock with feathers swart ;
The gates of heaven fly wide apart.

" Now crows the cock with feathers white ;
I can abide no longer to-night."

Whenever they heard the watch-dogs wail,
They gave the children bread and ale.

Whenever they heard the watch-dogs bay,
They feared lest the dead were on their
    way.

Whenever they heard the watch-dogs bark,
    I myself was young !
They feared the dead out there in the
    dark.
    Fair words gladden so many a heart.

INTERLUDE

TOUCHED by the pathos of these rhymes,
The Theologian said : " All praise
Be to the ballads of old times
And to the bards of simple ways,

Who walked with Nature hand in hand,
Whose country was their Holy Land,
Whose singing robes were homespun brown
From looms of their own native town,
Which they were not ashamed to wear,
And not of silk or sendal gay,
Nor decked with fanciful array
Of cockle-shells from Outre-Mer."

To whom the Student answered ; " Yes ;
All praise and honor ! I confess
That bread and ale, home-baked, home-
    brewed,
Are wholesome and nutritious food,
But not enough for all our needs ;
Poets — the best of them — are birds
Of passage ; where their instinct leads
They range abroad for thoughts and words,
And from all climes bring home the seeds
That germinate in flowers or weeds.
They are not fowls in barnyards born
To cackle o'er a grain of corn ;
And, if you shut the horizon down
To the small limits of their town,
What do you do but degrade your bard
Till he at last becomes as one
Who thinks the all-encircling sun
Rises and sets in his back yard ? "

The Theologian said again :
" It may be so ; yet I maintain
That what is native still is best,
And little care I for the rest.
'T is a long story ; time would fail
To tell it, and the hour is late ;
We will not waste it in debate,
But listen to our Landlord's tale."

And thus the sword of Damocles
Descending not by slow degrees,
But suddenly, on the Landlord fell,
Who blushing, and with much demur
And many vain apologies,
Plucking up heart, began to tell
The Rhyme of one Sir Christopher.

THE LANDLORD'S TALE

THE RHYME OF SIR CHRISTOPHER

IT was Sir Christopher Gardiner,
Knight of the Holy Sepulchre,
From Merry England over the sea,
Who stepped upon this continent

As if his august presence lent
A glory to the colony.

You should have seen him in the street
Of the little Boston of Winthrop's time.
His rapier dangling at his feet,
Doublet and hose and boots complete,
Prince Rupert hat with ostrich plume,
Gloves that exhaled a faint perfume,
Luxuriant curls and air sublime,
And superior manners now obsolete !

He had a way of saying things
That made one think of courts and kings,
And lords and ladies of high degree ;
So that not having been at court
Seemed something very little short
Of treason or lese-majesty,
Such an accomplished knight was he.

His dwelling was just beyond the town,
At what he called his country-seat ;
For, careless of Fortune's smile or frown,
And weary grown of the world and its
    ways,
He wished to pass the rest of his days
In a private life and a calm retreat.

But a double life was the life he led,
And, while professing to be in search
Of a godly course, and willing, he said,
Nay, anxious to join the Puritan church,
He made of all this but small account,
And passed his idle hours instead
With roystering Morton of Merry Mount,
That pettifogger from Furnival's Inn,
Lord of misrule and riot and sin,
Who looked on the wine when it was red.

This country-seat was little more
Than a cabin of logs ; but in front of the
    door
A modest flower-bed thickly sown
With sweet alyssum and columbine
Made those who saw it at once divine
The touch of some other hand than his
    own.
And first it was whispered, and then it was
    known,
That he in secret was harboring there
A little lady with golden hair,
Whom he called his cousin, but whom he
    had wed
In the Italian manner, as men said,
And great was the scandal everywhere.

But worse than this was the vague sur-
    mise,
Though none could vouch for it or aver,
That the Knight of the Holy Sepulchre
Was only a Papist in disguise ;
And the more to imbitter their bitter lives,
And the more to trouble the public mind,
Came letters from England, from two other
    wives,
Whom he had carelessly left behind ;
Both of them letters of such a kind
As made the governor hold his breath ;
The one imploring him straight to send
The husband home, that he might amend ;
The other asking his instant death,
As the only way to make an end.

The wary governor deemed it right,
When all this wickedness was revealed,
To send his warrant signed and sealed,
And take the body of the knight.
Armed with this mighty instrument,
The marshal, mounting his gallant steed,
Rode forth from town at the top of his
    speed,
And followed by all his bailiffs bold,
As if on high achievement bent,
To storm some castle or stronghold,
Challenge the warders on the wall,
And seize in his ancestral hall
A robber-baron grim and old.

But when through all the dust and heat
He came to Sir Christopher's country-seat,
No knight he found, nor warder there,
But the little lady with golden hair,
Who was gathering in the bright sunshine
The sweet alyssum and columbine ;
While gallant Sir Christopher, all so gay,
Being forewarned, through the postern gate
Of his castle wall had tripped away,
And was keeping a little holiday
In the forests, that bounded his estate.

Then as a trusty squire and true
The marshal searched the castle through,
Not crediting what the lady said ;
Searched from cellar to garret in vain,
And, finding no knight, came out again
And arrested the golden damsel instead,
And bore her in triumph into the town,
While from her eyes the tears rolled down
On the sweet alyssum and columbine,
That she held in her fingers white and
    fine

The governor's heart was moved to see
So fair a creature caught within
The snares of Satan and of sin,
And he read her a little homily
On the folly and wickedness of the lives
Of women half cousins and half wives ;
But, seeing that naught his words availed,
He sent her away in a ship that sailed
For Merry England over the sea,
To the other two wives in the old countree,
To search her further, since he had failed
To come at the heart of the mystery.

Meanwhile Sir Christopher wandered away
Through pathless woods for a month and a
    day,
Shooting pigeons, and sleeping at night
With the noble savage, who took delight
In his feathered hat and his velvet vest,
His gun and his rapier and the rest.
But as soon as the noble savage heard
That a bounty was offered for this gay bird,
He wanted to slay him out of hand,
And bring in his beautiful scalp for a show,
Like the glossy head of a kite or crow,
Until he was made to understand
They wanted the bird alive, not dead ;
Then he followed him whithersoever he fled,
Through forest and field, and hunted him
    down,
And brought him prisoner into the town.

Alas ! it was a rueful sight,
To see this melancholy knight
In such a dismal and hapless case ;
His hat deformed by stain and dent,
His plumage broken, his doublet rent,
His beard and flowing locks forlorn,
Matted, dishevelled, and unshorn,
His boots with dust and mire besprent ;
But dignified in his disgrace,
And wearing an unblushing face.
And thus before the magistrate
He stood to hear the doom of fate.
In vain he strove with wonted ease
To modify and extenuate
His evil deeds in church and state,
For gone was now his power to please ;
And his pompous words had no more weight
Than feathers flying in the breeze.

With suavity equal to his own
The governor lent a patient ear
To the speech evasive and high-flown,
In which he endeavored to make clear

That colo.ial laws were too severe
When applied to a gallant cavalier,
A gentleman born, and so well known,
And accustomed to move in a higher sphere.

All this the Puritan governor heard,
And deigned in answer never a word ;
But in summary manner shipped away,
In a vessel that sailed from Salem Bay,
This splendid and famous cavalier,
With his Rupert hat and his popery,
To Merry England over the sea,
As being unmeet to inhabit here.

Thus endeth the Rhyme of Sir Christo-
      pher,
Knight of the Holy Sepulchre,
The first who furnished this barren land
With apples of Sodom and ropes of sand.

FINALE

THESE are the tales those merry guests
Told to each other, well or ill ;
Like summer birds that lift their crests
Above the borders of their nests
And twitter, and again are still.

These are the tales, or new or old,
In idle moments idly told ;
Flowers of the field with petals thin,
Lilies that neither toil nor spin,
And tufts of wayside weeds and gorse
Hung in the parlor of the inn
Beneath the sign of the Red Horse.

And still, reluctant to retire,
The friends sat talking by the fire
And watched the smouldering embers
      burn
To ashes, and flash up again
Into a momentary glow,
Lingering like them when forced to go,
And going when they would remain ;
For on the morrow they must turn
Their faces homeward, and the pain

Of parting touched with its unrest
A tender nerve in every breast.

But sleep at last the victory won ;
They must be stirring with the sun,
And drowsily good night they said,
And went still gossiping to bed,
And left the parlor wrapped in gloom.
The only live thing in the room
Was the old clock, that in its pace
Kept time with the revolving spheres
And constellations in their flight,
And struck with its uplifted mace
The dark, unconscious hours of night,
To senseless and unlistening ears.

Uprose the sun ; and every guest,
Uprisen, was soon equipped and dressed
For journeying home and city-ward ;
The old stage-coach was at the door,
With horses harnessed, long before
The sunshine reached the withered sward
Beneath the oaks, whose branches hoar
Murmured : " Farewell forevermore."

" Farewell ! " the portly Landlord cried ;
" Farewell ! " the parting guests replied,
But little thought that nevermore
Their feet would pass that threshold o'er ;
That nevermore together there
Would they assemble, free from care,
To hear the oaks' mysterious roar,
And breathe the wholesome country air.

Where are they now ? What lands and skies
Paint pictures in their friendly eyes ?
What hope deludes, what promise cheers,
What pleasant voices fill their ears ?
Two are beyond the salt sea waves,
And three already in their graves.
Perchance the living still may look
Into the pages of this book,
And see the days of long ago
Floating and fleeting to and fro,
As in the well-remembered brook
They saw the inverted landscape gleam,
And their own faces like a dream
Look up upon them from below.

FLOWER–DE–LUCE

The poems in this division were published under the title *Flower-de-Luce* in 1867. The title poem was written March 20, 1866.

FLOWER–DE–LUCE

BEAUTIFUL lily, dwelling by still rivers,
  Or solitary mere,
Or where the sluggish meadow-brook delivers
  Its waters to the weir !

Thou laughest at the mill, the whir and worry
  Of spindle and of loom,
And the great wheel that toils amid the hurry
  And rushing of the flume.

Born in the purple, born to joy and pleasance,
  Thou dost not toil nor spin,
But makest glad and radiant with thy presence
  The meadow and the lin.

The wind blows, and uplifts thy drooping banner,
  And round thee throng and run
The rushes, the green yeomen of thy manor,
  The outlaws of the sun.

The burnished dragon-fly is thy attendant,
  And tilts against the field,
And down the listed sunbeam rides resplendent
  With steel-blue mail and shield.

Thou art the Iris, fair among the fairest,
  Who, armed with golden rod
And winged with the celestial azure, bearest
  The message of some God.

Thou art the Muse, who far from crowded cities
  Hauntest the sylvan streams,
Playing on pipes of reed the artless ditties
  That come to us as dreams.

O flower-de-luce, bloom on, and let the river
  Linger to kiss thy feet !
O flower of song, bloom on, and make forever
  The world more fair and sweet.

PALINGENESIS

In a letter dated March 20, 1859, Mr. Longfellow says: " For my own part, I am delighted to hear the birds again. Spring always reminds me of the *Palingenesis*, or re-creation, of the old alchemists, who believed that form is indestructible and that out of the ashes of a rose the rose itself could be reconstructed, — if they could only discover the great secret of Nature. It is done every spring beneath our windows and before our eyes; and is always so wonderful and so beautiful ! " The poem, which was printed in the *Atlantic* for July, 1864, appears to have been written, or at any rate revised, just before publication.

I LAY upon the headland-height, and listened
To the incessant sobbing of the sea
  In caverns under me,
And watched the waves, that tossed and fled and glistened,
Until the rolling meadows of amethyst
  Melted away in mist.

Then suddenly, as one from sleep, I started ;
For round about me all the sunny capes
  Seemed peopled with the shapes
Of those whom I had known in days departed,
Apparelled in the loveliness which gleams
  On faces seen in dreams.

A moment only, and the light and glory
Faded away, and the disconsolate shore
  Stood lonely as before ;
And the wild-roses of the promontory
Around me shuddered in the wind, and shed
  Their petals of pale red.

There was an old belief that in the embers
Of all things their primordial form exists,
  And cunning alchemists

Could re-create the rose with all its members
From its own ashes, but without the bloom,
   Without the lost perfume.

Ah me ! what wonder-working, occult science
Can from the ashes in our hearts once more
   The rose of youth restore ?
What craft of alchemy can bid defiance
To time and change, and for a single hour
   Renew this phantom-flower ?

"Oh, give me back," I cried, "the vanished splendors,
The breath of morn, and the exultant strife,
   When the swift stream of life
Bounds o'er its rocky channel, and surrenders
The pond, with all its lilies, for the leap
   Into the unknown deep ! "

And the sea answered, with a lamentation,
Like some old prophet wailing, and it said,
   " Alas ! thy youth is dead !
It breathes no more, its heart has no pulsation ;
In the dark places with the dead of old
   It lies forever cold ! "

Then said I, " From its consecrated cerements
I will not drag this sacred dust again,
   Only to give me pain ;
But, still remembering all the lost endearments,
Go on my way, like one who looks before,
   And turns to weep no more."

Into what land of harvests, what plantations
Bright with autumnal foliage and the glow
   Of sunsets burning low ;
Beneath what midnight skies, whose constellations
Light up the spacious avenues between
   This world and the unseen !

Amid what friendly greetings and caresses,
What households, though not alien, yet not mine,
   What bowers of rest divine ;

To what temptations in lone wildernesses,
What famine of the heart, what pain and loss,
   The bearing of what cross !

I do not know ; nor will I vainly question
Those pages of the mystic book which hold
   The story still untold,
But without rash conjecture or suggestion
Turn its last leaves in reverence and good heed,
   Until "The End " I read.

THE BRIDGE OF CLOUD

Burn, O evening hearth, and waken
   Pleasant visions, as of old !
Though the house by winds be shaken,
   Safe I keep this room of gold !

Ah, no longer wizard Fancy
   Builds her castles in the air,
Luring me by necromancy
   Up the never-ending stair !

But, instead, she builds me bridges
   Over many a dark ravine,
Where beneath the gusty ridges
   Cataracts dash and roar unseen.

And I cross them, little heeding
   Blast of wind or torrent's roar,
As I follow the receding
   Footsteps that have gone before.

Naught avails the imploring gesture,
   Naught avails the cry of pain !
When I touch the flying vesture,
   'T is the gray robe of the rain.

Baffled I return, and, leaning
   O'er the parapets of cloud,
Watch the mist that intervening
   Wraps the valley in its shroud.

And the sounds of life ascending
   Faintly, vaguely, meet the ear,
Murmur of bells and voices blending
   With the rush of waters near.

Well I know what there lies hidden,
   Every tower and town and farm,
And again the land forbidden
   Reassumes its vanished charm.

Well I know the secret places,
  And the nests in hedge and tree ;
At what doors are friendly faces,
  In what hearts are thoughts of me.

Through the mist and darkness sinking,
  Blown by wind and beaten by shower,
Down I fling the thought I 'm thinking,
  Down I toss this Alpine flower.

HAWTHORNE

MAY 23, 1864

The date is that of the burial of Hawthorne. The poem was written just a month later. Mr. Longfellow wrote to Mr. Fields: "I send you a poem, premising that I have not seen Holmes's article in the *Atlantic*. I hope we have not been singing and saying the same things. I have only tried to describe the state of mind I was in on that day. Did you not feel so likewise?" In sending a copy of the lines at the same time to Mrs. Hawthorne, he wrote: "I feel how imperfect and inadequate they are ; but I trust you will pardon their deficiencies for the love I bear his memory."

How beautiful it was, that one bright day
In the long week of rain !
Though all its splendor could not chase
    away
  The omnipresent pain.

The lovely town was white with apple-
    blooms,
  And the great elms o'erhead
Dark shadows wove on their aerial looms
  Shot through with golden thread.

Across the meadows, by the gray old
    manse,
  The historic river flowed :
I was as one who wanders in a trance,
  Unconscious of his road.

The faces of familiar friends seemed
    strange ;
  Their voices I could hear,
And yet the words they uttered seemed to
    change
  Their meaning to my ear.

For the one face I looked for was not
    there,
  The one low voice was mute ;
Only an unseen presence filled the air,
  And baffled my pursuit.

Now I look back, and meadow, manse, and
    stream
  Dimly my thought defines ;
I only see — a dream within a dream —
  The hill-top hearsed with pines.

I only hear above his place of rest
  Their tender undertone,
The infinite longings of a troubled breast,
  The voice so like his own.

There in seclusion and remote from men
  The wizard hand lies cold,
Which at its topmost speed let fall the pen,
  And left the tale half told.

Ah ! who shall lift that wand of magic
    power,
  And the lost clew regain ?
The unfinished window in Aladdin's tower
  Unfinished must remain !

CHRISTMAS BELLS

I HEARD the bells on Christmas Day
Their old, familiar carols play,
    And wild and sweet
    The words repeat
Of peace on earth, good-will to men !

And thought how, as the day had come,
The belfries of all Christendom
    Had rolled along
    The unbroken song
Of peace on earth, good-will to men !

Till, ringing, singing on its way,
The world revolved from night to day,
    A voice, a chime,
    A chant sublime
Of peace on earth, good-will to men !

Then from each black, accursed mouth
The cannon thundered in the South,
    And with the sound
    The carols drowned
Of peace on earth, good-will to men !

It was as if an earthquake rent
The hearth-stones of a continent,
    And made forlorn
    The households born
Of peace on earth, good-will to men !

And in despair I bowed my head ;
"There is no peace on earth," I said ;
  "For hate is strong,
  And mocks the song
Of peace on earth, good-will to men ! "

Then pealed the bells more loud and deep :
"God is not dead ; nor doth he sleep !
  The Wrong shall fail,
  The Right prevail,
With peace on earth, good-will to men ! "

THE WIND OVER THE CHIMNEY

SEE, the fire is sinking low,
Dusky red the embers glow,
  While above them still I cower,
While a moment more I linger,
Though the clock, with lifted finger,
  Points beyond the midnight hour.

Sings the blackened log a tune
Learned in some forgotten June
  From a school-boy at his play,
When they both were young together,
Heart of youth and summer weather
  Making all their holiday.

And the night-wind rising, hark !
How above there in the dark,
  In the midnight and the snow,
Ever wilder, fiercer, grander,
Like the trumpets of Iskander,
  All the noisy chimneys blow !

Every quivering tongue of flame
Seems to murmur some great name,
  Seems to say to me, "Aspire ! "
But the night-wind answers, "Hollow
Are the visions that you follow,
  Into darkness sinks your fire ! "

Then the flicker of the blaze
Gleams on volumes of old days,
  Written by masters of the art,
Loud through whose majestic pages
Rolls the melody of ages,
  Throb the harp-strings of the heart.

And again the tongues of flame
Start exulting and exclaim :
  "These are prophets, bards, and seers ;
In the horoscope of nations,

Like ascendant constellations,
  They control the coming years."

But the night-wind cries : "Despair !
Those who walk with feet of air
  Leave no long-enduring marks ;
At God's forges incandescent
Mighty hammers beat incessant,
  These are but the flying sparks.

"Dust are all the hands that wrought ;
Books are sepulchres of thought ;
  The dead laurels of the dead
Rustle for a moment only,
Like the withered leaves in lonely
  Churchyards at some passing tread."

Suddenly the flame sinks down ;
Sink the rumors of renown ;
  And alone the night-wind drear
Clamors louder, wilder, vaguer, —
"'T is the brand of Meleager
  Dying on the hearth-stone here ! "

And I answer, — "Though it be,
Why should that discomfort me ?
  No endeavor is in vain ;
Its reward is in the doing,
And the rapture of pursuing
  Is the prize the vanquished gain."

THE BELLS OF LYNN

HEARD AT NAHANT

O CURFEW of the setting sun ! O Bells of
  Lynn !
O requiem of the dying day ! O Bells of
  Lynn !

From the dark belfries of yon cloud-cathe-
  dral wafted,
Your sounds aerial seem to float, O Bells of
  Lynn !

Borne on the evening wind across the crim-
  son twilight,
O'er land and sea they rise and fall, O Bells
  of Lynn !

The fisherman in his boat, far out beyond
  the headland,
Listens, and leisurely rows ashore, O Bells
  of Lynn !

Over the shining sands the wandering cattle homeward
Follow each other at your call, O Bells of Lynn !

The distant lighthouse hears, and with his flaming signal
Answers you, passing the watchword on, O Bells of Lynn !

And down the darkening coast run the tumultuous surges,
And clap their hands, and shout to you, O Bells of Lynn !

Till from the shuddering sea, with your wild incantations,
Ye summon up the spectral moon, O Bells of Lynn !

And startled at the sight, like the weird woman of Endor,
Ye cry aloud, and then are still, O Bells of Lynn !

KILLED AT THE FORD

HE is dead, the beautiful youth,
The heart of honor, the tongue of truth,
He, the life and light of us all,
Whose voice was blithe as a bugle-call,
Whom all eyes followed with one consent,
The cheer of whose laugh, and whose pleasant word,
Hushed all murmurs of discontent.

Only last night, as we rode along,
Down the dark of the mountain gap,
To visit the picket-guard at the ford,
Little dreaming of any mishap,
He was humming the words of some old song :
" Two red roses he had on his cap
And another he bore at the point of his sword."

Sudden and swift a whistling ball
Came out of a wood, and the voice was still ;
Something I heard in the darkness fall,
And for a moment my blood grew chill ;
I spake in a whisper, as he who speaks
In a room where some one is lying dead ;
But he made no answer to what I said.

We lifted him up to his saddle again,
And through the mire and the mist and the rain
Carried him back to the silent camp,
And laid him as if asleep on his bed ;
And I saw by the light of the surgeon's lamp
Two white roses upon his cheeks,
And one, just over his heart, blood-red !

And I saw in a vision how far and fleet
That fatal bullet went speeding forth,
Till it reached a town in the distant North,
Till it reached a house in a sunny street,
Till it reached a heart that ceased to beat
Without a murmur, without a cry ;
And a bell was tolled, in that far-off town,
For one who had passed from cross to crown,
And the neighbors wondered that she should die.

GIOTTO'S TOWER

How many lives, made beautiful and sweet
By self-devotion and by self-restraint,
Whose pleasure is to run without complaint
On unknown errands of the Paraclete,
Wanting the reverence of unshodden feet,
Fail of the nimbus which the artists paint
Around the shining forehead of the saint,
And are in their completeness incomplete !
In the old Tuscan town stands Giotto's tower,
The lily of Florence blossoming in stone, —
A vision, a delight, and a desire, —
The builder's perfect and centennial flower,
That in the night of ages bloomed alone,
But wanting still the glory of the spire.

TO-MORROW

'T IS late at night, and in the realm of sleep
My little lambs are folded like the flocks ;
From room to room I hear the wakeful clocks
Challenge the passing hour, like guards that keep

Their solitary watch on tower and steep ;
  Far off I hear the crowing of the cocks,
  And through the opening door that time
     unlocks
  Feel the fresh breathing of To-morrow
     creep.
To-morrow ! the mysterious, unknown
     guest,
  Who cries to me : "Remember Barme-
     cide,
  And tremble to be happy with the rest."
And I make answer : "I am satisfied ;
  I dare not ask ; I know not what is
     best ;
  God hath already said what shall be-
     tide."

DIVINA COMMEDIA

The six sonnets which follow were written during the progress of Mr. Longfellow's work in translating the *Divina Commedia*, and were published as poetical fly-leaves to the three parts. The first was written just after he had put the first two cantos of the *Inferno* into the hands of the printer. This, with the second, prefaced the *Inferno*. The third and fourth introduced the *Purgatorio*, and the fifth and sixth the *Paradiso*.

I

OFT have I seen at some cathedral door
  A laborer, pausing in the dust and heat,
  Lay down his burden, and with reverent
     feet
Enter, and cross himself, and on the floor
Kneel to repeat his paternoster o'er ;
  Far off the noises of the world retreat ;
  The loud vociferations of the street
  Become an undistinguishable roar.
So, as I enter here from day to day,
  And leave my burden at this minster
     gate,
  Kneeling in prayer, and not ashamed to
     pray,
The tumult of the time disconsolate
  To inarticulate murmurs dies away,
  While the eternal ages watch and wait.

II

How strange the sculptures that adorn these
     towers !
  This crowd of statues, in whose folded
     sleeves

Birds build their nests ; while canopied
     with leaves
Parvis and portal bloom like trellised
     bowers,
And the vast minster seems a cross of
     flowers !
But fiends and dragons on the gar-
     goyled eaves
Watch the dead Christ between the liv-
     ing thieves,
And, underneath, the traitor Judas low-
     ers !
Ah ! from what agonies of heart and brain,
  What exultations trampling on despair,
  What tenderness, what tears, what hate
     of wrong,
What passionate outcry of a soul in pain,
  Uprose this poem of the earth and air,
  This mediæval miracle of song !

III

I enter, and I see thee in the gloom
  Of the long aisles, O poet saturnine !
  And strive to make my steps keep pace
     with thine.
The air is filled with some unknown per-
     fume ;
The congregation of the dead make room
  For thee to pass ; the votive tapers
     shine ;
  Like rooks that haunt Ravenna's groves
     of pine
  The hovering echoes fly from tomb to
     tomb.
From the confessionals I hear arise
  Rehearsals of forgotten tragedies,
  And lamentations from the crypts be-
     low ;
And then a voice celestial that begins
  With the pathetic words, "Although
     your sins
  As scarlet be," and ends with "as the
     snow."

IV

With snow-white veil and garments as of
     flame,
  She stands before thee, who so long ago
  Filled thy young heart with passion and
     the woe
From which thy song and all its splen-
     dors came ;

And while with stern rebuke she speaks thy name,
The ice about thy heart melts as the snow
On mountain heights, and in swift over-flow
Comes gushing from thy lips in sobs of shame.
Thou makest full confession ; and a gleam,
As of the dawn on some dark forest cast,
Seems on thy lifted forehead to in-crease ;
Lethe and Eunoë — the remembered dream
And the forgotten sorrow — bring at last
That perfect pardon which is perfect peace.

V

I lift mine eyes, and all the windows blaze
With forms of Saints and holy men who died,
Here martyred and hereafter glorified ;
And the great Rose upon its leaves dis-plays
Christ's Triumph, and the angelic rounde-lays,
With splendor upon splendor multiplied ;
And Beatrice again at Dante's side
No more rebukes, but smiles her words of praise.
And then the organ sounds, and unseen choirs
Sing the old Latin hymns of peace and love
And benedictions of the Holy Ghost ;
And the melodious bells among the spires
O'er all the house-tops and through heaven above
Proclaim the elevation of the Host !

VI

O star of morning and of liberty !
O bringer of the light, whose splendor shines
Above the darkness of the Apennines,
Forerunner of the day that is to be !
The voices of the city and the sea,
The voices of the mountains and the pines,
Repeat thy song, till the familiar lines
Are footpaths for the thought of Italy !

Thy flame is blown abroad from all the heights,
Through all the nations, and a sound is heard,
As of a mighty wind, and men devout,
Strangers of Rome, and the new proselytes,
In their own language hear thy won-drous word,
And many are amazed and many doubt.

NOËL

ENVOYÉ À M. AGASSIZ, LA VEILLE DE NOËL 1864, AVEC UN PANIER DE VINS DIVERS

The basket of wine which Mr. Longfellow sent to his friend with these verses was accompanied by the follow-ing note : "A Merry Christmas and Happy New Year to all the house of Agassiz! I send also six good wishes in the shape of bottles. Or is it wine ? It is both ; good wine and good wishes and kind memories of you on this Christmas Eve."
A translation of the verses was printed by Mr. John E. Norcross of Philadelphia in a brochure, 1867.

L'Académie en respect,
Nonobstant l'incorrection
A la faveur du sujet,
    Ture-lure,
N'y fera point de rature ;
Noël ! ture-lure-lure.
                          GUI BARÔZAI.

QUAND les astres de Noël
Brillaient, palpitaient au ciel,
Six gaillards, et chacun ivre,
Chantaient gaîment dans le givre,
    " Bons amis,
Allons donc chez Agassiz ! "

Ces illustres Pèlerins
D'Outre-Mer adroits et fins,
Se donnant des airs de prêtre,
A l'envi se vantaient d'être
    " Bons amis
De Jean Rudolphe Agassiz ! "

Œil-de-Perdrix, grand farceur,
Sans reproche et sans pudeur,
Dans son patois de Bourgogne,
Bredouillait comme un ivrogne,
    " Bons amis,
J'ai dansé chez Agassiz ! "

Verzenay le Champenois,
Bon Français, point New-Yorquois,
Mais des environs d'Avize,
Fredonne à mainte reprise,
    " Bons amis,
J'ai chanté chez Agassiz ! "

À côté marchait un vieux
Hidalgo, mais non mousseux ;
Dans le temps de Charlemagne
Fut son père Grand d'Espagne !
　　" Bons amis,
J'ai diné chez Agassiz ! "

Derrière eux un Bordelais,
Gascon, s'il en fut jamais,
Parfumé de poésie
Riait, chantait, plein de vie,
　　" Bons amis,
J'ai soupé chez Agassiz ! "

Avec ce beau cadet roux,
Bras dessus et bras dessous,
Mine altière et couleur terne,
Vint le Sire de Sauterne ;
　　" Bons amis,
J'ai couché chez Agassiz ! "

Mais le dernier de ces preux,
Etait un pauvre Chartreux,
Qui disait, d'un ton robuste,

" Bénédictions sur le Juste !
　　Bons amis,
Bénissons Père Agassiz ! "

Ils arrivent trois à trois,
Montent l'escalier de bois
Clopin-clopant ! quel gendarme
Peut permettre ce vacarme,
　　Bons amis,
À la porte d'Agassiz !

" Ouvrez donc, mon bon Seigneur,
Ouvrez vite et n'ayez peur ;
Ouvrez, ouvrez, car nous sommes
Gens de bien et gentilshommes,
　　Bons amis
De la famille Agassiz ! "

Chut, ganaches ! taisez-vous !
C'en est trop de vos glouglous ;
Epargnez aux Philosophes
Vos abominables strophes !
　　Bons amis,
Respectez mon Agassiz !

BIRDS OF PASSAGE

FLIGHT THE THIRD

Contained in the volume entitled *Aftermath*, 1873.

FATA MORGANA

O SWEET illusions of Song,
　　That tempt me everywhere,
In the lonely fields, and the throng
　　Of the crowded thoroughfare !

I approach, and ye vanish away,
　　I grasp you, and ye are gone ;
But ever by night and by day,
　　The melody soundeth on.

As the weary traveller sees
　　In desert or prairie vast,
Blue lakes, overhung with trees,
　　That a pleasant shadow cast ;

Fair towns with turrets high,
　　And shining roofs of gold,
That vanish as he draws nigh,
　　Like mists together rolled, —

So I wander and wander along,
　　And forever before me gleams
The shining city of song,
　　In the beautiful land of dreams.

But when I would enter the gate
　　Of that golden atmosphere,
It is gone, and I wonder and wait
　　For the vision to reappear.

THE HAUNTED CHAMBER

EACH heart has its haunted chamber,
　　Where the silent moonlight falls !
On the floor are mysterious footsteps,
　　There are whispers along the walls !

And mine at times is haunted
　　By phantoms of the Past,
As motionless as shadows
　　By the silent moonlight cast.

A form sits by the window,
 That is not seen by day,
For as soon as the dawn approaches
 It vanishes away.

It sits there in the moonlight,
 Itself as pale and still,
And points with its airy finger
 Across the window-sill.

Without, before the window,
 There stands a gloomy pine,
Whose boughs wave upward and down-
  ward
 As wave these thoughts of mine.

And underneath its branches
 Is the grave of a little child,
Who died upon life's threshold,
 And never wept nor smiled.

What are ye, O pallid phantoms !
 That haunt my troubled brain ?
That vanish when day approaches,
 And at night return again ?

What are ye, O pallid phantoms !
 But the statues without breath,
That stand on the bridge overarching
 The silent river of death ?

THE MEETING

AFTER so long an absence
 At last we meet again :
Does the meeting give us pleasure,
 Or does it give us pain ?

The tree of life has been shaken,
 And but few of us linger now,
Like the Prophet's two or three berries
 In the top of the uppermost bough.

We cordially greet each other
 In the old, familiar tone ;
And we think, though we do not say it,
 How old and gray he is grown !

We speak of a Merry Christmas
 And many a Happy New Year ;
But each in his heart is thinking
 Of those that are not here.

We speak of friends and their fortunes,
 And of what they did and said,
Till the dead alone seem living,
 And the living alone seem dead.

And at last we hardly distinguish
 Between the ghosts and the guests ;
And a mist and shadow of sadness
 Steals over our merriest jests.

VOX POPULI

WHEN Mazárvan the Magician
 Journeyed westward through Cathay,
Nothing heard he but the praises
 Of Badoura on his way.

But the lessening rumor ended
 When he came to Khaledan,
There the folk were talking only
 Of Prince Camaralzaman.

So it happens with the poets :
 Every province hath its own ;
Camaralzaman is famous
 Where Badoura is unknown.

THE CASTLE-BUILDER

A GENTLE boy, with soft and silken locks,
 A dreamy boy, with brown and tender
  eyes,
A castle-builder, with his wooden blocks,
 And towers that touch imaginary skies.

A fearless rider on his father's knee,
 An eager listener unto stories told
At the Round Table of the nursery,
 Of heroes and adventures manifold.

There will be other towers for thee to build ;
 There will be other steeds for thee to
  ride ;
There will be other legends, and all filled
 With greater marvels and more glorified.

Build on, and make thy castles high and
  fair,
 Rising and reaching upward to the skies ;
Listen to voices in the upper air,
 Nor lose thy simple faith in mysteries.

CHANGED

"November 25, 1847. [In Portland.] After church,
walked with Fessenden to the 'gallows' that used to
be, — a fine hillside, looking down and over the cove."
This was the scene of *Changed*, but the poem was not
written till 1858, when the poet was on a visit to Port-
land.

FROM the outskirts of the town,
   Where of old the mile-stone stood,
Now a stranger, looking down,
I behold the shadowy crown
   Of the dark and haunted wood.

Is it changed, or am I changed?
   Ah ! the oaks are fresh and green,
But the friends with whom I ranged
Through their thickets are estranged
   By the years that intervene.

Bright as ever flows the sea,
   Bright as ever shines the sun,
But alas ! they seem to me
Not the sun that used to be,
   Not the tides that used to run.

THE CHALLENGE

I HAVE a vague remembrance
   Of a story, that is told
In some ancient Spanish legend
   Or chronicle of old.

It was when brave King Sanchez
   Was before Zamora slain,
And his great besieging army
   Lay encamped upon the plain.

Don Diego de Ordoñez
   Sallied forth in front of all,
And shouted loud his challenge
   To the warders on the wall.

All the people of Zamora,
   Both the born and the unborn,
As traitors did he challenge
   With taunting words of scorn.

The living, in their houses,
   And in their graves, the dead !

And the waters of their rivers,
   And their wine, and oil, and bread !

There is a greater army,
   That besets us round with strife,
A starving, numberless army,
   At all the gates of life.

The poverty-stricken millions
   Who challenge our wine and bread,
And impeach us all as traitors,
   Both the living and the dead.

And whenever I sit at the banquet,
   Where the feast and song are high,
Amid the mirth and the music
   I can hear that fearful cry.

And hollow and haggard faces
   Look into the lighted hall,
And wasted hands are extended
   To catch the crumbs that fall.

For within there is light and plenty,
   And odors fill the air ;
But without there is cold and darkness,
   And hunger and despair.

And there in the camp of famine
   In wind and cold and rain,
Christ, the great Lord of the army,
   Lies dead upon the plain !

THE BROOK AND THE WAVE

THE brooklet came from the mountain,
   As sang the bard of old,
Running with feet of silver
   Over the sands of gold !

Far away in the briny ocean
   There rolled a turbulent wave,
Now singing along the sea-beach,
   Now howling along the cave.

And the brooklet has found the billow,
   Though they flowed so far apart,
And has filled with its freshness and sweet
      ness
   That turbulent, bitter heart !

AFTERMATH

This poem, placed last in the book, gave title to the volume published in 1873, which contained the third part of *Tales of a Wayside Inn* and the third flight of *Birds of Passage.* The completion of the *Tales* on his sixty-sixth birthday may have given rise to this poem.

WHEN the summer fields are mown,
When the birds are fledged and flown,
And the dry leaves strew the path ;

With the falling of the snow,
With the cawing of the crow,
Once again the fields we mow
And gather in the aftermath.

Not the sweet, new grass with flowers
Is this harvesting of ours ;
Not the upland clover bloom ;
But the rowen mixed with weeds,
Tangled tufts from marsh and meads,
Where the poppy drops its seeds
In the silence and the gloom.

THE MASQUE OF PANDORA

THE MASQUE OF PANDORA

The title poem in the volume, *The Masque of Pandora and other Poems*, published in 1875. It was adapted for the stage, and set to music by Alfred Cellier, and was brought out in an adaptation by Bolton Rowe at the Boston Theatre in 1881. Mr. Longfellow wrote for Miss Blanche Roosevelt, who was principally concerned in putting it on the stage, and who took the part of Pandora, the following song and chorus : —

What place is this ? Oh tell me, I implore !
  Tell me what I am feeling, hearing, seeing ;
If this be life, oh give me more and more.
  Till I am filled with the delight of being.

What forms mysterious people this dark space ?
  What voices and what sounds of music greet me ?
And who are these, so fair in form and face,
  That with such gracious welcome come to meet me ?

CHORUS

Blow, bellows, blow ! and keep the flame from dying,
Till from the iron on our anvils lying
We forge the thunderbolts of Zeus supreme,
Whose smothered lightnings in the ashes gleam.

I

THE WORKSHOP OF HEPHÆSTUS

HEPHÆSTUS (*standing before the statue of Pandora*).

Not fashioned out of gold, like Hera's
    throne,
Nor forged of iron like the thunderbolts
Of Zeus omnipotent, or other works
Wrought by my hands at Lemnos or Olym-
    pus,
But moulded in soft clay, that unresisting
Yields itself to the touch, this lovely form
Before me stands, perfect in every part.
Not Aphrodite's self appeared more fair,
When first upwafted by caressing winds

She came to high Olympus, and the gods
Paid homage to her beauty. Thus her hair
Was cinctured ; thus her floating drapery
Was like a cloud about her, and her face
Was radiant with the sunshine and the sea.

THE VOICE OF ZEUS.

Is thy work done, Hephæstus ?

HEPHÆSTUS.
            It is finished !

THE VOICE.

Not finished till I breathe the breath of life
Into her nostrils, and she moves and speaks.

HEPHÆSTUS.

Will she become immortal like ourselves ?

THE VOICE.

The form that thou hast fashioned out of
    clay
Is of the earth and mortal ; but the spirit,
The life, the exhalation of my breath,
Is of diviner essence and immortal.
The gods shall shower on her their benefac
    tions,
She shall possess all gifts : the gift of song,
The gift of eloquence, the gift of beauty,
The fascination and the nameless charm
That shall lead all men captive.

HEPHÆSTUS.
        Wherefore ? wherefore ?

A wind shakes the house.

I hear the rushing of a mighty wind
Through all the halls and chambers of my
    house !

Her parted lips inhale it, and her bosom
Heaves with the inspiration. As a reed
Beside a river in the rippling current
Bends to and fro, she bows or lifts her head.
She gazes round about as if amazed ;
She is alive ; she breathes, but yet she
  speaks not !

PANDORA *descends from the pedestal*

CHORUS OF THE GRACES

AGLAIA.

In the workshop of Hephæstus
  What is this I see ?
Have the Gods to four increased us
  Who were only three ?
Beautiful in form and feature,
  Lovely,as the day,
Can there be so fair a creature
  Formed of common clay ?

THALIA.

O sweet, pale face ! O lovely eyes of
  azure,
Clear as the waters of a brook that run
Limpid and laughing in the summer sun !
O golden hair, that like a miser's trea-
  sure
In its abundance overflows the measure !
O graceful form, that cloudlike floatest
  on
With the soft, undulating gait of one
Who moveth as if motion were a plea-
  sure !
By what name shall I call thee ? Nymph
  or Muse,
Callirrhoë or Urania ? Some sweet name
Whose every syllable is a caress
Would best befit thee ; but I cannot
  choose,
  Nor do I care to choose ; for still the
  same,
Nameless or named, will be thy love-
  liness.

EUPHROSYNE.

Dowered with all celestial gifts,
  Skilled in every art
That ennobles and uplifts
  And delights the heart,
Fair on earth shall be thy fame
  As thy face is fair,
And Pandora be the name
  Thou henceforth shalt bear.

II

OLYMPUS

HERMES (*putting on his sandals*).

Much must he toil who serves the Immor-
  tal Gods,
And I, who am their herald, most of all.
No rest have I, nor respite. I no sooner
Unclasp the wingèd sandals from my feet,
Than I again must clasp them, and depart
Upon some foolish errand. But to-day
The errand is not foolish. Never yet
With greater joy did I obey the summons
That sends me earthward. I will fly so
  swiftly
That my caduceus in the whistling air
Shall make a sound like the Pandæan
  pipes,
Cheating the shepherds ; for to-day I go,
Commissioned by high-thundering Zeus, to
  lead
A maiden to Prometheus, in his tower,
And by my cunning arguments persuade
  him
To marry her. What mischief lies con-
  cealed
In this design I know not ; but I know
Who thinks of marrying hath already
  taken
One step upon the road to penitence.
Such embassies delight me. Forth I
  launch
On the sustaining air, nor fear to fall
Like Icarus, nor swerve aside like him
Who drove amiss Hyperion's fiery steeds.
I sink, I fly ! The yielding element
Folds itself round about me like an arm,
And holds me as a mother holds her child.

III

TOWER OF PROMETHEUS ON MOUNT CAUCASUS

PROMETHEUS.

I hear the trumpet of Alectryon
Proclaim the dawn. The stars begin to
  fade,
And all the heavens are full of prophecies
And evil auguries. Blood-red last night
I saw great Kronos rise ; the crescent
  moon

Sank through the mist, as if it were the scythe
His parricidal hand had flung far down
The western steeps. O ye Immortal Gods,
What evil are ye plotting and contriving ?

HERMES *and* PANDORA *at the threshold.*

PANDORA.

I cannot cross the threshold. An unseen
And icy hand repels me. These blank walls
Oppress me with their weight !

PROMETHEUS.

Powerful ye are,
But not omnipotent. Ye cannot fight
Against Necessity. The Fates control you,
As they do us, and so far we are equals !

PANDORA.

Motionless, passionless, companionless,
He sits there muttering in his beard. His voice
Is like a river flowing underground !

HERMES.

Prometheus, hail !

PROMETHEUS.

Who calls me ?

HERMES.

It is I.
Dost thou not know me ?

PROMETHEUS.

By thy wingèd cap
And wingèd heels I know thee. Thou art Hermes,
Captain of thieves ! Hast thou again been stealing
The heifers of Admetus in the sweet
Meadows of asphodel ? or Hera's girdle ?
Or the earth-shaking trident of Poseidon ?

HERMES.

And thou, Prometheus ; say, hast thou again
Been stealing fire from Helios' chariot-wheels
To light thy furnaces ?

PROMETHEUS.

Why comest thou hither
So early in the dawn ?

HERMES.

The Immortal Gods
Know naught of late or early. Zeus himself,
The omnipotent hath sent me.

PROMETHEUS.

For what purpose ?

HERMES.

To bring this maiden to thee.

PROMETHEUS.

I mistrust
The Gods and all their gifts. If they have sent her
It is for no good purpose.

HERMES.

What disaster
Could she bring on thy house, who is a woman ?

PROMETHEUS.

The Gods are not my friends, nor am I theirs.
Whatever comes from them, though in a shape
As beautiful as this, is evil only.
Who art thou ?

PANDORA.

One who, though to thee unknown,
Yet knoweth thee.

PROMETHEUS.

How shouldst thou know me, woman ?

PANDORA.

Who knoweth not Prometheus the humane ?

PROMETHEUS.

Prometheus the unfortunate ; to whom
Both Gods and men have shown themselves ungrateful.
When every spark was quenched on every hearth
Throughout the earth, I brought to man the fire
And all its ministrations. My reward
Hath been the rock and vulture.

HERMES.

But the Gods
At last relent and pardon.

PROMETHEUS.

They relent not ;
They pardon not ; they are implacable,
Revengeful, unforgiving !

HERMES.

As a pledge
Of reconciliation they have sent to thee
This divine being, to be thy companion,
And bring into thy melancholy house
The sunshine and the fragrance of her
    youth.

PROMETHEUS.

I need them not.   I have within myself
All that my heart desires ; the ideal beauty
Which the creative faculty of mind
Fashions and follows in a thousand shapes
More lovely than the real.   My own
    thoughts
Are my companions; my designs and labors
And aspirations are my only friends.

HERMES.

Decide not rashly.   The decision made
Can never be recalled.   The Gods implore
    not,
Plead not, solicit not ; they only offer
Choice and occasion, which once being
    passed
Return no more.   Dost thou accept the
    gift ?

PROMETHEUS.

No gift of theirs, in whatsoever shape
It comes to me, with whatsoever charm
To fascinate my sense, will I receive.
Leave me.

PANDORA.

Let us go hence.   I will not stay.

HERMES.

We leave thee to thy vacant dreams, and
    all
The silence and the solitude of thought,
The endless bitterness of unbelief,
The loneliness of existence without love.

CHORUS OF THE FATES

CLOTHO.

How the Titan, the defiant,
The self-centred, self-reliant,
Wrapped in visions and illusions,

Robs himself of life's best gifts !
Till by all the storm-winds shaken,
By the blast of fate o'ertaken,
Hopeless, helpless, and forsaken,
In the mists of his confusions
To the reefs of doom he drifts !

LACHESIS.

Sorely tried and sorely tempted,
From no agonies exempted,
In the penance of his trial,
And the discipline of pain ;
Often by illusions cheated,
Often baffled and defeated
In the tasks to be completed,
He, by toil and self-denial,
To the highest shall attain.

ATROPOS.

Tempt no more the noble schemer ;
Bear unto some idle dreamer
This new toy and fascination,
This new dalliance and delight !
To the garden where reposes
Epimetheus crowned with roses,
To the door that never closes
Upon pleasure and temptation,
Bring this vision of the night !

IV

THE AIR

HERMES (*returning to Olympus*).

As lonely as the tower that he inhabits,
As firm and cold as are the crags about
    him,
Prometheus stands.   The thunderbolts of
    Zeus
Alone can move him ; but the tender heart
Of Epimetheus, burning at white heat,
Hammers and flames like all his brother's
    forges !
Now as an arrow from Hyperion's bow,
My errand done, I fly, I float, I soar
Into the air, returning to Olympus.
O joy of motion ! O delight to cleave
The infinite realms of space, the liquid
    ether,
Through the warm sunshine and the cooling
    cloud,
Myself as light as sunbeam or as cloud !
With one touch of my swift and wingèd
    feet,

I spurn the solid earth, and leave it rock-
ing
As rocks the bough from which a bird takes
wing.

V

THE HOUSE OF EPIMETHEUS

EPIMETHEUS.

Beautiful apparition ! go not hence !
Surely thou art a Goddess, for thy voice
Is a celestial melody, and thy form
Self-poised as if it floated on the air !

PANDORA.

No Goddess am I, nor of heavenly birth,
But a mere woman fashioned out of clay
And mortal as the rest.

EPIMETHEUS.

    Thy face is fair ;
There is a wonder in thine azure eyes
That fascinates me. Thy whole presence
seems
A soft desire, a breathing thought of love.
Say, would thy star like Merope's grow dim
If thou shouldst wed beneath thee ?

PANDORA.

     Ask me not ;
I cannot answer thee. I only know
The Gods have sent me hither.

EPIMETHEUS.

     I believe,
And thus believing am most fortunate.
It was not Hermes led thee here, but Eros,
And swifter than his arrows were thine eyes
In wounding me. There was no moment's
space
Between my seeing thee and loving thee.
Oh, what a telltale face thou hast ! Again
I see the wonder in thy tender eyes.

PANDORA.

They do but answer to the love in thine,
Yet secretly I wonder thou shouldst love
me.
Thou knowest me not.

EPIMETHEUS.

    Perhaps I know thee better
Than had I known thee longer. Yet it
seems

That I have always known thee, and but
now
Have found thee.   Ah, I have been waiting
long.

PANDORA.

How beautiful is this house ! The atmos-
phere
Breathes rest and comfort, and the many
chambers
Seem full of welcomes.

EPIMETHEUS.

     They not only seem,
But truly are.   This dwelling and its mas-
ter
Belong to thee.

PANDORA.

    Here let me stay forever !
There is a spell upon me.

EPIMETHEUS.

     Thou thyself
Art the enchantress, and I feel thy power
Envelop me, and wrap my soul and sense
In an Elysian dream.

PANDORA.

    Oh, let me stay.
How beautiful are all things round about
me,
Multiplied by the mirrors on the walls !
What treasures hast thou here ! Yon oaken
chest,
Carven with figures and embossed with
gold,
Is wonderful to look upon ! What choice
And precious things dost thou keep hidden
in it ?

EPIMETHEUS.

I know not. 'T is a mystery.

PANDORA.

    Hast thou never
Lifted the lid ?

EPIMETHEUS.

    The oracle forbids.
Safely concealed there from all mortal eyes
Forever sleeps the secret of the Gods.
Seek not to know what they have hidden
from thee,
Till they themselves reveal it.

PANDORA.

As thou wilt.

EPIMETHEUS.

Let us go forth from this mysterious place.
The garden walks are pleasant at this
　　hour ;
The nightingales among the sheltering
　　boughs
Of populous and many-nested trees
Shall teach me how to woo thee, and shall
　　tell me
By what resistless charms or incantations
They won their mates.

PANDORA.

Thou dost not need a teacher.

They go out.

CHORUS OF THE EUMENIDES.

What the Immortals
Confide to thy keeping,
Tell unto no man ;
Waking or sleeping,
Closed be thy portals
To friend as to foeman.

Silence conceals it ;
The word that is spoken
Betrays and reveals it ;
By breath or by token
The charm may be broken.

With shafts of their splendors
The Gods unforgiving
Pursue the offenders,
The dead and the living !
Fortune forsakes them,
Nor earth shall abide them,
Nor Tartarus hide them ;
Swift wrath overtakes them.

With useless endeavor,
Forever, forever,
Is Sisyphus rolling
His stone up the mountain !
Immersed in the fountain,
Tantalus tastes not
The water that wastes not !
Through ages increasing
The pangs that afflict him,
With motion unceasing
The wheel of Ixion
Shall torture its victim !

VI

IN THE GARDEN

EPIMETHEUS.

Yon snow-white cloud that sails sublime in
　　ether
Is but the sovereign Zeus, who like a swan
Flies to fair-ankled Leda !

PANDORA.

Or perchance
Ixion's cloud, the shadowy shape of Hera,
That bore the Centaurs.

EPIMETHEUS.

The divine and human.

CHORUS OF BIRDS.

Gently swaying to and fro,
Rocked by all the winds that blow,
Bright with sunshine from above,
Dark with shadow from below,
Beak to beak and breast to breast
In the cradle of their nest,
Lie the fledglings of our love.

ECHO.

Love ! love !

EPIMETHEUS.

Hark ! listen ! Hear how sweetly over-
　　head
The feathered flute-players pipe their songs
　　of love,
And Echo answers, love and only love.

CHORUS OF BIRDS.

Every flutter of the wing,
Every note of song we sing,
Every murmur, every tone,
Is of love and love alone.

ECHO.

Love alone !

EPIMETHEUS.

Who would not love, if loving she might be
Changed like Callisto to a star in heaven ?

PANDORA.

Ah, who would love, if loving she might be
Like Semele consumed and burnt to
　　ashes ?

EPIMETHEUS.

Whence knowest thou these stories ?

PANDORA.

          Hermes taught me ;
He told me all the history of the Gods.

CHORUS OF REEDS.

Evermore a sound shall be
In the reeds of Arcady,
Evermore a low lament
Of unrest and discontent,
As the story is retold
Of the nymph so coy and cold,
Who with frightened feet outran
The pursuing steps of Pan.

EPIMETHEUS.

The pipe of Pan out of these reeds is
    made,
And when he plays upon it to the shep-
    herds
They pity him, so mournful is the sound.
Be thou not coy and cold as Syrinx was.

PANDORA.

Nor thou as Pan be rude and mannerless.

PROMETHEUS (without).

Ho ! Epimetheus !

EPIMETHEUS.

        'T is my brother's voice ;
A sound unwelcome and inopportune
As was the braying of Silenus' ass,
Once heard in Cybele's garden.

PANDORA.

          Let me go.
I would not be found here. I would not
    see him.

    She escapes among the trees.

CHORUS OF DRYADES.

Haste and hide thee,
Ere too late,
In these thickets intricate ;
Lest Prometheus
See and chide thee,
Lest some hurt
Or harm betide thee,
Haste and hide thee !

PROMETHEUS (entering).

Who was it fled from here ? I saw a
    shape
Flitting among the trees.

EPIMETHEUS.

        It was Pandora.

PROMETHEUS.

O Epimetheus ! Is it then in vain
That I have warned thee ? Let me now
    implore.
Thou harborest in thy house a dangerous
    guest.

EPIMETHEUS.

Whom the Gods love they honor with such
    guests.

PROMETHEUS.

Whom the Gods would destroy they first
    make mad.

EPIMETHEUS.

Shall I refuse the gifts they send to me ?

PROMETHEUS.

Reject all gifts that come from higher
    powers.

EPIMETHEUS.

Such gifts as this are not to be rejected.

PROMETHEUS.

Make not thyself the slave of any woman.

EPIMETHEUS.

Make not thyself the judge of any man.

PROMETHEUS.

I judge thee not ; for thou art more than
    man ;
Thou art descended from Titanic race,
And hast a Titan's strength and faculties
That make thee godlike ; and thou sittest
    here
Like Heracles spinning Omphale's flax,
And beaten with her sandals.

EPIMETHEUS.

        O my brother !
Thou drivest me to madness with thy taunts.

PROMETHEUS.

And me thou drivest to madness with thy
    follies.
Come with me to my tower on Caucasus :
See there my forges in the roaring caverns,
Beneficent to man, and taste the joy
That springs from labor. Read with me
    the stars,
And learn the virtues that lie hidden in
    plants,
And all things that are useful.

EPIMETHEUS.

                    O my brother !
I am not as thou art.   Thou dost inherit
Our father's strength, and I our mother's
    weakness :
The softness of the Oceanides,
The yielding nature that cannot resist.

PROMETHEUS.

Because thou wilt not.

EPIMETHEUS.

            Nay ; because I cannot.

PROMETHEUS.

Assert thyself ; rise up to thy full height ;
Shake from thy soul these dreams effemi-
    nate,
These passions born of indolence and ease.
Resolve, and thou art free. But breathe
    the air
Of mountains, and their unapproachable
    summits
Will lift thee to the level of themselves.

EPIMETHEUS.

The roar of forests and of waterfalls,
The rushing of a mighty wind, with loud
And undistinguishable voices calling,
Are in my ear !

PROMETHEUS.

            Oh, listen and obey.

EPIMETHEUS.

Thou leadest me as a child.   I follow thee.
            They go out.

CHORUS OF OREADES.

Centuries old are the mountains;
    Their foreheads wrinkled and rifted

Helios crowns by day,
Pallid Selene by night ;
From their bosoms uptossed
The snows are driven and drifted,
Like Tithonus' beard
Streaming dishevelled and white.

Thunder and tempest of wind
Their trumpets blow in the vastness ;
Phantoms of mist and rain,
Cloud and the shadow of cloud,
Pass and repass by the gates
Of their inaccessible fastness ;
Ever unmoved they stand,
Solemn, eternal, and proud.

VOICES OF THE WATERS.

Flooded by rain and snow
In their inexhaustible sources,
Swollen by affluent streams
Hurrying onward and hurled
Headlong over the crags,
The impetuous water-courses
Rush and roar and plunge
Down to the nethermost world.

Say, have the solid rocks
Into streams of silver been melted,
Flowing over the plains,
Spreading to lakes in the fields ?
Or have the mountains, the giants,
The ice-helmed, the forest-belted,
Scattered their arms abroad ;
Flung in the meadows their shields ?

VOICES OF THE WINDS.

High on their turreted cliffs
That bolts of thunder have shattered,
Storm-winds muster and blow
Trumpets of terrible breath ;
Then from the gateways rush,
And before them routed and scattered
Sullen the cloud-rack flies,
Pale with the pallor of death.

Onward the hurricane rides,
And flee for shelter the shepherds ;
White are the frightened leaves,
Harvests with terror are white ;
Panic seizes the herds,
And even the lions and leopards,
Prowling no longer for prey,
Crouch in their caverns with fright.

VOICES OF THE FORESTS.

Guarding the mountains around
Majestic the forests are standing,
Bright are their crested helms,
Dark is their armor of leaves ;
Filled with the breath of freedom
Each bosom subsiding, expanding,
Now like the ocean sinks,
Now like the ocean upheaves.

Planted firm on the rock,
With foreheads stern and defiant,
Loud they shout to the winds,
Loud to the tempest they call ;
Naught but Olympian thunders,
That blasted Titan and Giant,
Them can uproot and o'erthrow,
Shaking the earth with their fall.

CHORUS OF OREADES.

These are the Voices Three
Of winds and forests and fountains,
Voices of earth and of air,
Murmur and rushing of streams,
Making together one sound,
The mysterious voice of the mountains,
Waking the sluggard that sleeps,
Waking the dreamer of dreams.

These are the Voices Three,
That speak of endless endeavor,
Speak of endurance and strength,
Triumph and fulness of fame,
Sounding about the world,
An inspiration forever,
Stirring the hearts of men,
Shaping their end and their aim.

VII

THE HOUSE OF EPIMETHEUS

PANDORA.

Left to myself I wander as I will,
And as my fancy leads me, through this
house,
Nor could I ask a dwelling more complete
Were I indeed the Goddess that he deems
me.
No mansion of Olympus, framed to be
The habitation of the Immortal Gods,
Can be more beautiful. And this is mine,
And more than this, the love wherewith he
crowns me.

As if impelled by powers invisible
And irresistible, my steps return
Unto this spacious hall. All corridors
And passages lead hither, and all doors
But open into it. Yon mysterious chest
Attracts and fascinates me. Would I
knew
What there lies hidden ! But the oracle
Forbids. Ah me ! The secret then is
safe.
So would it be if it were in my keeping.
A crowd of shadowy faces from the
mirrors
That line these walls are watching me. I
dare not
Lift up the lid. A hundred times the act
Would be repeated, and the secret seen
By twice a hundred incorporeal eyes.
She walks to the other side of the hall.
My feet are weary, wandering to and fro,
My eyes with seeing and my heart with
waiting.
I will lie here and rest till he returns,
Who is my dawn, my day, my Helios.
Throws herself upon a couch, and falls asleep.

ZEPHYRUS.

Come from thy caverns dark and deep,
O son of Erebus and Night ;
All sense of hearing and of sight
Enfold in the serene delight
And quietude of sleep !

Set all thy silent sentinels
To bar and guard the Ivory Gate,
And keep the evil dreams of fate
And falsehood and infernal hate
Imprisoned in their cells.

But open wide the Gate of Horn,
Whence, beautiful as planets, rise
The dreams of truth, with starry eyes,
And all the wondrous prophecies
And visions of the morn.

CHORUS OF DREAMS FROM THE IVORY GATE.

Ye sentinels of sleep,
It is in vain ye keep
Your drowsy watch before the Ivory Gate ;
Though closed the portal seems,
The airy feet of dreams
Ye cannot thus in walls incarcerate.

We phantoms are and dreams
Born by Tartarean streams.

As ministers of the infernal powers ;
　O son of Erebus
　And Night, behold ! we thus
Elude your watchful warders on the towers !

　From gloomy Tartarus
　The Fates have summoned us
To whisper in her ear, who lies asleep,
　A tale to fan the fire
　Of her insane desire
To know a secret that the Gods would
　keep.

　This passion, in their ire,
　The Gods themselves inspire,
To vex mankind with evils manifold,
　So that disease and pain
　O'er the whole earth may reign,
And nevermore return the Age of Gold.

PANDORA (*waking*).

A voice said in my sleep : " Do not delay :
Do not delay ; the golden moments fly !
The oracle hath forbidden ; yet not thee
Doth it forbid, but Epimetheus only ! "
I am alone.　These faces in the mirrors
Are but the shadows and phantoms of my-
　self ;
They cannot help nor hinder.　No one sees
　me,
Save the all-seeing Gods, who, knowing
　good
And knowing evil, have created me
Such as I am, and filled me with desire
Of knowing good and evil like themselves.
　　　She approaches the chest.
I hesitate no longer.　Weal or woe,
Or life or death, the moment shall decide.

*She lifts the lid.　A dense mist rises from the
chest, and fills the room.　PANDORA falls
senseless on the floor.　Storm without.*

HORUS OF DREAMS FROM THE GATE OF HORN.

　Yes, the moment shall decide !
　It already hath decided ;
　And the secret once confided
　To the keeping of the Titan
　Now is flying far and wide,
　Whispered, told on every side,
　To disquiet and to frighten.

　Fever of the heart and brain,
　Sorrow, pestilence, and pain,
　Moans of anguish, maniac laughter,
　All the evils that hereafter

Shall afflict and vex mankind,
All into the air have risen
From the chambers of their prison;
Only Hope remains behind.

VIII

IN THE GARDEN

EPIMETHEUS.

The storm is past, but it hath left behind
　it
Ruin and desolation.　All the walks
Are strewn with shattered boughs ; the birds
　are silent ;
The flowers, downtrodden by the wind, lie
　dead ;
The swollen rivulet sobs with secret pain ;
The melancholy reeds whisper together
As if some dreadful deed had been com-
　mitted
They dare not name, and all the air is
　heavy
With an unspoken sorrow !　Premonitions,
Foreshadowings of some terrible disaster
Oppress my heart.　Ye Gods, avert the
　omen !

PANDORA, *coming from the house.*

O Epimetheus, I no longer dare
To lift mine eyes to thine, nor hear thy
　voice,
Being no longer worthy of thy love.

EPIMETHEUS.

What hast thou done ?

PANDORA.

　　Forgive me not, but kill me.

EPIMETHEUS.

What hast thou done ?

PANDORA.

　I pray for death, not pardon.

EPIMETHEUS.

What hast thou done ?

PANDORA.

　　　I dare not speak of it

EPIMETHEUS.

Thy pallor and thy silence terrify me !

PANDORA.

I have brought wrath and ruin on thy
house !
My heart hath braved the oracle that
guarded
The fatal secret from us, and my hand
Lifted the lid of the mysterious chest !

EPIMETHEUS.

Then all is lost ! I am indeed undone.

PANDORA.

I pray for punishment, and not for pardon.

EPIMETHEUS.

Mine is the fault, not thine. On me shall
fall
The vengeance of the Gods, for I betrayed
Their secret when, in evil hour, I said
It was a secret ; when, in evil hour,
I left thee here alone to this temptation.
Why did I leave thee ?

PANDORA.

Why didst thou return ?
Eternal absence would have been to me
The greatest punishment. To be left
alone
And face to face with my own crime, had
been
Just retribution. Upon me, ye Gods,
Let all your vengeance fall !

EPIMETHEUS.

On thee and me.
I do not love thee less for what is done,
And cannot be undone. Thy very weak-
ness
Hath brought thee nearer to me, and hence-
forth
My love will have a sense of pity in it,
Making it less a worship than before.

PANDORA.

Pity me not ; pity is degradation.
Love me and kill me.

EPIMETHEUS.

Beautiful Pandora !
Thou art a Goddess still !

PANDORA.

I am a woman ;
And the insurgent demon in my nature,

That made me brave the oracle, revolts
At pity and compassion. Let me die ;
What else remains for me ?

EPIMETHEUS.

Youth, hope, and love :
To build a new life on a ruined life,
To make the future fairer than the past,
And make the past appear a troubled
dream.
Even now in passing through the garden
walks
Upon the ground I saw a fallen nest
Ruined and full of rain ; and over me
Beheld the uncomplaining birds already
Busy in building a new habitation.

PANDORA.

Auspicious omen !

EPIMETHEUS.

May the Eumenides
Put out their torches and behold us not,
And fling away their whips of scorpions
And touch us not.

PANDORA.

Me let them punish.
Only through punishment of our evil deeds,
Only through suffering, are we reconciled
To the immortal Gods and to ourselves.

CHORUS OF THE EUMENIDES.

Never shall souls like these
Escape the Eumenides,
The daughters dark of Acheron and Night !
Unquenched our torches glare,
Our scourges in the air
Send forth prophetic sounds before they
smite.

Never by lapse of time
The soul defaced by crime
Into its former self returns again ;
For every guilty deed
Holds in itself the seed
Of retribution and undying pain.

Never shall be the loss
Restored, till Helios
Hath purified them with his heavenly fires ;
Then what was lost is won,
And the new life begun,
Kindled with nobler passions and desires.

THE HANGING OF THE CRANE

"One morning in the spring of 1867," writes Mr. T. B. Aldrich, " Mr. Longfellow came to the little home in Pinckney Street [Boston], where we had set up house-keeping in the light of our honeymoon. As we lingered a moment at the dining-room door, Mr. Longfellow turning to me said, 'Ah, Mr. Aldrich, your small round table will not always be closed. By and by you will find new young faces clustering about it; as years go on, leaf after leaf will be added until the time comes when the young guests will take flight, one by one, to build nests of their own elsewhere. Gradually the long table will shrink to a circle again, leaving two old peo-pie sitting there alone together. This is the story of life, the sweet and pathetic poem of the fireside. Make an idyl of it. I give the idea to you.' Several months afterward, I received a note from Mr. Longfellow in which he expressed a desire to use this *motif* in case I had done nothing in the matter. The theme was one peculiarly adapted to his sympathetic handling, and out of it grew *The Hanging of the Crane*." Just when the poem was written does not appear, but its first publica-tion was in the *New York Ledger*, March 28, 1874. Mr. Longfellow's old friend, Mr. Sam. Ward, had heard the poem, and offered to secure it for Mr. Robert Bonner, the proprietor of the *Ledger*, "touched," as he wrote to Mr. Longfellow, "by your kindness to poor ——, and haunted by the idea of increasing handsomely your noble charity fund." Mr. Bonner paid the poet the sum of three thousand dollars for this poem.

I

The lights are out, and gone are all the guests
That thronging came with merriment and jests
To celebrate the Hanging of the Crane
In the new house, — into the night are gone ;
But still the fire upon the hearth burns on,
And I alone remain.

O fortunate, O happy day,
When a new household finds its place
Among the myriad homes of earth,
Like a new star just sprung to birth,
And rolled on its harmonious way
Into the boundless realms of space !

So said the guests in speech and song,
As in the chimney, burning bright,
We hung the iron crane to-night,
And merry was the feast and long.

II

And now I sit and muse on what may be,
And in my vision see, or seem to see,
Through floating vapors interfused with light,
Shapes indeterminate, that gleam and fade,
As shadows passing into deeper shade
Sink and elude the sight.

For two alone, there in the hall,
Is spread the table round and small ;
Upon the polished silver shine
The evening lamps, but, more divine,
The light of love shines over all ;

Of love, that says not mine and thine,
But ours, for ours is thine and mine.

They want no guests, to come between
Their tender glances like a screen,
And tell them tales of land and sea,
And whatsoever may betide
The great, forgotten world outside ;
They want no guests ; they needs must be
Each other's own best company.

III

The picture fades ; as at a village fair
A showman's views, dissolving into air,
Again appear transfigured on the screen,
So in my fancy this ; and now once more,
In part transfigured, through the open door
Appears the selfsame scene.

Seated, I see the two again,
But not alone ; they entertain
A little angel unaware,
With face as round as is the moon,
A royal guest with flaxen hair,
Who, throned upon his lofty chair,
Drums on the table with his spoon,
Then drops it careless on the floor,
To grasp at things unseen before.

Are these celestial manners ? these
The ways that win, the arts that please ?
Ah yes ; consider well the guest,
And whatsoe'er he does seems best ;
He ruleth by the right divine
Of helplessness, so lately born
In purple chambers of the morn,
As sovereign over thee and thine.

He speaketh not ; and yet there lies
A conversation in his eyes ;
The golden silence of the Greek,
The gravest wisdom of the wise,
Not spoken in language, but in looks
More legible than printed books,
As if he could but would not speak.
And now, O monarch absolute,
Thy power is put to proof ; for, lo !
Resistless, fathomless, and slow,
The nurse comes rustling like the sea,
And pushes back thy chair and thee,
And so good night to King Canute.

IV

As one who walking in a forest sees
A lovely landscape through the parted
    trees,
  Then sees it not, for boughs that inter-
    vene ;
Or as we see the moon sometimes revealed
Through drifting clouds, and then again
    concealed,
    So I behold the scene.

There are two guests at table now ;
The king, deposed and older grown,
No longer occupies the throne, —
The crown is on his sister's brow ;
A Princess from the Fairy Isles,
The very pattern girl of girls,
All covered and embowered in curls,
Rose-tinted from the Isle of Flowers,
And sailing with soft, silken sails
From far-off Dreamland into ours.
Above their bowls with rims of blue
Four azure eyes of deeper hue
Are looking, dreamy with delight ;
Limpid as planets that emerge
Above the ocean's rounded verge,
Soft-shining through the summer night.
Steadfast they gaze, yet nothing see
Beyond the horizon of their bowls ;
Nor care they for the world that rolls
With all its freight of troubled souls
Into the days that are to be.

V

Again the tossing boughs shut out the
    scene,
Again the drifting vapors intervene,
  And the moon's pallid disk is hidden
    quite ;

And now I see the table wider grown,
As round a pebble into water thrown
  Dilates a ring of light.

I see the table wider grown,
I see it garlanded with guests,
As if fair Ariadne's Crown
Out of the sky had fallen down ;
Maidens within whose tender breasts
A thousand restless hopes and fears,
Forth reaching to the coming years,
Flutter awhile, then quiet lie,
Like timid birds that fain would fly,
But do not dare to leave their nests ; —
And youths, who in their strength elate
Challenge the van and front of fate,
Eager as champions to be
In the divine knight-errantry
Of youth, that travels sea and land
Seeking adventures, or pursues,
Through cities, and through solitudes
Frequented by the lyric Muse,
The phantom with the beckoning hand,
That still allures and still eludes.
O sweet illusions of the brain !
O sudden thrills of fire and frost !
The world is bright while ye remain,
And dark and dead when ye are lost !

VI

The meadow-brook, that seemeth to stand
    still,
Quickens its current as it nears the mill ;
  And so the stream of Time that linger-
    eth
In level places, and so dull appears,
Runs with a swifter current as it nears
    The gloomy mills of Death.

And now, like the magician's scroll,
That in the owner's keeping shrinks
With every wish he speaks or thinks,
Till the last wish consumes the whole,
The table dwindles, and again
I see the two alone remain.
The crown of stars is broken in parts ;
Its jewels, brighter than the day,
Have one by one been stolen away
To shine in other homes and hearts.
One is a wanderer now afar
In Ceylon or in Zanzibar,
Or sunny regions of Cathay ;
And one is in the boisterous camp
Mid clink of arms and horses' tramp,

And battle's terrible array.
I see the patient mother read,
With aching heart, of wrecks that float
Disabled on those seas remote,
Or of some great heroic deed
On battle-fields, where thousands bleed
To lift one hero into fame.
Anxious she bends her graceful head
Above these chronicles of pain,
And trembles with a secret dread
Lest there among the drowned or slain
She find the one beloved name.

VII

After a day of cloud and wind and rain
Sometimes the setting sun breaks out
    again,
And, touching all the darksome woods
    with light,
Smiles on the fields, until they laugh and
    sing,
Then like a ruby from the horizon's ring
    Drops down into the night.

What see I now ?   The night is fair,
The storm of grief, the clouds of care,
The wind, the rain, have passed away ;

The lamps are lit, the fires burn bright,
The house is full of life and light ;
It is the Golden Wedding day.
The guests come thronging in once more,
Quick footsteps sound along the floor,
The trooping children crowd the stair,
And in and out and everywhere
Flashes along the corridor
The sunshine of their golden hair.
On the round table in the hall
Another Ariadne's Crown
Out of the sky hath fallen down ;
More than one Monarch of the Moon
Is drumming with his silver spoon ;
The light of love shines over all.

O fortunate, O happy day !
The people sing, the people say.
The ancient bridegroom and the bride,
Smiling contented and serene
Upon the blithe, bewildering scene,
Behold, well pleased, on every side
Their forms and features multiplied,
As the reflection of a light
Between two burnished mirrors gleams,
Or lamps upon a bridge at night
Stretch on and on before the sight,
Till the long vista endless seems.

MORITURI SALUTAMUS

POEM FOR THE FIFTIETH AN-
NIVERSARY OF THE CLASS OF
1825 IN BOWDOIN COLLEGE

Tempora labuntur, tacitisque senescimus annis,
    Et fugiunt freno non remorante dies.
            OVID, *Fastorum*, Lib. vi.

In October, 1874, Mr. Longfellow was urged to write
a poem for the fiftieth anniversary of the graduation of
his college class to be held the next summer. At first
he said that he could not write the poem, so averse
was he from occasional poems, but a sudden thought
seems to have struck him, very likely upon seeing a
representation of Gerome's famous picture, and ten
days later he notes in his diary that he had finished the
writing. He not only wrote the poem, but what was a
rare act with him, read it before the audience gathered
in the church at Brunswick on the occasion of the anni-
versary. He expressed his relief when he found that
he could read his poem from the pulpit, and said, " Let
me cover myself as much as possible ; I wish it might
be entirely."

" O CÆSAR, we who are about to die
Salute you ! " was the gladiators' cry

In the arena, standing face to face
With death and with the Roman populace.

O ye familiar scenes, — ye groves of pine,
That once were mine and are no longer
    mine, —
Thou river, widening through the meadows
    green
To the vast sea, so near and yet unseen, —
Ye halls, in whose seclusion and repose
Phantoms of fame, like exhalations, rose
And vanished, — we who are about to die,
Salute you ; earth and air and sea and
    sky,
And the Imperial Sun that scatters down
His sovereign splendors upon grove and
    town.

Ye do not answer us ! ye do not hear !
We are forgotten ; and in your austere
And calm indifference, ye little care

Whether we come or go, or whence or
        where.
What passing generations fill these halls,
What passing voices echo from these walls,
Ye heed not ; we are only as the blast,
A moment heard, and then forever past.

Not so the teachers who in earlier days
Led our bewildered feet through learning's
        maze ;
They answer us — alas ! what have I said ?
What greetings come there from the voice-
        less dead ?
What salutation, welcome, or reply ?
What pressure from the hands that lifeless
        lie ?
They are no longer here ; they all are gone
Into the land of shadows, — all save one.
Honor and reverence, and the good repute
That follows faithful service as its fruit,
Be unto him, whom living we salute.

The great Italian poet, when he made
His dreadful journey to the realms of
        shade,
Met there the old instructor of his youth,
And cried in tones of pity and of ruth :
" Oh, never from the memory of my heart
Your dear, paternal image shall depart,
Who while on earth, ere yet by death
        surprised,
Taught me how mortals are immortalized ;
How grateful am I for that patient care
All my life long my language shall de-
        clare."

To-day we make the poet's words our own,
And utter them in plaintive undertone ;
Nor to the living only be they said,
But to the other living called the dead,
Whose dear, paternal images appear
Not wrapped in gloom, but robed in sun-
        shine here ;
Whose simple lives, complete and without
        flaw,
Were part and parcel of great Nature's
        law ;
Who said not to their Lord, as if afraid,
" Here is thy talent in a napkin laid,"
But labored in their sphere, as men who live
In the delight that work alone can give.
Peace be to them ; eternal peace and rest,
And the fulfilment of the great behest :
" Ye have been faithful over a few things,
Over ten cities shall ye reign as kings."

And ye who fill the places we once filled,
And follow in the furrows that we tilled,
Young men, whose generous hearts are
        beating high,
We who are old, and are about to die,
Salute you ; hail you ; take your hands in
        ours,
And crown you with our welcome as with
        flowers !

How beautiful is youth ! how bright it
        gleams
With its illusions, aspirations, dreams !
Book of Beginnings, Story without End,
Each maid a heroine, and each man a friend !
Aladdin's Lamp, and Fortunatus' Purse,
That holds the treasures of the universe !
All possibilities are in its hands,
No danger daunts it, and no foe with-
        stands ;
In its sublime audacity of faith,
" Be thou removed ! " it to the mountain
        saith,
And with ambitious feet, secure and proud,
Ascends the ladder leaning on the cloud !

As ancient Priam at the Scæan gate
Sat on the walls of Troy in regal state
With the old men, too old and weak to
        fight,
Chirping like grasshoppers in their de-
        light
To see the embattled hosts, with spear and
        shield,
Of Trojans and Achaians in the field ;
So from the snowy summits of our years
We see you in the plain, as each appears,
And question of you ; asking, " Who is he
That towers above the others ? Which may
        be
Atreides, Menelaus, Odysseus,
Ajax the great, or bold Idomeneus ? "

Let him not boast who puts his armor on
As he who puts it off, the battle done.
Study yourselves ; and most of all note
        well
Wherein kind Nature meant you to excel.
Not every blossom ripens into fruit ;
Minerva, the inventress of the flute,
Flung it aside, when she her face surveyed
Distorted in a fountain as she played ;
The unlucky Marsyas found it, and his
        fate
Was one to make the bravest hesitate.

Write on your doors the saying wise and
　　old,
"Be bold! be bold!" and everywhere,
　　" Be bold ;
Be not too bold !" Yet better the excess
Than the defect ; better the more than
　　less ;
Better like Hector in the field to die,
Than like a perfumed Paris turn and fly.

And now, my classmates ; ye remaining few
That number not the half of those we knew,
Ye, against whose familiar names not yet
The fatal asterisk of death is set,
Ye I salute ! The horologe of Time
Strikes the half-century with a solemn
　　chime,
And summons us together once again,
The joy of meeting not unmixed with pain.

Where are the others ? Voices from the
　　deep
Caverns of darkness answer me : " They
　　sleep ! "
I name no names ; instinctively I feel
Each at some well-remembered grave will
　　kneel,
And from the inscription wipe the weeds
　　and moss,
For every heart best knoweth its own loss.
I see their scattered gravestones gleaming
　　white
Through the pale dusk of the impending
　　night ;
O'er all alike the impartial sunset throws
Its golden lilies mingled with the rose ;
We give to each a tender thought, and pass
Out of the graveyards with their tangled
　　grass,
Unto these scenes frequented by our feet
When we were young, and life was fresh
　　and sweet.

What shall I say to you ? What can I say
Better than silence is ? When I survey
This throng of faces turned to meet my
　　own,
Friendly and fair, and yet to me unknown,
Transformed the very landscape seems to
　　be ;
It is the same, yet not the same to me.
So many memories crowd upon my brain,
So many ghosts are in the wooded plain,
I fain would steal away, with noiseless
　　tread,

As from a house where some one lieth dead.
I cannot go ; — I pause ; — I hesitate ;
My feet reluctant linger at the gate ;
As one who struggles in a troubled dream
To speak and cannot, to myself I seem.

Vanish the dream ! Vanish the idle fears !
Vanish the rolling mists of fifty years !
Whatever time or space may intervene,
I will not be a stranger in this scene.
Here every doubt, all indecision, ends ;
Hail, my companions, comrades, classmates,
　　friends !

Ah me ! the fifty years since last we met
Seem to me fifty folios bound and set
By Time, the great transcriber, on his
　　shelves,
Wherein are written the histories of our-
　　selves.
What tragedies, what comedies, are there ;
What joy and grief, what rapture and de-
　　spair !
What chronicles of triumph and defeat,
Of struggle, and temptation, and retreat !
What records of regrets, and doubts, and
　　fears !
What pages blotted, blistered by our tears !
What lovely landscapes on the margin
　　shine,
What sweet, angelic faces, what divine
And holy images of love and trust,
Undimmed by age, unsoiled by damp or
　　dust !

Whose hand shall dare to open and ex-
　　plore
These volumes, closed and clasped forever-
　　more ?
Not mine. With reverential feet I pass ;
I hear a voice that cries, " Alas ! alas !
Whatever hath been written shall remain,
Nor be erased nor written o'er again ;
The unwritten only still belongs to thee :
Take heed, and ponder well what that shall
　　be."

As children frightened by a thunder-cloud
Are reassured if some one reads aloud
A tale of wonder, with enchantment fraught,
Or wild adventure, that diverts their
　　thought,
Let me endeavor with a tale to chase
The gathering shadows of the time and
　　place,

And banish what we all too deeply feel
Wholly to say, or wholly to conceal.

In mediæval Rome, I know not where,
There stood an image with its arm in air,
And on its lifted finger, shining clear,
A golden ring with the device, "Strike
    here!"
Greatly the people wondered, though none
    guessed
The meaning that these words but half
    expressed,
Until a learned clerk, who at noonday
With downcast eyes was passing on his way,
Paused, and observed the spot, and marked
    it well,
Whereon the shadow of the finger fell;
And, coming back at midnight, delved, and
    found
A secret stairway leading underground.
Down this he passed into a spacious hall,
Lit by a flaming jewel on the wall;
And opposite, in threatening attitude,
With bow and shaft a brazen statue stood.
Upon its forehead, like a coronet,
Were these mysterious words of menace
    set:
"That which I am, I am; my fatal aim
None can escape, not even yon luminous
    flame!"

Midway the hall was a fair table placed,
With cloth of gold, and golden cups en-
    chased
With rubies, and the plates and knives were
    gold,
And gold the bread and viands manifold.
Around it, silent, motionless, and sad,
Were seated gallant knights in armor clad,
And ladies beautiful with plume and zone,
But they were stone, their hearts within
    were stone;
And the vast hall was filled in every part
With silent crowds, stony in face and heart.

Long at the scene, bewildered and amazed,
The trembling clerk in speechless wonder
    gazed;
Then from the table, by his greed made
    bold,
He seized a goblet and a knife of gold,
And suddenly from their seats the guests
    upsprang,
The vaulted ceiling with loud clamors rang,
The archer sped his arrow, at their call,

Shattering the lambent jewel on the wall,
And all was dark around and overhead; —
Stark on the floor the luckless clerk lay
    dead!

The writer of this legend then records
Its ghostly application in these words:
The image is the Adversary old,
Whose beckoning finger points to realms of
    gold;
Our lusts and passions are the downward
    stair
That leads the soul from a diviner air;
The archer, Death; the flaming jewel,
    Life;
Terrestrial goods, the goblet and the knife;
The knights and ladies, all whose flesh and
    bone
By avarice have been hardened into stone;
The clerk, the scholar whom the love of pelf
Tempts from his books and from his nobler
    self.

The scholar and the world! The endless
    strife,
The discord in the harmonies of life!
The love of learning, the sequestered nooks,
And all the sweet serenity of books;
The market-place, the eager love of gain,
Whose aim is vanity, and whose end is pain!

But why, you ask me, should this tale be
    told
To men grown old, or who are growing old?
It is too late! Ah, nothing is too late
Till the tired heart shall cease to palpitate.
Cato learned Greek at eighty; Sophocles
Wrote his grand Œdipus, and Simonides
Bore off the prize of verse from his com-
    peers,
When each had numbered more than four-
    score years,
And Theophrastus, at fourscore and ten,
Had but begun his "Characters of Men."
Chaucer, at Woodstock with the nightin-
    gales,
At sixty wrote the Canterbury Tales;
Goethe at Weimar, toiling to the last,
Completed Faust when eighty years were
    past.
These are indeed exceptions; but they show
How far the gulf-stream of our youth may
    flow
Into the arctic regions of our lives,
Where little else than life itself survives

As the barometer foretells the storm
While still the skies are clear, the weather
    warm,
So something in us, as old age draws near,
Betrays the pressure of the atmosphere.
The nimble mercury, ere we are aware,
Descends the elastic ladder of the air ;
The telltale blood in artery and vein
Sinks from its higher levels in the brain ;
Whatever poet, orator, or sage
May say of it, old age is still old age.
It is the waning, not the crescent moon ;
The dusk of evening, not the blaze of noon ;
It is not strength, but weakness ; not de-
    sire,
But its surcease ; not the fierce heat of
    fire,
The burning and consuming element,
But that of ashes and of embers spent,

In which some living sparks we still discern,
Enough to warm, but not enough to burn.

What then ?   Shall we sit idly down and
    say
The night hath come ; it is no longer day ?
The night hath not yet come ; we are not
    quite
Cut off from labor by the failing light ;
Something remains for us to do or dare ;
Even the oldest tree some fruit may bear ;
Not Œdipus Coloneus, or Greek Ode,
Or tales of pilgrims that one morning rode
Out of the gateway of the Tabard Inn,
But other something, would we but begin ;
For age is opportunity no less
Than youth itself, though in another dress,
And as the evening twilight fades away
The sky is filled with stars, invisible by day.

A BOOK OF SONNETS

THREE FRIENDS OF MINE

I

When I remember them, those friends of
    mine,
Who are no longer here, the noble three,
Who half my life were more than friends
    to me,
And whose discourse was like a generous
    wine,
I most of all remember the divine
Something, that shone in them, and made
    us see
The archetypal man, and what might be
The amplitude of Nature's first design.
In vain I stretch my hands to clasp their
    hands ;
I cannot find them.   Nothing now is left
But a majestic memory.   They mean-
    while
Wander together in Elysian lands,
Perchance remembering me, who am
    bereft
Of their dear presence, and, remember-
    ing, smile.

II

In Attica thy birthplace should have been,
Or the Ionian Isles, or where the seas

Encircle in their arms the Cyclades,
So wholly Greek wast thou in thy se-
    rene
And childlike joy of life, O Philhellene !
Around thee would have swarmed the
    Attic bees ;
Homer had been thy friend, or Socrates,
And Plato welcomed thee to his de-
    mesne.
For thee old legends breathed historic
    breath ;
Thou sawest Poseidon in the purple sea,
And in the sunset Jason's fleece of gold !
Oh, what hadst thou to do with cruel Death,
Who wast so full of life, or Death with
    thee,
That thou shouldst die before thou hadst
    grown old !

III

I stand again on the familiar shore,
And hear the waves of the distracted
    sea
Piteously calling and lamenting thee,
And waiting restless at thy cottage door.
The rocks, the sea-weed on the ocean floor,
The willows in the meadow, and the free
Wild winds of the Atlantic welcome me ;
Then why shouldst thou be dead, and
    come no more ?

Ah, why shouldst thou be dead, when com-
mon men
Are busy with their trivial affairs,
Having and holding ? Why, when thou
hadst read
Nature's mysterious manuscript, and then
Wast ready to reveal the truth it bears,
Why art thou silent ? Why shouldst
thou be dead ?

IV

River, that stealest with such silent pace
Around the City of the Dead, where lies
A friend who bore thy name, and whom
these eyes
Shall see no more in his accustomed
place,
Linger and fold him in thy soft embrace,
And say good night, for now the western
skies
Are red with sunset, and gray mists arise
Like damps that gather on a dead man's
face.
Good night ! good night ! as we so oft have
said
Beneath this roof at midnight, in the days
That are no more, and shall no more
return.
Thou hast but taken thy lamp and gone to
bed ;
I stay a little longer, as one stays
To cover up the embers that still burn.

V

The doors are all wide open ; at the gate
The blossomed lilacs counterfeit a blaze,
And seem to warm the air ; a dreamy
haze
Hangs o'er the Brighton meadows like a
fate,
And on their margin, with sea-tides elate,
The flooded Charles, as in the happier
days,
Writes the last letter of his name, and
stays
His restless steps, as if compelled to wait.
I also wait ; but they will come no more,
Those friends of mine, whose presence
satisfied
The thirst and hunger of my heart. Ah
me !
They have forgotten the pathway to my
door !

Something is gone from nature since they
died,
And summer is not summer, nor can be.

CHAUCER

An old man in a lodge within a park ;
The chamber walls depicted all around
With portraitures of huntsman, hawk,
and hound,
And the hurt deer. He listeneth to the
lark,
Whose song comes with the sunshine
through the dark
Of painted glass in leaden lattice bound ;
He listeneth and he laugheth at the
sound,
Then writeth in a book like any clerk.
He is the poet of the dawn, who wrote
The Canterbury Tales, and his old age
Made beautiful with song ; and as I read
I hear the crowing cock, I hear the note
Of lark and linnet, and from every page
Rise odors of ploughed field or flowery
mead.

SHAKESPEARE

A vision as of crowded city streets,
With human life in endless overflow ;
Thunder of thoroughfares ; trumpets
that blow
To battle ; clamor, in obscure retreats,
Of sailors landed from their anchored
fleets ;
Tolling of bells in turrets, and below
Voices of children, and bright flowers
that throw
O'er garden-walls their intermingled
sweets !
This vision comes to me when I unfold
The volume of the Poet paramount,
Whom all the Muses loved, not one
alone ; —
Into his hands they put the lyre of gold,
And, crowned with sacred laurel at their
fount,
Placed him as Musagetes on their throne.

MILTON

I pace the sounding sea-beach and behold
How the voluminous billows roll and run,

Upheaving and subsiding, while the sun
Shines through their sheeted emerald far
    unrolled,
And the ninth wave, slow gathering fold
    by fold
All its loose-flowing garments into one,
Plunges upon the shore, and floods the
    dun
Pale reach of sands, and changes them to
    gold.
So in majestic cadence rise and fall
    The mighty undulations of thy song,
    O sightless bard, England's Mæonides !
And ever and anon, high over all
    Uplifted, a ninth wave superb and
        strong,
    Floods all the soul with its melodious
        seas.

KEATS

THE young Endymion sleeps Endymion's
    sleep ;
    The shepherd-boy whose tale was left
        half told !
    The solemn grove uplifts its shield of
        gold
To the red rising moon, and loud and
    deep
The nightingale is singing from the steep ;
    It is midsummer, but the air is cold ;
    Can it be death ? Alas, beside the fold
A shepherd's pipe lies shattered near his
    sheep.
Lo ! in the moonlight gleams a marble
    white,
    On which I read : " Here lieth one whose
        name
    Was writ in water." And was this the
        meed
Of his sweet singing ? Rather let me
    write :
" The smoking flax before it burst to
    flame
Was quenched by death, and broken the
    bruised reed."

THE GALAXY

TORRENT of light and river of the air,
    Along whose bed the glimmering stars
        are seen
    Like gold and silver sands in some ravine
    Where mountain streams have left their
        channels bare !

The Spaniard sees in thee the pathway,
    where
    His patron saint descended in the sheen
    Of his celestial armor, on serene
    And quiet nights, when all the heavens
        were fair.
Not this I see, nor yet the ancient fable
    Of Phaeton's wild course, that scorched
        the skies
    Where'er the hoofs of his hot coursers
        trod ;
But the white drift of worlds o'er chasms
    of sable,
    The star-dust, that is whirled aloft and
        flies
    From the invisible chariot-wheels of God.

THE SOUND OF THE SEA

THE sea awoke at midnight from its sleep,
    And round the pebbly beaches far and
        wide
    I heard the first wave of the rising tide
Rush onward with uninterrupted sweep ;
A voice out of the silence of the deep,
    A sound mysteriously multiplied
    As of a cataract from the mountain's
        side,
Or roar of winds upon a wooded steep.
So comes to us at times, from the un-
    known
    And inaccessible solitudes of being,
    The rushing of the sea-tides of the soul ;
And inspirations, that we deem our own,
    Are some divine foreshadowing and fore-
        seeing
    Of things beyond our reason or control.

A SUMMER DAY BY THE SEA

THE sun is set ; and in his latest beams
    Yon little cloud of ashen gray and gold,
    Slowly upon the amber air unrolled,
    The falling mantle of the Prophet
        seems.
From the dim headlands many a light-house
    gleams,
    The street-lamps of the ocean ; and be-
        hold,
    O'erhead the banners of the night un-
        fold ;
    The day hath passed into the land of
        dreams.

O summer day beside the joyous sea !
  O summer day so wonderful and white,
  So full of gladness and so full of pain !
Forever and forever shalt thou be
  To some the gravestone of a dead delight,
  To some the landmark of a new domain.

THE TIDES

I SAW the long line of the vacant shore,
  The sea-weed and the shells upon the
    sand,
  And the brown rocks left bare on every
    hand,
As if the ebbing tide would flow no more.
Then heard I, more distinctly than before,
  The ocean breathe and its great breast
    expand,
  And hurrying came on the defenceless
    land
The insurgent waters with tumultuous
    roar.
All thought and feeling and desire, I said,
  Love, laughter, and the exultant joy of
    song
  Have ebbed from me forever ! Sud-
    denly o'er me
They swept again from their deep ocean bed,
  And in a tumult of delight, and strong
As youth, and beautiful as youth, upbore
    me.

A SHADOW

I SAID unto myself, if I were dead,
  What would befall these children ?
    What would be
  Their fate, who now are looking up to me
For help and furtherance ? Their lives,
    I said,
Would be a volume wherein I have read
  But the first chapters, and no longer see
  To read the rest of their dear history,
So full of beauty and so full of dread.
Be comforted ; the world is very old,
  And generations pass, as they have
    passed,
  A troop of shadows moving with the sun ;
Thousands of times has the old tale been
    told ;
  The world belongs to those who come
    the last,
  They will find hope and strength as we
    have done.

A NAMELESS GRAVE

A newspaper description of a burying ground in New-
port News, where, on the head-board of a soldier were
the words, " A Union Soldier mustered out," was sent
to Mr. Longfellow in 1864. Ten years passed before
the poet used the incident, for he wrote the sonnet No-
vember 30, 1874.

" A SOLDIER of the Union mustered out,"
  Is the inscription on an unknown grave
  At Newport. News, beside the salt-sea
    wave,
Nameless and dateless ; sentinel or scout
Shot down in skirmish, or disastrous rout
  Of battle, when the loud artillery drave
  Its iron wedges through the ranks of
    brave
And doomed battalions, storming the re-
    doubt.
Thou unknown hero sleeping by the sea
  In thy forgotten grave ! with secret
    shame
  I feel my pulses beat, my forehead burn,
When I remember thou hast given for
    me
  All that thou hadst, thy life, thy very
    name,
  And I can give thee nothing in return.

SLEEP

LULL me to sleep, ye winds, whose fitful
    sound
  Seems from some faint Æolian harp-
    string caught ;
  Seal up the hundred wakeful eyes of
    thought
As Hermes with his lyre in sleep pro-
    found
The hundred wakeful eyes of Argus bound ;
  For I am weary, and am overwrought
  With too much toil, with too much care
    distraught,
  And with the iron crown of anguish
    crowned.
Lay thy soft hand upon my brow and
    cheek,
  O peaceful Sleep ! until from pain re-
    leased
  I breathe again uninterrupted breath !
Ah, with what subtle meaning did the
    Greek
  Call thee the lesser mystery at the feast
  Whereof the greater mystery is death !

THE OLD BRIDGE AT FLORENCE

TADDEO GADDI built me. I am old,
　　Five centuries old. I plant my foot of
　　　stone
Upon the Arno, as St. Michael's own
Was planted on the dragon. Fold by
　　fold
Beneath me as it struggles, I behold
　　Its glistening scales. Twice hath it
　　　overthrown
　　My kindred and companions. Me alone
It moveth not, but is by me controlled.
I can remember when the Medici
　　Were driven from Florence ; longer still
　　　ago
The final wars of Ghibelline and Guelf.
Florence adorns me with her jewelry ;
　　And when I think that Michael Angelo
　　Hath leaned on me, I glory in myself.

IL PONTE VECCHIO DI FIRENZE

GADDI mi fece ; il Ponte Vecchio sono ;
　　Cinquecent' anni già sull' Arno pianto
　　Il piede, come il suo Michele Santo
Piantò sul draco. Mentre ch' io ragiono
Lo vedo torcere con flebil suono
　　Le rilucenti scaglie. Ha questi affranto
　　Due volte i miei maggior. Me solo in-
　　　tanto
Neppure muove, ed io non l' abbandono.
Io mi rammento quando fur cacciati
　　I Medici ; pur quando Ghibellino
　　E Guelfo fecer pace mi rammento.
Fiorenza i suoi giojelli m' ha prestati ;
　　E quando penso ch' Agnolo il divino
　　Su me posava, insuperbir mi sento.

NATURE

As a fond mother, when the day is o'er,
　　Leads by the hand her little child to
　　　bed,
　　Half willing, half reluctant to be led,
And leave his broken playthings on the
　　floor,
Still gazing at them through the open door,
　　Nor wholly reassured and comforted
　　By promises of others in their stead,
Which, though more splendid, may not
　　please him more ;

So Nature deals with us, and takes away
　　Our playthings one by one, and by the
　　　hand
　　Leads us to rest so gently, that we go
Scarce knowing if we wish to go or stay,
　　Being too full of sleep to understand
　　How far the unknown transcends the
　　　what we know.

IN THE CHURCHYARD AT TARRYTOWN

HERE lies the gentle humorist, who died
　　In the bright Indian Summer of his
　　　fame ;
　　A simple stone, with but a date and
　　　name,
Marks his secluded resting-place beside
The river that he loved and glorified.
　　Here in the autumn of his days he came,
　　But the dry leaves of life were all aflame
With tints that brightened and were
　　multiplied.
How sweet a life was his ; how sweet a
　　death !
　　Living, to wing with mirth the weary
　　　hours,
　　Or with romantic tales the heart to
　　　cheer ;
Dying, to leave a memory like the breath
　　Of summers full of sunshine and of
　　　showers,
　　A grief and gladness in the atmosphere.

ELIOT'S OAK

THOU ancient oak ! whose myriad leaves
　　are loud
　　With sounds of unintelligible speech,
　　Sounds as of surges on a shingly beach,
　　Or multitudinous murmurs of a crowd ;
With some mysterious gift of tongues
　　endowed,
　　Thou speakest a different dialect to
　　　each ;
　　To me a language that no man can
　　　teach,
　　Of a lost race, long vanished like a
　　　cloud.
For underneath thy shade, in days remote,
　　Seated like Abraham at eventide
　　Beneath the oaks of Mamre, the un-
　　　known

Apostle of the Indians, Eliot, wrote
His Bible in a language that hath died
And is forgotten, save by thee alone.

THE DESCENT OF THE MUSES

Mr. Longfellow was one day visiting Wellesley College, and was asked to write one of his poems. He begged for a few moments' delay, wrote this sonnet from memory, — it had not been printed, — and read it to the ladies.

NINE sisters, beautiful in form and face,
　Came from their convent on the shining
　　heights
Of Pierus, the mountain of delights,
　To dwell among the people at its base.
Then seemed the world to change. All
　　time and space,
　Splendor of cloudless days and starry
　　nights,
　And men and manners, and all sounds
　　and sights,
Had a new meaning, a diviner grace.
Proud were these sisters, but were not too
　　proud
　To teach in schools of little country
　　towns
Science and song, and all the arts that
　　please ;
So that while housewives span, and farmers
　　ploughed,
　Their comely daughters, clad in home-
　　spun gowns,
Learned the sweet songs of the Pierides.

VENICE

WHITE swan of cities, slumbering in thy
　　nest
　So wonderfully built among the reeds
　Of the lagoon, that fences thee and feeds,
As sayeth thy old historian and thy guest !
White water-lily, cradled and caressed
　By ocean streams, and from the silt and
　　weeds
　Lifting thy golden filaments and seeds,
Thy sun-illumined spires, thy crown and
　　crest !
White phantom city, whose untrodden
　　streets
　Are rivers, and whose pavements are the
　　shifting
　Shadows of palaces and strips of sky ;

I wait to see thee vanish like the fleets
　Seen in mirage, or towers of cloud up-
　　lifting
　In air their unsubstantial masonry.

THE POETS

O YE dead Poets, who are living still
　Immortal in your verse, though life be
　　fled,
　And ye, O living Poets, who are dead
Though ye are living, if neglect can kill,
Tell me if in the darkest hours of ill,
　With drops of anguish falling fast and
　　red
From the sharp crown of thorns upon
　　your head,
Ye were not glad your errand to fulfil ?
Yes ; for the gift and ministry of Song
　Have something in them so divinely
　　sweet,
It can assuage the bitterness of wrong ;
Not in the clamor of the crowded street,
　Not in the shouts and plaudits of the
　　throng,
But in ourselves, are triumph and defeat.

PARKER CLEAVELAND

WRITTEN ON REVISITING BRUNSWICK
IN THE SUMMER OF 1875

AMONG the many lives that I have known,
　None I remember more serene and sweet,
　More rounded in itself and more com-
　　plete,
Than his, who lies beneath this funeral
　　stone.
These pines, that murmur in low monotone,
　These walks frequented by scholastic
　　feet,
　Were all his world ; but in this calm
　　retreat
For him the Teacher's chair became a
　　throne.
With fond affection memory loves to dwell
　On the old days, when his example made
A pastime of the toil of tongue and pen ;
And now, amid the groves he loved so well
　That naught could lure him from their
　　grateful shade,
　He sleeps, but wakes elsewhere, for God
　　hath said, Amen !

THE HARVEST MOON

IT is the Harvest Moon ! On gilded
  vanes
  And roofs of villages, on woodland
    crests
  And their aerial neighborhoods of nests
Deserted, on the curtained window-panes
Of rooms where children sleep, on country
  lanes
  And harvest-fields, its mystic splendor
    rests !
  Gone are the birds that were our summer
    guests ;
  With the last sheaves return the labor-
    ing wains !
All things are symbols : the external
  shows
  Of Nature have their image in the
    mind,
  As flowers and fruits and falling of the
    leaves ;
The song-birds leave us at the summer's
  close,
  Only the empty nests are left behind,
  And pipings of the quail among the
    sheaves.

TO THE RIVER RHONE

THOU Royal River, born of sun and shower
  In chambers purple with the Alpine
    glow,
  Wrapped in the spotless ermine of the
    snow
  And rocked by tempests ! — at the ap-
    pointed hour
Forth, like a steel-clad horseman from a
  tower,
  With clang and clink of harness dost
    thou go
  To meet thy vassal torrents, that below
  Rush to receive thee and obey thy
    power.
And now thou movest in triumphal march,
  A king among the rivers ! On thy way
  A hundred towns await and welcome
    thee ;
Bridges uplift for thee the stately arch,
  Vineyards encircle thee with garlands
    gay,
  And fleets attend thy progress to the
    sea !

THE THREE SILENCES OF MOLINOS

TO JOHN GREENLEAF WHITTIER

Written to be read at the dinner given by the pub-
lishers of *The Atlantic Monthly* to Mr. Whittier in honor
of his seventieth birthday, December 18, 1877.

THREE Silences there are : the first of
  speech,
  The second of desire, the third of
    thought ;
  This is the lore a Spanish monk, dis-
    traught
  With dreams and visions, was the first to
    teach.
These Silences, commingling each with
  each,
  Made up the perfect Silence that he
    sought
  And prayed for, and wherein at times he
    caught
  Mysterious sounds from realms beyond
    our reach.
O thou, whose daily life anticipates
  The life to come, and in whose thought
    and word
  The spiritual world preponderates,
Hermit of Amesbury ! thou too hast heard
  Voices and melodies from beyond the
    gates,
  And speakest only when thy soul is
    stirred !

THE TWO RIVERS

I

SLOWLY the hour-hand of the clock moves
  round ;
  So slowly that no human eye hath power
  To see it move ! Slowly in shine or
    shower
  The painted ship above it, homeward
    bound,
Sails, but seems motionless, as if aground ;
  Yet both arrive at last ; and in his tower
  The slumberous watchman wakes and
    strikes the hour,
  A mellow, measured, melancholy sound.
Midnight ! the outpost of advancing day !
  The frontier town and citadel of night !
  The watershed of Time, from which the
    streams

Of Yesterday and To-morrow take their
way,
  One to the land of promise and of light,
  One to the land of darkness and of
    dreams !

II

O River of Yesterday, with current swift
  Through chasms descending, and soon
    lost to sight,
  I do not care to follow in their flight
  The faded leaves, that on thy bosom
    drift !
O River of To-morrow, I uplift
  Mine eyes, and thee I follow, as the night
Wanes into morning, and the dawning
    light
  Broadens, and all the shadows fade and
    shift !
I follow, follow, where thy waters run
  Through unfrequented, unfamiliar fields,
  Fragrant with flowers and musical with
    song ;
Still follow, follow ; sure to meet the sun,
  And confident, that what the future
    yields
  Will be the right, unless myself be
    wrong.

III

Yet not in vain, O River of Yesterday,
  Through chasms of darkness to the deep
    descending,
  I heard thee sobbing in the rain, and
    blending
  Thy voice with other voices far away.
I called to thee, and yet thou wouldst not
    stay,
  But turbulent, and with thyself contend-
    ing,
  And torrent-like thy force on pebbles
    spending,
  Thou wouldst not listen to a poet's lay.
Thoughts, like a loud and sudden rush of
    wings,
  Regrets and recollections of things past,
  With hints and prophecies of things to be,
And inspirations, which, could they be
    things,
  And stay with us, and we could hold
    them fast,
  Were our good angels, — these I owe to
    thee.

IV

And thou, O River of To-morrow, flowing
  Between thy narrow adamantine walls,
  But beautiful, and white with waterfalls,
  And wreaths of mist, like hands the path-
    way showing ;
I hear the trumpets of the morning blowing,
  I hear thy mighty voice, that calls and
    calls,
  And see, as Ossian saw in Morven's halls,
  Mysterious phantoms, coming, beckoning,
    going !
It is the mystery of the unknown
  That fascinates us ; we are children still,
  Wayward and wistful ; with one hand we
    cling
To the familiar things we call our own,
  And with the other, resolute of will,
  Grope in the dark for what the day will
    bring.

BOSTON

St. Botolph's Town ! Hither across the
    plains
  And fens of Lincolnshire, in garb austere,
  There came a Saxon monk, and founded
    here
  A Priory, pillaged by marauding Danes,
So that thereof no vestige now remains ;
  Only a name, that, spoken loud and clear,
  And echoed in another hemisphere,
  Survives the sculptured walls and painted
    panes.
St. Botolph's Town ! Far over leagues of
    land
  And leagues of sea looks forth its noble
    tower,
  And far around the chiming bells are
    heard ;
So may that sacred name forever stand
  A landmark, and a symbol of the power,
  That lies concentred in a single word.

ST. JOHN'S, CAMBRIDGE

The memorial chapel of St. John's, erected by Robert
Means Mason in connection with the Episcopal Theolo-
gical School, stands close by the home of Mr. Longfellow.

I STAND beneath the tree, whose branches
    shade
  Thy western window, Chapel of St.
    John !

And hear its leaves repeat their benison
  On him, whose hand thy stones memorial
    laid ;
Then I remember one of whom was said
  In the world's darkest hour, " Behold
    thy son ! "
And see him living still, and wandering on
  And waiting for the advent long delayed.
Not only tongues of the apostles teach
  Lessons of love and light, but these ex-
    panding
  And sheltering boughs with all their
    leaves implore,
And say in language clear as human speech,
  " The peace of God, that passeth under-
    standing,
  Be and abide with you forevermore ! "

MOODS

Oh that a Song would sing itself to me
  Out of the heart of Nature, or the heart
Of man, the child of Nature, not of Art,
  Fresh as the morning, salt as the salt sea,
With just enough of bitterness to be
  A medicine to this sluggish mood, and
    start
The life-blood in my veins, and so impart
  Healing and help in this dull lethargy !
Alas ! not always doth the breath of song
  Breathe on us. It is like the wind that
    bloweth
At its own will, not ours, nor tarrieth long ;
We hear the sound thereof, but no man
    knoweth
  From whence it comes, so sudden and
    swift and strong,
  Nor whither in its wayward course it
    goeth.

WOODSTOCK PARK

Here in a little rustic hermitage
  Alfred the Saxon King, Alfred the Great,
  Postponed the cares of king-craft to
    translate
The Consolations of the Roman sage.
Here Geoffrey Chaucer in his ripe old age
  Wrote the unrivalled Tales, which soon
    or late
  The venturous hand that strives to imitate
  Vanquished must fall on the unfinished
    page.

Two kings were they, who ruled by right
    divine,
  And both supreme ; one in the realm of
    Truth,
  One in the realm of Fiction and of Song.
What prince hereditary of their line,
  Uprising in the strength and flush of
    youth,
  Their glory shall inherit and prolong ?

THE FOUR PRINCESSES AT WILNA

A PHOTOGRAPH

Sweet faces, that from pictured casements
    lean
  As from a castle window, looking down
  On some gay pageant passing through a
    town,
  Yourselves the fairest figures in the
    scene ;
With what a gentle grace, with what serene
  Unconsciousness ye wear the triple
    crown
  Of youth and beauty and the fair re-
    nown
  Of a great name, that ne'er hath tarnished
    been !
From your soft eyes, so innocent and sweet,
  Four spirits, sweet and innocent as they,
  Gaze on the world below, the sky above ;
Hark ! there is some one singing in the
    street ;
  " Faith, Hope, and Love ! these three,"
    he seems to say ;
  " These three ; and greatest of the three
    is Love."

HOLIDAYS

The holiest of all holidays are those
  Kept by ourselves in silence and apart ;
  The secret anniversaries of the heart,
  When the full river of feeling over-
    flows ; —
The happy days unclouded to their close ;
  The sudden joys that out of darkness
    start
  As flames from ashes ; swift desires that
    dart
  Like swallows singing down each wind
    that blows !

White as the gleam of a receding sail,
  White as a cloud that floats and fades in
    air,
White as the whitest lily on a stream,
These tender memories are ; — a fairy tale
  Of some enchanted land we know not
    where,
But lovely as a landscape in a dream.

WAPENTAKE

TO ALFRED TENNYSON

POET ! I come to touch thy lance with mine ;
  Not as a knight, who on the listed field
  Of tourney touched his adversary's shield
In token of defiance, but in sign
Of homage to the mastery, which is thine,
  In English song ; nor will I keep con-
    cealed,
  And voiceless as a rivulet frost-congealed,
My admiration for thy verse divine.
Not of the howling dervishes of song,
  Who craze the brain with their delirious
    dance,
  Art thou, O sweet historian of the heart !
Therefore· to thee the laurel - leaves be-
    long,
  To thee our love and our allegiance,
  For thy allegiance to the poet's art.

THE BROKEN OAR

" November 13, 1864. Stay at home and ponder upon
Dante. I am frequently tempted to write upon my
work the inscription found upon an oar cast on the
coast of Iceland,—

  Oft war ek dasa durek ðro thick.
  Oft was I weary when I tugged at thee."

ONCE upon Iceland's solitary strand
  A poet wandered with his book and pen,
Seeking some final word, some sweet
    Amen,
Wherewith to close the volume in his
    hand.
The billows rolled and plunged upon the
    sand,
  The circling sea-gulls swept beyond his
    ken,
  And from the parting cloud-rack now and
    then
Flashed the red sunset over sea and land.
Then by the billows at his feet was tossed
  A broken oar ; and carved thereon he
    read :
  "Oft was I weary, when I toiled at
    thee ; "
And like a man, who findeth what was lost,
  He wrote the words, then lifted up his
    head,
  And flung his useless pen into the sea.

THE· CROSS OF SNOW

IN the long, sleepless watches of the night,
  A gentle face — the face of one long
    dead —
  Looks at me from the wall, where round
    its head
The night-lamp casts a halo of pale light.
Here in this room she died ; and soul more
    white
  Never through martyrdom of fire was led
  To its repose ; nor can in books be read
The legend of a life more benedight.
There is a mountain in the distant West
  That, sun-defying, in its deep ravines
  Displays a cross of snow upon its side.
Such is the cross I wear upon my breast
  These eighteen years, through all the
    changing scenes
  And seasons, changeless since the day
    she died.

BIRDS OF PASSAGE

FLIGHT THE FOURTH

The first draft of the first poem was made March 30, 1874. It did not satisfy the poet, for he wrote, April 2:

"I have been trying to write something about Sumner but to little purpose. I cannot collect my faculties."

CHARLES SUMNER

GARLANDS upon his grave
And flowers upon his hearse,
And to the tender heart and brave
The tribute of this verse.

His was the troubled life,
The conflict and the pain,
The grief, the bitterness of strife,
The honor without stain.

Like Winkelried, he took
Into his manly breast
The sheaf of hostile spears, and broke
A path for the oppressed.

Then from the fatal field
Upon a nation's heart
Borne like a warrior on his shield ! —
So should the brave depart.

Death takes us by surprise,
And stays our hurrying feet ;
The great design unfinished lies,
Our lives are incomplete.

But in the dark unknown
Perfect their circles seem,
Even as a bridge's arch of stone
Is rounded in the stream.

Alike are life and death,
When life in death survives,
And the uninterrupted breath
Inspires a thousand lives.

Were a star quenched on high,
For ages would its light,
Still travelling downward from the
     sky,
Shine on our mortal sight.

So when a great man dies,
For years beyond our ken,
The light he leaves behind him lies
Upon the paths of men.

TRAVELS BY THE FIRESIDE

Written October 7, 1874, as introduction to the series of volumes, *Poems of Places*, edited by Mr. Longfellow.

THE ceaseless rain is falling fast,
And yonder gilded vane,
Immovable for three days past,
Points to the misty main.

It drives me in upon myself
And to the fireside gleams,
To pleasant books that crowd my shelf,
And still more pleasant dreams.

I read whatever bards have sung
Of lands beyond the sea,
And the bright days when I was young
Come thronging back to me.

In fancy I can hear again
The Alpine torrent's roar,
The mule-bells on the hills of Spain,
The sea at Elsinore.

I see the convent's gleaming wall
Rise from its groves of pine,
And towers of old cathedrals tall,
And castles by the Rhine.

I journey on by park and spire,
Beneath centennial trees,
Through fields with poppies all on fire,
And gleams of distant seas.

I fear no more the dust and heat,
No more I feel fatigue,
While journeying with another's feet
O'er many a lengthening league.

Let others traverse sea and land,
And toil through various climes,
I turn the world round with my hand
Reading these poets' rhymes.

From them I learn whatever lies
Beneath each changing zone,
And see, when looking with their eyes,
Better than with mine own.

CADENABBIA

LAKE OF COMO

No sound of wheels or hoof-beat breaks
    The silence of the summer day,
As by the loveliest of all lakes
    I while the idle hours away.

I pace the leafy colonnade,
    Where level branches of the plane
Above me weave a roof of shade
    Impervious to the sun and rain.

At times a sudden rush of air
    Flutters the lazy leaves o'erhead,
And gleams of sunshine toss and flare
    Like torches down the path I tread.

By Somariva's garden gate
    I make the marble stairs my seat,
And hear the water, as I wait,
    Lapping the steps beneath my feet.

The undulation sinks and swells
    Along the stony parapets,
And far away the floating bells
    Tinkle upon the fisher's nets.

Silent and slow, by tower and town
    The freighted barges come and go,
Their pendent shadows gliding down
    By town and tower submerged below.

The hills sweep upward from the shore,
    With villas scattered one by one
Upon their wooded spurs, and lower
    Bellaggio blazing in the sun.

And dimly seen, a tangled mass
    Of walls and woods, of light and shade,
Stands, beckoning up the Stelvio Pass,
    Varenna with its white cascade.

I ask myself, Is this a dream?
    Will it all vanish into air?
Is there a land of such supreme
    And perfect beauty anywhere?

Sweet vision! Do not fade away:
    Linger, until my heart shall take
Into itself the summer day,
    And all the beauty of the lake;

Linger, until upon my brain
    Is stamped an image of the scene;
Then fade into the air again,
    And be as if thou hadst not been.

MONTE CASSINO

TERRA DI LAVORO

BEAUTIFUL valley! through whose verdant meads
    Unheard the Garigliano glides along; —
The Liris, nurse of rushes and of reeds,
    The river taciturn of classic song.

The Land of Labor and the Land of Rest,
    Where mediæval towns are white on all
The hillsides, and where every mountain's crest
    Is an Etrurian or a Roman wall.

There is Alagna, where Pope Boniface
    Was dragged with contumely from his throne;
Sciarra Colonna, was that day's disgrace
    The Pontiff's only, or in part thine own?

There is Ceprano, where a renegade
    Was each Apulian, as great Dante saith,
When Manfred by his men-at-arms betrayed
    Spurred on to Benevento and to death.

There is Aquinum, the old Volscian town,
    Where Juvenal was born, whose lurid light
Still hovers o'er his birthplace like the crown
    Of splendor seen o'er cities in the night.

Doubled the splendor is, that in its streets
    The Angelic Doctor as a school-boy played,
And dreamed perhaps the dreams, that he repeats
    In ponderous folios for scholastics made.

And there, uplifted, like a passing cloud
    That pauses on a mountain summit high,
Monte Cassino's convent rears its proud
    And venerable walls against the sky.

Well I remember how on foot I climbed
  The stony pathway leading to its gate ;
Above,   the   convent   bells   for   vespers
    chimed,
    Below,   the   darkening   town   grew   deso-
      late.

Well I remember the low arch and dark,
  The courtyard with its well, the terrace
    wide,
From   which,   far   down,   the   valley   like   a
    park,
  Veiled in the evening mists, was dim de-
    scried.

The day was dying, and with feeble hands
  Caressed the mountain-tops ; the vales
    between
Darkened ; the river in the meadow-lands
  Sheathed itself as a sword, and was not
    seen.

The silence of the place was like a sleep,
  So full of rest it seemed ; each passing
    tread
Was a reverberation from the deep
  Recesses of the ages that are dead.

For, more than thirteen centuries ago,
  Benedict fleeing from the gates of Rome,
A youth disgusted with its vice and woe,
  Sought in these mountain solitudes a
    home.

He founded here his Convent and his Rule
  Of prayer and work, and counted work
    as prayer ;
The pen became a clarion, and his school
  Flamed like a beacon in the midnight
    air.

What though Boccaccio, in his reckless
    way,
  Mocking the lazy brotherhood, deplores
The illuminated manuscripts, that lay
  Torn and neglected on the dusty floors ?

Boccaccio was a novelist, a child
  Of fancy and of fiction at the best !
This the urbane librarian said, and smiled
  Incredulous, as at some idle jest.

Upon such themes as these, with one young
    friar
  I sat conversing late into the night,

Till in its cavernous chimney the wood-fire
  Had   burnt   its   heart   out   like   an   an-
    chorite.

And then translated, in my convent cell,
  Myself yet not myself, in dreams I lay,
And, as a monk who hears the matin bell,
  Started   from   sleep ; — already   it   was
    day.

From the high window I beheld the scene
  On which Saint Benedict so oft had
    gazed, —
The mountains and the valley in the sheen
  Of the bright sun, — and stood as one
    amazed.

Gray mists were rolling, rising, vanishing ;
  The woodlands glistened with their jew-
    elled crowns ;
Far off the mellow bells began to ring
  For matins in the half-awakened towns.

The conflict of the Present and the Past,
  The ideal and the actual in our life,
As on a field of battle held me fast,
  Where this world and the next world
    were at strife.

For, as the valley from its sleep awoke,
  I saw the iron horses of the steam
Toss to the morning air their plumes of
    smoke,
  And woke, as one awaketh from a dream.

AMALFI

Sweet the memory is to me
Of a land beyond the sea,
Where the waves and mountains meet,
Where amid her mulberry-trees
Sits Amalfi in the heat,
Bathing ever her white feet
In the tideless summer seas.

In the middle of the town,
From its fountains in the hills,
Tumbling through the narrow gorge,
The Canneto rushes down,
Turns the great wheels of the mills,
Lifts the hammers of the forge.

'T is a stairway, not a street,
That ascends the deep ravine,

Where the torrent leaps between
Rocky walls that almost meet.
Toiling up from stair to stair
Peasant girls their burdens bear ;
Sunburnt daughters of the soil,
Stately figures tall and straight,
What inexorable fate
Dooms them to this life of toil ?

Lord of vineyards and of lands,
Far above the convent stands.
On its terraced walk aloof
Leans a monk with folded hands.
Placid, satisfied, serene,
Looking down upon the scene
Over wall and red-tiled roof ;
Wondering unto what good end
All this toil and traffic tend,
And why all men cannot be
Free from care and free from pain,
And the sordid love of gain,
And as indolent as he.

Where are now the freighted barks
From the marts of east and west ?
Where the knights in iron sarks
Journeying to the Holy Land,
Glove of steel upon the hand,
Cross of crimson on the breast ?
Where the pomp of camp and court ?
Where the pilgrims with their prayers ?
Where the merchants with their wares,
And their gallant brigantines
Sailing safely into port
Chased by corsair Algerines ?

Vanished like a fleet of cloud,
Like a passing trumpet-blast,
Are those splendors of the past,
And the commerce and the crowd !
Fathoms deep beneath the seas
Lie the ancient wharves and quays,
Swallowed by the engulfing waves ;
Silent streets and vacant halls,
Ruined roofs and towers and walls ;
Hidden from all mortal eyes
Deep the sunken city lies :
Even cities have their graves !

This is an enchanted land !
Round the headlands far away
Sweeps the blue Salernian bay
With its sickle of white sand :
Further still and furthermost
On the dim discovered coast

Pæstum with its ruins lies,
And its roses all in bloom
Seem to tinge the fatal skies
Of that lonely land of doom.

On his terrace, high in air,
Nothing doth the good monk care
For such worldly themes as these.
From the garden just below
Little puffs of perfume blow,
And a sound is in his ears
Of the murmur of the bees
In the shining chestnut trees ;
Nothing else he heeds or hears.
All the landscape seems to swoon
In the happy afternoon ;
Slowly o'er his senses creep
The encroaching waves of sleep,
And he sinks as sank the town,
Unresisting, fathoms down,
Into caverns cool and deep !

Walled about with drifts of snow,
Hearing the fierce north-wind blow,
Seeing all the landscape white
And the river cased in ice,
Comes this memory of delight,
Comes this vision unto me
Of a long-lost Paradise
In the land beyond the sea.

THE SERMON OF ST. FRANCIS

Up soared the lark into the air,
A shaft of song, a winged prayer,
As if a soul released from pain
Were flying back to heaven again.

St. Francis heard : it was to him
An emblem of the Seraphim ;
The upward motion of the fire,
The light, the heat, the heart's desire.

Around Assisi's convent gate
The birds, God's poor who cannot wait,
From moor and mere and darksome
    wood
Come flocking for their dole of food.

"O brother birds," St. Francis said,
"Ye come to me and ask for bread,
But not with bread alone to-day
Shall ye be fed and sent away.

" Ye shall be fed, ye happy birds,
With manna of celestial words ;
Not mine, though mine they seem to be,
Not mine, though they be spoken through me.

" Oh, doubly are ye bound to praise
The great Creator in your lays ;
He giveth you your plumes of down,
Your crimson hoods, your cloaks of brown.

" He giveth you your wings to fly
And breathe a purer air on high,
And careth for you everywhere,
Who for yourselves so little care ! "

With flutter of swift wings and songs
Together rose the feathered throngs,
And singing scattered far apart ;
Deep peace was in St. Francis' heart.

He knew not if the brotherhood
His homily had understood ;
He only knew that to one ear
The meaning of his words was clear.

BELISARIUS

I AM poor and old and blind ;
The sun burns me, and the wind
    Blows through the city gate,
And covers me with dust
From the wheels of the august
    Justinian the Great.

It was for him I chased
The Persians o'er wild and waste,
    As General of the East ;
Night after night I lay
In their camps of yesterday ;
    Their forage was my feast.

For him, with sails of red,
And torches at mast-head,
    Piloting the great fleet,
I swept the Afric coasts
And scattered the Vandal hosts,
    Like dust in a windy street.

For him I won again
The Ausonian realm and reign,
    Rome and Parthenope ;
And all the land was mine
From the summits of Apennine
    To the shores of either sea.

For him, in my feeble age,
I dared the battle's rage,
    To save Byzantium's state,
When the tents of Zabergan
Like snow-drifts overran
    The road to the Golden Gate.

And for this, for this, behold !
Infirm and blind and old,
    With gray, uncovered head,
Beneath the very arch
Of my triumphal march,
    I stand and beg my bread !

Methinks I still can hear,
Sounding distinct and near,
    The Vandal monarch's cry,
As, captive and disgraced,
With majestic step he paced, —
    " All, all is Vanity ! "

Ah ! vainest of all things
Is the gratitude of kings ;
    The plaudits of the crowd
Are but the clatter of feet
At midnight in the street,
    Hollow and restless and loud.

But the bitterest disgrace
Is to see forever the face
    Of the Monk of Ephesus !
The unconquerable will
This, too, can bear ; — I still
    Am Belisarius !

SONGO RIVER

Songo River is a winding stream which connects Lake Sebago with Long Lake in Cumberland County, Maine. Among the early literary plans of Mr. Longfellow was one for a prose tale, the scene of which was to be laid near Lake Sebago. This poem was written September 18, 1875, after a visit to the river in the summer then closing.

NOWHERE such a devious stream,
Save in fancy or in dream,
Winding   slow   through   bush   and
        brake,
Links together lake and lake.

Walled with woods or sandy shelf,
Ever doubling on itself
Flows the stream, so still and slow
That it hardly seems to flow.

Never errant knight of old,
Lost in woodland or on wold,
Such a winding path pursued
Through the sylvan solitude.

Never school-boy, in his quest
After hazel-nut or nest,
Through the forest in and out
Wandered loitering thus about.

In the mirror of its tide
Tangled thickets on each side
Hang inverted, and between
Floating cloud or sky serene.

Swift or swallow on the wing
Seems the only living thing,
Or the loon, that laughs and flies
Down to those reflected skies.

Silent stream ! thy Indian name
Unfamiliar is to fame ;

For thou hidest here alone,
Well content to be unknown.

But thy tranquil waters teach
Wisdom deep as human speech,
Moving without haste or noise
In unbroken equipoise.

Though thou turnest no busy mill,
And art ever calm and still,
Even thy silence seems to say
To the traveller on his way : —

"Traveller, hurrying from the heat
Of the city, stay thy feet !
Rest awhile, nor longer waste
Life with inconsiderate haste !

"Be not like a stream that brawls
Loud with shallow waterfalls,
But in quiet self-control
Link together soul and soul."

KÉRAMOS

*Turn, turn, my wheel !   Turn round and
    round
Without a pause, without a sound :
    So spins the flying world away !
This clay, well mixed with marl and sand,
Follows the motion of my hand ;
For some must follow, and some command,
    Though all are made of clay !*

Thus sang the Potter at his task
Beneath the blossoming hawthorn-tree,
While o'er his features, like a mask,
The quilted sunshine and leaf-shade
Moved, as the boughs above him swayed,
And clothed him, till he seemed to be
A figure woven in tapestry,
So sumptuously was he arrayed
In that magnificent attire
Of sable tissue flaked with fire.
Like a magician he appeared,
A conjurer without book or beard ;
And while he plied his magic art —
For it was magical to me —
I stood in silence and apart,
And wondered more and more to see
That shapeless, lifeless mass of clay
Rise up to meet the master's hand,
And now contract and now expand,
And even his slightest touch obey ;

While ever in a thoughtful mood
He sang his ditty, and at times
Whistled a tune between the rhymes,
As a melodious interlude.

*Turn, turn, my wheel ! All things must change
To something new, to something strange ;
    Nothing that is can pause or stay ;
The moon will wax, the moon will wane,
The mist and cloud will turn to rain,
The rain to mist and cloud again,
    To-morrow be to-day.*

Thus still the Potter sang, and still,
By some unconscious act of will,
The melody and even the words
Were intermingled with my thought,
As bits of colored thread are caught
And woven into nests of birds.
And thus to regions far remote,
Beyond the ocean's vast expanse,
This wizard in the motley coat
Transported me on wings of song,
And by the northern shores of France
Bore me with restless speed along.

What land is this that seems to be
A mingling of the land and sea ?
This land of sluices, dikes, and dunes ?

This water-net, that tessellates
The landscape ? this unending maze
Of gardens, through whose latticed gates
The imprisoned pinks and tulips gaze ;
Where in long summer afternoons
The sunshine, softened by the haze,
Comes streaming down as through a screen ;
Where over fields and pastures green
The painted ships float high in air,
And over all and everywhere
The sails of windmills sink and soar
Like wings of sea-gulls on the shore ?

What land is this ?   Yon pretty town
Is Delft, with all its wares displayed ;
The pride, the market-place, the crown
And centre of the Potter's trade.
See ! every house and room is bright
With glimmers of reflected light
From plates that on the dresser shine ;
Flagons to foam with Flemish beer,
Or sparkle with the Rhenish wine,
And pilgrim flasks with fleurs-de-lis,
And ships upon a rolling sea,
And tankards pewter topped, and queer
With comic mask and musketeer !
Each hospitable chimney smiles
A welcome from its painted tiles ;
The parlor walls, the chamber floors,
The stairways and the corridors,
The borders of the garden walks,
Are beautiful with fadeless flowers,
That never droop in winds or showers,
And never wither on their stalks.

Turn, turn, my wheel !   All life is brief;
What now is bud will soon be leaf,
*   What now is leaf will soon decay ;*
The wind blows east, the wind blows west ;
The blue eggs in the robin's nest
Will soon have wings and beak and breast,
*   And flutter and fly away.*

Now southward through the air I glide,
The song my only pursuivant,
And see across the landscape wide
The blue Charente, upon whose tide
The belfries and the spires of Saintes
Ripple and rock from side to side,
As, when an earthquake rends its walls,
A crumbling city reels and falls.

Who is it in the suburbs here,
This Potter, working with such cheer,
In this mean house, this mean attire,
His manly features bronzed with fire,

Whose figulines and rustic wares
Scarce find him bread from day to day ?
This madman, as the people say,
Who breaks his tables and his chairs
To feed his furnace fires, nor cares
Who goes unfed if they are fed,
Nor who may live if they are dead ?
This alchemist with hollow cheeks
And sunken, searching eyes, who seeks,
By mingled earths and ores combined
With potency of fire, to find
Some new enamel, hard and bright,
His dream, his passion, his delight ?

O Palissy ! within thy breast
Burned the hot fever of unrest ;
Thine was the prophet's vision, thine
The exultation, the divine
Insanity of noble minds,
That never falters nor abates,
But labors and endures and waits,
Till all that it foresees it finds,
Or what it cannot find creates !

Turn, turn, my wheel !   This earthen jar
A touch can make, a touch can mar ;
*   And shall it to the Potter say,*
What makest thou ?   Thou hast no hand ?
As men who think to understand
A world by their Creator planned,
*   Who wiser is than they.*

Still guided by the dreamy song,
As in a trance I float along
Above the Pyrenean chain,
Above the fields and farms of Spain,
Above the bright Majorcan isle
That lends its softened name to art, —
A spot, a dot upon the chart,
Whose little towns, red-roofed with tile,
Are ruby-lustred with the light
Of blazing furnaces by night,
And crowned by day with wreaths of smoke.
Then eastward, wafted in my flight
On my enchanter's magic cloak,
I sail across the Tyrrhene Sea
Into the land of Italy,
And o'er the windy Apennines,
Mantled and musical with pines.

The palaces, the princely halls,
The doors of houses and the walls
Of churches and of belfry towers,
Cloister and castle, street and mart,
Are garlanded and gay with flowers
That blossom in the fields of art

Here Gubbio's workshops gleam and glow
With brilliant, iridescent dyes,
The dazzling whiteness of the snow,
The cobalt blue of summer skies ;
And vase and scutcheon, cup and plate,
In perfect finish emulate
Faenza, Florence, Pesaro.

Forth from Urbino's gate there came
A youth with the angelic name
Of Raphael, in form and face
Himself angelic, and divine
In arts of color and design.
From him Francesco Xanto caught
Something of his transcendent grace,
And into fictile fabrics wrought
Suggestions of the master's thought.
Nor less Maestro Giorgio shines
With madre-perl and golden lines
Of arabesques, and interweaves
His birds and fruits and flowers and leaves
About some landscape, shaded brown,
With olive tints on rock and town.

Behold this cup within whose bowl,
Upon a ground of deepest blue
With yellow-lustred stars o'erlaid,
Colors of every tint and hue
Mingle in one harmonious whole !
With large blue eyes and steadfast gaze,
Her yellow hair in net and braid,
Necklace and ear-rings all ablaze
With golden lustre o'er the glaze,
A woman's portrait ; on the scroll,
Cana, the Beautiful ! A name
Forgotten save for such brief fame
As this memorial can bestow, —
A gift some lover long ago
Gave with his heart to this fair dame.

A nobler title to renown
Is thine, O pleasant Tuscan town,
Seated beside the Arno's stream ;
For Luca della Robbia there
Created forms so wondrous fair,
They made thy sovereignty supreme.
These choristers with lips of stone,
Whose music is not heard, but seen,
Still chant, as from their organ-screen,
Their Maker's praise ; nor these alone,
But the more fragile forms of clay,
Hardly less beautiful than they,
These saints and angels that adorn
The walls of hospitals, and tell
The story of good deeds so well

That poverty seems less forlorn,
And life more like a holiday.

Here in this old neglected church,
That long eludes the traveller's search,
Lies the dead bishop on his tomb ;
Earth upon earth he slumbering lies,
Life-like and death-like in the gloom ;
Garlands of fruit and flowers in bloom
And foliage deck his resting-place ;
A shadow in the sightless eyes,
A pallor on the patient face,
Made perfect by the furnace heat ;
All earthly passions and desires
Burnt out by purgatorial fires ;
Seeming to say, " Our years are fleet,
And to the weary death is sweet."

But the most wonderful of all
The ornaments on tomb or wall
That grace the fair Ausonian shores
Are those the faithful earth restores,
Near some Apulian town concealed,
In vineyard or in harvest field, —
Vases and urns and bas-reliefs,
Memorials of forgotten griefs,
Or records of heroic deeds
Of demigods and mighty chiefs :
Figures that almost move and speak,
And, buried amid mould and weeds,
Still in their attitudes attest
The presence of the graceful Greek, —
Achilles in his armor dressed,
Alcides with the Cretan bull,
And Aphrodite with her boy,
Or lovely Helena of Troy,
Still living and still beautiful.

Turn, turn, my wheel ! 'T is nature's plan
The child should grow into the man,
*   The man grow wrinkled, old, and gray*
In youth the heart exults and sings,
The pulses leap, the feet have wings ;
In age the cricket chirps, and brings
*   The harvest-home of day.*

And now the winds that southward blow,
And cool the hot Sicilian isle,
Bear me away. I see below
The long line of the Libyan Nile,
Flooding and feeding the parched lands
With annual ebb and overflow,
A fallen palm whose branches lie
Beneath the Abyssinian sky,
Whose roots are in Egyptian sands.

On either bank huge water-wheels,
Belted with jars and dripping weeds,
Send forth their melancholy moans,
As if, in their gray mantles hid,
Dead anchorites of the Thebaid
Knelt on the shore and told their beads,
Beating their breasts with loud appeals
And penitential tears and groans.

This city, walled and thickly set
With glittering mosque and minaret,
Is Cairo, in whose gay bazaars
The dreaming traveller first inhales
The perfume of Arabian gales,
And sees the fabulous earthen jars,
Huge as were those wherein the maid
Morgiana found the Forty Thieves
Concealed in midnight ambuscade ;
And seeing, more than half believes
The fascinating tales that run
Through all the Thousand Nights and One,
'Told by the fair Scheherezade.

More strange and wonderful than these
Are the Egyptian deities,
Ammon, and Emeth, and the grand
Osiris, holding in his hand
The lotus ; Isis, crowned and veiled ;
The sacred Ibis, and the Sphinx ;
Bracelets with blue enamelled links ;
The Scarabee in emerald mailed,
Or spreading wide his funeral wings ;
Lamps that perchance their night-watch
        kept
O'er Cleopatra while she slept, —
All plundered from the tombs of kings.

Turn, turn, my wheel!   The human race,
Of every tongue, of every place,
        Caucasian, Coptic, or Malay,
All that inhabit this great earth,
Whatever be their rank or worth,
Are kindred and allied by birth,
        And made of the same clay.

O'er desert sands, o'er gulf and bay,
O'er Ganges and o'er Himalay,
Bird-like I fly, and flying sing,
To flowery kingdoms of Cathay,
And bird-like poise on balanced wing
Above the town of King-te-tching,
A burning town, or seeming so, —
Three thousand furnaces that glow
Incessantly, and fill the air
With smoke uprising, gyre on gyre,

And painted by the lurid glare,
Of jets and flashes of red fire.

As leaves that in the autumn fall,
Spotted and veined with various hues,
Are swept along the avenues,
And lie in heaps by hedge and wall,
So from this grove of chimneys whirled
To all the markets of the world,
These porcelain leaves are wafted on,
Light yellow leaves with spots and stains
Of violet and of crimson dye,
Or tender azure of a sky
Just washed by gentle April rains,
And beautiful with celadon.

Nor less the coarser household wares,
The willow pattern, that we knew
In childhood, with its bridge of blue
Leading to unknown thoroughfares ;
The solitary man who stares
At the white river flowing through
Its arches, the fantastic trees
And wild perspective of the view ;
And intermingled among these
The tiles that in our nurseries
Filled us with wonder and delight,
Or haunted us in dreams at night.

And yonder by Nankin, behold !
The Tower of Porcelain, strange and old,
Uplifting to the astonished skies
Its ninefold painted balconies,
With balustrades of twining leaves,
And roofs of tile, beneath whose eaves
Hang porcelain bells that all the time
Ring with a soft, melodious chime ;
While the whole fabric is ablaze
With varied tints, all fused in one
Great mass of color, like a maze
Of flowers illumined by the sun.

Turn, turn, my wheel!   What is begun
At daybreak must at dark be done,
        To-morrow will be another day ;
To-morrow the hot furnace flame
Will search the heart and try the frame,
And stamp with honor or with shame
        These vessels made of clay.

Cradled and rocked in Eastern seas,
The islands of the Japanese
Beneath me lie ; o'er lake and plain
The stork, the heron, and the crane
Through the clear realms of azure drift,

And on the hillside I can see
The villages of Imari,
Whose thronged and flaming workshops lift
Their twisted columns of smoke on high,
Cloud cloisters that in ruins lie,
With sunshine streaming through each rift,
And broken arches of blue sky.

All the bright flowers that fill the land,
Ripple of waves on rock or sand,
The snow on Fusiyama's cone,
The midnight heaven so thickly sown
With constellations of bright stars,
The leaves that rustle, the reeds that make
A whisper by each stream and lake,
The saffron dawn, the sunset red,
Are painted on these lovely jars ;
Again the skylark sings, again
The stork, the heron, and the crane
Float through the azure overhead,
The counterfeit and counterpart
Of Nature reproduced in Art.

Art is the child of Nature ; yes,
Her darling child, in whom we trace
The features of the mother's face,
Her aspect and her attitude ;
All her majestic loveliness
Chastened and softened and subdued
Into a more attractive grace,
And with a human sense imbued.

He is the greatest artist, then,
Whether of pencil or of pen,
Who follows Nature. Never man,
As artist or as artisan,
Pursuing his own fantasies,
Can touch the human heart, or please.
Or satisfy our nobler needs,
As he who sets his willing feet
In Nature's footprints, light and fleet,
And follows fearless where she leads.

Thus mused I on that morn in May,
Wrapped in my visions like the Seer,
Whose eyes behold not what is near,
But only what is far away,
When, suddenly sounding peal on peal,
The church - bell from the neighboring town
Proclaimed the welcome hour of noon.
The Potter heard, and stopped his wheel,
His apron on the grass threw down,
Whistled his quiet little tune,
Not overloud nor overlong,
And ended thus his simple song :

Stop, stop, my wheel! Too soon, too soon
The noon will be the afternoon,
Too soon to-day be yesterday ;
Behind us in our path we cast
The broken potsherds of the past,
And all are ground to dust at last,
And trodden into clay!

BIRDS OF PASSAGE

FLIGHT THE FIFTH

Collected in the volume entitled *Kéramos and other Poems*, 1878. Elmwood, in the first poem, was the home of James Russell Lowell.

THE HERONS OF ELMWOOD

WARM and still is the summer night,
  As here by the river's brink I wander ;
White overhead are the stars, and white
  The glimmering lamps on the hillside yonder.

Silent are all the sounds of day ;
  Nothing I hear but the chirp of crickets,
And the cry of the herons winging their way
  O'er the poet's house in the Elmwood thickets.

Call to him, herons, as slowly you pass
  To your roosts in the haunts of the exiled thrushes,
Sing him the song of the green morass,
  And the tides that water the reeds and rushes.

Sing him the mystical Song of the Hern,
  And the secret that baffles our utmost seeking ;
For only a sound of lament we discern,
  And cannot interpret the words you are speaking.

Sing of the air, and the wild delight
　Of wings that uplift and winds that up-
　　hold you,
The joy of freedom, the rapture of flight
　Through the drift of the floating mists
　　that infold you ;

Of the landscape lying so far below,
　With its towns and rivers and desert
　　places ;
And the splendor of light above, and the
　　glow
　Of the limitless, blue, ethereal spaces.

Ask him if songs of the Troubadours,
　Or of Minnesingers in old black-letter,
Sound in his ears more sweet than yours,
　And if yours are not sweeter and wilder
　　and better.

Sing to him, say to him, here at his gate,
　Where the boughs of the stately elms are
　　meeting,
Some one hath lingered to meditate,
　And send him unseen this friendly greet-
　　ing ;

That many another hath done the same,
　Though not by a sound was the silence
　　broken ;
The surest pledge of a deathless name
　Is the silent homage of thoughts un-
　　spoken.

A DUTCH PICTURE

SIMON DANZ has come home again,
　From cruising about with his buccaneers ;
He has singed the beard of the King of
　　Spain,
And carried away the Dean of Jaen
　And sold him in Algiers.

In his house by the Maese, with its roof of
　　tiles,
　And weathercocks flying aloft in air,
There are silver tankards of antique styles,
Plunder of convent and castle, and piles
　Of carpets rich and rare.

In his tulip-garden there by the town,
　Overlooking the sluggish stream,

With his Moorish cap and dressing-gown,
The old sea-captain, hale and brown,
　Walks in a waking dream.

A smile in his gray mustachio lurks
　Whenever he thinks of the King of Spain,
And the listed tulips look like Turks,
And the silent gardener as he works
　Is changed to the Dean of Jaen.

The windmills on the outermost
　Verge of the landscape in the haze,
To him are towers on the Spanish coast,
With whiskered sentinels at their post,
　Though this is the river Maese.

But when the winter rains begin,
　He sits and smokes by the blazing brands,
And old seafaring men come in,
Goat-bearded, gray, and with double chin,
　And rings upon their hands.

They sit there in the shadow and shine
　Of the flickering fire of the winter night ;
Figures in color and design
Like those by Rembrandt of the Rhine,
　Half darkness and half light.

And they talk of ventures lost or won,
　And their talk is ever and ever the
　　same,
While they drink the red wine of Tarragon,
From the cellars of some Spanish Don,
　Or convent set on flame.

Restless at times with heavy strides
　He paces his parlor to and fro ;
He is like a ship that at anchor rides,
And swings with the rising and falling
　　tides,
　And tugs at her anchor-tow.

Voices mysterious far and near,
　Sound of the wind and sound of the sea,
Are calling and whispering in his ear,
" Simon Danz ! Why stayest thou here ?
　Come forth and follow me ! "

So he thinks he shall take to the sea again
　For one more cruise with his buccaneers,
To singe the beard of the King of Spain,
And capture another Dean of Jaen
　And sell him in Algiers.

CASTLES IN SPAIN

How much of my young heart, O Spain,
  Went out to thee in days of yore !
What dreams romantic filled my brain,
And summoned back to life again
The Paladins of Charlemagne,
  The Cid Campeador !

And shapes more shadowy than these,
  In the dim twilight half revealed ;
Phœnician galleys on the seas,
The Roman camps like hives of bees,
The Goth uplifting from his knees
  Pelayo on his shield.

It was these memories perchance,
  From annals of remotest eld,
That lent the colors of romance
To every trivial circumstance,
And changed the form and countenance
  Of all that I beheld.

Old towns, whose history lies hid
  In monkish chronicle or rhyme, —
Burgos, the birthplace of the Cid,
Zamora and Valladolid,
Toledo, built and walled amid
  The wars of Wamba's time ;

The long, straight line of the highway,
  The distant town that seems so near,
The peasants in the fields, that stay
Their toil to cross themselves and pray,
When from the belfry at midday
  The Angelus they hear ;

White crosses in the mountain pass,
  Mules gay with tassels, the loud din
Of muleteers, the tethered ass
That crops the dusty wayside grass,
And cavaliers with spurs of brass
  Alighting at the inn ;

White hamlets hidden in fields of wheat,
  White cities slumbering by the sea,
White sunshine flooding square and street,
Dark mountain ranges, at whose feet
The river beds are dry with heat, —
  All was a dream to me.

Yet something sombre and severe
  O'er the enchanted landscape reigned ;
A terror in the atmosphere

As if King Philip listened near,
Or Torquemada, the austere,
  His ghostly sway maintained.

The softer Andalusian skies
  Dispelled the sadness and the gloom ;
There Cadiz by the seaside lies,
And Seville's orange-orchards rise,
Making the land a paradise
  Of beauty and of bloom.

There Cordova is hidden among
  The palm, the olive, and the vine ;
Gem of the South, by poets sung,
And in whose mosque Almanzor hung
As lamps the bells that once had rung
  At Compostella's shrine.

But over all the rest supreme,
  The star of stars, the cynosure,
The artist's and the poet's theme,
The young man's vision, the old man's
    dream, —
Granada by its winding stream,
  The city of the Moor !

And there the Alhambra still recalls
  Aladdin's palace of delight :
Allah il Allah ! through its halls
Whispers the fountain as it falls,
The Darro darts beneath its walls,
  The hills with snow are white.

Ah yes, the hills are white with snow,
  And cold with blasts that bite and
    freeze ;
But in the happy vale below
The orange and pomegranate grow,
And wafts of air toss to and fro
  The blossoming almond trees.

The Vega cleft by the Xenil,
  The fascination and allure
Of the sweet landscape chains the will ;
The traveller lingers on the hill,
His parted lips are breathing still
  The last sigh of the Moor.

How like a ruin overgrown
  With flowers that hide the rents of
    time,
Stands now the Past that I have known ;
Castles in Spain, not built of stone
But of white summer clouds, and blown
  Into this little mist of rhyme !

VITTORIA COLONNA

Vittoria Colonna, on the death of her husband, the Marchese di Pescara, retired to her castle at Ischia (Inarimé), and there wrote the Ode upon his death which gained her the title of Divine. H. W. L.

ONCE more, once more, Inarimé,
  I see thy purple halls ! — once more
I hear the billows of the bay
  Wash the white pebbles on thy shore.

High o'er the sea-surge and the sands,
  Like a great galleon wrecked and cast
Ashore by storms, thy castle stands,
  A mouldering landmark of the Past.

Upon its terrace-walk I see
  A phantom gliding to and fro ;
It is Colonna, — it is she
  Who lived and loved so long ago.

Pescara's beautiful young wife,
  The type of perfect womanhood,
Whose life was love, the life of life,
  That time and change and death with-
    stood.

For death, that breaks the marriage band
  In others, only closer pressed
The wedding-ring upon her hand
  And closer locked and barred her breast.

She knew the life-long martyrdom,
  The weariness, the endless pain
Of waiting for some one to come
  Who nevermore would come again.

The shadows of the chestnut trees,
  The odor of the orange blooms,
The song of birds, and, more than these,
  The silence of deserted rooms ;

The respiration of the sea,
  The soft caresses of the air,
All things in nature seemed to be
  But ministers of her despair ;

Till the o'erburdened heart, so long
  Imprisoned in itself, found vent
And voice in one impassioned song
  Of inconsolable lament.

Then as the sun, though hidden from sight,
  Transmutes to gold the leaden mist,

Her life was interfused with light,
  From realms that, though unseen, exist.

Inarimé ! Inarimé !
  Thy castle on the crags above
In dust shall crumble and decay,
  But not the memory of her love.

THE REVENGE OF RAIN-IN-THE-FACE

IN that desolate land and lone,
Where the Big Horn and Yellowstone
  Roar down their mountain path,
By their fires the Sioux Chiefs
Muttered their woes and griefs
  And the menace of their wrath.

" Revenge ! " cried Rain-in-the-Face,
" Revenge upon all the race
  Of the White Chief with yellow hair
And the mountains dark and high
From their crags reëchoed the cry
  Of his anger and despair.

In the meadow, spreading wide
By woodland and river-side
  The Indian village stood ;
All was silent as a dream,
Save the rushing of the stream
  And the blue-jay in the wood.

In his war paint and his beads,
Like a bison among the reeds,
  In ambush the Sitting Bull
Lay with three thousand braves
Crouched in the clefts and caves,
  Savage, unmerciful !

Into the fatal snare
The White Chief with yellow hair
  And his three hundred men
Dashed headlong, sword in hand ;
But of that gallant band
  Not one returned again.

The sudden darkness of death
Overwhelmed them like the breath
  And smoke of a furnace fire :
By the river's bank, and between
The rocks of the ravine,
  They lay in their bloody attire.

But the foemen fled in the night,
And Rain-in-the-Face, in his flight,
    Uplifted high in air
As a ghastly trophy, bore
The brave heart, that beat no more,
    Of the White Chief with yellow hair.

Whose was the right and the wrong ?
Sing it, O funeral song,
    With a voice that is full of tears,
And say that our broken faith
Wrought all this ruin and scathe,
    In the Year of a Hundred Years.

TO THE RIVER YVETTE

O LOVELY river of Yvette !
    O darling river ! like a bride,
Some dimpled, bashful, fair Lisette,
    Thou goest to wed the Orge's tide.

Maincourt, and lordly Dampierre,
    See and salute thee on thy way,
And, with a blessing and a prayer,
    Ring the sweet bells of St. Forget.

The valley of Chevreuse in vain
    Would hold thee in its fond embrace ;
Thou glidest from its arms again
    And hurriest on with swifter pace.

Thou wilt not stay ; with restless feet,
    Pursuing still thine onward flight,
Thou goest as one in haste to meet
    Her sole desire, her heart's delight.

O lovely river of Yvette !
    O darling stream ! on balanced wings
The wood-birds sang the chansonnette
    That here a wandering poet sings.

THE EMPEROR'S GLOVE

" Combien faudrait-il de peaux d'Espagne pour faire
un gant de cette grandeur ? " A play upon the words
gant, a glove, and *Gand*, the French for Ghent. H. W.
L.

ON St. Bavon's tower, commanding
    Half of Flanders, his domain,
Charles the Emperor once was standing,
While beneath him on the landing
    Stood Duke Alva and his train.

Like a print in books of fables,
    Or a model made for show,
With its pointed roofs and gables,
Dormer windows, scrolls and labels,
    Lay the city far below.

Through its squares and streets and alleys
    Poured the populace of Ghent ;
As a routed army rallies,
Or as rivers run through valleys,
    Hurrying to their homes they went.

" Nest of Lutheran misbelievers ! "
    Cried Duke Alva as he gazed ;
" Haunt of traitors and deceivers,
Stronghold of insurgent weavers,
    Let it to the ground be razed ! "

On the Emperor's cap the feather
    Nods, as laughing he replies :
" How many skins of Spanish leather,
Think you, would, if stitched together,
    Make a glove of such a size ? "

A BALLAD OF THE FRENCH
FLEET

OCTOBER, 1746

MR. THOMAS PRINCE *loquitur*

Written at the instance of the Rev. E. E. Hale, when
efforts were making to save from destruction the Old
South Meeting House in Boston. Mr. Hale sent Mr.
Longfellow a passage out of Hutchinson's history, and
referred him to Prince's Thanksgiving sermon, given at
the Old South in 1746.

A FLEET with flags arrayed
    Sailed from the port of Brest,
And the Admiral's ship displayed
    The signal : " Steer southwest."
For this Admiral D'Anville
    Had sworn by cross and crown
To ravage with fire and steel
    Our helpless Boston Town.

There were rumors in the street,
    In the houses there was fear
Of the coming of the fleet,
    And the danger hovering near.
And while from mouth to mouth
    Spread the tidings of dismay,
I stood in the Old South,
    Saying humbly : " Let us pray !

" O Lord ! we would not advise ;
    But if in thy Providence
A tempest should arise
To drive the French Fleet hence,
And scatter it far and wide,
    Or sink it in the sea,
We should be satisfied,
    And thine the glory be."

This was the prayer I made,
    For my soul was all on flame,
And even as I prayed
    The answering tempest came ;
It came with a mighty power,
    Shaking the windows and walls,
And tolling the bell in the tower,
    As it tolls at funerals.

The lightning suddenly
    Unsheathed its flaming sword,
And I cried : " Stand still, and see
    The salvation of the Lord ! "
The heavens were black with cloud,
    The sea was white with hail,
And ever more fierce and loud
    Blew the October gale.

The fleet it overtook,
    And the broad sails in the van
Like the tents of Cushan shook,
    Or the curtains of Midian.
Down on the reeling decks
    Crashed the o'erwhelming seas ;
Ah, never were there wrecks
    So pitiful as these !

Like a potter's vessel broke
    The great ships of the line ;
They were carried away as a smoke,
    Or sank like lead in the brine.
O Lord ! before thy path
    They vanished and ceased to be,
When thou didst walk in wrath
    With thine horses through the sea !

THE LEAP OF ROUSHAN BEG

Mounted on Kyrat strong and fleet,
His chestnut steed with four white feet,
    Roushan Beg, called Kurroglou,
Son of the road and bandit chief,
Seeking refuge and relief,
    Up the mountain pathway flew.

Such was Kyrat's wondrous speed,
Never yet could any steed
    Reach the dust-cloud in his course.
More than maiden, more than wife,
More than gold and next to life
    Roushan the Robber loved his horse.

In the land that lies beyond
Erzeroum and Trebizond,
    Garden-girt his fortress stood ;
Plundered khan, or caravan
Journeying north from Koordistan,
    Gave him wealth and wine and food

Seven hundred and fourscore
Men at arms his livery wore,
    Did his bidding night and day ;
Now, through regions all unknown,
He was wandering, lost, alone,
    Seeking without guide his way.

Suddenly the pathway ends,
Sheer the precipice descends,
    Loud the torrent roars unseen ;
Thirty feet from side to side
Yawns the chasm ; on air must ride
    He who crosses this ravine.

Following close in his pursuit,
At the precipice's foot
    Reyhan the Arab of Orfah
Halted with his hundred men,
Shouting upward from the glen,
    " La Illáh illa Alláh ! "

Gently Roushan Beg caressed
Kyrat's forehead, neck, and breast ;
    Kissed him upon both his eyes,
Sang to him in his wild way,
As upon the topmost spray
    Sings a bird before it flies.

" O my Kyrat, O my steed,
Round and slender as a reed,
    Carry me this peril through !
Satin housings shall be thine,
Shoes of gold, O Kyrat mine,
    O thou soul of Kurroglou !

" Soft thy skin as silken skein,
Soft as woman's hair thy mane,
    Tender are thine eyes and true ;
All thy hoofs like ivory shine,
Polished bright ; O life of mine,
    Leap, and rescue Kurroglou ! "

Kyrat, then, the strong and fleet,
Drew together his four white feet,
  Paused a moment on the verge,
  Measured with his eye the space,
  And into the air's embrace
Leaped as leaps the ocean surge.

As the ocean surge o'er sand
Bears a swimmer safe to land,
  Kyrat safe his rider bore ;
Rattling down the deep abyss
Fragments of the precipice
  Rolled like pebbles on a shore.

Roushan's tasselled cap of red
Trembled not upon his head,
  Careless sat he and upright ;
Neither hand nor bridle shook,
Nor his head he turned to look,
  As he galloped out of sight.

Flash of harness in the air,
Seen a moment like the glare
  Of a sword drawn from its sheath ;
Thus the phantom horseman passed,
And the shadow that he cast
  Leaped the cataract underneath.

Reyhan the Arab held his breath
While this vision of life and death
  Passed above him. " Allahu ! "
Cried he. " In all Koordistan
Lives there not so brave a man
  As this Robber Kurroglou ! "

HAROUN AL RASCHID

ONE day, Haroun Al Raschid read
A book wherein the poet said : —

" Where are the kings, and where the rest
Of those who once the world possessed ?

" They 're gone with all their pomp and show,
They 're gone the way that thou shalt go.

" O thou who choosest for thy share
The world, and what the world calls fair,

" Take all that it can give or lend,
But know that death is at the end ! "

Haroun Al Raschid bowed his head :
Tears fell upon the page he read.

KING TRISANKU

VISWAMITRA the Magician,
  By his spells and incantations,
Up to Indra's realms elysian
  Raised Trisanku, king of nations.

Indra and the gods offended
  Hurled him downward, and descending
In the air he hung suspended,
  With these equal powers contending.

Thus by aspirations lifted,
  By misgivings downward driven,
Human hearts are tossed and drifted
  Midway between earth and heaven.

A WRAITH IN THE MIST

" Sir, I should build me a fortification, if I came to
live here." — BOSWELL'S *Johnson.*

ON the green little isle of Inchkenneth,
  Who is it that walks by the shore,
So gay with his Highland blue bonnet,
  So brave with his targe and claymore ?

His form is the form of a giant,
  But his face wears an aspect of pain ;
Can this be the Laird of Inchkenneth ?
  Can this be Sir Allan McLean ?

Ah, no ! It is only the Rambler,
  The Idler, who lives in Bolt Court,
And who says, were he Laird of Inchkenneth,
  He would wall himself round with a fort.

THE THREE KINGS

THREE Kings came riding from far away,
  Melchior and Gaspar and Baltasar ;
Three Wise Men out of the East were they,
And they travelled by night and they slept
    by day,
  For their guide was a beautiful, wonder-
    ful star.

The star was so beautiful, large, and clear,
  That all the other stars of the sky
Became a white mist in the atmosphere,
And by this they knew that the coming was
    near
  Of the Prince foretold in the prophecy.

Three caskets they bore on their saddle-
bows,
Three caskets of gold with golden keys ;
Their robes were of crimson silk with rows
Of bells and pomegranates and furbelows,
Their turbans like blossoming almond-
trees.

And so the Three Kings rode into the West,
Through the dusk of night, over hill and
dell,
And sometimes they nodded with beard on
breast,
And sometimes talked, as they paused to
rest,
With the people they met at some way-
side well.

"Of the child that is born," said Baltasar,
"Good people, I pray you, tell us the
news ;
For we in the East have seen his star,
And have ridden fast, and have ridden far,
To find and worship the King of the
Jews."

And the people answered, "You ask in vain ;
We know of no king but Herod the
Great ! "
They thought the Wise Men were men in-
sane,
As they spurred their horses across the
plain,
Like riders in haste, and who cannot
wait.

And when they came to Jerusalem,
Herod the Great, who had heard this
thing,
Sent for the Wise Men and questioned
them ;
And said, " Go down unto Bethlehem,
And bring me tidings of this new king."

So they rode away ; and the star stood still,
The only one in the gray of morn ;
Yes, it stopped, — it stood still of its own
free will,
Right over Bethlehem on the hill,
The city of David, where Christ was born.

And the Three Kings rode through the gate
and the guard,
Through the silent street, till their horses
turned

And neighed as they entered the great inn-
yard ;
But the windows were closed, and the
doors were barred,
And only a light in the stable burned.

And cradled there in the scented hay,
In the air made sweet by the breath of
kine,
The little child in the manger lay,
The child, that would be king one day
Of a kingdom not human but divine.

His mother Mary of Nazareth
Sat watching beside his place of rest,
Watching the even flow of his breath,
For the joy of life and the terror of death
Were mingled together in her breast.

They laid their offerings at his feet :
The gold was their tribute to a King,
The frankincense, with its odor sweet,
Was for the Priest, the Paraclete,
The myrrh for the body's burying.

And the mother wondered and bowed her
head,
And sat as still as a statue of stone ;
Her heart was troubled yet comforted,
Remembering what the Angel had said
Of an endless reign and of David's
throne.

Then the Kings rode out of the city gate,
With a clatter of hoofs in proud array ;
But they went not back to Herod the Great,
For they knew his malice and feared his
hate,
And returned to their homes by another
way.

SONG

STAY, stay at home, my heart, and rest ;
Home-keeping hearts are happiest,
For those that wander they know not where
Are full of trouble and full of care ;
To stay at home is best.

Weary and homesick and distressed,
They wander east, they wander west,
And are baffled and beaten and blown about
By the winds of the wilderness of doubt ;
To stay at home is best.

Then stay at home, my heart, and rest ;
The bird is safest in its nest ;
O'er all that flutter their wings and fly
A hawk is hovering in the sky ;
    To stay at home is best.

THE WHITE CZAR

The White Czar is Peter the Great. Batyushka, *Father dear*, and Gosudar, *Sovereign*, are titles the Russian people are fond of giving to the Czar in their popular songs. H. W. L.

Dost thou see on the rampart's height
That wreath of mist, in the light
Of the midnight moon ? Oh, hist !
It is not a wreath of mist ;
It is the Czar, the White Czar,
    Batyushka ! Gosudar !

He has heard, among the dead,
The artillery roll o'erhead ;
The drums and the tramp of feet
Of his soldiery in the street ;
He is awake ! the White Czar,
    Batyushka ! Gosudar !

He has heard in the grave the cries
Of his people : "Awake ! arise !"
He has rent the gold brocade
Whereof his shroud was made ;
He is risen ! the White Czar,
    Batyushka ! Gosudar !

From the Volga and the Don
He has led his armies on,
Over river and morass,
Over desert and mountain pass ;
The Czar, the Orthodox Czar,
    Batyushka ! Gosudar !

He looks from the mountain-chain
Toward the seas, that cleave in twain
The continents ; his hand
Points southward o'er the land
Of Roumili ! O Czar,
    Batyushka ! Gosudar !

And the words break from his lips :
"I am the builder of ships,
And my ships shall sail these seas
To the Pillars of Hercules !
I say it ; the White Czar,
    Batyushka ! Gosudar !

"The Bosphorus shall be free ;
It shall make room for me ;
And the gates of its water-streets
Be unbarred before my fleets.
I say it ; the White Czar,
    Batyushka ! Gosudar !

"And the Christian shall no more
Be crushed, as heretofore,
Beneath thine iron rule,
O Sultan of Istamboul !
I swear it ! I the Czar,
    Batyushka ! Gosudar !"

DELIA

Sweet as the tender fragrance that sur-
    vives,
When martyred flowers breathe out their
    little lives,
Sweet as a song that once consoled our pain,
But never will be sung to us again,
Is thy remembrance. Now the hour of
    rest
Hath come to thee. Sleep, darling ; it is
    best.

ULTIMA THULE

The collection of poems under this title was published in 1880. The volume bore on the title-page these lines from Horace (Lib. I., Carmen XXX., *Ad Apollinem*) : —
    Precor, integrâ
Cum mente, nec turpem senectam
Degere, nec citharâ carentem.

The dedication is to his life-long friend, George Washington Greene, who himself dedicated his *Life of Nathanael Greene* to Mr. Longfellow in words which give a glowing picture of the aspirations of the two in the days of their young manhood.

DEDICATION

TO G. W. G.

WITH favoring winds, o'er sunlit seas,
We sailed for the Hesperides,
The land where golden apples grow ;
But that, ah ! that was long ago.

How far since then the ocean streams
Have swept us from that land of dreams,
That land of fiction and of truth,
The lost Atlantis of our youth !

Whither, ah, whither ?   Are not these
The tempest-haunted Orcades,
Where sea-gulls scream, and breakers roar,
And wreck and sea-weed line the shore ?

Ultima Thule !   Utmost Isle !
Here in thy harbors for a while
We lower our sails ; a while we rest
From the unending, endless quest.

POEMS

BAYARD TAYLOR

DEAD he lay among his books !
The peace of God was in his looks.

As the statues in the gloom
Watch o'er Maximilian's tomb,

So those volumes from their shelves
Watched him, silent as themselves.

Ah ! his hand will nevermore
Turn their storied pages o'er ;

Nevermore his lips repeat
Songs of theirs, however sweet.

Let the lifeless body rest !
He is gone, who was its guest ;

Gone, as travellers haste to leave
An inn, nor tarry until eve.

Traveller ! in what realms afar,
In what planet, in what star,

In what vast, aerial space,
Shines the light upon thy face ?

In what gardens of delight
Rest thy weary feet to-night ?

Poet ! thou, whose latest verse
Was a garland on thy hearse ;

Thou hast sung, with organ tone,
In Deukalion's life, thine own ;

On the ruins of the Past
Blooms the perfect flower at last.

Friend ! but yesterday the bells
Rang for thee their loud farewells ;

And to-day they toll for thee,
Lying dead beyond the sea ;

Lying dead among thy books,
The peace of God in all thy looks !

THE CHAMBER OVER THE GATE

Written October 30, 1878. Suggested to the poet
when writing a letter of condolence to the Bishop of
Mississippi, whose son, the Rev. Duncan C. Green, had
died at his post at Greenville, Mississippi, September
15, during the prevalence of yellow fever.

Is it so far from thee
Thou canst no longer see,
In the Chamber over the Gate,
That old man desolate,
Weeping and wailing sore
For his son, who is no more ?
  O Absalom, my son !

Is it so long ago
That cry of human woe
From the walled city came,
Calling on his dear name,
That it has died away
In the distance of to-day ?
  O Absalom, my son !

There is no far or near,
There is neither there nor here,
There is neither soon nor late,
In that Chamber over the Gate,
Nor any long ago
To that cry of human woe,
  O Absalom, my son !

From the ages that are past
The voice sounds like a blast,

Over seas that wreck and drown,
Over tumult of traffic and town ;
And from ages yet to be
Come the echoes back to me,
    O Absalom, my son !

Somewhere at every hour
The watchman on the tower
Looks forth, and sees the fleet
Approach of the hurrying feet
Of messengers, that bear
The tidings of despair.
    O Absalom, my son !

He goes forth from the door,
Who shall return no more.
With him our joy departs ;
The light goes out in our hearts ;
In the Chamber over the Gate
We sit disconsolate.
    O Absalom, my son !

That 't is a common grief
Bringeth but slight relief ;
Ours is the bitterest loss,
Ours is the heaviest cross ;
And forever the cry will be
" Would God I had died for thee,
    O Absalom, my son ! "

FROM MY ARM-CHAIR

TO THE CHILDREN OF CAMBRIDGE

WHO PRESENTED TO ME, ON MY SEVENTY-SECOND BIRTHDAY, FEBRUARY 27, 1879, THIS CHAIR MADE FROM THE WOOD OF THE VILLAGE BLACKSMITH'S CHESTNUT TREE.

Mr. Longfellow had this poem, which he wrote on the same day, printed on a sheet, and was accustomed to give a copy to each child who visited him and sat in the chair.

AM I a king, that I should call my own
    This splendid ebon throne ?
Or by what reason, or what right divine,
    Can I proclaim it mine ?

Only, perhaps, by right divine of song
    It may to me belong ;
Only because the spreading chestnut tree
    Of old was sung by me.

Well I remember it in all its prime,
    When in the summer-time
The affluent foliage of its branches made
    A cavern of cool shade.

There, by the blacksmith's forge, beside
    the street,
    Its blossoms white and sweet
Enticed the bees, until it seemed alive,
    And murmured like a hive.

And when the winds of autumn, with a
    shout,
    Tossed its great arms about,
The shining chestnuts, bursting from the
    sheath,
    Dropped to the ground beneath.

And now some fragments of its branches
    bare,
    Shaped as a stately chair,
Have by my hearthstone found a home at
    last,
    And whisper of the past.

The Danish king could not in all his pride
    Repel the ocean tide,
But, seated in this chair, I can in rhyme
    Roll back the tide of Time.

I see again, as one in vision sees,
    The blossoms and the bees,
And hear the children's voices shout and
    call,
    And the brown chestnuts fall.

I see the smithy with its fires aglow,
    I hear the bellows blow,
And the shrill hammers on the anvil beat
    The iron white with heat !

And thus, dear children, have ye made for
    me
    This day a jubilee,
And to my more than threescore years and
    ten
    Brought back my youth again.

The heart hath its own memory, like the
    mind,
    And in it are enshrined
The precious keepsakes, into which is
    wrought
    The giver's loving thought.

Only your love and your remembrance could
    Give life to this dead wood,
And make these branches, leafless now so
    long,
    Blossom again in song.

JUGURTHA

How cold are thy baths, Apollo !
  Cried the African monarch, the splendid,
As down to his death in the hollow
  Dark dungeons of Rome he descended,
  Uncrowned, unthroned, unattended ;
How cold are thy baths, Apollo !

How cold are thy baths, Apollo !
  Cried the Poet, unknown, unbefriended,
As the vision, that lured him to follow,
  With the mist and the darkness blended,
  And the dream of his life was ended ;
How cold are thy baths, Apollo !

THE IRON PEN

Written June 20, 1879. The pen was made of a bit of iron from the prison of Bonnivard at Chillon ; the handle of wood from the Frigate Constitution, and bound with a circlet of gold, inset with three precious stones from Siberia, Ceylon, and Maine. It was a gift from Miss Helen Hamlin, of Bangor, Maine.

I THOUGHT this Pen would arise
From the casket where it lies —
  Of itself would arise and write
My thanks and my surprise.

When you gave it me under the pines,
I dreamed these gems from the mines
  Of Siberia, Ceylon, and Maine
Would glimmer as thoughts in the lines ;

That this iron link from the chain
Of Bonnivard might retain
  Some verse of the Poet who sang
Of the prisoner and his pain ;

That this wood from the frigate's mast
Might write me a rhyme at last,
  As it used to write on the sky
The song of the sea and the blast.

But motionless as I wait,
Like a Bishop lying in state
  Lies the Pen, with its mitre of gold,
And its jewels inviolate.

Then must I speak, and say
That the light of that summer day
  In the garden under the pines
Shall not fade and pass away.

I shall see you standing there,
Caressed by the fragrant air,
  With the shadow on your face,
And the sunshine on your hair.

I shall hear the sweet low tone
Of a voice before unknown,
  Saying, "This is from me to you —
From me, and to you alone."

And in words not idle and vain
I shall answer and thank you again
  For the gift, and the grace of the gift,
O beautiful Helen of Maine !

And forever this gift will be
As a blessing from you to me,
  As a drop of the dew of your youth
On the leaves of an aged tree.

ROBERT BURNS

I SEE amid the fields of Ayr
A ploughman, who, in foul and fair,
  Sings at his task
So clear, we know not if it is
The laverock's song we hear, or his,
  Nor care to ask.

For him the ploughing of those fields
A more ethereal harvest yields
  Than sheaves of grain ;
Songs flush with purple bloom the rye,
The plover's call, the curlew's cry,
  Sing in his brain.

Touched by his hand, the wayside weed
Becomes a flower ; the lowliest reed
  Beside the stream
Is clothed with beauty ; gorse and grass
And heather, where his footsteps pass,
  The brighter seem.

He sings of love, whose flame illumes
The darkness of lone cottage rooms ;
  He feels the force,
The treacherous undertow and stress
Of wayward passions, and no less
  The keen remorse.

At moments, wrestling with his fate,
His voice is harsh, but not with hate ;
  The brush-wood, hung
Above the tavern door, lets fall

Its bitter leaf, its drop of gall
    Upon his tongue.

But still the music of his song
Rises o'er all, elate and strong ;
    Its master-chords
Are Manhood, Freedom, Brotherhood,
Its discords but an interlude
    Between the words.

And then to die so young and leave
Unfinished what he might achieve !
    Yet better sure
Is this, than wandering up and down,
An old man in a country town,
    Infirm and poor.

For now he haunts his native land
As an immortal youth ; his hand
    Guides every plough ;
He sits beside each ingle-nook,
His voice is in each rushing brook,
    Each rustling bough.

His presence haunts this room to-night,
A form of mingled mist and light
    From that far coast.
Welcome beneath this roof of mine !
Welcome ! this vacant chair is thine,
    Dear guest and ghost !

HELEN OF TYRE

WHAT phantom is this that appears
Through the purple mists of the years,
    Itself but a mist like these ?
A woman of cloud and of fire ;
It is she ; it is Helen of Tyre,
    The town in the midst of the seas.

O Tyre ! in thy crowded streets
The phantom appears and retreats,
    And the Israelites that sell
Thy lilies and lions of brass,
Look up as they see her pass,
    And murmur " Jezebel ! "

Then another phantom is seen
At her side, in a gray gabardine,
    With beard that floats to his waist ;
It is Simon Magus, the Seer ;
He speaks, and she pauses to hear
    The words he utters in haste.

He says : " From this evil fame,
From this life of sorrow and shame,
    I will lift thee and make thee mine ;
Thou hast been Queen Candace,
And Helen of Troy, and shalt be
    The Intelligence Divine ! "

Oh, sweet as the breath of morn,
To the fallen and forlorn
    Are whispered words of praise ;
For the famished heart believes
The falsehood that tempts and deceives,
    And the promise that betrays.

So she follows from land to land
The wizard's beckoning hand,
    As a leaf is blown by the gust,
Till she vanishes into night.
O reader, stoop down and write
    With thy finger in the dust.

O town in the midst of the seas,
With thy rafts of cedar trees,
    Thy merchandise and thy ships,
Thou, too, art become as naught,
A phantom, a shadow, a thought,
    A name upon men's lips.

ELEGIAC

DARK is the morning with mist ; in the
        narrow mouth of the harbor
Motionless lies the sea, under its curtain
        of cloud ;
Dreamily glimmer the sails of ships on the
        distant horizon,
    Like to the towers of a town, built on
        the verge of the sea.

Slowly and stately and still, they sail forth
        into the ocean ;
    With them sail my thoughts over the
        limitless deep,
Farther and farther away, borne on by un-
        satisfied longings,
    Unto Hesperian isles, unto Ausonian
        shores.

Now they have vanished away, have dis-
        appeared in the ocean ;
    Sunk are the towers of the town into the
        depths of the sea !

All have vanished but those that, moored
    in the neighboring roadstead,
Sailless at anchor ride, looming so large
    in the mist.

Vanished, too, are the thoughts, the dim,
    unsatisfied longings ;
Sunk are the turrets of cloud into the
    ocean of dreams ;
While in a haven of rest my heart is riding
    at anchor,
    Held by the chains of love, held by the
      anchors of trust !

Were I a pilgrim in search of peace,
    Were I a pastor of Holy Church,
More than a Bishop's diocese
Should I prize this place of rest and re-
    lease
From further longing and further search.

Here would I stay, and let the world
    With its distant thunder roar and
    roll ;
Storms do not rend the sail that is furled ;
Nor like a dead leaf, tossed and whirled
    In an eddy of wind, is the anchored souL

OLD ST. DAVID'S AT RADNOR

At the time of the Centennial Exhibition at Phila-
delphia in 1876, Mr. Longfellow, who was a visitor,
established himself with his family at Rosemont, a few
miles from the city, in the immediate neighborhood of
which is the old church of St. David's, the outgrowth of
an English mission of Queen Anne's time.

WHAT an image of peace and rest
    Is this little church among its graves !
All is so quiet ; the troubled breast,
The wounded spirit, the heart oppressed,
    Here may find the repose it craves.

See, how the ivy climbs and expands
    Over this humble hermitage,
And seems to caress with its little hands
The rough, gray stones, as a child that
    stands
    Caressing the wrinkled cheeks of age !

You cross the threshold ; and dim and small
    Is the space that serves for the Shep-
    herd's Fold ;
The narrow aisle, the bare, white wall,
The pews, and the pulpit quaint and tall,
    Whisper and say : " Alas ! we are old."

Herbert's chapel at Bemerton
    Hardly more spacious is than this ;
But poet and pastor, blent in one,
Clothed with a splendor, as of the sun,
    That lowly and holy edifice.

It is not the wall of stone without
    That makes the building small or great,
But the soul's light shining round about,
And the faith that overcometh doubt,
    And the love that stronger is than hate.

FOLK–SONGS

THE SIFTING OF PETER

IN St. Luke's Gospel we are told
How Peter in the days of old
    Was sifted ;
And now, though ages intervene,
Sin is the same, while time and scene
    Are shifted.

Satan desires us, great and small,
As wheat to sift us, and we all
    Are tempted ;
Not one, however rich or great,
Is by his station or estate
    Exempted.

No house so safely guarded is
But he, by some device of his,
    Can enter ;
No heart hath armor so complete
But he can pierce with arrows fleet
    Its centre.

For all at last the cock will crow,
Who hear the warning voice, but go
    Unheeding,
Till thrice and more they have denied
The Man of Sorrows, crucified
    And bleeding.

One look of that pale, suffering face
Will make us feel the deep disgrace
    Of weakness ;
We shall be sifted till the strength
Of self-conceit be changed at length
    To meekness.

Wounds of the soul, though healed, will
    ache ;
The reddening scars remain, and make
    Confession ;
Lost innocence returns no more ;
We are not what we were before
    Transgression.

But noble souls, through dust and heat,
Rise from disaster and defeat
    The stronger ;
And conscious still of the divine
Within them, lie on earth supine
    No longer.

MAIDEN AND WEATHERCOCK

MAIDEN.

O WEATHERCOCK on the village spire,
With your golden feathers all on fire,
Tell me, what can you see from your
    perch
Above there over the tower of the church ?

WEATHERCOCK.

I can see the roofs and the streets below,
And the people moving to and fro,
And beyond, without either roof or street,
The great salt sea, and the fishermen's
    fleet.

I can see a ship come sailing in
Beyond the headlands and harbor of Lynn,
And a young man standing on the deck,
With a silken kerchief round his neck.

Now he is pressing it to his lips,
And now he is kissing his finger-tips,
And now he is lifting and waving his
    hand,
And blowing the kisses toward the land.

MAIDEN.

Ah, that is the ship from over the sea,
That is bringing my lover back to me,
Bringing my lover so fond and true,
Who does not change with the wind like
    you.

WEATHERCOCK.

If I change with all the winds that blow,
It is only because they made me so,
And people would think it wondrous strange,
If I, a Weathercock, should not change.

O pretty Maiden, so fine and fair,
With your dreamy eyes and your golden
    hair,
When you and your lover meet to-day
You will thank me for looking some other
    way.

THE WINDMILL

BEHOLD ! a giant am I !
    Aloft here in my tower,
    With my granite jaws I devour
The maize, and the wheat, and the rye,
    And grind them into flour.

I look down over the farms ;
    In the fields of grain I see
    The harvest that is to be,
And I fling to the air my arms,
    For I know it is all for me.

I hear the sound of flails
    Far off, from the threshing-floors
    In barns, with their open doors,
And the wind, the wind in my sails,
    Louder and louder roars.

I stand here in my place,
    With my foot on the rock below,
    And whichever way it may blow,
I meet it face to face
    As a brave man meets his foe.

And while we wrestle and strive,
    My master, the miller, stands
    And feeds me with his hands ;
For he knows who makes him thrive,
    Who makes him lord of lands.

On Sundays I take my rest ;
    Church-going bells begin
    Their low, melodious din ;
I cross my arms on my breast,
    And all is peace within.

THE TIDE RISES, THE TIDE FALLS

THE tide rises, the tide falls,
The twilight darkens, the curlew calls ;
Along the sea-sands damp and brown
The traveller hastens toward the town,
    And the tide rises, the tide falls.

Darkness settles on roofs and walls,
But the sea, the sea in the darkness calls ;
The little waves, with their soft, white
hands,
Efface the footprints in the sands,
And the tide rises, the tide falls.

The morning breaks ; the steeds in their
stalls
Stamp and neigh, as the hostler calls ;
The day returns, but nevermore
Returns the traveller to the shore,
And the tide rises, the tide falls.

SONNETS

MY CATHEDRAL

Like two cathedral towers these stately
pines
Uplift their fretted summits tipped with
cones ;
The arch beneath them is not built with
stones,
Not Art but Nature traced these lovely
lines,
And carved this graceful arabesque of
vines ;
No organ but the wind here sighs and
moans,
No sepulchre conceals a martyr's bones,
No marble bishop on his tomb reclines.
Enter ! the pavement, carpeted with leaves,
Gives back a softened echo to thy tread !
Listen ! the choir is singing ; all the birds,
In leafy galleries beneath the eaves,
Are singing ! listen, ere the sound be
fled,
And learn there may be worship without
words.

THE BURIAL OF THE POET

RICHARD HENRY DANA

In the old churchyard of his native town,
And in the ancestral tomb beside the
wall,
We laid him in the sleep that comes to
all,
And left him to his rest and his re-
nown.

The snow was falling, as if Heaven dropped
down
White flowers of Paradise to strew his
pall ; —
The dead around him seemed to wake,
and call
His name, as worthy of so white a crown.
And now the moon is shining on the
scene,
And the broad sheet of snow is written
o'er
With shadows cruciform of leafless trees,
As once the winding-sheet of Saladin
With chapters of the Koran ; but, ah !
more
Mysterious and triumphant signs are
these.

NIGHT

Into the darkness and the hush of night
Slowly the landscape sinks, and fades
away,
And with it fade the phantoms of the day,
The ghosts of men and things, that haunt
the light.
The crowd, the clamor, the pursuit, the
flight,
The unprofitable splendor and display,
The agitations, and the cares that prey
Upon our hearts, all vanish out of sight.
The better life begins ; the world no more
Molests us ; all its records we erase
From the dull commonplace book of our
lives,
That like a palimpsest is written o'er
With trivial incidents of time and place,
And lo ! the ideal, hidden beneath, revives.

L'ENVOI

THE POET AND HIS SONGS

As the birds come in the Spring,
We know not from where ;
As the stars come at evening
From depths of the air ;

As the rain comes from the cloud,
And the brook from the ground ;
As suddenly, low or loud,
Out of silence a sound ;

As the grape comes to the vine,
  The fruit to the tree ;
As the wind comes to the pine,
  And the tide to the sea ;

As come the white sails of ships
  O'er the ocean's verge ;
As comes the smile to the lips,
  The foam to the surge ;

So come to the Poet his songs,
  All hitherward blown

From the misty realm, that belongs
  To the vast Unknown.

His, and not his, are the lays
  He sings ; and their fame
Is his, and not his ; and the praise
  And the pride of a name.

For voices pursue him by day,
  And haunt him by night,
And he listens, and needs must obey,
  When the Angel says, " Write ! "

IN THE HARBOR

Shortly after Mr. Longfellow's death, the collection
entitled *In the Harbor*, *Ultima Thule*, *Part II.*, was
published, bearing upon the title-page for a motto the
final stanza in the dedicatory poem which introduces
Ultima Thule.

BECALMED

BECALMED upon the sea of Thought,
Still unattained the land it sought,
My mind, with loosely-hanging sails,
Lies waiting the auspicious gales.

On either side, behind, before,
The ocean stretches like a floor, —
A level floor of amethyst,
Crowned by a golden dome of mist.

Blow, breath of inspiration, blow !
Shake and uplift this golden glow !
And fill the canvas of the mind
With wafts of thy celestial wind.

Blow, breath of song ! until I feel
The straining sail, the lifting keel,
The life of the awakening sea,
Its motion and its mystery !

THE POET'S CALENDAR

JANUARY

JANUS am I ; oldest of potentates ;
  Forward I look, and backward, and be-
    low
I count, as god of avenues and gates,
  The years that through my portals come
    and go.

I block the roads, and drift the fields with
    snow ;
  I chase the wild-fowl from the frozen
    fen ;
My frosts congeal the rivers in their flow,
  My fires light up the hearths and hearts
    of men.

FEBRUARY

I am lustration ; and the sea is mine !
  I wash the sands and headlands with my
    tide ;
My brow is crowned with branches of the
    pine ;
  Before my chariot - wheels the fishes
    glide.
By me all things unclean are purified,
  By me the souls of men washed white
    again ;
E'en the unlovely tombs of those who died
  Without a dirge, I cleanse from every
    stain.

MARCH

I Martius am ! Once first, and now the
    third !
  To lead the Year was my appointed
    place ;
A mortal dispossessed me by a word,
  And set there Janus with the double
    face.

Hence I make war on all the human race ;
   I shake the cities with my hurricanes ;
I flood the rivers and their banks efface,
   And drown the farms and hamlets with
      my rains.

APRIL

I open wide the portals of the Spring
   To welcome the procession of the flowers,
With their gay banners, and the birds that
      sing
   Their song of songs from their aerial
      towers.
I soften with my sunshine and my showers
   The heart of earth ; with thoughts of
      love I glide
Into the hearts of men ; and with the
      Hours
   Upon the Bull with wreathèd horns I
      ride.

MAY

Hark ! The sea-faring wild-fowl loud pro-
      claim
   My coming, and the swarming of the
      bees.
These are my heralds, and behold ! my
      name
   Is written in blossoms on the hawthorn-
      trees.
I tell the mariner when to sail the seas ;
   I waft o'er all the land from far away
The breath and bloom of the Hesperides,
   My birthplace. I am Maia. I am May.

JUNE

Mine is the Month of Roses ; yes, and
      mine
   The Month of Marriages ! All pleasant
      sights
And scents, the fragrance of the blossoming
      vine,
   The foliage of the valleys and the
      heights.
Mine are the longest days, the loveliest
      nights ;
   The mower's scythe makes music to my
      ear ;
I am the mother of all dear delights ;
   I am the fairest daughter of the year.

JULY

My emblem is the Lion, and I breathe
   The breath of Libyan deserts o'er the
      land ;
My sickle as a sabre I unsheathe,
   And bent before me the pale harvests
      stand.
The lakes and rivers shrink at my com-
      mand,
   And there is thirst and fever in the air ;
The sky is changed to brass, the earth to
      sand ;
   I am the Emperor whose name I bear.

AUGUST

The Emperor Octavian, called the August,
   I being his favorite, bestowed his name
Upon me, and I hold it still in trust,
   In memory of him and of his fame.
I am the Virgin, and my vestal flame
   Burns less intensely than the Lion's
      rage ;
Sheaves are my only garlands, and I claim
   The golden Harvests as my heritage.

SEPTEMBER

I bear the Scales, where hang in equipoise
   The night and day ; and when unto my
      lips
I put my trumpet, with its stress and noise
   Fly the white clouds like tattered sails
      of ships ;
The tree-tops lash the air with sounding
      whips ;
   Southward the clamorous sea-fowl wing
      their flight ;
The hedges are all red with haws and hips,
   The Hunter's Moon reigns empress of
      the night.

OCTOBER

My ornaments are fruits ; my garments
      leaves,
   Woven like cloth of gold, and crimson
      dyed ;
I do not boast the harvesting of sheaves,
   O'er orchards and o'er vineyards I pre-
      side.

Though on the frigid Scorpion I ride,
  The dreamy air is full, and overflows
With tender memories of the summer-tide,
  And mingled voices of the doves and
    crows.

NOVEMBER

The Centaur, Sagittarius, am I,
  Born of Ixion's and the cloud's embrace ;
With sounding hoofs across the earth I
    fly,
  A steed Thessalian with a human face.
Sharp winds the arrows are with which I
    chase
  The leaves, half dead already with
    affright ;
I shroud myself in gloom ; and to the race
  Of mortals bring nor comfort nor de-
    light.

DECEMBER

Riding upon the Goat, with snow-white
    hair,
  I come, the last of all. This crown of
    mine
Is of the holly ; in my hand I bear
  The thyrsus, tipped with fragrant cones
    of pine.
I celebrate the birth of the Divine,
  And the return of the Saturnian reign ; —
My songs are carols sung at every shrine,
  Proclaiming " Peace on earth, good will
    to men."

AUTUMN WITHIN

  It is autumn ; not without,
    But within me is the cold.
  Youth and spring are all about ;
    It is I that have grown old.

  Birds are darting through the air,
    Singing, building without rest ;
  Life is stirring everywhere,
    Save within my lonely breast.

  There is silence : the dead leaves
    Fall and rustle and are still ;
  Beats no flail upon the sheaves,
    Comes no murmur from the mill.

THE FOUR LAKES OF MADISON

Four limpid lakes, — four Naiades
Or sylvan deities are these,
  In flowing robes of azure dressed ;
Four lovely handmaids, that uphold
Their shining mirrors, rimmed with gold,
  To the fair city in the West.

By day the coursers of the sun
Drink of these waters as they run
  Their swift diurnal round on high ;
By night the constellations glow
Far down the hollow deeps below,
  And glimmer in another sky.

Fair lakes, serene and full of light,
Fair town, arrayed in robes of white,
  How visionary ye appear !
All like a floating landscape seems
In cloud-land or the land of dreams,
  Bathed in a golden atmosphere !

VICTOR AND VANQUISHED

As one who long hath fled with panting
    breath
  Before his foe, bleeding and near to
    fall,
  I turn and set my back against the
    wall,
  And look thee in the face, triumphant
    Death.
I call for aid, and no one answereth ;
  I am alone with thee, who conquerest
    all ;
  Yet me thy threatening form doth not
    appall,
  For thou art but a phantom and a wraith.
Wounded and weak, sword broken at the
    hilt,
  With armor shattered, and without a
    shield,
  I stand unmoved ; do with me what thou
    wilt ;
I can resist no more, but will not yield.
  This is no tournament where cowards
    tilt ;
  The vanquished here is victor of the
    field.

MOONLIGHT

As a pale phantom with a lamp
  Ascends some ruin's haunted stair,
So glides the moon along the damp
  Mysterious chambers of the air.

Now hidden in cloud, and now revealed,
  As if this phantom, full of pain,
Were by the crumbling walls concealed,
  And at the windows seen again.

Until at last, serene and proud
  In all the splendor of her light,
She walks the terraces of cloud,
  Supreme as Empress of the Night.

I look, but recognize no more
  Objects familiar to my view ;
The very pathway to my door
  Is an enchanted avenue.

All things are changed. One mass of shade,
  The elm-trees drop their curtains down ;
By palace, park, and colonnade
  I walk as in a foreign town.

The very ground beneath my feet
  Is clothed with a diviner air ;
While marble paves the silent street
  And glimmers in the empty square.

Illusion ! Underneath there lies
  The common life of every day ;
Only the spirit glorifies
  With its own tints the sober gray.

In vain we look, in vain uplift
  Our eyes to heaven, if we are blind ;
We see but what we have the gift
  Of seeing ; what we bring we find.

THE CHILDREN'S CRUSADE

[A FRAGMENT]

I

WHAT is this I read in history,
Full of marvel, full of mystery,
Difficult to understand ?
Is it fiction, is it truth ?
Children in the flower of youth,

Heart in heart, and hand in hand,
Ignorant of what helps or harms,
Without armor, without arms,
Journeying to the Holy Land !

Who shall answer or divine ?
Never since the world was made
Such a wonderful crusade
Started forth for Palestine.
Never while the world shall last
Will it reproduce the past ;
Never will it see again
Such an army, such a band,
Over mountain, over main,
Journeying to the Holy Land.

Like a shower of blossoms blown
From the parent trees were they ;
Like a flock of birds that fly
Through the unfrequented sky,
Holding nothing as their own,
Passed they into lands unknown,
Passed to suffer and to die.

O the simple, child-like trust !
O the faith that could believe
What the harnessed, iron-mailed
Knights of Christendom had failed,
By their prowess, to achieve,
They, the children, could and must !

Little thought the Hermit, preaching
Holy Wars to knight and baron,
That the words dropped in his teaching,
His entreaty, his beseeching,
Would by children's hands be gleaned,
And the staff on which he leaned
Blossom like the rod of Aaron.

As a summer wind upheaves
The innumerable leaves
In the bosom of a wood, —
Not as separate leaves, but massed
All together by the blast, —
So for evil or for good
His resistless breath upheaved
All at once the many-leaved,
Many-thoughted multitude.

In the tumult of the air
Rock the boughs with all the nests
Cradled on their tossing crests ;
By the fervor of his prayer
Troubled hearts were everywhere
Rocked and tossed in human breasts.

For a century, at least,
His prophetic voice had ceased ;
But the air was heated still
By his lurid words and will,
As from fires in far-off woods,
In the autumn of the year,
An unwonted fever broods
In the sultry atmosphere.

II

In Cologne the bells were ringing,
In Cologne the nuns were singing
Hymns and canticles divine ;
Loud the monks sang in their stalls,
And the thronging streets were loud
With the voices of the crowd ; —
Underneath the city walls
Silent flowed the river Rhine.

From the gates, that summer day,
Clad in robes of hodden gray,
With the red cross on the breast,
Azure-eyed and golden-haired,
Forth the young crusaders fared ;
While above the band devoted
Consecrated banners floated,
Fluttered many a flag and streamer,
And the cross o'er all the rest !
Singing lowly, meekly, slowly,
"Give us, give us back the holy
Sepulchre of the Redeemer ! "
On the vast procession pressed,
Youths and maidens. . . .

III

Ah ! what master hand shall paint
How they journeyed on their way,
How the days grew long and dreary,
How their little feet grew weary,
How their little hearts grew faint !

Ever swifter day by day
Flowed the homeward river ; ever
More and more its whitening current
Broke and scattered into spray,
Till the calmly-flowing river
Changed into a mountain torrent,
Rushing from its glacier green
Down through chasm and black ravine.

Like a phœnix in its nest,
Burned the red sun in the West,

Sinking in an ashen cloud ;
In the East, above the crest
Of the sea-like mountain chain,
Like a phœnix from its shroud,
Came the red sun back again.

Now around them, white with snow,
Closed the mountain peaks.   Below,
Headlong from the precipice
Down into the dark abyss,
Plunged the cataract, white with foam ;
And it said, or seemed to say :
"Oh return, while yet you may,
Foolish children, to your home,
There the Holy City is ! "

But the dauntless leader said :
"Faint not, though your bleeding feet
O'er these slippery paths of sleet
Move but painfully and slowly ;
Other feet than yours have bled ;
Other tears than yours been shed.
Courage ! lose not heart or hope ;
On the mountains' southern slope
Lies Jerusalem the Holy ! "
As a white rose in its pride,
By the wind in summer-tide
Tossed and loosened from the branch,
Showers its petals o'er the ground,
From the distant mountain's side,
Scattering all its snows around,
With mysterious, muffled sound,
Loosened, fell the avalanche.
Voices, echoes far and near,
Roar of winds and waters blending,
Mists uprising, clouds impending,
Filled them with a sense of fear,
Formless, nameless, never ending.

•   •   •   •   •   •   •

SUNDOWN

THE summer sun is sinking low ;
Only the tree-tops redden and glow :
Only the weathercock on the spire
Of the neighboring church is a flame of fire
    All is in shadow below.

O beautiful, awful summer day,
What hast thou given, what taken away ?
Life and death, and love and hate,
Homes made happy or desolate,
    Hearts made sad or gay !

On the road of life one mile-stone more !
In the book of life one leaf turned o'er !
Like a red seal is the setting sun
On the good and the evil men have done, —
    Naught can to-day restore !

CHIMES

SWEET chimes ! that in the loneliness of
    night
    Salute the passing hour, and in the dark
    And silent chambers of the household
      mark
    The movements of the myriad orbs of
      light !
Through my closed eyelids, by the inner
    sight,
    I see the constellations in the arc
    Of their great circles moving on, and
      hark !
I almost hear them singing in their flight.
Better than sleep it is to lie awake,
    O'er-canopied by the vast starry dome
Of the immeasurable sky ; to feel
The slumbering world sink under us, and
    make
    Hardly an eddy, — a mere rush of foam
    On the great sea beneath a sinking keel.

FOUR BY THE CLOCK

    " Nahant, September 8, 1880, four o'clock in the
morning."

FOUR by the clock ! and yet not day ;
But the great world rolls and wheels away,
With its cities on land, and its ships at
    sea,
Into the dawn that is to be !

Only the lamp in the anchored bark
Sends its glimmer across the dark,
And the heavy breathing of the sea
Is the only sound that comes to me.

AUF WIEDERSEHEN

IN MEMORY OF J. T. F.

    In April, 1881, Mr. Longfellow notes in his diary:
" A sorrowful and distracted week. Fields died on Sun-
day, the 24th. Palfrey died on Tuesday. Two intimate
friends in one week ! " The poem was written April
30, 1881.

UNTIL we meet again ! That is the mean-
    ing
Of the familiar words, that men repeat
    At parting in the street.
Ah yes, till then ! but when death inter-
    vening
Rends us asunder, with what ceaseless pain
    We wait for the Again !

The friends who leave us do not feel the
    sorrow
Of parting, as we feel it, who must stay
    Lamenting day by day,
And knowing, when we wake upon the
    morrow,
We shall not find in its accustomed place
    The one beloved face.

It were a double grief, if the departed,
Being released from earth, should still re-
    tain
    A sense of earthly pain ;
It were a double grief, if the true-hearted,
Who loved us here, should on the farther
    shore
    Remember us no more.

Believing, in the midst of our afflictions,
That death is a beginning, not an end,
    We cry to them, and send
Farewells, that better might be called pre-
    dictions,
Being fore-shadowings of the future, thrown
    Into the vast Unknown.

Faith overleaps the confines of our rea-
    son,
And if by faith, as in old times was said,
    Women received their dead
Raised up to life, then only for a season
Our partings are, nor shall we wait in vain
    Until we meet again !

ELEGIAC VERSE

    Written at various times, mostly between April and
July, 1881. In the notes at the end of the volume will
be found further examples.

I

PERADVENTURE of old, some bard in Ionian
    Islands,
    Walking alone by the sea, hearing the
      wash of the waves,

Learned the secret from them of the beauti-
    ful verse elegiac,
Breathing into his song motion and sound
    of the sea.

For as the wave of the sea, upheaving in
    long undulations,
Plunges loud on the sands, pauses, and
    turns, and retreats,
So the Hexameter, rising and singing, with
    cadence sonorous,
Falls ; and in refluent rhythm back the
    Pentameter flows.

II

Not in his youth alone, but in age, may the
    heart of the poet
Bloom into song, as the gorse blossoms
    in autumn and spring.

III

Not in tenderness wanting, yet rough are
    the rhymes of our poet ;
Though it be Jacob's voice, Esau's, alas !
    are the hands.

IV

Let us be grateful to writers for what is
    left in the inkstand ;
When to leave off is an art only attained
    by the few.

V

How can the Three be One ? you ask me ;
    I answer by asking,
Hail and snow and rain, are they not
    three, and yet one ?

VI

By the mirage uplifted, the land floats
    vague in the ether,
Ships and the shadows of ships hang in
    the motionless air ;
So by the art of the poet our common life
    is uplifted,
So, transfigured, the world floats in a
    luminous haze.

VII

Like a French poem is Life ; being only
    perfect in structure
When with the masculine rhymes mingled
    the feminine are.

VIII

Down from the mountain descends the
    brooklet, rejoicing in freedom ;
Little it dreams of the mill hid in the
    valley below ;
Glad with the joy of existence, the child
    goes singing and laughing,
Little dreaming what toils lie in the
    future concealed.

IX

As the ink from our pen, so flow our
    thoughts and our feelings
When we begin to write, however slug-
    gish before.

X

Like the Kingdom of Heaven, the Fountain
    of Youth is within us ;
If we seek it elsewhere, old shall we
    grow in the search.

XI

If you would hit the mark, you must aim
    a little above it ;
Every arrow that flies feels the attraction
    of earth.

XII

Wisely the Hebrews admit no Present tense
    in their language ;
While we are speaking the word, it is
    already the Past.

XIII

In the twilight of age all things seem
    strange and phantasmal,
As between daylight and dark ghost-like
    the landscape appears.

XIV

Great is the art of beginning, but greater
   the art is of ending ;
Many a poem is marred by a superfluous
   verse.

THE CITY AND THE SEA

THE panting City cried to the Sea,
" I am faint with heat, — Oh breathe on
   me ! "

And the Sea said, " Lo, I breathe ! but my
   breath
To some will be life, to others death ! "

As to Prometheus, bringing ease
In pain, come the Oceanides,

So to the City, hot with the flame
Of the pitiless sun, the east wind came.

It came from the heaving breast of the
   deep,
Silent as dreams are, and sudden as sleep.

Life-giving, death-giving, which will it be ;
O breath of the merciful, merciless Sea ?

MEMORIES

OFT I remember those whom I have known
   In other days, to whom my heart was
     led
   As by a magnet, and who are not dead,
   But absent, and their memories over-
     grown
With other thoughts and troubles of my
   own,
   As graves with grasses are, and at their
     head
The stone with moss and lichens so o'er-
   spread,
Nothing is legible but the name alone.
And is it so with them ?   After long years,
   Do they remember me in the same way,
   And is the memory pleasant as to me ?
I fear to ask ; yet wherefore are my fears ?
   Pleasures, like flowers, may wither and
     decay,
   And yet the root perennial may be.

HERMES TRISMEGISTUS

As Seleucus narrates, Hermes describes the principles
that rank as wholes in two myriads of books ; or, as we
are informed by Manetho, he perfectly unfolded these
principles in three myriads six thousand five hundred
and twenty-five volumes. . . .
  . . . Our ancestors dedicated the inventions of their
wisdom to this deity, inscribing all their own writings
with the name of Hermes. — IAMBLICUS.

STILL through Egypt's desert places
   Flows the lordly Nile,
From its banks the great stone faces
   Gaze with patient smile.
Still the pyramids imperious
   Pierce the cloudless skies,
And the Sphinx stares with mysterious,
   Solemn, stony eyes.

But where are the old Egyptian
   Demi-gods and kings ?
Nothing left but an inscription
   Graven on stones and rings.
Where are Helios and Hephæstus,
   Gods of eldest eld ?
Where is Hermes Trismegistus,
   Who their secrets held ?

Where are now the many hundred
   Thousand books he wrote ?
By the Thaumaturgists plundered,
   Lost in lands remote ;
In oblivion sunk forever,
   As when o'er the land
Blows a storm-wind, in the river
   Sinks the scattered sand.

Something unsubstantial, ghostly,
   Seems this Theurgist,
In deep meditation mostly
   Wrapped, as in a mist.
Vague, phantasmal, and unreal
   To our thought he seems,
Walking in a world ideal,
   In a land of dreams.

Was he one, or many, merging
   Name and fame in one,
Like a stream, to which, converging,
   Many streamlets run ?
Till, with gathered power proceeding,
   Ampler sweep it takes,
Downward the sweet waters leading
   From unnumbered lakes.

By the Nile I see him wandering,
  Pausing now and then,
On the mystic union pondering
  Between gods and men ;
Half believing, wholly feeling,
  With supreme delight,
How the gods, themselves concealing,
  Lift men to their height.

Or in Thebes, the hundred-gated,
  In the thoroughfare
Breathing, as if consecrated,
  A diviner air ;
And amid discordant noises,
  In the jostling throng,
Hearing far, celestial voices
  Of Olympian song.

Who shall call his dreams fallacious ?
  Who has searched or sought
All the unexplored and spacious
  Universe of thought ?
Who, in his own skill confiding,
  Shall with rule and line
Mark the border-land dividing
  Human and divine ?

Trismegistus ! three times greatest !
  How thy name sublime
Has descended to this latest
  Progeny of time !
Happy they whose written pages
  Perish with their lives,
If amid the crumbling ages
  Still their name survives !

Thine, O priest of Egypt, lately
  Found I in the vast,
Weed-encumbered, sombre, stately,
  Grave-yard of the Past ;
And a presence moved before me
  On that gloomy shore,
As a waft of wind, that o'er me
  Breathed, and was no more.

TO THE AVON

FLOW on, sweet river ! like his verse
Who lies beneath this sculptured hearse ;
Nor wait beside the churchyard wall
For him who cannot hear thy call.

Thy playmate once ; I see him now
A boy with sunshine on his brow,
And hear in Stratford's quiet street
The patter of his little feet.

I see him by thy shallow edge
Wading knee-deep amid the sedge ;
And lost in thought, as if thy stream
Were the swift river of a dream.

He wonders whitherward it flows ;
And fain would follow where it goes,
To the wide world, that shall erelong
Be filled with his melodious song.

Flow on, fair stream ! That dream is o'er ;
He stands upon another shore ;
A vaster river near him flows,
And still he follows where it goes.

PRESIDENT GARFIELD

" E venni dal martirio a questa pace."
  Paradiso, XV. 148.

THESE words the poet heard in Paradise,
  Uttered by one who, bravely dying here,
  In the true faith was living in that
    sphere
Where the celestial cross of sacrifice
Spread its protecting arms athwart the
    skies ;
  And set thereon, like jewels crystal
    clear,
  The souls magnanimous, that knew not
    fear,
  Flashed their effulgence on his dazzled
    eyes.
Ah me ! how dark the discipline of pain,
  Were not the suffering followed by the
    sense
Of infinite rest and infinite release !
This is our consolation ; and again
  A great soul cries to us in our suspense,
  " I came from martyrdom unto this
    peace ! "

MY BOOKS

SADLY as some old mediæval knight
  Gazed at the arms he could no longer
    wield,
  The sword two-handed and the shining
    shield
Suspended in the hall, and full in sight,

While secret longings for the lost delight
　Of tourney or adventure in the field
Came over him, and tears but half con-
　　cealed
Trembled and fell upon his beard of
　　white,
So I behold these books upon their shelf,
　My ornaments and arms of other days ;
Not wholly useless, though no longer
　used,
For they remind me of my other self,
　Younger and stronger, and the pleasant
　　ways
In which I walked, now clouded and
　confused.

MAD RIVER

IN THE WHITE MOUNTAINS

TRAVELLER.

WHY dost thou wildly rush and roar,
　Mad River, O Mad River ?
Wilt thou not pause and cease to pour
Thy hurrying, headlong waters o'er
　This rocky shelf forever ?

What secret trouble stirs thy breast ?
　Why all this fret and flurry ?
Dost thou not know that what is best
In this too restless world is rest
　From over-work and worry ?

THE RIVER.

What wouldst thou in these mountains
　　seek,
　O stranger from the city ?
Is it perhaps some foolish freak
Of thine, to put the words I speak
　Into a plaintive ditty ?

TRAVELLER.

Yes ; I would learn of thee thy song,
　With all its flowing numbers,
And in a voice as fresh and strong
As thine is, sing it all day long,
　And hear it in my slumbers.

THE RIVER.

A brooklet nameless and unknown
　Was I at first, resembling
A little child, that all alone
Comes venturing down the stairs of stone,
　Irresolute and trembling.

Later, by wayward fancies led,
　For the wide world I panted ;
Out of the forest, dark and dread,
Across the open fields I fled,
　Like one pursued and haunted.

I tossed my arms, I sang aloud,
　My voice exultant blending
With thunder from the passing cloud,
The wind, the forest bent and bowed,
　The rush of rain descending.

I heard the distant ocean call,
　Imploring and entreating ;
Drawn onward, o'er this rocky wall
I plunged, and the loud waterfall
　Made answer to the greeting.

And now, beset with many ills,
　A toilsome life I follow ;
Compelled to carry from the hills
These logs to the impatient mills
　Below there in the hollow.

Yet something ever cheers and charms
　The rudeness of my labors ;
Daily I water with these arms
The cattle of a hundred farms,
　And have the birds for neighbors.

Men call me Mad, and well they may,
　When, full of rage and trouble,
I burst my banks of sand and clay,
And sweep their wooden bridge away,
　Like withered reeds or stubble.

Now go and write thy little rhyme,
　As of thine own creating.
Thou seest the day is past its prime ;
I can no longer waste my time ;
　The mills are tired of waiting.

POSSIBILITIES

WHERE are the Poets, unto whom belong
　The Olympian heights ; whose singing
　　shafts were sent
　Straight to the mark, and not from bows
　　half bent,
　But with the utmost tension of the thong ?
Where are the stately argosies of song,
　Whose rushing keels made music as they
　　went
　Sailing in search of some new continent,

With all sail set, and steady winds and
    strong?
Perhaps there lives some dreamy boy, un-
    taught
In schools, some graduate of the field or
    street,
Who shall become a master of the art,
An admiral sailing the high seas of thought,
Fearless and first, and steering with his
    fleet
For lands not yet laid down in any chart.

DECORATION DAY

SLEEP, comrades, sleep and rest
    On this Field of the Grounded Arms,
Where foes no more molest,
    Nor sentry's shot alarms!

Ye have slept on the ground before,
    And started to your feet
At the cannon's sudden roar,
    Or the drum's redoubling beat.

But in this camp of Death
    No sound your slumber breaks;
Here is no fevered breath,
    No wound that bleeds and aches.

All is repose and peace,
    Untrampled lies the sod;
The shouts of battle cease,
    It is the truce of God!

Rest, comrades, rest and sleep!
    The thoughts of men shall be
As sentinels to keep
    Your rest from danger free.

Your silent tents of green
    We deck with fragrant flowers;
Yours has the suffering been,
    The memory shall be ours.

A FRAGMENT

AWAKE! arise! the hour is late!
    Angels are knocking at thy door!
They are in haste and cannot wait,
    And once departed come no more.

Awake! arise! the athlete's arm
    Loses its strength by too much rest;
The fallow land, the untilled farm
    Produces only weeds at best.

LOSS AND GAIN

WHEN I compare
What I have lost with what I have gained,
What I have missed with what attained,
    Little room do I find for pride.

I am aware
How many days have been idly spent;
How like an arrow the good intent
    Has fallen short or been turned aside.

But who shall dare
To measure loss and gain in this wise?
Defeat may be victory in disguise;
    The lowest ebb is the turn of the tide.

INSCRIPTION ON THE SHANK- LIN FOUNTAIN

O TRAVELLER, stay thy weary feet;
Drink of this fountain, pure and sweet;
    It flows for rich and poor the same.
Then go thy way, remembering still
The wayside well beneath the hill,
    The cup of water in his name.

THE BELLS OF SAN BLAS

*The last poem written by Mr. Longfellow. The last
verse but one is dated March 12, 1882. The final verse
was added March 15. Mr. Longfellow died March 24.
The poem was suggested by an article in Harper's
Magazine, which the poet had just read.*

WHAT say the Bells of San Blas
To the ships that southward pass
    From the harbor of Mazatlan?
To them it is nothing more
Than the sound of surf on the shore, —
    Nothing more to master or man.

But to me, a dreamer of dreams,
To whom what is and what seems
    Are often one and the same, —
The Bells of San Blas to me
Have a strange, wild melody,
    And are something more than a name.

For bells are the voice of the church;
They have tones that touch and search
    The hearts of young and old;
One sound to all, yet each
Lends a meaning to their speech,
    And the meaning is manifold.

They are a voice of the Past,
Of an age that is fading fast,
    Of a power austere and grand ;
When the flag of Spain unfurled
Its folds o'er this western world,
    And the Priest was lord of the land.

The chapel that once looked down
On the little seaport town
    Has crumbled into the dust ;
And on oaken beams below
The bells swing to and fro,
    And are green with mould and rust.

"Is, then, the old faith dead,"
They say, "and in its stead
    Is some new faith proclaimed,
That we are forced to remain
Naked to sun and rain,
    Unsheltered and ashamed ?

"Once in our tower aloof
We rang over wall and roof
    Our warnings and our complaints ;
And round about us there
The white doves filled the air,
    Like the white souls of the saints.

"The saints ! Ah, have they grown
Forgetful of their own ?
    Are they asleep, or dead,
That open to the sky
Their ruined Missions lie,
    No longer tenanted ?

"Oh, bring us back once more
The vanished days of yore,
    When the world with faith was filled ;
Bring back the fervid zeal,
The hearts of fire and steel,
    The hands that believe and build.

"Then from our tower again
We will send over land and main
    Our voices of command,
Like exiled kings who return
To their thrones. and the people learn
    That the Priest is lord of the land !"

O Bells of San Blas, in vain
Ye call back the Past again !
    The Past is deaf to your prayer ;
Out of the shadows of night
The world rolls into light ;
    It is daybreak everywhere.

FRAGMENTS

October 22, 1838.

NEGLECTED record of a mind neglected,
Unto what " lets and stops " art thou sub-
    jected !
The day with all its toils and occupations,
The night with its reflections and sensations,
The future, and the present, and the past, —
All I remember, feel, and hope at last,
All shapes of joy and sorrow, as they pass, —
Find but a dusty image in this glass.

August 18, 1847.

O faithful, indefatigable tides,
That evermore upon God's errands go, —
Now seaward bearing tidings of the land, —
Now landward bearing tidings of the sea, —
And filling every frith and estuary,
Each arm of the great sea, each little creek,
Each thread and filament of water-courses,
Full with your ministration of delight !
Under the rafters of this wooden bridge
I see you come and go ; sometimes in haste
To reach your journey's end, which being
    done
With feet unrested ye return again
And recommence the never-ending task ;
Patient, whatever burdens ye may bear,
And fretted only by the impeding rocks.

December 18, 1847.

Soft through the silent air descend the
    feathery snow-flakes ;
White are the distant hills, white are the
    neighboring fields ;
Only the marshes are brown, and the river
    rolling among them
Weareth the leaden hue seen in the eyes of
    the blind.

August 4, 1856.

A lovely morning, without the glare of the
sun, the sea in great commotion, chafing
and foaming.

So from the bosom of darkness our days
    come roaring and gleaming,
    Chafe and break into foam, sink into
    darkness again.
But on the shores of Time each leaves some
    trace of its passage,
    Though the succeeding wave washes it
    out from the sand.

CHRISTUS: A MYSTERY

There is no one of Mr. Longfellow's writings which may be said to have so dominated his literary life. The study of Dante and the translation of the *Divina Commedia* subtended a wider arc in time, but from the nature of things the interpretation of a great work was subordinate to the development of a theme which was interior to the poet's thought and emotion. Yet even in point of time, that which elapsed between the first conception of *Christus* and its final accomplishment was scarcely less than that which extended from the day when Mr. Longfellow opened Dante to the end of his life, — for so long did he live in companionship with the great seer.

The first indication of actual work upon the subject does not appear until the end of 1849, when he seems to have decided to take up first the second division. He had dismissed his volume of poems, *The Seaside and the Fireside*, "another stone rolled over the hilltop!" and proceeded in his diary, November 19: "And now I long to try a loftier strain, the sublimer Song whose broken melodies have for so many years breathed through my soul in the better hours of life, and which I trust and believe will ere long unite themselves into a symphony not all unworthy the sublime theme, but furnishing 'some equivalent expression for the trouble and wrath of life, for its sorrow and its mystery.'" On December 10th, he wrote: "A bleak and dismal day. Wrote in the morning *The Challenge of Thor* as Prologue or *Introitus* to the second part of *Christus.*" This he laid aside, taking it up again ten years later, when he proposed to write the *Saga of King Olaf.* It is probable that he had in mind the opposition of northern paganism to the Christianity of sacerdotalism, and the supremacy of the latter. But the theme of the drama was constantly before him in one shape or another. In his diary, under date of January 10, 1850, he records: "In the evening, pondered and meditated upon sundry scenes of *Christus.* In such meditation one tastes the delight of the poetic vision, without the pain of putting it into words." The scheme of his first venture had evidently been more or less determined upon, for a few weeks later he notes: "February 28. And so ends the winter and the vacation. Not quite satisfactorily to me. Yet something I have done. Some half dozen scenes or more are written of *The Golden Legend,* which is Part Second of *Christus;* and the whole is much clearer in my mind as to handling, division, and the form and pressure of the several parts." It is to be noted that already in 1839 there had crossed his mind the notion of writing a drama based upon the legend of *Der Arme Heinrich,* and that he had perceived the value of Elsie. "I have a heroine," he says, "as sweet as Imogen, could I but paint her so."

The *Golden Legend* was published near the close of 1851, but the author gave no intimation of the relation which the work held to a larger plan. He had taken for the core of his poem the story of *Der Arme Heinrich* as told by Hartmann von der Aue, a minnesinger of the twelfth century, to be found in Mailáth's *Altdeutsche Gedichte,* published in Stuttgart in 1809, and it was not till after the book was issued that he caught sight of Jacobus de Voragine's *Legenda Aurea.* His own account of his work may be read in brief in a letter which he wrote to an English correspondent at this time. "I am glad to know," he says, "that you find something to like in *The Golden Legend.* I have endeavored to show in it, among other things, that through the darkness and corruption of the Middle Ages ran a bright, deep stream of Faith, strong enough for all the exigen-

cies of life and death. In order to do this I had to introduce some portion of this darkness and corruption as a background. I am sure you will be glad to know that the monk's sermon is not wholly of my own invention. The worst passage in it is from a sermon of Fra Gabriella Barletta, an Italian preacher of the fifteenth century. The Miracle Play is founded on the Apocryphal Gospels of James and the Infancy of Christ. Both this and the sermon show how sacred themes were handled in 'the days of long ago.'"

It is a strong illustration of the importance which Mr. Longfellow attached to *The Golden Legend* as a portion of a larger, more inclusive work, that we find him regretting, while his book was in full tide of success, that he had not taken a theme more fit to his purpose which had been chosen by another poet. "We stayed at home," he writes, April 2, 1852, "reading *The Saint's Tragedy,* the story of St. Elizabeth of Hungary put into dramatic form with great power. I wish I had hit upon this theme for my *Golden Legend,* the mediæval part of my Trilogy. It is nobler and more characteristic than my obscure legend. Strange that while I was writing a dramatic poem illustrating the Middle Ages, Kingsley should have been doing the same, and that we should have chosen precisely the same period, about 1230. His poem was published first, but I never saw it, or a review of it, till two days ago." Whether or not Mr. Longfellow would have wrought at the other theme with any more satisfaction to himself, *The Golden Legend* has taken its place as a faithful exponent of the phase of Christianity which it described. "Longfellow," says a competent authority, "in his *Golden Legend* has entered more closely into the temper of the monk, for good and for evil, than ever yet theological writer or historian, though they may have given their life's labor to the analysis."

Christus was, however, pressing upon the poet's mind; the completion of the second division only made him more desirous of fulfilling the noble theme. *The Golden Legend* had been published a few weeks when he wrote in his diary one Sunday: "Dec. 28, 1851. The weather, which has been intensely cold, suddenly changes to rain; and avalanches of snow thunder from the college-roofs all sermon-time. A grand accompaniment to Mr. Ellis, who was preaching about the old prophets, — an excellent discourse. Ah me! how many things there are to meditate upon in this great world! And all this meditation, — of what avail is it, if it does not end in some action? The great theme of my poem haunts me ever; but I cannot bring it into act."

It was nearly a score of years before another number of the Trilogy was ready, though it is probable that Mr. Longfellow was in the neighborhood of *The New England Tragedies* when he was diverted for the time by the attractive theme of *The Courtship of Miles Standish.* As far back as 1839 he had thought of a drama on Cotton Mather. It is curious that he should have mentioned that and a drama on "the old poetic legend of *Der Arme Heinrich*" in the same sentence as possible themes, a couple of years before the conception of *Christus* came to him. In the spring of 1856 he was contemplating a tragedy which should take in the Puritans and the Quakers, and preparing for it by looking over books on the two sects, "particularly," he says, "Besse's *Sufferings of the Quakers,* — a strange record of violent persecution for merest trifles." He notes on April 2d of that year: "Wrote a scene in my new drama, *The Old Colony,* just to break ground," and a month later: "May 1. At home all day pondering the New England Tragedy, and writing notes and bits of scenes." He was still experimenting on it in July and in November, but then he seems to have made a new start and to have begun *The Courtship of Miles Standish* as a drama.

On the 27th of August, 1857, he had finished the first rough draft of *Wenlock Christison*, and later resumed his *Miles Standish* as an idyl. For a while this poem excluded the tragedy, but he took up the latter when the *Courtship* was completed and began a revision. On the 17th of August, 1858, he notes : " The morning, as usual, worm - eaten with the writing of letters. I am now going to try a scene in *Wenlock Christison*. I write accordingly scene second of act first. Just as I finish the bells ring noon. There is a distant booming of cannon. F. comes in and says, 'The Queen's message has arrived by the Atlantic cable.' " " December 13. I have been at work on *Wenlock Christison*, moulding and shaping it."

It was ten years after this that *The New England Tragedies* emerged from the printing-office. Ten copies at first were printed to guard against accident to the manuscript copy, as the author was about leaving home for a considerable absence in Europe. In October of the same year, 1868, the book was published simultaneously in Boston and London. It would seem as if this whole division of the Trilogy caused the poet great doubt, and that he held back from publication out of distrust of his work. He makes but little reference to it in his diary, recording once that he read a portion to Mr. Fields, who received it rather coldly. In this case more emphatically than in the case of *The Golden Legend*, the relation of the part to the whole was uppermost in the poet's mind. It may be that he intended at first to wait until he could write the first part before publishing the third, but finally gave out the modern portion, as before, with no intimation of its place in a larger plan. But *The New England Tragedies* had no such intrinsic attractiveness as *The Golden Legend*, and in absence of any explanation of the author's ulterior design was taken on its own ground with comparative indifference. The title of *Wenlock Christison* given to the former of the two tragedies was changed, when the book was published, to *John Endicott*.

Although Mr. Longfellow projected a third drama, the scene to be laid among the Moravians of Bethlehem, by which he hoped to be able to harmonize the discord of *The New England Tragedies* and thus give a not unfitting close to the work, he never wrote this drama, and it is most probable that Mr. Longfellow finally regarded the *Tragedies* as satisfying the requirements of the Trilogy, and was thenceforth impelled by an increased desire to complete his task by the preparation of the first and most difficult number. In the latter part of 1870 he began to make essays in it, and early in January, 1871, he writes in his diary : " The subject of *The Divine Tragedy* has taken entire possession of me. All day pondering upon and arranging it."

The Divine Tragedy was published thus at the close of 1871, and in the autumn of 1872 *Christus* appeared as a complete work. It is an interesting illustration of the place which the work held in his mind that he should now incorporate in it the poem of *Blind Bartimeus*, which, when he wrote it, he was disposed to refer in imagination to a monk of the middle ages. The design of the poet now stood revealed.

INTROITUS

The ANGEL *bearing the* PROPHET HABAKKUK
through the air.

PROPHET.

WHY dost thou bear me aloft,
O Angel of God, on thy pinions
O'er realms and dominions ?
Softly I float as a cloud
In air, for thy right hand upholds me,
Thy garment enfolds me !

ANGEL.

Lo ! as I passed on my way
In the harvest-field I beheld thee,
When no man compelled thee,
Bearing with thine own hands
This food to the famishing reapers,
A flock without keepers !

The fragrant sheaves of the wheat
Made the air above them sweet ;
Sweeter and more divine
Was the scent of the scattered grain,
That the reaper's hand let fall
To be gathered again
By the hand of the gleaner !
Sweetest, divinest of all,
Was the humble deed of thine,
And the meekness of thy demeanor !

PROPHET.

Angel of Light,
I cannot gainsay thee,
I can but obey thee !

ANGEL.

Beautiful was it in the Lord's sight,
To behold his Prophet
Feeding those that toil,
The tillers of the soil.
But why should the reapers eat of it
And not the Prophet of Zion
In the den of the lion ?
The Prophet should feed the Prophet !
Therefore I thee have uplifted,
And bear thee aloft by the hair
Of thy head, like a cloud that is drifted
Through the vast unknown of the air !

Five days hath the Prophet been lying
In Babylon, in the den
Of the lions, death-defying,
Defying hunger and thirst ;
But the worst
Is the mockery of men !
Alas ! how full of fear
Is the fate of Prophet and Seer !
Forevermore, forevermore,
It shall be as it hath been heretofore ;
The age in which they live
Will not forgive

The splendor of the everlasting light,
That makes their foreheads bright,
Nor the sublime
Fore-running of their time!

PROPHET.

Oh tell me, for thou knowest,
Wherefore and by what grace,
Have I, who am least and lowest,
Been chosen to this place,
To this exalted part?

ANGEL.

Because thou art
The Struggler; and from thy youth
Thy humble and patient life
Hath been a strife
And battle for the Truth;
Nor hast thou paused nor halted,
Nor ever in thy pride
Turned from the poor aside,
But with deed and word and pen
Hast served thy fellow-men;
Therefore art thou exalted!

PROPHET.

By thine arrow's light
Thou goest onward through the night,
And by the clear
Sheen of thy glittering spear!
When will our journey end?

ANGEL.

Lo, it is ended!
Yon silver gleam
Is the Euphrates' stream.
Let us descend
Into the city splendid,
Into the City of Gold!

PROPHET.

Behold!
As if the stars had fallen from their places
Into the firmament below,
The streets, the gardens, and the vacant
        spaces
With light are all aglow;
And hark!
As we draw near,
What sound is it I hear
Ascending through the dark?

ANGEL.

The tumultuous noise of the nations,
Their rejoicings and lamentations,

The pleadings of their prayer,
The groans of their despair,
The cry of their imprecations.
Their wrath, their love, their hate!

PROPHET.

Surely the world doth wait
The coming of its Redeemer!

ANGEL.

Awake from thy sleep, O dreamer!
The hour is near, though late;
Awake! write the vision sublime,
The vision, that is for a time,
Though it tarry, wait; it is nigh;
In the end it will speak and not lie.

PART ONE

THE DIVINE TRAGEDY

THE FIRST PASSOVER

I

VOX CLAMANTIS

JOHN THE BAPTIST.

REPENT! repent! repent!
For the kingdom of God is at hand,
And all the land
Full of the knowledge of the Lord shall be
As the waters cover the sea,
And encircle the continent!

Repent! repent! repent!
For lo, the hour appointed,
The hour so long foretold
By the Prophets of old,
Of the coming of the Anointed,
The Messiah, the Paraclete,
The Desire of the Nations, is nigh!
He shall not strive nor cry,
Nor his voice be heard in the street;
Nor the bruised reed shall He break,
Nor quench the smoking flax;
And many of them that sleep
In the dust of earth shall awake,
On that great and terrible day,
And the wicked shall wail and weep,
And be blown like a smoke away,
And be melted away like wax.
Repent! repent! repent!

O Priest, and Pharisee,
Who hath warned you to flee
From the wrath that is to be?
From the coming anguish and ire?
The axe is laid at the root
Of the trees, and every tree
That bringeth not forth good fruit
Is hewn down and cast into the fire!

Ye Scribes, why come ye hither?
In the hour that is uncertain,
In the day of anguish and trouble,
He that stretcheth the heavens as a curtain
And spreadeth them out as a tent,
Shall blow upon you, and ye shall wither,
And the whirlwind shall take you away as
    stubble!
Repent! repent! repent!

PRIEST.

Who art thou, O man of prayer!
In raiment of camel's hair,
Begirt with leathern thong,
That here in the wilderness,
With a cry as of one in distress,
Preachest unto this throng?
Art thou the Christ?

JOHN.

Priest of Jerusalem,
In meekness and humbleness,
I deny not, I confess
I am not the Christ!

PRIEST.

What shall we say unto them
That sent us here? Reveal
Thy name, and naught conceal!
Art thou Elias?

JOHN.
No!

PRIEST.

Art thou that Prophet, then,
Of lamentation and woe,
Who, as a symbol and sign
Of impending wrath divine
Upon unbelieving men,
Shattered the vessel of clay
In the Valley of Slaughter?

JOHN.
Nay.

I am not he thou namest!

PRIEST.

Who art thou, and what is the word
That here thou proclaimest?

JOHN.

I am the voice of one
Crying in the wilderness alone:
Prepare ye the way of the Lord;
Make his paths straight
In the land that is desolate!

PRIEST.

If thou be not the Christ,
Nor yet Elias, nor he
That, in sign of the things to be,
Shattered the vessel of clay
In the Valley of Slaughter,
Then declare unto us, and say
By what authority now
Baptizest thou?

JOHN.

I indeed baptize you with water
Unto repentance; but He,
That cometh after me,
Is mightier than I and higher;
The latchet of whose shoes
I am not worthy to unloose;
He shall baptize you with fire,
And with the Holy Ghost!
Whose fan is in his hand;
He will purge to the uttermost
His floor, and garner his wheat,
But will burn the chaff in the brand
And fire of unquenchable heat!
Repent! repent! repent!

II

MOUNT QUARANTANIA

I

LUCIFER.

Not in the lightning's flash, nor in the
    thunder,
Not in the tempest, nor the cloudy storm,
    Will I array my form;
But part invisible these boughs asunder,
And move and murmur, as the wind up-
    heaves
    And whispers in the leaves.

Not as a terror and a desolation,
Not in my natural shape, inspiring fear
   And dread, will I appear ;
But in soft tones of sweetness and persua-
   sion,
A sound as of the fall of mountain streams,
   Or voices heard in dreams.

He sitteth there in silence, worn and wasted
With famine, and uplifts his hollow eyes
   To the unpitying skies ;
For forty days and nights he hath not tasted
Of food or drink, his parted lips are pale,
   Surely his strength must fail.

Wherefore dost thou in penitential fasting
Waste and consume the beauty of thy
   youth ?
Ah, if thou be in truth
The Son of the Unnamed, the Everlasting,
Command these stones beneath thy feet to
   be
   Changed into bread for thee !

CHRISTUS.

'T is written : Man shall not live by bread
   alone,
But by each word that from God's mouth
   proceedeth !

II

LUCIFER.

Too weak, alas ! too weak is the temptation
For one whose soul to nobler things aspires
   Than sensual desires !
Ah, could I, by some sudden aberration,
Lead and delude to suicidal death
   This Christ of Nazareth !

Unto the holy Temple on Moriah,
With its resplendent domes, and manifold
   Bright pinnacles of gold,
Where they await thy coming, O Messiah !
Lo, I have brought thee ! Let thy glory
   here
   Be manifest and clear.

Reveal thyself by royal act and gesture
Descending with the bright triumphant host
   Of all the highermost
Archangels, and about thee as a vesture
The shining clouds, and all thy splendors
   show
   Unto the world below !

Cast thyself down, it is the hour appointed ;
And God hath given his angels charge and
   care
   To keep thee and upbear
Upon their hands his only Son, the Anointed,
Lest he should dash his foot against a stone
   And die, and be unknown.

CHRISTUS.

'T is written : Thou shalt not tempt the
   Lord thy God !

III

LUCIFER.

I cannot thus delude him to perdition !
But one temptation still remains untried,
   The trial of his pride,
The thirst of power, the fever of ambition !
Surely by these a humble peasant's son
   At last may be undone !

Above the yawning chasms and deep abysses,
Across the headlong torrents, I have brought
   Thy footsteps, swift as thought ;
And from the highest of these precipices,
The Kingdoms of the world thine eyes be-
   hold,
   Like a great map unrolled.

From far-off Lebanon, with cedars crested,
To where the waters of the Asphalt Lake
   On its white pebbles break,
And the vast desert, silent, sand-invested,
These kingdoms all are mine, and thine
   shall be,
   If thou wilt worship me !

CHRISTUS.

Get thee behind me, Satan ! thou shalt wor-
   ship
The Lord thy God ; Him only shalt thou
   serve !

ANGELS MINISTRANT.

The sun goes down ; the evening shadows
   lengthen,
The fever and the struggle of the day
   Abate and pass away ;
Thine Angels Ministrant, we come to
   strengthen
And comfort thee, and crown thee with the
   palm,
   The silence and the calm.

III

THE MARRIAGE IN CANA

THE MUSICIANS.

Rise up, my love, my fair one,
Rise up, and come away,
For lo ! the winter is past,
The rain is over and gone,
The flowers appear on the earth,
The time of the singing of birds is come,
And the voice of the turtle is heard in
    our land.

THE BRIDEGROOM.

Sweetly the minstrels sing the Song of
    Songs !
My heart runs forward with it, and I say :
Oh set me as a seal upon thine heart,
And set me as a seal upon thine arm ;
For love is strong as life, and strong as
    death,
And cruel as the grave is jealousy !

THE MUSICIANS.

I sleep, but my heart awaketh ;
'T is the voice of my beloved
Who knocketh, saying : Open to me,
My sister, my love, my dove,
For my head is filled with dew,
My locks with the drops of the night !

THE BRIDE.

Ah yes, I sleep, and yet my heart awaketh.
It is the voice of my beloved who knocks.

THE BRIDEGROOM.

O beautiful as Rebecca at the fountain,
O beautiful as Ruth among the sheaves !
O fairest among women ! O undefiled !
Thou art all fair, my love, there 's no spot
    in thee !

THE MUSICIANS.

My beloved is white and ruddy,
The chiefest among ten thousand ;
His locks are black as a raven,
His eyes are the eyes of doves,
Of doves by the rivers of water,
His lips are like unto lilies,
Dropping sweet-smelling myrrh.

ARCHITRICLINUS.

Who is that youth with the dark azure
    eyes,
And hair, in color like unto the wine,
Parted upon his forehead, and behind
Falling in flowing locks ?

PARANYMPHUS.

          The Nazarene
Who preacheth to the poor in field and
    village
The coming of God's Kingdom.

ARCHITRICLINUS.

          How serene
His aspect is ! manly yet womanly.

PARANYMPHUS.

Most beautiful among the sons of men !
Oft known to weep, but never known to
    laugh.

ARCHITRICLINUS.

And tell me, she with eyes of olive tint,
And skin as fair as wheat, and pale brown
    hair,
The woman at his side ?

PARANYMPHUS.

          His mother, Mary.

ARCHITRICLINUS.

And the tall figure standing close behind
    them,
Clad all in white, with face and beard like
    ashes,
As if he were Elias, the White Witness,
Come from his cave on Carmel to fore-
    tell
The end of all things ?

PARANYMPHUS.

          That is Manahem
The Essenian, he who dwells among the
    palms
Near the Dead Sea.

ARCHITRICLINUS.

          He who foretold to Herod
He should one day be King ?

PARANYMPHUS.

          The same.

ARCHITRICLINUS.

          Then why
Doth he come here to sadden with his
    presence

Our marriage feast, belonging to a sect
Haters of women, and that taste not wine ?

THE MUSICIANS.

My undefiled is but one,
The only one of her mother,
The choice of her that bare her ;
The daughters saw her and blessed her ;
The queens and the concubines praised
    her ;
Saying, Lo ! who is this
That looketh forth as the morning ?

MANAHEM, *aside.*

The Ruler of the Feast is gazing at me,
As if he asked, why is that old man here
Among the revellers ? And thou, the
    Anointed !
Why art thou here ? I see as in a vision
A figure clothed in purple, crowned with
    thorns ;
I see a cross uplifted in the darkness,
And hear a cry of agony, that shall echo
Forever and forever through the world !

ARCHITRICLINUS.

Give us more wine. These goblets are all
    empty.

MARY *to* CHRISTUS.

They have no wine !

CHRISTUS.

          O woman, what have I
To do with thee ? Mine hour is not yet
come.

MARY *to the servants.*

Whatever he shall say to you, that do.

CHRISTUS.

Fill up these pots with water.

THE MUSICIANS.

Come, my beloved,
Let us go forth into the field,
Let us lodge in the villages ;
Let us get up early to the vineyards,
Let us see if the vine flourish,
Whether the tender grape appear,
And the pomegranates bud forth.

CHRISTUS.

          Draw out now
And bear unto the Ruler of the Feast.

MANAHEM, *aside.*

O thou, brought up among the Essenians,
Nurtured in abstinence, taste not the wine !
It is the poison of dragons from the vine-
    yards
Of Sodom, and the taste of death is in it !

ARCHITRICLINUS *to the* BRIDEGROOM.

All men set forth good wine at the be-
    ginning,
And when men have well drunk, that which
    is worse ;
But thou hast kept the good wine until
    now.

MANAHEM, *aside.*

The things that have been and shall be no
    more,
The things that are, and that hereafter
    shall be,
The things that might have been, and yet
    were not,
The fading twilight of great joys departed,
The daybreak of great truths as yet un-
    risen,
The intuition and the expectation
Of something, which, when come, is not the
    same,
But only like its forecast in men's dreams,
The longing, the delay, and the delight,
Sweeter for the delay ; youth, hope, love,
    death,
And disappointment which is also death,
All these make up the sum of human life ;
A dream within a dream, a wind at night
Howling across the desert in despair,
Seeking for something lost it cannot find.
Fate or foreseeing, or whatever name
Men call it, matters not ; what is to be
Hath been fore-written in the thought
    divine
From the beginning. None can hide
    from it,
But it will find him out ; nor run from it,
But it o'ertaketh him ! The Lord hath
    said it.

THE BRIDEGROOM *to the* BRIDE, *on the balcony.*

When Abraham went with Sarah into
    Egypt,
The land was all illumined · with her
    beauty ;
But thou dost make the very night itself
Brighter than day ! Behold, in glad pro-
    cession,

Crowding the threshold of the sky above us,
The stars come forth to meet thee with
    their lamps ;
And the soft winds, the ambassadors of
    flowers,
From neighboring gardens and from fields
    unseen,
Come laden with odors unto thee, my
    Queen!

THE MUSICIANS.

Awake, O north-wind,
And come, thou wind of the South.
Blow, blow upon my garden,
That the spices thereof may flow out.

IV

IN THE CORNFIELDS

PHILIP.

Onward through leagues of sun-illumined
    corn,
As if through parted seas, the pathway
    runs,
And crowned with sunshine as the Prince
    of Peace
Walks the beloved Master, leading us,
As Moses led our fathers in old times
Out of the land of bondage ! We have
    found
Him of whom Moses and the Prophets
    wrote,
Jesus of Nazareth, the Son of Joseph.

NATHANAEL.

Can any good come out of Nazareth ?
Can this be the Messiah ?

PHILIP.

                        Come and see.

NATHANAEL.

The summer sun grows hot : I am anhun-
    gered.
How cheerily the Sabbath-breaking quail
Pipes in the corn, and bids us to his Feast
Of Wheat Sheaves ! How the bearded,
    ripening ears
Toss in the roofless temple of the air ;
As if the unseen hand of some High-Priest
Waved them before Mount Tabor as an
    altar !
It were no harm, if we should pluck and eat.

PHILIP.

How wonderful it is to walk abroad
With the Good Master ! Since the miracle
He wrought at Cana, at the marriage feast,
His fame hath gone abroad through all the
    land,
And when we come to Nazareth, thou shalt
    see
How his own people will receive their
    Prophet,
And hail him as Messiah ! See, he turns
And looks at thee.

CHRISTUS.

                    Behold an Israelite
In whom there is no guile.

NATHANAEL.

        Whence knowest thou me ?

CHRISTUS.

Before that Philip called thee, when thou
    wast
Under the fig-tree, I beheld thee.

NATHANAEL.

                            Rabbi !
Thou art the Son of God, thou art the King
Of Israel !

CHRISTUS.

            Because I said I saw thee
Under the fig-tree, before Philip called thee,
Believest thou ? Thou shalt see greater
    things.
Hereafter thou shalt see the heavens un-
    closed,
The angels of God ascending and descend-
    ing
Upon the Son of Man !

PHARISEES, passing.

        Hail, Rabbi !

CHRISTUS.

                    Hail!

PHARISEES.

Behold how thy disciples do a thing
Which is not lawful on the Sabbath-day,
And thou forbiddest them not !

CHRISTUS.

                    Have ye not read
What David did when he anhungered was,

And all they that were with him? How
    he entered
Into the house of God, and ate the shew-
    bread,
Which was not lawful, saving for the
    priests?
Have ye not read, how on the Sabbath-days
The priests profane the Sabbath in the
    Temple,
And yet are blameless? But I say to you,
One in this place is greater than the
    Temple!
And had ye known the meaning of the
    words,
I will have mercy and not sacrifice,
The guiltless ye would not condemn. The
    Sabbath
Was made for man, and not man for the
    Sabbath.
    Passes on with the disciples.

PHARISEES.

This is, alas! some poor demoniac
Wandering about the fields, and uttering
His unintelligible blasphemies
Among the common people, who receive
As prophecies the words they comprehend
    not!
Deluded folk! The incomprehensible
Alone excites their wonder. There is none
So visionary, or so void of sense,
But he will find a crowd to follow him!

V

NAZARETH

CHRISTUS, *reading in the Synagogue.*

The Spirit of the Lord God is upon me.
He hath anointed me to preach good tidings
Unto the poor; to heal the broken-hearted;
To comfort those that mourn, and to throw
    open
The prison doors of captives, and proclaim
The Year Acceptable of the Lord, our God!
    He closes the book and sits down.

A PHARISEE.

Who is this youth? He hath taken the
    Teacher's seat!
Will he instruct the Elders?

A PRIEST.

                Fifty years
Have I been Priest here in the Synagogue,

And never have I seen so young a man
Sit in the Teacher's seat!

CHRISTUS.

                Behold, to-day
This scripture is fulfilled. One is appointed
And hath been sent to them that mourn in
    Zion,
To give them beauty for ashes, and the oil
Of joy for mourning! They shall build
    again
The old waste-places; and again raise up
The former desolations, and repair
The cities that are wasted! As a bride-
    groom
Decketh himself with ornaments; as a bride
Adorneth herself with jewels, so the Lord
Hath clothed me with the robe of righteous-
    ness!

A PRIEST.

He speaks the Prophet's words; but with
    an air
As if himself had been foreshadowed in
    them!

CHRISTUS.

For Zion's sake I will not hold my peace,
And for Jerusalem's sake I will not rest
Until its righteousness be as a brightness,
And its salvation as a lamp that burneth!
Thou shalt be called no longer the For-
    saken,
Nor any more thy land the Desolate.
The Lord hath sworn, by his right hand
    hath sworn,
And by his arm of strength: I will no more
Give to thine enemies thy corn as meat;
The sons of strangers shall not drink thy
    wine.
Go through, go through the gates! Pre-
    pare a way
Unto the people! Gather out the stones!
Lift up a standard for the people!

A PRIEST.

                      Ah!
These are seditious words!

CHRISTUS.

              And they shall call them
The holy people; the redeemed of God!
And thou, Jerusalem, shalt be called Sought
    out,
A city not forsaken!

A PHARISEE.
                    Is not this
The carpenter Joseph's son ? Is not his
    mother
Called Mary ? and his brethren and his
    sisters
Are they not with us ? Doth he make
    himself
To be a Prophet ?

CHRISTUS.
                    No man is a Prophet
In his own country, and among his kin.
In his own house no Prophet is accepted.
I say to you, in the land of Israel
Were many widows in Elijah's day,
When for three years and more the heavens
    were shut,
And a great famine was throughout the
    land ;
But unto no one was Elijah sent
Save to Sarepta, to a city of Sidon,
And to a woman there that was a widow.
And many lepers were there in the land
Of Israel, in the time of Eliseus
The Prophet, and yet none of them was
    cleansed,
Save Naaman the Syrian !

A PRIEST.
                    Say no more !
Thou comest here into our Synagogue
And speakest to the Elders and the Priests,
As if the very mantle of Elijah
Had fallen upon thee ! Art thou not
    ashamed ?

A PHARISEE.
We want no Prophets here ! Let him be
    driven
From Synagogue and city ! Let him go
And prophesy to the Samaritans !

AN ELDER.
The world is changed. We Elders are as
    nothing !
We are but yesterdays, that have no part
Or portion in to-day ! Dry leaves that
    rustle,
That make a little sound, and then are
    dust !

A PHARISEE.
A carpenter's apprentice ! a mechanic,
Whom we have seen at work here in the
    town

Day after day ; a stripling without learn-
    ing,
Shall he pretend to unfold the Word of God
To men grown old in study of the Law ?
                    CHRISTUS is thrust out.

VI

THE SEA OF GALILEE

PETER and ANDREW mending their nets.

PETER.
Never was such a marvellous draught of
    fishes
Heard of in Galilee ! The market-places
Both of Bethsaida and Capernaum
Are full of them ! Yet we had toiled all
    night
And taken nothing, when the Master said :
Launch out into the deep, and cast your
    nets ;
And doing this, we caught such multitudes,
Our nets like spiders' webs were snapped
    asunder,
And with the draught we filled two ships
    so full
That they began to sink. Then I knelt
    down
Amazed, and said : O Lord, depart from me,
I am a sinful man. And he made answer :
Simon, fear not ; henceforth thou shalt
    catch men !
What was the meaning of those words ?

ANDREW.
                    I know not.
But here is Philip, come from Nazareth.
He hath been with the Master. Tell us,
    Philip,
What tidings dost thou bring ?

PHILIP.
                    Most wonderful !
As we drew near to Nain, out of the gate
Upon a bier was carried the dead body
Of a young man, his mother's only son,
And she a widow, who with lamentation
Bewailed her loss, and the much people
    with her ;
And when the Master saw her he was
    filled
With pity ; and he said to her : Weep not !
And came and touched the bier, and they
    that bare it

Stood still ; and then he said : Young man,
arise !
And he that had been dead sat up, and
soon
Began to speak ; and he delivered him
Unto his mother. And there came a fear
On all the people, and they glorified
The Lord, and said, rejoicing : A great
Prophet
Is risen up among us ! and the Lord
Hath visited his people !

PETER.

A great Prophet ?
Ay, greater than a Prophet : greater even
Than John the Baptist !

PHILIP.

Yet the Nazarenes
Rejected him.

PETER.

The Nazarenes are dogs !
As natural brute beasts, they growl at
things
They do not understand ; and they shall
perish,
Utterly perish in their own corruption.
The Nazarenes are dogs !

PHILIP.

They drave him forth
Out of their Synagogue, out of their city,
And would have cast him down a precipice,
But, passing through the midst of them, he
vanished
Out of their hands.

PETER.

Wells are they without water,
Clouds carried with a tempest, unto whom
The mist of darkness is reserved forever !

PHILIP.

Behold he cometh. There is one man with
him
I am amazed to see !

ANDREW.

What man is that ?

PHILIP.

Judas Iscariot ; he that cometh last,
Girt with a leathern apron. No one
knoweth

His history ; but the rumor of him is
He had an unclean spirit in his youth.
It hath not left him yet.

CHRISTUS, *passing.*

Come unto me,
All ye that labor and are heavy laden,
And I will give you rest ! Come unto me,
And take my yoke upon you and learn of me,
For I am meek, and I am lowly in heart,
And ye shall all find rest unto your souls !

PHILIP.

Oh, there is something in that voice that
reaches
The innermost recesses of my spirit !
I feel that it might say unto the blind :
Receive your sight ! and straightway they
would see !
I feel that it might say unto the dead,
Arise ! and they would hear it and obey !
Behold, he beckons to us !

CHRISTUS, *to* PETER *and* ANDREW.

Follow me !

PETER.

Master, I will leave all and follow thee.

VII

THE DEMONIAC OF GADARA

A GADARENE.

He hath escaped, hath plucked his chains
asunder,
And broken his fetters ; always night and
day
Is in the mountains here, and in the tombs,
Crying aloud, and cutting himself with
stones,
Exceeding fierce, so that no man can tame
him !

THE DEMONIAC *from above, unseen.*

O Aschmedai ! O Aschmedai, have pity !

A GADARENE.

Listen ! It is his voice ! Go warn the people
Just landing from the lake !

THE DEMONIAC.

O Aschmedai !
Thou angel of the bottomless pit, have
pity !

It was enough to hurl King Solomon,
On whom be peace ! two hundred leagues
    away
Into the country, and to make him scul-
    lion
In the kitchen of the King of Maschke-
    men !
Why dost thou hurl me here among these
    rocks,
And cut me with these stones ?

A GADARENE.
               He raves and mutters
He knows not what.

THE DEMONIAC, *appearing from a tomb among
the rocks.*
          The wild cock Tarnegal
Singeth to me, and bids me to the banquet,
Where all the Jews shall come ; for they
    have slain
Behemoth the great ox, who daily cropped
A thousand hills for food, and at a draught
Drank up the river Jordan, and have slain
The huge Leviathan, and stretched his
    skin
Upon the high walls of Jerusalem,
And made them shine from one end of the
    world
Unto the other ; and the fowl Barjuchne,
Whose outspread wings eclipse the sun,
    and make
Midnight at noon o'er all the continents !
And we shall drink the wine of Paradise
From Adam's cellars.

A GADARENE.
              O thou unclean spirit !

THE DEMONIAC, *hurling down a stone.*
This is the wonderful Barjuchne's egg,
That fell out of her nest, and broke to
    pieces
And swept away three hundred cedar-
    trees,
And threescore villages ! — Rabbi Eliezer,
How thou didst sin there in that seaport
    town
When thou hadst carried safe thy chest of
    silver
Over the seven rivers for her sake !
I too have sinned beyond the reach of
    pardon.
Ye hills and mountains, pray for mercy on
    me !

Ye stars and planets, pray for mercy on
    me !
Ye sun and moon, oh pray for mercy on
    me !
    CHRISTUS *and his disciples pass.*

A GADARENE.
There is a man here of Decapolis,
Who hath an unclean spirit ; so that none
Can pass this way. He lives among the
    tombs
Up there upon the cliffs, and hurls down
    stones
On those who pass beneath.

CHRISTUS.
              Come out of him,
Thou unclean spirit !

THE DEMONIAC.
             What have I to do
With thee, thou Son of God ? Do not
    torment us.

CHRISTUS.
What is thy name ?

THE DEMONIAC.
          Legion ; for we are many.
Cain, the first murderer ; and the King
    Belshazzar,
And Evil Merodach of Babylon,
And Admatha, the death-cloud, prince of
    Persia ;
And Aschmedai, the angel of the pit,
And many other devils. We are Legion.
Send us not forth beyond Decapolis ;
Command us not to go into the deep !
There is a herd of swine here in the pas-
    tures,
Let us go into them.

CHRISTUS.
              Come out of him,
Thou unclean spirit !

A GADARENE.
           See, how stupefied,
How motionless he stands ! He cries no
    more ;
He seems bewildered and in silence stares
As one who, walking in his sleep, awakes
And knows not where he is, and looks
    about him,
And at his nakedness, and is ashamed.

THE DEMONIAC.

Why am I here alone among the tombs ?
What have they done to me, that I am
    naked ?
Ah, woe is me !

CHRISTUS.

                    Go home unto thy friends
And tell them how great things the Lord
    hath done
For thee, and how He had compassion on
    thee !

A SWINEHERD, *running.*

The herds ! the herds ! O most unlucky
    day !
They were all feeding quiet in the sun,
When suddenly they started, and grew
    savage
As the wild boars of Tabor, and together
Rushed down a precipice into the sea !
They are all drowned !

PETER.

            Thus righteously are punished
The apostate Jews, that eat the flesh of
    swine,
And broth of such abominable things !

GREEKS OF GADARA.

We sacrifice a sow unto Demeter
At the beginning of harvest, and another
To Dionysus at the vintage-time.
Therefore we prize our herds of swine, and
    count them
Not as unclean, but as things consecrate
To the immortal gods. O great magician,
Depart out of our coasts ; let us alone,
We are afraid of thee.

PETER.

                    Let us depart ;
For they that sanctify and purify
Themselves in gardens, eating flesh of swine,
And the abomination, and the mouse,
Shall be consumed together, saith the Lord !

VIII

TALITHA CUMI

JAIRUS *at the feet of* CHRISTUS.

O Master ! I entreat thee ! I implore thee !
My daughter lieth at the point of death ;

I pray thee come and lay thy hands upon
    her,
And she shall live !

CHRISTUS.

Who was it touched my garments ?

SIMON PETER.

Thou seest the multitude that throng and
    press thee,
And sayest thou : Who touched me ?
    'T was not I.

CHRISTUS.

Some one hath touched my garments ; I
    perceive
That virtue is gone out of me.

A WOMAN.

                    O Master !
Forgive me ! For I said within myself,
If I so much as touch his garment's hem,
I shall be whole.

CHRISTUS.

            Be of good comfort, daughter!
Thy faith hath made thee whole. Depart
    in peace.

A MESSENGER *from the house.*

Why troublest thou the Master ? Hearest
    thou not
The flute-players, and the voices of the wo-
    men
Singing their lamentation ? She is dead !

THE MINSTRELS AND MOURNERS.

We have girded ourselves with sackcloth !
We have covered our heads with ashes !
For our young men die, and our maidens
Swoon in the streets of the city ;
And into their mother's bosom
They pour out their souls like water !

CHRISTUS, *going in.*

Give place. Why make ye this ado, and
    weep ?
She is not dead, but sleepeth.

THE MOTHER, *from within.*

                    Cruel Death !
To take away from me this tender blos-
    som !
To take away my dove, my lamb, my dar-
    ling !

THE MINSTRELS AND MOURNERS.

He hath led me and brought into darkness,
Like the dead of old in dark places !
He hath bent his bow, and hath set me
Apart as a mark for his arrow !
He hath covered himself with a cloud,
That our prayer should not pass through
    and reach him !

THE CROWD.

He stands beside her bed ! He takes her
    hand !
Listen, he speaks to her !

CHRISTUS, *within.*
                    Maiden, arise !

THE CROWD.

See, she obeys his voice ! She stirs ! She
    lives !
Her mother holds her folded in her arms !
O miracle of miracles ! O marvel !

IX

THE TOWER OF MAGDALA

MARY MAGDALENE.

Companionless, unsatisfied, forlorn,
I sit here in this lonely tower, and look
Upon the lake below me, and the hills
That swoon with heat, and see as in a
    vision
All my past life unroll itself before me.
The princes and the merchants come to
    me,
Merchants of Tyre and Princes of Damas-
    cus,
And pass, and disappear, and are no more ;
But leave behind their merchandise and
    jewels,
Their perfumes, and their gold, and their
    disgust.
I loathe them, and the very memory of them
Is unto me as thought of food to one
Cloyed with the luscious figs of Dalmanu-
    tha !
What if hereafter, in the long hereafter
Of endless joy or pain, or joy in pain,
It were my punishment to be with them
Grown hideous and decrepit in their sins,
And hear them say : Thou that hast brought
    us here,
Be unto us as thou hast been of old !

I look upon this raiment that I wear,
These silks, and these embroideries, and
    they seem
Only as cerements wrapped about my
    limbs !
I look upon these rings thick set with pearls,
And emerald and amethyst and jasper,
And they are burning coals upon my flesh !
This serpent on my wrist becomes alive !
Away, thou viper ! and away, ye garlands,
Whose odors bring the swift remembrance
    back
Of the unhallowed revels in these cham-
    bers !
But yesterday, — and yet it seems to me
Something remote, like a pathetic song
Sung long ago by minstrels in the street, —
But yesterday, as from this tower I gazed,
Over the olive and the walnut trees
Upon the lake and the white ships, and
    wondered
Whither and whence they steered, and who
    was in them,
A fisher's boat drew near the landing-place
Under the oleanders, and the people
Came up from it, and passed beneath the
    tower,
Close under me. In front of them, as
    leader,
Walked one of royal aspect, clothed in
    white,
Who lifted up his eyes, and looked at me,
And all at once the air seemed filled and
    living
With a mysterious power, that streamed
    from him,
And overflowed me with an atmosphere
Of light and love. As one entranced I
    stood,
And when I woke again, lo ! he was gone ;
So that I said : Perhaps it is a dream.
But from that very hour the seven demons
That had their habitation in this body
Which men call beautiful, departed from
    me !

This morning, when the first gleam of the
    dawn
Made Lebanon a glory in the air,
And all below was darkness, I beheld
An angel, or a spirit glorified,
With wind-tossed garments walking on the
    lake.
The face I could not see, but I distin-
    guished

The attitude and gesture, and I knew
'T was he that healed me. And the gusty
    wind
Brought to mine ears a voice, which seemed
    to say :
Be of good cheer ! 'T is I ! Be not afraid !
And from the darkness, scarcely heard, the
    answer :
If it be thou, bid me come unto thee
Upon the water ! And the voice said :
    Come !
And then I heard a cry of fear : Lord,
    save me !
As of a drowning man. And then the
    voice :
Why didst thou doubt, O thou of little
    faith !
At this all vanished, and the wind was
    hushed,
And the great sun came up above the hills,
And the swift-flying vapors hid themselves
In caverns among the rocks ! Oh, I must
    find him
And follow him, and be with him forever !

Thou box of alabaster, in whose walls
The souls of flowers lie pent, the precious
    balm
And spikenard of Arabian farms, the spirits
Of aromatic herbs, ethereal natures
Nursed by the sun and dew, not all un-
    worthy
To bathe his consecrated feet, whose step
Makes every threshold holy that he crosses ;
Let us go forth upon our pilgrimage,
Thou and I only ! Let us search for him
Until we find him, and pour out our souls
Before his feet, till all that 's left of us
Shall be the broken caskets that once held
    us !

X

THE HOUSE OF SIMON THE PHARISEE

A GUEST *at table.*

Are ye deceived ? Have any of the Rulers
Believed on him ? or do they know indeed
This man to be the very Christ ? Howbeit
We know whence this man is, but when the
    Christ
Shall come, none knoweth whence he is.

CHRISTUS.

Whereunto shall I liken, then, the men
Of this generation ? and what are they
    like ?
They are like children sitting in the mar-
    kets,
And calling unto one another, saying :
We have piped unto you, and ye have not
    danced ;
We have mourned unto you, and ye have
    not wept !
This say I unto you, for John the Baptist
Came neither eating bread nor drinking
    wine ;
Ye say he hath a devil. The Son of Man
Eating and drinking cometh, and ye say :
Behold a gluttonous man, and a wine-bib-
    ber ;
Behold a friend of publicans and sinners !

A GUEST *aside to* SIMON.

Who is that woman yonder, gliding in
So silently behind him ?

SIMON.
                    It is Mary,
Who dwelleth in the Tower of Magdala.

THE GUEST.

See, how she kneels there weeping, and her
    tears
Fall on his feet ; and her long, golden hair
Waves to and fro and wipes them dry again.
And now she kisses them, and from a box
Of alabaster is anointing them
With precious ointment, filling all the house
With its sweet odor !

SIMON, *aside.*
                    Oh, this man, forsooth,
Were he indeed a Prophet, would have
    known
Who and what manner of woman this may
    be
That toucheth him ! would know she is a
    sinner !

CHRISTUS.

Simon, somewhat have I to say to thee.

SIMON.
Master, say on.

CHRISTUS.
                    A certain creditor
Had once two debtors ; and the one of them
Owed him five hundred pence ; the other,
    fifty.

They having naught to pay withal, he
    frankly
Forgave them both. Now tell me which of
    them
Will love him most?

SIMON.

                He, I suppose, to whom
He most forgave.

CHRISTUS.

            Yea, thou hast rightly judged.
Seest thou this woman? When thine
    house I entered,
Thou gavest me no water for my feet,
But she hath washed them with her tears,
    and wiped them
With her own hair. Thou gavest me no
    kiss ;
This woman hath not ceased, since I came
    in,
To kiss my feet. My head with oil didst
    thou
Anoint not ; but this woman hath anointed
My feet with ointment. Hence I say to
    thee,
Her sins, which have been many, are for-
    given,
For she loved much.

THE GUESTS.

                On, who, then, is this man
That pardoneth also sins without atone-
    ment ?

CHRISTUS.

Woman, thy faith hath saved thee ! Go in
    peace !

THE SECOND PASSOVER

I

BEFORE THE GATES OF MACHÆRUS

MANAHEM.

WELCOME, O wilderness, and welcome,
    night
And solitude, and ye swift-flying stars
That drift with golden sands the barren
    heavens,
Welcome once more ! The Angels of the
    Wind

Hasten across the desert to receive me ;
And sweeter than men's voices are to me
The voices of these solitudes ; the sound
Of unseen rivulets, and the far-off cry
Of bitterns in the reeds of water-pools.
And lo ! above me, like the Prophet's arrow
Shot from the eastern window, high in air
The clamorous cranes go singing through
    the night.
O ye mysterious pilgrims of the air,
Would I had wings that I might follow
    you !

I look forth from these mountains, and be-
    hold
The omnipotent and omnipresent night,
Mysterious as the future and the fate
That hangs o'er all men's lives ! I see be-
    neath me
The desert stretching to the Dead Sea shore,
And westward, faint and far away, the
    glimmer
Of torches on Mount Olivet, announcing
The rising of the Moon of Passover.
Like a great cross it seems, on which sus-
    pended,
With head bowed down in agony, I see
A human figure ! Hide, O merciful heaven,
The awful apparition from my sight !

And thou, Machærus, lifting high and black
Thy dreadful walls against the rising moon,
Haunted by demons and by apparitions,
Lilith, and Jezerhara, and Bedargon,
How grim thou showest in the uncertain
    light,
A palace and a prison, where King Herod
Feasts with Herodias, while the Baptist
    John
Fasts, and consumes his unavailing life !
And in thy court-yard grows the untithed
    rue,
Huge as the olives of Gethsemane,
And ancient as the terebinth of Hebron,
Coeval with the world. Would that its
    leaves
Medicinal could purge thee of the demons
That now possess thee, and the cunning fox
That burrows in thy walls, contriving mis-
    chief !

            Music is heard from within.

Angels of God ! Sandalphon, thou that
    weavest
The prayers of men into immortal garlands,

And thou, Metatron, who dost gather up
Their songs, and bear them to the gates of
    heaven,
Now gather up together in your hands
The prayers that fill this prison, and the
    songs
That echo from the ceiling of this palace,
And lay them side by side before God's
    feet !

He enters the castle.

II

HEROD'S BANQUET-HALL

MANAHEM.

Thou hast sent for me, O King, and I am
here.

HEROD.

Who art thou ?

MANAHEM.
           Manahem, the Essenian.

HEROD.

I recognize thy features, but what mean
These torn and faded garments ? On thy
    road
Have demons crowded thee, and rubbed
    against thee,
And given thee weary knees ? A cup of
    wine !

MANAHEM.

The Essenians drink no wine.

HEROD.
           What wilt thou, then ?

MANAHEM.

Nothing.

HEROD.

Not even a cup of water ?

MANAHEM.
              Nothing.

Why hast thou sent for me ?

HEROD.
         Dost thou remember
One day when I, a schoolboy in the streets
Of the great city, met thee on my way
To school, and thou didst say to me : Here-
    after
Thou shalt be king ?

MANAHEM.

Yea, I remember it.

HEROD.

Thinking thou didst not know me, I re-
    plied :
I am of humble birth ; whereat thou, smil-
    ing,
Didst smite me with thy hand, and saidst
    again :
Thou shalt be King ; and let the friendly
    blows
That Manahem hath given thee on this day
Remind thee of the fickleness of fortune.

MANAHEM.

What more ?

HEROD.

No more.

MANAHEM.
         Yea, for I said to thee :
It shall be well with thee if thou love jus-
    tice
And clemency towards thy fellow-men.
Hast thou done this, O King ?

HEROD.
           Go, ask my people.

MANAHEM.

And then, foreseeing all thy life, I added :
But these thou wilt forget ; and at the end
Of life the Lord will punish thee.

HEROD.
             The end !
When will that come ? For this I sent to
    thee.
How long shall I still reign ? Thou dost
    not answer !
Speak ! shall I reign ten years ?

MANAHEM.
         Thou shalt reign twenty,
Nay, thirty years. I cannot name the end.

HEROD.

Thirty ? I thank thee, good Essenian !
This is my birthday, and a happier one
Was never mine. We hold a banquet here.
See, yonder are Herodias and her daughter.

MANAHEM, *aside.*

'T is said that devils sometimes take the
    shape

Of ministering angels, clothed with air,
That they may be inhabitants of earth,
And lead man to destruction. Such are
these.

HEROD.
Knowest thou John the Baptist ?

MANAHEM.
Yea, I know him ;
Who knows him not ?

HEROD.
Know, then, this John the Baptist
Said that it was not lawful I should marry
My brother Philip's wife, and John the
Baptist
Is here in prison. In my father's time
Matthias Margaloth was put to death
For tearing the golden eagle from its sta-
tion
Above the Temple Gate, — a slighter
crime
Than John is guilty of. These things are
warnings
To intermeddlers not to play with eagles,
Living or dead. I think the Essenians
Are wiser, or more wary, are they not ?

MANAHEM.
The Essenians do not marry.

HEROD.
Thou hast given
My words a meaning foreign to my
thought.

MANAHEM.
Let me go hence, O King !

HEROD.
Stay yet awhile,
And see the daughter of Herodias dance.
Cleopatra of Jerusalem, my mother,
In her best days, was not more beautiful.
Music. THE DAUGHTER OF HERODIAS *dances.*

HEROD.
Oh, what was Miriam dancing with her
timbrel,
Compared to this one ?

MANAHEM, *aside.*
O thou Angel of Death,
Dancing at funerals among the women,

When men bear out the dead ! The air is
hot
And stifles me ! Oh for a breath of air !
Bid me depart, O King !

HEROD.
Not yet. Come hither.
Salome, thou enchantress ! Ask of me
Whate'er thou wilt ; and even unto the
half
Of all my kingdom, I will give it thee,
As the Lord liveth !

DAUGHTER OF HERODIAS, *kneeling.*
Give me here the head
Of John the Baptist on this silver charger !

HEROD.
Not that, dear child ! I dare not ; for the
people
Regard John as a prophet.

DAUGHTER OF HERODIAS.
Thou hast sworn it.

HEROD.
For mine oath's sake, then. Send unto the
prison ;
Let him die quickly. Oh, accursed oath !

MANAHEM.
Bid me depart, O King !

HEROD.
Good Manahem,
Give me thy hand. I love the Essenians.
He 's gone and hears me not ! The guests
are dumb,
Awaiting the pale face, the silent witness.
The lamps flare ; and the curtains of the
doorways
Wave to and fro as if a ghost were
passing !
Strengthen my heart, red wine of Ascalon !

III

UNDER THE WALLS OF MACHÆRUS

MANAHEM, *rushing out.*
Away from this Palace of sin !
The demons, the terrible powers
Of the air, that haunt its towers
And hide in its water-spouts,

Deafen me with the din
Of their laughter and their shouts
For the crimes that are done within !

Sink back into the earth,
Or vanish into the air,
Thou castle of despair !
Let it all be but a dream
Of the things of monstrous birth,
Of the things that only seem !
White Angel of the Moon,
Onafiel ! be my guide
Out of this hateful place
Of sin and death, nor hide
In yon black cloud too soon
Thy pale and tranquil face !
A trumpet is blown from the walls.
Hark ! hark ! It is the breath
Of the trump of doom and death,
From the battlements overhead
Like a burden of sorrow cast
On the midnight and the blast,
A wailing for the dead,
That the gusts drop and uplift !
O Herod, thy vengeance is swift !
O Herodias, thou hast been
The demon, the evil thing,
That in place of Esther the Queen,
In place of the lawful bride,
Hast lain at night by the side
Of Ahasuerus the king !
The trumpet again.
The Prophet of God is dead !
At a drunken monarch's call,
At a dancing-woman's beck,
They have severed that stubborn neck
And into the banquet-hall
Are bearing the ghastly head !
A body is thrown from the tower.
A torch of lurid red
Lights the window with its glow ;
And a white mass as of snow
Is hurled into the abyss
Of the black precipice,
That yawns for it below !
O hand of the Most High,
O hand of Adonai !
Bury it, hide it away
From the birds and beasts of prey,
And the eyes of the homicide,
More pitiless than they,
As thou didst bury of yore
The body of him that died
On the mountain of Peor !

Even now I behold a sign,
A threatening of wrath divine,
A watery, wandering star,
Through whose streaming hair, and the
white
Unfolding garments of light,
That trail behind it afar,
The constellations shine !
And the whiteness and brightness appear
Like the Angel bearing the Seer
By the hair of his head, in the might
And rush of his vehement flight.
And I listen until I hear
From fathomless depths of the sky
The voice of his prophecy
Sounding louder and more near !

Malediction ! malediction !
May the lightnings of heaven fall
On palace and prison wall,
And their desolation be
As the day of fear and affliction,
As the day of anguish and ire,
With the burning and fuel of fire,
In the Valley of the Sea !

IV

NICODEMUS AT NIGHT

NICODEMUS.

The streets are silent. The dark houses
seem
Like sepulchres, in which the sleepers lie
Wrapped in their shrouds, and for the mo-
ment dead.
The lamps are all extinguished ; only one
Burns steadily, and from the door its light
Lies like a shining gate across the street.
He waits for me. Ah, should this be at last
The long-expected Christ ! I see him there
Sitting alone, deep-buried in his thought,
As if the weight of all the world were rest-
ing
Upon him, and thus bowed him down. O
Rabbi,
We know thou art a Teacher come from
God,
For no man can perform the miracles
Thou dost perform, except the Lord be with
him.
Thou art a Prophet, sent here to proclaim
The Kingdom of the Lord. Behold in me

A Ruler of the Jews, who long have waited
The coming of that kingdom. Tell me of it.

CHRISTUS.

Verily, verily I say unto thee,
Except a man be born again, he cannot
Behold the Kingdom of God!

NICODEMUS.

Be born again?
How can a man be born when he is old?
Say, can he enter for a second time
Into his mother's womb, and so be born?

CHRISTUS.

Verily I say unto thee, except
A man be born of water and the spirit,
He cannot enter into the Kingdom of God.
For that which of the flesh is born, is
flesh;
And that which of the spirit is born, is
spirit.

NICODEMUS.

We Israelites from the Primeval Man
Adam Ahelion derive our bodies;
Our souls are breathings of the Holy Ghost.
No more than this we know, or need to
know.

CHRISTUS.

Then marvel not, that I said unto thee
Ye must be born again.

NICODEMUS.

The mystery
Of birth and death we cannot comprehend.

CHRISTUS.

The wind bloweth where it listeth, and we
hear
The sound thereof, but know not whence it
cometh,
Nor whither it goeth. So is every one
Born of the spirit!

NICODEMUS, *aside.*

How can these things be?
He seems to speak of some vague realm of
shadows,
Some unsubstantial kingdom of the air!
It is not this the Jews are waiting for,
Nor can this be the Christ, the Son of
David,
Who shall deliver us!

CHRISTUS.

Art thou a master
Of Israel, and knowest not these things?
We speak that we do know, and testify
That we have seen, and ye will not receive
Our witness. If I tell you earthly things,
And ye believe not, how shall ye believe,
If I should tell you of things heavenly?
And no man hath ascended up to heaven,
But He alone that first came down from
heaven,
Even the Son of Man which is in heaven!

NICODEMUS, *aside.*

This is a dreamer of dreams; a visionary,
Whose brain is overtasked, until he deems
The unseen world to be a thing substantial,
And this we live in, an unreal vision!
And yet his presence fascinates and fills me
With wonder, and I feel myself exalted
Into a higher region, and become
Myself in part a dreamer of his dreams,
A seer of his visions!

CHRISTUS.

And as Moses
Uplifted the serpent in the wilderness,
So must the Son of Man be lifted up;
That whosoever shall believe in Him
Shall perish not, but have eternal life.
He that believes in Him is not condemned;
He that believes not, is condemned already.

NICODEMUS, *aside.*

He speaketh like a Prophet of the Lord!

CHRISTUS.

This is the condemnation; that the light
Is come into the world, and men loved
darkness
Rather than light, because their deeds are
evil!

NICODEMUS, *aside.*

Of me he speaketh! He reproveth me,
Because I come by night to question him!

CHRISTUS.

For every one that doeth evil deeds
Hateth the light, nor cometh to the light,
Lest he should be reproved.

NICODEMUS, *aside.*

Alas, how truly
He readeth what is passing in my heart!

CHRISTUS.

But he that doeth truth comes to the light,
So that his deeds may be made manifest,
That they are wrought in God.

NICODEMUS.

Alas! alas!

V

BLIND BARTIMEUS

BARTIMEUS.

Be not impatient, Chilion ; it is pleasant
To sit here in the shadow of the walls
Under the palms, and hear the hum of
bees,
And rumor of voices passing to and fro,
And drowsy bells of caravans on their way
To Sidon or Damascus. This is still
The City of Palms, and yet the walls thou
seest
Are not the old walls, not the walls where
Rahab
Hid the two spies, and let them down by
cords
Out of the window, when the gates were
shut,
And it was dark. Those walls were over-
thrown
When Joshua's army shouted, and the
priests
Blew with their seven trumpets.

CHILION.

When was that ?

BARTIMEUS.

O my sweet rose of Jericho, I know not.
Hundreds of years ago. And over there
Beyond the river, the great prophet Elijah
Was taken by a whirlwind up to heaven
In chariot of fire, with fiery horses.
That is the plain of Moab ; and beyond
it
Rise the blue summits of Mount Abarim,
Nebo and Pisgah and Peor, where Moses
Died, whom the Lord knew face to face,
and whom
He buried in a valley, and no man
Knows of his sepulchre unto this day.

CHILION.

Would thou couldst see these places, as I
see them.

BARTIMEUS.

I have not seen a glimmer of the light
Since thou wast born. I never saw thy face,
And yet I seem to see it ; and one day
Perhaps shall see it ; for there is a Prophet
In Galilee, the Messiah, the Son of David,
Who heals the blind, if I could only find
him.
I hear the sound of many feet approaching,
And voices, like the murmur of a crowd !
What seest thou ?

CHILION.

A young man clad in white
Is coming through the gateway, and a
crowd
Of people follow.

BARTIMEUS.

Can it be the Prophet !
O neighbors, tell me who it is that passes ?

ONE OF THE CROWD.

Jesus of Nazareth.

BARTIMEUS, crying.

O Son of David !
Have mercy on me !

MANY OF THE CROWD.

Peace, Blind Bartimeus !
Do not disturb the Master.

BARTIMEUS, crying more vehemently.

Son of David,
Have mercy on me !

ONE OF THE CROWD.

See, the Master stops.
Be of good comfort ; rise, He calleth thee !

BARTIMEUS, casting away his cloak.

Chilion ! good neighbors ! lead me on.

CHRISTUS.

What wilt thou
That I should do to thee ?

BARTIMEUS.

Good Lord ! my sight —
That I receive my sight !

CHRISTUS.

Receive thy sight !
Thy faith hath made thee whole !

THE CROWD.

He sees again !

CHRISTUS *passes on. The crowd gathers round* BARTIMEUS.

BARTIMEUS.

I see again ; but sight bewilders me !
Like a remembered dream, familiar things
Come back to me. I see the tender sky
Above me, see the trees, the city walls,
And the old gateway, through whose echo-
ing arch
I groped so many years ; and you, my
neighbors ;
But know you by your friendly voices only.
How beautiful the world is ! and how
wide !
Oh, I am miles away, if I but look !
Where art thou, Chilion ?

CHILION.

Father, I am here.

BARTIMEUS.

Oh let me gaze upon thy face, dear child !
For I have only seen thee with my hands !
How beautiful thou art ! I should have
known thee ;
Thou hast her eyes whom we shall see
hereafter !
O God of Abraham ! Elion ! Adonai !
Who art thyself a Father, pardon me
If for a moment I have thee postponed
To the affections and the thoughts of
earth,
Thee, and the adoration that I owe thee,
When by thy power alone these darkened
eyes
Have been unsealed again to see thy light !

VI

JACOB'S WELL

A SAMARITAN WOMAN.

The sun is hot ; and the dry east-wind
blowing
Fills all the air with dust. The birds are
silent ;
Even the little fieldfares in the corn
No longer twitter ; only the grasshoppers
Sing their incessant song of sun and sum-
mer.

I wonder who those strangers were I met
Going into the city ? Galileans
They seemed to me in speaking, when they
asked
The short way to the market-place. Per-
haps
They are fishermen from the lake ; or
travellers,
Looking to find the inn. And here is some
one
Sitting beside the well ; another stranger ;
A Galilean also by his looks.
What can so many Jews be doing here
Together in Samaria ? Are they going
Up to Jerusalem to the Passover ?
Our Passover is better here at Sychem,
For here is Ebal ; here is Gerizim,
The mountain where our father Abra-
ham
Went up to offer Isaac ; here the tomb
Of Joseph, — for they brought his bones
from Egypt
And buried them in this land, and it is
holy.

CHRISTUS.

Give me to drink.

SAMARITAN WOMAN.

How can it be that thou,
Being a Jew, askest to drink of me
Which am a woman of Samaria ?
You Jews despise us ; have no dealings
with us ;
Make us a byword ; call us in derision
The silly folk of Sychar. Sir, how is it
Thou askest drink of me ?

CHRISTUS.

If thou hadst known
The gift of God, and who it is that sayeth
Give me to drink, thou wouldst have asked
of Him ;
He would have given thee the living water.

SAMARITAN WOMAN.

Sir, thou hast naught to draw with, and the
well
Is deep ! Whence hast thou living water ?
Say, art thou greater than our father
Jacob,
Which gave this well to us, and drank
thereof
Himself, and all his children and his
cattle ?

CHRISTUS.

Ah, whosoever drinketh of this water
Shall thirst again ; but whosoever drinketh
The water I shall give him shall not thirst
Forevermore, for it shall be within him
A well of living water, springing up
Into life everlasting.

SAMARITAN WOMAN.
                    Every day
I must go to and fro, in heat and cold,
And I am weary.   Give me of this water,
That I may thirst not, nor come here to
    draw.

CHRISTUS.

Go call thy husband, woman, and come
    hither.

SAMARITAN WOMAN.

I have no husband, Sir.

CHRISTUS.

                    Thou hast well said
I have no husband.   Thou hast had five
    husbands ;
And he whom now thou hast is not thy
    husband.

SAMARITAN WOMAN.

Surely thou art a Prophet, for thou readest
The hidden things of life !   Our fathers
    worshipped
Upon this mountain Gerizim ; and ye say
The only place in which men ought to wor-
    ship
Is at Jerusalem.

CHRISTUS.

                    Believe me, woman,
The hour is coming, when ye neither shall
Upon this mount. nor at Jerusalem,
Worship the Father ; for the hour is coming,
And is now come, when the true worship-
    pers
Shall worship the Father in spirit and in
    truth !
The Father seeketh such to worship Him.
God is a spirit ; and they that worship Him
Must worship Him in spirit and in truth.

SAMARITAN WOMAN.

Master, I know that the Messiah cometh,
Which is called Christ ; and He will tell
    us all things.

CHRISTUS.

I that speak unto thee am He !

THE DISCIPLES, returning
                    Behold,
The Master sitting by the well, and talk-
    ing
With a Samaritan woman ! With a woman
Of Sychar, the silly people, always boast-
    ing
Of their Mount Ebal, and Mount Gerizim,
Their Everlasting Mountain, which they
    think
Higher and holier than our Mount Moriah !
Why, once upon the Feast of the New
    Moon,
When our great Sanhedrim of Jerusalem
Had all its watch-fires kindled on the hills
To warn the distant villages, these people
Lighted up others to mislead the Jews,
And make a mockery of their festival !
See, she has left the Master ; and is run-
    ning
Back to the city !

SAMARITAN WOMAN.
                    Oh, come see a man
Who hath told me all things that I ever
    did !
Say, is not this the Christ ?

THE DISCIPLES.
                    Lo, Master, here
Is food, that we have brought thee from
    the city.
We pray thee eat it.

CHRISTUS.
                    I have food to eat
Ye know not of.

THE DISCIPLES, to each other.
                    Hath any man been here,
And brought Him aught to eat, while we
    were gone ?

CHRISTUS.

The food I speak of is to do the will
Of Him that sent me, and to finish his
    work.
Do ye not say, Lo ! there are yet four
    months
And cometh harvest ?   I say unto you,
Lift up your eyes, and look upon the fields,
For they are white already unto harvest !

VII

THE COASTS OF CÆSAREA PHILIPPI

CHRISTUS, *going up the mountain.*

Who do the people say I am ?

JOHN.

Some say
That thou art John the Baptist ; some,
Elias ;
And others Jeremiah.

JAMES.

Or that one
Of the old Prophets is arisen again.

CHRISTUS.

But who say ye I am ?

PETER.

Thou art the Christ !
Thou art the Son of God !

CHRISTUS.

Blessed art thou,
Simon Barjona ! Flesh and blood hath
not
Revealed it unto thee, but even my Father,
Which is in Heaven. And I say unto thee
That thou art Peter ; and upon this rock
I build my Church, and all the gates of
Hell
Shall not prevail against it. But take heed
Ye tell to no man that I am the Christ.
For I must go up to Jerusalem,
And suffer many things, and be rejected
Of the Chief Priests, and of the Scribes and
Elders,
And must be crucified, and the third day
Shall rise again !

PETER.

Be it far from thee, Lord !
This shall not be !

CHRISTUS.

Get thee behind me, Satan !
Thou savorest not the things that be of
God,
But those that be of men ! If any will
Come after me, let him deny himself,
And daily take his cross, and follow me.

For whosoever will save his life shall lose
it,
And whosoever will lose his life shall find
it.
For wherein shall a man be profited
If he shall gain the whole world, and shall
lose
Himself or be a castaway ?

JAMES, *after a long pause.*

Why doth
The Master lead us up into this mountain ?

PETER.

He goeth up to pray.

JOHN.

See, where He standeth
Above us on the summit of the hill !
His face shines as the sun ! and all his
raiment
Exceeding white as snow, so as no fuller
On earth can white them ! He is not
alone ;
There are two with Him there ; two men
of eld,
Their white beards blowing on the moun-
tain air,
Are talking with him.

JAMES.

I am sore afraid !

PETER.

Who and whence are they ?

JOHN.

Moses and Elias !

PETER.

O Master ! it is good for us to be here !
If thou wilt, let us make three taberna-
cles ;
For thee one, and for Moses and Elias !

JOHN.

Behold a bright cloud sailing in the sun !
It overshadows us. A golden mist
Now hides them from us, and envelops us
And all the mountain in a luminous shadow !
I see no more. The nearest rocks are hid-
den.

VOICE *from the cloud.*

Lo ! this is my beloved Son ! Hear Him !

PETER.

It is the voice of God. He speaketh to us,
As from the burning bush He spake to
Moses !

JOHN.

The cloud-wreaths roll away. The veil is
lifted ;
We see again. Behold ! He is alone.
It was a vision that our eyes beheld,
And it hath vanished into the unseen.

CHRISTUS, *coming down from the mountain.*

I charge ye, tell the vision unto no one,
Till the Son of Man be risen from the dead !

PETER, *aside.*

Again He speaks of it ! What can it mean,
This rising from the dead ?

JAMES.

Why say the Scribes
Elias must first come ?

CHRISTUS.

He cometh first,
Restoring all things. But I say to you,
That this Elias is already come.
They knew him not, but have done unto
him
Whate'er they listed, as is written of him.

PETER, *aside.*

It is of John the Baptist He is speaking.

JAMES.

As we descend, see, at the mountain's foot,
A crowd of people ; coming, going, throng-
ing
Round the disciples, that we left behind us,
Seeming impatient, that we stay so long.

PETER.

It is some blind man, or some paralytic
That waits the Master's coming to be
healed.

JAMES.

I see a boy, who struggles and demeans him
As if an unclean spirit tormented him !

A CERTAIN MAN, *running forward.*

Lord ! I beseech thee, look upon my son.
He is mine only child ; a lunatic,
And sorely vexed ; for oftentimes he falleth

Into the fire and oft into the water.
Wherever the dumb spirit taketh him
He teareth him. He gnasheth with his
teeth,
And pines away. I spake to thy disciples
That they should cast him out, and they
could not.

CHRISTUS.

O faithless generation and perverse !
How long shall I be with you, and suffer
you ?
Bring thy son hither.

BYSTANDERS.

How the unclean spirit
Seizes the boy, and tortures him with pain !
He falleth to the ground and wallows,
foaming !
He cannot live.

CHRISTUS.

How long is it ago
Since this came unto him ?

THE FATHER.

Even of a child.
Oh, have compassion on us, Lord, and help
us,
If thou canst help us.

CHRISTUS.

If thou canst believe.
For unto him that verily believeth,
All things are possible.

THE FATHER.

Lord, I believe !
Help thou mine unbelief !

CHRISTUS.

Dumb and deaf spirit,
Come out of him, I charge thee, and no
more
Enter thou into him !
*The boy utters a loud cry of pain, and then lies
still.*

BYSTANDERS.

How motionless
He lieth there. No life is left in him.
His eyes are like a blind man's, that see not.
The boy is dead !

OTHERS.

Behold ! the Master stoops,

And takes him by the hand, and lifts him up.
He is not dead.

DISCIPLES.

But one word from those lips,
But one touch of that hand, and he is healed !
Ah, why could we not do it ?

THE FATHER.

My poor child !
Now thou art mine again. The unclean spirit
Shall never more torment thee ! Look at me !
Speak unto me ! Say that thou knowest me !

DISCIPLES to CHRISTUS, *departing.*

Good Master, tell us, for what reason was it
We could not cast him out ?

CHRISTUS.

Because of your unbelief !

VIII

THE YOUNG RULER

CHRISTUS.

Two men went up into the temple to pray.
The one was a self-righteous Pharisee,
The other a Publican. And the Pharisee
Stood and prayed thus within himself ! O God,
I thank thee I am not as other men,
Extortioners, unjust, adulterers,
Or even as this Publican. I fast
Twice in the week, and also I give tithes
Of all that I possess ! The Publican,
Standing afar off, would not lift so much
Even as his eyes to heaven, but smote his breast,
Saying : God be merciful to me a sinner !
I tell you that this man went to his house
More justified than the other. Every one
That doth exalt himself shall be abased,
And he that humbleth himself shall be exalted !

CHILDREN, *among themselves.*

Let us go nearer ! He is telling stories !
Let us go listen to them.

AN OLD JEW.

Children, children !
What are ye doing here ? Why do ye crowd us ?
It was such little vagabonds as you,
That followed Elisha, mocking him and crying :
Go up, thou bald-head ! But the bears — the bears
Came out of the wood, and tare them !

A MOTHER.

Speak not thus !
We brought them here, that He might lay his hands
On them, and bless them.

CHRISTUS.

Suffer little children
To come unto me, and forbid them not ;
Of such is the kingdom of heaven ; and their angels
Look always on my Father's face.

Takes them in his arms and blesses them.

A YOUNG RULER, *running.*

Good Master !
What good thing shall I do, that I may have
Eternal life ?

CHRISTUS.

Why callest thou me good ?
There is none good but one, and that is God.
If thou wilt enter into life eternal,
Keep the commandments.

YOUNG RULER.

Which of them ?

CHRISTUS.

Thou shalt not
Commit adultery ; thou shalt not kill ;
Thou shalt not steal ; thou shalt not bear false witness ;
Honor thy father and thy mother ; and love
Thy neighbor as thyself.

YOUNG RULER.

From my youth up
All these things have I kept. What lack I yet ?

JOHN.

With what divine compassion in his eyes
The Master looks upon this eager youth,
As if He loved him !

CHRISTUS.

Wouldst thou perfect be,
Sell all thou hast, and give it to the poor,
And come, take up thy cross, and follow me,
And thou shalt have thy treasure in the
heavens.

JOHN.

Behold, how sorrowful he turns away !

CHRISTUS.

Children ! how hard it is for them that trust
In riches to enter into the kingdom of God !
'T is easier for a camel to go through
A needle's eye, than for the rich to enter
The kingdom of God !

JOHN.

Ah, who then can be saved ?

CHRISTUS.

With men this is indeed impossible,
But unto God all things are possible !

PETER.

Behold, we have left all, and followed thee.
What shall we have therefor ?

CHRISTUS.

Eternal life.

IX

AT BETHANY

MARTHA *busy about household affairs.* MARY
sitting at the feet of CHRISTUS.

MARTHA.

She sitteth idly at the Master's feet,
And troubles not herself with household
cares.
'T is the old story. When a guest arrives
She gives up all to be with him ; while I
Must be the drudge, make ready the guest-
chamber,
Prepare the food, set everything in order,
And see that naught is wanting in the house.
She shows her love by words, and I by
works.

MARY.

O Master ! when thou comest, it is always
A Sabbath in the house. I cannot work ;
I must sit at thy feet ; must see thee, hear
thee !
I have a feeble, wayward, doubting heart,
Incapable of endurance or great thoughts,
Striving for something that it cannot reach,
Baffled and disappointed, wounded, hungry ;
And only when I hear thee am I happy,
And only when I see thee am at peace !
Stronger than I, and wiser, and far better
In every manner, is my sister Martha.
Thou seest how well she orders everything
To make thee welcome ; how she comes
and goes,
Careful and cumbered ever with much
serving,
While I but welcome thee with foolish
words !
Whene'er thou speakest to me, I am
happy ;
When thou art silent, I am satisfied.
Thy presence is enough. I ask no more.
Only to be with thee, only to see thee,
Sufficeth me. My heart is then at rest.
I wonder I am worthy of so much.

MARTHA.

Lord, dost thou care not that my sister
Mary
Hath left me thus to wait on thee alone ?
I pray thee, bid her help me.

CHRISTUS.

Martha, Martha,
Careful and troubled about many things
Art thou, and yet one thing alone is need-
ful !
Thy sister Mary hath chosen that good
part,
Which never shall be taken away from her !

X

BORN BLIND

A JEW.

Who is this beggar blinking in the sun ?
Is it not he who used to sit and beg
By the Gate Beautiful ?

ANOTHER.

It is the same.

A THIRD.

It is not he, but like him, for that beggar
Was blind from birth. It cannot be the
same.

THE BEGGAR.

Yea, I am he.

A JEW.

How have thine eyes been opened ?

THE BEGGAR.

A man that is called Jesus made a clay
And put it on mine eyes, and said to me :
Go to Siloam's Pool and wash thyself.
I went and washed, and I received my
sight.

A JEW.

Where is He ?

THE BEGGAR.
I know not.

PHARISEES.
What is this crowd
Gathered about a beggar ? What has hap-
pened ?

A JEW.

Here is a man who hath been blind from
birth,
And now he sees. He says a man called
Jesus
Hath healed him.

PHARISEES.
As God liveth, the Nazarene !
How was this done ?

THE BEGGAR.
Rabboni, he put clay
Upon mine eyes ; I washed, and now I
see.

PHARISEES.
When did he this ?

THE BEGGAR.
Rabboni, yesterday.

PHARISEES.

The Sabbath day. This man is not of God
Because he keepeth not the Sabbath day !

A JEW.

How can a man that is a sinner do
Such miracles ?

PHARISEES.
What dost thou say of him
That hath restored thy sight ?

THE BEGGAR.
He is a Prophet.

A JEW.

This is a wonderful story, but not true.
A beggar's fiction. He was not born blind,
And never has been blind !

OTHERS.
Here are his parents.
Ask them.

PHARISEES.
Is this your son ?

THE PARENTS.
Rabboni, yea ;
We know this is our son.

PHARISEES.
Was he born blind ?

THE PARENTS.

He was born blind.

PHARISEES.
Then how doth he now see ?

THE PARENTS, *aside.*

What answer shall we make ? If we con-
fess
It was the Christ, we shall be driven forth
Out of the Synagogue ! We know, Rab-
boni,
This is our son, and that he was born
blind ;
But by what means he seeth, we know not,
Or who his eyes hath opened, we know
not.
He is of age ; ask him ; we cannot say ;
He shall speak for himself.

PHARISEES.
Give God the praise !
We know the man that healed thee is a
sinner !

THE BEGGAR.

Whether He be a sinner, I know not ;
One thing I know ; that whereas I was
blind,
I now do see.

PHARISEES.

How opened he thine eyes ?
What did he do ?

THE BEGGAR.

I have already told you.
Ye did not hear : why would ye hear
again ?
Will ye be his disciples ?

PHARISEES.

God of Moses !
Are we demoniacs, are we halt or blind,
Or palsy-stricken, or lepers, or the like,
That we should join the Synagogue of
Satan,
And follow jugglers ? Thou art his dis-
ciple,
But we are disciples of Moses ; and we
know
That God spake unto Moses ; but this
fellow,
We know not whence he is !

THE BEGGAR.

Why, herein is
A marvellous thing ! Ye know not whence
He is,
Yet He hath opened mine eyes ! We know
that God
Heareth not sinners ; but if any man
Doeth God's will, and is his worshipper,
Him doth He hear. Oh, since the world
began
It was not heard that any man hath
opened
The eyes of one that was born blind. If
He
Were not of God, surely He could do no-
thing !

PHARISEES.

Thou, who wast altogether born in sins
And in iniquities, dost thou teach us ?
Away with thee out of the holy places,
Thou reprobate, thou beggar, thou blas-
phemer !
THE BEGGAR *is cast out.*

XI

SIMON MAGUS AND HELEN OF TYRE

*On the house-top at Endor. Night. A lighted
lantern on a table.*

SIMON.

Swift are the blessed Immortals to the
mortal
That perseveres ! So doth it stand re-
corded
In the divine Chaldæan Oracles
Of Zoroaster, once Ezekiel's slave,
Who in his native East betook himself
To lonely meditation, and the writing
On the dried skins of oxen the Twelve
Books
Of the Avesta and the Oracles !
Therefore I persevere ; and I have brought
thee
From the great city of Tyre, where men
deride
The things they comprehend not, to this
plain
Of Esdraelon, in the Hebrew tongue
Called Armageddon, and this town of Endor,
Where men believe ; where all the air is full
Of marvellous traditions, and the Enchan-
tress
That summoned up the ghost of Samuel
Is still remembered. Thou hast seen the
land ;
Is it not fair to look on ?

HELEN.

It is fair,
Yet not so fair as Tyre.

SIMON.

Is not Mount Tabor
As beautiful as Carmel by the Sea ?

HELEN.

It is too silent and too solitary ;
I miss the tumult of the streets ; the sounds
Of traffic, and the going to and fro
Of people in gay attire, with cloaks of
purple,
And gold and silver jewelry !

SIMON.

Inventions
Of Ahriman, the spirit of the dark,
The Evil Spirit !

HELEN.
I regret the gossip
Of friends and neighbors at the open door
On summer nights.

SIMON.
An idle waste of time.

HELEN.
The singing and the dancing, the delight
Of music and of motion. Woe is me,
To give up all these pleasures, and to lead
The life we lead !

SIMON.
Thou canst not raise thyself
Up to the level of my higher thought,
And though possessing thee, I still remain
Apart from thee, and with thee, am alone
In my high dreams.

HELEN.
Happier was I in Tyre.
Oh, I remember how the gallant ships
Came sailing in, with ivory, gold, and silver,
And apes and peacocks ; and the singing
sailors,
And the gay captains with their silken
dresses,
Smelling of aloes, myrrh, and cinnamon !

SIMON.
But the dishonor, Helen ! Let the ships
Of Tarshish howl for that !

HELEN.
And what dishonor ?
Remember Rahab, and how she became
The ancestress of the great Psalmist David ;
And wherefore should not I, Helen of Tyre,
Attain like honor ?

SIMON.
Thou art Helen of Tyre,
And hast been Helen of Troy, and hast
been Rahab,
The Queen of Sheba, and Semiramis,
And Sara of seven husbands, and Jezebel,
And other women of the like allurements ;
And now thou art Minerva, the first Æon,
The Mother of Angels !

HELEN.
And the concubine
Of Simon the Magician ! Is it honor

For one who has been all these noble dames,
To tramp about the dirty villages
And cities of Samaria with a juggler ?
A charmer of serpents ?

SIMON.
He who knows himself
Knows all things in himself. I have
charmed thee,
Thou beautiful asp : yet am I no magician.
I am the Power of God, and the Beauty of
God !
I am the Paraclete, the Comforter !

HELEN.
Illusions ! Thou deceiver, self-deceived !
Thou dost usurp the titles of another ;
Thou art not what thou sayest.

SIMON.
Am I not ?
Then feel my power.

HELEN.
Would I had ne'er left Tyre !
He looks at her, and she sinks into a deep sleep.

SIMON.
Go, see it in thy dreams, fair unbeliever !
And leave me unto mine, if they be dreams,
That take such shapes before me, that I see
them ;
These effable and ineffable impressions
Of the mysterious world, that come to me
From the elements of Fire and Earth and
Water,
And the all-nourishing Ether ! It is written,
Look not on Nature, for her name is fatal !
Yet there are Principles, that make ap-
parent
The images of unapparent things,
And the impression of vague characters
And visions most divine appear in ether.
So speak the Oracles ; then wherefore
fatal ?
I take this orange-bough, with its five
leaves,
Each equidistant on the upright stem ;
And I project them on a plane below,
In the circumference of a circle drawn
About a centre where the stem is planted,
And each still equidistant from the other ;
As if a thread of gossamer were drawn
Down from each leaf, and fastened with a
pin.

Now if from these five points a line be
      traced
To each alternate point, we shall obtain
The Pentagram, or Solomon's Pentangle,
A charm against all witchcraft, and a sign,
Which on the banner of Antiochus
Drove back the fierce barbarians of the
      North,
Demons esteemed, and gave the Syrian
      King
The sacred name of Soter, or of Savior.
Thus Nature works mysteriously with
      man ;
And from the Eternal One, as from a
      centre,
All things proceed, in fire, air, earth, and
      water,
And all are subject to one law, which
      broken
Even in a single point, is broken in all ;
Demons rush in, and chaos comes again.

By this will I compel the stubborn spirits,
That guard the treasures, hid in caverns
      deep
On Gerizim, by Uzzi the High-Priest,
The ark and holy vessels, to reveal
Their secret unto me, and to restore
These precious things to the Samaritans.
A mist is rising from the plain below me,
And as I look, the vapors shape themselves
Into strange figures, as if unawares
My lips had breathed the Tetragrammaton,
And from their graves, o'er all the battle-
      fields
Of Armageddon, the long-buried captains
Had started, with their thousands, and ten
      thousands,
And rushed together to renew their wars,
Powerless, and weaponless, and without a
      sound !
Wake, Helen, from thy sleep ! The air
      grows cold ;
Let us go down.

HELEN, *awaking.*
            Oh, would I were at home !

SIMON.
Thou sayest that I usurp another's titles.
In youth I saw the Wise Men of the East,
Magalath and Pangalath and Saracen,
Who followed the bright star, but home
      returned
For fear of Herod by another way.

Oh shining worlds above me ! in what deep
Recesses of your realms of mystery
Lies hidden now that star ? and where are
      they
That brought the gifts of frankincense and
      myrrh ?

HELEN.
The Nazarene still liveth.

SIMON.
            We have heard
His name in many towns, but have not
      seen Him.
He flits before us ; tarries not ; is gone
When we approach, like something unsub-
      stantial,
Made of the air, and fading into air.
He is at Nazareth, He is at Nain,
Or at the Lovely Village on the Lake,
Or sailing on its waters.

HELEN.
            So say those
Who do not wish to find Him.

SIMON.
            Can this be
The King of Israel, whom the Wise Men
      worshipped ?
Or does He fear to meet me ? It would
      seem so.
We should soon learn which of us twain
      usurps
The titles of the other, as thou sayest.
            They go down.

THE THIRD PASSOVER

I

THE ENTRY INTO JERUSALEM

THE SYRO - PHŒNICIAN WOMAN *and her*
DAUGHTER *on the house-top at Jerusalem.*

THE DAUGHTER, *singing.*
BLIND Bartimeus at the gates
Of Jericho in darkness waits ;
He hears the crowd ; — he hears a breath
Say, It is Christ of Nazareth !
And calls, in tones of agony,
ʼΙησοῦ, ἐλέησόν με !

The thronging multitudes increase ;
Blind Bartimeus, hold thy peace !

But still, above the noisy crowd,
The beggar's cry is shrill and loud ;
Until they say, He calleth thee !
Θάρσει · ἔγειραι, φωνεῖ σε !

Then saith the Christ, as silent stands
The crowd, What wilt thou at my hands ?
And he replies, Oh, give me light !
Rabbi, restore the blind man's sight !
And Jesus answers, Ὕπαγε ·
Ἡ πίστις σου σέσωκέ σε !

Ye that have eyes, yet cannot see,
In darkness and in misery,
Recall those mighty voices three,
Ἰησοῦ, ἐλέησόν με !
Θάρσει · ἔγειραι, ὕπαγε !
Ἡ πίστις σου σέσωκέ σε !

THE MOTHER.

Thy faith hath saved thee !   Ah, how true
   that is !
For I had faith ; and when the Master
   came
Into the coasts of Tyre and Sidon, fleeing
From those who sought to slay Him, I went
   forth
And cried unto Him, saying : Have mercy
   on me,
O Lord, thou Son of David ! for my
   daughter
Is grievously tormented with a devil.
But He passed on, and answered not a word.
And his disciples said, beseeching Him :
Send her away !   She crieth after us !
And then the Master answered them and
   said :
I am not sent but unto the lost sheep
Of the House of Israel !   Then I wor-
   shipped Him,
Saying : Lord, help me !   And He an-
   swered me,
It is not meet to take the children's bread
And cast it unto dogs !   Truth, Lord, I said ;
And yet the dogs may eat the crumbs
   which fall
From off their master's table ; and He
   turned,
And answered me ; and said to me : O
   woman,
Great is thy faith ; then be it unto thee
Even as thou wilt.   And from that very
   hour
Thou wast made whole, my darling ! my
   delight !

THE DAUGHTER.

There came upon my dark and troubled
   mind
A calm, as when the tumult of the city
Suddenly ceases, and I lie and hear
The silver trumpets of the Temple blowing
Their welcome to the Sabbath.   Still I
   wonder,
That one who was so far away from me,
And could not see me, by his thought alone
Had power to heal me.   Oh that I could see
   Him !

THE MOTHER.

Perhaps thou wilt ; for I have brought
   thee here
To keep the holy Passover, and lay
Thine offering of thanksgiving on the altar.
Thou mayst both see and hear Him.
   Hark !

VOICES *afar off*.
Hosanna !

THE DAUGHTER.

A crowd comes pouring through the city
   gate !
O mother, look !

VOICES *in the street*.
             Hosanna to the Son
Of David !

THE DAUGHTER.

           A great multitude of people
Fills all the street ; and riding on an ass
Comes one of noble aspect, like a king !
The people spread their garments in the
   way,
And scatter branches of the palm-trees !

VOICES.
                  Blessed
Is He that cometh in the name of the
   Lord !
Hosanna in the highest !

OTHER VOICES.
             Who is this ?

VOICES.
Jesus of Nazareth !

THE DAUGHTER.
           Mother, it is He !

VOICES.

He hath called Lazarus of Bethany
Out of his grave, and raised him from the
dead !
Hosanna in the highest !

PHARISEES.

Ye perceive
That nothing we prevail. Behold, the
world
Is all gone after him !

THE DAUGHTER.

What majesty,
What power is in that care-worn counte-
nance !
What sweetness, what compassion ! I no
longer
Wonder that He hath healed me !

VOICES.

Peace in heaven,
And glory in the highest !

PHARISEES.

Rabbi ! Rabbi !
Rebuke thy followers !

CHRISTUS.

Should they hold their peace
The very stones beneath us would cry
out !

THE DAUGHTER.

All hath passed by me like a dream of won-
der !
But I have seen Him, and have heard his
voice,
And I am satisfied ! I ask no more !

II

SOLOMON'S PORCH

GAMALIEL THE SCRIBE.

When Rabban Simeon, upon whom be
peace !
Taught in these Schools, he boasted that
his pen
Had written no word that he could call his
own,
But wholly and always had been conse-
crated

To the transcribing of the Law and Pro-
phets.
He used to say, and never tired of saying,
The world itself was built upon the Law.
And ancient Hillel said, that whosoever
Gains a good name, gains something for
himself,
But he who gains a knowledge of the Law
Gains everlasting life. And they spake
truly.
Great is the Written Law ; but greater still
The Unwritten, the Traditions of the
Elders,
The lovely words of Levites, spoken first
To Moses on the Mount, and handed down
From mouth to mouth, in one unbroken
sound
And sequence of divine authority,
The voice of God resounding through the
ages.

The Written Law is water ; the Unwritten
Is precious wine ; the Written Law is salt,
The Unwritten costly spice ; the Written
Law
Is but the body ; the Unwritten, the soul
That quickens it and makes it breathe and
live.
I can remember, many years ago,
A little bright-eyed school-boy, a mere
stripling,
Son of a Galilean carpenter,
From Nazareth, I think, who came one day
And sat here in the Temple with the Scribes,
Hearing us speak, and asking many ques-
tions,
And we were all astonished at his quickness.
And when his mother came, and said : Be-
hold
Thy father and I have sought thee, sorrow-
ing ;
He looked as one astonished, and made an-
swer,
How is it that ye sought me ? Wist ye not
That I must be about my Father's busi-
ness ?
Often since then I see him here among us,
Or dream I see him, with his upraised face
Intent and eager, and I often wonder
Unto what manner of manhood he hath
grown !
Perhaps a poor mechanic, like his father,
Lost in his little Galilean village
And toiling at his craft, to die unknown
And be no more remembered among men.

CHRISTUS *in the outer court.*

The Scribes and Pharisees sit in Moses'
　　seat ;
All, therefore, whatsoever they command
　　you,
Observe and do ; but follow not their
　　works ;
They say and do not. They bind heavy
　　burdens
And very grievous to be borne, and lay
　　them
Upon men's shoulders, but they move them
　　not
With so much as a finger !

GAMALIEL, *looking forth.*

　　　　　　　　　　　Who is this
Exhorting in the outer courts so loudly ?

CHRISTUS.

Their works they do for to be seen of men.
They make broad their phylacteries, and
　　enlarge
The borders of their garments, and they
　　love
The uppermost rooms at feasts, and the
　　chief seats
In Synagogues, and greetings in the
　　markets,
And to be called of all men Rabbi, Rabbi !

GAMALIEL.

It is that loud and turbulent Galilean,
That came here at the Feast of Dedication,
And stirred the people up to break the
　　Law !

CHRISTUS.

Woe unto you, ye Scribes and Pharisees,
Ye hypocrites ! for ye shut up the kingdom
Of heaven, and neither go ye in yourselves
Nor suffer them that are entering to go in !

GAMALIEL.

How eagerly the people throng and listen,
As if his ribald words were words of wis-
　　dom !

CHRISTUS.

Woe unto you, ye Scribes and Pharisees,
Ye hypocrites ! for ye devour the houses
Of widows, and for pretence ye make long
　　prayers ;
Therefore shall ye receive the more dam-
　　nation.

GAMALIEL.

This brawler is no Jew, — he is a vile
Samaritan, and hath an unclean spirit !

CHRISTUS.

Woe unto you, ye Scribes and Pharisees,
Ye hypocrites ! ye compass sea and land
To make one proselyte, and when he is made
Ye make him twofold more the child of
　　hell
Than you yourselves are !

GAMALIEL.

　　　　　　　O my father's father !
Hillel of blessed memory, hear and judge !

CHRISTUS.

Woe unto you, ye Scribes and Pharisees,
Ye hypocrites ! for ye pay tithe of mint,
Of anise, and of cumin, and omit
The weightier matters of the law of God,
Judgment and faith and mercy ; and all
　　these
Ye ought to have done, nor leave undone
　　the others !

GAMALIEL.

O Rabban Simeon ! how must thy bones
Stir in their grave to hear such blas-
　　phemies !

CHRISTUS.

Woe unto you, ye Scribes and Pharisees,
Ye hypocrites ! for ye make clean and
　　sweet
The outside of the cup and of the platter,
But they within are full of all excess !

GAMALIEL.

Patience of God ! canst thou endure so
　　long ?
Or art thou deaf, or gone upon a journey ?

CHRISTUS.

Woe unto you, ye Scribes and Pharisees,
Ye hypocrites ! for ye are very like
To whited sepulchres, which indeed appear
Beautiful outwardly, but are within
Filled full of dead men's bones and all un-
　　cleanness !

GAMALIEL.

Am I awake ? Is this Jerusalem ?
And are these Jews that throng and stare
　　and listen ?

CHRISTUS.

Woe unto you, ye Scribes and Pharisees,
Ye hypocrites! because ye build the tombs
Of prophets, and adorn the sepulchres
Of righteous men, and say: If we had
    lived
When lived our fathers, we would not have
    been
Partakers with them in the blood of Pro-
    phets.
So ye be witnesses unto yourselves,
That ye are children of them that killed the
    Prophets!
Fill ye up then the measure of your fathers.
I send unto you Prophets and Wise Men,
And Scribes, and some ye crucify, and
    some
Scourge in your Synagogues, and perse-
    cute
From city to city; that on you may come
The righteous blood that hath been shed on
    earth,
From the blood of righteous Abel to the
    blood
Of Zacharias, son of Barachias,
Ye slew between the Temple and the altar!

GAMALIEL.

Oh, had I here my subtle dialectician,
My little Saul of Tarsus, the tent-maker,
Whose wit is sharper than his needle's
    point,
He would delight to foil this noisy wran-
    gler!

CHRISTUS.

Jerusalem! Jerusalem! O thou
That killest the Prophets, and that stonest
    them
Which are sent unto thee, how often would I
Have gathered together thy children, as a
    hen
Gathereth her chickens underneath her
    wing,
And ye would not! Behold, your house is
    left
Unto you desolate!

THE PEOPLE.
                This is a Prophet!
This is the Christ that was to come!

GAMALIEL.
                Ye fools!
Think ye, shall Christ come out of Galilee?

III

LORD, IS IT I?

CHRISTUS.
One of you shall betray me.

THE DISCIPLES.
                Is it I?
Lord, is it I?

CHRISTUS.
            One of the Twelve it is
That dippeth with me in this dish his hand;
He shall betray me. Lo, the Son of Man
Goeth indeed as it is written of Him;
But woe shall be unto that man by whom
He is betrayed! Good were it for that
    man
If he had ne'er been born!

JUDAS ISCARIOT.
                Lord, is it I?

CHRISTUS.
Ay, thou hast said. And that thou doest,
    do quickly.

JUDAS ISCARIOT, going out.
Ah, woe is me!

CHRISTUS.
            All ye shall be offended
Because of me this night; for it is written:
Awake, O sword against my shepherd!
    Smite
The shepherd, saith the Lord of hosts, and
    scattered
Shall be the sheep! — But after I am
    risen
I go before you into Galilee.

PETER.
O Master! though all men shall be of-
    fended
Because of thee, yet will not I be!

CHRISTUS.
                Simon,
Behold how Satan hath desired to have you,
That he may sift you as one sifteth wheat!
Whither I go thou canst not follow me —
Not now; but thou shalt follow me here-
    after.

PETER.

Wherefore can I not follow thee ?   I am
    ready
To go with thee to prison and to death.

CHRISTUS.

Verily say I unto thee, this night,
Ere the cock crow, thou shalt deny me
    thrice !

PETER.

Though I should die, yet will I not deny
    thee.

CHRISTUS.

When first I sent you forth without a
    purse,
Or scrip, or shoes, did ye lack anything ?

THE DISCIPLES.

Not anything.

CHRISTUS.

                    But he that hath a purse,
Now let him take it, and likewise his
    scrip ;
And he that hath no sword, let him go sell
His clothes and buy one.   That which hath
    been written
Must be accomplished now : He hath
    poured out
His soul even unto death ; he hath been
    numbered
With the transgressors, and himself hath
    borne
The sin of many, and made intercession
For the transgressors.   And here have an
    end
The things concerning me.

PETER.

                    Behold, O Lord,
Behold, here are two swords !

CHRISTUS.

                    It is enough.

IV

THE GARDEN OF GETHSEMANE

CHRISTUS.

My spirit is exceeding sorrowful
Even unto death ! Tarry ye here and
    watch.
            He goes apart.

PETER.

Under this ancient olive-tree, that spreads
Its broad centennial branches like a tent,
Let us lie down and rest.

JOHN.

                    What are those torches,
That glimmer on Brook Kedron there
    below us ?

JAMES.

It is some marriage feast ; the joyful maid-
    ens
Go out to meet the bridegroom.

PETER.

                    I am weary.
The struggles of this day have overcome
    me.
            They sleep.

CHRISTUS, *falling on his face.*

Father ! all things are possible to thee, —
Oh let this cup pass from me !   Neverthe-
    less
Not as I will, but as thou wilt, be done !
            Returning to the Disciples.
What ! could ye not watch with me for one
    hour ?
Oh watch and pray, that ye may enter not
Into temptation.   For the spirit indeed
Is willing, but the flesh is weak !

JOHN.

                    Alas !
It is for sorrow that our eyes are heavy. —
I see again the glimmer of those torches
Among the olives ; they are coming hither.

JAMES.

Outside the garden wall the path divides ;
Surely they come not hither.
            They sleep again.

CHRISTUS, *as before.*

                    O my Father !
If this cup may not pass away from me,
Except I drink of it, thy will be done.
            Returning to the Disciples.
Sleep on ; and take your rest !

JOHN.

                    Beloved Master,
Alas ! we know not what to answer thee !
It is for sorrow that our eyes are heavy. —
Behold, the torches now encompass us.

JAMES.

They do but go about the garden wall,
Seeking for some one, or for something lost.
They sleep again.

CHRISTUS, *as before.*

If this cup may not pass away from me,
Except I drink of it, thy will be done.
Returning to the Disciples.
It is enough ! Behold, the Son of Man
Hath been betrayed into the hands of sin-
ners !
The hour is come. Rise up, let us be go-
ing ;
For he that shall betray me is at hand.

JOHN.

Ah me ! See, from his forehead, in the
torchlight,
Great drops of blood are falling to the
ground !

PETER.

What lights are these ? What torches
glare and glisten
Upon the swords and armor of these men ?
And there among them Judas Iscariot !
*He smites the servant of the High-Priest with his
sword.*

CHRISTUS.

Put up thy sword into its sheath ; for they
That take the sword shall perish with the
sword.
The cup my Father hath given me to drink,
Shall I not drink it ? Think'st thou that
I cannot
Pray to my Father, and that He shall give
me
More than twelve legions of angels pres-
ently ?

JUDAS *to* CHRISTUS, *kissing him.*

Hail, Master ! hail !

CHRISTUS.

Friend, wherefore art thou come ?
Whom seek ye ?

CAPTAIN OF THE TEMPLE.
Jesus of Nazareth.

CHRISTUS.
I am he.
Are ye come hither as against a thief,

With swords and staves to take me ?
When I daily
Was with you in the Temple, ye stretched
forth
No hands to take me ! But this is your
hour,
And this the power of darkness. If ye
seek
Me only, let these others go their way.
The Disciples depart. CHRISTUS *is bound and
led away. A certain young man follows Him,
having a linen cloth cast about his body. They
lay hold of him, and the young man flees from
them naked.*

V

THE PALACE OF CAIAPHAS

PHARISEES.

What do we ? Clearly something must
we do,
For this man worketh many miracles.

CAIAPHAS.

I am informed that he is a mechanic ;
A carpenter's son ; a Galilean peasant,
Keeping disreputable company.

PHARISEES.

The people say that here in Bethany
He hath raised up a certain Lazarus,
Who had been dead three days.

CAIAPHAS.
Impossible !
There is no resurrection of the dead ;
This Lazarus should be taken, and put to
death
As an impostor. If this Galilean
Would be content to stay in Galilee,
And preach in country towns, I should not
heed him.
But when he comes up to Jerusalem
Riding in triumph, as I am informed,
And drives the money-changers from the
Temple,
That is another matter.

PHARISEES.
If we thus
Let him alone, all will believe on him,
And then the Romans come and take
away
Our place and nation.

CAIAPHAS.

Ye know nothing at all.
Simon Ben Camith, my great predecessor,
On whom be peace! would have dealt
presently
With such a demagogue. I shall no less.
The man must die. Do ye consider not
It is expedient that one man should die,
Not the whole nation perish? What is
death?
It differeth from sleep but in duration.
We sleep and wake again; an hour or two
Later or earlier, and it matters not,
And if we never wake it matters not;
When we are in our graves we are at peace,
Nothing can wake us or disturb us more.
There is no resurrection.

PHARISEES, aside.

O most faithful
Disciple of Hircanus Maccabæus,
Will nothing but complete annihilation
Comfort and satisfy thee?

CAIAPHAS.

While ye are talking
And plotting, and contriving how to take
him,
Fearing the people, and so doing naught,
I, who fear not the people, have been act-
ing;
Have taken this Prophet, this young Naza-
rene,
Who by Beelzebub the Prince of devils
Casteth out devils, and doth raise the dead,
That might as well be dead, and left in
peace.
Annas my father-in-law hath sent him
hither.
I hear the guard. Behold your Galilean!
CHRISTUS is brought in bound.

SERVANT, in the vestibule.

Why art thou up so late, my pretty damsel?

DAMSEL.

Why art thou up so early, pretty man?
It is not cock-crow yet, and art thou stir-
ring?

SERVANT.

What brings thee here?

DAMSEL.

What brings the rest of you?

SERVANT.

Come here and warm thy hands.

DAMSEL to PETER.

Art thou not also
One of this man's disciples?

PETER.

I am not.

DAMSEL.

Now surely thou art also one of them;
Thou art a Galilean, and thy speech
Bewrayeth thee.

PETER.

Woman, I know him not!

CAIAPHAS to CHRISTUS, in the Hall.

Who art thou? Tell us plainly of thyself
And of thy doctrines, and of thy disciples.

CHRISTUS.

Lo, I have spoken openly to the world,
I have taught ever in the Synagogue,
And in the Temple, where the Jews resort;
In secret have said nothing. Wherefore
then
Askest thou me of this? Ask them that
heard me
What I have said to them. Behold, they
know
What I have said!

OFFICER, striking him.

What, fellow! answerest thou
The High-Priest so?

CHRISTUS.

If I have spoken evil,
Bear witness of the evil; but if well,
Why smitest thou me?

CAIAPHAS.

Where are the witnesses?
Let them say what they know.

THE TWO FALSE WITNESSES.

We heard him say:
I will destroy this Temple made with hands,
And will within three days build up another
Made without hands.

SCRIBES and PHARISEES.

He is o'erwhelmed with shame
And cannot answer!

CAIAPHAS.

Dost thou answer nothing?
What is this thing they witness here against
thee?

SCRIBES *and* PHARISEES.

He holds his peace.

CAIAPHAS.

Tell us, art thou the Christ?
I do adjure thee by the living God,
Tell us, art thou indeed the Christ?

CHRISTUS.

I am.
Hereafter shall ye see the Son of Man
Sit on the right hand of the power of God,
And come in clouds of heaven!

CAIAPHAS, *rending his clothes.*

It is enough.
He hath spoken blasphemy! What further
need
Have we of witnesses? Now ye have heard
His blasphemy. What think ye? Is he
guilty?

SCRIBES *and* PHARISEES.

Guilty of death!

KINSMAN OF MALCHUS *to* PETER, *in the vestibule.*

Surely I know thy face,
Did I not see thee in the garden with him?

PETER.

How couldst thou see me? I swear unto
thee
I do not know this man of whom ye speak!
The cock crows.
Hark! the cock crows! That sorrowful,
pale face
Seeks for me in the crowd, and looks at me,
As if He would remind me of those words:
Ere the cock crow thou shalt deny me
thrice!
Goes out weeping. CHRISTUS *is blindfolded and
buffeted.*

AN OFFICER, *striking him with his palm.*

Prophesy unto us, thou Christ, thou
Prophet!
Who is it smote thee?

CAIAPHAS.

Lead him unto Pilate!

VI

PONTIUS PILATE

PILATE.

Wholly incomprehensible to me,
Vainglorious, obstinate, and given up
To unintelligible old traditions,
And proud, and self-conceited are these
Jews!
Not long ago, I marched the legions down
From Cæsarea to their winter-quarters
Here in Jerusalem, with the effigies
Of Cæsar on their ensigns, and a tumult
Arose among these Jews, because their
Law
Forbids the making of all images!
They threw themselves upon the ground
with wild
Expostulations, bared their necks, and
cried
That they would sooner die than have their
Law
Infringed in any manner; as if Numa
Were not as great as Moses, and the Laws
Of the Twelve Tables as their Pentateuch!

And then, again, when I desired to span
Their valley with an aqueduct, and bring
A rushing river in to wash the city
And its inhabitants, — they all rebelled
As if they had been herds of unwashed
swine!
Thousands and thousands of them got
together
And raised so great a clamor round my
doors,
That, fearing violent outbreak, I desisted,
And left them to their wallowing in the
mire.

And now here comes the reverend Sanhe-
drim
Of lawyers, priests, and Scribes and Phari-
sees,
Like old and toothless mastiffs, that can
bark
But cannot bite, howling their accusations
Against a mild enthusiast, who hath
preached
I know not what new doctrine, being King
Of some vague kingdom in the other world,
That hath no more to do with Rome and
Cæsar

Than I have with the patriarch Abra-
ham !
Finding this man to be a Galilean
I sent him straight to Herod, and I hope
That is the last of it ; but if it be not,
I still have power to pardon and release
him,
As is the custom at the Passover,
And so accommodate the matter smoothly,
Seeming to yield to them, yet saving him ;
A prudent and sagacious policy
For Roman Governors in the Provinces.

Incomprehensible, fanatic people !
Ye have a God, who seemeth like your-
selves
Incomprehensible, dwelling apart,
Majestic, cloud - encompassed, clothed in
darkness !
One whom ye fear, but love not ; yet ye
have
No Goddesses to soften your stern lives,
And make you tender unto human weak-
ness,
While we of Rome have everywhere
around us
Our amiable divinities, that haunt
The woodlands, and the waters, and fre-
quent
Our households, with their sweet and
gracious presence !
I will go in, and while these Jews are
wrangling,
Read my Ovidius on the Art of Love.

VII

BARABBAS IN PRISON

BARABBAS, *to his fellow-prisoners.*

Barabbas is my name,
Barabbas, the Son of Shame,
Is the meaning I suppose ;
I'm no better than the best,
And whether worse than the rest
Of my fellow-men, who knows ?

I was once, to say it in brief,
A highwayman, a robber-chief,
In the open light of day.
So much I am free to confess ;
But all men, more or less,
Are robbers in their way.

From my cavern in the crags,
From my lair of leaves and flags,
I could see, like ants, below,
The camels with their load
Of merchandise, on the road
That leadeth to Jericho.

And I struck them unaware,
As an eagle from the air
Drops down upon bird or beast ;
And I had my heart's desire
Of the merchants of Sidon and Tyre
And Damascus and the East.

But it is not for that I fear ;
It is not for that I am here
In these iron fetters bound ;
Sedition ! that is the word
That Pontius Pilate heard,
And he liketh not the sound.

What think ye, would he care
For a Jew slain here or there,
Or a plundered caravan ?
But Cæsar ! — ah, that is a crime,
To the uttermost end of time
Shall not be forgiven to man.

Therefore was Herod wroth
With Matthias Margaloth,
And burned him for a show !
Therefore his wrath did smite
Judas the Gaulonite,
And his followers, as ye know.

For that cause and no more,
Am I here, as I said before ;
For one unlucky night,
Jucundus, the captain of horse,
Was upon us with all his force,
And I was caught in the fight.

I might have fled with the rest,
But my dagger was in the breast
Of a Roman equerry ;
As we rolled there in the street,
They bound me, hands and feet ;
And this is the end of me.

Who cares for death ? Not I !
A thousand times I would die,
Rather than suffer wrong !
Already those women of mine
Are mixing the myrrh and the wine
I shall not be with you long.

VIII

ECCE HOMO

PILATE, *on the tessellated pavement in front of his palace.*

Ye have brought unto me this man, as
  one
Who doth pervert the people ; and be-
  hold !
I have examined him, and found no fault
Touching the things whereof ye do accuse
  him.
No, nor yet Herod ; for I sent you to him,
And nothing worthy of death he findeth in
  him.
Ye have a custom at the Passover,
That one condemned to death shall be re-
  leased.
Whom will ye, then, that I release to you ?
Jesus Barabbas, called the Son of Shame,
Or Jesus, Son of Joseph, called the Christ ?

THE PEOPLE, *shouting.*

Not this man, but Barabbas !

PILATE.

                What then will ye
That I should do with him that is called
  Christ ?

THE PEOPLE.

Crucify him !

PILATE.

                Why, what evil hath he done ?
Lo, I have found no cause of death in him ;
I will chastise him, and then let him go.

THE PEOPLE, *more vehemently.*

Crucify him ! crucify him !

A MESSENGER, *to* PILATE.

                Thy wife sends
This message to thee, — Have thou naught
  to do
With that just man ; for I this day in
  dreams
Have suffered many things because of him.

PILATE, *aside.*

The Gods speak to us in our dreams ! I
  tremble
At what I have to do ! O Claudia,

How shall I save him ? Yet one effort
  more,
Or he must perish !
      Washes his hands before them.
                I am innocent
Of the blood of this just person ; see ye to
  it !

THE PEOPLE.

Let his blood be on us and on our children !

VOICES, *within the palace.*

Put on thy royal robes ; put on thy crown,
And take thy sceptre ! Hail, thou King of
  the Jews !

PILATE.

I bring him forth to you, that ye may know
I find no fault in him. Behold the man !
CHRISTUS *is led in with the purple robe and crown
        of thorns.*

CHIEF PRIESTS *and* OFFICERS.

Crucify him ! crucify him !

PILATE.

                Take ye him ;
I find no fault in him.

CHIEF PRIESTS.

                We have a Law,
And by our Law he ought to die ; because
He made himself to be the Son of God.

PILATE, *aside.*

Ah ! there are Sons of God, and demi-gods
More than ye know, ye ignorant High-
  Priests !

To CHRISTUS.

Whence art thou ?

CHIEF PRIESTS.

                Crucify him ! crucify him !

PILATE, *to* CHRISTUS.

Dost thou not answer me ? Dost thou not
  know
That I have power enough to crucify thee ?
That I have also power to set thee free ?

CHRISTUS.

Thou couldest have no power at all against
  me
Except that it were given thee from above ;

Therefore hath he that sent me unto thee
The greater sin.

CHIEF PRIESTS.

     If thou let this man go,
Thou art not Cæsar's friend. For whoso-
  ever
Maketh himself a King, speaks against
  Cæsar.

PILATE.

Ye Jews, behold your King !

CHIEF PRIESTS.

      Away with him !
Crucify him !

PILATE.

    Shall I crucify your King ?

CHIEF PRIESTS.

We have no King but Cæsar !

PILATE.

      Take him, then,
Take him, ye cruel and bloodthirsty Priests,
More merciless than the plebeian mob,
Who pity and spare the fainting gladi-
  ator
Blood-stained in Roman amphitheatres, —
Take him, and crucify him if ye will ;
But if the immortal Gods do ever min-
  gle
With the affairs of mortals, which I doubt
  not,
And hold the attribute of justice dear,
They will commission the Eumenides
To scatter you to the four winds of
  heaven,
Exacting tear for tear, and blood for
  blood.
Here, take ye this inscription, Priests, and
  nail it
Upon the cross, above your victim's head :
Jesus of Nazareth, King of the Jews.

CHIEF PRIESTS.

Nay, we entreat ! write not, the King of
  the Jews ;
But that he said : I am the King of the
  Jews !

PILATE.

Enough. What I have written, I have
  written.

IX

ACELDAMA

JUDAS ISCARIOT.

Lost ! lost ! Forever lost ! I have betrayed
The innocent blood ! O God ! if thou art
  love,
Why didst thou leave me naked to the
  tempter ?
Why didst thou not commission thy swift
  lightning
To strike me dead ? or why did I not per-
  ish
With those by Herod slain, the innocent
  children
Who went with playthings in their little
  hands
Into the darkness of the other world,
As if to bed ? Or wherefore was I born,
If thou in thy foreknowledge didst perceive
All that I am, and all that I must be ?
I know I am not generous, am not gentle,
Like other men ; but I have tried to be,
And I have failed. I thought by following
  Him
I should grow like Him ; but the unclean
  spirit
That from my childhood up hath tortured
  me
Hath been too cunning and too strong for
  me.
Am I to blame for this ? Am I to blame
Because I cannot love, and ne'er have
  known
The love of woman or the love of chil-
  dren ?
It is a curse and a fatality,
A mark, that hath been set upon my fore-
  head,
That none shall slay me, for it were a
  mercy
That I were dead, or never had been born.

Too late ! too late ! I shall not see Him
  more
Among the living. That sweet, patient
  face
Will never more rebuke me, nor those
  lips
Repeat the words : One of you shall betray
  me !
It stung me into madness. How I loved,
Yet hated Him ! But in the other world

I will be there before Him, and will wait
Until he comes, and fall down on my
  knees
And kiss his feet, imploring pardon, par-
  don !

I heard Him say : All sins shall be for-
  given,
Except the sin against the Holy Ghost.
That shall not be forgiven in this world,
Nor in the world to come. Is that my
  sin ?
Have I offended so there is no hope
Here nor hereafter ? That I soon shall
  know.
O God, have mercy ! Christ have mercy
  on me !
  Throws himself headlong from the cliff.

X

THE THREE CROSSES

MANAHEM, THE ESSENIAN.

Three crosses in this noonday night up-
  lifted,
Three human figures that in mortal pain
Gleam white against the supernatural dark-
  ness ;
Two thieves, that writhe in torture, and
  between them
The Suffering Messiah, the Son of Joseph,
Ay, the Messiah Triumphant, Son of
  David !
A crown of thorns on that dishonored
  head !
Those hands that healed the sick now
  pierced with nails,
Those feet that wandered homeless through
  the world
Now crossed and bleeding, and at rest for-
  ever !
And the three faithful Maries, over-
  whelmed
By this great sorrow, kneeling, praying,
  weeping !
O Joseph Caiaphas, thou great High-
  Priest,
How wilt thou answer for this deed of
  blood ?

SCRIBES *and* ELDERS.

Thou that destroyest the Temple, and dost
  build it

In three days, save thyself ; and if thou be
The Son of God, come down now from the
  cross.

CHIEF PRIESTS.

Others he saved, himself he cannot save !
Let Christ the King of Israel descend
That we may see and believe !

SCRIBES *and* ELDERS.

            In God he trusted ;
Let Him deliver him, if He will have him,
And we will then believe.

CHRISTUS.

            Father ! forgive them ;
They know not what they do.

THE IMPENITENT THIEF.

            If thou be Christ,
Oh save thyself and us !

THE PENITENT THIEF.

            Remember me,
Lord, when thou comest into thine own
  kingdom.

CHRISTUS.

This day shalt thou be with me in Paradise.

MANAHEM.

Golgotha ! Golgotha ! Oh the pain and
  darkness !
Oh the uplifted cross, that shall forever
Shine through the darkness, and shall con-
  quer pain
By the triumphant memory of this hour !

SIMON MAGUS.

O Nazarene ! I find thee here at last !
Thou art no more a phantom unto me !
This is the end of one who called himself
The Son of God ! Such is the fate of those
Who preach new doctrines. 'T is not
  what he did,
But what he said, hath brought him unto
  this.
I will speak evil of no dignitaries.
This is my hour of triumph, Nazarene !

THE YOUNG RULER.

This is the end of him who said to me :
Sell that thou hast, and give unto the poor !
This is the treasure in heaven he promised
  me !

CHRISTUS.

Eloi, Eloi, lama sabacthani!

A SOLDIER, *preparing the hyssop.*

He calleth for Elias !

ANOTHER.

Nay, let be !
See if Elias now will come to save him !

CHRISTUS.

I thirst.

A SOLDIER.

Give him the wormwood !

CHRISTUS, *with a loud cry, bowing his head.*

It is finished !

XI

THE TWO MARIES

MARY MAGDALENE.

We have arisen early, yet the sun
O'ertakes us ere we reach the sepulchre,
To wrap the body of our blessed Lord
With our sweet spices.

MARY, MOTHER OF JAMES.

Lo, this is the garden,
And yonder is the sepulchre. But who
Shall roll away the stone for us to enter ?

MARY MAGDALENE.

It hath been rolled away ! The sepulchre
Is open ! Ah, who hath been here before
us,
When we rose early, wishing to be first ?

MARY, MOTHER OF JAMES.

I am affrighted !

MARY MAGDALENE.

Hush ! I will stoop down
And look within. There is a young man
sitting
On the right side, clothed in a long white
garment !
It is an angel !

THE ANGEL.

Fear not ; ye are seeking
Jesus of Nazareth, which was crucified.
Why do ye seek the living among the dead ?
He is no longer here ; he is arisen !

Come see the place where the Lord lay !
Remember
How He spake unto you in Galilee,
Saying : The Son of Man must be delivered
Into the hands of sinful men ; by them
Be crucified, and the third day rise again !
But go your way, and say to his disciples,
He goeth before you into Galilee ;
There shall ye see Him as He said to you.

MARY, MOTHER OF JAMES.

I will go swiftly for them.

MARY MAGDALENE, *alone, weeping.*

They have taken
My Lord away from me, and now I know
not
Where they have laid Him ! Who is
there to tell me ?
This is the gardener. Surely he must know.

CHRISTUS.

Woman, why weepest thou ? Whom seek-
est thou ?

MARY MAGDALENE.

They have taken my Lord away ; I cannot
find Him.
O Sir, if thou have borne him hence, I
pray thee
Tell me where thou hast laid Him.

CHRISTUS.

Mary !

MARY MAGDALENE.

Rabboni !

XII

THE SEA OF GALILEE

NATHANAEL, *in the ship.*

All is now ended.

JOHN.

Nay, He is arisen,
I ran unto the tomb, and stooping down
Looked in, and saw the linen grave-clothes
lying,
Yet dared not enter.

PETER.

I went in, and saw
The napkin that had been about his head,

Not lying with the other linen clothes,
But wrapped together in a separate place.

THOMAS.

And I have seen Him. I have seen the print
Of nails upon his hands, and thrust my hands
Into his side. I know He is arisen ;
But where are now the kingdom and the glory
He promised unto us? We have all dreamed
That we were princes, and we wake to find
We are but fishermen.

PETER.

Who should have been
Fishers of men !

JOHN.

We have come back again
To the old life, the peaceful life, among
The white towns of the Galilean lake.

PETER.

They seem to me like silent sepulchres
In the gray light of morning ! The old life,
Yea, the old life ! for we have toiled all night
And have caught nothing.

JOHN.

Do ye see a man
Standing upon the beach and beckoning ?
'T is like an apparition. He hath kindled
A fire of coals, and seems to wait for us.
He calleth.

CHRISTUS, *from the shore.*

Children, have ye any meat ?

PETER.

Alas ! We have caught nothing.

CHRISTUS.

Cast the net
On the right side of the ship, and ye shall find.

PETER.

How that reminds me of the days gone by,
And one who said : Launch out into the deep,
And cast your nets !

NATHANAEL.

We have but let them down
And they are filled, so that we cannot draw them !

JOHN.

It is the Lord !

PETER, *girding his fisher's coat about him.*

He said : When I am **risen**
I will go before you into Galilee !
He casts himself into the lake.

JOHN.

There is no fear in love ; for perfect love
Casteth out fear. Now then, if ye are men,
Put forth your strength ; we are not far from shore ;
The net is heavy, but breaks not. All is safe.

PETER, *on the shore.*

Dear Lord ! I heard thy voice and could not wait.
Let me behold thy face, and kiss thy feet !
Thou art not dead, thou livest ! Again I see thee.
Pardon, dear Lord ! I am a sinful man ;
I have denied thee thrice. Have mercy on me !

THE OTHERS, *coming to land.*

Dear Lord ! stay with us ! cheer us ! comfort us !
Lo ! we again have found thee ! Leave us not !

CHRISTUS.

Bring hither of the fish that ye have caught,
And come and eat !

JOHN.

Behold ! He breaketh bread
As He was wont. From his own blessed hands
Again we take it.

CHRISTUS.

Simon, son of Jonas,
Lovest thou me, more than these others ?

PETER.

Yea,
More, Lord, than all men ; even more than these.
Thou knowest that I love thee.

CHRISTUS.
Feed my lambs.

THOMAS, *aside.*

How more than we do ? He remaineth ever
Self-confident and boastful as before.
Nothing will cure him.

CHRISTUS.
Simon, son of Jonas,
Lovest thou me ?

PETER.
Yea, dearest Lord, I love thee.
Thou knowest that I love thee.

CHRISTUS.
Feed my sheep.

THOMAS, *aside.*

Again, the selfsame question, and the answer
Repeated with more vehemence. Can the
Master
Doubt if we love Him ?

CHRISTUS.
Simon, son of Jonas,
Lovest thou me ?

PETER, *grieved.*

Dear Lord ! thou knowest all things.
Thou knowest that I love thee.

CHRISTUS.
Feed my sheep.
When thou wast young thou girdedst thyself, and walkedst
Whither thou wouldst ; but when thou
shalt be old,
Thou shalt stretch forth thy hands, and
other men
Shall gird and carry thee whither thou
wouldst not.
Follow thou me !

JOHN, *aside.*
It is a prophecy
Of what death he shall die.

PETER, *pointing to* JOHN.
Tell me, O Lord,
And what shall this man do ?

CHRISTUS.
And if I will
He tarry till I come, what is it to thee ?
Follow thou me !

PETER.
Yea, I will follow thee, dear Lord and
Master !
Will follow thee through fasting and temptation,
Through all thine agony and bloody sweat,
Thy cross and passion, even unto death !

EPILOGUE

SYMBOLUM APOSTOLORUM

PETER.

I BELIEVE in God the Father Almighty ;

JOHN.

Maker of Heaven and Earth ;

JAMES.

And in Jesus Christ his only Son, our
Lord ;

ANDREW.

Who was conceived by the Holy Ghost,
born of the Virgin Mary ;

PHILIP.

Suffered under Pontius Pilate, was crucified,
dead, and buried ;

THOMAS.

And the third day He rose again from the
dead ;

BARTHOLOMEW.

He ascended into Heaven, and sitteth on
the right hand of God, the Father
Almighty ;

MATTHEW.

From thence He shall come to judge the
quick and the dead.

JAMES, THE SON OF ALPHEUS.

I believe in the Holy Ghost ; the holy
Catholic Church ;

SIMON ZELOTES.

The communion of Saints ; the forgiveness
of sins ;

JUDE.

The resurrection of the body ;

MATTHIAS.

And the Life Everlasting.

FIRST INTERLUDE

THE ABBOT JOACHIM

A ROOM IN THE CONVENT OF FLORA
IN CALABRIA.   NIGHT

JOACHIM.

THE wind is rising ; it seizes and shakes
The doors and window-blinds and makes
Mysterious moanings in the halls ;
The convent-chimneys seem almost
The trumpets of some heavenly host,
Setting its watch upon our walls !
Where it listeth, there it bloweth ;
We hear the sound, but no man knoweth
Whence it cometh or whither it goeth,
And thus it is with the Holy Ghost.
O breath of God ! O my delight
In many a vigil of the night,
Like the great voice in Patmos heard
By John, the Evangelist of the Word,
I hear thee behind me saying : Write
In a book the things that thou hast seen,
The things that are, and that have been,
And the things that shall hereafter be !

This convent, on the rocky crest
Of the Calabrian hills, to me
A Patmos is wherein I rest ;
While round about me like a sea
The white mists roll, and overflow
The world that lies unseen below
In darkness and in mystery.
Here in the Spirit, in the vast
Embrace of God's encircling arm,
Am I uplifted from all harm ;
The world seems something far away,
Something belonging to the Past,
A hostelry, a peasant's farm,
That lodged me for a night or day,
In which I care not to remain,
Nor having left, to see again.

Thus, in the hollow of God's hand
I dwelt on sacred Tabor's height,
When as a simple acolyte
I journeyed to the Holy Land,
A pilgrim for my master's sake,
And saw the Galilean Lake,
And walked through many a village street
That once had echoed to his feet.
There first I heard the great command,

The voice behind me saying : Write !
And suddenly my soul became
Illumined by a flash of flame,
That left imprinted on my thought
The image I in vain had sought,
And which forever shall remain ;
As sometimes from these windows high,
Gazing at midnight on the sky
Black with a storm of wind and rain,
I have beheld a sudden glare
Of lightning lay the landscape bare,
With tower and town and hill and plain
Distinct, and burnt into my brain,
Never to be effaced again !

And I have written.   These volumes
     three,
The Apocalypse, the Harmony
Of the Sacred Scriptures, new and old,
And the Psalter with Ten Strings, enfold
Within their pages, all and each,
The Eternal Gospel that I teach.
Well I remember the Kingdom of Heaven
Hath been likened to a little leaven
Hidden in two measures of meal,
Until it leavened the whole mass ;
So likewise will it come to pass
With the doctrines that I here conceal.

Open and manifest to me
The truth appears, and must be told ;
All sacred mysteries are threefold ;
Three Persons in the Trinity,
Three ages of Humanity,
And Holy Scriptures likewise three,
Of Fear, of Wisdom, and of Love ;
For Wisdom that begins in Fear
Endeth in Love ; the atmosphere
In which the soul delights to be,
And finds that perfect liberty
Which cometh only from above.

In the first Age, the early prime
And dawn of all historic time,
The Father reigned ; and face to face
He spake with the primeval race.
Bright Angels, on his errands sent,
Sat with the patriarch in his tent ;
His prophets thundered in the street ;
His lightnings flashed, his hailstorms beat ;
In earthquake and in flood and flame,
In tempest and in cloud He came !
The fear of God is in his Book ;
The pages of the Pentateuch
Are full of the terror of his name.

Then reigned the Son ; his Covenant
Was peace on earth, good-will to man ;
With Him the reign of Law began.
He was the Wisdom and the Word,
And sent his Angels Ministrant,
Unterrified and undeterred,
To rescue souls forlorn and lost,
The troubled, tempted, tempest-tost
To heal, to comfort, and to teach.
The fiery tongues of Pentecost
His symbols were, that they should preach
In every form of human speech,
From continent to continent.
He is the Light Divine, whose rays
Across the thousand years unspent
Shine through the darkness of our days,
And touch with their celestial fires
Our churches and our convent spires.
His Book is the New Testament.

These Ages now are of the Past ;
And the Third Age begins at last.
The coming of the Holy Ghost,
The reign of Grace, the reign of Love
Brightens the mountain-tops above,
And the dark outline of the coast.
Already the whole land is white
With convent walls, as if by night
A snow had fallen on hill and height !
Already from the streets and marts
Of town and traffic, and low cares,
Men climb the consecrated stairs
With weary feet, and bleeding hearts ;
And leave the world, and its delights,
Its passions, struggles, and despairs,
For contemplation and for prayers
In cloister-cells of cœnobites.

Eternal benedictions rest
Upon thy name, Saint Benedict !
Founder of convents in the West,
Who built on Mount Cassino's crest
In the Land of Labor, thine eagle's nest !
May I be found not derelict
In aught of faith or godly fear,
If I have written, in many a page,
The Gospel of the coming age,
The Eternal Gospel men shall hear.
Oh may I live resembling thee,
And die at last as thou hast died ;
So that hereafter men may see,
Within the choir, a form of air,
Standing with arms outstretched in prayer,
As one that hath been crucified !

My work is finished ; I am strong
In faith and hope and charity ;
For I have written the things I see,
The things that have been and shall be,
Conscious of right, nor fearing wrong ;
Because I am in love with Love,
And the sole thing I hate is Hate ;
For Hate is death ; and Love is life,
A peace, a splendor from above ;
And Hate, a never-ending strife,
A smoke, a blackness from the abyss
Where unclean serpents coil and hiss !
Love is the Holy Ghost within ;
Hate the unpardonable sin !
Who preaches otherwise than this,
Betrays his Master with a kiss !

PART TWO

THE GOLDEN LEGEND

PROLOGUE

THE SPIRE OF STRASBURG CATHE-DRAL

Night and storm. LUCIFER, *with the Powers of the Air, trying to tear down the Cross.*

LUCIFER.

HASTEN ! hasten !
O ye spirits !
From its station drag the ponderous
Cross of iron, that to mock us
Is uplifted high in air !

VOICES.

Oh, we cannot !
For around it
All the Saints and Guardian Angels
Throng in legions to protect it ;
They defeat us everywhere !

THE BELLS.

Laudo Deum verum !
Plebem voco !
Congrego clerum !

LUCIFER.

Lower ! lower !
Hover downward !
Seize the loud, vociferous bells, and
Clashing, clanging, to the pavement
Hurl them from their windy tower !

VOICES.

All thy thunders
Here are harmless !
For these bells have been anointed,
And baptized with holy water !
They defy our utmost power.

THE BELLS.

Defunctos ploro !
Pestem fugo !
Festa decoro !

LUCIFER.

Shake the casements !
Break the painted
Panes, that flame with gold and crimson ;
Scatter them like leaves of Autumn,
Swept away before the blast !

VOICES.

Oh, we cannot !
The Archangel
Michael flames from every window,
With the sword of fire that drove us
Headlong, out of heaven, aghast !

THE BELLS.

Funera plango !
Fulgura frango !
Sabbata pango !

LUCIFER.

Aim your lightnings
At the oaken,
Massive, iron-studded portals !
Sack the house of God, and scatter
Wide the ashes of the dead !

VOICES.

Oh, we cannot !
The Apostles
And the Martyrs, wrapped in mantles,
Stand as warders at the entrance,
Stand as sentinels o'erhead !

THE BELLS.

Excito lentos !
Dissipo ventos !
Paco cruentos !

LUCIFER.

Baffled ! baffled !
Inefficient,
Craven spirits ! leave this labor
Unto Time, the great Destroyer !
Come away, ere night is gone !

VOICES.

Onward ! onward !
With the night-wind,
Over field and farm and forest,
Lonely homestead, darksome hamlet,
Blighting all we breathe upon !
They sweep away. Organ and Gregorian Chant.

CHOIR.

Nocte surgentes
Vigilemus omnes !

I

THE CASTLE OF VAUTSBERG ON THE RHINE

A chamber in a tower. PRINCE HENRY, *sitting
alone, ill and restless. Midnight.*

PRINCE HENRY.

I cannot sleep ! my fervid brain
Calls up the vanished Past again,
And throws its misty splendors deep
Into the pallid realms of sleep !
A breath from that far-distant shore
Comes freshening ever more and more,
And wafts o'er intervening seas
Sweet odors from the Hesperides !
A wind, that through the corridor
Just stirs the curtain, and no more,
And, touching the æolian strings,
Faints with the burden that it brings !
Come back ! ye friendships long departed !
That like o'erflowing streamlets started,
And now are dwindled, one by one,
To stony channels in the sun !
Come back ! ye friends, whose lives are
        ended,
Come back, with all that light attended,
Which seemed to darken and decay
When ye arose and went away !

They come, the shapes of joy and woe,
The airy crowds of long ago,
The dreams and fancies known of yore,
That have been, and shall be no more.
They change the cloisters of the night
Into a garden of delight ;
They make the dark and dreary hours
Open and blossom into flowers !
I would not sleep ! I love to be
Again in their fair company ;
But ere my lips can bid them stay,
They pass and vanish quite away !

Alas'! our memories may retrace
Each circumstance of time and place,
Season and scene come back again,
And outward things unchanged remain ;
The rest we cannot reinstate ;
Ourselves we cannot re-create,
Nor set our souls to the same key
Of the remembered harmony !

Rest ! rest ! Oh, give me rest and peace !
The thought of life that ne'er shall cease
Has something in it like despair,
A weight I am too weak to bear !
Sweeter to this afflicted breast
The thought of never-ending rest !
Sweeter the undisturbed and deep
Tranquillity of endless sleep !
A flash of lightning, out of which LUCIFER *appears, in the garb of a travelling Physician.*

LUCIFER.

All hail, Prince Henry !

PRINCE HENRY, *starting.*

Who is it speaks ?
Who and what are you ?

LUCIFER.

One who seeks
A moment's audience with the Prince.

PRINCE HENRY.

When came you in ?

LUCIFER.

A moment since.
I found your study door unlocked,
And thought you answered when I knocked.

PRINCE HENRY.

I did not hear you.

LUCIFER.

You heard the thunder ;
It was loud enough to waken the dead.
And it is not a matter of special wonder
That, when God is walking overhead,
You should not hear my feeble tread.

PRINCE HENRY.

What may your wish or purpose be ?

LUCIFER.

Nothing or everything, as it pleases
Your Highness. You behold in me

Only a travelling Physician ;
One of the few who have a mission
To cure incurable diseases,
Or those that are called so.

PRINCE HENRY.

Can you bring
The dead to life ?

LUCIFER.

Yes ; very nearly.
And, what is a wiser and better thing,
Can keep the living from ever needing
Such an unnatural, strange proceeding,
By showing conclusively and clearly
That death is a stupid blunder merely,
And not a necessity of our lives.
My being here is accidental ;
The storm, that against your casement
        drives,
In the little village below waylaid me.
And there I heard with a secret delight,
Of your maladies physical and mental,
Which neither astonished nor dismayed
        me.
And I hastened hither, though late in the
        night,
To proffer my aid !

PRINCE HENRY, *ironically.*

For this you came !
Ah, how can I ever hope to requite
This honor from one so erudite ?

LUCIFER.

The honor is mine, or will be when
I have cured your disease.

PRINCE HENRY.

But not till then.

LUCIFER.

What is your illness ?

PRINCE HENRY.

It has no name.
A smouldering, dull, perpetual flame,
As in a kiln, burns in my veins,
Sending up vapors to the head ;
My heart has become a dull lagoon,
Which a kind of leprosy drinks and
        drains ;
I am accounted as one who is dead,
And, indeed, I think that I shall be soon.

LUCIFER.

And has Gordonius the Divine,
In his famous Lily of Medicine, —
I see the book lies open before you, —
No remedy potent enough to restore you ?

PRINCE HENRY.

None whatever !

LUCIFER.

The dead are dead,
And their oracles dumb, when questionèd
Of the new diseases that human life
Evolves in its progress, rank and rife.
Consult the dead upon things that were,
But the living only on things that are.
Have you done this, by the appliance
And aid of doctors ?

PRINCE HENRY.

Ay, whole schools
Of doctors, with their learned rules ;
But the case is quite beyond their science.
Even the doctors of Salern
Send me back word they can discern
No cure for a malady like this,
Save one which in its nature is
Impossible and cannot be !

LUCIFER.

That sounds oracular !

PRINCE HENRY.

Unendurable !

LUCIFER.

What is their remedy ?

PRINCE HENRY.

You shall see ;
Writ in this scroll is the mystery.

LUCIFER, reading.

" Not to be cured, yet not incurable !
The only remedy that remains
Is the blood that flows from a maiden's
veins,
Who of her own free will shall die,
And give her life as the price of yours ! "

That is the strangest of all cures,
And one, I think, you will never try ;
The prescription you may well put by,
As something impossible to find

Before the world itself shall end !
And yet who knows ? One cannot say
That into some maiden's brain that kind
Of madness will not find its way.
Meanwhile permit me to recommend,
As the matter admits of no delay,
My wonderful Catholicon,
Of very subtile and magical powers !

PRINCE HENRY.

Purge with your nostrums and drugs infer-
nal
The spouts and gargoyles of these towers,
Not me ! My faith is utterly gone
In every power but the Power Supernal !
Pray tell me, of what school are you ?

LUCIFER.

Both of the Old and of the New !
The school of Hermes Trismegistus,
Who uttered his oracles sublime
Before the Olympiads, in the dew
Of the early dusk and dawn of time,
The reign of dateless old Hephæstus !
As northward, from its Nubian springs,
The Nile, forever new and old,
Among the living and the dead,
Its mighty, mystic stream has rolled ;
So, starting from its fountain-head
Under the lotus-leaves of Isis,
From the dead demigods of eld,
Through long, unbroken lines of kings
Its course the sacred art has held,
Unchecked, unchanged by man's devices.
This art the Arabian Geber taught,
And in alembics, finely wrought,
Distilling herbs and flowers, discovered
The secret that so long had hovered
Upon the misty verge of Truth,
The Elixir of Perpetual Youth,
Called Alcohol, in the Arab speech !
Like him, this wondrous lore I teach !

PRINCE HENRY.

What ! an adept ?

LUCIFER.

Nor less, nor more !

PRINCE HENRY.

I am a reader of your books,
A lover of that mystic lore !
With such a piercing glance it looks
Into great Nature's open eye,
And sees within it trembling lie

The portrait of the Deity !
And yet, alas ! with all my pains,
The secret and the mystery
Have baffled and eluded me,
Unseen the grand result remains !

LUCIFER, *showing a flask.*

Behold it here ! this little flask
Contains the wonderful quintessence,
The perfect flower and efflorescence,
Of all the knowledge man can ask !
Hold it up thus against the light !

PRINCE HENRY.

How limpid, pure, and crystalline,
How quick, and tremulous, and bright
The little wavelets dance and shine,
As were it the Water of Life in sooth !

LUCIFER.

It is ! It assuages every pain,
Cures all disease, and gives again
To age the swift delights of youth.
Inhale its fragrance.

PRINCE HENRY.

It is sweet.
A thousand different odors meet
And mingle in its rare perfume,
Such as the winds of summer waft
At open windows through a room !

LUCIFER.

Will you not taste it ?

PRINCE HENRY.

Will one draught
Suffice ?

LUCIFER.

If not, you can drink more.

PRINCE HENRY.

Into this crystal goblet pour
So much as safely I may drink.

LUCIFER, *pouring.*

Let not the quantity alarm you ;
You may drink all ; it will not harm you.

PRINCE HENRY.

I am as one who on the brink
Of a dark river stands and sees
The waters flow, the landscape dim
Around him waver, wheel, and swim,
And, ere he plunges, stops to think

Into what whirlpools he may sink ;
One moment pauses, and no more,
Then madly plunges from the shore !
Headlong into the mysteries
Of life and death I boldly leap,
Nor fear the fateful current's sweep,
Nor what in ambush lurks below !
For death is better than disease !

An ANGEL *with an œolian harp hovers in the
air.*

ANGEL.

Woe ! woe ! eternal woe !
Not only the whispered prayer
Of love,
But the imprecations of hate,
Reverberate
For ever and ever through the air
Above !
This fearful curse
Shakes the great universe !

LUCIFER, *disappearing.*

Drink ! drink !
And thy soul shall sink
Down into the dark abyss,
Into the infinite abyss,
From which no plummet nor rope
Ever drew up the silver sand of hope !

PRINCE HENRY, *drinking.*

It is like a draught of fire !
Through every vein
I feel again
The fever of youth, the soft desire ;
A rapture that is almost pain
Throbs in my heart and fills my brain !
O joy ! O joy ! I feel
The band of steel
That so long and heavily has pressed
Upon my breast
Uplifted, and the malediction
Of my affliction
Is taken from me, and my weary breast
At length finds rest.

THE ANGEL.

It is but the rest of the fire, from which
the air has been taken !
It is but the rest of the sand, when the
hour-glass is not shaken !
It is but the rest of the tide between the
ebb and the flow !
It is but the rest of the wind between the
flaws that blow !

With fiendish laughter,
Hereafter,
This false physician
Will mock thee in thy perdition.

PRINCE HENRY.

Speak ! speak !
Who says that I am ill ?
I am not ill !   I am not weak !
The trance, the swoon, the dream, is o'er !
I feel the chill of death no more !
At length,
I stand renewed in all my strength !
Beneath me I can feel
The great earth stagger and reel,
As if the feet of a descending God
Upon its surface trod,
And like a pebble it rolled beneath his
    heel !
This, O brave physician ! this
Is thy great Palingenesis !
            Drinks again.

THE ANGEL.

Touch the goblet no more !
It will make thy heart sore
To its very core !
Its perfume is the breath
Of the Angel of Death,
And the light that within it lies
Is the flash of his evil eyes.
Beware ! Oh, beware !
For sickness, sorrow, and care
All are there !

PRINCE HENRY, *sinking back.*

O thou voice within my breast !
Why entreat me, why upbraid me,
When the steadfast tongues of truth
And the flattering hopes of youth
Have all deceived me and betrayed me ?
Give me, give me rest, oh rest !
Golden visions wave and hover,
Golden vapors, waters streaming,
Landscapes moving, changing, gleaming !
I am like a happy lover,
Who illumines life with dreaming !
Brave physician ! Rare physician !
Well hast thou fulfilled thy mission !
            His head falls on his book.

THE ANGEL, *receding.*

Alas ! alas !
Like a vapor the golden vision
Shall fade and pass,

And thou wilt find in thy heart again
Only the blight of pain,
And bitter, bitter, bitter contrition !

COURT-YARD OF THE CASTLE.

HUBERT *standing by the gateway.*

HUBERT.

How sad the grand old castle looks !
O'erhead, the unmolested rooks
Upon the turret's windy top
Sit, talking of the farmer's crop ;
Here in the court-yard springs the grass,
So few are now the feet that pass ;
The stately peacocks, bolder grown,
Come hopping down the steps of stone,
As if the castle were their own ;
And I, the poor old seneschal,
Haunt, like a ghost, the banquet-hall.
Alas ! the merry guests no more
Crowd through the hospitable door ;
No eyes with youth and passion shine,
No cheeks glow redder than the wine ;
No song, no laugh, no jovial din
Of drinking wassail to the pin ;
But all is silent, sad, and drear,
And now the only sounds I hear
Are the hoarse rooks upon the walls,
And horses stamping in their stalls !
            A horn sounds.
What ho ! that merry, sudden blast
Reminds me of the days long past !
And, as of old resounding, grate
The heavy hinges of the gate,
And, clattering loud, with iron clank,
Down goes the sounding bridge of plank,
As if it were in haste to greet
The pressure of a traveller's feet !

Enter WALTER *the Minnesinger.*

WALTER.

How now, my friend ! This looks quite
    lonely !
No banner flying from the walls,
No pages and no seneschals,
No warders, and one porter only !
Is it you, Hubert ?

HUBERT.

            Ah ! Master Walter !

WALTER.

Alas ! how forms and faces alter !

I did not know you.　You look older !
Your hair has grown much grayer and
　　　thinner,
And you stoop a little in the shoulder !

HUBERT.

Alack !　I am a poor old sinner,
And, like these towers, begin to moulder ;
And you have been absent many a year !

WALTER.

How is the Prince ?

HUBERT.

　　　　　　He is not here ;
He has been ill : and now has fled.

WALTER.

Speak it out frankly : say he 's dead !
Is it not so ?

HUBERT.

　　　　　No ; if you please,
A strange, mysterious disease
Fell on him with a sudden blight.
Whole hours together he would stand
Upon the terrace, in a dream,
Resting his head upon his hand,
Best pleased when he was most alone,
Like Saint John Nepomuck in stone,
Looking down into a stream.
In the Round Tower, night after night,
He sat and bleared his eyes with books ;
Until one morning we found him there
Stretched on the floor, as if in a swoon
He had fallen from his chair.
We hardly recognized his sweet looks !

WALTER.

Poor Prince !

HUBERT.

　　　　I think he might have mended ;
And he did mend ; but very soon
The priests came flocking in, like rooks,
With all their crosiers and their crooks,
And so at last the matter ended.

WALTER.

How did it end ?

HUBERT.

　　　　Why, in Saint Rochus
They made him stand, and wait his doom ;
And, as if he were condemned to the tomb,

Began to mutter their hocus-pocus.
First, the Mass for the Dead they chanted,
Then three times laid upon his head
A shovelful of churchyard clay,
Saying to him, as he stood undaunted,
" This is a sign that thou art dead,
So in thy heart be penitent ! "
And forth from the chapel door he went
Into disgrace and banishment,
Clothed in a cloak of hodden gray,
And bearing a wallet, and a bell,
Whose sound should be a perpetual knell
To keep all travellers away.

WALTER.

Oh, horrible fate !　Outcast, rejected,
As one with pestilence infected !

HUBERT.

Then was the family tomb unsealed,
And broken helmet, sword, and shield,
Buried together, in common wreck,
As is the custom, when the last
Of any princely house has passed,
And thrice, as with a trumpet-blast,
A herald shouted down the stair
The words of warning and despair, —
" O Hoheneck !　O Hoheneck ! "

WALTER.

Still in my soul that cry goes on, —
Forever gone ! forever gone !
Ah, what a cruel sense of loss,
Like a black shadow, would fall across
The hearts of all, if he should die !
His gracious presence upon earth
Was as a fire upon a hearth ;
As pleasant songs, at morning sung,
The words that dropped from his sweet
　　　tongue
Strengthened our hearts ; or heard at night,
Made all our slumbers soft and light.
Where is he ?

HUBERT.

　　　　In the Odenwald.
Some of his tenants, unappalled
By fear of death, or priestly word, —
A holy family, that make
Each meal a Supper of the Lord, —
Have him beneath their watch and ward,
For love of him, and Jesus' sake !
Pray you come in.　For why should I
With out-door hospitality
My prince's friend thus entertain ?

WALTER.

I would a moment here remain.
But you, good Hubert, go before,
Fill me a goblet of May-drink,
As aromatic as the May
From which it steals the breath away,
And which he loved so well of yore ;
It is of him that I would think.
You shall attend me, when I call,
In the ancestral banquet-hall.
Unseen companions, guests of air,
You cannot wait on, will be there ;
They taste not food, they drink not wine,
But their soft eyes look into mine,
And their lips speak to me, and all
The vast and shadowy banquet-hall
Is full of looks and words divine !

Leaning over the parapet.

The day is done ; and slowly from the
  scene
The stooping sun up-gathers his spent
  shafts,
And puts them back into his golden
  quiver !
Below me in the valley, deep and green
As goblets are, from which in thirsty
  draughts
We drink its wine, the swift and mantling
  river
Flows on triumphant through these lovely
  regions,
Etched with the shadows of its sombre
  margent,
And soft, reflected clouds of gold and ar-
  gent !
Yes, there it flows, forever, broad and
  still
As when the vanguard of the Roman
  legions
First saw it from the top of yonder
  hill !
How beautiful it is ! Fresh fields of
  wheat,
Vineyard, and town, and tower with flutter-
  ing flag,
The consecrated chapel on the crag,
And the white hamlet gathered round its
  base,
Like Mary sitting at her Saviour's feet,
And looking up at his beloved face !
O friend ! O best of friends ! Thy absence
  more
Than the impending night darkens the land-
  scape o'er !

II

A FARM IN THE ODENWALD

A garden; morning; PRINCE HENRY *seated,
  with a book.* ELSIE *at a distance gathering
  flowers.*

PRINCE HENRY, *reading.*

One morning, all alone,
Out of his convent of gray stone,
Into the forest older, darker, grayer,
His lips moving as if in prayer,
His head sunken upon his breast
As in a dream of rest,
Walked the Monk Felix. All about
The broad, sweet sunshine lay without,
Filling the summer air ;
And within the woodlands as he trod,
The dusk was like the Truce of God
With worldly woe and care ;
Under him lay the golden moss ;
And above him the boughs of hoary trees
Waved, and made the sign of the cross,
And whispered their Benedicites ;
And from the ground
Rose an odor sweet and fragrant
Of the wild-flowers and the vagrant
Vines that wandered,
Seeking the sunshine, round and round.

These he heeded not, but pondered
On the volume in his hand,
Wherein amazed he read :
" A thousand years in thy sight
Are but as yesterday when it is past,
And as a watch in the night ! "
And with his eyes downcast
In humility he said :
" I believe, O Lord,
What is written in thy Word,
But alas ! I do not understand ! "

And lo ! he heard
The sudden singing of a bird,
A snow-white bird, that from a cloud
Dropped down,
And among the branches brown
Sat singing,
So sweet, and clear, and loud,
It seemed a thousand harp-strings ringing.
And the Monk Felix closed his book,
And long, long,
With rapturous look,
He listened to the song,

And hardly breathed or stirred,
Until he saw, as in a vision,
The land Elysian,
And in the heavenly city heard
Angelic feet
Fall on the golden flagging of the street.
And he would fain
Have caught the wondrous bird,
But strove in vain ;
For it flew away, away,
Far over hill and dell,
And instead of its sweet singing
He heard the convent bell
Suddenly in the silence ringing
For the service of noonday.
And he retraced
His pathway homeward sadly and in haste.

In the convent there was a change !
He looked for each well-known face,
But the faces were new and strange ;
New figures sat in the oaken stalls,
New voices chanted in the choir ;
Yet the place was the same place,
The same dusky walls
Of cold, gray stone,
The same cloisters and belfry and spire.

A stranger and alone
Among that brotherhood
The Monk Felix stood.
"Forty years," said a Friar,
" Have I been Prior
Of this convent in the wood,
But for that space
Never have I beheld thy face ! "

The heart of the Monk Felix fell :
And he answered, with submissive tone,
" This morning, after the hour of Prime,
I left my cell,
And wandered forth alone,
Listening all the time
To the melodious singing
Of a beautiful white bird,
Until I heard
The bells of the convent ringing
Noon from their noisy towers.
It was as if I dreamed ;
For what to me had seemed
Moments only, had been hours ! "

"Years ! " said a voice close by.
It was an aged monk who spoke,
From a bench of oak

Fastened against the wall ; —
He was the oldest monk of all.
For a whole century
Had he been there,
Serving God in prayer,
The meekest and humblest of his creatures.
He remembered well the features
Of Felix, and he said,
Speaking distinct and slow :
"One hundred years ago,
When I was a novice in this place,
There was here a monk, full of God's
grace,
Who bore the name
Of Felix, and this man must be the same."

And straightway
They brought forth to the light of day
A volume old and brown,
A huge tome, bound
In brass and wild- boar's hide,
Wherein were written down
The names of all who had died
In the convent, since it was edified.
And there they found,
Just as the old monk said,
That on a certain day and date,
One hundred years before,
Had gone forth from the convent gate
The Monk Felix, and never more
Had entered that sacred door.
He had been counted among the dead !
And they knew, at last,
That, such had been the power
Of that celestial and immortal song,
A hundred years had passed,
And had not seemed so long
As a single hour !

ELSIE *comes in with flowers.*

ELSIE.
Here are flowers for you,
But they are not all for you.
Some of them are for the Virgin
And for Saint Cecilia.

PRINCE HENRY.
As thou standest there,
Thou seemest to me like the angel
That brought the immortal roses
To Saint Cecilia's bridal chamber.

ELSIE.
But these will fade.

PRINCE HENRY.

Themselves will fade,
But not their memory,
And memory has the power
To re-create them from the dust.
They remind me, too,
Of martyred Dorothea,
Who from celestial gardens sent
Flowers as her witnesses
To him who scoffed and doubted.

ELSIE.

Do you know the story
Of Christ and the Sultan's daughter?
That is the prettiest legend of them all.

PRINCE HENRY.

Then tell it to me.
But first come hither.
Lay the flowers down beside me,
And put both thy hands in mine.
Now tell me the story.

ELSIE.

Early in the morning
The Sultan's daughter
Walked in her father's garden,
Gathering the bright flowers,
All full of dew.

PRINCE HENRY.

Just as thou hast been doing
This morning, dearest Elsie.

ELSIE.

And as she gathered them
She wondered more and more
Who was the Master of the Flowers,
And made them grow
Out of the cold, dark earth.
"In my heart," she said,
"I love him; and for him
Would leave my father's palace,
To labor in his garden."

PRINCE HENRY.

Dear, innocent child!
How sweetly thou recallest
The long-forgotten legend,
That in my early childhood
My mother told me!
Upon my brain
It reappears once more,
As a birth-mark on the forehead

When a hand suddenly
Is laid upon it, and removed!

ELSIE.

And at midnight,
As she lay upon her bed,
She heard a voice
Call to her from the garden,
And, looking forth from her window,
She saw a beautiful youth
Standing among the flowers.
It was the Lord Jesus;
And she went down to Him,
And opened the door for Him;
And He said to her, "O maiden!
Thou hast thought of me with love,
And for thy sake
Out of my Father's kingdom
Have I come hither:
I am the Master of the Flowers.
My garden is in Paradise,
And if thou wilt go with me,
Thy bridal garland
Shall be of bright red flowers."
And then He took from his finger
A golden ring,
And asked the Sultan's daughter
If she would be his bride.
And when she answered Him with love,
His wounds began to bleed,
And she said to him,
"O Love! how red thy heart is,
And thy hands are full of roses."
"For thy sake," answered He,
"For thy sake is my heart so red,
For thee I bring these roses;
I gathered them at the cross
Whereon I died for thee!
Come, for my Father calls.
Thou art my elected bride!"
And the Sultan's daughter
Followed Him to his Father's garden.

PRINCE HENRY.

Wouldst thou have done so, Elsie.

ELSIE.

Yes, very gladly.

PRINCE HENRY.

Then the Celestial Bridegroom
Will come for thee also.
Upon thy forehead He will place
Not his crown of thorns,
But a crown of roses.

In thy bridal chamber,
Like Saint Cecilia,
Thou shalt hear sweet music,
And breathe the fragrance
Of flowers immortal !
Go now and place these flowers
Before her picture.

A ROOM IN THE FARM-HOUSE.

Twilight. URSULA *spinning.* GOTTLIEB
asleep in his chair.

URSULA.

Darker and darker !   Hardly a glimmer
Of light comes in at the window-pane ;
Or is it my eyes are growing dimmer ?
I cannot disentangle this skein,
Nor wind it rightly upon the reel.
Elsie !

GOTTLIEB, *starting.*

The stopping of thy wheel
Has awakened me out of a pleasant dream.
I thought I was sitting beside a stream,
And heard the grinding of a mill,
When suddenly the wheels stood still,
And a voice cried " Elsie " in my ear !
It startled me, it seemed so near.

URSULA.

I was calling her : I want a light.
I cannot see to spin my flax.
Bring the lamp, Elsie.   Dost thou hear ?

ELSIE, *within.*

In a moment !

GOTTLIEB.

Where are Bertha and Max ?

URSULA.

They are sitting with Elsie at the door.
She is telling them stories of the wood,
And the Wolf, and little Red Ridinghood.

GOTTLIEB.

And where is the Prince ?

URSULA

In his room overhead ;
I heard him walking across the floor,
As he always does, with a heavy tread.

ELSIE *comes in with a lamp.* MAX *and* BERTHA
*follow her ; and they all sing the Evening Song
on the lighting of the lamps.*

EVENING SONG

O gladsome light
Of the Father Immortal,
And of the celestial
Sacred and blessed
Jesus, our Saviour !

Now to the sunset
Again hast thou brought us ;
And, seeing the evening
Twilight, we bless thee,
Praise thee, adore thee !

Father omnipotent !
Son, the Life-giver !
Spirit, the Comforter !
Worthy at all times
Of worship and wonder !

PRINCE HENRY, *at the door.*

Amen !

URSULA.

Who was it said Amen ?

ELSIE

It was the Prince : he stood at the door,
And listened a moment, as we chanted
The evening song.   He is gone again.
I have often seen him there before.

URSULA.

Poor Prince !

GOTTLIEB.

I thought the house was haunted !
Poor Prince, alas ! and yet as mild
And patient as the gentlest child !

MAX.

I love him because he is so good,
And makes me such fine bows and ar-
rows,
To shoot at the robins and the sparrows.
And the red squirrels in the wood !

BERTHA.

I love him, too !

GOTTLIEB.

Ah, yes ! we all
Love him, from the bottom of our hearts ;
He gave us the farm, the house, and the
grange,
He gave us the horses and the carts,
And the great oxen in the stall,

The vineyard, and the forest range !
We have nothing to give him but our
love !

BERTHA.

Did he give us the beautiful stork above
On the chimney-top, with its large, round
nest ?

GOTTLIEB.

No, not the stork ; by God in heaven,
As a blessing, the dear white stork was
given,
But the Prince has given us all the rest.
God bless him, and make him well again.

ELSIE.

Would I could do something for his sake,
Something to cure his sorrow and pain !

GOTTLIEB.

That no one can ; neither thou nor I,
Nor any one else.

ELSIE.
And must he die ?

URSULA.

Yes ; if the dear God does not take
Pity upon him, in his distress,
And work a miracle !

GOTTLIEB.
Or unless
Some maiden, of her own accord,
Offers her life for that of her lord,
And is willing to die in his stead.

ELSIE.
I will !

URSULA.

Prithee, thou foolish child, be still !
Thou shouldst not say what thou dost not
mean !

ELSIE.

I mean it truly !

MAX.

O father ! this morning,
Down by the mill, in the ravine,
Hans killed a wolf, the very same
That in the night to the sheepfold came,
And ate up my lamb, that was left out-
side.

GOTTLIEB.

I am glad he is dead. It will be a warning
To the wolves in the forest, far and wide.

MAX.

And I am going to have his hide !

BERTHA.

I wonder if this is the wolf that ate
Little Red Ridinghood !

URSULA.
Oh, no !
That wolf was killed a long while ago.
Come, children, it is growing late.

MAX.

Ah, how I wish I were a man,
As stout as Hans is, and as strong !
I would do nothing else, the whole day
long,
But just kill wolves.

GOTTLIEB.
Then go to bed,
And grow as fast as a little boy can.
Bertha is half asleep already.
See how she nods her heavy head,
And her sleepy feet are so unsteady
She will hardly be able to creep upstairs.

URSULA.

Good night, my children. Here 's the
light.
And do not forget to say your prayers
Before you sleep.

GOTTLIEB.
Good night !

MAX *and* BERTHA.
Good night !

They go out with ELSIE.

URSULA, *spinning.*

She is a strange and wayward child,
That Elsie of ours. She looks so old,
And thoughts and fancies weird and wild
Seem of late to have taken hold
Of her heart, that was once so docile and
mild !

GOTTLIEB.

She is like all girls.

URSULA.
Ah no, forsooth !
Unlike all I have ever seen.

For she has visions and strange dreams,
And in all her words and ways, she seems
Much older than she is in truth.
Who would think her but fifteen ?
And there has been of late such a change !
My heart is heavy with fear and doubt
That she may not live till the year is out.
She is so strange, — so strange, — so
    strange !

GOTTLIEB.

I am not troubled with any such fear ;
She will live and thrive for many a year.

ELSIE'S CHAMBER.

Night. ELSIE *praying.*

ELSIE.

My Redeemer and my Lord,
I beseech thee, I entreat thee,
Guide me in each act and word,
That hereafter I may meet thee,
Watching, waiting, hoping, yearning,
With my lamp well trimmed and burning !

Interceding
With these bleeding
Wounds upon thy hands and side,
For all who have lived and errèd
Thou hast suffered, thou hast died,
Scourged, and mocked, and crucified,
And in the grave hast thou been buried !

If my feeble prayer can reach thee,
O my Saviour, I beseech thee,
Even as thou hast died for me,
More sincerely
Let me follow where thou leadest,
Let me, bleeding as thou bleedest,
Die, if dying I may give
Life to one who asks to live,
And more nearly,
Dying thus, resemble thee !

THE CHAMBER OF GOTTLIEB AND URSULA.

Midnight. ELSIE *standing by their bedside,*
weeping.

GOTTLIEB.

The wind is roaring ; the rushing rain
Is loud upon roof and window-pane,
As if the Wild Huntsman of Rodenstein,
Boding evil to me and mine,
Were abroad to-night with his ghostly
    train !

In the brief lulls of the tempest wild,
The dogs howl in the yard ; and hark !
Some one is sobbing in the dark,
Here in the chamber !

ELSIE.

It is I.

URSULA.

Elsie ! what ails thee, my poor child ?

ELSIE.

I am disturbed and much distressed,
In thinking our dear Prince must die ;
I cannot close mine eyes, nor rest.

GOTTLIEB.

What wouldst thou ? In the Power Divine
His healing lies, not in our own ;
It is in the hand of God alone.

ELSIE.

Nay, He has put it into mine,
And into my heart !

GOTTLIEB.

    Thy words are wild !

URSULA.

What dost thou mean ? my child ! m
    child !

ELSIE.

That for our dear Prince Henry's sake
I will myself the offering make,
And give my life to purchase his.

URSULA.

Am I still dreaming, or awake ?
Thou speakest carelessly of death,
And yet thou knowest not what it is.

ELSIE.

'T is the cessation of our breath.
Silent and motionless we lie ;
And no one knoweth more than this.
I saw our little Gertrude die ;
She left off breathing, and no more
I smoothed the pillow beneath her head.
She was more beautiful than before.
Like violets faded were her eyes ;
By this we knew that she was dead.
Through the open window looked the skies
Into the chamber where she lay,
And the wind was like the sound of wings,
As if angels came to bear her away.

Ah ! when I saw and felt these things,
I found it difficult to stay ;
I longed to die, as she had died,
And go forth with her, side by side.
The Saints are dead, the Martyrs dead,
And Mary, and our Lord ; and I
Would follow in humility
The way by them illuminèd !

URSULA.

My child ! my child ! thou must not die !

ELSIE.

Why should I live ?   Do I not know
The life of woman is full of woe ?
Toiling on and on and on,
With breaking heart, and tearful eyes,
And silent lips, and in the soul
The secret longings that arise,
Which this world never satisfies !
Some more, some less, but of the whole
Not one quite happy, no, not one !

URSULA.

It is the malediction of Eve !

ELSIE.

In place of it, let me receive
The benediction of Mary, then.

GOTTLIEB.

Ah, woe is me !   Ah, woe is me !
Most wretched am I among men !

URSULA.

Alas ! that I should live to see
Thy death, beloved, and to stand
Above thy grave !   Ah, woe the day !

ELSIE.

Thou wilt not see it.   I shall lie
Beneath the flowers of another land,
For at Salerno, far away
Over the mountains, over the sea,
It is appointed me to die !
And it will seem no more to thee
Than if at the village on market-day
I should a little longer stay
Than I am wont.

URSULA.

Even as thou sayest !
And how my heart beats, when thou stayest !
I cannot rest until my sight

Is satisfied with seeing thee.
What then, if thou wert dead ?

GOTTLIEB.

Ah me !
Of our old eyes thou art the light !
The joy of our old hearts art thou !
And wilt thou die ?

URSULA.

Not now ! not now !

ELSIE.

Christ died for me, and shall not I
Be willing for my Prince to die ?
You both are silent ; you cannot speak.
This said I at our Saviour's feast
After confession, to the priest,
And even he made no reply.
Does he not warn us all to seek
The happier, better land on high,
Where flowers immortal never wither ;
And could he forbid me to go thither ?

GOTTLIEB.

In God's own time, my heart's delight !
When He shall call thee, not before !

ELSIE.

I heard Him call.   When Christ ascended
Triumphantly, from star to star,
He left the gates of heaven ajar.
I had a vision in the night,
And saw Him standing at the door
Of his Father's mansion, vast and splen-
did,
And beckoning to me from afar.
I cannot stay !

GOTTLIEB.

She speaks almost
As if it were the Holy Ghost
Spake through her lips, and in her stead !
What if this were of God ?

URSULA.

Ah, then
Gainsay it dare we not.

GOTTLIEB.

Amen !
Elsie ! the words that thou hast said
Are strange and new for us to hear,
And fill our hearts with doubt and fear.
Whether it be a dark temptation
Of the Evil One, or God's inspiration,

We in our blindness cannot say.
We must think upon it, and pray ;
For evil and good it both resembles.
If it be of God, his will be done !
May He guard us from the Evil One !
How hot thy hand is ! how it trembles !
Go to thy bed, and try to sleep.

URSULA.

Kiss me.   Good night ; and do not weep !
ELSIE *goes out.*

Ah, what an awful thing is this !
I almost shuddered at her kiss,
As if a ghost had touched my cheek,
I am so childish and so weak !
As soon as I see the earliest gray
Of morning glimmei in the east,
I will go over to the priest,
And hear what the good man has to say !

A VILLAGE CHURCH.

A woman kneeling at the confessional.

THE PARISH PRIEST, *from within.*

Go, sin no more !   Thy penance o'er,
A new and better life begin !
God maketh thee forever free
From the dominion of thy sin !
Go, sin no more !   He will restore
The peace that filled thy heart before,
And pardon thine iniquity !

*The woman goes out.   The Priest comes forth,
    and walks slowly up and down the church.*

O blessed Lord ! how much I need
Thy light to guide me on my way !
So many hands, that, without heed,
Still touch thy wounds, and make them
    bleed !
So many feet, that, day by day,
Still wander from thy fold astray !
Unless thou fill me with thy light,
I cannot lead thy flock aright ;
Nor, without thy support, can bear
The burden of so great a care,
But am myself a castaway !
A pause.
The day is drawing to its close ;
And what good deeds, since first it rose,
Have I presented, Lord, to thee,
As offerings of my ministry ?
What wrong repressed, what right main-
    tained,
What struggle passed, what victory gained,
What good attempted and attained ?

Feeble, at best, is my endeavor !
I see, but cannot reach, the height
That lies forever in the light,
And yet forever and forever,
When seeming just within my grasp,
I feel my feeble hands unclasp,
And sink discouraged into night !
For thine own purpose, thou hast sent
The strife and the discouragement !
A pause.
Why stayest thou, Prince of Hoheneck ?
Why keep me pacing to and fro
Amid these aisles of sacred gloom,
Counting my footsteps as I go,
And marking with each step a tomb ?
Why should the world for thee make room,
And wait thy leisure and thy beck ?
Thou comest in the hope to hear
Some word of comfort and of cheer.
What can I say ?   I cannot give
The counsel to do this and live ;
But rather, firmly to deny
The tempter, though his power be strong,
And, inaccessible to wrong,
Still like a martyr live and die !
A pause.
The evening air grows dusk and brown ;
I must go forth into the town,
To visit beds of pain and death,
Of restless limbs, and quivering breath,
And sorrowing hearts, and patient eyes
That see, through tears, the sun go down,
But never more shall see it rise.
The poor in body and estate,
The sick and the disconsolate,
Must not on man's convenience wait.
Goes out.

Enter LUCIFER, *as a Priest.*

LUCIFER, *with a genuflexion, mocking.*

This is the Black Pater-noster.
God was my foster,
He fostered me
Under the book of the Palm-tree !
St. Michael was my dame.
He was born at Bethlehem,
He was made of flesh and blood.
God send me my right food,
My right food, and shelter too,
That I may to yon kirk go,
To read upon yon sweet book
Which the mighty God of heaven shook.
Open, open, hell's gates !
Shut, shut, heaven's gates !

All the devils in the air
The stronger be, that hear the Black
    Prayer !
        Looking round the church.
What a darksome and dismal place !
I wonder that any man has the face
To call such a hole the House of the Lord,
And the Gate of Heaven, — yet such is the
    word.
Ceiling, and walls, and windows old,
Covered with cobwebs, blackened with
    mould ;
Dust on the pulpit, dust on the stairs,
Dust on the benches, and stalls, and chairs !
The pulpit, from which such ponderous ser-
    mons
Have fallen down on the brains of the Ger-
    mans,
With about as much real edification
As if a great Bible, bound in lead,
Had fallen, and struck them on the head ;
And I ought to remember that sensation !
Here stands the holy-water stoup !
Holy-water it may be to many,
But to me, the veriest Liquor Gehennæ !
It smells like a filthy fast-day soup !
Near it stands the box for the poor,
With its iron padlock, safe and sure.
I and the priest of the parish know
Whither all these charities go ;
Therefore, to keep up the institution,
I will add my little contribution !
        He puts in money.
Underneath this mouldering tomb,
With statue of stone, and scutcheon of
    brass,
Slumbers a great lord of the village.
All his life was riot and pillage,
But at length, to escape the threatened
    doom
Of the everlasting penal fire,
He died in the dress of a mendicant friar,
And bartered his wealth for a daily mass.
But all that afterwards came to pass,
And whether he finds it dull or pleasant,
Is kept a secret for the present,
At his own particular desire.

And here, in a corner of the wall,
Shadowy, silent, apart from all,
With its awful portal open wide,
And its latticed windows on either side,
And its step well worn by the bended
    knees
Of one or two pious centuries,

Stands the village confessional !
Within it, as an honored guest,
I will sit down awhile and rest !
        Seats himself in the confessional.
Here sits the priest ; and faint and low,
Like the sighing of an evening breeze,
Comes through these painted lattices
The ceaseless sound of human woe ;
Here, while her bosom aches and throbs
With deep and agonizing sobs,
That half are passion, half contrition,
The luckless daughter of perdition
Slowly confesses her secret shame !
The time, the place, the lover's name !
Here the grim murderer, with a groan,
From his bruised conscience rolls the stone,
Thinking that thus he can atone
For ravages of sword and flame !

Indeed, I marvel, and marvel greatly,
How a priest can sit here so sedately,
Reading, the whole year out and in,
Naught but the catalogue of sin,
And still keep any faith whatever
In human virtue ! Never ! never !

I cannot repeat a thousandth part
Of the horrors and crimes and sins and
    woes
That arise, when with palpitating throes
The graveyard in the human heart
Gives up its dead, at the voice of the
    priest,
As if he were an archangel, at least.
It makes a peculiar atmosphere,
This odor of earthly passions and crimes,
Such as I like to breathe, at times,
And such as often brings me here
In the hottest and most pestilential sea-
    son.
To-day, I come for another reason ;
To foster and ripen an evil thought
In a heart that is almost to madness
    wrought,
And to make a murderer out of a prince,
A sleight of hand I learned long since !
He comes. In the twilight he will not see
The difference between his priest and me !
In the same net was the mother caught !

PRINCE HENRY, *entering and kneeling at the
        confessional.*
Remorseful, penitent, and lowly,
I come to crave, O Father holy,
Thy benediction on my head.

LUCIFER.

The benediction shall be said
After confession, not before !
'T is a God-speed to the parting guest,
Who stands already at the door,
Sandalled with holiness, and dressed
In garments pure from earthly stain.
Meanwhile, hast thou searched well thy
    breast ?
Does the same madness fill thy brain ?
Or have thy passion and unrest
Vanished forever from thy mind ?

PRINCE HENRY.

By the same madness still made blind,
By the same passion still possessed,
I come again to the house of prayer,
A man afflicted and distressed !
As in a cloudy atmosphere,
Through unseen sluices of the air,
A sudden and impetuous wind
Strikes the great forest white with fear,
And every branch, and bough, and spray
Points all its quivering leaves one way,
And meadows of grass, and fields of grain,
And the clouds above, and the slanting
    rain,
And smoke from chimneys of the town,
Yield themselves to it, and bow down,
So does this dreadful purpose press
Onward, with irresistible stress,
And all my thoughts and faculties,
Struck level by the strength of this,
From their true inclination turn,
And all stream forward to Salern !

LUCIFER.

Alas ! we are but eddies of dust,
Uplifted by the blast, and whirled
Along the highway of the world
A moment only, then to fall
Back to a common level all,
At the subsiding of the gust !

PRINCE HENRY.

O holy Father ! pardon in me
The oscillation of a mind
Unsteadfast, and that cannot find
Its centre of rest and harmony !
For evermore before mine eyes
This ghastly phantom flits and flies,
And as a madman through a crowd,
With frantic gestures and wild cries,
It hurries onward, and aloud
Repeats its awful prophecies !

Weakness is wretchedness ! To be strong
Is to be happy ! I am weak,
And cannot find the good I seek,
Because I feel and fear the wrong !

LUCIFER.

Be not alarmed ! The Church is kind,
And in her mercy and her meekness
She meets half-way her children's weakness,
Writes their transgressions in the dust !
Though in the Decalogue we find
The mandate written, "Thou shalt not
    kill ! "
Yet there are cases when we must.
In war, for instance, or from scathe
To guard and keep the one true Faith
We must look at the Decalogue in the light
Of an ancient statute, that was meant
For a mild and general application,
To be understood with the reservation
That in certain instances the Right
Must yield to the Expedient !
Thou art a Prince. If thou shouldst die,
What hearts and hopes would prostrate lie !
What noble deeds, what fair renown,
Into the grave with thee go down !
What acts of valor and courtesy
Remain undone, and die with thee !
Thou art the last of all thy race !
With thee a noble name expires,
And vanishes from the earth's face
The glorious memory of thy sires !
She is a peasant. In her veins
Flows common and plebeian blood ;
It is such as daily and hourly stains
The dust and the turf of battle plains,
By vassals shed, in a crimson flood,
Without reserve, and without reward,
At the slightest summons of their lord !
But thine is precious ; the fore-appointed
Blood of kings, of God's anointed !
Moreover, what has the world in store
For one like her, but tears and toil ?
Daughter of sorrow, serf of the soil,
A peasant's child and a peasant's wife,
And her soul within her sick and sore
With the roughness and barrenness of life
I marvel not at the heart's recoil
From a fate like this, in one so tender,
Nor at its eagerness to surrender
All the wretchedness, want, and woe
That await it in this world below,
Nor the unutterable splendor
Of the world of rest beyond the skies.
So the Church sanctions the sacrifice :

Therefore inhale this healing balm,
And breathe this fresh life into thine ;
Accept the comfort and the calm
She offers, as a gift divine ;
Let her fall down and anoint thy feet
With the ointment costly and most sweet
Of her young blood, and thou shalt live.

PRINCE HENRY.

And will the righteous Heaven forgive ?
No action, whether foul or fair,
Is ever done, but it leaves somewhere
A record, written by fingers ghostly,
As a blessing or a curse, and mostly
In the greater weakness or greater strength
Of the acts which follow it, till at length
The wrongs of ages are redressed,
And the justice of God made manifest !

LUCIFER.

In ancient records it is stated
That, whenever an evil deed is done,
Another devil is created
To scourge and torment the offending one !
But evil is only good perverted,
And Lucifer, the bearer of Light,
But an angel fallen and deserted,
Thrust from his Father's house with a curse
Into the black and endless night.

PRINCE HENRY.

If justice rules the universe,
From the good actions of good men
Angels of light should be begotten,
And thus the balance restored again.

LUCIFER.

Yes ; if the world were not so rotten,
And so given over to the Devil !

PRINCE HENRY.

But this deed, is it good or evil ?
Have I thine absolution free
To do it, and without restriction ?

LUCIFER.

Ay ; and from whatsoever sin
Lieth around it and within,
From all crimes in which it may involve
    thee,
I now release thee and absolve thee !

PRINCE HENRY.

Give me thy holy benediction.

LUCIFER, *stretching forth his hand and muttering.*

Maledictione perpetua
Maledicat vos
Pater eternus !

THE ANGEL, *with the œolian harp.*

Take heed ! take heed !
Noble art thou in thy birth,
By the good and the great of earth
Hast thou been taught !
Be noble in every thought
And in every deed !
Let not the illusion of thy senses
Betray thee to deadly offences.
Be strong ! be good ! be pure !
The right only shall endure,
All things else are but false pretences.
I entreat thee, I implore,
Listen no more
To the suggestions of an evil spirit,
That even now is there,
Making the foul seem fair,
And selfishness itself a virtue and a merit,

A ROOM IN THE FARM-HOUSE.

GOTTLIEB.

It is decided ! For many days,
And nights as many, we have had
A nameless terror in our breast,
Making us timid, and afraid
Of God, and his mysterious ways !
We have been sorrowful and sad ;
Much have we suffered, much have prayed
That he would lead us as is best,
And show us what his will required.
It is decided ; and we give
Our child, O Prince, that you may live !

URSULA.

It is of God.   He has inspired
This purpose in her ; and through pain,
Out of a world of sin and woe,
He takes her to Himself again.
The mother's heart resists no longer ;
With the Angel of the Lord in vain
It wrestled, for he was the stronger.

GOTTLIEB.

As Abraham offered long ago
His son unto the Lord, and even
The Everlasting Father in heaven

Gave his, as a lamb unto the slaughter,
So do I offer up my daughter !

URSULA *hides her face.*

ELSIE.

My life is little,
Only a cup of water,
But pure and limpid.
Take it, O my Prince !
Let it refresh you,
Let it restore you.
It is given willingly,
It is given freely ;
May God bless the gift !

PRINCE HENRY.

And the giver !

GOTTLIEB.

Amen !

PRINCE HENRY.

I accept it !

GOTTLIEB.

Where are the children ?

URSULA.

They are already asleep.

GOTTLIEB.

What if they were dead ?

IN THE GARDEN.

ELSIE.

I have one thing to ask of you.

PRINCE HENRY.

What is it ?
It is already granted.

ELSIE.

Promise me,
When we are gone from here, and on our
        way
Are journeying to Salerno, you will not,
By word or deed, endeavor to dissuade me
And turn me from my purpose ; but re-
        member
That as a pilgrim to the Holy City
Walks unmolested, and with thoughts of
        pardon
Occupied wholly, so would I approach

The gates of Heaven, in this great jubi-
        lee,
With my petition, putting off from me
All thoughts of earth, as shoes from off
        my feet.
Promise me this.

PRINCE HENRY.

Thy words fall from thy lips
Like roses from the lips of Angelo : and
        angels
Might stoop to pick them up !

ELSIE.

Will you not promise ?

PRINCE HENRY.

If ever we depart upon this journey,
So long to one or both of us, I promise.

ELSIE.

Shall we not go, then ? Have you lifted
        me
Into the air, only to hurl me back
Wounded upon the ground ? and offered
        me
The waters of eternal life, to bid me
Drink the polluted puddles of this world ?

PRINCE HENRY.

O Elsie ! what a lesson thou dost teach
        me !
The life which is, and that which is to
        come,
Suspended hang in such nice equipoise
A breath disturbs the balance ; and that
        scale
In which we throw our hearts preponder-
        ates,
And the other, like an empty one, flies
        up,
And is accounted vanity and air !
To me the thought of death is terrible,
Having such hold on life. To thee it is
        not
So much even as the lifting of a latch ;
Only a step into the open air
Out of a tent already luminous
With light that shines through its trans-
        parent walls !
O pure in heart ! from thy sweet dust
        shall grow
Lilies, upon whose petals will be written
" Ave Maria " in characters of gold !

III

A STREET IN STRASBURG

Night. PRINCE HENRY *wandering alone,
wrapped in a cloak.*

PRINCE HENRY.

Still is the night. The sound of feet
Has died away from the empty street,
And like an artisan, bending down
His head on his anvil, the dark town
Sleeps, with a slumber deep and sweet.
Sleepless and restless, I alone,
In the dusk and damp of these walls of
stone,
Wander and weep in my remorse !

CRIER OF THE DEAD, *ringing a bell.*

Wake ! wake !
All ye that sleep !
Pray for the Dead !
Pray for the Dead !

PRINCE HENRY.

Hark ! with what accents loud and hoarse
This warder on the walls of death
Sends forth the challenge of his breath !
I see the dead that sleep in the grave !
They rise up and their garments wave,
Dimly and spectral, as they rise,
With the light of another world in their
eyes !

CRIER OF THE DEAD.

Wake ! wake !
All ye that sleep !
Pray for the Dead !
Pray for the Dead !

PRINCE HENRY.

Why for the dead, who are at rest ?
Pray for the living, in whose breast
The struggle between right and wrong
Is raging terrible and strong,
As when good angels war with devils !
This is the Master of the Revels,
Who, at Life's flowing feast, proposes
The health of absent friends, and pledges,
Not in bright goblets crowned with roses,
And tinkling as we touch their edges,
But with his dismal, tinkling bell,
That mocks and mimics their funeral
knell !

CRIER OF THE DEAD.

Wake ! wake !
All ye that sleep !
Pray for the Dead !
Pray for the Dead !

PRINCE HENRY.

Wake not, beloved ! be thy sleep
Silent as night is, and as deep !
There walks a sentinel at thy gate
Whose heart is heavy and desolate,
And the heavings of whose bosom number
The respirations of thy slumber,
As if some strange, mysterious fate
Had linked two hearts in one, and mine
Went madly wheeling about thine,
Only with wider and wilder sweep !

CRIER OF THE DEAD, *at a distance.*

Wake ! wake !
All ye that sleep !
Pray for the Dead !
Pray for the Dead !

PRINCE HENRY.

Lo ! with what depth of blackness thrown
Against the clouds, far up the skies
The walls of the cathedral rise,
Like a mysterious grove of stone,
With fitful lights and shadows blending,
As from behind, the moon, ascending,
Lights its dim aisles and paths unknown !
The wind is rising ; but the boughs
Rise not and fall not with the wind,
That through their foliage sobs and
soughs ;
Only the cloudy rack behind,
Drifting onward, wild and ragged,
Gives to each spire and buttress jagged
A seeming motion undefined.
Below on the square, an armèd knight,
Still as a statue and as white,
Sits on his steed, and the moonbeams
quiver
Upon the points of his armor bright
As on the ripples of a river.
He lifts the visor from his cheek,
And beckons, and makes as he would
speak.

WALTER *the Minnesinger.*

Friend ! can you tell me where alight
Thuringia's horsemen for the night ?
For I have lingered in the rear,
And wander vainly up and down.

PRINCE HENRY.

I am a stranger in the town,
As thou art ; but the voice I hear
Is not a stranger to mine ear.
Thou art Walter of the Vogelweid !

WALTER.

Thou hast guessed rightly ; and thy name
Is Henry of Hoheneck !

PRINCE HENRY.

Ay, the same.

WALTER, *embracing him.*

Come closer, closer to my side !
What brings thee hither ?   What potent
      charm
Has drawn thee from thy German farm
Into the old Alsatian city ?

PRINCE HENRY.

A tale of wonder and of pity !
A wretched man, almost by stealth
Dragging my body to Salern,
In the vain hope and search for health,
And destined never to return.
Already thou hast heard the rest.
But what brings thee, thus armed and dight
In the equipments of a knight ?

WALTER.

Dost thou not see upon my breast
The cross of the Crusaders shine ?
My pathway leads to Palestine.

PRINCE HENRY.

Ah, would that way were also mine !
O noble poet ! thou whose heart
Is like a nest of singing-birds
Rocked on the topmost bough of life,
Wilt thou, too, from our sky depart,
And in the clangor of the strife
Mingle the music of thy words ?

WALTER.

My hopes are high, my heart is proud,
And like a trumpet long and loud,
Thither my thoughts all clang and ring !
My life is in my hand, and lo !
I grasp and bend it as a bow,
And shoot forth from its trembling string
An arrow, that shall be, perchance,
Like the arrow of the Israelite king
Shot from the window toward the east,
That of the Lord's deliverance !

PRINCE HENRY.

My life, alas ! is what thou seest !
O enviable fate ! to be
Strong, beautiful, and armed like thee
With lyre and sword, with song and steel ;
A hand to smite, a heart to feel !
Thy heart, thy hand, thy lyre, thy sword,
Thou givest all unto thy Lord ;
While I, so mean and abject grown,
Am thinking of myself alone.

WALTER.

Be patient : Time will reinstate
Thy health and fortunes.

PRINCE HENRY.

'Tis too late !
I cannot strive against my fate !

WALTER.

Come with me ; for my steed is weary ;
Our journey has been long and dreary,
And, dreaming of his stall, he dints
With his impatient hoofs the flints.

PRINCE HENRY, *aside.*

I am ashamed, in my disgrace,
To look into that noble face !
To-morrow, Walter, let it be.

WALTER.

To-morrow, at the dawn of day,
I shall again be on my way.
Come with me to the hostelry,
For I have many things to say.
Our journey into Italy
Perchance together we may make ;
Wilt thou not do it for my sake ?

PRINCE HENRY.

A sick man's pace would but impede
Thine eager and impatient speed.
Besides, my pathway leads me round
To Hirschau, in the forest's bound,
Where I assemble man and steed,
And all things for my journey's need.
      They go out.

LUCIFER, *flying over the city.*

Sleep, sleep, O city ! till the light
Wake you to sin and crime again,
Whilst on your dreams, like dismal rain,
I scatter downward through the night
My maledictions dark and deep.
I have more martyrs in your walls

Than God has ; and they cannot sleep ;
They are my bondsmen and my thralls ;
Their wretched lives are full of pain,
Wild agonies of nerve and brain ;
And every heart-beat, every breath,
Is a convulsion worse than death !
Sleep, sleep, O city ! though within
The circuit of your walls there be
No habitation free from sin,
And all its nameless misery ;
The aching heart, the aching head,
Grief for the living and the dead,
And foul corruption of the time,
Disease, distress, and want, and woe,
And crimes, and passions that may grow
Until they ripen into crime !

SQUARE IN FRONT OF THE CATHEDRAL.

Easter Sunday. FRIAR CUTHBERT *preaching to the crowd from a pulpit in the open air.* PRINCE HENRY *and* ELSIE *crossing the square.*

PRINCE HENRY.

This is the day, when from the dead
Our Lord arose ; and everywhere,
Out of their darkness and despair,
Triumphant over fears and foes,
The hearts of his disciples rose,
When to the women, standing near,
The Angel in shining vesture said,
"The Lord is risen ; he is not here ! "
And, mindful that the day is come,
On all the hearths in Christendom
The fires are quenched, to be again
Rekindled from the sun, that high
Is dancing in the cloudless sky.
The churches are all decked with flowers,
The salutations among men
Are but the Angel's words divine,
"Christ is arisen ! " and the bells
Catch the glad murmur, as it swells,
And chant together in their towers.
All hearts are glad ; and free from care
The faces of the people shine.
See what a crowd is in the square,
Gayly and gallantly arrayed !

ELSIE.

Let us go back ; I am afraid !

PRINCE HENRY.

Nay, let us mount the church-steps here,
Under the doorway's sacred shadow ;
We can see all things, and be freer
From the crowd that madly heaves and
presses !

ELSIE.

What a gay pageant ! what bright dresses !
It looks like a flower-besprinkled meadow.
What is that yonder on the square ?

PRINCE HENRY.

A pulpit in the open air,
And a Friar, who is preaching to the crowd
In a voice so deep and clear and loud,
That, if we listen, and give heed,
His lowest words will reach the ear.

FRIAR CUTHBERT, *gesticulating and cracking a postilion's whip.*

What ho ! good people ! do you not hear ?
Dashing along at the top of his speed,
Booted and spurred, on his jaded steed,
A courier comes with words of cheer.
Courier ! what is the news, I pray ?
"Christ is arisen ! "   Whence come you ?
    "From court."
Then I do not believe it ; you say it in
    sport.
        Cracks his whip again.
Ah, here comes another, riding this way ;
We soon shall know what he has to say.
Courier ! what are the tidings to-day ?
"Christ is arisen ! "   Whence come you ?
    "From town."
Then I do not believe it ; away with you,
    clown.
        Cracks his whip more violently.
And here comes a third, who is spurring
    amain ;
What news do you bring, with your loose-
    hanging rein,
Your spurs wet with blood, and your bridle
    with foam ?
"Christ is arisen ! "   Whence come you ?
    "From Rome."
Ah, now I believe.   He is risen, indeed.
Ride on with the news, at the top of your
    speed !
        Great applause among the crowd.
To come back to my text !   When the
    news was first spread
That Christ was arisen indeed from the
    dead,
Very great was the joy of the angels in
    heaven ;
And as great the dispute as to who should
    carry
The tidings thereof to the Virgin Mary,
Pierced to the heart with sorrows seven.
Old Father Adam was first to propose,

As being the author of all our woes ;
But he was refused, for fear, said they,
He would stop to eat apples on the way !
Abel came next, but petitioned in vain,
Because he might meet with his brother
    Cain !
Noah, too, was refused, lest his weakness
    for wine
Should delay him at every tavern-sign ;
And John the Baptist could not get a vote,
On account of his old-fashioned camel's-
    hair coat ;
And the Penitent Thief, who died on the
    cross,
Was reminded that all his bones were
    broken !
Till at last, when each in turn had spoken,
The company being still at loss,
The Angel, who rolled away the stone,
Was sent to the sepulchre, all alone.
And filled with glory that gloomy prison,
And said to the Virgin, " The Lord is
    arisen ! "
    The Cathedral bells ring.
But hark ! the bells are beginning to
    chime ;
And I feel that I am growing hoarse.
I will put an end to my discourse,
And leave the rest for some other time.
For the bells themselves are the best of
    preachers ;
Their brazen lips are learned teachers,
From their pulpits of stone, in the upper air,
Sounding aloft, without crack or flaw,
Shriller than trumpets under the Law,
Now a sermon, and now a prayer.
The clangorous hammer is the tongue,
This way, that way, beaten and swung,
That from mouth of brass, as from Mouth
    of Gold,
May be taught the Testaments, New and
    Old.
And above it the great cross-beam of wood
Representeth the Holy Rood,
Upon which, like the bell, our hopes are
    hung.
And the wheel wherewith it is swayed and
    rung
Is the mind of man, that round and round
Sways, and maketh the tongue to sound !
And the rope, with its twisted cordage three,
Denoteth the Scriptural Trinity
Of Morals, and Symbols, and History ;
And the upward and downward motion show
That we touch upon matters high and low ;

And the constant change and transmutation
Of action and of contemplation,
Downward, the Scripture brought from on
    high,
Upward, exalted again to the sky ;
Downward, the literal interpretation,
Upward, the Vision and Mystery !

And now, my hearers, to make an end,
I have only one word more to say ;
In the church, in honor of Easter day
Will be presented a Miracle Play ;
And I hope you will all have the grace to
    attend.
Christ bring us at last to his felicity !
Pax vobiscum ! et Benedicite !

IN THE CATHEDRAL.

CHANT.

Kyrie Eleison !
Christe Eleison !

ELSIE.

I am at home here in my Father's house ?
These paintings of the Saints upon the walls
Have all familiar and benignant faces.

PRINCE HENRY.

The portraits of the family of God !
Thine own hereafter shall be placed among
    them.

ELSIE.

How very grand it is and wonderful !
Never have I beheld a church so splendid !
Such columns, and such arches, and such
    windows,
So many tombs and statues in the chapels,
And under them so many confessionals.
They must be for the rich. I should not
    like
To tell my sins in such a church as this.
Who built it ?

PRINCE HENRY.

            A great master of his craft,
Erwin von Steinbach ; but not he alone,
For many generations labored with him.
Children that came to see these Saints in
    stone,
As day by day out of the blocks they rose,
Grew old and died, and still the work went
    on,

And on, and on, and is not yet completed.
The generation that succeeds our own
Perhaps may finish it.   The architect
Built his great heart into these sculptured
    stones,
And with him toiled his children, and their
    lives
Were builded, with his own, into the walls,
As offerings unto God.   You see that statue
Fixing its joyous, but deep-wrinkled eyes
Upon the Pillars of the Angels yonder.
That is the image of the master, carved
By the fair hand of his own child, Sabina.

ELSIE.

How beautiful is the column that he looks
    at !

PRINCE HENRY.

That, too, she sculptured.   At the base of
    it
Stand the Evangelists ; above their heads
Four Angels blowing upon marble trumpets,
And over them the blessed Christ, sur-
    rounded
By his attendant ministers, upholding
The instruments of his passion.

ELSIE.

                            O my Lord !
Would I could leave behind me upon earth
Some monument to thy glory, such as this !

PRINCE HENRY.

A greater monument than this thou leavest
In thine own life, all purity and love !
See, too, the Rose, above the western portal
Resplendent with a thousand gorgeous
    colors,
The perfect flower of Gothic loveliness !

ELSIE.

And, in the gallery, the long line of statues,
Christ with his twelve Apostles watching
    us !

A BISHOP *in armor, booted and spurred, passes
    with his train.*

PRINCE HENRY.

But come away ; we have not time to look.
The crowd already fills the church, and
    yonder
Upon a stage, a herald with a trumpet,
Clad like the Angel Gabriel, proclaims
The Mystery that will now be represented.

THE NATIVITY

A MIRACLE-PLAY

INTROITUS

PRÆCO.

Come, good people, all and each,
Come and listen to our speech !
In your presence here I stand,
With a trumpet in my hand,
To announce the Easter Play,
Which we represent to-day !
First of all we shall rehearse,
In our action and our verse,
The Nativity of our Lord,
As written in the old record
Of the Protevangelion,
So that he who reads may run !
            Blows his trumpet.

I. HEAVEN.

MERCY, *at the feet of God.*

Have pity, Lord ! be not afraid
To save mankind, whom thou hast made
Nor let the souls that were betrayed
    Perish eternally !

JUSTICE.

It cannot be, it must not be !
When in the garden placed by thee,
The fruit of the forbidden tree
    He ate, and he must die !

MERCY.

Have pity, Lord ! let penitence
Atone for disobedience,
Nor let the fruit of man's offence
    Be endless misery !

JUSTICE.

What penitence proportionate
Can e'er be felt for sin so great ?
Of the forbidden fruit he ate,
    And damnèd must he be !

GOD.

He shall be saved, if that within
The bounds of earth one free from sin
Be found, who for his kith and kin
    Will suffer martyrdom.

THE FOUR VIRTUES.

Lord ! we have searched the world around,
From centre to the utmost bound,
But no such mortal can be found ;
    Despairing, back we come.

WISDOM.

No mortal, but a God made man,
Can ever carry out this plan,
Achieving what none other can,
    Salvation unto all !

GOD.

Go, then, O my beloved Son !
It can by thee alone be done ;
By thee the victory shall be won
    O'er Satan and the Fall !

Here the ANGEL GABRIEL *shall leave Paradise
and fly towards the earth; the jaws of Hell
open below, and the Devils walk about, making
a great noise.*

II.   MARY AT THE WELL.

MARY.

Along the garden walk, and thence
Through the wicket in the garden fence,
    I steal with quiet pace,
My pitcher at the well to fill,
That lies so deep and cool and still
    In this sequestered place.

These sycamores keep guard around ;
I see no face, I hear no sound,
    Save bubblings of the spring,
And my companions, who, within,
The threads of gold and scarlet spin,
    And at their labor sing.

THE ANGEL GABRIEL.

Hail, Virgin Mary, full of grace !

Here MARY *looketh around her, trembling, and
then saith :*

MARY.

Who is it speaketh in this place,
    With such a gentle voice ?

GABRIEL.

The Lord of heaven is with thee now !
Blessed among all women thou,
    Who art his holy choice !

MARY, *setting down the pitcher.*

What can this mean ?   No one is near,
And yet, such sacred words I hear,
    I almost fear to stay.

Here the ANGEL, *appearing to her, shall say :*

GABRIEL.

Fear not, O Mary ! but believe !
For thou, a Virgin, shalt conceive
    A child this very day.

Fear not, O Mary ! from the sky
The majesty of the Most High
    Shall overshadow thee !

MARY.

Behold the handmaid of the Lord !
According to thy holy word,
    So be it unto me !

*Here the Devils shall again make a great noise,
under the stage.*

III.   THE ANGELS OF THE SEVEN PLANETS,
    BEARING THE STAR OF BETHLEHEM.

THE ANGELS.

The Angels of the Planets Seven,
Across the shining fields of heaven
    The natal star we bring !
Dropping our sevenfold virtues down
As priceless jewels in the crown
    Of Christ, our new-born King.

RAPHAEL.

I am the Angel of the Sun,
Whose flaming wheels began to run
    When God's almighty breath
Said to the darkness and the Night,
Let there be light ! and there was light !
    I bring the gift of Faith.

ONAFIEL.

I am the Angel of the Moon,
Darkened to be rekindled soon
    Beneath the azure cope !
Nearest to earth, it is my ray
That best illumes the midnight way ;
    I bring the gift of Hope !

ANAEL.

The Angel of the Star of Love,
The Evening Star, that shines above
    The place where lovers be,

Above all happy hearths and homes,
On roofs of thatch, or golden domes,
　　I give him Charity !

ZOBIACHEL.

The Planet Jupiter is mine !
The mightiest star of all that shine,
　　Except the sun alone !
He is the High Priest of the Dove,
And sends, from his great throne above,
　　Justice, that shall atone !

MICHAEL.

The Planet Mercury, whose place
Is nearest to the sun in space,
　　Is my allotted sphere !
And with celestial ardor swift
I bear upon my hands the gift
　　Of heavenly Prudence here !

URIEL.

I am the Minister of Mars,
The strongest star among the stars !
　　My songs of power prelude
The march and battle of man's life,
And for the suffering and the strife,
　　I give him Fortitude !

ORIFEL.

The Angel of the uttermost
Of all the shining, heavenly host,
　　From the far-off expanse
Of the Saturnian, endless space
I bring the last, the crowning grace,
　　The gift of Temperance !
*A sudden light shines from the windows of the
　　stable in the village below.*

IV.　THE WISE MEN OF THE EAST.

The stable of the Inn.　The VIRGIN *and* CHILD.
Three Gypsy Kings, GASPAR, MELCHIOR, *and*
BELSHAZZAR, *shall come in.*

GASPAR.

Hail to thee, Jesus of Nazareth !
Though in a manger thou draw breath,
Thou art greater than Life and Death,
　　Greater than Joy or Woe !
This cross upon the line of life
Portendeth struggle, toil, and strife,
And through a region with peril rife
　　In darkness shalt thou go !

MELCHIOR.

Hail to thee, King of Jerusalem !
Though humbly born in Bethlehem,
A sceptre and a diadem
　　Await thy brow and hand !
The sceptre is a simple reed,
The crown will make thy temples bleed,
And in thine hour of greatest need,
　　Abashed thy subjects stand !

BELSHAZZAR.

Hail to thee, Christ of Christendom !
O'er all the earth thy kingdom come !
From distant Trebizond to Rome
　　Thy name shall men adore !
Peace and good-will among all men,
The Virgin has returned again,
Returned the old Saturnian reign
　　And Golden Age once more.

THE CHILD CHRIST.

Jesus, the Son of God, am I,
Born here to suffer and to die
According to the prophecy,
　　That other men may live !

THE VIRGIN.

And now these clothes, that wrapped Him,
　　take
And keep them precious, for his sake ;
Our benediction thus we make,
　　Naught else have we to give.
*She gives them swaddling-clothes, and they de-
　　part.*

V.　THE FLIGHT INTO EGYPT.

Here JOSEPH *shall come in, leading an ass, on
　　which are seated* MARY *and the* CHILD.

MARY.

Here will we rest us, under these
O'erhanging branches of the trees,
Where robins chant their Litanies
　　And canticles of joy.

JOSEPH.

My saddle-girths have given way
With trudging through the heat to-day ;
To you I think it is but play
　　To ride and hold the boy.

MARY.

Hark ! how the robins shout and sing,
As if to hail their infant King !

I will alight at yonder spring
To wash his little coat.

JOSEPH.

And I will hobble well the ass,
Lest, being loose upon the grass,
He should escape ; for, by the mass,
He's nimble as a goat.

Here MARY *shall alight and go to the spring.*

MARY.

O Joseph ! I am much afraid,
For men are sleeping in the shade ;
I fear that we shall be waylaid,
And robbed and beaten sore !

Here a band of robbers shall be seen sleeping, two of whom shall rise and come forward.

DUMACHUS.

Cock's soul ! deliver up your gold !

JOSEPH.

I pray you, Sirs, let go your hold !
You see that I am weak and old,
Of wealth I have no store.

DUMACHUS.

Give up your money !

TITUS.

Prithee cease.
Let these people go in peace.

DUMACHUS.

First let them pay for their release,
And then go on their way.

TITUS.

These forty groats I give in fee,
If thou wilt only silent be.

MARY.

May God be merciful to thee
Upon the Judgment Day !

JESUS.

When thirty years shall have gone by,
I at Jerusalem shall die,
By Jewish hands exalted high
On the accursed tree,
Then on my right and my left side,
These thieves shall both be crucified,

And Titus thenceforth shall abide
In paradise with me.

Here a great rumor of trumpets and horses, like the noise of a king with his army, and the robbers shall take flight.

VI.   THE SLAUGHTER OF THE INNOCENTS.

KING HEROD.

Potz-tausend !   Himmel-sacrament !
Filled am I with great wonderment
At this unwelcome news !
Am I not Herod ?   Who shall dare
My crown to take, my sceptre bear,
As king among the Jews ?

Here he shall stride up and down and flourish his sword.

What ho !   I fain would drink a can
Of the strong wine of Canaan !
The wine of Helbon bring
I purchased at the Fair of Tyre,
As red as blood, as hot as fire,
And fit for any king !

He quaffs great goblets of wine.

Now at the window will I stand,
While in the street the armèd band
The little children slay ;
The babe just born in Bethlehem
Will surely slaughtered be with them,
Nor live another day !

Here a voice of lamentation shall be heard in the street.

RACHEL.

O wicked king !   O cruel speed !
To do this most unrighteous deed !
My children all are slain !

HEROD.

Ho seneschal ! another cup !
With wine of Sorek fill it up !
I would a bumper drain !

RAHAB.

May maledictions fall and blast
Thyself and lineage, to the last
Of all thy kith and kin !

HEROD.

Another goblet ! quick ! and stir
Pomegranate juice and drops of myrrh
And calamus therein !

SOLDIERS, *in the street.*

Give up thy child into our hands !
It is King Herod who commands
   That he should thus be slain !

THE NURSE MEDUSA.

O monstrous men ! What have ye done !
It is King Herod's only son
   That ye have cleft in twain !

HEROD.

Ah, luckless day ! What words of fear
Are these that smite upon my ear
   With such a doleful sound !
What torments rack my heart and head !
Would I were dead ! would I were dead,
   And buried in the ground !

He falls down and writhes as though eaten by
  worms. Hell opens, and SATAN *and* ASTA-
  ROTH *come forth, and drag him down.*

VII. JESUS AT PLAY WITH HIS SCHOOL-
           MATES.

JESUS.

The shower is over. Let us play,
And make some sparrows out of clay,
   Down by the river's side.

JUDAS.

See, how the stream has overflowed
Its banks, and o'er the meadow road
   Is spreading far and wide !

They draw water out of the river by channels, and
  form little pools. JESUS *makes twelve sparrows*
  of clay, and the other boys do the same.

JESUS.

Look ! look how prettily I make
These little sparrows by the lake
   Bend down their necks and drink !
Now will I make them sing and soar
So far, they shall return no more
   Unto this river's brink.

JUDAS.

That canst thou not ! They are but clay,
They cannot sing, nor fly away
   Above the meadow lands !

JESUS.

Fly, fly ! ye sparrows ! you are free !
And while you live, remember me,
   Who made you with my hands.

Here JESUS *shall clap his hands, and the spar-*
  rows shall fly away, chirruping.

JUDAS.

Thou art a sorcerer, I know ;
Oft has my mother told me so,
   I will not play with thee !

    He strikes JESUS *in the right side.*

JESUS.

Ah, Judas ! thou hast smote my side,
And when I shall be crucified,
   There shall I piercèd be !

    Here JOSEPH *shall come in and say:*

JOSEPH.

Ye wicked boys ! why do ye play,
And break the holy Sabbath day?
What, think ye, will your mothers say
   To see you in such plight !
In such a sweat and such a heat,
With all that mud upon your feet !
There 's not a beggar in the street
   Makes such a sorry sight !

VIII. THE VILLAGE SCHOOL.

The RABBI BEN ISRAEL, *sitting on a high stool,*
  with a long beard, and a rod in his hand.

RABBI.

I am the Rabbi Ben Israel,
Throughout this village known full well,
And, as my scholars all will tell,
   Learned in things divine ;
The Cabala and Talmud hoar
Than all the prophets prize I more,
For water is all Bible lore,
   But Mishna is strong wine.

My fame extends from West to East,
And always, at the Purim feast,
I am as drunk as any beast
   That wallows in his sty ;
The wine it so elateth me,
That I no difference can see
Between " Accursed Haman be ! "
   And " Blessed be Mordecai ! "

Come hither, Judas Iscariot ;
Say, if thy lesson thou hast got
From the Rabbinical Book or not.
   Why howl the dogs at night ?

JUDAS.

In the Rabbinical Book, it saith
The dogs howl, when with icy breath

Great Sammael, the Angel of Death,
  Takes through the town his flight !

RABBI.

Well, boy ! now say, if thou art wise,
When the Angel of Death, who is full of
    eyes,
Comes where a sick man dying lies,
  What doth he to the wight ?

JUDAS.

He stands beside him, dark and tall,
Holding a sword, from which doth fall
Into his mouth a drop of gall,
  And so he turneth white.

RABBI.

And now, my Judas, say to me
What the great Voices Four may be,
That quite across the world do flee,
  And are not heard by men ?

JUDAS.

The Voice of the Sun in heaven's dome,
The Voice of the Murmuring of Rome,
The Voice of a Soul that goeth home,
  And the Angel of the Rain !

RABBI.

Right are thine answers every one !
Now little Jesus, the carpenter's son,
Let us see how thy task is done ;
  Canst thou thy letters say ?

JESUS.

Aleph.

RABBI.

      What next ? Do not stop yet !
Go on with all the alphabet.
Come, Aleph, Beth ; dost thou forget ?
  Cock's soul ! thou 'dst rather play !

JESUS.

What Aleph means I fain would know,
Before I any farther go !

RABBI.

Oh, by Saint Peter ! wouldst thou so ?
  Come hither, boy, to me.
As surely as the letter Jod
Once cried aloud, and spake to God,
So surely shalt thou feel this rod,
  And punished shalt thou be !

Here RABBI BEN ISRAEL *shall lift up his rod to
strike* JESUS, *and his right arm shall be paralyzed.*

IX.   CROWNED WITH FLOWERS.

JESUS *sitting among his playmates crowned with
    flowers as their King.*

BOYS.

We spread our garments on the ground !
With fragrant flowers thy head is crowned
While like a guard we stand around,
  And hail thee as our King !
Thou art the new King of the Jews !
Nor let the passers-by refuse
To bring that homage which men use
  To majesty to bring.

*Here a traveller shall go by, and the boys shall
    lay hold of his garments and say:*

BOYS.

Come hither ! and all reverence pay
Unto our monarch, crowned to-day !
Then go rejoicing on your way,
  In all prosperity !

TRAVELLER.

Hail to the King of Bethlehem,
Who weareth in his diadem
The yellow crocus for the gem
  Of his authority !

*He passes by ; and others come in, bearing on a
    litter a sick child.*

BOYS.

Set down the litter and draw near !
The King of Bethlehem is here !
What ails the child, who seems to fear
  That we shall do him harm ?

THE BEARERS.

He climbed up to the robin's nest,
And out there darted, from his rest,
A serpent with a crimson crest,
  And stung him in the arm.

JESUS.

Bring him to me, and let me feel
The wounded place ; my touch can heal
The sting of serpents, and can steal
  The poison from the bite !

He touches the wound, and the boy begins to cry.

Cease to lament ! I can foresee
That thou hereafter known shalt be,
Among the men who follow me,
  As Simon the Canaanite !

EPILOGUE.

In the after part of the day
Will be represented another play,
Of the Passion of our Blessed Lord,
Beginning directly after Nones !
At the close of which we shall accord,
By way of benison and reward,
The sight of a holy Martyr's bones !

IV

THE ROAD TO HIRSCHAU

PRINCE HENRY and ELSIE, *with their attendants
on horseback.*

ELSIE.

Onward and onward the highway runs to
the distant city, impatiently bearing
Tidings of human joy and disaster, of love
and of hate, of doing and daring !

PRINCE HENRY.

This life of ours is a wild æolian harp of
many a joyous strain,
But under them all there runs a loud per-
petual wail, as of souls in pain.

ELSIE.

Faith alone can interpret life, and the heart
that aches and bleeds with the stigma
Of pain, alone bears the likeness of Christ,
and can comprehend its dark enigma.

PRINCE HENRY.

Man is selfish, and seeketh pleasure with
little care of what may betide,
Else why am I travelling here beside thee,
a demon that rides by an angel's
side ?

ELSIE.

All the hedges are white with dust, and the
great dog under the creaking wain
Hangs his head in the lazy heat, while on-
ward the horses toil and strain.

PRINCE HENRY.

Now they stop at the wayside inn, and the
wagoner laughs with the landlord's
daughter,
While out of the dripping trough the horses
distend their leathern sides with
water.

ELSIE.

All through life there are wayside inns,
where man may refresh his soul with
love ;
Even the lowest may quench his thirst at
rivulets fed by springs from above.

PRINCE HENRY.

Yonder, where rises the cross of stone, our
journey along the highway ends,
And over the fields, by a bridle path, down
into the broad green valley de-
scends.

ELSIE.

I am not sorry to leave behind the beaten
road with its dust and heat ;
The air will be sweeter far, and the turf
will be softer under our horses'
feet.
They turn down a green lane.

ELSIE.

Sweet is the air with the budding haws,
and the valley stretching for miles
below
Is white with blossoming cherry-trees, as if
just covered with lightest snow.

PRINCE HENRY.

Over our heads a white cascade is gleam-
ing against the distant hill ;
We cannot hear it, nor see it move, but it
hangs like a banner when winds are
still.

ELSIE.

Damp and cool is this deep ravine, and
cool the sound of the brook by our
side !
What is this castle that rises above us, and
lords it over a land so wide ?

PRINCE HENRY.

It is the home of the Counts of Calva ; well
have I known these scenes of old,
Well I remember each tower and turret,
remember the brooklet, the wood,
and the wold.

ELSIE.

Hark ! from the little village below us the
bells of the church are ringing for
rain !
Priests and peasants in long procession
come forth and kneel on the arid
plain.

PRINCE HENRY.

They have not long to wait, for I see in
    the south uprising a little cloud,
That before the sun shall be set will cover
    the sky above us as with a shroud.
They pass on.

THE CONVENT OF HIRSCHAU IN THE BLACK
FOREST.

The Convent cellar. FRIAR CLAUS *comes in
with a light and a basket of empty flagons.*

FRIAR CLAUS.

I always enter this sacred place
With a thoughtful, solemn, and reverent
    pace,
Pausing long enough on each stair
To breathe an ejaculatory prayer,
And a benediction on the vines
That produce these various sorts of
    wines !
For my part, I am well content
That we have got through with the tedious
    Lent !
Fasting is all very well for those
Who have to contend with invisible foes ;
But I am quite sure it does not agree
With a quiet, peaceable man like me,
Who am not of that nervous and meagre
    kind,
That are always distressed in body and
    mind !
And at times it really does me good
To come down among this brotherhood,
Dwelling forever underground,
Silent, contemplative, round and sound ;
Each one old, and brown with mould,
But filled to the lips with the ardor of
    youth,
With the latent power and love of truth,
And with virtues fervent and manifold.

I have heard it said, that at Easter-tide
When buds are swelling on every side,
And the sap begins to move in the vine,
Then in all cellars, far and wide,
The oldest as well as the newest wine
Begins to stir itself, and ferment,
With a kind of revolt and discontent
At being so long in darkness pent,
And fain would burst from its sombre tun
To bask on the hillside in the sun ;
As in the bosom of us poor friars,
The tumult of half-subdued desires

For the world that we have left behind
Disturbs at times all peace of mind !
And now that we have lived through Lent,
My duty it is, as often before,
To open awhile the prison-door,
And give these restless spirits vent.

Now here is a cask that stands alone,
And has stood a hundred years or more,
Its beard of cobwebs, long and hoar,
Trailing and sweeping along the floor,
Like Barbarossa, who sits in his cave,
Taciturn, sombre, sedate, and grave,
Till his beard has grown through the table
    of stone !
It is of the quick and not of the dead !
In its veins the blood is hot and red,
And a heart still beats in those ribs of oak
That time may have tamed, but has not
    broke !
It comes from Bacharach on the Rhine,
Is one of the three best kinds of wine,
And costs some hundred florins the ohm ;
But that I do not consider dear,
When I remember that every year
Four butts are sent to the Pope of Rome.
And whenever a goblet thereof I drain,
The old rhyme keeps running in my brain :

    At Bacharach on the Rhine,
    At Hochheim on the Main,
    And at Würzburg on the Stein,
    Grow the three best kinds of wine !

They are all good wines, and better far
Than those of the Neckar, or those of the
    Ahr.
In particular, Würzburg well may boast
Of its blessed wine of the Holy Ghost,
Which of all wines I like the most.
This I shall draw for the Abbot's drink-
    ing,
Who seems to be much of my way of think-
    ing.
Fills a flagon.
Ah ! how the streamlet laughs and sings !
What a delicious fragrance springs
From the deep flagon, while it fills,
As of hyacinths and daffodils !
Between this cask and the Abbot's lips
Many have been the sips and slips ;
Many have been the draughts of wine,
On their way to his, that have stopped at
    mine ;
And many a time my soul has hankered

For a deep draught out of his silver tan-
kard,
When it should have been busy with other
affairs,
Less with its longings and more with its
prayers.
But now there is no such awkward con-
dition,
No danger of death and eternal perdition ;
So here's to the Abbot and Brothers all,
Who dwell in this convent of Peter and
Paul !

He drinks.

O cordial delicious ! O soother of pain !
It flashes like sunshine into my brain !
A benison rest on the Bishop who sends
Such a fudder of wine as this to his friends !
And now a flagon for such as may ask
A draught from the noble Bacharach cask,
And I will be gone, though I know full well
The cellar's a cheerfuller place than the
cell.
Behold where he stands, all sound and good,
Brown and old in his oaken hood ;
Silent he seems externally
As any Carthusian monk may be ;
But within, what a spirit of deep unrest !
What a seething and simmering in his
breast !
As if the heaving of his great heart
Would burst his belt of oak apart !
Let me unloose this button of wood,
And quiet a little his turbulent mood.

Sets it running.

See ! how its currents gleam and shine,
As if they had caught the purple hues
Of autumn sunsets on the Rhine,
Descending and mingling with the dews ;
Or as if the grapes were stained with the
blood
Of the innocent boy, who, some years back,
Was taken and crucified by the Jews,
In that ancient town of Bacharach ;
Perdition upon those infidel Jews,
In that ancient town of Bacharach !
The beautiful town, that gives us wine
With the fragrant odor of Muscadine !
I should deem it wrong to let this pass
Without first touching my lips to the glass,
For here in the midst of the current I stand
Like the stone Pfalz in the midst of the
river,
Taking toll upon either hand,
And much more grateful to the giver.

He drinks.

Here, now, is a very inferior kind,
Such as in any town you may find,
Such as one might imagine would suit
The rascal who drank wine out of a boot.
And, after all, it was not a crime,
For he won thereby Dorf Hüffelsheim.
A jolly old toper ! who at a pull
Could drink a postilion's jack-boot full,
And ask with a laugh, when that was
done,
If the fellow had left the other one !
This wine is as good as we can afford
To the friars, who sit at the lower board,
And cannot distinguish bad from good,
And are far better off than if they could,
Being rather the rude disciples of beer
Than of anything more refined and dear !

Fills the flagon and departs.

THE SCRIPTORIUM.

FRIAR PACIFICUS *transcribing and illuminating.*

FRIAR PACIFICUS.

It is growing dark ! Yet one line more,
And then my work for to-day is o'er.
I come again to the name of the Lord !
Ere I that awful name record,
That is spoken so lightly among men,
Let me pause awhile, and wash my pen ;
Pure from blemish and blot must it be
When it writes that word of mystery !

Thus have I labored on and on,
Nearly through the Gospel of John.
Can it be that from the lips
Of this same gentle Evangelist,
That Christ himself perhaps has kissed,
Came the dread Apocalypse !
It has a very awful look,
As it stands there at the end of the book,
Like the sun in an eclipse.
Ah me ! when I think of that vision divine,
Think of writing it, line by line,
I stand in awe of the terrible curse,
Like the trump of doom, in the closing
verse !
God forgive me ! if ever I
Take aught from the book of that Prophecy,
Lest my part too should be taken away
From the Book of Life on the Judgment
Day.
This is well written, though I say it !
I should not be afraid to display it
In open day, on the selfsame shelf

With the writings of St. Thecla herself,
Or of Theodosius, who of old
Wrote the Gospels in letters of gold!
That goodly folio standing yonder,
Without a single blot or blunder,
Would not bear away the palm from
    mine,
If we should compare them line for line.

There, now, is an initial letter!
Saint Ulric himself never made a better!
Finished down to the leaf and the snail,
Down to the eyes on the peacock's tail!
And now, as I turn the volume over,
And see what lies between cover and cover,
What treasures of art these pages hold,
All ablaze with crimson and gold,
God forgive me! I seem to feel
A certain satisfaction steal
Into my heart, and into my brain,
As if my talent had not lain
Wrapped in a napkin, and all in vain.
Yes, I might almost say to the Lord,
Here is a copy of thy Word,
Written out with much toil and pain;
Take it, O Lord, and let it be
As something I have done for thee!
                He looks from the window.
How sweet the air is! How fair the
    scene!
I wish I had as lovely a green
To paint my landscapes and my leaves!
How the swallows twitter under the eaves!
There, now, there is one in her nest;
I can just catch a glimpse of her head and
    breast,
And will sketch her thus, in her quiet
    nook,
For the margin of my Gospel book.
                He makes a sketch.
I can see no more. Through the valley
    yonder
A shower is passing; I hear the thunder
Mutter its curses in the air,
The devil's own and only prayer!
The dusty road is brown with rain,
And, speeding on with might and main,
Hitherward rides a gallant train.
They do not parley, they cannot wait,
But hurry in at the convent gate.
What a fair lady! and beside her
What a handsome, graceful, noble rider!
Now she gives him her hand to alight;
They will beg a shelter for the night.
I will go down to the corridor,

And try to see that face once more;
It will do for the face of some beautiful
    Saint,
Or for one of the Maries I shall paint.
                Goes out.

THE CLOISTERS.

The ABBOT ERNESTUS pacing to and fro.

ABBOT.

Slowly, slowly up the wall
Steals the sunshine, steals the shade;
Evening damps begin to fall,
Evening shadows are displayed.
Round me, o'er me, everywhere,
All the sky is grand with clouds,
And athwart the evening air
Wheel the swallows home in crowds.
Shafts of sunshine from the west
Paint the dusky windows red;
Darker shadows, deeper rest,
Underneath and overhead.
Darker, darker, and more wan,
In my breast the shadows fall;
Upward steals the life of man,
As the sunshine from the wall.
From the wall into the sky,
From the roof along the spire;
Ah, the souls of those that die
Are but sunbeams lifted higher.
                Enter PRINCE HENRY.

PRINCE HENRY.

Christ is arisen!

ABBOT.

                    Amen! He is arisen!
His peace be with you!

PRINCE HENRY.

                    Here it reigns forever!
The peace of God, that passeth understand-
    ing,
Reigns in these cloisters and these corri-
    dors.
Are you Ernestus, Abbot of the convent?

ABBOT.

I am.

PRINCE HENRY.

            And I Prince Henry of Hoheneck,
Who crave your hospitality to-night.

ABBOT.

You are thrice welcome to our humble
    walls.
You do us honor ; and we shall requite it,
I fear, but poorly, entertaining you
With Paschal eggs, and our poor convent
    wine,
The remnants of our Easter holidays.

PRINCE HENRY.

How fares it with the holy monks of Hir-
    schau ?
Are all things well with them ?

ABBOT.

                    All things are well.

PRINCE HENRY.

A noble convent ! I have known it long
By the report of travellers. I now see
Their commendations lag behind the truth.
You lie here in the valley of the Nagold
As in a nest : and the still river, gliding
Along its bed, is like an admonition
How all things pass. Your lands are rich
    and ample,
And your revenues large. God's benedic-
    tion
Rests on your convent.

ABBOT.

                    By our charities
We strive to merit it. Our Lord and Mas-
    ter,
When He departed, left us in his will,
As our best legacy on earth, the poor !
These we have always with us ; had we
    not,
Our hearts would grow as hard as are these
    stones.

PRINCE HENRY.

If I remember right, the Counts of Calva
Founded your convent.

ABBOT.

                    Even as you say.

PRINCE HENRY.

And, if I err not, it is very old.

ABBOT.

Within these cloisters lie already buried
Twelve holy Abbots. Underneath the
    flags

On which we stand, the Abbot William
    lies,
Of blessed memory.

PRINCE HENRY.

                    And whose tomb is that,
Which bears the brass escutcheon ?

ABBOT.

                    A benefactor's.
Conrad, a Count of Calva, he who stood
Godfather to our bells.

PRINCE HENRY.

                    Your monks are learned
And holy men, I trust.

ABBOT.

                    There are among them
Learned and holy men. Yet in this age
We need another Hildebrand, to shake
And purify us like a mighty wind.
The world is wicked, and sometimes I won-
    der
God does not lose his patience with it
    wholly,
And shatter it like glass ! Even here, at
    times,
Within these walls, where all should be at
    peace,
I have my trials. Time has laid his hand
Upon my heart, gently, not smiting it,
But as a harper lays his open palm
Upon his harp, to deaden its vibrations.
Ashes are on my head, and on my lips
Sackcloth, and in my breast a heaviness
And weariness of life, that makes me ready
To say to the dead Abbots under us,
"Make room for me !" Only I see the
    dusk
Of evening twilight coming, and have not
Completed half my task ; and so at times
The thought of my shortcomings in this
    life
Falls like a shadow on the life to come.

PRINCE HENRY.

We must all die, and not the old alone ;
The young have no exemption from that
    doom.

ABBOT.

Ah, yes ! the young may die, but the old
    must !
That is the difference.

PRINCE HENRY.

           I have heard much laud
Of your transcribers. Your Scriptorium
Is famous among all ; your manuscripts
Praised for their beauty and their excel-
    lence.

ABBOT.

That is indeed our boast. If you desire
    it,
You shall behold these treasures. And
    meanwhile
Shall the Refectorarius bestow
Your horses and attendants for the night.
    They go in. The Vesper-bell rings.

THE CHAPEL.

*Vespers ; after which the monks retire, a chorister
leading an old monk who is blind.*

PRINCE HENRY.

They are all gone, save one who lingers,
Absorbed in deep and silent prayer.
As if his heart could find no rest,
At times he beats his heaving breast
With clenchèd and convulsive fingers,
Then lifts them trembling in the air.
A chorister, with golden hair,
Guides hitherward his heavy pace.
Can it be so ? Or does my sight
Deceive me in the uncertain light ?
Ah no ! I recognize that face,
Though Time has touched it in his flight,
And changed the auburn hair to white.
It is Count Hugo of the Rhine,
The deadliest foe of all our race,
And hateful unto me and mine !

THE BLIND MONK.

Who is it that doth stand so near
His whispered words I almost hear ?

PRINCE HENRY.

I am Prince Henry of Hoheneck,
And you, Count Hugo of the Rhine !
I know you, and I see the scar,
The brand upon your forehead, shine
And redden like a baleful star !

THE BLIND MONK.

Count Hugo once, but now the wreck
Of what I was. O Hoheneck !

The passionate will, the pride, the wrath
That bore me headlong on my path,
Stumbled and staggered into fear,
And failed me in my mad career,
As a tired steed some evil-doer,
Alone upon a desolate moor,
Bewildered, lost, deserted, blind,
And hearing loud and close behind
The o'ertaking steps of his pursuer.
Then suddenly from the dark there came
A voice that called me by my name,
And said to me, " Kneel down and pray ! "
And so my terror passed away,
Passed utterly away forever.
Contrition, penitence, remorse,
Came on me, with o'erwhelming force ;
A hope, a longing, an endeavor,
By days of penance and nights of prayer,
To frustrate and defeat despair !
Calm, deep, and still is now my heart,
With tranquil waters overflowed ;
A lake whose unseen fountains start,
Where once the hot volcano glowed.
And you, O Prince of Hoheneck !
Have known me in that earlier time,
A man of violence and crime,
Whose passions brooked no curb nor check
Behold me now, in gentler mood,
One of this holy brotherhood.
Give me your hand ; here let me kneel ;
Make your reproaches sharp as steel ;
Spurn me, and smite me on each cheek ;
No violence can harm the meek,
There is no wound Christ cannot heal !
Yes ; lift your princely hand, and take
Revenge, if 't is revenge you seek ;
Then pardon me, for Jesus' sake !

PRINCE HENRY.

Arise, Count Hugo ! let there be
No further strife nor enmity
Between us twain ; we both have erred !
Too rash in act, too wroth in word,
From the beginning have we stood
In fierce, defiant attitude,
Each thoughtless of the other's right,
And each reliant on his might.
But now our souls are more subdued ;
The hand of God, and not in vain,
Has touched us with the fire of pain.
Let us kneel down and side by side
Pray, till our souls are purified,
And pardon will not be denied !
    They kneel.

THE REFECTORY.

Gaudiolum of Monks at midnight. LUCIFER *disguised as a Friar.*

FRIAR PAUL *sings.*

Ave ! color vini clari,
Dulcis potus, non amari,
Tua nos inebriari
    Digneris potentia !

FRIAR CUTHBERT.

Not so much noise, my worthy frères,
You 'll disturb the Abbot at his prayers.

FRIAR PAUL *sings.*

O ! quam placens in colore !
O ! quam fragrans in odore !
O ! quam sapidum in ore !
    Dulce linguæ vinculum !

FRIAR CUTHBERT.

I should think your tongue had broken its
    chain !

FRIAR PAUL *sings.*

Felix venter quem intrabis !
Felix guttur quod rigabis !
Felix os quod tu lavabis !
    Et beata labia !

FRIAR CUTHBERT.

Peace ! I say, peace !
Will you never cease !
You will rouse up the Abbot, I tell you
    again !

FRIAR JOHN.

No danger ! to-night he will let us alone,
As I happen to know he has guests of his
    own.

FRIAR CUTHBERT.

Who are they ?

FRIAR JOHN.

    A German Prince and his train,
Who arrived here just before the rain.
There is with him a damsel fair to see,
As slender and graceful as a reed !
When she alighted from her steed,
It seemed like a blossom blown from a
    tree.

FRIAR CUTHBERT.

None of your pale-faced girls for me !
None of your damsels of high degree !

FRIAR JOHN.

Come, old fellow, drink down to your peg !
But do not drink any further, I beg !

FRIAR PAUL, *sings.*

In the days of gold,
The days of old,
Crosier of wood
And bishop of gold !

FRIAR CUTHBERT.

What an infernal racket and riot !
Can you not drink your wine in quiet ?
Why fill the convent with such scandals,
As if we were so many drunken Vandals ?

FRIAR PAUL, *continues.*

Now we have changed
That law so good
To crosier of gold
And bishop of wood !

FRIAR CUTHBERT.

Well, then, since you are in the mood
To give your noisy humors vent,
Sing and howl to your heart's content !

CHORUS OF MONKS.

Funde vinum, funde !
Tanquam sint fluminis undæ,
Nec quæras unde,
Sed fundas semper abunde !

FRIAR JOHN.

What is the name of yonder friar,
With an eye that glows like a coal of fire,
And such a black mass of tangled hair ?

FRIAR PAUL.

He who is sitting there,
With a rollicking,
Devil may care,
Free and easy look and air,
As if he were used to such feasting and
    frolicking ?

FRIAR JOHN.

The same.

FRIAR PAUL.

He's a stranger. You had better ask his
        name,
And where he is going and whence he came.

FRIAR JOHN.

Hallo! Sir Friar!

FRIAR PAUL.

You must raise your voice a little higher,
He does not seem to hear what you say.
Now, try again! He is looking this way.

FRIAR JOHN.

Hallo! Sir Friar,
We wish to inquire
Whence you came, and where you are go-
        ing,
And anything else that is worth the know-
        ing.
So be so good as to open your head.

LUCIFER.

I am a Frenchman born and bred,
Going on a pilgrimage to Rome.
My home
Is the convent of St. Gildas de Rhuys,
Of which, very like, you never have heard.

MONKS.

Never a word!

LUCIFER.

You must know, then, it is in the diocese
Called the Diocese of Vannes,
In the province of Brittany.
From the gray rocks of Morbihan
It overlooks the angry sea ;
The very sea-shore where,
In his great despair,
Abbot Abelard walked to and fro,
Filling the night with woe,
And wailing aloud to the merciless seas
The name of his sweet Heloise,
Whilst overhead
The convent windows gleamed as red
As the fiery eyes of the monks within,
Who with jovial din
Gave themselves up to all kinds of sin !
Ha! that is a convent! that is an abbey !
Over the doors,
None of your death-heads carved in wood,
None of your Saints looking pious and
        good,
None of your Patriarchs old and shabby !

But the heads and tusks of boars,
And the cells
Hung all round with the fells
Of the fallow-deer.
And then what cheer !
What jolly, fat friars,
Sitting round the great, roaring fires,
Roaring louder than they,
With their strong wines,
And their concubines,
And never a bell,
With its swagger and swell,
Calling you up with a start of affright
In the dead of night,
To send you grumbling down dark stairs,
To mumble your prayers ;
But the cheery crow
Of cocks in the yard below,
After daybreak, an hour or so,
And the barking of deep-mouthed hounds,
These are the sounds
That, instead of bells, salute the ear.
And then all day
Up and away
Through the forest, hunting the deer !
Ah, my friends ! I 'm afraid that here
You are a little too pious, a little too tame,
And the more is the shame.
'T is the greatest folly
Not to be jolly ;
That's what I think !
Come, drink, drink,
Drink, and die game !

MONKS.

And your Abbot What 's-his-name ?

LUCIFER.

Abelard !

MONKS.

Did he drink hard ?

LUCIFER.

Oh, no ! Not he !
He was a dry old fellow,
Without juice enough to get thoroughly
        mellow.
There he stood,
Lowering at us in sullen mood,
As if he had come into Brittany
Just to reform our brotherhood !
        A roar of laughter.
But you see
It never would do !
For some of us knew a thing or two,

In the Abbey of St. Gildas de Rhuys!
For instance, the great ado
With old Fulbert's niece,
The young and lovely Heloise.

FRIAR JOHN.

Stop there, if you please,
Till we drink to the fair Heloise.

ALL, *drinking and shouting.*

Heloise! Heloise!
The Chapel-bell tolls.

LUCIFER, *starting.*

What is that bell for? Are you such asses
As to keep up the fashion of midnight
masses?

FRIAR CUTHBERT.

It is only a poor, unfortunate brother,
Who is gifted with most miraculous powers
Of getting up at all sorts of hours,
And, by way of penance and Christian
meekness,
Of creeping silently out of his cell
To take a pull at that hideous bell;
So that all the monks who are lying awake
May murmur some kind of prayer for his
sake,
And adapted to his peculiar weakness!

FRIAR JOHN.

From frailty and fall —

ALL.

Good Lord, deliver us all!

FRIAR CUTHBERT.

And before the bell for matins sounds,
He takes his lantern, and goes the rounds,
Flashing it into our sleepy eyes,
Merely to say it is time to arise.
But enough of that. Go on, if you please,
With your story about St. Gildas de Rhuys.

LUCIFER.

Well, it finally came to pass
That, half in fun and half in malice,
One Sunday at Mass
We put some poison into the chalice.
But, either by accident or design,
Peter Abelard kept away
From the chapel that day,
And a poor young friar, who in his stead
Drank the sacramental wine,

Fell on the steps of the altar, dead!
But look! do you see at the window there
That face, with a look of grief and despair,
That ghastly face, as of one in pain?

MONKS.

Who? where?

LUCIFER.

As I spoke, it vanished away again.

FRIAR CUTHBERT.

It is that nefarious
Siebald the Refectorarius.
That fellow is always playing the scout,
Creeping and peeping and prowling about;
And then he regales
The Abbot with scandalous tales.

LUCIFER.

A spy in the convent? One of the brothers
Telling scandalous tales of the others?
Out upon him, the lazy loon!
I would put a stop to that pretty soon,
In a way he should rue it.

MONKS.

How shall we do it?

LUCIFER.

Do you, brother Paul,
Creep under the window, close to the wall,
And open it suddenly when I call.
Then seize the villain by the hair,
And hold him there,
And punish him soundly, once for all.

FRIAR CUTHBERT.

As St. Dunstan of old,
We are told,
Once caught the Devil by the nose!

LUCIFER.

Ha! ha! that story is very clever,
But has no foundation whatsoever.
Quick! for I see his face again
Glaring in at the window-pane;
Now! now! and do not spare your blows.
FRIAR PAUL *opens the window suddenly, and
seizes* SIEBALD.
They beat him.

FRIAR SIEBALD.

Help! help! are you going to slay me?

FRIAR PAUL.

That will teach you again to betray me !

FRIAR SIEBALD.

Mercy ! mercy !

FRIAR PAUL, *shouting and beating.*

Rumpas bellorum lorum
Vim confer amorum
Morum verorum rorum
Tu plena polorum !

LUCIFER.

Who stands in the doorway yonder,
Stretching out his trembling hand,
Just as Abelard used to stand,
The flash of his keen, black eyes
Forerunning the thunder ?

THE MONKS, *in confusion.*

The Abbot ! the Abbot !

FRIAR CUTHBERT.

    And what is the wonder !
He seems to have taken you by surprise.

FRIAR FRANCIS.

Hide the great flagon
From the eyes of the dragon !

FRIAR CUTHBERT.

Pull the brown hood over your face !
This will bring us into disgrace !

ABBOT.

What means this revel and carouse ?
Is this a tavern and drinking-house ?
Are you Christian monks, or heathen devils,
To pollute this convent with your revels ?
Were Peter Damian still upon earth,
To be shocked by such ungodly mirth,
He would write your names, with pen of
 gall,
In his Book of Gomorrah, one and all !
Away, you drunkards ! to your cells,
And pray till you hear the matin-bells ;
You, Brother Francis, and you, Brother
 Paul !
And as a penance mark each prayer
With the scourge upon your shoulders
 bare ;
Nothing atones for such a sin
But the blood that follows the discipline.
And you, Brother Cuthbert, come with me
Alone into the sacristy ;

You, who should be a guide to your bro-
 thers,
And are ten times worse than all the others,
For you I 've a draught that has long been
 brewing,
You shall do a penance worth the doing !
Away to your prayers, then, one and all !
I wonder the very convent wall
Does not crumble and crush you in its fall !

THE NEIGHBORING NUNNERY.

The ABBESS IRMINGARD *sitting with* ELSIE *in
the moonlight.*

IRMINGARD.

The night is silent, the wind is still,
The moon is looking from yonder hill
Down upon convent, and grove, and garden ;
The clouds have passed away from her face,
Leaving behind them no sorrowful trace,
Only the tender and quiet grace
Of one whose heart has been healed with
 pardon !

And such am I. My soul within
Was dark with passion and soiled with sin.
But now its wounds are healed again ;
Gone are the anguish, the terror, and pain ;
For across that desolate land of woe,
O'er whose burning sands I was forced to
 go,
A wind from heaven began to blow ;
And all my being trembled and shook,
As the leaves of the tree, or the grass of
 the field,
And I was healed, as the sick are healed,
When fanned by the leaves of the Holy
 Book !

As thou sittest in the moonlight there,
Its glory flooding thy golden hair,
And the only darkness that which lies
In the haunted chambers of thine eyes,
I feel my soul drawn unto thee,
Strangely, and strongly, and more and
 more,
As to one I have known and loved before ;
For every soul is akin to me
That dwells in the land of mystery !
I am the Lady Irmingard,
Born of a noble race and name !
Many a wandering Suabian bard,
Whose life was dreary, and bleak, and hard,
Has found through me the way to fame.

Brief and bright were those days, and the
    night
Which followed was full of a lurid light.
Love, that of every woman's heart
Will have the whole, and not a part,
That is to her, in Nature's plan,
More than ambition is to man,
Her light, her life, her very breath,
With no alternative but death,
Found me a maiden soft and young,
Just from the convent's cloistered school,
And seated on my lowly stool,
Attentive while the minstrels sung.

Gallant, graceful, gentle, tall,
Fairest, noblest, best of all,
Was Walter of the Vogelweid ;
And, whatsoever may betide,
Still I think of him with pride !
His song was of the summer-time,
The very birds sang in his rhyme ;
The sunshine, the delicious air,
The fragrance of the flowers, were there ;
And I grew restless as I heard,
Restless and buoyant as a bird,
Down soft, aerial currents sailing,
O'er blossomed orchards, and fields in
    bloom,
And through the momentary gloom
Of shadows o'er the landscape trailing,
Yielding and borne I knew not where,
But feeling resistance unavailing.

And thus, unnoticed and apart,
And more by accident than choice,
I listened to that single voice
Until the chambers of my heart
Were filled with it by night and day.
One night, — it was a night in May, —
Within the garden, unawares,
Under the blossoms in the gloom,
I heard it utter my own name
With protestations and wild prayers ;
And it rang through me, and became
Like the archangel's trump of doom,
Which the soul hears, and must obey ;
And mine arose as from a tomb.
My former life now seemed to me
Such as hereafter death may be,
When in the great Eternity
We shall awake and find it day.

It was a dream, and would not stay ;
A dream, that in a single night
Faded and vanished out of sight.

My father's anger followed fast
This passion, as a freshening blast
Seeks out and fans the fire, whose rage
It may increase, but not assuage.
And he exclaimed : " No wandering bard
Shall win thy hand, O Irmingard !
For which Prince Henry of Hoheneck
By messenger and letter sues."

Gently, but firmly, I replied :
" Henry of Hoheneck I discard !
Never the hand of Irmingard
Shall lie in his as the hand of a bride ! "
This said I, Walter, for thy sake ;
This said I, for I could not choose.
After a pause, my father spake
In that cold and deliberate tone
Which turns the hearer into stone,
And seems itself the act to be
That follows with such dread certainty :
" This or the cloister and the veil ! "
No other words than these he said,
But they were like a funeral wail ;
My life was ended, my heart was dead.

That night from the castle-gate went
    down,
With silent, slow, and stealthy pace,
Two shadows, mounted on shadowy steeds,
Taking the narrow path that leads
Into the forest dense and brown.
In the leafy darkness of the place,
One could not distinguish form nor face,
Only a bulk without a shape,
A darker shadow in the shade ;
One scarce could say it moved or stayed.
Thus it was we made our escape !
A foaming brook, with many a bound,
Followed us like a playful hound ;
Then leaped before us, and in the hollow
Paused, and waited for us to follow,
And seemed impatient, and afraid
That our tardy flight should be betrayed
By the sound our horses' hoof-beats made.
And when we reached the plain below,
We paused a moment and drew rein
To look back at the castle again ;
And we saw the windows all aglow
With lights, that were passing to and fro ;
Our hearts with terror ceased to beat ;
The brook crept silent to our feet ;
We knew what most we feared to know.
Then suddenly horns began to blow ;
And we heard a shout, and a heavy
    tramp,

And our horses snorted in the damp
Night-air of the meadows green and wide,
And in a moment, side by side,
So close, they must have seemed but one,
The shadows across the moonlight run,
And another came, and swept behind,
Like the shadow of clouds before the
    wind !

How I remember that breathless flight
Across the moors, in the summer night !
How under our feet the long, white road
Backward like a river flowed,
Sweeping with it fences and hedges,
Whilst farther away and overhead,
Paler than I, with fear and dread,
The moon fled with us as we fled
Along the forest's jagged edges !

All this I can remember well ;
But of what afterwards befell
I nothing further can recall
Than a blind, desperate, headlong fall ;
The rest is a blank and darkness all.
When I awoke out of this swoon,
The sun was shining, not the moon,
Making a cross upon the wall
With the bars of my windows narrow and
    tall ;
And I prayed to it, as I had been wont to
    pray,
From early childhood, day by day,
Each morning, as in bed I lay !
I was lying again in my own room !
And I thanked God, in my fever and pain,
That those shadows on the midnight plain
Were gone, and could not come again !
I struggled no longer with my doom !

This happened many years ago.
I left my father's home to come
Like Catherine to her martyrdom,
For blindly I esteemed it so.
And when I heard the convent door
Behind me close, to ope no more,
I felt it smite me like a blow.
Through all my limbs a shudder ran,
And on my bruisèd spirit fell
The dampness of my narrow cell
As night-air on a wounded man,
Giving intolerable pain.

But now a better life began.
I felt the agony decrease
By slow degrees, then wholly cease,

Ending in perfect rest and peace !
It was not apathy, nor dulness,
That weighed and pressed upon my
    brain,
But the same passion I had given
To earth before, now turned to heaven
With all its overflowing fulness.

Alas ! the world is full of peril !
The path that runs through the fairest
    meads,
On the sunniest side of the valley, leads
Into a region bleak and sterile !
Alike in the high-born and the lowly,
The will is feeble, and passion strong.
We cannot sever right from wrong ;
Some falsehood mingles with all truth ;
Nor is it strange the heart of youth
Should waver and comprehend but slowly
The things that are holy and unholy !
But in this sacred, calm retreat,
We are all well and safely shielded
From winds that blow, and waves that
    beat,
From the cold, and rain, and blighting
    heat,
To which the strongest hearts ha
    yielded.
Here we stand as the Virgins Seven,
For our celestial bridegroom yearning ;
Our hearts are lamps forever burning,
With a steady and unwavering flame,
Pointing upward, forever the same,
Steadily upward toward the heaven !

The moon is hidden behind a cloud ;
A sudden darkness fills the room,
And thy deep eyes, amid the gloom,
Shine like jewels in a shroud.
On the leaves is a sound of falling rain ;
A bird, awakened in its nest,
Gives a faint twitter of unrest,
Then smooths its plumes and sleeps
    again.
No other sounds than these I hear ;
The hour of midnight must be near.
Thou art o'erspent with the day's fatigue
Of riding many a dusty league ;
Sink, then, gently to thy slumber ;
Me so many cares encumber.
So many ghosts, and forms of fright,
Have started from their graves to-night,
They have driven sleep from mine eyes
    away :
I will go down to the chapel and pray.

V

A COVERED BRIDGE AT LUCERNE

PRINCE HENRY.

God's blessing on the architects who build
The bridges o'er swift rivers and abysses
Before impassable to human feet,
No less than on the builders of cathedrals,
Whose massive walls are bridges thrown across
The dark and terrible abyss of Death.
Well has the name of Pontifex been given
Unto the Church's head, as the chief builder
And architect of the invisible bridge
That leads from earth to heaven.

ELSIE.
How dark it grows!
What are these paintings on the walls around us?

PRINCE HENRY.
The Dance Macaber!

ELSIE.
What?

PRINCE HENRY.
The Dance of Death!
All that go to and fro must look upon it,
Mindful of what they shall be, while beneath,
Among the wooden piles, the turbulent river
Rushes, impetuous as the river of life,
With dimpling eddies, ever green and bright,
Save where the shadow of this bridge falls on it.

ELSIE.
Oh yes! I see it now!

PRINCE HENRY.
The grim musician
Leads all men through the mazes of that dance,
To different sounds in different measures moving;
Sometimes he plays a lute, sometimes a drum,
To tempt or terrify.

ELSIE.
What is this picture?

PRINCE HENRY.
It is a young man singing to a nun,
Who kneels at her devotions, but in kneeling
Turns round to look at him; and Death, meanwhile,
Is putting out the candles on the altar!

ELSIE.
Ah, what a pity 't is that she should listen
Unto such songs, when in her orisons
She might have heard in heaven the angels singing!

PRINCE HENRY.
Here he has stolen a jester's cap and bells,
And dances with the Queen.

ELSIE.
A foolish jest!

PRINCE HENRY.
And here the heart of the new-wedded wife,
Coming from church with her beloved lord,
He startles with the rattle of his drum.

ELSIE.
Ah, that is sad! And yet perhaps 't is best
That she should die, with all the sunshine on her,
And all the benedictions of the morning,
Before this affluence of golden light
Shall fade into a cold and clouded gray,
Then into darkness!

PRINCE HENRY.
Under it is written,
"Nothing but death shall separate thee and me!"

ELSIE.
And what is this, that follows close upon it?

PRINCE HENRY.
Death, playing on a dulcimer. Behind him,
A poor old woman, with a rosary,
Follows the sound, and seems to wish her feet
Were swifter to o'ertake him. Underneath,
The inscription reads, "Better is Death than Life."

ELSIE.

Better is Death than Life ! Ah yes ! to
   thousands
Death plays upon a dulcimer, and sings
That song of consolation, till the air
Rings with it, and they cannot choose but
   follow
Whither he leads. And not the old alone,
But the young also hear it, and are still.

PRINCE HENRY.

Yes, in their sadder moments. 'T is the
   sound
Of their own hearts they hear, half full of
   tears,
Which are like crystal cups, half filled with
   water,
Responding to the pressure of a finger
With music sweet and low and melan-
   choly.
Let us go forward, and no longer stay
In this great picture-gallery of Death !
I hate it ! ay, the very thought of it !

ELSIE.

Why is it hateful to you ?

PRINCE HENRY.

            For the reason
That life, and all that speaks of life, is
   lovely,
And death, and all that speaks of death, is
   hateful.

ELSIE.

The grave itself is but a covered bridge,
Leading from light to light, through a brief
   darkness !

PRINCE HENRY, *emerging from the bridge.*

I breathe again more freely ! Ah, how
   pleasant
To come once more into the light of day,
Out of that shadow of death ! To hear
   again
The hoof-beats of our horses on firm
   ground,
And not upon those hollow planks, resound-
   ing
With a sepulchral echo, like the clods
On coffins in a churchyard ! Yonder lies
The Lake of the Four Forest-Towns, ap-
   parelled
In light, and lingering, like a village
   maiden,

Hid in the bosom of her native mountains,
Then pouring all her life into another's,
Changing her name and being ! Over-
   head,
Shaking his cloudy tresses loose in air,
Rises Pilatus, with his windy pines.

They pass on.

THE DEVIL'S BRIDGE.

PRINCE HENRY *and* ELSIE *crossing with attend-
ants.*

GUIDE.

This bridge is called the Devil's Bridge.
With a single arch, from rid e to ridge,
It leaps across the terrible chasm
Yawning beneath us, black and deep,
As if, in some convulsive spasm,
The summits of the hills had cracked,
And made a road for the cataract
That raves and rages down the steep !

LUCIFER, *under the bridge.*

Ha ! ha !

GUIDE.

Never any bridge but this
Could stand across the wild abyss ;
All the rest, of wood or stone,
By the Devil's hand were overthrown.
He toppled crags from the precipice,
And whatsoe'er was built by day
In the night was swept away ;
None could stand but this alone.

LUCIFER, *under the bridge.*

Ha ! ha !

GUIDE.

I showed you in the valley a bowlder
Marked with the imprint of his shoulder ;
As he was bearing it up this way,
A peasant, passing, cried, " Herr Jé !"
And the Devil dropped it in his fright,
And vanished suddenly out of sight !

LUCIFER, *under the bridge.*

Ha ! ha !

GUIDE.

Abbot Giraldus of Einsiedel,
For pilgrims on their way to Rome,
Built this at last, with a single arch,
Under which, on its endless march,
Runs the river, white with foam,
Like a thread through the eye of a needle.
And the Devil promised to let it stand,

Under compact and condition
That the first living thing which crossed
Should be surrendered into his hand,
And be beyond redemption lost.

LUCIFER, *under the bridge.*
Ha! ha! perdition!

GUIDE.
At length, the bridge being all completed,
The Abbot, standing at its head,
Threw across it a loaf of bread,
Which a hungry dog sprang after,
And the rocks reëchoed with the peals of
laughter
To see the Devil thus defeated!
They pass on.

LUCIFER, *under the bridge.*
Ha! ha! defeated!
For journeys and for crimes like this
I let the bridge stand o'er the abyss!

THE ST. GOTHARD PASS.

PRINCE HENRY.
This is the highest point. Two ways the
rivers
Leap down to different seas, and as they
roll
Grow deep and still, and their majestic
presence
Becomes a benefaction to the towns
They visit, wandering silently among
them,
Like patriarchs old among their shining
tents.

ELSIE.
How bleak and bare it is! Nothing but
mosses
Grow on these rocks.

PRINCE HENRY.
Yet are they not forgotten;
Beneficent Nature sends the mists to feed
them.

ELSIE.
See yonder little cloud, that, borne aloft
So tenderly by the wind, floats fast away
Over the snowy peaks! It seems to me
The body of St. Catherine, borne by an-
gels!

PRINCE HENRY.
Thou art St. Catherine, and invisible
angels
Bear thee across these chasms and preci-
pices,
Lest thou shouldst dash thy feet against a
stone!

ELSIE.
Would I were borne unto my grave, as she
was,
Upon angelic shoulders! Even now
I seem uplifted by them, light as air!
What sound is that?

PRINCE HENRY.
The tumbling avalanches!

ELSIE.
How awful, yet how beautiful!

PRINCE HENRY.
These are
The voices of the mountains! Thus they
ope
Their snowy lips, and speak unto each
other,
In the primeval language, lost to man.

ELSIE.
What land is this that spreads itself beneath
us?

PRINCE HENRY.
Italy! Italy!

ELSIE.
Land of the Madonna
How beautiful it is! It seems a garden
Of Paradise!

PRINCE HENRY.
Nay, of Gethsemane
To thee and me, of passion and of prayer!
Yet once of Paradise. Long years ago
I wandered as a youth among its bowers,
And never from my heart has faded quite
Its memory, that, like a summer sunset,
Encircles with a ring of purple light
All the horizon of my youth.

GUIDE.
O friends!
The days are short, the way before us
long;
We must not linger, if we think to reach
The inn at Bellinzona before vespers!
They pass on.

AT THE FOOT OF THE ALPS.

A halt under the trees at noon.

PRINCE HENRY.

Here let us pause a moment in the trembling
Shadow and sunshine of the roadside trees,
And, our tired horses in a group assembling,
Inhale long draughts of this delicious breeze.
Our fleeter steeds have distanced our attendants ;
They lag behind us with a slower pace ;
We will await them under the green pendants
Of the great willows in this shady place.
Ho, Barbarossa ! how thy mottled haunches
Sweat with this canter over hill and glade !
Stand still, and let these overhanging branches
Fan thy hot sides and comfort thee with shade !

ELSIE.

What a delightful landscape spreads before us,
Marked with a whitewashed cottage here and there !
And, in luxuriant garlands drooping o'er us,
Blossoms of grape-vines scent the sunny air.

PRINCE HENRY.

Hark ! what sweet sounds are those, whose accents holy
Fill the warm noon with music sad and sweet !

ELSIE.

It is a band of pilgrims, moving slowly
On their long journey, with uncovered feet.

PILGRIMS, *chanting the Hymn of St. Hildebert.*

Me receptet Sion illa,
Sion David, urbs tranquilla,
Cujus faber auctor lucis,
Cujus portæ lignum crucis,
Cujus claves lingua Petri,
Cujus cives semper læti,
Cujus muri lapis vivus,
Cujus custos Rex festivus !

LUCIFER, *as a Friar in the procession.*

Here am I, too, in the pious band,
In the garb of a barefooted Carmelite dressed !

The soles of my feet are as hard and tanned
As the conscience of old Pope Hildebrand,
The Holy Satan, who made the wives
Of the bishops lead such shameful lives.
All day long I beat my breast,
And chant with a most particular zest
The Latin hymns, which I understand
Quite as well, I think, as the rest.
And at night such lodging in barns and sheds,
Such a hurly-burly in country inns,
Such a clatter of tongues in empty heads,
Such a helter-skelter of prayers and sins !
Of all the contrivances of the time
For sowing broadcast the seeds of crime,
There is none so pleasing to me and mine
As a pilgrimage to some far-off shrine !

PRINCE HENRY.

If from the outward man we judge the inner,
And cleanliness is godliness, I fear
A hopeless reprobate, a hardened sinner,
Must be that Carmelite now passing near.

LUCIFER.

There is my German Prince again,
Thus far on his journey to Salern,
And the lovesick girl, whose heated brain
Is sowing the cloud to reap the rain ;
But it 's a long road that has no turn !
Let them quietly hold their way,
I have also a part in the play.
But first I must act to my heart's content
This mummery and this merriment,
And drive this motley flock of sheep
Into the fold, where drink and sleep
The jolly old friars of Benevent.
Of a truth, it often provokes me to laugh
To see these beggars hobble along,
Lamed and maimed, and fed upon chaff,
Chanting their wonderful piff and paff,
And, to make up for not understanding the song,
Singing it fiercely, and wild, and strong !
Were it not for my magic garters and staff,
And the goblets of goodly wine I quaff,
And the mischief I make in the idle throng,
I should not continue the business long.

PILGRIMS, *chanting.*

In hâc urbe, lux solennis,
Ver æternum, pax perennis ;
In hâc odor implens cælos,
In hâc semper festum melos !

PRINCE HENRY.

Do you observe that monk among the train,
Who pours from his great throat the roaring bass,
As a cathedral spout pours out the rain,
And this way turns his rubicund, round face?

ELSIE.

It is the same who, on the Strasburg square,
Preached to the people in the open air.

PRINCE HENRY.

And he has crossed o'er mountain, field, and fell,
On that good steed, that seems to bear him well,
The hackney of the Friars of Orders Gray,
His own stout legs! He, too, was in the play,
Both as King Herod and Ben Israel.
Good morrow, Friar!

FRIAR CUTHBERT.

Good morrow, noble Sir!

PRINCE HENRY.

I speak in German, for, unless I err,
You are a German.

FRIAR CUTHBERT.

I cannot gainsay you.
But by what instinct, or what secret sign,
Meeting me here, do you straightway divine
That northward of the Alps my country lies?

PRINCE HENRY.

Your accent, like St. Peter's, would betray you,
Did not your yellow beard and your blue eyes.
Moreover, we have seen your face before,
And heard you preach at the Cathedral door
On Easter Sunday, in the Strasburg square.
We were among the crowd that gathered there,
And saw you play the Rabbi with great skill,
As if, by leaning o'er so many years
To walk with little children, your own will
Had caught a childish attitude from theirs,
A kind of stooping in its form and gait,

And could no longer stand erect and straight.
Whence come you now?

FRIAR CUTHBERT.

From the old monastery
Of Hirschau, in the forest; being sent
Upon a pilgrimage to Benevent,
To see the image of the Virgin Mary,
That moves its holy eyes, and sometimes speaks,
And lets the piteous tears run down its cheeks,
To touch the hearts of the impenitent.

PRINCE HENRY.

Oh, had I faith, as in the days gone by,
That knew no doubt, and feared no mystery!

LUCIFER, *at a distance.*

Ho, Cuthbert! Friar Cuthbert!

FRIAR CUTHBERT.

Farewell, Prince!
I cannot stay to argue and convince.

PRINCE HENRY.

This is indeed the blessed Mary's land,
Virgin and Mother of our dear Redeemer!
All hearts are touched and softened at her name,
Alike the bandit, with the bloody hand,
The priest, the prince, the scholar, and the peasant,
The man of deeds, the visionary dreamer,
Pay homage to her as one ever present!
And even as children, who have much offended
A too indulgent father, in great shame,
Penitent, and yet not daring unattended
To go into his presence, at the gate
Speak with their sister, and confiding wait
Till she goes in before and intercedes;
So men, repenting of their evil deeds,
And yet not venturing rashly to draw near
With their requests an angry father's ear,
Offer to her their prayers and their confession,
And she for them in heaven makes intercession.
And if our Faith had given us nothing more
Than this example of all womanhood,
So mild, so merciful, so strong, so good,
So patient, peaceful, loyal, loving, pure,

This were enough to prove it higher and
    truer
Than all the creeds the world had known
    before.

PILGRIMS, *chanting afar off.*

Urbs cœlestis, urbs beata,
Supra petram collocata,
Urbs in portu satis tuto
De longinquo te saluto,
Te saluto, te suspiro,
Te affecto, te requiro !

THE INN AT GENOA.

A terrace overlooking the sea. Night.

PRINCE HENRY.

It is the sea, it is the sea,
In all its vague immensity,
Fading and darkening in the distance !
Silent, majestical, and slow,
The white ships haunt it to and fro,
With all their ghostly sails unfurled,
As phantoms from another world
Haunt the dim confines of existence !
But ah ! how few can comprehend
Their signals, or to what good end
From land to land they come and go !
Upon a sea more vast and dark
The spirits of the dead embark,
All voyaging to unknown coasts.
We wave our farewells from the shore,
And they depart, and come no more,
Or come as phantoms and as ghosts.

Above the darksome sea of death
Looms the great life that is to be,
A land of cloud and mystery,
A dim mirage, with shapes of men
Long dead, and passed beyond our ken.
Awe-struck we gaze, and hold our breath
Till the fair pageant vanisheth,
Leaving us in perplexity,
And doubtful whether it has been
A vision of the world unseen,
Or a bright image of our own
Against the sky in vapors thrown.

LUCIFER, *singing from the sea.*

Thou didst not make it, thou canst not
    mend it,
But thou hast the power to end it !
The sea is silent, the sea is discreet,

Deep it lies at thy very feet ;
There is no confessor like unto Death !
Thou canst not see him, but he is near ;
Thou needst not whisper above thy breath,
And he will hear ;
He will answer the questions,
The vague surmises and suggestions,
That fill thy soul with doubt and fear !

PRINCE HENRY.

The fisherman, who lies afloat,
With shadowy sail, in yonder boat,
Is singing softly to the Night !
But do I comprehend aright
The meaning of the words he sung
So sweetly in his native tongue ?
Ah yes ! the sea is still and deep.
All things within its bosom sleep !
A single step, and all is o'er ;
A plunge, a bubble, and no more ;
And thou, dear Elsie, wilt be free
From martyrdom and agony.

ELSIE, *coming from her chamber upon the terrace.*

The night is calm and cloudless,
And still as still can be,
And the stars come forth to listen
To the music of the sea.
They gather, and gather, and gather,
Until they crowd the sky,
And listen, in breathless silence,
To the solemn litany.
It begins in rocky caverns,
As a voice that chants alone
To the pedals of the organ
In monotonous undertone ;
And anon from shelving beaches,
And shallow sands beyond,
In snow-white robes uprising
The ghostly choirs respond.
And sadly and unceasing
The mournful voice sings on,
And the snow-white choirs still answer
Christe eleison !

PRINCE HENRY.

Angel of God ! thy finer sense perceives
Celestial and perpetual harmonies !
Thy purer soul, that trembles and believes,
Hears the archangel's trumpet in the
    breeze,
And where the forest rolls, or ocean heaves,
Cecilia's organ sounding in the seas,
And tongues of prophets speaking in the
    leaves.

But I hear discord only and despair,
And whispers as of demons in the air !

AT SEA.

IL PADRONE.

The wind upon our quarter lies,
And on before the freshening gale,
That fills the snow-white lateen sail,
Swiftly our light felucca flies.
Around, the billows burst and foam ;
They lift her o'er the sunken rock,
They beat her sides with many a shock,
And then upon their flowing dome
They poise her, like a weathercock !
Between us and the western skies
The hills of Corsica arise ;
Eastward, in yonder long blue line,
The summits of the Apennine,
And southward, and still far away,
Salerno, on its sunny bay
You cannot see it, where it lies.

PRINCE HENRY.

Ah, would that never more mine eyes
Might see its towers by night or day !

ELSIE.

Behind us, dark and awfully,
There comes a cloud out of the sea,
That bears the form of a hunted deer,
With hide of brown, and hoofs of black,
And antlers laid upon its back,
And fleeing fast and wild with fear,
As if the hounds were on its track !

PRINCE HENRY.

Lo ! while we gaze, it breaks and falls
In shapeless masses, like the walls
Of a burnt city.   Broad and red
The fires of the descending sun
Glare through the windows, and o'erhead,
Athwart the vapors, dense and dun,
Long shafts of silvery light arise,
Like rafters that support the skies !

ELSIE.

See ! from its summit the lurid levin
Flashes downward without warning,
As Lucifer, son of the morning,
Fell from the battlements of heaven !

IL PADRONE.

I must entreat you, friends, below !
The angry storm begins to blow,

For the weather changes with the moon.
All this morning, until noon,
We had baffling winds, and sudden flaws
Struck the sea with their cat's-paws.
Only a little hour ago
I was whistling to Saint Antonio
For a capful of wind to fill our sail,
And instead of a breeze he has sent a
    gale.
Last night I saw Saint Elmo's stars,
With their glimmering lanterns, all at play
On the tops of the masts and the tips of the
    spars,
And I knew we should have foul weather
    to-day.
Cheerily, my hearties ! yo heave ho !
Brail up the mainsail, and let her go
As the winds will and Saint Antonio !

Do you see that Livornese felucca,
That vessel to the windward yonder,
Running with her gunwale under ?
I was looking when the wind o'ertook her.
She had all sail set, and the only wonder
Is that at once the strength of the blast
Did not carry away her mast.
She is a galley of the Gran Duca,
That, through the fear of the Algerines,
Convoys those lazy brigantines,
Laden with wine and oil from Lucca.
Now all is ready, high and low ;
Blow, blow, good Saint Antonio !

Ha ! that is the first dash of the rain,
With a sprinkle of spray above the rails,
Just enough to moisten our sails,
And make them ready for the strain.
See how she leaps, as the blasts o'ertake her,
And speeds away with a bone in her mouth !
Now keep her head toward the south,
And there is no danger of bank or breaker.
With the breeze behind us, on we go ;
Not too much, good Saint Antonio !

VI

THE SCHOOL OF SALERNO

*A travelling Scholastic affixing his Theses to the
    gate of the College.*

SCHOLASTIC.

There, that is my gauntlet, my banner, my
    shield,
Hung up as a challenge to all the field !

One hundred and twenty-five propositions,
Which I will maintain with the sword of
   the tongue
Against all disputants, old and young.
Let us see if doctors or dialecticians
Will dare to dispute my definitions,
Or attack any one of my learned theses.
Here stand I ; the end shall be as God
   pleases.
I think I have proved, by profound re-
   searches,
The error of all those doctrines so vicious
Of the old Areopagite Dionysius,
That are making such terrible work in the
   churches,
By Michael the Stammerer sent from the
   East,
And done into Latin by that Scottish beast,
Johannes Duns Scotus, who dares to main-
   tain,
In the face of the truth, the error infer-
   nal,
That the universe is and must be eternal ;
At first laying down, as a fact fundamen-
   tal,
That nothing with God can be accidental ;
Then asserting that God before the crea-
   tion
Could not have existed, because it is plain
That, had He existed, He would have cre-
   ated ;
Which is begging the question that should
   be debated,
And moveth me less to anger than laugh-
   ter.
All nature, he holds, is a respiration
Of the Spirit of God, who, in breathing,
   hereafter
Will inhale it into his bosom again,
So that nothing but God alone will remain.
And therein he contradicteth himself ;
For he opens the whole discussion by stat-
   ing,
That God can only exist in creating.
That question I think I have laid on the
   shelf !

*He goes out. Two Doctors come in disputing,
   and followed by pupils.*

DOCTOR SERAFINO.

I, with the Doctor Seraphic, maintain,
That a word which is only conceived in the
   brain
Is a type of eternal Generation ;
The spoken word is the Incarnation.

DOCTOR CHERUBINO.

What do I care for the Doctor Seraphic,
With all his wordy chaffer and traffic ?

DOCTOR SERAFINO.

You make but a paltry show of resistance ;
Universals have no real existence !

DOCTOR CHERUBINO.

Your words are but idle and empty chatter ;
Ideas are eternally joined to matter !

DOCTOR SERAFINO.

May the Lord have mercy on your position,
You wretched, wrangling culler of herbs !

DOCTOR CHERUBINO.

May he send your soul to eternal perdition,
For your Treatise on the Irregular Verbs !
They rush out fighting. Two Scholars come in.

FIRST SCHOLAR.

Monte Cassino, then, is your College.
What think you of ours here at Salern ?

SECOND SCHOLAR.

To tell the truth, I arrived so lately,
I hardly yet have had time to discern.
So much, at least, I am bound to acknow-
   ledge :
The air seems healthy, the buildings stately,
And on the whole I like it greatly.

FIRST SCHOLAR.

Yes, the air is sweet ; the Calabrian hills
Send us down puffs of mountain air ;
And in summer-time the sea-breeze fills
With its coolness cloister, and court, and
   square.
Then at every season of the year
There are crowds of guests and travellers
   here ;
Pilgrims, and mendicant friars, and traders
From the Levant, with figs and wine,
And bands of wounded and sick Crusaders,
Coming back from Palestine.

SECOND SCHOLAR.

And what are the studies you pursue ?
What is the course you here go through ?

FIRST SCHOLAR.

The first three years of the college course
Are given to Logic alone, as the source
Of all that is noble, and wise, and true.

SECOND SCHOLAR.

That seems rather strange, I must confess,
In a Medical School ; yet, nevertheless,
You doubtless have reasons for that.

FIRST SCHOLAR.
Oh yes !
For none but a clever dialectician
Can hope to become a great physician ;
That has been settled long ago.
Logic makes an important part
Of the mystery of the healing art ;
For without it how could you hope to show
That nobody knows so much as you know ?
After this there are five years more
Devoted wholly to medicine,
With lectures on chirurgical lore,
And dissections of the bodies of swine,
As likest the human form divine.

SECOND SCHOLAR.

What are the books now most in vogue ?

FIRST SCHOLAR.

Quite an extensive catalogue ;
Mostly, however, books of our own ;
As Gariopontus' Passionarius,
And the writings of Matthew Platearius ;
And a volume universally known
As the Regimen of the School of Salern,
For Robert of Normandy written in terse
And very elegant Latin verse.
Each of these writings has its turn.
And when at length we have finished these,
Then comes the struggle for degrees,
With all the oldest and ablest critics ;
The public thesis and disputation,
Question, and answer, and explanation
Of a passage out of Hippocrates,
Or Aristotle's Analytics.
There the triumphant Magister stands !
A book is solemnly placed in his hands,
On which he swears to follow the rule
And ancient forms of the good old School ;
To report if any confectionarius
Mingles his drugs with matters various,
And to visit his patients twice a day,
And once in the night, if they live in town,
And if they are poor, to take no pay.
Having faithfully promised these,
His head is crowned with a laurel crown ;
A kiss on his cheek, a ring on his hand,
The Magister Artium et Physices
Goes forth from the school like a lord of
    the land.

And now, as we have the whole morning
    before us,
Let us go in, if you make no objection,
And listen awhile to a learned prelection
On Marcus Aurelius Cassiodorus.
    They go in. Enter LUCIFER *as a Doctor.*

LUCIFER.

This is the great School of Salern !
A land of wrangling and of quarrels,
Of brains that seethe, and hearts that burn,
Where every emulous scholar hears,
In every breath that comes to his ears,
The rustling of another's laurels !
The air of the place is called salubrious ;
The neighborhood of Vesuvius lends it
An odor volcanic, that rather mends it,
And the buildings have an aspect lugubrious,
That inspires a feeling of awe and terror
Into the heart of the beholder,
And befits such an ancient homestead of
    error,
Where the old falsehoods moulder and
    smoulder,
And yearly by many hundred hands
Are carried away, in the zeal of youth,
And sown like tares in the field of truth,
To blossom and ripen in other lands.

What have we here, affixed to the gate ?
The challenge of some scholastic wight,
Who wishes to hold a public debate
On sundry questions wrong or right !
Ah, now this is my great delight !
For I have often observed of late
That such discussions end in a fight.
Let us see what the learned wag maintains
With such a prodigal waste of brains.
    Reads.
" Whether angels in moving from place to
    place
Pass through the intermediate space.
Whether God himself is the author of evil,
Or whether that is the work of the Devil.
When, where, and wherefore Lucifer fell,
And whether he now is chained in hell."
I think I can answer that question well !
So long as the boastful human mind
Consents in such mills as this to grind,
I sit very firmly upon my throne !
Of a truth it almost makes me laugh,
To see men leaving the golden grain
To gather in piles the pitiful chaff
That old Peter Lombard thrashed with his
    brain,

To have it caught up and tossed again
On the horns of the Dumb Ox of Cologne !

But my guests approach ! there is in the air
A fragrance, like that of the Beautiful Garden
Of Paradise, in the days that were !
An odor of innocence and of prayer,
And of love, and faith that never fails,
Such as the fresh young heart exhales
Before it begins to wither and harden !
I cannot breathe such an atmosphere !
My soul is filled with a nameless fear,
That, after all my trouble and pain,
After all my restless endeavor,
The youngest, fairest soul of the twain,
The most ethereal, most divine,
Will escape from my hands for ever and ever.
But the other is already mine !
Let him live to corrupt his race,
Breathing among them, with every breath,
Weakness, selfishness, and the base
And pusillanimous fear of death.
I know his nature, and I know
That of all who in my ministry
Wander the great earth to and fro,
And on my errands come and go,
The safest and subtlest are such as he.

Enter PRINCE HENRY *and* ELSIE, *with attendants.*

PRINCE HENRY.

Can you direct us to Friar Angelo ?

LUCIFER.

He stands before you.

PRINCE HENRY.
                        Then you know our purpose
I am Prince Henry of Hoheneck, and this
The maiden that I spake of in my letters.

LUCIFER.

It is a very grave and solemn business !
We must not be precipitate. Does she
Without compulsion, of her own free will,
Consent to this ?

PRINCE HENRY.
                        Against all opposition,
Against all prayers, entreaties, protestations.
She will not be persuaded.

LUCIFER.
                        That is strange !
Have you thought well of it ?

ELSIE.
                        I come not here
To argue, but to die. Your business is not
To question, but to kill me. I am ready.
I am impatient to be gone from here
Ere any thoughts of earth disturb again
The spirit of tranquillity within me.

PRINCE HENRY.

Would I had not come here ! Would I were dead,
And thou wert in thy cottage in the forest,
And hadst not known me ! Why have I done this ?
Let me go back and die.

ELSIE.
                        It cannot be ;
Not if these cold, flat stones on which we tread
Were coulters heated white, and yonder gateway
Flamed like a furnace with a sevenfold heat.
I must fulfil my purpose.

PRINCE HENRY.
                        I forbid it !
Not one step further. For I only meant
To put thus far thy courage to the proof.
It is enough. I, too, have strength to die,
For thou hast taught me !

ELSIE.
                        O my Prince ! remember
Your promises. Let me fulfil my errand.
You do not look on life and death as I do.
There are two angels, that attend unseen
Each one of us, and in great books record
Our good and evil deeds. He who writes down
The good ones, after every action closes
His volume, and ascends with it to God.
The other keeps his dreadful day-book open
Till sunset, that we may repent ; which doing,
The record of the action fades away,
And leaves a line of white across the page.
Now if my act be good, as I believe,

It cannot be recalled.   It is already
Sealed up in heaven, as a good deed accomplished.
The rest is yours.   Why wait you?   I am ready.
                To her attendants.
Weep not, my friends! rather rejoice with me.
I shall not feel the pain, but shall be gone,
And you will have another friend in heaven.
Then start not at the creaking of the door
Through which I pass.   I see what lies beyond it.
                To PRINCE HENRY.
And you, O Prince! bear back my benison
Unto my father's house, and all within it.
This morning in the church I prayed for them,
After confession, after absolution,
When my whole soul was white, I prayed for them.
God will take care of them, they need me not.
And in your life let my remembrance linger,
As something not to trouble and disturb it,
But to complete it, adding life to life.
And if at times beside the evening fire
You see my face among the other faces,
Let it not be regarded as a ghost
That haunts your house, but as a guest that loves you.
Nay, even as one of your own family,
Without whose presence there were something wanting.
I have no more to say.   Let us go in.

                PRINCE HENRY.

Friar Angelo!   I charge you on your life,
Believe not what she says, for she is mad,
And comes here not to die, but to be healed.

                ELSIE.

Alas! Prince Henry!

                LUCIFER.

                Come with me; this way.
ELSIE *goes in with* LUCIFER, *who thrusts* PRINCE
        HENRY *back and closes the door.*

                PRINCE HENRY.

Gone! and the light of all my life gone with her!
A sudden darkness falls upon the world!

Oh, what a vile and abject thing am I
That purchase length of days at such a cost!
Not by her death alone, but by the death
Of all that's good and true and noble in me!
All manhood, excellence, and self-respect,
All love, and faith, and hope, and heart are dead!
All my divine nobility of nature
By this one act is forfeited forever.
I am a Prince in nothing but in name!
                To the attendants.
Why did you let this horrible deed be done?
Why did you not lay hold on her, and keep her
From self-destruction?   Angelo! murderer!
        Struggles at the door, but cannot open it.

                ELSIE, *within.*
Farewell, dear Prince! farewell!

                PRINCE HENRY.
                        Unbar the door!

                LUCIFER.
It is too late!

                PRINCE HENRY.
                It shall not be too late!
        They burst the door open and rush in.

THE FARM-HOUSE IN THE ODENWALD.

URSULA *spinning.   A summer afternoon.   A
        table spread.*

                URSULA.

I have marked it well, — it must be true, —
Death never takes one alone, but two!
Whenever he enters in at a door,
Under roof of gold or roof of thatch,
He always leaves it upon the latch,
And comes again ere the year is o'er.
Never one of a household only!
Perhaps it is a mercy of God,
Lest the dead there under the sod,
In the land of strangers, should be lonely!
Ah me! I think I am lonelier here!
It is hard to go, — but harder to stay!
Were it not for the children, I should pray
That Death would take me within the year!
And Gottlieb! — he is at work all day,

In the sunny field, or the forest murk,
But I know that his thoughts are far away,
I know that his heart is not in his work !
And when he comes home to me at night
He is not cheery, but sits and sighs,
And I see the great tears in his eyes,
And try to be cheerful for his sake.
Only the children's hearts are light.
Mine is weary, and ready to break.
God help us ! I hope we have done right ;
We thought we were acting for the best !
        Looking through the open door.
Who is it coming under the trees ?
A man, in the Prince's livery dressed !
He looks about him with doubtful face,
As if uncertain of the place.
He stops at the beehives ; — now he sees
The garden gate ; — he is going past !
Can he be afraid of the bees ?
No ; he is coming in at last !
He fills my heart with strange alarm !
        Enter a Forester.

FORESTER.

Is this the tenant Gottlieb's farm ?

URSULA.

This is his farm, and I his wife.
Pray sit. What may your business be !

FORESTER.

News from the Prince !

URSULA.

                    Of death or life ?

FORESTER.

You put your questions eagerly !

URSULA.

Answer me, then !   How is the Prince ?

FORESTER.

I left him only two hours since
Homeward returning down the river,
As strong and well as if God, the Giver,
Had given him back his youth again.

URSULA, *despairing.*

Then Elsie, my poor child, is dead !

FORESTER.

That, my good woman, I have not said.
Don't cross the bridge till you come to it,
Is a proverb old, and of excellent wit.

URSULA.

Keep me no longer in this pain !

FORESTER.

It is true your daughter is no more ; —
That is, the peasant she was before.

URSULA.

Alas ! I am simple and lowly bred,
I am poor, distracted, and forlorn.
And it is not well that you of the court
Should mock me thus, and make a sport
Of a joyless mother whose child is dead,
For you, too, were of mother born !

FORESTER.

Your daughter lives, and the Prince is well !
You will learn erelong how it all befell.
Her heart for a moment never failed ;
But when they reached Salerno's gate,
The Prince's nobler self prevailed,
And saved her for a noble fate.
And he was healed, in his despair,
By the touch of St. Matthew's sacred
        bones ;
Though I think the long ride in the open
        air,
That pilgrimage over stocks and stones,
In the miracle must come in for a share !

URSULA.

Virgin ! who lovest the poor and lowly,
If the loud cry of a mother's heart
Can ever ascend to where thou art,
Into thy blessed hands and holy
Receive my prayer of praise and thanks-
        giving !
Let the hands that bore our Saviour bear it
Into the awful presence of God ;
For thy feet with holiness are shod,
And if thou bearest it He will hear it.
Our child who was dead again is living !

FORESTER.

I did not tell you she was dead ;
If you thought so 't was no fault of mine ;
At this very moment, while I speak,
They are sailing homeward down the
        Rhine,
In a splendid barge, with golden prow,
And decked with banners white and red
As the colors on your daughter's cheek.
They call her the Lady Alicia now ;
For the Prince in Salerno made a vow
That Elsie only would he wed.

URSULA.

Jesu Maria ! what a change !
All seems to me so weird and strange !

FORESTER.

I saw her standing on the deck,
Beneath an awning cool and shady ;
Her cap of velvet could not hold
The tresses of her hair of gold,
That flowed and floated like the stream,
And fell in masses down her neck.
As fair and lovely did she seem
As in a story or a dream
Some beautiful and foreign lady.
And the Prince looked so grand and
    proud,
And waved his hand thus to the crowd
That gazed and shouted from the shore,
All down the river, long and loud.

URSULA.

We shall behold our child once more ;
She is not dead ! She is not dead !
God, listening, must have overheard
The prayers, that, without sound or word,
Our hearts in secrecy have said !
Oh, bring me to her ; for mine eyes
Are hungry to behold her face ;
My very soul within me cries ;
My very hands seem to caress her,
To see her, gaze at her, and bless her ;
Dear Elsie, child of God and grace !
    Goes out toward the garden.

FORESTER.

There goes the good woman out of her
    head ;
And Gottlieb's supper is waiting here ;
A very capacious flagon of beer,
And a very portentous loaf of bread.
One would say his grief did not much op-
    press him.
Here 's to the health of the Prince, God
    bless him !

He drinks.

Ha ! it buzzes and stings like a hornet !
And what a scene there, through the
    door !
The forest behind and the garden be-
    fore,
And midway an old man of threescore,
With a wife and children that caress
    him.

Let me try still further to cheer and adorn
    it
With a merry, echoing blast of my cornet !
    Goes out blowing his horn.

THE CASTLE OF VAUTSBERG ON THE
RHINE.

PRINCE HENRY *and* ELSIE *standing on the ter-
    race at evening.*

The sound of bells heard from a distance.

PRINCE HENRY.

We are alone. The wedding guests
Ride down the hill, with plumes and cloaks,
And the descending dark invests
The Niederwald, and all the nests
Among its hoar and haunted oaks.

ELSIE.

What bells are those, that ring so slow,
So mellow, musical, and low ?

PRINCE HENRY.

They are the bells of Geisenheim,
That with their melancholy chime
Ring out the curfew of the sun.

ELSIE.

Listen, beloved.

PRINCE HENRY.

They are done !
Dear Elsie ! many years ago
Those same soft bells at eventide
Rang in the ears of Charlemagne,
As, seated by Fastrada's side
At Ingelheim, in all his pride
He heard their sound with secret pain.

ELSIE.

Their voices only speak to me
Of peace and deep tranquillity,
And endless confidence in thee !

PRINCE HENRY.

Thou knowest the story of her ring,
How, when the court went back to Aix,
Fastrada died ; and how the king
Sat watching by her night and day,
Till into one of the blue lakes,
Which water that delicious land,
They cast the ring, drawn from her hand :
And the great monarch sat serene

And sad beside the fated shore,
Nor left the land forevermore.

ELSIE.

That was true love.

PRINCE HENRY.

For him the queen
Ne'er did what thou hast done for me.

ELSIE.

Wilt thou as fond and faithful be ?
Wilt thou so love me after death ?

PRINCE HENRY.

In life's delight, in death's dismay,
In storm and sunshine, night and day,
In health, in sickness, in decay,
Here and hereafter, I am thine !
Thou hast Fastrada's ring. Beneath
The calm, blue waters of thine eyes,
Deep in thy steadfast soul it lies,
And, undisturbed by this world's breath,
With magic light its jewels shine !
This golden ring, which thou hast worn
Upon thy finger since the morn,
Is but a symbol and a semblance,
An outward fashion, a remembrance,
Of what thou wearest within unseen,
O my Fastrada, O my queen !
Behold ! the hill-tops all aglow
With purple and with amethyst ;
While the whole valley deep below
Is filled, and seems to overflow,
With a fast-rising tide of mist.
The evening air grows damp and chill ;
Let us go in.

ELSIE.

Ah, not so soon.
See yonder fire ! It is the moon
Slow rising o'er the eastern hill.
It glimmers on the forest tips,
And through the dewy foliage drips
In little rivulets of light,
And makes the heart in love with night.

PRINCE HENRY.

Oft on this terrace, when the day
Was closing, have I stood and gazed,
And seen the landscape fade away,
And the white vapors rise and drown
Hamlet and vineyard, tower and town,
While far above the hill-tops blazed.
But then another hand than thine
Was gently held and clasped in mine ;

Another head upon my breast
Was laid, as thine is now, at rest.
Why dost thou lift those tender eyes
With so much sorrow and surprise ?
A minstrel's, not a maiden's hand,
Was that which in my own was pressed.
A manly form usurped thy place,
A beautiful, but bearded face,
That now is in the Holy Land,
Yet in my memory from afar
Is shining on us like a star.
But linger not. For while I speak,
A sheeted spectre white and tall,
The cold mist climbs the castle wall,
And lays his hand upon thy cheek !

They go in.

EPILOGUE

THE TWO RECORDING ANGELS AS-CENDING

THE ANGEL OF GOOD DEEDS, *with closed book.*

God sent his messenger the rain,
And said unto the mountain brook,
" Rise up, and from thy caverns look
And leap, with naked, snow-white feet,
From the cool hills into the heat
Of the broad, arid plain."

God sent his messenger of faith,
And whispered in the maiden's heart,
" Rise up, and look from where thou
          art,
And scatter with unselfish hands
Thy freshness on the barren sands
And solitudes of Death."

O beauty of holiness,
Of self-forgetfulness, of lowliness !
O power of meekness,
Whose very gentleness and weakness
Are like the yielding, but irresistible air !
Upon the pages
Of the sealed volume that I bear,
The deed divine
Is written in characters of gold,
That never shall grow old,
But through all ages
Burn and shine,
With soft effulgence !
O God ! it is thy indulgence
That fills the world with the bliss
Of a good deed like this !

THE ANGEL OF EVIL DEEDS, *with open book.*

Not yet, not yet
Is the red sun wholly set,
But evermore recedes,
While open still I bear
The Book of Evil Deeds,
To let the breathings of the upper air
Visit its pages and erase
The records from its face !
Fainter and fainter as I gaze
In the broad blaze
The glimmering landscape shines,
And below me the black river
Is hidden by wreaths of vapor !
Fainter and fainter the black lines
Begin to quiver
Along the whitening surface of the paper ;
Shade after shade
The terrible words grow faint and fade,
And in their place
Runs a white space !

Down goes the sun !
But the soul of one,
Who by repentance
Hath escaped the dreadful sentence,
Shines bright below me as I look.
It is the end !
With closèd Book
'To God do I ascend.
Lo ! over the mountain steeps
A dark, gigantic shadow sweeps
Beneath my feet ;
A blackness inwardly brightening
With sullen heat,
As a storm-cloud lurid with lightning.
And a cry of lamentation,
Repeated and again repeated,
Deep and loud
As the reverberation
Of cloud answering unto cloud,
Swells and rolls away in the distance,
As if the sheeted
Lightning retreated,
Baffled and thwarted by the wind's resist-
ance.

It is Lucifer,
The son of mystery ;
And since God suffers him to be,
He, too, is God's minister,
And labors for some good
By us not understood !

SECOND INTERLUDE

MARTIN LUTHER

A CHAMBER IN THE WARTBURG. MORN-
ING. MARTIN LUTHER WRITING

MARTIN LUTHER.

Our God, a Tower of Strength is He,
A goodly wall and weapon ;
From all our need He helps us free,
That now to us doth happen.
    The old evil foe
    Doth in earnest grow,
    In grim armor dight,
    Much guile and great might ;
On earth there is none like him.

OH yes ; a tower of strength indeed,
A present help in all our need,
A sword and buckler is our God.
Innocent men have walked unshod
O'er burning ploughshares, and have trod
Unharmed on serpents in their path,
And laughed to scorn the Devil's wrath !

Safe in this Wartburg tower I stand
Where God hath led me by the hand,
And look down, with a heart at ease,
Over the pleasant neighborhoods,
Over the vast Thuringian Woods,
With flash of river, and gloom of trees,
With castles crowning the dizzy heights,
And farms and pastoral delights,
And the morning pouring everywhere
Its golden glory on the air.
Safe, yes, safe am I here at last,
Safe from the overwhelming blast
Of the mouths of Hell, that followed me
        fast,
And the howling demons of despair
That hunted me like a beast to his lair.

    Of our own might we nothing can ;
    We soon are unprotected ;
    There fighteth for us the right Man,
    Whom God himself elected.
        Who is He ; ye exclaim ?
        Christus is his name,
        Lord of Sabaoth,
        Very God in troth ;
    The field He holds forever.

Nothing can vex the Devil more
Than the name of Him whom we adore.

Therefore doth it delight me best
To stand in the choir among the rest,
With the great organ trumpeting
Through its metallic tubes, and sing :
Et verbum caro factum est !
These words the Devil cannot endure,
For he knoweth their meaning well !
Him they trouble and repel,
Us they comfort and allure,
And happy it were, if our delight
Were as great as his affright !

Yea, music is the Prophets' art ;
Among the gifts that God hath sent,
One of the most magnificent !
It calms the agitated heart ;
Temptations, evil thoughts, and all
The passions that disturb the soul,
Are quelled by its divine control,
As the Evil Spirit fled from Saul,
And his distemper was allayed,
When David took his harp and played.

> This world may full of Devils be,
> All ready to devour us;
> Yet not so sore afraid are we,
> They shall not overpower us.
>   This World's Prince, howe'er
>   Fierce he may appear,
>   He can harm us not,
>   He is doomed, God wot!
> One little word can slay him!

Incredible it seems to some
And to myself a mystery,
That such weak flesh and blood as we,
Armed with no other shield or sword,
Or other weapon than the Word,
Should combat and should overcome
A spirit powerful as he !
He summons forth the Pope of Rome
With all his diabolic crew,
His shorn and shaven retinue
Of priests and children of the dark ;
Kill ! kill ! they cry, the Heresiarch,
Who rouseth up all Christendom
Against us ; and at one fell blow
Seeks the whole Church to overthrow !
Not yet ; my hour is not yet come.

Yesterday in an idle mood,
Hunting with others in the wood,
I did not pass the hours in vain,
For in the very heart of all
The joyous tumult raised around,
Shouting of men, and baying of hound,

And the bugle's blithe and cheery call,
And echoes answering back again,
From crags of the distant mountain
    chain, —
In the very heart of this, I found
A mystery of grief and pain.
It was an image of the power
Of Satan, hunting the world about,
With his nets and traps and well-trained
    dogs,
His bishops and priests and theologues,
And all the rest of the rabble rout,
Seeking whom he may devour !
Enough I have had of hunting hares,
Enough of these hours of idle mirth,
Enough of nets and traps and gins !
The only hunting of any worth
Is where I can pierce with javelins
The cunning foxes and wolves and bears,
The whole iniquitous troop of beasts,
The Roman Pope and the Roman priests
That sorely infest and afflict the earth !

Ye nuns, ye singing birds of the air !
The fowler hath caught you in his snare,
And keeps you safe in his gilded cage,
Singing the song that never tires,
To lure down others from their nests ;
How ye flutter and beat your breasts,
Warm and soft with young desires
Against the cruel, pitiless wires,
Reclaiming your lost heritage !
Behold ! a hand unbars the door,
Ye shall be captives held no more.

> The Word they shall perforce let stand,
> And little thanks they merit!
> For He is with us in the land,
> With gifts of his own Spirit!
>   Though they take our life,
>   Goods, honors, child and wife,
>   Let these pass away,
>   Little gain have they;
> The Kingdom still remaineth !

Yea, it remaineth forevermore,
However Satan may rage and roar,
Though often he whispers in my ears :
What if thy doctrines false should be ?
And wrings from me a bitter sweat.
Then I put him to flight with jeers,
Saying : Saint Satan ! pray for me ;
If thou thinkest I am not saved yet !

And my mortal foes that lie in wait
In every avenue and gate !

As to that odious monk John Tetzel,
Hawking about his hollow wares
Like a huckster at village fairs,
And those mischievous fellows, Wetzel,
Campanus, Carlstadt, Martin Cellarius,
And all the busy, multifarious
Heretics, and disciples of Arius,
Half-learned, dunce-bold, dry and hard,
They are not worthy of my regard,
Poor and humble as I am.

But ah ! Erasmus of Rotterdam,
He is the vilest miscreant
That ever walked this world below !
A Momus, making his mock and mow,
At Papist and at Protestant,
Sneering at St. John and St. Paul,
At God and Man, at one and all ;
And yet as hollow and false and drear,
As a cracked pitcher to the ear,
And ever growing worse and worse !
Whenever I pray, I pray for a curse
On Erasmus, the Insincere !

Philip Melancthon ! thou alone
Faithful among the faithless known,
Thee I hail, and only thee !
Behold the record of us three !
    Res et verba Philippus,
    Res sine verbis Lutherus ;
    Erasmus verba sine re !

My Philip, prayest thou for me ?
Lifted above all earthly care,
From these high regions of the air,
Among the birds that day and night
Upon the branches of tall trees
Sing their lauds and litanies,
Praising God with all their might,
My Philip, unto thee I write.

My Philip ! thou who knowest best
All that is passing in this breast ;
The spiritual agonies,
The inward deaths, the inward hell,
And the divine new births as well,
That surely follow after these,
As after winter follows spring ;
My Philip, in the night-time sing
This song of the Lord I send to thee ;
And I will sing it for thy sake,
Until our answering voices make
A glorious antiphony,
And choral chant of victory !

PART THREE

THE NEW ENGLAND TRAGEDIES

JOHN ENDICOTT

DRAMATIS PERSONÆ

JOHN ENDICOTT	Governor.
JOHN ENDICOTT	His son.
RICHARD BELLINGHAM	Deputy Governor.
JOHN NORTON	Minister of the Gospel.
EDWARD BUTTER	Treasurer.
WALTER MERRY	Tithing-man.
NICHOLAS UPSALL	An old citizen.
SAMUEL COLE	Landlord of the Three Mariners.
SIMON KEMPTHORN } RALPH GOLDSMITH }	Sea-Captains.
WENLOCK CHRISTISON } EDITH, his daughter } EDWARD WHARTON }	Quakers.

Assistants, Halberdiers, Marshal, etc.

The Scene is in Boston in the year 1665.

PROLOGUE

TO-NIGHT we strive to read, as we may best,
This city, like an ancient palimpsest ;
And bring to light, upon the blotted page,
The mournful record of an earlier age,
That, pale and half effaced, lies hidden
    away
Beneath the fresher writing of to-day.

Rise, then, O buried city that hast been ;
Rise up, rebuilded in the painted scene,
And let our curious eyes behold once more
The pointed gable and the pent-house door,
The Meeting-house with leaden-latticed
    panes,
The narrow thoroughfares, the crooked
    lanes !

Rise, too, ye shapes and shadows of the
    Past,
Rise from your long-forgotten graves at
    last ;
Let us behold your faces, let us hear
The words ye uttered in those days of fear !
Revisit your familiar haunts again, —
The scenes of triumph, and the scenes of
    pain,
And leave the footprints of your bleeding
    feet
Once more upon the pavement of the
    street !

Nor let the Historian blame the Poet
here,
If he perchance misdate the day or year,
And group events together, by his art,
That in the Chronicles lie far apart ;
For as the double stars, though sundered
far,
Seem to the naked eye a single star,
So facts of history, at a distance seen,
Into one common point of light convene.

" Why touch upon such themes ? " perhaps
some friend
May ask, incredulous ; " and to what good
end ?
Why drag again into the light of day
The errors of an age long passed away ? "
I answer : " For the lesson that they
teach :
The tolerance of opinion and of speech.
Hope, Faith, and Charity remain, — these
three ;
And greatest of them all is Charity."

Let us remember, if these words be true,
That unto all men Charity is due ;
Give what we ask ; and pity, while we
blame,
Lest we become copartners in the shame,
Lest we condemn, and yet ourselves par-
take,
And persecute the dead for conscience'
sake.

Therefore it is the author seeks and strives
To represent the dead as in their lives,
And lets at times his characters unfold
Their thoughts in their own language,
strong and bold ;
He only asks of you to do the like ;
To hear him first, and, if you will, then
strike.

ACT I

SCENE I. — *Sunday afternoon. The interior of
the Meeting-house. On the pulpit, an hour-
glass ; below, a box for contributions.* JOHN
NORTON *in the pulpit.* GOVERNOR ENDICOTT
*in a canopied seat, attended by four halberd-
iers. The congregation singing.*

The Lord descended from above,
And bowed the heavens high ;
And underneath his feet He cast
The darkness of the sky.

On Cherubim and Seraphim
Right royally He rode,
And on the wings of mighty winds
Came flying all abroad.

NORTON (*rising and turning the hour-glass on the
pulpit*).
I heard a great voice from the temple say-
ing
Unto the Seven Angels, Go your ways ;
Pour out the vials of the wrath of God
Upon the earth. And the First Angel went
And poured his vial on the earth ; and
straight
There fell a noisome and a grievous sore
On them which had the birth-mark of the
Beast,
And them which worshipped and adored
his image.
On us hath fallen this grievous pestilence.
There is a sense of terror in the air ;
And apparitions of things horrible
Are seen by many. From the sky above us
The stars fall ; and beneath us the earth
quakes !
The sound of drums at midnight from afar,
The sound of horsemen riding to and fro,
As if the gates of the invisible world
Were opened, and the dead came forth to
warn us, —
All these are omens of some dire disaster
Impending over us, and soon to fall.
Moreover, in the language of the Prophet,
Death is again come up into our windows,
To cut off little children from without,
And young men from the streets. And in
the midst
Of all these supernatural threats and warn-
ings
Doth Heresy uplift its horrid head ;
A vision of Sin more awful and appalling
Than any phantasm, ghost, or apparition,
As arguing and portending some enlarge-
ment
Of the mysterious Power of Darkness !

EDITH, *barefooted, and clad in sackcloth, with
her hair hanging loose upon her shoulders, walks
slowly up the aisle, followed by* WHARTON *and
other Quakers. The congregation starts up in
confusion.*

EDITH (*to* NORTON, *raising her hand*).
Peace !

NORTON.
Anathema maranatha ! The Lord cometh !

EDITH.

Yea, verily He cometh, and shall judge
The shepherds of Israel who do feed them-
    selves,
And leave their flocks to eat what they
    have trodden
Beneath their feet.

NORTON.

            Be silent, babbling woman !
St. Paul commands all women to keep
    silence
Within the churches.

EDITH.

            Yet the women prayed
And prophesied at Corinth in his day ;
And, among those on whom the fiery
    tongues
Of Pentecost descended, some were women !

NORTON.

The Elders of the Churches, by our law,
Alone have power to open the doors of
    speech
And silence in the Assembly. I command
    you !

EDITH.

The law of God is greater than your laws !
Ye build your church with blood, your town
    with crime ;
The heads thereof give judgment for re-
    ward ;
The priests thereof teach only for their
    hire ;
Your laws condemn the innocent to death ;
And against this I bear my testimony !

NORTON.

What testimony ?

EDITH.

            That of the Holy Spirit,
Which, as your Calvin says, surpasseth
    reason.

NORTON.

The laborer is worthy of his hire.

EDITH.

Yet our great Master did not teach for
    hire,
And the Apostles without purse or scrip
Went forth to do his work. Behold this
    box

Beneath thy pulpit. Is it for the poor ?
Thou canst not answer. It is for the
    Priest ;
And against this I bear my testimony.

NORTON.

Away with all these Heretics and Quakers !
Quakers, forsooth ! Because a quaking
    fell
On Daniel, at beholding of the Vision,
Must ye needs shake and quake ? Because
    Isaiah
Went stripped and barefoot, must ye wail
    and howl ?
Must ye go stripped and naked ? must ye
    make
A wailing like the dragons, and a mourn-
    ing
As of the owls ? Ye verify the adage
That Satan is God's ape ! Away with
    them !

*Tumult. The Quakers are driven out with vio-
    lence, EDITH following slowly. The congrega-
    tion retires in confusion.*

Thus freely do the Reprobates commit
Such measure of iniquity as fits them
For the intended measure of God's wrath,
And even in violating God's commands
Are they fulfilling the divine decree !
The will of man is but an instrument
Disposed and predetermined to its action
According unto the decree of God,
Being as much subordinate thereto
As is the axe unto the hewer's hand !

He descends from the pulpit, and joins GOVERNOR
    ENDICOTT, *who comes forward to meet him.*

The omens and the wonders of the time,
Famine, and fire, and shipwreck, and dis-
    ease,
The blast of corn, the death of our young
    men,
Our sufferings in all precious, pleasant
    things,
Are manifestations of the wrath divine,
Signs of God's controversy with New Eng-
    land.
These emissaries of the Evil One,
These servants and ambassadors of Satan,
Are but commissioned executioners
Of God's vindictive and deserved displea-
    sure.
We must receive them as the Roman
    Bishop
Once received Attila, saying, I rejoice
You have come safe, whom I esteem to be

The scourge of God, sent to chastise his
    people.
This very heresy, perchance, may serve
The purposes of God to some good end.
With you I leave it ; but do not neglect
The holy tactics of the civil sword.

ENDICOTT.

And what more can be done ?

NORTON.

                        The hand that cut
The Red Cross from the colors of the king
Can cut the red heart from this heresy.
Fear not.   All blasphemies immediate
And heresies turbulent must be suppressed
By civil power.

ENDICOTT.

        But in what way suppressed ?

NORTON.

The Book of Deuteronomy declares
That if thy son, thy daughter, or thy wife,
Ay, or the friend which is as thine own
    soul,
Entice thee secretly, and say to thee,
Let us serve other gods, then shall thine
    eye
Not pity him, but thou shalt surely kill
    him,
And thine own hand shall be the first upon
    him
To slay him.

ENDICOTT.

                Four already have been slain ;
And others banished upon pain of death.
But they come back again to meet their
    doom,
Bringing the linen for their winding-sheets.
We must not go too far.   In truth, I
    shrink
From shedding of more blood.   The peo-
    ple murmur
At our severity.

NORTON.

                Then let them murmur !
Truth is relentless ; justice never wavers ;
The greatest firmness is the greatest
    mercy ;
The noble order of the Magistracy
Cometh immediately from God, and yet
This noble order of the Magistracy
Is by these Heretics despised and out-
    raged.

ENDICOTT.

To-night they sleep in prison.   If they die,
They cannot say that we have caused their
    death.
We do but guard the passage, with the
    sword
Pointed towards them ; if they dash upon
    it,
Their blood will be on their own heads, not
    ours.

NORTON.

Enough.   I ask no more.   My predecessor
Coped only with the milder heresies
Of Antinomians and of Anabaptists.
He was not born to wrestle with these
    fiends.
Chrysostom in his pulpit ; Augustine
In disputation ; Timothy in his house !
The lantern of St. Botolph's ceased to burn
When from the portals of that church he
    came
To be a burning and a shining light
Here in the wilderness.   And, as he lay
On his death-bed, he saw me in a vision
Ride on a snow-white horse into this town.
His vision was prophetic ; thus I came,
A terror to the impenitent, and Death
On the pale horse of the Apocalypse
To all the accursed race of Heretics !
                            [Exeunt.

SCENE II. — A street.   On one side, NICHO-
    LAS UPSALL'S house ; on the other, WALTER
    MERRY'S, with a flock of pigeons on the roof.
    UPSALL seated in the porch of his house.

UPSALL.

O day of rest !   How beautiful, how fair,
How welcome to the weary and the old !
Day of the Lord ! and truce to earthly
    cares !
Day of the Lord, as all our days should
    be !
Ah, why will man by his austerities
Shut out the blessed sunshine and the light,
And make of thee a dungeon of despair !

WALTER MERRY (entering and looking round
                    him).

All silent as a graveyard !   No one stir-
    ring ;
No footfall in the street, no sound of
    voices !
By righteous punishment and perseverance,
And perseverance in that punishment,

At last I have brought this contumacious town
To strict observance of the Sabbath day.
Those wanton gospellers, the pigeons yonder,
Are now the only Sabbath-breakers left.
I cannot put them down. As if to taunt me,
They gather every Sabbath afternoon
In noisy congregation on my roof,
Billing and cooing. Whir! take that, ye Quakers.

Throws a stone at the pigeons. Sees UPSALL.

Ah! Master Nicholas!

UPSALL.
Good afternoon,
Dear neighbor Walter.

MERRY.
Master Nicholas,
You have to-day withdrawn yourself from meeting.

UPSALL.

Yea, I have chosen rather to worship God
Sitting in silence here at my own door.

MERRY.

Worship the Devil! You this day have broken
Three of our strictest laws. First, by abstaining
From public worship. Secondly, by walking
Profanely on the Sabbath.

UPSALL.
Not one step.
I have been sitting still here, seeing the pigeons
Feed in the street and fly about the roofs.

MERRY.

You have been in the street with other intent
Than going to and from the Meeting-house.
And, thirdly, you are harboring Quakers here.
I am amazed!

UPSALL.
Men sometimes, it is said,
Entertain angels unawares.

MERRY.
Nice angels!
Angels in broad-brimmed hats and russet cloaks,
The color of the Devil's nutting-bag! They came
Into the Meeting-house this afternoon
More in the shape of devils than of angels.
The women screamed and fainted; and the boys
Made such an uproar in the gallery
I could not keep them quiet.

UPSALL.
Neighbor Walter,
Your persecution is of no avail.

MERRY.
'T is prosecution, as the Governor says,
Not persecution.

UPSALL.
Well, your prosecution;
Your hangings do no good.

MERRY.
The reason is,
We do not hang enough. But, mark my words,
We'll scour them; yea, I warrant ye, we'll scour them!
And now go in and entertain your angels,
And don't be seen here in the street again
Till after sundown! — There they are again!

Exit UPSALL. MERRY *throws another stone at the pigeons, and then goes into his house.*

SCENE III. — *A room in* UPSALL'S *house. Night.* EDITH, WHARTON, *and other Quakers seated at a table.* UPSALL *seated near them. Several books on the table.*

WHARTON.

William and Marmaduke, our martyred brothers,
Sleep in untimely graves, if aught untimely
Can find place in the providence of God,
Where nothing comes too early or too late.
I saw their noble death. They to the scaffold
Walked hand in hand. Two hundred armèd men
And many horsemen guarded them, for fear
Of rescue by the crowd, whose hearts were stirred.

EDITH.

O holy martyrs !

WHARTON.

When they tried to speak,
Their voices by the roll of drums were
drowned.
When they were dead they still looked
fresh and fair,
The terror of death was not upon their
faces.
Our sister Mary, likewise, the meek woman,
Has passed through martyrdom to her re-
ward ;
Exclaiming, as they led her to her death,
"These many days I've been in Paradise."
And, when she died, Priest Wilson threw
the hangman
His handkerchief, to cover the pale face
He dared not look upon.

EDITH.

As persecuted,
Yet not forsaken ; as unknown, yet known ;
As dying, and behold we are alive ;
As sorrowful, and yet rejoicing always ;
As having nothing, yet possessing all !

WHARTON.

And Leddra, too, is dead. But from his
prison,
The day before his death, he sent these
words
Unto the little flock of Christ : "Whatever
May come upon the followers of the
Light, —
Distress, affliction, famine, nakedness,
Or perils in the city or the sea,
Or persecution, or even death itself, —
I am persuaded that God's armor of Light,
As it is loved and lived in, will preserve
you.
Yea, death itself ; through which you will
find entrance
Into the pleasant pastures of the fold,
Where you shall feed forever as the herds
That roam at large in the low valleys of
Achor.
And as the flowing of the ocean fills
Each creek and branch thereof, and then
retires,
Leaving behind a sweet and wholesome
savor ;
So doth the virtue and the life of God
Flow evermore into the hearts of those

Whom he hath made partakers of his
nature ;
And, when it but withdraws itself a little,
Leaves a sweet savor after it, that many
Can say they are made clean by every word
That He hath spoken to them in their
silence."

EDITH (rising and breaking into a kind of chant).

Truly we do but grope here in the dark,
Near the partition-wall of Life and Death,
At every moment dreading or desiring
To lay our hands upon the unseen door !
Let us, then, labor for an inward stillness, —
An inward stillness and an inward healing ;
That perfect silence where the lips and
heart
Are still, and we no longer entertain
Our own imperfect thoughts and vain opin-
ions,
But God alone speaks in us, and we wait
In singleness of heart, that we may know
His will, and in the silence of our spirits,
That we may do His will, and do that only !

A long pause, interrupted by the sound of a drum
approaching ; then shouts in the street, and a
loud knocking at the door.

MARSHAL.

Within there ! Open the door !

MERRY.

Will no one answer ?

MARSHAL.

In the King's name ! Within there !

MERRY.

Open the door !

UPSALL (from the window).

It is not barred. Come in. Nothing pre-
vents you.
The poor man's door is ever on the latch.
He needs no bolt nor bar to shut out
thieves ;
He fears no enemies, and has no friends
Importunate enough to need a key.

Enter JOHN ENDICOTT, the MARSHAL, MERRY,
and a crowd. Seeing the Quakers silent and
unmoved, they pause, awe-struck. ENDICOTT
opposite EDITH.

MARSHAL.

In the King's name do I arrest you all !
Away with them to prison. Master Upsall,

You are again discovered harboring here
These ranters and disturbers of the peace.
You know the law.

UPSALL.

        I know it, and am ready
To suffer yet again its penalties.

EDITH (*to* ENDICOTT).

Why dost thou persecute me, Saul of Tarsus ?

ACT II

SCENE I. — JOHN ENDICOTT'S *room.* *Early morning.*

JOHN ENDICOTT.

" Why dost thou persecute me, Saul of Tarsus ? "
All night these words were ringing in mine ears !
A sorrowful sweet face ; a look that pierced me
With meek reproach ; a voice of resignation
That had a life of suffering in its tone ;
And that was all ! And yet I could not sleep,
Or, when I slept, I dreamed that awful dream !
I stood beneath the elm-tree on the Common
On which the Quakers have been hanged, and heard
A voice, not hers, that cried amid the darkness,
" This is Aceldama, the field of blood !
I will have mercy, and not sacrifice ! "
    Opens the window, and looks out.
The sun is up already ; and my heart
Sickens and sinks within me when I think
How may tragedies will be enacted
Before his setting. As the earth rolls round,
It seems to me a huge Ixion's wheel,
Upon whose whirling spokes we are bound fast,
And must go with it ! Ah, how bright the sun
Strikes on the sea and on the masts of vessels,
That are uplifted in the morning air,
Like crosses of some peaceable crusade !
It makes me long to sail for lands unknown,

No matter whither ! Under me, in shadow,
Gloomy and narrow lies the little town,
Still sleeping, but to wake and toil awhile,
Then sleep again. How dismal looks the prison,
How grim and sombre in the sunless street, —
The prison where she sleeps, or wakes and waits
For what I dare not think of, — death, perhaps !
A word that has been said may be unsaid :
It is but air. But when a deed is done
It cannot be undone, nor can our thoughts
Reach out to all the mischiefs that may follow.
'T is time for morning prayers. I will go down.
My father, though severe, is kind and just ;
And when his heart is tender with devotion, —
When from his lips have fallen the words, " Forgive us
As we forgive," — then will I intercede
For these poor people, and perhaps may save them.   [*Exit.*

SCENE II. — *Dock Square. On one side, the tavern of the Three Mariners. In the background, a quaint building with gables ; and, beyond it, wharves and shipping.* CAPTAIN KEMPTHORN *and others seated at a table before the door.* SAMUEL COLE *standing near them.*

KEMPTHORN.

Come, drink about ! Remember Parson Melham,
And bless the man who first invented flip !
    They drink.

COLE.

Pray, Master Kempthorn, where were you last night ?

KEMPTHORN.

On board the Swallow, Simon Kempthorn, master,
Up for Barbadoes, and the Windward Islands.

COLE.

The town was in a tumult.

KEMPTHORN.

        And for what ?

COLE.

Your Quakers were arrested.

KEMPTHORN.

How my Quakers?

COLE.

Those you brought in your vessel from Bar-
badoes.
They made an uproar in the Meeting-house
Yesterday, and they 're now in prison for
it.
I owe you little thanks for bringing them
To the Three Mariners.

KEMPTHORN.

They have not harmed you.
I tell you, Goodman Cole, that Quaker
girl
Is precious as a sea-bream's eye. I tell
you
It was a lucky day when first she set
Her little foot upon the Swallow's deck,
Bringing good luck, fair winds, and pleasant
weather.

COLE.

I am a law-abiding citizen;
I have a seat in the new Meeting-house,
A cow-right on the Common; and, besides,
Am corporal in the Great Artillery.
I rid me of the vagabonds at once.

KEMPTHORN.

Why should you not have Quakers at your
tavern
If you have fiddlers?

COLE.

Never! never! never!
If you want fiddling you must go else-
where,
To the Green Dragon and the Admiral
Vernon,
And other such disreputable places.
But the Three Mariners is an orderly
house,
Most orderly, quiet, and respectable.
Lord Leigh said he could be as quiet here
As at the Governor's. And have I not
King Charles's Twelve Good Rules, all
framed and glazed,
Hanging in my best parlor?

KEMPTHORN.

Here 's a health
To good King Charles. Will you not drink
the King?
Then drink confusion to old Parson Palmer.

COLE.

And who is Parson Palmer? I don't know
him.

KEMPTHORN.

He had his cellar underneath his pulpit,
And so preached o'er his liquor, just as you
do.

A drum within.

COLE.

Here comes the Marshal.

MERRY (*within*).

Make room for the Marshal.

KEMPTHORN.

How pompous and imposing he appears!
His great buff doublet bellying like a main-
sail,
And all his streamers fluttering in the
wind.
What holds he in his hand?

COLE.

A proclamation.

Enter the MARSHAL, *with a proclamation; and*
MERRY, *with a halberd. They are preceded
by a drummer, and followed by the hangman,
with an armful of books, and a crowd of people,
among whom are* UPSALL *and* JOHN ENDI-
COTT. *A pile is made of the books.*

MERRY.

Silence, the drum! Good citizens, attend
To the new laws enacted by the Court.

MARSHAL (*reads*).

"Whereas a cursed sect of Heretics
Has lately risen, commonly called Quakers,
Who take upon themselves to be commis-
sioned
Immediately of God, and furthermore
Infallibly assisted by the Spirit
To write and utter blasphemous opinions,
Despising Government and the order of
God
In Church and Commonwealth, and speak-
ing evil
Of Dignities, reproaching and reviling

The Magistrates and Ministers, and seeking
To turn the people from their faith, and thus
Gain proselytes to their pernicious ways ; —
This Court, considering the premises,
And to prevent like mischief as is wrought
By their means in our land, doth hereby order,
That whatsoever master or commander
Of any ship, bark, pink, or catch shall bring
To any roadstead, harbor, creek, or cove
Within this Jurisdiction any Quakers,
Or other blasphemous Heretics, shall pay
Unto the Treasurer of the Commonwealth
One hundred pounds, and for default thereof
Be put in prison, and continue there
Till the said sum be satisfied and paid."

COLE.

Now, Simon Kempthorn, what say you to that ?

KEMPTHORN.

I pray you, Cole, lend me a hundred pounds !

MARSHAL (*reads*).

" If any one within this Jurisdiction
Shall henceforth entertain, or shall conceal
Quakers, or other blasphemous Heretics,
Knowing them so to be, every such person
Shall forfeit to the country forty shillings
For each hour's entertainment or concealment,
And shall be sent to prison, as aforesaid,
Until the forfeiture be wholly paid."
Murmurs in the crowd.

KEMPTHORN.

Now, Goodman Cole, I think your turn has come !

COLE.

Knowing them so to be !

KEMPTHORN.

At forty shillings
The hour, your fine will be some forty pounds !

COLE.

Knowing them so to be ! That is the law.

MARSHAL (*reads*).

" And it is further ordered and enacted,
If any Quaker or Quakers shall presume
To come henceforth into this Jurisdiction,
Every male Quaker for the first offence
Shall have one ear cut off ; and shall be kept
At labor in the Workhouse, till such time
As he be sent away at his own charge.
And for the repetition of the offence
Shall have his other ear cut off, and then
Be branded in the palm of his right hand.
And every woman Quaker shall be whipt
Severely in three towns ; and every Quaker,
Or he or she, that shall for a third time
Herein again offend, shall have their tongues
Bored through with a hot iron, and shall be
Sentenced to Banishment on pain of Death."
Loud murmurs. The voice of CHRISTISON *in the crowd.*

O patience of the Lord ! How long, how long,
Ere thou avenge the blood of Thine Elect ?

MERRY.

Silence, there, silence ! Do not break the peace !

MARSHAL (*reads*).

" Every inhabitant of this Jurisdiction
Who shall defend the horrible opinions
Of Quakers, by denying due respect
To equals and superiors, and withdrawing
From Church Assemblies, and thereby approving
The abusive and destructive practices
Of this accursed sect, in opposition
To all the orthodox received opinions
Of godly men, shall be forthwith committed
Unto close prison for one month ; and then
Refusing to retract and to reform
The opinions as aforesaid, he shall be
Sentenced to Banishment on pain of Death.
By the Court. Edward Rawson, Secretary."
Now, hangman, do your duty. Burn those books.
Loud murmurs in the crowd. The pile of books is lighted.

UPSALL.

I testify against these cruel laws !
Forerunners are they of some judgment on us ;

And, in the love and tenderness I bear
Unto this town and .people, I beseech you,
O Magistrates, take heed, lest ye be found
As fighters against God !

JOHN ENDICOTT (*taking* UPSALL'S *hand*).
Upsall, I thank you
For speaking words such as some younger
man,
I, or another, should have said before you.
Such laws as these are cruel and oppres-
sive ;
A blot on this fair town, and a disgrace
To any Christian people.

MERRY (*aside, listening behind them*).
Here 's sedition !
I never thought that any good would come
Of this young popinjay, with his long hair
And his great boots, fit only for the Rus-
sians
Or barbarous Indians, as his father says !

THE VOICE.
Woe to the bloody town !   And rightfully
Men call it the Lost Town !   The blood of
Abel
Cries from the ground, and at the final
judgment
The Lord will say, " Cain, Cain ! where is
thy brother ? "

MERRY.
Silence there in the crowd !

UPSALL (*aside*).
'T is Christison !
THE VOICE.
O foolish people, ye that think to burn
And to consume the truth of God, I tell
you
That every flame is a loud tongue of fire
To publish it abroad to all the world
Louder than tongues of men !

KEMPTHORN (*springing to his feet*).
Well said, my hearty !
There 's a brave fellow !   There 's a man of
pluck !
A man who 's not afraid to say his say,
Though a whole town 's against him.   Rain,
rain, rain,
Bones of St. Botolph, and put out this fire !
The drum beats. Exeunt all but MERRY, KEMP-
THORN, *and* COLE.

MERRY.
And now that matter 's ended, Goodman
Cole,
Fetch me a mug of ale, your strongest ale.

KEMPTHORN (*sitting down*).
And me another mug of flip ; and put
Two gills of brandy in it.
[*Exit* COLE.
MERRY.
No ; no more.
Not a drop more, I say.   You 've had
enough.

KEMPTHORN.
And who are you, sir ?

MERRY.
I 'm a Tithing-man,
And Merry is my name.

KEMPTHORN.
A merry name !
I like it ; and I 'll drink your merry health
Till all is blue.

MERRY.
And then you will be clapped
Into the stocks, with the red letter D
Hung round about your neck for drunken-
ness.
You 're a free-drinker, — yes, and a free-
thinker !

KEMPTHORN.
And you are Andrew Merry, or Merry
Andrew.

MERRY.
My name is Walter Merry, and not An-
drew.

KEMPTHORN.
Andrew or Walter, you 're a merry fellow ;
I 'll swear to that.

MERRY.
No swearing, let me tell you.
The other day one Shorthose had his tongue
Put into a cleft stick for profane swearing.
COLE *brings the ale.*

KEMPTHORN.
Well, where 's my flip ?   As sure as my
name 's Kempthorn —

MERRY.
Is your name Kempthorn ?

KEMPTHORN.
That 's the name I go by.

MERRY.
What, Captain Simon Kempthorn of the Swallow ?

KEMPTHORN.
No other.

MERRY (*touching him on the shoulder*).
Then you 're wanted.   I arrest you In the King's name.

KEMPTHORN.
And where 's your warrant ?

MERRY (*unfolding a paper, and reading*).
Here.
Listen to me.   " Hereby you are required, In the King's name, to apprehend the body Of Simon Kempthorn, mariner, and him Safely to bring before me, there to answer All such objections as are laid to him, Touching the Quakers."   Signed, John Endicott.

KEMPTHORN.
Has it the Governor's seal ?

MERRY.
Ay, here it is.

KEMPTHORN.
Death's head and cross-bones.   That 's a pirate's flag !

MERRY.
Beware how you revile the Magistrates ; You may be whipped for that.

KEMPTHORN.
Then mum 's the word.
Exeunt MERRY *and* KEMPTHORN.

COLE.
There 's mischief brewing !   Sure, there 's mischief brewing !
I feel like Master Josselyn when he found The hornet's nest, and thought it some strange fruit,
Until the seeds came out, and then he dropped it.   [*Exit.*

SCENE III. — *A room in the Governor's house.*
Enter GOVERNOR ENDICOTT *and* MERRY.

ENDICOTT.
My son, you say ?

MERRY.
Your Worship's eldest son.

ENDICOTT.
Speaking against the laws ?

MERRY.
Ay, worshipful sir.

ENDICOTT.
And in the public market-place ?

MERRY.
I saw him With my own eyes, heard him with my own ears.

ENDICOTT.
Impossible !

MERRY.
He stood there in the crowd With Nicholas Upsall, when the laws were read
To-day against the Quakers, and I heard him
Denounce and vilipend them as unjust, And cruel, wicked, and abominable.

ENDICOTT.
Ungrateful son !   O God ! thou layest upon me
A burden heavier than I can bear !
Surely the power of Satan must be great Upon the earth, if even the elect
Are thus deceived and fall away from grace !

MERRY.
Worshipful sir ! I meant no harm —

ENDICOTT.
'T is well.
You 've done your duty, though you 've done it roughly,
And every word you 've uttered since you came
Has stabbed me to the heart !

MERRY.
I do beseech Your Worship's pardon !

ENDICOTT.

He whom I have nurtured
And brought up in the reverence of the
    Lord !
The child of all my hopes and my affec-
    tions !
He upon whom I leaned as a sure staff
For my old age !   It is God's chastisement
For leaning upon any arm but His !

MERRY.

Your Worship ! —

ENDICOTT.

And this comes from holding parley
With the delusions and deceits of Satan.
At once, forever, must they be crushed out,
Or all the land will reek with heresy !
Pray, have you any children ?

MERRY.
                    No, not any.

ENDICOTT.

Thank God for that.   He has delivered
    you
From a great care.   Enough ; my private
    griefs
Too long have kept me from the public ser-
    vice.

Exit MERRY.   ENDICOTT *seats himself at the
    table and arranges his papers.*

The hour has come ; and I am eager now
To sit in judgment on these Heretics.
        A knock.
Come in.   Who is it ?   (*Not looking up*).

JOHN ENDICOTT.
        It is I.

ENDICOTT (*restraining himself*).
                    Sit down !

JOHN ENDICOTT (*sitting down*).

I come to intercede for these poor people
Who are in prison, and await their trial.

ENDICOTT.

It is of them I wish to speak with you.
I have been angry with you, but 't is
    passed.
For when I hear your footsteps come or go,
See in your features your dead mother's
    face,
And in your voice detect some tone of hers,

All anger vanishes, and I remember
The days that are no more, and come no
    more,
When as a child you sat upon my knee,
And prattled of your playthings, and the
    games
You played among the pear trees in the
    orchard !

JOHN ENDICOTT.

Oh, let the memory of my noble mother
Plead with you to be mild and merciful !
For mercy more becomes a Magistrate
Than the vindictive wrath which men call
    justice !

ENDICOTT.

The sin of heresy is a deadly sin.
'T is like the falling of the snow, whose
    crystals
The traveller plays with, thoughtless of his
    danger,
Until he sees the air so full of light
That it is dark ; and blindly staggering on-
    ward,
Lost and bewildered, he sits down to rest ;
There falls a pleasant drowsiness upon
    him,
And what he thinks is sleep, alas ! is death.

JOHN ENDICOTT.

And yet who is there that has never
    doubted ?
And doubting and believing, has not said,
" Lord, I believe ; help thou my unbe-
    lief " ?

ENDICOTT.

In the same way we trifle with our doubts,
Whose shining shapes are like the stars de-
    scending ;
Until at last, bewildered and dismayed,
Blinded by that which seemed to give us
    light,
We sink to sleep, and find that it is death,
        Rising.
Death to the soul through all eternity !
Alas that I should see you growing up
To man's estate, and in the admonition
And nurture of the Law, to find you now
Pleading for Heretics !

JOHN ENDICOTT (*rising*).
                    In the sight of God,
Perhaps all men are Heretics.   Who dares
To say that he alone has found the truth ?

We cannot always feel and think and act
As those who go before us.   Had you done
      so,
You would not now be here.

ENDICOTT.

Have you forgotten
The doom of Heretics, and the fate of
      those
Who aid and comfort them ?   Have you
      forgotten
That in the market-place this very day
You trampled on the laws ?   What right
      have you,
An inexperienced and untravelled youth,
To sit in judgment here upon the acts
Of older men and wiser than yourself,
Thus stirring up sedition in the streets,
And making me a byword and a jest ?

JOHN ENDICOTT.

Words of an inexperienced youth like me
Were powerless if the acts of older men
Went not before them.   'T is these laws
      themselves
Stir up sedition, not my judgment of them.

ENDICOTT.

Take heed, lest I be called, as Brutus was,
To be the judge of my own son !   P .gone !
When you are tired of feeding upon husks,
Return again to duty and submission,
But not till then.

JOHN ENDICOTT.

I hear and I obey !
                            [*Exit.*

ENDICOTT.

Oh happy, happy they who have no chil-
      dren !
He 's gone ! I hear the hall door shut be-
      hind him.
It sends a dismal echo through my heart,
As if forever it had closed between us,
And I should look upon his face no more !
Oh, this will drag me down into my
      grave, —
To that eternal resting-place wherein
Man lieth down, and riseth not again !
Till the heavens be no more he shall not
      wake,
Nor be roused from his sleep ; for Thou
      dost change
His countenance, and sendest him away !
                            [*Exit.*

ACT III

SCENE I. — *The Court of Assistants.* ENDICOTT,
      BELLINGHAM, ATHERTON, *and other magis-
      trates.* KEMPTHORN, MERRY, *and constables.
      Afterwards* WHARTON, EDITH, *and* CHRIS-
      TISON.

ENDICOTT.

Call Captain Simon Kempthorn.

MERRY.

Simon Kempthorn,
Come to the bar !

KEMPTHORN *comes forward.*

ENDICOTT.

You are accused of bringing
Into this Jurisdiction, from Barbadoes,
Some persons of that sort and sect of
      people
Known by the name of Quakers, and main-
      taining
Most dangerous and heretical opinions ;
Purposely coming here to propagate
Their heresies and errors ; bringing with
      them
And spreading sundry books here, which
      contain
Their doctrines most corrupt and blasphe-
      mous,
And contrary to the truth professed among
      us.
What say you to this charge ?

KEMPTHORN.

I do acknowledge,
Among the passengers on board the Swal-
      low
Were certain persons saying Thee and
      Thou.
They seemed a harmless people, mostways
      silent,
Particularly when they said their prayers.

ENDICOTT.

Harmless and silent as the pestilence !
You 'd better have brought the fever or the
      plague
Among us in your ship !   Therefore, this
      Court,
For preservation of the Peace and Truth,
Hereby commands you speedily to trans-
      port,
Or cause to be transported speedily,

The aforesaid persons hence unto Bar-
    badoes,
From whence they came ; you paying all
    the charges
Of their imprisonment.

KEMPTHORN.
                    Worshipful sir,
No ship e'er prospered that has carried
    Quakers
Against their will ! I knew a vessel
    once —

ENDICOTT.
And for the more effectual performance
Hereof you are to give security
In bonds amounting to one hundred pounds.
On your refusal, you will be committed
To prison till you do it.

KEMPTHORN.
                    But you see
I cannot do it. The law, sir, of Barbadoes
Forbids the landing Quakers on the island.

ENDICOTT.
Then you will be committed.   Who comes
    next ?

MERRY.
There is another charge against the Cap-
    tain.

ENDICOTT.
What is it ?

MERRY.
    Profane swearing, please your Worship.
He cursed and swore from Dock Square to
    the Court-house.

ENDICOTT.
Then let him stand in the pillory for one
    hour.
            [*Exit* KEMPTHORN *with constable.*
Who 's next ?

MERRY.
    The Quakers.

ENDICOTT.
            Call them.
MERRY.
                    Edward Wharton,
Come to the bar !

WHARTON.
            Yea, even to the bench.

ENDICOTT.
Take off your hat.

WHARTON.
            My hat offendeth not.
If it offendeth any, let him take it ;
For I shall not resist.

ENDICOTT.
                Take off his hat.
Let him be fined ten shillings for contempt.
    MERRY *takes off* WHARTON'S *hat.*

WHARTON.
What evil have I done ?

ENDICOTT.
                Your hair 's too long ;
And in not putting off your hat to us
You 've disobeyed and broken that com-
    mandment
Which sayeth " Honor thy father and thy
    mother."

WHARTON.
John Endicott, thou art become too proud ;
And lovest him who putteth off the hat,
And honoreth thee by bowing of the body,
And sayeth " Worshipful sir ! "   'T is time
    for thee
To give such follies over, for thou mayest
Be drawing very near unto thy grave.

ENDICOTT.
Now, sirrah, leave your canting.   Take the
    oath.

WHARTON.
Nay, sirrah me no sirrahs !

ENDICOTT.
                    Will you swear ?

WHARTON.
Nay, I will not.

ENDICOTT.
                You made a great disturbance
And uproar yesterday in the Meeting-
    house,
Having your hat on.

WHARTON.
                I made no disturbance ;
For peacefully I stood, like other people.
I spake no words ; moved against none my
    hand :

But by the hair they haled me out, and
    dashed
Their books into my face.

ENDICOTT.

          You, Edward Wharton,
On pain of death, depart this Jurisdiction
Within ten days. Such is your sentence.
Go.

WHARTON.

John Endicott, it had been well for thee
If this day's doings thou hadst left undone.
But, banish me as far as thou hast power,
Beyond the guard and presence of my God
Thou canst not banish me!

ENDICOTT.

         Depart the Court ;
We have no time to listen to your babble.
Who's next ?   [*Exit* WHARTON.

MERRY.

This woman, for the same offence.
EDITH *comes forward.*

ENDICOTT.

What is your name ?

EDITH.

       'T is to the world unknown,
But written in the Book of Life.

ENDICOTT.

          Take heed
It be not written in the Book of Death !
What is it ?

EDITH.

    Edith Christison.

ENDICOTT (*with eagerness*).

         The daughter
Of Wenlock Christison?

EDITH.

       I am his daughter.

ENDICOTT.

Your father hath given us trouble many
    times.
A bold man and a violent, who sets
At naught the authority of our Church and
    State,
And is in banishment on pain of death.
Where are you living ?

EDITH.

    In the Lord.

ENDICOTT.

           Make answer
Without evasion. Where ?

EDITH.

         My outward being
Is in Barbadoes.

ENDICOTT.

       Then why come you here ?

EDITH.

I come upon an errand of the Lord.

ENDICOTT.

'T is not the business of the Lord you 're
    doing;
It is the Devil's. Will you take the oath ?
Give her the Book.

MERRY *offers the book.*

EDITH.

         You offer me this Book
To swear on; and it saith, "Swear not at
    all,
Neither by heaven, because it is God's
    Throne,
Nor by the earth, because it is his foot-
    stool ! "
I dare not swear.

ENDICOTT.

       You dare not ? Yet you Quakers
Deny this Book of Holy Writ, the Bible,
To be the Word of God.

EDITH (*reverentially*).

         Christ is the Word,
The everlasting oath of God. I dare not.

ENDICOTT.

You own yourself a Quaker,— do you not ?

EDITH.

I own that in derision and reproach
I am so called.

ENDICOTT.

       Then you deny the Scripture
To be the rule of life.

EDITH.

Yea, I believe
The Inner Light, and not the Written Word,
To be the rule of life.

ENDICOTT.

And you deny
That the Lord's Day is holy.

EDITH.

Every day
Is the Lord's Day. It runs through all our lives,
As through the pages of the Holy Bible,
"Thus saith the Lord."

ENDICOTT.

You are accused of making
An horrible disturbance, and affrighting
The people in the Meeting-house on Sunday.
What answer make you?

EDITH.

I do not deny
That I was present in your Steeple-house
On the First Day; but I made no disturbance.

ENDICOTT.

Why came you there?

EDITH.

Because the Lord commanded.
His word was in my heart, a burning fire
Shut up within me and consuming me,
And I was very weary with forbearing;
I could not stay.

ENDICOTT.

'T was not the Lord that sent you;
As an incarnate devil did you come!

EDITH.

On the First Day, when, seated in my chamber,
I heard the bells toll, calling you together,
The sound struck at my life, as once at his,
The holy man, our Founder, when he heard
The far-off bells toll in the Vale of Beavor.
It sounded like a market bell to call
The folk together, that the Priest might set

His wares to sale. And the Lord said within me,
"Thou must go cry aloud against that Idol,
And all the worshippers thereof." I went
Barefooted, clad in sackcloth, and I stood
And listened at the threshold; and I heard
The praying and the singing and the preaching,
Which were but outward forms, and without power.
Then rose a cry within me, and my heart
Was filled with admonitions and reproofs.
Remembering how the Prophets and Apostles
Denounced the covetous hirelings and diviners,
I entered in, and spake the words the Lord
Commanded me to speak. I could no less.

ENDICOTT.

Are you a Prophetess?

EDITH.

Is it not written,
"Upon my handmaidens will I pour out
My spirit, and they shall prophesy"?

ENDICOTT.

Enough;
For out of your own mouth are you condemned!
Need we hear further?

THE JUDGES.

We are satisfied.

ENDICOTT.

It is sufficient. Edith Christison,
The sentence of the Court is, that you be
Scourged in three towns, with forty stripes save one,
Then banished upon pain of death!

EDITH.

Your sentence
Is truly no more terrible to me
Than had you blown a feather into the air,
And, as it fell upon me, you had said,
"Take heed it hurt thee not!" God's will be done!

WENLOCK CHRISTISON (unseen in the crowd).

Woe to the city of blood! The stone shall cry

Out of the wall ; the beam from out the timber
Shall answer it ! Woe unto him that buildeth
A town with blood, and stablisheth a city
By his iniquity !

ENDICOTT.

Who is it makes
Such outcry here ?

CHRISTISON (coming forward).

I, Wenlock Christison !

ENDICOTT.

Banished on pain of death, why come you here ?

CHRISTISON.

I come to warn you that you shed no more
The blood of innocent men ! It cries aloud
For vengeance to the Lord !

ENDICOTT.

Your life is forfeit
Unto the law ; and you shall surely die,
And shall not live.

CHRISTISON.

Like unto Eleazer,
Maintaining the excellence of ancient years
And the honor of his gray head, I stand before you ;
Like him disdaining all hypocrisy,
Lest, through desire to live a little longer,
I get a stain to my old age and name !

ENDICOTT.

Being in banishment, on pain of death,
You come now in among us in rebellion.

CHRISTISON.

I come not in among you in rebellion,
But in obedience to the Lord of Heaven.
Not in contempt to any Magistrate,
But only in the love I bear your souls,
As ye shall know hereafter, when all men
Give an account of deeds done in the body !
God's righteous judgments ye cannot escape.

ONE OF THE JUDGES.

Those who have gone before you said the same,
And yet no judgment of the Lord hath fallen
Upon us.

CHRISTISON.

He but waiteth till the measure
Of your iniquities shall be filled up,
And ye have run your race. Then will his wrath
Descend upon you to the uttermost !
For thy part, Humphrey Atherton, it hangs
Over thy head already. It shall come
Suddenly, as a thief doth in the night,
And in the hour when least thou thinkest of it !

ENDICOTT.

We have a law, and by that law you die.

CHRISTISON.

I, a free man of England and freeborn,
Appeal unto the laws of mine own nation !

ENDICOTT.

There 's no appeal to England from this Court !
What ! do you think our statutes are but paper ?
Are but dead leaves that rustle in the wind ?
Or litter to be trampled under foot ?
What say ye, Judges of the Court, — what say ye ?
Shall this man suffer death ? Speak your opinions.

ONE OF THE JUDGES.

I am a mortal man, and die I must,
And that erelong ; and I must then appear
Before the awful judgment-seat of Christ,
To give account of deeds done in the body.
My greatest glory on that day will be,
That I have given my vote against this man.

CHRISTISON.

If, Thomas Danforth, thou hast nothing more
To glory in upon that dreadful day
Than blood of innocent people, then thy glory
Will be turned into shame ! The Lord hath said it !

ANOTHER JUDGE.

I cannot give consent, while other men
Who have been banished upon pain of death
Are now in their own houses here among us.

ENDICOTT.

Ye that will not consent, make record of it.

I thank my God that I am not afraid
To give my judgment. Wenlock Christison,
You must be taken back from hence to
prison,
Thence to the place of public execution,
There to be hanged till you be dead — dead,
—dead !

CHRISTISON.

If ye have power to take my life from
me, —
Which I do question, — God hath power to
raise
The principle of life in other men,
And send them here among you. There
shall be
No peace unto the wicked, saith my God.
Listen, ye Magistrates, for the Lord hath
said it !
The day ye put his servitors to death,
That day the Day of your own Visitation,
The Day of Wrath, shall pass above your
heads,
And ye shall be accursed forevermore !

To EDITH, *embracing her.*

Cheer up, dear heart ! they have not power
to harm us.

[*Exeunt* CHRISTISON *and* EDITH *guarded. The
Scene closes.*

SCENE II. — *A street. Enter* JOHN ENDICOTT
and UPSALL.

JOHN ENDICOTT.

Scourged in three towns ! and yet the busy
people
Go up and down the streets on their affairs
Of business or of pleasure, as if nothing
Had happened to disturb them or their
thoughts !
When bloody tragedies like this are acted,
The pulses of a nation should stand still ;
The town should be in mourning, and the
people
Speak only in low whispers to each other.

UPSALL.

I know this people ; and that underneath
A cold outside there burns a secret fire
That will find vent, and will not be put out,
Till every remnant of these barbarous laws
Shall be to ashes burned, and blown away.

JOHN ENDICOTT.

Scourged in three towns ! It is incredible

Such things can be ! I feel the blood within
me
Fast mounting in rebellion, since in vain
Have I implored compassion of my father !

UPSALL.

You know your father only as a father ;
I know him better as a Magistrate.
He is a man both loving and severe ;
A tender heart ; a will inflexible.
None ever loved him more than I have
loved him.
He is an upright man and a just man
In all things save the treatment of the
Quakers.

JOHN ENDICOTT.

Yet I have found him cruel and unjust
Even as a father. He has driven me forth
Into the street ; has shut his door upon me,
With words of bitterness. I am as home-
less
As these poor Quakers are.

UPSALL.

Then come with me.
You shall be welcome for your father's
sake,
And the old friendship that has been be-
tween us.
He will relent erelong. A father's anger
Is like a sword without a handle, piercing
Both ways alike, and wounding him that
wields it
No less than him that it is pointed at.

[*Exeunt.*

SCENE III. *The prison. Night.* EDITH *read-
ing the Bible by a lamp.*

EDITH.

" Blessed are ye when men shall persecute
you,
And shall revile you, and shall say against
you
All manner of evil falsely for my sake !
Rejoice, and be exceeding glad, for great
Is your reward in heaven. For so the pro-
phets,
Which were before you, have been perse-
cuted."

Enter JOHN ENDICOTT.

JOHN ENDICOTT.

Edith !

EDITH.

Who is it that speaketh?

JOHN ENDICOTT.

Saul of Tarsus :
As thou didst call me once.

EDITH (*coming forward*).

Yea, I remember.
Thou art the Governor's son.

JOHN ENDICOTT.

I am ashamed
Thou shouldst remember me.

EDITH.

Why comest thou
Into this dark guest-chamber in the night?
What seekest thou?

JOHN ENDICOTT.

Forgiveness!

EDITH.

I forgive
All who have injured me. What hast thou
done?

JOHN ENDICOTT.

I have betrayed thee, thinking that in this
I did God service. Now, in deep contri-
tion,
I come to rescue thee.

EDITH.

From what?

JOHN ENDICOTT.

From prison.

EDITH.

I am safe here within these gloomy walls.

JOHN ENDICOTT.

From scourging in the streets, and in three
towns!

EDITH.

Remembering who was scourged for me, I
shrink not
Nor shudder at the forty stripes save one.

JOHN ENDICOTT.

Perhaps from death itself!

EDITH.

I fear not death,
Knowing who died for me.

JOHN ENDICOTT (*aside*).

Surely some divine
Ambassador is speaking through those lips
And looking through those eyes! I cannot
answer!

EDITH.

If all these prison doors stood opened wide
I would not cross the threshold, — not one
step.
There are invisible bars I cannot break;
There are invisible doors that shut me in,
And keep me ever steadfast to my pur-
pose.

JOHN ENDICOTT.

Thou hast the patience and the faith of
Saints!

EDITH.

Thy Priest hath been with me this day to
save me,
Not only from the death that comes to all,
But from the second death!

JOHN ENDICOTT.

The Pharisee!
My heart revolts against him and his
creed!
Alas! the coat that was without a seam
Is rent asunder by contending sects;
Each bears away a portion of the garment,
Blindly believing that he has the whole!

EDITH.

When Death, the Healer, shall have touched
our eyes
With moist clay of the grave, then shall we
see
The truth as we have never yet beheld it.
But he that overcometh shall not be
Hurt of the second death. Has he forgot-
ten
The many mansions in our father's house?

JOHN ENDICOTT.

There is no pity in his iron heart!
The hands that now bear stamped upon
their palms
The burning sign of Heresy, hereafter
Shall be uplifted against such accusers,

And then the imprinted letter and its mean-
ing
Will not be Heresy, but Holiness !

EDITH.

Remember, thou condemnest thine own
father !

JOHN ENDICOTT.

I have no father ! He has cast me off.
I am as homeless as the wind that moans
And wanders through the streets. Oh,
come with me !
Do not delay. Thy God shall be my God,
And where thou goest I will go.

EDITH.
I cannot.
Yet will I not deny it, nor conceal it ;
From the first moment I beheld thy face
I felt a tenderness in my soul towards thee.
My mind has since been inward to the
Lord,
Waiting his word. It has not yet been
spoken.

JOHN ENDICOTT.

I cannot wait. Trust me. Oh, come with
me !

EDITH.

In the next room, my father, an old man,
Sitteth imprisoned and condemned to
death,
Willing to prove his faith by martyrdom ;
And thinkest thou his daughter would do
less ?

JOHN ENDICOTT.

Oh, life is sweet, and death is terrible !

EDITH.

I have too long walked hand in hand with
death
To shudder at that pale familiar face.
But leave me now. I wish to be alone.

JOHN ENDICOTT.

Not yet. Oh, let me stay.

EDITH.
Urge me no more.

JOHN ENDICOTT.

Alas ! good-night. I will not say good-by !

EDITH.

Put this temptation underneath thy feet.
To him that overcometh shall be given
The white stone with the new name written
on it,
That no man knows save him that doth
receive it,
And I will give thee a new name, and call
thee
Paul of Damascus and not Saul of Tarsus.

[*Exit* ENDICOTT. EDITH *sits down again to
read the Bible.*

ACT IV

SCENE I. — *King Street, in front of the town-
house.* KEMPTHORN *in the pillory.* MERRY
and a crowd of lookers-on.

KEMPTHORN (*sings*).

The world is full of care,
Much like unto a bubble ;
Women and care. and care and women,
And women and care and trouble.

Good Master Merry, may I say confound ?

MERRY.

Ay, that you may.

KEMPTHORN.

Well, then, with your permission,
Confound the Pillory !

MERRY.
That 's the very thing
The joiner said who made the Shrewsbury
stocks.
He said, Confound the stocks, because they
put him
Into his own. He was the first man in
them.

KEMPTHORN.

For swearing, was it ?

MERRY.
No, it was for charging ;
He charged the town too much ; and so the
town,
To make things square, set him in his own
stocks,
And fined him five pound sterling, — just
enough
To settle his own bill.

KEMPTHORN.

And served him right ;
But, Master Merry, is it not eight bells ?

MERRY.

Not quite.

KEMPTHORN.

For, do you see ? I 'm getting tired
Of being perched aloft here in this cro'
    nest
Like the first mate of a whaler, or a Middy
Mast-headed, looking out for land ! Sail
    ho !
Here comes a heavy-laden merchantman
With the lee clews eased off, and running
    free
Before the wind. A solid man of Boston.
A comfortable man, with dividends,
And the first salmon, and the first green
    peas.

A gentleman passes.

He does not even turn his head to look.
He 's gone without a word. Here comes
    another,
A different kind of craft on a taut bow-
    line, —
Deacon Giles Firmin the apothecary,
A pious and a ponderous citizen,
Looking as rubicund and round and splen-
    did
As the great bottle in his own shop win-
    dow !

DEACON FIRMIN *passes.*

And here 's my host of the Three Mariners,
My creditor and trusty taverner,
My corporal in the Great Artillery !
He 's not a man to pass me without speak-
    ing.

COLE *looks away and passes.*

Don't yaw so ; keep your luff, old hypo-
    crite !
Respectable, ah yes, respectable,
You, with your seat in the new Meeting-
    house,
Your cow - right on the Common ! But
    who 's this ?
I did not know the Mary Ann was in !
And yet this is my old friend, Captain
    Goldsmith,
As sure as I stand in the bilboes here.
Why, Ralph, my boy !

Enter RALPH GOLDSMITH.

GOLDSMITH.

Why, Simon, is it you ?
Set in the bilboes ?

KEMPTHORN.

Chock-a-block, you see,
And without chafing-gear.

GOLDSMITH.

And what 's it for ?

KEMPTHORN.

Ask that starbowline with the boat-hook
    there,
That handsome man.

MERRY (*bowing*).

For swearing.

KEMPTHORN.

In this town
They put sea-captains in the stocks for
    swearing,
And Quakers for not swearing. So look
    out.

GOLDSMITH.

I pray you set him free ; he meant no
    harm ;
'T is an old habit he picked up afloat.

MERRY.

Well, as your time is out, you may come
    down.
The law allows you now to go at large
Like Elder Oliver's horse upon the Com-
    mon.

KEMPTHORN.

Now, hearties, bear a hand ! Let go and
    haul.

KEMPTHORN *is set free, and comes forward, shak-*
ing GOLDSMITH'S *hand.*

KEMPTHORN.

Give me your hand, Ralph.   Ah, how good
    it feels !
The hand of an old friend.

GOLDSMITH.

God bless you, Simon !

KEMPTHORN.

Now let us make a straight wake for the
    tavern

Of the Three Mariners, Samuel Cole com-
  mander ;
Where we can take our ease, and see the
  shipping,
And talk about old times.

GOLDSMITH.

First I must pay
My duty to the Governor, and take him
His letters and dispatches. Come with
  me.

KEMPTHORN.

I'd rather not. I saw him yesterday.

GOLDSMITH.

Then wait for me at the Three Nuns and
  Comb.

KEMPTHORN.

I thank you. That 's too near to the town
  pump.
I will go with you to the Governor's,
And wait outside there, sailing off and
  on ;
If I am wanted, you can hoist a signal.

MERRY.

Shall I go with you and point out the way ?

GOLDSMITH.

Oh no, I thank you. I am not a stran-
  ger
Here in your crooked little town.

MERRY.

How now, sir ?
Do you abuse our town?   [Exit.

GOLDSMITH.

Oh, no offence.

KEMPTHORN.

Ralph, I am under bonds for a hundred
  pound.

GOLDSMITH.

Hard lines. What for ?

KEMPTHORN.

To take some Quakers back
I brought here from Barbadoes in the
  Swallow.
And how to do it I don't clearly see,
For one of them is banished, and another
Is sentenced to be hanged ! What shall I
  do ?

GOLDSMITH.

Just slip your hawser on some cloudy
  night ;
Sheer off, and pay it with the topsail,
  Simon !   [Exeunt.

SCENE II. — *Street in front of the prison. In
the background a gateway and several flights
of steps leading up terraces to the Governor's
house. A pump on one side of the street.*
JOHN ENDICOTT, MERRY, UPSALL, *and others.
A drum beats.*

JOHN ENDICOTT.

Oh shame, shame, shame !

MERRY.

Yes, it would be a shame
But for the damnable sin of Heresy !

JOHN ENDICOTT.

A woman scourged and dragged about our
  streets !

MERRY.

Well, Roxbury and Dorchester must take
Their share of shame. She will be whipped
  in each !
Three towns, and Forty Stripes save one ;
  that makes
Thirteen in each.

JOHN ENDICOTT.

And are we Jews or Christians ?
See where she comes, amid a gaping crowd !
And she a child. Oh, pitiful ! pitiful !
There 's blood upon her clothes, her hands,
  her feet !

Enter MARSHAL *and a drummer,* EDITH,
*stripped to the waist, followed by the hangman
with a scourge, and a noisy crowd.*

EDITH.

Here let me rest one moment. I am tired.
Will some one give me water ?

MERRY.

At his peril.

UPSALL.

Alas ! that I should live to see this day !

A WOMAN.

Did I forsake my father and my mother
And come here to New England to see
  this ?

EDITH.

I am athirst. Will no one give me water?

JOHN ENDICOTT (*making his way through the crowd with water*).
In the Lord's name!

EDITH (*drinking*).
In his name I receive it!
Sweet as the water of Samaria's well
This water tastes. I thank thee. Is it thou?
I was afraid thou hadst deserted me.

JOHN ENDICOTT.

Never will I desert thee, nor deny thee.
Be comforted.

MERRY.
O Master Endicott,
Be careful what you say.

JOHN ENDICOTT.
Peace, idle babbler!

MERRY.

You 'll rue these words!

JOHN ENDICOTT.
Art thou not better now?

EDITH.

They 've struck me as with roses.

JOHN ENDICOTT.
Ah, these wounds!
These bloody garments!

EDITH.
It is granted me
To seal my testimony with my blood.

JOHN ENDICOTT.

O blood-red seal of man's vindictive wrath!
O roses of the garden of the Lord!
I, of the household of Iscariot,
I have betrayed in thee my Lord and Master!

WENLOCK CHRISTISON *appears above, at the window of the prison, stretching out his hands through the bars.*

CHRISTISON.

Be of good courage, O my child! my child!
Blessed art thou when men shall persecute thee!

Fear not their faces, saith the Lord, fear not,
For I am with thee to deliver thee.

A CITIZEN.

Who is it crying from the prison yonder?

MERRY.

It is old Wenlock Christison.

CHRISTISON.
Remember
Him who was scourged, and mocked, and crucified!
I see his messengers attending thee.
Be steadfast, oh, be steadfast to the end!

EDITH (*with exultation*).

I cannot reach thee with these arms, O father!
But closely in my soul do I embrace thee
And hold thee. In thy dungeon and thy death
I will be with thee, and will comfort thee!

MARSHAL.

Come, put an end to this. Let the drum beat.
The drum beats. Exeunt all but JOHN ENDI-COTT, UPSALL, *and* MERRY.

CHRISTISON.

Dear child, farewell! Never shall I behold
Thy face again with these bleared eyes of flesh;
And never wast thou fairer, lovelier, dearer
Than now, when scourged and bleeding, and insulted
For the truth's sake. O pitiless, pitiless town!
The wrath of God hangs over thee; and the day
Is near at hand when thou shalt be abandoned
To desolation and the breeding of nettles.
The bittern and the cormorant shall lodge
Upon thine upper lintels, and their voice
Sing in thy windows. Yea, thus saith the Lord!

JOHN ENDICOTT.

Awake! awake! ye sleepers, ere too late,
And wipe these bloody statutes from your books!   [*Exit.*

MERRY.

Take heed ; the walls have ears !

UPSALL.

At last, the heart
Of every honest man must speak or break !
Enter GOVERNOR ENDICOTT *with his halberdiers.*

ENDICOTT.

What is this stir and tumult in the street ?

MERRY.

Worshipful sir, the whipping of a girl,
And her old father howling from the prison.

ENDICOTT (*to his halberdiers*).
Go on.

CHRISTISON.

Antiochus ! Antiochus !
O thou that slayest the Maccabees ! The
Lord
Shall smite thee with incurable disease,
And no man shall endure to carry thee !

MERRY.

Peace, old blasphemer !

CHRISTISON.

I both feel and see
The presence and the waft of death go
forth
Against thee, and already thou dost look
Like one that 's dead !

MERRY (*pointing*).

And there is your own son,
Worshipful sir, abetting the sedition.

ENDICOTT.

Arrest him. Do not spare him.

MERRY (*aside*).

His own child !
There is some special providence takes care
That none shall be too happy in this world !
His own first-born.

ENDICOTT.

O Absalom, my son !
[*Exeunt ; the Governor with his halberdiers as-
cending the steps of his house.*

SCENE III. — *The Governor's private room.
Papers upon the table.* ENDICOTT *and* BEL-
LINGHAM.

ENDICOTT.

There is a ship from England has come in,

Bringing dispatches and much news from
home.
His Majesty was at the Abbey crowned ;
And when the coronation was complete
There passed a mighty tempest o'er the city,
Portentous with great thunderings and
lightnings.

BELLINGHAM.

After his father's, if I well remember,
There was an earthquake, that foreboded
evil.

ENDICOTT.

Ten of the Regicides have been put to death !
The bodies of Cromwell, Ireton, and Brad-
shaw
Have been dragged from their graves, and
publicly
Hanged in their shrouds at Tyburn.

BELLINGHAM.

Horrible !

ENDICOTT.

Thus the old tyranny revives again !
Its arm is long enough to reach us here,
As you will see. For, more insulting still
Than flaunting in our faces dead men's
shrouds,
Here is the King's Mandamus, taking from
us,
From this day forth, all power to punish
Quakers.

BELLINGHAM.

That takes from us all power ; we are but
puppets,
And can no longer execute our laws.

ENDICOTT.

His Majesty begins with pleasant words,
"Trusty and well-beloved, we greet you
well ; "
Then with a ruthless hand he strips from
me
All that which makes me what I am ; as if
From some old general in the field, grown
gray
In service, scarred with many wounds,
Just at the hour of victory, he should strip
His badge of office and his well-gained
honors,
And thrust him back into the ranks again.

Opens the Mandamus and hands it to BELLING-
HAM ; *and, while he is reading,* ENDICOTT
walks up and down the room.

Here, read it for yourself ; you see his
    words
Are pleasant words — considerate — not
    reproachful —
Nothing could be more gentle — or more
    royal ;
But then the meaning underneath the
    words,
Mark that. He says all people known as
    Quakers
Among us, now condemned to suffer death
Or any corporal punishment whatever,
Who are imprisoned, or may be obnoxious
To the like condemnation, shall be sent
Forthwith to England, to be dealt with
    there
In such wise as shall be agreeable
Unto the English law and their demerits.
Is it not so ?

BELLINGHAM *(returning the paper)*.
          Ay, so the paper says.

ENDICOTT.

It means we shall no longer rule the Prov-
    ince ;
It means farewell to law and liberty,
Authority, respect for Magistrates,
The peace and welfare of the Common-
    wealth.
If all the knaves upon this continent
Can make appeal to England, and so
    thwart
The ends of truth and justice by delay,
Our power is gone forever. We are nothing
But ciphers, valueless save when we follow
Some unit ; and our unit is the King !
'T is he that gives us value.

BELLINGHAM.
          I confess
Such seems to be the meaning of this
    paper,
But being the King's Mandamus, signed
    and sealed,
We must obey, or we are in rebellion.

ENDICOTT.

I tell you, Richard Bellingham, — I tell
    you,
That this is the beginning of a struggle
Of which no mortal can foresee the end.
I shall not live to fight the battle for you,
I am a man disgraced in every way ;

This order takes from me my self-respect
And the respect of others. 'T is my doom,
Yes, my death - warrant, but must be
    obeyed !
Take it, and see that it is executed
So far as this, that all be set at large ;
But see that none of them be sent to Eng-
    land
To bear false witness, and to spread reports
That might be prejudicial to ourselves.
          [Exit BELLINGHAM.
There 's a dull pain keeps knocking at my
    heart,
Dolefully saying, " Set thy house in order,
For thou shalt surely die, and shalt not
    live ! "
For me the shadow on the dial-plate
Goeth not back, but on into the dark !
                 [Exit.

SCENE IV. — *The street. A crowd, reading
a placard on the door of the Meeting-house.*
NICHOLAS UPSALL *among them. Enter* JOHN
NORTON.

NORTON.
What is this gathering here ?

UPSALL.
          One William Brand,
An old man like ourselves, and weak in
    body,
Has been so cruelly tortured in his prison,
The people are excited, and they threaten
To tear the prison down.

NORTON.
          What has been done ?

UPSALL.
He has been put in irons, with his neck
And heels tied close together, and so left
From five in the morning until nine at
    night.

NORTON.
What more was done ?

UPSALL.
          He has been kept five days
In prison without food, and cruelly beaten,
So that his limbs were cold, his senses
    stopped.

NORTON.
What more ?

UPSALL.

And is this not enough?

NORTON.

Now hear me.
This William Brand of yours has tried to beat
Our Gospel Ordinances black and blue;
And, if he has been beaten in like manner,
It is but justice, and I will appear
In his behalf that did so. I suppose
That he refused to work.

UPSALL.

He was too weak.
How could an old man work, when he was starving?

NORTON.

And what is this placard?

UPSALL.

The Magistrates,
To appease the people and prevent a tumult,
Have put up these placards throughout the town,
Declaring that the jailer shalt be dealt with
Impartially and sternly by the Court.

NORTON (tearing down the placard).

Down with this weak and cowardly concession,
This flag of truce with Satan and with Sin!
I fling it in his face! I trample it
Under my feet! It is his cunning craft,
The masterpiece of his diplomacy,
To cry and plead for boundless toleration.
But toleration is the first-born child
Of all abominations and deceits.
There is no room in Christ's triumphant army
For tolerationists. And if an Angel
Preach any other gospel unto you
Than that ye have received, God's malediction
Descend upon him! Let him be accursed!
[Exit.

UPSALL.

Now, go thy ways, John Norton! go thy ways,
Thou Orthodox Evangelist, as men call thee!
But even now there cometh out of England,

Like an o'ertaking and accusing conscience,
An outraged man, to call thee to account
For the unrighteous murder of his son!
[Exit.

SCENE V. — The Wilderness. Enter EDITH.

EDITH.

How beautiful are these autumnal woods!
The wilderness doth blossom like the rose,
And change into a garden of the Lord!
How silent everywhere! Alone and lost.
Here in the forest, there comes over me
An inward awfulness. I recall the words
Of the Apostle Paul: "In journeyings often,
Often in perils in the wilderness,
In weariness, in painfulness, in watchings,
In hunger and thirst, in cold and nakedness;"
And I forget my weariness and pain,
My watchings, and my hunger and my thirst.
The Lord hath said that He will seek his flock
In cloudy and dark days, and they shall dwell
Securely in the wilderness, and sleep
Safe in the woods! Whichever way I turn,
I come back with my face towards the town.
Dimly I see it, and the sea beyond it.
O cruel town! I know what waits me there,
And yet I must go back; for ever louder
I hear the inward calling of the Spirit,
And must obey the voice. O woods, that wear
Your golden crown of martyrdom, blood-stained,
From you I learn a lesson of submission,
And am obedient even unto death,
If God so wills it. [Exit.

JOHN ENDICOTT (within).

Edith! Edith! Edith!

He enters.

It is in vain! I call, she answers not;
I follow, but I find no trace of her!
Blood! blood! The leaves above me and around me
Are red with blood! The pathways of the forest,
The clouds that canopy the setting sun

And even the little river in the meadows
Are stained with it ! Where'er I look, I
  see it !
Away, thou horrible vision ! Leave me !
  leave me !
Alas ! you winding stream, that gropes its
  way
Through mist and shadow, doubling on it-
  self,
At length will find, by the unerring law
Of nature, what it seeks. O soul of man,
Groping through mist and shadow, and re-
  coiling
Back on thyself, are, too, thy devious ways
Subject to law ? and when thou seemest to
  wander
The farthest from thy goal, art thou still
  drawing
Nearer and nearer to it, till at length
Thou findest, like the river, what thou
  seekest ?   [*Exit.*

ACT V

Scene I. — *Daybreak. Street in front of* Up-
sall's *house. A light in the window. Enter*
John Endicott.

JOHN ENDICOTT.

O silent, sombre, and deserted streets,
To me ye 're peopled with a sad procession,
And echo only to the voice of sorrow !
O houses full of peacefulness and sleep,
Far better were it to awake no more
Than wake to look upon such scenes again !
There is a light in Master Upsall's window.
The good man is already risen, for sleep
Deserts the couches of the old.
    Knocks at Upsall's *door.*

UPSALL (*at the window*).
               Who 's there ?

JOHN ENDICOTT.

Am I so changed you do not know my
  voice ?

UPSALL.
I know you. Have you heard what things
  have happened ?

JOHN ENDICOTT.

I have heard nothing.

UPSALL.
    Stay ; I will come down.

JOHN ENDICOTT.

I am afraid some dreadful news awaits me !
I do not dare to ask, yet am impatient
To know the worst. Oh, I am very weary
With waiting and with watching and pur-
  suing !
    Enter Upsall.

UPSALL.

Thank God, you have come back ! I 've
  much to tell you.
Where have you been ?

JOHN ENDICOTT.

         You know that I was seized,
Fined, and released again. You know that
  Edith,
After her scourging in three towns, was
  banished
Into the wilderness, into the land
That is not sown ; and there I followed
  her,
But found her not. Where is she ?

UPSALL.

               She is here.

JOHN ENDICOTT.

Oh, do not speak that word, for it means
  death !

UPSALL.

No, it means life. She sleeps in yonder
  chamber.
Listen to me. When news of Leddra's
  death
Reached England, Edward Burroughs, hav-
  ing boldly
Got access to the presence of the King,
Told him there was a vein of innocent
  blood
Opened in his dominions here, which
  threatened
To overrun them all. The King replied,
" But I will stop that vein ! " and he forth-
  with
Sent his Mandamus to our Magistrates,
That they proceed no further in this busi-
  ness.
So all are pardoned, and all set at large.

JOHN ENDICOTT.

Thank God ! This is a victory for truth !
Our thoughts are free. They cannot be
  shut up
In prison walls, nor put to death on scaf-
  folds !

UPSALL.

Come in ; the morning air blows sharp and
    cold
Through the damp streets.

JOHN ENDICOTT.

                  It is the dawn of day
That chases the old darkness from our
    sky,
And fills the land with liberty and light.
                          [*Exeunt.*

SCENE II. — *The parlor of the Three Mariners.*
    Enter KEMPTHORN.

KEMPTHORN.

A dull life this, — a dull life anyway !
Ready for sea ; the cargo all aboard,
Cleared for Barbadoes, and a fair wind
    blowing
From nor'-nor'-west ; and I, an idle lubber,
Laid neck and heels by that confounded
    bond !
I said to Ralph, says I, "What's to be
    done ? "
Says he : "Just slip your hawser in the
    night ;
Sheer off, and pay it with the topsail, Si-
    mon."
But that won't do ; because, you see, the
    owners
Somehow or other are mixed up with it.
Here are King Charles's Twelve Good
    Rules, that Cole
Thinks as important as the Rule of Three.
                Reads.
"Make no comparisons ; make no long
    meals."
Those are good rules and golden for a
    landlord
To hang in his best parlor, framed and
    glazed !
"Maintain no ill opinions ; urge no
    healths."
I drink the King's, whatever he may say,
And, as to ill opinions, that depends.
Now of Ralph Goldsmith I 've a good opin-
    ion,
And of the bilboes I 've an ill opinion ;
And both of these opinions I 'll maintain
As long as there 's a shot left in the locker.
Enter EDWARD BUTTER *with an ear-trumpet.*

BUTTER.

Good morning, Captain Kempthorn.

KEMPTHORN.

                          Sir, to you.
You 've the advantage of me.   I don't
    know you.
What may I call your name ?

BUTTER.

                  That 's not your name ?

KEMPTHORN.

Yes, that 's my name.   What 's yours ?

BUTTER.

                  My name is Butter.
I am the treasurer of the Commonwealth.

KEMPTHORN.

Will you be seated ?

BUTTER.

        What say ?   Who 's conceited ?

KEMPTHORN.

Will you sit down ?

BUTTER.

        Oh, thank you.

KEMPTHORN.

                          Spread yourself
Upon this chair, sweet Butter.

BUTTER (*sitting down*).

                          A fine morning.
KEMPTHORN.

Nothing 's the matter with it that I know
    of.
I have seen better, and I have seen worse.
The wind 's nor'west.   That 's fair for them
    that sail.

BUTTER.

You need not speak so loud ; I understand
    you.
You sail to-day.

KEMPTHORN.

                  No, I don't sail to-day.
So, be it fair or foul, it matters not.
Say, will you smoke ?   There 's choice
    tobacco here.

BUTTER.

No, thank you.   It 's against the law to
    smoke.

KEMPTHORN.

Then, will you drink ? There 's good ale
at this inn.

BUTTER.

No, thank you. It 's against the law to
drink.

KEMPTHORN.

Well, almost everything 's against the law
In this good town. Give a wide berth to
one thing,
You 're sure to fetch up soon on something
else.

BUTTER.

And so you sail to-day for dear Old Eng-
land.
I am not one of those who think a sup
Of this New England air is better worth
Than a whole draught of our Old Eng-
land's ale.

KEMPTHORN.

Nor I. Give me the ale and keep the air.
But, as I said, I do not sail to-day.

BUTTER.

Ah yes ; you sail to-day.

KEMPTHORN.

I 'm under bonds
To take some Quakers back to the Bar-
badoes ;
And one of them is banished, and another
Is sentenced to be hanged.

BUTTER.

No, all are pardoned,
All are set free, by order of the Court ;
But some of them would fain return to
England.
You must not take them. Upon that con-
dition
Your bond is cancelled.

KEMPTHORN.

Ah, the wind has shifted !
I pray you, do you speak officially ?

BUTTER.

I always speak officially. To prove it,
Here is the bond.
Rising and giving a paper.

KEMPTHORN.

And here 's my hand upon it.
And, look you, when I say I 'll do a thing
The thing is done. Am I now free to go ?

BUTTER.

What say ?

KEMPTHORN.

I say, confound the tedious man
With his strange speaking-trumpet ! Can
I go ?

BUTTER.

You 're free to go, by order of the Court.
Your servant, sir.   [*Exit.*

KEMPTHORN (*shouting from the window*).

Swallow, ahoy ! Hallo !
If ever a man was happy to leave Boston,
That man is Simon Kempthorn of the
Swallow !

Reënter BUTTER.

BUTTER.

Pray, did you call ?

KEMPTHORN.

Call ? Yes, I hailed the Swallow.

BUTTER.

That 's not my name. My name is Edward
Butter.
You need not speak so loud.

KEMPTHORN (*shaking hands*).

Good-by ! Good-by !

BUTTER.

Your servant, sir.

KEMPTHORN.

And yours a thousand times !
[*Exeunt.*

SCENE III. — GOVERNOR ENDICOTT'S *private
room. An open window.* ENDICOTT *seated
in an arm-chair.* BELLINGHAM *standing
near.*

ENDICOTT.

O lost, O loved ! wilt thou return no more ?
O loved and lost, and loved the more when
lost !
How many men are dragged into their
graves
By their rebellious children ! I now feel

The agony of a father's breaking heart
In David's cry, " O Absalom, my son ! "

BELLINGHAM.

Can you not turn your thoughts a little
    while
To public matters ?   There are papers
    here
That need attention.

ENDICOTT.

            Trouble me no more !
My business now is with another world.
Ah, Richard Bellingham ! I greatly fear
That in my righteous zeal I have been
    led
To doing many things which, left undone,
My mind would now be easier.   Did I
    dream it,
Or has some person told me, that John
    Norton
Is dead ?

BELLINGHAM.

    You have not dreamed it.   He is dead,
And gone to his reward.   It was no dream.

ENDICOTT.

Then it was very sudden ; for I saw him
Standing where you now stand, not long
    ago.

BELLINGHAM.

By his own fireside, in the afternoon,
A faintness and a giddiness came o'er
    him ;
And, leaning on the chimney-piece, he
    cried,
" The hand of God is on me ! " and fell
    dead.

ENDICOTT.

And did not some one say, or have I
    dreamed it,
That Humphrey Atherton is dead ?

BELLINGHAM.

            Alas !
He too is gone, and by a death as sudden.
Returning home one evening, at the place
Where usually the Quakers have been
    scourged,
His horse took fright, and threw him to the
    ground,
So that his brains were dashed about the
    street.

ENDICOTT.

I am not superstitious, Bellingham,
And yet I tremble lest it may have been
A judgment on him.

BELLINGHAM.

            So the people think.
They say his horse saw standing in the
    way
The ghost of William Leddra, and was
    frightened.
And furthermore, brave Richard Daven-
    port,
The captain of the Castle, in the storm
Has been struck dead by lightning.

ENDICOTT.

            Speak no more.
For as I listen to your voice it seems
As if the Seven Thunders uttered their
    voices,
And the dead bodies lay about the streets
Of the disconsolate city !   Bellingham,
I did not put those wretched men to
    death.
I did but guard the passage with the
    sword
Pointed towards them, and they rushed
    upon it !
Yet now I would that I had taken no part
In all that bloody work.

BELLINGHAM.

            The guilt of it
Be on their heads, not ours.

ENDICOTT.

            Are all set free ?

BELLINGHAM.

All are at large.

ENDICOTT.

            And none have been sent back
To England to malign us with the King ?

BELLINGHAM.

The ship that brought them sails this very
    hour,
But carries no one back.

        A distant cannon.

ENDICOTT.

            What is that gun ?

BELLINGHAM.

Her parting signal.   Through the window
  there,
Look, you can see her sails, above the
  roofs,
Dropping below the Castle, outward bound.

ENDICOTT.

O white, white, white ! Would that my
  soul had wings
As spotless as those shining sails to fly
  with !
Now lay this cushion straight.   I thank
  you.   Hark !
I thought I heard the hall door open and
  shut !
I thought I heard the footsteps of my boy !

BELLINGHAM.

It was the wind.   There 's no one in the
  passage.

ENDICOTT.

O Absalom, my son ! I feel the world
Sinking beneath me, sinking, sinking, sink-
  ing !
Death knocks ! I go to meet him ! Wel-
  come, Death !

*Rises, and sinks back dead ; his head falling
  aside upon his shoulder.*

BELLINGHAM.

O ghastly sight ! Like one who has been
  hanged !
Endicott ! Endicott ! He makes no an-
  swer !

Raises ENDICOTT's *head.*

He breathes no more ! How bright this
  signet-ring
Glitters upon his hand, where he has worn
  it
Through such long years of trouble, as if
  Death
Had given him this memento of affection,
And whispered in his ear, " Remember
  me ! "
How placid and how quiet is his face,
Now that the struggle and the strife are
  ended !
Only the acrid spirit of the times
Corroded this true steel.   Oh, rest in
  peace,
Courageous heart ! Forever rest in peace !

GILES COREY OF THE SALEM FARMS

DRAMATIS PERSONÆ

GILES COREY	*Farmer.*
JOHN HATHORNE	*Magistrate.*
COTTON MATHER	*Minister of the Gospel.*
JONATHAN WALCOT	*A youth.*
RICHARD GARDNER	*Sea-Captain.*
JOHN GLOYD	*Corey's hired man.*
MARTHA	*Wife of Giles Corey.*
TITUBA	*An Indian woman.*
MARY WALCOT	*One of the Afflicted.*

The Scene is in Salem in the year 1692.

PROLOGUE

DELUSIONS of the days that once have
  been,
Witchcraft and wonders of the world un-
  seen,
Phantoms of air, and necromantic arts
That crushed the weak and awed the
  stoutest hearts, —
These are our theme to-night ; and vaguely
  here,
Through the dim mists that crowd the at-
  mosphere,
We draw the outlines of weird figures cast
In shadow on the background of the
  Past.

Who would believe that in the quiet town
Of Salem, and amid the woods that crown
The neighboring hillsides, and the sunny
  farms
That fold it safe in their paternal arms, —
Who would believe that in those peaceful
  streets,
Where the great elms shut out the sum-
  mer heats,
Where quiet reigns, and breathes through
  brain and breast
The benediction of unbroken rest, —
Who would believe such deeds could find a
  place
As these whose tragic history we retrace ?

'T was but a village then : the goodman
  ploughed
His ample acres under sun or cloud ;
The goodwife at her doorstep sat and spun,
And gossiped with her neighbors in the
  sun ;
The only men of dignity and state

Were then the Minister and the Magistrate,
Who ruled their little realm with iron rod,
Less in the love than in the fear of God ;
And who believed devoutly in the Powers
Of Darkness, working in this world of ours,
In spells of Witchcraft, incantations dread,
And shrouded apparitions of the dead.

Upon this simple folk " with fire and
    flame,"
Saith the old Chronicle, " the Devil came ;
Scattering his firebrands and his poisonous
    darts,
To set on fire of Hell all tongues and
    hearts !
And 't is no wonder ; for, with all his host,
There most he rages where he hateth most,
And is most hated ; so on us he brings
All these stupendous and portentous
    things ! "

Something of this our scene to-night will
    show ;
And ye who listen to the Tale of Woe,
Be not too swift in casting the first stone,
Nor think New England bears the guilt
    alone.
This sudden burst of wickedness and crime
Was but the common madness of the time,
When in all lands, that lie within the sound
Of Sabbath bells, a Witch was burned or
    drowned.

ACT I

SCENE I. — *The woods near Salem Village.
Enter* TITUBA, *with a basket of herbs.*

TITUBA.

Here 's monk's-hood, that breeds fever in
    the blood ;
And deadly nightshade, that makes men see
    ghosts ;
And henbane, that will shake them with
    convulsions ;
And meadow-saffron and black hellebore,
That rack the nerves, and puff the skin
    with dropsy ;
And bitter-sweet, and briony, and eye-
    bright,
That cause eruptions, nosebleed, rheuma-
    tisms ;
I know them, and the places where they
    hide
In field and meadow ; and I know their
    secrets,

And gather them because they give me
    power
Over all men and women. Armed with
    these,
I, Tituba, an Indian and a slave,
Am stronger than the captain with his sword,
Am richer than the merchant with his
    money,
Am wiser than the scholar with his books,
Mightier than Ministers and Magistrates,
With all the fear and reverence that attend
    them !
For I can fill their bones with aches and
    pains,
Can make them cough with asthma, shake
    with palsy,
Can make their daughters see and talk
    with ghosts,
Or fall into delirium and convulsions.
I have the Evil Eye, the Evil Hand ;
A touch from me and they are weak with
    pain,
A look from me, and they consume and die.
The death of cattle and the blight of corn,
The shipwreck, the tornado, and the fire, —
These are my doings, and they know it not.
Thus I work vengeance on mine enemies,
Who, while they call me slave, are slaves to
    me !

Exit TITUBA. *Enter* MATHER, *booted and
spurred, with a riding-whip in his hand.*

MATHER.

Methinks that I have come by paths un-
    known
Into the land and atmosphere of Witches ;
For, meditating as I journeyed on,
Lo ! I have lost my way ! If I remember
Rightly, it is Scribonius the learned
That tells the story of a man who, praying
For one that was possessed by Evil Spirits,
Was struck by Evil Spirits in the face ;
I, journeying to circumvent the Witches
Surely by Witches have been led astray.
I am persuaded there are few affairs
In which the Devil doth not interfere.
We cannot undertake a journey even,
But Satan will be there to meddle with it
By hindering or by furthering. He hath
    led me
Into this thicket, struck me in the face
With branches of the trees, and so entan-
    gled
The fetlocks of my horse with vines and
    brambles,

That I must needs dismount, and search on
    foot
For the lost pathway leading to the village.

Reënter TITUBA.

What shape is this ?   What monstrous ap-
    parition,
Exceeding fierce, that none may pass that
    way ?
Tell me, good woman, if you are a
    woman —

TITUBA.

I am a woman, but I am not good.
I am a Witch !

MATHER.

        Then tell me, Witch and woman,
For you must know the pathways through
    this wood,
Where lieth Salem Village ?

TITUBA.

                Reverend sir,
The village is near by.   I 'm going there
With these few herbs.   I 'll lead you.   Fol-
    low me.

MATHER.

First say, who are you ?   I am loath to
    follow
A stranger in this wilderness, for fear
Of being misled, and left in some morass.
Who are you ?

TITUBA.

         I am Tituba the Witch,
Wife of John Indian.

MATHER.

            You are Tituba ?
I know you then.   You have renounced the
    Devil,
And have become a penitent confessor.
The Lord be praised !   Go on, I 'll follow
    you.
Wait only till I fetch my horse, that stands
Tethered among the trees, not far from
    here.

TITUBA.

Let me get up behind you, reverend sir.

MATHER.

The Lord forbid !   What would the people
    think,
If they should see the Reverend Cotton
    Mather
Ride into Salem with a Witch behind him ?
The Lord forbid !

TITUBA.

        I do not need a horse !
I can ride through the air upon a stick,
Above the tree-tops and above the houses,
And no one see me, no one overtake me !

                  [*Exeunt.*

SCENE II. — *A room at* JUSTICE HATHORNE'S.
A clock in the corner.   Enter HATHORNE *and*
MATHER.

HATHORNE.

You are welcome, reverend sir, thrice wel-
    come here
Beneath my humble roof.

MATHER.

           I thank your Worship.

HATHORNE.

Pray you be seated.   You must be fatigued
With your long ride through unfrequented
    woods.

They sit down.

MATHER.

You know the purport of my visit here, —
To be advised by you, and counsel with
    you,
And with the Reverend Clergy of the vil-
    lage,
Touching these witchcrafts that so much
    afflict you ;
And see with mine own eyes the wonders
    told
Of spectres and the shadows of the dead,
That come back from their graves to speak
    with men.

HATHORNE.

Some men there are, I have known such,
    who think
That the two worlds — the seen and the un-
    seen,
The world of matter and the world of
    spirit —
Are like the hemispheres upon our maps,
And touch each other only at a point.
But these two worlds are not divided
    thus,
Save for the purposes of common speech.
They form one globe, in which the parted
    seas
All flow together and are intermingled,
While the great continents remain dis-
    tinct.

MATHER.

I doubt it not. The spiritual world
Lies all about us, and its avenues
Are open to the unseen feet of phantoms
That come and go, and we perceive them
    not,
Save by their influence, or when at times
A most mysterious Providence permits
    them
To manifest themselves to mortal eyes.

HATHORNE.

You, who are always welcome here among
    us,
Are doubly welcome now. We need your
    wisdom,
Your learning in these things, to be our
    guide.
The Devil hath come down in wrath upon
    us,
And ravages the land with all his hosts.

MATHER.

The Unclean Spirit said, "My name is
    Legion !"
Multitudes in the Valley of Destruction !
But when our fervent, well - directed
    prayers,
Which are the great artillery of Heaven,
Are brought into the field, I see them scat-
    tered
And driven like autumn leaves before the
    wind.

HATHORNE.

You, as a Minister of God, can meet them
With spiritual weapons ; but, alas !
I, as a Magistrate, must combat them
With weapons from the armory of the
    flesh.

MATHER.

These wonders of the world invisible, —
These spectral shapes that haunt our habi-
    tations, —
The multiplied and manifold afflictions
With which the aged and the dying saints
Have their death prefaced and their age
    imbittered, —
Are but prophetic trumpets that proclaim
The Second Coming of our Lord on earth.
The evening wolves will be much more
    abroad,
When we are near the evening of the
    world.

HATHORNE.

When you shall see, as I have hourly seen,
The sorceries and the witchcrafts that tor-
    ment us,
See children tortured by invisible spirits,
And wasted and consumed by powers un-
    seen,
You will confess the half has not been told
    you.

MATHER.

It must be so. The death-pangs of the
    Devil
Will make him more a Devil than before ;
And Nebuchadnezzar's furnace will be
    heated
Seven times more hot before its putting
    out.

HATHORNE.

Advise me, reverend sir. I look to you
For counsel and for guidance in this matter.
What further shall we do ?

MATHER.

                    Remember this,
That as a sparrow falls not to the ground
Without the will of God, so not a Devil
Can come down from the air without his
    leave.
We must inquire.

HATHORNE.

                    Dear sir, we have inquired ;
Sifted the matter thoroughly through and
    through,
And then resifted it.

MATHER.

                    If God permits
These Evil Spirits from the unseen regions
To visit us with surprising informations,
We must inquire what cause there is for
    this,
But not receive the testimony borne
By spectres as conclusive proof of guilt
In the accused.

HATHORNE.

                    Upon such evidence
We do not rest our case. The ways are
    many
In which the guilty do betray themselves.

MATHER.

Be careful. Carry the knife with such ex-
    actness,

That on one side no innocent blood be
    shed
By too excessive zeal, and on the other
No shelter given to any work of darkness.

HATHORNE.

For one, I do not fear excess of zeal.
What do we gain by parleying with the
    Devil ?
You reason, but you hesitate to act !
Ah, reverend sir ! believe me, in such
    cases
The only safety is in acting promptly.
'T is not the part of wisdom to delay
In things where not to do is still to do
A deed more fatal than the deed we shrink
    from.
You are a man of books and meditation,
But I am one who acts.

MATHER.

           God give us wisdom
In the directing of this thorny business,
And guide us, lest New England should
    become
Of an unsavory and sulphurous odor
In the opinion of the world abroad !

    The clock strikes.

I never hear the striking of a clock
Without a warning and an admonition
That time is on the wing, and we must
    quicken
Our tardy pace in journeying Heaven-
    ward,
As Israel did in journeying Canaan-ward !

    They rise.

HATHORNE.

Then let us make all haste ; and I will
    show you
In what disguises and what fearful shapes
The Unclean Spirits haunt this neighbor-
    hood,
And you will pardon my excess of zeal.

MATHER.

Ah, poor New England ! He who hurri-
    canoed
The house of Job is making now on thee
One last assault, more deadly and more
    snarled
With unintelligible circumstances
Than any thou hast hitherto encountered !

                 [*Exeunt.*

SCENE III. — *A room in* WALCOT'S *house.*
MARY WALCOT *seated in an arm-chair.* TI-
TUBA *with a mirror.*

MARY.

Tell me another story, Tituba.
A drowsiness is stealing over me
Which is not sleep ; for, though I close
    mine eyes,
I am awake, and in another world.
Dim faces of the dead and of the absent
Come floating up before me, — floating,
    fading,
And disappearing.

TITUBA.

          Look into this glass.
What see you ?

MARY.

          Nothing but a golden vapor.
Yes, something more. An island, with the
    sea
Breaking all round it, like a blooming
    hedge.
What land is this ?

TITUBA.

          It is San Salvador,
Where Tituba was born. What see you
    now ?

MARY.

A man all black and fierce.

TITUBA.

            That is my father.
He was an Obi man, and taught me
    magic, —
Taught me the use of herbs and images.
What is he doing ?

MARY.

          Holding in his hand
A waxen figure. He is melting it
Slowly before a fire.

TITUBA.

      And now what see you ?

MARY.

A woman lying on a bed of leaves,
Wasted and worn away. Ah, she is dying !

TITUBA.

That is the way the Obi men destroy

The people they dislike !   That is the way
Some one is wasting and consuming you.

MARY.

You terrify me, Tituba !   Oh, save me
From those who make me pine and waste
      away !
Who are they ?   Tell me.

TITUBA.
                        That I do not know,
But you will see them.   They will come to
      you.

MARY.

No, do not let them come !   I cannot bear
      it !
I am too weak to bear it !   I am dying.
            Falls into a trance.

TITUBA.

Hark ! there is some one coming !
      Enter HATHORNE, MATHER, *and* WALCOT.

WALCOT.
                        There she lies,
Wasted and worn by devilish incantations !
O my poor sister !

MATHER.
                  Is she always thus ?

WALCOT.

Nay, she is sometimes tortured by con-
      vulsions.

MATHER.

Poor child !   How thin she is !   How wan
      and wasted !

HATHORNE.

Observe her.   She is troubled in her sleep.

MATHER.

Some fearful vision haunts her.

HATHORNE.
                        You now see
With your own eyes, and touch with your
      own hands,
The mysteries of this Witchcraft.

MATHER.
                        One would need
The hands of Briareus and the eyes of
      Argus
To see and touch them all.

HATHORNE.
                  You now have entered
The realm of ghosts and phantoms, — the
      vast realm
Of the unknown and the invisible,
Through whose wide-open gates there blows
      a wind
From the dark valley of the shadow of
      Death,
That freezes us with horror.

MARY (*starting*).
                        Take her hence !
Take her away from me.   I see her there !
She 's coming to torment me !

WALCOT (*taking her hand*).
                        O my sister !
What frightens you ?   She neither hears
      nor sees me.
She 's in a trance.

MARY.
            Do you not see her there ?

TITUBA.
My child, who is it ?

MARY.
                  Ah, I do not know.
I cannot see her face.

TITUBA.
                  How is she clad ?

MARY.
She wears a crimson bodice.   In her hand
She holds an image, and is pinching it
Between her fingers.   Ah, she tortures
      me !
I see her face now.   It is Goodwife Bishop !
Why does she torture me ?   I never
      harmed her !
And now she strikes me with an iron rod !
Oh, I am beaten !

MATHER.
                  This is wonderful !
I can see nothing !   Is this apparition
Visibly there, and yet we cannot see it ?

HATHORNE.
It is.   The spectre is invisible
Unto our grosser senses, but she sees it.

MARY.

Look ! look ! there is another clad in gray !
She holds a spindle in her hand, and
    threatens
To stab me with it ! It is Goodwife
    Corey !
Keep her away ! Now she is coming at
    me !
O mercy ! mercy !

WALCOT (*thrusting with his sword*).
                        There is nothing there !

MATHER (*to* HATHORNE).
Do you see anything ?

HATHORNE.
                The laws that govern
The spiritual world prevent our seeing
Things palpable and visible to her.
These spectres are to us as if they were
    not.
Mark her ; she wakes.
        TITUBA *touches her, and she awakes.*

MARY.
            Who are these gentlemen ?

WALCOT.
They are our friends. Dear Mary, are you
better ?
            MARY.
Weak, very weak.
Taking a spindle from her lap, and holding it up.
            How came this spindle here ?

TITUBA.
You wrenched it from the hand of Good-
    wife Corey
When she rushed at you.

HATHORNE.
            Mark that, reverend sir !

MATHER.
It is most marvellous, most inexplicable !

TITUBA (*picking up a bit of gray cloth from the
            floor*).
And here, too, is a bit of her gray dress,
That the sword cut away.

MATHER.
                Beholding this,
It were indeed by far more credulous

To be incredulous than to believe.
None but a Sadducee, who doubts of all
Pertaining to the spiritual world,
Could doubt such manifest and damning
    proofs !

HATHORNE.
Are you convinced ?

MATHER (*to* MARY).
            Dear child, be comforted !
Only by prayer and fasting can you drive
These Unclean Spirits from you. An old
    man
Gives you his blessing. God be with you,
    Mary !

ACT II

SCENE I. — GILES COREY'S *farm. Morning.
Enter* COREY, *with a horseshoe and a hammer.*

COREY.
The Lord hath prospered me. The rising
    sun
Shines on my Hundred Acres and my
    woods
As if he loved them. On a morn like this
I can forgive mine enemies, and thank God
For all his goodness unto me and mine.
My orchard groans with russets and pear-
    mains ;
My ripening corn shines golden in the sun ;
My barns are crammed with hay, my cattle
    thrive ;
The birds sing blithely on the trees around
    me !
And blither than the birds my heart within
    me.
But Satan still goes up and down the earth ;
And to protect this house from his assaults,
And keep the powers of darkness from my
    door,
This horseshoe will I nail upon the thresh-
    old.
        Nails down the horseshoe.
There, ye night-hags and witches that tor-
    ment
The neighborhood, ye shall not enter
    here ! —
What is the matter in the field ? — John
    Gloyd !
The cattle are all running to the woods ! —
John Gloyd ! Where is the man ?
        Enter JOHN GLOYD.

Look there !
What ails the cattle ?   Are they all be-
    witched ?
They run like mad.

GLOYD.

They have been overlooked.

COREY.

The Evil Eye is on them sure enough.
Call all the men.   Be quick.   Go after
    them !

Exit GLOYD *and enter* MARTHA.

MARTHA.

What is amiss ?

COREY.

The cattle are bewitched.
They are broken loose and making for the
    woods.

MARTHA.

Why will you harbor such delusions, Giles ?
Bewitched ?   Well, then it was John Gloyd
    bewitched them ;
I saw him even now take down the bars
And turn them loose !   They 're only frolic-
    some.

COREY.

The rascal !

MARTHA.

I was standing in the road,
Talking with Goodwife Proctor, and I saw
    him.

COREY.

With Proctor's wife ?   And   what   says
Goodwife Proctor ?

MARTHA.

Sad things indeed ; the saddest you can
    hear
Of Bridget Bishop.   She 's cried out upon !

COREY.

Poor soul !   I 've known her forty year or
    more.
She was the widow Wasselby ; and then
She married Oliver, and Bishop next.
She 's had three husbands.   I remember
    well
My games of shovel-board at Bishop's
    tavern
In the old merry days, and she so gay
With her red paragon bodice and her rib-
    bons !
Ah, Bridget Bishop always was a Witch !

MARTHA.

They 'll little help her now, — her caps and
    ribbons,
And her red paragon bodice, and her
    plumes,
With which she flaunted in the Meeting-
    house !
When next she goes there, it will be for
    trial.

COREY.

When will that be ?

MARTHA.

This very day at ten.

COREY.

Then get you ready.   We will go and see
    it.
Come ; you shall ride behind me on the pil-
    lion.

MARTHA.

Not I.   You know I do not like such things.
I wonder you should.   I do not believe
In Witches nor in Witchcraft.

COREY.

Well, I do.
There 's a strange fascination in it all,
That draws me on and on, I know not why.

MARTHA.

What do we know of spirits good or ill,
Or of their power to help us or to harm us ?

COREY.

Surely what 's in the Bible must be true.
Did not an Evil Spirit come on Saul ?
Did not the Witch of Endor bring the ghost
Of Samuel from his grave ?   The Bible
    says so.

MARTHA.

That happened very long ago.

COREY.

With God
There is no long ago.

MARTHA.

There is with us.

COREY.

And Mary Magdalene had seven devils,
And he who dwelt among the tombs a
    legion !

MARTHA.

God's power is infinite. I do not doubt it.
If in His providence He once permitted
Such things to be among the Israelites,
It does not follow He permits them now,
And among us who are not Israelites.
But we will not dispute about it, Giles.
Go to the village, if you think it best,
And leave me here ; I 'll go about my
    work.   [*Exit into the house.*

COREY.

And I will go and saddle the gray mare.
The last word always. That is woman's
    nature.
If an old man will marry a young wife,
He must make up his mind to many things.
It 's putting new cloth into an old garment,
When the strain comes, it is the old gives
    way.
            Goes to the door.
Oh Martha ! I forgot to tell you some-
    thing.
I 've had a letter from a friend of mine,
A certain Richard Gardner of Nantucket,
Master and owner of a whaling-vessel ;
He writes that he is coming down to see us.
I hope you 'll like him.

MARTHA.
                I will do my best.

COREY.

That 's a good woman. Now I will be
    gone.
I 've not seen Gardner for this twenty
    year ;
But there is something of the sea about
    him, —
Something so open, generous, large, and
    strong,
It makes me love him better than a bro-
    ther.   [*Exit.*
MARTHA *comes to the door.*

MARTHA.

Oh these old friends and cronies of my hus-
    band,
These captains from Nantucket and the
    Cape,
That come and turn my house into a tavern
With their carousing ! Still, there 's some-
    thing frank
In these seafaring men that makes me
    like them.

Why, here 's a horseshoe nailed upon the
    doorstep !
Giles has done this to keep away the
    Witches.
I hope this Richard Gardner will bring with
    him
A gale of good sound common-sense to
    blow
The fog of these delusions from his brain !

COREY (*within*).

Ho ! Martha ! Martha !
            Enter COREY.
            Have you seen my saddle ?

MARTHA.

I saw it yesterday.

COREY.
            Where did you see it ?

MARTHA.

On a gray mare, that somebody was riding
Along the village road.

COREY.
            Who was it ? Tell me.

MARTHA.

Some one who should have stayed at home.

COREY (*restraining himself*).
                        I see !
Don't vex me, Martha. Tell me where it
    is.

MARTHA.

I 've hidden it away.

COREY.
            Go fetch it me.

MARTHA.
Go find it.

COREY.

        No. I 'll ride down to the village
Bare-back ; and when the people stare and
    say,
"Giles Corey, where 's your saddle ? " I
    will answer,
" A Witch has stolen it." How shall you
    like that ?

MARTHA.

I shall not like it.

COREY.

Then go fetch the saddle.
[*Exit* MARTHA.

If an old man will marry a young wife,
Why then — why then — why then — he
must spell Baker !
Enter MARTHA *with the saddle, which she throws
down.*

MARTHA.

There ! .There 's the saddle.

COREY.

Take it up.

MARTHA.

I won't !

COREY.

Then let it lie there. I 'll ride to the vil-
lage,
And say you are a Witch.

MARTHA.

No, not that, Giles.

She takes up the saddle.

COREY.

Now come with me, and saddle the gray
mare
With your own hands ; and you shall see
me ride
Along the village road as is becoming
Giles Corey of the Salem Farms, your hus-
band !   [*Exeunt.*

SCENE II. —*The Green in front of the Meeting-
house in Salem Village. People coming and
going. Enter* GILES COREY.

COREY.

A melancholy end !   Who would have
thought
That Bridget Bishop e'er would come to
this ?
Accused, convicted, and condemned to death
For Witchcraft !   And so good a woman
too !

A FARMER.

Good morrow, neighbor Corey.

COREY (*not hearing him*).

Who is safe ?
How do I know but under my own roof
I too may harbor Witches, and some Devil
Be plotting and contriving against me ?

FARMER.

He does not hear.   Good morrow, neighbor
Corey !

COREY.

Good morrow.

FARMER.

Have you seen John Proctor lately ?

COREY.

No, I have not.

FARMER.

Then do not see him, Corey.

COREY.

Why should I not ?

FARMER.

Because he 's angry with you.
So keep out of his way.   Avoid a quarrel.

COREY.

Why does he seek to fix a quarrel on me ?

FARMER.

He says you burned his house.

COREY.

I burn his house ?
If he says that, John Proctor is a liar !
The night his house was burned I was in
bed,
And I can prove it !   Why, we are old
friends !
He could not say that of me.

FARMER.

He did say it.
I heard him say it.

COREY.

Then he shall unsay it.

FARMER.

He said you did it out of spite to him
For taking part against you in the quar-
rel
You had with your John Gloyd about his
wages.
He says you murdered Goodell ; that you
trampled
Upon his body till he breathed no more.
And so beware of him ; that 's my advice !
[*Exit*

COREY.

By Heaven ! this is too much ! I 'll seek
    him out,
And make him eat his words, or strangle
    him.
I 'll not be slandered at a time like this,
When every word is made an accusation,
When every whisper kills, and every man
Walks with a halter round his neck !

Enter GLOYD *in haste.*

                        What now ?

GLOYD.

I came to look for you.   The cattle —

COREY.

                        Well,
What of them ?   Have you found them ?

GLOYD.

                        They are dead.
I followed them through the woods, across
    the meadows ;
Then they all leaped into the Ipswich River,
And swam across, but could not climb the
    bank,
And so were drowned.

COREY.

            You are to blame for this ;
For you took down the bars, and let them
    loose.

GLOYD.

That I deny.   They broke the fences down.
You know they were bewitched.

COREY.

            Ah, my poor cattle !
The Evil Eye was on them ; that is true.
Day of disaster !   Most unlucky day !
Why did I leave my ploughing and my
    reaping
To plough and reap this Sodom and Gomor-
    rah ?
Oh, I could drown myself for sheer vexa-
    tion !   [*Exit.*

GLOYD.

He 's going for his cattle.   He won't find
    them.
By this time they have drifted out to sea.
They will not break his fences any more,
Though they may break his heart.   And
    what care I ?   [*Exit.*

SCENE III. — COREY'S *kitchen   A table with*
    supper. MARTHA *knitting.*

MARTHA.

He 's come at last.   I hear him in the pas-
    sage.
Something has gone amiss with him to-day ;
I know it by his step, and by the sound
The door made as he shut it.   He is angry.

Enter COREY *with his riding-whip.   As he speaks*
    he takes off his hat and gloves, and throws them
    down violently.

COREY.

I say if Satan ever entered man
He 's in John Proctor !

MARTHA.

            Giles, what is the matter ?
You frighten me.

COREY.

            I say if any man
Can have a Devil in him, then that man
Is Proctor, — is John Proctor, and no
    other !

MARTHA.

Why, what has he been doing ?

COREY.

                        Everything !
What do you think I heard there in the
    village ?

MARTHA.

I 'm sure I cannot guess.   What did you
    hear ?

COREY.

He says I burned his house !

MARTHA.

                        Does he say that ?

COREY.

He says I burned his house.   I was in bed
And fast asleep that night ; and I can
    prove it.

MARTHA.

If he says that, I think the Father of Lies
Is surely in the man.

COREY.

                        He does say that,
And that I did it to wreak vengeance on
    him
For taking sides against me in the quarrel
I had with that John Gloyd about his wages.

And God knows that I never bore him mal-
    ice
For that, as I have told him twenty times !

MARTHA.

It is John Gloyd has stirred him up to this.
I do not like that Gloyd. I think him
    crafty,
Not to be trusted, sullen, and untruthful.
Come, have your supper. You are tired
    and hungry.

COREY.

I 'm angry, and not hungry.

MARTHA.

             Do eat something.
You 'll be the better for it.

COREY (*sitting down*).

              I 'm not hungry.

MARTHA.

Let not the sun go down upon your wrath.

COREY.

It has gone down upon it, and will rise
To-morrow, and go down again upon it.
They have trumped up against me the old
    story
Of causing Goodell's death by trampling on
    him.

MARTHA.

Oh, that is false. I know it to be false.

COREY.

He has been dead these fourteen years or
    more.
Why can't they let him rest ? Why must
    they drag him
Out of his grave to give me a bad name ?
I did not kill him. In his bed he died,
As most men die, because his hour had
    come.
I have wronged no man. Why should
    Proctor say
Such things about me ? I will not forgive
    him
Till he confesses he has slandered me.
Then, I 've more trouble. All my cattle
    gone.

MARTHA.

They will come back again.

COREY.

             Not in this world.
Did I not tell you they were overlooked ?
They ran down through the woods, into the
    meadows,
And tried to swim the river, and were
    drowned.
It is a heavy loss.

MARTHA.

             I 'm sorry for it.

COREY.

All my dear oxen dead. I loved them,
    Martha,
Next to yourself. I liked to look at them,
And watch the breath come out of their wide
    nostrils,
And see their patient eyes. Somehow I
    thought
It gave me strength only to look at them.
And how they strained their necks against
    the yoke
If I but spoke, or touched them with the
    goad !
They were my friends ; and when Gloyd
    came and told me
They were all drowned, I could have
    drowned myself
From sheer vexation ; and I said as much
To Gloyd and others.

MARTHA.

             Do not trust John Gloyd
With anything you would not have re-
    peated.

COREY.

As I came through the woods this after-
    noon,
Impatient at my loss, and much perplexed
With all that I had heard there in the vil-
    lage,
The yellow leaves lit up the trees about me
Like an enchanted palace, and I wished
I knew enough of magic or of Witchcraft
To change them into gold. Then suddenly
A tree shook down some crimson leaves
    upon me,
Like drops of blood, and in the path before
    me
Stood Tituba the Indian, the old crone.

MARTHA.

Were you not frightened ?

COREY.

No, I do not think
I know the meaning of that word. Why
frightened ?
I am not one of those who think the Lord
Is waiting till He catches them some day
In the back yard alone ! What should I
fear ?
She started from the bushes by the path,
And had a basket full of herbs and roots
For some witch-broth or other, — the old
hag !

MARTHA.

She has been here to-day.

COREY.

With hand outstretched
She said : "Giles Corey, will you sign the
Book ? "
"Avaunt !" I cried : "Get thee behind
me, Satan ! "
At which she laughed and left me. But a
voice
Was whispering in my ear continually :
"Self-murder is no crime. The life of
man
Is his, to keep it or to throw away ! "

MARTHA.

'T was a temptation of the Evil One !
Giles, Giles ! why will you harbor these
dark thoughts ?

COREY (rising).

I am too tired to talk. I 'll go to bed.

MARTHA.

First tell me something about Bridget
Bishop.
How did she look ? You saw her ? You
were there ?

COREY.

I 'll tell you that to-morrow, not to-night.
I 'll go to bed.

MARTHA.

First let us pray together.

COREY.

I cannot pray to-night.

MARTHA.

Say the Lord's Prayer,
And that will comfort you.

COREY.

I cannot say,
"As we forgive those that have sinned
against us,"
When I do not forgive them.

MARTHA (kneeling on the hearth).

God forgive you !

COREY.

I will not make believe ! I say, to-night
There 's something thwarts me when I wish
to pray,
And thrusts into my mind, instead of
prayers,
Hate and revenge, and things that are not
prayers.
Something of my old self, — my old, bad
life, —
And the old Adam in me, rises up,
And will not let me pray. I am afraid
The Devil hinders me. You know I say
Just what I think, and nothing more nor
less,
And, when I pray, my heart is in my
prayer.
I cannot say one thing and mean another.
If I can't pray, I will not make believe !
[Exit COREY. MARTHA continues kneeling.

ACT III

SCENE I. — GILES COREY's kitchen. Morning.
COREY and MARTHA sitting at the breakfast-
table.

COREY (rising).

Well, now I 've told you all I saw and
heard
Of Bridget Bishop ; and I must be gone.

MARTHA.

Don't go into the village, Giles, to-day.
Last night you came back tired and out of
humor.

COREY.

Say, angry ; say, right angry. I was never
In a more devilish temper in my life.
All things went wrong with me.

MARTHA.

You were much vexed ;
So don't go to the village.

COREY (*going*).
                        No, I won't.
I won't go near it.   We are going to mow
The Ipswich meadows for the aftermath,
The crop of sedge and rowens.

MARTHA.
                        Stay a moment.
I want to tell you what I dreamed last
    night.
Do you believe in dreams ?

COREY.
                        Why, yes and no.
When they come true, then I believe in
    them ;
When they come false, I don't believe in
    them.
But let me hear.   What did you dream
    about ?

MARTHA.
I dreamed that you and I were both in
    prison ;
That we had fetters on our hands and feet ;
That we were taken before the Magis-
    trates,
And tried for Witchcraft, and condemned
    to death !
I wished to pray ; they would not let me
    pray ;
You tried to comfort me, and they forbade
    it.
But the most dreadful thing in all my dream
Was that they made you testify against
    me !
And then there came a kind of mist be-
    tween us ;
I could not see you ; and I woke in terror.
I never was more thankful in my life
Than when I found you sleeping at my
    side !

COREY (*with tenderness*).
It was our talk last night that made you
    dream.
I 'm sorry for it.   I 'll control myself
Another time, and keep my temper down !
I do not like such dreams. — Remember,
    Martha,
I 'm going to mow the Ipswich River
    meadows ;
If Gardner comes, you 'll tell him where
    to find me.   [*Exit.*

MARTHA.
So this delusion grows from bad to worse.
First, a forsaken and forlorn old woman,
Ragged and wretched, and without a
    friend ;
Then something higher.   Now it 's Bridget
    Bishop ;
God only knows whose turn it will be next !
The Magistrates are blind, the people mad !
If they would only seize the Afflicted Chil-
    dren,
And put them in the Workhouse, where
    they should be,
There 'd be an end of all this wickedness.
                                [*Exit.*

SCENE II. — *A street in Salem Village.   Enter*
    MATHER *and* HATHORNE.

MATHER.
Yet one thing troubles me.

HATHORNE.
                        And what is that ?

MATHER.
May not the Devil take the outward shape
Of innocent persons ?   Are we not in dan-
    ger,
Perhaps, of punishing some who are not
    guilty ?

HATHORNE.
As I have said, we do not trust alone
To spectral evidence.

MATHER.
                        And then again,
If any shall be put to death for Witch-
    craft,
We do but kill the body, not the soul.
The Unclean Spirits that possessed them
    once
Live still, to enter into other bodies.
What have we gained ?   Surely, there 's
    nothing gained.

HATHORNE.
Doth not the Scripture say, " Thou shalt
    not suffer
A Witch to live ? "

MATHER.
                        The Scripture sayeth it,
But speaketh to the Jews ; and we are
    Christians.
What say the laws of England ?

HATHORNE.

They make Witchcraft
Felony without the benefit of Clergy.
Witches are burned in England. You
have read —
For you read all things, not a book escapes
you —
The famous Demonology of King James?

MATHER.

A curious volume. I remember also
The plot of the Two Hundred, with one
Fian,
The Registrar of the Devil, at their head,
To drown his Majesty on his return
From Denmark ; how they sailed in sieves
or riddles
Unto North Berwick Kirk in Lothian,
And, landing there, danced hand in hand,
and sang,
" Goodwife, go ye before ! goodwife, go ye !
If ye 'll not go before, goodwife, let me ! "
While Geilis Duncan played the Witches'
Reel
Upon a jews-harp.

HATHORNE.

Then you know full well
The English law, and that in England
Witches,
When lawfully convicted and attainted,
Are put to death.

MATHER.

When lawfully convicted ;
That is the point.

HATHORNE.

You heard the evidence
Produced before us yesterday at the trial
Of Bridget Bishop.

MATHER.

One of the Afflicted,
I know, bore witness to the apparition
Of ghosts unto the spectre of this Bishop,
Saying, " You murdered us ! " of the truth
whereof
There was in matter of fact too much sus-
picion.

HATHORNE.

And when she cast her eyes on the Af-
flicted,
They were struck down ; and this in such a
manner

There could be no collusion in the busi-
ness.
And when the accused but laid her hand
upon them,
As they lay in their swoons, they straight
revived,
Although they stirred not when the others
touched them.

MATHER.

What most convinced me of the woman's
guilt
Was finding hidden in her cellar wall
Those poppets made of rags, with headless
pins
Stuck into them point outwards, and
whereof
She could not give a reasonable account.

HATHORNE.

When you shall read the testimony given
Before the Court in all the other cases,
I am persuaded you will find the proof
No less conclusive than it was in this.
Come, then, with me, and I will tax your
patience
With reading of the documents so far
As may convince you that these sorcerers
Are lawfully convicted and attainted.
Like doubting Thomas, you shall lay your
hand
Upon these wounds, and you will doubt no
more.   [Exeunt.

SCENE III. — A room in COREY'S house. MAR-
THA and two Deacons of the church.

MARTHA.

Be seated. I am glad to see you here.
I know what you are come for. You are
come
To question me, and learn from my own
lips
If I have any dealings with the Devil ;
In short, if I 'm a Witch.

DEACON (sitting down).

Such is our purpose.
How could you know beforehand why we
came ?

MARTHA.

'T was only a surmise.

DEACON.

We came to ask you,
You being with us in church covenant,
What part you have, if any, in these
matters.

MARTHA.

And I make answer, No part whatsoever.
I am a farmer's wife, a working woman ;
You see my spinning-wheel, you see my
loom,
You know the duties of a farmer's wife,
And are not ignorant that my life among
you
Has been without reproach until this day.
Is it not true ?

DEACON.

So much we 're bound to own ;
And say it frankly, and without reserve.

MARTHA.

I 've heard the idle tales that are abroad ;
I 've heard it whispered that I am a Witch ;
I cannot help it. I do not believe
In any Witchcraft. It is a delusion.

DEACON.

How can you say that it is a delusion,
When all our learned and good men believe
it ? —
Our Ministers and worshipful Magistrates ?

MARTHA.

Their eyes are blinded, and see not the
truth.
Perhaps one day they will be open to it.

DEACON.

You answer boldly. The Afflicted Chil-
dren
Say you appeared to them.

MARTHA.

And did they say
What clothes I came in ?

DEACON.

No, they could not tell.
They said that you foresaw our visit here,
And blinded them, so that they could not
see
The clothes you wore.

MARTHA.

The cunning, crafty girls !
I say to you, in all sincerity,

I never have appeared to any one
In my own person. If the Devil takes
My shape to hurt these children, or afflict
them,
I am not guilty of it. And I say
It 's all a mere delusion of the senses.

DEACON.

I greatly fear that you will find too late
It is not so.

MARTHA (rising).

They do accuse me falsely.
It is delusion, or it is deceit.
There is a story in the ancient Scriptures
Which much I wonder comes not to your
minds.
Let me repeat it to you.

DEACON.

We will hear it.

MARTHA.

It came to pass that Naboth had a vineyard
Hard by the palace of the King called
Ahab.
And Ahab, King of Israel, spake to Naboth,
And said to him, Give unto me thy vine-
yard,
That I may have it for a garden of herbs,
And I will give a better vineyard for it,
Or, if it seemeth good to thee, its worth
In money. And then Naboth said to Ahab,
The Lord forbid it me that I should give
The inheritance of my fathers unto thee.
And Ahab came into his house displeased
And heavy at the words which Naboth
spake,
And laid him down upon his bed, and
turned
His face away ; and he would eat no bread.
And Jezebel, the wife of Ahab, came
And said to him, Why is thy spirit sad ?
And he said unto her, Because I spake
To Naboth, to the Jezreelite, and said,
Give me thy vineyard ; and he answered,
saying,
I will not give my vineyard unto thee.
And Jezebel, the wife of Ahab, said,
Dost thou not rule the realm of Israel ?
Arise, eat bread, and let thy heart be
merry ;
I will give Naboth's vineyard unto thee.
So she wrote letters in King Ahab's name,
And sealed them with his seal, and sent the
letters
Unto the elders that were in his city

Dwelling with Naboth, and unto the nobles ;
And in the letters wrote, Proclaim a fast ;
And set this Naboth high among the
    people,
And set two men, the sons of Belial,
Before him, to bear witness and to say,
Thou didst blaspheme against God and the
    King ;
And carry him out and stone him, that he
    die !
And the elders and the nobles in the city
Did even as Jezebel, the wife of Ahab,
Had sent to them and written in the letters.

And then it came to pass, when Ahab
    heard
Naboth was dead, that Ahab rose to go
Down unto Naboth's vineyard, and to take
Possession of it.   And the word of God
Came to Elijah, saying to him, Arise,
Go down to meet the King of Israel
In Naboth's vineyard, whither he hath gone
To take possession.   Thou shalt speak to
    him,
Saying, Thus saith the Lord !   What ! hast
    thou killed
And also taken possession ?   In the place
Wherein the dogs have licked the blood of
    Naboth
Shall the dogs lick thy blood, — ay, even
    thine !
Both of the Deacons start from their seats.
And Ahab then, the King of Israel,
Said, Hast thou found me, O mine enemy ?
Elijah the Prophet answered, I have found
    thee !
So will it be with those who have stirred up
The Sons of Belial here to bear false wit-
    ness
And swear away the lives of innocent peo-
    ple ;
Their enemy will find them out at last,
The Prophet's voice will thunder, I have
    found thee !   [*Exeunt.*

SCENE IV. — *Meadows on Ipswich River. COREY
and his men mowing ; COREY in advance.*

COREY.

Well done, my men.   You see, I lead the
    field !
I 'm an old man, but I can swing a scythe
Better than most of you, though you be
    younger.
        Hangs his scythe upon a tree.

GLOYD (*aside to the others*).

How strong he is !   It 's supernatural.
No man so old as he is has such strength.
The Devil helps him !

COREY (*wiping his forehead*).
                Now we 'll rest awhile,
And take our nooning.   What 's the mat-
    ter with you ?
You are not angry with me, — are you,
    Gloyd ?
Come, come, we will not quarrel.   Let 's be
    friends.
It 's an old story, that the Raven said,
" Read the Third of Colossians and fif-
    teenth."

GLOYD.

You 're handier at the scythe, but I can
    beat you
At wrestling.

COREY.

        Well, perhaps so.   I don't know.
I never wrestled with you.   Why, you 're
    vexed !
Come, come, don't bear a grudge.

GLOYD.
                You are afraid.

COREY.

What should I be afraid of ?   All bear
    witness
The challenge comes from him.   Now,
    then, my man.
    They wrestle, and GLOYD is thrown.

ONE OF THE MEN.

That 's a fair fall.

ANOTHER.

    'T was nothing but a foil !

OTHERS.

You 've hurt him !

COREY (*helping GLOYD rise*).

        No ; this meadow-land is soft
You 're not hurt, — are you, Gloyd ?

GLOYD (*rising*).

        No, not much hurt.

COREY.

Well, then, shake hands ; and there 's an
    end of it.

How do you like that Cornish hug, my lad ?
And now we 'll see what 's in our basket
    here.

GLOYD (*aside*).

The Devil and all his imps are in that
    man !
The clutch of his ten fingers burns like
    fire !

COREY (*reverentially taking off his hat*).

God bless the food He hath provided for
    us,
And make us thankful for it, for Christ's
    sake !

He lifts up a keg of cider, and drinks from it.

GLOYD.

Do you see that ? Don't tell me it 's not
    Witchcraft.
Two of us could not lift that cask as he
    does !

COREY *puts down the keg, and opens a basket. A
    voice is heard calling.*

VOICE.

Ho ! Corey, Corey !

COREY.

            What is that ? I surely
Heard some one calling me by name !

VOICE.

            Giles Corey !

Enter a boy, running, and out of breath.

BOY.

Is Master Corey here ?

COREY.

            Yes, here I am.

BOY.

O Master Corey !

COREY.

Well ?

BOY.

    Your wife — your wife —

COREY.

What 's happened to my wife ?

BOY.

            She 's sent to prison !

COREY.

The dream ! the dream ! O God, be mer-
    ciful !

BOY.

She sent me here to tell you.

COREY (*putting on his jacket*).

            Where 's my horse ?
Don't stand there staring, fellows. Where 's
    my horse ?   [*Exit* COREY.

GLOYD.

Under the trees there. Run, old man, run,
    run !
You 've got some one to wrestle with you
    now
Who 'll trip your heels up, with your Cor-
    nish hug.
If there 's a Devil, he has got you now.
Ah, there he goes ! His horse is snorting
    fire !

ONE OF THE MEN.

John Gloyd, don't talk so ! It 's a shame
    to talk so !
He 's a good master, though you quarrel
    with him.

GLOYD.

If hard work and low wages make good
    masters,
Then he is one. But I think otherwise.
Come, let us have our dinner and be merry,
And talk about the old man and the
    Witches.
I know some stories that will make you
    laugh.
        They sit down on the grass, and eat.
Now there are Goody Cloyse and Goody
    Good,
Who have not got a decent tooth between
    them,
And yet these children — the Afflicted
    Children —
Say that they bite them, and show marks
    of teeth
Upon their arms !

ONE OF THE MEN.

            That makes the wonder greater.
That 's Witchcraft. Why; if they had teeth
    like yours,
'T would be no wonder if the girls were
    bitten !

GLOYD.

And then those ghosts that come out of
their graves
And cry, "You murdered us! you mur-
dered us!"

ONE OF THE MEN.

And all those Apparitions that stick pins
Into the flesh of the Afflicted Children!

GLOYD.

Oh those Afflicted Children! They know
well
Where the pins come from. I can tell you
that.
And there 's old Corey, he has got a horse-
shoe
Nailed on his doorstep to keep off the
Witches,
And all the same his wife has gone to
prison.

ONE OF THE MEN.

Oh, she 's no Witch. I 'll swear that Good-
wife Corey
Never did harm to any living creature.
She 's a good woman, if there ever was
one.

GLOYD.

Well, we shall see. As for that Bridget
Bishop, .
She has been tried before ; some years
ago
A negro testified he saw her shape
Sitting upon the rafters in a barn,
And holding in its hand an egg ; and while
He went to fetch his pitchfork, she had
vanished.
And now be quiet, will you ? I am tired,
And want to sleep here on the grass a
little.

They stretch themselves on the grass.

ONE OF THE MEN.

There may be Witches riding through the
air
Over our heads on broomsticks at this mo-
ment,
Bound for some Satan's Sabbath in the
woods
To be baptized.

GLOYD.

I wish they 'd take you with them,
And hold you under water head and ears,

Till you were drowned ; and that would
stop your talking,
If nothing else will. Let me sleep, I say.

ACT IV

SCENE I. — *The Green in front of the village
Meeting-house. An excited crowd gathering.
Enter* JOHN GLOYD.

A FARMER.

Who will be tried to-day ?

A SECOND.

I do not know.
Here is John Gloyd. Ask him ; he knows.

FARMER.

John Gloyd,
Whose turn is it to-day ?

GLOYD.

It 's Goodwife Corey's.

FARMER.

Giles Corey's wife ?

GLOYD.

The same. She is not mine.
It will go hard with her with all her pray-
ing.
The hypocrite ! She 's always on her
knees ;
But she prays to the Devil when she prays.
Let us go in.

A trumpet blows.

FARMER.

Here come the Magistrates.

SECOND FARMER.

Who 's the tall man in front ?

GLOYD.

Oh, that is Hathorne,
A Justice of the Court, and Quartermaster
In the Three County Troop. He 'll sift
the matter.
That 's Corwin with him ; and the man in
black
Is Cotton Mather, Minister of Boston.

Enter HATHORNE *and other Magistrates on
horseback, followed by the Sheriff, constables.
and attendants on foot. The Magistrates dis-
mount, and enter the Meeting-house, with the
rest.*

FARMER.

The Meeting-house is full. I never saw
So great a crowd before.

GLOYD.

No matter. Come.
We shall find room enough by elbowing
Our way among them. Put your shoulder
to it.

FARMER.

There were not half so many at the trial
Of Goodwife Bishop.

GLOYD.

Keep close after me.
I 'll find a place for you. They 'll want me
there.
I am a friend of Corey's, as you know,
And he can't do without me just at present.
                     [*Exeunt.*

SCENE II. — *Interior of the Meeting-house.*
MATHER *and the Magistrates seated in front
of the pulpit. Before them a raised platform.*
MARTHA *in chains.* COREY *near her.* MARY
WALCOT *in a chair. A crowd of spectators,
among them* GLOYD. *Confusion and murmurs
during the scene.*

HATHORNE*.*

Call Martha Corey*:*

MARTHA.

I am here.

HATHORNE.

Come forward.
She ascends the platform.
The Jurors of our Sovereign Lord and Lady
The King and Queen, here present, do ac-
cuse you
Of having on the tenth of June last past,
And divers other times before and after,
Wickedly used and practised certain arts
Called Witchcrafts, Sorceries, and Incanta-
tions,
Against one Mary Walcot, single woman,
Of Salem Village ; by which wicked arts
The aforesaid Mary Walcot was tor-
mented,
Tortured, afflicted, pined, consumed, and
wasted,
Against the peace of our Sovereign Lord
and Lady

The King and Queen, as well as of the
Statute
Made and provided in that case. What
say you ?

MARTHA.

Before I answer, give me leave to pray.

HATHORNE.

We have not sent for you, nor are we here,
To hear you pray, but to examine you
In whatsoever is alleged against you.
Why do you hurt this person ?

MARTHA.

I do not.
I am not guilty of the charge against me.

MARY.

Avoid, she-devil ! You may torment me
now !
Avoid, avoid, Witch !

MARTHA.

I am innocent.
I never had to do with any Witchcraft
Since I was born. I am a gospel woman.

MARY.

You are a gospel Witch !

MARTHA (*clasping her hands*).

Ah me ! ah me !
Oh, give me leave to pray !

MARY (*stretching out her hands*).

She hurts me now.
See, she has pinched my hands !

HATHORNE.

Who made these marks
Upon her hands ?

MARTHA.

I do not know. I stand
Apart from her. I did not touch her hands.

HATHORNE.

Who hurt her then ?

MARTHA.

I know not.

HATHORNE.

Do you think
She is bewitched ?

MARTHA.

Indeed I do not think so.
I am no Witch, and have no faith in
Witches.

HATHORNE.

Then answer me : When certain persons
came
To see you yesterday, how did you know
Beforehand why they came ?

MARTHA.

I had had speech ;
The children said I hurt them, and I
thought
These people came to question me about it.

HATHORNE.

How did you know the children had been
told
To note the clothes you wore ?

MARTHA.

My husband told me
What others said about it.

HATHORNE.

Goodman Corey,
Say, did you tell her ?

COREY.

I must speak the truth ;
I did not tell her. It was some one else.

HATHORNE.

Did you not say your husband told you so ?
How dare you tell a lie in this assembly ?
Who told you of the clothes ? Confess the
truth.

MARTHA *bites her lips, and is silent.*
You bite your lips, but do not answer me !

MARY.

Ah, she is biting me ! Avoid, avoid !

HATHORNE.

You said your husband told you.

MARTHA.

Yes, he told me
The children said I troubled them.

HATHORNE.

Then tell me,
Why do you trouble them ?

MARTHA.

I have denied it.

MARY.

She threatened me ; stabbed at me with
her spindle ;
And, when my brother thrust her with his
sword,
He tore her gown, and cut a piece away.
Here are they both, the spindle and the
cloth.
Shows them.

HATHORNE.

And there are persons here who know the
truth
Of what has now been said. What answer
make you ?

MARTHA.

I make no answer. Give me leave to pray.

HATHORNE.

Whom would you pray to ?

MARTHA.

To my God and Father.

HATHORNE.

Who is your God and Father ?

MARTHA.

The Almighty !

HATHORNE.

Doth he you pray to say that he is God ?
It is the Prince of Darkness, and not God.

MARY.

There is a dark shape whispering in her
ear.

HATHORNE.

What does it say to you ?

MARTHA.

I see no shape.

HATHORNE.

Did you not hear it whisper ?

MARTHA.

I heard nothing.

MARY.

What torture !   Ah, what agony I suffer !
Falls into a swoon.

HATHORNE.

You see this woman cannot stand before
    you.
If you would look for mercy, you must look
In God's way, by confession of your guilt.
Why does your spectre haunt and hurt this
    person ?

MARTHA.

I do not know.   He who appeared of old
In Samuel's shape, a saint and glorified,
May come in whatsoever shape he chooses.
I cannot help it.   I am sick at heart !

COREY.

O Martha, Martha ! let me hold your hand.

HATHORNE.

No ; stand aside, old man.

MARY (*starting up*).
                    Look there !   Look there !
I see a little bird, a yellow bird,
Perched on her finger ; and it pecks at me.
Ah, it will tear mine eyes out !

MARTHA.
                    I see nothing.

HATHORNE.

'T is the Familiar Spirit that attends her.

MARY.

Now it has flown away.   It sits up there
Upon the rafters.   It is gone ; is vanished.

MARTHA.

Giles, wipe these tears of anger from mine
    eyes.
Wipe the sweat from my forehead.   I am
    faint.
She leans against the railing.

MARY.

Oh, she is crushing me with all her weight !

HATHORNE.

Did you not carry once the Devil's Book
To this young woman ?

MARTHA.
                    Never.

HATHORNE.
                    Have you signed it,
Or touched it ?

MARTHA.
                    No ; I never saw it.

HATHORNE.

Did you not scourge her with an iron rod ?

MARTHA.

No, I did not.   If any Evil Spirit
Has taken my shape to do these evil deeds,
I cannot help it.   I am innocent.

HATHORNE.

Did you not say the Magistrates were
    blind ?
That you would open their eyes ?

MARTHA (*with a scornful laugh*).
                    Yes, I said that ;
If you call me a sorceress, you are blind !
If you accuse the innocent, you are blind !
Can the innocent be guilty ?

HATHORNE.
                    Did you not
On one occasion hide your husband's saddle
To hinder him from coming to the Ses-
    sions ?

MARTHA.

I thought it was a folly in a farmer
To waste his time pursuing such illusions.

HATHORNE.

What was the bird that this young woman
    saw
Just now upon your hand ?

MARTHA.
                    I know no bird.

HATHORNE.

Have you not dealt with a Familiar Spirit ?

MARTHA.

No, never, never !

HATHORNE.
                    What then was the Book
You showed to this young woman, and
    besought her
To write in it ?

MARTHA.
Where should I have a book ?
I showed her none, nor have none.

MARY.
The next Sabbath
Is the Communion Day, but Martha Corey
Will not be there !

MARTHA.
Ah, you are all against me.
What can I do or say ?

HATHORNE.
You can confess.

MARTHA.
No, I cannot, for I am innocent.

HATHORNE.
We have the proof of many witnesses
That you are guilty.

MARTHA.
Give me leave to speak.
Will you condemn me on such evidence, —
You who have known me for so many
years ?
Will you condemn me in this house of God,
Where I so long have worshipped with you
all ?
Where I have eaten the bread and drunk
the wine
So many times at our Lord's Table with
you ?
Bear witness, you that hear me ; you all
know
That I have led a blameless life among
you,
That never any whisper of suspicion
Was breathed against me till this accusa-
tion.
And shall this count for nothing ? Will
you take
My life away from me, because this girl,
Who is distraught, and not in her right
mind,
Accuses me of things I blush to name ?

HATHORNE.
What ! is it not enough ? Would you
hear more ?
Giles Corey !

COREY.
I am here.

HATHORNE.
Come forward, then.
COREY *ascends the platform.*
Is it not true, that on a certain night
You were impeded strangely in your
prayers ?
That something hindered you ? and that
you left
This woman here, your wife, kneeling
alone
Upon the hearth ?

COREY.
Yes ; I cannot deny it.

HATHORNE.
Did you not say the Devil hindered you ?

COREY.
I think I said some words to that effect.

HATHORNE.
Is it not true, that fourteen head of cattle,
To you belonging, broke from their en-
closure
And leaped into the river, and were
drowned ?

COREY.
It is most true.

HATHORNE.
And did you not then say
That they were overlooked ?

COREY.
So much I said.
I see ; they're drawing round me closer,
closer,
A net I cannot break, cannot escape from !
(Aside.)

HATHORNE.
Who did these things ?

COREY.
I do not know who did them.

HATHORNE.
Then I will tell you. It is some one near
you ;
You see her now ; this woman, your own
wife.

COREY.
I call the heavens to witness, it is false !
She never harmed me, never hindered me

In anything but what I should not do.
And I bear witness in the sight of heaven,
And in God's house here, that I never knew
    her
As otherwise than patient, brave, and true,
Faithful, forgiving, full of charity,
A virtuous and industrious and good wife !

HATHORNE.

Tut, tut, man ; do not rant so in your
    speech ;
You are a witness, not an advocate !
Here, Sheriff, take this woman back to
    prison.

MARTHA.

O Giles, this day you 've sworn away my
    life !

MARY.

Go, go and join the Witches at the door.
Do you not hear the drum ?   Do you not
    see them ?
Go quick.   They 're waiting for you.   You
    are late.
            [Exit MARTHA ; COREY following.

COREY.

The dream ! the dream ! the dream !

HATHORNE.

                    What does he say ?
Giles Corey, go not hence.   You are your-
    self
Accused of Witchcraft and of Sorcery
By many witnesses.   Say, are you guilty ?

COREY.

I know my death is foreordained by you, —
Mine and my wife's.   Therefore I will not
    answer.

During the rest of the scene he remains silent.

HATHORNE.

Do you refuse to plead ? — 'T were better
    for you
To make confession, or to plead Not
    Guilty. —
Do you not hear me ? — Answer, are you
    guilty ?
Do you not know a heavier doom awaits
    you,
If you refuse to plead, than if found
    guilty ?
Where is John Gloyd ?

GLOYD (*coming forward*).
                    Here am I.

HATHORNE.

                    Tell the Court ;
Have you not seen the supernatural power
Of this old man ?   Have you not seen him
    do
Strange feats of strength ?

GLOYD.

                    I 've seen him lead the field,
On a hot day, in mowing, and against
Us younger men ; and I have wrestled with
    him.
He threw me like a feather.   I have seen
    him
Lift up a barrel with his single hands,
Which two strong men could hardly lift to-
    gether,
And, holding it above his head, drink from
    it.

HATHORNE.

That is enough ; we need not question
    further.
What answer do you make to this, Giles
    Corey ?

MARY.

See there !   See there !

HATHORNE.

            What is it ?   I see nothing.

MARY.

Look ! Look !   It is the ghost of Robert
    Goodell,
Whom fifteen years ago this man did mur-
    der
By stamping on his body !   In his shroud
He comes here to bear witness to the
    crime !

The crowd shrinks back from COREY in horror.

HATHORNE.

Ghosts of the dead and voices of the liv-
    ing
Bear witness to your guilt, and you must
    die !
It might have been an easier death.   Your
    doom
Will be on your own head, and not on ours.
Twice more will you be questioned of these
    things ;

Twice more have room to plead or to confess.
If you are contumacious to the Court,
And if, when questioned, you refuse to answer,
Then by the Statute you will be condemned
To the *peine forte et dure !* To have your body
Pressed by great weights until you shall be dead !
And may the Lord have mercy on your soul !

ACT V

Scene I. — Corey's *farm as in Act II., Scene I. Enter* Richard Gardner, *looking round him.*

GARDNER.

Here stands the house as I remember it,
The four tall poplar-trees before the door ;
The house, the barn, the orchard, and the well,
With its moss-covered bucket and its trough ;
The garden, with its hedge of currant-bushes ;
The woods, the harvest-fields ; and, far beyond,
The pleasant landscape stretching to the sea.
But everything is silent and deserted !
No bleat of flocks, no bellowing of herds,
No sound of flails, that should be beating now ;
Nor man nor beast astir. What can this mean ?

Knocks at the door.

What ho ! Giles Corey ! Hillo-ho ! Giles Corey ! —
No answer but the echo from the barn,
And the ill-omened cawing of the crow,
That yonder wings his flight across the fields,
As if he scented carrion in the air.

Enter Tituba *with a basket.*

What woman 's this, that, like an apparition,
Haunts this deserted homestead in broad day ?
Woman, who are you ?

TITUBA.

I 'm Tituba.
I am John Indian's wife. I am a Witch.

GARDNER.

What are you doing here ?

TITUBA.

I am gathering herbs, —
Cinquefoil, and saxifrage, and pennyroyal.

GARDNER (*looking at the herbs*).

This is not cinquefoil, it is deadly nightshade !
This is not saxifrage, but hellebore !
This is not pennyroyal, it is henbane !
Do you come here to poison these good people ?

TITUBA.

I get these for the Doctor in the Village.
Beware of Tituba. I pinch the children ;
Make little poppets and stick pins in them,
And then the children cry out they are pricked.
The Black Dog came to me, and said,
"Serve me !"
I was afraid. He made me hurt the children.

GARDNER.

Poor soul ! She 's crazed, with all these Devil's doings.

TITUBA.

Will you, sir, sign the Book ?

GARDNER.

No, I 'll not sign it.
Where is Giles Corey ? Do you know Giles Corey ?

TITUBA.

He 's safe enough. He 's down there in the prison.

GARDNER.

Corey in prison ? What is he accused of ?

TITUBA.

Giles Corey and Martha Corey are in prison
Down there in Salem Village. Both are Witches.
She came to me and whispered, "Kill the children !"
Both signed the Book !

GARDNER.

Begone, you imp of darkness !
You Devil's dam !

TITUBA.

Beware of Tituba !

[*Exit.*

GARDNER.

How often out at sea on stormy nights,
When the waves thundered round me, and
    the wind
Bellowed, and beat the canvas, and my ship
Clove through the solid darkness, like a
    wedge,
I've thought of him, upon his pleasant
    farm,
Living in quiet with his thrifty housewife,
And envied him, and wished his fate were
    mine !
And now I find him shipwrecked utterly,
Drifting upon this sea of sorceries,
And lost, perhaps, beyond all aid of man !

[*Exit.*

SCENE II. — *The prison.* GILES COREY *at a
    table on which are some papers.*

COREY.

Now I have done with earth and all its
    cares ;
I give my worldly goods to my dear chil-
    dren ;
My body I bequeath to my tormentors,
And my immortal soul to Him who made
    it.
O God ! who in thy wisdom dost afflict me
With an affliction greater than most men
Have ever yet endured or shall endure,
Suffer me not in this last bitter hour
For any pains of death to fall from thee !

MARTHA *is heard singing.*

Arise, O righteous Lord !
    And disappoint my foes ;
They are but thine avenging sword,
    Whose wounds are swift to close.

COREY.

Hark, hark ! it is her voice ! She is not
    dead !
She lives ! I am not utterly forsaken !

MARTHA, *singing.*

By thine abounding grace,
    And mercies multiplied,

I shall awake, and see thy face ;
    I shall be satisfied.

COREY *hides his face in his hands.   Enter the*
    JAILER, *followed by* RICHARD GARDNER.

JAILER.

Here's a seafaring man, one Richard Gard-
    ner,
A friend of yours, who asks to speak with
    you.

COREY *rises.   They embrace.*

COREY.

I'm glad to see you, ay, right glad to see
    you.

GARDNER.

And I am most sorely grieved to see you
    thus.

COREY.

Of all the friends I had in happier days,
You are the first, ay, and the only one,
That comes to seek me out in my disgrace !
And you but come in time to say farewell.
They've dug my grave already in the field.
I thank you.   There is something in your
    presence,
I know not what it is, that gives me
    strength.
Perhaps it is the bearing of a man
Familiar with all dangers of the deep,
Familiar with the cries of drowning men,
With fire, and wreck, and foundering ships
    at sea !

GARDNER.

Ah, I have never known a wreck like
    yours !
Would I could save you !

COREY.

                    Do not speak of that.
It is too late.   I am resolved to die.

GARDNER.

Why would you die who have so much to
    live for ? —
Your daughters, and —

COREY.

                    You cannot say the word.
My daughters have gone from me.   They
    are married ;
They have their homes, their thoughts,
    apart from me ;

I will not say their hearts, — that were too
    cruel.
What would you have me do ?

GARDNER.
Confess and live.

COREY.
That 's what they said who came here yes-
    terday
To lay a heavy weight upon my conscience
By telling me that I was driven forth
As an unworthy member of their church.

GARDNER.
It is an awful death.

COREY.
'T is but to drown,
And have the weight of all the seas upon
    you.

GARDNER.
Say something ; say enough to fend off
    death
Till this tornado of fanaticism
Blows itself out.   Let me come in between
    you
And your severer self, with my plain sense ;
Do not be obstinate.

COREY.
I will not plead.
If I deny, I am condemned already,
In courts where ghosts appear as witnesses,
And swear men's lives away.   If I confess,
Then I confess a lie, to buy a life
Which is not life, but only death in life.
I will not bear false witness against any,
Not even against myself, whom I count
    least.

GARDNER (aside).
Ah, what a noble character is this !

COREY.
I pray you, do not urge me to do that
You would not do yourself.   I have already
The bitter taste of death upon my lips ;
I feel the pressure of the heavy weight
That will crush out my life within this hour ;
But if a word could save me, and that
    word
Were not the Truth ; nay, if it did but
    swerve
A hair's-breadth from the Truth, I would
    not say it !

GARDNER (aside).
How mean I seem beside a man like this !

COREY.
As for my wife, my Martha and my Mar-
    tyr, —
Whose virtues, like the stars, unseen by day,
Though numberless, do but await the dark
To manifest themselves unto all eyes, —
She who first won me from my evil ways,
And taught me how to live by her example,
By her example teaches me to die,
And leads me onward to the better life !

SHERIFF (without).
Giles Corey ! Come ! The hour has struck !

COREY.
I come !
Here is my body ; ye may torture it,
But the immortal soul ye cannot crush !
[Exeunt.

SCENE III. — A street in the Village. Enter
    GLOYD and others.

GLOYD.
Quick, or we shall be late !

A MAN.
That 's not the way.
Come here ; come up this lane.

GLOYD.
I wonder now
If the old man will die, and will not speak ?
He 's obstinate enough and tough enough
For anything on earth.
A bell tolls.
Hark !   What is that ?

A MAN.
The passing bell.   He 's dead !

GLOYD.
We are too late.
[Exeunt in haste.

SCENE IV. — A field near the graveyard. GILES
    COREY lying dead, with a great stone on his
    breast. The Sheriff at his head, RICHARD
    GARDNER at his feet. A crowd behind. The
    bell tolling. Enter HATHORNE and MATHER.

HATHORNE.
This is the Potter's Field.   Behold the fate
Of those who deal in Witchcrafts, and,
    when questioned,

Refuse to plead their guilt or innocence,
And stubbornly drag death upon them-
selves.

MATHER.

O sight most horrible ! In a land like this,
Spangled with Churches Evangelical,
Inwrapped in our salvations, must we seek
In mouldering statute - books of English
Courts
Some old forgotten Law, to do such deeds ?
Those who lie buried in the Potter's Field
Will rise again, as surely as ourselves
That sleep in honored graves with epitaphs ;
And this poor man, whom we have made a
victim,
Hereafter will be counted as a martyr !

FINALE

SAINT JOHN

SAINT JOHN *wandering over the face of the Earth.*

SAINT JOHN.

THE Ages come and go,
The Centuries pass as Years ;
My hair is white as the snow,
My feet are weary and slow,
The earth is wet with my tears !
The kingdoms crumble, and fall
Apart, like a ruined wall,
Or a bank that is undermined
By a river's ceaseless flow,
And leave no trace behind !
The world itself is old ;
The portals of Time unfold
On hinges of iron, that grate
And groan with the rust and the weight,
Like the hinges of a gate
That hath fallen to decay ;
But the evil doth not cease ;
There is war instead of peace,
Instead of Love there is hate ;
And still I must wander and wait,
Still I must watch and pray,
Not forgetting in whose sight,
A thousand years in their flight
Are as a single day.

The life of man is a gleam
Of light, that comes and goes
Like the course of the Holy Stream,
The cityless river, that flows
From fountains no one knows,
Through the Lake of Galilee,
Through forests and level lands,
Over rocks, and shallows, and sands
Of a wilderness wild and vast,
Till it findeth its rest at last
In the desolate Dead Sea !
But alas ! alas for me
Not yet this rest shall be !

What, then ! doth Charity fail ?
Is Faith of no avail ?
Is Hope blown out like a light
By a gust of wind in the night ?
The clashing of creeds, and the strife
Of the many beliefs, that in vain
Perplex man's heart and brain,
Are naught but the rustle of leaves
When the breath of God upheaves
The boughs of the Tree of Life,
And they subside again !
And I remember still
The words, and from whom they came,
Not he that repeateth the name,
But he that doeth the will !

And Him evermore I behold
Walking in Galilee,
Through the cornfield's waving gold,
In hamlet, in wood, and in wold,
By the shores of the Beautiful Sea.
He toucheth the sightless eyes ;
Before him the demons flee ;
To the dead He sayeth : Arise !
To the living : Follow me !
And that voice still soundeth on
From the centuries that are gone,
To the centuries that shall be !

From all vain pomps and shows,
From the pride that overflows,
And the false conceits of men ;
From all the narrow rules
And subtleties of Schools,
And the craft of tongue and pen ;
Bewildered in its search,
Bewildered with the cry :
Lo, here ! lo, there, the Church !
Poor, sad Humanity
Through all the dust and heat
Turns back with bleeding feet,
By the weary road it came,
Unto the simple thought
By the great Master taught,
And that remaineth still :
Not he that repeateth the name,
But he that doeth the will !

JUDAS MACCABÆUS

The writing of this tragedy followed immediately upon the dismissal of *The Divine Tragedy*, and was in a measure an offshoot from it. While the poet's mind was charged with the contemplation of Judaic scenes, there came back to him the thought of a tragedy based upon the history of Judas Maccabæus, which had first visited him twenty years before. In 1850 he had entered it in his note-book as a subject for a poem.

Now, he repeats the suggestion December 5, 1871, and five days later he records: "At home all day. Began the tragedy of *Judas Maccabæus*. The subject is a very striking one — the collision of Judaism and Hel-

lenism." Elsewhere, he raises the question: "The subject is tragic enough, but has it unity, and a catastrophe to end with?" He began the drama on the 10th of December; on the 12th *The Divine Tragedy* was published, and on the 21st he had finished his first draft of the new work. "The acts are not long," he writes, "but there are five of them." *Judas Maccabæus* formed one division of the volume *Three Books of Song*, which was published May 25, 1872; the other two divisions were *The Second Day* of *Tales of a Wayside Inn* and *A Handful of Translations*.

ACT I

THE CITADEL OF ANTIOCHUS AT JERUSALEM

SCENE I. — ANTIOCHUS ; JASON.

ANTIOCHUS.

O ANTIOCH, my Antioch, my city !
Queen of the East ! my solace, my delight !
The dowry of my sister Cleopatra
When she was wed to Ptolemy, and now
Won back and made more wonderful by
    me !
I love thee, and I long to be once more
Among the players and the dancing women
Within thy gates, and bathe in the Orontes,
Thy river and mine. O Jason, my High-
    Priest,
For I have made thee so, and thou art
    mine,
Hast thou seen Antioch the Beautiful ?

JASON.

Never, my Lord.

ANTIOCHUS.

    Then hast thou never seen
The wonder of the world. This city of
    David
Compared with Antioch is but a village,
And its inhabitants compared with Greeks
Are mannerless boors.

JASON.

    They are barbarians,
And mannerless.

ANTIOCHUS.

    They must be civilized.
They must be made to have more gods
    than one ;
And goddesses besides.

JASON.

They shall have more.

ANTIOCHUS.

They must have hippodromes, and games,
    and baths,
Stage-plays and festivals, and most of all
The Dionysia.

JASON.

They shall have them all.

ANTIOCHUS.

By Heracles ! but I should like to see
These Hebrews crowned with ivy, and
    arrayed
In skins of fawns, with drums and flutes
    and thyrsi,
Revel and riot through the solemn streets
Of their old town. Ha, ha ! It makes me
    merry
Only to think of it ! — Thou dost not
    laugh.

JASON.

Yea, I laugh inwardly.

ANTIOCHUS.

    The new Greek leaven
Works slowly in this Israelitish dough !
Have I not sacked the Temple, and on the
    altar
Set up the statue of Olympian Zeus
To Hellenize it ?

JASON.

Thou hast done all this.

ANTIOCHUS.

As thou wast Joshua once and now art
    Jason,
And from a Hebrew hast become a Greek,
So shall this Hebrew nation be translated,

Their very natures and their names be
    changed,
And all be Hellenized.

JASON.
                It shall be done.

ANTIOCHUS.
Their manners and their laws and way of
    living
Shall all be Greek.   They shall unlearn
    their language,
And learn the lovely speech of Antioch.
Where hast thou been to-day ?   Thou com-
    est late.

JASON.
Playing at discus with the other priests
In the Gymnasium.

ANTIOCHUS.
             Thou hast done well.
There 's nothing better for you lazy priests
Than discus-playing with the common peo-
    ple.
Now tell me, Jason, what these Hebrews
    call me
When they converse together at their
    games.

JASON.
Antiochus Epiphanes, my Lord ;
Antiochus the Illustrious.

ANTIOCHUS.
              Oh, not that ;
That is the public cry ; I mean the name
They give me when they talk among them-
    selves,
And think that no one listens ; what is
    that ?

JASON.
Antiochus Epimanes, my Lord !

ANTIOCHUS.
Antiochus the Mad !   Ay, that is it.
And who hath said it ?   Who hath set in
    motion
That sorry jest ?

JASON.
           The Seven Sons insane
Of a weird woman, like themselves insane.

ANTIOCHUS.
I like their courage, but it shall not save
    them.
They shall be made to eat the flesh of
    swine
Or they shall die.   Where are they ?

JASON.
              In the dungeons
Beneath this tower.

ANTIOCHUS.
         There let them stay and starve,
Till I am ready to make Greeks of them,
After my fashion.

JASON.
         They shall stay and starve. —
My Lord, the Ambassadors of Samaria
Await thy pleasure.

ANTIOCHUS.
           Why not my displeasure ?
Ambassadors are tedious.   They are men
Who work for their own ends, and not for
    mine ;
There is no furtherance in them.   Let them
    go
To Apollonius, my governor
There in Samaria, and not trouble me.
What do they want ?

JASON.
           Only the royal sanction
To give a name unto a nameless temple
Upon Mount Gerizim.

ANTIOCHUS.
           Then bid them enter.
This pleases me, and furthers my designs.
The occasion is auspicious.   Bid them
    enter.

SCENE II. — ANTIOCHUS ; JASON ; *the* SAMAR-
    ITAN AMBASSADORS.

ANTIOCHUS.
Approach.   Come forward ; stand not at
    the door
Wagging your long beards, but demean
    yourselves
As doth become Ambassadors.   What seek
    ye ?

AN AMBASSADOR.
An audience from the King.

ANTIOCHUS.
                    Speak, and be brief.
Waste not the time in useless rhetoric.
Words are not things.

AMBASSADOR (*reading*).
              " To King Antiochus,
The God, Epiphanes ; a Memorial
From the Sidonians, who live at Sichem."

ANTIOCHUS.
Sidonians ?

AMBASSADOR.
    Ay, my Lord.

ANTIOCHUS.
                    Go on, go on !
And do not tire thyself and me with bow-
    ing !

AMBASSADOR (*reading*).
" We are a colony of Medes and Persians."

ANTIOCHUS.
No, ye are Jews from one of the Ten
    Tribes ;
Whether Sidonians or Samaritans
Or Jews of Jewry, matters not to me ;
Ye are all Israelites, ye are all Jews.
When the Jews prosper, ye claim kindred
    with them ;
When the Jews suffer, ye are Medes and
    Persians ;
I know that in the days of Alexander
Ye claimed exemption from the annual
    tribute
In the Sabbatic Year, because, ye said,
Your fields had not been planted in that
    year.

AMBASSADOR (*reading*).
" Our fathers, upon certain frequent
    plagues,
And following an ancient superstition,
Were long accustomed to observe that day
Which by the Israelites is called the Sab-
    bath,
And in a temple on Mount Gerizim
Without a name, they offered sacrifice.
Now we, who are Sidonians, beseech thee,
Who art our benefactor and our savior,
Not to confound us with these wicked Jews,
But to give royal order and injunction
To Apollonius in Samaria,
Thy governor, and likewise to Nicanor,

Thy procurator, no more to molest us ;
And let our nameless temple now be named
The Temple of Jupiter Hellenius."

ANTIOCHUS.
This shall be done.   Full well it pleaseth
    me
Ye are not Jews, or are no longer Jews,
But Greeks ; if not by birth, yet Greeks by
    custom.
Your nameless temple shall receive the
    name
Of Jupiter Hellenius.   Ye may go !

SCENE III. — ANTIOCHUS ; JASON.

ANTIOCHUS.
My task is easier than I dreamed.   These
    people
Meet me half-way.   Jason, didst thou take
    note
How these Samaritans of Sichem said
They were not Jews ? that they were
    Medes and Persians,
They were Sidonians, anything but Jews ?
'T is of good augury.   The rest will follow
Till the whole land is Hellenized.

JASON.
                    My Lord,
These are Samaritans.   The tribe of Judah
Is of a different temper, and the task
Will be more difficult.

ANTIOCHUS.
              Dost thou gainsay me ?

JASON.
I know the stubborn nature of the Jew.
Yesterday, Eleazer, an old man,
Being fourscore years and ten, chose rather
    death
By torture than to eat the flesh of swine.

ANTIOCHUS.
The life is in the blood, and the whole
    nation
Shall bleed to death, or it shall change its
    faith !

JASON.
Hundreds have fled already to the moun-
    tains
Of Ephraim, where Judas Maccabæus
Hath raised the standard of revolt against
    thee.

ANTIOCHUS.

I will burn down their city, and will make
 it
Waste as a wilderness.   Its thoroughfares
Shall be but furrows in a field of ashes.
It shall be sown with salt as Sodom is !
This hundred and fifty-third Olympiad
Shall have a broad and blood-red seal upon
 it,
Stamped with the awful letters of my name,
Antiochus the God, Epiphanes ! —
Where are those Seven Sons ?

JASON.

     My Lord, they wait
Thy royal pleasure.

ANTIOCHUS.

They shall wait no longer !

ACT II

THE DUNGEONS IN THE CITADEL

SCENE I. — THE MOTHER *of the* SEVEN SONS
  alone, listening.

THE MOTHER.

Be strong, my heart ! Break not till they
 are dead.
All, all my Seven Sons ; then burst asunder,
And let this tortured and tormented soul
Leap and rush out like water through the
 shards
Of earthen vessels broken at a well.
O my dear children, mine in life and death,
I know not how ye came into my womb ;
I neither gave you breath, nor gave you
 life,
And neither was it I that formed the mem-
 bers
Of every one of you.   But the Creator,
Who made the world, and made the heavens
 above us,
Who formed the generation of mankind,
And found out the beginning of all things,
He gave you breath and life, and will again
Of his own mercy, as ye now regard
Not your own selves, but his eternal law.
I do not murmur, nay, I thank thee, God,
That I and mine have not been deemed un-
 worthy
To suffer for thy sake, and for thy law,
And for the many sins of Israel.

Hark ! I can hear within the sound of
 scourges !
I feel them more than ye do, O my sons !
But cannot come to you.   I, who was wont
To wake at night at the least cry ye made,
To whom ye ran at every slightest hurt, —
I cannot take you now into my lap
And soothe your pain, but God will take
 you all
Into his pitying arms, and comfort you,
And give you rest.

A VOICE (*within*).

   What wouldst thou ask of us ?
Ready are we to die, but we will never
Transgress the law and customs of our
 fathers.

THE MOTHER.

It is the voice of my first-born ! O brave
And noble boy ! Thou hast the privilege
Of dying first, as thou wast born the first.

THE SAME VOICE (*within*).

God looketh on us, and hath comfort in us ;
As Moses in his song of old declared,
He in his servants shall be comforted.

THE MOTHER.

I knew thou wouldst not fail ! — He speaks
 no more,
He is beyond all pain !

ANTIOCHUS (*within*).

    If thou eat not
Thou shalt be tortured throughout all the
 members
Of thy whole body.   Wilt thou eat then ?

SECOND VOICE (*within*).

       No.

THE MOTHER.

It is Adaiah's voice.   I tremble for him.
I know his nature, devious as the wind,
And swift to change, gentle and yielding
 always.
Be steadfast, O my son !

THE SAME VOICE (*within*).

     Thou, like a fury,
Takest us from this present life, but God,
Who rules the world, shall raise us up
 again
Into life everlasting.

THE MOTHER.

God, I thank thee
That thou hast breathed into that timid
heart
Courage to die for thee. O my Adaiah,
Witness of God ! if thou for whom I feared
Canst thus encounter death, I need not
fear ;
The others will not shrink.

THIRD VOICE (*within*).

Behold these hands
Held out to thee, O King Antiochus,
Not to implore thy mercy, but to show
That I despise them. He who gave them
to me
Will give them back again.

THE MOTHER.

O Avilan,
It is thy voice. For the last time I hear it ;
For the last time on earth, but not the last.
To death it bids defiance, and to torture.
It sounds to me as from another world,
And makes the petty miseries of this
Seem unto me as naught, and less than
naught.
Farewell, my Avilan ; nay, I should say
Welcome, my Avilan ; for I am dead
Before thee. I am waiting for the others.
Why do they linger ?

FOURTH VOICE (*within*).

It is good, O King,
Being put to death by men, to look for
hope
From God, to be raised up again by Him.
But thou — no resurrection shalt thou have
To life hereafter.

THE MOTHER.

Four ! already four !
Three are still living ; nay, they all are
living,
Half here, half there. Make haste, An-
tiochus,
To reunite us ; for the sword that cleaves
These miserable bodies makes a door
Through which our souls, impatient of re-
lease,
Rush to each other's arms.

FIFTH VOICE (*within*).

Thou hast the power ;
Thou doest what thou wilt. Abide awhile,

And thou shalt see the power of God, and
how
He will torment thee and thy seed.

THE MOTHER.

O hasten ;
Why dost thou pause ? Thou who hast
slain already
So many Hebrew women, and hast hung
Their murdered infants round their necks,
slay me,
For I too am a woman, and these boys
Are mine. Make haste to slay us all,
And hang my lifeless babes about my neck.

SIXTH VOICE (*within*).

Think not, Antiochus, that takest in hand
To strive against the God of Israel,
Thou shalt escape unpunished, for his wrath
Shall overtake thee and thy bloody house.

THE MOTHER.

One more, my Sirion, and then all is ended.
Having put all to bed, then in my turn
I will lie down and sleep as sound as they.
My Sirion, my youngest, best beloved !
And those bright golden locks, that I so oft
Have curled about these fingers, even now
Are foul with blood and dust, like a lamb's
fleece,
Slain in the shambles. — Not a sound I
hear.
This silence is more terrible to me
Than any sound, than any cry of pain,
That might escape the lips of one who dies.
Doth his heart fail him ? Doth he fall
away
In the last hour from God ? O Sirion,
Sirion,
Art thou afraid ? I do not hear thy voice.
Die as thy brothers died. Thou must not
live !

SCENE II. — THE MOTHER ; ANTIOCHUS ; SIRION.

THE MOTHER.

Are they all dead ?

ANTIOCHUS.

Of all thy Seven Sons
One only lives. Behold them where they
lie ;
How dost thou like this picture ?

THE MOTHER.

God in heaven !
Can a man do such deeds, and yet not die
By the recoil of his own wickedness ?
Ye murdered, bleeding, mutilated bodies
That were my children once, and still are
    mine,
I cannot watch o'er you as Rizpah watched
In sackcloth o'er the seven sons of Saul,
Till water drop upon you out of heaven
And wash this blood away !   I cannot
    mourn
As she, the daughter of Aiah, mourned the
    dead,
From the beginning of the barley-harvest
Until the autumn rains, and suffered not
The birds of air to rest on them by day,
Nor the wild beasts by night.   For ye have
    died
A better death, a death so full of life
That I ought rather to rejoice than
    mourn. —
Wherefore art thou not dead, O Sirion ?
Wherefore art thou the only living thing
Among thy brothers dead ?   Art thou
    afraid ?

ANTIOCHUS.

O woman, I have spared him for thy sake,
For he is fair to look upon and comely ;
And I have sworn to him by all the gods
That I would crown his life with joy and
    honor,
Heap treasures on him, luxuries, delights,
Make him my friend and keeper of my
    secrets,
If he would turn from your Mosaic Law
And be as we are ; but he will not listen.

THE MOTHER.

My noble Sirion !

ANTIOCHUS.

Therefore I beseech thee,
Who art his mother, thou wouldst speak
    with him,
And wouldst persuade him.   I am sick of
    blood.

THE MOTHER.

Yea, I will speak with him and will per-
    suade him.
O Sirion, my son ! have pity on me,
On me that bare thee, and that gave thee
    suck,

And fed and nourished thee, and brought
    thee up
With the dear trouble of a mother's care
Unto this age.   Look on the heavens above
    thee,
And on the earth and all that is therein ;
Consider that God made them out of things
That were not ; and that likewise in this
    manner
Mankind was made.   Then fear not this
    tormentor ;
But, being worthy of thy brethren, take
Thy death as they did, that I may receive
    thee
Again in mercy with them.

ANTIOCHUS.

I am mocked,
Yea, I am laughed to scorn.

SIRION.

Whom wait ye for ?
Never will I obey the King's command-
    ment,
But the commandment of the ancient Law,
That was by Moses given unto our fathers.
And thou, O godless man, that of all others
Art the most wicked, be not lifted up,
Nor puffed up with uncertain hopes, up-
    lifting
Thy hand against the servants of the Lord,
For thou hast not escaped the righteous
    judgment
Of the Almighty God, who seeth all things !

ANTIOCHUS.

He is no God of mine ; I fear Him not.

SIRION.

My brothers, who have suffered a brief
    pain,
Are dead ; but thou, Antiochus, shalt suffer
The punishment of pride.   I offer up
My body and my life, beseeching God
That He would speedily be merciful
Unto our nation, and that thou by plagues
Mysterious and by torments mayest confess
That He alone is God.

ANTIOCHUS.

Ye both shall perish
By torments worse than any that your
    God,
Here or hereafter, hath in store for me.

THE MOTHER.

My Sirion, I am proud of thee!

ANTIOCHUS.

Be silent!
Go to thy bed of torture in yon chamber,
Where lie so many sleepers, heartless mother!
Thy footsteps will not wake them, nor thy voice,
Nor wilt thou hear, amid thy troubled dreams,
Thy children crying for thee in the night!

THE MOTHER.

O Death, that stretchest thy white hands to me,
I fear them not, but press them to my lips,
That are as white as thine; for I am Death,
Nay, am the Mother of Death, seeing these sons
All lying lifeless. — Kiss me, Sirion.

ACT III

THE BATTLE-FIELD OF BETH-HORON

SCENE I. — JUDAS MACCABÆUS *in armor before his tent.*

JUDAS.

The trumpets sound; the echoes of the mountains
Answer them, as the Sabbath morning breaks
Over Beth-horon and its battle-field,
Where the great captain of the hosts of God,
A slave brought up in the brick-fields of Egypt,
O'ercame the Amorites. There was no day
Like that, before or after it, nor shall be.
The sun stood still; the hammers of the hail
Beat on their harness; and the captains set
Their weary feet upon the necks of kings,
As I will upon thine, Antiochus,
Thou man of blood! — Behold the rising sun
Strikes on the golden letters of my banner,
Be Elohim Yehovah! Who is like

To thee, O Lord, among the gods? —
Alas!
I am not Joshua, I cannot say,
"Sun, stand thou still on Gibeon, and thou Moon,
In Ajalon!" Nor am I one who wastes
The fateful time in useless lamentation;
But one who bears his life upon his hand
To lose it or to save it, as may best
Serve the designs of Him who giveth life.

SCENE II. — JUDAS MACCABÆUS; JEWISH FUGITIVES.

JUDAS.

Who and what are ye, that with furtive steps
Steal in among our tents?

FUGITIVES.

O Maccabæus,
Outcasts are we, and fugitives as thou art,
Jews of Jerusalem, that have escaped
From the polluted city, and from death.

JUDAS.

None can escape from death. Say that ye come
To die for Israel, and ye are welcome.
What tidings bring ye?

FUGITIVES.

Tidings of despair.
The Temple is laid waste; the precious vessels,
Censers of gold, vials and veils and crowns,
And golden ornaments, and hidden treasures,
Have all been taken from it, and the Gentiles
With revelling and with riot fill its courts,
And dally with harlots in the holy places.

JUDAS.

All this I knew before.

FUGITIVES.

Upon the altar
Are things profane, things by the law forbidden;
Nor can we keep our Sabbaths or our Feasts,
But on the festivals of Dionysus
Must walk in their processions, bearing ivy
To crown a drunken god.

JUDAS.

This too I know.
But tell me of the Jews.   How fare the
    Jews ?

FUGITIVES.

The coming of this mischief hath been sore
And grievous to the people.   All the land
Is full of lamentation and of mourning.
The Princes and the Elders weep and wail ;
The young men and the maidens are made
    feeble ;
The beauty of the women hath been
    changed.

JUDAS.

And are there none to die for Israel ?
'T is not enough to mourn.   Breastplate
    and harness
Are better things than sackcloth.   Let the
    women
Lament for Israel ; the men should die.

FUGITIVES.

Both men and women die ; old men and
    young :
Old Eleazer died : and Máhala
With all her Seven Sons.

JUDAS.

Antiochus,
At every step thou takest there is left
A bloody footprint in the street, by which
The avenging wrath of God will track thee
    out !
It is enough.   Go to the sutler's tents :
Those of you who are men, put on such ar-
    mor
As ye may find ; those of you who are
    women,
Buckle that armor on ; and for a watch-
    word
Whisper, or cry aloud, " The Help of
    God."

SCENE III. — JUDAS MACCABÆUS ; NICANOR.

NICANOR.

Hail, Judas Maccabæus !

JUDAS.

Hail ! — Who art thou
That comest here in this mysterious guise
Into our camp unheralded ?

NICANOR.

A herald
Sent from Nicanor.

JUDAS.

Heralds come not thus
Armed with thy shirt of mail from head to
    heel,
Thou glidest like a serpent silently
Into my presence.   Wherefore dost thou
    turn
Thy face from me ?   A herald speaks his
    errand
With forehead unabashed.   Thou art a
    spy
Sent by Nicanor.

NICANOR.

No disguise avails !
Behold my face ; I am Nicanor's self.

JUDAS.

Thou art indeed Nicanor.   I salute thee.
What brings thee hither to this hostile camp
Thus unattended ?

NICANOR.

Confidence in thee.
Thou hast the nobler virtues of thy race,
Without the failings that attend those vir-
    tues.
Thou canst be strong, and yet not tyran-
    nous,
Canst righteous be and not intolerant.
Let there be peace between us.

JUDAS.

What is peace ?
Is it to bow in silence to our victors ?
Is it to see our cities sacked and pillaged,
Our people slain, or sold as slaves, or flee-
    ing
At night - time by the blaze of burning
    towns ;
Jerusalem laid waste ; the Holy Temple
Polluted with strange gods ?   Are these
    things peace ?

NICANOR.

These are the dire necessities that wait
On war, whose loud and bloody enginery
I seek to stay.   Let there be peace between
Antiochus and thee

JUDAS.

Antiochus ?
What is Antiochus, that he should prate
Of peace to me, who am a fugitive ?
To-day he shall be lifted up ; to-morrow
Shall not be found, because he is returned
Unto his dust ; his thought has come to
    nothing.
There is no peace between us, nor can be,
Until this banner floats upon the walls
Of our Jerusalem.

NICANOR.

                    Between that city
And thee there lies a waving wall of
    tents
Held by a host of forty thousand foot,
And horsemen seven thousand.   What hast
    thou
To bring against all these ?

JUDAS.

                    The power of God,
Whose breath shall scatter your white tents
    abroad,
As flakes of snow.

NICANOR.

                    Your Mighty One in heaven
Will not do battle on the Seventh Day ;
It is his day of rest.

JUDAS.

                    Silence, blasphemer.
Go to thy tents.

NICANOR.

                    Shall it be war or peace ?

JUDAS.

War, war, and only war.   Go to thy tents
That shall be scattered, as by you were
    scattered
The torn and trampled pages of the Law,
Blown through the windy streets.

NICANOR.

                    Farewell, brave foe !

JUDAS.

Ho, there, my captains ! Have safe-con-
    duct given
Unto Nicanor's herald through the camp,
And come yourselves to me. — Farewell,
    Nicanor !

SCENE IV. — JUDAS MACCABÆUS ; CAPTAINS
         AND SOLDIERS.

JUDAS.

The hour is come. Gather the host to-
    gether
For battle.   Lo, with trumpets and with
    songs
The army of Nicanor comes against us.
Go forth to meet them, praying in your
    hearts,
And fighting with your hands.

CAPTAINS.

                    Look forth and see !
The morning sun is shining on their shields
Of gold and brass ; the mountains glisten
    with them,
And shine like lamps.   And we, who are so
    few
And poorly armed, and ready to faint with
    fasting,
How shall we fight against this multitude ?

JUDAS.

The victory of a battle standeth not
In multitudes, but in the strength that com-
    eth
From heaven above.   The Lord forbid that
    I
Should do this thing, and flee away from
    them.
Nay, if our hour be come, then let us die ;
Let us not stain our honor.

CAPTAINS.

                    'T is the Sabbath.
Wilt thou fight on the Sabbath, Macca-
    bæus ?

JUDAS.

Ay ; when I fight the battles of the Lord,
I fight them on his day, as on all others.
Have ye forgotten certain fugitives
That fled once to these hills, and hid
    themselves
In caves ?   How their pursuers camped
    against them
Upon the Seventh Day, and challenged
    them ?
And how they answered not, nor cast a
    stone,
Nor stopped the places where they lay con-
    cealed.

But meekly perished with their wives and
  children,
Even to the number of a thousand souls ?
We who are fighting for our laws and lives
Will not so perish.

CAPTAINS.

Lead us to the battle !

JUDAS.

And let our watchword be, " The Help of
  God ! "
Last night I dreamed a dream ; and in my
  vision
Beheld Onias, our High-Priest of old,
Who holding up his hands prayed for the
  Jews.
This done, in the like manner there ap-
  peared
An old man, and exceeding glorious,
With hoary hair, and of a wonderful
And excellent majesty.   And Onias said :
" This is a lover of the Jews, who prayeth
Much for the people and the Holy City, —
God's prophet Jeremias."   And the pro-
  phet
Held forth his right hand and gave unto
  me
A sword of gold ; and giving it he said :
" Take thou this holy sword, a gift from
  God,
And with it thou shalt wound thine adver-
  saries."

CAPTAINS.

The Lord is with us !

JUDAS.

Hark ! I hear the trumpets
Sound from Beth-horon ; from the battle-
  field
Of Joshua, where he smote the Amorites,
Smote the Five Kings of Eglon and of Jar-
  muth,
Of Hebron, Lachish, and Jerusalem,
As we to-day will smite Nicanor's hosts
And leave a memory of great deeds behind
  us.

CAPTAINS AND SOLDIERS.

The Help of God !

JUDAS.

Be Elohim Yehovah !
Lord, thou didst send thine Angel in the
  time

Of Esekias, King of Israel,
And in the armies of Sennacherib
Didst slay a hundred fourscore and five
  thousand.
Wherefore, O Lord of heaven, now also
  send
Before us a good angel for a fear,
And through the might of thy right arm let
  those
Be stricken with terror that have come this
  day
Against thy holy people to blaspheme !

ACT IV

THE OUTER COURTS OF THE TEMPLE
AT JERUSALEM

SCENE I. — JUDAS MACCABÆUS ; CAPTAINS ;
    JEWS.

JUDAS.

Behold, our enemies are discomfited.
Jerusalem has fallen ; and our banners
Float from her battlements, and o'er her
  gates
Nicanor's severed head, a sign of terror,
Blackens in wind and sun.

CAPTAINS.

O Maccabæus,
The citadel of Antiochus, wherein
The Mother with her Seven Sons was mur-
  dered,
Is still defiant.

JUDAS.

Wait.

CAPTAINS.

Its hateful aspect
Insults us with the bitter memories
Of other days.

JUDAS.

Wait ; it shall disappear
And vanish as a cloud.   First let us cleanse
The Sanctuary.   See, it is become
Waste like a wilderness.   Its golden gates
Wrenched from their hinges and consumed
  by fire ;
Shrubs growing in its courts as in a forest ;
Upon its altars hideous and strange idols ;
And strewn about its pavement at my feet

Its Sacred Books, half-burned and painted
 o'er
With images of heathen gods.

JEWS.
       Woe ! woe !
Our beauty and our glory are laid waste !
The Gentiles have profaned our holy
 places !
(Lamentation and alarm of trumpets.)

JUDAS.
This sound of trumpets, and this lamenta-
 tion,
The heart-cry of a people toward the
 heavens,
Stir me to wrath and vengeance. Go, my
 captains ;
I hold you back no longer. Batter down
The citadel of Antiochus, while here
We sweep away his altars and his gods.

SCENE II. — JUDAS MACCABÆUS ; JASON ;
 JEWS.

JEWS.
Lurking among the ruins of the Temple,
Deep in its inner courts, we found this man,
Clad as High-Priest.

JUDAS.
    I ask not who thou art,
I know thy face, writ over with deceit
As are these tattered volumes of the Law
With heathen images. A priest of God
Wast thou in other days, but thou art now
A priest of Satan. Traitor, thou art Jason.

JASON.
I am thy prisoner, Judas Maccabæus,
And it would ill become me to conceal
My name or office.

JUDAS.
    Over yonder gate
There hangs the head of one who was a
 Greek.
What should prevent me now, thou man of
 sin,
From hanging at its side the head of one
Who born a Jew hath made himself a
 Greek ?

JASON.
Justice prevents thee.

JUDAS.
    Justice ? Thou art stained
With every crime 'gainst which the Deca-
 logue
Thunders with all its thunder.

JASON.
      If not Justice,
Then Mercy, her handmaiden.

JUDAS.
     When hast thou
At any time, to any man or woman,
Or even to any little child, shown mercy ?

JASON.
I have but done what King Antiochus
Commanded me.

JUDAS.
   True, thou hast been the weapon
With which he struck ; but hast been such
 a weapon,
So flexible, so fitted to his hand,
It tempted him to strike. So thou hast
 urged him
To double wickedness, thine own and his.
Where is this King ? Is he in Antioch
Among his women still, and from his win-
 dows
Throwing down gold by handfuls, for the
 rabble
To scramble for ?

JASON.
   Nay, he is gone from there,
Gone with an army into the far East.

JUDAS.
And wherefore gone ?

JASON.
   I know not. For the space
Of forty days almost were horsemen seen
Running in air, in cloth of gold, and armed
With lances, like a band of soldiery ;
It was a sign of triumph.

JUDAS.
     Or of death.
Wherefore art thou not with him ?

JASON.
      I was left
For service in the Temple.

JUDAS.

To pollute it,
And to corrupt the Jews ; for there are men
Whose presence is corruption ; to be with
them
Degrades us and deforms the things we do.

JASON.

I never made a boast, as some men do,
Of my superior virtue, nor denied
The weakness of my nature, that hath made
me
Subservient to the will of other men.

JUDAS.

Upon this day, the five-and-twentieth day
Of the month Caslan, was the Temple here
Profaned by strangers, — by Antiochus
And thee, his instrument. Upon this day
Shall it be cleansed. Thou, who didst lend
thyself
Unto this profanation, canst not be
A witness of these solemn services.
There can be nothing clean where thou art
present.
The people put to death Callisthenes,
Who burned the Temple gates ; and if
they find thee
Will surely slay thee. I will spare thy life
To punish thee the longer. Thou shalt
wander
Among strange nations. Thou, that hast
cast out
So many from their native land, shalt
perish
In a strange land. Thou, that hast left so
many
Unburied, shalt have none to mourn for
thee,
Nor any solemn funerals at all,
Nor sepulchre with thy fathers. — Get thee
hence !

*Music. Procession of Priests and people, with
cithers, harps, and cymbals.* JUDAS MAC-
CABÆUS *puts himself at their head, and they
go into the inner courts.*

SCENE III. — JASON *alone.*

JASON.

Through the Gate Beautiful I see them
come,
With branches and green boughs and leaves
of palm,
And pass into the inner courts. Alas !

I should be with them, should be one of
them,
But in an evil hour, an hour of weakness,
That cometh unto all, I fell away
From the old faith, and did not clutch the
new,
Only an outward semblance of belief ;
For the new faith I cannot make mine own,
Not being born to it. It hath no root
Within me. I am neither Jew nor Greek,
But stand between them both, a renegade
To each in turn ; having no longer faith
In gods or men. Then what mysterious
charm,
What fascination is it chains my feet,
And keeps me gazing like a curious child
Into the holy places, where the priests
Have raised their altar ? — Striking stones
together,
They take fire out of them, and light the
lamps
In the great candlestick. They spread the
veils,
And set the loaves of shewbread on the
table.
The incense burns ; the well-remembered
odor
Comes wafted unto me, and takes me back
To other days. I see myself among them
As I was then ; and the old superstition
Creeps over me again ! — A childish
fancy ! —
And hark ! they sing with cithers and
with cymbals,
And all the people fall upon their faces,
Praying and worshipping ! — I will away
Into the East, to meet Antiochus
Upon his homeward journey, crowned with
triumph.
Alas ! to-day I would give everything
To see a friend's face, or to hear a voice
That had the slightest tone of comfort
in it !

ACT V

THE MOUNTAINS OF ECBATANA

SCENE I. — ANTIOCHUS ; PHILIP ; ATTEND-
ANTS.

ANTIOCHUS.

Here let us rest awhile. Where are we,
Philip ?
What place is this ?

PHILIP.
Ecbatana, my Lord ;
And yonder mountain range is the Orontes.

ANTIOCHUS.
The Orontes is my river at Antioch.
Why did I leave it ? Why have I been
    tempted
By coverings of gold and shields and breast-
    plates
To plunder Elymais, and be driven
From out its gates, as by a fiery blast
Out of a furnace ?

PHILIP.
These are fortune's changes.

ANTIOCHUS.
What a defeat it was ! The Persian horse-
    men
Came like a mighty wind, the wind Khamá-
    seen,
And melted us away, and scattered us
As if we were dead leaves, or desert sand.

PHILIP.
Be comforted, my Lord ; for thou hast
    lost
But what thou hadst not.

ANTIOCHUS.
I, who made the Jews
Skip like the grasshoppers, am made my-
    self
To skip among these stones.

PHILIP.
Be not discouraged.
Thy realm of Syria remains to thee ;
That is not lost nor marred.

ANTIOCHUS.
Oh, where are now
The splendors of my court, my baths and
    banquets ?
Where are my players and my dancing
    women ?
Where are my sweet musicians with their
    pipes,
That made me merry in the olden time ?
I am a laughing-stock to man and brute.
The very camels, with their ugly faces,
Mock me and laugh at me.

PHILIP.
Alas ! my Lord,
It is not so. If thou wouldst sleep awhile,
All would be well.

ANTIOCHUS.
Sleep from mine eyes is gone,
And my heart faileth me for very care.
Dost thou remember, Philip, the old fable
Told us when we were boys, in which the
    bear
Going for honey overturns the hive,
And is stung blind by bees ? I am that
    beast,
Stung by the Persian swarms of Elymais.

PHILIP.
When thou art come again to Antioch,
These thoughts will be as covered and for-
    gotten
As are the tracks of Pharaoh's chariot-
    wheels
In the Egyptian sands.

ANTIOCHUS.
Ah ! when I come
Again to Antioch ! When will that be ?
Alas ! alas !

SCENE II. — ANTIOCHUS ; PHILIP ; A MES-
    SENGER.

MESSENGER.
May the King live forever !

ANTIOCHUS.
Who art thou, and whence comest thou ?

MESSENGER.
My Lord,
I am a messenger from Antioch,
Sent here by Lysias.

ANTIOCHUS.
A strange foreboding
Of something evil overshadows me.
I am no reader of the Jewish Scriptures ;
I know not Hebrew ; but my High-Priest
    Jason,
As I remember, told me of a Prophet
Who saw a little cloud rise from the sea
Like a man's hand, and soon the heaven
    was black
With clouds and rain. Here, Philip, read ;
    I cannot ;

I see that cloud. It makes the letters dim
Before mine eyes.

PHILIP (*reading*).
"To King Antiochus,
The God, Epiphanes."

ANTIOCHUS.
Oh mockery!
Even Lysias laughs at me! — Go on, go on!

PHILIP (*reading*).
"We pray thee hasten thy return. The
realm
Is falling from thee. Since thou hast gone
from us
The victories of Judas Maccabæus
Form all our annals. First he overthrew
Thy forces at Beth-horon, and passed on,
And took Jerusalem, the Holy City.
And then Emmaus fell; and then Bethsura,
Ephron and all the towns of Galaad,
And Maccabæus marched to Carnion."

ANTIOCHUS.
Enough, enough! Go call my chariot-
men;
We will drive forward, forward, without
ceasing,
Until we come to Antioch. My captains,
My Lysias, Gorgias, Seron, and Nicanor,
Are babes in battle, and this dreadful Jew
Will rob me of my kingdom and my crown.
My elephants shall trample him to dust;
I will wipe out his nation, and will make
Jerusalem a common burying-place,
And every home within its walls a tomb!

*Throws up his hands, and sinks into the arms of
attendants, who lay him upon a bank.*

PHILIP.
Antiochus! Antiochus! Alas,
The King is ill! What is it, O my Lord?

ANTIOCHUS.
Nothing. A sudden and sharp spasm of
pain,
As if the lightning struck me, or the knife
Of an assassin smote me to the heart.
'T is passed, even as it came. Let us set
forward.

PHILIP.
See that the chariots be in readiness;
We will depart forthwith.

ANTIOCHUS.
A moment more.
I cannot stand. I am become at once
Weak as an infant. Ye will have to lead
me.
Jove, or Jehovah, or whatever name
Thou wouldst be named, — it is alike to
me, —
If I knew how to pray, I would entreat
To live a little longer.

PHILIP.
O my Lord,
Thou shalt not die; we will not let thee
die!

ANTIOCHUS.
How canst thou help it, Philip? Oh the
pain!
Stab after stab. Thou hast no shield
against
This unseen weapon. God of Israel,
Since all the other gods abandon me,
Help me. I will release the Holy City,
Garnish with goodly gifts the Holy Temple.
Thy people, whom I judged to be un-
worthy
To be so much as buried, shall be equal
Unto the citizens of Antioch.
I will become a Jew, and will declare
Through all the world that is inhabited
The power of God!

PHILIP.
He faints. It is like death.
Bring here the royal litter. We will bear
him
Into the camp, while yet he lives.

ANTIOCHUS.
O Philip,
Into what tribulation am I come!
Alas! I now remember all the evil
That I have done the Jews; and for this
cause
These troubles are upon me, and behold
I perish through great grief in a strange
land.

PHILIP.
Antiochus! my King!

ANTIOCHUS.
Nay, King no longer.
Take thou my royal robes, my signet ring,
My crown and sceptre, and deliver them

Unto my son, Antiochus Eupator ;
And unto the good Jews, my citizens,
In all my towns, say that their dying
    monarch
Wisheth them joy, prosperity, and health.
I who, puffed up with pride and arro-
    gance,

Thought all the kingdoms of the earth
    mine own,
If I would but outstretch my hand and
    take them,
Meet face to face a greater potentate,
King Death — Epiphanes — the Illustrious !
                             [Dies.

MICHAEL ANGELO : A FRAGMENT

Michel piu che mortal, Angel divino.
                    ARIOSTO.
Similamente operando all' artista
Ch' a l' abito dell' arte e man che trema.
              DANTE, *Par.* xiii. *st.* 77.

The notes at the end of this volume point out some of
the more interesting indications of the manner in which
the authorities used were made to contribute to the
realism of the poem. It was the poet's intention at one
time to insert in the poem translations of some of the
sonnets and other verses of Michael Angelo, and to
this he refers in his *Dedication* when he says —

              Flowers of song have thrust
Their roots among the loose disjointed stones.

These translations with one exception he withdrew
and published instead in the volume entitled *Kéramos
and other Poems ;* they may be found in their place
among the *Translations* in this edition. Another inti-
mation of the connection of his poetry with this study
appears in the poem *Vittoria Colonna,* written in 1877,
and published in *Flight the Fifth* of *Birds of Pas-
sage.*
   Michael Angelo was found in the poet's desk after
his death, and while in one or two instances some doubt
arose as to Mr. Longfellow's final choice of alternative
scenes, it was reasonably clear what his latest decision
was as to the sequence and form of the poem.
   The reader who is interested in the poet's develop-
ment of the theme and in his several experiments will
find the material at his hand in the poem as printed and
annotated in vol. vi. of the Riverside edition.

DEDICATION

NOTHING that is shall perish utterly,
  But perish only to revive again
  In other forms, as clouds restore in
    rain
  The exhalations of the land and sea.
Men build their houses from the masonry
  Of ruined tombs ; the passion and the
    pain
  Of hearts, that long have ceased to beat,
    remain
  To throb in hearts that are, or are to
    be.
So from old chronicles, where sleep in
    dust
  Names that once filled the world with
    trumpet tones,
  I build this verse ; and flowers of song
    have thrust
Their roots among the loose disjointed
    stones,
  Which to this end I fashion as I must.
  Quickened are they that touch the
    Prophet's bones.

PART FIRST

I

PROLOGUE AT ISCHIA

The Castle Terrace. VITTORIA COLONNA *and*
    JULIA GONZAGA.

VITTORIA.

WILL you then leave me, Julia, and so
    soon,
To pace alone this terrace like a ghost ?

JULIA.

To-morrow, dearest.

VITTORIA.

            Do not say to-morrow.
A whole month of to-morrows were too
    soon.
You must not go. You are a part of me.

JULIA.

I must return to Fondi.

VITTORIA.
The old castle
Needs not your presence. No one waits
for you.
Stay one day longer with me. They who
go
Feel not the pain of parting; it is they
Who stay behind that suffer. I was think-
ing
But yesterday how like and how unlike
Have been, and are, our destinies. Your
husband,
The good Vespasian, an old man, who
seemed
A father to you rather than a husband,
Died in your arms; but mine, in all the
flower
And promise of his youth, was taken from
me
As by a rushing wind. The breath of
battle
Breathed on him, and I saw his face no
more,
Save as in dreams it haunts me. As our
love
Was for these men, so is our sorrow for
them.
Yours a child's sorrow, smiling through its
tears;
But mine the grief of an impassioned
woman,
Who drank her life up in one draught of
love.

JULIA.
Behold this locket. This is the white hair
Of my Vespasian. This the flower-of-love,
This amaranth, and beneath it the device,
Non moritura. Thus my heart remains
True to his memory; and the ancient
castle,
Where we have lived together, where he
died,
Is dear to me as Ischia is to you.

VITTORIA.
I did not mean to chide you.

JULIA.
Let your heart
Find, if it can, some poor apology
For one who is too young, and feels too
keenly
The joy of life, to give up all her days
To sorrow for the dead. While I am true

To the remembrance of the man I loved
And mourn for still, I do not make a show
Of all the grief I feel, nor live secluded
And, like Veronica da Gámbara,
Drape my whole house in mourning, and
drive forth
In coach of sable drawn by sable horses,
As if I were a corpse. Ah, one to-day
Is worth for me a thousand yesterdays.

VITTORIA.
Dear Julia! Friendship has its jealousies
As well as love. Who waits for you at
Fondi?

JULIA.
A friend of mine and yours; a friend and
friar.
You have at Naples your Fra Bernardino;
And I at Fondi have my Fra Bastiano,
The famous artist, who has come from
Rome
To paint my portrait. That is not a sin.

VITTORIA.
Only a vanity.

JULIA.
He painted yours.

VITTORIA.
Do not call up to me those days departed,
When I was young, and all was bright
about me,
And the vicissitudes of life were things
But to be read of in old histories,
Though as pertaining unto me or mine
Impossible. Ah, then I dreamed your
dreams,
And now, grown older, I look back and
see
They were illusions.

JULIA.
Yet without illusions
What would our lives become, what we
ourselves?
Dreams or illusions, call them what you
will,
They lift us from the commonplace of life
To better things.

VITTORIA.
Are there no brighter dreams,
No higher aspirations, than the wish
To please and to be pleased?

JULIA.

For you there are :
I am no saint ; I feel the world we live in
Comes before that which is to be hereafter,
And must be dealt with first.

VITTORIA.

But in what way ?

JULIA.

Let the soft wind that wafts to us the odor
Of orange blossoms, let the laughing sea
And the bright sunshine bathing all the
world,
Answer the question.

VITTORIA.

And for whom is meant
This portrait that you speak of ?

JULIA.

For my friend
The Cardinal Ippolito.

VITTORIA.

For him ?

JULIA.

Yes, for Ippolito the Magnificent.
'T is always flattering to a woman's pride
To be admired by one whom all admire.

VITTORIA.

Ah, Julia, she that makes herself a dove
Is eaten by the hawk.   Be on your guard.
He is a Cardinal ; and his adoration
Should be elsewhere directed.

JULIA.

You forget
The horror of that night, when Barbarossa,
The Moorish corsair, landed on our coast
To seize me for the Sultan Soliman ;
How in the dead of night, when all were
sleeping,
He scaled the castle wall ; how I escaped,
And in my night-dress, mounting a swift
steed,
Fled to the mountains, and took refuge
there
Among the brigands.   Then of all my
friends
The Cardinal Ippolito was first
To come with his retainers to my rescue.
Could I refuse the only boon he asked
At such a time, my portrait ?

VITTORIA.

I have heard
Strange stories of the splendors of his pal-
ace,
And how, apparelled like a Spanish Prince,
He rides through Rome with a long reti-
nue
Of Ethiopians and Numidians
And Turks and Tartars, in fantastic dresses,
Making a gallant show.   Is this the way
A Cardinal should live ?

JULIA.

He is so young ;
Hardly of age, or little more than that ;
Beautiful, generous, fond of arts and let-
ters,
A poet, a musician, and a scholar ;
Master of many languages, and a player
On many instruments.   In Rome, his pal-
ace
Is the asylum of all men distinguished
In art or science, and all Florentines
Escaping from the tyranny of his cousin,
Duke Alessandro.

VITTORIA.

I have seen his portrait,
Painted by Titian.   You have painted it
In brighter colors.

JULIA.

And my Cardinal,
At Itri, in the courtyard of his palace,
Keeps a tame lion !

VITTORIA.

And so counterfeits
St. Mark, the Evangelist !

JULIA.

Ah, your tame lion
Is Michael Angelo.

VITTORIA.

You speak a name
That always thrills me with a noble sound,
As of a trumpet !   Michael Angelo !
A lion all men fear and none can tame ;
A man that all men honor, and the model
That all should follow ; one who works and
prays,
For work is prayer, and consecrates his
life
To the sublime ideal of his art,
Till art and life are one ; a man who holds

Such place in all men's thoughts, that when
    they speak
Of great things done, or to be done, his
    name
Is ever on their lips.

JULIA.
            You too can paint
The portrait of your hero, and in colors
Brighter than Titian's ; I might warn you
    also
Against the dangers that beset your path ;
But I forbear.

VITTORIA.
         If I were made of marble,
Of Fior di Persico or Pavonazzo,
He might admire me : being but flesh and
    blood,
I am no more to him than other women ;
That is am nothing.

JULIA.
         Does he ride through Rome
Upon his little mule, as he was wont,
With his slouched hat, and boots of Cor-
    dovan,
As when I saw him last ?

VITTORIA.
           Pray do not jest.
I cannot couple with his noble name
A trivial word ! Look, how the setting
    sun
Lights up Castel-a-mare and Sorrento,
And changes Capri to a purple cloud !
And there Vesuvius with its plume of
    smoke,
And the great city stretched upon the
    shore
As in a dream !

JULIA.
    Parthenope the Siren !

VITTORIA.
And yon long line of lights, those sunlit
    windows
Blaze like the torches carried in procession
To do her honor ! It is beautiful !

JULIA.
I have no heart to feel the beauty of it !
My feet are weary, pacing up and down
These level flags, and wearier still my
    thoughts

Treading the broken pavement of the Past.
It is too sad. I will go in and rest,
And make me ready for to-morrow's jour-
    ney.

VITTORIA.
I will go with you ; for I would not lose
One hour of your dear presence. 'T is
    enough
Only to be in the same room with you.
I need not speak to you, nor hear you
    speak ;
If I but see you, I am satisfied.
                  [*They go in.*

MONOLOGUE : THE LAST JUDGMENT

MICHAEL ANGELO'S *Studio. He is at work on
    the cartoon of the Last Judgment.*

MICHAEL ANGELO.
Why did the Pope and his ten Cardinals
Come here to lay this heavy task upon
    me ?
Were not the paintings on the Sistine
    ceiling
Enough for them ? They saw the Hebrew
    leader
Waiting, and clutching his tempestuous
    beard,
But heeded not. The bones of Julius
Shook in their sepulchre. I heard the
    sound ;
They only heard the sound of their own
    voices.

Are there no other artists here in Rome
To do this work, that they must needs seek
    me ?
Fra Bastian, my Fra Bastian, might have
    done it,
But he is lost to art. The Papal Seals,
Like leaden weights upon a dead man's
    eyes,
Press down his lids ; and so the burden
    falls
On Michael Angelo, Chief Architect
And Painter of the Apostolic Palace.
That is the title they cajole me with,
To make me do their work and leave my
    own ;
But having once begun, I turn not back.
Blow, ye bright angels, on your golden
    trumpets
To the four corners of the earth, and wake

The dead to judgment! Ye recording
angels,
Open your books and read! Ye dead,
awake!
Rise from your graves, drowsy and drugged
with death,
As men who suddenly aroused from sleep
Look round amazed, and know not where
they are!

In happy hours, when the imagination
Wakes like a wind at midnight, and the
soul
Trembles in all its leaves, it is a joy
To be uplifted on its wings, and listen
To the prophetic voices in the air
That call us onward. Then the work we do
Is a delight, and the obedient hand
Never grows weary. But how different
is it
In the disconsolate, discouraged hours,
When all the wisdom of the world appears
As trivial as the gossip of a nurse
In a sick-room, and all our work seems
useless.

What is it guides my hand, what thoughts
possess me,
That I have drawn her face among the
angels,
Where she will be hereafter? O sweet
dreams,
That through the vacant chambers of my
heart
Walk in the silence, as familiar phantoms
Frequent an ancient house, what will ye
with me?
'T is said that Emperors write their names
in green
When under age, but when of age in
purple.
So Love, the greatest Emperor of them all,
Writes his in green at first, but afterwards
In the imperial purple of our blood.
First love or last love, — which of these
two passions
Is more omnipotent? Which is more fair,
The star of morning, or the evening star?
The sunrise or the sunset of the heart?
The hour when we look forth to the un-
known,
And the advancing day consumes the
shadows,
Or that when all the landscape of our
lives

Lies stretched behind us, and familiar
places
Gleam in the distance, and sweet memo-
ries
Rise like a tender haze, and magnify
The objects we behold, that soon must
vanish?

What matters it to me, whose counte-
nance
Is like Laocoön's, full of pain? whose fore-
head
Is a ploughed harvest-field, where three-
score years
Have sown in sorrow and have reaped in
anguish?
To me, the artisan, to whom all women
Have been as if they were not, or at most
A sudden rush of pigeons in the air,
A flutter of wings, a sound, and then a
silence?
I am too old for love; I am too old
To flatter and delude myself with visions
Of never-ending friendship with fair
women,
Imaginations, fantasies, illusions,
In which the things that cannot be take
shape,
And seem to be, and for the moment are.
Convent bells ring.
Distant and near and low and loud the
bells,
Dominican, Benedictine, and Franciscan,
Jangle and wrangle in their airy towers,
Discordant as the brotherhoods themselves
In their dim cloisters. The descending
sun
Seems to caress the city that he loves,
And crowns it with the aureole of a saint.
I will go forth and breathe the air awhile.

II

SAN SILVESTRO

*A Chapel in the Church of San Silvestro on
Monte Cavallo.*

Vittoria Colonna, Claudio Tolommei, *and
others.*

VITTORIA.

Here let us rest awhile, until the crowd
Has left the church. I have already sent
For Michael Angelo to join us here.

MESSER CLAUDIO.

After Fra Bernardino's wise discourse
On the Pauline Epistles, certainly
Some words of Michael Angelo on Art
Were not amiss, to bring us back to earth.

MICHAEL ANGELO, *at the door.*

How like a Saint or Goddess she appears !
Diana or Madonna, which I know not,
In attitude and aspect formed to be
At once the artist's worship and despair !

VITTORIA.

Welcome, Maestro.   We were waiting for
    you.

MICHAEL ANGELO.

I met your messenger upon the way,
And hastened hither.

VITTORIA.

                It is kind of you
To come to us, who linger here like gossips
Wasting the afternoon in idle talk.
These are all friends of mine and friends
    of yours.

MICHAEL ANGELO.

If friends of yours, then are they friends of
    mine.
Pardon me, gentlemen.   But when I en-
    tered
I saw but the Marchesa.

VITTORIA.

                Take this seat
Between me and Ser Claudio Tolommei,
Who still maintains that our Italian tongue
Should be called Tuscan.   But for that
    offence
We will not quarrel with him.

MICHAEL ANGELO.

                            Eccellenza —

VITTORIA.

Ser Claudio has banished Eccellenza
And all such titles from the Tuscan tongue.

MESSER CLAUDIO.

'T is the abuse of them, and not the use,
I deprecate.

MICHAEL ANGELO.

        The use or the abuse,
It matters not.   Let them all go together,

As empty phrases and frivolities,
And common as gold-lace upon the collar
Of an obsequious lackey.

VITTORIA.

                    That may be,
But something of politeness would go with
    them ;
We should lose something of the stately
    manners
Of the old school.

MESSER CLAUDIO.

            Undoubtedly.

VITTORIA.

                    But that
Is not what occupies my thoughts at
    present,
Nor why I sent for you, Messer Michele.
It was to counsel me.   His Holiness
Has granted me permission, long desired,
To build a convent in this neighborhood,
Where the old tower is standing, from
    whose top
Nero looked down upon the burning city.

MICHAEL ANGELO.

It is an inspiration !

VITTORIA.

            I am doubtful
How I shall build; how large to make the
    convent,
And which way fronting.

MICHAEL ANGELO.

                Ah, to build, to build !
That is the noblest art of all the arts.
Painting and sculpture are but images,
Are merely shadows cast by outward
    things
On stone or canvas, having in themselves
No separate existence.   Architecture,
Existing in itself, and not in seeming
A something it is not, surpasses them
As substance shadow.   Long, long years
    ago,
Standing one morning near the Baths of
    Titus,
I saw the statue of Laocoön
Rise from its grave of centuries, like a
    ghost
Writhing in pain ; and as it tore away

The knotted serpents from its limbs, I
  heard,
Or seemed to hear, the cry of agony
From its white, parted lips. And still I
  marvel
At the three Rhodian artists, by whose
  hands
This miracle was wrought. Yet he beholds
Far nobler works who looks upon the ruins
Of temples in the Forum here in Rome.
If God should give me power in my old
  age
To build for Him a temple half as grand
As those were in their glory, I should
  count
My age more excellent than youth itself,
And all that I have hitherto accomplished
As only vanity.

VITTORIA.
      I understand you.
Art is the gift of God, and must be used
Unto His glory. That in art is highest
Which aims at this. When St. Hilarion
  blessed
The horses of Italicus, they won
The race at Gaza, for his benediction
O'erpowered all magic ; and the people
  shouted
That Christ had conquered Marnas. So
  that art
Which bears the consecration and the seal
Of holiness upon it will prevail
Over all others. Those few words of
  yours
Inspire me with new confidence to build.
What think you ? The old walls might
  serve, perhaps,
Some purpose still. The tower can hold
  the bells.

MICHAEL ANGELO.
If strong enough.

VITTORIA.
      If not, it can be strengthened.

MICHAEL ANGELO.
I see no bar nor drawback to this building,
And on our homeward way, if it shall please
  you,
We may together view the site.

VITTORIA.
            I thank you.
I did not venture to request so much.

MICHAEL ANGELO.
Let us now go to the old walls you spake
  of,
Vossignoria —

VITTORIA.
    What, again, Maestro ?

MICHAEL ANGELO.
Pardon me, Messer Claudio, if once more
I use the ancient courtesies of speech.
I am too old to change.

III

CARDINAL IPPOLITO

SCENE I. — *A richly furnished apartment in
  the Palace of* CARDINAL IPPOLITO. *Night.*

JACOPO NARDI, *an old man, alone.*

NARDI.
I am bewildered. These Numidian slaves,
In strange attire ; these endless antecham-
  bers ;
This lighted hall, with all its golden splen-
  dors,
Pictures, and statues ! Can this be the
  dwelling
Of a disciple of that lowly Man
Who had not where to lay his head ? These
  statues
Are not of Saints ; nor is this a Madonna,
This lovely face, that with such tender
  eyes
Looks down upon me from the painted can-
  vas.
My heart begins to fail me. What can
  he
Who lives in boundless luxury at Rome
Care for the imperilled liberties of Flor-
  ence,
Her people, her Republic ? Ah, the rich
Feel not the pangs of banishment. All
  doors
Are open to them, and all hands extended.
The poor alone are outcasts ; they who
  risked
All they possessed for liberty, and lost ;
And wander through the world without a
  friend,
Sick, comfortless, distressed, unknown, un-
  cared for.

SCENE II. — JACOPO NARDI ; CARDINAL IPPO-
LITO, *in Spanish cloak and slouched hat.*

IPPOLITO.

I pray you pardon me if I have kept you
Waiting so long alone.

NARDI.
     I wait to see
The Cardinal.

IPPOLITO.
    I am the Cardinal ;
And you ?

NARDI.
Jacopo Nardi.

IPPOLITO.
     You are welcome.
I was expecting you. Philippo Strozzi
Had told me of your coming.

NARDI.
     'T was his son
That brought me to your door.

IPPOLITO.
     Pray you, be seated.
You seem astonished at the garb I wear,
But at my time of life, and with my habits,
The petticoats of a Cardinal would be —
Troublesome ; I could neither ride nor
  walk,
Nor do a thousand things, if I were dressed
Like an old dowager. It were putting
  wine
Young as the young Astyanax into goblets
As old as Priam.

NARDI.
    Oh, your Eminence
Knows best what you should wear.

IPPOLITO.
    Dear Messer Nardi,
You are no stranger to me. I have read
Your excellent translation of the books
Of Titus Livius, the historian
Of Rome, and model of all historians
That shall come after him. It does you
  honor ;
But greater honor still the love you bear
To Florence, our dear country, and whose
  annals
I hope your hand will write, in happier
  days
Than we now see.

NARDI.
    Your Eminence will pardon
The lateness of the hour.

IPPOLITO.
    The hours I count not
As a sun-dial ; but am like a clock,
That tells the time as well by night as day.
So, no excuse. I know what brings you
  here.
You come to speak of Florence.

NARDI.
    And her woes.

IPPOLITO.

The duke, my cousin, the black Alessandro,
Whose mother was a Moorish slave, that
  fed
The sheep upon Lorenzo's farm, still lives
And reigns.

NARDI.
    Alas, that such a scourge
Should fall on such a city !

IPPOLITO.
    When he dies,
The Wild Boar in the gardens of Lorenzo,
The beast obscene, should be the monument
Of this bad man.

NARDI.
    He walks the streets at night
With revellers, insulting honest men.
No house is sacred from his lusts. The
  convents
Are turned by him to brothels, and the
  honor
Of woman and all ancient pious customs
Are quite forgotten now.   The offices
Of the Priori and Gonfalonieri
Have been abolished. All the magistrates
Are now his creatures. Liberty is dead.
The very memory of all honest living
Is wiped away, and even our Tuscan tongue
Corrupted to a Lombard dialect.

IPPOLITO.

And, worst of all, his impious hand has
  broken
The Martinella, — our great battle bell,
That, sounding through three centuries, has
  led
The Florentines to victory, — lest its voice

Should waken in their soul some memory
Of far-off times of glory.

NARDI.

What a change
Ten little years have made ! We all re-
member
Those better days, when Niccolà Capponi,
The Gonfaloniere, from the windows
Of the Old Palace, with the blast of trum-
pets,
Proclaimed to the inhabitants that Christ
Was chosen King of Florence ; and already
Christ is dethroned, and slain ; and in his
stead
Reigns Lucifer ! Alas, alas, for Florence !

IPPOLITO.

Lilies with lilies, said Savonarola ;
Florence and France ! But I say Florence
only,
Or only with the Emperor's hand to help us
In sweeping out the rubbish.

NARDI.

Little hope
Of help is there from him. He has be-
trothed
His daughter Margaret to this shameless
Duke.
What hope have we from such an Em-
peror ?

IPPOLITO.

Baccio Valori and Philippo Strozzi,
Once the Duke's friends and intimates, are
with us,
And Cardinals Salvati and Ridolfi.
We shall soon see, then, as Valori says,
Whether the Duke can best spare honest
men,
Or honest men the Duke.

NARDI.

We have determined
To send ambassadors to Spain, and lay
Our griefs before the Emperor, though I
fear
More than I hope.

IPPOLITO.

The Emperor is busy
With this new war against the Algerines,
And has no time to listen to complaints
From our ambassadors ; nor will I trust
them,

But go myself. All is in readiness
For my departure, and to-morrow morning
I shall go down to Itri, where I meet
Dante da Castiglione and some others,
Republicans and fugitives from Florence,
And then take ship at Gaëta. and go
To join the Emperor in his new crusade
Against the Turk. I shall have time
enough
And opportunity to plead our cause.

NARDI, *rising.*

It is an inspiration, and I hail it
As of good omen. May the power that
sends it
Bless our beloved country, and restore
Its banished citizens. The soul of Florence
Is now outside its gates. What lies within
Is but a corpse, corrupted and corrupting.
Heaven help us all. I will not tarry
longer,
For you have need of rest. Good-night.

IPPOLITO.

Good-night !

SCENE III. — CARDINAL IPPOLITO ; FRA SE-
BASTIANO ; *Turkish attendants.*

IPPOLITO.

Fra Bastiano, how your portly presence
Contrasts with that of the spare Florentine
Who has just left me !

FRA SEBASTIANO.

As we passed each other,
I saw that he was weeping.

IPPOLITO.

Poor old man !

FRA SEBASTIANO.

Who is he ?

IPPOLITO.

Jacopo Nardi. A brave soul ;
One of the Fuorusciti, and the best
And noblest of them all ; but he has made
me
Sad with his sadness. As I look on you
My heart grows lighter. I behold a man
Who lives in an ideal world, apart
From all the rude collisions of our life,
In a calm atmosphere.

FRA SEBASTIANO.

Your Eminence

Is surely jesting. If you knew the life
Of artists as I know it, you might think
Far otherwise.

IPPOLITO.

But wherefore should I jest?
The world of art is an ideal world, —
The world I love, and that I fain would
    live in;
So speak to me of artists and of art,
Of all the painters, sculptors, and musicians
That now illustrate Rome.

FRA SEBASTIANO.

Of the musicians,
I know but Goudimel, the brave maestro
And chapel-master of his Holiness,
Who trains the Papal choir.

IPPOLITO.

In church, this morning,
I listened to a mass of Goudimel,
Divinely chanted. In the Incarnatus,
In lieu of Latin words, the tenor sang
With infinite tenderness, in plain Italian,
A Neapolitan love-song.

FRA SEBASTIANO.

You amaze me.
Was it a wanton song?

IPPOLITO.

Not a divine one.
I am not over-scrupulous, as you know,
In word or deed, yet such a song as that,
Sung by the tenor of the Papal choir,
And in a Papal mass, seemed out of place;
There's something wrong in it.

FRA SEBASTIANO.

There's something wrong
In everything. We cannot make the world
Go right. 'T is not my business to reform
The Papal choir.

IPPOLITO.

Nor mine, thank Heaven!
Then tell me of the artists.

FRA SEBASTIANO.

Naming one
I name them all; for there is only one:
His name is Messer Michael Angelo.
All art and artists of the present day
Centre in him.

IPPOLITO.

You count yourself as nothing?

FRA SEBASTIANO.

Or less than nothing, since I am at best
Only a portrait-painter; one who draws
With greater or less skill, as best he may,
The features of a face.

IPPOLITO.

And you have had
The honor, nay, the glory, of portraying
Julia Gonzaga! Do you count as nothing
A privilege like that? See there the por-
    trait
Rebuking you with its divine expression.
Are you not penitent? He whose skilful
    hand
Painted that lovely picture has not right
To vilipend the art of portrait-painting.
But what of Michael Angelo?

FRA SEBASTIANO.

But lately
Strolling together down the crowded Corso,
We stopped, well pleased, to see your Em-
    inence
Pass on an Arab steed, a noble creature,
Which Michael Angelo, who is a lover
Of all things beautiful, and especially
When they are Arab horses, much ad-
    mired,
And could not praise enough.

IPPOLITO, to an attendant.

Hassan, to-morrow,
When I am gone, but not till I am gone, —
Be careful about that, — take Barbarossa
To Messer Michael Angelo the sculptor,
Who lives there at Macello dei Corvi,
Near to the Capitol; and take besides
Some ten mule-loads of provender, and
    say
Your master sends them to him as a
    present.

FRA SEBASTIANO.

A princely gift. Though Michael Angelo
Refuses presents from his Holiness,
Yours he will not refuse.

IPPOLITO.

You think him like
Thymœtes, who received the wooden horse
Into the walls of Troy. That book of
    Virgil

Have I translated in Italian verse,
And shall, some day, when we have leisure
        for it,
Be pleased to read you.   When I speak of
        Troy
I am reminded of another town
And of a lovelier Helen, our dear Coun-
        tess
Julia Gonzaga.   You remember, surely,
The adventure with the corsair Barbarossa,
And all that followed ?

        FRA SEBASTIANO.
                A most strange adventure ;
A tale as marvellous and full of wonder
As any in Boccaccio or Sacchetti ;
Almost incredible !

        IPPOLITO.
                Were I a painter
I should not want a better theme than
        that :
The lovely lady fleeing through the night
In wild disorder ; and the brigands' camp
With the red fire-light on their swarthy
        faces.
Could you not paint it for me ?

        FRA SEBASTIANO.
                        No, not I.
It is not in my line.

        IPPOLITO.
                Then you shall paint
The portrait of the corsair, when we bring
        him
A prisoner chained to Naples ; for I feel
Something like admiration for a man
Who dared this strange adventure.

        FRA SEBASTIANO.
                        I will do it.
But catch the corsair first.

        IPPOLITO.
                        You may begin
To-morrow with the sword.   Hassan, come
        hither ;
Bring me the Turkish scimitar that hangs
Beneath the picture yonder.   Now un-
        sheathe it.
'T is a Damascus blade ; you see the in-
        scription
In Arabic :   *La Allah ! illa Allah !* —
There is no God but God.

        FRA SEBASTIANO.
                        How beautiful
In fashion and in finish !   It is perfect.
The Arsenal of Venice cannot boast
A finer sword.

        IPPOLITO.
        You like it ?   It is yours.

        FRA SEBASTIANO.
You do not mean it.

        IPPOLITO.
                I am not a Spaniard,
To say that it is yours and not to mean it.
I have at Itri a whole armory
Full of such weapons.   When you paint the
        portrait
Of Barbarossa, it will be of use.
You have not been rewarded as you should
        be
For painting the Gonzaga.   Throw this
        bauble
Into the scale, and make the balance equal.
Till then suspend it in your studio ;
You artists like such trifles.

        FRA SEBASTIANO.
                I will keep it
In memory of the donor.   Many thanks.

        IPPOLITO.
Fra Bastian, I am growing tired of Rome,
The old dead city, with the old dead
        people ;
Priests everywhere, like shadows on a wall,
And morning, noon, and night the cease-
        less sound
Of convent bells.   I must be gone from
        here ;
Though Ovid somewhere says that Rome is
        worthy
To be the dwelling-place of all the Gods,
I must be gone from here.   To-morrow
        morning
I start for Itri, and go thence by sea
To join the Emperor, who is making war
Upon the Algerines ; perhaps to sink
Some Turkish galleys, and bring back in
        chains
The famous corsair.   Thus would I avenge
The beautiful Gonzaga.

        FRA SEBASTIANO.
                An achievement
Worthy of Charlemagne, or of Orlando.

Berni and Ariosto both shall add
A canto to their poems, and describe you
As Furioso and Innamorato.
Now I must say good-night.

IPPOLITO.

You must not go ;
First you shall sup with me. My seneschal,
Giovan Andrea dal Borgo a San Se-
polcro, —
I like to give the whole sonorous name,
It sounds so like a verse of the Æneid, —
Has brought me eels fresh from the Lake
of Fondi,
And Lucrine oysters cradled in their
shells ;
These, with red Fondi wine, the Cæcuban
That Horace speaks of, under a hundred
keys
Kept safe, until the heir of Posthumus
Shall stain the pavement with it, make a
feast
Fit for Lucullus, or Fra Bastian even ;
So we will go to supper, and be merry.

FRA SEBASTIANO.

Beware ! Remember that Bolsena's eels
And Vernage wine once killed a Pope of
Rome !

IPPOLITO.

'T was a French Pope ; and then so long
ago ;
Who knows ? — perhaps the story is not
true.

IV

BORGO DELLE VERGINE AT NAPLES

Room in the Palace of JULIA GONZAGA. *Night.*
JULIA GONZAGA, GIOVANNI VALDESSO.

JULIA.

Do not go yet.

VALDESSO.

The night is far advanced ;
I fear to stay too late, and weary you
With these discussions.

JULIA.

I have much to say.
I speak to you, Valdesso, with that frank-
ness
Which is the greatest privilege of friend-
ship, —

Speak as I hardly would to my confes-
sor,
Such is my confidence in you.

VALDESSO.

Dear Countess,
If loyalty to friendship be a claim
Upon your confidence, then I may claim it.

JULIA.

Then sit again, and listen unto things
That nearer are to me than life itself.

VALDESSO.

In all things I am happy to obey you,
And happiest then when you command me
most.

JULIA.

Laying aside all useless rhetoric,
That is superfluous between us two,
I come at once unto the point, and say,
You know my outward life, my rank and
fortune ;
Countess of Fondi, Duchess of Trajetto,
A widow rich and flattered, for whose hand
In marriage princes ask, and ask it only
To be rejected. All the world can offer
Lies at my feet. If I remind you of it
It is not in the way of idle boasting,
But only to the better understanding
Of what comes after.

VALDESSO.

God hath given you also
Beauty and intellect ; and the signal grace
To lead a spotless life amid temptations
That others yield to.

JULIA.

But the inward life, —
That you know not ; 't is known but to my-
self,
And is to me a mystery and a pain :
A soul disquieted and ill at ease,
A mind perplexed with doubts and appre-
hensions,
A heart dissatisfied with all around me,
And with myself, so that sometimes I
weep,
Discouraged and disgusted with the world.

VALDESSO.

Whene'er we cross a river at a ford,
If we would pass in safety, we must keep

Our eyes fixed steadfast on the shore be-
    yond,
For if we cast them on the flowing stream,
The head swims with it ; so if we would
    cross
The running flood of things here in the
    world,
Our souls must not look down, but fix their
    sight
On the firm land beyond.

JULIA.
                    I comprehend you.
You think I am too worldly ; that my head
Swims with the giddying whirl of life about
    me.
Is that your meaning ?

VALDESSO.
                    Yes ; your meditations
Are more of this world and its vanities
Than of the world to come.

JULIA.
                    Between the two
I am confused.

VALDESSO.
                    Yet have I seen you listen
Enraptured when Fra Bernardino preached
Of faith and hope and charity.

JULIA.
                    I listen,
But only as to music without meaning.
It moves me for the moment, and I think
How beautiful it is to be a saint,
As dear Vittoria is ; but I am weak
And wayward, and I soon fall back again
To my old ways, so very easily.
There are too many week-days for one
    Sunday.

VALDESSO.
Then take the Sunday with you through
    the week,
And sweeten with it all the other days.

JULIA.
In part I do so ; for to put a stop
To idle tongues, what men might say of
    me
If I lived all alone here in my palace,
And not from a vocation that I feel
For the monastic life, I now am living
With Sister Caterina at the convent
Of Santa Chiara, and I come here only

On certain days, for my affairs, or visits
Of ceremony, or to be with friends.
For I confess, to live among my friends
Is Paradise to me ; my Purgatory
Is living among people I dislike.
And so I pass my life in these two worlds,
This palace and the convent.

VALDESSO.
                    It was then
The fear of man, and not the love of God,
That led you to this step. Why will you
    not
Renounce the world, and give your heart
    to God,[1]

JULIA.
                    If God so commands it,
Wherefore hath He not made me capable
Of doing for Him what I wish to do
As easily as I could offer Him
This jewel from my hand, this gown I
    wear,
Or aught else that is mine ?

VALDESSO.
                    The hindrance lies
In that original sin, by which all fell.

JULIA.
Ah me, I cannot bring my troubled mind
To wish well to that Adam, our first parent,
Who by his sin lost Paradise for us,
And brought such ills upon us.

VALDESSO.
                    We ourselves,
When we commit a sin, lose Paradise,
As much as he did. Let us think of this,
And how we may regain it.

JULIA.
                    Teach me, then,
To harmonize the discord of my life,
And stop the painful jangle of these wires.

VALDESSO.
That is a task impossible, until
You tune your heart-strings to a higher key
Than earthly melodies.

JULIA.
                    How shall I do it ?
Point out to me the way of this perfection,

1 For some unexplained reason, the sentence has been
left incomplete ; apparently the omission was not more
than a half line.

And I will follow you ; for you have made
My soul enamored with it, and I cannot
Rest satisfied until I find it out.
But lead me privately, so that the world
Hear not my steps ; I would not give occa-
        sion
For talk among the people.

VALDESSO.
                        Now at last
I understand you fully.   Then, what need
Is there for us to beat about the bush ?
I know what you desire of me.

JULIA.
                        What rudeness !
If you already know it, why not tell me ?

VALDESSO.
Because I rather wait for you to ask it
With your own lips.

JULIA.
                        Do me the kindness, then,
To speak without reserve ; and with all
        frankness,
If you divine the truth, will I confess it.

VALDESSO.
I am content.

JULIA.
Then speak.

VALDESSO.
                        You would be free
From the vexatious thoughts that come and
        go
Through your imagination, and would have
        me
Point out some royal road and lady-like
Which you may walk in, and not wound
        your feet.
You would attain to the divine perfection,
And yet not turn your back upon the
        world ;
You would possess humility within,
But not reveal it in your outward actions ;
You would have patience, but without the
        rude
Occasions that require its exercise ;
You would despise the world, but in such
        fashion
The world should not despise you in return ;
Would clothe the soul with all the Chris-
        tian graces,
Yet not despoil the body of its gauds ;

Would feed the soul with spiritual food,
Yet not deprive the body of its feasts ;
Would seem angelic in the sight of God,
Yet not too saint-like in the eyes of men ;
In short, would lead a holy Christian life
In such a way that even your nearest friend
Would not detect therein one circumstance
To show a change from what it was before.
Have I divined your secret ?

JULIA.
                        You have drawn
The portrait of my inner self as truly
As the most skilful painter ever painted
A human face.

VALDESSO.
                        This warrants me in saying
You think you can win heaven by compro-
        mise,
And not by verdict.

JULIA.
                        You have often told me
That a bad compromise was better even
Than a good verdict.

VALDESSO.
                        Yes, in suits at law ;
Not in religion.   With the human soul
There is no compromise.   By faith alone
Can man be justified.

JULIA.
                        Hush, dear Valdesso ;
That is a heresy.   Do not, I pray you,
Proclaim it from the house-top, but preserve
        it
As something precious, hidden in your
        heart,
As I, who half believe and tremble at it.

VALDESSO.
I must proclaim the truth.

JULIA.
                        Enthusiast !
Why must you ?   You imperil both your-
        self
And friends by your imprudence.   Pray,
        be patient.
You have occasion now to show that virtue
Which you lay stress upon.   Let us return
To our lost pathway.   Show me by what
        steps
I shall walk in it.
                        [*Convent bells are heard.*

VALDESSO.

Hark ! the convent bells
Are ringing ; it is midnight ; I must leave
you.
And yet I linger.   Pardon me, dear Coun-
tess,
Since you to-night have made me your con-
fessor,
If I so far may venture, I will warn you
Upon one point.

JULIA.

What is it ?   Speak, I pray you,
For I have no concealments in my conduct ;
All is as open as the light of day.
What is it you would warn me of ?

VALDESSO.

Your friendship
With Cardinal Ippolito.

JULIA.

What is there
To cause suspicion or alarm in that,
More than in friendships that I entertain
With you and others ?   I ne'er sat with
him
Alone at night, as I am sitting now
With you, Valdesso.

VALDESSO.

Pardon me ; the portrait
That Fra Bastiano painted was for him.
Is that quite prudent ?

JULIA.

That is the same question
Vittoria put to me, when I last saw her.
I make you the same answer.   That was
not
A pledge of love, but of pure gratitude.
Recall the adventure of that dreadful night
When Barbarossa with two thousand Moors
Landed upon the coast, and in the dark-
ness
Attacked my castle.   Then, without delay,
The Cardinal came hurrying down from
Rome
To rescue and protect me.   Was it wrong
That in an hour like that I did not weigh
Too nicely this or that, but granted him
A boon that pleased him, and that flattered
me ?

VALDESSO.

Only beware lest, in disguise of friendship,
Another corsair, worse than Barbarossa,

Steal in and seize the castle, not by storm
But strategy.   And now I take my leave.

JULIA.

Farewell ; but ere you go, look forth and
see
How night hath hushed the clamor and the
stir
Of the tumultuous streets.   The cloudless
moon
Roofs the whole city as with tiles of silver ;
The dim, mysterious sea in silence sleeps,
And straight into the air Vesuvius lifts
His plume of smoke.   How beautiful it is !
[*Voices in the street.*

GIOVAN ANDREA.

Poisoned at Itri.

ANOTHER VOICE.

Poisoned ?   Who is poisoned ?

GIOVAN ANDREA.

The Cardinal Ippolito, my master.
Call it malaria.   It was very sudden.
[*Julia swoons.*

V

VITTORIA COLONNA

A room in the Torre Argentina.

VITTORIA COLONNA and JULIA GONZAGA.

VITTORIA.

Come to my arms and to my heart once
more ;
My soul goes out to meet you and embrace
you,
For we are of the sisterhood of sorrow.
I know what you have suffered.

JULIA.

Name it not.
Let me forget it.

VITTORIA.

I will say no more.
Let me look at you.   What a joy it is
To see your face, to hear your voice again !
You bring with you a breath as of the
morn,
A memory of the far-off happy days
When we were young.   When did you
come from Fondi ?

JULIA.

I have not been at Fondi since —

VITTORIA.
　　　　　　　　　　Ah me !
You need not speak the word : I understand you.

JULIA.

I came from Naples by the lovely valley,
The Terra di Lavoro.

VITTORIA.
　　　　　　　And you find me
But just returned from a long journey
northward.
I have been staying with that noble woman,
Renée of France, the Duchess of Ferrara.

JULIA.

Oh, tell me of the Duchess. I have heard
Flaminio speak her praises with such
　　warmth
That I am eager to hear more of her
And of her brilliant court.

VITTORIA.
　　　　　　　You shall hear all.
But first sit down and listen patiently
While I confess myself.

JULIA.
　　　　　　　What deadly sin
Have you committed ?

VITTORIA.
　　　　　　　Not a sin ; a folly.
I chid you once at Ischia, when you told
me
That brave Fra Bastian was to paint your
portrait.

JULIA.

Well I remember it.

VITTORIA.
　　　　　　　Then chide me now,
For I confess to something still more
　　strange.
Old as I am, I have at last consented
To the entreaties and the supplications
Of Michael Angelo —

JULIA.
　　　　　　　To marry him ?

VITTORIA.

I. pray you, do not jest with me ! You
　　know,
Or you should know, that never such a
　　thought
Entered my breast. I am already married.
The Marquis of Pescara is my husband,
And death has not divorced us.

JULIA.
　　　　　　　Pardon me.
Have I offended you ?

VITTORIA.
　　　　　　　No, but have hurt me.
Unto my buried lord I give myself,
Unto my friend the shadow of myself,
My portrait. It is not from vanity,
But for the love I bear him.

JULIA.
　　　　　　　I rejoice
To hear these words. Oh, this will be a
　　portrait
Worthy of both of you !　　　[*A knock.*

VITTORIA.
　　　　　　　Hark ! he is coming.

JULIA.

And shall I go or stay ?

VITTORIA.
　　　　　　　By all means, stay.
The drawing will be better for your presence ;
You will enliven me.

JULIA.
　　　　　　　I shall not speak ;
The presence of great men doth take from
me
All power of speech. I only gaze at them
In silent wonder, as if they were gods,
Or the inhabitants of some other planet.
　　　　Enter MICHAEL ANGELO.

VITTORIA.
Come in.

MICHAEL ANGELO.
　　　　　　　I fear my visit is ill-timed ;
I interrupt you.

VITTORIA.
　　　　　　　No ; this is a friend
Of yours as well as mine, — the Lady Julia
The Duchess of Trajetto.

MICHAEL ANGELO *to* JULIA.
                    I salute you.
'T is long since I have seen your face, my
    lady ;
Pardon me if I say that having seen it,
One never can forget it.

JULIA.
                    You are kind
To keep me in your memory.

MICHAEL ANGELO.
                    It is
The privilege of age to speak with frank-
    ness.
You will not be offended when I say
That never was your beauty more divine.

JULIA.
When Michael Angelo condescends to flat-
    ter
Or praise me, I am proud, and not offended.

VITTORIA.
Now this is gallantry enough for one ;
Show me a little.

MICHAEL ANGELO.
                    Ah, my gracious lady,
You know I have not words to speak your
    praise.
I think of you in silence.   You conceal
Your manifold perfections from all eyes,
And make yourself more saint-like day by
    day,
And day by day men worship you the more.
But now your hour of martyrdom has come.
You know why I am here.

VITTORIA.
                    Ah yes, I know it ;
And meet my fate with fortitude.   You
    find me
Surrounded by the labors of your hands :
The Woman of Samaria at the Well,
The Mater Dolorosa, and the Christ
Upon the Cross, beneath which you have
    written
Those memorable words of Alighieri,
" Men have forgotten how much blood it
    costs."

MICHAEL ANGELO.
And now I come to add one labor more,
If you will call that labor which is pleasure,
And only pleasure.

VITTORIA.
How shall I be seated ?

MICHAEL ANGELO, *opening his portfolio.*
Just as you are.   The light falls well upon
    you.

VITTORIA.
I am ashamed to steal the time from you
That should be given to the Sistine Chapel.
How does that work go on ?

MICHAEL ANGELO, *drawing.*
                    But tardily,
Old men work slowly.   Brain and hand
    alike
Are dull and torpid.   To die young is best,
And not to be remembered as old men
Tottering about in their decrepitude.

VITTORIA.
My dear Maestro ! have you, then, forgot-
    ten
The story of Sophocles in his old age ?

MICHAEL ANGELO.
What story is it ?

VITTORIA.
                    When his sons accused him,
Before the Areopagus, of dotage,
For all defence, he read there to his Judges
The Tragedy of Œdipus Coloneus, —
The work of his old age.

MICHAEL ANGELO.
                    'T is an illusion,
A fabulous story, that will lead old men
Into a thousand follies and conceits.

VITTORIA.
So you may show to cavillers your painting
Of the Last Judgment in the Sistine
    Chapel.

MICHAEL ANGELO.
Now you and Lady Julia shall resume
The conversation that I interrupted.

VITTORIA.
It was of no great import ; nothing more
Nor less than my late visit to Ferrara,
And what I saw there in the ducal palace.
Will it not interrupt you ?

MICHAEL ANGELO.

          Not the least.

VITTORIA.

Well, first, then, of Duke Ercole : a man
Cold in his manners, and reserved and si-
    lent,
And yet magnificent in all his ways ;
Not hospitable unto new ideas,
But from state policy, and certain reasons
Concerning the investiture of the duchy,
A partisan of Rome, and consequently
Intolerant of all the new opinions.

JULIA.

I should not like the Duke.   These silent
    men,
Who only look and listen, are like wells
That have no water in them, deep and
    empty.
How could the daughter of a king of France
Wed such a duke ?

MICHAEL ANGELO.

          The men that women marry,
And why they marry them, will always be
A marvel and a mystery to the world.

VITTORIA.

And then the Duchess, — how shall I de-
    scribe her,
Or tell the merits of that happy nature
Which pleases most when least it thinks of
    pleasing ?
Not beautiful, perhaps, in form and fea-
    ture,
Yet with an inward beauty, that shines
    through
Each look and attitude and word and ges-
    ture ;
A kindly grace of manner and behavior,
A something in her presence and her ways
That makes her beautiful beyond the reach
Of mere external beauty ; and in heart
So noble and devoted to the truth,
And so in sympathy with all who strive
After the higher life.

JULIA.

          She draws me to her
As much as her Duke Ercole repels me.

VITTORIA.

Then the devout and honorable women
That grace her court, and make it good to
    be there ;

Francesca Bucyronia, the true-hearted,
Lavinia della Rovere and the Orsini,
The Magdalena and the Cherubina,
And Anne de Parthenai, who sings so
    sweetly ;
All lovely women, full of noble thoughts
And aspirations after noble things.

JULIA.

Boccaccio would have envied you such
    dames.

VITTORIA.

No ; his Fiammettas and his Philomenas
Are fitter company for Ser Giovanni ;
I fear he hardly would have comprehended
The women that I speak of.

MICHAEL ANGELO.

          Yet he wrote
The story of Griseldis.   That is something
To set down in his favor.

VITTORIA.

          With these ladies
Was a young girl, Olympia Morata,
Daughter of Fulvio, the learned scholar,
Famous in all the universities :
A marvellous child, who at the spinning-
    wheel,
And in the daily round of household cares,
Hath learned both Greek and Latin ; and
    is now
A favorite of the Duchess and companion
Of Princess Anne.   This beautiful young
    Sappho
Sometimes recited to us Grecian odes
That she had written, with a voice whose
    sadness
Thrilled and o'ermastered me, and made
    me look
Into the future time, and ask myself
What destiny will be hers.

JULIA.

          A sad one, surely.
Frost kills the flowers that blossom out of
    season ;
And these precocious intellects portend
A life of sorrow or an early death.

VITTORIA.

About the court were many learned men ;
Chilian Sinapius from beyond the Alps,
And Celio Curione, and Manzolli,

The Duke's physician ; and a pale young
man,
Charles d'Espeville of Geneva, whom the
Duchess
Doth much delight to talk with and to read.
For he hath written a book of Institutes
The Duchess greatly praises, though some
call it
The Koran of the heretics.

JULIA.
And what poets
Were there to sing you madrigals, and
praise
Olympia's eyes and Cherubina's tresses ?

VITTORIA.
None ; for great Ariosto is no more.
The voice that filled those halls with mel-
ody
Has long been hushed in death.

JULIA.
You should have made
A pilgrimage unto the poet's tomb,
And laid a wreath upon it, for the words
He spake of you.

VITTORIA.
And of yourself no less,
And of our master, Michael Angelo.

MICHAEL ANGELO.
Of me ?

VITTORIA.
Have you forgotten that he calls you
Michael, less man than angel, and divine ?
You are ungrateful.

MICHAEL ANGELO.
A mere play on words.
That adjective he wanted for a rhyme,
To match with Gian Bellino and Urbino.

VITTORIA.
Bernardo Tasso is no longer there,
Nor the gay troubadour of Gascony,
Clement Marot, surnamed by flatterers
The Prince of Poets and the Poet of Princes,
Who, being looked upon with much dis-
favor
By the Duke Ercole, has fled to Venice.

MICHAEL ANGELO.
There let him stay with Pietro Aretino,
The Scourge of Princes, also called Divine.
The title is so common in our mouths,
That even the Pifferari of Abruzzi,
Who play their bag-pipes in the streets of
Rome
At the Epiphany, will bear it soon,
And will deserve it better than some poets.

VITTORIA.
What bee hath stung you ?

MICHAEL ANGELO.
One that makes no honey ;
One that comes buzzing in through every
window,
And stabs men with his sting. A bitter
thought
Passed through my mind, but it is gone
again ;
I spake too hastily.

JULIA.
I pray you, show me
What you have done.

MICHAEL ANGELO.
Not yet ; it is not finished.

PART SECOND

I

MONOLOGUE

A room in MICHAEL ANGELO'S *house.*

MICHAEL ANGELO.
Fled to Viterbo, the old Papal city
Where once an Emperor, humbled in his
pride,
Held the Pope's stirrup, as his Holiness
Alighted from his mule ! A fugitive
From Cardinal Caraffa's hate, who hurls
His thunders at the house of the Colonna,
With endless bitterness ! — Among the nuns
In Santa Caterina's convent hidden,
Herself in soul a nun ! And now she chides
me
For my too frequent letters, that disturb
Her meditations, and that hinder me
And keep me from my work ; now gra-
ciously

She thanks me for the crucifix I sent her,
And says that she will keep it : with one
 hand
Inflicts a wound, and with the other heals it.
 [*Reading.*
"Profoundly I believed that God would
 grant you
A supernatural faith to paint this Christ ;
I wished for that which now I see fulfilled
So marvellously, exceeding all my wishes.
Nor more could be desired, or even so much.
And greatly I rejoice that you have made
The angel on the right so beautiful ;
For the Archangel Michael will place you,
You, Michael Angelo, on that new day,
Upon the Lord's right hand ! And waiting
 that,
How can I better serve you than to pray
To this sweet Christ for you, and to beseech
 you
To hold me altogether yours in all things."

Well, I will write less often, or no more,
But wait her coming. No one born in
 Rome
Can live elsewhere ; but he must pine for
 Rome,
And must return to it. I, who am born
And bred a Tuscan and a Florentine,
Feel the attraction, and I linger here
As if I were a pebble in the pavement
Trodden by priestly feet. This I endure,
Because I breathe in Rome an atmosphere
Heavy with odors of the laurel leaves
That crowned great heroes of the sword
 and pen,
In ages past. I feel myself exalted
To walk the streets in which a Virgil
 walked,
Or Trajan rode in triumph ; but far more,
And most of all, because the great Colonna
Breathes the same air I breathe, and is to
 me
An inspiration. Now that she is gone,
Rome is no longer Rome till she return.
This feeling overmasters me. I know not
If it be love, this strong desire to be
Forever in her presence ; but I know
That I, who was the friend of solitude,
And ever was best pleased when most alone,
Now weary grow of my own company.
For the first time old age seems lonely to
 me.
 [*Opening the Divina Commedia.*
I turn for consolation to the leaves

Of the great master of our Tuscan tongue,
Whose words, like colored garnet-shirls in
 lava,
Betray the heat in which they were en-
 gendered.
A mendicant, he ate the bitter bread
Of others, but repaid their meagre gifts
With immortality. In courts of princes
He was a by-word, and in streets of towns
Was mocked by children, like the Hebrew
 prophet,
Himself a prophet. I too know the cry,
Go up, thou bald head ! from a generation
That, wanting reverence, wanteth the best
 food
The soul can feed on. There's not room
 enough
For age and youth upon this little planet.
Age must give way. There was not room
 enough
Even for this great poet. In his song
I hear reverberate the gates of Florence,
Closing upon him, never more to open ;
But mingled with the sound are melodies
Celestial from the gates of paradise.
He came and he is gone. The people
 knew not
What manner of man was passing by their
 doors,
Until he passed no more ; but in his vision
He saw the torments and beatitudes
Of souls condemned or pardoned, and hath
 left
Behind him this sublime Apocalypse.

I strive in vain to draw here on the margin
The face of Beatrice. It is not hers,
But the Colonna's. Each hath his ideal,
The image of some woman excellent,
That is his guide. No Grecian art, nor
 Roman,
Hath yet revealed such loveliness as hers.

II

VITERBO

VITTORIA COLONNA *at the convent window.*

VITTORIA.

Parting with friends is temporary death,
As all death is. We see no more their
 faces,
Nor hear their voices, save in memory.

But messages of love give us assurance
That we are not forgotten. Who shall say
That from the world of spirits comes no
    greeting,
No message of remembrance? It may be
The thoughts that visit us, we know not
    whence,
Sudden as inspiration, are the whispers
Of disembodied spirits, speaking to us
As friends, who wait outside a prison wall,
Through the barred windows speak to those
    within. [*A pause.*
As quiet as the lake that lies beneath me,
As quiet as the tranquil sky above me,
As quiet as a heart that beats no more,
This convent seems. Above, below, all
    peace!
Silence and solitude, the soul's best friends,
Are with me here, and the tumultuous
    world
Makes no more noise than the remotest
    planet [*A pause.*
O gentle spirit, unto the third circle
Of heaven among the blessed souls as-
    cended,
Who, living in the faith and dying for it,
Have gone to their reward, I do not sigh
For thee as being dead, but for myself
That I am still alive. Turn those dear eyes,
Once so benignant to me, upon mine,
That open to their tears such uncontrolled
And such continual issue. Still awhile
Have patience; I will come to thee at last.
A few more goings in and out these doors,
A few more chimings of these convent
    bells,
A few more prayers, a few more sighs and
    tears,
And the long agony of this life will end,
And I shall be with thee. If I am wanting
To thy well-being, as thou art to mine,
Have patience; I will come to thee at last.
Ye winds that loiter in these cloister
    gardens,
Or wander far above the city walls,
Bear unto him this message, that I ever
Or speak or think of him, or weep for him.

By unseen hands uplifted in the light
Of sunset, yonder solitary cloud
Floats, with its white apparel blown abroad,
And wafted up to heaven. It fades away,
And melts into the air. Ah, would that I
Could thus be wafted unto thee, Francesco,
A cloud of white, an incorporeal spirit!

III

MICHAEL ANGELO AND BENVENUTO
CELLINI

SCENE I. — MICHAEL ANGELO, BENVENUTO
CELLINI *in gay attire.*

BENVENUTO.

A good day and good year to the divine
Maestro Michael Angelo, the sculptor!

MICHAEL ANGELO.

Welcome, my Benvenuto.

BENVENUTO.
                That is what
My father said, the first time he beheld
This handsome face. But say farewell, not
    welcome.
I come to take my leave. I start for
    Florence
As fast as horse can carry me. I long
To set once more upon its level flags
These feet, made sore by your vile Roman
    pavements.
Come with me; you are wanted there in
    Florence.
The Sacristy is not finished.

MICHAEL ANGELO.
                Speak not of it!
How damp and cold it was! How my
    bones ached
And my head reeled, when I was working
    there!
I am too old. I will stay here in Rome,
Where all is old and crumbling, like myself,
To hopeless ruin. All roads lead to Rome.

BENVENUTO.

And all lead out of it.

MICHAEL ANGELO.
                There is a charm,
A certain something in the atmosphere,
That all men feel, and no man can de-
    scribe.

BENVENUTO.
Malaria?

MICHAEL ANGELO.
        Yes, malaria of the mind,
Out of this tomb of the majestic Past;
The fever to accomplish some great work
That will not let us sleep. I must go on
Until I die.

BENVENUTO.

Do you ne'er think of Florence ?

MICHAEL ANGELO.

               Yes ; whenever
I think of anything beside my work,
I think of Florence. I remember, too,
The bitter days I passed among the quarries
Of Seravezza and Pietrasanta ;
Road - building in the marshes ; stupid
    people,
And cold and rain incessant, and mad
    gusts
Of mountain wind, like howling Dervishes,
That spun and whirled the eddying snow
    about them
As if it were a garment ; aye, vexations
And troubles of all kinds, that ended only
In loss of time and money.

BENVENUTO.

              True, Maestro ;
But that was not in Florence. You should
    leave
Such work to others.   Sweeter memories
Cluster about you, in the pleasant city
Upon the Arno.

MICHAEL ANGELO.

           In my waking dreams
I see the marvellous dome of Brunelleschi,
Ghiberti's gates of bronze, and Giotto's
    tower ;
And Ghirlandajo's lovely Benci glides
With folded hands amid my troubled
    thoughts,
A splendid vision ! Time rides with the old
At a great pace.   As travellers on swift
    steeds
See the near landscape fly and flow behind
    them,
While the remoter fields and dim horizons
Go with them, and seem wheeling round to
    meet them,
So in old age things near us slip away,
And distant things go with us.   Pleasantly
Come back to me the days when, as a
    youth,
I walked with Ghirlandajo in the gardens
Of Medici, and saw the antique statues,
The forms august of gods and godlike men,
And the great world of art revealed itself
To my young eyes.   Then all that man
    hath done

Seemed possible to me.   Alas ! how little
Of all I dreamed of has my hand achieved !

BENVENUTO.

Nay, let the Night and Morning, let
    Lorenzo
And Julian in the Sacristy at Florence,
Prophets and Sibyls in the Sistine Chapel,
And the Last Judgment answer.   Is it
    finished ?

MICHAEL ANGELO.

The work is nearly done.   But this Last
    Judgment
Has been the cause of more vexation to me
Than it will be of honor.   Ser Biagio,
Master of ceremonies at the Papal court,
A man punctilious and over nice,
Calls it improper ; says that those nude
    forms,
Showing their nakedness in such shameless
    fashion,
Are better suited to a common bagnio,
Or wayside wine - shop, than a Papal
    Chapel.
To punish him I painted him as Minos
And leave him there as master of cere-
    monies
In the Infernal Regions.   What would you
Have done to such a man ?

BENVENUTO.

          I would have killed him.
When any one insults me, if I can
I kill him, kill him.

MICHAEL ANGELO.

           Oh, you gentlemen,
Who dress in silks and velvets, and wear
    swords,
Are ready with your weapons, and have all
A taste for homicide.

BENVENUTO.

          I learned that lesson
Under Pope Clement at the siege of Rome,
Some twenty years ago.   As I was standing
Upon the ramparts of the Campo Santo
With Alessandro Bene, I beheld
A sea of fog, that covered all the plain,
And hid from us the foe ; when suddenly,
A misty figure, like an apparition,
Rose up above the fog, as if on horseback.
At this I aimed my arquebus, and fired.
The figure vanished ; and there rose a cry

Out of the darkness, long and fierce and
    loud.
With imprecations in all languages.
It was the Constable of France, the Bourbon,
That I had slain.

MICHAEL ANGELO.
    Rome should be grateful to you.

BENVENUTO.
But has not been ; you shall hear pres-
    ently.
During the siege I served as bombardier,
There in St. Angelo.   His Holiness
One day was walking with his Cardinals
On the round bastion, while I stood above
Among my falconets.   All thought and
    feeling,
All skill in art and all desire of fame,
Were swallowed up in the delightful music
Of that artillery.   I saw far off,
Within the enemy's trenches on the Prati,
A Spanish cavalier in scarlet cloak ;
And firing at him with due aim and range,
I cut the gay Hidalgo in two pieces.
The eyes are dry that wept for him in
    Spain.
His Holiness, delighted beyond measure
With such display of gunnery, and amazed
To see the man in scarlet cut in two,
Gave me his benediction, and absolved me
From all the homicides I had committed
In service of the Apostolic Church,
Or should commit thereafter.   From that
    day
I have not held in very high esteem
The life of man.

MICHAEL ANGELO.
    And who absolved Pope Clement ?
Now let us speak of Art.

BENVENUTO.
    Of what you will.

MICHAEL ANGELO.
Say, have you seen our friend Fra Bastian
    lately,
Since by a turn of fortune he became
Friar of the Signet ?

BENVENUTO.
    Faith, a pretty artist
To pass his days in stamping leaden seals
On Papal bulls !

MICHAEL ANGELO.
    He has grown fat and lazy,
As if the lead clung to him like a sinker.
He paints no more since he was sent to
    Fondi
By Cardinal Ippolito to paint
The fair Gonzaga.   Ah, you should have
    seen him
As I did, riding through the city gate,
In his brown hood, attended by four horse-
    men,
Completely armed, to frighten the banditti.
I think he would have frightened them
    alone,
For he was rounder than the O of Giotto.

BENVENUTO.
He must have looked more like a sack of
    meal
Than a great painter.

MICHAEL ANGELO.
    Well, he is not great,
But still I like him greatly.   Benvenuto,
Have faith in nothing but in industry.
Be at it late and early ; persevere,
And work right on through censure and
    applause,
Or else abandon Art.

BENVENUTO.
    No man works harder
Than I do.   I am not a moment idle.

MICHAEL ANGELO.
And what have you to show me ?

BENVENUTO.
    This gold ring,
Made for his Holiness, — my latest work,
And I am proud of it.   A single diamond,
Presented by the Emperor to the Pope.
Targhetta of Venice set and tinted it ;
I have reset it, and retinted it
Divinely, as you see.   The jewellers
Say I 've surpassed Targhetta.

MICHAEL ANGELO.
    Let me see it.
A pretty jewel.

BENVENUTO.
    That is not the expression.
Pretty is not a very pretty word
To be applied to such a precious stone,

Given by an Emperor to a Pope, and set
By Benvenuto!

MICHAEL ANGELO.
Messer Benvenuto,
I lose all patience with you ; for the gifts
That God hath given you are of such a kind,
They should be put to far more noble uses
Than setting diamonds for the Pope of
    Rome.
You can do greater things.

BENVENUTO.
The God who made me
Knows why he made me what I am, — a
    goldsmith,
A mere artificer.

MICHAEL ANGELO.
Oh no ; an artist,
Richly endowed by nature, but who wraps
His talent in a napkin, and consumes
His life in vanities.

BENVENUTO.
Michael Angelo
May say what Benvenuto would not bear
From any other man. He speaks the truth.
I know my life is wasted and consumed
In vanities ; but I have better hours
And higher aspirations than you think.
Once, when a prisoner at St. Angelo,
Fasting and praying in the midnight dark-
    ness,
In a celestial vision I beheld
A crucifix in the sun, of the same sub-
    stance
As is the sun itself. And since that hour
There is a splendor round about my head,
That may be seen at sunrise and at sunset
Above my shadow on the grass. And now
I know that I am in the grace of God,
And none henceforth can harm me.

MICHAEL ANGELO.
None but one, —
None but yourself, who are your greatest
    foe.
He that respects himself is safe from
    others ;
He wears a coat of mail that none can
    pierce.

BENVENUTO.
I always wear one.

MICHAEL ANGELO.
O incorrigible !
At least, forget not the celestial vision.
Man must have something higher than
    himself
To think of.

BENVENUTO.
That I know full well. Now listen.
I have been sent for into France, where
    grow
The Lilies that illumine heaven and earth,
And carry in mine equipage the model
Of a most marvellous golden salt-cellar
For the king's table ; and here in my brain
A statue of Mars Armipotent for the foun-
    tain
Of Fontainebleau, colossal, wonderful.
I go a goldsmith, to return a sculptor.
And so farewell, great Master. Think of
    me
As one who, in the midst of all his follies,
Had also his ambition, and aspired
To better things.

MICHAEL ANGELO.
Do not forget the vision.

SCENE II. — MICHAEL ANGELO sitting down
    again to the Divina Commedia.

MICHAEL ANGELO.
Now in what circle of his poem sacred
Would the great Florentine have placed
    this man ?
Whether in Phlegethon, the river of blood,
Or in the fiery belt of Purgatory,
I know not, but most surely not with those
Who walk in leaden cloaks. Though he is
    one
Whose passions, like a potent alkahest,
Dissolve his better nature, he is not
That despicable thing, a hypocrite ·
He doth not cloak his vices, nor deny them.
Come back, my thoughts, from him to Par-
    adise.

IV

FRA SEBASTIANO DEL PIOMBO

SCENE I. — MICHAEL ANGELO ; FRA SEBAS-
    TIANO DEL PIOMBO.

MICHAEL ANGELO, not turning round.
Who is it ?

FRA SEBASTIANO.
                    Wait, for I am out of breath
In climbing your steep stairs.

MICHAEL ANGELO.
                    Ah my Bastiano,
If you went up and down as many stairs
As I do still, and climbed as many ladders,
It would be better for you. Pray sit down.
Your idle and luxurious way of living
Will one day take your breath away en-
    tirely,
And you will never find it.

FRA SEBASTIANO.
                    Well, what then?
That would be better, in my apprehension,
Than falling from a scaffold.

MICHAEL ANGELO.
                    That was nothing.
It did not kill me ; only lamed me slightly ;
I am quite well again.

FRA SEBASTIANO.
                    But why, dear Master,
Why do you live so high up in your house,
When you could live below and have a gar-
    den,
As I do?

MICHAEL ANGELO.
                    From this window I can look
On many gardens ; o'er the city roofs
See the Campagna and the Alban hills :
And all are mine.

FRA SEBASTIANO.
                    Can you sit down in them,
On summer afternoons, and play the lute,
Or sing, or sleep the time away?

MICHAEL ANGELO.
                    I never
Sleep in the day-time ; scarcely sleep at
    night ;
I have not time. Did you meet Benvenuto
As you came up the stair?

FRA SEBASTIANO.
                    He ran against me
On the first landing, going at full speed ;
Dressed like the Spanish captain in a play,
With his long rapier and his short red
    cloak.

Why hurry through the world at such a
    pace ?
Life will not be too long.

MICHAEL ANGELO.
                    It is his nature, —
A restless spirit, that consumes itself
With useless agitations. He o'erleaps
The goal he aims at. Patience is a plant
That grows not in all gardens. You are
    made
Of quite another clay.

FRA SEBASTIANO.
                    And thank God for it.
And now, being somewhat rested, I will
    tell you
Why I have climbed these formidable
    stairs.
I have a friend, Francesco Berni, here,
A very charming poet and companion,
Who greatly honors you and all your doings,
And you must sup with us.

MICHAEL ANGELO.
                    Not I, indeed.
I know too well what artists' suppers are.
You must excuse me.

FRA SEBASTIANO.
                    I will not excuse you.
You need repose from your incessant work ;
Some recreation, some bright hours of plea-
    sure.

MICHAEL ANGELO.
To me, what you and other men call plea-
    sure.
Is only pain. Work is my recreation,
The play of faculty ; a delight like that
Which a bird feels in flying, or a fish
In darting through the water, — nothing
    more.
I cannot go. The Sibylline leaves of life
Grow precious now, when only few remain.
I cannot go.

FRA SEBASTIANO.
                    Berni, perhaps, will read
A canto of the Orlando Innamorato.

MICHAEL ANGELO.
That is another reason for not going.
If aught is tedious and intolerable,
It is a poet reading his own verses.

FRA SEBASTIANO.

Berni thinks somewhat better of your verses
Than you of his. He says that you speak
      things,
And other poets words. So, pray you, come.

MICHAEL ANGELO.

If it were now the Improvisatore,
Luigi Pulci, whom I used to hear
With Benvenuto, in the streets of Florence,
I might be tempted. I was younger then,
And singing in the open air was pleasant.

FRA SEBASTIANO.

There is a Frenchman here, named Rabe-
      lais,
Once a Franciscan friar, and now a doctor,
And secretary to the embassy :
A learned man, who speaks all languages,
And wittiest of men ; who wrote a book
Of the Adventures of Gargantua,
So full of strange conceits one roars with
      laughter
At every page ; a jovial boon-companion
And lover of much wine. He too is coming.

MICHAEL ANGELO.

Then you will not want me, who am not
      witty,
And have no sense of mirth, and love not
      wine.
I should be like a dead man at your
      banquet.
Why should I seek this Frenchman, Rabe-
      lais ?
And wherefore go to hear Francesco Berni,
When I have Dante Alighieri here,
The greatest of all poets ?

FRA SEBASTIANO.

                       And the dullest ;
And only to be read in episodes.
His day is past. Petrarca is our poet.

MICHAEL ANGELO.

Petrarca is for women and for lovers,
And for those soft Abati, who delight
To wander down long garden walks in
      summer,
Tinkling their little sonnets all day long,
As lap-dogs do their bells.

FRA SEBASTIANO.

                     I love Petrarca.
How sweetly of his absent love he sings,

When journeying in the forest of Ar-
      dennes !
"I seem to hear her, hearing the boughs
      and breezes
And leaves and birds lamenting, and the
      waters
Murmuring flee along the verdant herb-
      age."

MICHAEL ANGELO.

Enough. It is all seeming, and no being.
If you would know how a man speaks in
      earnest,
Read here this passage, where St. Peter
      thunders
In Paradise against degenerate Popes
And the corruptions of the church, till all
The heaven about him blushes like a sunset.
I beg you to take note of what he says
About the Papal seals, for that concerns
Your office and yourself.

FRA SEBASTIANO, reading.

                       Is this the passage ?
" Nor I be made the figure of a seal
To privileges venal and mendacious ;
Whereat I often redden and flash with
      fire ! " —
That is not poetry.

MICHAEL ANGELO.

            What is it, then ?

FRA SEBASTIANO.

Vituperation ; gall that might have spirted
From Aretino's pen.

MICHAEL ANGELO.

            Name not that man !
A profligate, whom your Francesco Berni
Describes as having one foot in the brothel
And the other in the hospital ; who lives
By flattering or maligning, as best serves
His purpose at the time. He writes to
      me
With easy arrogance of my Last Judgment,
In such familiar tone that one would say
The great event already had transpired,
And he was present, and from observation
Informed me how the picture should be
      painted.

FRA SEBASTIANO.

What unassuming, unobtrusive men
These critics are ! Now, to have Aretino

Aiming his shafts at you brings back to
  mind
The Gascon archers in the square of Milan,
Shooting their arrows at Duke Sforza's
  statue,
By Leonardo, and the foolish rabble
Of envious Florentines, that at your David
Threw stones at night. But Aretino
  praised you.

MICHAEL ANGELO.

His praises were ironical. He knows
How to use words as weapons, and to wound
While seeming to defend. But look, Bas-
  tiano,
See how the setting sun lights up that pic-
  ture!

FRA SEBASTIANO.

My portrait of Vittoria Colonna.

MICHAEL ANGELO.

It makes her look as she will look here-
  after,
When she becomes a saint!

FRA SEBASTIANO.

          A noble woman!

MICHAEL ANGELO.

Ah, these old hands can fashion fairer
  shapes
In marble, and can paint diviner pictures,
Since I have known her.

FRA SEBASTIANO.

       And you like this picture;
And yet it is in oils, which you detest.

MICHAEL ANGELO.

When that barbarian Jan Van Eyck dis-
  covered
The use of oil in painting, he degraded
His art into a handicraft, and made it
Sign-painting, merely, for a country inn
Or wayside wine-shop. 'T is an art for
  women,
Or for such leisurely and idle people
As you are, Fra Bastiano. Nature paints
  not
In oils, but frescoes the great dome of
  heaven
With sunsets, and the lovely forms of
  clouds
And flying vapors.

FRA SEBASTIANO.

       And how soon they fade!
Behold yon line of roofs and belfries
  painted
Upon the golden background of the sky,
Like a Byzantine picture, or a portrait
Of Cimabue. See how hard the outline,
Sharp-cut and clear, not rounded into
  shadow.
Yet that is nature.

MICHAEL ANGELO.

        She is always right.
The picture that approaches sculpture
  nearest
Is the best picture.

FRA SEBASTIANO.

        Leonardo thinks
The open air too bright. We ought to
  paint
As if the sun were shining through a mist.
'T is easier done in oil than in distemper.

MICHAEL ANGELO.

Do not revive again the old dispute;
I have an excellent memory for forgetting,
But I still feel the hurt. Wounds are not
  healed
By the unbending of the bow that made
  them.

FRA SEBASTIANO.

So say Petrarca and the ancient proverb.

MICHAEL ANGELO.

But that is past. Now I am angry with
  you,
Not that you paint in oils, but that, grown
  fat
And indolent, you do not paint at all.

FRA SEBASTIANO.

Why should I paint? Why should I toil
  and sweat,
Who now am rich enough to live at ease,
And take my pleasure?

MICHAEL ANGELO.

       When Pope Leo died,
He who had been so lavish of the wealth
His predecessors left him, who received
A basket of gold-pieces every morning,
Which every night was empty, left behind
Hardly enough to pay his funeral.

FRA SEBASTIANO.

I care for banquets, not for funerals,
As did his Holiness.   I have forbidden
All tapers at my burial, and procession
Of priests and friars and monks ; and have
    provided
The cost thereof be given to the poor !

MICHAEL ANGELO.

You have done wisely, but of that I speak
    not.
Ghiberti left behind him wealth and chil-
    dren ;
But who to-day would know that he had
    lived,
If he had never made those gates of bronze
In the old Baptistery, — those gates of
    bronze,
Worthy to be the gates of Paradise.
His wealth is scattered to the winds ; his
    children
Are long since dead ; but those celestial
    gates
Survive, and keep his name and memory
    green.

FRA SEBASTIANO.

But why should I fatigue myself ? I think
That all things it is possible to paint
Have been already painted ; and if not,
Why, there are painters in the world at
    present
Who can accomplish more in two short
    months
Than I could in two years ; so it is well
That some one is contented to do nothing,
And leave the field to others.

MICHAEL ANGELO.

                   O blasphemer !
Not without reason do the people call you
Sebastian del Piombo, for the lead
Of all the Papal bulls is heavy upon you,
And wraps you like a shroud.

FRA SEBASTIANO.

                   Misericordia !
Sharp is the vinegar of sweet wine, and
    sharp
The words you speak, because the heart
    within you
Is sweet unto the core.

MICHAEL ANGELO.

                   How changed you are
From the Sebastiano I once knew,

When poor, laborious, emulous to excel,
You strove in rivalry with Baldassare
And Raphael Sanzio.

FRA SEBASTIANO.

                   Raphael is dead ;
He is but dust and ashes in his grave,
While I am living and enjoying life,
And so am victor.   One live Pope is worth
A dozen dead ones.

MICHAEL ANGELO.

                   Raphael is not dead ;
He doth but sleep ; for how can he be dead
Who lives immortal in the hearts of men ?
He only drank the precious wine of youth,
The outbreak of the grapes, before the
    vintage
Was trodden to bitterness by the feet of
    men.
The gods have given him sleep.   We never
    were
Nor could be foes, although our followers,
Who are distorted shadows of ourselves,
Have striven to make us so ; but each one
    worked
Unconsciously upon the other's thought,
Both giving and receiving.   He perchance
Caught strength from me, and I some
    greater sweetness
And tenderness from his more gentle
    nature.
I have but words of praise and admiration
For his great genius ; and the world is
    fairer
That he lived in it.

FRA SEBASTIANO.

                   We at least are friends ;
So come with me.

MICHAEL ANGELO.

                   No, no ; I am best pleased
When I 'm not asked to banquets.   I have
    reached
A time of life when daily walks are
    shortened,
And even the houses of our dearest friends,
That used to be so near, seem far away.

FRA SEBASTIANO.

Then we must sup without you.   We shall
    laugh
At those who toil for fame, and make their
    lives

A tedious martyrdom, that they may live
A little longer in the mouths of men !
And so, good-night.

MICHAEL ANGELO.
Good-night, my Fra Bastiano.

SCENE II. — MICHAEL ANGELO, *returning to his work.*

MICHAEL ANGELO.
How will men speak of me when I am
    gone,
When all this colorless, sad life is ended,
And I am dust ? They will remember
    only
The wrinkled forehead, the marred coun-
    tenance,
The rudeness of my speech, and my rough
    manners,
And never dream that underneath them all
There was a woman's heart of tenderness ;
They will not know the secret of my life,
Locked up in silence, or but vaguely hinted
In uncouth rhymes, that may perchance
    survive
Some little space in memories of men !
Each one performs his life-work, and then
    leaves it ;
Those that come after him will estimate
His influence on the age in which he lived.

V

PALAZZO BELVEDERE

TITIAN's *studio. A painting of Danaë with
a curtain before it.* TITIAN, MICHAEL AN-
GELO, *and* GIORGIO VASARI.

MICHAEL ANGELO.
So you have left at last your still lagoons,
Your City of Silence floating in the sea,
And come to us in Rome.

TITIAN.
                        I come to learn,
But I have come too late. I should have
    seen
Rome in my youth, when all my mind was
    open
To new impressions. Our Vasari here
Leads me about, a blind man, groping
    darkly

Among the marvels of the past. I touch
    them,
But do not see them.

MICHAEL ANGELO.
                    There are things in Rome
That one might walk barefooted here from
    Venice
But to see once, and then to die content.

TITIAN.
I must confess that these majestic ruins
Oppress me with their gloom. I feel as
    one
Who in the twilight stumbles among tombs,
And cannot read the inscriptions carved
    upon them.

MICHAEL ANGELO.
I felt so once ; but I have grown familiar
With desolation, and it has become
No more a pain to me, but a delight.

TITIAN.
I could not live here. I must have the sea,
And the sea-mist, with sunshine interwoven
Like cloth of gold ; must have beneath my
    windows
The laughter of the waves, and at my door
Their pattering footsteps, or I am not
    happy.

MICHAEL ANGELO.
Then tell me of your city in the sea,
Paved with red basalt of the Paduan hills.
Tell me of art in Venice. Three great
    names,
Giorgione, Titian, and the Tintoretto,
Illustrate your Venetian school, and send
A challenge to the world. The first is
    dead,
But Tintoretto lives.

TITIAN.
                    And paints with fire,
Sudden and splendid, as the lightning
    paints
The cloudy vault of heaven.

GIORGIO.
                        Does he still keep
Above his door the arrogant inscription
That once was painted there, — " The color
    of Titian,
With the design of Michael Angelo " ?

TITIAN.

Indeed, I know not. 'T was a foolish boast,
And does no harm to any but himself.
Perhaps he has grown wiser.

MICHAEL ANGELO.

              When you two
Are gone, who is there that remains behind
To seize the pencil falling from your fin-
     gers ?

GIORGIO.

Oh, there are many hands upraised already
To clutch at such a prize, and hardly wait
For death to loose your grasp, — a hun-
     dred of them :
Schiavone, Bonifazio, Campagnola,
Moretto, and Moroni ; who can count them,
Or measure their ambition ?

TITIAN.

           When we are gone,
The generation that comes after us
Will have far other thoughts than ours.
Our ruins
Will serve to build their palaces or tombs.
They will possess the world that we think
     ours,
And fashion it far otherwise.

MICHAEL ANGELO.

            I hear
Your son Orazio and your nephew Marco
Mentioned with honor.

TITIAN.

         Ay, brave lads, brave lads.
But time will show. There is a youth in
     Venice,
One Paul Cagliari, called the Veronese,
Still a mere stripling, but of such rare
     promise
That we must guard our laurels, or may
     lose them.

MICHAEL ANGELO.

These are good tidings ; for I sometimes
     fear
That, when we die, with us all art will die.
'T is but a fancy. Nature will provide
Others to take our places. I rejoice
To see the young spring forward in the race,
Eager as we were, and as full of hope
And the sublime audacity of youth.

TITIAN.

Men die and are forgotten. The great
     world
Goes on the same. Among the myriads
Of men that live, or have lived, or shall
     live,
What is a single life, or thine or mine,
That we should think all nature would
     stand still
If we were gone ? We must make room
     for others.

MICHAEL ANGELO.

And now, Maestro, pray unveil your picture
Of Danaë, of which I hear such praise.

TITIAN, *drawing back the curtain.*

What think you ?

MICHAEL ANGELO.

            That Acrisius did well
To lock such beauty in a brazen tower,
And hide it from all eyes.

TITIAN.

           The model truly
Was beautiful.

MICHAEL ANGELO.

        And more, that you were present,
And saw the showery Jove from high Olym-
     pus
Descend in all his splendor.

TITIAN.

           From your lips
Such words are full of sweetness.

MICHAEL ANGELO.

            You have caught
These golden hues from your Venetian sun-
     sets.

TITIAN.

Possibly.

MICHAEL ANGELO.

        Or from sunshine through a shower
On the lagoons, or the broad Adriatic.
Nature reveals herself in all our arts.
The pavements and the palaces of cities
Hint at the nature of the neighboring hills.
Red lavas from the Euganean quarries
Of Padua pave your streets ; your palaces
Are the white stones of Istria, and gleam
Reflected in your waters and your pictures.
And thus the works of every artist show

Something of his surroundings and his habits.
The uttermost that can be reached by color
Is here accomplished. Warmth and light and softness
Mingle together. Never yet was flesh
Painted by hand of artist, dead or living,
With such divine perfection.

TITIAN.
                    I am grateful
For so much praise from you, who are a master ;
While mostly those who praise and those who blame
Know nothing of the matter, so that mainly
Their censure sounds like praise, their praise like censure.

MICHAEL ANGELO.
Wonderful ! wonderful !   The charm of color
Fascinates me the more that in myself
The gift is wanting.   I am not a painter.

GIORGIO.
Messer Michele, all the arts are yours,
Not one alone ; and therefore I may venture
To put a question to you.

MICHAEL ANGELO.
                    Well, speak on.
GIORGIO.
Two nephews of the Cardinal Farnese
Have made me umpire in dispute between them
Which is the greater of the sister arts,
Painting or sculpture. Solve for me the doubt.

MICHAEL ANGELO.
Sculpture and painting have a common goal,
And whosoever would attain to it,
Whichever path he take, will find that goal
Equally hard to reach.

GIORGIO.
                    No doubt, no doubt ;
But you evade the question.

MICHAEL ANGELO.
                    When I stand
In presence of this picture, I concede

That painting has attained its uttermost ;
But in the presence of my sculptured figures
I feel that my conception soars beyond
All limit I have reached.

GIORGIO.
                    You still evade me.

MICHAEL ANGELO.
Giorgio Vasari, I have often said
That I account that painting as the best
Which most resembles sculpture.   Here before us
We have the proof. Behold these rounded limbs !
How from the canvas they detach themselves,
Till they deceive the eye, and one would say,
It is a statue with a screen behind it !

TITIAN.
Signori, pardon me ; but all such questions
Seem to me idle.

MICHAEL ANGELO.
                    Idle as the wind.
And now, Maestro, I will say once more
How admirable I esteem your work,
And leave you, without further interruption.

TITIAN.
Your friendly visit hath much honored me.

GIORGIO.
Farewell.

MICHAEL ANGELO *to* GIORGIO, *going out.*
                    If the Venetian painters knew
But half as much of drawing as of color,
They would indeed work miracles in art,
And the world see what it hath never seen.

VI

PALAZZO CESARINI

SCENE I. — VITTORIA COLONNA, *seated in an arm-chair;* JULIA GONZAGA, *standing near her.*

JULIA.
It grieves me that I find you still so weak
And suffering.

VITTORIA.

No, not suffering ; only dying.
Death is the chillness that precedes the
    dawn ;
We shudder for a moment, then awake
In the broad sunshine of the other life.
I am a shadow, merely, and these hands,
These cheeks, these eyes, these tresses that
    my husband
Once thought so beautiful, and I was proud
    of
Because he thought them so, are faded
    quite, —
All beauty gone from them.

JULIA.

Ah, no, not that.
Paler you are, but not less beautiful.

VITTORIA, *folding her hands.*

O gentle spirit, unto the third circle
Of heaven among the blessed souls as-
    cended,
Who living for the faith and dying for it,
Have gone to their reward, I do not mourn
For thee as being dead, but for myself
That I am still alive.   A little longer
Have patience with me, and if I am want-
    ing
To thy well-being as thou art to mine,
Have patience ; I will come to thee ere
    long.

JULIA.

Do not give way to these foreboding
    thoughts.

VITTORIA.

Hand me the mirror.   I would fain behold
What change comes o'er our features when
    we die.
Thank you.   And now sit down beside me
    here.
How glad I am that you have come to-day,
Above all other days, and at the hour
When most I need you.

JULIA.

Do you ever need me ?

VITTORIA.

Always, and most of all to-day and now.
Do you remember, Julia, when we walked,
One afternoon, upon the castle terrace
At Ischia, on the day before you left me ?

JULIA.

Well I remember ; but it seems to me
Something unreal that has never been,
Something that I have read of in a book,
Or heard of some one else.

VITTORIA.

Ten years and more
Have passed since then ; and many things
    have happened
In those ten years, and many friends have
    died :
Marco Flaminio, whom we all admired
And loved as our Catullus ; dear Valdesso,
The noble champion of free thought and
    speech ;
And Cardinal Ippolito, your friend.

JULIA.

Oh, do not speak of him ! His sudden
    death
O'ercomes me now, as it o'ercame me then.
Let me forget it ; for my memory
Serves me too often as an unkind friend,
And I remember things I would forget,
While I forget the things I would re-
    member.

VITTORIA.

Forgive me ; I will speak of him no more.
The good Fra Bernardino has departed,
Has fled from Italy, and crossed the Alps,
Fearing Caraffa's wrath, because he taught
That He who made us all without our help
Could also save us without aid of ours.
Renée of France, the Duchess of Ferrara,
That Lily of the Loire, is bowed by winds
That blow from Rome ; Olympia Morata
Banished from court because of this new
    doctrine.
Therefore be cautious.   Keep your secret
    thought
Locked in your breast.

JULIA.

I will be very prudent.
But speak no more, I pray ; it wearies
    you.

VITTORIA.

Yes, I am very weary   Read to me.

JULIA.

Most willingly.   What shall I read ?

VITTORIA.
                    Petrarca's
Triumph of Death. The book lies on the
      table,
Beside the casket there. Read where you
      find
The leaf turned down. 'T was there I left
      off reading.

JULIA reads.
" Not as a flame that by some force is
      spent,
   But one that of itself consumeth quite,
   Departed hence in peace the soul con-
      tent,
In fashion of a soft and lucent light
   Whose nutriment by slow gradation
      goes,
   Keeping until the end its lustre bright.
Not pale, but whiter than the sheet of
      snows
   That without wind on some fair hill-top
      lies,
   Her weary body seemed to find re-
      pose.
Like a sweet slumber in her lovely eyes,
   When now the spirit was no longer
      there,
   Was what is dying called by the un-
      wise.
E'en Death itself in her fair face seemed
      fair."

Is it of Laura that he here is speaking ? —
She doth not answer, yet is not asleep ;
Her eyes are full of light and fixed on
      something
Above her in the air. I can see naught
Except the painted angels on the ceiling.
Vittoria ! speak ! What is it ? Answer
      me ! —
She only smiles, and stretches out her
      hands.
                    [The mirror falls and breaks.

VITTORIA.
Call my confessor ! —
Not disobedient to the heavenly vision !
Pescara ! my Pescara !   [Dies.

JULIA.
                    Holy Virgin !
Her body sinks together, — she is dead !
      [Kneels, and hides her face in Vittoria's lap.

SCENE II. — JULIA GONZAGA, MICHAEL AN-
      GELO.

JULIA.
Hush ! make no noise.

MICHAEL ANGELO.
                    How is she ?

JULIA.
                    Never better.

MICHAEL ANGELO.
Then she is dead !

JULIA.
                    Alas ! yes, she is dead !
Even death itself in her fair face seems
      fair.

MICHAEL ANGELO.
How wonderful ! The light upon her face
Shines from the windows of another world.
Saints only have such faces. Holy Angels !
Bear her like sainted Catherine to her
      rest !   [Kisses Vittoria's hand.

PART THIRD

I

MONOLOGUE

Macello de' Corvi. A room in MICHAEL AN-
      GELO'S *house.*

MICHAEL ANGELO, *standing before a model of
      St. Peter's.*

MICHAEL ANGELO.
Better than thou I cannot, Brunelleschi,
And less than thou I will not ! If the
      thought
Could, like a windlass, lift the ponderous
      stones
And swing them to their places ; if a
      breath
Could blow this rounded dome into the
      air,
As if it were a bubble, and these statues
Spring at a signal to their sacred stations,
As sentinels mount guard upon a wall,
Then were my task completed. Now,
      alas !
Naught am I but a Saint Sebaldus, holding
Upon his hand the model of a church,

As German artists paint him ; and what
    years,
What weary years, must drag themselves
    along,
Ere this be turned to stone ! What hin-
    drances
Must block the way ; what idle inter-
    ferences
Of Cardinals and Canons of St. Peter's,
Who nothing know of art beyond the color
Of cloaks and stockings, nor of any build-
    ing
Save that of their own fortunes ! And what
    then ?
I must then the short-coming of my
    means
Piece out by stepping forward, as the Spar-
    tan
Was told to add a step to his short sword.
                                    [A pause.
And is Fra Bastian dead ? Is all that light
Gone out ? that sunshine darkened ? all
    that music
And merriment, that used to make our
    lives
Less melancholy, swallowed up in silence
Like madrigals sung in the street at night
By passing revellers ? It is strange in-
    deed
That he should die before me. 'T is against
The laws of nature that the young should
    die,
And the old live ; unless it be that some
Have long been dead who think themselves
    alive,
Because not buried. Well, what matters
    it,
Since now that greater light, that was my
    sun,
Is set, and all is darkness, all is darkness !
Death's lightnings strike to right and left
    of me,
And, like a ruined wall, the world around
    me
Crumbles away, and I am left alone.
I have no friends, and want none. My
    own thoughts
Are now my sole companions, — thoughts
    of her,
That like a benediction from the skies
Come to me in my solitude and soothe me.
When men are old, the incessant thought
    of Death
Follows them like their shadow ; sits with
    them

At every meal ; sleeps with them when
    they sleep ;
And when they wake already is awake,
And standing by their bedside. Then, what
    folly
It is in us to make an enemy
Of this importunate follower, not a friend !
To me a friend, and not an enemy,
Has he become since all my friends are
    dead.

II

VIGNA DI PAPA GIULIO

SCENE I. — POPE JULIUS III. *seated by the
    Fountain of Acqua Vergine, surrounded by
    Cardinals.*

JULIUS.

Tell me, why is it ye are discontent,
You, Cardinals Salviati and Marcello,
With Michael Angelo ? What has he
    done,
Or left undone, that ye are set against
    him ?
When one Pope dies, another is soon made ;
And I can make a dozen Cardinals,
But cannot make one Michael Angelo.

CARDINAL SALVIATI.

Your Holiness, we are not set against him ;
We but deplore his incapacity.
He is too old.

JULIUS.

            You, Cardinal Salviati,
Are an old man. Are you incapable ?
'T is the old ox that draws the straightest
    furrow.

CARDINAL MARCELLO.

Your Holiness remembers he was charged
With the repairs upon St. Mary's bridge ;
Made cofferdams, and heaped up load on
    load
Of timber and travertine ; and yet for
    years
The bridge remained unfinished, till we
    gave it
To Baccio Bigio.

JULIUS.

            Always Baccio Bigio !
Is there no other architect on earth ?

Was it not he that sometime had in charge
The harbor of Ancona ?

CARDINAL MARCELLO.

Ay, the same.

JULIUS.

Then let me tell you that your Baccio
   Bigio
Did greater damage in a single day
To that fair harbor than the sea had done
Or would do in ten years. And him you
   think
To put in place of Michael Angelo,
In building the Basilica of St. Peter !
The ass that thinks himself a stag discovers
His error when he comes to leap the ditch.

CARDINAL MARCELLO.

He does not build ; he but demolishes
The labors of Bramante and San Gallo.

JULIUS.

Only to build more grandly.

CARDINAL MARCELLO.

But time passes ;
Year after year goes by, and yet the work
Is not completed. Michael Angelo
Is a great sculptor, but no architect.
His plans are faulty.

JULIUS.

I have seen his model,
And have approved it. But here comes
   the artist.
Beware of him. He may make Persians
   of you,
To carry burdens on your backs forever.

SCENE II. — *The same:* MICHAEL ANGELO.

JULIUS.

Come forward, dear Maestro. In these
   gardens
All ceremonies of our court are banished.
Sit down beside me here.

MICHAEL ANGELO, *sitting down.*

How graciously
Your Holiness commiserates old age
And its infirmities !

JULIUS.

Say its privileges.
Art I respect. The building of this palace

And laying out of these pleasant garden
   walks
Are my delight, and if I have not asked
Your aid in this, it is that I forbear
To lay new burdens on you at an age
When you need rest. Here I escape
   from Rome
To be at peace. The tumult of the city
Scarce reaches here.

MICHAEL ANGELO.

How beautiful it is,
And quiet almost as a hermitage !

JULIUS.

We live as hermits here ; and from these
   heights
O'erlook all Rome and see the yellow Tiber
Cleaving in twain the city, like a sword,
As far below there as St. Mary's bridge.
What think you of that bridge ?

MICHAEL ANGELO.

I would advise
Your Holiness not to cross it, or not often ;
It is not safe.

JULIUS.

It was repaired of late.

MICHAEL ANGELO.

Some morning you will look for it in vain ;
It will be gone. The current of the river
Is undermining it.

JULIUS.

But you repaired it.

MICHAEL ANGELO.

I strengthened all its piers, and paved its
   road
With travertine. He who came after me
Removed the stone and sold it, and filled in
The space with gravel.

JULIUS.

Cardinal Salviati
And Cardinal Marcello, do you listen ?
This is your famous Nanni Baccio Bigio.

MICHAEL ANGELO, *aside.*

There is some mystery here. These Car-
   dinals
Stand lowering at me with unfriendly eyes.

JULIUS.

Now let us come to what concerns us more
Than bridge or gardens.　Some complaints
are made
Concerning the Three Chapels in St. Pe-
ter's ;
Certain supposed defects or imperfections,
You doubtless can explain.

MICHAEL ANGELO.

This is no longer
The golden age of art.　Men have become
Iconoclasts and critics.　They delight not
In what an artist does, but set themselves
To censure what they do not comprehend.
You will not see them bearing a Madonna
Of Cimabue to the church in triumph,
But tearing down the statue of a Pope
To cast it into cannon.　Who are they
That bring complaints against me ?

JULIUS.

Deputies
Of the Commissioners ; and they complain
Of insufficient light in the Three Chapels.

MICHAEL ANGELO.

Your Holiness, the insufficient light
Is somewhere else, and not in the Three
Chapels.
Who are the deputies that make com-
plaint ?

JULIUS.

The Cardinals Salviati and Marcello,
Here present.

MICHAEL ANGELO, rising.

With permission, Monsignori,
What is it ye complain of ?

CARDINAL MARCELLO.

We regret
You have departed from Bramante's plan,
And from San Gallo's.

MICHAEL ANGELO.

Since the ancient time
No greater architect has lived on earth
Than Lazzari Bramante.　His design,
Without confusion, simple, clear, well-
lighted,
Merits all praise, and to depart from it
Would be departing from the truth.　San
Gallo,

Building about with columns, took all light
Out of this plan ; left in the choir dark
corners
For infinite ribaldries, and lurking places
For rogues and robbers ; so that when the
church
Was shut at night, not five and twenty
men
Could find them out.　It was San Gallo,
then,
That left the church in darkness, and not I.

CARDINAL MARCELLO.

Excuse me ; but in each of the Three
Chapels
Is but a single window.

MICHAEL ANGELO.

Monsignore,
Perhaps you do not know that in the vault-
ing
Above there are to go three other windows.

CARDINAL SALVIATI.

How should we know ?　You never told
us of it.

MICHAEL ANGELO.

I neither am obliged, nor will I be,
To tell your Eminence or any other
What I intend or ought to do.　Your office
Is to provide the means, and see that
thieves
Do not lay hands upon them.　The designs
Must all be left to me.

CARDINAL MARCELLO.

Sir architect,
You do forget yourself, to speak thus
rudely
In presence of his Holiness, and to us
Who are his Cardinals.

MICHAEL ANGELO, putting on his hat.

I do not forget
I am descended from the Counts Canossa,
Linked with the Imperial line, and with
Matilda,
Who gave the Church Saint Peter's Patri-
mony.
I, too, am proud to give unto the Church
The labor of these hands, and what of life
Remains to me.　My father Buonarotti
Was Podestà of Chiusi and Caprese.
I am not used to have men speak to me

As if I were a mason, hired to build
A garden wall, and paid on Saturdays
So much an hour.

CARDINAL SALVIATI, *aside.*

   No wonder that Pope Clement
Never sat down in presence of this man,
Lest he should do the same ; and always
 bade him
Put on his hat, lest he unasked should
 do it !

MICHAEL ANGELO.

If any one could die of grief and shame,
I should. This labor was imposed upon
 me ;
I did not seek it ; and if I assumed it,
'T was not for love of fame or love of gain,
But for the love of God. Perhaps old age
Deceived me, or self-interest, or ambition ;
I may be doing harm instead of good.
Therefore, I pray your Holiness, release
 me ;
Take off from me the burden of this work ;
Let me go back to Florence.

JULIUS.

     Never, never,
While I am living.

MICHAEL ANGELO.

   Doth your Holiness
Remember what the Holy Scriptures say
Of the inevitable time, when those
Who look out of the windows shall be
 darkened,
And the almond-tree shall flourish ?

JULIUS.

     That is in
Ecclesiastes.

MICHAEL ANGELO.

  And the grasshopper
Shall be a burden, and desire shall fail,
Because man goeth unto his long home.
Vanity of Vanities, saith the Preacher ;
 all
Is vanity.

JULIUS.

  Ah, were to do a thing
As easy as to dream of doing it,
We should not want for artists. But the
 men
Who carry out in act their great designs
Are few in number ; aye, they may be
 counted

Upon the fingers of this hand. Your place
Is at St. Peter's.

MICHAEL ANGELO.

   I have had my dream,
And cannot carry out my great conception,
And put it into act.

JULIUS.

   Then who can do it ?
You would but leave it to some Baccio
 Bigio
To mangle and deface.

MICHAEL ANGELO.

   Rather than that,
I will still bear the burden on my shoulders
A little longer. If your Holiness
Will keep the world in order, and will leave
The building of the church to me, the work
Will go on better for it. Holy Father,
If all the labors that I have endured,
And shall endure, advantage not my soul,
I am but losing time.

JULIUS, *laying his hands on* MICHAEL ANGELO'S
shoulders.

   You will be gainer
Both for your soul and body.

MICHAEL ANGELO.

   Not events
Exasperate me, but the funest conclusions
I draw from these events ; the sure decline
Of art, and all the meaning of that word ;
All that embellishes and sweetens life,
And lifts it from the level of low cares
Into the purer atmosphere of beauty ;
The faith in the Ideal ; the inspiration
That made the canons of the church of Se-
 ville
Say, " Let us build, so that all men here-
 after
Will say that we were madmen." Holy
 Father,
I beg permission to retire from here.

JULIUS.

Go ; and my benediction be upon you.

SCENE III. — POPE JULIUS *and the* CARDINALS.

JULIUS.

My Cardinals, this Michael Angelo
Must not be dealt with as a common mason.

He comes of noble blood, and for his crest
Bears two bull's horns ; and he has given
    us proof
That he can toss with them.   From this
    day forth
Unto the end of time, let no man utter
The name of Baccio Bigio in my presence.
All great achievements are the natural
    fruits
Of a great character.   As trees bear not
Their fruits of the same size and quality,
But each one in its kind with equal ease,
So are great deeds as natural to great men
As mean things are to small ones.   By his
    work
We know the master.   Let us not perplex
    him.

III

BINDO ALTOVITI

A street in Rome. BINDO ALTOVITI, *standing
at the door of his house.* MICHAEL ANGELO,
passing.

BINDO.
Good-morning, Messer Michael Angelo !

MICHAEL ANGELO.
Good-morning, Messer Bindo Altoviti !

BINDO.
What brings you forth so early ?

MICHAEL ANGELO.
                    The same reason
That keeps you standing sentinel at your
    door, —
The air of this delicious summer morning.
What news have you from Florence ?

BINDO.
                    Nothing new ;
The same old tale of violence and wrong.
Since the disastrous day at Monte Murlo,
When in procession, through San Gallo's
    gate,
Bareheaded, clothed in rags, on sorry
    steeds,
Philippo Strozzi and the good Valori
Amid the shouts of an ungrateful people
Were led as prisoners down the streets of
    Florence,
Hope is no more, and liberty no more.
Duke Cosimo, the tyrant, reigns supreme.

MICHAEL ANGELO.
Florence is dead : her houses are but
    tombs ;
Silence and solitude are in her streets.

BINDO.
Ah yes ; and often I repeat the words
You wrote upon your statue of the Night,
There in the Sacristy of San Lorenzo :
" Grateful to me is sleep ; to be of stone
More grateful, while the wrong and shame
    endure ;
To see not, feel not, is a benediction ;
Therefore awake me not ; oh, speak in
    whispers."

MICHAEL ANGELO.
Ah, Messer Bindo, the calamities,
The fallen fortunes, and the desolation
Of Florence are to me a tragedy
Deeper than words, and darker than de-
    spair.
I, who have worshipped freedom from my
    cradle,
Have loved her with the passion of a lover,
And clothed her with all lovely attributes
That the imagination can conceive,
Or the heart conjure up, now see her dead,
And trodden in the dust beneath the feet
Of an adventurer !   It is a grief
Too great for me to bear in my old age.

BINDO.
I say no news from Florence : I am wrong
For Benvenuto writes that he is coming
To be my guest in Rome.

MICHAEL ANGELO.
                    Those are good tidings
He hath been many years away from us.

BINDO.
Pray you, come in.

MICHAEL ANGELO.
                    I have not time to stay,
And yet I will.   I see from here your house
Is filled with works of art.   That bust in
    bronze
Is of yourself.   Tell me, who is the master
That works in such an admirable way,
And with such power and feeling ?

BINDO.
                    Benvenuto.

MICHAEL ANGELO.

Ah? Benvenuto? 'T is a masterpiece!
It pleases me as much, and even more,
Than the antiques about it; and yet they
Are of the best one sees. But you have
placed it
By far too high. The light comes from
below,
And injures the expression. Were these
windows
Above and not beneath it, then indeed
It would maintain its own among these
works
Of the old masters, noble as they are.
I will go in and study it more closely.
I always prophesied that Benvenuto,
With all his follies and fantastic ways,
Would show his genius in some work of
art
That would amaze the world, and be a
challenge
Unto all other artists of his time.

[*They go in.*

IV

IN THE COLISEUM

MICHAEL ANGELO *and* TOMASO DE' CAVA-
LIERI.

CAVALIERI.

What do you here alone, Messer Michele?

MICHAEL ANGELO.

I come to learn.

CAVALIERI.
You are already master,
And teach all other men.

MICHAEL ANGELO.
Nay, I know nothing;
Not even my own ignorance, as some
Philosopher hath said. I am a school-boy
Who hath not learned his lesson, and who
stands
Ashamed and silent in the awful presence
Of the great master of antiquity
Who built these walls cyclopean.

CAVALIERI.
Gaudentius
His name was, I remember. His reward

Was to be thrown alive to the wild beasts
Here where we now are standing.

MICHAEL ANGELO.
Idle tales.

CAVALIERI.
But you are greater than Gaudentius was,
And your work nobler.

MICHAEL ANGELO.
Silence, I beseech you.

CAVALIERI.
Tradition says that fifteen thousand men
Were toiling for ten years incessantly
Upon this amphitheatre.

MICHAEL ANGELO.
Behold
How wonderful it is! The queen of
flowers,
The marble rose of Rome! Its petals torn
By wind and rain of thrice five hundred
years;
Its mossy sheath half rent away, and sold
To ornament our palaces and churches,
Or to be trodden under feet of man
Upon the Tiber's bank; yet what remains
Still opening its fair bosom to the sun,
And to the constellations that at night
Hang poised above it like a swarm of bees.

CAVALIERI.
The rose of Rome, but not of Paradise;
Not the white rose our Tuscan poet saw,
With saints for petals. When this rose
was perfect
Its hundred thousand petals were not
saints,
But senators in their Thessalian caps,
And all the roaring populace of Rome;
And even an Empress and the Vestal
Virgins,
Who came to see the gladiators die,
Could not give sweetness to a rose like this.

MICHAEL ANGELO.
I spake not of its uses, but its beauty.

CAVALIERI.
The sand beneath our feet is saturate
With blood of martyrs; and these rifted
stones
Are awful witnesses against a people
Whose pleasure was the pain of dying men

MICHAEL ANGELO.

Tomaso Cavalieri, on my word,
You should have been a preacher, not a
    painter!
Think you that I approve such cruelties,
Because I marvel at the architects
Who built these walls, and curved these
    noble arches?
Oh, I am put to shame, when I consider
How mean our work is, when compared
    with theirs!
Look at these walls about us and above us!
They have been shaken by earthquakes,
    have been made
A fortress, and been battered by long
    sieges;
The iron clamps, that held the stones
    together,
Have been wrenched from them; but they
    stand erect
And firm, as if they had been hewn and
    hollowed
Out of the solid rock, and were a part
Of the foundations of the world itself.

CAVALIERI.

Your work, I say again, is nobler work,
In so far as its end and aim are nobler;
And this is but a ruin, like the rest.
Its vaulted passages are made the caverns
Of robbers, and are haunted by the ghosts
Of murdered men.

MICHAEL ANGELO.

                A thousand wild flowers bloom
From every chink, and the birds build their
    nests
Among the ruined arches, and suggest
New thoughts of beauty to the architect.
Now let us climb the broken stairs that
    lead
Into the corridors above, and study
The marvel and the mystery of that art
In which I am a pupil, not a master.

All things must have an end; the world
    itself
Must have an end, as in a dream I saw it.
There came a great hand out of heaven,
    and touched
The earth, and stopped it in its course.
    The seas
Leaped, a vast cataract, into the abyss;
The forests and the fields slid off, and
    floated

Like wooded islands in the air. The dead
Were hurled forth from their sepulchres;
    the living
Were mingled with them, and themselves
    were dead, —
All being dead; and the fair, shining
    cities
Dropped out like jewels from a broken
    crown.
Naught but the core of the great globe re-
    mained,
A skeleton of stone. And over it
The wrack of matter drifted like a cloud,
And then recoiled upon itself, and fell
Back on the empty world, that with the
    weight
Reeled, staggered, righted, and then head-
    long plunged
Into the darkness, as a ship, when struck
By a great sea, throws off the waves at
    first
On either side, then settles and goes down
Into the dark abyss, with her dead crew.

CAVALIERI.

But the earth does not move.

MICHAEL ANGELO.

                Who knows? who knows?
There are great truths that pitch their
    shining tents
Outside our walls, and though but dimly
    seen
In the gray dawn, they will be manifest
When the light widens into perfect day.
A certain man, Copernicus by name,
Sometime professor here in Rome, has
    whispered
It is the earth, and not the sun, that moves.
What I beheld was only in a dream,
Yet dreams sometimes anticipate events,
Being unsubstantial images of things
As yet unseen.

V

MACELLO DE' CORVI

MICHAEL ANGELO, BENVENUTO CELLINI.

MICHAEL ANGELO.

So, Benvenuto, you return once more
To the Eternal City. 'T is the centre
To which all gravitates. One finds no rest

Elsewhere than here. There may be other cities
That please us for a while, but Rome alone
Completely satisfies. It becomes to all
A second native land by predilection,
And not by accident of birth alone.

BENVENUTO.

I am but just arrived, and am now lodging
With Bindo Altoviti. I have been
To kiss the feet of our most Holy Father,
And now am come in haste to kiss the hands
Of my miraculous Master.

MICHAEL ANGELO.

And to find him
Grown very old.

BENVENUTO.

You know that precious stones
Never grow old.

MICHAEL ANGELO.

Half sunk beneath the horizon,
And yet not gone. Twelve years are a long while.
Tell me of France.

BENVENUTO.

It were too long a tale
To tell you all. Suffice in brief to say
The King received me well, and loved me well ;
Gave me the annual pension that before me
Our Leonardo had, nor more nor less,
And for my residence the Tour de Nesle,
Upon the river-side.

MICHAEL ANGELO.

A princely lodging.

BENVENUTO.

What in return I did now matters not,
For there are other things, of greater moment,
I wish to speak of. First of all, the letter
You wrote me, not long since, about my bust
Of Bindo Altoviti, here in Rome. You said,
" My Benvenuto, I for many years
Have known you as the greatest of all goldsmiths,

And now I know you as no less a sculptor."
Ah, generous Master ! How shall I e'er thank you
For such kind language ?

MICHAEL ANGELO.

By believing it.
I saw the bust at Messer Bindo's house,
And thought it worthy of the ancient masters,
And said so. That is all.

BENVENUTO.

It is too much ;
And I should stand abashed here in your presence,
Had I done nothing worthier of your praise
Than Bindo's bust.

MICHAEL ANGELO.

What have you done that 's better ?

BENVENUTO.

When I left Rome for Paris, you remember
I promised you that if I went a goldsmith
I would return a sculptor. I have kept
The promise I then made.

MICHAEL ANGELO.

Dear Benvenuto,
I recognized the latent genius in you,
But feared your vices.

BENVENUTO.

I have turned them all
To virtues. My impatient, wayward nature,
That made me quick in quarrel, now has served me
Where meekness could not, and where patience could not,
As you shall hear now. I have cast in bronze
A statue of Perseus, holding thus aloft
In his left hand the head of the Medusa,
And in his right the sword that severed it ;
His right foot planted on the lifeless corse ;
His face superb and pitiful, with eyes
Down-looking on the victim of his vengeance.

MICHAEL ANGELO.

I see it as it should be.

BENVENUTO.
                    As it will be
When it is placed upon the Ducal Square,
Half-way between your David and the Judith
Of Donatello.

MICHAEL ANGELO.
          Rival of them both !

BENVENUTO.
But ah, what infinite trouble have I had
With Bandinello, and that stupid beast,
The major-domo of Duke Cosimo,
Francesco Ricci, and their wretched agent
Gorini, who came crawling round about me
Like a black spider, with his whining voice
That sounded like the buzz of a mosquito !
Oh, I have wept in utter desperation,
And wished a thousand times I had not
    left
My Tour de Nesle, nor e'er returned to
    Florence,
Nor thought of Perseus.   What malignant
    falsehoods
They told the Grand Duke, to impede my
    work,
And make me desperate !

MICHAEL ANGELO.
                    The nimble lie
Is like the second-hand upon a clock ;
We see it fly, while the hour-hand of truth
Seems to stand still, and yet it moves unseen,
And wins at last, for the clock will not
    strike
Till it has reached the goal.

BENVENUTO.
                    My obstinacy
Stood me in stead, and helped me to o'ercome
The hindrances that envy and ill-will
Put in my way.

MICHAEL ANGELO.
          When anything is done
People see not the patient doing of it,
Nor think how great would be the loss to
    man
If it had not been done.   As in a building
Stone rests on stone, and wanting the foundation
All would be wanting, so in human life

Each action rests on the foregone event,
That made it possible, but is forgotten
And buried in the earth.

BENVENUTO.
          Even Bandinello,
Who never yet spake well of anything,
Speaks well of this ; and yet he told the
    Duke
That, though I cast small figures well
    enough,
I never could cast this.

MICHAEL ANGELO.
          But you have done it,
And proved Ser Bandinello a false prophet.
That is the wisest way.

BENVENUTO.
          And ah, that casting !
What a wild scene it was, as late at night,
A night of wind and rain, we heaped the
    furnace
With pine of Serristori, till the flames
Caught in the rafters over us, and threatened
To send the burning roof upon our heads ;
And from the garden side the wind and
    rain
Poured in upon us, and half quenched our
    fires.
I was beside myself with desperation.
A shudder came upon me, then a fever ;
I thought that I was dying, and was forced
To leave the work-shop, and to throw myself
Upon my bed, as one who has no hope.
And as I lay there, a deformed old man
Appeared before me, and with dismal voice,
Like one who doth exhort a criminal
Led forth to death, exclaimed, " Poor Benvenuto,
Thy work is spoiled !   There is no remedy ! "
Then with a cry so loud it might have
    reached
The heaven of fire, I bounded to my feet,
And rushed back to my workmen.   They
    all stood
Bewildered and desponding ; and I looked
Into the furnace, and beheld the mass
Half molten only, and in my despair
I fed the fire with oak, whose terrible heat
Soon made the sluggish metal shine and
    sparkle.

Then followed a bright flash, and an explosion,
As if a thunderbolt had fallen among us.
The covering of the furnace had been rent
Asunder, and the bronze was flowing over ;
So that I straightway opened all the sluices
To fill the mould. The metal ran like lava,
Sluggish and heavy ; and I sent my workmen
To ransack the whole house, and bring together
My pewter plates and pans, two hundred of them,
And cast them one by one into the furnace
To liquefy the mass, and in a moment
The mould was filled ! I fell upon my knees
And thanked the Lord ; and then we ate and drank
And went to bed, all hearty and contented.
It was two hours before the break of day.
My fever was quite gone.

MICHAEL ANGELO.

A strange adventure,
That could have happened to no man alive
But you, my Benvenuto.

BENVENUTO.

As my workmen said
To major-domo Ricci afterward
When he inquired of them : " 'T was not a man,
But an express great devil."

MICHAEL ANGELO.

And the statue ?

BENVENUTO.

Perfect in every part, save the right foot
Of Perseus, as I had foretold the Duke.
There was just bronze enough to fill the mould ;
Not a drop over, not a drop too little.
I looked upon it as a miracle
Wrought by the hand of God.

MICHAEL ANGELO.

And now I see
How you have turned your vices into virtues.

BENVENUTO.

But wherefore do I prate of this ? I came
To speak of other things. Duke Cosimo
Through me invites you to return to Florence,
And offers you great honors, even to make you
One of the Forty-Eight, his Senators.

MICHAEL ANGELO.

His Senators ! That is enough. Since Florence
Was changed by Clement Seventh from a Republic
Into a Dukedom, I no longer wish
To be a Florentine. That dream is ended.
The Grand Duke Cosimo now reigns supreme ;
All liberty is dead. Ah, woe is me !
I hoped to see my country rise to heights
Of happiness and freedom yet unreached
By other nations, but the climbing wave
Pauses, lets go its hold, and slides again
Back to the common level, with a hoarse
Death-rattle in its throat. I am too old
To hope for better days. I will stay here
And die in Rome. The very weeds, that grow
Among the broken fragments of her ruins,
Are sweeter to me than the garden flowers
Of other cities ; and the desolate ring
Of the Campagna round about her walls
Fairer than all the villas that encircle
The towns of Tuscany.

BENVENUTO.

But your old friends !

MICHAEL ANGELO.

All dead by violence. Baccio Valori
Has been beheaded ; Guicciardini poisoned ;
Philippo Strozzi strangled in his prison.
Is Florence then a place for honest men
To flourish in ? What is there to prevent
My sharing the same fate ?

BENVENUTO.

Why, this : if all
Your friends are dead, so are your enemies.

MICHAEL ANGELO.

Is Aretino dead ?

BENVENUTO.

He lives in Venice,
And not in Florence.

MICHAEL ANGELO.
                    'T is the same to me.
This wretched mountebank, whom flatterers
Call the Divine, as if to make the word
Unpleasant in the mouths of those who
          speak it
And in the ears of those who hear it, sends
          me
A letter written for the public eye,
And with such subtle and infernal malice,
I wonder at his wickedness. 'T is he
Is the express great devil, and not you.
Some years ago he told me how to paint
The scenes of the Last Judgment.

BENVENUTO.
                    I remember.
MICHAEL ANGELO.
Well, now he writes to me that, as a Chris-
          tian,
He is ashamed of the unbounded freedom
With which I represent it.

BENVENUTO.
                    Hypocrite !
MICHAEL ANGELO.
He says I show mankind that I am want-
          ing
In piety and religion, in proportion
As I profess perfection in my art.
Profess perfection ? Why, 't is only men
Like Bugiardini who are satisfied
With what they do. I never am content,
But always see the labor of my hand
Fall short of my conception.

BENVENUTO.
                         I perceive
The malice of this creature. He would
          taint you
With heresy, and in a time like this !
'T is infamous !

MICHAEL ANGELO.
               I represent the angels
Without their heavenly glory, and the
          saints
Without a trace of earthly modesty.

BENVENUTO.
Incredible audacity !

MICHAEL ANGELO.
                    The heathen
Veiled their Diana with some drapery,

And when they represented Venus naked
They made her by her modest attitude
Appear half clothed. But I, who am a
          Christian,
Do so subordinate belief to art
That I have made the very violation
Of modesty in martyrs and in virgins
A spectacle at which all men would gaze
With half-averted eyes even in a brothel.

BENVENUTO.
He is at home there, and he ought to know
What men avert their eyes from in such
          places ;
From the Last Judgment chiefly, I imagine.

MICHAEL ANGELO.
But divine Providence will never leave
The boldness of my marvellous work un-
          punished ;
And the more marvellous it is, the more
'T is sure to prove the ruin of my fame !
And finally, if in this composition
I had pursued the instructions that he gave
          me
Concerning heaven and hell and paradise,
In that same letter, known to all the
          world,
Nature would not be forced, as she is now,
To feel ashamed that she invested me
With such great talent ; that I stand
          myself
A very idol in the world of art.
He taunts me also with the Mausoleum
Of Julius, still unfinished, for the reason
That men persuaded the inane old man
It was of evil augury to build
His tomb while he was living ; and he
          speaks
Of heaps of gold this Pope bequeathed to
          me,
And calls it robbery ; — that is what he
          says.
What prompted such a letter ?

BENVENUTO.
                         Vanity.
He is a clever writer, and he likes
To draw his pen, and flourish it in the face
Of every honest man, as swordsmen do
Their rapiers on occasion, but to show
How skilfully they do it. Had you fol-
          lowed
The advice he gave, or even thanked him
          for it,

You would have seen another style of
fence.
'T is but his wounded vanity, and the wish
To see his name in print. So give it not
A moment's thought; it will soon be for-
gotten.

MICHAEL ANGELO.

I will not think of it, but let it pass
For a rude speech thrown at me in the
street,
As boys threw stones at Dante.

BENVENUTO.

And what answer
Shall I take back to Grand Duke Cosimo?
He does not ask your labor or your service;
Only your presence in the city of Florence,
With such advice upon his work in hand
As he may ask, and you may choose to
give.

MICHAEL ANGELO.

You have my answer. Nothing he can
offer
Shall tempt me to leave Rome. My work
is here,
And only here, the building of St. Peter's.
What other things I hitherto have done
Have fallen from me, are no longer mine;
I have passed on beyond them, and have
left them
As milestones on the way. What lies be-
fore me,
That is still mine, and while it is unfinished
No one shall draw me from it, or persuade
me,
By promises of ease, or wealth, or honor,
Till I behold the finished dome uprise
Complete, as now I see it in my thought.

BENVENUTO.

And will you paint no more?

MICHAEL ANGELO.

No more.

BENVENUTO.

'T is well.
Sculpture is more divine, and more like
Nature,
That fashions all her works in high relief,
And that is sculpture. This vast ball, the
Earth,
Was moulded out of clay, and baked in
fire;
Men, women, and all animals that breathe

Are statues and not paintings. Even the
plants,
The flowers, the fruits, the grasses, were
first sculptured,
And colored later. Painting is a lie,
A shadow merely.

MICHAEL ANGELO.

Truly, as you say,
Sculpture is more than painting. It is
greater
To raise the dead to life than to create
Phantoms that seem to live. The most
majestic
Of the three sister arts is that which builds;
The eldest of them all, to whom the others
Are but the handmaids and the servitors,
Being but imitation, not creation.
Henceforth I dedicate myself to her.

BENVENUTO.

And no more from the marble hew those
forms
That fill us all with wonder?

MICHAEL ANGELO.

Many statues
Will there be room for in my work. Their
station
Already is assigned them in my mind.
But things move slowly. There are hin-
drances,
Want of material, want of means, delays
And interruptions, endless interference
Of Cardinal Commissioners, and disputes
And jealousies of artists, that annoy me.
But I will persevere until the work
Is wholly finished, or till I sink down
Surprised by Death, that unexpected guest,
Who waits for no man's leisure, but steps in,
Unasked and unannounced, to put a stop
To all our occupations and designs.
And then perhaps I may go back to Flor-
ence;
This is my answer to Duke Cosimo.

VI

MICHAEL ANGELO'S STUDIO

MICHAEL ANGELO and URBINO.

MICHAEL ANGELO, *pausing in his work.*

Urbino, thou and I are both old men.
My strength begins to fail me.

URBINO.

Eccellenza,
That is impossible. Do I not see you
Attack the marble blocks with the same
    fury
As twenty years ago ?

MICHAEL ANGELO.

'T is an old habit.
I must have learned it early from my nurse
At Setignano, the stone-mason's wife ;
For the first sounds I heard were of the
    chisel
Chipping away the stone.

URBINO.

At every stroke
You strike fire with your chisel.

MICHAEL ANGELO.

Aye, because
The marble is too hard.

URBINO.

It is a block
That Topolino sent you from Carrara.
He is a judge of marble.

MICHAEL ANGELO.

I remember.
With it he sent me something of his mak-
    ing, —
A Mercury, with long body and short legs,
As if by any possibility
A messenger of the gods could have short
    legs.
It was no more like Mercury than you
    are,
But rather like those little plaster figures
That peddlers hawk about the villages
As images of saints. But luckily
For Topolino, there are many people
Who see no difference between what is
    best
And what is only good, or not even good ;
So that poor artists stand in their esteem
On the same level with the best, or higher.

URBINO.

How Eccellenza laughed !

MICHAEL ANGELO.

Poor Topolino !
All men are not born artists, nor will labor
E'er make them artists.

URBINO.

No, no more
Than Emperors, or Popes, or Cardinals.
One must be chosen for it. I have been
Your color-grinder six and twenty years,
And am not yet an artist.

MICHAEL ANGELO.

Some have eyes
That see not ; but in every block of mar-
    ble
I see a statue, — see it as distinctly
As if it stood before me shaped and per-
    fect
In attitude and action. I have only
To hew away the stone walls that imprison
The lovely apparition, and reveal it
To other eyes as mine already see it.
But I grow old and weak. What wilt thou
    do
When I am dead, Urbino ?

URBINO.

Eccellenza,
I must then serve another master.

MICHAEL ANGELO.

Never !
Bitter is servitude at best. Already
So many years hast thou been serving me ;
But rather as a friend than as a servant.
We have grown old together. Dost thou
    think
So meanly of this Michael Angelo
As to imagine he would let thee serve,
When he is free from service ? Take this
    purse,
Two thousand crowns in gold.

URBINO.

Two thousand crowns !

MICHAEL ANGELO.

Ay, it will make thee rich. Thou shalt not
    die
A beggar in a hospital.

URBINO.

Oh, Master !

MICHAEL ANGELO.

I cannot have them with me on the jour-
    ney
That I am undertaking. The last garment
That men will make for me will have no
    pockets.

URBINO, *kissing the hand of* MICHAEL ANGELO.
My generous master !

MICHAEL ANGELO.
Hush !

URBINO.
My Providence !

MICHAEL ANGELO.
Not a word more. Go now to bed, old
man.
Thou hast served Michael Angelo. Re-
member,
Henceforward thou shalt serve no other
master.

VII

THE OAKS OF MONTE LUCA

MICHAEL ANGELO, *alone in the woods.*

MICHAEL ANGELO.
How still it is among these ancient oaks !
Surges and undulations of the air
Uplift the leafy boughs, and let them fall
With scarce a sound. Such sylvan quie-
tudes
Become old age. These huge centennial
oaks,
That may have heard in infancy the trum-
pets
Of Barbarossa's cavalry, deride
Man's brief existence, that with all his
strength
He cannot stretch beyond the hundredth
year.
This little acorn, turbaned like the Turk,
Which with my foot I spurn, may be an
oak
Hereafter, feeding with its bitter mast
The fierce wild-boar, and tossing in its
arms
The cradled nests of birds, when all the
men
That now inhabit this vast universe,
They and their children, and their chil-
dren's children,
Shall be but dust and mould, and nothing
more.
Through openings in the trees I see below
me
The valley of Clitumnus, with its farms

And snow-white oxen grazing in the shade
Of the tall poplars on the river's brink.
O Nature, gentle mother, tender nurse !
I, who have never loved thee as I ought,
But wasted all my years immured in cities,
And breathed the stifling atmosphere of
streets,
Now come to thee for refuge. Here is peace.
Yonder I see the little hermitages
Dotting the mountain side with points of
light,
And here St. Julian's convent, like a nest
Of curlews, clinging to some windy cliff.
Beyond the broad, illimitable plain
Down sinks the sun, red as Apollo's quoit,
That, by the envious Zephyr blown aside,
Struck Hyacinthus dead, and stained the
earth
With his young blood, that blossomed into
flowers.
And now, instead of these fair deities,
Dread demons haunt the earth ; hermits
inhabit
The leafy homes of sylvan Hamadryads ;
And jovial friars, rotund and rubicund,
Replace the old Silenus with his ass.

Here underneath these venerable oaks,
Wrinkled and brown and gnarled like them
with age,
A brother of the monastery sits,
Lost in his meditations. What may be
The questions that perplex, the hopes that
cheer him ? —
Good-evening, holy father.

MONK.
God be with you.

MICHAEL ANGELO.
Pardon a stranger if he interrupt
Your meditations.

MONK.
It was but a dream. —
The old, old dream, that never will come
true ;
The dream that all my life I have been
dreaming,
And yet is still a dream.

MICHAEL ANGELO.
All men have dreams,
I have had mine ; but none of them came
true ;

They were but vanity.   Sometimes I think
The happiness of man lies in pursuing,
Not in possessing ; for the things possessed
Lose half their value.   Tell me of your
dream.

MONK.

The yearning of my heart, my sole desire,
That like the sheaf of Joseph stands up-
right,
While all the others bend and bow to it ;
The passion that torments me, and that
breathes
New meaning into the dead forms of
prayer,
Is that with mortal eyes I may behold
The Eternal City.

MICHAEL ANGELO.
Rome ?

MONK.
There is but one ;
The rest are merely names.   I think of it
As the Celestial City, paved with gold,
And sentinelled with angels.

MICHAEL ANGELO.
Would it were.
I have just fled from it.   It is beleaguered
By Spanish troops, led by the Duke of Alva.

MONK.
But still for me 't is the Celestial City,
And I would see it once before I die.

MICHAEL ANGELO.
Each one must bear his cross.

MONK.
Were it a cross
That had been laid upon me, I could bear
it,
Or fall with it.   It is a crucifix ;
I am nailed hand and foot, and I am dying !

MICHAEL ANGELO.
What would you see in Rome ?

MONK.
His Holiness.

MICHAEL ANGELO.
Him that was once the Cardinal Caraffa ?
You would but see a man of fourscore
years,
With sunken eyes, burning like carbuncles,

Who sits at table with his friends for hours,
Cursing the Spaniards as a race of Jews
And miscreant Moors.   And with what
soldiery
Think you he now defends the Eternal
City ?

MONK.
With legions of bright angels.

MICHAEL ANGELO.
So he calls them ;
And yet in fact these bright angelic legions
Are only German Lutherans.

MONK, *crossing himself.*
Heaven protect us !

MICHAEL ANGELO.
What further would you see ?

MONK.
The Cardinals,
Going in their gilt coaches to High Mass.

MICHAEL ANGELO.
Men do not go to Paradise in coaches.

MONK.
The catacombs, the convents, and the
churches ;
The ceremonies of the Holy Week
In all their pomp, or, at the Epiphany,
The feast of the Santissimo Bambino
At Ara Cœli.   But I shall not see them.

MICHAEL ANGELO.
These pompous ceremonies of the Church
Are but an empty show to him who knows
The actors in them.   Stay here in your
convent,
For he who goes to Rome may see too
much.
What would you further ?

MONK.
I would see the painting
Of the Last Judgment in the Sistine Chapel.

MICHAEL ANGELO.
The smoke of incense and of altar candles
Has blackened it already.

MONK.
Woe is me !
Then I would hear Allegri's Miserere,
Sung by the Papal choir.

MICHAEL ANGELO.
                    A dismal dirge !
I am an old, old man, and I have lived
In Rome for thirty years and more, and
    know
The jarring of the wheels of that great
    world,
Its jealousies, its discords, and its strife.
Therefore I say to you, remain content
Here in your convent, here among your
    woods,
Where only there is peace. Go not to
    Rome.
There was of old a monk of Wittenberg
Who went to Rome ; you may have heard
    of him ;
His name was Luther ; and you know
    what followed.
                    [*The convent bell rings.*

MONK, *rising.*

It is the convent bell ; it rings for vespers.
Let us go in ; we both will pray for peace.

VIII

THE DEAD CHRIST

MICHAEL ANGELO's *Studio.* MICHAEL AN-
GELO *with a light, working upon the Dead
Christ. Midnight.*

MICHAEL ANGELO.

O Death, why is it I cannot portray
Thy form and features ? Do I stand too
    near thee ?
Or dost thou hold my hand, and draw me
    back,
As being thy disciple, not thy master ?
Let him who knows not what old age is
    like
Have patience till it comes, and he will
    know.
I once had skill to fashion Life and Death
And Sleep, which is the counterfeit of
    Death ;
And I remember what Giovanni Strozzi
Wrote underneath my statue of the Night
In San Lorenzo, ah, so long ago !
Grateful to me is sleep ! More grateful
    now
Than it was then ; for all my friends are
    dead ;
And she is dead, the noblest of them all.

I saw her face, when the great sculptor
    Death,
Whom men should call Divine, had at a
    blow
Stricken her into marble ; and I kissed
Her cold white hand. What was it held
    me back
From kissing her fair forehead, and those
    lips,
Those dead, dumb lips ? Grateful to me
    is sleep !

            Enter GIORGIO VASARI.

GIORGIO.

Good-evening, or good-morning, for I know
    not
Which of the two it is.

MICHAEL ANGELO.
                    How came you in ?
GIORGIO.
Why, by the door, as all men do.

MICHAEL ANGELO.
                            Ascanio
Must have forgotten to bolt it.

GIORGIO.
                        Probably.
Am I a spirit, or so like a spirit,
That I could slip through bolted door or
    window ?
As I was passing down the street, I saw
A glimmer of light, and heard the well-
    known chink
Of chisel upon marble. So I entered,
To see what keeps you from your bed so
    late.

MICHAEL ANGELO, *coming forward with the
    lamp.*

You have been revelling with your boon
    companions,
Giorgio Vasari, and you come to me
At an untimely hour.

GIORGIO.
                The Pope hath sent me.
His Holiness desires to see again
The drawing you once showed him of the
    dome
Of the Basilica.

MICHAEL ANGELO.
    We will look for it.

GIORGIO.

What is the marble group that glimmers
    there
Behind you ?

MICHAEL ANGELO.

    Nothing, and yet everything, —
As one may take it. It is my own tomb
That I am building.

GIORGIO.

        Do not hide it from me.
By our long friendship and the love I bear
    you,
Refuse me not !

MICHAEL ANGELO, *letting fall the lamp.*

    Life hath become to me
An empty theatre, — its lights extinguished,
The music silent, and the actors gone ;
And I alone sit musing on the scenes
That once have been. I am so old that
    Death
Oft plucks me by the cloak, to come with
    him ;
And some day, like this lamp, shall I fall
    down,
And my last spark of life will be ex-
    tinguished.
Ah me ! ah me ! what darkness of despair !
So near to death, and yet so far from God.

TRANSLATIONS

In accordance with the plan determined upon for this edition, the Translations are collected from the separate volumes put forth by Mr. Longfellow and re-arranged here. Translating played an important part in the development of Mr. Longfellow's powers. Before he had begun to write those poems which at once attested his poetic calling, and while he was busying himself with study and prose expression, he was finding an outlet for his metrical thought and emotion in the translation of lyrics and pastoral verse, and occasionally of epic and dramatic fragments. Tasks thus early begun passed easily into pleasant avocations, and to the end of his life he found an ever grateful occupation in recasting the foreign thought of other men in moulds of his own. It has been deemed most expedient to group these translations by the several literatures from which they are derived, following in each group a chronological order of composition, as far as possible. As the first most important work in this field by Mr. Longfellow was in a translation from the Spanish, the group from the literature of Spain takes precedence.

The successive publication of *Coplas de Manrique* indicates the importance attached to it by Mr. Longfellow, and both the treatment which it received at his hands and the formal statement of his theory of translation have an interest, for the contrast which they afford to his later judgment and practice.

The preface to the book, dated Bowdoin College, August 9, 1833, besides a brief notice of Don Jorge Manrique and some characterization of the poem which will be found in the notes, contained the following remarks on the translator's task : —

"The object of this little work is to place in the hands of the lovers of Spanish literature the most beautiful moral poem of that language. The original is printed with the translation, that in the estimate of those at least who are versed in the Spanish tongue the author may not suffer for the imperfections of the translator.

"The great art of translating well lies in the power of rendering literally the words of a foreign author while at the same time we preserve the spirit of the original. But how far one of these requisites of a good translation may be sacrificed to the other — how far a translator is at liberty to embellish the original

before him, while clothing it in a new language, is a question which has been decided differently by persons of different tastes. The sculptor, when he transfers to the inanimate marble the form and features of a living being, may be said not only to copy, but to translate. But the sculptor cannot represent in marble the beauty and expression of the human eye; and in order to remedy this defect as far as possible, he is forced to transgress the rigid truth of nature. By sinking the eye deeper, and making the brow more prominent above it, he produces a stronger light and shade, and thus gives to the statue more of the spirit and life of the original than he could have done by an exact copy. So, too, the translator. As there are certain beauties of thought and expression in a good original, which cannot be fully represented in the less flexible material of another language, he, too, at times may be permitted to transgress the rigid truth of language, and remedy the defect, as far as such a defect can be remedied, by slight and judicious embellishments.

"By this principle I have been guided in the following translations. I have rendered literally the words of the original, when it could be done without injuring their spirit; and when this could not be done, I have occasionally used the embellishment of an additional epithet, or a more forcible turn of expression: How far I have succeeded in my purpose, the reader shall determine."

It may be added that the translator did not keep to the exact metre and rhyme of the Spanish original, but adopted what he regarded as an equivalent stanza. He afterward adopted a much stricter rule of translation indicated by the couplet from Spenser prefixed to his version of Dante : —

"I follow here the footing of thy feete,
    That with thy meaning so I may the rather meete."

Besides the translations preserved by Mr. Longfellow in successive volumes, there are several published in periodicals and elsewhere which are directly traceable to his pen, and are included in the Appendix to this volume, including one found among his manuscripts. As a fitting prelude to the entire series, the poem, not a translation, which was used for a similar purpose in the posthumous collection *In the Harbor*, is here given at the outset.

PRELUDE

As treasures that men seek,
 Deep buried in sea-sands,
Vanish if they but speak,
 And elude their eager hands, —

So ye escape and slip,
 O songs, and fade away,
When the word is on my lip
 To interpret what ye say.

Were it not better, then,
 To let the treasures rest
Hid from the eyes of men
 Locked in their iron chest?

I have but marked the place,
 But half the secret told,
That, following this slight trace,
 Others may find the gold.

FROM THE SPANISH

COPLAS DE MANRIQUE

OH let the soul her slumbers break,
Let thought be quickened, and awake ;
Awake to see
How soon this life is past and gone,
And death comes softly stealing on,
How silently !

Swiftly our pleasures glide away,
Our hearts recall the distant day
With many sighs ;
The moments that are speeding fast
We heed not, but the past, — the past,
More highly prize.

Onward its course the present keeps,
Onward the constant current sweeps,
Till life is done ;
And, did we judge of time aright,
The past and future in their flight
Would be as one.

Let no one fondly dream again,
That Hope and all her shadowy train
Will not decay ;
Fleeting as were the dreams of old,
Remembered like a tale that 's told,
They pass away.

Our lives are rivers, gliding free
To that unfathomed, boundless sea,
The silent grave !
Thither all earthly pomp and boast
Roll, to be swallowed up and lost
In one dark wave.

Thither the mighty torrents stray,
Thither the brook pursues its way,
And tinkling rill.
There all are equal ; side by side
The poor man and the son of pride
Lie calm and still.

I will not here invoke the throng
Of orators and sons of song,
The deathless few ;
Fiction entices and deceives,
And, sprinkled o'er her fragrant leaves,
Lies poisonous dew.

To One alone my thoughts arise,
The Eternal Truth, the Good and Wise,
To Him I cry,
Who shared on earth our common lot,
But the world comprehended not
His deity.

This world is but the rugged road
Which leads us to the bright abode
Of peace above ;
So let us choose that narrow way,
Which leads no traveller's foot astray
From realms of love.

Our cradle is the starting-place,
Life is the running of the race,
We reach the goal
When, in the mansions of the blest,
Death leaves to its eternal rest
The weary soul.

Did we but use it as we ought,
This world would school each wandering
    thought
To its high state.
Faith wings the soul beyond the sky,
Up to that better world on high,
For which we wait.

Yes, the glad messenger of love,
To guide us to our home above,
The Saviour came ;

Born amid mortal cares and fears,
He suffered in this vale of tears
A death of shame.

Behold of what delusive worth
The bubbles we pursue on earth,
The shapes we chase
Amid a world of treachery !
They vanish ere death shuts the eye,
And leave no trace.

Time steals them from us, chances strange,
Disastrous accident, and change,
That come to all ;
Even in the most exalted state,
Relentless sweeps the stroke of fate ;
The strongest fall.

Tell me, the charms that lovers seek
In the clear eye and blushing cheek,
The hues that play
O'er rosy lip and brow of snow,
When hoary age approaches slow,
Ah, where are they ?

The cunning skill, the curious arts,
The glorious strength that youth imparts
In life's first stage ;
These shall become a heavy weight,
When Time swings wide his outward gate
To weary age.

The noble blood of Gothic name,
Heroes emblazoned high to fame,
In long array ;
How, in the onward course of time,
The landmarks of that race sublime
Were swept away !

Some, the degraded slaves of lust,
Prostrate and trampled in the dust,
Shall rise no more ;
Others, by guilt and crime, maintain
The scutcheon, that, without a stain,
Their fathers bore.

Wealth and the high estate of pride,
With what untimely speed they glide,
How soon depart !
Bid not the shadowy phantoms stay,
The vassals of a mistress they,
Of fickle heart.

These gifts in Fortune's hands are found;
Her swift revolving wheel turns round,
And they are gone !

No rest the inconstant goddess knows,
But changing, and without repose,
Still hurries on.

Even could the hand of avarice save
Its gilded baubles, till the grave
Reclaimed its prey,
Let none on such poor hopes rely ;
Life, like an empty dream, flits by,
And where are they ?

Earthly desires and sensual lust
Are passions springing from the dust,
They fade and die ;
But, in the life beyond the tomb,
They seal the immortal spirit's doom
Eternally !

The pleasures and delights, which mask
In treacherous smiles life's serious task,
What are they all
But the fleet coursers of the chase,
And death an ambush in the race,
Wherein we fall ?

No foe, no dangerous pass, we heed,
Brook no delay, but onward speed
With loosened rein ;
And, when the fatal snare is near,
We strive to check our mad career,
But strive in vain.

Could we new charms to age impart,
And fashion with a cunning art
The human face,
As we can clothe the soul with light,
And make the glorious spirit bright
With heavenly grace,

How busily each passing hour
Should we exert that magic power !
What ardor show,
To deck the sensual slave of sin,
Yet leave the freeborn soul within,
In weeds of woe !

Monarchs, the powerful and the strong,
Famous in history and in song
Of olden time,
Saw, by the stern decrees of fate,
Their kingdoms lost, and desolate
Their race sublime.

Who is the champion ? who the strong ?
Pontiff and priest, and sceptred throng ?
On these shall fall

As heavily the hand of Death,
As when it stays the shepherd's breath
Beside his stall.

I speak not of the Trojan name,
Neither its glory nor its shame
Has met our eyes ;
Nor of Rome's great and glorious dead,
Though we have heard so oft, and read,
Their histories.

Little avails it now to know
Of ages passed so long ago,
Nor how they rolled ;
Our theme shall be of yesterday,
Which to oblivion sweeps away,
Like days of old.

Where is the King, Don Juan ?   Where
Each royal prince and noble heir
Of Aragon ?
Where are the courtly gallantries ?
The deeds of love and high emprise,
In battle done ?

Tourney and joust, that charmed the
      eye,
And scarf, and gorgeous panoply,
And nodding plume,
What were they but a pageant scene ?
What but the garlands, gay and green,
That deck the tomb ?

Where are the high-born dames, and
      where
Their gay attire, and jewelled hair,
And odors sweet ?
Where are the gentle knights, that came
To kneel, and breathe love's ardent
      flame,
Low at their feet ?

Where is the song of Troubadour ?
Where are the lute and gay tambour
They loved of yore ?
Where is the mazy dance of old,
The flowing robes, inwrought with gold,
The dancers wore ?

And he who next the sceptre swayed,
Henry, whose royal court displayed
Such power and pride ;
Oh, in what winning smiles arrayed,
The world its various pleasures laid
His throne beside !

But oh, how false and full of guile
That world, which wore so soft a smile
But to betray !
She, that had been his friend before,
Now from the fated monarch tore
Her charms away.

The countless gifts, the stately walls,
The royal palaces, and halls,
All filled with gold ;
Plate with armorial bearings wrought,
Chambers with ample treasures fraught
Of wealth untold ;

The noble steeds, and harness bright,
And gallant lord, and stalwart knight,
In rich array,
Where shall we seek them now ?   Alas !
Like the bright dewdrops on the grass,
They passed away.

His brother, too, whose factious zeal
Usurped the sceptre of Castile,
Unskilled to reign ;
What a gay, brilliant court had he,
When all the flower of chivalry
Was in his train !

But he was mortal ; and the breath
That flamed from the hot forge of Death
Blasted his years ;
Judgment of God ! that flame by thee,
When raging fierce and fearfully,
Was quenched in tears !

Spain's haughty Constable, the true
And gallant Master, whom we knew
Most loved of all ;
Breathe not a whisper of his pride,
He on the gloomy scaffold died,
Ignoble fall !

The countless treasures of his care,
His villages and villas fair,
His mighty power,
What were they all but grief and shame,
Tears and a broken heart, when came
The parting hour ?

His other brothers, proud and high,
Masters, who, in prosperity,
Might rival kings ;
Who made the bravest and the best
The bondsmen of their high behest,
Their underlings ;

What was their prosperous estate,
When high exalted and elate
With power and pride ?
What, but a transient gleam of light,
A flame, which, glaring at its height,
Grew dim and died ?

So many a duke of royal name,
Marquis and count of spotless fame,
And baron brave,
That might the sword of empire wield,
All these, O Death, hast thou concealed
In the dark grave !

Their deeds of mercy and of arms,
In peaceful days, or war's alarms,
When thou dost show,
O Death, thy stern and angry face,
One stroke of thy all-powerful mace
Can overthrow.

Unnumbered hosts, that threaten nigh,
Pennon and standard flaunting high,
And flag displayed ;
High battlements intrenched around,
Bastion, and moated wall, and mound,
And palisade,

And covered trench, secure and deep,
All these cannot one victim keep,
O Death, from thee,
When thou dost battle in thy wrath,
And thy strong shafts pursue their path
Unerringly.

O World ! so few the years we live,
Would that the life which thou dost give
Were life indeed !
Alas ! thy sorrows fall so fast,
Our happiest hour is when at last
The soul is freed.

Our days are covered o'er with grief,
And sorrows neither few nor brief
Veil all in gloom ;
Left desolate of real good,
Within this cheerless solitude
No pleasures bloom.

Thy pilgrimage begins in tears,
And ends in bitter doubts and fears,
Or dark despair ;
Midway so many toils appear,
That he who lingers longest here
Knows most of care.

Thy goods are bought with many a groan,
By the hot sweat of toil alone,
And weary hearts ;
Fleet-footed is the approach of woe,
But with a lingering step and slow
Its form departs.

And he, the good man's shield and shade,
To whom all hearts their homage paid,
As Virtue's son,
Roderic Manrique, he whose name
Is written on the scroll of Fame,
Spain's champion ;

His signal deeds and prowess high
Demand no pompous eulogy,
Ye saw his deeds !
Why should their praise in verse be sung ?
The name, that dwells on every tongue,
No minstrel needs.

To friends a friend ; how kind to all
The vassals of this ancient hall
And feudal fief !
To foes how stern a foe was he !
And to the valiant and the free
How brave a chief !

What prudence with the old and wise :
What grace in youthful gayeties ;
In all how sage !
Benignant to the serf and slave,
He showed the base and falsely brave
A lion's rage.

His was Octavian's prosperous star,
The rush of Cæsar's conquering car
At battle's call ;
His, Scipio's virtue ; his, the skill
And the indomitable will
Of Hannibal.

His was a Trajan's goodness, his
A Titus' noble charities
And righteous laws ;
The arm of Hector, and the might
Of Tully, to maintain the right
In truth's just cause ;

The clemency of Antonine,
Aurelius' countenance divine,
Firm, gentle, still ;
The eloquence of Adrian,
And Theodosius' love to man,
And generous will ;

In tented field and bloody fray,
An Alexander's vigorous sway
And stern command ;
The faith of Constantine ; ay, more,
The fervent love Camillus bore
His native land.

He left no well-filled treasury,
He heaped no pile of riches high,
Nor massive plate ;
He fought the Moors, and, in their fall,
City and tower and castled wall
Were his estate.

Upon the hard-fought battle-ground,
Brave steeds and gallant riders found
A common grave ;
And there the warrior's hand did gain
The rents, and the long vassal train,
That conquest gave.

And if of old his halls displayed
The honored and exalted grade
His worth had gained,
So, in the dark, disastrous hour,
Brothers and bondsmen of his power
His hand sustained.

After high deeds, not left untold,
In the stern warfare which of old
'T was his to share,
Such noble leagues he made that more
And fairer regions than before
His guerdon were.

These are the records, half effaced,
Which, with the hand of youth, he traced
On history's page ;
But with fresh victories he drew
Each fading character anew
In his old age.

By his unrivalled skill, by great
And veteran service to the state,
By worth adored,
He stood, in his high dignity,
The proudest knight of chivalry,
Knight of the Sword.

He found his cities and domains
Beneath a tyrant's galling chains
And cruel power ;
But, by fierce battle and blockade,
Soon his own banner was displayed
From every tower.

By the tried valor of his hand,
His monarch and his native land
Were nobly served ;
Let Portugal repeat the story,
And proud Castile, who shared the glory
His arms deserved.

And when so oft, for weal or woe,
His life upon the fatal throw
Had been cast down ;
When he had served, with patriot zeal,
Beneath the banner of Castile,
His sovereign's crown ;

And done such deeds of valor strong,
That neither history nor song
Can count them all ;
Then, on Ocaña's castled rock,
Death at his portal came to knock,
With sudden call,

Saying, "Good Cavalier, prepare
To leave this world of toil and care
With joyful mien ;
Let thy strong heart of steel this day
Put on its armor for the fray,
The closing scene.

" Since thou hast been, in battle-strife,
So prodigal of health and life,
For earthly fame,
Let virtue nerve thy heart again ;
Loud on the last stern battle-plain
They call thy name.

" Think not the struggle that draws near
Too terrible for man, nor fear
To meet the foe ;
Nor let thy noble spirit grieve,
Its life of glorious fame to leave
On earth below.

" A life of honor and of worth
Has no eternity on earth,
'T is but a name ;
And yet its glory far exceeds
That base and sensual life, which leads
To want and shame.

"The eternal life, beyond the sky,
Wealth cannot purchase, nor the high
And proud estate ;
The soul in dalliance laid, the spirit
Corrupt with sin, shall not inherit
A joy so great.

" But the good monk, in cloistered cell,
Shall gain it by his book and bell,
His prayers and tears ;
And the brave knight, whose arm en-
    dures
Fierce battle, and against the Moors
His standard rears.

" And thou, brave knight, whose hand has
    poured
The life-blood of the Pagan horde
O'er all the land,
In heaven shalt thou receive, at length,
The guerdon of thine earthly strength
And dauntless hand.

" Cheered onward by this promise sure,
Strong in the faith entire and pure
Thou dost profess,
Depart, thy hope is certainty,
The third, the better life on high
Shalt thou possess."

" O Death, no more, no more delay ;
My spirit longs to flee away,
And be at rest ;
The will of Heaven my will shall be,
I bow to the divine decree,
To God's behest.

" My soul is ready to depart,
No thought rebels, the obedient heart
Breathes forth no sigh ;
The wish on earth to linger still
Were vain, when 't is God's sovereign
    will
That we shall die.

" O thou, that for our sins didst take
A human form, and humbly make
Thy home on earth ;
Thou, that to thy divinity
A human nature didst ally
By mortal birth,

" And in that form didst suffer here
Torment, and agony, and fear,
So patiently ;
By thy redeeming grace alone,
And not for merits of my own,
Oh, pardon me ! "

As thus the dying warrior prayed,
Without one gathering mist or shade
Upon his mind ;

Encircled by his family,
Watched by affection's gentle eye
So soft and kind ;

His soul to Him who gave it rose ;
God lead it to its long repose,
Its glorious rest !
And, though the warrior's sun has set,
Its light shall linger round us yet,
Bright, radiant, blest.

SONNETS

I

THE GOOD SHEPHERD

(EL BUEN PASTOR)

BY LOPE DE VEGA

The five following sonnets are from the *Coplas de Manrique* volume, where they were printed with the Spanish text on the opposite pages. Two other sonnets in that volume, not retained when the volume was merged in *Voices of the Night*, will be found in the Appendix. The two Lope de Vega sonnets are from his *Rimas Sacras*.

SHEPHERD ! who with thine amorous, sylvan
    song
  Hast broken the slumber that encom-
    passed me,
  Who mad'st thy crook from the accursed
    tree,
  On which thy powerful arms were
    stretched so long !
Lead me to mercy's ever-flowing foun-
    tains ;
  For thou my shepherd, guard, and guide
    shalt be ;
  I will obey thy voice, and wait to see
  Thy feet all beautiful upon the moun-
    tains.
Hear, Shepherd ! thou who for thy flock
    art dying,
  Oh, wash away these scarlet sins, for
    thou
  Rejoicest at the contrite sinner's vow.
Oh, wait ! to thee my weary soul is cry-
    ing,
  Wait for me ! Yet why ask it, when I
    see,
  With feet nailed to the cross, thou 'rt
    waiting still for me !

II

TO-MORROW

(MAÑANA)

BY LOPE DE VEGA

LORD, what am I, that, with unceasing care,
　Thou didst seek after me, that thou didst
　　wait,
　Wet with unhealthy dews, before my
　　gate,
　And pass the gloomy nights of winter
　　there ?
Oh, strange delusion, that I did not greet
　Thy blest approach! and oh, to Heaven
　　how lost,
　If my ingratitude's unkindly frost
　Has chilled the bleeding wounds upon
　　thy feet!
How oft my guardian angel gently cried,
　"Soul, from thy casement look, and thou
　　shalt see
　How he persists to knock and wait for
　　thee!"
And, oh! how often to that voice of sorrow,
　"To-morrow we will open," I replied,
　And when the morrow came I answered
　　still, "To-morrow."

III

THE NATIVE LAND

(EL PATRIO CIELO)

BY FRANCISCO DE ALDANA

CLEAR fount of light! my native land on
　high,
　Bright with a glory that shall never
　　fade!
　Mansion of truth! without a veil or
　　shade,
　Thy holy quiet meets the spirit's eye.
There dwells the soul in its ethereal es-
　sence,
　Gasping no longer for life's feeble
　　breath ;
　But, sentinelled in heaven, its glorious
　　presence
　With pitying eye beholds, yet fears not,
　　death.

Beloved country ! banished from thy shore,
　A stranger in this prison-house of clay,
　The exiled spirit weeps and sighs for
　　thee !
Heavenward the bright perfections I adore
　Direct, and the sure promise cheers the
　　way,
　That, whither love aspires, there shall
　　my dwelling be.

IV

THE IMAGE OF GOD

(LA IMÁGEN DE DIOS)

BY FRANCISCO DE ALDANA

O LORD ! who seest, from yon starry
　height,
　Centred in one the future and the past,
　Fashioned in thine own image, see how
　　fast
　The world obscures in me what once was
　　bright !
Eternal Sun ! the warmth which thou hast
　given,
　To cheer life's flowery April, fast de-
　　cays ;
　Yet, in the hoary winter of my days,
　Forever green shall be my trust in
　　Heaven.
Celestial King ! oh let thy presence pass
　Before my spirit, and an image fair
　Shall meet that look of mercy from on
　　high,
As the reflected image in a glass
　Doth meet the look of him who seeks it
　　there,
　And owes its being to the gazer's eye.

V

THE BROOK

(Á UN ARROYUELO)

ANONYMOUS

LAUGH of the mountain ! — lyre of bird
　and tree !
　Pomp of the meadow ! mirror of the
　　morn !

The soul of April, unto whom are born
The rose and jessamine, leaps wild in
    thee!
Although, where'er thy devious current
    strays,
The lap of earth with gold and silver
    teems,
To me thy clear proceeding brighter
    seems
Than golden sands, that charm each
    shepherd's gaze.
How without guile thy bosom, all trans-
    parent
As the pure crystal, lets the curious eye
Thy secrets scan, thy smooth, round peb-
    bles count!
How, without malice murmuring, glides thy
    current!
O sweet simplicity of days gone by!
Thou shun'st the haunts of man, to dwell
    in limpid fount!

ANCIENT SPANISH BALLADS

In the chapter with this title in *Outre-Mer*, besides
illustrations from Byron and Lockhart are the three
following examples, contributed by Mr. Longfellow.

I

RIO VERDE, Rio Verde!
    Many a corpse is bathed in thee,
Both of Moors and eke of Christians,
    Slain with swords most cruelly.

And thy pure and crystal waters
    Dappled are with crimson gore;
For between the Moors and Christians
    Long has been the fight and sore.

Dukes and counts fell bleeding near thee,
    Lords of high renown were slain,
Perished many a brave hidalgo
    Of the noblemen of Spain.

II

"King Alfonso the Eighth, having exhausted his
treasury in war, wishes to lay a tax of five farthings
upon each of the Castilian hidalgos, in order to defray
the expenses of a journey from Burgos to Cuenca. This
proposition of the king was met with disdain by the
noblemen who had been assembled on the occasion."

DON NUNO, Count of Lara,
    In anger and in pride,
Forgot all reverence for the king,
    And thus in wrath replied:

"Our noble ancestors," quoth he,
    "Ne'er such a tribute paid;
Nor shall the king receive of us
    What they have once gainsaid.

"The base-born soul who deems it just
    May here with thee remain;
But follow me, ye cavaliers,
    Ye noblemen of Spain."

Forth followed they the noble Count,
    They marched to Glera's plain;
Out of three thousand gallant knights
    Did only three remain.

They tied the tribute to their spears,
    They raised it in the air,
And they sent to tell their lord the king
    That his tax was ready there.

"He may send and take by force," said
    they,
    "This paltry sum of gold;
But the goodly gift of liberty
    Cannot be bought and sold."

III

"One of the finest of the historic ballads is that
which describes Bernardo's march to Roncesvalles. He
sallies forth 'with three thousand Leonese and more,'
to protect the glory and freedom of his native land.
From all sides, the peasantry of the land flock to the
hero's standard."

THE peasant leaves his plough afield,
    The reaper leaves his hook,
And from his hand the shepherd-boy
    Lets fall the pastoral crook.

The young set up a shout of joy,
    The old forget their years,
The feeble man grows stout of heart,
    No more the craven fears.

All rush to Bernard's standard,
    And on liberty they call;
They cannot brook to wear the yoke,
    When threatened by the Gaul.

"Free were we born," 't is thus they cry,
    "And willingly pay we
The duty that we owe our king,
    By the divine decree.

"But God forbid that we obey
    The laws of foreign knaves,

Tarnish the glory of our sires,
And make our children slaves.

"Our hearts have not so craven grown,
So bloodless all our veins,
So vigorless our brawny arms,
As to submit to chains.

"Has the audacious Frank, forsooth,
Subdued these seas and lands?
Shall he a bloodless victory have?
No, not while we have hands.

"He shall learn that the gallant Leonese
Can bravely fight and fall,
But that they know not how to yield;
They are Castilians all.

"Was it for this the Roman power
Of old was made to yield
Unto Numantia's valiant hosts
On many a bloody field?

"Shall the bold lions that have bathed
Their paws in Libyan gore,
Crouch basely to a feebler foe,
And dare the strife no more?

"Let the false king sell town and tower,
But not his vassals free;
For to subdue the free-born soul
No royal power hath he!"

VIDA DE SAN MILLAN

BY GONZALO DE BERCEO

AND when the kings were in the field, —
their squadrons in array, —
With lance in rest they onward pressed to
mingle in the fray;
But soon upon the Christians fell a terror
of their foes, —
These were a numerous army, — a little
handful those.

And while the Christian people stood in
this uncertainty,
Upward to heaven they turned their eyes,
and fixed their thoughts on high;
And there two figures they beheld, all
beautiful and bright,
Even than the pure new-fallen snow their
garments were more white.

They rode upon two horses more white
than crystal sheen,
And arms they bore such as before no
mortal man had seen;
The one, he held a crosier, — a pontiff's
mitre wore;
The other held a crucifix, — such man ne'er
saw before.

Their faces were angelical, celestial forms
had they, —
And downward through the fields of air
they urged their rapid way;
They looked upon the Moorish host with
fierce and angry look,
And in their hands, with dire portent, their
naked sabres shook.

The Christian host, beholding this, straight-
way take heart again;
They fall upon their bended knees, all rest-
ing on the plain,
And each one with his clenchèd fist to
smite his breast begins,
And promises to God on high he will for-
sake his sins.

And when the heavenly knights drew near
unto the battle-ground,
They dashed among the Moors and dealt
unerring blows around;
Such deadly havoc there they made the
foremost ranks along,
A panic terror spread unto the hindmost of
the throng.

Together with these two good knights, the
champions of the sky,
The Christians rallied and began to smite
full sore and high;
The Moors raised up their voices and by
the Koran swore
That in their lives such deadly fray they
ne'er had seen before.

Down went the misbelievers, — fast sped
the bloody fight, —
Some ghastly and dismembered lay, and
some half dead with fright:
Full sorely they repented that to the field
they came,
For they saw that from the battle they
should retreat with shame.

Another thing befell them, — they dreamed
    not of such woes, —
The very arrows that the Moors shot from
    their twanging bows
Turned back against them in their flight
    and wounded them full sore,
And every blow they dealt the foe was
    paid in drops of gore.

.   .   .   .

Now he that bore the crosier, and the papal
    crown had on,
Was the glorified Apostle, the brother of
    Saint John ;
And he that held the crucifix, and wore the
    monkish hood,
Was the holy San Millan of Cogolla's neigh-
    borhood.

SAN MIGUEL, THE CONVENT

(SAN MIGUEL DE LA TUMBA)

BY GONZALO DE BERCEO

SAN MIGUEL DE LA TUMBA is a convent
    vast and wide ;
The sea encircles it around, and groans on
    every side :
It is a wild and dangerous place, and many
    woes betide
The monks who in that burial-place in pen-
    itence abide.

Within those dark monastic walls, amid the
    ocean flood,
Of pious, fasting monks there dwelt a holy
    brotherhood ;
To the Madonna's glory there an altar high
    was placed,
And a rich and costly image the sacred
    altar graced.

Exalted high upon a throne, the Virgin
    Mother smiled,
And, as the custom is, she held within her
    arms the Child ;
The kings and wise men of the East were
    kneeling by her side ;
Attended was she like a queen whom God
    had sanctified.

.   .   .   .

Descending low before her face a screen of
    feathers hung, —
A *moscader*, or fan for flies, 't is called in
    vulgar tongue ;

From the feathers of the peacock's wing
    't was fashioned bright and fair,
And glistened like the heaven above when
    all its stars are there.

It chanced that, for the people's sins, fell
    the lightning's blasting stroke :
Forth from all four the sacred walls the
    flames consuming broke ;
The sacred robes were all consumed, missal
    and holy book ;
And hardly with their lives the monks their
    crumbling walls forsook.

.   .   .   .

But though the desolating flame raged
    fearfully and wild,
It did not reach the Virgin Queen, it did not
    reach the Child ;
It did not reach the feathery screen before
    her face that shone,
Nor injure in a farthing's worth the image
    or the throne.

The image it did not consume, it did not
    burn the screen ;
Even in the value of a hair they were not
    hurt, I ween ;
Not even the smoke did reach them, nor in-
    jure more the shrine
Than the bishop hight Don Tello has been
    hurt by hand of mine.

.   .   .   .

SONG

SHE is a maid of artless grace,
Gentle in form, and fair of face.

Tell me, thou ancient mariner,
    That sailest on the sea,
If ship, or sail, or evening star
    Be half so fair as she !

Tell me, thou gallant cavalier,
    Whose shining arms I see,
If steel, or sword, or battle-field
    Be half so fair as she !

Tell me, thou swain, that guard'st thy
    flock
    Beneath the shadowy tree,
If flock, or vale, or mountain-ridge
    Be half so fair as she !

SANTA TERESA'S BOOK–MARK

(LETRILLA QUE LLEVABA POR REGISTRO EN SU BREVIARIO)

BY SANTA TERESA DE AVILA

LET nothing disturb thee,
Nothing affright thee ;
All things are passing ;
God never changeth ;
Patient endurance
Attaineth to all things ;
Who God possesseth
In nothing is wanting ;
Alone God sufficeth.

FROM THE CANCIONEROS

The main repository of these poems is Ochoa's *Tesoro de los Romanceros y Cancioneros Españoles*, Paris, 1838. See also *Antológia Española*. Mr. Longfellow published his translations in the volume entitled *Aftermath*, 1873. His acquaintance with these Spanish popular songs was an early one, for there is an entry in his journal, when at Dresden, February 1, 1829 : "At the Public Library in the morning till one o'clock. Found a very curious old Spanish book, treating of the troubadour poetry of Spain, entitled the *Cancionero General*."

I

EYES SO TRISTFUL, EYES SO TRISTFUL

(OJOS TRISTES, OJOS TRISTES)

BY DIEGO DE SALDAÑA

EYES so tristful, eyes so tristful,
Heart so full of care and cumber,
I was lapped in rest and slumber,
Ye have made me wakeful, wistful !
In this life of labor endless
Who shall comfort my distresses ?
Querulous my soul and friendless
In its sorrow shuns caresses.
Ye have made me, ye have made me
Querulous of you, that care not,
Eyes so tristful, yet I dare not
Say to what ye have betrayed me.

II

SOME DAY, SOME DAY

(ALGUNA VEZ)

BY CRISTÓBAL DE GASTILLEJO

SOME day, some day,
O troubled breast,
Shalt thou find rest.
If Love in thee

To grief give birth,
Six feet of earth
Can more than he ;
There calm and free
And unoppressed
Shalt thou find rest.

The unattained
In life at last,
When life is passed,
Shall all be gained ;
And no more pained,
No more distressed,
Shalt thou find rest.

III

COME, O DEATH, SO SILENT FLYING

(VEN, MUERTE TAN ESCONDIDA)

BY EL COMMENDADOR ESCRIVA

COME, O Death, so silent flying
That unheard thy coming be,
Lest the sweet delight of dying
Bring life back again to me.
For thy sure approach perceiving.
In my constancy and pain
I new life should win again,
Thinking that I am not living.
So to me, unconscious lying,
All unknown thy coming be,
Lest the sweet delight of dying
Bring life back again to me.
Unto him who finds thee hateful,
Death, thou art inhuman pain ;
But to me, who dying gain,
Life is but a task ungrateful.
Come, then, with my wish complying,
All unheard thy coming be,
Lest the sweet delight of dying
Bring life back again to me.

IV

GLOVE OF BLACK IN WHITE HAND BARE

GLOVE of black in white hand bare,
And about her forehead pale
Wound a thin, transparent veil,
That doth not conceal her hair ;
Sovereign attitude and air,
Cheek and neck alike displayed,
With coquettish charms arrayed,
Laughing eyes and fugitive ; —
This is killing men that live,
'T is not mourning for the dead.

FROM THE SWEDISH AND DANISH

Mr. Longfellow spent the summer of 1835 in Sweden, where he occupied himself with the study of the language and literature, and with travel and observations of Swedish character. "The Swedish language," he wrote, "is soft and musical, with an accent like the lowland Scotch. It is an easy language to read, but difficult to speak with correctness, owing to some grammatical peculiarities. . . . Sweden has one great poet, and only one. That is Tegnér, Bishop of Wexiö, who is still living. His noblest work is *Frithiof's Saga*, a heroic poem, founded on an old tradition." After his return to America, Mr. Longfellow wrote an article on the poem for the *North American Review*, giving in it the translations which are placed first in this section.

His friend Mr. Samuel Ward four years later urged him to translate another of Tegnér's poems, of which Mr. Longfellow had shown him a brief specimen ; and in reply Mr. Longfellow wrote, under date of October 24, 1841 : "How strange! While you are urging me to translate *Nattvardsbarnen* [*The Children of the Lord's Supper*] comes a letter from Bishop Tegnér himself, saying that of all the translations he has seen of *Frithiof*, my fragments are the only attempts 'that have *fully* satisfied him.' 'The only fault,' he says, 'that I can find with your translation is, that it is not complete. I take the liberty of urging you to complete the task, that I may be able to say that *Frithiof* has

been translated into at least one language.' Highly complimentary is the Bishop to my humble endeavor. . . . After this kind letter, can I do less than over-set the *Nattvardsbarnen ?*" In his willingness, he at once set about the translation, and wrote his friend, November 6th : "It is Saturday night, and eight by the village clock. I have just finished the translation of *The Children of the Lord's Supper ;* and with the very ink that wrote the last words of it, I commence this letter to you. That it is with the same pen, too, this chirography sufficiently makes manifest. With your permission I will mend that. The poem is indeed very beautiful ; and in parts so touching that more than once in translating it I was blinded with tears. Perhaps my weakness makes the poet strong. You shall soon judge." In the introduction to the volume containing the poem, Mr. Longfellow made the following remarks regarding his translation : —

"The translation is literal, perhaps to a fault. In no instance have I done the author a wrong by introducing into his work any supposed improvements or embellishments of my own. I have preserved even the measure, that inexorable hexameter, in which, it must be confessed, the motions of the English muse are not unlike those of a prisoner dancing to the music of his chains, and perhaps, as Dr. Johnson said of the dancing dog, 'the wonder is not that she should do it so well, but that she should do it at all.'"

PASSAGES FROM FRITHIOF'S SAGA

BY ESAIAS TEGNÉR

I

FRITHIOF'S HOMESTEAD

THREE miles extended around the fields of the homestead, on three sides
Valleys and mountains and hills, but on the fourth side was the ocean.
Birch woods crowned the summits, but down the slope of the hillsides
Flourished the golden corn, and man-high was waving the rye-field.
Lakes, full many in number, their mirror held up for the mountains,
Held for the forests up, in whose depths the high-horned reindeer
Had their kingly walk, and drank of a hundred brooklets.
But in the valleys widely around, there fed on the greensward
Herds with shining hides and udders that longed for the milk-pail.
'Mid these scattered, now here and now there, were numberless flocks of
Sheep with fleeces white, as thou seest the white-looking stray clouds,
Flock-wise spread o'er the heavenly vault, when it bloweth in spring-time.

Coursers two times twelve, all mettlesome, fast fettered storm-winds,
Stamping stood in the line of stalls, and tugged at their fodder.
Knotted with red were their manes, and their hoofs all white with steel shoes.
Th' banquet-hall, a house by itself, was timbered of hard fir.
Not five hundred men (at ten times twelve to the hundred)
Filled up the roomy hall, when assembled for drinking, at Yule-tide.
Thorough the hall, as long as it was, went a table of holm-oak,
Polished and white, as of steel ; the columns twain of the High-seat
Stood at the end thereof, two gods carved out of an elm-tree ;
Odin with lordly look, and Frey with the sun on his frontlet.
Lately between the two, on a bear-skin (the skin it was coal-black,
Scarlet-red was the throat, but the paws were shodden with silver),
Thorsten sat with his friends, Hospitality sitting with Gladness.
Oft, when the moon through the cloud-rack flew, related the old man
Wonders from distant lands he had seen, and cruises of Vikings
Far away on the Baltic, and Sea of the West, and the White Sea.

Hushed sat the listening bench, and their
glances hung on the graybeard's
Lips, as a bee on the rose ; but the Scald
was thinking of Brage,
Where, with his silver beard, and runes on
his tongue, he is seated
Under the leafy beech, and tells a tradition
by Mimer's
Ever-murmuring wave, himself a living
tradition.
Midway the floor (with thatch was it
strewn) burned ever the fire-flame
Glad on its stone-built hearth ; and thor-
ough the wide-mouthed smoke-flue
Looked the stars, those heavenly friends,
down into the great hall.
Round the walls, upon nails of steel, were
hanging in order
Breastplate and helmet together, and here
and there among them
Downward lightened a sword, as in winter
evening a star shoots.
More than helmets and swords the shields
in the hall were resplendent,
White as the orb of the sun, or white as
the moon's disk of silver.
·Ever and anon went a maid round the
board, and filled up the drink-horns,
Ever she cast down her eyes and blushed ;
in the shield her reflection
Blushed, too, even as she ; this gladdened
the drinking champions.

II

A SLEDGE-RIDE ON THE ICE

KING RING with his queen to the banquet
did fare,
On the lake stood the ice so mirror-clear.

"Fare not o'er the ice," the stranger
cries ;
"It will burst, and full deep the cold bath
lies."

"The king drowns not easily," Ring out-
spake ;
"He who's afraid may go round the lake."

Threatening and dark looked the stranger
round,
His steel shoes with haste on his feet he
bound.

The sledge-horse starts forth strong and
free ;
He snorteth flames, so glad is he.

"Strike out," screamed the king, "my
trotter good,
Let us see if thou art of Sleipner's blood."

They go as a storm goes over the lake,
No heed to his queen doth the old man
take.

But the steel-shod champion standeth not
still,
He passeth them by as swift as he will.

He carves many runes in the frozen tide,
Fair Ingeborg o'er her own name doth
glide.

III

FRITHIOF'S TEMPTATION

SPRING is coming, birds are twittering,
forests leaf, and smiles the sun,
And the loosened torrents downward, sing-
ing, to the ocean run ;
Glowing like the cheek of Freya, peeping
rosebuds 'gin to ope,
And in human hearts awaken love of life,
and joy, and hope.

Now will hunt the ancient monarch, and
the queen shall join the sport :
Swarming in its gorgeous splendor, is as-
sembled all the court ;
Bows ring loud, and quivers rattle, stallions
paw the ground alway,
And, with hoods upon their eyelids, scream
the falcons for their prey.

See, the Queen of the chase advances !
Frithiof, gaze not at the sight !
Like a star upon a spring-cloud sits she on
her palfrey white.
Half of Freya, half of Rota, yet more
beauteous than these two,
And from her light hat of purple wave
aloft the feathers blue.

Gaze not at her eyes' blue heaven, gaze
not at her golden hair !
Oh beware ! her waist is slender, full her
bosom is, beware !

Look not at the rose and lily on her cheek
    that shifting play,
List not to the voice beloved, whispering
    like the wind of May.

Now the huntsman's band is ready. Hur-
    rah ! over hill and dale !
Horns ring, and the hawks right upward
    to the hall of Odin sail.
All the dwellers in the forest seek in fear
    their cavern homes,
But, with spear outstretched before her,
    after them the Valkyr comes.

. . . .

Then threw Frithiof down his mantle, and
    upon the greensward spread,
And the ancient king so trustful laid on
    Frithiof's knee his head,
Slept as calmly as the hero sleepeth, after
    war's alarm,
On his shield, or as an infant sleeps upon
    its mother's arm.

As he slumbers, hark ! there sings a coal-
    black bird upon the bough ;
" Hasten, Frithiof, slay the old man, end
    your quarrel at a blow :
Take his queen, for she is thine, and once
    the bridal kiss she gave,
Now no human eye beholds thee, deep and
    silent is the grave."

Frithiof listens ; hark ! there sings a snow-
    white bird upon the bough :
" Though no human eye beholds thee,
    Odin's eye beholds thee now.
Coward ! wilt thou murder sleep, and a
    defenceless old man slay !
Whatsoe'er thou winn'st, thou canst not
    win a hero's fame this way."

Thus the two wood-birds did warble :
    Frithiof took his war-sword good,
With a shudder hurled it from him, far
    into the gloomy wood.
Coal-black bird flies down to Nastrand, but
    on light, unfolded wings,
Like the tone of harps, the other, sounding
    towards the sun, upsprings.

Straight the ancient king awakens. " Sweet
    has been my sleep," he said ;
" Pleasantly sleeps one in the shadow,
    guarded by a brave man's blade.

But where is thy sword, O stranger ?
    Lightning's brother, where is he ?
Who thus parts you, who should never
    from each other parted be ! "

"It avails not," Frithiof answered ; " in
    the North are other swords :
Sharp, O monarch ! is the sword's tongue,
    and it speaks not peaceful words ;
Murky spirits dwell in steel blades, spirits
    from the Niffelhem ;
Slumber is not safe before them, silver
    locks but anger them."

IV

FRITHIOF'S FAREWELL

No more shall I see
In its upward motion
The smoke of the Northland. Man is a
    slave :
The fates decree.
On the waste of the ocean
There is my fatherland, there is my grave.

Go not to the strand,
Ring, with thy bride,
After the stars spread their light through
    the sky.
Perhaps in the sand,
Washed up by the tide,
The bones of the outlawed Viking may lie.

Then, quoth the king,
" 'T is mournful to hear
A man like a whimpering maiden cry.
The death-song they sing
Even now in mine ear.
What avails it ? He who is born must
    die."

THE CHILDREN OF THE LORD'S SUPPER

BY ESAIAS TEGNÉR

PENTECOST, day of rejoicing, had come.
    The church of the village
Gleaming stood in the morning's sheen.
    On the spire of the belfry,
Decked with a brazen cock, the friendly
    flames of the Spring-sun

Glanced like the tongues of fire, beheld by
Apostles aforetime.
Clear was the heaven and blue, and May,
with her cap crowned with roses,
Stood in her holiday dress in the fields, and
the wind and the brooklet
Murmured gladness and peace, God's-
peace ! with lips rosy-tinted
Whispered the race of the flowers, and
merry on balancing branches
Birds were singing their carol, a jubilant
hymn to the Highest.
Swept and clean was the churchyard.
Adorned like a leaf-woven arbor
Stood its old-fashioned gate ; and within
upon each cross of iron
Hung was a fragrant garland, new twined
by the hands of affection.
Even the dial, that stood on a mound among
the departed,
(There full a hundred years had it stood,)
was embellished with blossoms.
Like to the patriarch hoary, the sage of his
kith and the hamlet,
Who on his birthday is crowned by children
and children's children,
So stood the ancient prophet, and mute
with his pencil of iron
Marked on the tablet of stone, and mea-
sured the time and its changes,
While all around at his feet, an eternity
slumbered in quiet.
Also the church within was adorned, for
this was the season
When the young, their parents' hope, and
the loved-ones of heaven,
Should at the foot of the altar renew the
vows of their baptism.
Therefore each nook and corner was swept
and cleaned, and the dust was
Blown from the walls and ceiling, and
from the oil-painted benches.
There stood the church like a garden ; the
Feast of the Leafy Pavilions
Saw we in living presentment. From noble
arms on the church wall
Grew forth a cluster of leaves, and the
preacher's pulpit of oak-wood
Budded once more anew, as aforetime the
rod before Aaron.
Wreathed thereon was the Bible with
leaves, and the dove, washed with
silver,
Under its canopy fastened, had on it a
necklace of wind-flowers.

But in front of the choir, round the altar-
piece painted by Hörberg,
Crept a garland gigantic ; and bright-curl-
ing tresses of angels
Peeped, like the sun from a cloud, from
out of the shadowy leaf-work.
Likewise the lustre of brass, new-polished,
blinked from the ceiling,
And for lights there were lilies of Pentecost
set in the sockets.

Loud rang the bells already ; the throng-
ing crowd was assembled
Far from valleys and hills, to list to the
holy preaching.
Hark ! then roll forth at once the mighty
tones of the organ,
Hover like voices from God, aloft like
invisible spirits.
Like as Elias in heaven, when he cast from
off him his mantle,
So cast off the soul its garments of earth ;
and with one voice
Chimed in the congregation, and sang an
anthem immortal
Of the sublime Wallín, of David's harp in
the North-land
Tuned to the choral of Luther ; the song
on its mighty pinions
Took every living soul, and lifted it gently
to heaven,
And each face did shine like the Holy One's
face upon Tabor.
Lo ! there entered then into the church the
Reverend Teacher.
Father he hight and he was in the parish ;
a Christianly plainness
Clothed from his head to his feet the old
man of seventy winters.
Friendly was he to behold, and glad as the
heralding angel
Walked he among the crowds, but still a
contemplative grandeur
Lay on his forehead as clear as on moss-
covered gravestone a sunbeam.
As in his inspiration (an evening twilight
that faintly
Gleams in the human soul, even now, from
the day of creation)
Th' Artist, the friend of heaven, imagines
Saint John when in Patmos,
Gray, with his eyes uplifted to heaven, so
seemed then the old man ;
Such was the glance of his eye, and such
were his tresses of silver.

All the congregation arose in the pews that
were numbered.
But with a cordial look, to the right and
the left hand, the old man
Nodding all hail and peace, disappeared in
the innermost chancel.

Simply and solemnly now proceeded the
Christian service,
Singing and prayer, and at last an ardent
discourse from the old man.
Many a moving word and warning, that out
of the heart came,
Fell like the dew of the morning, like
manna on those in the desert.
Then, when all was finished, the Teacher
reëntered the chancel,
Followed therein by the young. The boys
on the right had their places,
Delicate figures, with close-curling hair
and cheeks rosy-blooming.
But on the left of these there stood the
tremulous lilies,
Tinged with the blushing light of the dawn,
the diffident maidens, —
Folding their hands in prayer, and their
eyes cast down on the pavement.
Now came, with question and answer, the
catechism. In the beginning
Answered the children with troubled and
faltering voice, but the old man's
Glances of kindness encouraged them soon,
and the doctrines eternal
Flowed, like the waters of fountains, so
clear from lips unpolluted.
Each time the answer was closed, and as
oft as they named the Redeemer,
Lowly louted the boys, and lowly the maid-
ens all courtesied.
Friendly the Teacher stood, like an angel
of light there among them,
And to the children explained the holy, the
highest, in few words,
Thorough, yet simple and clear, for sublim-
ity always is simple,
Both in sermon and song, a child can seize
on its meaning.
E'en as the green-growing bud unfolds
when Springtide approaches,
Leaf by leaf puts forth, and, warmed by
the radiant sunshine,
Blushes with purple and gold, till at last the
perfected blossom
Opens its odorous chalice, and rocks with
its crown in the breezes,

So was unfolded here the Christian lore of
salvation,
Line by line from the soul of childhood. The
fathers and mothers
Stood behind them in tears, and were glad
at the well-worded answer.

Now went the old man up to the altar ;
— and straightway transfigured
(So did it seem unto me) was then the af-
fectionate Teacher.
Like the Lord's Prophet sublime, and awful
as Death and as Judgment
Stood he, the God-commissioned, the
soul-searcher, earthward descend-
ing.
Glances, sharp as a sword, into hearts that
to him were transparent
Shot he ; his voice was deep, was low like
the thunder afar off.
So on a sudden transfigured he stood there,
he spake and he questioned.

"This is the faith of the Fathers, the
faith the Apostles delivered,
This is moreover the faith whereunto I
baptized you, while still ye
Lay on your mothers' breasts, and nearer
the portals of heaven.
Slumbering received you then the Holy
Church in its bosom ;
Wakened from sleep are ye now, and the
light in its radiant splendor
Downward rains from the heaven ; — to-day
on the threshold of childhood
Kindly she frees you again, to examine and
make your election,
For she knows naught of compulsion, and
only conviction desireth.
This is the hour of your trial, the turning-
point of existence,
Seed for the coming days ; without revo-
cation departeth
Now from your lips the confession. Bethink
ye, before ye make answer !
Think not, oh think not with guile to de-
ceive the questioning Teacher.
Sharp is his eye to-day, and a curse ever
rests upon falsehood.
Enter not with a lie on Life's journey ; the
multitude hears you,
Brothers and sisters and parents, what dear
upon earth is and holy
Standeth before your sight as a witness ;
the Judge everlasting

Looks from the sun down upon you, and
    angels in waiting beside him
Grave your confession in letters of fire
    upon tablets eternal.
Thus, then, — believe ye in God, in the
    Father who this world created ?
Him who redeemed it, the Son, and the
    Spirit where both are united ?
Will ye promise me here, (a holy promise !)
    to cherish
God more than all things earthly, and every
    man as a brother ?
Will ye promise me here, to confirm your
    faith by your living,
Th' heavenly faith of affection ! to hope, to
    forgive, and to suffer,
Be what it may your condition, and walk
    before God in uprightness ?
Will ye promise me this before God and
    man ?" — With a clear voice
Answered the young men Yes ! and Yes !
    with lips softly-breathing
Answered the maidens eke. Then dis-
    solved from the brow of the Teacher
Clouds with the lightnings therein, and he
    spake in accents more gentle,
Soft as the evening's breath, as harps by
    Babylon's rivers.

"Hail, then, hail to you all ! To the
    heirdom of heaven be ye welcome !
Children no more from this day, but by
    covenant brothers and sisters !
Yet, — for what reason not children ? Of
    such is the kingdom of heaven.
Here upon earth an assemblage of children,
    in heaven one Father,
Ruling them all as his household, — for-
    giving in turn and chastising,
That is of human life a picture, as Scripture
    has taught us.
Blest are the pure before God ! Upon pur-
    ity and upon virtue
Resteth the Christian Faith ; she herself
    from on high is descended.
Strong as a man and pure as a child, is the
    sum of the doctrine,
Which the Divine One taught, and suffered
    and died on the cross for.
Oh, as ye wander this day from childhood's
    sacred asylum
Downward, and ever downward, and deeper
    in Age's chill valley,
Oh, how soon will ye come, — too soon ! —
    and long to turn backward

Up to its hill-tops again, to the sun-illu-
    mined, where Judgment
Stood like a father before you, and Pardon,
    clad like a mother,
Gave you her hand to kiss, and the loving
    heart was forgiven,
Life was a play and your hands grasped
    after the roses of heaven !
Seventy years have I lived already ; the
    Father eternal
Gave me gladness and care ; but the loveli-
    est hours of existence,
When I have steadfastly gazed in their
    eyes, I have instantly known them,
Known them all again ; — they were my
    childhood's acquaintance.
Therefore take from henceforth, as guides
    in the paths of existence,
Prayer, with her eyes raised to heaven,
    and Innocence, bride of man's child-
    hood.
Innocence, child beloved, is a guest from
    the world of the blessed,
Beautiful, and in her hand a lily ; on life's
    roaring billows
Swings she in safety, she heedeth them not,
    in the ship she is sleeping.
Calmly she gazes around in the turmoil of
    men ; in the desert
Angels descend and minister unto her ; she
    herself knoweth
Naught of her glorious attendance ; but
    follows faithful and humble,
Follows so long as she may her friend ; oh
    do not reject her,
For she cometh from God and she holdeth
    the keys of the heavens.
Prayer is Innocence' friend ; and willingly
    flieth incessant
'Twixt the earth and the sky, the carrier-
    pigeon of heaven.
Son of Eternity, fettered in Time, and an
    exile, the Spirit
Tugs at his chains evermore, and struggles
    like flame ever upward.
Still he recalls with emotion his Father's
    manifold mansions,
Thinks of the land of his fathers, where blos-
    somed more freshly the flowerets,
Shone a more beautiful sun, and he played
    with the wingèd angels.
Then grows the earth too narrow, too close ;
    and homesick for heaven
Longs the wanderer again ; and the
    Spirit's longings are worship ;

Worship is called his most beautiful hour,
    and its tongue is entreaty.
Ah! when the infinite burden of life de-
    scendeth upon us,
Crushes to earth our hope, and, under the
    earth, in the graveyard,
Then it is good to pray unto God; for his
    sorrowing children
Turns He ne'er from his door, but He heals
    and helps and consoles them.
Yet is it better to pray when all things are
    prosperous with us,
Pray in fortunate days, for life's most
    beautiful Fortune
Kneels before the Eternal's throne; and
    with hands interfolded,
Praises thankful and moved the only giver
    of blessings.
Or do ye know, ye children, one blessing
    that comes not from Heaven?
What has mankind forsooth, the poor! that
    it has not received?
Therefore, fall in the dust and pray! The
    seraphs adoring
Cover with pinions six their face in the
    glory of Him who
Hung his masonry pendent on naught, when
    the world He created.
Earth declareth his might, and the firma-
    ment utters his glory.
Races blossom and die, and stars fall
    downward from heaven,
Downward like withered leaves; at the
    last stroke of midnight, millenniums
Lay themselves down at his feet, and He
    sees them, but counts them as no-
    thing.
Who shall stand in his presence? The
    wrath of the Judge is terrific,
Casting the insolent down at a glance.
    When He speaks in his anger
Hillocks skip like the kid, and mountains
    leap like the roebuck.
Yet, — why are ye afraid, ye children?
    This awful avenger,
Ah! is a merciful God! God's voice was
    not in the earthquake,
Not in the fire, nor the storm, but it was
    in the whispering breezes.
Love is the root of creation; God's essence;
    worlds without number
Lie in his bosom like children; He made
    them for this purpose only.
Only to love and to be loved again, He
    breathed forth his spirit

Into the slumbering dust, and upright
    standing, it laid its
Hand on its heart, and felt it was warm
    with a flame out of heaven.
Quench, oh quench not that flame! It is
    the breath of your being.
Love is life, but hatred is death. Not
    father nor mother
Loved you, as God has loved you; for
    't was that you may be happy
Gave He his only Son. When He bowed
    down his head in the death-hour
Solemnized Love its triumph; the sacrifice
    then was completed.
Lo! then was rent on a sudden the veil of
    the temple, dividing
Earth and heaven apart, and the dead from
    their sepulchres rising
Whispered with pallid lips and low in the
    ears of each other
Th' answer, but dreamed of before, to cre-
    ation's enigma, — Atonement!
Depths of Love are Atonement's depths,
    for Love is Atonement.
Therefore, child of mortality, love thou
    the merciful Father;
Wish what the Holy One wishes, and not
    from fear, but affection;
Fear is the virtue of slaves; but the heart
    that loveth is willing;
Perfect was before God, and perfect is
    Love, and Love only.
Lovest thou God as thou oughtest, then
    lovest thou likewise thy brethren;
One is the sun in heaven, and one, only one,
    is Love also.
Bears not each human figure the godlike
    stamp on his forehead?
Readest thou not in his face thine origin?
    Is he not sailing
Lost like thyself on an ocean unknown, and
    is he not guided
By the same stars that guide thee? Why
    shouldst thou hate then thy bro-
    ther?
Hateth he thee, forgive! For 't is sweet
    to stammer one letter
Of the Eternal's language; — on earth it
    is callèd Forgiveness!
Knowest thou Him, who forgave, with the
    crown of thorns on his temples?
Earnestly prayed for his foes, for his mur-
    derers? Say, dost thou know Him?
Ah! thou confessest his name, so follow
    likewise his example,

Think of thy brother no ill, but throw a veil over his failings,
Guide the erring aright ; for the good, the heavenly shepherd
Took the lost lamb in his arms, and bore it back to its mother.
This is the fruit of Love, and it is by its fruits that we know it.
Love is the creature's welfare, with God ; but Love among mortals
Is but an endless sigh ! He longs, and endures, and stands waiting,
Suffers and yet rejoices, and smiles with tears on his eyelids.
Hope, — so is called upon earth his recompense, — Hope, the befriending,
Does what she can, for she points evermore up to heaven, and faithful
Plunges her anchor's peak in the depths of the grave, and beneath it
Paints a more beautiful world, a dim, but a sweet play of shadows !
Races, better than we, have leaned on her wavering promise,
Having naught else but Hope. Then praise we our Father in heaven,
Him, who has given us more ; for to us has Hope been transfigured,
Groping no longer in night ; she is Faith, she is living assurance.
Faith is enlightened Hope ; she is light, is the eye of affection,
Dreams of the longing interprets, and carves their visions in marble.
Faith is the sun of life ; and her countenance shines like the Hebrew's,
For she has looked upon God ; the heaven on its stable foundation
Draws she with chains down to earth, and the New Jerusalem sinketh
Splendid with portals twelve in golden vapors descending.
There enraptured she wanders, and looks at the figures majestic,
Fears not the wingèd crowd, in the midst of them all is her homestead.
Therefore love and believe ; for works will follow spontaneous
Even as day does the sun ; the Right from the Good is an offspring,
Love in a bodily shape ; and Christian works are no more than
Animate Love and Faith, as flowers are the animate Springtide.

Works do follow us all unto God ; there stand and bear witness
Not what they seemed, — but what they were only. Blessed is he who
Hears their confession secure ; they are mute upon earth until death's hand
Opens the mouth of the silent. Ye children, does Death e'er alarm you ?
Death is the brother of Love, twin-brother is he, and is only
More austere to behold. With a kiss upon lips that are fading
Takes he the soul and departs, and, rocked in the arms of affection,
Places the ransomed child, new born, 'fore the face of its father.
Sounds of his coming already I hear, — see dimly his pinions,
Swart as the night, but with stars strewn upon them ! I fear not before him.
Death is only release, and in mercy is mute. On his bosom
Freer breathes, in its coolness, my breast ; and face to face standing
Look I on God as He is, a sun unpolluted by vapors ;
Look on the light of the ages I loved, the spirits majestic,
Nobler, better than I ; they stand by the throne all transfigured,
Vested in white, and with harps of gold, and are singing an anthem,
Writ in the climate of heaven, in the language spoken by angels.
You, in like manner, ye children beloved, He one day shall gather,
Never forgets He the weary ; — then welcome, ye loved ones hereafter !
Meanwhile forget not the keeping of vows, forget not the promise,
Wander from holiness onward to holiness ; earth shall ye heed not ;
Earth is but dust and heaven is light ; I have pledged you to heaven.
God of the universe, hear me ! thou fountain of Love everlasting,
Hark to the voice of thy servant ! I send up my prayer to thy heaven !
Let me hereafter not miss at thy throne one spirit of all these,
Whom thou hast given me here ! I have loved them all like a father.
May they bear witness for me, that I taught them the way of salvation,

Faithful, so far as I knew, of thy word ;
    again may they know me,
Fall on their Teacher's breast, and before
    thy face may I place them,
Pure as they now are, but only more tried,
    and exclaiming with gladness,
Father, lo! I am here, and the children,
    whom thou hast given me ! "

Weeping he spake in these words ; and
    now at the beck of the old man
Knee against knee they knitted a wreath
    round the altar's enclosure.
Kneeling he read then the prayers of the
    consecration, and softly
With him the children read ; at the close,
    with tremulous accents,
Asked he the peace of Heaven, a benedic-
    tion upon them.
Now should have ended his task for the
    day ; the following Sunday
Was for the young appointed to eat of the
    Lord's holy Supper.
Sudden, as struck from the clouds, stood
    the Teacher silent and laid his
Hand on his forehead, and cast his looks
    upward ; while thoughts high and
    holy
Flew through the midst of his soul, and his
    eyes glanced with wonderful bright-
    ness.
" On the next Sunday, who knows ! perhaps
    I shall rest in the graveyard !
Some one perhaps of yourselves, a lily
    broken untimely,
Bow down his head to the earth ; why de-
    lay I ? the hour is accomplished.
Warm is the heart ; — I will ! for to-day
    grows the harvest of heaven.
What I began accomplish I now ; what
    failing therein is
I, the old man, will answer to God and the
    reverend father.
Say to me only, ye children, ye denizens
    new-come in heaven,
Are ye ready this day to eat of the bread
    of Atonement ?
What it denoteth, that know ye full well,
    I have told it you often.
Of the new covenant symbol it is, of Atone-
    ment a token,
Stablished between earth and heaven.
    Man by his sins and transgressions
Far has wandered from God. from his es-
    sence.   'T was in the beginning

Fast by the Tree of Knowledge he fell, and
    it hangs its crown o'er the
Fall to this day ; in the Thought is the Fall ;
    in the Heart the Atonement.
Infinite is the fall, — the Atonement infinite
    likewise.
See ! behind me, as far as the old man re-
    members, and forward,
Far as Hope in her flight can reach with
    her wearied pinions,
Sin and Atonement incessant go through the
    lifetime of mortals,
Sin is brought forth full-grown ; but Atone-
    ment sleeps in our bosoms
Still as the cradled babe ; and dreams of
    heaven and of angels,
Cannot awake to sensation ; is like the
    tones in the harp's strings,
Spirits imprisoned, that wait evermore the
    deliverer's finger.
Therefore, ye children beloved, descended
    the Prince of Atonement,
Woke the slumberer from sleep, and she
    stands now with eyes all resplen-
    dent,
Bright as the vault of the sky, and battles
    with Sin and o'ercomes her.
Downward to earth He came and, trans-
    figured, thence reascended,
Not from the heart in like wise, for there
    He still lives in the Spirit,
Loves and atones evermore. So long as
    Time is, is Atonement.
Therefore with reverence take this day her
    visible token.
Tokens are dead if the things live not.
    The light everlasting
Unto the blind is not, but is born of the
    eye that has vision.
Neither in bread nor in wine, but in the
    heart that is hallowed
Lieth forgiveness enshrined ; the intention
    alone of amendment
Fruits of the earth ennobles to heavenly
    things, and removes all
Sin and the guerdon of sin.   Only Love
    with his arms wide extended,
Penitence weeping and praying ; the Will
    that is tried, and whose gold flows
Purified forth from the flames ; in a word,
    mankind by Atonement
Breaketh Atonement's bread, and drinketh
    Atonement's wine-cup.
But he who cometh up hither, unworthy,
    with hate in his bosom,

Scoffing at men and at God, is guilty of
    Christ's blessed body,
And the Redeemer's blood ! To himself
    he eateth and drinketh
Death and doom ! And from this, preserve
    us, thou heavenly Father !
Are ye ready, ye children, to eat of the
    bread of Atonement ? "
Thus with emotion he asked, and together
    answered the children,
" Yes ! " with deep sobs interrupted. Then
    read he the due supplications,
Read the Form of Communion, and in
    chimed the organ and anthem :
' O Holy Lamb of God, who takest away
    our transgressions,
Hear us ! give us thy peace ! have mercy,
    have mercy upon us ! "
Th' old man, with trembling hand, and
    heavenly pearls on his eyelids,
Filled now the chalice and paten, and dealt
    round the mystical symbols.
Oh, then seemed it to me as if God, with
    the broad eye of midday,
Clearer looked in at the windows, and all
    the trees in the churchyard
Bowed down their summits of green, and
    the grass on the graves 'gan to
    shiver.
But in the children (I noted it well ; I
    knew it) there ran a
Tremor of holy rapture along through
    their ice-cold members.
Decked like an altar before them, there
    stood the green earth, and above it
Heaven opened itself, as of old before
    Stephen ; they saw there
Radiant in glory the Father, and on his
    right hand the Redeemer.
Under them hear they the clang of harp-
    strings, and angels from gold clouds
Beckon to them like brothers, and fan with
    their pinions of purple.

Closed was the Teacher's task, and with
    heaven in their hearts and their
    faces,
Up rose the children all, and each bowed
    him, weeping full sorely,
Downward to kiss that reverend hand, but
    all of them pressed he
Moved to his bosom, and laid, with a
    prayer, his hands full of blessings,
Now on the holy breast, and now on the
    innocent tresses.

KING CHRISTIAN

(KONG CHRISTIAN STOD VED HØIEN MAST)

A NATIONAL SONG OF DENMARK

Written during a visit to Copenhagen in September,
1835. The poet first heard the air from some strolling
musician in a coffee-house, and looking up the words
by Johannes Evald in his lyrical drama *Fiskerne* (*The
Fishermen*), Act ii. Sc. v., translated them.

KING CHRISTIAN stood by the lofty mast
    In mist and smoke ;
His sword was hammering so fast,
Through Gothic helm and brain it passed ;
Then sank each hostile hulk and mast,
    In mist and smoke.
" Fly ! " shouted they, " fly, he who can !
Who braves of Denmark's Christian
    The stroke ? "

Nils Juel gave heed to the tempest's
    roar,
    Now is the hour !
He hoisted his blood-red flag once more,
And smote upon the foe full sore,
And shouted loud, through the tempest's
    roar,
    " Now is the hour ! "
" Fly ! " shouted they, " for shelter fly !
Of Denmark's Juel who can defy
    The power ? "

North Sea ! a glimpse of Wessel rent
    Thy murky sky !
Then champions to thine arms were
    sent ;
Terror and Death glared where he went ;
From the waves was heard a wail, that
    rent
    Thy murky sky !
From Denmark thunders Tordenskiol',
Let each to Heaven commend his soul,
    And fly !

Path of the Dane to fame and might !
    Dark-rolling wave !
Receive thy friend, who, scorning flight,
Goes to meet danger with despite,
Proudly as thou the tempest's might,
    Dark-rolling wave !
And amid pleasures and alarms,
And war and victory, be thine arms
    My grave !

THE ELECTED KNIGHT

(Den Udkaarne Ridder)

This strange and somewhat mystical ballad is from Nyerup and Rahbek's *Danske Viser fra Middelalderen.* It seems to refer to the first preaching of Christianity in the North, and to the institution of Knight-Errantry. The three maidens I suppose to be Faith, Hope, and Charity. The irregularities of the original have been carefully preserved in the translation. H. W. L.

Sir Oluf he rideth over the plain,
    Full seven miles broad and seven miles
        wide,
But never, ah never can meet with the
      man
    A tilt with him dare ride.

He saw under the hillside
    A Knight full well equipped ;
His steed was black, his helm was barred ;
    He was riding at full speed.

He wore upon his spurs
    Twelve little golden birds ;
Anon he spurred his steed with a clang,
    And there sat all the birds and sang.

He wore upon his mail
    Twelve little golden wheels ;
Anon in eddies the wild wind blew,
    And round and round the wheels they
    flew.

He wore before his breast
    A lance that was poised in rest ;
And it was sharper than diamond-stone,
    It made Sir Oluf's heart to groan.

He wore upon his helm
    A wreath of ruddy gold ;
And that gave him the Maidens Three,
    The youngest was fair to behold.

Sir Oluf questioned the Knight eftsoon
    If he were come from heaven down ;
"Art thou Christ of Heaven," quoth
    he,
    "So will I yield me unto thee."

"I am not Christ the Great,
    Thou shalt not yield thee yet ;
I am an Unknown Knight,
    Three modest Maidens have me be-
    dight."

"Art thou a Knight elected,
    And have three maidens thee bedight ;
So shalt thou ride a tilt this day,
    For all the Maidens' honor !"

The first tilt they together rode
    They put their steeds to the test ;
The second tilt they together rode
    They proved their manhood best.

The third tilt they together rode
    Neither of them would yield ;
The fourth tilt they together rode
    They both fell on the field.

Now lie the lords upon the plain,
    And their blood runs unto death ;
Now sit the Maidens in the high tower,
    The youngest sorrows till death.

CHILDHOOD

(Da jeg var lille)

BY JENS IMMANUEL BAGGESEN

There was a time when I was very small,
    When my whole frame was but an ell in
      height ;
Sweetly, as I recall it, tears do fall,
    And therefore I recall it with delight.

I sported in my tender mother's arms,
    And rode a-horseback on best father's
      knee ;
Alike were sorrows, passions and alarms,
    And gold, and Greek, and love, unknown
      to me.

Then seemed to me this world far less in
      size,
    Likewise it seemed to me less wicked
      far ;
Like points in heaven, I saw the stars
      arise,
    And longed for wings that I might catch
      a star.

I saw the moon behind the island fade,
    And thought, "Oh, were I on that island
      there,
I could find out of what the moon is made,
    Find out how large it is, how round, how
      fair !"

Wondering, I saw God's sun, through
    western skies,
Sink in the ocean's golden lap at night,
And yet upon the morrow early rise,
    And paint the eastern heaven with crim-
    son light;

And thought of God, the gracious Heavenly
    Father,
Who made me, and that lovely sun on
    high,
And all those pearls of heaven thick-strung
    together,
    Dropped, clustering, from his hand o'er
    all the sky.

With childish reverence, my young lips did
    say
    The prayer my pious mother taught to
    me :
" O gentle God ! oh, let me strive alway
    Still to be wise, and good, and follow
    thee ! "

So prayed I for my father and my mother,
    And for my sister, and for all the
    town ;
The king I knew not, and the beggar-bro-
    ther,
    Who, bent with age, went, sighing, up
    and down.

They perished, the blithe days of boy-
    hood perished,
    And all the gladness, all the peace I
    knew !
Now have I but their memory, fondly cher-
    ished ; —
    God ! may I never lose that too !

FROM THE GERMAN

The first ten of the following poems are all from the
volume *Voices of the Night*, into which they were brought
for the most part from *Hyperion*. The winter of 1836,
spent by Mr. Longfellow in Germany, appears to have
been the time when most of his translations from Ger-
man poetry were made.

THE HAPPIEST LAND

THERE sat one day in quiet,
    By an alehouse on the Rhine,
Four hale and hearty fellows,
    And drank the precious wine.

The landlord's daughter filled their cups,
    Around the rustic board ;
Then sat they all so calm and still,
    And spake not one rude word.

But when the maid departed,
    A Swabian raised his hand,
And cried, all hot and flushed with wine,
    " Long live the Swabian land !

" The greatest kingdom upon earth
    Cannot with that compare ;
With all the stout and hardy men
    And the nut-brown maidens there."

" Ha ! " cried a Saxon, laughing,
    And dashed his beard with wine ;
" I had rather live in Lapland,
    Than that Swabian land of thine !

" The goodliest land on all this earth,
    It is the Saxon land !
There have I as many maidens
    As fingers on this hand ! "

" Hold your tongues ! both Swabian **and**
    Saxon ! "
    A bold Bohemian cries ;
" If there 's a heaven upon this earth,
    In Bohemia it lies.

" There the tailor blows the flute,
    And the cobbler blows the horn,
And the miner blows the bugle,
    Over mountain gorge and bourn."

. . . . . .
And then the landlord's daughter
    Up to heaven raised her hand,
And said, " Ye may no more contend, —
    There lies the happiest land ! "

THE WAVE

(DIE WELLE)

BY CHRISTOPH AUGUST TIEDGE

" WHITHER, thou turbid wave ?
Whither, with so much haste,
As if a thief wert thou ? "

" I am the Wave of Life,
Stained with my margin's dust ;
From the struggle and the strife
Of the narrow stream I fly

To the Sea's immensity,
To wash from me the slime
Of the muddy banks of Time."

THE DEAD

BY ERNST STOCKMANN

How they so softly rest,
All they the holy ones,
Unto whose dwelling-place
Now doth my soul draw near!
How they so softly rest,
All in their silent graves,
Deep to corruption
Slowly down-sinking!

And they no longer weep,
Here, where complaint is still!
And they no longer feel,
Here, where all gladness flies!
And by the cypresses
Softly o'ershadowed,
Until the Angel
Calls them, they slumber!

THE BIRD AND THE SHIP

(SCHIFF UND VOGEL)

BY WILHELM MÜLLER

" THE rivers rush into the sea,
By castle and town they go ;
The winds behind them merrily
Their noisy trumpets blow.

"The clouds are passing far and high,
We little birds in them play ;
And everything, that can sing and fly,
Goes with us, and far away.

" I greet thee, bonny boat! Whither, or
whence,
With thy fluttering golden band ?" —
"I greet thee, little bird! To the wide
sea
I haste from the narrow land.

" Full and swollen is every sail ;
I see no longer a hill,
I have trusted all to the sounding gale,
And it will not let me stand still.

" And wilt thou, little bird, go with us ?
Thou mayest stand on the mainmast tall,
For full to sinking is my house
With merry companions all." —

" I need not and seek not company,
Bonny boat, I can sing all alone ;
For the mainmast tall too heavy am I,
Bonny boat, I have wings of my own.

" High over the sails, high over the mast,
Who shall gainsay these joys ?
When thy merry companions are still, at
last,
Thou shalt hear the sound of my voice.

" Who neither may rest, nor listen may,
God bless them every one !
I dart away, in the bright blue day,
And the golden fields of the sun.

" Thus do I sing my weary song,
Wherever the four winds blow ;
And this same song, my whole life long,
Neither Poet nor Printer may know."

WHITHER?

(WOHIN ?)

BY WILHELM MÜLLER

I HEARD a brooklet gushing
From its rocky fountain near,
Down into the valley rushing,
So fresh and wondrous clear.

I know not what came o'er me,
Nor who the counsel gave ;
But I must hasten downward,
All with my pilgrim-stave ;

Downward, and ever farther,
And ever the brook beside ;
And ever fresher murmured,
And ever clearer, the tide.

Is this the way I was going ?
Whither, O brooklet, say !
Thou hast, with thy soft murmur,
Murmured my senses away.

What do I say of a murmur ?
That can no murmur be ;

'T is the water-nymphs, that are singing
Their roundelays under me.

Let them sing, my friend, let them murmur,
And wander merrily near ;
The wheels of a mill are going
In every brooklet clear.

BEWARE !

(HÜT DU DICH !)

I KNOW a maiden fair to see,
Take care !
She can both false and friendly be,
Beware ! Beware !
Trust her not,
She is fooling thee !

She has two eyes, so soft and brown,
Take care !
She gives a side-glance and looks down,
Beware ! Beware !
Trust her not,
She is fooling thee !

And she has hair of a golden hue,
Take care !
And what she says, it is not true,
Beware ! Beware !
Trust her not,
She is fooling thee !

She has a bosom as white as snow,
Take care !
She knows how much it is best to show,
Beware ! Beware !
Trust her not,
She is fooling thee !

She gives thee a garland woven fair,
Take care !
It is a fool's-cap for thee to wear,
Beware ! Beware !
Trust her not,
She is fooling thee !

SONG OF THE BELL

First published in *Hyperion*, Book III. chapter iii.
The scene of the chapter is laid at Interlachen. "The
evening sun was setting," writes the author, "when I

first beheld thee. The sun of life will set ere I forget
thee ! Surely it was a scene like this that inspired the
soul of the Swiss poet, in his *Song of the Bell.*"

BELL ! thou soundest merrily,
When the bridal party
To the church doth hie !
Bell ! thou soundest solemnly,
When, on Sabbath morning,
Fields deserted lie !

Bell ! thou soundest merrily ;
Tellest thou at evening,
Bed-time draweth nigh !
Bell ! thou soundest mournfully,
Tellest thou the bitter
Parting hath gone by !

Say ! how canst thou mourn ?
How canst thou rejoice ?
Thou art but metal dull !
And yet all our sorrowings,
And all our rejoicings,
Thou dost feel them all !

God hath wonders many,
Which we cannot fathom,
Placed within thy form !
When the heart is sinking,
Thou alone canst raise it,
Trembling in the storm !

THE CASTLE BY THE SEA

(DAS SCHLOSS AM MEERE)

BY JOHANN LUDWIG UHLAND

" HAST thou seen that lordly castle,
That Castle by the Sea ?
Golden and red above it
The clouds float gorgeously.

" And fain it would stoop downward
To the mirrored wave below ;
And fain it would soar upward
In the evening's crimson glow."

" Well have I seen that castle,
That Castle by the Sea,
And the moon above it standing,
And the mist rise solemnly."

" The winds and the waves of ocean,
Had they a merry chime ?

Didst thou hear, from those lofty chambers
  The harp and the minstrel's rhyme ? "

" The winds and the waves of ocean,
  They rested quietly,
But I heard on the gale a sound of wail,
  And tears came to mine eye."

" And sawest thou on the turrets
  The King and his royal bride ?
And the wave of their crimson mantles ?
  And the golden crown of pride ?

" Led they not forth, in rapture,
  A beauteous maiden there ?
Resplendent as the morning sun,
  Beaming with golden hair ? "

" Well saw I the ancient parents,
  Without the crown of pride ;
They were moving slow, in weeds of woe,
  No maiden was by their side ! "

THE BLACK KNIGHT

(DER SCHWARZE RITTER)

BY JOHANN LUDWIG UHLAND

'T WAS Pentecost, the Feast of Gladness,
When woods and fields put off all sadness,
  Thus began the King and spake :
" So from the halls
Of ancient Hofburg's walls,
  A luxuriant Spring shall break."

Drums and trumpets echo loudly,
Wave the crimson banners proudly,
  From balcony the King looked on ;
In the play of spears,
Fell all the cavaliers,
  Before the monarch's stalwart son.

To the barrier of the fight
Rode at last a sable Knight.
  " Sir Knight ! your name and scutcheon,
    say ! "
" Should I speak it here,
Ye would stand aghast with fear ;
  I am a Prince of mighty sway ! "

When he rode into the lists,
The arch of heaven grew black with mists,
  And the castle 'gan to rock ;

At the first blow,
Fell the youth from saddle-bow,
  Hardly rises from the shock.

Pipe and viol call the dances,
Torch-light through the high halls glances ;
  Waves a mighty shadow in ;
With manner bland
Doth ask the maiden's hand,
  Doth with her the dance begin.

Danced in sable iron sark,
Danced a measure weird and dark,
  Coldly clasped her limbs around ;
From breast and hair
Down fall from her the fair
  Flowerets, faded, to the ground.

To the sumptuous banquet came
Every Knight and every Dame ;
  'Twixt son and daughter all distraught,
With mournful mind
The ancient King reclined,
  Gazed at them in silent thought.

Pale the children both did look,
But the guest a beaker took :
  " Golden wine will make you whole ! "
The children drank,
Gave many a courteous thank :
  " Oh, that draught was very cool ! "

Each the father's breast embraces,
Son and daughter ; and their faces
  Colorless grow utterly ;
Whichever way
Looks the fear-struck father gray,
  He beholds his children die.

" Woe ! the blessed children both
Takest thou in the joy of youth ;
  Take me, too, the joyless father ! "
Spake the grim Guest,
From his hollow, cavernous breast :
  " Roses in the spring I gather ! "

SONG OF THE SILENT LAND

(LIED : INS STILLE LAND)

BY JOHANN GAUDENZ VON SALIS-SEEWIS

INTO the Silent Land !
Ah ! who shall lead us thither ?

Clouds in the evening sky more darkly
    gather,
And shattered wrecks lie thicker on the
    strand.
Who leads us with a gentle hand
Thither, oh, thither,
Into the Silent Land?

Into the Silent Land!
To you, ye boundless regions
Of all perfection! Tender morning-visions
Of beauteous souls! The Future's pledge
    and band!
Who in Life's battle firm doth stand,
Shall bear Hope's tender blossoms
Into the Silent Land!

O Land! O Land!
For all the broken-hearted
The mildest herald by our fate allotted,
Beckons, and with inverted torch doth stand
To lead us with a gentle hand
To the land of the great Departed,
Into the Silent Land!

THE LUCK OF EDENHALL

(DAS GLÜCK VON EDENHALL)

BY JOHANN LUDWIG UHLAND

OF Edenhall, the youthful Lord
Bids sound the festal trumpet's call;
He rises at the banquet board,
And cries, 'mid the drunken revellers all,
" Now bring me the Luck of Edenhall!"

The butler hears the words with pain,
The house's oldest seneschal,
Takes slow from its silken cloth again
The drinking-glass of crystal tall;
They call it the Luck of Edenhall.

Then said the Lord : " This glass to praise,
Fill with red wine from Portugal!"
The graybeard with trembling hand obeys;
A purple light shines over all,
It beams from the Luck of Edenhall.

Then speaks the Lord, and waves it light :
" This glass of flashing crystal tall
Gave to my sires the Fountain-Sprite;
She wrote in it, *If this glass doth fall,*
Farewell then, O Luck of Edenhall!

" 'T was right a goblet the Fate should be
Of the joyous race of Edenhall!
Deep draughts drink we right willingly;
And willingly ring, with merry call,
Kling! klang! to the Luck of Edenhall!"

First rings it deep, and full, and mild,
Like to the song of a nightingale;
Then like the roar of a torrent wild;
Then mutters at last like the thunder's fall,
The glorious Luck of Edenhall.

" For its keeper takes a race of might,
The fragile goblet of crystal tall;
It has lasted longer than is right;
Kling! klang!—with a harder blow than
    all
Will I try the Luck of Edenhall!"

As the goblet ringing flies apart,
Suddenly cracks the vaulted hall;
And through the rift, the wild flames start;
The guests in dust are scattered all,
With the breaking Luck of Edenhall!

In storms the foe, with fire and sword;
He in the night had scaled the wall,
Slain by the sword lies the youthful Lord,
But holds in his hand the crystal tall,
The shattered Luck of Edenhall.

On the morrow the butler gropes alone,
The graybeard in the desert hall,
He seeks his Lord's burnt skeleton,
He seeks in the dismal ruin's fall
The shards of the Luck of Edenhall.

" The stone wall," saith he, " doth fall
    aside,
Down must the stately columns fall;
Glass is this earth's Luck and Pride;
In atoms shall fall this earthly ball
One day like the Luck of Edenhall!"

THE TWO LOCKS OF HAIR

(DER JUNGGESELL)

BY GUSTAV PFIZER

A YOUTH, light-hearted and content,
  I wander through the world;
Here, Arab-like, is pitched my tent
  And straight again is furled.

Yet oft I dream, that once a wife
Close in my heart was locked,
And in the sweet repose of life
A blessed child I rocked.

I wake ! Away that dream, — away !
Too long did it remain !
So long, that both by night and day
It ever comes again.

The end lies ever in my thought ;
To a grave so cold and deep
The mother beautiful was brought ;
Then dropt the child asleep.

But now the dream is wholly o'er,
I bathe mine eyes and see ;
And wander through the world once
more,
A youth so light and free.

Two locks — and they are wondrous fair —
Left me that vision mild ;
The brown is from the mother's hair,
The blond is from the child.

And when I see that lock of gold,
Pale grows the evening-red ;
And when the dark lock I behold,
I wish that I were dead.

THE HEMLOCK TREE

O HEMLOCK tree ! O hemlock tree ! how
faithful are thy branches !
Green not alone in summer time,
But in the winter's frost and rime !
O hemlock tree ! O hemlock tree ! how
faithful are thy branches !

O maiden fair ! O maiden fair ! how faith-
less is thy bosom !
To love me in prosperity,
And leave me in adversity !
O maiden fair ! O maiden fair ! how faith-
less is thy bosom !

The nightingale the nightingale, thou tak'st
for thine example !
So long as summer laughs she sings,
But in the autumn spreads her wings.
The nightingale, the nightingale, thou tak'st
for thine example !

The meadow brook, the meadow brook, is
mirror of thy falsehood !
It flows so long as falls the rain,
In drought its springs soon dry again.
The meadow brook, the meadow brook, is
mirror of thy falsehood !

ANNIE OF THARAW

(ANKE VON THARAU)

BY SIMON DACH

ANNIE of Tharaw, my true love of old,
She is my life, and my goods, and my gold.

Annie of Tharaw her heart once again
To me has surrendered in joy and in pain.

Annie of Tharaw, my riches, my good,
Thou, O my soul, my flesh, and my blood !

Then come the wild weather, come sleet or
come snow,
We will stand by each other, however it
blow.

Oppression, and sickness, and sorrow, and
pain
Shall be to our true love as links to the chain.

As the palm-tree standeth so straight and
so tall,
The more the hail beats, and the more the
rains fall, —

So love in our hearts shall grow mighty
and strong,
Through crosses, through sorrows, through
manifold wrong.

Shouldst thou be torn from me to wander
alone
In a desolate land where the sun is scarce
known, —

Through forests I 'll follow, and where the
sea flows,
Through ice, and through iron, through
armies of foes.

Annie of Tharaw, my light and my sun,
The threads of our two lives are woven in
one.

Whate'er I have bidden thee thou hast
    obeyed,
Whatever forbidden thou hast not gainsaid.

How in the turmoil of life can love stand,
Where there is not one heart, and one
    mouth, and one hand ?

Some seek for dissension, and trouble, and
    strife ;
Like a dog and a cat live such man and
    wife.

Annie of Tharaw, such is not our love ;
Thou art my lambkin, my chick, and my
    dove.

Whate'er my desire is, in thine may be
    seen ;
I am king of the household, and thou art
    its queen.

It is this, O my Annie, my heart's sweetest
    rest,
That makes of us twain but one soul in
    one breast.

This turns to a heaven the hut where we
    dwell ;
While wrangling soon changes a home to a
    hell.

THE STATUE OVER THE CA-
THEDRAL DOOR

(DAS STEINBILD AM DOME)

BY JULIUS MOSEN

FORMS of saints and kings are standing
    The cathedral door above ;
Yet I saw but one among them
    Who hath soothed my soul with love.

In his mantle, — wound about him,
    As their robes the sowers wind, —
Bore he swallows and their fledglings,
    Flowers and weeds of every kind.

And so stands he calm and childlike,
    High in wind and tempest wild ;
Oh, were I like him exalted,
    I would be like him a child !

And my songs, — green leaves and blos-
    soms, —
    To the doors of heaven would bear,
Calling even in storm and tempest,
    Round me still these birds of air.

THE LEGEND OF THE CROSS-
BILL

(DER KREUZSCHNABEL, No. 3)

BY JULIUS MOSEN

ON the cross the dying Saviour
    Heavenward lifts his eyelids calm,
Feels, but scarcely feels, a trembling
    In his pierced and bleeding palm.

And by all the world forsaken,
    Sees He how with zealous care
At the ruthless nail of iron
    A little bird is striving there.

Stained with blood and never tiring,
    With its beak it doth not cease,
From the cross 't would free the Saviour,
    Its Creator's Son release.

And the Saviour speaks in mildness :
    " Blest be thou of all the good !
Bear, as token of this moment,
    Marks of blood and holy rood ! "

And that bird is called the crossbill ;
    Covered all with blood so clear,
In the groves of pine it singeth
    Songs, like legends, strange to hear.

THE SEA HATH ITS PEARLS

BY HEINRICH HEINE

THE sea hath its pearls,
    The heaven hath its stars ;
But my heart, my heart,
    My heart hath its love.

Great are the sea and the heaven,
    Yet greater is my heart ;
And fairer than pearls and stars
    Flashes and beams my love.

Thou little, youthful maiden,
Come unto my great heart ;
My heart, and the sea, and the heaven
Are melting away with love !

POETIC APHORISMS

FROM THE SINNGEDICHTE OF FRIE-
DRICH VON LOGAU

MONEY

WHEREUNTO is money good ?
Who has it not wants hardihood,
Who has it has much trouble and care,
Who once has had it has despair.

THE BEST MEDICINES

Joy and Temperance and Repose
Slam the door on the doctor's nose.

SIN

Man-like is it to fall into sin,
Fiend-like is it to dwell therein,
Christ-like is it for sin to grieve,
God-like is it all sin to leave.

POVERTY AND BLINDNESS

A blind man is a poor man, and blind a
poor man is ;
For the former seeth no man, and the latter
no man sees.

LAW OF LIFE

Live I, so live I,
To my Lord heartily,
To my Prince faithfully,
To my Neighbor honestly,
Die I, so die I.

CREEDS

Lutheran, Popish, Calvinistic, all these
creeds and doctrines three
Extant are ; but still the doubt is, where
Christianity may be.

THE RESTLESS HEART

A mill-stone and the human heart are
driven ever round ;
If they have nothing else to grind, they
must themselves be ground.

CHRISTIAN LOVE

Whilom Love was like a fire, and warmth
and comfort it bespoke ;
But, alas ! it now is quenched, and only
bites us, like the smoke.

ART AND TACT

Intelligence and courtesy not always are
combined ;
Often in a wooden house a golden room we
find.

RETRIBUTION

Though the mills of God grind slowly, yet
they grind exceeding small ;
Though with patience he stands waiting,
with exactness grinds he all.

TRUTH

When by night the frogs are croaking,
kindle but a torch's fire,
Ha ! how soon they all are silent ! Thus
Truth silences the liar.

RHYMES

If perhaps these rhymes of mine should
sound not well in strangers' ears,
They have only to bethink them that it
happens so with theirs ;
For so long as words, like mortals, call a
fatherland their own,
They will be most highly valued where they
are best and longest known.

SILENT LOVE

WHO love would seek,
Let him love evermore
And seldom speak ;
For in love's domain
Silence must reign ;
Or it brings the heart
Smart
And pain.

BLESSED ARE THE DEAD

(SELIG SIND, DIE IN DEM HERRN STERBEN)

BY SIMON DACH

OH, how blest are ye whose toils are
ended !
Who, through death, have unto God as-
cended !

Ye have arisen
From the cares which keep us still in
prison.

We are still as in a dungeon living,
Still oppressed with sorrow and misgiv-
ing ;
Our undertakings
Are but toils, and troubles, and heart-
breakings.

Ye, meanwhile, are in your chambers sleep-
ing,
Quiet, and set free from all our weeping ;
No cross nor trial
Hinders your enjoyments with denial.

Christ has wiped away your tears for
ever ;
Ye have that for which we still endeavor.
To you are chanted
Songs which yet no mortal ear have haunted.

Ah ! who would not, then, depart with glad-
ness,
To inherit heaven for earthly sadness ?
Who here would languish
Longer in bewailing and in anguish ?

Come, O Christ, and loose the chains that
bind us !
Lead us forth, and cast this world behind
us !
With thee, the Anointed,
Finds the soul its joy and rest appointed.

WANDERER'S NIGHT–SONGS

(WANDRERS NACHTLIED AND EIN GLEICHES)

BY JOHANN WOLFGANG VON GOETHE

I

THOU that from the heavens art,
Every pain and sorrow stillest,
And the doubly wretched heart
Doubly with refreshment fillest,
I am weary with contending !
Why this rapture and unrest ?
Peace descending
Come, ah, come into my breast !

II

O'er all the hill-tops
Is quiet now,
In all the tree-tops
Hearest thou
Hardly a breath ;
The birds are asleep in the trees :
Wait ; soon like these
Thou too shalt rest.

REMORSE

(MUT AND UNMUT)

BY AUGUST VON PLATEN

How I started up in the night, in the night,
Drawn on without rest or reprieval !
The streets, with their watchmen, were lost
to my sight,
As I wandered so light
In the night, in the night,
Through the gate with the arch mediæval.

The mill-brook rushed from the rocky
height,
I leaned o'er the bridge in my yearn-
ing ;
Deep under me watched I the waves in
their flight,
As they glided so light
In the night, in the night,
Yet backward not one was returning.

O'erhead were revolving, so countless and
bright,
The stars in melodious existence ;
And with them the moon, more serenely
bedight ;
They sparkled so light
In the night, in the night,
Through the magical, measureless distance.

And upward I gazed in the night, in the
night,
And again on the waves in their fleeting ;
Ah woe ! thou hast wasted thy days in
delight,
Now silence thou light,
In the night, in the night,
The remorse in thy heart that is beating.

FORSAKEN

SOMETHING the heart must have to cherish,
    Must love and joy and sorrow learn,
Something with passion clasp, or perish,
    And in itself to ashes burn.

So to this child my heart is clinging,
    And its frank eyes, with look intense,
Me from a world of sin are bringing
    Back to a world of innocence.

Disdain must thou endure forever ;
    Strong may thy heart in danger be !
Thou shalt not fail ! but ah, be never
    False as thy father was to me.

Never will I forsake thee, faithless,
    And thou thy mother ne'er forsake,
Until her lips are white and breathless,
    Until in death her eyes shall break.

ALLAH

BY SIEGFRIED AUGUST MAHLMANN

ALLAH gives light in darkness,
    Allah gives rest in pain,
Cheeks that are white with weeping
    Allah paints red again.

The flowers and the blossoms wither,
    Years vanish with flying feet ;
But my heart will live on forever,
    That here in sadness beat.

Gladly to Allah's dwelling
    Yonder would I take flight ;
There will the darkness vanish,
    There will my eyes have sight.

FROM THE ANGLO–SAXON

THE GRAVE

For thee was a house built
Ere thou wast born,
For thee was a mould meant
Ere thou of mother camest.
But it is not made ready,
Nor its depth measured,

Nor is it seen
How long it shall be.
Now I bring thee
Where thou shalt be ;
Now I shall measure thee,
And the mould afterwards.

Thy house is not
Highly timbered,
It is unhigh and low ;
When thou art therein,
The heel-ways are low,
The side-ways unhigh.
The roof is built
Thy breast full nigh,
So thou shalt in mould
Dwell full cold,
Dimly and dark.

Doorless is that house,
And dark it is within ;
There thou art fast detained
And Death hath the key.
Loathsome is that earth-house,
And grim within to dwell.
There thou shalt dwell,
And worms shall divide thee.

Thus thou art laid,
And leavest thy friends ;
Thou hast no friend,
Who will come to thee,
Who will ever see
How that house pleaseth thee ;
Who will ever open
The door for thee,
And descend after thee ;
For soon thou art loathsome
And hateful to see.

BEOWULF'S EXPEDITION TO HEORT

THUS then, much care-worn,
The son of Healfden
Sorrowed evermore,
Nor might the prudent hero
His woes avert.
The war was too hard,
Too loath and longsome,
That on the people came,
Dire wrath and grim,
Of night-woes the worst.

This from home heard
Higelac's Thane,
Good among the Goths,
Grendel's deeds.
He was of mankind
In might the strongest,
At that day
Of this life,
Noble and stalwart.
He bade him a sea-ship,
A goodly one, prepare.
Quoth he, the war-king,
Over the swan's road,
Seek he would
The mighty monarch,
Since he wanted men.
For him that journey
His prudent fellows
Straight made ready,
Those that loved him.
They excited their souls,
The omen they beheld.
Had the good-man
Of the Gothic people
Champions chosen,
Of those that keenest
He might find,
Some fifteen men.
The sea-wood sought he.
The warrior showed,
Sea-crafty man!
The land-marks,
And first went forth.
The ship was on the waves,
Boat under the cliffs.
The barons ready
To the prow mounted.
The streams they whirled
The sea against the sands.
The chieftains bore
On the naked breast
Bright ornaments,
War-gear, Goth-like.
The men shoved off,
Men on their willing way,
The bounden wood.
 Then went over the sea-waves,
Hurried by the wind,
The ship with foamy neck,
Most like a sea-fowl,
Till about one hour
Of the second day
The curved prow
Had passed onward

So that the sailors
The land saw,
The shore-cliffs shining,
Mountains steep,
And broad sea-noses.
Then was the sea-sailing
Of the Earl at an end.
 Then up speedily
The Weather people
On the land went,
The sea-bark moored,
Their mail-sarks shook,
Their war-weeds.
God thanked they,
That to them the sea-journey
Easy had been.
 Then from the wall beheld
The warden of the Scyldings,
He who the sea-cliffs
Had in his keeping,
Bear o'er the balks
The bright shields,
The war-weapons speedily.
Him the doubt disturbed
In his mind's thought,
What these men might be.
 Went then to the shore,
On his steed riding,
The Thane of Hrothgar.
Before the host he shook
His warden's-staff in hand,
In measured words demanded:
 "What men are ye
War-gear wearing,
Host in harness,
Who thus the brown keel
Over the water-street
Leading come
Hither over the sea?
I these boundaries
As shore-warden hold,
That in the Land of the Danes
Nothing loathsome
With a ship-crew
Scathe us might. . . .
Ne'er saw I mightier
Earl upon earth
Than is your own,
Hero in harness.
Not seldom this warrior
Is in weapons distinguished;
Never his beauty belies him,
His peerless countenance!
Now would I fain

Your origin know,
Ere ye forth
As false spies
Into the Land of the Danes
Farther fare.
Now, ye dwellers afar-off !
Ye sailors of the sea :
Listen to my
One-fold thought.
Quickest is best
To make known
Whence your coming may be."

THE SOUL'S COMPLAINT AGAINST THE BODY

FROM THE ANGLO-SAXON

MUCH it behoveth
Each one of mortals,
That he his soul's journey
In himself ponder,
How deep it may be.
When Death cometh,
The bonds he breaketh
By which were united
The soul and the body.

Long it is thenceforth
Ere the soul taketh

From God himself
Its woe or its weal ;
As in the world erst,
Even in its earth-vessel,
It wrought before.

The soul shall come
Wailing with loud voice,
After a sennight,
The soul, to find
The body
That it erst dwelt in ; —
Three hundred winters,
Unless ere that worketh
The Eternal Lord,
The Almighty God,
The end of the world.

Crieth then, so care-worn,
With cold utterance,
And speaketh grimly,
The ghost to the dust :
" Dry dust ! thou dreary one !
How little didst thou labor for me !
In the foulness of earth
Thou all wearest away
Like to the loam !
Little didst thou think
How thy soul's journey
Would be thereafter,
When from the body
It should be led forth."

FROM THE FRENCH

SONG

FROM THE PARADISE OF LOVE

The first work which Mr. Longfellow printed in the way of translation of French poetry was in connection with his article on *Origin and Progress of the French Language*, which he contributed to the *North American Review* for April, 1831. He used a portion of this paper in the chapter, *The Trouvères*, in *Outer-Mer*, introducing his translation of some early lyrics by these words : " The favorite theme of the ancient lyric poets of the North of France is the wayward passion of love. They all delight to sing *les douces dolors et li mal plaisant de fine amor.*' With such feelings the beauties of the opening spring are naturally associated. Almost every love-ditty of the old poets commences with some such exordium as this : ' When the snows of winter have passed away, when the soft and gentle spring returns, and the flower and leaf shoot in the groves, and the little birds warble to their mates in their own sweet language, — then will I sing my lady-love !' Another favorite introduction to these little rhapsodies of romantic passion is the approach of morning and its sweet-voiced herald, the lark. The minstrel's song to his lady-love frequently commences with an allusion to the hour

When the rosebud opes its een,
  And the bluebells droop and die,
And upon the leaves so green
  Sparkling dew-drops lie.

"The following is at once the simplest and prettiest piece of this kind which I have met with among the early lyric poets of the North of France. It is taken from an anonymous poem, entitled *The Paradise of Love*. A lover, having passed the 'live-long night in tears as he was wont,' goes forth to beguile his sorrows with the fragrance and beauty of morning. The carol of the vaulting skylark salutes his ear, and to this merry musician he makes his complaint."

HARK! hark!
Pretty lark!
Little heedest thou my pain!
But if to these longing arms
Pitying Love would yield the charms
    Of the fair
    With smiling air,
Blithe would beat my heart again.

Hark! hark!
Pretty lark!
Little heedest thou my pain!
Love may force me still to bear,
While he lists, consuming care;
    But in anguish
    Though I languish,
Faithful shall my heart remain.

Hark! hark!
Pretty lark!
Little heedest thou my pain!
Then cease, Love, to torment me so;
But rather than all thoughts forego
    Of the fair
    With flaxen hair,
Give me back her frowns again.

Hark! hark!
Pretty lark!
Little heedest thou my pain!

SONG

Given in *The Trouvères*, a chapter of *Outre-Mer*, as another example of the lyrics of the early poets of the North of France.

AND whither goest thou, gentle sigh,
    Breathed so softly in my ear?
    Say, dost thou bear his fate severe
To Love's poor martyr doomed to die?
Come, tell me quickly, — do not lie;
    What secret message bring'st thou here?
And whither goest thou, gentle sigh,
    Breathed so softly in my ear?
May Heaven conduct thee to thy will,
    And safely speed thee on thy way;
    This only I would humbly pray, —

Pierce deep, — but oh! forbear to kill.
And whither goest thou, gentle sigh,
    Breathed so softly in my ear?

THE RETURN OF SPRING

(RENOUVEAU)

BY CHARLES D'ORLEANS

Now Time throws off his cloak again
Of ermined frost, and wind, and rain,
And clothes him in the embroidery
Of glittering sun and clear blue sky.
With beast and bird the forest rings,
Each in his jargon cries or sings;
And Time throws off his cloak again
Of ermined frost, and wind, and rain.

River, and fount, and tinkling brook
Wear in their dainty livery
Drops of silver jewelry;
In new-made suit they merry look;
And Time throws off his cloak again
Of ermined frost, and wind, and rain.

SPRING

BY CHARLES D'ORLEANS

GENTLE Spring! in sunshine clad,
    Well dost thou thy power display!
For Winter maketh the light heart sad,
    And thou, thou makest the sad heart gay.
He sees thee, and calls to his gloomy train,
    The sleet, and the snow, and the wind, and the rain;
And they shrink away, and they flee in fear,
    When thy merry step draws near.

Winter giveth the fields and the trees, so old,
    Their beards of icicles and snow;
And the rain, it raineth so fast and cold,
    We must cower over the embers low;
And, snugly housed from the wind and weather,
Mope like birds that are changing feather.
But the storm retires, and the sky grows clear,
    When thy merry step draws near.

Winter maketh the sun in the gloomy sky
  Wrap him round with a mantle of cloud ;
But, Heaven be praised, thy step is nigh ;
  Thou tearest away the mournful shroud,
And the earth looks bright, and Winter
    surly,
Who has toiled for naught both late and
    early,
Is banished afar by the new-born year,
When thy merry step draws near.

THE CHILD ASLEEP

(VERSLETS À MON PREMIER NÉ)

BY CLOTILDE DE SURVILLE

SWEET babe ! true portrait of thy father's
    face,
  Sleep on the bosom that thy lips have
    pressed !
Sleep, little one ; and closely, gently place
  Thy drowsy eyelid on thy mother's
    breast.

Upon that tender eye, my little friend,
  Soft sleep shall come, that cometh not to
    me !
I watch to see thee, nourish thee, defend ;
  'T is sweet to watch for thee, alone for
    thee !

His arms fall down ; sleep sits upon his
    brow ;
  His eye is closed ; he sleeps, nor dreams
    of harm.
Wore not his cheek the apple's ruddy glow,
  Would you not say he slept on Death's
    cold arm ?

Awake, my boy ! I tremble with affright !
  Awake, and chase this fatal thought ! Un-
    close
Thine eye but for one moment on the
    light !
  Even at the price of thine, give me re-
    pose !

Sweet error ! he but slept, I breathe again ;
  Come, gentle dreams, the hour of sleep
    beguile !
Oh, when shall he, for whom I sigh in vain,
  Beside me watch to see thy waking
    smile ?

DEATH OF ARCHBISHOP TURPIN

FROM THE CHANSON DE ROLAND

THE Archbishop, whom God loved in high
    degree,
Beheld his wounds all bleeding fresh and
    free ;
And then his cheek more ghastly grew and
    wan,
And a faint shudder through his members
    ran.
Upon the battle-field his knee was bent ;
Brave Roland saw, and to his succor went,
Straightway his helmet from his brow un-
    laced,
And tore the shining hauberk from his
    breast.
Then raising in his arms the man of God,
Gently he laid him on the verdant sod.
" Rest, Sire," he cried,— " for rest thy suf-
    fering needs."
The priest replied, "Think but of warlike
    deeds !
The field is ours ; well may we boast this
    strife !
But death steals on, — there is no hope of
    life ;
In paradise, where Almoners live again,
There are our couches spread, there shall
    we rest from pain."

Sore Roland grieved ; nor marvel I, alas !
That thrice he swooned upon the thick green
    grass.
When he revived, with a loud voice cried he,
" O Heavenly Father ! Holy Saint Marie !
Why lingers death to lay me in my grave !
Beloved France ! how have the good and
    brave
Been torn from thee, and left thee weak
    and poor ! "
Then thoughts of Aude, his lady-love, came
    o'er
His spirit, and he whispered soft and slow,
" My gentle friend ! — what parting full of
    woe !
Never so true a liegeman shalt thou see ; —
Whate'er my fate, Christ's benison on thee !
Christ, who did save from realms of woe
    beneath,
The Hebrew Prophets from the second
    death."

Then to the Paladins, whom well he knew,
He went, and one by one unaided drew
To Turpin's side, well skilled in ghostly
   lore ; —
No heart had he to smile, but, weeping
   sore,
He blessed them in God's name, with faith
   that he
Would soon vouchsafe to them a glad
   eternity.

The Archbishop, then, on whom God's
   benison rest,
Exhausted, bowed his head upon his
   breast ; —
His mouth was full of dust and clotted
   gore,
And many a wound his swollen visage bore.
Slow beats his heart, his panting bosom
   heaves,
Death comes apace, — no hope of cure re-
   lieves.
Towards heaven he raised his dying hands
   and prayed
That God, who for our sins was mortal
   made,
Born of the Virgin, scorned and crucified,
In paradise would place him by his side.

Then Turpin died in service of Charlon,
In battle great and eke great orison ; —
'Gainst Pagan host alway strong champion ;
God grant to him his holy benison.

THE BLIND GIRL OF CASTÈL CUILLÈ

BY JACQUES JASMIN

Only the Lowland tongue of Scotland might
Rehearse this little tragedy aright ;
Let me attempt it with an English quill ;
And take, O Reader, for the deed the will.

On the 30th of September, 1849, Mr. Longfellow
wrote in his diary : " I think I shall translate Jasmin's
Blind Girl of Castèl Cuillè,—a beautiful poem, unknown
to English ears and hearts, but well deserving to be
made known."

I

At the foot of the mountain height
Where is perched Castèl Cuillè,
When the apple, the plum, and the almond
   tree
In the plain below were growing white,

This is the song one might perceive
On a Wednesday morn of St. Joseph's
   Eve :

The roads should blossom, the roads should bloom,
So fair a bride shall leave her home !
Should blossom and bloom with garlands gay,
So fair a bride shall pass to-day !

This old Te Deum, rustic rites attending,
   Seemed from the clouds descending ;
   When lo ! a merry company
Of rosy village girls, clean as the eye,
   Each one with her attendant swain,
Came to the cliff, all singing the same
   strain ;
Resembling there, so near unto the sky,
Rejoicing angels, that kind heaven had
   sent
For their delight and our encouragement.
   Together blending,
   And soon descending
   The narrow sweep
   Of the hillside steep,
   They wind aslant
   Towards Saint Amant,
   Through leafy alleys
   Of verdurous valleys
   With merry sallies,
   Singing their chant :

The roads should blossom, the roads should bloom,
So fair a bride shall leave her home !
Should blossom and bloom with garlands gay,
So fair a bride shall pass to-day !

It is Baptiste, and his affianced maiden,
With garlands for the bridal laden !

The sky was blue ; without one cloud of
   gloom,
   The sun of March was shining brightly,
   And to the air the freshening wind gave
     lightly
Its breathings of perfume.

When one beholds the dusky hedges blos-
   som,
   A rustic bridal, ah ! how sweet it is !
   To sounds of joyous melodies,
That touch with tenderness the trembling
   bosom,
   A band of maidens
   Gayly frolicking,
   A band of youngsters

Wildly rollicking !
  Kissing,
  Caressing,
With fingers pressing,
  Till in the veriest
Madness of mirth, as they dance,
  They retreat and advance,
    Trying whose laugh shall be loud-
      est and merriest ;
  While the bride, with roguish eyes,
Sporting with them, now escapes and
    cries :
  "Those who catch me
    Married verily
    This year shall be !"

And all pursue with eager haste,
And all attain what they pursue,
And touch her pretty apron fresh and
  new,
And the linen kirtle round her waist.

Meanwhile, whence comes it that
    among
These youthful maidens fresh and fair,
So joyous, with such laughing air,
Baptiste stands sighing, with silent
  tongue ?
And yet the bride is fair and young !
Is it Saint Joseph would say to us all,
That love, o'er-hasty, precedeth a fall ?
  Oh no ! for a maiden frail, I trow,
  Never bore so lofty a brow !
What lovers ! they give not a single caress !
To see them so careless and cold to-day,
  These are grand people, one would
    say.
What ails Baptiste ? what grief doth him
  oppress ?

It is, that, half-way up the hill,
In yon cottage, by whose walls
Stand the cart-house and the stalls,
Dwelleth the blind orphan still,
Daughter of a veteran old ;
And you must know, one year ago,
That Margaret, the young and tender,
Was the village pride and splendor,
And Baptiste her lover bold.
Love, the deceiver, them ensnared ;
For them the altar was prepared ;
But alas ! the summer's blight,
The dread disease that none can stay,
The pestilence that walks by night,
Took the young bride's sight away.

All at the father's stern command was
    changed ;
Their peace was gone, but not their love
    estranged.
Wearied at home, erelong the lover fled ;
  Returned but three short days ago,
  The golden chain they round him
    throw,
  He is enticed, and onward led
  To marry Angela, and yet
  Is thinking ever of Margaret.

Then suddenly a maiden cried,
  "Anna, Theresa, Mary, Kate !
Here comes the cripple Jane !"   And by a
    fountain's side
  A woman, bent and gray with years,
  Under the mulberry trees appears,
  And all towards her run, as fleet
  As had they wings upon their feet.

It is that Jane, the cripple Jane,
Is a soothsayer, wary and kind.
She telleth fortunes, and none complain.
  She promises one a village swain,
  Another a happy wedding-day,
  And the bride a lovely boy straight-
    way.
  All comes to pass as she avers ;
  She never deceives, she never errs.

But for this once the village seer
  Wears a countenance severe,
And from beneath her eyebrows thin and
    white
  Her two eyes flash like cannons bright
  Aimed at the bridegroom in waistcoat
    blue,
  Who, like a statue, stands in view ;
  Changing color, as well he might,
  When the beldame wrinkled and gray
  Takes the young bride by the hand,
  And, with the tip of her reedy wand
  Making the sign of the cross, doth
    say : —
  "Thoughtless Angela, beware !
  Lest, when thou weddest this false
    bridegroom,
  Thou diggest for thyself a tomb !"
And she was silent ; and the maidens fair
Saw from each eye escape a swollen tear ;
But on a little streamlet silver-clear,
  What are two drops of turbid rain ?
  Saddened a moment, the bridal train
  Resumed the dance and song again ;

The bridegroom only was pale with fear ; —
  And down green alleys
  Of verdurous valleys,
  With merry sallies,
  They sang the refrain : —

The roads should blossom, the roads should bloom,
So fair a bride shall leave her home !
Should blossom and bloom with garlands gay,
So fair a bride shall pass to-day !

II

And by suffering worn and weary,
But beautiful as some fair angel yet,
  Thus lamented Margaret,
In her cottage lone and dreary : —

  " He has arrived ! arrived at last !
Yet Jane has named him not these three
  days past ;
  Arrived ! yet keeps aloof so far !
And knows that of my night he is the star !
Knows that long months I wait alone, be-
  nighted,
And count the moments since he went
  away !
Come ! keep the promise of that happier
  day,
That I may keep the faith to thee I
  plighted !
What joy have I without thee ? what de-
  light ?
Grief wastes my life, and makes it misery ;
Day for the others ever, but for me
  Forever night ! forever night !
When he is gone 't is dark ! my soul is
  sad !
I suffer ! O my God ! come, make me glad.
When he is near, no thoughts of day in-
  trude ;
Day has blue heavens, but Baptiste has
  blue eyes !
Within them shines for me a heaven of
  love,
A heaven all happiness, like that above,
  No more of grief ! no more of lassi-
  tude !
Earth I forget, — and heaven, and all dis-
  tresses,
When seated by my side my hand he
  presses ;
But when alone, remember all !
Where is Baptiste ? he hears not when I
  call !

A branch of ivy, dying on the ground,
  I need some bough to twine around !
In pity come ! be to my suffering kind !
True love, they say, in grief doth more
  abound !
  What then — when one is blind ?

  " Who knows ? perhaps I am forsaken !
Ah ! woe is me ! then bear me to my
  grave !
  O God ! what thoughts within me
  waken !
Away ! he will return ! I do but rave !
He will return ! I need not fear !
He swore it by our Saviour dear ;
He could not come at his own will ;
Is weary, or perhaps is ill !
Perhaps his heart, in this disguise,
Prepares for me some sweet sur-
  prise !
But some one comes ! Though blind, my
  heart can see !
And that deceives me not ! 't is he ! 't is
  he ! "
  And the door ajar is set,
  And poor, confiding Margaret
Rises, with outstretched arms, but sightless
  eyes ;
'T is only Paul, her brother, who thus
  cries : —
  " Angela the bride has passed !
I saw the wedding guests go by ;
Tell me, my sister, why were we not
  asked ?
For all are there but you and I ! "

  " Angela married ! and not sent
To tell her secret unto me !
Oh, speak ! who may the bridegroom
  be ? "
  " My sister, 't is Baptiste, thy
  friend ! "

A cry the blind girl gave, but nothing
  said ;
A milky whiteness spreads upon her
  cheeks ;
  An icy hand, as heavy as lead,
Descending, as her brother speaks,
Upon her heart, that has ceased to
  beat,
Suspends awhile its life and heat.
She stands beside the boy, now sore dis-
  tressed,
A wax Madonna as a peasant dressed.

At length, the bridal song again
Brings her back to her sorrow and
    pain.

"Hark! the joyous airs are ringing!
Sister, dost thou hear them singing?
How merrily they laugh and jest!
Would we were bidden with the rest!
I would don my hose of homespun
    gray,
And my doublet of linen striped and
    gay;
Perhaps they will come; for they do
    not wed
Till to-morrow at seven o'clock, it is
    said!"
"I know it!" answered Margaret;
Whom the vision, with aspect black as jet,
Mastered again; and its hand of ice
Held her heart crushed, as in a vice!
"Paul, be not sad! 'T is a holiday;
To-morrow put on thy doublet gay!
But leave me now for awhile alone."
Away, with a hop and a jump, went
    Paul,
And, as he whistled along the hall,
Entered Jane, the crippled crone.

"Holy Virgin! what dreadful heat!
I am faint, and weary, and out of
    breath!
But thou art cold, — art chill as
    death;
My little friend! what ails thee,
    sweet?"
"Nothing! I heard them singing home the
    bride;
And, as I listened to the song,
I thought my turn would come erelong,
Thou knowest it is at Whitsuntide.
Thy cards forsooth can never lie,
To me such joy they prophesy,
Thy skill shall be vaunted far and
    wide
When they behold him at my side.
And poor Baptiste, what sayest thou?
It must seem long to him; — methinks I see
    him now!"
Jane, shuddering, her hand doth press:
"Thy love I cannot all approve;
We must not trust too much to happi-
    ness; —
Go, pray to God, that thou mayest love him
    less!"
"The more I pray, the more I love!

It is no sin, for God is on my side!"
It was enough; and Jane no more replied.

Now to all hope her heart is barred and
    cold;
But to deceive the beldame old
She takes a sweet, contented air;
Speak of foul weather or of fair,
At every word the maiden smiles!
Thus the beguiler she beguiles;
So that, departing at the evening's close,
She says, "She may be saved! she
    nothing knows!"

Poor Jane, the cunning sorceress!
Now that thou wouldst, thou art no pro-
    phetess!
This morning, in the fulness of thy heart,
Thou wast so, far beyond thine art!

III

Now rings the bell, nine times reverber-
    ating,
And the white daybreak, stealing up the
    sky,
Sees in two cottages two maidens waiting,
    How differently!

Queen of a day, by flatterers caressed,
    The one puts on her cross and crown,
    Decks with a huge bouquet her breast,
    And flaunting, fluttering up and down,
    Looks at herself, and cannot rest.
    The other, blind, within her little
        room,
    Has neither crown nor flower's per-
        fume;
But in their stead for something gropes
        apart,
    That in a drawer's recess doth lie,
And, 'neath her bodice of bright scarlet
        dye,
    Convulsive clasps it to her heart.

The one, fantastic, light as air,
    'Mid kisses ringing,
    And joyous singing,
Forgets to say her morning prayer!

The other, with cold drops upon her brow,
    Joins her two hands, and kneels upon the
        floor,
And whispers, as her brother opes the door,
    "O God! forgive me now!"

And then the orphan, young and blind,
Conducted by her brother's hand,
Towards the church, through paths un-
scanned,
With tranquil air, her way doth wind.
Odors of laurel, making her faint and pale,
Round her at times exhale,
And in the sky as yet no sunny ray,
But brumal vapors gray.

Near that castle, fair to see,
Crowded with sculptures old, in every
part,
Marvels of nature and of art,
And proud of its name of high degree,
A little chapel, almost bare
At the base of the rock, is builded
there ;
All glorious that it lifts aloof,
Above each jealous cottage roof,
Its sacred summit, swept by autumn gales,
And its blackened steeple high in air,
Round which the osprey screams and
sails.

" Paul, lay thy noisy rattle by ! "
Thus Margaret said. " Where are we ? we
ascend ! "
" Yes ; seest thou not our journey's end ?
Hearest not the osprey from the belfry
cry ?
The hideous bird, that brings ill luck, we
know !
Dost thou remember when our father said,
The night we watched beside his bed,
' O daughter, I am weak and low ;
Take care of Paul ; I feel that I am dy-
ing ! '
And thou, and he, and I, all fell to crying ?
Then on the roof the osprey screamed
aloud ;
And here they brought our father in his
shroud.
There is his grave ; there stands the cross
we set ;
Why dost thou clasp me so, dear Mar-
garet ?
Come in ! the bride will be here soon :
Thou tremblest ! O my God ! thou art go-
ing to swoon ! "

She could no more, — the blind girl, weak
and weary !
A voice seemed crying from that grave so
dreary,

" What wouldst thou do, my daughter ? " —
and she started,
And quick recoiled, aghast, faint-
hearted ;
But Paul, impatient, urges evermore
Her steps towards the open door ;
And when, beneath her feet, the unhappy
maid
Crushes the laurel near the house immor-
tal,
And with her head, as Paul talks on again,
Touches the crown of filigrane
Suspended from the low-arched portal,
No more restrained, no more afraid,
She walks, as for a feast arrayed,
And in the ancient chapel's sombre night
They both are lost to sight.

At length the bell,
With booming sound,
Sends forth, resounding round,
Its hymeneal peal o'er rock and down the
dell.
It is broad day, with sunshine and with
rain ;
And yet the guests delay not long,
For soon arrives the bridal train,
And with it brings the village throng.

In sooth, deceit maketh no mortal gay,
For lo ! Baptiste on this triumphant day,
Mute as an idiot, sad as yester-morning,
Thinks only of the beldame's words of
warning.

And Angela thinks of her cross, I wis ;
To be a bride is all ! the pretty lisper
Feels her heart swell to hear all round her
whisper,
" How beautiful ! how beautiful she is ! "

But she must calm that giddy head,
For already the Mass is said ;
At the holy table stands the priest ;
The wedding ring is blessed ; Baptiste re-
ceives it ;
Ere on the finger of the bride he leaves
it,
He must pronounce one word at
least !
'T is spoken ; and sudden at the grooms-
man's side
" 'T is he ! " a well-known voice has cried.
And while the wedding guests all hold their
breath,

Opes the confessional, and the blind girl,
    see !
"Baptiste," she said, "since thou hast
    wished my death,
As holy water be my blood for thee ! "
And calmly in the air a knife suspended !
Doubtless her guardian angel near attended,
    For anguish did its work so well,
    That, ere the fatal stroke descended,
        Lifeless she fell !

    At eve, instead of bridal verse,
    The De Profundis filled the air ;
    Decked with flowers a simple hearse
To the churchyard forth they bear ;
Village girls in robes of snow
Follow, weeping as they go ;
Nowhere was a smile that day,
No, ah no ! for each one seemed to say : —

The road should mourn and be veiled in gloom,
So fair a corpse shall leave its home !
Should mourn and should weep, ah, well-away !
So fair a corpse shall pass to day !

A CHRISTMAS CAROL

**FROM THE NOEI BOURGUIGNON DE GUI
BARÔZAI**

I HEAR along our street
Pass the minstrel throngs ;
Hark ! they play so sweet,
On their hautboys, Christmas songs !
    Let us by the fire
    Ever higher
Sing them till the night expire !

In December ring
Every day the chimes ;
Loud the gleemen sing
In the streets their merry rhymes.
    Let us by the fire
    Ever higher
Sing them till the night expire.

Shepherds at the grange,
Where the Babe was born,
Sang, with many a change,
Christmas carols until morn.
    Let us by the fire
    Ever higher
Sing them till the night expire !

These good people sang
Songs devout and sweet ;
While the rafters rang,
There they stood with freezing feet.
    Let us by the fire
    Ever higher
Sing them till the night expire.

Nuns in frigid cells
At this holy tide,
For want of something else,
Christmas songs at times have tried.
    Let us by the fire
    Ever higher
Sing them till the night expire !

Washerwomen old,
To the sound they beat,
Sing by rivers cold,
With uncovered heads and feet.
    Let us by the fire
    Ever higher
Sing them till the night expire.

Who by the fireside stands
Stamps his feet and sings ;
But he who blows his hands
Not so gay a carol brings.
    Let us by the fire
    Ever higher
Sing them till the night expire !

CONSOLATION

**TO M. DUPERRIER, GENTLEMAN OF AIX
IN PROVENCE, ON THE DEATH OF HIS
DAUGHTER**

BY FRANÇOIS DE MALHERBE

WILL then, Duperrier, thy sorrow be eter-
    nal ?
    And shall the sad discourse
Whispered within thy heart, by tenderness
    paternal,
    Only augment its force ?

Thy daughter's mournful fate, into the tomb
    descending
    By death's frequented ways,
Has it become to thee a labyrinth never
    ending,
    Where thy lost reason strays ?

I know the charms that made her youth a
  benediction :
Nor should I be content,
As a censorious friend, to solace thine afflic-
  tion
By her disparagement.

But she was of the world, which fairest
  things exposes
To fates the most forlorn ;
A rose, she too hath lived as long as live
  the roses,
The space of one brief morn.

. . . .
Death has his rigorous laws, unparalleled,
  unfeeling ;
All prayers to him are vain ;
Cruel, he stops his ears, and, deaf to our
  appealing,
He leaves us to complain.

The poor man in his hut, with only thatch
  for cover,
Unto these laws must bend ;
The sentinel that guards the barriers of the
  Louvre
Cannot our kings defend.

To murmur against death, in petulant defi-
  ance,
Is never for the best ;
To will what God doth will, that is the only
  science
That gives us any rest.

TO CARDINAL RICHELIEU

BY FRANÇOIS DE MALHERBE

Thou mighty Prince of Church and State,
Richelieu ! until the hour of death,
Whatever road man chooses, Fate
Still holds him subject to her breath.
Spun of all silks, our days and nights
Have sorrows woven with delights ;
And of this intermingled shade
Our various destiny appears,
Even as one sees the course of years
Of summers and of winters made.

Sometimes the soft, deceitful hours
Let us enjoy the halcyon wave ;
Sometimes impending peril lowers
Beyond the seaman's skill to save.

The Wisdom, infinitely wise,
That gives to human destinies
Their foreordained necessity,
Has made no law more fixed below,
Than the alternate ebb and flow
Of Fortune and Adversity.

THE ANGEL AND THE CHILD

(L'Ange et l'Enfant ; Elégie à une Mère)

BY JEAN REBOUL, THE BAKER OF NISMES

An angel with a radiant face,
  Above a cradle bent to look,
Seemed his own image there to trace,
  As in the waters of a brook.

" Dear child ! who me resemblest so,"
  It whispered, " come, oh come with me !
Happy together let us go,
  The earth unworthy is of thee !

" Here none to perfect bliss attain ;
  The soul in pleasure suffering lies ;
Joy hath an undertone of pain,
  And even the happiest hours their sighs.

" Fear doth at every portal knock ;
  Never a day serene and pure
From the o'ershadowing tempest's shock
  Hath made the morrow's dawn secure.

" What, then, shall sorrows and shall fears
  Come to disturb so pure a brow ?
And with the bitterness of tears
  These eyes of azure troubled grow ?

" Ah no ! into the fields of space,
  Away shalt thou escape with me ;
And Providence will grant thee grace
  Of all the days that were to be.

" Let no one in thy dwelling cower,
  In sombre vestments draped and veiled ;
But let them welcome thy last hour,
  As thy first moments once they hailed.

" Without a cloud be there each brow ;
  There let the grave no shadow cast ;
When one is pure as thou art now,
  The fairest day is still the last."

And waving wide his wings of white,
  The angel, at these words, had sped
Towards the eternal realms of light ! —
  Poor mother ! see, thy son is dead !

ON THE TERRACE OF THE AIGALADES

BY JOSEPH MÉRY

FROM this high portal, where upsprings
The rose to touch our hands in play,
We at a glance behold three things, —
The Sea, the Town, and the Highway.

And the Sea says : My shipwrecks fear ;
I drown my best friends in the deep ;
And those who braved my tempests, here
Among my sea-weeds lie asleep !

The Town says : I am filled and fraught
With tumult and with smoke and care ;
My days with toil are overwrought,
And in my nights I gasp for air.

The Highway says : My wheel-tracks guide
To the pale climates of the North ;
Where my last milestone stands abide
The people to their death gone forth.

Here in the shade this life of ours,
Full of delicious air, glides by
Amid a multitude of flowers
As countless as the stars on high ;

These red-tiled roofs, this fruitful soil,
Bathed with an azure all divine,
Where springs the tree that gives us oil,
The grape that giveth us the wine ;

Beneath these mountains stripped of trees,
Whose tops with flowers are covered o'er,
Where springtime of the Hesperides
Begins, but endeth nevermore ;

Under these leafy vaults and walls,
That unto gentle sleep persuade ;
This rainbow of the waterfalls,
Of mingled mist and sunshine made ;

Upon these shores, where all invites,
We live our languid life apart ;
This air is that of life's delights,
The festival of sense and heart ;

This limpid space of time prolong,
Forget to-morrow in to-day,
And leave unto the passing throng
The Sea, the Town, and the Highway.

TO MY BROOKLET

(À MON RUISSEAU)

BY JEAN FRANÇOIS DUCIS

THOU brooklet, all unknown to song,
  Hid in the covert of the wood !
Ah, yes, like thee I fear the throng,
  Like thee I love the solitude.

O brooklet, let my sorrows past
  Lie all forgotten in their graves,
Till in my thoughts remain at last
  Only thy peace, thy flowers, thy waves.

The lily by thy margin waits ; —
  The nightingale, the marguerite ;
In shadow here he meditates
  His nest, his love, his music sweet.

Near thee the self-collected soul
  Knows naught of error or of crime ;
Thy waters, murmuring as they roll,
  Transform his musings into rhyme.

Ah, when, on bright autumnal eves,
  Pursuing still thy course, shall I
List the soft shudder of the leaves,
  And hear the lapwing's plaintive cry ?

BARRÉGES

BY LEFRANC DE POMPIGNAN

I LEAVE you, ye cold mountain chains,
  Dwelling of warriors stark and frore !
  You, may these eyes behold no more,
Save on the horizon of our plains.

Vanish, ye frightful, gloomy views !
  Ye rocks that mount up to the clouds !
  Of skies, enwrapped in misty shrouds,
Impracticable avenues !

Ye torrents, that with might and main
  Break pathways through the rocky walls,
  With your terrific waterfalls
Fatigue no more my weary brain !

Arise, ye landscapes full of charms,
　Arise, ye pictures of delight !
　Ye brooks, that water in your flight
The flowers and harvests of our farms !

You I perceive, ye meadows green,
　Where the Garonne the lowland fills,
　Not far from that long chain of hills,
With intermingled vales between.

Yon wreath of smoke, that mounts so high,
　Methinks from my own hearth must come;
　With speed, to that beloved home,
Fly, ye too lazy coursers, fly !

And bear me thither, where the soul
　In quiet may itself possess,
　Where all things soothe the mind's dis-
　　tress,
Where all things teach me and console.

WILL EVER THE DEAR DAYS COME BACK AGAIN ?

WILL ever the dear days come back again,
　Those days of June, when lilacs were in
　　bloom,
　And bluebirds sang their sonnets in the
　　gloom
Of leaves that roofed them in from sun
　or rain ?
I know not ; but a presence will remain
　Forever and forever in this room,
　Formless, diffused in air ; like a per-
　　fume, —
A phantom of the heart, and not the brain.
Delicious days ! when every spoken word
　Was like a footfall nearer and more near,
　And a mysterious knocking at the gate
Of the heart's secret places, and we heard
　In the sweet tumult of delight and fear
　A voice that whispered, " Open, I cannot
　　wait ! "

AT LA CHAUDEAU

BY XAVIER MARMIER

At La Chaudeau, — 't is long since then :
I was young, — my years twice ten ;
All things smiled on the happy boy,
Dreams of love and songs of joy,
Azure of heaven and wave below,
　　At La Chaudeau.

To La Chaudeau I come back old :
My head is gray, my blood is cold ;
Seeking along the meadow ooze,
Seeking beside the river Seymouse,
The days of my spring-time of long ago
　　At La Chaudeau.

At La Chaudeau nor heart nor brain
Ever grows old with grief and pain ;
A sweet remembrance keeps off age ;
A tender friendship doth still assuage
The burden of sorrow that one may know
　　At La Chaudeau.

At La Chaudeau, had fate decreed
To limit the wandering life I lead,
Peradventure I still, forsooth,
Should have preserved my fresh green
　youth
Under the shadows the hill-tops throw
　　At La Chaudeau.

At La Chaudeau, live on, my friends,
Happy to be where God intends ;
And sometimes, by the evening fire,
Think of him whose sole desire
Is again to sit in the old château
　　At La Chaudeau.

A QUIET LIFE

LET him who will, by force or fraud in-
　nate,
　Of courtly grandeurs gain the slippery
　　height ;
I, leaving not the home of my delight,
　Far from the world and noise will medi-
　　tate.
Then, without pomps or perils of the great,
　I shall behold the day succeed the night ;
Behold the alternate seasons take their
　flight,
　And in serene repose old age await.
And so, whenever Death shall come to
　close
　The happy moments that my days com-
　　pose,
I, full of years, shall die, obscure, alone !
How wretched is the man, with honors
　crowned,
　Who, having not the one thing needful
　　found,
　Dies, known to all, but to himself un-
　　known.

THE WINE OF JURANÇON

BY CHARLES CORAN

LITTLE sweet wine of Jurançon,
  You are dear to my memory still !
With mine host and his merry song,
  Under the rose-tree I drank my fill.

Twenty years after, passing that way,
  Under the trellis I found again
Mine host, still sitting there *au frais*,
  And singing still the same refrain.

The Jurançon, so fresh and bold,
  Treats me as one it used to know ;
Souvenirs of the days of old
  Already from the bottle flow.

With glass in hand our glances met ;
  We pledge, we drink. How sour it is !
Never Argenteuil piquette
  Was to my palate sour as this !

And yet the vintage was good, in sooth ;
  The self-same juice, the self-same cask !
It was you, O gayety of my youth,
  That failed in the autumnal flask !

FRIAR LUBIN

(LE FRÈRE LUBIN)

BY CLEMENT MAROT

Mr. Longfellow gave this lyric in his paper on *Origin and Progress of the French Language*, and afterward printed it in *The Poets and Poetry of Europe*. In one of the scenes of *Michael Angelo*, which he appears to have set aside when revising that dramatic poem, he makes Rabelais sing it. The *envoy* which closes the poem here is omitted in the scene.

To gallop off to town post-haste,
  So oft, the times I cannot tell ;
To do vile deed, nor feel disgraced, —
  Friar Lubin will do it well.
But a sober life to lead,
  To honor virtue, and pursue it,
That 's a pious, Christian deed, —
  Friar Lubin cannot do it.

To mingle, with a knowing smile,
  The goods of others with his own,
And leave you without cross or pile,
  Friar Lubin stands alone.

To say 't is yours is all in vain,
  If once he lays his finger to it ;
For as to giving back again,
  Friar Lubin cannot do it.

With flattering words and gentle tone,
  To woo and win some guileless maid,
Cunning pander need you none, —
  Friar Lubin knows the trade.
Loud preacheth he sobriety,
  But as for water, doth eschew it ;
Your dog may drink it, — but not he ;
  Friar Lubin cannot do it.

ENVOY

When an evil deed 's to do
Friar Lubin is stout and true ;
Glimmers a ray of goodness through it,
Friar Lubin cannot do it.

RONDEL

BY JEAN FROISSART

LOVE, love, what wilt thou with this heart
    of mine ?
  Naught see I fixed or sure in thee !
I do not know thee, — nor what deeds are
    thine :
Love, love, what wilt thou with this heart
    of mine ?
  Naught see I fixed or sure in thee !

Shall I be mute, or vows with prayers
    combine ?
  Ye who are blessed in loving, tell it me :
Love, love, what wilt thou with this heart
    of mine ?
  Naught see I permanent or sure in thee !

MY SECRET

BY FÉLIX ARVERS

MY soul its secret has, my life too has its
    mystery,
A love eternal in a moment's space con-
    ceived ;
Hopeless the evil is, I have not told its
    history,
And she who was the cause nor knew it nor
    believed.

Alas ! I shall have passed close by her un-
    perceived,
Forever at her side, and yet forever lonely,
I shall unto the end have made life's jour-
    ney, only
Daring to ask for naught, and having
    naught received.
For her, though God has made her gentle
    and endearing,
She will go on her way distraught and
    without hearing
These murmurings of love that round her
    steps ascend,
Piously faithful still unto her austere duty,
Will say, when she shall read these lines
    full of her beauty,
"Who can this woman be ? " and will not
comprehend.

FROM THE ITALIAN

THE CELESTIAL PILOT

PURGATORIO II. 13–51.

Mr. Longfellow's biographer, in speaking of the poet's
methods with his college class when engaged upon the
study of Dante, says: " The Professor read the book
into English to his class, with a running commentary
and illustration. For his purpose he had bound an in-
terleaved copy of the author ; the blank pages of which
he gradually filled with notes and with translations of
noteworthy passages. In this way were written those
passages from the *Divina Commedia* which were first
printed in the *Voices of the Night.*"

AND now, behold ! as at the approach of
    morning,
Through the gross vapors, Mars grows
    fiery red
Down in the west upon the ocean floor,
Appeared to me, — may I again behold
    it !
A light along the sea, so swiftly com-
    ing,
Its motion by no flight of wing is equalled.
And when therefrom I had withdrawn a
    little
Mine eyes, that I might question my con-
    ductor,
Again I saw it brighter grown and larger.
Thereafter, on all sides of it, appeared
I knew not what of white, and under-
    neath,
Little by little, there came forth another.
My master yet had uttered not a word,

While the first whiteness into wings un-
    folded ;
But, when he clearly recognized the
    pilot,
He cried aloud : "Quick, quick, and bow
    the knee !
Behold the Angel of God ! fold up thy
    hands !
Henceforward shalt thou see such offi-
    cers !
See, how he scorns all human arguments,
So that no oar he wants, nor other sail
Than his own wings, between so distant
    shores !
See, how he holds them, pointed straight to
    heaven,
Fanning the air with the eternal pinions,
That do not moult themselves like mortal
    hair ! "
And then, as nearer and more near us
    came
The Bird of Heaven, more glorious he
    appeared,
So that the eye could not sustain his
    presence,
But down I cast it ; and he came to shore
With a small vessel, gliding swift and
    light,
So that the water swallowed naught
    thereof.
Upon the stern stood the Celestial Pilot !
Beatitude seemed written in his face !
And more than a hundred spirits sat
    within.
"*In exitu Israel de Ægypto !*"
Thus sang they all together in one voice,
With whatso in that Psalm is after writ-
    ten.
Then made he sign of holy rood upon them,
Whereat all cast themselves upon the
    shore,
And he departed swiftly as he came.

THE TERRESTRIAL PARADISE

PURGATORIO XXVIII. I–33.

LONGING already to search in and round
The heavenly forest, dense and living-
    green,
Which tempered to the eyes the new-
    born day.
Withouten more delay I left the bank,

Crossing the level country slowly, slowly,
    Over the soil, that everywhere breathed
        fragrance.
A gently-breathing air, that no mutation
    Had in itself, smote me upon the fore-
        head
    No heavier blow than of a pleasant breeze,
Whereat the tremulous branches readily
    Did all of them bow downward towards
        that side
    Where its first shadow casts the Holy
        Mountain ;
Yet not from their upright direction bent
    So that the little birds upon their tops
    Should cease the practice of their tune-
        ful art ;
But, with full-throated joy, the hours of
        prime
    Singing received they in the midst of
        foliage
    That made monotonous burden to their
        rhymes,
Even as from branch to branch it gather-
        ing swells,
    Through the pine forests on the shore of
        Chiassi,
    When Æolus unlooses the Sirocco.
Already my slow steps had led me on
    Into the ancient wood so far, that I
    Could see no more the place where I
        had entered.
And lo ! my further course cut off a river,
    Which, tow'rds the left hand, with its
        little waves,
    Bent down the grass, that on its margin
        sprang.
All waters that on earth most limpid are,
    Would seem to have within themselves
        some mixture,
    Compared with that, which nothing doth
        conceal,
Although it moves on with a brown, brown
        current,
    Under the shade perpetual, that never
    Ray of the sun lets in, nor of the moon.

BEATRICE

PURGATORIO XXX. 13-33, 85-99, XXXI.
    13-21.

EVEN as the Blessed, at the final summons,
    Shall rise up quickened, each one from
        his grave,

Wearing again the garments of the flesh,
So, upon that celestial chariot,
    A hundred rose *ad vocem tanti senis*,
    Ministers and messengers of life eter-
        nal.
They all were saying, "*Benedictus qui
    venis*,"
    And scattering flowers above and round
        about,
" *Manibus o date lilia plenis*."
Oft have I seen, at the approach of day,
    The orient sky all stained with roseate
        hues,
    And the other heaven with light serene
        adorned,
And the sun's face uprising, overshad-
        owed,
    So that, by temperate influence of va-
        pors,
    The eye sustained his aspect for long
        while ;
Thus in the bosom of a cloud of flowers,
    Which from those hands angelic were
        thrown up,
    And down descended inside and with-
        out,
With crown of olive o'er a snow-white
        veil,
    Appeared a lady, under a green mantle,
    Vested in colors of the living flame.

.   .   .   .

Even as the snow, among the living raf-
        ters
    Upon the back of Italy, congeals,
    Blown on and beaten by Sclavonian
        winds,
And then, dissolving, filters through it-
        self,
    Whene'er the land, that loses shadow,
        breathes,
    Like as a taper melts before a fire,
Even such I was, without a sigh or tear,
    Before the song of those who chime for-
        ever
    After the chiming of the eternal
        spheres ;
But, when I heard in those sweet melo-
        dies
    Compassion for me, more than had they
        said,
    " Oh wherefore, lady, dost thou thus con-
        sume him ? "
The ice, that was about my heart congealed,
    To air and water changed, and, in my
        anguish,

Through lips and eyes came gushing
   from my breast.

. . . .

Confusion and dismay, together min-
   gled,
Forced such a feeble "Yes!" out of my
   mouth,
To understand it one had need of
   sight.
Even as a cross-bow breaks, when 't is dis-
   charged,
Too tensely drawn the bow-string and
   the bow,
And with less force the arrow hits the
   mark ;
So I gave way beneath this heavy burden,
   Gushing forth into bitter tears and
   sighs,
And the voice, fainting, flagged upon its
   passage.

TO ITALY

BY VINCENZO DA FILICAJA

ITALY! Italy! thou who 'rt doomed to
   wear
The fatal gift of beauty, and possess
The dower funest of infinite wretched-
   ness
Written upon thy forehead by de-
   spair ;
Ah! would that thou wert stronger, or less
   fair,
That they might fear thee more, or love
   thee less,
Who in the splendor of thy loveliness
Seem wasting, yet to mortal combat
   dare !
Then from the Alps I should not see de-
   scending
Such torrents of armed men, nor Gallic
   horde
Drinking the wave of Po, distained with
   gore,
Nor should I see thee girded with a
   sword
Not thine, and with the stranger's arm
   contending,
Victor or vanquished, slave forever-
   more.

SEVEN SONNETS AND A CAN-ZONE

The following translations are from the poems of Michael Angelo as revised by his nephew, Michael Angelo the Younger, and were made before the publication of the original text by Guasti. H. W. L.

I

THE ARTIST

NOTHING the greatest artist can conceive
   That every marble block doth not confine
   Within itself ; and only its design
   The hand that follows intellect can
   achieve.
The ill I flee, the good that I believe,
   In thee, fair lady, lofty and divine,
   Thus hidden lie ; and so that death be
   mine,
   Art of desired success doth me bereave.
Love is not guilty, then, nor thy fair face,
   Nor fortune, cruelty, nor great disdain,
   Of my disgrace, nor chance nor destiny,
If in thy heart both death and love find
   place
   At the same time, and if my humble
   brain,
   Burning, can nothing draw but death
   from thee.

II

FIRE

NOT without fire can any workman mould
   The iron to his preconceived design,
   Nor can the artist without fire refine
   And purify from all its dross the gold ;
Nor can revive the phœnix, we are told,
   Except by fire.   Hence, if such death be
   mine,
   I hope to rise again with the divine,
   Whom death augments, and time cannot
   make old.
O sweet, sweet death !   O fortunate fire
   that burns
   Within me still to renovate my days,
   Though I am almost numbered with the
   dead !
If by its nature unto heaven returns
   This element, me, kindled in its blaze,
   Will it bear upward when my life is fled.

III

YOUTH AND AGE

OH give me back the days when loose and
  free
   To my blind passion were the curb and
   rein,
   Oh give me back the angelic face again,
   With which all virtue buried seems to
   be !
Oh give my panting footsteps back to me,
   That are in age so slow and fraught with
   pain,
   And fire and moisture in the heart and
   brain,
   If thou wouldst have me burn and weep
   for thee !
If it be true thou livest alone, Amor,
   On the sweet - bitter tears of human
   hearts,
   In an old man thou canst not wake de-
   sire ;
Souls that have almost reached the other
   shore
   Of a diviner love should feel the darts,
   And be as tinder to a holier fire.

IV

OLD AGE

THE course of my long life hath reached at
   last,
   In fragile bark o'er a tempestuous sea,
   The common harbor, where must ren-
   dered be
   Account of all the actions of the past.
The impassioned phantasy, that, vague and
   vast,
   Made art an idol and a king to me,
   Was an illusion, and but vanity
   Were the desires that lured me and
   harassed.
The dreams of love, that were so sweet of
   yore,
   What are they now, when two deaths
   may be mine, —
One sure, and one forecasting its alarms ?
Painting and sculpture satisfy no more
   The soul now turning to the Love Di-
   vine,
   That oped, to embrace us, on the cross its
   arms.

V

TO VITTORIA COLONNA

LADY, how can it chance — yet this we
   see
   In long experience — that will longer
   last
   A living image carved from quarries
   vast
   Than its own maker, who dies pres-
   ently ?
Cause yieldeth to effect if this so be,
   And even Nature is by Art surpassed ;
   This know I, who to Art have given the
   past,
   But see that Time is breaking faith with
   me.
Perhaps on both of us long life can I
   Either in color or in stone bestow,
   By now portraying each in look and
   mien ;
So that a thousand years after we die,
   How fair thou wast, and I how full of
   woe,
   And wherefore I so loved thee, may be
   seen.

VI

TO VITTORIA COLONNA

WHEN the prime mover of my many sighs
   Heaven took through death from out her
   earthly place,
   Nature, that never made so fair a face,
   Remained ashamed, and tears were in all
   eyes.
O fate, unheeding my impassioned cries !
   O hopes fallacious ! O thou spirit of
   grace,
   Where art thou now ? Earth holds in
   its embrace
   Thy lovely limbs, thy holy thoughts the
   skies.
Vainly did cruel death attempt to stay
   The rumor of thy virtuous renown,
   That Lethe's waters could not wash away !
A thousand leaves, since he hath stricken
   thee down,
   Speak of thee, nor to thee could Heaven
   convey,
   Except through death, a refuge and a
   crown.

VII

DANTE

WHAT should be said of him cannot be
  said ;
  By too great splendor is his name at-
    tended ;
  To blame is easier those who him of-
    fended,
  Than reach the faintest glory round him
    shed.
This man descended to the doomed and
    dead
  For our instruction ; then to God as-
    cended ;
  Heaven opened wide to him its portals
    splendid,
  Who from his country's, closed against
    him, fled.
Ungrateful land !   To its own prejudice
  Nurse of his fortunes ; and this showeth
    well
  That the most perfect most of grief shall
    see.
Among a thousand proofs let one suffice,
  That as his exile hath no parallel,
  Ne'er walked the earth a greater man
    than he.

VIII

CANZONE

AH me ! ah me ! when thinking of the
    years,
  The vanished years, alas, I do not find
  Among them all one day that was my
    own !
Fallacious hopes, desires of the unknown,
  Lamenting, loving, burning, and in
    tears,
  (For human passions all have stirred my
    mind,)
Have held me, now I feel and know, con-
    fined
Both from the true and good still far
    away.
  I perish day by day ;
The sunshine fails, the shadows grow more
    dreary,
And I am near to fall, infirm and weary.

THE NATURE OF LOVE

BY GUIDO GUINIZELLI

To noble heart Love doth for shelter
    fly,
As seeks the bird the forest's leafy shade ;
Love was not felt till noble heart beat
    high,
Nor before love the noble heart was made.
  Soon as the sun's broad flame
Was formed, so soon the clear light filled the
    air ;
  Yet was not till he came :
So love springs up. in noble breasts, and
    there
  Has its appointed space,   .
As heat in the bright flames finds its allotted
    place.
Kindles in noble heart the fire of love,
As hidden virtue in the precious stone :
This virtue comes not from the stars
    above,
Till round it the ennobling sun has shone ;
  But when his powerful blaze
Has drawn forth what was vile, the stars
    impart
  Strange virtue in their rays ;
And thus when Nature doth create the
    heart
  Noble and pure and high,
Like virtue from the star, love comes from
    woman's eye.

FROM THE PORTUGUESE

SONG

BY GIL VICENTE

IF thou art sleeping, maiden,
  Awake, and open thy door.
'T is the break of day, and we must away,
  O'er meadow, and mount, and moor.

Wait not to find thy slippers,
  But come with thy naked feet :
We shall have to pass through the dewy
    grass,
  And waters wide and fleet.

FROM EASTERN SOURCES

THE FUGITIVE

A TARTAR SONG

I

"HE is gone to the desert land !
I can see the shining mane
Of his horse on the distant plain,
As he rides with his Kossak band !

"Come back, rebellious one !
Let thy proud heart relent ;
Come back to my tall, white tent,
Come back, my only son !

"Thy hand in freedom shall
Cast thy hawks, when morning breaks,
On the swans of the Seven Lakes,
On the lakes of Karajal.

"I will give thee leave to stray
And pasture thy hunting steeds
In the long grass and the reeds
Of the meadows of Karaday.

"I will give thee my coat of mail,
Of softest leather made,
With choicest steel inlaid ;
Will not all this prevail ? "

II

"This hand no longer shall
Cast my hawks, when morning breaks,
On the swans of the Seven Lakes,
On the lakes of Karajal.

"I will no longer stray
And pasture my hunting steeds
In the long grass and the reeds
Of the meadows of Karaday.

"Though thou give me thy coat of mail,
Of softest leather made,
With choicest steel inlaid,
All this cannot prevail.

"What right hast thou, O Khan,
To me, who am mine own,
Who am slave to God alone,
And not to any man ?

"God will appoint the day
When I again shall be
By the blue, shallow sea,
Where the steel-bright sturgeons play.

"God, who doth care for me,
In the barren wilderness,
On unknown hills, no less
Will my companion be.

"When I wander lonely and lost
In the wind ; when I watch at night
Like a hungry wolf, and am white
And covered with hoar-frost ;

"Yea, wheresoever I be,
In the yellow desert sands,
In mountains or unknown lands,
Allah will care for me ! "

III

Then Sobra, the old, old man, —
Three hundred and sixty years
Had he lived in this land of tears,
Bowed down and said, " O Khan !

"If you bid me, I will speak.
There 's no sap in dry grass,
No marrow in dry bones ! Alas,
The mind of old men is weak !

"I am old, I am very old :
I have seen the primeval man,
I have seen the great Genghis Khan,
Arrayed in his robes of gold.

"What I say to you is the truth ;
And I say to you, O Khan,
Pursue not the star-white man,
Pursue not the beautiful youth.

"Him the Almighty made,
And brought him forth of the light
At the verge and end of the night,
When men on the mountain prayed.

"He was born at the break of day,
When abroad the angels walk ;
He hath listened to their talk,
And he knoweth what they say·

"Gifted with Allah's grace,
Like the moon of Ramazan

When it shines in the skies, O Khan,
Is the light of his beautiful face.

" When first on earth he trod,
The first words that he said
Were these, as he stood and prayed,
' There is no God but God ! '

" And he shall be king of men,
For Allah hath heard his prayer,
And the Archangel in the air,
Gabriel, hath said, Amen ! "

THE SIEGE OF KAZAN

BLACK are the moors before Kazan,
And their stagnant waters smell of
blood :
I said in my heart, with horse and man,
I will swim across this shallow flood.

Under the feet of Argamack,
Like new moons were the shoes he bare,
Silken trappings hung on his back,
In a talisman on his neck, a prayer.

My warriors, thought I, are following me ;
But when I looked behind, alas !
Not one of all the band could I see,
All had sunk in the black morass !

Where are our shallow fords ? and where
The power of Kazan with its fourfold
gates ?
From the prison windows our maidens fair
Talk of us still through the iron grates.

We cannot hear them ; for horse and man
Lie buried deep in the dark abyss !
Ah ! the black day hath come down on
Kazan !
Ah ! was ever a grief like this ?

THE BOY AND THE BROOK

DOWN from yon distant mountain height
The brooklet flows through the village
street ;
A boy comes forth to wash his hands,
Washing, yes, washing, there he stands,
In the water cool and sweet.

Brook, from what mountain dost thou
come ?
O my brooklet cool and sweet !
I come from yon mountain high and cold
Where lieth the new snow on the old,
And melts in the summer heat.

Brook, to what river dost thou go ?
O my brooklet cool and sweet !
I go to the river there below
Where in bunches the violets grow,
And sun and shadow meet.

Brook, to what garden dost thou go ?
O my brooklet cool and sweet !
I go to the garden in the vale
Where all night long the nightingale
Her love-song doth repeat.

Brook, to what fountain dost thou go ?
O my brooklet cool and sweet !
I go to the fountain at whose brink
The maid that loves thee comes to drink,
And whenever she looks therein,
I rise to meet her, and kiss her chin,
And my joy is then complete.

TO THE STORK

WELCOME, O Stork ! that dost wing
Thy flight from the far-away !
Thou hast brought us the signs of Spring,
Thou hast made our sad hearts gay.

Descend, O Stork ! descend
Upon our roof to rest ;
In our ash-tree, O my friend,
My darling, make thy nest.

To thee, O Stork, I complain,
O Stork, to thee I impart
The thousand sorrows, the pain
And aching of my heart.

When thou away didst go,
Away from this tree of ours,
The withering winds did blow,
And dried up all the flowers.

Dark grew the brilliant sky,
Cloudy and dark and drear ;
They were breaking the snow on high,
And winter was drawing near.

From Varaca's rocky wall,
  From the rock of Varaca unrolled,
The snow came and covered all,
  And the green meadow was cold.

O Stork, our garden with snow
  Was hidden away and lost,
And the rose-trees that in it grow
  Were withered by snow and frost.

FROM THE LATIN

VIRGIL'S FIRST ECLOGUE

MELIBŒUS.

TITYRUS, thou in the shade of a spreading
    beech tree reclining
Meditatest, with slender pipe, the Muse of
    the woodlands.
We our country's bounds and pleasant pas-
    tures relinquish,
We our country fly ; thou, Tityrus, stretched
    in the shadow,
Teachest the woods to resound with the
    name of the fair Amaryllis.

TITYRUS.

O Melibœus, a god for us this leisure
    created,
For he will be unto me a god forever ; his
    altar
Oftentimes shall imbue a tender lamb from
    our sheepfolds.
He, my heifers to wander at large, and
    myself, as thou seest,
On my rustic reed to play what I will, hath
    permitted.

MELIBŒUS.

Truly I envy not, I marvel rather ; on all
    sides
In all the fields is such trouble.   Behold,
    my goats I am driving,
Heartsick, further away ; this one scarce,
    Tityrus, lead I ;
For having here yeaned twins just now
    among the dense hazels,
Hope of the flock, ah me ! on the naked
    flint she hath left them.
Often this evil to me, if my mind had not
    been insensate,
Oak trees stricken by heaven predicted, as
    now I remember ;

Often the sinister crow from the hollow
    ilex predicted.
Nevertheless, who this god may be, O
    Tityrus, tell me.

TITYRUS.

O Melibœus, the city that they call Rome,
    I imagined,
Foolish I ! to be like this of ours, where
    often we shepherds
Wonted are to drive down of our ewes the
    delicate offspring.
Thus whelps like unto dogs had I known,
    and kids to their mothers,
Thus to compare great things with small
    had I been accustomed.
But this among other cities its head as far
    hath exalted
As the cypresses do among the lissome
    viburnums.

MELIBŒUS.

And what so great occasion of seeing Rome
    hath possessed thee ?

TITYRUS.

Liberty, which, though late, looked upon
    me in my inertness,
After the time when my beard fell whiter
    from me in shaving,
Yet she looked upon me, and came to me
    after a long while,
Since Amaryllis possesses and Galatea hath
    left me.
For I will even confess that while Galatea
    possessed me
Neither care of my flock nor hope of
    liberty was there.
Though from my wattled folds there went
    forth many a victim,
And the unctuous cheese was pressed for
    the city ungrateful,
Never did my right hand return home
    heavy with money.

MELIBŒUS.

I have wondered why sad thou invokedst
    the gods, Amaryllis,
And for whom thou didst suffer the apples
    to hang on the branches !
Tityrus hence was absent !   Thee, Tityrus,
    even the pine trees,
Thee the very fountains, the very copses
    were calling.

TITYRUS.

What could I do? No power had I to
 escape from my bondage,
Nor had I power elsewhere to recognize
 gods so propitious.
Here I beheld that youth, to whom each
 year, Melibœus,
During twice six days ascends the smoke
 of our altars.
Here first gave he response to me soliciting
 favor:
" Feed as before your heifers, ye boys, and
 yoke up your bullocks."

MELIBŒUS.

Fortunate old man! So then thy fields
 will be left thee,
And large enough for thee, though naked
 stone and the marish
All thy pasture-lands with the dreggy rush
 may encompass.
No unaccustomed food thy gravid ewes
 shall endanger,
Nor of the neighboring flock the dire con-
 tagion infect them.
Fortunate old man! Here among familiar
 rivers,
And these sacred founts, shalt thou take
 the shadowy coolness.
On this side, a hedge along the neighboring
 cross-road,
Where Hyblæan bees ever feed on the
 flower of the willow,
Often with gentle susurrus to fall asleep
 shall persuade thee.
Yonder, beneath the high rock, the pruner
 shall sing to the breezes,
Nor meanwhile shall thy heart's delight,
 the hoarse wood-pigeons,
Nor the turtle-dove cease to mourn from
 aerial elm trees.

TITYRUS.

Therefore the agile stags shall sooner feed
 in the ether,
And the billows leave the fishes bare on the
 sea-shore,
Sooner, the border-lands of both overpassed,
 shall the exiled
Parthian drink of the Soane, or the German
 drink of the Tigris,
Than the face of him shall glide away from
 my bosom!

MELIBŒUS.

But we hence shall go, a part to the thirsty
 Africs,
Part to Scythia come, and the rapid Cretan
 Oaxes,
And to the Britons from all the universe
 utterly sundered.
Ah, shall I ever, a long time hence, the
 bounds of my country
And the roof of my lowly cottage covered
 with greensward
Seeing, with wonder behold, — my king-
 doms, a handful of wheat-ears!
Shall an impious soldier possess these lands
 newly cultured,
And these fields of corn a barbarian? Lo,
 whither discord
Us wretched people hath brought! for
 whom our fields we have planted!
Graft, Melibœus, thy pear trees now, put in
 order thy vineyards.
Go, my goats, go hence, my flocks so happy
 aforetime.
Never again henceforth outstretched in my
 verdurous cavern
Shall I behold you afar from the bushy
 precipice hanging.
Songs no more shall I sing; not with me,
 ye goats, as your shepherd,
Shall ye browse on the bitter willow or
 blooming laburnum.

TITYRUS.

Nevertheless, this night together with me
 canst thou rest thee
Here on the verdant leaves; for us there
 are mellowing apples,
Chestnuts soft to the touch, and clouted
 cream in abundance;
And the high roofs now of the villages
 smoke in the distance,
And from the lofty mountains are falling
 larger the shadows.

OVID IN EXILE

AT TOMIS, IN BESSARABIA, NEAR THE
MOUTHS OF THE DANUBE

TRISTIA, BOOK III., ELEGY X.

SHOULD any one there in Rome remember
 Ovid the exile,
 And, without me, my name still in the
 city survive;

Tell him that under stars which never set in the ocean
I am existing still, here in a barbarous land.

Fierce Sarmatians encompass me round, and the Bessi and Getæ ;
Names how unworthy to be sung by a genius like mine !

Yet when the air is warm, intervening Ister defends us :
He, as he flows, repels inroads of war with his waves.

But when the dismal winter reveals its hideous aspect,
When all the earth becomes white with a marble-like frost ;

And when Boreas is loosed, and the snow hurled under Arcturus,
Then these nations, in sooth, shudder and shiver with cold.

Deep lies the snow, and neither the sun nor the rain can dissolve it ;
Boreas hardens it still, makes it forever remain.

Hence, ere the first has melted away, another succeeds it.
And two years it is wont, in many places, to lie.

And so great is the power of the North-wind awakened, it levels
Lofty towers with the ground, roofs uplifted bears off.

Wrapped in skins, and with trousers sewed, they contend with the weather,
And their faces alone of the whole body are seen.

Often their tresses, when shaken, with pendent icicles tinkle,
And their whitened beards shine with the gathering frost.

Wines consolidate stand, preserving the form of the vessels ;
No more draughts of wine, — pieces presented they drink.

Why should I tell you how all the rivers are frozen and solid,
And from out of the lake frangible water is dug ?

Ister, — no narrower stream than the river that bears the papyrus, —
Which through its many mouths mingles its waves with the deep ;

Ister, with hardening winds, congeals its cerulean waters,
Under a roof of ice winding its way to the sea.

There where ships have sailed, men go on foot ; and the billows,
Solid made by the frost, hoof-beats of horses indent.

Over unwonted bridges, with water gliding beneath them,
The Sarmatian steers drag their barbarian carts.

Scarcely shall I be believed ; yet when naught is gained by a falsehood,
Absolute credence then should to a witness be given.

I have beheld the vast Black Sea of ice all compacted,
And a slippery crust pressing its motionless tides.

'T is not enough to have seen, I have trodden this indurate ocean ;
Dry shod passed my foot over its uppermost wave.

If thou hadst had of old such a sea as this is, Leander !
Then thy death had not been charged as a crime to the Strait.

Nor can the curvèd dolphins uplift themselves from the water ;
All their struggles to rise merciless winter prevents ;

And though Boreas sound with roar of wings in commotion,
In the blockaded gulf never a wave will there be ;

And the ships will stand hemmed in by the frost, as in marble,
Nor will the oar have power through the stiff waters to cleave.

Fast-bound in the ice have I seen the fishes adhering,
Yet notwithstanding this some of them still were alive.

Hence, if the savage strength of omnipotent Boreas freezes
Whether the salt-sea wave, whether the refluent stream, —

Straightway, — the Ister made level by arid blasts of the North-wind, —
Comes the barbaric foe borne on his swift-footed steed ;

Foe, that powerful made by his steed and his far-flying arrows,
All the neighboring land void of inhabitants makes.

Some take flight, and none being left to defend their possessions,
Unprotected, their goods pillage and plunder become ;

Cattle and creaking carts, the little wealth of the country,
And what riches beside indigent peasants possess.

Some as captives are driven along, their hands bound behind them,
Looking backward in vain toward their Lares and lands.

Others, transfixed with barbèd arrows, in agony perish.
For the swift arrow-heads all have in poison been dipped.

What they cannot carry or lead away they demolish,
And the hostile flames burn up the innocent cots.

Even when there is peace, the fear of war is impending ;
None, with the ploughshare pressed, furrows the soil any more.

Either this region sees, or fears a foe that it sees not,
And the sluggish land slumbers in utter neglect.

No sweet grape lies hidden here in the shade of its vine-leaves,
No fermenting must fills and o'erflows the deep vats.

Apples the region denies ; nor would Acontius have found here
Aught upon which to write words for his mistress to read.

Naked and barren plains without leaves or trees we behold here, —
Places, alas ! unto which no happy man would repair.

Since then this mighty orb lies open so wide upon all sides,
Has this region been found only my prison to be ?

TRISTIA, BOOK III., ELEGY XII.

Now the zephyrs diminish the cold, and the year being ended,
Winter Mæotian seems longer than ever before ;

And the Ram that bore unsafely the burden of Helle,
Now makes the hours of the day equal with those of the night.

Now the boys and the laughing girls the violet gather,
Which the fields bring forth, nobody sowing the seed.

Now the meadows are blooming with flowers of various colors,
And with untaught throats carol the garrulous birds.

Now the swallow, to shun the crime of her merciless mother,
Under the rafters builds cradles and dear little homes ;

And the blade that lay hid, covered up in
the furrows of Ceres,
Now from the tepid ground raises its
delicate head.

Where there is ever a vine, the bud shoots
forth from the tendrils,
But from the Getic shore distant afar is
the vine !

Where there is ever a tree, on the tree the
branches are swelling,
But from the Getic land distant afar is
the tree !

Now it is holiday there in Rome, and to
games in due order
Give place the windy wars of the vocifer-
ous bar.

Now they are riding the horses ; with light
arms now they are playing,
Now with the ball, and now round rolls
the swift-flying hoop :

Now, when the young athlete with flowing
oil is anointed,
He in the Virgin's Fount bathes, over-
wearied, his limbs.

Thrives the stage ; and applause, with
voices at variance, thunders,
And the Theatres three for the three
Forums resound.

Four times happy is he, and times without
number is happy,
Who the city of Rome, uninterdicted, en-
joys.

But all I see is the snow in the vernal sun-
shine dissolving,
And the waters no more delved from the
indurate lake.

Nor is the sea now frozen, nor as before
o'er the Ister
Comes the Sarmatian boor driving his
stridulous cart.

Hitherward, nevertheless, some keels al-
ready are steering,
And on this Pontic shore alien vessels
will be.

Eagerly shall I run to the sailor, and, having
saluted,
Who he may be, I shall ask ; wherefore
and whence he hath come.

Strange indeed will it be, if he come not
from regions adjacent,
And incautious unless ploughing the
neighboring sea.

Rarely a mariner over the deep from Italy
passes,
Rarely he comes to these shores, wholly
of harbors devoid.

Whether he knoweth Greek, or whether in
Latin he speaketh,
Surely on this account he the more wel-
come will be.

Also perchance from the mouth of the
Strait and the waters Propontic,
Unto the steady South-wind, some one is
spreading his sails.

Whosoever he is, the news he can faithfully
tell me,
Which may become a part and an ap-
proach to the truth.

He, I pray, may be able to tell me the
triumphs of Cæsar,
Which he has heard of, and vows paid
to the Latian Jove ;

And that thy sorrowful head, Germania,
thou, the rebellious,
Under the feet, at last, of the Great
Captain hast laid.

Whoso shall tell me these things, that not
to have seen will afflict me,
Forthwith unto my house welcomed as
guest shall he be.

Woe is me ! Is the house of Ovid in Scy-
thian lands now ?
And doth punishment now give me its
place for a home ?

Grant, ye gods, that Cæsar make this not
my house and my homestead,
But decree it to be only the inn of my
pain.

APPENDIX

I. JUVENILE POEMS

WHEN Mr. Longfellow made his first collection of poems in *Voices of the Night*, he included a group of *Earlier Poems*, but printed only seven out of a number which bore his initials or are directly traceable to him. He chose these, doubtless, not as specimens of his youthful work, but because, of all that he had written ten years or more before, they only appeared to him to have poetic qualities which he could regard with any complacency. It is not likely that any readers will be found to contravene his judgment in the omission of the other verses, but since this edition is intended for the student as well as for the general reader, it has been thought best to print here those poetical exercises which curious investigators have recovered from the obscurity in which Mr. Longfellow was entirely willing to leave them. They are printed in as nearly chronological order as may be.

THE BATTLE OF LOVELL'S POND

Mr. Longfellow's first verses, so far as known, printed in the Portland *Gazette*, November 17, 1820.

COLD, cold is the north wind and rude is the blast
That sweeps like a hurricane loudly and fast,
As it moans through the tall waving pines lone and drear,
Sighs a requiem sad o'er the warrior's bier.

The war-whoop is still, and the savage's yell
Has sunk into silence along the wild dell;
The din of the battle, the tumult, is o'er,
And the war-clarion's voice is now heard no more.

The warriors that fought for their country, and bled,
Have sunk to their rest; the damp earth is their bed;
No stone tells the place where their ashes repose,
Nor points out the spot from the graves of their foes.

They died in their glory, surrounded by fame,
And Victory's loud trump their death did proclaim;
They are dead; but they live in each Patriot's breast,
And their names are engraven on honor's bright crest.
.   HENRY.

TO IANTHE

WHEN upon the western cloud
Hang day's fading roses,
When the linnet sings aloud
And the twilight closes, —
As I mark the moss-grown spring
By the twisted holly,
Pensive thoughts of thee shall bring
Love's own melancholy.

Lo, the crescent moon on high
Lights the half-choked fountain;
Wandering winds steal sadly by
From the hazy mountain.
Yet that moon shall wax and wane,
Summer winds pass over, —
Ne'er the heart shall love again
Of the slighted lover!

When the russet autumn brings
Blighting to the forest,
Twisted close the ivy clings
To the oak that's hoarest;
So the love of other days
Cheers the broken-hearted;
But if once our love decays
'T is for aye departed.

When the hoar-frost nips the leaf,
Pale and sear it lingers,
Wasted in its beauty brief
By decay's cold fingers;
Yet unchanged it ne'er again
Shall its bloom recover; —
Thus the heart shall aye remain
Of the slighted lover.

Love is like the songs we hear
O'er the moonlit ocean;
Youth, the spring-time of a year
Passed in Love's devotion!
Roses of their bloom bereft
Breathe a fragrance sweeter;
Beauty has no fragrance left
Though its bloom is fleeter.

Then when tranquil evening throws
Twilight shades above thee,
And when early morning glows, —
Think on those that love thee!
For an interval of years
We ere long must sever,
But the hearts that love endears
Shall be parted never.

THANKSGIVING

WHEN first in ancient time, from Jubal's tongue
The tuneful anthem filled the morning air,
To sacred hymnings and elysian song
His music-breathing shell the minstrel woke.
Devotion breathed aloud from every chord:
The voice of praise was heard in every tone,
And prayer and thanks to Him, the Eternal One,
To Him, that with bright inspiration touched
The high and gifted lyre of heavenly song,
And warmed the soul with new vitality.
A stirring energy through Nature breathed:
The voice of adoration from her broke,
Swelling aloud in every breeze, and heard
Long in the sullen waterfall, what time
Soft Spring or hoary Autumn threw on earth
Its bloom or blighting; when the summer smiled;
Or Winter o'er the year's sepulchre mourned.

The Deity was there; a nameless spirit
Moved in the breasts of men to do him homage;
And when the morning smiled, or evening pale
Hung weeping o'er the melancholy urn,
They came beneath the broad, o'erarching trees,
And in their tremulous shadow worshipped oft,
Where pale the vine clung round their simple al-
    tars,
And gray moss mantling hung. Above was heard
The melody of winds, breathed out as the green trees
Bowed to their quivering touch in living beauty;
And birds sang forth their cheerful hymns. Below,
The bright and widely wandering rivulet
Struggled and gushed amongst the tangled roots
That choked its reedy fountain, and dark rocks
Worn smooth by the constant current. Even there
The listless wave, that stole with mellow voice
Where reeds grew rank on the rushy-fringed brink,
And the green sedge bent to the wandering wind,
Sang with a cheerful song of sweet tranquillity.
Men felt the heavenly influence; and it stole
Like balm into their hearts, till all was peace:
And even the air they breathed, the light they saw,
Became religion; for the ethereal spirit
That to soft music wakes the chords of feeling,
And mellows everything to beauty, moved
With cheering energy within their breasts
And made all holy there, for all was love.
The morning stars, that sweetly sang together;
The moon, that hung at night in the mid-sky;
Dayspring and eventide; and all the fair
And beautiful forms of nature, had a voice
Of eloquent worship. Ocean, with its tides
Swelling and deep, where low the infant storm
Hung on his dun, dark cloud, and heavily beat
The pulses of the sea, sent forth a voice
Of awful adoration to the spirit
That, wrapt in darkness, moved upon its face.
And when the bow of evening arched the east,
Or, in the moonlight pale, the curling wave
Kissed with a sweet embrace the sea-worn beach,
And soft the song of winds came o'er the waters,
The mingled melody of wind and wave
Touched like a heavenly anthem on the ear;
For it arose a tuneful hymn of worship.
And have *our* hearts grown cold? Are there on earth
No pure reflections caught from heavenly light?
Have our mute lips no hymn, our souls no song?
Let him that in the summer-day of youth
Keeps pure the holy fount of youthful feeling,
And him that in the nightfall of his years
Lies down in his last sleep, and shuts in peace
His dim, pale eyes on life's short wayfaring,
Praise Him that rules the destiny of man.

AUTUMNAL NIGHTFALL

ROUND Autumn's mouldering urn
Loud mourns the chill and cheerless gale,
When nightfall shades the quiet vale
    And stars in beauty burn.

'T is the year's eventide.
The wind, like one that sighs in pain
O'er joys that ne'er will bloom again
    Mourns on the far hillside.

And yet my pensive eye
Rests on the faint blue mountain long;
And for the fairy-land of song,
    That lies beyond, I sigh.

The moon unveils her brow;
In the mid-sky her urn glows bright,
And in her sad and mellowing light
    The valley sleeps below.

Upon the hazel gray
The lyre of Autumn hangs unstrung
And o'er its tremulous chords are flung
    The fringes of decay.

I stand deep musing here,
Beneath the dark and motionless beech,
Whilst wandering winds of nightfall reach
    My melancholy ear.

The air breathes chill and free:
A spirit in soft music calls
From Autumn's gray and moss-grown halls,
    And round her withered tree.

The hoar and mantled oak,
With moss and twisted ivy brown,
Bends in its lifeless beauty down
    Where weeds the fountain choke.

That fountain's hollow voice
Echoes the sound of precious things;
Of early feeling's tuneful springs
    Choked with our blighted joys.

Leaves, that the night-wind bears
To earth's cold bosom with a sigh,
Are types of our mortality,
    And of our fading years.

The tree that shades the plain,
Wasting and hoar as time decays,
Spring shall renew with cheerful days, —
    But not my joys again.

ITALIAN SCENERY

NIGHT rests in beauty on Mont Alto.
Beneath its shade the beauteous Arno sleeps
In Vallombrosa's bosom, and dark trees
Bend with a calm and quiet shadow down
Upon the beauty of that silent river.

Still in the west a melancholy smile
Mantles the lips of day, and twilight pale
Moves like a spectre in the dusky sky,
While eve's sweet star on the fast-fading year
Smiles calmly. Music steals at intervals
Across the water, with a tremulous swell,
From out the upland dingle of tall firs;
And a faint footfall sounds, where, dim and dark,
Hangs the gray willow from the river's brink,
O'ershadowing its current. Slowly there
The lover's gondola drops down the stream,
Silent, save when its dipping oar is heard,
Or in its eddy sighs the rippling wave.
Mouldering and moss-grown through the lapse of years,
In motionless beauty stands the giant oak;
Whilst those that saw its green and flourishing youth
Are gone and are forgotten. Soft the fount,
Whose secret springs the star-light pale discloses,
Gushes in hollow music; and beyond
The broader river sweeps its silent way,
Mingling a silver current with that sea,
Whose waters have no tides, coming nor going.
On noiseless wing along that fair blue sea
The halcyon flits; and, where the wearied storm
Left a loud moaning, all is peace again.

A calm is on the deep. The winds that came
O'er the dark sea-surge with a tremulous breathing,
And mourned on the dark cliff where weeds grew rank,
And to the autumnal death-dirge the deep sea
Heaved its long billows, with a cheerless song
Have passed away to the cold earth again,
Like a wayfaring mourner. Silently

Up from the calm sea's dim and distant verge,
Full and unveiled, the moon's broad disk emerges.
On Tivoli, and where the fairy hues
Of autumn glow upon Abruzzi's woods,
The silver light is spreading. Far above,
Encompassed with their thin, cold atmosphere,
The Apennines uplift their snowy brows,
Glowing with colder beauty, where unheard
The eagle screams in the fathomless ether,
And stays his wearied wing. Here let us pause.
The spirit of these solitudes — the soul
That dwells within these steep and difficult places —
Speaks a mysterious language to mine own,
And brings unutterable musings. Earth
Sleeps in the shades of nightfall, and the sea
Spreads like a thin blue haze beneath my feet ;
Whilst the gray columns and the mouldering tombs
Of the Imperial City, hidden deep
Beneath the mantle of their shadows, rest.

My spirit looks on earth. A heavenly voice
Comes silently : " Dreamer, is earth thy dwelling ?
Lo ! nursed within that fair and fruitful bosom,
Which has sustained thy being, and within
The colder breast of Ocean, lie the germs
Of thine own dissolution ! E'en the air,
That fans the clear blue sky, and gives thee strength,
Up from the sullen lake of mouldering reeds,
And the wide waste of forest, where the osier
Thrives in the damp and motionless atmosphere,
Shall bring the dire and wasting pestilence,
And blight thy cheek. Dream thou of higher things :
This world is not thy home ! " And yet my eye
Rests upon earth again. How beautiful,
Where wild Velino heaves its sullen waves
Down the high cliff of gray and shapeless granite,
Hung on the curling mist, the moonlight bow
Arches the perilous river ! A soft light
Silvers the Albanian mountains, and the haze
That rests upon their summits mellows down
The austerer features of their beauty. Faint
And dim-discovered glow the Sabine hills ;
And, listening to the sea's monotonous shell,
High on the cliffs of Terracina stands
The castle of the royal Goth in ruins.

But night is in her wane : day's early flush
Glows like a hectic on her fading cheek,
Wasting its beauty. And the opening dawn
With cheerful lustre lights the royal city,
Where, with its proud tiara of dark towers,
It sleeps upon its own romantic bay.

THE LUNATIC GIRL

Most beautiful, most gentle ! Yet how lost
To all that gladdens the fair earth ; the eye
That watched her being ; the maternal care
That kept and nourished her ; and the calm light
That steals from our own thoughts, and softly rests
On youth's green valleys and smooth-sliding waters.
Alas ! few suns of life, and fewer winds,
Had withered or had wasted the fresh rose
That bloomed upon her cheek : but one chill frost
Came in that early autumn, when ripe thought
Is rich and beautiful, and blighted it ;
And the fair stalk grew languid day by day,
And drooped — and drooped — and shed its many leaves.
'T is said that some have died of love ; and some,
That once from beauty's high romance had caught
Love's passionate feelings and heart-wasting cares,
Have spurned life's threshold with a desperate foot ;
And others have gone mad, — and she was one !
Her lover died at sea ; and they had felt
A coldness for each other when they parted,
But love returned again : and to her ear

Came tidings that the ship which bore her lover
Had sullenly gone down at sea, and all were lost.
I saw her in her native vale, when high
The aspiring lark up from the reedy river
Mounted on cheerful pinion ; and she sat
Casting smooth pebbles into a clear fountain,
And marking how they sunk ; and oft she sighed
For him that perished thus in the vast deep.
She had a sea-shell, that her lover brought
From the far-distant ocean ; and she pressed
Its smooth, cold lips unto her ear, and thought
It whispered tidings of the dark blue sea ;
And sad, she cried, " The tides are out ! — and now
I see his corse upon the stormy beach ! "
Around her neck a string of rose-lipped shells,
And coral, and white pearl, was loosely hung ;
And close beside her lay a delicate fan,
Made of the halcyon's blue wing ; and when
She looked upon it, it would calm her thoughts
As that bird calms the ocean, — for it gave
Mournful, yet pleasant, memory. Once I marked,
When through the mountain hollows and green woods,
That bent beneath its footsteps, the loud wind
Came with a voice as of the restless deep,
She raised her head, and on her pale, cold cheek
A beauty of diviner seeming came ;
And then she spread her hands, and smiled, as if
She welcomed a long-absent friend, — and then
Shrunk timorously back again, and wept.
I turned away : a multitude of thoughts,
Mournful and dark, were crowding on my mind ;
And as I left that lost and ruined one, —
A living monument that still on earth
There is warm love and deep sincerity, —
She gazed upon the west, where the blue sky
Held, like an ocean, in its wide embrace
Those fairy islands of bright cloud, that lay
So calm and quietly in the thin ether.
And then she pointed where, alone and high,
One little cloud sailed onward, like a lost
And wandering bark, and fainter grew, and fainter,
And soon was swallowed up in the blue depths ;
And, when it sunk away, she turned again
With sad despondency and tears to earth.

Three long and weary months — yet not a whisper
Of stern reproach for that cold parting ! Then
She sat no longer by her favorite fountain :
She was at rest forever.

THE VENETIAN GONDOLIER

Here rest the weary oar ! — soft airs
    Breathe out in the o'erarching sky ;
And Night — sweet Night — serenely wears
    A smile of peace : her noon is nigh.

Where the tall fir in quiet stands,
    And waves, embracing the chaste shores,
Move over sea-shells and bright sands,
    Is heard the sound of dipping oars.

Swift o'er the wave the light bark springs,
    Love's midnight hour draws lingering near ;
And list ! — his tuneful viol strings
    The young Venetian Gondolier.

Lo ! on the silver-mirrored deep,
    On earth, and her embosomed lakes,
And where the silent rivers sweep,
    From the thin cloud fair moonlight breaks

Soft music breathes around, and dies
    On the calm bosom of the sea ;
Whilst in her cell the novice sighs
    Her vespers to her rosary.

At their dim altars bow fair forms,
  In tender charity for those,
That, helpless left to life's rude storms,
  Have never found this calm repose.

The bell swings to its midnight chime,
  Relieved against the deep blue sky.
Haste! — dip the oar again — 't is time
  To seek Genevra's balcony.

THE ANGLER'S SONG

FROM the river's plashy bank,
Where the sedge grows green and rank,
  And the twisted woodbine springs,
Upward speeds the morning lark
To its silver cloud — and hark!
  On his way the woodman sings.

On the dim and misty lakes
Gloriously the morning breaks,
  And the eagle 's on his cloud : —
Whilst the wind, with sighing, wooes
To its arms the chaste cold ooze,
  And the rustling reeds pipe loud.

Where the embracing ivy holds
Close the hoar elm in its folds,
  In the meadow's fenny land,
And the winding river sweeps
Through its shallows and still deeps, —
  Silent with my rod I stand.

But when sultry suns are high
Underneath the oak I lie
  As it shades the water's edge,
And I mark my line, away
In the wheeling eddy, play,
  Tangling with the river sedge.

When the eye of evening looks
On green woods and winding brooks,
  And the wind sighs o'er the lea, —
Woods and streams, — I leave you then,
While the shadow in the glen
  Lengthens by the greenwood tree.

LOVER'S ROCK

They showed us, near the outlet of Sebago, the Lover's
Rock, from which an Indian maid threw herself down into
the lake, when the guests were coming together to the mar-
riage festival of her false-hearted lover." — *Leaf from a Trav-
eller's Journal.*

THERE is a love that cannot die ! —
  And some their doom have met
Heart-broken — and gone as stars go by,
  That rise, and burn, and set.
Their days were in Spring's fallen leaf —
Tender — and young — and bright — and brief.

There is a love that cannot die ! —
  Aye — it survives the grave ;
When life goes out with many a sigh,
  And earth takes what it gave,
Its light is on the home of those
That heed not when the cold wind blows.

With us there are sad records left
  Of life's declining day :
How true hearts here were broken and cleft,
  And how they passed away.
And yon dark rock that swells above
Its blue lake — has a tale of love.

'T is of an Indian maid, whose fate
  Was saddened by the burst
Of passion, that made desolate
  The heart it filled at first.
Her lover was false-hearted, — yet
Her love she never could forget.

It was a summer-day, and bright
  The sun was going down :
The wave lay blushing in rich light
  Beneath the dark rock's frown,
And under the green maple's shade
Her lover's bridal feast was made.

She stood upon the rocky steep,
  Grief had her heart unstrung,
And far across the lake's blue sweep
  Was heard the dirge she sung.
It ceased — and in the deep cold wave
The Indian Girl has made her grave.

DIRGE OVER A NAMELESS GRAVE

BY yon still river, where the wave
  Is winding slow at evening's close,
The beech, upon a nameless grave.
  Its sadly-moving shadow throws.

O'er the fair woods the sun looks down
  Upon the many-twinkling leaves,
And twilight's mellow shades are brown,
  Where darkly the green turf upheaves.

The river glides in silence there,
  And hardly waves the sapling tree :
Sweet flowers are springing, and the air
  Is full of balm — but where is she !

They bade her wed a son of pride,
  And leave the hope she cherished long :
She loved but one — and would not hide
  A love which knew a wrong.

And months went sadly on — and years :
  And she was wasting day by day :
At length she died — and many tears
  Were shed, that she should pass away.

Then came a gray old man, and knelt
  With bitter weeping by her tomb :
And others mourned for him, who felt
  That he had sealed a daughter's doom.

The funeral train has long past on,
  And time wiped dry the father's tear !
Farewell — lost maiden ! — there is one
  That mourns thee yet — and he is here.

A SONG OF SAVOY

As the dim twilight shrouds
  The mountain's purple crest,
And Summer's white and folded clouds
  Are glowing in the west,
Loud shouts come up the rocky dell,
And voices hail the evening-bell.

Faint is the goatherd's song,
  And sighing comes the breeze ;
The silent river sweeps along
  Amid its bending trees —
And the full moon shines faintly there,
And music fills the evening air.

Beneath the waving firs
　The tinkling cymbals sound ;
And as the wind the foliage stirs,
　I see the dancers bound
Where the green branches, arched above,
Bend over this fair scene of love.

And he is there, that sought
　My young heart long ago !
But he has left me — though I thought
　He ne'er could leave me so.
Ah ! lover's vows — how frail are they !
And his — were made but yesterday.

Why comes he not ? I call
　In tears upon him yet ;
'T were better ne'er to love at all,
　Than love, and then forget !
Why comes he not ? Alas ! I should
Reclaim him still, if weeping could.

But see — he leaves the glade,
　And beckons me away :
He comes to seek his mountain maid !
　I cannot chide his stay.
Glad sounds along the valley swell,
And voices hail the evening-bell.

THE INDIAN HUNTER

When the summer harvest was gathered in,
And the sheaf of the gleaner grew white and thin,
And the ploughshare was in its furrow left,
Where the stubble land had been lately cleft,
An Indian hunter, with unstrung bow,
Looked down where the valley lay stretched below.

He was a stranger there, and all that day
Had been out on the hills, a perilous way,
But the foot of the deer was far and fleet,
And the wolf kept aloof from the hunter's feet.
And bitter feelings passed o'er him then,
As he stood by the populous haunts of men.

The winds of autumn came over the woods
As the sun stole out from their solitudes ;
The moss was white on the maple's trunk,
And dead from its arms the pale vine shrunk.
And ripened the mellow fruit hung, and red
Were the tree's withered leaves round it shed.

The foot of the reaper moved slow on the lawn
And the sickle cut down the yellow corn —
The mower sung loud by the meadow-side,
Where the mists of evening were spreading wide,
And the voice of the herdsmen came up the lea,
And the dance went round by the greenwood tree.

Then the hunter turned away from that scene,
Where the home of his fathers once had been,
And heard by the distant and measured stroke,
That the woodman hewed down the giant oak,
And burning thoughts flashed over his mind
Of the white man's faith, and love unkind.

The moon of the harvest grew high and bright,
As her golden horn pierced the cloud of white —
A footstep was heard in the rustling brake,
Where the beech overshadowed the misty lake,
And a mourning voice, and a plunge from shore, —
And the hunter was seen on the hills no more.

When years had passed on, by that still lakeside
The fisher looked down through the silver tide,
And there, on the smooth yellow sand displayed,

A skeleton wasted and white was laid,
And 't was seen, as the waters moved deep and slow,
That the hand was still grasping a hunter's bow.

ODE WRITTEN FOR THE COMMEMORATION AT FRYEBURG, MAINE, OF LOVEWELL'S FIGHT.

Air — Bruce's Address.

I

Many a day and wasted year
Bright has left its footsteps here,
Since was broke the warrior's spear,
　And our fathers bled.
Still the tall trees, arching, shake
Where the fleet deer by the lake,
As he dash'd through birch and brake.
　From the hunter fled.

II

In these ancient woods so bright,
That are full of life and light,
Many a dark, mysterious rite
　The stern warriors kept.
But their altars are bereft,
Fall'n to earth, and strewn and cleft,
And a holier faith is left
　Where their fathers slept.

III

From their ancient sepulchres,
Where amid the giant firs,
Moaning loud, the high wind stirs,
　Have the red men gone.
Tow'rd the setting sun that makes
Bright our western hills and lakes,
Faint and few, the remnant takes
　Its sad journey on.

IV

Where the Indian hamlet stood,
In the interminable wood,
Battle broke the solitude,
　And the war-cry rose ;
Sudden came the straggling shot
Where the sun looked on the spot
That the trace of war would blot
　Ere the day's faint close.

V

Low the smoke of battle hung ;
Heavy down the lake it swung,
Till the death wail loud was sung
　When the night shades fell ;
And the green pine, waving dark,
Held within its shattered bark
Many a lasting scathe and mark,
　That a tale could tell.

VI

And the story of that day
Shall not pass from earth away,
Nor the blighting of decay
　Waste our liberty ;
But within the river's sweep
Long in peace our vale shall sleep
And free hearts the record keep
　Of this jubilee.

JECKOYVA

The Indian chief, Jeckoyva, as tradition says, perished alone on the mountain which now bears his name. Night overtook him whilst hunting among the cliffs, and he was not heard of till after a long time, when his half-decayed corpse was found at the foot of a high rock, over which he must have fallen. Mount Jeckoyva is near the White Hills. H. W. L.

THEY made the warrior's grave beside
The dashing of his native tide :
And there was mourning in the glen —
The strong wail of a thousand men —
　O'er him thus fallen in his pride,
Ere mist of age — or blight or blast
Had o'er his mighty spirit past.

They made the warrior's grave beneath
The bending of the wild elm's wreath,
When the dark hunter's piercing eye
Had found that mountain rest on high,
　Where, scattered by the sharp wind's breath,
Beneath the ragged cliff were thrown
The strong belt and the mouldering bone.

Where was the warrior's foot, when first
The red sun on the mountain burst ?
Where — when the sultry noon-time came
On the green vales with scorching flame,
　And made the woodlands faint with thirst ?
'T was where the wind is keen and loud,
And the gray eagle breasts the cloud.

Where was the warrior's foot when night
Veiled in thick cloud the mountain-height ?
None heard the loud and sudden crash —
None saw the fallen warrior dash
　Down the bare rock so high and white !
But he that drooped not in the chase
Made on the hills his burial-place.

They found him there, when the long day
Of cold desertion passed away,
And traces on that barren cleft
Of struggling hard with death were left —
　Deep marks and footprints in the clay !
And they have laid this feathery helm
By the dark river and green elm.

THE SEA-DIVER

MY way is on the bright blue sea,
　My sleep upon its rocking tide ;
And many an eye has followed me
　Where billows clasp the worn seaside.

My plumage bears the crimson blush,
　When ocean by the sun is kissed !
When fades the evening's purple flush,
　My dark wing cleaves the silver mist.

Full many a fathom down beneath
　The bright arch of the splendid deep
My ear has heard the sea-shell breathe
　O'er living myriads in their sleep.

They rested by the coral throne,
　And by the pearly diadem ;
Where the pale sea-grape had o'ergrown
　The glorious dwellings made for them.

At night upon my storm-drench'd wing,
　I poised above a helmless bark,
And soon I saw the shattered thing
　Had passed away and left no mark.

And when the wind and storm were done,
　A ship, that had rode out the gale,
Sunk down, without a signal-gun,
　And none was left to tell the tale.

I saw the pomp of day depart —
　The cloud resign its golden crown,
When to the ocean's beating heart
　The sailor's wasted corse went down.

Peace be to those whose graves are made
　Beneath the bright and silver sea !
Peace — that their relics there were laid
　With no vain pride and pageantry.

MUSINGS

I SAT by my window one night,
　And watched how the stars grew high ;
And the earth and skies were a splendid sight
　To a sober and musing eye.

From heaven the silver moon shone down
　With gentle and mellow ray,
And beneath the crowded roofs of the town
　In broad light and shadow lay.

A glory was on the silent sea,
　And mainland and island too,
Till a haze came over the lowland lea,
　And shrouded that beautiful blue.

Bright in the moon the autumn wood
　Its crimson scarf unrolled,
And the trees like a splendid army stood
　In a panoply of gold !

I saw them waving their banners high,
　As their crests to the night wind bowed,
And a distant sound on the air went by,
　Like the whispering of a crowd.

Then I watched from my window how fast
　The lights all around me fled,
As the wearied man to his slumber passed
　And the sick one to his bed.

All faded save one, that burned
　With distant and steady light ;
But that, too, went out — and I turned
　Where my own lamp within shone bright !

Thus, thought I, our joys must die,
　Yes — the brightest from earth we win :
Till each turns away, with a sigh,
　To the lamp that burns brightly within.

SONG

WHERE, from the eye of day,
　The dark and silent river
Pursues through tangled woods a way
　O'er which the tall trees quiver ;

The silver mist, that breaks
　From out that woodland cover,
Betrays the hidden path it takes,
　And hangs the current over !

So oft the thoughts that burst
　From hidden springs of feeling,
Like silent streams, unseen at first,
　From our cold hearts are stealing :

But soon the clouds that veil
The eye of Love, when glowing,
Betray the long unwhispered tale
Of thoughts in darkness flowing !

SONG OF THE BIRDS

WITH what a hollow dirge its voice did fill
The vast and empty hollow of the night ! —
It had perched itself upon a tall old tree,
That hung its tufted and thick clustering leaves
Midway across the brook ; and sung most sweetly,
In all the merry and heart-broken sadness
Of those that love hath crazed. Clearly it ran
Through all the delicate compass of its voice : —
And then again, as from a distant hollow,
I heard its sweet tones like an echo sounding,
And coming, like the memory of a friend
From a far distant country — or the silent land
Of the mourned and the dead, to which we all are pass-
ing ;
It seemed the song of some poor broken heart,
Haunted forever with love's cruel fancies ! —
Of one that has loved much yet never known
The luxury of being loved again !

But when the morning broke, and the green woods
Were all alive with birds — with what a clear
And ravishing sweetness sung the plaintive thrush ;
I love to hear its delicate rich voice,
Chanting through all the gloomy day, when loud
Amid the trees is dropping the big rain,
And gray mists wrap the hills ; — for aye the sweeter
Its song is, when the day is sad and dark. And thus,
When the bright fountains of a woman's love
Are gently running over, if a cloud
But darken, with its melancholy shadow,
The bright flowers round our way, her heart
Doth learn new sweetness, and her rich voice falls
With more delicious music on our ears.

II. UNACKNOWLEDGED AND UNCOL-
LECTED TRANSLATIONS

THE history of Mr. Longfellow's work in
translation has been given in the Introductory
Note to the *Translations* in the present volume.
As indicated there, a number of poems were
contributed by Mr. Longfellow to periodicals as
well as to his two collections, *The Poets and
Poetry of Europe* and *Poems of Places*, which
were signed by him, but for some reason were
not included in any of the volumes of poetry
which he put forth from time to time. Such
poems have been recovered and placed in their
proper groups. Besides these signed poems,
however, there are a number which may be
traced without question to Mr. Longfellow's
pen, and in accordance with the plan of this
edition they have been reserved for the Appen-
dix, and are here given.

LET ME GO WARM

BY LUIS DE GÓNGORA Y ARGOTE

Published in *The New England Magazine*, July, 1831, and
afterwards in *The Poets and Poetry of Europe.*

LET me go warm and merry still ;
And let the world laugh, an' it will.

Let others muse on earthly things, —
The fall of thrones, the fate of kings,
And those whose fame the world doth fill ;
Whilst muffins sit enthroned in trays,
And orange-punch in winter sways
The merry sceptre of my days ; —
And let the world laugh, an' it will.

He that the royal purple wears
From golden plate a thousand cares
Doth swallow as a gilded pill :
On feasts like these I turn my back,
Whilst puddings in my roasting-jack
Beside the chimney hiss and crack ; —
And let the world laugh, an' it will.

And when the wintry tempest blows,
And January's sleets and snows
Are spread o'er every vale and hill,
With one to tell a merry tale
O'er roasted nuts and humming ale,
I sit, and care not for the gale ; —
And let the world laugh, an' it will.

Let merchants traverse seas and lands,
For silver mines and golden sands ;
Whilst I beside some shadowy rill,
Just where its bubbling fountain swells,
Do sit and gather stones and shells,
And hear the tale the blackbird tells ; —
And let the world laugh, an' it will.

For Hero's sake the Grecian lover
The stormy Hellespont swam over :
I cross, without the fear of ill,
The wooden bridge that slow bestrides
The Madrigal's enchanting sides,
Or barefoot wade through Yepes' tides ; —
And let the world laugh, an' it will.

But since the Fates so cruel prove,
That Pyramus should die of love,
And love should gentle Thisbe kill ;
My Thisbe be an apple-tart,
The sword I plunge into her heart
The tooth that bites the crust apart, —
And let the world laugh, an' it will.

THE NATIVITY OF CHRIST

BY LUIS DE GÓNGORA Y ARGOTE

TO-DAY from the Aurora's bosom
A pink has fallen, — a crimson blossom :
And oh, how glorious rests the hay
On which the fallen blossom lay.

When silence gently had unfurled
Her mantle over all below,
And, crowned with winter's frost and snow,
Night swayed the sceptre of the world,
Amid the gloom descending slow,
Upon the monarch's frozen bosom
A pink has fallen, — a crimson blossom.

The only flower the Virgin bore
(Aurora fair,) within her breast,
She gave to earth, yet still possessed
Her virgin blossom as before :
The hay that colored drop caressed, —
Received upon its faithful bosom
That single flower, — a crimson blossom.

The manger, unto which 't was given,
Even amid wintry snows and cold,
Within its fostering arms to fold

The blushing flower that fell from Heaven,
Was as a canopy of gold, —
A downy couch, — where on its bosom
That flower hath fallen, — that crimson blossom.

THE ASSUMPTION OF THE VIRGIN

BY LUIS PONCE DE LEON

LADY ! thine upward flight
The opening heavens receive with joyful song:
Blest, who thy garments bright
May seize, amid the throng,
And to the sacred mount float peacefully along.

Bright angels are around thee,
They that have served thee from thy birth are there:
Their hands with stars have crowned thee ;
Thou, — peerless Queen of air,
As sandals to thy feet the silver moon dost wear.

Celestial dove ! so meek
And mild and fair ! — oh, let thy peaceful eye
This thorny valley seek,
Where such sweet blossoms lie,
But where the sons of Eve in pain and sorrow sigh.

For if the imprisoned soul
Could catch the brightness of that heavenly way,
'T would own its sweet control
And gently pass away,
Drawn by its magnet power to an eternal day.

THE DISEMBODIED SPIRIT

BY HERNANDO DE HERRERA

PURE Spirit ! that within a form of clay
Once veiled the brightness of thy native sky ;
In dreamless slumber sealed thy burning eye,
Nor heavenward sought to wing thy flight away !
He that chastised thee did at length unclose
Thy prison doors, and give thee sweet release ; —
Unloosed the mortal coil, eternal peace
Received thee to its stillness and repose.
Look down once more from thy celestial dwelling,
Help me to rise and be immortal there, —
An earthly vapor melting into air ; —
For my whole soul, with secret ardor swelling,
From earth's dark mansion struggles to be free,
And longs to soar away and be at rest with thee.

IDEAL BEAUTY

BY HERNANDO DE HERRERA

O LIGHT serene ! present in him who breathes
That love divine, which kindles yet restrains
The high-born soul — that in its mortal chains
Heavenward aspires for love's immortal wreaths !
Rich golden locks, within whose clustered curls
Celestial and eternal treasures lie !
A voice that breathes angelic harmony
Among bright coral and unspotted pearls !
What marvellous beauty ! Of the high estate
Of immortality, within this light
Transparent veil of flesh, a glimpse is given ;
And in the glorious form, I contemplate,
(Although its brightness blinds my feeble sight,)
The immortal still I seek and follow on to Heaven !

THE LOVER'S COMPLAINT

BY HERNANDO DE HERRERA

BRIGHT Sun ! that, flaming through the mid-day sky,
Fillest with light heaven's blue, deep-vaulted arch,
Say, hast thou seen in thy celestial march
One hue to rival this blue, tranquil eye ?
Thou Summer Wind, of soft and delicate touch,
Fanning me gently with thy cool, fresh pinion,
Say, hast thou found, in all thy wide dominion,
Tresses of gold, that can delight so much ?
Moon, honor of the night ! Thou glorious choir
Of wandering Planets and eternal Stars !
Say, have ye seen two peerless orbs like these ?
Answer me, Sun, Air, Moon, and Stars of fire —
Hear ye my woes, that know no bounds nor bars ?
See ye these cruel stars, that brighten and yet freeze ?

ART AND NATURE

BY FRANCISCO DE MEDRANO

THE works of human artifice soon tire
The curious eye ; the fountain's sparkling rill,
And gardens, when adorned by human skill,
Reproach the feeble hand, the vain desire.
But oh ! the free and wild magnificence
Of Nature, in her lavish hours, doth steal,
In admiration silent and intense,
The soul of him who hath a soul to feel.
The river moving on its ceaseless way,
The verdant reach of meadows fair and green,
And the blue hills, that bound the sylvan scene,
These speak of grandeur, that defies decay, —
Proclaim the Eternal Architect on high,
Who stamps on all his works his own eternity.

THE TWO HARVESTS

BY FRANCISCO DE MEDRANO

BUT yesterday these few and hoary sheaves
Waved in the golden harvest ; from the plain
I saw the blade shoot upward, and the grain
Put forth the unripe ear and tender leaves.
Then the glad upland smiled upon the view,
And to the air the broad green leaves unrolled,
A peerless emerald in each silken fold,
And on each palm a pearl of morning dew.
And thus sprang up and ripened in brief space
All that beneath the reaper's sickle died,
All that smiled beauteous in the summer-tide.
And what are we ? a copy of that race,
The later harvest of a longer year !
And oh ! how many fall before the ripened ear !

CLEAR HONOR OF THE LIQUID ELEMENT

BY LUIS DE GÓNGORA Y ARGOTE

CLEAR honor of the liquid element,
Sweet rivulet of shining silver sheen !
Whose waters steal along the meadows green,
With gentle step, and murmur of content !
When she, for whom I bear each fierce extreme,
Beholds herself in thee, — then Love doth trace
The snow and crimson of that lovely face
In the soft gentle movement of thy stream.
Then smoothly flow as now ; and set not free
The crystal curb and undulating rein
Which now thy current's headlong speed restrain ;
Lest broken and confused the image rest
Of such rare charms on the deep-heaving breast
Of him who holds and sways the trident of the sea.

PRAISE OF LITTLE WOMEN

JUAN RUIZ DE HITA

I WISH to make my sermon brief, — to shorten my oration, —
For a never-ending sermon is my utter detestation:
I like short women, — suits at law without procrastination, —
And am always most delighted with things of short duration.

A babbler is a laughing-stock; he 's a fool who 's always grinning;
But little women love so much, one falls in love with sinning.
There are women who are very tall, and yet not worth the winning,
And in the change of short for long repentance finds beginning.

To praise the little women Love besought me in my musing;
To tell their noble qualities is quite beyond refusing:
So I 'll praise the little women, and you 'll find the thing amusing:
They are, I know, as cold as snow, whilst flames around diffusing.

They 're cold without, whilst warm within the flame of Love is raging;
They 're gay and pleasant in the street, — soft, cheerful, and engaging;
They 're thrifty and discreet at home, — the cares of life assuaging;
All this and more; — try, and you 'll find how true is my presaging.

In a little precious stone what splendor meets the eyes!
In a little lump of sugar how much of sweetness lies!
So in a little woman love grows and multiplies:
You recollect the proverb says, — A word unto the wise.

A pepper-corn is very small, but seasons every dinner
More than all other condiments, although 't is sprinkled thinner:
Just so a little woman is, if Love will let you win her, —
There 's not a joy in all the world you will not find within her.

And as within the little rose you find the richest dyes,
And in a little grain of gold much price and value lies,
As from a little balsam much odor doth arise,
So in a little woman there 's a taste of paradise.

Even as the little ruby its secret worth betrays,
Color, and price, and virtue, in the clearness of its rays, —
Just so a little woman much excellence displays,
Beauty, and grace, and love, and fidelity always.

The skylark and the nightingale, though small and light of wing,
Yet warble sweeter in the grove than all the birds that sing:
And so a little woman, though a very little thing,
Is sweeter far than sugar, and flowers that bloom in spring.

The magpie and the golden thrush have many a thrilling note,
Each as a gay musician doth strain his little throat, —
A merry little songster in his green and yellow coat:
And such a little woman is, when Love doth make her dote.

There 's naught can be compared to her, throughout the wide creation;
She is a paradise on earth, — our greatest consolation, —
So cheerful, gay, and happy, so free from all vexation:
In fine, she 's better in the proof than in anticipation.

If as her size increases are woman's charms decreased,
Then surely it is good to be from all the great released.
Now of two evils choose the less, — said a wise man of the East:
By consequence, of womankind be sure to choose the least.

MILAGROS DE NUESTRA SEÑORA

BY GONZALO DE BERCEO

I, GONZALO DE BERCEO, in the gentle summer-tide,
Wending upon a pilgrimage, came to a meadow's side:
All green was it and beautiful, with flowers far and wide, —
A pleasant spot, I ween, wherein the traveller might abide.

Flowers with the sweetest odors filled all the sunny air,
And not alone refreshed the sense, but stole the mind from care;
On every side a fountain gushed, whose waters pure and fair,
Ice-cold beneath the summer sun, but warm in winter were.

There on the thick and shadowy trees, amid the foliage green,
Were the fig and the pomegranate, the pear and apple, seen;
And other fruits of various kinds, the tufted leaves between,
None were unpleasant to the taste, and none decayed, I ween.

The verdure of the meadow green, the odor of the flowers,
The grateful shadows of the trees, tempered with fragrant showers,
Refreshed me in the burning heat of the sultry noontide hours:
Oh, one might live upon the balm and fragrance of those bowers!

Ne'er had I found on earth a spot that had such power to please,
Such shadows from the summer sun, such odors on the breeze:
I threw my mantle on the ground, that I might rest at ease,
And stretched upon the greensward lay in the shadow of the trees.

There soft reclining in the shade, all cares beside me flung,
I heard the soft and mellow notes that through the woodland rung:
Ear never listened to a strain, from instrument or tongue,
So mellow and harmonious as the songs above me sung.

SONG OF THE RHINE

FORTH rolled the Rhine-stream strong and deep
Beneath Helvetia's Alpine steep,
And joined in youthful company
Its fellow-travellers to the sea.

In Germany embraced the Rhine,
The Neckar, the Mosel, the Lahn, and the Main,
And strengthened by each rushing tide,
Onward he marched in kingly pride.

But soon from his enfeebled grasp
The satraps of his power,
The current's flowing veins unclasped —
He moves in pride no more.

Forth the confederate waters broke
On that rebellious day,
And, bursting from their monarch's yoke,
Each chose a separate way.

Wahl, Issel, Leck, and Wecht, all, all
Flowed sidewards o'er the land,
And a nameless brook, by Leyden's wall,
The Rhine sank in sand.

ELEGY WRITTEN IN THE RUINS OF AN OLD CASTLE

BY FRIEDRICH VON MATTHISSON

SILENT, in the veil of evening twilight,
Rests the plain; the woodland song is still,
Save that here, amid these mouldering ruins,
Chirps a cricket, mournfully and shrill.
Silence sinks from skies without a shadow,
Slowly wind the herds from field and meadow,
And the weary hind to the repose
Of his father's lowly cottage goes.

Here, upon this hill, by forests bounded,
'Mid the ruins of departed days,
By the awful shapes of Eld surrounded,
Sadness! unto thee my song I raise!
Sadly think I what in gray old ages
Were these wrecks of lordly heritages:
A majestic castle, like a crown,
Placed upon the mountain's brow of stone.

There, where round the column's gloomy ruins,
Sadly whispering, clings the ivy green,
And the evening twilight's mournful shimmer
Blinks the empty window-space between,
Blessed, perhaps, a father's tearful eye
Once the noblest son of Germany;
One whose heart, with high ambition rife,
Warmly swelled to meet the coming strife.

"Go in peace!" thus spake the hoary warrior,
As he girded on his sword of fame;
"Come not back again, or come as victor:
Oh, be worthy of thy father's name!"
And the noble youth's bright eyes were throwing
Deadly flashes forth; his cheeks were glowing,
As with full-blown branches the red rose
In the purple light of morning glows.

Then, a cloud of thunder, flew the champion,
Even as Richard Lion-Heart, to fight;
Like a wood of pines in storm and tempest,
Bowed before his path the hostile might.
Gently, as a brook through flowers descendeth.
Homeward to the castle-crag he wendeth, —
To his father's glad, yet tearful face, —
To the modest maiden's chaste embrace.

Oh, with anxious longing, looks the fair one
From her turret down the valley drear!
Shield and breastplate glow in gold of evening,
Steeds fly forward, the beloved draws near!
Him the faithful right-hand mute extending,
Stands she, pallid looks with blushes blending.

Oh, but what that soft, soft eye doth say,
Sings not Petrarch's, nor e'en Sappho's lay!

Merrily echoed there the sound of goblets,
Where the rank grass, waving in the gale,
O'er the nests of owls is blackly spreading,
Till the silver glance of stars grew pale.
Tales of hard-won battle fought afar,
Wild adventures in the Holy War,
Wakened in the breast of hardy knight
The remembrance of his fierce delight.

Oh, what changes! Awe and night o'ershadow
Now the scene of all that proud array;
Winds of evening, full of sadness, whisper,
Where the strong ones revelled and were gay;
Thistles lonely nod, in places seated
Where for shield and spear the boy entreated,
When aloud the war-horn's summons rang,
And to horse in speed the father sprang.

Ashes are the bones of these, — the mighty!
Deep they lie within earth's gloomy breast;
Hardly the half-sunken funeral tablets
Now point out the places where they rest!
Many to the winds were long since scattered, —
Like their tombs, their memories sunk and shattered
O'er the brilliant deeds of ages gone
Sweep the cloud-folds of Oblivion!

Thus depart life's pageantry and glory!
Thus flit by the visions of vain might!
Thus sinks, in the rapid lapse of ages,
All that earth doth bear, to empty night!
Laurels, that the victor's brow encircle,
High deeds, that in brass and marble sparkle,
Urns devoted unto Memory,
And the songs of Immortality!

All, all, that with longing and with rapture
Here on earth a noble heart doth warm,
Vanishes like sunshine in the autumn,
When the horizon's verge is veiled in storm.
Friends at evening part with warm embraces, —
Morning looks upon the death-pale faces;
Even the joys that Love and Friendship find
Leave on earth no lasting trace behind.

Gentle Love! how all thy fields of roses
Bounded close by thorny deserts lie!
And a sudden tempest's awful shadow
Oft doth darken Friendship's brightest sky!
Vain are titles, honor, might, and glory!
On the monarch's temples proud and hoary,
And the way-worn pilgrim's trembling head,
Doth the grave one common darkness spread!

THE STARS

BY MARTIN OPITZ

NIGHT comes stealing from the East,
Frees from labor man and beast,
Brings to all the wished-for rest,
And the sorrow to my breast.

Shines the moonlight clear and cold,
Shine the little stars of gold;
Glad are all things far and wide; —
I alone in grief abide.

Two are missing, two in vain
Seek I in the starry train;
And these stars that do not rise
Are my darling's lovely, eyes.

Naught I heed the moonlight clear,
Dim to me the stars appear.
Since is hidden from my sight
Kunigund, my heaven of light.

But when in their splendor shine
Over me those suns divine,
Then it seemeth best to me
Neither moon nor stars should be.

RONDEL

BY CHARLES D'ORLEANS

HENCE away, begone, begone,
  Carking care and melancholy!
  Think ye thus to govern me
All my life long, as ye have done ?
That shall ye not, I promise ye,
  Reason shall have the mastery.
So hence away, begone, begone,
  Carking care and melancholy !

If ever ye return this way,
  With your mournful company,
A curse be on ye, and the day
  That brings ye moping back to me !
Hence away, begone, I say,
  Carking care and melancholy !

THE BANKS OF THE CHER

BY ANTOINE-MARIN LE MIÈRRE

IN that province of our France
Proud of being called its garden,
In those fields where once by chance
Pepin's father with his lance
Made the Saracen sue for pardon ;
There between the old château
Which two hundred years ago
Was the centre of the League,
Whose infernal, black intrigue
Almost fatal was, 't is reckoned,
To young Francis, called the Second,
And that pleasant city's wall
Of this canton capital,
City memorable in story,
And whose fruits preserved with care
Make the riches and the glory
Of the gourmands everywhere ! —
Now, a more prosaic head
Without verbiage might have said,
There between Tours and Amboise
In the province of Touraine ;
But the poet, and with cause,
Loves to ponder and to pause ;
Ever more his soul delighteth
In the language that he writeth,
Finer far than other people's ;
So, while he describes the steeples,
One might travel through Touraine,
Far as Tours and back again.

On the borders of the Cher
Is a valley green and fair,
Where the eye, that travels fast,
Tires with the horizon vast ;
There, since five and forty lustres,
From the bosom of the stream,
Like the castle of a dream,
High into the fields of air
The château of Chenonceaux
Lifts its glittering vanes in clusters.
Six stone arches of a bridge

Into channels six divide
The swift river in its flow,
And upon their granite ridge
Hold this beautiful château,
Flanked with turrets on each side.
Time, that grand old man with wings,
Who destroys all earthly things,
Hath not tarnished yet one stone,
White as ermine is alone,
Of this palace of dead kings.

One in speechless wonder sees
In the rampart-walls of Blois,
To the shame of the Valois,
Marble stained with blood of Guise ;
By the crimes that it can show,
By its war-beleaguered gates,
Famous be that black château ;
Thou art famous for thy fêtes
And thy feastings, Chenonceaux !
Ah, most beautiful of places,
With what pleasure thee I see ;
Everywhere the selfsame traces,
Residence of all the Graces
And Love's inn and hostelry !

Here that second Agrippina,
The imperious Catharina,
Jealous of all pleasant things,
To her cruel purpose still
Subjugating every will,
Kept her sons as underlings
Fastened to her apron-strings.

Here, divested of his armor,
As gallant as he was brave,
Francis First to some fair charmer
Many an hour of dalliance gave.
Here, beneath these ceilings florid,
Chose Diana her retreat, —
Not Diana of the groves
With the crescent on her forehead,
Who, as swiftest arrow fleet,
Flies before all earthly loves ;
But that charming mortal dame,
She the Poiterine alone,
She the Second Henry's flame,
Who with her celestial zone
Loves and Laughters made secure
From banks of Cher to banks of Eure.

Cher, whose stream, obscure and troubled,
Flowed before with many a halt,
By this palace is ennobled,
Since it bathes its noble vault.
Even the boatman, hurrying fast,
Pauses, mute with admiration
To behold a pile so vast
Rising like an exhalation
From the stream ; and with his mast
Lowered salutes it, gliding past.

TO THE FOREST OF GASTINE

BY PIERRE DE RONSARD

STRETCHED in thy shadows I rehearse,
  Gastine, thy solitudes,
Even as the Grecians in their verse
  The Erymanthian woods.

For I, alas ! cannot conceal
  From any future race
The pleasure, the delight, I feel
  In thy green dwelling-place.

Thou who beneath thy sheltering bowers
  Dost make me visions see ;
Thou who dost cause that at all hours
  The Muses answer me ;

Thou who from each importunate care
  Dost free me with a look,
When lost I roam I know not where
  Conversing with a book !

Forever may thy thickets hold
  The amorous brigade
Of Satyrs and of Sylvans bold,
  That make the Nymphs afraid ;

In thee the Muses evermore
  Their habitation claim,
And never may thy woods deplore
  The sacrilegious flame.

FONTENAY

BY GUILLAUME AMFRYE DE CHAULIEU

O AMIABLE solitude,
Sojourn of silence and of peace !
Asylum where forever cease
All tumult and inquietude !

I, who have chanted many a time
To tender accents of my lyre
All that one suffers from the fire
Of love and beauty in its prime, —

Shall I, whose gratitude requites
All blessing I from thee receive, —
Shall I, unsung, in silence leave
Thy benefactions and delights ?

Thou bringest back my youthful dream ;
Calmest my agitated breast,
And of my idleness and rest
Makest a happiness extreme.

Amid these hamlets and these woods
Again do I begin to live,
And to the winds all memory give
Of sorrows and solicitudes.

. . . .
What smiling pictures and serene
Each day reveals to sight and sense,
Of treasures with which Providence
Embellishes this rural scene !

How sweet it is in yonder glade
To see, when noonday burns the plain,
The flocks around the shepherd swain
Reposing in the elm-tree's shade !

To hear at eve our flageolets
Answered by all the hills around,
And all the villages resound
With hautbois and with canzonets !

Alas ! these peaceful days, perforce,
With too great swiftness onward press ;
My indolence and idleness
Are powerless to suspend their course.

Old age comes stealing on apace ;
And cruel Death shall soon or late
Execute the decree of fate
That gives me to him without grace.

O Fontenay ! forever dear !
Where first I saw the light of day,

I soon from life shall steal away
To sleep with my forefathers here.

Ye Muses, that have nourished me
In this delightful spot of earth ;
Beautiful trees, that saw my birth,
Erelong ye too my death shall see !

Meanwhile let me in patience wait
Beneath thy shadowy woods, nor grieve
That I so soon their shade must leave
For that dark manor desolate,

Whither not one shall follow me
Of all these trees that my own hand
Hath planted, and for pastime planned,
Saving alone the cypress-tree !

PRAY FOR ME

BY CHARLES-HUBERT MILLEVOYE

IN the hamlet desolate,
Brooding o'er his woes in vain,
Lay a young man, doomed by fate,
Wasted by disease and pain.
" People of the chaumière,"
Said he, " 't is the hour of prayer ;
Ringing are the bells ! all ye
Who are praying, pray for me !

" When you see the waterfall
Covered with dark boughs in spring,
You will say, He 's free from all,
All his pain and suffering.
Then returning to this shore
Sing your simple plaint once more,
And when ring the bells, all ye
Who are praying, pray for me.

" Falsehood I could not endure,
Was the enemy of hate ;
Of an honest life and pure
The end approaches, and I wait.
Short my pilgrimage appears ;
In the springtime of my years
I am dying ; and all ye
Who are praying, pray for me.

" Best of friends and only friend,
Worthy of all love and praise,
Thine my life was to the end ;
Ah, 't was but a life of days.
People of the chaumière,
Pity, at the hour of prayer,
Her who comes with bended knee,
Saying also, Pray for me ! "

VIRE

BY GUSTAVE LE VAVASSEUR

IT is good to rhyming go
From the valleys of Vire to the valleys of Bures.
For a poet of Normandy the Low
It is good to rhyming go !
One is inspired and all aglow
With the old singers of voice so pure.
It is good to rhyming go
From the valleys of Vire to the valleys of Bures !

Do you know one Thomas Sonnet ?
He was a medical man of Vire ;
And turned very well a roundelay,
Do you know this Thomas Sonnet ?

To the sick he used to say,
"Never drink bad wine, my dear!"
Do you know this Thomas Sonnet?
He was a medical man of Vire.

Do you know one Master Le Houx?
He was an advocate of Vire;
The taste of dry and sweet he knew;
Do you know this Master Le Houx?
From the holly boughs his name he drew
Which as tavern-signs one sees appear.
Do you know this Master Le Houx?
He was an advocate of Vire.

Do you know one Master Olivier?
He was an ancient fuller of Vire;
He only fulled his tub, they say;
Do you know this Master Olivier?
As to his trade, it was only play;
He knew how to sing and drink and leer;
Do you know this Master Olivier?
He was an ancient fuller of Vire.

Olivier, Le Houx, Le Sonnet
Are Peace, and Tavern, and Poesy;
Every good rhymer knows to-day
Olivier, Le Houx, Le Sonnet.
Dame Reason throws her cap away
If the rhyme well chosen be;
Olivier, Le Houx, Le Sonnet
Are Peace, and Tavern, and Poesy.

Vire is a delicious place,
Vire is a little Norman town.
'T is not the home of a godlike race,
Vire is a delicious place;
But what gives it its crowning grace
Is the peace that there comes down.
Vire is a delicious place,
Vire is a little Norman town.

There are taverns by the score
And solid are the drinkers there.
More than in Evreux of yore,
There are taverns by the score.
One sees there empty brains no more,
But empty glasses everywhere.
There are taverns by the score,
And solid are the drinkers there.

'T is the fresh cradle of the Song,
And mother of the Vaudeville;
Lawyers as cupbearers throng,
'T is the fresh cradle of the Song.
The fullers pierce the puncheons strong,
The doctors drink abroad their fill;
'T is the fresh cradle of the Song
And mother of the Vaudeville.

It is good to rhyming go
From the valleys of Vire to the valleys of Bures!
For a poet of Normandy the Low,
It is good to rhyming go!
One is inspired and all aglow
With the old singers of voice so pure.
It is good to rhyming go
From the valleys of Vire to the valleys of Bures!

A FLORENTINE SONG

If I am fair 't is for myself alone,
I do not wish to have a sweetheart near me,
Nor would I call another's heart my own,
Nor have a gallant lover to revere me.
For surely I will plight my faith to none,
Though many an amorous cit would jump to hear me

For I have heard that lovers prove deceivers,
When once they find that maidens are believers.

Yet should I find one that in truth could please me,
One whom I thought my charms had power to move;
Why then, I do confess, the whim might seize me,
To taste for once the porringer of love.
Alas! there is one pair of eyes that tease me;
And then that mouth! — he seems a star above,
He is so good, so gentle, and so kind,
And so unlike the sullen, clownish hind.

What love may be, indeed I cannot tell,
Nor if I e'er have known his cunning arts;
But true it is, there 's one I *like* so well,
That when he looks at me my bosom starts.
And, if we meet, my heart begins to swell;
And the green fields around, when he departs,
Seem like a nest from which the bird has flown;
Can this be love? — say — ye who love have known

A NEAPOLITAN CANZONET

One morning, on the sea-shore as I strayed,
My heart dropped in the sand beside the sea;
I asked of yonder mariners, who said
They saw it in thy bosom, — worn by thee.
And I am come to seek that heart of mine,
For I have none, and thou, alas, hast two;
If this be so, dost know what thou shalt do? —
Still keep my heart, and give me, give me thine.

CHRISTMAS CAROL

One of the Neapolitan *Pastorali de' Zampognari.*

When Christ was born in Bethlehem,
'T was night, but seemed the noon of day;
The stars, whose light
Was pure and bright,
Shone with unwavering ray;
But one, one glorious star
Guided the Eastern Magi from afar.

Then peace was spread throughout the land:
The lion fed beside the tender lamb;
And with the kid,
To pasture led,
The spotted leopard fed;
In peace, the calf and bear,
The wolf and lamb reposed together there.

As shepherds watched their flocks by night,
An angel, brighter than the sun's own light,
Appeared in air,
And gently said,
Fear not, — be not afraid,
For lo! beneath your eyes,
Earth has become a smiling paradise.

A SOLDIER'S SONG

Paraphrase of a Neapolitan popular song.

"Who knocks, — who knocks at my door,
    Who knocks, and who can it be?"
"Thy own true lover, betrothed forever,
    So open the door to me."

"My mother is not at home,
    So I cannot open to thee."
"Why make me wait so long at the gate,
    For mercy's sake open to me."

"Thou canst not come in so late,
 From the window I 'll listen to thee."
"My cloak is old, and the wind blows cold,
 So open the door to me."

TELL ME, TELL ME, THOU PRETTY BEE

BY GIOVANNI MELI

TELL me, tell me, thou pretty bee,
Whither so early thy flight may be ?
Not a neighboring mountain height
Yet blushes with the morning light ;
Still the dew on spray and blossom
Trembling shines in the meadow's bosom ;
Why do I see thee, then, unfold
Thy soft and dainty wings of gold ; —
Those little wings are weary quite,
Still thou holdest thy onward flight, —
Then tell me, tell me, thou pretty bee,
Whither so early thy flight may be.

Thou seekest honey ? — if it be so,
Fold up thy wings, — no farther go ;
I 'll show thee a safe and sacred spot,
Where all the year round 't will fail thee not.
Knowest thou the maid for whom I sigh, —
Her of the bright and beaming eye ?
Endless sweetness shalt thou sip,
Honied stores upon her lip.
On those lips of brightest red,
Lips of the beloved maid,
Sweetest honey lies for thee ; —
Sip it, — sip it ; — this is she.

SICILIAN CANZONET

WHAT shall I do, sweet Nici, tell me,
I burn, — I burn, — I can no more !
I know not how the thing befell me,
But I 'm in love, and all is o'er.
One look, — alas ! one glance of thine,
One single glance my death shall be ;
Even this poor heart no more is mine,
For, Nici, it belongs to thee.

How shall I then my grief repress,
How shall this soul in anguish live ?
I fear a *no*, — desire a *yes*, —
But which the answer thou wilt give ?
No, — Love, — not so deceived am I ;
Soft pity dwells in those bright eyes,
And no tyrannic cruelty
Within that gentle bosom lies.

Then, fairest Nici, speak and say
If I must know thy love or hate ;
Oh, do not leave me thus, I pray,
But speak, — be quick, — I cannot wait.
Quick, — I entreat thee ; — if not so,
This weary soul no more shall sigh ; —
So tell me quickly, — *yes* or *no*,
Which, — which shall be my destiny.

THE GLEANER OF SAPRI

BY LUIGI MERCANTINI

Published in the *Supplement to The Poets and Poetry of Europe.* "This poet," says Mr. Longfellow, "is a professor in the University of Palermo. The following simple and striking poem from his pen has reference to the ill-fated expedition of Carlo Pisacane, on the shores of the kingdom of Naples in the summer of 1857, in which, says Dall' Ongaro, 'he fell with his followers like Leonidas with his three hundred.'"

THEY were three hundred, they were young and strong,
 And they are dead !
One morning as I went to glean the grain,
I saw a bark in middle of the main ;
It was a bark came steaming to the shore,
And hoisted for its flag the tricolor.
At Ponza's isle it stopped beneath the lea,
It stayed awhile, and then put out to sea,
Put out to sea, and came unto our strand ;
Landed with arms, but not as foemen land.
They were three hundred, they were young and strong,
 And they are dead !

Landed with arms, but not as foemen land,
For they stooped down and kissed the very sand.
And one by one I looked them in the face ;
A tear and smile in each one I could trace !
"Thieves from their dens are these," some people said,
And yet they took not even a loaf of bread !
I heard them utter but a single cry :
"We for our native land have come to die ! "
They were three hundred, they were young and strong,
 And they are dead !

With eyes of azure, and with hair of gold,
A young man marched in front of them ; and bold
I made myself, and having seized his hand,
Asked him, "Where goest, fair captain of the band ? "
He looked at me and answered, "Sister mine,
I go to die for this fair land of thine ! "
I felt my heart was trembling through and through,
Nor could I say to him, "God comfort you ! "
They were three hundred, they were young and strong,
 And they are dead !

That morning I forgot to glean the grain,
And set myself to follow in their train.
Twice over they encountered the gens-d'armes,
Twice over they despoiled them of their arms ;
But when we came before Certosa's wall
We heard the drums beat and the trumpets call,
And 'mid the smoke, the firing, and the glare,
More than a thousand fell upon them there.
They were three hundred, they were young and strong,
 And they are dead !

They were three hundred, and they would not fly ;
They seemed three thousand, and they wished to die,
But wished to die with weapons in their hands ;
Before them ran with blood the meadow lands.
I prayed for them, but ere the fight was o'er,
Swooned suddenly away, and looked no more ;
For in their midst I could no more behold
Those eyes of azure and that hair of gold !
They were three hundred, they were young and strong,
 And they are dead !

III. NOTES AND ILLUSTRATIONS

Page 9. *Hymn of the Moravian Nuns of Bethlehem.*

[This poem was suggested by the following sentence in an article upon Pulaski in the *North American Review*, for April, 1825 : "The standard of his legion was formed of a piece of crimson silk embroidered by the Moravian Nuns of Bethlehem in Pennsylvania." The historic facts in regard to the banner appear to be that Pulaski ordered it of the Moravian sisters at Bethlehem, who helped to support their house by needlework. This banner is preserved in the cabinet of the Maryland Historical Society at Baltimore ; it is twenty inches square and made to be carried on a lance. It is of double silk, now so much faded and discolored by time as to make it impossible to determine its original color. On both sides designs are embroidered with what was yellow silk, shaded with green, and deep silk fringe bordering. On one side are the letters "U. S.," and in a circle around them the words, " *Unitas Virtus Fortior* " ; on the other side, in the centre, is embroidered an all-seeing eye and the words " *Non Alius Regit.*" Pulaski received a mortal wound at the siege of Savannah, and dying on one of the vessels of the fleet when he was on his way north, was buried at sea. It is said that Lafayette lay sick at Bethlehem, and that it was on a visit to his brother officer that Pulaski ordered the flag. Its size, in any event, would have precluded its use as a shroud.]

Page 11. *The Skeleton in Armor.*
[The historic groundwork upon which Mr. Longfellow built his legend is in two parts, the Newport tower and the Fall River skeleton. The passage from Rafn, to which Mr. Longfellow refers as affording a poet sufficient basis upon which to build, is as follows : —

" There is no mistaking in this instance the style in which the more ancient stone edifices of the North were constructed, — the style which belongs to the Roman or Ante-Gothic architecture, and which, especially after the time of Charlemagne, diffused itself from Italy over the whole of the West and North of Europe, where it continued to predominate until the close of the twelfth century, — that style which some authors have, from one of its most striking characteristics, called the round arch style, the same which in England is denominated Saxon and sometimes Norman architecture.

" On the ancient structure in Newport there are no ornaments remaining which might possibly have served to guide us in assigning the probable date of its erection. That no vestige whatever is found of the pointed arch, nor any approximation to it, is indicative of an earlier rather than of a later period. From such characteristics as remain, however, we can scarcely form any other inference than one, in which I am persuaded that all who are familiar with Old-Northern architecture will concur, THAT THIS BUILDING WAS ERECTED AT A PERIOD DECIDEDLY NOT LATER THAN THE TWELFTH CENTURY. This remark applies, of course, to the original building only, and not to the alterations that it subsequently received ; for there are several such alterations in the upper part of the building which cannot be mistaken, and which were most likely occasioned by its being adapted in modern times to various uses ; for example, as the substructure of a windmill, and latterly as a hay magazine. To the same times may be referred the windows, the fireplace, and the apertures made above the columns. That this building could not have been erected for a windmill, is what an architect will easily discern."

Dr. Palfrey, in his *History of New England*, so cogently presented the reasons for believing this tower to have been constructed by Governor Arnold, that most students have since been disposed to accept this explanation ; but there have not been wanting those who maintained other views, as witness an article by R. G. Hatfield in *Scribner's Monthly* for March, 1879, in which the author maintains that the old mill at Newport ought to be called the Vinland Baptistery ; and also an article by Mr. S. Edward Forbes who maintains that the structure had nothing in common with the Chesterton mill in Warwickshire, with which it is commonly compared.

With regard to the Fall River skeleton, which with its appurtenances was unfortunately burned before it could be satisfactorily examined by experts, the following description taken from *The American Monthly Magazine* for January, 1836, will give the reader as full an account as is now possible :

" In digging down a hill near the village, a large mass of earth slid off, leaving in the bank and partially uncovered a human skull, which on examination was found to belong to a body buried in a sitting posture ; the head being about one foot below what had been for many years the surface of the ground. The surrounding earth was carefully removed, and the body found to be enveloped in a covering of coarse bark of a dark color. Within this envelope were found the remains of another of coarse cloth, made of fine bark, and about the texture of a Manilla coffee bag. On the breast was a plate of brass, thirteen inches long, six broad at the upper end, and five in the lower. This plate appears to have been cast, and is from one eighth to three thirty-seconds of an inch in thickness. It is so much corroded that whether or not anything was engraved upon it has not yet been ascertained. It is oval in form, the edges being irregular, apparently made so by corrosion. Below the breastplate, and entirely encircling the body, was a belt composed of brass tubes, each four and a half inches in length, and three sixteenths of an inch in diameter, arranged longitudinally and close together, the length of the tube being the width of the belt. The tubes are of thin brass, cast upon hollow reeds, and were fastened together by pieces of sinew. Near the right knee was a quiver of arrows. The arrows are of brass, thin, flat, and triangular in shape, with a round hole cut through near the base. The shaft was fastened to the head by inserting the latter in an opening at the end of the wood and then tying with a sinew through the round hole, a mode of constructing the weapon never practised by the Indians, not even with their arrows of thin shell. Parts of the shaft still remain on some of them. When first discovered, the arrows were in a sort of quiver of bark, which fell to pieces when exposed to the air."

The more generally received opinion amongst archæologists makes the skeleton to be that of an Indian.]

Page 13. *Skoal!*
In Scandinavia, this is the customary salutation when drinking a health. I have slightly changed the orthography of the word, in order to preserve the correct pronunciation [*skaal*].
Page 24. *As Lope says.*

La cólera
De un Español sentado no se templa,
Sino le representan en dos horas
Hasta el final juicio desde el Génesis.
LOPE DE VEGA.

Page 25. *Abrenuncio Satanas!*
" Digo, Señora, respondió Sancho, lo que tengo dicho, que de los azotes abernuncio. Abrenuncio, habeis de decir, Sancho, y no como decis, dijo el Duque." — *Don Quixote*, Part II., ch. 35.
Page 29. *Fray Carrillo.*
The allusion here is to a Spanish Epigram.

Siempre Fray Carrillo estás
Cansándonos acá fuera ;
Quien en tu celda estuviera
Para no verte jamas !
BÖHL DE FABER, *Floresta*, No. 611.

Page 29. *Padre Francisco.*
This is from an Italian popular song.

" Padre Francesco,
Padre Francesco ! "
— Cosa volete del Padre Francesco ? —
" V'è una bella ragazzina
Che si vuole confessar ! "
Fatte l' entrare, fatte l' entrare !
Che la voglio confessare.
KOPISCH, *Volksthümliche Poesien aus allen Mundarten Italiens und seiner Inseln*, p. 194.

Page 30. *Ave ! cujus calcem clare.*
From a monkish hymn of the twelfth century, in Sir Alexander Croke's *Essay on the Origin, Progress, and Decline of Rhyming Latin Verse*, p. 109.
Page 33. *The Gold of the Busné.*
Busné is the name given by the Gypsies to all who are not of their race.
Page 33. *Count of the Calés.*
The Gypsies call themselves Calés. See Borrow's valuable and extremely interesting work, *The Zincali ; or an Account of the Gypsies in Spain.* London, 1841.
Page 35. *Asks if his money-bags would rise.*
" ¿ Y volviéndome á un lado, ví á un Avariento, que estaba preguntando á otro, (que por haber sido embalsamado, y estar léxos sus tripas no hablaba, porque no habian llegado si habian de resucitar aquel dia todos los enterrados) si resucitarian unos bolsones suyos ? " —*El Sueño de las Calaveras.*
Page 35. *And amen ! said my Cid the Campeador.*
A line from the ancient *Poema del Cid.*

Amen, dixo Mio Cid el Campeador.
Line 3044.

Page 35. *The river of his thoughts.*
This expression is from Dante : —

Si che chiaro
Per essa scenda della mente il fiume.

Byron has likewise used the expression.

[She was his life,
The ocean to the river of his thoughts,
Which terminated all.
The Dream.]

Page 35. *Mari Franca.*
A common Spanish proverb, used to turn aside a question one does not wish to answer :—

Porque casó Mari Franca
Quatro leguas de Salamanca.

Page 36. *Ay, soft, emerald eyes.*
The Spaniards, with good reason, consider this color of the eye as beautiful, and celebrate it in song ; as, for example, in the well-known *Villancico :* —

Ay ojuelos verdes,
Ay los mis ojuelos,
Ay hagan los cielos
Que de mí te acuerdes !

.   .   .   .   .
Tengo confianza
De mis verdes ojos.
BÖHL DE FABER, *Floresta*, No. 255.

Dante speaks of Beatrice's eyes as emeralds. *Purgatorio*, xxxi. 116. Lami says, in his *Annotazioni*, " Erano i suoi occhi d' un turchino verdiccio, simile a quel del mare."
Page 36. *The Avenging Child.*
See the ancient Ballads of *El Infante Vengador*, and *Calaynos.*
Page 36. *All are sleeping.*
From the Spanish. Böhl de Faber. *Floresta*, No. 282.
Page 42. *Good night.*
From the Spanish ; as are likewise the songs immediately following, and that which commences the first scene of Act III. (by Lopez Maldonado).
Page 48. *The evil eye.*
" In the Gitano language, casting the evil eye is called *Querelar nasula*, which simply means making sick, and which, according to the common superstition, is accomplished by casting an evil look at people, especially children, who, from the tenderness of their constitution, are supposed to be more easily blighted than those of a more mature age. After receiving the evil glance, they fall sick, and die in a few hours.
" The Spaniards have very little to say respecting the evil eye, though the belief in it is very prevalent, especially in Andalusia, amongst the lower orders. A stag's horn is considered a good safeguard, and on that account a small horn, tipped with silver, is frequently attached to the children's necks by means of a cord braided from the hair of a black mare's tail. Should the evil glance be cast, it is imagined that the horn receives it, and instantly snaps asunder. Such horns may be purchased in some of the silversmiths' shops at Seville." — Borrow's *Zincali*, vol. i., ch. 9.
Page 48. *On the top of a mountain I stand.*
This and the following scraps of song are from Borrow's *Zincali.*

The Gypsy words in the same scene may be thus interpreted : —

John-Dorados, pieces of gold.
Pigeon, a simpleton.
In your morocco, stripped.
Doves, sheets.
Moon, a shirt.
Chirelin, a thief.
Murcigalleros, those who steal at nightfall.
Rastilleros, footpads.
Hermit, a highway-robber.
Planets, candles.
Commandments, the fingers.
St. Martin asleep, to rob a person asleep.
Lanterns, eyes.
Goblin, police officer.
Papagayo, a spy.
Vineyards and Dancing John, to take flight.

Page 52. *If thou art sleeping, maiden.*

From the Spanish ; as is likewise the song of the Contrabandista on the same page.

Page 55. *All the Foresters of Flanders.*

The title of Foresters was given to the early governors of Flanders, appointed by the kings of France. Lyderick du Bucq, in the days of Clotaire the Second, was the first of them ; and Beaudoin Bras-de-Fer, who stole away the fair Judith, daughter of Charles the Bald, from the French court, and married her in Bruges, was the last. After him the title of Forester was changed to that of Count. Philippe d'Alsace, Guy de Dampierre, and Louis de Crécy, coming later, in the order of time, were therefore rather Counts than Foresters. Philippe went twice to the Holy Land as a Crusader, and died of the plague at St. Jean-d'Acre, shortly after the capture of the city by the Christians. Guy de Dampierre died in the prison of Compiégne. Louis de Crécy was son and successor of Robert de Béthune, who strangled his wife, Yolande de Bourgogne, with the bridle of his horse, for having poisoned, at the age of eleven years, Charles, his son by his first wife, Blanche d'Anjou.

Page 55. *Stately dames, like queens attended.*

When Philippe-le-Bel, king of France, visited Flanders with his queen, she was so astonished at the magnificence of the dames of Bruges, that she exclaimed : " Je croyais être seule reine ici, mais il paraît que ceux de Flandre qui se trouvent dans nos prisons sont tous des princes, car leurs femmes sont habillées comme des princesses et des reines."

When the burgomasters of Ghent, Bruges, and Ypres went to Paris to pay homage to King John, in 1351, they were received with great pomp and distinction ; but, being invited to a festival, they observed that their seats at table were not furnished with cushions ; whereupon, to make known their displeasure at this want of regard to their dignity, they folded their richly embroidered cloaks and seated themselves upon them. On rising from table, they left their cloaks behind them, and, being informed of their apparent forgetfulness, Simon van Eertrycke, burgomaster of Bruges, replied, " We Flemings are not in the habit of carrying away our cushions after dinner."

Page 55. *Knights who bore the Fleece of Gold.*

Philippe de Bourgogne, surnamed Le Bon, espoused Isabella of Portugal on the 10th of January, 1430 ; and on the same day instituted the famous order of the Fleece of Gold.

Page 55. *I beheld the gentle Mary.*

Marie de Valois, Duchess of Burgundy, was left by the death of her father, Charles le Téméraire, at the age of twenty, the richest heiress of Europe. She came to Bruges, as Countess of Flanders, in 1477, and in the same year was married by proxy to the Archduke Maximilian. According to the custom of the time, the Duke of Bavaria, Maximilian's substitute, slept with the princess. They were both in complete dress, separated by a naked sword, and attended by four armed guards. Marie was adored by her subjects for her gentleness and her many other virtues.

Maximilian was son of the Emperor Frederick the Third, and is the same person mentioned afterwards in the poem of *Nuremberg* as the Kaiser Maximilian, and the hero of Pfinzing's poem of *Teuerdank.* Having been imprisoned by the revolted burghers of Bruges, they refused to release him till he consented to kneel in the public square, and to swear on the Holy Evangelists and the body of Saint Donatus that he would not take vengeance upon them for their rebellion.

Page 55. *The bloody battle of the Spurs of Gold.*

This battle, the most memorable in Flemish history, was fought under the walls of Courtray, on the 11th of July, 1302, between the French and the Flemings, the former commanded by Robert, Comte d'Artois, and the latter by Guillaume de Juliers, and Jean, Comte de Namur. The French army was completely routed, with a loss of twenty thousand infantry and seven thousand cavalry ; among whom were sixty-three princes, dukes, and counts, seven hundred lords-banneret, and eleven hundred noblemen. The flower of the French nobility perished on that day ; to which history has given the name of the *Journée des Eperons d'Or*, from the great number of golden spurs found on the field of battle. Seven hundred of them were hung up as a trophy in the church of Notre Dame de Courtray ; and, as the cavaliers of that day wore but a single spur each, these vouched to God for the violent and bloody death of seven hundred of his creatures.

Page 55. *Saw the fight at Minnewater.*

When the inhabitants of Bruges were digging a canal at Minnewater, to bring the waters of the Lys from Deynze to their city, they were attacked and routed by the citizens of Ghent, whose commerce would have been much injured by the canal. They were led by Jean Lyons, captain of a military company at Ghent, called the *Chaperons Blancs.* He had great sway over the turbulent populace, who, in those prosperous times of the city, gained an easy livelihood by laboring two or three days in the week, and had the remaining four or five to devote to public affairs. The fight at Minnewater was followed by open rebellion against Louis de Maele, the Count of Flanders and Protector of Bruges. His superb château of Wondelghem was pillaged and burnt; and the insurgents forced the gates of Bruges, and entered in triumph, with Lyons mounted at their head. A few days afterwards he died suddenly, perhaps by poison.

Meanwhile the insurgents received a check at the village of Nevèle; and two hundred of them perished in the church, which was burned by the Count's orders. One of the chiefs, Jean de Lannoy, took refuge in the belfry. From the summit of the tower he held forth his purse filled with gold, and begged for deliverance. It was in vain. His enemies cried to him from below to save himself as best he might; and, half suffocated with smoke and flame, he threw himself from the tower and perished at their feet. Peace was soon afterwards established, and the Count retired to faithful Bruges.

Page 55. *The Golden Dragon's nest.*

The Golden Dragon, taken from the church of St. Sophia, at Constantinople, in one of the Crusades, and placed on the belfry of Bruges, was afterwards transported to Ghent by Philip van Artevelde, and still adorns the belfry of that city.

The inscription on the alarm-bell at Ghent is, "*Mynen naem is Roland; als ik klep is er brand, and als ik luy is er victorie in het land.*" My name is Roland; when I toll there is fire, and when I ring there is victory in the land.

Page 57. *That their great imperial city stretched its hand through every clime.*

An old popular proverb of the town runs thus: —

> *Nurnberg's Hand*
> *Geht durch alle Land.*

> Nuremberg's Hand
> Goes through every land.

Page 57. *Sat the poet Melchior singing Kaiser Maximilian's praise.*

Melchior Pfinzing was one of the most celebrated German poets of the sixteenth century. The hero of his *Teuerdank* was the reigning Emperor, Maximilian; and the poem was to the Germans of that day what the *Orlando Furioso* was to the Italians. Maximilian is mentioned before, in the *Belfry of Bruges*. See preceding page.

Page 57. *In the church of sainted Sebald sleeps enshrined his holy dust.*

The tomb of Saint Sebald, in the church which bears his name, is one of the richest works of art in Nuremberg. It is of bronze, and was cast by Peter Vischer and his sons, who labored upon it thirteen years. It is adorned with nearly one hundred figures, among which those of the Twelve Apostles are conspicuous for size and beauty.

Page 57. *In the church of sainted Lawrence stands a pix of sculpture rare.*

This pix, or tabernacle for the vessels of the sacrament, is by the hand of Adam Kraft. It is an exquisite piece of sculpture in white stone, and rises to the height of sixty-four feet. It stands in the choir, whose richly painted windows cover it with varied colors.

Page 58. *Wisest of the Twelve Wise Masters.*

The Twelve Wise Masters was the title of the original corporation of the Mastersingers. Hans Sachs, the cobbler of Nuremberg, though not one of the original Twelve, was the most renowned of the Mastersingers, as well as the most voluminous. He flourished in the sixteenth century; and left behind him thirty-four folio volumes of manuscript, containing two hundred and eight plays, one thousand and seven hundred comic tales, and between four and five thousand lyric poems.

Page 58. *As in Adam Puschman's song.*

Adam Puschman, in his poem on the death of Hans Sachs, describes him as he appeared in a vision: —

> An old man,
> Gray and white, and dove-like,
> Who had, in sooth, a great beard,
> And read in a fair, great book,
> Beautiful with golden clasps.

Page 58. *As the old man, gray and dove-like.*

[In a letter to Freiligrath, written in the spring of 1844, Mr. Longfellow says: "Here I send you a poem on Nuremberg. . . . I trust I have not mistranslated wie ein *Taub Jermas*. It certainly stands for *eine Taube* or *ein Tauber*, and is *dove* and not *deaf*, though old Hans Sachs was deaf. But that Puschman describes afterwards when he says: —

> Dann sein Red und
> Gehör begunnt
> Ihne abzugehn, etc.

Therefore *dove-like* it is and shall be, for F. says 'I would have it so at any rate!' and at any rate I will."]

Page 64. *Who, unharmed, on his tusks once caught the bolts of the thunder.*

"A delegation of warriors from the Delaware tribe having visited the governor of Virginia, during the Revolution, on matters of business, after these had been discussed and settled in council, the governor asked them some questions relative to their country, and, among others, what they knew or had heard of the animal whose bones were found at the Saltlicks on the Ohio. Their chief speaker immediately put himself into an attitude of oratory, and, with a pomp suited to what he conceived the elevation of his subject, informed him that it was a tradition handed down from their fathers, 'that in ancient times a herd of these tremendous animals came to the Big-bone licks, and began an universal destruction of the bear, deer, elks, buffaloes, and other animals which had been created for the use of the Indians: that the Great Man above, looking down and seeing this, was so enraged that he seized his lightning, descended on the earth, seated himself on a neighboring mountain, on a rock of which his seat and the print of his feet are still to be seen, and hurled his bolts among them till the whole were slaughtered, except the big bull, who, presenting his forehead to the shafts, shook them off as they fell; but missing one at length, it wounded him in the side; whereon, springing round, he bounded over the Ohio, over the Wabash, the Illinois, and finally over the great lakes, where he is living at this day.' " —Jefferson's *Notes on Virginia*, Query VI.

Page 66. *Once some ancient Scald.*

[In commenting on this poem in his diary, Mr. Longfellow writes: "What is said of the Scald refers, of course, only to some of the melodies, which may possibly be as old as the days of Hakon Jarl, or older. Hamlet and Yorick are only symbolical of any old king and his jester."]

Page 66. *Vogelweid the Minnesinger.*

Walter von der Vogelweid, or Bird-Meadow, was one of the principal Minnesingers of the thirteenth century. He triumphed over Heinrich von Ofterdingen in that poetic contest at Wartburg Castle, known in literary history as the War of Wartburg.

Page 69. *Like imperial Charlemagne.*

Charlemagne may be called by preëminence the monarch of farmers. According to the German tradition, in seasons of great abundance, his spirit crosses the Rhine on a golden bridge at Bingen, and blesses the cornfields and the vineyards. During his lifetime, he did not disdain, says Montesquieu, " to sell the eggs from the farmyards of his domains, and the superfluous vegetables of his gardens; while he distributed among his people the wealth of the Lombards and the immense treasures of the Huns."

Page 72. *List to a Tale of Love in Acadie, home of the happy.*

[In the earliest records Acadie is called Cadie; afterwards it was called Arcadia, Accadia, or L'Acadie. The name is probably a French adaptation of a word common among the Micmac Indians, signifying place or region, and used as an affix to other words to indicate the place where various things, such as cranberries, eels, seals, were found in abundance. The French turned this Indian term into Cadie or Acadie; the English into Quoddy, in which form it remains when applied to the Quoddy Indians, to Quoddy Head, the last point of the United States next to Acadia, and in the compound Passamaquoddy, or Pollock-Ground.]

Page 74. *Lucky was he who found that stone in the nest of the swallow.*

[" If the eyes of one of the young of a swallow be put out, the mother bird will bring from the sea-shore a little stone, which will immediately restore its sight; fortunate is the person who finds this little stone in the nest, for it is a miraculous remedy." Pluquet, *Contes Populaires*, quoted by Wright, *Literature and Superstitions of England in the Middle Ages*, I. 128.]

Page 74. *"Sunshine of Saint Eulalie" was one called.*

Si le soleil rit le jour Sainte-Eulalie
Il y aura pommes et cidre à folie."
PLUQUET *in* WRIGHT, I. 131.

Page 75. *Flashed like a plane-tree the Persian adorned with mantles and jewels.*

See Evelyn's Silva, II. 53. [The story runs back to Herodotus, VII. 31, the "Persian" being Xerxes.]

Page 77. *For he told them tales.*

[The stories of the *Loup-garou*, or were-wolf, and the *Létiche*, and the miraculous properties of spiders, clover, and horseshoes, may be found in Pluquet, *Contes Populaires*, who conjectures that the white fleet ermine fox gave rise to the story of the *Létiche*.]

Page 77. *Well I remember a story.*

[This is an old Florentine story; in an altered form it is the theme of Rossini's opera of *La Gazza Ladra*.]

Page 85. *Thou art too fair to be left to braid St. Catherine's tresses.*

There is a Norman saying of a maid who does not marry — *Elle restera pour coiffer Sainte Katherine.*

Page 86. *On the Acadian coast, and the prairies of fair Opelousas.*

[Between the 1st of January and the 13th of May, 1765, about six hundred and fifty Acadians had arrived at New Orleans. The existence of a French population there attracted the exiles, and they were sent by the authorities to form settlements in Attakapas and Opelousas. They afterward established themselves on both sides of the Mississippi from the German Coast to Baton Rouge and even as high as Pointe Coupée. Hence the name of Acadian Coast, which a portion of the banks of the river still bears. See Gayarré's *History of Louisiana, the French Dominion*, vol. II.]

Page 102.

Behold, at last,
Each tall and tapering mast
Is swung into its place.

I wish to anticipate a criticism on this passage, by stating that sometimes, though not usually, vessels are launched fully sparred and rigged. I have availed myself of the exception as better suited to my purposes than the general rule; but the reader will see that it is neither a blunder nor a poetic license. On this subject a friend in Portland, Maine, writes me thus: —

"In this State, and also, I am told, in New York, ships are sometimes rigged upon the stocks, in order to save time, or to make a show. There was a fine large ship launched last summer at Ellsworth, fully sparred and rigged. Some years ago a ship was launched here, with her rigging, spars, sails, and cargo aboard. She sailed the next day and — was never heard of again! I hope this will not be the fate of your poem!"

Page 105. *Sir Humphrey Gilbert sailed.*

" When the wind abated and the vessels were near enough, the Admiral was seen constantly sitting in the stern, with a book in his hand. On the 9th of September he was seen for the last time, and was heard by the people of the *Hind* to say, ' We are as near heaven by sea as by land.' In the following night, the lights of the ship suddenly disappeared. The people in the other vessel kept a good lookout for him during the remainder of the voyage. On the 22d of September they arrived, through much tempest and peril, at Falmouth. But nothing more was seen or heard of the Admiral." — Belknap's *American Biography*, i. 203.

Page 107.

These severe afflictions
Not from the ground arise.

" Although affliction cometh not forth of the dust, neither doth trouble spring out of the ground." — *Job* v. 6.

Page 109. *Witlaf, a king of the Saxons.*
[In an entry in Mr. Longfellow's diary is the source from which the legend was derived. "Here is the part of King Witlaf's charter to the Abbey of Croyland relating to his drinking-horn, cited in Maitland's *Dark Ages*. I also offer to the refectory the horn of my table, that the elders of the monastery may drink out of it on the festivals of the Saints, and may sometimes amid their benedictions remember the soul of the donor, Witlaf."
In point of fact, Witlaf was one of the Angle kings of Mercia, who made a gallant stand against the Saxon invaders. It was while falling back before Egbert that Witlaf took sanctuary at Croyland, where he was for four months kept hidden by Siward, third Abbot of Croyland. At the end of three years Siward's influence procured the restoration of Witlaf, who became tributary to Egbert. In gratitude to the monks, Witlaf greatly added to the grants and privileges of the house.]

Page 113. THE SONG OF HIAWATHA. This Indian Edda — if I may so call it — is founded on a tradition, prevalent among the North American Indians, of a personage of miraculous birth, who was sent among them to clear their rivers, forests, and fishing-grounds, and to teach them the arts of peace. He was known among different tribes by the several names of Michabou, Chiabo, Manabozo, Tarenya-wagon and Hiawatha. Mr. Schoolcraft gives an account of him in his *Algic Researches*, vol. I. p. 134; and in his *History, Condition, and Prospects of the Indian Tribes of the United States*, Part III. p. 314, may be found the Iroquois form of the tradition, derived from the verbal narrations of an Onondaga chief.

Into this old tradition I have woven other curious Indian legends, drawn chiefly from the various and valuable writings of Mr. Schoolcraft, to whom the literary world is greatly indebted for his indefatigable zeal in rescuing from oblivion so much of the legendary lore of the Indians.

The scene of the poem is among the Ojibways on the southern shore of Lake Superior, in the region between the Pictured Rocks and the Grand Sable.

VOCABULARY

Adjidau'mo, *the red squirrel.*
Ahdeek', *the reindeer.*
Ahkose'win, *fever.*
Ahmeek', *the beaver.*
Algon'quin, *Ojibway.*
Annemee'kee, *the thunder.*
Apuk'wa, *a bulrush.*
Baim-wa'wa, *the sound of the thunder.*
Bemah'gut, *the grapevine.*
Be'na, *the pheasant.*
Big-Sea-Water, *Lake Superior.*
Bukada'win, *famine.*
Cheemaun', *a birch canoe.*
Chetowaik', *the plover.*
Chibia'bos, *a musician; friend of Hiawatha; ruler in the Land of Spirits.*
Dahin'da, *the bull-frog.*
Dush-kwo-ne'she, *or* Kwo-ne'she, *the dragon-fly.*
Esa, *shame upon you.*
Ewa-yea', *lullaby.*
Ghee'zis, *the sun.*
Gitche Gu'mee, *the Big Sea-Water, Lake Superior.*
Gitche Man'ito, *the Great Spirit, the Master of Life.*
Gushkewau', *the darkness.*
Hiawa'tha, *the Wise Man, the Teacher; son of Mudjekeewis, the West-Wind, and Wenonah, daughter of Nokomis.*
Ia'goo, *a great boaster and story-teller.*
Inin'ewug, *men, or pawns in the Game of the Bowl.*
Ishkoodah', *fire; a comet.*
Jee'bi, *a ghost, a spirit.*
Joss'akeed, *a prophet.*
Kabibonok'ka, *the North-Wind.*
Kagh, *the hedgehog.*
Ka'go, *do not.*
Kahgahgee', *the raven.*
Kaw, *no.*
Kayoshk', *the sea-gull.*
Kaween', *no indeed.*
Kee'go, *a fish.*
Keeway'din, *the Northwest Wind, the Home-Wind.*
Kena'beek, *a serpent.*
Keneu', *the great war-eagle.*
Keno'zha, *the pickerel.*
Ko'ko-ko' ho, *the owl.*
Kuntasoo', *the Game of Plum-stones.*
Kwa'sind, *the Strong Man.*
Kwo-ne'she, *or* Dush-kwo-ne'she, *the dragon-fly.*
Mahnahbe'zee, *the swan.*
Mahng, *the loon.*
Mahn-go-tay'see, *loon-hearted brave.*
Mahnomo'nee, *wild rice.*
Ma'ma, *the woodpecker.*
Maskeno'zha, *the pike.*
Me'da, *a medicine-man.*
Meenah'ga, *the blueberry.*
Megissog'won, *the great Pearl-Feather, a magician and the Manito of Wealth.*
Meshinau'wa, *a pipe-bearer.*
Minjekah'wun, *Hiawatha's mittens.*
Minneha'ha, *Laughing Water; a waterfall on a stream running into the Mississippi, between Fort Snelling and the Falls of St. Anthony.*
Minneha'ha, *Laughing Water; wife of Hiawatha.*
Minne-wa'wa, *a pleasant sound, as of the wind in the trees.*
Mishe-Mo'kwa, *the Great Bear.*
Mishe-Nah'ma, *the Great Sturgeon.*
Miskodeed', *the Spring Beauty, the Claytonia Virginica.*
Monda'min, *Indian Corn.*
Moon of Bright Nights, *April.*
Moon of Leaves, *May.*
Moon of Strawberries, *June.*
Moon of the Falling Leaves, *September.*
Moon of Snow-Shoes, *November.*
Mudjekee'wis, *the West-Wind; father of Hiawatha.*
Mudway-aush'ka, *sound of waves on a shore.*
Mushkoda'sa, *the grouse.*
Na'gow Wudj'oo, *the Sand Dunes of Lake Superior.*
Nah'ma, *the sturgeon.*

Nah'ma-wusk, *spearmint.*
Nee-ba-naw'baigs, *water spirits.*
Nenemoo'sha, *sweetheart.*
Nepah'win, *sleep.*
Noko'mis, *a grandmother ; mother of Wenonah.*
No'sa, *my father.*
Nush'ka, *look ! look !*
Odah'min, *the strawberry.*
Okahah'wis, *the fresh-water herring.*
Ome'mee, *the pigeon.*
Ona'gon, *a bowl.*
Onaway', *awake.*
Ope'chee, *the robin.*
Osse'o, *Son of the Evening Star.*
Owais'sa, *the bluebird.*
Oweenee', *wife of Osseo.*
Ozawa'beek, *a round piece of brass or copper in the Game of the Bowl.*
Pah'-puk-kee'na, *the grasshopper.*
Pau'guk, *death.*
Pau-Puk-Kee'wis, *the handsome Yenadizze, the Storm-Fool.*
Pauwa'ting, *Sault Sainte Marie.*
Pe'boan, *Winter.*
Pem'ican, *meat of the deer or buffalo dried and pounded.*
Pezheekee', *the bison.*
Pishnekuh', *the brant.*
Pone'mah, *hereafter.*
Pugasaing', *Game of the Bowl.*
Puggawau'gun, *a war-club.*
Puk-Wudj'ies, *little wild men of the woods ; pygmies.*
Sah'wa, *the perch.*
Sebowish'a, *rapids.*
Segwun', *Spring.*
Sha'da, *the pelican.*
Shahbo'min, *the gooseberry.*
Shah-shah, *long ago.*
Shaugoda'y , *a coward.*
Shawgashee', *the crawfish.*
Shawonda'see, *the South-Wind.*
Shaw-shaw, *the swallow.*
Shesh'ebwug, *ducks ; pieces in the Game of the Bowl.*
Shin'gebis, *the diver or grebe.*
Showain' neme'shin, *pity me.*
Shuh-shuh'gah, *the blue heron.*
Soan-ge-ta'ha, *strong hearted.*
Subbeka'she, *the spider.*
Sugge'ma, *the mosquito.*
To'tem, *family coat of arms.*
Ugh, *yes.*
Ugudwash', *the sun-fish.*
Unktahee', *the God of Water.*
Wabas'so, *the rabbit ; the North.*
Wabe'no, *a magician, a juggler.*
Wabe'no-wusk, *yarrow.*
Wa-bun, *the East-Wind.*
Wa'bun An'nung, *the Star of the East, the Morning Star.*
Wahono'win, *a cry of lamentation.*
Wah-wah-tay'see, *the fire-fly.*
Wam'pum, *beads of shell.*
Waubewy'on, *a white skin wrapper.*
Wa'wa, *the wild goose.*
Waw'beek, *a rock.*
Waw-be-wa'wa, *the white goose.*
Wawonais'sa, *the whippoorwill.*
Way-muk-kwa'na, *the caterpillar.*
Wen'digoes, *giants.*
Weno'nah, *Hiawatha's mother, daughter of Nokomis.*
Yenadiz'ze, *an idler and gambler ; an Indian dandy.*

Page 114. *In the Vale of Tawasentha.*
This valley, now called Norman's Kill, is in Albany County, New York.

Page 115. *On the Mountains of the Prairie.*
Mr. Catlin, in his *Letters and Notes on the Manners, Customs, and Condition of the North*

American Indians, vol. II. p. 160, gives an interesting account of the *Côteau des Prairies,* and the Red Pipestone Quarry. He says : —

"Here (according to their traditions) happened the mysterious birth of the red pipe, which has blown its fumes of peace and war to the remotest corners of the continent ; which has visited every warrior, and passed through its reddened stem the irrevocable oath of war and desolation. And here, also, the peace-breathing calumet was born, and fringed with the eagle's quills, which has shed its thrilling fumes over the land, and soothed the fury of the relentless savage.

"The Great Spirit at an ancient period here called the Indian nations together, and, standing on the precipice of the red pipe-stone rock, broke from its wall a piece, and made a huge pipe by turning it in his hand, which he smoked over them, and to the North, the South, the East, and the West, and told them that this stone was red, — that it was their flesh, — that they must use it for their pipes of peace, — that it belonged to them all, and that the war-club and scalping-knife must not be raised on its ground. At the last whiff of his pipe his head went into a great cloud, and the whole surface of the rock for several miles was melted and glazed ; two great ovens were opened beneath, and two women (guardian spirits of the place) entered them in a blaze of fire ; and they are heard there yet (Tso-mec-cos-tee and Tso-me-cos-te-won-dee), answering to the invocations of the high-priests or medicine-men, who consult them when they are visitors to this sacred place."

Page 116. *Hark you, Bear ! you are a coward.*
This anecdote is from Heckewelder. In his account of the Indian Nations, he describes an Indian hunter as addressing a bear in nearly these words. "I was present," he says, "at the delivery of this curious invective ; when the hunter had despatched the bear, I asked him how he thought that poor animal could understand what he said to it. 'Oh,' said he in answer, 'the bear understood me very well ; did you not observe how *ashamed* he looked while I was upbraiding him ? ' " — *Transactions of the American Philosophical Society,* vol. I. p. 240.

Page 118. *Sent the robin, the Opechee.*
[In his first edition, Mr. Longfellow printed, *Sent the Opechee, the robin,* but apparently was corrected in the pronunciation of the Indian word. A similar change was made by him in the line, *All the Wendigoes, the giants,* which at first read, *All the giants, the Wendigoes.*]

Page 120. *Hush ! the Naked Bear will hear thee !*
Heckewelder, in a letter published in the *Transactions of the American Philosophical Society,* vol. IV. p. 260, speaks of this tradition as prevalent among the Mohicans and Delawares. "Their reports," he says, "run thus : that among all animals that had been formerly in this country, this was the most ferocious ; that it was much larger than the largest of the common bears, and remarkably long - bodied ; all

over (except a spot of hair on its back of a white color) naked. . . .

"The history of this animal used to be a subject of conversation among the Indians, especially when in the woods a-hunting. I have also heard them say to their children when crying: 'Hush! the naked bear will hear you, be upon you, and devour you.'"

Page 123. *Where the Falls of Minnehaha*, etc.

"The scenery about Fort Snelling is rich in beauty. The Falls of St. Anthony are familiar to travellers, and to readers of Indian sketches. Between the fort and these falls are the ' Little Falls,' forty feet in height, on a stream that empties into the Mississippi. The Indians called them Mine-hah-hah, or 'laughing waters.'" — Mrs. Eastman's *Dacotah, or Legends of the Sioux*, Introd. p. ii.

Page 138. *Sand Hills of the Nagow Wudjoo.*

A description of the *Grand Sable*, or great sand-dunes of Lake Superior, is given in Foster and Whitney's *Report on the Geology of the Lake Superior Land District*, Part II. p. 131.

"The Grand Sable possesses a scenic interest little inferior to that of the Pictured Rocks. The explorer passes abruptly from a coast of consolidated sand to one of loose materials ; and although in the one case the cliffs are less precipitous, yet in the other they attain a higher altitude. He sees before him a long reach of coast, resembling a vast sand-bank, more than three hundred and fifty feet in height, without a trace of vegetation. Ascending to the top, rounded hillocks of blown sand are observed, with occasional clumps of trees, standing out like oases in the desert."

Page 138. *Onaway! Awake, beloved!*

The original of this song may be found in *Littell's Living Age*, vol. XXXV. p. 45.

Page 139. *Or the Red Swan floating, flying.*

The fanciful tradition of the Red Swan may be found in Schoolcraft's *Algic Researches*, vol. II. p. 9.

Page 143. *When I think of my beloved.*

The original of this song may be found in *Oneota*, p. 15.

Page 143. *Sing the mysteries of Mondamin.*

The Indians hold the maize, or Indian corn, in great veneration. "They esteem it so important and divine a grain," says Schoolcraft, "that their story-tellers invented various tales, in which this idea is symbolized under the form of a special gift from the Great Spirit. The Odjibwa-Algonquins, who call it Mon-da-min, that is, this Spirit's grain or berry, have a pretty story of the kind, in which the stalk in full tassel is represented as descending from the sky, under the guise of a handsome youth, in answer to the prayers of a young man at his fast of virility, or coming to manhood.

"It is well known that corn-planting and corn-gathering, at least among all the still *uncolonized* tribes, are left entirely to the females and children, and a few superannuated old men. It is not generally known, perhaps, that this labor is not compulsory. and that it is assumed by the females as a just equivalent, in their view, for the onerous and continuous labor of the other sex, in providing meats, and skins for clothing, by the chase, and in defending their villages against their enemies, and keeping intruders off their territories. A good Indian housewife deems this a part of her prerogative, and prides herself to have a store of corn to exercise her hospitality, or duly honor her husband's hospitality in the entertainment of the lodge guests." — *Oneóta*, p. 82.

Page 143. *Thus the fields shall be more fruitful.*

"A singular proof of this belief, in both sexes, of the mysterious influence of the steps of a woman on the vegetable and insect creation, is found in an ancient custom, which was related to me, respecting corn-planting. It was the practice of the hunter's wife, when the field of corn had been planted, to choose the first dark or overclouded evening to perform a secret circuit, *sans habillement*, around the field. For this purpose she slipped out of the lodge in the evening, unobserved, to some obscure nook, where she completely. disrobed. Then, taking her matchecota, or principal garment, in one hand, she dragged it around the field. This was thought to insure a prolific crop, and to prevent the assaults of insects and worms upon the grain. It was supposed they could not creep over the charmed line." — *Oneóta*. p. 83.

Page 144. *With his prisoner-string he bound him.*

"These cords," says Mr. Tanner, "are made of the bark of the elm-tree, by boiling and then immersing it in cold water. . . . The leader of a war party commonly carries several fastened about his waist, and if, in the course of the fight, any one of his young men takes a prisoner, it is his duty to bring him immediately to the chief, to be tied, and the latter is responsible for his safe keeping." — *Narrative of Captivity and Adventures*, p. 412.

Page 145.

Wagemin, the thief of cornfields,
Paimosaid, who steals the maize-ear.

"If one of the young female huskers finds a *red* ear of corn, it is typical of a brave admirer, and is regarded as a fitting present to some young warrior. But if the ear be *crooked*, and tapering to a point, no matter what color, the whole circle is set in a roar, and *wa-ge-min* is the word shouted aloud. It is the symbol of a thief in the cornfield. It is considered as the image of an old man stooping as he enters the lot. Had the chisel of Praxiteles been employed to produce this image, it could not more vividly bring to the minds of the merry group the idea of a pilferer of their favorite mondámin. . . .

"The literal meaning of the term is, a mass, or crooked ear of grain ; but the ear of corn so called is a conventional type of a little old man pilfering ears of corn in a cornfield. It is in this manner that a single word or term, in these curious languages, becomes the fruitful parent of many ideas. And we can thus perceive why it is that the word *wagemin* is alone competent to excite merriment in the husking circle.

" This term is taken as a basis of the cereal chorus, or corn song, as sung by the Northern Algonquin tribes. It is coupled with the phrase *Paimosaid*, — a permutative form of the Indian substantive, made from the verb *pim-o-sa*, to walk. Its literal meaning is, *he who walks*, or *the walker ;* but the ideas conveyed by it are, he who walks by night to pilfer corn. It offers, therefore, a kind of parallelism in expression to the preceding term." — *Oneóta*, p. 254.

Page 149. *Pugasaing, with thirteen pieces.*

This Game of the Bowl is the principal game of hazard among the Northern tribes of Indians. Mr. Schoolcraft gives a particular account of it in *Oneóta*, p. 85. "This game," he says, "is very fascinating to some portions of the Indians. They stake at it their ornaments, weapons, clothing, canoes, horses, everything in fact they possess ; and have been known, it is said, to set up their wives and children, and even to forfeit their own liberty. Of such desperate stakes I have seen no examples, nor do I think the game itself in common use. It is rather confined to certain persons, who hold the relative rank of gamblers in Indian society, — men who are not noted as hunters or warriors, or steady providers for their families. Among these are persons who bear the term of *Ienadizze-wug*, that is, wanderers about the country, braggadocios, or fops. It can hardly be classed with the popular games of amusement, by which skill and dexterity are acquired. I have generally found the chiefs and graver men of the tribes, who encouraged the young men to play ball, and are sure to be present at the customary sports, to witness, and sanction, and applaud them, speak lightly and disparagingly of this game of hazard. Yet it cannot be denied that some of the chiefs, distinguished in war and the chase, at the West, can be referred to as lending their example to its fascinating power."

See also his *History, Conditions, and Prospects of the Indian Tribes*, Part II. p. 72.

Page 154. *To the Pictured Rocks of sandstone.*

The reader will find a long description of the Pictured Rocks in Foster and Whitney's *Report on the Geology of the Lake Superior Land District*, Part II. p. 124. From this I make the following extract : —

"The Pictured Rocks may be described, in general terms, as a series of sandstone bluffs extending along the shore of Lake Superior for about five miles, and rising, in most places, vertically from the water, without any beach at the base, to a height varying from fifty to nearly two hundred feet. Were they simply a line of cliffs, they might not, so far as relates to height or extent, be worthy of a rank among great natural curiosities, although such an assemblage of rocky strata, washed by the waves of the great lake, would not, under any circumstances, be destitute of grandeur. To the voyager, coasting along their base in his frail canoe, they would, at all times, be an object of dread;

the recoil of the surf, the rock-bound coast, affording for miles no place of refuge, — the lowering sky, the rising wind, — all these would excite his apprehension, and induce him to ply a vigorous oar until the dreaded wall was passed. But in the Pictured Rocks there are two features which communicate to the scenery a wonderful and almost unique character. These are, first, the curious manner in which the cliffs have been excavated and worn away by the action of the lake, which for centuries has dashed an ocean-like surf against their base ; and, second, the equally curious manner in which large portions of the surface have been colored by bands of brilliant hues.

"It is from the latter circumstance that the name, by which these cliffs are known to the American traveller, is derived ; while that applied to them by the French voyageurs (' Les Portails ') is derived from the former, and by far the most striking peculiarity.

"The term *Pictured Rocks* has been in use for a great length of time ; but when it was first applied we have been unable to discover. It would seem that the first travellers were more impressed with the novel and striking distribution of colors on the surface than with the astonishing variety of form into which the cliffs themselves have been worn. . . .

"Our voyageurs had many legends to relate of the pranks of the *Menni-bojou* in these caverns, and, in answer to our inquiries, seemed disposed to fabricate stories without end of the achievements of this Indian deity."

Page 162. *Toward the sun his hands were lifted.*

In this manner, and with such salutations, was Father Marquette received by the Illinois. See his *Voyages et Découvertes*, Section V.

Page 166. *Full of the name and the fame of the Puritan maiden Priscilla.*

[Among the names of the Mayflower company are those of " Mr. William Mullines and his wife, and 2 children, Joseph and Priscila ; and a servant, Robart Carter."]

Page 167. *She is alone in the world.*

[" Mr. Molines, and his wife, his sone and his servant, dyed the first winter. Only his daughter Priscila survived and married with John Alden, who are both living and have 11 children." — Bradford : *History of Plymouth Plantation*.]

Page 169. *Gathering still, as he went, the Mayflowers blooming around him.*

[The Mayflower is the well-known *Epigœa repens*, sometimes also called the Trailing Arbutus. The name *Mayflower* was familiar in England, as the application of it to the historic vessel shows, but it was applied by the English, and still is, to the hawthorn. Its use here in connection with *Epigœa repens*, dates from a very early day, some claiming that the first Pilgrims so used it, in affectionate memory of the vessel and its English flower association.]

Page 175. *With Stephen and Richard and Gilbert.*

[These names are not taken at random. Ste

phen Hopkins, Richard Warren, and Gilbert Winslow were all among the Mayflower passengers, and were alive at this time.]

Page 183. *After the Puritan way, and the laudable custom of Holland.*

["May 12 was the first marriage in this place, which, according to the laudable custome of the Low-Cuntries, in which they had lived, was thought most requisite to be performed by the magistrate, as being a civill thing, upon which many questions aboute inheritances doe depende, with other things most proper to their cognizans, and most consonante to the scripturs, Ruth 4, and no wher found in the gospell to be layed on the ministers as a part of their office." — Bradford: *History of Plymouth Plantation*, p. 101.]

Page 186.
That of our vices we can frame A ladder.

The words of St. Augustine are, "De vitiis nostris scalam nobis facimus, si vitia ipsa calcamus." — Sermon III. *De Ascensione.*

Page 187. *In Mather's Magnalia Christi.*

[The passage in Mather upon which the poem is based is found in Book I. chapter vi., and is in the form of a letter to Mather from the Rev. James Pierpont, Pastor of New Haven.]

Page 190. *And the Emperor but a Macho.*

Macho, in Spanish, signifies a mule. *Golondrina* is the feminine form for *Golondrino*, a swallow, and also a cant name for a deserter.

Page 192. OLIVER BASSELIN.

Oliver Basselin, the "*Père joyeux du Vaudeville,*" flourished in the fifteenth century, and gave to his convivial songs the name of his native valleys, in which he sang them, Vaux-de-Vire. This name was afterwards corrupted into the modern *Vaudeville.*

Page 193. VICTOR GALBRAITH.

Victor Galbraith was a bugler in a company of volunteer cavalry; and was shot in Mexico for some breach of discipline. It is a common superstition among soldiers, that no balls will kill them unless their names are written on them. The old proverb says: "Every bullet has its billet."

Page 194. *I remember the sea-fight far away.*

This was the engagement between the Enterprise and Boxer off the harbor of Portland, in which both captains were slain. They were buried side by side in the cemetery on Mount-joy. [The fight took place in 1813. The Enterprise was an American brig, the Boxer an English one. The fight, which could be seen from the shore, lasted for three quarters of an hour, when the Enterprise came into the harbor, bringing her captive with her.]

Page 197. *The palm, the lily, and the spear.*

"At Pisa the church of San Francisco contains a chapel dedicated lately to Santa Filomena; over the altar is a picture, by Sabatelli, representing the Saint as a beautiful, nymphlike figure, floating down from heaven, attended by two angels bearing the lily, palm, and javelin, and beneath, in the foreground, the sick and maimed, who are healed by her interces-

sion." — Mrs. Jameson, *Sacred and Legendary Art*, II. 298.

Page 200. *Sandalphon, the Angel of Prayer.*

["Rabbi Eliezer hath said: 'There is an Angel who standeth on earth and reacheth with his head to the door of Heaven. It is taught in the Mishna that he is called Sandalphon.'"

"There are three [angels] who weave or make garlands out of the prayers of the Israelites . . . the third is Sandalphon."

"There be Angels which are of Wind and there be Angels which are of Fire."

"The holy and blessed God creates every day a multitude of angels in heaven, who, after they have sung a hymn before Him, do perish. . . . Except Michael and Gabriel . . . and Sandalphon and their equals, who remain in their glory wherewith they were invested in the six days' creation."

"The prophet Elias is the Angel Sandalphon, who twisteth or bindeth garlands out of the prayers, for his Lord."

The above passages from J. P. Stehelin's *The Traditions of the Jews* were marked by Mr. Longfellow, and evidently furnished the material upon which he based his poem.]

Page 205.
Writ near a century ago By the great Major Molineaux Whom Hawthorne has immortal made.

[The lines are as follows: —

What do you think ?
Here is good drink,
Perhaps you may not know it ;
If not in haste,
Do stop and taste !
You merry folk will show it.

On another pane appears the Major's name, Wm. Molineux Jr. Esq., and the date, June 24, 1774. The allusion is to Hawthorne's tale, *My Kinsman, Major Molineux.* Hawthorne, writing to Mr. Longfellow after the publication of the *Tales*, says, "It gratifies my mind to find my own name shining in your verse, — even as if I had been gazing up at the moon and detected my own features in its profile."]

Page 207. *The midnight ride of Paul Revere.*

[It is possible that Mr. Longfellow derived the story from Paul Revere's account of the incident in a letter to Dr. Jeremy Belknap, printed in Mass. Hist. Coll. V. Mr. Frothingham, in his *Siege of Boston*, pp. 57–59, gives the story mainly according to a memorandum of Richard Devens, Revere's friend and associate. The publication of Mr. Longfellow's poem called out a protracted discussion both as to the church from which the signals were hung, and as to the friend who hung the lanterns. The subject is discussed and authorities cited in *Memorial History of Boston*, III. 101.]

Page 209. THE FALCON OF SER FEDERIGO.

[The story is found in the *Decameron*, Fifth day, ninth tale. As Boccaccio, however, was not the first to tell it, so Mr. Longfellow is not the only one after him to repeat it. So remote a source as *Pantschatantra* (Benfey, II. 247) contains it, and La Fontaine includes it in his *Contes et Nouvelles* under the title of *Le Faucon*. Tennyson has treated the subject dramatically in *The Falcon*. See also Delisle de la Drévetière, who turned Boccaccio's story into a comedy in three acts.]

Page 214. THE LEGEND OF RABBI BEN LEVI.

[Varnhagen refers to three several sources of this legend in the books *Col Bo*, *Ben Sira*, and *Ketuboth*, but it is most likely that Mr. Longfellow was indebted for the story to his friend Emmanuel Vitalis Scherb.]

Page 215. KING ROBERT OF SICILY.

[This story is one of very wide distribution. It is given in *Gesta Romanorum* as the story of Jovinian. Frere in his *Old Deccan Days, or Hindoo Fairy Legends current in Southern India*, recites it in the form of *The Wanderings of Vicram Maharajah*. Varnhagen pursues the legend through a great variety of forms. Leigh Hunt, among moderns, has told the story in *A Jar of Honey from Mt. Hybla*, from which source Mr. Longfellow seems to have drawn. Dante refers to the King in *Paradiso*, Canto VIII.]

Page 240. THE BIRDS OF KILLINGWORTH.

[Killingworth in Connecticut was named from the English town Kenilworth in Warwickshire, and had the same orthography in the early records, but was afterwards corrupted into its present form. Sixty or seventy years ago, according to Mr. Henry Hull, writing from personal recollection, " the men of the northern part of the town did yearly in the spring choose two leaders, and then the two sides were formed : the side that got beaten should pay the bills. Their special game was the hawk, the owl, the crow, the blackbird, and any other bird supposed to be mischievous to the corn. Some years each side would bring them in by the bushel. This was followed up for only a few years, for the birds began to grow scarce." The story, based upon such a slight suggestion, was Mr. Longfellow's own invention.]

Page 245. THE BELL OF ATRI.

[See Gualteruzzi's *Cento Novelle Antiche*.]

Page 247. KAMBALU.

[See Boni's edition of *Il Milione di Marco Polo*, II. 35 and I. 14.]

Page 255. LADY WENTWORTH.

[The incidents of this tale are recounted by C. W. Brewster, *Rambles about Portsmouth*, I. 101. After the publication of Mr. Longfellow's poem, Mr. Thomas Wentworth Higginson wrote to one of Mr. Longfellow's kinsmen a version of the story sent him by Mrs. Mary Anne Williams, who had the story from her grandmother, *née* Mary Wentworth, who was niece to Governor Wentworth, and a child at the time of the incident. "I have seen Mr. Longfellow's poem," writes Mrs. Williams, " but I should think he would be afraid some of the old fellows would appear to him for making it appear that any others than the family were pres-

ent to witness what they considered a great degradation. Only the brothers and brothers in law were present, and Mr. Brown ; and the bride, who had been his housekeeper for seven years, was then 35, and attired in a calico dress and a white apron. The family stood in wholesome awe of the sturdy old governor, so treated Patty with civility, but it was hard work for the stately old dames, and she was dropped after his death." Governor Wentworth was born July 24, 1696, and his marriage was on March 15, 1760.]

Page 265. CHARLEMAGNE.

[In his diary, under date of May 12, 1872, Mr. Longfellow writes : " Wrote a short poem on Charlemagne from a story in an old chronicle, *De Factis Caroli Magni*, quoted by Cantù, *Storia degli Italiani*, II. 122. I first heard it from Charles Perkins, in one of his lectures."]

Page 270. ELIZABETH.

[As intimated in the Interlude which follows, the tale of *Elizabeth* was founded on a prose tale by Mrs. Lydia Maria Child, entitled *The Youthful Emigrant*, which fell under Mr. Longfellow's eye in a Portland paper. Besides this he had recourse to *A Call to the Unfaithful Professors of Truth*, by John Estaugh, with Preface by his widow. E. E.'s Testimony concerning her husband J. E. Several expressions in the poem are derived from this little book.]

Page 282. THE MOTHER'S GHOST.

[A Danish ballad to be found in Grundtvig's *Danmarks gamle Folkeviser*, II. 478, was the basis of this poem.]

Page 310.

" *O Cæsar, we who are about to die*
Salute you ! "

[This use of the phrase *Morituri Salutamus* agrees with the treatment of Gérôme in his painting, beneath which he wrote the words, *Ave Cæsar, Imperator, Morituri te Salutant*. The reference to a gladiatorial combat, however, is doubted by some scholars, who quote Suetonius and Dion Cassius as using the phrase in connection with the great sea-fight exhibition given by the Emperor on Lacus Fucinus. The combatants were condemned criminals, and they were to fight until one of the parties was killed, unless saved by the interposition of the Emperor.]

Page 311. *All save one.*

[Professor Alpheus Spring Packard, since deceased.]

Page 314. *In Attica thy birthplace should have been.*

[Cornelius Conway Felton, at one time Professor of Greek, and afterward President, at Harvard College.]

Page 314. *Piteously calling and lamenting thee.*

[Jean Louis Rodolphe Agassiz, the eminent naturalist, whose summer home at Nahant was near Mr. Longfellow's, while they were also fellow-townsmen in Cambridge.]

Page 315. *A friend who bore thy name.*

[Charles Sumner, one of Mr. Longfellow's closest friends.]

Page 318. *Here lies the gentle humorist.*
[Washington Irving. It is interesting to
note the influence which this writer had upon
Mr. Longfellow, as shown not only in his early
prose, but in his direct testimony. In present-
ing the resolutions upon the death of Irving at
a meeting of the Massachusetts Historical Soci-
ety, December 5, 1859, Mr. Longfellow said:
"Every reader has his first book ; I mean to
say, one book among all others which in early
youth first fascinates his imagination, and at
once excites and satisfies the desires of his
mind. To me, this first book was the Sketch-
Book of Washington Irving. I was a school-
boy when it was published, and read each suc-
ceeding number with ever increasing wonder
and delight, spell-bound by its pleasant humor,
its melancholy tenderness, its atmosphere of
revery, — nay, even by its gray-brown covers,
the shaded letters of its titles, and the fair
clear type, which seemed an outward symbol of
its style. How many delightful books the same
author has given us, written before and since,
— volumes of history and of fiction ; most of
which illustrate his native land, and some of
which illuminate it and make the Hudson, I
will not say as classic, but as romantic as the
Rhine ! Yet still the charm of the Sketch-
Book remains unbroken ; the old fascination
remains about it ; and whenever I open its
pages, I open also that mysterious door which
leads back into the haunted chambers of
youth." . . .]
Page 319. PARKER CLEAVELAND.
[A distinguished naturalist who was senior
professor at Bowdoin College, where Mr. Long-
fellow was first a student and afterward an in-
structor. The father of the poet was an inti-
mate friend of Professor Cleaveland, and when
the son went to Brunswick he found in the
older man one of his most cherished associates.
When he went back to give his poem, *Morituri
Salutamus*, he made his stay at the Cleaveland
mansion, with the daughter of the deceased
professor.]
Page 323. *Poet ! I come to touch thy lance
with mine.*
"When any came to take the government of
the Hundred or Wapentake in a day and place
appointed, as they were accustomed to meete,
all the better sort met him with lances, and he
alighting from his horse, all rise up to him, and
he setting or holding his lance upright, all the
rest come with their lances, according to the
auncient custome in confirming league and pub-
like peace and obedience, and touch his lance
or weapon, and thereof called Wapentake, for
the Saxon or old English *wapun* is weapon,
and *tac, tactus*, a touching, thereby this meeting
called Wapentake, or touching of weapon, be-
cause that by that signe and ceremonie of touch-
ing weapon or the lance, they were sworne and
confederate." — Master Lamberd in *Minshew*.
Page 336. *Of the White Chief with yellow
hair.*
[General George A. Custer, who was surprised

and with his entire force put to death by the
Sioux, June 25, 1876.]
Page 342. *Watch o'er Maximilian's tomb.*
In the Hofkirche at Innsbruck.
Page 343. FROM MY ARM-CHAIR.
[This chair bears the inscription,

To
THE AUTHOR
of
THE VILLAGE BLACKSMITH,
This chair, made from the wood of the
spreading chestnut-tree,
is presented as
An expression of grateful regard and veneration by
The children of Cambridge,
Who with their friends join in best wishes
and congratulations
on
This Anniversary.
February 27, 1879.

In 1880, when the city of Cambridge celebrated
the two hundred and fiftieth anniversary of
the founding of the town, December 28th,
there was a children's festival at Sanders Thea-
tre in the morning, and the chair stood on the
platform in full view of the thousand children
assembled. Mr. George Riddle read the poem ;
then, to the surprise of all, the poet himself
came forward and made this little speech : —
"My dear young Friends, — I do not rise to
make an address to you, but to excuse myself
from making one. I know the proverb says that
he who excuses himself accuses himself, and I
am willing on this occasion to accuse myself, for
I feel very much as I suppose some of you do
when you are suddenly called upon in your
class-room, and are obliged to say that you are
not prepared. I am glad to see your faces and
to hear your voices. I am glad to have this op-
portunity of thanking you in prose, as I have
already done in verse, for the beautiful present
you made me some two years ago. Perhaps
some of you have forgotten it, but I have not ;
and I am afraid — yes, I am afraid — that fifty
years hence, when you celebrate the three hun-
dredth anniversary of this occasion, this day
and all that belongs to it will have passed from
your memory : for an English philosopher has
said that the ideas as well as children of our
youth often die before us, and our minds repre-
sent to us those tombs to which we are ap-
proaching, where though the brass and marble
remain, yet the inscriptions are effaced by time,
and the imagery moulders away."]
Page 355.

*So the Hexameter, rising and singing, with ca-
dence sonorous,*
*Falls ; and in refluent rhythm back the Pentame-
ter flows.*

[Schiller's lines will be recalled : —

In Hexameter steigt des Springquells flüssige Säule :
In Pentameter drauf fällt sie melodisch herab.

In his diary, under date of February 24, 1847, Mr. Longfellow writes : —
"Walking down to Felton's this morning, seduced by the magnetic influence of the air and the approach to classic ground, I composed the following, a pendant to Schiller's, —

In Hexameter headlong the cataract plunges,
In Pentameter up whirls the eddying mist.

In my afternoon's walk I changed it and added three more.

I

In Hexameter plunges the headlong cataract downward,
In Pentameter up whirls the eddying mist.

II

In Hexameter rolls sonorous the peal of the organ ;
In Pentameter soft rises the chant of the choir.

III

In Hexameter gallops delighted a beggar on horseback ;
In Pentameter, whack ! tumbles he off of his steed.

IV

In Hexameter sings serenely a Harvard Professor ;
In Pentameter him damns censorious Poe."]

Page 408. THE GOLDEN LEGEND.
The old *Legenda Aurea*, or Golden Legend, was originally written in Latin, in the thirteenth century, by Jacobus de Voragine, a Dominican friar, who afterwards became Archbishop of Genoa, and died in 1292.
He called his book simply *Legends of the Saints*. The epithet of Golden was given it by his admirers ; for, as Wynkin de Worde says, "Like as passeth gold in value all other metals, so this Legend exceedeth all other books." But Edward Leigh, in much distress of mind, calls it "a book written by a man of a leaden heart for the basenesse of the errours, that are without wit or reason, and of a brazen forehead, for his impudent boldnesse in reporting things so fabulous and incredible."
This work, the great text-book of the legendary lore of the Middle Ages, was translated into French in the fourteenth century by Jean de Vignay, and in the fifteenth into English by William Caxton. It has lately been made more accessible by a new French translation : *La Legende Dorée, traduite du Latin, par M. G. B.* Paris, 1850. There is a copy of the original, with the *Gesta Longobardorum* appended, in the Harvard College Library, Cambridge, printed at Strasburg, 1496. The title-page is wanting ; and the volume begins with the *Tabula Legendorum*.
I have called this poem the *Golden Legend*, because the story upon which it is founded seems to me to surpass all other legends in beauty and significance. It exhibits, amid the corruptions of the Middle Ages, the virtue of disinterestedness and self-sacrifice, and the power of Faith, Hope, and Charity, sufficient for all the exigencies of life and death. The story is told, and perhaps invented, by Hartmann von der Aue, a Minnesinger of the twelfth century. The original may be found in Mailáth's *Altdeutsche Gedichte*, with a modern German version. There is another in Marbach's *Volksbücher*, No. 32.
[Mr. S. Arthur Bent has annotated *The Golden Legend* with fulness and care, and the reader is referred to his volume for more extended notes than are here expedient.]
Page 409.
*For these bells have been anointed,
And baptized with holy water !*
The consecration and baptism of bells is one of the most curious ceremonies of the Church in the Middle Ages. The Council of Cologne ordained as follows : —
"Let the bells be blessed, as the trumpets of the Church militant, by which the people are assembled to hear the word of God ; the clergy to announce his mercy by day, and his truth in their nocturnal vigils : that by their sound the faithful may be invited to prayers, and that the spirit of devotion in them may be increased. The fathers have also maintained that demons, affrighted by the sound of bells calling Christians to prayers, would flee away ; and when they fled, the persons of the faithful would be secure : that the destruction of lightnings and whirlwinds would be averted, and the spirits of the storm defeated." — *Edinburgh Encyclopædia*, Art. "Bells."
See also Scheible's *Kloster*, vi. 776.
Page 418. EVENING SONG.
[Mr. Bent, in his annotated edition of *The Golden Legend*, remarks that this is modelled upon the choral songs which the Reformed Church of Germany adopted from existing popular chorals, which had long been in use in the social and public observances of the German people.]
Page 420. *Who would think her but fifteen ?*
[In *Der Arme Heinrich*, Elsie is but eight years of age.]
Page 421. *It is the malediction of Eve !*
"Nec esses plus quam femina, quæ nunc etiam viros transcendis, et quæ maledictionem Evæ in benedictionem vertisti Mariæ." — *Epistola Abœlardi Heloissæ.*
Page 429. *To come back to my text !*
In giving this sermon of Friar Cuthbert as a specimen of the *Risus Paschales*, or streetpreaching of the monks at Easter, I have exaggerated nothing. This very anecdote, offensive as it is, comes from a discourse of Father Barletta, a Dominican friar of the fifteenth century, whose fame as a popular preacher was so great that it gave rise to the proverb, —
*Nescit predicare
Qui nescit Barlettare.*
"Among the abuses introduced in this century," says Tiraboschi, "was that of exciting from the pulpit the laughter of the hearers ; as if that were the same thing as converting them. We have examples of this, not only in Italy, but also in France, where the sermons of Menot and Maillard, and of others, who would make a better appearance on the stage than in the pulpit, are still celebrated for such follies."

If the reader is curious to see how far the freedom of speech was carried in these popular sermons, he is referred to Scheible's *Kloster*, vol. I., where he will find extracts from Abraham a Sancta Clara, Sebastian Frank, and others; and in particular an anonymous discourse called *Der Gräuel der Verwüstung*, The Abomination of Desolation, preached at Ottakring, a village west of Vienna, November 25, 1782, in which the license of language is carried to its utmost limit.

See also *Prédicatoriana, ou Révélations singulières et amusantes sur les Prédicateurs; par G. P. Philomneste.* (Menin.) This work contains extracts from the popular sermons of St. Vincent Ferrier, Barletta, Menot, Maillard, Marini, Raulin, Valladier, De Besse, Camus, Père André, Bening, and the most eloquent of all, Jacques Brydaine.

My authority for the spiritual interpretation of bell-ringing, which follows, is Durandus, *Ration. Divin, Offic.*, Lib. I., cap. 4.

Page 431. THE NATIVITY: a Miracle-Play.

A singular chapter in the history of the Middle Ages is that which gives account of the early Christian Drama, the Mysteries, Moralities, and Miracle-Plays, which were at first performed in churches, and afterwards in the streets, on fixed or movable stages. For the most part, the Mysteries were founded on the historic portions of the Old and New Testaments, and the Miracle-Plays on the lives of Saints; a distinction not always observed, however, for in Mr. Wright's *Early Mysteries and other Latin Poems of the Twelfth and Thirteenth Centuries*, the Resurrection of Lazarus is called a Miracle, and not a Mystery. The Moralities were plays in which the Virtues and Vices were personified.

The earliest religious play which has been preserved is the *Christos Paschon* of Gregory Nazianzen, written in Greek, in the fourth century. Next to this come the remarkable Latin plays of Roswitha, the Nun of Gandersheim, in the tenth century, which, though crude and wanting in artistic construction, are marked by a good deal of dramatic power and interest. A handsome edition of these plays, with a French translation, has been lately published, entitled *Théâtre de Rotsvitha, Religieuse allemande du Xe Siècle. Par Charles Magnin.* Paris, 1845.

The most important collections of English Mysteries and Miracle-Plays are those known as the Townley, the Chester, and the Coventry Plays. The first of these collections has been published by the Surtees Society, and the other two by the Shakespeare Society. In his Introduction to the Coventry Mysteries, the editor, Mr. Halliwell, quotes the following passage from Dugdale's *Antiquities of Warwickshire:* —

"Before the suppression of the monasteries, this city was very famous for the pageants, that were played therein, upon Corpus-Christi day; which, occasioning very great confluence of people thither, from far and near, was of no small benefit thereto; which pageants being acted with mighty state and reverence by the friars of this house had theaters for the severall scenes, very large and high, placed upon wheels, and drawn to all the eminent parts of the city, for the better advantage of spectators: and contain'd the story of the New Testament, composed into old English Rithme, as appeareth by an ancient MS. intituled *Ludus Corporis Christi, or Ludus Conventriæ.* I have been told by some old people, who in their younger years were eyewitnesses of these pageants so acted, that the yearly confluence of people to see that shew was extraordinary great, and yielded no small advantage to this city."

The representation of religious plays has not yet been wholly discontinued by the Roman Church. At Ober-Ammergau, in the Tyrol, a grand spectacle of this kind is exhibited once in ten years. A very graphic description of that which took place in the year 1850 is given by Miss Anna Mary Howitt, in her *Art-Student in Munich*, vol. I., chap. 4.

Mr. Bayard Taylor, in his *Eldorado*, gives a description of a Mystery he saw performed at San Lionel, in Mexico. See vol. II., chap. 11.

In 1852 there was a representation of this kind by Germans in Boston: and I have now before me the copy of a play-bill, announcing the performance, on June 10, 1852, in Cincinnati, of the *Great Biblico-Historical Drama, the Life of Jesus Christ*, with the characters and the names of the performers.

Page 432. *Here the Angel Gabriel shall leave Paradise.*

[A stage of three stories was often erected, the topmost representing Paradise (hence in Germany this word is used for the upper gallery of a theatre, *anglicé,* "the Gods"); on the middle stage was the Earth; below were the "Jaws of Hell," sometimes represented by the opening and shutting of the mouth of an enormous dragon. Goethe introduces the Jaws of Hell to the stage machinery of *Faust* (V. 6). — S. A. Bent.]

Page 439. *The Scriptorium.*

A most interesting volume might be written on the Calligraphers and Chrysographers, the transcribers and illuminators of manuscripts in the Middle Ages. These men were for the most part monks, who labored, sometimes for pleasure and sometimes for penance, in multiplying copies of the classics and the Scriptures.

"Of all bodily labors which are proper for us," says Cassiodorus, the old Calabrian monk, "that of copying books has always been more to my taste than any other. The more so, as in this exercise the mind is instructed by the reading of the Holy Scriptures, and it is a kind of homily to the others, whom these books may reach. It is preaching with the hand, by converting the fingers into tongues; it is publishing to men in silence the words of salvation: in fine, it is fighting against the demon with pen and ink. As many words as a transcriber writes, so many wounds the demon receives. In a word, a recluse, seated in his chair to copy books, travels into different provinces without moving from the spot, and the labor of his hands is felt even where he is not."

Nearly every monastery was provided with its Scriptorium. Nicolas de Clairvaux, St. Bernard's secretary, in one of his letters describes his cell, which he calls Scriptoriolum, where he copied books. And Mabillon, in his *Etudes Monastiques*, says that in his time were still to be seen at Citeaux "many of those little cells, where the transcribers and bookbinders worked."

Silvestre's *Paléographie Universelle* contains a vast number of fac-similes of the most beautiful illuminated manuscripts of all ages and all countries; and Montfaucon, in his *Palæographia Græca*, gives the names of over three hundred calligraphers. He also gives an account of the books they copied, and the colophons with which, as with a satisfactory flourish of the pen, they closed their long-continued labors. Many of these are very curious; expressing joy, humility, remorse; entreating the reader's prayers and pardon for the writer's sins; and sometimes pronouncing a malediction on any one who should steal the book. A few of these I subjoin : —

"As pilgrims rejoice, beholding their native land, so are transcribers made glad, beholding the end of a book."

"Sweet is it to write the end of any book."

"Ye who read, pray for me, who have written this book, the humble and sinful Theodulus."

"As many therefore as shall read this book, pardon me, I beseech you, if aught I have erred in accent acute and grave, in apostrophe, in breathing soft or aspirate; and may God save you all! Amen."

"If anything is well, praise the transcriber; if ill, pardon his unskilfulness."

"Ye who read, pray for me, the most sinful of all men, for the Lord's sake."

"The hand that has written this book shall decay, alas! and become dust, and go down to the grave, the corrupter of all bodies. But all ye who are of the portion of Christ, pray that I may obtain the pardon of my sins. Again and again I beseech you with tears, brothers and fathers, accept my miserable supplication, O holy choir! I am called John, woe is me! I am called Hiereus, or Sacerdos, in name only, not in unction."

"Whoever shall carry away this book, without permission of the Pope, may he incur the malediction of the Holy Trinity, of the Holy Mother of God, of Saint John the Baptist, of the one hundred and eighteen holy Nicene Fathers, and of all the Saints; the fate of Sodom and Gomorrah; and the halter of Judas! Anathema, amen."

"Keep safe, O Trinity, Father, Son and Holy Ghost, my three fingers, with which I have written this book."

"Mathusalas Machir transcribed this divinest book in toil, infirmity, and dangers many."

"Bacchius Barbardorius and Michael Sophianus wrote this book in sport and laughter, being the guests of their noble and common friend Vincentius Pinellus, and Petrus Nunnius, a most learned man."

This last colophon Montfaucon does not suffer to pass without reproof. "Other calligraphers," he remarks, "demand only the prayers of their readers, and the pardon of their sins; but these glory in their wantonness."

Page 443. *Drink down to your peg !*

One of the canons of Archbishop Anselm, promulgated at the beginning of the twelfth century, ordains "that priests go not to drinking-bouts, nor drink to pegs." In the times of the hard-drinking Danes, King Edgar ordained that pins or nails should be fastened into the drinking-cups or horns at stated distances, and whosoever should drink beyond those marks at one draught should be obnoxious to a severe punishment.

Sharpe, in his *History of the Kings of England*, says: "Our ancestors were formerly famous for compotation; their liquor was ale, and one method of amusing themselves in this way was with the peg-tankard. I had lately one of them in my hand. It had on the inside a row of eight pins, one above another, from top to bottom. It held two quarts, and was a noble piece of plate, so that there was a gill of ale, half a pint Winchester measure, between each peg. The law was, that every person that drank was to empty the space between pin and pin, so that the pins were so many measures to make the company all drink alike, and to swallow the same quantity of liquor. This was a pretty sure method of making all the company drunk, especially if it be considered that the rule was, that whoever drank short of his pin, or beyond it, was obliged to drink again, and even as deep as to the next pin."

Page 444. *The convent of St. Gildas de Rhuys.*

Abelard, in a letter to his friend Philintus, gives a sad picture of this monastery. "I live," he says, "in a barbarous country, the language of which I do not understand; I have no conversation but with the rudest people. my walks are on the inaccessible shore of a sea, which is perpetually stormy. my monks are only known by their dissoluteness, and living without any rule or order. could you see the abby, Philintus, you would not call it one. the doors and walls are without any ornament, except the heads of wild boars and hinds feet, which are nailed up against them, and the hides of frightful animals. the cells are hung with the skins of deer. the monks have not so much as a bell to wake them, the cocks and dogs supply that defect. in short, they pass their whole days in hunting; would to heaven that were their greatest fault ! or that their pleasure terminated there! I endeavor in vain to recall them to their duty; they all combine against me, and I only expose myself to continual vexations and dangers. I imagine I see every moment a naked sword hang over my head. sometimes they surround me, and load me with infinite abuses; sometimes they abandon me, and I am left alone to my own tormenting thoughts. I make it my endeavor to merit by my sufferings, and to appease an angry God. sometimes I grieve for the loss of the house of the Paraclete, and wish to see it again. ah Philintus, does not the love of Heloise still burn in my heart ? I have not yet triumphed over that unhappy passion. in the midst of my retirement I sigh, I weep, I pine, I speak the dear name Heloise, and am pleased to hear the sound." — *Letters of the Celebrated Abelard and Heloise. Translated by Mr. John Hughes. Glasgow, 1751.*

Page 452. *Were it not for my magic garters and staff.*

The method of making the Magic Garters and the Magic Staff is thus laid down in *Les Secrets Merveilleux du Petit Albert*, a French translation of *Alberti Parvi Lucii Libellus de Mirabilibus Naturæ Arcanis:* —

" Gather some of the herb called motherwort, when the sun is entering the first degree of the sign of Capricorn ; let it dry a little in the shade, and make some garters of the skin of a young hare ; that is to say, having cut the skin of the hare into strips two inches wide, double them, sew the before-mentioned herb between, and wear them on your legs. No horse can long keep up with a man on foot, who is furnished with these garters." — Page 128.

" Gather, on the morrow of All-Saints, a strong branch of willow, of which you will make a staff, fashioned to your liking. Hollow it out, by removing the pith from within, after having furnished the lower end with an iron ferule. Put into the bottom of the staff the two eyes of a young wolf, the tongue and heart of a dog, three green lizards, and the hearts of three swallows. These must all be dried in the sun, between two papers, having been first sprinkled with pulverized saltpetre. Besides all these, put into the staff seven leaves of vervain, gathered on the eve of St. John the Baptist, with a stone of divers colors, which you will find in the nest of the lapwing, and stop the end of the staff with a pomel of box, or of any other material you please, and be assured that this staff will guarantee you from the perils and mishaps which too often befall travellers, either from robbers, wild beasts, mad dogs, or venomous animals. It will also procure you the good-will of those with whom you lodge." Page 130.

Page 455. *Saint Elmo's stars.*

So the Italian sailors called the phosphorescent gleams that sometimes play about the masts and rigging of ships.

Page 455. *The School of Salerno.*

For a history of the celebrated schools of Salerno and Monte-Cassino, the reader is referred to Sir Alexander Croke's Introduction to the *Regimen Sanitatis Salernitanum* ; and to Kurt Sprengel's *Geschichte der Arzneikunde*, i. 463, or Jourdan's French translation of it, *Histoire de la Médecine*, ii. 354.

Page 504. *He must spell Baker.*

A local expression for doing anything difficult. In the old spelling-books, Baker was the first word of two syllables, and when a child

came to it he thought he had a hard task before him.

Page 525.

> *To King Antiochus,*
> *The God, Epiphanes : a Memorial*
> *From the Sidonians, who live at Sichem.*

[The reader will notice in *The Divine Tragedy* the ease with which Mr. Longfellow adjusted the Scriptural phraseology to the demands of blank verse. So here, he has been able to use without change the words found in Josephus, *Antiquities of the Jews*, Book XII. Chapter V. in Whiston's translation. The text of the Memorial is slightly condensed, but otherwise is almost a transcript from Whiston.]

Page 526. The Dungeons in the Citadel. [This powerful scene is a dramatization of II. Maccabees, chapter 7, with the effective change by which the mother is shown apart from the sons, and the torture is made inferential.]

Page 538.

> *And I at Fondi have my Fra Bastiano,*
> *The famous artist, who has come from Rome*
> *To paint my portrait.*

[In 1533 Cardinal Ippolito de Medici sent Sebastian with an armed force to paint the portrait of Julia Gonzaga. It was accomplished in a month and sent to Francis I. of France.

" The real portrait of Giulia Gonzaga is supposed to exist in two different collections. In the National Gallery, we have the likeness of a lady in the character of St. Agatha, as symbolized by a nimbus and pincers. Natural pose and posture and dignified mien indicate rank. The treatment is free and bold, but the colors are not blended with the care which Sebastian would surely have bestowed in such a case. In the Staedel Museum at Frankfort, the person represented is of a noble and elegant carriage, seated, in rich attire, and holding a fan made of feathers. A pretty landscape is seen through an opening, and a rich green hanging falls behind the figure. The handling curiously reminds us of Bronzino. It is well known that the likeness of Giulia was sent to Francis the First in Paris, and was registered in Lépicié's catalogue. The canvas of the National Gallery was purchased from the Borghese palace, the panel at Frankfort from the heirlooms of the late King of Holland. A third female portrait by Del Piombo deserves to be recorded in connection with this inquiry, — that of Lord Radnor at Longford Castle, in which a lady with a crimson mantle and pearl head-dress stands in profile, resting her hands on the back of a chair. On a shawl which falls from the chair we read, '*Sunt laquei veneris cave*.' The shape is slender as that of Vittoria Colonna in the Santangelo palace at Naples, but the color is too brown in light and too red in shadow to yield a pleasing effect, and were it proved that this is really Giulia Gonzaga the picture would not deserve Vasari's eulogy." — Crowe and Cavalcaselle: *History of Painting in North Italy*.]

Page 540.

> *Why did the Pope and his ten Cardinals*
> *Come here to lay this heavy task upon me?*

[The Last Judgment was begun in 1534 when Paul III., Alessandro Farnese, was Pope.]

Page 540.

The bones of Julius
Shook in their sepulchre.

[Julius II., who became Pope in 1503. The Julius who appears in this poem is Julius III.]

Page 541. SAN SILVESTRO.

[A miniature painter, Francesco d' Ollanda, was sent to Italy between 1530 and 1540 by the King of Portugal, and wrote an account of his experience. In this account he describes two Sundays which he spent with Michael Angelo and Vittoria Colonna at San Silvestro. His narrative, which is given by Grimm in his *Life of Michael Angelo*, II. 293-305, furnished Mr. Longfellow the material from which to construct this scene.]

Page 552.

The Marquis of Pescara is my husband,
And death has not divorced us.

[Vittoria Colonna was born in 1490, betrothed to the Marquis de Pescara in 1495, and married to him in 1509. Pescara was killed in fighting against the French under the walls of Ravenna in 1512. It is not known when or where Vittoria Colonna first met Michael Angelo, but all authorities agree that it must have been about the year 1536, when he was over sixty years of age. She did not escape the espionage of the Inquisition, but was compelled in 1541 to fly to the convent at Viterbo. Three years later, she went to the convent of Benedictines of St. Anne in Rome, and just before her death, in 1547, she was taken to the house of Giuliano Cesarini, the husband of Giulia Colonna, her only relative in Rome. It was after she fled to the convent that she began to write sonnets to and receive them from Michael Angelo, whose love for her was not capable of being concealed. Hartford, in his *Life of Michael Angelo Buonarotti*, includes a life also of Vittoria Colonna.]

Page 559.

It was the Constable of France, the Bourbon
That I had slain.

[See the seventh chapter of *Memoirs of Benvenuto Cellini* for his narrative of this incident.]

Page 572.

They complain
Of insufficient light in the Three Chapels.

[Grimm, II. 415, relates this bout between Michael Angelo and the cardinals.]

Page 578. *And ah! that casting.*

[Cellini gives an animated account of this incident in the forty-first chapter of his *Memoirs.*]

Page 587. COPLAS DE MANRIQUE.

This poem of Manrique is a great favorite in Spain. No less than four poetic Glosses, or running commentaries, upon it have been published, no one of which, however, possesses great poetic merit. That of the Carthusian monk, Rodrigo de Valdepeñas, is the best. It is known as the *Glosa del Cartujo*. There is also a prose Commentary by Luis de Aranda.

The following stanzas of the poem were found in the author's pocket, after his death on the field of battle.

O World! so few the years we live,
Would that the life which thou dost give
Were life indeed!
Alas! thy sorrows fall so fast,
Our happiest hour is when at last
The soul is freed.

Our days are covered o'er with grief,
And sorrows neither few nor brief
Veil all in gloom;
Left desolate of real good,
Within this cheerless solitude
No pleasures bloom.

Thy pilgrimage begins in tears,
And ends in bitter doubts and fears,
Or dark despair;
Midway so many toils appear,
That he who lingers longest here
Knows most of care.

Thy goods are bought with many a groan,
By the hot sweat of toil alone,
And weary hearts;
Fleet-footed is the approach of woe,
But with a lingering step and slow
Its form departs.

Page 600. THE CHILDREN OF THE LORD'S SUPPER.

There is one poem in this volume to which a few introductory remarks may be useful.[1] It is *The Children of the Lord's Supper*, from the Swedish of Bishop Tegnér, a poem which enjoys no inconsiderable reputation in the North of Europe, and for its beauty and simplicity merits the attention of English readers. It is an Idyl, descriptive of scenes in a Swedish village, and belongs to the same class of poems as the *Luise* of Voss and the *Hermann und Dorothea* of Goethe. But the Swedish poet has been guided by a surer taste than his German predecessors. His tone is pure and elevated, and he rarely, if ever, mistakes what is trivial for what is simple. [From this point, Mr. Longfellow proceeded with a description of rural life in Sweden which may be found in his paper *Frithiof's Saga* in vol. I. of his prose works, Riverside Edition.]

Page 601. *The Feast of the Leafy Pavilions.*

In Swedish, *Löfhyddohögtiden*, the Leafhuts'-high-tide.

Page 601. *Hörberg.*

The peasant-painter of Sweden. He is known chiefly by his altar-pieces in the village churches.

Page 601. *Wallin.*

A distinguished pulpit-orator and poet. He is particularly remarkable for the beauty and sublimity of his psalms.

Page 607. *Nils Juel gave heed to the tempest's roar.*

Nils Juel was a celebrated Danish Admiral, and Peder Wessel a Vice Admiral, who for his great prowess received the popular title of Tordenskiold, or Thundershield. In childhood he was a tailor's apprentice, and rose to his high

[1] It will be observed that the note here given originally stood as Introduction to the poem when it was first published.

rank before the age of twenty-eight, when he was killed in a duel.

Page 623. *The blind girl of Castèl-Cuillè.*

Jasmin, the author of this beautiful poem, is to the South of France what Burns is to the South of Scotland, — the representative of the heart of the people, — one of those happy bards who are born with their mouths full of birds (*la bouco pleno d' aouzelous*). He has written his own biography in a poetic form, and the simple narrative of his poverty, his struggles, and his triumphs is very touching. He still lives at Agen, —n the Garonne ; and long may he live there to delight his native land with native songs !

[When first printing this note, Mr. Longfellow added a long description of Jasmin and his way of life from Louisa Stuart Costello's *Béarn and the Pyrenees*. In more recent days Miss H. W. Preston has written sympathetically on the same subject. See *The Atlantic Monthly*, January, February, 1876.]

Page 628. *A Christmas Carol.*

[A description of Christmas in Burgundy from M. Fertiault's *Coup d'Œil sur les Noels en Bourgogne*, to the Paris edition of *Les Noels Bourguignons de Bernard de la Mennoye (Gui Barôzai)*, 1842, was quoted by Mr. Longfellow when first printing this poem.]

IV. A CHRONOLOGICAL LIST OF MR. LONGFELLOW'S POEMS

In the following list the poems are set down under date of the years in which they were composed. When the date of composition is undetermined, the poem, marked by an asterisk, is placed against the year of its publication. Translations are distinguished by italics.

1820. The Battle of Lovell's Pond.
1824. To Ianthe.
Thanksgiving.
Antumnal Nightfall.
Italian Scenery.
An April Day.
Autumn.
Woods in Winter.
1825. The Lunatic Girl.
The Venetian Gondolier.
The Angler's Song.
Sunrise on the Hills.
Hymn of the Moravian Nuns of Bethlehem.
Lover's Rock.
Dirge over a Nameless Grave.
A Song of Savoy.
The Indian Hunter.
Ode written for the Commemoration at Fryeburg, Maine, of Lovewell's Fight.
Jeckoyva.
The Sea-Diver.
Musings.
The Spirit of Poetry.
Burial of the Minnisink.
1826. Song: "Where, from the eye of day."
Song of the Birds.

1830. *Song:* "Hark, hark!"
Song: "And whither goest thou, gentle sigh."
The Return of Spring.
Rondel: "Hence away, begone, begone."
Spring.
The Child Asleep.
Friar Lubin.
1831. * *Let me go warm.*
* *The Disembodied Spirit.*
* *Ideal Beauty.*
* *The Lover's Complaint.*
The Nativity of Christ.
The Assumption of the Virgin.
1832. A Florentine Song.
A Neapolitan Canzonet.
Christmas Carol.
A Soldier's Song.
Tell me, tell me, thou pretty Bee.
Sicilian Canzonet.
Coplas de Manrique.
The Good Shepherd.
To-Morrow.
The Native Land.
The Image of God.
The Brook.
* *Vida de San Millan.*
* *San Miguel, The Convent.*
Death of Archbishop Turpin.
Art and Nature.
The Two Harvests.
1833. * *Ancient Spanish Ballads.*
* *Clear Honor of the Liquid Element.*
* *Praise of Little Women.*
* *Milagros de Nuestra Señora.*
1834. * *Song of the Rhine.*
1835. *King Christian.*
* *Song:* "She is a maid of artless grace.'
1836. *Song of the Bell.*
The Castle by the Sea.
Song of the Silent Land.
1837. *Passages from Frithiof's Saga.*
Flowers.
1838. A Psalm of Life.
The Reaper and the Flowers.
The Light of Stars.
"Neglected record of a mind neglected.'
The Grave.
The Soul's Complaint against the Body.
Beowulf's Expedition to Heort.
1839. The Wreck of the Hesperus.
The Village Blacksmith.
Prelude.
Hymn to the Night.
Footsteps of Angels.
The Beleaguered City.
Midnight Mass for the Dying Year.
L'Envoi to Voices of the Night.
* *The Celestial Pilot.*
* *The Terrestrial Paradise.*
* *Beatrice.*
* *The Happiest Land.*
* *The Wave.*
* *The Dead.*
* *The Bird and the Ship.*
* *Whither.*
* *Beware.*

* *The Black Knight.*

1840. It is not always May.
The Spanish Student.
The Skeleton in Armor.

1841. Endymion.
The Rainy Day.
God's Acre.
To the River Charles.
Blind Bartimeus.
The Goblet of Life.
Maidenhood.
Excelsior.
The Children of the Lord's Supper.
The Luck of Edenhall.
The Two Locks of Hair.
* *The Elected Knight.*

1842. To William E. Channing.
The Slave's Dream.
The Good Part, that shall not be taken
away.
The Slave in the Dismal Swamp.
The Slave singing at Midnight.
The Witnesses.
The Quadroon Girl.
* The Warning.
The Belfry of Bruges.
Mezzo Cammin.

1843. *Translation of Dante*, begun.
The Statue over the Cathedral Door.
The Legend of the Cross-Bill.
The Sea hath its Pearls.

1844. A Gleam of Sunshine.
The Arsenal at Springfield.
Nuremberg.
The Norman Baron.
Rain in Summer.
Sea Weed.
The Day is Done.
The Hemlock Tree.
Annie of Tharaw.
* *Childhood.*
* *Elegy: "Silent in the veil of evening
twilight."*

1845. To a Child.
The Occultation of Orion.
The Bridge.
To the Driving Cloud.
Carillon.
Afternoon in February.
To an Old Danish Song-Book.
Walter von der Vogelweid.
Drinking Song.
The Old Clock on the Stairs.
The Arrow and the Song.
The Evening Star.
Autumn.
* Dante.
Curfew.
Birds of Passage.
The Haunted Chamber.
Evangeline, begun.
* *Poetic Aphorisms.*
* *Silent Love.*
* *Blessed are the Dead.*
Wanderer's Night Songs.
* *The Nature of Love.*
* *Song: "If thou art sleeping, maiden."*

* *Rondel.*

1846. The Builders.
Pegasus in Pound.
Twilight.

1847. Tegnér's Drapa.
Evangeline, finished.
"O faithful, indefatigable tides."
"Soft through the silent air."

1848. Hymn for my Brother's Ordination.
The Secret of the Sea.
* Sir Humphrey Gilbert.
The Fire of Drift-Wood.
The Castle-Builder.
Resignation.
Sand of the Desert.
The Open Window.
King Witlaf's Drinking-Horn.

1849. Dedication : The Seaside and the Fire-
side.
The Building of the Ship.
Chrysaor.
The Challenge of Thor (Tales of a Way-
side Inn).
The Lighthouse.
Gaspar Becerra.
Sonnet on Mrs. Kemble's Readings from
Shakespeare.
Children.
The Singers.
The Brook and the Wave.
Suspiria.
The Blind Girl of Castèl-Cuillè.
A Christmas Carol.

1850. The Golden Legend, begun.
Michael Angelo : portion of III., iv.
The Ladder of St. Augustine.
The Phantom Ship.

1851. In the Churchyard at Cambridge.
The Golden Legend, finished.

1852. The Warden of the Cinque Ports.
Haunted Houses.
The Emperor's Bird's-Nest.
Daylight and Moonlight.
The Jewish Cemetery at Newport.

1853. The Two Angels.

1854. The Rope Walk.
The Golden Mile-Stone.
Catawba Wine.
Prometheus.
Epimetheus.
Hiawatha, begun.

1855. Hiawatha, finished.
Oliver Basselin.
Victor Galbraith.
My Lost Youth.

1856. John Endicott, begun.
So from the Bosom of Darkness.

1857. John Endicott, finished.
Santa Filomena.
The Discoverer of the North Cape.
Daybreak.
The Fiftieth Birthday of Agassiz.
Sandalphon.
The Courtship of Miles Standish, be-
gun.

1858. The Courtship of Miles Standish, fin-
ished.

1859.   The Children's Hour.
        Enceladus.
        Snow-Flakes.
        The Bells of Lynn.
        * *My Secret.*
1860.   Paul Revere's Ride (Tales of a Wayside
            Inn).
        The Saga of King Olaf, excepting The
            Challenge of Thor (Tales of a Way-
            side Inn).
        A Day of Sunshine.
1861.   Interlude : A strain of music closed the
            tale (Tales of a Wayside Inn).
1862.   Prelude : The Wayside Inn.
        The Legend of Rabbi Ben Levi (Tales
            of a Wayside Inn).
        King Robert of Sicily (Tales of a Way-
            side Inn).
        Torquemada (Tales of a Wayside Inn).
        The Cumberland.
1863.   * Five Interludes to First Part of Tales
            of a Wayside Inn.
        The Falcon of Ser Federigo (Tales of
            a Wayside Inn).
        The Birds of Killingworth (Tales of a
            Wayside Inn).
        * Finale to Part First of Tales of a
            Wayside Inn.
        * Something left Undone.
        * Weariness.
1864.   Palingenesis.
        The Bridge of Cloud.
        Hawthorne.
        Christmas Bells.
        The Wind over the Chimney.
        Divina Commedia : Sonnets, I., II.
        Noël.
        Kambalu (Tales of a Wayside Inn).
1865.   Divina Commedia : Sonnet III.
        To Italy.
1866.   Flower-de-Luce.
        Killed at the Ford.
        Giotto's Tower.
        To-Morrow.
        Divina Commedia : Sonnets V., VI.
        Translation of Dante, finished.
1867.   Divina Commedia : Sonnet IV.
1868.   Giles Corey of the Salem Farms.
1869.   *The Gleaner of Sapri.*
1870.   Prelude to Part Second of Tales of a
            Wayside Inn.
        The Bell of Atri (Tales of a Wayside
            Inn).
        Fata Morgana.
        The Meeting.
        Vox Populi.
        Prelude to Translations.
        The Divine Tragedy, begun.
        Consolation.
        * *To Cardinal Richelieu.*
        The Angel and the Child.
        Wanderer's Night Songs.
        The Fugitive.
        * *The Siege of Kazan.*
        The Boy and the Brook.
        * *To the Stork.*
        * *Santa Teresa's Book-Mark.*

        Remorse.
1871.   The Cobbler of Hagenau (Tales of a
            Wayside Inn).
        The Ballad of Carmilhan (Tales of a
            Wayside Inn).
        Lady Wentworth (Tales of a Wayside
            Inn).
        The Legend Beautiful (Tales of a Way-
            side Inn).
        The Baron of St. Castine (Tales of a
            Wayside Inn).
        Judas Maccabæus.
        The Abbot Joachim : First Interlude
            to Christus.
        Martin Luther : Second Interlude to
            Christus.
        St. John : Finale to Christus.
        The Divine Tragedy, finished.
1872.   * Introitus to Christus.
        * Interludes and Finale to Part Second
            of Tales of a Wayside Inn.
        Michael Angelo, first draft.
        Azrael (Tales of a Wayside Inn).
        Charlemagne (Tales of a Wayside
            Inn).
        Emma and Eginhard (Tales of a Way-
            side Inn).
1873.   * Prelude, Interludes and Finale to
            Part Third of Tales of a Wayside
            Inn.
        Elizabeth (Tales of a Wayside Inn).
        The Monk of Casal-Maggiore (Tales of
            a Wayside Inn).
        Scanderbeg (Tales of a Wayside Inn).
        The Mother's Ghost (Tales of a Wayside
            Inn).
        The Rhyme of Sir Christopher (Tales
            of a Wayside Inn).
        Michael Angelo : Monologue, The Last
            Judgment ; Monologue, Part Second.
            Palazzo Cesarini ; The Oaks of Monte
            Luca.
        * The Challenge.
        * Aftermath.
        The Hanging of the Crane.
        Chaucer.
        Shakespeare.
        Milton.
        Keats.
        * *From the Cancioneros.*
1874.   Charles Sumner.
        Travels by the Fireside.
        Cadenabbia.
        Autumn Within.
        Monte Cassino.
        Morituri Salutamus.
        Three Friends of Mine.
        The Galaxy.
        The Sound of the Sea.
        A Summer Day by the Sea.
        The Tides.
        A Nameless Grave.
        The Old Bridge at Florence.
        Il Ponte Vecchio di Firenze.
        Michael Angelo : Vittoria Colonna
            Palazzo Belvedere ; Bindo Altoviti ;
            In the Coliseum.

Seven Sonnets and a Canzone.
1875. Amalfi.
The Sermon of St. Francis.
Belisarius.
Songo River.
The Masque of Pandora.
* A Shadow.
Sleep.
Parker Cleaveland.
1876. The Herons of Elmwood.
To the Avon.
A Dutch Picture.
The Revenge of Rain-in-the-Face.
To the River Yvette.
A Wraith in the Mist.
Nature.
In the Churchyard at Tarrytown.
Eliot's Oak.
The Descent of the Muses.
Venice.
The Poets.
The Harvest Moon.
To the River Rhone.
The Two Rivers.
Boston.
St. John's, Cambridge.
Moods.
Woodstock Park.
The Four Princesses at Wilna.
The Broken Oar.
The Four Lakes of Madison.
Victor and Vanquished.
On the Terrace of the Aigalades.
To my Brooklet.
Barréges.
1877. Kéramos.
Castles in Spain.
Vittoria Colonna.
A Ballad of the French Fleet.
The Leap of Roushan Beg.
Haroun al Raschid.
King Trisanku.
The Three Kings.
Song : "Stay, stay at home, my heart, and rest."
The Three Silences of Molinos.
Holidays.
Wapentake.
* *The Banks of the Cher.*
* *To the Forest of Gastine.*
* *Fontenay.*
* *Pray for me.*
* *Vire.*
1878. * The Emperor's Glove.

The Poet's Calendar : March.
The White Czar.
* Delia.
Bayard Taylor.
The Chamber over the Gate.
Moonlight.
* *Forsaken.*
* *Virgil's First Eclogue.*
* *Ovid in Exile.*
1879. The Cross of Snow.
From my Arm Chair.
Jugurtha.
The Iron Pen.
Robert Burns.
Helen of Tyre.
The Sifting of Peter.
The Tide rises, the Tide falls.
My Cathedral.
The Burial of the Poet.
Night.
The Children's Crusade.
Sundown.
Chimes.
A Quiet Life.
1880. Dedication to Ultima Thule.
* Elegiac.
Old St. David's at Radnor.
Maiden and Weathercock.
The Windmill.
L'Envoi to Ultima Thule.
The Poet's Calendar, January, February, April–December.
Four by the Clock.
1881. Michael Angelo : Viterbo.
Auf Wiedersehen.
Elegiac Verse.
The City and the Sea.
Memories.
Hermes Trismegistus.
President Garfield.
My Books.
* Song for the Masque of Pandora.
1882. * Becalmed.
Mad River.
Possibilities.
Decoration Day.
* A Fragment.
* Loss and Gain.
Inscription on the Shanklin Fountain.
The Bells of San Blas.
* *Will ever the dear days come back again?*
* *At La Chaudeau.*
* *The Wine of Jurançon.*
(Undetermined) *The Stars.*

INDEX OF FIRST LINES

A BLIND man is a poor man, and poor a blind man is, 616.
A fleet with flags arrayed, 337.
After so long an absence, 295.
A gentle boy, with soft and silken locks, 295.
A handful of red sand, from the hot clime, 108.
Ah, how short are the days! How soon the night overtakes us, 270.
Ah, Love, 43.
Ah me! ah me! when thinking of the years, 637.
Ah! thou moon that shinest, 42.
Ah! what pleasant visions haunt me, 104.
A little bird in the air, 230.
Allah gives light in darkness, 618.
All are architects of Fate, 108.
All are sleeping, weary heart, 36, 37.
All day has the battle raged, 234.
All houses wherein men have lived and died, 188.
All the old gods are dead, 226.
Am I a king, that I should call my own, 343.
A mill-stone and the human heart are driven ever round, 616.
A mist was driving down the British Channel, 188.
Among the many lives that I have known, 319.
An angel with a radiant face, 629.
And King Olaf heard the cry, 219.
And now, behold! as at the approach of morning, 633.
And thou, O River of To-morrow, flowing, 321.
And when the kings were in the field, — their squadrons in array, 595.
And whither goest thou, gentle sigh, 621.
Annie of Tharaw, my true love of old, 614.
An old man in a lodge within a park, 315.
Arise, O righteous Lord, 520.
As a fond mother, when the day is o'er, 318.
As a pale phantom with a lamp, 352.
A soldier of the Union mustered out, 317.
As one who long hath fled with panting breath, 351.
As one who, walking in the twilight gloom, 99.
As the birds come in the Spring, 348.
As the dim twilight shrouds, 648.
As treasures that men seek, 587.
As unto the bow the cord is, 135.
At anchor in Hampton Roads we lay, 202.
At Atri, in Abruzzo, a small town, 245.
At Drontheim, Olaf the King, 227.
At La Chaudeau, — 't is long since then, 631.
At Stralsund, by the Baltic Sea, 252.
At the foot of the mountain height, 623.
A vision as of crowded city streets, 315.

Awake! arise! the hour is late, 359.
Awake, O north-wind, 368.
A wind came up out of the sea, 199.
A youth, light-hearted and content, 613.

Barabbas is my name, 400.
Baron Castine of St. Castine, 259.
Beautiful lily, dwelling by still rivers, 287.
Beautiful valley! through whose verdant meads, 325.
Becalmed upon the sea of Thought, 349.
Behold! a giant am I, 347.
Bell! thou soundest merrily, 611.
Beside the ungathered rice he lay, 20.
Between the dark and the daylight, 201.
Beware! the Israelite of old, who tore, 23.
Black are the moors before Kazan, 639.
Black shadows fall, 184.
Blind Bartimeus at the gates, 17, 391.
Bright Sun! that, flaming through the mid-day sky, 652.
Build me straight, O worthy Master, 99.
Burn, O evening hearth, and waken, 288.
But yesterday these few and hoary leaves, 652.
By his evening fire the artist, 110.
By the shore of Gitche Gumee, 162.
By yon still river, where the wave, 648.

Can it be the sun descending, 139.
Centuries old are the mountains, 304.
Christ to the young man said: Yet one thing more, 113.
Clear fount of light! my native land on high, 593.
Clear honor of the liquid element, 652.
Cold, cold is the north wind and rude is the blast, 645.
Come from thy caverns dark and deep, 305.
Come, my beloved, 367.
Come, O Death, so silent flying, 597.
Come, old friend! sit down and listen, 67.
Come to me, O ye children, 200.

Dark is the morning with mist; in the narrow mouth of the harbor, 345.
Dead he lay among his books, 342.
Dear child! how radiant on thy mother's knee, 60.
Don Nuno, Count of Lara, 594.
Dost thou see on the rampart's height, 341.
Dowered with all celestial gifts, 298.
Down from yon distant mountain height, 639.
Downward through the evening twilight, 119.

Each heart has its haunted chamber, 294.
Even as the Blessed, at the final summons, 634.
Evermore a sound shall be, 303.

Every flutter of the wing, 302.
Eyes so tristful, eyes so tristful, 597.

Far and wide among the nations, 155.
Filled is Life's goblet to the brim, 17.
Flooded by rain and snow, 304.
Flow on, sweet river ! like his verse, 357.
Forms of saints and kings are standing, 615.
For thee was a house built, 618.
Forth from the curtain of clouds, from the tent of purple and scarlet, 182.
Forth rolled the Rhine - stream strong and deep, 653.
Forth upon the Gitche Gumee, 130.
Four by the clock ! and yet not day, 354.
Four limpid lakes, — four Naiades, 351.
From the outskirts of the town, 296.
From the river's plashy bank, 648.
From this high portal, where upsprings, 630.
Full of wrath was Hiawatha, 151.

Gaddi mi fece : il Ponte Vecchio sono, 318.
Garlands upon his grave, 324.
Gentle Spring ! in sunshine clad, 621.
Gently swaying to and fro, 302.
Give me of your bark, O Birch-tree, 128.
Gloomy and dark art thou, O chief of the mighty Omahas, 64.
Glove of black in white hand bare, 597.
God sent his messenger the rain, 462.
God sent his Singers upon earth, 112.
Good night ! good night, beloved, 42.
Guarding the mountains around, 305.

Hadst thou stayed, I must have fled, 257.
Half of my life is gone, and I have let, 68.
Hark, hark, 621.
Haste and hide thee, 303.
Hast thou seen that lordly castle, 611.
Have I dreamed ? or was it real, 186.
Have you read in the Talmud of old, 200.
He is dead, the beautiful youth, 291.
He is gone to the desert land ! 638.
Hence away, begone, begone, 655.
Here in a little rustic hermitage, 322.
Here lies the gentle humorist, who died, 318.
Here rest the weary oar ! — soft airs, 647.
High on their turreted cliffs, 304.
Honor be to Mudjekeewis ! 116.
How beautiful is the rain, 59.
How beautiful it was, that one bright day, 289.
How cold are thy baths, Apollo ! 344.
How I started up in the night, in the night, 617.
How many lives, made beautiful and sweet, 291.
How much of my young heart, O Spain, 335.
How strange it seems !   These Hebrews in their graves, 191.
How strange the sculptures that adorn these towers, 292.
How the Titan, the defiant, 300.
How they so softly rest, 610.

I am poor and old and blind, 328.
I am the God Thor, 218.
I enter, and I see thee in the gloom, 292.
If I am fair 't is for myself alone, 657.

If perhaps these rhymes of mine should sound not well in strangers' ears, 616.
If thou art sleeping, maiden, 52, 637.
I, Gonzalo de Berceo, in the gentle summer-tide, 653.
I have a vague remembrance, 296.
I have read, in some old, marvelous tale. 6.
I hear along our street, 628.
I heard a brooklet gushing, 610.
I heard a voice, that cried, 111.
I heard the bells on Christmas Day, 289.
I heard the trailing garments of the Night, 2.
I know a maiden fair to see, 611.
I lay upon the headland-height, and listened, 287.
I leave you, ye cold mountain chains, 630.
I lift mine eyes, and all the windows blaze, 293.
I like that ancient Saxon phrase, which calls, 16.
In Attica thy birthplace should have been, 314.
In broad daylight, and at noon, 191.
In dark fens of the Dismal Swamp, 21.
In his chamber, weak and dying, 58.
In his lodge beside a river, 160.
In Mather's Magnalia Christi, 187.
In Ocean's wide domains, 22.
In St. Luke's Gospel we are told, 346.
Intelligence and courtesy not always are combined, 616.
In that building long and low, 195.
In that desolate land and lone, 336.
In that province of our France, 655.
In the ancient town of Bruges, 54.
In the convent of Drontheim, 235.
In the hamlet desolate, 656.
In the heroic days when Ferdinand, 236.
In the long, sleepless watches of the night, 323.
In the market-place of Bruges stands the belfry old and brown, 54.
In the old churchyard of his native town, 348.
In the Old Colony days, in Plymouth the land of the Pilgrims, 165.
In the valley of the Pegnitz, where across broad meadow-lands, 57.
In the Valley of the Vire, 192.
In the village churchyard she lies, 189.
In the workshop of Hephæstus, 298.
In those days said Hiawatha, 145.
In those days the Evil Spirits, 147.
Into the city of Kambalu, 247.
Into the darkness and the hush of night, 348.
Into the open air John Alden, perplexed and bewildered, 171.
Into the Silent Land, 612.
I pace the sounding sea-beach and behold, 315.
I said unto myself, if I were dead, 317.
I sat by my window one night, 650.
I saw, as in a dream sublime, 62.
I saw the long line of the vacant shore, 317.
I see amid the fields of Ayr, 344.
I shot an arrow into the air, 68.
Is it so far from thee, 342.
I sleep, but my heart awaketh, 366.
I stand again on the familiar shore, 314.
I stand beneath the tree, whose branches shade, 321.
I stood on the bridge at midnight, 63.

I stood upon the hills, when heaven's wide arch, 9.

Italy! Italy! thou who 'rt doomed to wear, 635.

I thought this Pen would arise, 344.

It is autumn ; not without, 351.

It is good to rhyming go, 656.

It is the Harvest Moon! On gilded vanes, 320.

I trust that somewhere and somehow, 249.

It was Einar Tamberskelver, 233.

It was fifty years ago, 199.

It was Sir Christopher Gardiner, 284.

It was the schooner Hesperus, 13.

It was the season, when through all the land, 240.

I wish to make my sermon brief, — to shorten my oration, 653.

Janus am I ; oldest of potentates, 349.

Joy and Temperance and Repose, 616.

Just above yon sandy bar, 104.

Just in the gray of the dawn, as the mists uprose from the meadows, 174.

King Christian stood by the lofty mast, 607.

King Ring with his queen to the banquet did fare, 599.

King Solomon, before his palace gate, 264.

Labor with what zeal we will, 203.

Lady, how can it chance — yet this we see, 636.

Lady! thine upward flight, 652.

Laugh of the mountain ! — lyre of bird and tree ! 593.

Leafless are the trees; their purple branches, 195.

Let him who will, by force or fraud innate, 631.

Let me go warm and merry still, 651.

Let nothing disturb thee, 597.

Like two cathedral towers these stately pines, 348.

Listen, my children, and you shall hear, 207.

Little sweet wine of Jurançon, 632.

Live I, so live I, 616.

Lo! in the painted oriel of the West, 69.

Longing already to search in and round, 634.

Lord, what am I, that, with unceasing care, 593.

Loud he sang the psalm of David, 22.

Loud sang the Spanish cavalier, 48.

Loud the angry wind was wailing, 226.

Loudly the sailors cheered, 231.

Love, love, what wilt thou with this heart of mine ? 632.

Lull me to sleep, ye winds, whose fitful sound, 317.

Lutheran, Popish, Calvinistic, all these creeds and doctrines three, 616.

Maiden! with the meek, brown eyes, 18.

Man-like is it to fall into sin, 616.

Many a day and wasted year, 649.

Meanwhile the stalwart Miles Standish was marching steadily northward, 178.

Month after month passed away, and in Autumn the ships of the merchants, 180.

Most beautiful, most gentle ! yet how lost, 647.

Mounted on Kyrat strong and fleet, 338.

Much it behoveth, 620.

My beloved is white and ruddy, 366.

My soul its secret has, my life too has its mystery, 632.

My undefiled is but one, 367,

My way is on the bright blue sea, 650.

Neglected record of a mind neglected, 360.

Never shall souls like these, 307.

Never stoops the soaring vulture, 156.

Night comes stealing from the East, 654.

Night rests in beauty on Mont Alto, 646.

Nine sisters, beautiful in form and face, 319.

No more shall I see, 600.

Northward over Drontheim, 230.

No sound of wheels or hoof-beat breaks, 325.

Not fashioned out of gold, like Hera's throne, 297.

Nothing that is shall perish utterly, 537.

Nothing the greatest artist can conceive, 635.

Nothing was heard in the room but the hurrying pen of the stripling, 166.

Not without fire can any workman mould, 635.

Now from all King Olaf's farms, 221.

Nowhere such a devious stream, 328.

Now the zephyrs diminish the cold, and the year being ended, 643.

Now Time throws off his cloak again, 621.

O amiable solitude, 656.

O Cæsar, we who are about to die, 310.

O curfew of the setting sun ! O bells of Lynn ! 290.

O'er all the hill-tops, 617.

O faithful, indefatigable tides, 360.

Of Edenhall, the youthful Lord, 613.

Of Prometheus, how undaunted, 185.

Often I think of the beautiful town, 194.

Oft have I seen at some cathedral door, 292.

Oft I remember those whom I have known, 356.

O gift of God ! O perfect day, 202.

O gladsome light, 418.

O hemlock tree ! O hemlock tree ! how faithful are thy branches, 614.

Oh, give me back the days when loose and free, 636.

Oh, how blest are ye whose toils are ended, 616.

Oh let the soul her slumbers break, 587.

Oh that a Song would sing itself to me, 322.

Oh, the long and dreary Winter, 158.

Olaf the King, one summer morn, 223.

Olger the Dane and Desiderio, 265.

O Light serene ! present in him who breathes, 652.

O little feet ! that such long years, 203.

O Lord! who seest, from yon starry height, 593.

O lovely river of Yvette, 337.

Once into a quiet village, 110.

Once more, once more, Inarimé, 336.

Once on a time, some centuries ago, 275.

Once the Emperor Charles of Spain, 189.

Once upon Iceland's solitary strand, 323.

One Autumn night, in Sudbury town, 204.

One day, Haroun Al Raschid read, 339.

One hundred years ago, and something more, 255.
One morning, all alone, 415.
One morning, on the sea shore as I strayed, 657.
One summer morning, when the sun was hot, 209.
On King Olaf's bridal night, 224.
On St. Bavon's tower, commanding, 337.
On sunny slope and beechen swell, 10.
On the cross the dying Saviour, 615.
On the gray sea-sands, 232.
On the green little isle of Inchkenneth, 339.
On the Mountains of the Prairie, 115.
On the shores of Gitche Gumee, 132.
On the top of a mountain I stand, 48.
O precious evenings! all too swiftly sped, 112.
O River of Yesterday, with current swift, 321.
O star of morning and of liberty, 293.
O sweet illusions of Song, 294.
Othere, the old sea-captain, 198.
O traveller, stay thy weary feet, 359.
Our God, a Tower of Strength is He, 463.
Out of childhood into manhood, 121.
Out of the bosom of the Air, 202.
O weathercock on the village spire, 347.
O ye dead Poets, who are living still, 319.

Padre Francisco, 29.
Pentecost, day of rejoicing, had come. The church of the village, 600.
Peradventure of old, some bard in Ionian Islands, 354.
Pleasant it was, when woods were green, 1.
Poet! I come to touch thy lance with mine, 323.
Pure Spirit! that within a form of clay, 652.

Quand les astres de Noël, 293.
Queen Sigrid the Haughty sat proud and aloft, 220.

Rabbi Ben Levi, on the Sabbath, read, 214.
Rio Verde, Rio Verde, 594.
Rise up, my love, my fair one, 366.
River! that in silence windest, 16.
River, that stealest with such silent pace, 315.
Robert of Sicily, brother of Pope Urbane, 215.
Round Autumn's mouldering urn, 646.

Sadly as some old mediæval knight, 357.
Safe at anchor in Drontheim bay, 229.
Saint Augustine! well hast thou said, 186.
St. Botolph's Town! Hither across the plains, 321.
San Miguel de la Tumba is a convent vast and wide, 596.
See, the fire is sinking low, 290.
She dwells by Great Kenhawa's side, 21.
She is a maid of artless grace, 596.
Shepherd! who with thine amorous, sylvan song, 592.
Short of stature, large of limb, 225.
Should any one there in Rome remember Ovid the exile, 641.
Should you ask me, whence these stories, 113.
Silent, in the veil of evening twilight, 654.
Simon Danz has come home again, 334.
Sing, O Song of Hiawatha, 143.
Sir Oluf he rideth over the plain, 608.

Sleep, comrades, sleep and rest, 359.
Slowly, slowly up the wall, 440.
Slowly the hour-hand of the clock moves round, 320.
So from the bosom of darkness our days come roaring and gleaming, 360.
Soft through the silent air descend the feathery snow-flakes, 360.
Solemnly, mournfully, 69.
Some day, some day, 597.
Something the heart must have to cherish, 618.
Somewhat back from the village street, 67.
So the strong will prevailed, and Alden went on his errand, 168.
Southward with fleet of ice, 105.
Spake full well, in language quaint and olden, 5.
Speak! speak! thou fearful guest, 11.
Spring is coming, birds are twittering, forests leaf, and smiles the sun, 599.
Stars of the summer night, 26.
Stay, stay at home, my heart, and rest, 340.
Still through Egypt's desert places, 356.
Stretched in thy shadows I rehearse, 655.
Strike the sails! King Olaf said, 233.
Svend Dyring he rideth adown the glade, 282.
Sweet as the tender fragrance that survives, 341.
Sweet babe! true portrait of thy father's face, 622.
Sweet chimes! that in the loneliness of night, 354.
Sweet faces, that from pictured casements lean, 322.
Sweet the memory is to me, 326.

Taddeo Gaddi built me. I am old, 318.
Take them, O Death! and bear away, 112.
Tell me not, in mournful numbers, 3.
Tell me, tell me, thou pretty bee, 658.
The Ages come and go, 522.
The Archbishop, whom God loved in high degree, 622.
The battle is fought and won, 280.
The brooklet came from the mountain, 296.
The ceaseless rain is falling fast, 324.
The course of my long life hath reached at last 636.
The day is cold, and dark, and dreary, 16.
The day is done, and the darkness, 64.
The day is ending, 65.
The doors are all wide open; at the gate, 315.
The guests were loud, the ale was strong, 222.
The holiest of all holidays are those, 322.
The lights are out, and gone are all the guests 308.
The Lord descended from above, 466.
The night is come, but not too soon, 4.
The nuns in the cloister, 42.
The old house by the lindens, 109.
The pages of thy book I read, 20.
The panting City cried to the Sea, 356.
The peasant leaves his plough afield, 594.
There is a love that cannot die, 648.
There is a quiet spirit in these woods, 10.
There is a Reaper, whose name is Death, 3.
There is no flock, however watched and tended, 107.

There sat one day in quiet, 609.
There was a time when I was very small, 608.
The rising moon has hid the stars, 15.
The rivers rush into the sea, 610.
The rocky ledge runs far into the sea, 106.
The sea awoke at midnight from its sleep, 316.
The sea hath its pearls, 615.
These are the Voices Three, 305.
These words the poet heard in Paradise, 357.
The shades of night were falling fast, 19.
The Slaver in the broad lagoon, 22.
The summer sun is sinking low, 353.
The sun is bright, — the air is clear, 15.
The sun is set ; and in his latest beams, 316.
The tide rises, the tide falls, 347.
The twilight is sad and cloudy, 105.
The wind is rising ; it seizes and shakes, 407.
The works of human artifice soon tire, 652.
The world is full of care, 484.
They made the warrior's grave beside, 650.
The young Endymion sleeps Endymion's sleep, 316.
They were three hundred, they were young and strong, 658.
This is the Arsenal. From floor to ceiling, 56.
This is the forest primeval. The murmuring pines and the hemlocks, 71.
This is the place. Stand still, my steed, 55.
This song of mine, 196.
Thora of Rimol ! hide me ! hide me, 220.
Thorberg Skafting, master-builder, 228.
Thou ancient oak ! whose myriad leaves are loud, 318.
Thou brooklet, all unknown to song, 630.
Thou comest, Autumn, heralded by the rain, 69.
Though the mills of God grind slowly, yet they grind exceeding small, 616.
Thou mighty Prince of Church and State, 629.
Thou Royal River, born of sun and shower, 320.
Thou that from the heavens art, 617.
Three Kings came riding from far away, 339.
Three miles extended around the fields of the homestead, on three sides, 598.
Three Silences there are : the first of speech, 320.
Thus for a while he stood, and mused by the shore of the ocean, 177.
Thus sang the Potter at his task, 329.
Thus, then, much care-worn, 618.
'T is late at night, and in the realm of sleep, 291.
Tityrus, thou in the shade of a spreading beech-tree reclining, 640.
To-day from the Aurora's bosom, 651.
To gallop off to town post-haste, 632.
To noble heart Love doth for shelter fly, 637.
Torrent of light and river of the air, 316.
Turn, turn, my wheel ! Turn round and round, 329.
Tuscan, that wanderest through the realms of gloom, 69.
'T was Pentecost, the Feast of Gladness, 612.
Two angels, one of Life and one of Death, 190.
Two good friends had Hiawatha, 127.

Under a spreading chestnut-tree, 14.
Under Mount Etna he lies, 201.
Under the walls of Monterey, 193.

Until we meet again ! That is the meaning, 354.
Up soared the lark into the air, 327.

Viswamitra the Magician, 339.
Vogelweid the Minnesinger, 66.

Warm and still is the summer night, 333.
Welcome, my old friend, 65.
Welcome, O Stork ! that dost wing, 639.
We sat within the farm-house old, 106.
What an image of peace and rest, 346.
What is this I read in history, 352.
What phantom is this that appears, 345.
What say the Bells of San Blas, 359.
What shall I do, sweet Nici, tell me, 658.
What should be said of him cannot be said, 637.
What the Immortals, 302.
When Alcuin taught the sons of Charlemagne, 266.
When by night the frogs are croaking, kindle but a torch's fire, 616.
When Christ was born in Bethlehem, 657.
When descends on the Atlantic, 103.
Whene'er a noble deed is wrought, 197.
When first in ancient time, from Jubal's tongue, 645.
When I compare, 359.
When I remember them, those friends of mine, 314.
When Mazárvan the Magician, 295.
When the dying flame of day, 9.
When the hours of Day are numbered, 4.
When the prime mover of my many sighs, 636.
When the summer fields are mown, 297.
When the summer harvest was gathered in, 649.
When the warm sun, that brings, 7.
When upon the western cloud, 645.
When winter winds are piercing chill, 8.
Where are the Poets, unto whom belong, 358.
Where from the eye of day, 650.
Whereunto is money good, 616.
Whilom Love was like a fire, and warmth and comfort it bespoke, 616.
White swan of cities, slumbering in thy nest, 319.
Whither, thou turbid wave, 609.
Who knocks, — who knocks at my door, 657.
Who love would seek, 616.
Why dost thou wildly rush and roar, 358.
Will ever the dear days come back again, 631.
Will then, Duperrier, thy sorrow be eternal ? 628.
With favoring winds, o'er sunlit seas, 342.
With snow-white veil and garments as of flame, 292.
With what a glory comes and goes the year, 8.
With what a hollow dirge, its voice did fill, 651.
Witlaf, a king of the Saxons. 109.
Worn with speed is my good steed, 52.

Ye sentinels of sleep, 305.
Yes, the moment shall decide, 306.
Yes, the Year is growing old. 6.
Yet not in vain, O River of Yesterday, 321.
Ye voices, that arose. 11.
You shall hear how Hiawatha, 124.
You shall hear how Pau-Puk-Keewis, 137, 149.

INDEX OF TITLES

The titles of major works and of general divisions are set in small capitals.

Abbot Joachim, The, 407.
Aftermath, 297.
Afternoon in February, 65.
Allah, 618.
Amalfi, 326.
Ancient Spanish Ballads, 594.
Angel and the Child, The, 629.
Angler's Song, The, 648.
Annie of Tharaw, 614.
April Day, An, 7.
Arrow and the Song, The, 68.
Arsenal at Springfield, The, 56.
Art and Nature, 652.
Artist, The, 635.
Assumption of the Virgin, The, 652.
At La Chaudeau, 631.
Auf Wiedersehen, 354.
Autumn: "Thou comest, Autumn, heralded by the rain," 69.
Autumn: "With what a glory comes and goes the year, 8.
Autumnal Nightfall, 646.
Autumn Within, 351.
Avon, To the, 357.
Azrael, 264.

Ballad of Carmilhan, The, 252.
Ballad of the French Fleet, A, 337.
BALLADS AND OTHER POEMS, 11.
Banks of the Cher, The, 655.
Baron of St. Castine, The, 259.
Barréges, 630.
Battle of Lovell's Pond, The, 645.
Bayard Taylor, 342.
Beatrice, 634.
Becalmed, 349.
Beleaguered City, The, 5.
BELFRY OF BRUGES AND OTHER POEMS, THE, 53.
Belfry of Bruges, The, 54.
Belisarius, 328.
Bell of Atri, The, 245.
Bells of Lynn, The, 290.
Bells of San Blas, The, 359.
Beowulf's Expedition to Heort, 618.
Beware, 611.
Bird and the Ship, The, 610.
Birds of Killingworth, The, 240.
BIRDS OF PASSAGE, 184.
Birds of Passage, 184.
Black Knight, The, 612.
Blessed are the Dead, 616.
Blind Bartimeus, 17.
BLIND GIRL OF CASTÈL-CUILLÈ, THE, 623.
BOOK OF SONNETS, A, 314.
Boston, 321.
Boy and the Brook, The, 639.
Bridge, The, 63.
Bridge of Cloud, The, 288.
Broken Oar, The, 323.
Brook, The, 593.
Brook and the Wave, The, 296.
Brooklet, To my, 630.
BUILDING OF THE SHIP, THE, 99.
Builders, The, 108.
Burial of the Minnisink, 10.
Burial of the Poet, The, 348.

Cadenabbia, 325.
Canzone, 637.
Carillon, 54.
Castle-Builder, The, 295.
Castle by the Sea, The, 611.
Castles in Spain, 335.
Catawba Wine, 196.
Celestial Pilot, The, 633.
Challenge, The, 296.
Chamber over the Gate, The, 342.
Changed, 296.
Channing, To William E., 20.
Charlemagne, 265.
Charles Sumner, 324.
Chaucer, 315.
Chaudeau, At La, 631.
Child Asleep, The, 622.
Child, To a, 60.
Childhood, 608.
Children, 200.
CHILDREN OF THE LORD'S SUPPER, THE, 600.
Children's Crusade, The, 352.
Children's Hour, The, 201.
Chimes, 354.
Christmas Bells, 289.
Christmas Carol, 628.
Christmas Carol, A, 657.
CHRISTUS: A MYSTERY, 361.
Chrysaor, 104.
City and the Sea, The, 356.
Clear Honor of the Liquid Element, 652.
Cobbler of Hagenau, The, 249.
Come, O Death, so silent flying, 597.
Consolation, 628.
COPLAS DE MANRIQUE, 587.
COURTSHIP OF MILES STANDISH, THE, 164.
Cross of Snow, The, 323.
Cumberland, The, 202.
Curfew, 69.

Danish Song-Book, To an Old, 65.
Dante: "Tuscan, that wanderest through the realms of gloom," 69.
Dante: "What should be said of him cannot be said," 637.
Daybreak, 199.
Day is Done, The, 64.
Daylight and Moonlight, 191.
Day of Sunshine, A, 202.
Dead, The, 610.
Death of Archbishop Turpin, 622.
Decoration Day, 359.
Dedication (Michael Angelo), 537.
Dedication (The Seaside and the Fireside), 99.
Delia, 341.
Descent of the Muses, The, 319.
Dirge over a Nameless Grave, 648.
Discoverer of the North Cape, The, 198.
Disembodied Spirit, The, 652.
Divina Commedia, 292.
DIVINE TRAGEDY, THE, 363.
Drinking Song, 67.
Driving Cloud, To the, 64.
Dutch Picture, A, 334.

EARLIER POEMS, 7.
Elected Knight, The, 608.

Elegiac, 345.
Elegiac Verse, 354.
Elegy, 654.
Eliot's Oak, 318.
Elizabeth, 270.
Emma and Eginhard, 266.
Emperor's Bird's-Nest, The, 189.
Emperor's Glove, The, 337.
Enceladus, 201.
Endymion, 15.
Epimetheus, or the Poet's Afterthought, 186.
EVANGELINE : A TALE OF ACADIE, 70.
Evening Star, The, 69.
Excelsior, 19.
Eyes so tristful, eyes so tristful, 597.

Falcon of Ser Federigo, The, 209.
Fata Morgana, 294.
Fiftieth Birthday of Agassiz, 199.
Fire, 635.
Fire of Driftwood, The, 106.
Florentine Song, A, 657.
FLOWER-DE-LUCE, 287.
Flower-de-Luce, 287.
Flowers, 5.
Fontenay, 656.
Footsteps of Angels, 4.
Forest of Gastine, To the, 655.
Forsaken, 618.
Four by the Clock, 354.
Four Lakes of Madison, The, 351.
Four Princesses at Wilna, The, 322.
Fragment, A, 359.
FRAGMENTS, 360.
Friar Lubin, 632.
Frithiof's Farewell, 600.
Frithiof's Homestead, 598.
Frithiof's Temptation, 599.
From my Arm-Chair, 343.
From the Cancioneros, 597.
Fugitive, The, 638.

Galaxy, The, 316.
Gaspar Becerra, 110.
Giles Corey of the Salem Farms, 495.
Giotto's Tower, 291.
Gleam of Sunshine, A, 55.
Gleaner of Sapri, The, 658.
Glove of Black in White Hand Bare, 597.
Goblet of Life, The, 17.
God's-Acre, 16.
GOLDEN LEGEND, THE, 408.
Golden Milestone, The, 195.
Good Part that shall not be taken away, The, 21.
Good Shepherd, The, 592.
Grave, The, 618.

HANGING OF THE CRANE, THE, 308.
Happiest Land, The, 609.
Haroun Al Raschid, 339.
Harvest Moon, The, 320.
Haunted Chamber, The, 294.
Haunted Houses, 188.
Hawthorne, 289.
Helen of Tyre, 345.
Hemlock Tree, 614.
Hermes Trismegistus, 356.
Herons of Elmwood, The, 333.
Holidays, 322.
Hymn for my Brother's Ordination, 112.
Hymn of the Moravian Nuns of Bethlehem, 9.
Hymn to the Night, 2.

Ianthe, To, 645.
Ideal Beauty, 652.
Image of God, The, 593.
Indian Hunter, The, 649.

Inscription on the Shanklin Fountain, 359.
In the Churchyard at Cambridge, 189.
In the Churchyard at Tarrytown, 318.
IN THE HARBOR, 349.
Iron Pen, The, 344.
Italian Scenery, 646.
Italy, To, 635.
It is not always May, 15.

Jeckoyva, 650.
Jewish Cemetery at Newport, The, 191.
John Endicott. 465.
JUDAS MACCABÆUS, 523.
Jugurtha, 344.
JUVENILE POEMS, 645.

Kambalu, 247.
Keats, 316.
KÉRAMOS, 329.
Killed at the Ford, 291.
King Christian, 607.
King Robert of Sicily, 215.
King Trisanku, 339.
King Witlaf's Drinking-Horn, 109.

Ladder of St. Augustine, The, 186.
Lady Wentworth, 255.
Leap of Roushan Beg, The, 338.
Legend Beautiful, The, 257.
Legend of the Cross-Bill, The, 615.
Legend of Rabbi Ben Levi, The, 214.
L'Envoi (Ultima Thule), 348.
L'Envoi (Voices of the Night), 11.
Let me go Warm, 651.
Lighthouse, The, 106.
Light of Stars, The, 4.
Loss and Gain, 359.
Lover's Complaint, The, 652.
Lover's Rock, 648.
Luck of Edenhall, The, 613.
Lunatic Girl, 647.

Mad River, 358.
Maiden and Weathercock, 347.
Maidenhood, 18.
Martin Luther, 463.
MASQUE OF PANDORA, THE, 297.
Meeting, The, 295.
Memories, 356.
Mezzo Cammin, 68.
MICHAEL ANGELO : A FRAGMENT, 537.
Midnight Mass for the Dying Year, 6.
Milagros de Nuestra Señora, 653.
Milton, 315.
Monk of Casal-Maggiore, The, 275.
Monte Cassino, 325.
Moods, 322.
Moonlight, 352.
Morituri Salutamus, 310.
Mother's Ghost, The, 282.
Musings, 650.
My Books, 357.
My Cathedral, 348.
My Lost Youth, 193.
My Secret, 632.

Nameless Grave, A, 317.
Native Land, The, 593.
Nativity of Christ, The, 651.
Nature, 318.
Nature of Love, The, 637.
Neapolitan Canzonet, A, 657.
Neglected Record of a Mind Neglected, 360.
NEW ENGLAND TRAGEDIES, THE, 465.
Night, 348.
Noël, 293.
Norman Baron, The, 58.

Nuremberg, 57.

Occultation of Orion, The, 62.
Ode written for the Commemoration at Fryeburg, Maine,
  of Lovewell's Fight, 649.
O Faithful, Indefatigable Tides, 360.
Old Age, 636.
Old Bridge at Florence, The, 318.
Old Clock on the Stairs, The, 67.
Old St. David's at Radnor, 346.
Oliver Basselin, 192.
Open Window, The, 109.
Ovid in Exile, 641.

Palingenesis, 287.
Parker Cleaveland, 319.
PASSAGES FROM FRITHIOF'S SAGA, 598.
Paul Revere's Ride, 207.
Pegasus in Pound, 110.
Phantom Ship, The, 187.
POEMS ON SLAVERY, 20.
Poet and his Songs, The, 348.
Poetic Aphorisms, 616.
Poets, The, 319.
Poet's Calendar, The, 349.
Ponte Vecchio di Firenze, Il, 318.
Possibilities, 358.
Praise of Little Women, 653.
Pray for me, 656.
Prelude (Voices of the Night), 1.
President Garfield, 357.
Prometheus, or the Poet's Forethought, 185.
Psalm of Life, A, 2.

Quadroon Girl, The, 22.
Quiet Life, A, 631.

Rain in Summer, 59.
Rainy Day, The, 16.
Reaper and the Flowers, The, 3.
Remorse, 617.
Resignation, 107.
Return of Spring, The, 621.
Revenge of Rain-in-the-Face, The, 336.
Rhyme of Sir Christopher, The, 284.
River Charles, To the, 16.
River Rhone, To the, 320.
River Yvette, To the, 337.
Robert Burns, 344.
Rondel : "Hence away, begone, begone," 655.
Rondel : "Love, love, what wilt thou with this heart of
  mine ? " 632.
Ropewalk, The, 195.

SAGA OF KING OLAF, THE, 218.
St. John, 522.
St. John's, Cambridge, 321.
Sandalphon, 200.
Sand of the Desert in an Hour-Glass, 108.
San Miguel, the Convent, 596.
Santa Filomena, 197.
Santa Teresa's Book-Mark, 597.
Scanderbeg, 280.
Sea-Diver, The, 650.
Sea hath its Pearls, The, 615.
SEASIDE AND THE FIRESIDE, THE, 98.
Seaweed, 103.
Secret of the Sea, The, 104.
Sermon of St. Francis, The, 327.
Seven Sonnets and a Canzone, 635.
Shadow, A, 317.
Shakespeare, 315.
Sicilian Canzonet, 658.
Siege of Kazan, The, 639.
Sifting of Peter, The, 346.
Silent Love, 616.
Singers, The, 112.
Sir Humphrey Gilbert, 105.

Skeleton in Armor, The, 11.
Slave in the Dismal Swamp, The, 21.
Slave's Dream, The, 20.
Slave Singing at Midnight, The, 22.
Sledge-Ride on the Ice, A, 599.
Sleep, 317.
Snow-Flakes, 202.
So from the Bosom of Darkness, 360.
Soft through the Silent Air, 360.
Soldier's Song, A, 657.
Some Day, Some Day, 597.
Something left Undone, 203.
Song : And whither goest thou, gentle sigh, 621.
Song : Hark, hark ! 621.
Song : If thou art sleeping, maiden, 637.
Song : She is a maid of artless grace, 596.
Song : Stay, stay at home, my heart, 340.
Song : Where, from the eye of day, 650.
SONG OF HIAWATHA, THE, 113.
Song of Savoy, A, 648.
Song of the Bell, 611.
Song of the Birds, 651.
Song of the Rhine, 653.
Song of the Silent Land, 612.
Songo River, 328.
SONNETS.
  Art and Nature, 652.
  Artist, The, 635.
  Autumn, 69.
  Boston, 321.
  Broken Oar, The, 323.
  Brook, The, 593.
  Burial of the Poet, The, 348.
  Chaucer, 315.
  Chimes, 354.
  Clear Honor of the Liquid Element, 652.
  Cross of Snow, The, 323.
  Dante, 69.
  Dante, 637.
  Dedication to Michael Angelo, 537.
  Descent of the Muses, The, 319.
  Disembodied Spirit, The, 652.
  Divina Commedia, 292.
  Eliot's Oak, 318.
  Evening Star, The, 69.
  Fire, 635.
  Four Princesses at Wilna, The, 322.
  Galaxy, The, 316.
  Giotto's Tower, 291.
  Good Shepherd, The, 592.
  Harvest Moon, The, 320.
  Holidays, 322.
  How strange the sculptures that adorn these towers,
    292.
  Ideal Beauty, 652.
  I enter, and I see thee in the gloom, 292.
  I lift mine eyes, and all the windows blaze, 293.
  Image of God, The, 593.
  In the Churchyard at Tarrytown, 318.
  Italy, To, 635.
  Keats, 316.
  Lover's Complaint, The, 652.
  Memories, 356.
  Mezzo Cammin, 68.
  Milton, 315.
  Moods, 322.
  Mrs. Kemble's Readings from Shakespeare, On, 112.
  My Books, 357.
  My Cathedral, 348.
  My Secret, 632.
  Nameless Grave, A, 317.
  Native Land, The, 593.
  Nature, 318.
  Night, 348.
  Oft have I seen at some Cathedral Door, 292.
  Old Age, 636.
  Old Bridge at Florence, The, 318.
  O Star of Morning and of Liberty ! 293.

Parker Cleaveland. 319.
Poets, The, 319.
Ponte Vecchio di Firenze, Il, 318.
Possibilities, 358.
President Garfield. 357.
Quiet Life, A, 631.
Return of Spring, The, 621.
River Rhone, To the, 320.
St. John's, Cambridge, 321.
Shadow, A, 317.
Shakespeare, 315.
Sleep, 317.
Sound of the Sea, The, 316.
Summer Day by the Sea, A, 316.
Three Friends of Mine, 314.
Three Silences of Molinos, The, 320.
Tides, The, 317.
To-Morrow, 291.
To-Morrow, 593.
Two Harvests, The, 652.
Two Rivers, The, 320.
Venice, 319.
Victor and Vanquished, 351.
Vittoria Colonna, To, 636.
Vittoria Colonna, To, 636.
Wapentake, 323.
Will ever the dear Days come back again, 631.
With Snow-white Veil and Garments as of Flame, 292.
Woodstock Park, 322.
Youth and Age, 635.
Soul's Complaint against the Body, The, 620.
Sound of the Sea, The, 316.
SPANISH STUDENT, The, 23.
Spirit of Poetry, The, 10.
Spring, 621.
Stars, The, 654.
Statue over the Cathedral Door, The, 615.
Stork, To the, 639.
Summer Day by the Sea, A, 316.
Sundown, 353.
Sunrise on the Hills, 9.
Suspiria, 112.
Symbolum Apostolorum, 406.

TALES OF A WAYSIDE INN, 204.
Tegnér's Drapa, 111.
Tell me, tell me, thou pretty Bee, 658.
Terrace of the Aigalades, On the, 630.
Terrestrial Paradise, The, 634.
Thanksgiving, 645.
Three Friends of Mine, 314.
Three Kings, The, 339.
Three Silences of Molinos, The, 320.
Tide Rises, the Tide Falls, The, 347.
Tides, The, 317.
To a Child, 60.
To an Old Danish Song-Book, 65.
To Cardinal Richelieu, 629.
To Ianthe, 645.

To Italy, 635.
To-Morrow, 291.
To-Morrow (Mañana), 593.
To my Brooklet, 630.
Torquemada, 236.
To the Avon, 357.
To the Driving Cloud, 64.
To the Forest of Gastine, 655.
To the River Charles, 16.
To the River Rhone, 320.
To the River Yvette, 337.
To the Stork, 639.
To William E. Channing, 20.
To Vittoria Colonna, 636.
To Vittoria Colonna, 636.
TRANSLATIONS, 586.
Travels by the Fireside, 324.
Twilight, 105.
Two Angels, The, 190.
Two Harvests, The, 652.
Two Locks of Hair. The, 613.
Two Rivers, The, 320.

ULTIMA THULE, 341.

Venetian Gondolier, The, 647.
Venice, 319.
Victor and Vanquished, 351.
Victor Galbraith, 193.
Vida de San Millan, 595.
Village Blacksmith, The, 14.
Vire, 656.
Virgil's First Eclogue, 640.
Vittoria Colonna, 336.
Vittoria Colonna, To, 636.
Vittoria Colonna, To, 636.
VOICES OF THE NIGHT, 1.
Vox Populi, 295.

Walter von der Vogelweid, 66.
Wanderer's Night-Songs, 617.
Wapentake, 323.
Warden of the Cinque Ports, The, 188.
Warning, The, 23.
Wave, The, 609.
Weariness, 203.
White Czar, The, 341.
Whither, 610.
Will ever the dear Days come back again, 631.
Windmill, The, 347.
Wind over the Chimney, The, 290.
Wine of Jurançon, The, 632.
Witnesses, The, 22.
Woods in Winter, 8.
Woodstock Park, 322.
Wraith in the Mist, A, 339.
Wreck of the Hesperus, The, 13.

Youth and Age, 636.